THE LAW AND ETHICS OF LAWYERING

THIRD EDITION

by

GEOFFREY C. HAZARD, JR.
Trustee Professor
University of Pennsylvania Law School

SUSAN P. KONIAK
Professor of Law
Boston University School of Law

ROGER C. CRAMTON
Robert S. Stevens Professor of Law
Cornell Law School

NEW YORK, NEW YORK
FOUNDATION PRESS

1999

 TEXT IS PRINTED ON 10% POST
CONSUMER RECYCLED PAPER

1st Reprint — 2001

To those we love
To those no longer with us who helped make us who we are
To the memory of Robert M. Cover

*

PREFACE

This book seeks to fulfill its title. Thus, first of all it contains cases. Cases are at the same time sources of legal doctrine in the law governing law practice, a mirror of the minds of judges in interpreting what lawyers do, and "war stories" of difficult situations that lawyers confront. This book also contains statutes and rules of professional conduct. Statutes reflect public sentiment about right and wrong in transactions in which lawyers are involved, such as managing a service enterprise, buying and selling property, administering criminal justice and paying taxes. The rules of professional conduct are formulated primarily by lawyers. Hence, those rules are a mirror of the minds of lawyers in interpreting their own work. All of these legal sources project visions of the practice of law, but the visions are not the same. Therein lies an important part of the tale.

The book also contains source materials on ethics and morals, from Plato and since. The practice of law is not fully intelligible without reference to these great philosophical issues in ethics and to ethical standards of the community at large. Community ethical standards inform the minds of clients and opposite parties with whom a lawyer deals, the minds of officials and other lawyers with whom lawyers must work, and the minds of jurors, judges and disciplinary committees before whom a lawyer may be called to account. Neither is the practice of law fully intelligible without reference to the inner mind of each of us who engages in law practice. Every act a lawyer does, or fails to do, appears somehow in her own mind's eye. The accumulation of these impressions is not only professional experience but personal identity as well. Every lawyer should continually ask herself: What kind of memories will this leave with me? Contemplating the morality of practicing law does not come too soon in law school. Indeed if not started then it may come too late, or never.

The materials in the book also reflect the variousness of lawyers' situations in practice. Some of the cases and rules involve big firm corporate practice. Others involve small firm lawyers and sole practitioners and such transactions as drafting a will, handling a divorce or defending an accused in a criminal proceeding. Situation in practice makes a difference in the kind of matters a lawyer handles and therefore the kind of ethical problems she encounters. Situation in practice also makes a difference in the kinds of political, economic and moral resources a lawyer has for dealing with ethical problems. Moreover, each practice context has its own set of constraints and customs, a distinctive legal culture that may be in some tension with more general professional norms. In these respects, lawyers are very different from each other. Yet they are alike in being governed by a common body of law and professional lore and being obliged, in the end, to resolve ethical dilemmas alone on the basis of personal judgments.

The book covers a wide range not only in the foregoing respects but in fields of legal subject matter. We include distillates of agency law, criminal law and procedure, civil procedure, evidence law, tort law, contract law, securities law and corporation law, and make reference to tax law and the law of wills, estate planning and marital dissolution. This cannot be avoided if the problems of legal ethics are to be adequately comprehended. The stuff of law practice includes all legal subjects, and law practice performed competently and ethically requires dealing with unfamiliar areas of law. In the "pervasive method" of teaching legal ethics, ethical problems are implanted in the context of a body of some other law in some other course. This book represents the "pervasive method" in reverse.

We live in a period when the law of lawyering is growing and changing rapidly. During the almost six years since the prior edition of this book went to press, the profession and the public have discussed the conduct of lawyers in events of great public moment, such as the O. J. Simpson Case and the Clinton Impeachment Proceeding. Judicial decisions have applied old rules to new situations and on occasion elaborated new law. Rule-makers have been busy at the national level, where ABA actions and rule amendments have been frequent and ongoing, the American Law Institute has completed work on a new Restatement of the Law Governing Lawyers and federal authorities have taken new actions. Rule-making has also been active at the state level, where a number of jurisdictions have adopted new ethics codes.

This edition constitutes a substantial revision that maintains the qualities and themes of prior editions. Much new material, including a new section on the law and ethics of negotiation, has been added. Deletion and condensation have kept the book about the same length. For more extensive discussion of our goals and methods in teaching this subject, see Roger C. Cramton and Susan P. Koniak, Rule, Story and Commitment in the Teaching of Legal Ethics, 38 Wm. & Mary L. Rev. 145 (1996), and Susan P. Koniak and Geoffrey C. Hazard, Jr., Paying Attention to the Signs, 58 Law & Contemp. Prob. 117 (1996).

G.C.H., Jr.
S.P.K.
R.C.C.

July 1999

NOTE ON EDITORIAL PRACTICES

The editorial practices followed in the book require brief explanation. In general we have reprinted cases rather fully in a desire to provide class material that retains the detail and texture of the originals. We have not carried this approach so far as to preserve passages that are repetitious or irrelevant. Authorities cited in principal cases have been pruned out, leaving only those citations that build an understanding of the course as a whole or that a curious student might want to examine. Our notes contain important citations to cases and secondary sources, but these are placed in footnotes so as not to interrupt the flow of the text. We have discussed and cited all of the materials that we think a careful instructor or diligent student might want to examine for class purposes.

Omissions from principal cases or quoted materials are indicated in all instances, with the exceptions noted below. Periods (. . .) signal the omission of words, sentences or citations from within a paragraph (although in some instances citations are omitted without indication). A centered ellipsis (. . .) indicates the omission of a paragraph or more. Most of the footnotes in principal cases and quoted materials have been discarded. Those footnotes which have been included retain their original numbers. Notation of the elimination of dissenting opinions is provided. In a few instances we have corrected obvious typographical errors in the original, or changed italic to roman typeface or vice versa. Editorial material within reprinted cases or quoted material is placed within brackets.

Short-hand references are used for a number of sources and publications that are cited extensively:

American Bar Association, Model Rules of Professional Conduct (1983 and subsequent amendments): referred to as "Model Rules" collectively and cited individually as "Rule x" or "M.R. x."

American Bar Association, Model Code of Professional Responsibility (1969): referred to as "Model Code" or cited individually as "DR x" or "EC x."

American Bar Association, Committee on Ethics and Professional Responsibility, Formal Opinions: referred to as "ABA Formal Op. x (date)."

ABA/BNA Lawyers Manual of Professional Conduct (bi-weekly loose-leaf publication): "ABA/BNA Law.Man.Prof.Cond. § x."

American Law Institute, Restatement Third of the Law Governing Lawyers (currently available in two Proposed Final Drafts and one Tentative Draft, but to be published in 2000): referred to as "Restatement § x" (other Restatements are cited more fully).

Geoffrey C. Hazard, Jr. & W. William Hodes, The Law of Lawyering (Prentice-Hall, 3d ed. 1998, with annual supplements): "Hazard & Hodes § x."

Charles W. Wolfram, Modern Legal Ethics (West, 1986): "Wolfram, Modern Legal Ethics, p. x."

ACKNOWLEDGMENTS

We thank the hundreds of students and lawyers in our professional experience who have helped us to try and understand this subject. Special thanks for this edition go to Rachel Black and Marc Foster, students at the Cornell Law School; Nicole P. Armenta, Rachel M. Jones, Mary Ann Peterson and Elizabeth A. Reed, students at Harvard Law School; and Professors George M. Cohen, University of Virginia School of Law and Ted Schneyer, University of Arizona College of Law, who provided many helpful suggestions for the improvement of this edition. Jack Glezen at Cornell provided exceptional assistance in the preparation of the manuscript for both the second and third editions.

Continued thanks go to Professor Charles W. Wolfram of Cornell Law School, whose detailed comments on a tentative version of the second edition were extremely helpful. Special thanks for that edition also go to Susan Evans, Julia Lee, Richard McCaffrey and Lenore Neerbasch, students at the Cornell Law School, and Christine Biancheria at the University of Pittsburgh School of Law.

We also owe continued thanks to many who contributed to the first edition: LuAnn Driscoll, Ruth Jencks, Karen Knochel, Darleen Mocello, Carolyn Rohan, Barbara Salopek and Hillary Sonet, who typed various portions of the manuscript. We thank Kathleen C. Cleary, Andrew B. Klaber, Kristen A. Lee, Daniel Lee and Lauren Schlecker, research assistants at the University of Pittsburgh School of Law, who worked so earnestly on the first edition. Especially, we thank Margaret M. Egler, J.D. 1988, University of Pittsburgh, for her tireless efforts, critical eye, good spirit and sincere dedication to this project.

We thank each other for a lovely law partnership.

G.C.H., Jr.
S.P.K.
R.C.C.

We thank the authors and holders of copyrights for permission to publish excerpts, as follows:

American Bar Association, Formal Opinion 342 (November 24, 1975). Copyright © by the American Bar Association and reprinted with its permission.

Association of the Bar of the City of New York, Committee on Professional and Judicial Ethics, Inquiry Reference 80-23. Reprinted with permission.

Sissela Bok, Lying: Moral Choice in Public and Private Life (1978). Copyright © 1978 by Sissela Bok and reprinted with her permission and the permission of Pantheon Books.

Sissela Bok, Secrets (1982). Copyright © 1983 by Sissela Bok and reprinted with her permission and the permission of Pantheon Books.

Louis D. Brandeis, "The Opportunity in the Law" (1905), in Brandeis, Business: A Profession (1914).

Steven Brill, "The Stench of Room 202." Reprinted with permission from the April 1987 issue of The American Lawyer. Copyright © 1987 The American Lawyer.

Steven Brill, "When a Lawyer Lies." Reprinted with permission from the December 19, 1979 issue of Esquire Magazine. Copyright © 1979 Esquire Magazine.

John C. Coffee, Jr., "Class Wars: The Dilemma of the Mass Tort Class Action," 95 Colum. L. Rev. 1343 (1995). Reprinted with permission. Copyright © Columbia Law Review.

John C. Coffee, Jr., "Understanding the Plaintiff's Attorney: The Implications of Economic Theory for Private Enforcement of Law Through Class and Derivative Actions," 86 Colum. L. Rev. 669 (1986). Reprinted with permission. Copyright © Columbia Law Review.

Robert M. Cover, "Violence and the Word," 95 Yale L.J. 1601 (1986). Reprinted with permission of the Yale Law Journal Company and Fred B. Rothman & Company.

Roger C. Cramton, "The Lawyer as Whistleblower: Confidentiality and the Government Lawyer," 5 Geo. J. Legal Ethics 292 (1991). Reprinted with permission. Copyright © 1991 Georgetown Journal of Legal Ethics and Georgetown University.

Roger C. Cramton, "On Giving Meaning to 'Professionalism.'" Reprinted with permission from Teaching and Learning Professionalism: Proceedings of a Symposium of the ABA Section on Legal Education and Admission to the Bar and the ABA Center for Professional Responsibility, Oak Brook, Illinois, October 2-4, 1996. Copyright © 1997 American Bar Association.

Norman Dorsen and Leon Friedman, Disorder in the Courtroom (1973). Copyright © 1973 by Association of the Bar of the City of New York. Reprinted with permission.

Monroe H. Freedman, "Perjury: The Lawyer's Trilemma," 1 Litigation 26 (No. 1 Winter, 1975). Reprinted with permission of the Section of Litigation, American Bar Association.

James J. Fuld, "Lawyers' Standards and Responsibilities in Rendering Opinions," 33 Bus. Law. 1295 (1978). Copyright © 1978 by the American Bar Association and reprinted with its permission and the permission of its Section of Business Law. All rights reserved.

William J. Genego, "The Future of Effective Assistance of Counsel: Performance Standards and Competent Representation," 22 American Crim. L. Rev. 181 (1984). Copyright © 1984 jointly by American Criminal Law Review and the author and reprinted with the permission of both.

Carol Gilligan, In a Different Voice (1982). Copyright © 1980 by Carol Gilligan. Reprinted with permission of the publisher, Harvard University Press.

Erving Goffman, Asylums: Essays on the Social Situation of Mental Patients and Other Inmates (1961). Copyright © 1961 by Erving Goffman. Reprinted with permission.

Robert W. Gordon, "The Ideal and the Actual in the Law," in Gawalt, ed., The New High Priests: Lawyers in Post-Civil War America (1984). Reprinted with permission.

Geoffrey C. Hazard, Jr., Ethics in the Practice of Law (1978). Reprinted with permission of Yale University Press.

Geoffrey C. Hazard, Jr., "How Far May a Lawyer Go in Assisting a Client in Legally Wrongful Conduct?," 35 U. Miami L. Rev. 669 (1981). Reprinted with the permission of the University of Miami Law Review.

Geoffrey C. Hazard, Jr., "Rectification of Client Fraud: Death and Revival of a Professional Norm," 33 Emory L. J. 271 (1984). Reprinted with permission of the Emory Law Journal.

Geoffrey C. Hazard, Jr., "Securing Courtroom Decorum," 80 Yale L. J. 433 (1970). Reprinted with permission of the Yale Law Journal Company and Fred B. Rothman & Company.

Geoffrey C. Hazard, Jr., "Triangular Lawyer Relationships: An Exploratory Analysis," 1 Geo. J. of Leg. Ethics 15 (1987). Reprinted with permission of the Georgetown Journal of Legal Ethics.

Oliver W. Holmes, Jr., "The Path of Law," in Collected Legal Papers (1920), also appears in 10 Harv. L. Rev. 457 (1897).

Robert Keeton, Trial Tactics and Methods (2d ed. 1973). Copyright © 1973 by Little, Brown and Company and reprinted with its permission.

Duncan Kennedy, Legal Education and the Reproduction of Hierarchy (1983). Reprinted with permission of the author.

Susan P. Koniak, "The Law Between the Bar and the State," 70 N. C. L. Rev. 1389 (1992). Reprinted with permission of North Carolina Law Review.

Susan P. Koniak and George M. Cohen, "In Hell There Will Be Lawyers Without Clients or Law," reprinted with permission of the authors and Deborah L. Rhode from a book to be published under the editorship of Deborah L. Rhode. Copyright © 1999 Susan P. Koniak and George M. Cohen.

David Luban, Lawyers and Justice: An Ethical Study xiv-xv, 297-98 (1988). Copyright © 1988 Princeton University Press.

David Luban, "Paternalism and the Legal Profession," 1981 Wis. L. Rev. 454. Reprinted with the permission of the Wisconsin Law Review.

Stewart Macaulay, "Law Schools and the World Outside Their Doors II: Some Notes on Two Recent Studies of the Chicago Bar," 32 J. Legal Educ. 506 (1982). Reprinted with permission of the author and the Association of American Law Schools.

Jonathan R. Macey and Geoffrey P. Miller, "The Plaintiffs' Attorney's Role in Class Action and Derivative Litigation: Economic Analysis and Recommendations for Reform," 58 U. Chi, L. Rev. 1 (1991). Reprinted with permission of the University of Chicago Law Review.

Morton Mintz, At Any Cost: Corporate Greed, Women, and the Dalkon Shield. Copyright © 1985 by Morton Mintz. Reprinted with permission of Pantheon Books, a division of Random House, Inc.

Plato, "Gorgias," in The Dialogues of Plato, translated by Benjamin Jowett (1898). Copyright © 1898 by D. Appleton and Company.

Richard A. Posner, "Law School Should Be Two Years, Not Three." Reprinted with permission from Harvard Law Record, January 16, 1998.

Deborah L. Rhode, "Perspectives on Professional Women," 40 Stan. L. Rev. 1163 (1988). Copyright © 1988 by the Board of Trustees of the Leland Stanford Junior University. Reprinted with permission.

Douglas E. Rosenthal, Lawyer and Client, Who's in Charge? Copyright © 1974 by the Russell Sage Foundation and reprinted with its permission.

Alvin B. Rubin, "A Causerie on Lawyers' Ethics in Negotiation," 35 La. L. Rev. 577 (1975). Copyright © Louisiana Law Review. Reprinted with permission.

Patrick J. Schiltz, "On Being a Happy, Healthy, and Ethical Member of an Unhappy, Unhealthy, and Unethical Profession," 54 Vand. L. Rev. 871-951 (1999). Adapted and reprinted by permission of the author and the Vanderbilt Law Review. Copyright © 1999. Vanderbilt Law Review. All rights reserved.

Geraldine Segal, Blacks in the Law (University of Pennsylvania Press 1985). Reprinted with permission.

William H. Simon, "The Ideology of Advocacy," 1978 Wisconsin Law Review 30. Copyright © 1978 Wisconsin Law Review. Reprinted with the permission of the Wisconsin Law Review.

Stuart Taylor, Jr., "Ethics and the Law: A Case History," New York Times Magazine (January 9, 1983). Reprinted with permission. Copyright © 1983 by the New York Times Company.

Richard Wasserstrom, "Lawyers and Revolution," 30 U. Pitt. L. Rev. 125 (1968). Reprinted with permission of University of Pittsburgh Law Review.

Richard Wasserstrom, "Lawyers as Professionals: Some Moral Issues," 5 Human Rights 1 (1975). Reprinted with permission.

Stephen Wexler, "Practicing Law for Poor People," 79 Yale L. J. 1049-1067 (1970). Reprinted with permission of the Yale Law Journal Company and Fred B. Rothman & Company.

David B. Wilkins and G. Mitu Gulati, "Why Are There So Few Black Lawyers in Corporate Law Firms?," 85 Cal. L. Rev. 493 (1996). Reprinted with permission of the authors and the California Law Review.

Charles W. Wolfram, Modern Legal Ethics 33-38 (1986). Reprinted with permission of the author and West Publishing Company. Copyright © 1986 West Publishing Company.

*

SUMMARY OF CONTENTS

*

TABLE OF CONTENTS

Page

*

TABLE OF CASES

Principal cases are in bold type. Non-principal cases are in roman type. References are to Pages.

TABLE OF OTHER AUTHORITIES

*

THE LAW AND ETHICS
OF LAWYERING

*

CHAPTER 1

RELATIONSHIP OF LAW, LAWYERS AND ETHICS

A. INTRODUCTION

This book is about the law and ethics of lawyering.[1] Each of these terms has depth, complexity and multiple shades of meaning. Law and ethics, which are related yet distinct concepts, are part of a general subject that includes all aspects of the concept of obligation. As used here, *ethics* refers to imperatives regarding the welfare of others that are recognized as binding upon a person's conduct in some more immediate and binding sense than *law* and in some more general and impersonal sense than *morals*. While acknowledging the place in the philosophical universe of ethical theories that deny the existence of an imperative regarding the welfare of others, such as ethical egoism, our concern here is with the relationship between rules that are believed to exist and the conduct to which they are thought to refer.

Ethical rules are not merely moral sentiments that have attained a certain publicity and formality nor are they merely a subspecies of legislation—rules that differ from law only in that their enforcement is relatively informal. Ethics rules emerge from a process of subjective deliberation leading to a decision about what one ought to do and from interpersonal exchanges establishing what a group believes one should have done. In the real world of acting, judging and being judged, ethics is best regarded as all of these—deliberation about how one should act given the existence of rules established by a consensus that one shares substantially if not unreservedly.

This book, however, is not about ethics generally but about the law and ethics of lawyering, a variegated set of activities that cannot be reduced to the two paradigms of the advocate in litigation and the counselor or advisor in the law office. Common elements of a lawyer's role and function, however, suggest two general problems. First, a lawyer's training and activity as a legal technician demythologizes the law. The lawyer, more than the lay person, is conscious of the ambiguities of the law's commands, the frequently specious or conflicting character of its policy and the frailties of its interpreters. The lawyer's professional function consists largely of providing counsel for clients about how, on the one hand, to escape or

---

1. Some of the material in this introduction is drawn, with permission of the publisher, Yale University Press, from Geoffrey C. Hazard, Jr., Ethics in the Practice of Law 1–3, 11–14, and 19–21 (1978).

mitigate the incidence of the law's obligations, or, on the other, to enlarge or detail its enforcement. The essence of these activities is the manipulation of governmental authority and the language and social processes through which that authority is exercised. The lawyer as counselor gives at least lip service to the idea that the law's obligations are real, but she is bound to advise on the extent to which they are mere formalities or even less. What view should she take of rules that address her own conduct? Are they legal regulations whose burdens the lawyer may minimize or obviate by technical advice delivered professionally to herself, or are they strictures of conscience whose only meaning is in their observation?

A second problem of legal ethics arises from the fact that a client is in the picture. Ethics, seriously discussed as in Western philosophy, usually speak in terms that require treating all other persons on an equal footing. That is, ethical norms are cast as universals in which in principle every "other" is entitled to equal respect and consideration in the calculation of the actor's alternatives and course of action. On the other hand, professional ethics give priority to an "other" who is a client and in general require subordination of everyone else's interests to that of the client. Indeed, the central problem in professional ethics can be described as the tension between the client's preferred position resulting from the professional connection and the position of equality that everyone else is accorded by general principles of morality and legality.

Although many modern moral philosophers frame rules of behavior in universal (Kantian) terms, only in a rigorous system taken seriously is there an expectation that they will be applied without regard to special circumstances. In other religious and philosophic traditions, as well as in folk ethics, it is accepted that a person owes one kind of duty to a member of her family (or village or working group) and another to those with whom a relationship is more remote. The possibility of such discrimination opens up a range of questions: How does one rank the various "others" (spouse, child, cousin, next-door neighbor, fellow worker, compatriot, etc.) and how does one rank different kinds of obligations (to refrain from killing, to refrain from stealing, to forbear, to counsel forbearance by others, to come to another's aid, to sacrifice one's self for another, etc.). These questions pose great philosophic difficulties for all universalistic ethical conceptions, a fact that may explain why these conceptions are usually expressed in wholly abstract terms. They pose similar difficulties in practical application, so that folk ethics is a mishmash of homilies, legalistic formulations of various duty relationships and resignation to subjective ethical choice.

We lead our daily lives by making ethical discriminations in these terms, but we are left defenseless against charges of inconsistency, casuistry and discrimination. The burden of these charges can be lifted by attributing responsibility to the force of circumstances. Thus we say that no one volunteers to have to distinguish between her spouse and child, employer and customer, or neighbor and the building inspector. When events conscript us into doing so, we make ethical distinctions because we must in order to continue to function. At the level of principle, therefore, many modern conceptions of ethics posit a system of universals, while in day-by-day application ethics involves a more complicated scheme of distinctions and excuses based on role, relationships and practical necessity.

The rules governing a lawyer's office are neither a system of universal rules nor a set of injunctions to be virtuous in responding to situational exigencies. Rules of legal ethics are not universal because they give a preferred position to clients; the office of lawyer begins with having to make distinctions among persons. At least in an immediate sense, the rules are not based on practical necessity, for no one is compelled to become a lawyer and, ordinarily at least, no lawyer is compelled to take a particular case. While in some situations a lawyer is supposed to act with perfect neutrality among others, a lawyer usually intervenes in relationships between others with a predisposition to treat the one who is her client with greater solicitude than she treats the other, regardless of the merits of their respective positions.

According to any "nonlegal" ethics, intervention on these terms is difficult to justify. It violates the principle of equal treatment inherent in all forms of universalist ethics. It lacks the involuntarism that is present in the ethical dilemmas of everyday life. For the lawyer does not merely encounter choices between the conflicting interests of others but makes a business out of such encounters, and takes partisan positions for money. Thus, her vocation violates the concepts of ethics held both by philosophers and in folklore.

If the profession were uniformly an elite, it would be unlikely to have adopted a formal code and so the problem of disobeying that code would not arise. Shared norms would be enforced by informal means such as peer pressure. Our relatively heterogeneous legal profession, however, seems to require positive legislation to resolve questions of conduct about which a consensus is lacking. But positive legislation is inevitably simplistic to some degree, and thus an incomplete guide in delicate situations. A truly conscientious and self-confident practitioner would not feel bound to follow the letter of the law when her personal judgment dictated a different course. Hence, the concept of a principled violation of the rules of ethics introduces what is in fact a triple standard—conscience for some, code for others and lip-service for still others. This state of affairs, whether desirable or not, necessarily results from the admission that conduct can be at the same time unlawful and right.

The profession's codes of legal ethics govern a number of matters that are very important to the public interest but either trivially obvious or largely irrelevant to ethics as such. These include:

- Rules requiring that a lawyer be truthful and honest.
- Rules regulating competition among lawyers (advertising, solicitation, etc.), which are subsumed under the rubric of assisting "the legal profession in fulfilling its duty to make legal counsel available."
- Rules regulating competition from outside the profession. The substance of these rules is that lawyers should prevent nonlawyers from

doing anything that is the "practice of law," whatever that may include.

Putting these aside, the ethics codes—and the bulk of this book—deal with essentially four problems:

- Prohibited assistance: What kinds of things is a lawyer prohibited from doing for a client?

- Competence: What measures will assure competent lawyering?

- Confidentiality: What information learned by a lawyer should she treat as secret, and from whom, and under what conditions may the secrecy be lifted?

- Conflicts of interest: When and to what extent is a lawyer prohibited from acting because there is a conflict of interest between her clients or between herself and a client?

These are all tough problems, and not only for lawyers. What is perhaps not fully appreciated, by lawyers and lay people alike, is that similar problems arise in everyday life. If this fact were appreciated by lawyers, they might be able to perceive and to discuss the problems free of the introverted assumption that lawyers alone can appreciate their complex and stressful nature. If lay people recognized the similarity, they might regard the lawyers' ethical dilemmas with greater comprehension and perhaps even greater sympathy.

Many illustrations might be suggested from other walks of life, at work and at home, of problems involving prohibited assistance, confidentiality and conflict of interest. A few will suffice to make the point. Thus, regarding prohibited assistance: Do you help a friend by lying to the police? Omit adverse information when asked to evaluate a former student or employee? Help sell stock that may be overvalued? Maintain the "character of a neighborhood" by not renting to an African American? Regarding confidentiality: What should a parent do who knows that a child has stolen something from a store? A pediatrician who discovers physical abuse of a child by its parents? A teacher who finds out that a student has been using drugs? An accountant who knows that a client is understating income for tax purposes? Regarding conflicts of interest: Does a parent send a healthy child to college rather than send a sick one to the Mayo Clinic? A plant manager trim on safety systems to keep her company financially afloat? A doctor order hospitalization because medical insurance will not otherwise cover the patient? A supervisor commend a subordinate who may become a rival?

If there is any peculiarity about these problems as they are confronted by lawyers, it is that a lawyer confronts them every day and is supposed to resolve them in a fashion that is compatible with a conception of her professional role. The ethics codes and the law of lawyering undertake to tell her how she should do so.

B. WHO AMONG US?

1. ADVERSARY ETHICS

Spaulding v. Zimmerman

Supreme Court of Minnesota, 1962.
263 Minn. 346, 116 N.W.2d 704.

■ GALLAGHER, JUSTICE.

Appeal from an order of the District Court of Douglas County vacating and setting aside a prior order of such court dated May 8, 1957, approving a settlement made on behalf of David Spaulding on March 5, 1957, at which time he was a minor of the age of 20 years; and in connection therewith, vacating and setting aside releases executed by him and his parents, a stipulation of dismissal, an order for dismissal with prejudice, and a judgment entered pursuant thereto.

The prior action was brought against defendants by Theodore Spaulding, as father and natural guardian of David Spaulding, for injuries sustained by David in an automobile accident, arising out of a collision which occurred August 24, 1956, between an automobile driven by John Zimmerman, in which David was a passenger, and one owned by John Ledermann and driven by Florian Ledermann.

On appeal defendants contend that the court was without jurisdiction to vacate the settlement solely because their counsel then possessed information, unknown to plaintiff herein, that at the time he was suffering from an aorta aneurysm which may have resulted from the accident, because (1) no mutual mistake of fact was involved; (2) no duty rested upon them to disclose information to plaintiff which they could assume had been disclosed to him by his own physicians; (3) insurance limitations as well as physical injuries formed the basis for the settlement; and (4) plaintiff's motion to vacate the order for settlement and to set aside the releases was barred by the limitations provided in Rule 60.02 of Rules of Civil Procedure.[2]

After the accident, David's injuries were diagnosed by his family physician, Dr. James H. Cain, as a severe crushing injury of the chest with multiple rib fractures; a severe cerebral concussion, probably with petechial hemorrhages of the brain; and bilateral fractures of the clavicles. At Dr. Cain's suggestion, on January 3, 1957, David was examined by Dr. John F. Pohl, an orthopedic specialist, who made X-ray studies of his chest. Dr. Pohl's detailed report of this examination included the following:

2. [Editors' note:] Minnesota Rule 60.02 is substantially identical to Rule 60(b) of the Federal Rules of Civil Procedure.

"... The lung fields are clear. The heart and aorta are normal."

Nothing in such report indicated the aorta aneurysm with which David was then suffering. On March 1, 1957, at the suggestion of Dr. Pohl, David was examined from a neurological viewpoint by Dr. Paul S. Blake, and in the report of this examination there was no finding of the aorta aneurysm.

In the meantime, on February 22, 1957, at defendants' request, David was examined by Dr. Hewitt Hannah, a neurologist. On February 26, 1957, the latter reported to Messrs. Field, Arvesen, & Donoho, attorneys for defendant John Zimmerman, as follows:

"The one feature of the case which bothers me more than any other part of the case is the fact that this boy of 20 years of age has an aneurysm, which means a dilatation of the aorta and the arch of the aorta. Whether this came out of this accident I cannot say with any degree of certainty and I have discussed it with the Roentgenologist and a couple of Internists.... Of course an aneurysm or dilatation of the aorta in a boy of this age is a serious matter as far as his life. This aneurysm may dilate further and it might rupture with further dilatation and this would cause his death.

"It would be interesting also to know whether the X-ray of his lungs, taken immediately following the accident, shows this dilatation or not. If it was not present immediately following the accident and is now present, then we could be sure that it came out of the accident."

Prior to the negotiations for settlement, the contents of the above report were made known to counsel for defendants Florian and John Ledermann.

The case was called for trial on March 4, 1957, at which time the respective parties and their counsel possessed such information as to David's physical condition as was revealed to them by their respective medical examiners as above described. It is thus apparent that neither David nor his father, the nominal plaintiff in the prior action, was then aware that David was suffering the aorta aneurysm but on the contrary believed that he was recovering from the injuries sustained in the accident.

On the following day an agreement for settlement was reached wherein, in consideration of the payment of $6,500, David and his father agreed to settle in full for all claims arising out of the accident.

Richard S. Roberts, counsel for David, thereafter presented to the court a petition for approval of the settlement, wherein David's injuries were described as:

"... severe crushing of the chest, with multiple rib fractures, severe cerebral concussion, with petechial hemorrhages of the brain, bilateral fractures of the clavicles."

Attached to the petition were affidavits of David's physicians, Drs. James H. Cain and Paul S. Blake, wherein they set forth the same diagnoses they had made upon completion of their respective examinations of David as above described. At no time was there information disclosed to the court that David was then suffering from an aorta aneurysm which may have been the result of the accident. Based upon the petition for settlement and such affidavits of Drs. Cain and Blake, the court on May 8, 1957, made its order approving the settlement.

Early in 1959, David was required by the army reserve, of which he was a member, to have a physical checkup. For this, he again engaged the services of Dr. Cain. In this checkup, the latter discovered the aorta aneurysm. He then reexamined the X-rays which had been taken shortly after the accident and at this time discovered that they disclosed the beginning of the process which produced the aneurysm. He promptly sent David to Dr. Jerome Grismer for an examination and opinion. The latter confirmed the finding of the aorta aneurysm and recommended immediate surgery therefor. This was performed by him at Mount Sinai Hospital in Minneapolis on March 10, 1959.

Shortly thereafter, David, having attained his majority, instituted the present action for additional damages due to the more serious injuries including the aorta aneurysm which he alleges proximately resulted from the accident. As indicated above, the prior order for settlement was vacated. In a memorandum made a part of the order vacating the settlement, the court stated:

"The facts material to a determination of the motion are without substantial dispute. The only disputed facts appear to be whether ... Mr. Roberts, former counsel for plaintiff, discussed plaintiff's injuries with Mr. Arvesen, counsel for defendant Zimmerman, immediately before the settlement agreement, and, further, whether or not there is a causal relationship between the accident and the aneurysm.

"Contrary to the ... suggestion in the affidavit of Mr. Roberts that he discussed the minor's injuries with Mr. Arvesen, the Court finds that no such discussion of the specific injuries claimed occurred prior to the settlement agreement on March 5, 1957.

"... the Court finds that although the aneurysm now existing is causally related to the accident, such finding is for the purpose of the motions only and is based solely upon the opinion expressed by Dr. Cain (Exhibit 'F'), which, so far as the Court can find from the numerous affidavits and statements of fact by counsel, stands without dispute.

"The mistake concerning the existence of the aneurysm was not mutual. For reasons which do not appear, plaintiff's doctor failed to ascertain its existence. By reason of the failure of plaintiff's counsel to use available rules of discovery, plaintiff's doctor and all his representatives did not learn that defendants and their agents knew of its existence and possible serious consequences. Except for the character of the concealment in the light of plaintiff's minority, the Court would, I believe, be justified in denying plaintiff's motion to vacate, leaving him to whatever questionable remedy he may have against his doctor and against his lawyer.

"That defendants' counsel concealed the knowledge they had is not disputed. The essence of the application of the above rule is the character of the concealment. Was it done under circumstances that defendants must be charged with knowledge that plaintiff did not know of the injury? If so, an enriching advantage was gained for defendants at plaintiff's expense. There is no doubt of the good faith of both defendants' counsel. There is no doubt that during the course of the negotiations, when the parties were in an adversary relationship, no rule required or duty rested upon defendants or their representatives to disclose this knowledge. However, once the agreement to settle was reached, it is difficult to characterize the parties' relationship as adverse. At this point all parties were interested in securing Court approval....

"When the adversary nature of the negotiations concluded in a settlement, the procedure took on the posture of a joint application to the Court, at least so far as the facts upon which the Court could and must approve settlement is concerned. It is here that the true nature of the concealment appears, and defendants' failure to act affirmatively, after having been given a copy of the application for approval, can only be defendants' decision to take a calculated risk that the settlement would be final...."

1.   The principles applicable to the court's authority to vacate settlements made on behalf of minors and approved by it appear well established. With reference thereto, we have held that the court in its discretion may vacate such a settlement, even though it is not induced by fraud or bad faith, where it is shown that in the accident the minor sustained separate and distinct injuries which were not known or considered by the court at the time settlement was approved....

2.   From the foregoing it is clear that in the instant case the court did not abuse its discretion in setting aside the settlement which it had approved on plaintiff's behalf while he was still a minor. It is undisputed that neither he nor his counsel nor his medical attendants were aware that at the time settlement was made he was suffering from an aorta aneurysm which may have resulted from the accident. The seriousness of this disability is indicated by Dr. Hannah's report indicating the imminent danger of death therefrom. This was known by counsel for both defendants but was not disclosed to the court at the time it was petitioned to approve the settlement. While no canon of ethics or legal obligation may have required them to inform plaintiff or his counsel with respect thereto, or to advise the court therein, it did become obvious to them at the time, that the settlement then made did not contemplate or take into consideration the disability described. This fact opened the way for the court to later exercise its discretion in vacating the settlement and under the circumstances described we cannot say that there was any abuse of discretion on the part of the court in so doing under Rule 60.02(6) of Rules of Civil Procedure [which permits the court to set aside a judgment on motion

made more than a year after entry for "any other reason justifying relief from the operation of the judgment"] . . . .

■ ROGOSHESKE, J., [who served as the trial judge in the case and was subsequently elevated to the Supreme Court,] took no part in the consideration or decision of this case.

———

Disclosure of Adverse Evidence

What was Zimmerman's duty to Spaulding? What responsibility did the defense-paid doctor have to Spaulding? What were Zimmerman's lawyers' responsibilities to Zimmerman? To the doctor they hired? To Spaulding?

Fed.R.Civ.P. 35(a) provides that upon motion showing good cause a court may order a party to submit to a physical or mental examination. Rule 35(b) provides that the medical report from any such examination (or any examination agreed to by the parties without court order) shall be supplied to the party examined upon that party's request. In general, the turnover obligation exists whether the examination is ordered by the court or agreed to by the parties. Similar rules apply in state courts.

Spaulding's lawyers could have obtained a copy of the defense expert's report if they had asked the right questions or made the right motions. Does the negligence of Spaulding's lawyers (or of one or more of his doctors) excuse or mitigate the silence of Zimmerman's lawyers (or the doctor they hired)?

The result in *Spaulding* turns on the special responsibilities of a court toward a minor and the special responsibilities of lawyers to the court. If Spaulding had attained the age of majority, the court would have left Spaulding to seek redress against his doctor and his lawyer. Does this game-like framework, in which clients are bound by the actions of their lawyers, lose sight of David Spaulding? Why doesn't the court base its ruling on the seriousness of the undisclosed facts rather than on Spaulding's minority?

Absent special circumstances, such as mutual mistake, fraud on the court or concealment from the court, courts will not set aside a judgment because a lawyer has concealed adverse evidence from the opposing party. In Brown v. County of Genesee,[3] an employment discrimination case, plaintiff Brown through her lawyer made it clear to defense counsel during settlement negotiations that Brown "would not settle unless [she] were paid at a rate of pay she would have received had she been hired on June 16, 1982." Both Brown and her lawyer believed the highest rate of pay to which this would entitle her was Step C pay; and they therefore settled for Step C pay. In fact, she would have been eligible for Step D pay, a higher rate. At the time of settlement, defense counsel "did not know, but he believed it probable that Brown and her counsel" mistakenly believed that

---

3.   872 F.2d 169 (6th Cir.1989).

Step C was the ceiling for employees hired on June 16, 1982. Defense counsel said nothing to correct Brown and her lawyer's mistaken belief. The district court vacated the settlement, but the Sixth Circuit reversed, holding that, "absent some misrepresentation or fraudulent conduct, [the defendant] had no duty to advise [Brown or her counsel] of any such factual error. . . ." The court pointed out that Brown's counsel could have discovered the correct information about the pay scales by either examining public documents or asking the right questions in discovery: "The failure of Brown's counsel . . . cannot be imputed to the [defendant] as unethical or fraudulent."[4]

Apparently only one case, Virzi v. Grand Trunk Warehouse & Cold Storage Co.,[5] states that a lawyer has a duty to reveal adverse information to an opposing party in civil litigation. In *Virzi* the court set aside a $35,000 settlement in a personal injury action because the plaintiff's lawyer had concealed the fact that the plaintiff, viewed by both parties as an excellent witness, had died of causes unrelated to the lawsuit. The court said:

> Candor and honesty necessarily require disclosure of such a significant fact as the death of one's client. Opposing counsel does not have to deal with his adversary as he would deal in the marketplace. Standards of ethics require greater honesty, greater candor, and greater disclosure, even though it might not be in the interest of the client or his estate.[6]

As in *Spaulding,* however, the specific holding in *Virzi* rests on a concealment from the court, rather than on a failure to disclose to an adverse party: Because the plaintiff's lawyer did not move for a substitution of parties under Rule 25 of the Federal Rules of Civil Procedure, the court "enter[ed] an order of settlement for a non-existent party." Causing the court to do this constituted concealment and justified setting aside the settlement.[7]

In civil litigation, is a lawyer who knows of evidence that would establish the claim or defense of the opposing party (a) required to remain silent, (b) required to disclose the adverse evidence, or (c) permitted to take either path? Suppose a lawyer represents an apartment house landlord. A tenant has sued on behalf of his infant child, who sustained serious injury from falling either through a negligently created gap in a porch railing or

4. 872 F.2d at 175.

5. 571 F.Supp. 507 (E.D.Mich.1983).

6. 571 F.Supp. at 512. ABA Formal Op. 94–387 (Sept. 26, 1994) rejects *Virzi*'s dictum that a duty of candor exists in third-party negotiations: a lawyer may negotiate and settle a legal claim that the lawyer knows is barred by the statute of limitations without communicating this information to the adverse party. The lawyer has an obligation to pursue the client's interest in a settlement and is prohibited from volunteering the information without the client's consent, citing M.R. 1.3 (diligence) and M.R. 1.6 (confidentiality of information). A dissent chided the majority for encouraging "sharp practice."

7. ABA Formal Op. 94–397 (Sept. 18, 1995) agrees with the result in *Virzi* but on somewhat different grounds. When the lawyer's client dies, the claim is transferred to a new party–the personal representative, who may or may not be the lawyer's client. Entering into a settlement agreement under these circumstances would misrepresent the lawyer's changed position.

down the porch stairs. The landlord's lawyer has discovered an eyewitness, unknown to the tenant, who will support the claim that the infant fell through the gap. Without this witness the case will be dismissed for failure of proof. An ethics opinion on these facts concluded that "the conduct of the defendant's attorney [in moving to dismiss the plaintiff's case without disclosing] is not professionally improper. The fact of infancy does not call for a different reply."[8]

Consider a further hypothetical, also based on a well-known ethics opinion.[9] At a sentencing hearing, the judge asks the prosecutor whether the convicted defendant has a prior criminal record. The prosecutor replies that he does not. Defense counsel, who knows that her client has been convicted of two armed robberies in another jurisdiction, remains silent. The trial judge, "because this is a first offense," gives the defendant a suspended sentence. Did defense counsel act properly? Should she have volunteered information about the prior conviction? What if she had argued for a suspended sentence on the basis of the defendant's "clean record?" For "a clean record in this state."[10]

Procedural rules impose duties on litigating parties that alter the responsibilities of their lawyers. The 1993 amendments of Rule 26 illustrate the effect of procedural rules on the disclosure obligations of lawyers. The procedural rules impose requirements on parties that lawyers are required to implement; as such, the rules displace the lawyer's general obligation under the professional duty of confidentiality not to volunteer adverse information to an opposing party. The controversial amendment requires mutual disclosure of "discoverable information relevant to disputed facts alleged with particularity in the pleadings." Each party is required, "without awaiting a discovery request," to provide to other parties the following information "relevant to disputed facts alleged with particularity in the pleadings:" (1) identity of "each individual likely to have discoverable information;" (2) a copy or description of "all documents, data compilations, and tangible things in the possession, custody, or control of the party that are relevant to disputed facts; and (3) information concerning damages and insurance. Rule 26(a)(1). With reference to expert wit-

---

8. New York County Lawyer's Ass'n Comm. on Prof. Ethics, Op. 309 (1933). Why the double negative in the Committee's formulation? In his autobiography, Samuel Williston recounts a situation in which he, as a young lawyer, sat silently (and uncomfortably) as an opposing witness was unable to supply a crucial fact established by a document in Williston's possession. Samuel B. Williston, Life and Law 271 (1940), discussed in Charles P. Curtis, It's Your Law 17 (1954).

9. ABA Formal Op. 287 (June 27, 1953).

10. The majority of the ethics committee, relying on Canon 37 of the Canons of Professional Ethics, concluded that, if the law-yer's information came from her client, she should remain silent. A concurring member stated that the same position should be taken even if the lawyer's information came from her own work rather than from the client. Two dissenting members stated that Canons 15, 22, 29 and 41, taken together, "require the lawyer to see that his client gives to the court the truth about [the client's] criminal record or the lawyer must do so himself." Does Model Rule 1.6, extending the duty of confidentiality to all "information relating to the representation of a client," resolve the clash between Canon 37 and the other canons cited?

nesses, parties must disclose the identity and report of any person" who may be used at trial to present evidence" as an expert witness. Moreover, under Rule 26(g), a lawyer must sign all disclosure and discovery requests and responses. This signature constitutes "a certification that to the best of the signer's knowledge, information and belief, formed *after a reasonable inquiry*, the disclosure is complete and correct as of the time it is made." (Emphasis added.) False answers, whether knowingly or negligently made, violate the discovery rules. Under the amended rule, would Zimmerman's lawyers have been required to disclose to Spaulding their information concerning the extent of Spaulding's injuries?

The continuing controversy over advance disclosure, viewed by many trial lawyers as inconsistent with the adversary system, reflects the tension between the lawyer's partisan role and the rulemakers' desire to have disputes decided on the basis of accurate and complete information. Federal district courts have an option to depart by local rule from the disclosure provisions of Rule 26; about one-half of federal district courts, including most metropolitan areas, have done so. The local rules cover the entire range between the old regime of no up-front required disclosure (disclosure only after proper request by the opposing party) and various degrees of up-front disclosure.[11] The Civil Rules Advisory Committee is currently reconsidering disclosure and discovery practice.[12] Concern about loss of national uniformity in federal procedure, in combination with continuing hostility to required disclosure, has resulted in a new proposed Rule 26 (August 1998). If adopted, the amended rule would restore national uniformity and largely limit initial disclosure obligations to identification of witnesses and documents that support the claims or defenses of the party. A party would no longer be obligated to disclose witnesses or documents that would harm its position. Final adoption of a revised Rule 26 is not expected before December 2000.

Procedural rules, however, provide no help to the Spauldings or Browns of this world, whose lawyers fail to ask the right questions. Normally, the legal system does not protect a party in civil litigation from the laziness, incompetence or failure of the party's lawyer. In Link v. Wabash R. Co.,[13] upholding an involuntary dismissal of an injured railroad worker's federal tort claim for failure of his lawyer to attend a pretrial conference, Justice Harlan stated:

> There is certainly no merit to the contention that dismissal of petitioner's claim because of his counsel's unexcused conduct imposes an unjust penalty on the client. Petitioner voluntarily chose this attorney as his representative in the action, and he cannot now avoid the consequences of the acts or omissions of this freely selected agent. Any other notion would be wholly inconsistent with our system of represen-

11. See Lauren K. Robel, Mandatory Disclosure and Local Abrogation: In Search of a Theory of Optional Rules, 14 Rev. of Litig. 49 (1994).

12. See T. Willging et al., Discovery and Disclosure Practice, Problems, and Proposals for Change (Fed. Jud'l Center 1997).

13. 370 U.S. 626 (1962).

tative litigation, in which each party is deemed bound by the acts of his lawyer-agent and is considered to have "notice of all facts, notice of which can be charged upon the attorney."[14]

2.   Introduction to Ethical Codes

Three times in its history the American Bar Association (ABA) has issued a model code for regulation of the conduct of lawyers and a fourth review is underway in 1998–2000. As a voluntary organization of lawyers, the ABA's actions do not have the force of law. However, the ABA has long been recognized as the leading national organization of lawyers, and it has succeeded in convincing state courts, state legislatures, federal courts and federal agencies to adopt some form of its model codes, giving the codes, as so adopted, the effect of law. The rules as adopted by individual states contain many significant departures from the ABA recommended texts; the reader should not assume, for example, that the current text of the ABA Model Rules of Professional Conduct is "law" in any state.

Canons of Professional Ethics

In the 19th century the states left regulation of the profession to common law precedent and occasional statutory pronouncements. Alabama adopted the first formal code of ethics in 1887, codifying a series of published lectures on ethics by David Hoffman of Baltimore and George Sharswood of Philadelphia. A number of other states followed Alabama's lead in the ensuing two decades.

The ABA in 1908 adopted the Canons of Professional Ethics, alluded to in *Spaulding*. As with most state ethics codes of the era, the Canons owed a great debt to the Hoffman and Sharswood antecedents. The Canons originally numbered 32, but expanded to 47 by the end of the 1930s. Even at 47, the Canons were brief, written in broad language with a high moral tone. Criticism of the Canons centered on the need for more specificity. Despite their ambiguities, bar associations and state courts gave the Canons wide recognition. They remained in force in the states until the early 1970s.

Model Code of Professional Responsibility

In 1964 Lewis F. Powell, Jr., then president of the ABA, appointed a committee to examine the Canons and suggest revisions. This committee proposed the Model Code of Professional Responsibility, which the ABA

---

14.   370 U.S. at 633–34. Justice Black, dissenting, complained that visiting "the sins or faults or delinquencies of a lawyer ... upon his client ... is to ignore the practicalities and realities of the lawyer-client relationship." 370 U.S. at 646. The injured worker, having lost his damage claim due to his lawyer's failure, is left with the possibility of a malpractice remedy against the lawyer. Some courts, however, are willing to give the client a second chance in some circumstances. See, e.g., Carroll v. Abbott Laboratories, Inc., 32 Cal.3d 892, 187 Cal. Rptr. 592, 654 P.2d 775, (1982) (client may obtain relief from an involuntary dismissal based on his lawyer's "positive misconduct" or "excusable neglect," but not for "inexcusable neglect" as in the failure in this case to respond to discovery requests).

adopted in 1969. Almost every state thereafter adopted some form of the Model Code. The Model Code also became operative in federal courts because most federal district courts adopted the Model Code by local court rule.

The 1969 Model Code has a much more complicated format than the 1909 Canons. The Model Code contains nine Canons, which function as chapter headings. Each Canon contains both Ethical Considerations [ECs] and Disciplinary Rules [DRs]. The Preamble and Preliminary Statement of the Model Code explains its structure as follows:

> The Canons are statements of axiomatic norms, expressing in general terms the standards of professional conduct expected of lawyers in their relationships with the public, with the legal system, and with the legal profession. They embody the general concepts from which the Ethical Considerations and the Disciplinary Rules are derived.

> The Ethical Considerations are aspirational in character and represent the objectives toward which every member of the profession should strive. They constitute a body of principles upon which the lawyer can rely for guidance in many specific situations.

> The Disciplinary Rules, unlike the Ethical Considerations, are mandatory in character. The Disciplinary Rules state the minimum level of conduct below which no lawyer can fall without being subject to disciplinary action.... An enforcing agency, in applying the Disciplinary Rules, may find interpretive guidance in the basic principles embodied in the Canons and in the objectives, reflected in the Ethical Considerations.

This statement suggests greater clarity to the Model Code's structure than in fact exists. For example, although the Ethical Considerations (ECs) supposedly are aspirational statements, some sound like commands, e.g., EC 5–15: "A lawyer should never...." Other ECs elaborate on the Disciplinary Rules (DRs) by providing concrete examples of what the latter mean, e.g., EC 3–8 and EC 5–24. Not surprisingly, courts and bar disciplinary bodies have sometimes applied Ethical Considerations as though they were Disciplinary Rules.

Aside from problems of structure, the Model Code has been criticized for embodying outdated assumptions about what lawyers do and how they do it. The Model Code primarily reflects a vision of lawyers in a courtroom, as equal advocates competing under the watchful eye of a judge, who stands ready to correct overzealousness by either party. This vision provides little practical guidance to a lawyer negotiating a transaction, drafting documents, or counseling clients, or even one engaged in pretrial matters. The Model Code also envisions lawyers operating alone in practice or with a few partners, equal in status and responsibility. Of course, lawyers today practice in large organizations—large law firms, government offices, corporations—with hierarchical structures in which lawyers at various levels have different degrees of responsibility and control over their work. Finally, the Model Code imagines a client as an individual, not a collection of individuals nor an inanimate legal entity such as a corporation or a government agency. Thus, the Model Code leaves a lawyer representing a corporation or a class with little enlightenment on such basic issues as the identity of the client.

Model Rules of Professional Conduct

ABA President William Spann in 1977 appointed a Commission on the Evaluation of Professional Responsibility, popularly known as the Kutak Commission after its Chairman Robert J. Kutak, to recommend changes to the Model Code of Professional Responsibility. The Kutak Commission concluded that the ethics rules needed a new formulation with a cleaner structure and a basis in a modern conception of the lawyer's role. The Kutak Commission, unlike the committee that drafted the Model Code, worked largely in the open: The Commission held public hearings and circulated its working drafts to the bar and public alike for comment. The resulting debate over the professional responsibility of lawyers was unprecedented in scope and intensity. In 1983, the ABA House of Delegates, after amending several key provisions of the Kutak final draft, adopted the Model Rules of Professional Conduct, with a recommendation to states and to federal courts and agencies that the Model Rules replace their respective versions of the Model Code.[15]

The format of the Model Rules follows that used by the Restatements of Law produced by the American Law Institute: black-letter rules followed by explanatory comments. The Rules also reflect a more modern concept of a lawyer's role. For example, M.R. 1.13 addresses the lawyer who represents an entity as distinct from an individual; M.R. 2.1 addresses the lawyer as advisor; M.R. 2.2, the lawyer as intermediary; M.R. 2.3, the lawyer as evaluator of a matter for the use of third parties; M.R. 5.1 describes the responsibilities of a partner or supervisory lawyer; M.R. 5.2 is the counterpart rule for the lawyer who is a subordinate.

As of July 1999, 41 states and the District of Columbia had adopted some version of the Model Rules. Some states—for example, New York, North Carolina and Oregon—have decided to retain their version of the Model Code although often with numerous adjustments based on provisions in the Model Rules. California's code is unique; it has elements of both the Model Rules and the Model Code, but omits significant material found in both. The federal courts, including the Supreme Court, cite both the Model Rules and the Model Code as authority in decisions concerning a lawyer's professional conduct.

---

15. The legislative history of the Model Rules is discussed by Ted Schneyer, Professionalism as Bar Politics: The Making of the Model Rules of Professional Conduct, 1989 Law & Soc. Inquiry 677. For a more detailed history, see ABA Center for Professional Responsibility, The Legislative History of the Model Rules of Professional Conduct (1987).

ABA Ethics 2000 Commission

In 1998 the ABA launched a broad review of the Model Rules of Professional Conduct. A special commission, referred to as the "Ethics 2000 Commission," is gathering information, holding hearings, and publishing drafts of possible revisions. Important revisions of the rules dealing with confidentiality and conflict of interest have already been considered by the Commission. It remains unclear whether the project will result in a package of amendments to the existing Model Rules or recommendation of a new code in its entirety. The Commission is expected to report to the ABA in 2000.

Ethics Rules in Federal Courts

No special set of ethics rules for federal courts currently exist. For many years individual federal courts drew on general principles to decide legal ethics questions as they arose. In the twentieth century, accompanying the promulgation of recommended codes by the ABA and state adoption of amended versions, federal district courts issued a variety of local rules on the subject.[16] Moreover, the federal courts of appeals have exercised great freedom in deciding ethics issues.[17] Most of these local rules adopt either the ethics code in effect in the state in which the district court sits or one or another of the ABA model codes. The resulting disuniformity—from the state in which the federal court sits and among federal courts across the nation—led the Standing Committee on Rules and Practice of the U.S. Judicial Conference, after an extensive study, to refer proposed Federal Rules of Attorney Conduct to the five rule advisory committees of the Conference.[18] The ten rules, if later approved by the Standing Committee, the Judicial Conference and the Supreme Court, would replace nearly 100 disparate local rules. The proposed rules adopt an *Erie* approach in that the basic standard of Rule 1 is to apply the ethics code of the state in which the district court sits as default standards for federal court proceedings. The other nine rules provide a uniform national rule for certain matters that are thought to be of special significance to the integrity of federal courts or reflect special federal policies. These nine rules, if adopted, would provide a uniform ethics rule in federal courts, perhaps different from the state rule, on the following matters: confidentiality and its exceptions; conflicts of interest; candor toward the tribunal; lawyer as witness; truthfulness of

---

16. Under Fed.R.Civ.P. 83, federal district courts may establish their own rules for lawyers practicing in the federal court. See, e.g., United States v. Walsh, 699 F.Supp. 469, 472 (D.N.J.1988) (Model Rule 1.11 applies in district court, not Rule 1.11 as amended in New Jersey's version of the Rules).

17. See Ted Schneyer, Nostalgia in the Fifth Circuit: Holding the Line on Litigation Conflicts Though Federal Common Law, 16 Rev.Litig. 537 (1997); and Bruce A. Green, Whose Rules of Professional Con-

duct Should Govern Lawyers in Federal Court and How Should The Rules Be Created?, 64 Geo.Wash.L.Rev. 460 (1996).

18. For the text of the proposed rules, see 14 ABA*BNA Law. Man. Prof. Conduct 82 (March 4, 1998), with an explanatory comment at p. 78. For the prior study, see Daniel Coquillette and M. Leary, Working Papers of the Committee on Rules of Practice and Procedure: Special Studies of Federal Rules Governing Attorney Conduct, Administrative Conf. of the U.S. Courts (Sept.1997).

statements to others; and lawyers' communications with persons represented by counsel.

Other Sources of Ethical Guidance

In May 1998 the American Law Institute approved the final draft of the Restatement (Third) of the Law Governing Lawyers. It will be referred to in this book as "the Restatement" with references to other restatements given their full titles. Until the final text is published, the Restatement is available only in the form of a series of proposed final drafts. The Restatement has already been cited in a large number of judicial decisions and is likely to have a substantial influence. A number of its provisions will be quoted or discussed at relevant places in these materials.

The ABA has generated two other important sets of rules governing the conduct of lawyers: the ABA Standards Relating to the Administration of Criminal Justice and the Model Code of Judicial Conduct. The Standards, which have not been embodied in formal rules of courts or agencies, do not have the same force of law as the adopted versions of the Model Code or Model Rules. However, state and federal courts frequently rely on the Standards as authority for proper conduct by prosecutors and defense counsel. The Model Code of Judicial Conduct, originally adopted by the ABA in 1972, applies to judges and has been adopted in most states and the federal courts. A thorough revision in 1990 resulted in a new Model Code of Judicial Conduct, which has now resulted in revised codes in many states and in a new code applicable to federal judges. The regulation of judges in these codes imposes controls on relationships between judges and lawyers.

Ethics opinions are another source of guidance. The ABA Standing Committee on Ethics and Professional Responsibility issues formal and informal opinions on ethical questions. These opinions do not have the force of law, but they are sometimes cited by courts. In theory a formal opinion responds to a question of general interest, whereas an informal opinion is a response to a question "comparatively narrow in scope."[19] Some ethics opinions limit themselves to "ethics" and refuse to take a position on matters of "law."

State and local bars also issue ethics opinions. Some states publish editions of the state ethical code with annotations that include state and local ethics opinions. State and local bar ethics opinions may provide guidance and usually offer a good defense to a disciplinary charge, but they do not have the status of law. Court decisions provide the only truly authoritative interpretation of ethics rules.

---

19. ABA, Opinions of the Committee on Professional Ethics 6 (1967); ABA Standing Committee on Ethics and Professional Responsibility, Rules of Procedure 3. See Wolfram, Modern Legal Ethics 65–67 (1986) for a general discussion of ethics committees and opinions. The ethics opinions of the ABA are reviewed and criticized in Ted Finman and Ted Schneyer, The Role of Bar Association Ethics Opinions in Regulating Lawyer Conduct, 29 UCLA L. Rev. 67 (1981) (analyzing 21 opinions issued under 1969 Model Code).

Other voluntary associations of lawyers promulgate ethical codes applicable to their members. The Federal Bar Association, composed primarily of lawyers engaged in the practice of federal law, adopted the Model Rules of Professional Conduct for Federal Lawyers in 1990. The Association of American Trial Lawyers, composed primarily of claimants' lawyers, became dissatisfied with the process and emerging content of the ABA's Model Rules; it published a competing ethics code in 1982, the American Lawyer's Code of Conduct (ALCC). Organizations of specialized practitioners often publish special rules for their members (e.g., matrimonial lawyers). Several major law book publishers issue annual volumes compiling most of the ethics codes we have mentioned.[20]

Ethics Rules and *Spaulding*

The Canons of Professional Ethics were in effect in Minnesota when the *Spaulding* case was decided. The court stated that "no canon of ethics or legal obligation may have required [defense counsel] to inform plaintiff [of the aneurysm]." Is that a correct statement? Read the following provisions of the Canons of Professional Ethics in your standards supplement: Canon 15 (How Far a Lawyer May Go in Supporting a Client's Cause), Canon 22 (Candor and Fairness), Canon 31 (Responsibility for Litigation), Canon 37 (Confidences of a Client), Canon 41 (Discovery of Imposition and Deception) and Canon 44 (Withdrawal From Employment as Attorney or Counsel).

Minnesota adopted a version of the Model Rules of Professional Conduct in 1985. If the Model Rules had been in effect at the time, and Spaulding had been an adult rather than a minor, would the defense lawyers be required, permitted or prohibited from disclosing his life-threatening condition to him? See especially Model Rules 1.2(d), 1.3, 1.4, 1.6, 1.16, 2.1, 3.3, 4.1, and 8.4. These rules and their comments should be read carefully at this time.

3.   REFLECTIONS ON SPAULDING

What Really Happened in *Spaulding*?

The opinion in the *Spaulding* case provides a sparse recital of facts that leaves many questions unanswered. A recent study of the appellate record, supplemented by interviews with surviving lawyers and family members, reveals the following additional facts:[21]

- The accident occurred late in the day in August 1956 at a rural intersection. Visibility in both directions was partially obscured by

---

20. Thomas D. Morgan and Ronald D. Rotunda, 1999 Selected Standards of Professional Responsibility (Foundation Press); Stephen Gillers and Roy D. Simon, Jr., 1998 Regulation of Lawyers: Statutes and Standards (Little, Brown & Co.); John S. Dzienkowski, Selected Statutes, Rules and Standards on the Legal Profession (West Publishing Co.1998).

21. See Roger C. Cramton & Lori P. Knowles, Professional Secrecy and Its Exceptions: *Spaulding v. Zimmerman* Revisited, 83 Minn.L.Rev. 63–65 (1998).

tall corn in the adjoining fields. There were no stop signs at the intersection. Twelve persons were in the two colliding cars; all were injured and two were killed.

- David Spaulding and his father were passengers in the Zimmerman car. They were employees of a road construction firm operated by the Zimmerman family and were being driven home at the end of the work day. The other occupants of the car were also employees. John Zimmerman's brother was killed in the accident.

- The Ledermann vehicle, driven by Florian Ledermann, age 15, driving his father's car on a farm permit, contained the Ledermann family, which was on its way to the county fair where daughter Elaine, age 12, also killed in the crash, was to participate in the 4–H dress review. Their father's injuries left him unable to operate the family farm.

- Spaulding's lawyer, Roberts, was a young lawyer at the beginning of his career. Arveson, the lawyer for the Zimmerman family and its liability insurer, was an experienced trial lawyer and so was the lawyer for the Ledermann family and its insurer.

- The individual defendants were neither informed of Dr. Hannah's report nor consulted about whether the aneurysm should be disclosed to Spaulding. Dr. Hannah's report was sent to representatives of the insurers, but it is not clear that its disclosure was the subject of meaningful consultation as distinct from routine forwarding. The defense lawyers apparently made the decision not to disclose themselves.

- The claims of all the victims of the accident were settled at the same time. The settlements were paid by contributions from the insurers of both cars and were within the policy limits. David Spaulding received $6,500 of the total payments of $40,000.

- At the time of the accident, contributory negligence was a complete bar to recovery and Minnesota lawyers were adjusting to a new regime of broad discovery in civil cases based on the Federal Rules of Civil Procedure.

- After remand to the trial court, the case settled. Spaulding received an additional award of unknown amount.

How do these facts affect the likelihood of whether, if consulted by their lawyers, the Zimmerman and Ledermann families would have informed Spaulding of his physical condition?

Professional Failure

Spaulding is a good illustration of the pervasiveness of professional failure. Each of the participating professionals may have been been guilty of professional failure. The law deals with professional failure primarily through malpractice liability and professional discipline. Yet its prevention rests in large part on internalized standards of professional conduct that are written in the hearts and minds of each lawyer and are reinforced by the monitoring and criticism of other lawyers. How should individual lawyers and law firms deal with problems of professional failure, inevitable to some degree in any professional practice? Who among us can claim that we have never, out of carelessness or inattention, made a mistake that hurt others? Yet individual conscience, quality control measures in law firms, and surrounding institutional arrangements can have dramatic effects in reducing the frequency and magnitude of the harms caused by professional failure. Charles Bosk, in addressing professional failure on the part of surgeons, argues that practice structures and professional ideologies have a large role in causing departures from competency, such as norms that support silence about substance abuse by medical colleagues.[22]

Lawyer conduct in *Spaulding*, for example, was influenced by the built-in conflict of interest of defense insurance counsel (who calls the shots, the insured defendant or the liability insurer?) and by the common professional attitude that clients are only interested in winning (so why consult them about whether Spaulding's condition should be disclosed to him?).[23] Bosk's thesis is suggested by his title: ''Forgive and Remember'': Professionals need to forgive themselves and each other for their inevitable failures, while striving to correct through memory and reform the circumstances and conditions that lead to professional failure.

Richard Pemberton, then a young lawyer in the firm representing the Ledermann family but later a leader of the Minnesota bar, believes he was asked to brief and argue the case in the Minnesota Supreme Court because his senior partner found the task a distasteful one, as did Pemberton.

> [W]hen I briefed and argued the *Spaulding* case in the Supreme Court, I was within the first few months of legal practice and was attempting to defend a senior partner's handling of the matter in the trial court. After 20 years of practice, I would like to think that I would have disclosed the aneurysm of the aorta as an act of humanity and without regard to the legalities involved, just as I surely would now. You might suggest to your students in the course on professional responsibility that a pretty good rule for them to practice respecting professional conduct is to do the right thing.[24]

What was ''the right thing'' for the defense lawyers in *Spaulding* to do?

C.   PERSPECTIVES ON MORALITY OF THE LAWYER'S ROLE

1.   LAWYER AS FRIEND?

In examining the question, ''Can a lawyer be a good person?'', Professor Charles Fried has sought to justify the lawyer's disregard for the

---

22. Charles L. Bosk, Forgive and Remember: Managing Medical Failure (1979) (discussing the way surgeons recognize, manage, control and sometimes deny professional failure).

23. See Cramton & Knowles, supra, at 91–96.

24. Quoted in Cramton & Knowles, supra, at 126.

interests of others by drawing an analogy to friendship:[25]

> [M]y analogy shall be to friendship, where the freedom to choose and to be chosen expresses our freedom to hold something of ourselves in reserve, in reserve even from the universalizing claims of morality. These personal ties and the claims they engender may be all-consuming, as with a close friend or family member, or they may be limited, special-purpose claims, as in the case of the client or patient. The special-purpose claim is one in which the beneficiary, the client, is entitled to all the special consideration within the limits of the relationship which we accord to a friend or a loved one. It is not that the claims of the client are less intense or demanding: they are only more limited in their scope. After all, the ordinary concept of friendship provides only an analogy. . . .
>
> . . .
>
> If[, however,] personal integrity lies at the foundation of the lawyer's right to treat his client as a friend, then surely consideration for personal integrity—his own and others'—must limit what he can do in friendship. Consideration for personal integrity forbids me to lie, cheat, or humiliate, whether in my own interests or those of a friend, so surely they prohibit such conduct on behalf of a client, one's legal friend. . . . [26]

Lawyers, of course, may easily be distinguished from "real" friends. For example, unlike friends, lawyers are paid and are granted a special franchise by the state to give legal advice, and friendship is an "open" contract that the parties are continuously free to redefine or revoke.[27] Do such distinctions suggest different moral responsibilities for lawyers? William Simon describes Fried's portrayal of the lawyer-client relationship as more like prostitution than friendship.[28]

What would a good friend of Zimmerman's have advised him to do?

2. Lawyer's Partisan and Amoral Role

Richard Wasserstrom "Lawyers as Professionals: Some Moral Issues"
5 Human Rights 1 (1975).[29]

In this paper I examine two moral criticisms of lawyers which, if well-founded, are fundamental. . . .

25. Charles Fried, The Lawyer as Friend: The Moral Foundations of the Lawyer–Client Relation, 85 Yale L.J. 1060 (1976).

26. Id. at 1071, 1083.

27. For a critique of Fried's analogy to friendship, see Edward A. Dauer and Arthur A. Leff, Correspondence, 86 Yale L.J. 573 (1977).

28. William H. Simon, The Ideology of Advocacy, 1978 Wis.L.Rev. 29, 108.

29. Copyright © 1975 by the American Bar Association, Section of Individual Rights

The first criticism centers around the lawyer's stance toward the world at large. The accusation is that the lawyer-client relationship renders the lawyer at best systematically amoral and at worst more than occasionally immoral in his or her dealings with the rest of mankind.

The second criticism focuses upon the relationship between the lawyer and the client. Here the charge is that it is the lawyer-client relationship which is morally objectionable because it is a relationship in which the lawyer dominates and in which the lawyer typically, and perhaps inevitably, treats the client in both an impersonal and a paternalistic fashion.

Although I am undecided about the ultimate merits of either criticism, I am convinced that each is deserving of careful articulation and assessment, and that each contains insights that deserve more acknowledgment than they often receive. My ambition is, therefore, more to exhibit the relevant considerations and to stimulate additional reflection, than it is to provide any very definite conclusions.

I.

... [T]he first issue I propose to examine concerns the ways the professional-client relationship affects the professional's stance toward the world at large. The primary question that is presented is whether there is adequate justification for the kind of moral universe that comes to be inhabited by the lawyer as he or she goes through professional life. For at best the lawyer's world is a simplified moral world; often it is an amoral one; and more than occasionally, perhaps, an overtly immoral one.

... [O]ne central feature of the professions in general and of law in particular is that there is a special, complicated relationship between the professional, and the client or patient. For each of the parties in this relationship, but especially for the professional, the behavior that is involved is to a very significant degree, what I call, role-differentiated behavior. . . .

. . .

... [W]here the attorney-client relationship exists, it is often appropriate and many times even obligatory for the attorney to do things that, all other things being equal, an ordinary person need not, and should not do. What is characteristic of this role of a lawyer is the lawyer's required indifference to a wide variety of ends and consequences that in other contexts would be of undeniable moral significance. Once a lawyer represents a client, the lawyer has a duty to make his or her expertise fully available in the realization of the end sought by the client, irrespective, for the most part, of the moral worth to which the end will be put or the character of the client who seeks to utilize it. Provided that the end sought is not illegal, the lawyer is, in essence, an amoral technician whose peculiar skills and knowledge in respect to the law are available to those with whom the relationship of client is established. The question, as I have indicated, is

and Responsibilities, and Southern Methodist University.

whether this particular and pervasive feature of professionalism is itself justifiable. At a minimum, I do not think any of the typical, simple answers will suffice.

One such answer focuses upon and generalizes from the criminal defense lawyer.... The received view within the profession (and to a lesser degree within the society at large) is that having once agreed to represent the client, the lawyer is under an obligation to do his or her best to defend that person at trial, irrespective, for instance, even of the lawyer's belief in the client's innocence....

But ... the irrelevance of the guilt or innocence of an accused client by no means exhausts the altered perspective of the lawyer's conscience, even in criminal cases. For in the course of defending an accused, an attorney may have, as a part of his or her duty of representation, the obligation to invoke procedures and practices which are themselves morally objectionable and of which the lawyer in other contexts might thoroughly disapprove. And these situations, I think, are somewhat less comfortable to confront. For example, in California, the case law permits a defendant in a rape case to secure in some circumstances an order from the court requiring the complaining witness, that is the rape victim, to submit to a psychiatric examination before trial.[2] For no other crime is such a pretrial remedy available. In no other case can the victim of a crime be required to undergo psychiatric examination at the request of the defendant on the ground that the results of the examination may help the defendant prove that the offense did not take place. I think such a rule is wrong and is reflective of the sexist bias of the law in respect to rape.... Nonetheless, it appears to be part of the role-differentiated obligation of a lawyer for a defendant charged with rape to seek to take advantage of this particular rule of law— irrespective of the independent moral view he or she may have of the rightness or wrongness of such a rule.

Nor, it is important to point out, is this peculiar, strikingly amoral behavior limited to the lawyer involved with the workings of the criminal law. Most clients come to lawyers to get the lawyers to help them do things that they could not easily do without the assistance provided by the lawyer's special competence....

And in each case, the role-differentiated character of the lawyer's way of being tends to render irrelevant what would otherwise be morally relevant considerations. Suppose that a client desires to make a will disinheriting her children because they opposed the war in Vietnam. Should the lawyer refuse to draft the will because the lawyer thinks this a bad reason to disinherit one's children? Suppose a client can avoid the payment of taxes through a loophole only available to a few wealthy taxpayers. Should the lawyer refuse to tell the client of a loophole because

---

2. Ballard v. Superior Court, 49 Cal.Rptr. 302 (Cal.1966). [Editors' note:] Cal. Pen. Code § 1112, effective Jan. 1, 1981, prohibited a trial court from ordering any witness or victim in any sexual assault prosecution to submit to a psychiatric or psychological examination for the purpose of assessing credibility. The constitutionality of the statute was upheld in People v. Armbruster, 210 Cal.Rptr. 11 (3d Dist.1985).

the lawyer thinks it an unfair advantage for the rich? Suppose a client wants to start a corporation that will manufacture, distribute and promote a harmful but not illegal substance, e.g., cigarettes. Should the lawyer refuse to prepare the articles of incorporation for the corporation? In each case, the accepted view within the profession is that these matters are just of no concern to the lawyer *qua* lawyer. The lawyer need not of course agree to represent the client (and that is equally true for the unpopular client accused of a heinous crime), but there is nothing wrong with representing a client whose aims and purposes are quite immoral. And having agreed to do so, the lawyer is required to provide the best possible assistance, without regard to his or her disapproval of the objective that is sought.

The lesson, on this view, is clear. The job of the lawyer, so the argument typically concludes, is not to approve or disapprove of the character of his or her client, the cause for which the client seeks the lawyer's assistance, or the avenues provided by the law to achieve that which the client wants to accomplish. . . . And the difficulty I have with all of this is that the arguments for such a way of life seem to be not quite so convincing to me as they do to many lawyers. I am, that is, at best uncertain that it is a good thing for lawyers to be so professional—for them to embrace so completely this role-differentiated way of approaching matters.

. . .

. . . [F]or most lawyers, most of the time, pursuing the interests of one's clients is an attractive and satisfying way to live in part just because the moral world of the lawyer is a simpler, less complicated, and less ambiguous world than the moral world of ordinary life. . . .

But there is, of course, also an argument which seeks to demonstrate that it is good and not merely comfortable for lawyers to behave this way.

It is good, so the argument goes, that the lawyer's behavior and concomitant point of view are role-differentiated because the lawyer *qua* lawyer participates in a complex institution which functions well only if the individuals adhere to their institutional roles.

For example, when there is a conflict between individuals, or between the state and an individual, there is a well-established institutional mechanism by which to get that dispute resolved. That mechanism is the trial in which each side is represented by a lawyer whose job it is both to present his or her client's case in the most attractive, forceful light and to seek to expose the weaknesses and defects in the case of the opponent.

When an individual is charged with having committed a crime, the trial is the mechanism by which we determine in our society whether or not the person is in fact guilty. Just imagine what would happen if lawyers were to refuse, for instance, to represent persons whom they thought to be guilty. . . . The private judgment of individual lawyers would in effect be substituted for the public, institutional judgment of the judge and jury. The amorality of lawyers helps to guarantee that every criminal defendant will have his or her day in court.

Nor is the amorality of the institutional role of the lawyer restricted to the defense of those accused of crimes. . . . The attorney may think it wrong to disinherit one's children because of their views about the Vietnam war, but here the attorney's complaint is really with the laws of inheritance and not with his or her client. The attorney may think the tax provision an unfair, unjustifiable loophole, but once more the complaint is really with the Internal Revenue Code and not with the client who seeks to take advantage of it. . . . If lawyers were to substitute their own private views of what ought to be legally permissible and impermissible for those of the legislature, this would constitute a surreptitious and undesirable shift from a democracy to an oligarchy of lawyers. For given the fact that lawyers are needed to effectuate the wishes of clients, the lawyer ought to make his or her skills available to those who seek them without regard for the particular objectives of the client.

As I indicated earlier, I do believe that the amoral behavior of the *criminal* defense lawyer is justifiable. But I think that [justification] depends at least as much upon the special needs of an accused as upon any more general defense of a lawyer's role-differentiated behavior. As a matter of fact I think it likely that many persons such as myself have been misled by the special features of the criminal case. Because a deprivation of liberty is so serious, because the prosecutorial resources of the state are so vast, and because, perhaps, of a serious skepticism about the rightness of punishment even where wrongdoing has occurred, it is easy to accept the view that it makes sense to charge the defense counsel with the job of making the best possible case for the accused—without regard, so to speak, for the merits. This coupled with the fact that it is an adversarial proceeding succeeds, I think, in justifying the amorality of the criminal defense counsel. But this does not, however, justify a comparable perspective on the part of lawyers generally. Once we leave the peculiar situation of the criminal defense lawyer, I think it quite likely that the role-differentiated amorality of the lawyer is almost certainly excessive and at times inappropriate. . . .

Moreover, even if I am wrong about all this, four things do seem to me to be true and important.

First, all of the arguments that support the role-differentiated amorality of the lawyer on institutional grounds can succeed only if the enormous degree of trust and confidence in the institutions themselves is itself justified. . . . To the degree to which the institutional rules and practices are unjust, unwise or undesirable, to that same degree is the case for the role-differentiated behavior of the lawyer weakened if not destroyed.

Second, it is clear that there are definite character traits that the professional such as the lawyer must take on if the system is to work. What is less clear is that they are admirable ones. Even if the role-differentiated amorality of the professional lawyer is justified by the virtues of the adversary system, this also means that the lawyer *qua* lawyer will be encouraged to be competitive rather than cooperative; aggressive rather than accommodating; ruthless rather than compassionate; and pragmatic rather than principled.... It is surely neither accidental nor unimportant that these are the same character traits that are emphasized and valued by the capitalist ethic—and on precisely analogous grounds. Because the ideals of professionalism and capitalism are the dominant ones within our culture, it is harder than most of us suspect even to take seriously the suggestion that radically different styles of living, kinds of occupational outlooks, and types of social institutions might be possible, let alone preferable.

Third, there is a special feature of the role-differentiated behavior of the lawyer that distinguishes it from the comparable behavior of other professionals. What I have in mind can be brought out through the following question: Why is it that it seems far less plausible to talk critically about the amorality of the doctor, for instance, who treats all patients irrespective of their moral character than it does to talk critically about the comparable amorality of the lawyer? ...

... The lawyer lives with and within a dilemma that is not shared by other professionals. If the lawyer actually believes everything that he or she asserts on behalf of the client, then it appears to be proper to regard the lawyer as in fact embracing and endorsing the points of view that he or she articulates. If the lawyer does not in fact believe what is urged by way of argument, if the lawyer is only playing a role, then it appears to be proper to tax the lawyer with hypocrisy and insincerity. To be sure, actors in a play take on roles and say things that the characters, not the actors, believe. But we know it is a play and that they are actors. The law courts are not, however, theaters, and the lawyers both talk about justice and they genuinely seek to persuade. The fact that the lawyer's words, thoughts, and convictions are, apparently, for sale and at the service of the client helps us, I think, to understand the peculiar hostility which is more than occasionally uniquely directed by lay persons toward lawyers....

Fourth, ... we do pay a social price for that way of thought and action. For to become and to be a professional, such as a lawyer, is to incorporate within oneself ways of behaving and ways of thinking that shape the whole person. It is especially hard, if not impossible, because of the nature of the professions, for one's professional way of thinking not to dominate one's entire adult life.... In important respects, one's professional role becomes and is one's dominant role, so that for many persons at least they become their professional being. This is at a minimum a heavy price to pay for the professions as we know them in our culture, and especially so for lawyers. Whether it is an inevitable price is, I think, an open question, largely because the problem has not begun to be fully perceived as such by the professionals in general, the legal profession in particular, or by the educational institutions that train professionals.

II.

The role-differentiated behavior of the professional also lies at the heart of the second of the two moral issues I want to discuss, namely, the character of the interpersonal relationship that exists between the lawyer and the client.* As I indicated at the outset, the charge that I want to examine here is that the relationship between the lawyer and the client is typically, if not inevitably, a morally defective one in which the client is not treated with the respect and dignity that he or she deserves.

. . .

... [O]ne pervasive, and I think necessary, feature of the relationship between any professional and the client or patient is that it is in some sense a relationship of inequality. This relationship of inequality is intrinsic to the existence of professionalism. For the professional is, in some respects at least, always in a position of dominance vis-á-vis the client, and the client in a position of dependence vis-á-vis the professional. . . .

To begin with, there is the fact that one characteristic of professions is that the professional is the possessor of expert knowledge of a sort not readily or easily attainable by members of the community at large. Hence, in the most straightforward of all senses the client, typically, is dependent upon the professional's skill or knowledge because the client does not possess the same knowledge.

Moreover, virtually every profession has its own technical language, a private terminology which can only be fully understood by the members of the profession. The presence of such a language plays the dual role of creating and affirming the membership of the professionals within the profession and of preventing the client from fully discussing or understanding his or her concerns in the language of the profession.

In addition, because the matters for which professional assistance is sought usually involve things of great personal concern to the client, it is the received wisdom within the professions that the client lacks the perspective necessary to pursue in a satisfactory way his or her own best interests, and that the client requires a detached, disinterested representative to look after his or her interests. . . .

Finally, as I have indicated, to be a professional is to have been acculturated in a certain way. It is to have satisfactorily passed through a lengthy and allegedly difficult period of study and training. It is to have done something hard. Something that not everyone can do. Almost all professions encourage this way of viewing oneself; as having joined an elect group by virtue of hard work and mastery of the mysteries of the profession. In addition, the society at large treats members of a profession as members of an elite by paying them more than most people for the work they do with their heads rather than their hands, and by according them a substantial amount of social prestige and power by virtue of their membership in a profession. It is hard, I think, if not impossible, for a person to emerge from professional training and participate in a profession without

---

* [Editors' note:] The moral aspects of the lawyer-client relationship are considered below in Chapter 6. See p. 451 infra for further discussion of Richard Wasserstrom's views.

the belief that he or she is a special kind of person, both different from and somewhat better than those nonprofessional members of the social order. It is equally hard for the other members of society not to hold an analogous view of the professionals. And these beliefs surely contribute, too, to the dominant role played by a professional in any professional-client relationship.

· · ·

... It is, I believe, indicative of the state of legal education and of the profession that there has been to date extremely little self-conscious concern even with the possibility that these dimensions of the attorney-client relationship are worth examining—to say nothing of being capable of alteration. That awareness is, surely, the prerequisite to any serious assessment of the moral character of the attorney-client relationship as a relationship among adult human beings.

Wasserstrom and Role Morality

How would Wasserstrom have a lawyer deal with Zimmerman to accord Zimmerman the "respect and dignity that he ... deserves"? Do Wasserstrom's observations apply to all lawyers or only to lawyers who represent individuals who are inexperienced and unsophisticated in selecting and monitoring lawyers?

Wasserstrom accepts the role-based morality of the criminal defense lawyer while rejecting such morality for lawyers in other situations. Are his arguments distinguishing the criminal lawyer persuasive? Are not his arguments against the role-morality of other lawyers equally applicable to the criminal defense lawyer? For example, are trust and confidence in the criminal justice system more warranted than trust and confidence in the civil system? Should we be less concerned with the character traits nourished by role-morality in criminal defense lawyers than with the traits fostered in civil litigators?

Suppose Zimmerman was a criminal defendant who possessed knowledge that, if disclosed, would save another's life but would also result in Zimmerman's imprisonment. Would the morality of his lawyer's action in keeping the information secret differ from that lawyer's morality in doing the same in the civil case?

In Nebraska v. Harper,[22] Harper, who had been convicted of poisoning several people, claimed that his trial counsel had provided ineffective representation because the lawyer had "permitted" Harper to tell the court the kind of poison he had administered to victims who were still alive. This disclosure allowed the victims to get appropriate medical treatment. The trial court allowed the disclosure but excluded from evidence the fact that

22.   336 N.W.2d 597 (Neb.1983).

Harper had provided the information. In rejecting the claim of ineffective assistance of counsel, the court said:

> [R]efusal ... to disclose would have only served as an aggravating circumstance. To now suggest that [the lawyer] should not have permitted Harper to disclose ... is totally without basis. The lives of three individuals hung in the balance. Effective assistance of counsel does not require such callous behavior as [now] suggested by Harper.[23]

Wasserstrom describes a lawyer's moral universe as defined by client interests and restricted only by the dictates of law. He says that conduct permissible under law includes immoral behavior that should not be condoned. His argument assumes that the boundary between lawful and unlawful conduct is discernible, discerned and respected by most lawyers. The problem, according to Wasserstrom and most other commentators on this subject, is not that lawyers are lawless but that compliance with law does not ensure "moral" behavior. Yet Wasserstrom acknowledges, in a part of his article not reprinted here, that the Watergate scandal, which involved many lawyers, prompted renewed concern about legal ethics. The lawyers involved in Watergate, however, committed acts that were illegal as well as immoral. Does the amorality of role-differentiated lawyer behavior lead to lawlessness?

Do lawyers pay a personal price when their role as technicians in the service of client interests leads them to do things they find morally repugnant? There is a substantial literature dealing with the personal consequences of cognitive dissonance as experienced by lawyers.[24]

For a number of reasons lawyers, at least when representing relatively unsophisticated individual clients, have considerable influence or control over decisions concerning the representation. Many clients seek their lawyer's approval or place great importance on what their lawyer thinks. The lawyer's control over information and its legal significance provides opportunities for manipulation of the client, who may be led to conform his goals to those the lawyer presents. In addition, many lawyers fail to have candid conversations with their clients about the moral and other "nonlegal" aspects of the representation; as suggested by William Simon in an excerpt that follows, lawyers representing individuals may find it convenient to make assumptions that their clients' only goals are self-interested ones. Thus the reality of representation is filled with decisional gaps that lawyers fill often from habit, rather than necessity, and often without consultation or meaningful reflection. In making decisions about the ends of a representation, "[t]he values or ends the lawyer chooses are likely to be ... the readily assumed, the safe, the self-evident: more money, freedom from incarceration or procedural delay," even though "for many clients, such goods are neither what they want nor what they need."[25]

---

23. 336 N.W.2d at 600.

24. See, e.g., Patrick J. Schiltz, On Being a Happy, Healthy and Ethical Member of an Unhappy, Unhealthy, and Unethical Profession, 52 Vand. L. Rev. 871 (1999) (containing extensive citations to this large literature).

25. Warren Lehman, The Pursuit of a Client's Interest, 77 Mich.L.Rev. 1078, 1087 (1979).

The "Standard Conception" of Lawyer Role

Leading moral philosophers and legal ethicists have examined what is often referred to as the "standard conception" of professional role outlined by Wasserstrom.[26] It is a model of "total commitment to client" that can be traced back to Samuel Johnson: "A lawyer is to do for his client all that his client might fairly do for himself, if he [had his lawyer's knowledge and skill]. If, by a superiority of attention, of knowledge, of skill, and a better method of communication, [the lawyer] has the advantage of his adversary, it is an advantage to which he is entitled."[27] The standard conception is also encapsulated in a saying of Elihu Root: "The client never wants to be told he can't do what he wants to do; he wants to be told how to do it, and it is the lawyer's business to tell him how."[28] The "standard conception" rests on the two principles of partisanship and nonaccountability:[29]

> *Partisanship.* A lawyer must, within the established constraints on professional behavior, maximize the likelihood that the client's objectives will be attained.

> *Nonaccountability.* In representing a client, a lawyer is neither legally, professionally nor morally accountable for the means used or the ends achieved.

The first principle requires the lawyer to be a partisan for the client; the second purports to excuse the lawyer, when acting in this prescribed role, from legal, professional and moral accountability for what the lawyer does on behalf of the client.

David Luban attacks the premises of the standard conception in his book, *Lawyers and Justice.* First, the lawyer's one-sided partisan zeal is founded on professional obligations to the client, but these obligations are more ambiguous and uncertain than commonly recognized. Second, the

26. Ted Schneyer and others have challenged the proposition that the "standard conception" is required by the ethics codes, pointing out the enormous discretion the codes vest in the lawyer and the ethics provisions and other law that require or permit the lawyer to recognize the interests of tribunals or third persons in some situations. Luban concedes that lawyers possess substantial choice concerning how they define their own roles, but argues that as a practical matter a hired-gun ideology is dominant in many sectors of practice. See Ted Schneyer, Moral Philosophy's Standard Misconception of Legal Ethics, 1984 Wis.L.Rev. 1529; and Schneyer, Some Sympathy for the Hired Gun, 41 J.Legal Educ. 11 (1991).

27. Samuel Johnson, in Boswell, The Journal of a Tour to the Hebrides with Samuel Johnson 13–14 (Temple Classics ed., 1930).

28. See David Luban, Lawyers and Justice: An Ethical Study (1988); and David Luban, Partisanship, Betrayal and Autonomy in the Lawyer–Client Relationship: A Reply to Stephen Ellmann, 90 Colum.L.Rev. 1004 (1990). Similar arguments have been made by other moral philosophers. See, e.g., Alvin H. Goldman, The Moral Foundations of Professional Ethics (1980); and the essays in David Luban (ed.), The Good Lawyer: Lawyers' Roles and Lawyers' Ethics (1984).

29. The principles of advocacy were originally stated by Professor Murray Schwartz in slightly different words and have been discussed by a number of other authors. See Murray L. Schwartz, The Professionalism and Accountability of Lawyers, 66 Cal. L.Rev. 669, 673 (1978), and Schwartz, The Zeal of the Civil Advocate, 1983 Am.Bar Found. Research J. 543; and Gerald Postema, Moral Responsibility in Professional Ethics, 55 N.Y.U. L. Rev. 63 (1980).

obligations themselves—loyalty, confidentiality, competence, diligence and avoidance of conflicting interests—are justified as essential to the lawyer's role as the client's advocate-agent in legal proceedings; but lawyers do many things (e.g., planning, counseling, advising) that do not fit this model. Third, the "adversary system excuse" is only as good as the adversary system. The "standard conception" of adversarial ethics, Luban argues, is that the system justifies a lawyer doing everything that is legally permissible to advance a client's interest, notwithstanding how morally repugnant those things may be. But the system can justify immoral conduct only to the extent that it itself is morally justified. Luban provides an elaboration of Wasserstrom's point that "support[ing] the role-differentiated amorality of the lawyer on institutional grounds can succeed only if the enormous degree of trust and confidence in the institutions themselves is itself justified."

Supporters of the lawyer's adversary role, such as Monroe Freedman and Stephen Pepper, defend the standard conception on a variety of grounds: first, it serves client autonomy, including the protection of the basic freedoms provided for in the Bill of Rights; second, a better range of moral outcomes may result overall if lawyers simply play their assigned adversarial roles in the legal system without assuming the paternalistic role of "lawyer as statesman;" and third, the legitimate expectations of clients, who retain lawyers with the traditional role in mind, justify the lawyers' conforming to the morality of the expected adversarial role. Underlying these views is a more affirmative position on the efficacy of the current adversary system.[30]

3. PERSPECTIVE OF THE BAD MAN

Oliver Wendell Holmes, Jr. "The Path of the Law," Collected Legal Papers
Pp. 167–169, 171–175 (1920).
Appears also in 10 Harv.L.Rev. 457–462 (1897).

When we study law we are not studying a mystery but a well-known profession. We are studying what we shall want in order to appear before judges, or to advise people in such a way as to keep them out of court. The reason why it is a profession, why people will pay lawyers to argue for them or to advise them, is that in societies like ours the command of the public force is intrusted to the judges in certain cases, and the whole power of the state will be put forth, if necessary, to carry out their judgments and decrees. People want to know under what circumstances and how far they

---

30. See, e.g., Monroe H. Freedman, Understanding Lawyers' Ethics (1990) (defending adversarial ethics as essential to the vindication of individual autonomy and individual rights); Stephen L. Pepper, The Lawyer's Amoral Ethical Role: A Defense, A Problem, and Some Possibilities, 1986 Am. Bar Found.Research J. 613 (lawyer's adversarial role is essential to provide people with meaningful access to law in all its forms).

will run the risk of coming against what is so much stronger than themselves, and hence it becomes a business to find out when this danger is to be feared. The object of our study, then, is prediction, the prediction of the incidence of the public force through the instrumentality of the courts.

... If you want to know the law and nothing else, you must look at it as a bad man, who cares only for the material consequences which such knowledge enables him to predict, not as a good one, who finds his reasons for conduct, whether inside the law or outside of it, in the vaguer sanctions of conscience. The theoretical importance of the distinction is no less, if you would reason on your subject aright. The law is full of phraseology drawn from morals, and by the mere force of language continually invites us to pass from one domain to the other without perceiving it, as we are sure to do unless we have the boundary constantly before our minds....

The confusion with which I am dealing besets confessedly legal conceptions. Take the fundamental question. What constitutes the law? You will find some text writers telling you that it is something different from what is decided by the courts of Massachusetts or England, that it is a system of reason, that it is a deduction from principles of ethics or admitted axioms or what not, which may or may not coincide with the decisions. But if we take the view of our friend the bad man we shall find that he does not care two straws for the axioms or deductions, but that he does want to know what the Massachusetts or English courts are likely to do in fact. I am much of his mind. The prophecies of what the court will do in fact, and nothing more pretentious, are what I mean by the law.

Take again a notion which as popularly understood is the widest conception which the law contains—the notion of legal duty, to which already I have referred. We fill the word with all the content which we draw from morals. But what does it mean to a bad man? Mainly, and in the first place, a prophecy that if he does certain things he will be subjected to disagreeable consequences by way of imprisonment or compulsory payment of money. But from his point of view, what is the difference between being fined and being taxed a certain sum for doing, a certain thing? ...

———

Lawyer as Bad Man

Holmes says the bad man's perspective is necessary "if you want to know the law and *nothing else*...." What are the consequences for the lawyer of adopting this perspective? Is it possible to keep the bad man's perspective in one's office and not have it intrude on the rest of one's life?[31] What are the consequences of this view for the client?

31. See Thomas L. Shaffer, Faith and the Professions 71–110 (1987) (discussing whether it is possible or desirable to separate professional morality from personal morality). See also Shaffer, The Theology of the Two Kingdoms, 17 Valparaiso L.Rev. 17 (1983).

How would Holmes have advised Zimmerman's lawyers to counsel Zimmerman?

Holmes' "bad man" presumably would be interested not only in what the courts of Massachusetts would say but also in the likelihood that a prosecutor or private person would bring his actions before a court. If the courts would hold the client liable, but the local prosecutor is unlikely to discover the violation, should the lawyer so inform the client? How should the likelihood of prosecution affect the advice the lawyer gives the client? If Holmes' lawyer found out that the judge could be bought, should she tell her client this too?[32]

Critique of the Bad Man's Perspective

William Simon's restatement and critique of the "lawyer as bad man" is cast in terms of the acceptance by many lawyers of a world view that seeks to advance a client's individual dignity and personal autonomy.[33] The lawyer enhances a client's autonomy by shaping fact and by applying and manipulating legal rules to advance the client's goals. The problem, however, is that the client cannot give a satisfactory account of his situation without the lawyer's knowledge of legal relevance. The lawyer for her part has no way of divining the client's goals, or ends, by herself, since they are subjective and peculiar to the individual. Any speculation by the lawyer would reveal merely the interference of the lawyer's own biases or ends. The instrumentalist lawyer's dilemma is that she cannot advise her client without referring to ends, yet she cannot refer to ends without jeopardizing her client's own autonomy via the lawyer's biases.

The lawyer's strategy for dealing with this dilemma is to impute certain basic ends to the client, and then to work to advance these ends, even though this weakens the premise of the absolute individuality of the client's ends. Thus, the personal injury claimant is presumed to be interested only in the largest award, and the criminal defendant is presumed to be interested only in being relieved of all responsibility for his conduct. Imputed ends are invariably extremely selfish ones, primarily involving "maximization of freedom of movement and the accumulation of wealth" (p. 54).

This approach offers one way to avoid potentially "dangerous" (and time-consuming) inquiries into a client's ends from the beginning, and, if the ends selected are shared, the lawyer does advance the client's actual needs to some degree while advancing the ends that the lawyer imputes to him.

---

32. Other materials on the morality of the lawyer's role, not previously cited, include: Douglas E. Rosenthal, Lawyer & Client: Who's In Charge? (1974); Alan H. Goldman, The Moral Foundations of Professional Ethics, ch. 3 (1980); Thomas L. Shaffer, Legal Ethics and the Good Client, 36 Cath. U.L.Rev. 319 (1987); William F. Simon, Ethical Discretion in Lawyering, 101 Harv. L.Rev. 1083 (1988).

33. William H. Simon, The Ideology of Advocacy, 1978 Wisconsin L. Rev. 30, 52 ff.

... [T]he naive [client], face to face with the alien force of the state [is] threatened with a massive disruption of his life. Confronted with the need to act in this strange situation, the client must make sense of it as best he can. The lawyer puts [herself] forth quite plausibly as the client's best hope of mastering his predicament. If [the client] is to avoid being overwhelmed by chaos, he must acquiesce in his lawyer's definition of the situation. He must think in a manner which gives coherence to the advice he is given. He may begin to do this quite unconsciously. If he is at all aware of the change, he is likely to see it as a defensive posture forced on him by the hostile intentions of opposing parties.... His only strategy of survival requires that he see himself as the lawyers and the officials see him, as an abstraction, a hypothetical person with only a few crude, discrete ends. He must assume that his subtler ends, his long-range plans, and his social relationships are irrelevant to the situation at hand. This is the profound and unintended meaning of Holmes's remark:

> If you want to know the law and nothing else, you must look at it as a bad man, who cares only for the material consequences which such knowledge enables him to predict, not as a good one, who finds his reasons for conduct, whether inside the law or outside of it, in the vaguer sanctions of conscience.

The role of the bad man, conceived as an analytical device for the lawyer, becomes, under pressure of circumstances, a psychological reality for the client.

. . .

Despite its complete irrationality, this [strategy of imposing ends on the client] has become so widely accepted that many lawyers have come to equate the manipulation of the client ... with neutral advice to the client on his rights. For instance, lawyers constantly express astonishment at the willingness of intelligent laymen, aware of their rights, to make inculpatory statements to the authorities. They can think of no other explanation for this phenomenon besides confusion or pressure from the interrogators, and they thus conclude that no one can be expected to make an "informed decision" on such matters without the assistance of counsel. But the lawyer's assistance does not take the form of neutral information or the alleviation of pressure. Along with [her] knowledge of the law, the lawyer brings [her] own prejudices and [her] own psychological pressures. These derive from the conception of the roles of lawyer and client which is implicit in ... the strategy of imputed ends. As Justice Jackson put it, "[A]ny lawyer worth his salt will tell the suspect in no uncertain terms to make no statement to the police under any circumstances."[66] [Under this ap-

---

66. Watts v. Indiana, 338 U.S. 49, 59 (1949); cf. Justice Jackson's remark on his experience of civil practice in Jamestown, N.Y., " ... a lawyer there, if he was con-sulted on a matter, usually dominated the matter, no matter who the businessman was." E. Gerhart, America's Advocate: Robert M. Jackson 63 (1958).

proach, the] lawyer is not an advisor, but a lobbyist for a peculiar theory of human nature.

The Legal Realism Problem

The positivist interpretation of law in part reacted against a natural law interpretation, which held that law expresses inevitable and therefore "natural" justice. Does the legal system deliver natural justice? Or, at best, moderately effective controls on "bad men"? If the latter, shouldn't a lawyer advise her client on that basis? Every sensitive person wishes for more caring conduct toward others than the "bad man" delivers. But how can legal process deliver or compel such conduct?[34] How do you feel about pursuing a vocation that, unlike medicine or teaching, is not generally considered a "caring profession"?

Holmes is celebrated as a precursor of "legal realism," today a widely held jurisprudential position. Legal realism places great emphasis on the indeterminacy and manipulability of law. If only law—not morality—limits a lawyer's conduct, moral input or constraint in the lawyer-client relationship is reduced or eliminated.[35] For example, a lawyer's emphasis on "law" may lead corporate clients to evaluate planned conduct only in terms of economic costs and legal risks even when the conduct threatens harm to others. Moral analysis, using such terms as "right" and "wrong" or "fair" or "unfair" are avoided. An amoral, realist lawyer thus may encourage an industrial client to engage in as much pollution as the lawyer believes the client can get away with, viewing the "law" solely as a prediction of the risks and benefits of what officials are likely to do, including the likelihood of being caught and of stiff sanctions being applied.

A rare glimpse of lawyer-client dialogue on the likelihood that a law will be enforced came to light early in the Clinton administration when it became known that Attorney General-designate Zoe Baird and her husband, a Yale law professor, had hired illegal aliens to care for their son. Their lawyer, an immigration specialist, had advised them it was unlikely they would be fined by the Immigration Service for this "technical violation" of existing law.[36] The President, members of Congress and other Washington insiders–legal realists all–initially took the view that violation of a law that was largely unenforced was not a serious matter, only to discover that this explanation was unacceptable to the public. Baird's nomination was withdrawn and the subsequent "Nanny" debate then contributed to defeat of several other high-level appointments. Should the advice given by Ms. Baird's lawyer have dealt with potential consequences other than a fine? Included moral and political concerns?[37]

---

34. For a sophisticated modern presentation of a positivist perspective, see Joseph Raz, The Authority of Law: Essays on Morality and Law 250–61 (1979) (defending the view that a positivist lawyer would have a qualified respect for law that would lead her to obey most laws of a reasonably just and good society).

35. See Pepper, supra, at 625 et seq.

36. See "Baird Hired Illegal Aliens After Lawyer Said Fine Unlikely," Wash.Post, Jan. 15, 1993, at p. 5A.

37. For discussion of the lawyer's role in advising about the law enforcement roulette, see Jamie G. Heller, Legal Counsel-

One response to the legal realism problem is to encourage lawyers to engage in moral dialogue with clients, who retain responsibility for determining the objectives of representation. A second response is to ask lawyers to reject the premise that assisting a client by unjust means or toward an unjust goal is morally permissible. No one believes that everything legally right is also morally right.[38] A good society wants people not only to make their own choices, but to make *good* choices. From this perspective, increasing individual autonomy is good only if the consequences are good or neutral, but not when the act chosen is bad, such as telling a lie, humiliating a truthful witness or causing other serious harm to third persons.

4. RELATIONAL FEMINISM

Carol Gilligan, In a Different Voice

Pp. 25–29 (1982).[39]

The dilemma that these eleven-year-olds were asked to resolve was one in the series devised by [Lawrence] Kohlberg to measure moral development in adolescence by presenting a conflict between moral norms and exploring the logic of its resolution. In this particular dilemma, a man named Heinz considers whether or not to steal a drug which he cannot afford to buy in order to save the life of his wife. In the standard format of Kohlberg's interviewing procedure, the description of the dilemma itself—Heinz's predicament, the wife's disease, the druggist's refusal to lower his price—is followed by the question, "Should Heinz steal the drug?" The reasons for and against stealing are then explored through a series of questions that vary the parameters of the dilemma in a way designed to reveal the underlying structure of moral thought.

Jake, at eleven, is clear from the outset that Heinz should steal the drug. Constructing the dilemma, as Kohlberg did, as a conflict between the values of property and life, he discerns the logical priority of life and uses that logic to justify his choice.

> For one thing, a human life is worth more than money, and if the druggist only makes $1,000, he is still going to live, but if Heinz doesn't steal the drug, his wife is going to die. (*Why is life worth more than money* ?) Because the druggist can get a thousand dollars later from rich people with cancer, but Heinz can't get his wife again. (*Why not* ?) Because people are all different and so you couldn't get Heinz's wife again.

ing in the Administrative State: How to Let the Client Decide, 103 Yale L.J. 2503 (1994).

38. This argument, frequently encountered, is spelled out in David Luban, The Lysistratian Prerogative: A Response to Stephen Pepper, 1986 Am.Bar Found. Research J. 637.

39. Copyright © 1982 by Carol G. Gilligan. Published by Harvard University Press. Reprinted by Permission.

Asked whether Heinz should steal the drug if he does not love his wife, Jake replies that he should, saying that not only is there "a difference between hating and killing," but also, if Heinz were caught, "the judge would probably think it was the right thing to do." Asked about the fact that, in stealing, Heinz would be breaking the law, he says that "the laws have mistakes and you can't go writing up a law for everything that you can imagine."

· · ·

[In contrast to Jake's answers are Amy's.] Asked if Heinz should steal the drug, she replies. . . .

> Well, I don't think so. I think there might be other ways besides stealing it, like if he could borrow the money or make a loan or something, but he really shouldn't steal the drug—but his wife shouldn't die either.

Asked why he should not steal the drug, she considers neither property nor law but rather the effect that theft could have on the relationship between Heinz and his wife:

> If he stole the drug, he might save his wife then, but if he did, he might have to go to jail, and then his wife might get sicker again, and he couldn't get more of the drug, and it might not be good. So, they should really just talk it out and find some other way to make the money.

Seeing in the dilemma not a math problem with humans but a narrative of relationships that extends over time, Amy envisions the wife's continuing need for her husband and the husband's continuing concern for his wife and seeks to respond to the druggist's need in a way that would sustain rather than sever connection. . . . Since Amy's moral judgment is grounded in the belief that "if somebody has something that would keep somebody alive, then it's not right not to give it to them," she considers the problem in the dilemma to arise not from the druggist's assertion of rights but from his failure of response.

. . . Failing to see the dilemma as a self-contained problem in moral logic, she does not discern the internal structure of its resolution; . . . she constructs the problem differently. . . .

Instead, seeing a world comprised of relationships rather than people standing alone, a world that coheres through human connection rather than through systems of rules, she finds the puzzle in the dilemma to lie in the failure of the druggist to respond to the wife. Saying that "it is not right for someone to die when their life could be saved," she assumes that if the druggist were to see the consequences of his refusal to lower his price, he would realize that "he should just give it to the wife and then have the husband pay back the money later." Thus she considers the solution to the dilemma to lie in making the wife's condition more salient to the druggist or, that failing, in appealing to others who are in a position to help.

Just as Jake is confident the judge would agree that stealing is the right thing for Heinz to do, so Amy is confident that, "if Heinz and the druggist had talked it out long enough, they could reach something besides stealing." . . .

––––––––

Putting People First

How would Jake analyze the moral predicament of the lawyers in *Spaulding* ? How would Amy? Can you improve on their analyses?

A prominent psychologist, Mihaly Csikszentmihalyi, has reflected on Gilligan's alternative vision of moral development and selfhood:[40]

> Mr. Kohlberg's moral hierarchy was reasonably convincing and widely accepted, but it led to some disturbing results. When girls were asked to justify their moral choices, they often failed to arrive at the "highest" form of moral reasoning. Instead of using abstract rules of justice to decide whether an action was right or wrong, they kept wondering who would suffer by the action. They would then rate as best the choice that led to the least harm. If Mr. Kohlberg's argument was correct, it seemed that women's moral reasoning was underdeveloped. This was a conclusion that many famous psychologists, including Freud and Piaget, had held to be true all along.

> Ms. Gilligan did not reject Mr. Kohlberg's findings, but simply reinterpreted them. Basically, she asked: why should we believe that the sequence of moral stages through which boys pass constitutes moral development *tout court* ? What comes later does not necessarily represent a higher order of morality. Perhaps the girls' abiding concern for human relatedness and personal responsibility is not a lower form of reasoning, but an equally sophisticated and vital perspective, complementing the more masculine concern for rights and justice.

> In retrospect, this hardly seems like a revolutionary concept. Of course, it is often the case with new ideas that after they have been stated, people will say: "Why didn't I think of it? It was so obvious." But Ms. Gilligan, either because she focused on a very concrete and clear issue (the hierarchy of moral arguments), or because she delved into it with great zest and eloquence, or because she happened to be writing at the right historical moment, was able to make her ideas the common currency of the academic world.

. . .

> One disturbing finding that seems to emerge [in a later book by Gilligan and others] is that as girls become involved in the institutional roles of the world as men—the more they advance in school, or in the

––––––––

40. Mihaly Csikszentmihalyi, More Ways Than One to Be Good, Book Review,   N.Y.Times Book Review 6 (May 28, 1989).

professions—their "voices" change into masculine baritones. The concern with care and personal involvement is never totally expunged, but increasingly it gets displaced by recourse to impersonal justice. In the old days, psychologists would have interpreted this to mean that women learn higher forms of moral reasoning as they move into the complexity of the "real" world. Now, thanks to Ms. Gilligan's insights, we cannot be so sure.[41]

D. Pitfalls for the Unwary

1. Shaping and Using Law and Facts

Both legal education and legal practice attune lawyers to the ambiguity of law and facts. The first-year law student who reads the proverbial statute prohibiting vehicles in the park[1] might think she knows what the statute means, but the law professor quickly demonstrates how slippery words can be. Does the statute include motorcycles? Bicycles? Baby carriages? An army truck used as a war memorial? A similar process occurs in law firms when new associates find out the many ways to characterize their client's behavior. Facts that seem clearly to show negligence reemerge under a partner's skillful hands as facts demonstrating great care and caution. Taking advantage of ambiguity that exists and creating ambiguity where none appeared before are skills that every lawyer cultivates. Beyond some line, however, exercise of these skills may lead to trouble.

In Matter of Krueger[2] the client, while living in Illinois, retained Krueger, a Wisconsin lawyer, to represent him in a divorce proceeding. Krueger counseled the client to rent a room in Wisconsin to satisfy the residency requirement for a divorce action under Wisconsin law. The client did so for two weeks. Krueger thereafter filed for the client a divorce petition alleging that the client had been a resident of Wisconsin for more than six months and of the county in question for more than 30 days. The court-appointed referee in a disciplinary proceeding found that the client initially gave Krueger some reason to believe that he could meet Wisconsin's residency requirements; the referee also found "that diverse opinions could exist concerning the client's residency at the time the action was commenced." Krueger did not tell his client to testify falsely but did tell him how to "manifest an intention to continue his Wisconsin residency, despite the presence of facts indicating a specific intention to abandon a

---

41. See also Mary F. Belenky et al., Women's Ways of Knowing: The Development of Self, Voice and Mind (1986). Gilligan's thesis and methodology have been criticized by other feminists: See, e.g., Cynthia F. Ep-

stein, Deceptive Distinctions: Sex, Gender, and the Social Order 76–94 (1988).

1. Herbert L.A. Hart, The Concept of Law 121 (1961).

2. 307 N.W.2d 184 (Wis.1981).

Wisconsin domicile...." Krueger was publicly reprimanded for unprofessional conduct.

What did Krueger do wrong? Should Krueger have refused to tell the client what the courts would consider as evidence of an intention to stay in Wisconsin once Krueger had reason to believe the client would not stay? Is it proper to keep such information from a client? What did Krueger do that went beyond giving realistic advice about Wisconsin domicile law?

Legal philosophy today generally interprets law as uncertain and malleable to a greater degree than the positivist approach, which replaced natural law thinking and legal formalism early in the twentieth century. Most proponents of legal positivism asserted that law in its various forms—common and statutory—was discoverable, i.e., had an inherent meaning apart from the will of its reader or interpreter. Judges could be right or wrong about what the law was. Legal realism, which understood law as "what courts do", supplanted positivism as the dominant jurisprudential perspective. Law was what judges said it was; the lawyer's job was to predict what that might be. See the Holmes' excerpt printed above at p. 31. What judges did and would do—in other words, what the law was and would be—could be understood as a function of the societal values held by judges, who as products of their environment would act in a manner consistent with historical and cultural norms. Understanding those norms, the values of the society that produced judges, was the key to understanding law. More recently, Critical Legal Studies takes the realist critique of positivism one step further. Law is to be understood as the product of neither rational thought nor shared societal values. Law is power exercised by judges as state officials. Their will—their commitment to their own values and the use of power—determines the content of law.

If law is the exercise of power or a prediction of what courts will do, why was Krueger wrong to help his client act in a way that would produce a more favorable ruling by the courts? How does a lawyer interpret the requirement of Canon 7 of the Model Code that representation of a client remain "within the bounds of the law" when many modern concepts of law reject the notion that law has bounds? Where is the line between presenting evidence in the light most favorable to one's client, permitted under EC 7–6, and making false statements about the facts, prohibited by M.R. 3.3 and DR 7–102(A)(5)?

2. ARE LAWYERS IMMUNE FROM LAW'S PROHIBITIONS?

INTRODUCTORY NOTE

When lawyers act not as advocates but as counselors, advisors, negotiators, etc., the law treats them very much as it treats lay persons performing similar roles. Hence, the same law that applies to all people regardless of profession governs lawyers most of the time. The law makes an exception, however, for advocates, who act not in the real world but in a staged world with its own set of rules—the theater of a court—where the lawyer is governed by the special rules governing the adjudicatory process. The suspension of aspects of general law (and the substitution of special rules) for the advocate arises not from membership in the profession but from the courtroom theater and the lawyer's part in it.

The fact that an advocate operates under some special rules in a courtroom operates as a source of confusion for many lawyers and as an excuse for misconduct by others.[3] The extent to which laws of general application apply to lawyers outside the courtroom will be considered in depth in the next chapter. The special rules that govern the advocate in court are considered in Chapter 5. The following case examines the line between the paradigms of in-court behavior and office conduct.

Commonwealth v. Stenhach

Superior Court of Pennsylvania, 1986.
356 Pa.Super. 5, 514 A.2d 114, appeal denied, 517 Pa. 589, 534 A.2d 769 (1987).

■ HESTER, JUDGE:

Two criminal defense attorneys have appealed from convictions for hindering prosecution and tampering with evidence arising from their conduct while representing a defendant in a murder trial. Appellants George and Walter Stenhach were young public defenders appointed to represent Richard Buchanan, a man charged with first degree murder. Following Buchanan's directions, appellants recovered a rifle stock used in the homicide. Allegedly believing that disclosure of the rifle stock would be legally and ethically prohibited, appellants did not deliver it to the prosecutor until ordered to do so by the court during the prosecution's case. After Buchanan's conviction of third degree murder, appellants were charged with hindering prosecution, 18 Pa.C.S. § 5105(a)(3), tampering with physical evidence, § 4910(1), criminal conspiracy, § 903, and criminal solicitation, § 902. A jury found both appellants guilty of hindering prosecution, a third degree felony, and tampering, a second degree misdemeanor. In addition, George was convicted of solicitation, and Walter of conspiracy. Each was sentenced to twelve months probation and a fine of $750.

Their appeal raises questions relating to the interplay of the fifth and sixth amendments to the United States Constitution, the statutory attorney-client privilege, and the Pennsylvania Code of Professional Responsibility, in which appellants challenge their duty to deliver evidence to the prosecution. Appellants also raise a due process challenge to the criminal statutes which prohibit hindering prosecution and tampering with evidence

---

3. "One of the least supportable excesses of M. Freedman, Lawyer's Ethics in an Adversary System (1975), is the extension of arguments for client-oriented lawyer action from the area of advocacy to the entirely different field of client counseling. As a glaring example, arguments for a lawyer's exclusive focus on the interests of his or her client that Professor Freedman develops, in the context of the criminal defense function, he then applies without qualification to lawyers who advise clients about non-criminal law matters when issuing securities, id. at 20–24." Wolfram, Modern Legal Ethics 697 n. 45 (1986).

when these statutes are applied to criminal defense attorneys, claiming the statutes are unconstitutionally overbroad; the statutory defense of justification; and allegations of numerous trial errors in evidentiary and other rulings. Amicus curiae briefs by the Pennsylvania Trial Lawyers Association, the National Association of Criminal Defense Lawyers and the Public Defender Association of Pennsylvania all support reversal of the judgments of sentence.

We reject appellants' argument that their retention of physical evidence was proper under existing law. We hold, however, that the statutes under which they were convicted are unconstitutionally overbroad as applied to criminal defense attorneys. Accordingly, we do not address appellants' claims of trial error, but order appellants discharged.

Background

In March, 1982, Theodore Young was killed in Potter County. The following day Richard Buchanan and an accomplice were arrested and charged with first degree murder. Appellant George Stenhach, part-time Public Defender of Potter County, undertook Buchanan's defense immediately. He petitioned for appointment of an investigator to assist in Buchanan's defense, and former police officer Daniel Weidner was appointed as Buchanan's investigator. During a confidential conference among Stenhach, Weidner and Buchanan, Buchanan described the death of Theodore Young. He said that Young had attacked him with two knives and that during the attack, Young had died after he was shot, hit by Buchanan's car, then struck by Buchanan's rifle, causing the stock of the rifle to break off. Buchanan and his accomplice had then disposed of the weapons and other items relating to Young's death. During the conference, Weidner and Buchanan prepared a map identifying the location of some of these items.

Appellant Walter Stenhach, George's younger brother, was practicing law in partnership with George, and assisted in Buchanan's defense. Appellants George and Walter Stenhach had graduated from law school in 1978 and 1980, respectively, and had been admitted to practice in Pennsylvania in 1979 and 1981. They discussed the information received from Buchanan, and decided to pursue the theory of self-defense and to attempt to gather evidence supporting that theory. Accordingly, they ordered Weidner to search for the items Buchanan had described, and to retrieve as many as he could find.

On the same day, Weidner found the broken rifle stock and brought it back to appellants' office. He did not find the barrel, which was eventually discovered by the prosecutor and introduced into evidence at Buchanan's trial. Weidner was unable to locate the knives allegedly used by the victim, and no knives were ever found. When Weidner delivered the rifle stock to appellants, they stored it inside a paper bag in a desk drawer in their office.

Weidner had been a police officer for twenty years and was performing his first defense investigation in the Buchanan case. He expressed his concern as many as twenty times during the five months before Buchanan's trial that appellants were violating the law by withholding the rifle stock.

Based on their research of case law, the Constitution, Pennsylvania statutes and the Pennsylvania Code of Professional Responsibility, appellants repeatedly told Weidner that the weapon was protected by the attorney-client privilege and that Weidner and appellants had a legal duty to preserve Buchanan's confidential communications which led to discovery of the weapon.

On the fourth day of Buchanan's murder trial, during an in-camera hearing, the prosecutor questioned Weidner about the rifle stock. Appellants objected on the ground that an answer would violate the attorney-client privilege. The trial judge overruled the objection, holding the privilege inapplicable to physical evidence, and ordered Weidner to answer. After Weidner testified how he had located and retrieved the rifle stock, the judge ordered its production, and appellants brought it from their office. The stock was not entered into evidence during Buchanan's trial by the prosecution or by the defense.

After Buchanan's conviction, the prosecutor, District Attorney Leber, charged appellants with hindering prosecution and tampering with evidence for withholding the rifle stock. Due to Leber's role as a prospective witness against appellants, a prosecutor was appointed by the state attorney general's office.

At appellants' trial, the primary witnesses for the Commonwealth were Buchanan, Leber and Weidner. Due to Buchanan's invocation of his fifth amendment privilege while his conviction was on direct appeal, the trial court allowed the transcript of Buchanan's testimony in his murder trial to be read into evidence against appellants to establish the evidentiary nature of the rifle stock in question. Leber testified concerning its concealment, its production, and the effect on the prosecution of Buchanan. Weidner testified about discovery and seizure of the evidence as well as appellants' acts and statements regarding continuing retention of the weapon after its discovery.

Appellants in turn testified about the various authorities which allegedly justified their belief that they were obligated to retain the rifle stock to protect their client. They attempted to offer the expert testimony of law professor John Burkoff to establish a justification defense based on the ethical standards applicable to attorney conduct. The trial judge did not permit Burkoff to testify, nor did he instruct the jury on the defense of justification.

Following conviction and sentencing, this appeal was filed. Appellants argue four issues. First, they challenge the trial court's interpretation of the statutes as requiring production of the physical evidence without a court order. Second, they argue they were denied due process of law in that the hindering prosecution and evidence tampering statutes are unconstitutionally vague or overbroad as applied to defense attorneys when literal compliance would require them to violate their statutory, ethical and constitutional duties to their clients. Third, they claim the trial court erred in refusing to permit presentation of a justification defense. Fourth, they argue that the trial court committed reversible error [in failing to sustain a number of appellants' objections] . . . .

Duty to Deliver

Appellants' first argument is that they had no duty to turn over the rifle stock to the prosecutor until ordered to do so by the court. We reject this argument. Although we have no Pennsylvania cases on point, the decisions in other jurisdictions appear to be virtually unanimous in requiring a criminal defense attorney to deliver physical evidence in his possession to the prosecution without court order. It is true that most of the cases arose in the context of appeals from criminal convictions challenging the effectiveness of counsel who had turned over physical evidence, or in the context of litigation of discovery orders or in the context of contempt proceedings against attorneys who failed to produce evidence. The sole case in which an attorney was charged with a criminal offense resulted in the only holding that the concealed evidence was protected by the attorney-client privilege. We join the overwhelming majority of states which hold that physical evidence of crime in the possession of a criminal defense attorney is not subject to a privilege but must be delivered to the prosecution.

Turning to the law in other jurisdictions, we note the much-quoted case of State v. Olwell, 64 Wash.2d 828, 394 P.2d 681 (1964). A criminal defense attorney had been held in contempt of court following his refusal to answer questions or produce weapons at a coroner's inquest, in defiance of a subpoena duces tecum. [The subpoena sought production of the defendant's weapon, a knife.] The appellate court reversed the finding of contempt, holding that the subpoena was defective on its face for invading the confidential relationship between attorney and client so that refusal to testify against the client was not contemptuous. Id. at 833, 394 P.2d 681. The court went on to state that the attorney was required to produce the weapon on his own motion, and that the jury was not to learn the source of the evidence.

> We do not, however, by so holding, mean to imply that evidence can be permanently withheld by the attorney under the claim of the attorney-client privilege. Here, we must consider the balancing process between the attorney-client privilege and the public interest in criminal investigation. We are in agreement that the attorney-client privilege is applicable to the knife held by appellant, but do not agree that the privilege warrants the attorney, as an officer of the court, from withholding it after being properly requested to produce the same. The attorney should not be a depository for criminal evidence (such as a knife, other weapons, stolen property, etc.), which in itself has little, if any, material value for the purposes of aiding counsel in the preparation of the defense of his client's case. Such evidence given the attorney during legal consultation for information purposes and used by the attorney in preparing the defense of his client's case whether or not the case ever goes to trial, could clearly be withheld for a reasonable

period of time. It follows that the attorney, after a reasonable period, should, as an officer of the court, on his own motion turn the same over to the prosecution.

We think the attorney-client privilege should and can be preserved even though the attorney surrenders the evidence he has in his possession. The prosecution, upon receipt of such evidence from an attorney, where charge against the attorney's client is contemplated (presently or in the future), should be well aware of the existence of the attorney-client privilege. Therefore, the state when attempting to introduce such evidence at the trial, should take extreme precautions to make certain that the source of the evidence is not disclosed in the presence of the jury and prejudicial error is not committed. By thus allowing the prosecution to recover such evidence, the public interest is served, and by refusing the prosecution an opportunity to disclose the source of the evidence, the client's privilege is preserved and a balance is reached between these conflicting interests.

Id. at 833–34, 394 P.2d 681. We have quoted at length from Olwell because most of the cases which follow cite or quote it and raise the same issues addressed in the above passage.

People v. Meredith, 29 Cal.3d 682, 175 Cal.Rptr. 612, 631 P.2d 46 (1981), reached similar conclusions. A murder defendant told his attorney where he had abandoned physical evidence of the crime [the wallet of the murder victim, which the defendant had taken from the victim, attempted to burn, and left in a burn barrel behind his residence]. The attorney's investigator retrieved the evidence, the attorney examined it and then turned it over to the police, and the evidence was admitted at trial along with testimony of the investigator describing the location of the evidence. On appeal from his conviction, the defendant conceded the admissibility of the physical evidence, but challenged the admissibility of the testimony regarding its location. The court held that the testimony did not violate the attorney-client privilege. "When defense counsel alters or removes physical evidence, he necessarily deprives the prosecution of the opportunity to observe that evidence in its original condition or location. . . . To extend the attorney-client privilege to a case in which the defense removed evidence might encourage defense counsel to race the police to seize critical evidence." Id. 175 Cal.Rptr. at 612, 631 P.2d at 46.

In People v. Lee, 83 Cal.Rptr. 715, 3 Cal.App.3d 514 (1970), the court also concluded that physical evidence in the possession of an attorney was not privileged [shoes stained with the victim's blood delivered to the defense lawyer by the client's wife]. . . .

Morrell v. State, 575 P.2d 1200 (Alaska Supreme Ct.1978), is another direct appeal from a criminal conviction raising the issue of ineffectiveness of trial counsel following his delivery of incriminating physical evidence to the police [a kidnapping plan prepared by the defendant in advance of the crime]. A third party had discovered the evidence and brought it to the attorney. Unsure of his duties, he sought guidance from the ethics committee of the state bar association. The committee advised him to return the evidence to the finder, explaining the laws pertaining to concealment of evidence. Counsel did so, and assisted the third party in delivering the evidence to the police. The court held that counsel was not ineffective, stating:

> As [appellant] notes, authority in this area is surprisingly sparse. The existing authority seems to indicate, however, that a criminal defense attorney has an obligation to turn over to the prosecution physical evidence which comes into his possession, especially where the evidence comes into the attorney's possession through acts of a third party who is neither a client of the attorney nor an agent of a client. After turning over such evidence, an attorney may have either a right or a duty to remain silent as to the circumstances under which he obtained such evidence. . . .

Id. at 1207. After reviewing cases involving duties of attorneys in possession of incriminating physical evidence, the court summarized their holdings

> From the foregoing cases emerges the rule that a criminal defense attorney must turn over to the prosecution real evidence that the attorney obtains from his client. Further, if the evidence is obtained from a non-client third party who is not acting for the client, then the privilege to refuse to testify concerning the manner in which the evidence was obtained is inapplicable.

Id. at 1210.

Another case in which defense counsel, who had received physical evidence incriminating his client from a third party, sought the advice of the state bar association ethics committee is Hitch v. Pima County Superior Court, 146 Ariz. 588, 708 P.2d 72 (Supreme Ct.1985). The committee's opinion advised him he had a legal obligation to deliver the evidence to the prosecution. He informed the court of the evidence and the ethics committee opinion, whereupon the court ordered him to turn over the evidence and to withdraw from the case. His client, prior to trial, appealed that order.

The Arizona Supreme Court, referring to "Ethical Standard to Guide [A Lawyer] Who Receives Physical Evidence Implicating His Client in Criminal Conduct," proposed by the Ethics Committee of the Criminal Justice Section of the American Bar Association, 29 Crim.L.Rptr. 2465–66 (August 26, 1981), held that the attorney might return the evidence to its source if he could do so without destroying the evidence, or he must turn it over to the prosecution. Counsel's reasonable belief that the third-party source, a friend of the client, might cause destruction or concealment of the evidence necessitated its delivery to the prosecution. The court also rejected the procedure utilized in the District of Columbia whereby such evidence is given to the local bar association for subsequent delivery to the prosecutor. The court believed that such anonymous transmittal would frequently destroy the evidentiary significance of the physical item, which often depends upon where and under what circumstances it was found. Citing

People v. Nash, 110 Mich.App. 428, 447, 313 N.W.2d 307, 314 (1981), the court stated that "it is simpler and more direct for defendant's attorney to turn the matter over to the state as long as it is understood that the prosecutor may not mention in front of the jury the fact that the evidence came from the defendant or his attorney." Hitch, supra, 708 P.2d at 79. Finding no dereliction in the attorney's representation of his client, the court held that he need not withdraw unless "the client [believes] his attorney no longer has his best interest in mind." Id.

The only case we have found involving criminal prosecution of an attorney for failure to deliver physical evidence is *People v. Belge,* 83 Misc.2d 186, 372 N.Y.S.2d 798 (1975). Representing a murder defendant and relying on an insanity defense, counsel investigated his client's claim that he had committed other murders and discovered one of the bodies hidden in a cemetery. He left the body *in situ* and did not reveal his discovery until his client's trial. After the murder trial, counsel was indicted for the offenses of failure to assure that a decent burial be accorded the dead and failure to report to authorities the death of a person without medical attendance. Not surprisingly,

> Public indignation reached the fever pitch.... A hue and cry went up from the press and other news media.... However, the [Constitution] attempts to preserve the dignity of the individual and to do that guarantees him the services of an attorney who will bring to the bar and to the bench every conceivable protection from the inroads of the state against such rights as are vested in the [C]onstitution for one accused of crime. Among those substantial constitutional rights is that a defendant does not have to incriminate himself. His attorneys were bound to uphold that concept and [to] maintain what has been called a sacred trust of confidentiality.

372 N.Y.S.2d at 801–02. The court held that counsel had "conducted himself as an officer of this Court with all the zeal at his command to protect the constitutional rights of his client," id. at 803, and dismissed the indictment.

The court did state, however, that the attorney's conduct in balancing his client's rights against the public interest in the administration of justice was, "in a sense, obstruction of justice." The court believed the grand jury was "grasping at straws," and that if instead of charging the attorney with violation of a "pseudo-criminal statute," it had charged him with obstruction of justice under a proper statute, the court would have been faced with a much more difficult decision. Id.

With the exception of *Belge,* id., the foregoing cases provide a consistent body of law, which we adopt. To summarize, a criminal defense attorney in possession of physical evidence incriminating his client may, after a reasonable time for examination, return it to its source if he can do so without hindering the apprehension, prosecution, conviction or punishment of another and without altering, destroying or concealing it or impairing its verity or availability in any pending or imminent investigation or proceeding. Otherwise, he must deliver it to the prosecution on his own motion. In the latter event, the prosecution is entitled to use the physical evidence as well as information pertaining to its condition, location and discovery but may not disclose to a fact-finder the source of the evidence. We thus reject appellants' contention that their conduct was proper and that they had no duty to deliver the rifle stock to the prosecution until they were ordered to do so.

Due Process: Overbreadth

Appellants' second argument is that the statutes against hindering prosecution and tampering with evidence are unconstitutionally vague or overbroad as applied to attorneys engaged in the representation of criminal defendants, and hence their enforcement against appellants was a denial of due process. We agree. Our discussion of appellants' first argument, while holding that defense attorneys have an affirmative duty to deliver physical evidence to the prosecution, clearly demonstrates that there are conflicting concerns facing defense attorneys in possession of incriminating physical evidence. Moreover, we are not aware of *any* case in *any* state in which an attorney was convicted of a crime for conduct similar to that of appellants. . . .

Both overbroad and vague statutes deny due process in two ways: they do not give fair notice to people of ordinary intelligence that their contemplated activity may be unlawful, and they do not set reasonably clear guidelines for law enforcement officials and courts, thus inviting arbitrary and discriminatory enforcement. . . .

We hold that the statutes at issue in this case are overbroad when applied to attorneys representing criminal defendants. The literal language of each section is relatively clear. Section 5105(a)(3) states that a person is guilty of hindering prosecution "if, with intent to hinder the . . . conviction . . . of another for crime, he . . . conceals . . . evidence of the crime . . . regardless of its admissibility in evidence. . . ." Section 4910 provides that a person is guilty of tampering with physical evidence "if, believing that an official proceeding . . . is pending . . ., he . . . conceals or removes any record, document or thing with intent to impair its verity or availability in such proceeding. . . ." The clarity of the language is delusive, for it prohibits conduct which cannot constitutionally be prohibited along with conduct which clearly can. In certain circumstances, an attorney might conceal evidence with the intent of impairing its availability in his client's criminal trial and with the intent of hindering his client's conviction.

An example of such circumstances might involve an attorney whose client gives him a handwritten account of involvement in the crime he is charged with committing. If the attorney were to destroy the statement or retain it in his file, he would be guilty of violating the literal terms of the statutes against hindering prosecution and tampering with evidence. Yet no one would suggest the attorney should give the document to the prosecutor; indeed, to do so would be an egregious violation of the attorney's duties to his client.

The functions of the attorney counseling a criminal defendant have a constitutional dimension. In opposing unreasonable searches and seizures, in preventing self-incrimination and in rendering effective assistance of counsel, the defense attorney is charged with the protection of fourth, fifth and sixth amendment rights. In performing these functions, the defense attorney might run afoul of the statutes against hindering prosecution and tampering with evidence; thus he may not have adequate notice of what conduct might be a crime, and he is subject to the threat of arbitrary and discriminatory prosecution.

Beyond the obvious example stated above, there is little or no guidance for an attorney to know when he has crossed the invisible line into an area of criminal behavior. There are no prior cases in this jurisdiction in which a criminal defense attorney has been convicted of violating these statutes. We have discussed many of the similar cases from other jurisdictions, none of which addresses the precise issues facing us in this case. Although we focused on the uniformity we found in those cases as to disposition of physical evidence, they express a great deal of doubt and reflect great diversity as to the grayer areas of ethical usage of evidence of all sorts. Attorneys face a distressing paucity of dispositive precedent to guide them in balancing their duty of zealous representation against their duty as officers of the court. Volumes are filled with other potential sources of guidance, such as ethical codes and comments thereto, both proposed and adopted, advisory opinions by ethics committees and myriad articles in legal periodicals. The plethora of writings exemplifies the profession's concern with the problem, and although they may help to clarify some of the issues, they fail to answer many of the difficult questions in this area of legal practice.

In the cases discussed in the preceding section, we find many statements which belie the seeming consistency in their approach to the problem. *People v. Belge,* supra, of course, dismissing the indictment against an attorney who had withheld evidence, focused on the rights of a criminal defendant rather than the society's interest in criminal law enforcement:

> A trial is in part a search for truth, but it is only partly a search for truth. The mantle of innocence is flung over the defendant to such an extent that he is safeguarded by rules of evidence which frequently keep out absolute truth, much to the chagrin of juries. Nevertheless, this has been a part of our system since our laws were taken from the laws of England and over these many years has been found to best protect a balance between the rights of the individual and the rights of society.

Belge, supra, 372 N.Y.S.2d at 801. Another example is In re Gartley, supra, wherein this court stated:

Not only is effective assistance of counsel a constitutional mandate, it is also necessary to an adversary system of justice. Assuredly, counsel's assistance can be made safely and readily available only when the client is free from the apprehension of disclosure.

. . .

Finally, *Hitch v. Pima County Superior Court*, supra, although holding that an attorney has a duty to deliver incriminating evidence to the prosecutor, added:

> We note also that the lawyer's role as a zealous advocate is an important one, not only for the client but for the administration of justice. We have chosen an adversary system of justice in which, in theory, the state and the defendant meet as equals—"strength against strength, resource against resource, argument against argument." United States v. Bagley, [473 U.S. 667, 694] n. 2 (1985) (Marshall, J., dissenting). In order to close the gap between theory and practice and thereby ensure that the system is working properly, a defendant must have an attorney who will fight against the powerful resources of the state. It is only when this occurs that we can be assured that the system is functioning properly and only the guilty are convicted.

Hitch, supra, 708 P.2d at 76.

Two cases cited in the previous section involved attorneys who had sought advisory opinions from ethics committees when confronted with problems related to disposition of physical evidence. Their action was salutary, but underscores the dilemma facing criminal defense attorneys in similar situations. Not only is the resort to guidance from an ethics committee a time-consuming process,[2] it is a process totally inconsistent with the precision which must attend a valid criminal statute to inform its subjects of what specific behavior is proscribed.

Another symbol of the dilemma is its extensive treatment in legal periodicals. Of the many articles which have been cited by the parties in this case, we have found several to be helpful and noteworthy.[3] Nonetheless, the writings exemplify a variety of approaches and suggestions, and indicate that an evidentiary problem related to incriminating evidence might arise in divers contexts in the representation of criminal defendants. It is not incumbent upon attorneys to digest the legal periodicals in order

---

2. The court in *Hitch*, supra, explained the result of seeking advice in that case:

> We note that the prosecution in this matter has been delayed for over a year while this issue is being resolved. We believe that the recourse to the State Bar Ethics Committee, while proper and commendable, resulted in an excessive delay. We hope that in the future the State Bar Ethics Committee will be more prompt in responding to requests for opinions when, as here, a criminal prosecution is held in abeyance awaiting the opinion of the Committee.

Id. 708 P.2d at 79 n. 3.

3. See Comment, Ethics, Law and Loyalty: The Attorney's Duty to Turn Over Incriminating Physical Evidence, 32 Stan.L.Rev. 977 (1980); Comment, The Right of a Criminal Defense Attorney to Withhold Physical Evidence Received from His Client, 38 U.Chi.L.Rev. 211 (1970); Comment, Disclosure of Incriminating Physical Evidence: The Defense Attorney's Dilemma, 52 U.Colo.L.Rev. 419 (1981).

to conform their conduct to a criminal statute. The statutes involved in this case embrace conduct which is constitutionally protected as well as conduct which may validly be prohibited, and there is no line between the two which can be ascertained with any assurance whatsoever.

Even if it were possible, it is not the function of this court to provide an advisory opinion as to various examples of attorney conduct not involved in this case which might or might not violate the statutes we are reviewing. We note that other jurisdictions have enacted criminal statutes which address the unique role of defense attorneys in the administration of criminal justice and do not subject them to rules identical with those applicable to the public. See Clark v. State, 159 Tex.Cr.R. 187, 261 S.W.2d 339 (1953) (statute specifically excluded from liability one who aids an offender in preparing his defense). We note, also, as the Pennsylvania Supreme Court iterated in Estate of Pedrick, that the courts have the power, outside the context of criminal sanctions, to regulate the conduct of attorneys practicing before them, and that the Pennsylvania Supreme Court has established a Disciplinary Board together with comprehensive rules for dealing with apparent attorney misconduct. 505 Pa. [530,] 542, 482 A.2d [215,] 221.

For these reasons, we hold that the statutes which prohibit hindering prosecution and tampering with physical evidence are unconstitutionally overbroad when applied to attorneys representing criminal defendants.

Accordingly, the judgments of sentence are vacated and appellants discharged.

———

Did the Lawyers in *Stenhach* Commit a Crime?

The court in *Stenhach* rejects the argument that the lawyers had no duty to turn over the evidence. The court not only "adopts" the rule of other jurisdictions that a lawyer has a responsibility under the ethics rules to turn over incriminating physical evidence, but speaks as though this duty were in force when the lawyers in this case acted. Why is the court confident that lawyers can observe the line between ethical and unethical conduct but not between criminal and legal conduct? Why isn't the court concerned about the potential "chilling effect" of the disciplinary rules? Does the dismissal of the criminal charges against the Stenhachs beg the question of why lawyers should be treated differently from everyone else?

The lawyers claimed that they had conducted exhaustive research and concluded they were "obligated" to retain the rifle stock. However, as the court's review of the case law shows, all the decided cases, with the exception of *Belge*,[4] had held that there was a duty to turn over such evidence. Does *Belge*, insofar as its relies on norms flowing from the attorney-client privilege to interpret public health statutes as not applying

———

4. See the discussion of the *Dead Bodies Case*, p. 57 below.

to lawyers in their professional role, support the Stenhachs' claim of immunity? Despite the consistency of court decisions in this area, lawyers have long been confused about their duties as to incriminating physical evidence. A Virginia lawyer was disciplined by a federal court in In re Ryder,[5] a leading case, for removing from his client's safe deposit box a sawed-off shot gun and the proceeds of a bank robbery and placing those items in a safe deposit box under the lawyer's own name. Ryder had consulted with several other lawyers, including a former judge, as to what he should do with the evidence. All those consulted were uncertain, but none recommended the "correct" course of conduct, i.e., turning the evidence over to law enforcement officials. Neither did any suggest that Ryder might be criminally liable as an accomplice for retaining and concealing money stolen from the bank. The confusion might be attributed to the fact that *Ryder* was one of the first opinions decided on this question, but this fact does not explain why no one considered the stolen-property statute as even potentially applicable.

This failure to consider general criminal statutes may be due to the assumption that lawyers are immune from laws of general applicability, but even so *Ryder* does not explain the continuing confusion of lawyers like the Stenhach brothers. In 1980 a commentator wrote:

> The attorney [in possession of incriminating physical evidence] has little guidance on how to resolve [her conflicting responsibilities as an officer of the court and as an advocate of the client]. Neither the attorney-client privilege nor ethical rules nor statutes nor constitutional doctrines give a clear signal to the attorney seeking both to maintain loyalty to her client and to be properly candid with the court. The attorney in possession of incriminating physical evidence confronts a series of rules most of which indicate the importance of the value of loyalty to the client but none of which quite provides the loyal attorney with a *safe harbor* from discipline or criminal penalties.[6]

Some writers continue to bemoan the confusion in this area.[7] The confusion may have less to do with conflicting legal standards, however, than with a perceived conflict between what the law actually requires and what lawyers believe to be their duty, i.e., not to harm or betray their clients.[8]

---

5. 263 F.Supp. 360 (E.D.Va.1967), aff'd, 381 F.2d 713 (4th Cir.1967).

6. Note, Ethics, Law, and Loyalty: The Attorney's Duty to Turn Over Incriminating Physical Evidence, 32 Stan.L.Rev. 977, 980 (1980) (emphasis added).

7. See, e.g., Norman Lefstein, Incriminating Physical Evidence, The Defense Attorney's Dilemma, and the Need for Rules, 64 N.C.L.Rev. 897 (1986).

8. The tension between professional norms that appear to require certain lawyer conduct and general criminal statutes that prohibit the same conduct, is dealt with in

Restatement § 8: "[t]he traditional and appropriate activities of lawyers in representing clients consistent with the requirements of the applicable lawyer code are relevant factors for the tribunal in assessing [the] propriety of a lawyer's conduct under the law of crimes." The comments provide little illumination of how this murky principle should differentiate between the general rule that criminal laws "are drafted assuming the applicability of such law," and the exceptional case in which a court should construe a criminal provision "so as to make it consistent with

Spaulding v. Zimmerman, supra, assumes that a lawyer has no duty to disclose adverse evidence to the opposing party in the absence of a proper request. Why is a different approach applied to physical evidence of crime?

3.   LAWYERS AND INCRIMINATING EVIDENCE

Ethics Rules and Criminal Statutes

The Model Rules take the clear position that general criminal law trumps the lawyer's general duty of loyalty to client. Rule 3.4(a) states, "A lawyer shall not *unlawfully* obstruct another party's access to evidence, or *unlawfully* alter, destroy or conceal a document or other material having potential evidentiary value. A lawyer shall not counsel or assist another person to do any such act." (Emphasis added.) Rules 1.2(d) and 8.4(b) and (c), which prohibit lawyer conduct that is "criminal or fraudulent," also subject lawyers to general criminal law.[9]

The question then is: What does law require?

First, criminal laws in all jurisdictions make the concealment or destruction of evidence criminal although the circumstances that trigger the statutes vary from one state to another. Some states prohibit destruction only when a person "knows" a legal proceeding is ongoing or about to be instituted; other states prohibit destruction when a person "believes" a proceeding is pending or about to be instituted; and still other states prohibit destruction with intent to prevent the production of the evidence.[10] These statutes generally make no exception for lawyers. But see Clark v. State,[11] holding that the Texas concealment statute contains an implied exclusion for lawyers, and the approval of this approach in *Stenhach*.

Contraband statutes, which make the possession of certain items illegal, exist in all jurisdictions and make no exceptions for criminal defense lawyers.[12] Prohibited items generally include instrumentalities of crime

---

an applicable lawyer code provision ... [when the court can do so] consistent with precedent and with accepted norms governing construction of a criminal statute." Restatement § 8, cmt. c.

9.   The Model Rules' predecessor, the Model Code, is to the same effect while using different language. DR 7–102(A)(3) provides that "a lawyer shall not conceal or knowingly fail to disclose that which he is required by law to reveal"; and DR 7–109(A) states, "A lawyer shall not suppress any evidence that he or his client has a legal obligation to reveal or produce." Finally, DR 7–102(A)(8) directs that "a lawyer shall not knowingly engage in other illegal conduct or conduct contrary to a Disciplinary Rule."

10.   See, e.g., Model Penal Code § 242.3 (1962); 18 U.S.C. § 1001; West's Ann.Cal. Pen.Code § 135; Minn.Stat.Ann. § 609.63(1), (7); N.Y.—McKinney's Penal Law § 205.50.

11.   261 S.W.2d 339 (Tex.Crim.App.1953).

12.   At least one commentator has suggested that the contraband statutes be amended to provide an exception for lawyers. Note, Ethics, Law, and Loyalty: The Attorney's Duty to Turn Over Incriminating Physical Evidence, 32 Stan.L.Rev. 977, 995 (1980). This commentator also suggests an exception for lawyers under the concealment and destruction of evidence statutes, arguing that a lawyer's duty of loyalty to a client should preclude having to provide the prosecution with physical evidence.

(such as a murder weapon), illegal weapons and drugs and other controlled substances.[13]

Judicial decisions, as pointed out in *Stenhach*, are unanimous in holding that the ethics rules, read in conjunction with the concealment and contraband laws, require a lawyer to deliver physical evidence when those laws would be violated by retaining the evidence. There is some question, as *Stenhach* demonstrates, whether courts will uphold the use of criminal sanctions against criminal defense lawyers whose conduct violates these laws, but none that lawyers may be disciplined for such conduct under the ethics rules. But see *Stenhach II*, discussed below.

Case Law on a Lawyer's Obligations as to Incriminating Evidence[14]

Generally, a lawyer must not act or assist in the destruction or unlawful concealment of evidence.[15] This means that a lawyer must not take affirmative steps to conceal evidence, such as those taken by the lawyers in *Stenhach*.[16] If a lawyer leaves evidence where she finds it, she cannot be compelled to reveal information gained from a privileged communication. However, once physical evidence[17] is taken from its original resting place, the lawyer must not do anything that would conceal or destroy either the evidence itself or evidence of its location or condition.

Once a lawyer possesses physical evidence, she must not return that evidence to its source (whether the client or a third person) if she has reason to believe that the evidence will be destroyed or unlawfully concealed or that the chain of evidence will be broken. In light of the risk of subsequent destruction or concealment, the majority of jurisdictions require the lawyer to hand over to the proper authorities *all* physical evidence.[18]

Two caveats limit this rule. The first concerns evidence created as part of a defense, such as a statement by a defendant prepared for his lawyer on

---

13. See, e.g., Model Pen.Code § 5.06–.07 (1962) (possession of criminal instruments and weapons); West's Ann.Cal.Pen.Code § 12020 (Supp.1980) (possession of illegal weapons); West's Ann.Cal.Health & Safety Code § 11377 (Supp.1980) (possession of drugs and controlled substances); Uniform Controlled Substances Act § 401(c).

14. The lawyer's responsibilities as to evidence in civil cases are discussed in Chapter 5 below at pp. 381–84 (false evidence) and 455 (improper means).

15. The word "unlawful" distinguishes what might be called "lawful concealment", i.e., the legal steps an attorney may take to suppress evidence inadmissible under evidence rules or obtained through a violation of the client's constitutional rights or the legal steps a lawyer may take to prevent the opposing party in a civil case from gaining access to privileged material.

16. See, e.g., Hitch v. Pima County Superior Court, 708 P.2d 72 (Ariz.1985); People v. Meredith, 631 P.2d 46 (Cal.1981).

17. Throughout this discussion we are speaking of *physical* evidence. A bright line exists between the lawyer's possession of physical evidence and her knowledge of testimonial evidence. The lawyer has a duty to keep the testimonial evidence of past criminal activity confidential.

18. See, e.g., State ex rel. Sowers v. Olwell, 394 P.2d 681 (Wash.1964); People v. Lee, 83 Cal.Rptr. 715 (1970); Morrell v. State, 575 P.2d 1200 (Alaska 1978).

what the defendant knew about the bank's security system. Such evidence falls under the protective umbrella of the attorney-client privilege and thus need not be turned over to authorities as physical evidence. The fact that certain communications between client and lawyer are in physical form does not change their privileged status. If the client prepared a written statement for some purpose other than assisting in the defense, e.g., the client kept a journal of her criminal activities as they took place, the document qualifies as physical evidence and is not protected by the attorney-client privilege. In Morrell v. State,[19] where a third party gave the defense lawyer kidnap plans written out by the defendant prior to the crime, the court held that the lawyer acted properly in returning the plans to the third party and advising him to turn them over to the police.[20]

The second caveat involves evidence that the state could not compel a defendant to produce against his will. If a personal diary, for example, is constitutionally protected against compulsory production by an accused, the protection continues once possession is transferred to the accused's lawyer.[21] Some earlier cases, including *Ryder,* extended protection to "merely evidentiary articles" that are not contraband or the fruits or instrumentalities of crime. The Supreme Court's later repudiation of the "mere evidence" rule narrowed sharply the category of protected physical evidence, whether retained by the client or given to the client's lawyer.[22]

Even if a lawyer must eventually turn over all physical evidence, courts allow the lawyer to retain the evidence for a "reasonable" period of time for investigatory purposes. As long as the defense then stipulates to the "chain of possession, location or condition of the evidence," the prosecution may not disclose to the jury from whom or in what manner the evidence was obtained.[23] Requiring the defense to stipulate to the evidence's original location and source prevents the defendant from "destroying" the evidence by negating its probative value. On the other hand, restricting the prosecu-

---

19. 575 P.2d 1200 (Alaska 1978).

20. Accord: State v. Carlin, 640 P.2d 324 (Kan.App.1982) (lawyer ordered to surrender an incriminating tape recording made by the client). The Texas criminal court of appeals strained accepted doctrine in the *Baby Brandon* case. Henderson v. State, 962 S.W.2d 544 (Tex.Crim.App.1997). After an infant boy had been left by his parents with a babysitter, both disappeared. In the subsequent kidnaping investigation, the prosecutor learned that the principal suspect, the babysitter, who at one point had told police that she had accidentally killed Brandon, had prepared a map for her attorney indicating the location of the body. A subpoena to the babysitter's lawyer for the map was enforced on appeal on the theory that the child, who had been missing 18 days when the subpoena was enforced, might still be alive and that the attorney-client privilege had to yield to the strong

public interest of protecting a child from death or serious injury. The holding rests on the dubious assumption that the boy was still alive and hence the map was part of a continuing rather than past crime.

21. See, e.g., State v. Superior Court, 625 P.2d 316 (Ariz.1981).

22. Warden v. Hayden, 387 U.S. 294, 306–307 (1967), repudiated the "mere evidence" rule. See the discussion of fourth amendment protection of diaries or letters in Chapter 4 below at p. 238.

23. People v. Meredith, supra, 631 P.2d at 54; see also *Olwell*, supra. See also Commonwealth v. Ferri, 599 A.2d 208, 211–13 (Pa.Super.1991) (if defendant fails to stipulate the authenticity of physical evidence delivered to his lawyer, the lawyer may testify concerning the chain of custody).

tion's disclosure of the source of the evidence protects a privileged communication—the client's statement to the lawyer of the source or location of the evidence. The physical evidence itself is not privileged. As the court in People v. Meredith said:

> To bar admission of testimony concerning the original condition and location of the evidence ... permits the defense to "destroy" critical information; it is as if ... the wallet in this case bore a tag bearing the words "located in the trash can by Scott's residence," and the defense by taking the wallet, destroyed this tag.[24]

The District of Columbia version of the Model Rules provides that a lawyer shall not counsel or assist concealment or destruction of evidence "if the lawyer reasonably should know that the evidence is or may be the subject of discovery or subpoena in any pending or imminent proceeding."[25] The comments to the D.C. rules, which include a summary of federal and D.C. criminal provisions relating to physical evidence, rely on a D.C. ethics opinion stating that the "test is whether destruction of [a] document is directed at concrete litigation that is either pending or almost certain to be filed":

> Because of the duty of confidentiality under Rule 1.6, the lawyer is generally forbidden to volunteer information about physical evidence received from a client without the client's consent after consultation.[26]

The D.C. Rules also contain a unique procedure:

> In some cases, the Office of Bar Counsel will accept physical evidence from a lawyer and then turn it over to the appropriate persons; in those cases this procedure is usually the best means of delivering evidence to the proper authorities without disclosing the client's confidences.[27]

The comment then cautions lawyers that advance thought should be given "before accepting evidence from a client" because "Bar Counsel may refuse to accept evidence," leaving the lawyer with limited options. The comment, viewed as a whole, appears to state that a lawyer may do what the Stenhachs did: receive physical evidence from the client and hold it in secrecy until an official request is made for it. Isn't that prohibited concealment? Other courts have rejected this procedure because it may result in erasing the chain of evidence so completely as to render the evidence meaningless:[28]

> Not all items have evidentiary significance in and of themselves. In this case, for instance, the watch is not inculpatory per se; rather, it is the fact that the [victim's] watch was found in defendant's jacket that

---

24. 631 P.2d at 53.

25. D.C. Rules of Professional Conduct, Rule 3.4(a) (adopted March 1, 1990 by the D.C. Court of Appeals). The rules are reprinted in Thomas D. Morgan and Ronald D. Rotunda, 1999 Selected Standards on Professional Responsibility.

26. D.C. Rules of Professional Conduct, Comment [5] to Rule 3.4.

27. Id.

28. Hitch v. Pima County, 708 P.2d 72 (Ariz.1985).

makes the watch material evidence. By returning the watch anonymously to the police, this significance is lost. Assuming investigating officials are even able to determine to what case the evidence belongs, they may never be able to reconstruct where it was originally discovered or under what circumstances.[29]

Do the rules change when a lawyer obtains the evidence from a third person rather than from a client? When the source is the client or the client's agent, the attorney-client privilege usually prevents the prosecution from compelling the lawyer to testify as to the origin of the evidence as long as the defense makes an appropriate stipulation as to the evidence's original location and condition. When the source is a third person, however, the courts hold that the evidentiary privilege no longer applies. See, e.g., *Olwell*, supra.

Given the case law, how could the lawyers in *Stenhach* have conducted extensive research, as they testified they did, and still have reached the conclusion they did? Apparently they approached their research with the goal of building a legal argument to justify retention of the rifle stock. What question might they have asked instead?

The *Dead Bodies* Case[30]

This case has gained a special place in the annals of legal ethics. A murder defendant, Robert Garrow, confessed to his lawyers, Belge and Armani, that he had committed the crime charged, as well as three other murders. The police had not yet discovered the bodies of two of those victims. Following Garrow's directions, the two lawyers found the bodies of Alicia Hauk, a 16–year–old high school student, and Susan Petz, a 21–year–old Boston University journalism student. Petz had disappeared after going camping in the Adirondacks with Dan Porter, a third murder victim whose body the police had already discovered. Hauk had disappeared a month before Petz and Porter. The lawyers photographed the two women's bodies but told no one of their discovery.

Petz's parents, knowing that police suspected Garrow of the murder of their daughter's camping partner, feared that she too was dead. They pleaded with Garrow's lawyers, Belge and Armani, for knowledge about their daughter, but the lawyers remained silent. Six months later, Garrow testified at his trial about the Hauk and Petz murders as part of an ultimately unsuccessful insanity defense. At a press conference Belge and Armani acknowledged they had known the location of the two women's bodies for many months but had remained silent. The lawyers, however, had offered to help the police solve the Petz and Hauk cases in exchange for a plea bargain promise that Garrow would be committed to a mental hospital, an offer the prosecutor had rejected.

---

29. 708 P.2d at 78–79.

30. People v. Belge, 376 N.Y.S.2d 771 (4th Dept.1975), aff'd, 359 N.E.2d 377 (N.Y. 1976). The facts stated in the text are drawn from the reported opinions and from Tom Alibrandi with Frank H. Armani, Privileged Information (1984).

Community outrage over the case resulted in criminal charges against one of the lawyers, Belge, for violating a New York law that requires a decent burial for the dead and the reporting of any death that occurs without medical attention. The trial court granted a motion to dismiss based on attorney-client privilege. The appeals' court affirmed, holding that the privilege "effectively shielded the defendant attorney from his actions which would otherwise have violated the Public Health Law." The court, however, expressed its "serious concern" with the argument that the privilege is absolute: "We believe that an attorney must protect his client's interests, but also must observe basic human standards of decency, having due regard to the need that the legal system accord justice to the interests of society and its individual members."[31] After the appellate court's decision, the Committee on Professional Ethics of the New York State Bar Association issued an opinion stating that the ethical rules required the lawyers' silence.[32]

The court in *Stenhach* notes that *Belge* dismissed a criminal prosecution against a lawyer who had failed to take affirmative steps to disclose physical evidence to law enforcement officials. *Belge*, however, is distinguishable on other grounds. The lawyers in that case never had possession of the evidence nor did they conceal or alter the evidence: They looked at the bodies in their original resting places and left them there.

Did the lawyers in *Belge* act immorally? Would an anonymous tip of the location of the bodies have satisfied professional, legal and moral duties? Would disclosure have been proper if the uncertainty concerning her daughter had constituted a grave threat to Mrs. Petz's life?

Why are the moral intuitions of many lay people so much at odds with those of lawyers in situations like that involved in the *Dead Bodies Case?* The anguish of parents who do not know whether a child is alive or dead is easy to understand. Moreover, the decent treatment of the dead is a powerful moral theme in all civilizations. In the Western tradition, one need mention only *Antigone*. Lawyers, who share these cultural values, nevertheless generally believe that the values underlying confidentiality and the partisan representation of clients in the adversary system outweigh considerations of "ordinary morality." The differentiated role morality associated with being a lawyer displaces the more general moral principles that otherwise would prevail.

The tension between ordinary morality and professional morality has a further element: In situations like that in the *Dead Bodies Case*, the concern of lay people is not just the lawyer's passive role in keeping secrets. Lawyers, such as those who represented the killer in the *Dead Bodies Case*, do more than merely remain silent: They provide active assistance in helping clients (in this situation, a guilty and repulsive person) avoid disclosure and accountability. An effective lawyer, even if aware of a client's guilt, will try to reshape reality to make the client appear innocent

31. 376 N.Y.S.2d 771, 772.

32. N.Y. State Bar Ass'n Comm. on Prof. Ethics Op. 479 (1978).

or, at least, not guilty beyond a reasonable doubt. This active participation in suppressing or distorting truth burdens lawyers in the public eye with a kind of moral complicity in a client's antisocial ends. Do you agree?

Why Lawyers Are Not Prosecuted for Concealing Evidence

Prosecutors have shown little interest in prosecuting lawyers for violating the evidence or contraband statutes. Although there may be many reasons for this, including collegial sympathy, the primary reasons include the following: (1) Most of the evidence statutes require proof of "specific" or "willful" intent, e.g., intent to hinder the prosecution, and prosecutors appreciate that defense lawyers will claim to have concealed with intent only to fulfill their professional responsibility; (2) prosecutors tend to exercise their discretion against bringing charges against one who acted without malicious intent or bad faith, even if the statute does not require evil purpose; and (3) prosecutors may share the assumption that lawyers are somehow immune from liability.[33]

Stenhach II

In Office of Disciplinary Counsel v. Stenhach,[34] the Pennsylvania disciplinary board unanimously refused to discipline the Stenhach brothers for their conduct. The board found that the Stenhachs, who "resolved in favor of their client doubts as to the bounds of law," acted in good faith and were guilty only of "zealous advocacy." The board's opinion, however, provides little comfort to Pennsylvania lawyers who receive and retain physical evidence of a crime. At the time the Stenhachs acted, the board emphasized, no Pennsylvania decision had held that physical evidence must be turned over to authorities; but the turnover rule first announced in *Stenhach I* changed the law of Pennsylvania prospectively. Further, the board observed, the prosecutor, who knew or should have known that the Stenhachs had acquired physical evidence, did not seek to compel its production. The Stenhachs' action did not impair the integrity of the criminal process because the prosecution neither needed nor used the rifle stock as evidence in the case.

Is the rule in Pennsylvania after Stenhach II that a lawyer may retain incriminating evidence so long as it is not vital to the prosecution? Since the time that the Stenhach brothers acted, Pennsylvania has adopted a version of the Model Rules that includes a provision substantially similar to M.R. 3.4(a). Does this clarify the rule in Pennsylvania? Does a lawyer in Pennsylvania who retains the murder weapon or any other material evi-

---

33. For discussion of the ways in which criminal law regulates lawyers and the criminal law's relationship to professional norms, see Bruce A. Green, The Criminal Regulation of Lawyers, 67 Fordham L.Rev. 327 (1998) (recommending that courts in interpreting criminal statutes be more accommodating to professional norms and

that prosecutors should exercise more restraint in situations in which a lawyer has relied in good faith on professional norms).

34. No. 479, slip op. at 25–27 (Pa.Super.Ct.Disciplinary Board, Aug. 8, 1989) (*Stenhach II*).

dence that incriminates the client run a serious risk of being disciplined for such conduct? If so, what explains Stenhach II ?

Should Nixon Have Burned the Tapes?

The Watergate burglary took place on June 17, 1972. Shortly thereafter, criminal investigators discovered evidence indicating that some persons connected with the Nixon administration were implicated. Over a year later, during the course of an investigation conducted by a Senate committee, an aide to President Richard Nixon revealed that tapes existed of all conversations in the president's office. The committee sought to compel production of relevant tapes, but the courts ultimately held the committee's subpoena to be unauthorized by statute.[35] A criminal investigation of Watergate, however, began soon after the Watergate burglary. In April 1974, a special prosecutor, who had taken over the criminal investigation, issued a second subpoena seeking production of the tapes. The Supreme Court upheld the validity of the second subpoena in July 1974 against plausible claims of executive privilege.[36]

Nixon later claimed that he should have destroyed the tapes: "I had bad advice from well-intentioned lawyers who had sort of the cockeyed notion that I would be destroying evidence."[37] Was Nixon given sound advice? At what point, if at all, would destruction of the tapes have violated the federal obstruction of justice statute, infra, p. 72, or the D.C. ethics rule, supra, p. 56. What moral or practical reasons support advice not to destroy the tapes?

Document Retention and Destruction

Cases stating a lawyer's obligation to turn over physical evidence of crime to a prosecutor generally involve the instrumentalities or fruits of crime (e.g., a bloody knife or stolen property) or contraband (things that it is unlawful to possess, such as an illegal drug). What about corporate documents prepared in the ordinary course of business? As will be seen in Chapter 4, business records are usually not protected by the attorney-client privilege and thus can be discovered by appropriate legal process or seized by exercise of a valid search warrant. If the only copies of such documents are transferred to the organization's lawyer, they are entitled to no greater protection in the hands of the lawyer than they would receive if retained by the client. See United States v. Fisher, infra, at p. 227. We have not found cases applying the turnover doctrine to preexisting client business records transferred to a lawyer, presumably because discovery and seizure devices adequately protect law enforcement interests in this context. The lawyer's responsibilities with respect to corporate documents primarily concern the prevention of destruction and avoidance of concealment.

35. Senate Select Committee v. Nixon, 366 F.Supp. 51 (D.D.C.1973).

36. United States v. Nixon, 418 U.S. 683 (1974). President Nixon resigned on Aug. 9, 1974, only four days after transcripts of the subpoenaed conversations were released.

37. John Herbers, Former Aide Interviews Nixon, N.Y. Times, Apr. 9, 1984, at p. 8.

Lawyers who handle civil matters for white-collar clients are unlikely to encounter dead bodies, sawed-off shotguns or paper bags of $100 bills. They nevertheless encounter serious questions concerning concealment or destruction of physical evidence. For example, a company official might seek advice as to what documents may be "harmful" in a rumored antitrust investigation. A pharmaceutical company might ask whether it may destroy test results that reveal harmful side effects of a drug that the company has marketed. Even if destruction of documents is not a crime, there are practical questions that must be considered. Documents may offer protection against false accusations (e.g., President Nixon might have wanted to retain the tapes because they would protect him against accusations that others implicated in the Watergate coverup might make against him). Destruction has other consequences:

> The destruction of a document to prevent its use at trial precludes that party from later introducing secondary evidence to prove the document's contents, but does not bar the opposing party from doing so. Moreover, the intentional destruction of a document to prevent its use at trial, even when not illegal, creates an adverse inference that a party's whole case is weak. Finally, any questions asked of a client under oath concerning the destruction must be answered honestly to avoid outright perjury. It is possible that the answers will be as damaging as the actual contents of the destroyed documents.[38]

38. Note, Legal Ethics and the Destruction of Evidence, 88 Yale L.J. 1665, 1675 (1979). See also John M. Fedders & Lauryn H. Guttenplan, Document Retention and Destruction: Practical, Legal and Ethical Considerations, 56 Notre Dame L. 5 (1980).

Chapter 2

CONFORMITY TO THE LAW

I have been asked many times as regard to particular practices or agreements as to whether they were legal or illegal under the Sherman [antitrust] law. One gentleman said to me: "We do not know where we can go." To which I replied, "I think your lawyers ... can tell you where a fairly safe course lies. If you are walking along a precipice no human being can tell you how near you can go to that precipice without falling over, because you may stumble on a loose stone, you may slip and go over; but anybody can tell you where you can walk perfectly safe within convenient distance of that precipice." The difficulty which men have felt ... has been rather that they wanted to go to the limit rather than that they have wanted to go safely.[1]

Louis D. Brandeis

A. CRIMINAL LAW

1. FRAUD AND CRIMINAL COMPLICITY

United States v. Benjamin

United States Court of Appeals, Second Circuit, 1964.
328 F.2d 854.

■ Before MOORE, FRIENDLY and KAUFMAN, CIRCUIT JUDGES.

■ FRIENDLY, CIRCUIT JUDGE.

This appeal concerns another of those sickening financial frauds which so sadly memorialize the rapacity of the perpetrators and the gullibility, and perhaps also the cupidity, of the victims. It is unusual in that the vehicle, American Equities Corporation, owned nothing at all—and, in a happier sense, in that the SEC was able to nip the fraud quite early in the bud. The appellants are Milton Mende, the principal promoter, Martin Benjamin, his lawyer, and Bernard Howard, a certified public accountant. After trial in the District Court for the Southern District of New York before Judge Palmieri without a jury, all three were convicted of conspiring willfully by use of interstate commerce to sell unregistered securities and to defraud in the sale of securities, in violation of the Securities Act of 1933, §§ 5(a) and (c), and 17(a), 15 U.S.C. §§ 77e(a) and (c), and 77q(a), sections

---

1. Louis D. Brandeis, Hearings before Sen. Comm. on Interstate Commerce, S.Res.No. 98, 62nd Cong., 1st Sess. 1161 (1911), quot- ed in Harry First, Business Crimes 27 (1990).

which are implemented criminally by § 24 of the Act, 15 U.S.C. § 77x. Mende and Benjamin were convicted also on three substantive counts for using the mails in furtherance of the fraudulent schemes in violation of 18 U.S.C. § 1341. As their sentences on the latter counts were the same as those on the conspiracy count and run concurrently with them, and as we are satisfied that their conspiracy conviction was proper, we need not concern ourselves with the mail fraud counts. Lawn v. United States, 355 U.S. 339, 362 (1958).

Since the principal claim of Howard and Benjamin relates to the sufficiency of the evidence against them, it is necessary to give some description of what went on. The scheme began in December, 1960, when Mende, then in Nevada, arranged to be put in touch with a Reno attorney, McDonald, who was reported to have some "old corporations prior to 1933" for sale. Mende's interest in corporations of such vintage was due to § 3(a)(1) of the Securities Act of 1933, 15 U.S.C. § 77c(a)(1), which confers an exemption from the need for registration on

> "Any security which, prior to or within sixty days after May 27, 1933, has been sold or disposed of by the issuer or bona fide offered to the public, but this exemption shall not apply to any new offering of any such security by an issuer or underwriter subsequent to such sixty days."

He was especially attracted by a 1919 shell, then bearing the rather appropriate name of Star Midas Mining Co., Inc. Authorized to issue 1,500,000 shares with a par value of 10¢ per share, Star Midas had approximately 964,000 shares outstanding, nearly all owned by a so-called "Mahoney group." It had no assets. After arranging to purchase the Mahoney holdings for $5,000 plus a $1,500 fee, Mende instructed McDonald to change the corporate name to American Equities Corporation and to increase the authorized capital to $1,500,000 by raising the par value to $1 per share. Before closing the purchase, the funds for which were not yet available, Mende, with McDonald's cooperation, bought stock certificates and a seal reflecting these changes. The purchase was not completed until February 23, 1961, when McDonald, having previously caused appropriate resolutions to be adopted and new officers and directors of Mende's selection to be named, turned over to Reiss and Kovaleski, as Mende's representatives, the books and records of the corporation and stock certificates for the 890,000 shares owned by the selling group. At this time the name of the corporation was changed.

Mende had not waited to acquire the American Equities shares before starting to sell them. In mid-January, 1961, he ordered an additional supply of stock certificates from a Los Angeles printer. By entering a bid to buy shares he arranged for American Equities to appear in the pink and white sheets of the National Quotation Service at a price of something over $5 per share. Robert Drattell, president of Lawrence Securities, Inc., which was inactive because of financial difficulties, testified that Benjamin then sought to interest him in selling shares of a corporation whose alleged assets corresponded with those later shown in statements of American

Equities. Benjamin indicated that if Drattell would cooperate, he might be in a position to find some way to make capital available to Lawrence Securities. Later in January, Benjamin had Drattell come to a New York hotel to meet Mende, who told Drattell and Reiter, another broker, in Benjamin's presence, that American Equities "was a holding corporation that had property, various types of property all over the United States, assets of about six and a half million dollars, liabilities of about three million dollars." Mende whetted Drattell's appetite, as Benjamin had already done, by indicating he would help to get Lawrence Securities back on its feet. Drattell said he "would need letters of opinion" and "certified financial statements," and also would need to see the transfer records which, Mende told him, were kept by "a certified public accountant out on the Coast."

Benjamin speedily filled one of Drattell's demands by handing him a signed opinion, dated January 28, 1961, headed "To Whom It May Concern: American Equities Corporation." It recited that the corporation was organized in May, 1919, "and there was at that time issued to the public, 963,067 Shares." It went on to say that in Benjamin's opinion "the aforesaid shares are presently free and tradeable pursuant to" § 3(a)(1) of the Securities Act which it quoted, and reiterated:

> "In view of the foregoing section, and further in view of the fact that the original issuance of the 963,067 Shares in May of 1919, falls directly within Section 3(1) of the Securities Act of 1933, and is therefore, in my opinion, free and tradeable." [sic]

[In January 1961 Benjamin went to Los Angeles with two brokers and met with Mende and Drattell. Mende distributed shares of American Equities to the three brokers. Drattell used his shares to obtain a bank loan, part of the proceeds of which were distributed to Mende and Mende's wife; the remaining proceeds went into the depleted capital account of Drattell's brokerage firm. When the group returned to New York, they brought an unidentified "Pro Forma Balance Sheet," dated November 30, 1960, that had been prepared by a confederate of Mende. They also brought] . . . a sheet of descriptive material [on yellow-lined paper], a draft of which the judge could reasonably have found to have been written out by Benjamin. The first numbered paragraph of this recited that American Equities was "a diversified investment company formed in the State of Nevada in 1919" and that its holdings consisted of "8 Apartment Houses, 2 Hotels, 2 Office Buildings (all located in Detroit area, Michigan)" with a "gross income from the properties" of $1,061,406.51 and net income of $200,000. This was completely false; the company owned no real estate in Detroit or elsewhere. Three subsequent paragraphs gave facts and figures as to the Outpost Inn, in Arizona, Biesmeyer Boat & Plastic Co., also of Arizona, and Stanford Trailer and Marine Supply Co., of California; the description did not say just what was American Equities' interest in these companies. . . . [In fact, American Equities had no ownership interest in any of these companies, although Mende had signed options to buy interests in two of them but had paid nothing.]

In mid-January, Benjamin invited Howard, a certified public accountant who had served Benjamin and his clients, to do some work for American Equities. Howard testified he received the November 30, 1960, "Pro Forma Balance Sheet," a yellow handwritten sheet of paper listing certain real estate holdings in Detroit, and balance sheets of corporations which Mende and Benjamin claimed were "owned or controlled" by American Equities. From these materials and without any examination of books and records, he prepared a paper dated February 10, 1961, and on the following day gave copies of this to Mende who handed one to Reiter. The latter testified that this was in Howard's presence.

The paper has a cover, on the stationery of Howard as a Certified Public Accountant, which bears the legend:

American Equities Corporation
December 31, 1960.

Auditors Report.

This is followed by a two-page letter in which Howard advises the company that "After an examination of the books and records of the diversified holdings of your corporation for the period ended December 31, 1960," he is submitting a report of the company as at that date, consisting of "Exhibit 'A'—Pro-forma Balance Sheet as at December 31, 1960." Next comes a section entitled "COMMENTS" informing the company that it is "a diversified investment corporation with the following holdings." These were substantially the same as in the description accompanying the November 30 statement, with the Outpost Inn, Biesmeyer, Stanford and also California Molded Products now clearly listed among them. ...[The comments also stated] that "The assets are shown at actual cost and are calculated at the most conservative value," although "A recent appraisal of the real estate in Detroit shows an increase of approximately $2,500,000.00 over book value, which has not been reflected in the statement"; that "The accounts receivable, loans receivable, loans payable, and mortgages payable were not verified by direct communication" and inventories were taken as submitted by the management; and, finally, that "The statement reflects an accurate and true picture of the corporation's net worth after taking into consideration the proposed loan by the officers." The "Pro–Forma Balance Sheet as at December 31, 1960" showed total assets of $7,769,-657.11 and a net worth of $3,681,049.70—this including $963,067.00 in the capital stock account. Howard received $200 for his two days of service in preparing the report.

. . .

American Equities stock continued to be sold until March 22, 1961, when, as a result of the SEC's action, trading stopped.

Howard's principal claim is that the evidence against him was insufficient to show the state of mind required for a criminal conviction. He says he was performing an accountant's duties innocently if inefficiently—and for a negligible compensation, that he sheltered himself with the label "pro forma," and that he did not know his reports were to help in stock peddling but thought they were to be used solely for management purposes. His own testimony belies the last claim; he admitted knowing that the promoters intended to use the stock as collateral for loans or as part of or collateral for the purchase price in various acquisitions and that his statements were shown to prospective lenders or sellers. Since his reports were little more than a regurgitation of material handed him by the "management" and related to properties that, as he had reason to know, were not owned, the judge could properly have regarded his claim that he thought them needed for "management" purposes as incredible in the last degree. But the evidence we have summarized shows directly that he knew his reports were being used with brokers who were selling the stock. Drattell, whom he knew to be a broker interested in American Equities, telephoned him in regard to his reports, and, on Reiter's testimony, he saw Mende hand a copy of his first report to Reiter whom he knew to be similarly interested.

The argument that reports which depicted American Equities as owner of properties and companies it neither owned nor had any firm arrangements to acquire were not false because they were stated to be "pro forma" involves a complete misconception of the duties of an accountant in issuing a report thus entitled. Although pro forma statements "purport to give effect to transactions actually consummated or expected to be consummated at a date subsequent to that of the date of the statements," "auditors consider it proper to submit their report and opinion on such statements only when the nature of the transactions effected is clearly described in the statements, and when satisfactory evidence of their bona fides is available, such as actual subsequent consummation or signed firm contracts." Montgomery, Auditing Theory and Practice (6th ed. 1940), 62–63; see also Prentice–Hall Encyclopedic Dictionary of Business Finance (1960), 485. It would be insulting an honorable profession to suppose that a certified public accountant may take the representations of a corporation official as to companies it proposes to acquire, combine their balance sheets without any investigation as to the arrangements for their acquisition or suitable provision reflecting payment of the purchase price, and justify the meaningless result simply by an appliqué of two Latin words.

It is true that the Government had not merely to show that the statements were false but to present evidence from which the judge could be convinced beyond reasonable doubt of Howard's culpable state of mind. But, as Judge Hough said for this court years ago, "when that state of mind is a knowledge of false statements, while there is no allowable inference of knowledge from the mere fact of falsity, there are many cases where from the actor's special situation and continuity of conduct an inference that he *did* know the untruth of what he said or wrote may legitimately be drawn." Bentel v. United States, 13 F.2d 327, 329 (2 Cir.1926). Any accountant must know that his obligations in certifying "pro forma" statements are not satisfied by any such arithmetical exercise as Howard performed. But, as our description of the reports has indicated, there were further false assertions, some of them clearly known to Howard to be such; these constituted a basis for holding him that was independent of the falsity of the total report, as well as for discrediting his assertions of ignorance as to what was required of him. The Michigan real estate was represented to Howard not as properties to be acquired but as already owned; he claimed to have seen deeds for these properties but admitted that American Equities was not named as grantee. The statements that certain assets had not been "verified by direct communication" implied that with this qualification all assets had been verified by suitable means; they had not been. Howard made no examination of American Equities' books, which, indeed, were not available when he rendered his first report; even a most cursory inspection would have revealed that nothing had been paid when the capital stock account was written up ten-fold. His statement purported to reflect "an accurate and true picture of the corporation's net worth after taking into consideration the proposed loan by the officers"; at best it would have been accurate only if the corporation had had at least some contractual basis for the assertion of ownership, and even then only if proper provision had been made for the cost.... Perhaps most damning of all was the making of a profit and loss statement including a positive assertion that the six companies were "acquired within the last few months," when Howard knew that at least some of them had not been acquired at all.

... Judge Learned Hand said in a similar context, " ... the cumulation of instances, each explicable only by extreme credulity or professional inexpertness, may have a probative force immensely greater than any one of them alone." United States v. White, 124 F.2d 181, 185 (2 Cir.1941).

In fact, however, the Government was not required to go that far. "Willful," the Supreme Court has told us, "is a word of many meanings, its construction often being influenced by its context." Spies v. United States, 317 U.S. 492, 497 (1943), citing United States v. Murdock, 290 U.S. 389, 394–396 (1933). We think that in the context of § 24 of the Securities Act as applied to § 17(a), the Government can meet its burden by proving that a defendant deliberately closed his eyes to facts he had a duty to see, compare Spurr v. United States, 174 U.S. 728 (1899) and American Law Institute, Model Penal Code, § 2.02(7), commentary in Tent.Draft No. 4, pages 129–30 (1955), or recklessly stated as facts things of which he was ignorant. Judge Hough so ruled in Bentel v. United States, supra; although that case and the similar ruling in Slakoff v. United States, 8 F.2d 9 (3 Cir.1925), were under the mail fraud statute, § 215 of the then Criminal Code, 35 Stat. 1130 (1909), the ancestor of 18 U.S.C. § 1341, which does not use the term "willfully," the Congress that passed the Securities Act scarcely meant to make life easier for defrauders. Other circuits have gone further and have held the willfulness requirement of the Securities Act to be satisfied in fraud cases by proof of representations which due diligence would have shown to be untrue. Stone v. United States, 113 F.2d 70, 75 (6 Cir.1940); United States v. Schaefer, 299 F.2d 625, 629, 632 (7 Cir.1962). In our complex society the accountant's certificate and the lawyer's opinion can be instruments for inflicting pecuniary loss more potent than the chisel or the crowbar. Of course, Congress did not mean that any mistake of law or misstatement of fact should subject an attorney or an accountant to criminal liability simply because more skillful practitioners would not have made them. But Congress equally could not have intended that men holding themselves out as members of these ancient professions should be able to escape criminal liability on a plea of ignorance when they have shut their eyes to what was plainly to be seen or have represented a knowledge they knew they did not possess. . . .

Much of what we have said as to Howard is relevant also to Benjamin's claim of insufficiency of the evidence as to his culpable state of mind. Benjamin brought Howard into the scheme; he had written out the list of assets which Howard later used in his first report; as Howard testified, Benjamin had told him to take the statements of the various companies "and just put them into a consolidated form"; and his work in connection with several of the proposed "acquisitions" gave him actual knowledge of the falsity both of the November 30 statement and of Howard's reports. But there was much more than this. His opinion letter made a positive statement that he believed all the shares of American Equities were exempt from registration, although he must have known that control of the corporation, not yet even named "American Equities Corporation," was being acquired by Mende and that the statute explicitly denied exemption to any new offerings by persons in control, a limitation of which his testimony before the SEC showed he was well aware. Yet there is abundant evidence that Benjamin knew Mende was putting American Equities shares on the market. Among the instances was the transaction outlined above with Drattell in late January wherein Benjamin received a confirmation of a purchase of 5,000 shares from "Martin Benjamin Trustee" for $9,000—at a time when the pink sheets were quoting the stock at $5 per share or more—and the distribution of part of the proceeds to Mende and his wife; yet Benjamin prepared a letter whereby the transfer agent certified these shares to be "free stock and . . . not investment stock." . . . [Benjamin's] proffer of financial aid if Drattell would undertake some distribution of American Equities afforded further basis for inferring knowledge of the intended fraud, as did his efforts falsely to minimize Mende's role when he and others were examined by the SEC. This and other evidence made a case at least as strong as that held sufficient with respect to another lawyer in United States v. Crosby, 294 F.2d 928, 938 (2 Cir.1961).

. . .

Mende, as the central figure in the scheme, has not challenged the sufficiency of the evidence introduced against him. He raises several points on appeal; all seem so patently without substance as not to require discussion. We here mention only his claim that McDonald's testimony should have been excluded under the attorney-client privilege, and we do that solely to state its complete lack of merit. The relation between Mende and McDonald was not that of client and attorney but of buyer and seller; what Mende was seeking from McDonald was not legal advice but a pre-1933 corporate shell.

Affirmed.

———

Proof of Criminal Liability

The court holds Benjamin criminally liable for activities, such as drafting an opinion letter for his client, Mende, and trying to minimize his client's role in the affair. What made those acts—routinely undertaken by lawyers—criminal on Benjamin's part?

Criminal law operates on a basic premise that bad acts alone are not enough to establish criminal liability; an actor must also have had a culpable state of mind, the mens rea. Various states of mind satisfy the mens rea requirement, however, depending on the crime. For example, some crimes require a specific intent to do harm; others provide that negligence satisfies the mens rea component.[2] In *Benjamin* what state of mind did the government have to prove to establish the requisite mens rea?

What distinguishes mere incompetence or misplaced confidence in a client's story from the conduct of Howard and Benjamin?

What a Lawyer "Knows"—Mens Rea

Benjamin's extensive participation in the fraudulent scheme resulted in his conviction as a full member of a criminal conspiracy (primary liability). More often, lawyers are charged with aiding and abetting a client's crime or fraud (secondary liability.) In either event, the question is whether the lawyer did so with a culpable state of mind and whether his actions facilitated the criminal scheme. Most jurisdictions hold that mere knowledge of another's criminal purpose does not suffice to make a person guilty of aiding and abetting the other's criminal conduct. One must associate oneself with the venture, participate in it as something one desires to bring about and seek by one's acts to make the venture succeed.[3] The court, however, may infer an intent to facilitate commission of the crime from an actor's knowledge that a principal would use the aid to commit a crime. What a lawyer knows about her client's criminal purpose is therefore critical.

Aside from criminal law sanctions, both the Model Code and the Model Rules make it unethical for a lawyer to facilitate a client's criminal or fraudulent purpose. Model Rule 1.2(d) states that a lawyer may not "counsel a client to engage, or assist a client, in conduct that the lawyer

---

2. Strict liability offenses provide an exception to the basic criminal law requirement of a culpable mental state. The crimes charged against Howard and Benjamin were not strict liability crimes and so required a showing of mens rea.

3. See United States v. Peoni, 100 F.2d 401 (2d Cir.1938). For a general discussion of the various mental states required for ac-complice liability, see Wayne R. LaFave and Austin Scott, Jr., Criminal Law § 6.7(b) at 579 (2d ed.1986). Some jurisdictions hold that knowledge or reason to know of another's intent to commit a crime establishes the mens rea. See, e.g., Mowery v. State, 105 S.W.2d 239 (Tex.Crim.App. 1937).

knows is criminal or fraudulent." DR 7–102(A)(7) of the Model Code bans a lawyer from actions that "counsel or assist his client in conduct that the lawyer knows to be illegal or fraudulent." Does the reach of these formulations differ? When will a lawyer be held to have known that her client is engaged in or contemplating criminal activity?

Benjamin reflects a general belief by courts that lawyers and accountants have a greater responsibility to know their client's actions and goals than do nonprofessionals in similar situations. The courts base this greater responsibility on an assumption that lawyers and other similarly situated professionals are more familiar with applicable legal limits and thus are more sensitive to facts that suggest transgression of those limits. Note that this assumption runs counter to that suggested by the paradigm of the criminal defense lawyer, who is permitted and even expected to act in court as though a client were innocent no matter what reasons the lawyer may have to believe or know otherwise. Relying on the criminal defense paradigm, lawyers often say that their job is not to judge the client but to believe in him. However, as *Benjamin* makes clear, lawyers who, while acting as counselors or advisors, "shut their eyes to what was plainly to be seen" or represent that they know something that they do not know, not only act improperly but risk criminal sanctions.[4] Thus a Colorado lawyer who received a car from his client in payment of a legal fee was found guilty of receiving stolen property.[5]

What a Lawyer Does—Actus Reus

The criminal law contains a corollary to the principle that bad acts alone are insufficient for criminal liability: Bad thoughts without an act are also insufficient. For criminal liability to attach, an act (actus reus) must be performed with the required culpable state of mind. Aiding and abetting a client's unlawful activity may result in professional discipline in addition to criminal liability.[6]

As *Benjamin* shows, an act routine in law practice—including the act of giving advice—may constitute the requisite actus reus, resulting in criminal liability if combined with the required culpable state of mind (which may be mere knowledge that a client intends to use the advice to further a criminal purpose). In United States v. Feaster,[7] for example, the court upheld a charge of aiding preparation of a false tax return in a case in which a lawyer advised an undercover agent, posing as a client, on how to

---

4. See Comment, Model Penal Code Section 2.02(7) and Wilful Blindness, 102 Yale L.J. 2231 (1993). What a lawyer as advocate "knows" about the truthfulness of a client's assertions is discussed infra in Chapter 5.

5. People v. Zelinger, 504 P.2d 668 (Colo. 1972) (lawyer failed to make appropriate further inquiry after receiving, under suspicious circumstances, a car in payment of a legal fee).

6. See People v. Kenelly, 648 P.2d 1065 (Colo.1982) (lawyer fashioned an agreement whereby client would receive money in return for being unavailable to testify at criminal trial); In re La Duca, 299 A.2d 405 (N.J.1973) (lawyer aided client in extorting ransom for return of stolen property).

7. 843 F.2d 1392 (6th Cir.1988) (unreported opinion, text available on WESTLAW).

avoid paying taxes. In another case a lawyer's advice to a client to destroy documents if a proceeding was instituted resulted in conviction of conspiracy to obstruct a future judicial proceeding.[8] Drafting documents with unlawful terms may also constitute assisting in illegal conduct.[9]

Sanford Kadish discusses the assistance element of criminal complicity:

> Various terms are used to capture the central notions of assistance and influence. Assistance is sometimes expressed as helping, aiding, or abetting. Liability never turns, however, on the choice among these terms. All embrace ways in which one person may help another commit a crime, including furnishing means, whether material or informational, providing opportunities, and lending a helping hand in preparation or execution. Influence is expressed in a greater variety of terms, sometimes with overlapping meanings, sometimes with different connotations. [The author then discusses the terms "advise," "persuade," "command," "encourage," "induce," "provoke" and "solicit."]
>
> These differences in emphasis and connotation rarely have legal significance. All of these terms describe ways of influencing a person to choose to act in a particular way and therefore constitute a ground of complicity. Occasionally, however, the precise form of influence affects the legal conclusion, most often where statutes employ one or more of these terms restrictively.[10]

Prepaid Legal Services for Those Engaged in Crime

In 1989 a Florida attorney was convicted of both conspiracy to import marijuana and to defraud the Internal Revenue Service by concealing the proceeds of narcotics law violations.[11] According to the government's case the lawyer collected a $10,000 fee from each person on board a boat before it left on a drug-smuggling trip. If no one was caught, the lawyer kept the money; if anyone was arrested, the lawyer would represent that person without further charge.

In In re Disbarment Proceedings,[12] several lawyers were disbarred for making advance agreements with the operators of an illegal numbers racket to represent subordinates who were arrested. The court said:

> An attorney who agrees in advance to defend persons if and when arrested for criminal offenses whose future commission is a planned certainty, or from whose conduct such an agreement may be inferred, forfeits all right to practice law.... An attorney may defend persons

---

8. United States v. Perlstein, 126 F.2d 789 (3d Cir.1942).

9. See, e.g., In re Giordano, 229 A.2d 524 (N.J.1967) (discipline for usurious loan contract); Leardi v. Brown, 474 N.E.2d 1094 (Mass.1985) (lawyer violates consumer protection law by including unconscionable provision in residential lease). The problem of inclusion of illegal or unenforce-

able provisions in documents drafted for one party to a consumer transaction is considered below in Chapter 11 at p. 1127.

10. Sanford H. Kadish, Complicity, Cause and Blame: A Study in the Interpretation of Doctrine, 73 Calif.L.Rev. 323, 343 (1985).

11. Wall St.J., July 20, 1989, at p. B5.

12. 184 A. 59 (Pa.1936).

accused of participating in the numbers racket as writers, pick-up men, or bankers, and their clients need not be limited. It is not the number of persons defended that counts, but it is the regularity, character, and purpose of employment. When the purpose is to guide and aid a combination of persons engaged in crime, an attorney becomes part of the criminal system. Where a large number of cases of the same kind of crime are regularly defended by the same lawyer, where the defendants do not know and never have seen the lawyer prior to the moment of representation, and where the attorney's fees are paid by men known to be the leaders of a criminal system, a court may not only infer knowledge on his part of the criminal combination, but, from the frequency of his performance and knowledge, conclude that he becomes an actual participant therein. . . .[13]

2.   OTHER CRIMES

Aside from liability for aiding and abetting, lawyers who know or suspect that their clients are engaged in criminal activity may also suffer sanctions under a variety of criminal statutes. The following notes describe some of the crimes to which lawyers risk exposure.[14]

Obstruction of Justice[15]

Obstruction of justice is a crime of large importance to lawyers.[16] The federal obstruction of justice statute, 18 U.S.C. § 1503, provides: "Whoever corruptly . . . endeavors to influence, intimidate, or impede any . . . officer . . . of any court of the United States . . . in the discharge of his duty . . . or corruptly . . . influences, obstructs or impedes, or endeavors to influence, obstruct, or impede, the due administration of justice, shall be fined . . . or imprisoned . . . or both." Conduct commonly treated as obstruction of justice includes: attempting to alter or prevent the testimony of a witness,[17] interfering with a grand jury investigation[18] and destroying evidence sought

---

13. Id. at 66.

14. Perjury is discussed in Chapter 5 infra. The Foreign Corrupt Practices Act (FCPA), 15 U.S.C. § 78m(b)(2)-(3), should be mentioned. The "books and records" provisions of the FCPA requires that every company with publicly traded securities maintain books and records that "accurately and fairly reflect" the company's transactions. The current statute imposes liability for making a third-party payment "while knowing that all or a portion of such money or thing of value" would be paid to a foreign official for a corrupt purpose. 15 U.S.C. § 78dd–1(a)(3). Lawyers who represent publicly held corporations may be guilty of aiding and abetting violations if they know of unreported transactions and have assisted the client in the failure to report.

15. See generally Bruce A. Green, The Criminal Regulation of Lawyers, 67 Fordham L.Rev. 327 (1998) (arguing that prosecutors give insufficient attention to profession's norms in charging lawyers with crimes growing out of client representation; several of the cases discussed in this section are considered).

16. Obstruction of justice served as the central charge against the Watergate defendants, many of whom were lawyers. See United States v. Haldeman, 559 F.2d 31 nn. 2–3 (D.C.Cir.1976).

17. United States v. Tedesco, 635 F.2d 902, 907 (1st Cir.1980).

18. See also United States v. Cueto, 151 F.3d 620 (7th Cir.1998) (lawyer's "corrupt intent" in using legal processes to derail a investigation of his client's illegal gambling

by a court or grand jury.[19]

Even if the means used to obstruct justice are not in themselves unlawful, obstruction may be found. The crime of obstruction of justice "reaches all corrupt conduct capable of producing an effect that prevents justice from being duly administered, regardless of the means employed."[20] For example, in United States v. Cintolo[21] a lawyer was convicted of obstructing justice by his advice to his client although giving advice is not in itself unlawful. The lawyer advised his client to refuse to testify before the grand jury even though the client had a valid grant of immunity. The prosecution introduced tape-recorded conversations between the lawyer and others that revealed the lawyer's purpose was to keep the grand jury from finding out about the criminal activities of others, some of whom the lawyer-defendant apparently represented. In fact, the lawyer regularly reported on his client's inclination to testify and was aware of plans to kill the client should the client decide to testify. The court stated:

> [M]eans, though lawful in themselves, can cross the line of illegality if (i) employed with a corrupt motive, (ii) to hinder the due administration of justice, so long as (iii) the means have the capacity to obstruct.

> The appellant and amici [Massachusetts Association of Criminal Defense Lawyers and National Network for the Right to Counsel] pay lip service to this principle, but maintain that different considerations come into play where criminal defense lawyers are concerned. In those [situations], they assert, a corrupt motive may not be found in conduct which is, itself, not independently illegal....

> [T]he conversion of innocent acts to guilty ones by the addition of improper intent—is what this case is all about.... Nothing in the caselaw ... suggests that lawyers should be plucked gently from the madding crowd and sheltered from the rigors of 18 U.S.C. § 1503....[22]

Sometimes, however, the government's attempt to criminalize everyday lawyering activities goes too far. This was the case with a 1996 health care provision that made it a crime to assist an elderly person to transfer assets in order to qualify for Medicaid, conduct that itself was not made

---

enterprise, in which the lawyer also had a financial interest, supported conviction for obstruction of justice). Most of Cueto's activities involved ordinary lawyer tasks, such as writing letters to state officials complaining about the conduct of the investigation, bringing a state court action against an FBI agent, obtaining a preliminary injunction against the agent's investigatory activities, and questioning the agent in the state court proceeding about the details of the investigation.

19.   United States v. Faudman, 640 F.2d 20 (6th Cir.1981).

20.   United States v. Silverman, 745 F.2d 1386, 1393 (11th Cir.1984); see also State v. Cogdell, 257 S.E.2d 748 (S.C.1979).

21.   818 F.2d 980 (1st Cir.1987).

22.   818 F.2d at 992–93, 995–96. Lawyer Cintolo served 13 months in prison and was suspended indefinitely, but not disbarred, from the practice of law. In 1995, supported, according to a Boston newspaper, by a virtual Who's Who of Boston defense lawyers, the Massachusetts Board of Bar Overseers permitted Cintolo to rejoin the ranks of practicing lawyers See Ralph Ranalli, Boston Herald, June 21, 1995, at p. 12.

illegal.[23] When the restriction on advising clients concerning a legal option was attacked in the courts, Attorney General Reno refused to defend it and a federal court struck it down as violating the free speech rights of lawyers.[24]

In President Clinton's impeachment proceedings, one specific charge of obstruction of justice involved witness tampering—the President's alleged attempt to encourage his secretary to testify falsely. One of the President's defenses to this charge was that at the time of the conversation between the President and his secretary in which he allegedly sought to encourage her to testify falsely, she was not on any witness list in any proceeding. Under the federal obstruction of justice statute, however, the person's status on a witness list is not determinative. In United States v. Vitti,[25] the court considered this question under 18 U.S.C. § 1512(b)(1), which makes it a crime to "corruptly persuade[] another person, or attempt[] to do so, or engage in misleading conduct toward another person, with intent to— influence ... the testimony of any person in any official proceeding." The court rejected the defendant's argument that the government had to prove that his actions were likely to affect the other person's testimony. Under the omnibus section of the obstruction statute, 18 U.S.C. § 1503, the government must show that the conduct was likely to affect the administration of justice.[26]. However, under the more specific provision on witness tampering in § 1512 no such showing need be made. If the government can show a "likely affect" under § 1503, it is unnecessary to show that the witness was already on a witness list when the obstruction occurred, and under§ 1512, if the government can show the corrupt intent of the defendant, the witness need not be willing to testify or on any list; "[t]here need not be an ongoing investigation or even an intent to investigate."[27]

Mail Fraud

The mail and wire fraud statutes, 18 U.S.C. §§ 1341, 1343, prohibit the use of the mail or of electronic transmissions to execute "any scheme or artifice to defraud, or for the purpose of obtaining money or property by false or fraudulent pretenses...." The material mailed need not itself be false; liability attaches regardless of the truth or falsity of the material if the communication of that material aids the execution of a fraud.[28] Mailings occurring after receipt of the proceeds obtained by fraud are covered if the mailings "were designed to lull the victims into a false sense of security, postpone their ultimate complaint to the authorities, and there-

---

23. Health Insurance Portability Act of 1996 § 10, as amended by Balanced Budget Act of 1997 § 4734 (applying it only to lawyers and other professional adviseers).

24. New York State Bar Ass'n v. Reno, 999 F.Supp. 710 (S.D.N.Y.1998).

25. 125 F.3d 89 (2d Cir.1997).

26. See United States v. Aguilar, 515 U.S. 593 (1995).

27. Vitti, supra, at 103 (quoting United States v. Romero, 54 F.3d 56 (2d Cir.1995).

28. United States v. Talbott, 590 F.2d 192 (6th Cir.1978); United States v. Reid, 533 F.2d 1255 (D.C.Cir.1976).

fore make the apprehension of the defendants less likely than if no mailings had taken place.''[29]

The mail fraud statute reaches fraudulent schemes to deprive people of intangible civic rights in addition to money and goods. For example, federal prosecutors use the mail fraud statute to convict corrupt state and federal government officials (many of them lawyers) of defrauding citizens of their right to honest government services. Typically, those cases involve a government official who has used public office for personal gain. The government also successfully prosecutes cases against private persons for schemes involving the corruption of public servants.[30] Moreover, the courts interpret the ''intangible rights'' theory to protect the public's right to an honest election process[31] and to allow prosecution of employees and union officials who accepted kickbacks or used confidential information for personal gain.[32]

In Carpenter v. United States,[33] the Wall Street Journal's ''Heard on the Street'' columnist, one Winans, was charged with giving two securities brokers advance notice of his column. The brokers and their clients bought and sold securities based on the probable impact of the column on the market. The lower court convicted Winans and his codefendants of violating the federal securities laws and the mail and wire fraud statutes. The Supreme Court divided 4–4 on the securities laws convictions, but unanimously affirmed the fraud convictions. The Court rejected the defendants' argument that their scheme did not deprive the Wall Street Journal of property: the ''intangible nature'' of commercial information ''does not make it any less 'property' protected by the mail and wire fraud statutes.''[34]

The *Carpenter* case has large implications for lawyers who use client information for personal gain. In United States v. O'Hagan,[35] a partner in a Minneapolis firm learned that a firm client was about to make a tender offer for the stock of Pillsbury Co. He purchased call options in Pillsbury common stock and, after the tender offer was made public, sold his stock options, receiving profits of over $4.3 million. A divided court applied the SEC's misappropriation theory to uphold an insider-trading securities violation against the lawyer, even though he was a corporate outsider. The Court also upheld O'Hagan's mail fraud conviction—unanimously. The lesson is clear: A lawyer who appropriates information of the law firm or the client and uses it for personal gain, in violation of this relationship of trust and confidence, is guilty of mail fraud. The lawyer may well be guilty

---

29. United States v. Maze, 414 U.S. 395, 403 (1974).

30. See, e.g., United States v. Rauhoff, 525 F.2d 1170 (7th Cir.1975) (bribing state secretary of state).

31. See, e.g., United States v. Girdner, 754 F.2d 877 (10th Cir.1985); and United States v. Clapps, 732 F.2d 1148 (3d Cir. 1984) (convictions for using the mails to falsify votes).

32. See, e.g., United States v. Bryza, 522 F.2d 414 (7th Cir.1975).

33. 484 U.S. 19 (1987).

34. Id. at 25.

35. 521 U.S. 642 (1997).

of other crimes, including insider trading under federal securities laws and, at the state level, fraud and theft.[36]

The broad reach of the mail fraud statute became visible to lawyers when Armand D'Amato, the brother of former Senator D'Amato, was charged with and convicted of mail fraud for submitting "disguised" bills to a defense contractor, Unisys, for legal lobbying services, i.e., encouraging his brother, an important member of the Senate Appropriations Committee, to support the purchase by the Defense Department of Unisys's radar missile control systems.[37] The marketing vice-president of a Unisys division retained D'Amato through purchase orders stating that D'Amato's firm would "[p]rovide technical services to produce ... reports on senatorial proceedings," but it was understood that D'Amato was not expected to, and would not, produce any reports. The arrangement also concealed D'Amato's personal involvement: the firm was paid by checks payable to "J. Forchelli," one of D'Amato's partners. D'Amato's firm was paid a total of $88,000 for about 100 hours' work by D'Amato.

D'Amato's conviction was reversed by the Second Circuit largely on scienter grounds: the government had failed to establish that D'Amato was aware that the marketing vice president lacked authority to instruct D'Amato to disguise his services in billing Unisys; or that the payments were unlawful; or that the Unisys officer personally profited from the concealed arrangement. Whether D'Amato's services were worth the amount paid or were excessive was not a basis for inferring fraudulent intent: "The mail fraud statute does not criminalize the charging of an allegedly excessive fee, where, as here, a corporate agent with at least apparent authority to do so agreed to the fee, received no personal benefit from the fee, and was not deceived by the payee." [38]

Did D'Amato's conduct deserve the application of federal prosecutorial power? Although the conviction was ultimately reversed, lawyer D'Amato suffered the embarrassment, cost and anxiety of years of indictment, trial, conviction and appeal; and the result might have been different if the lobbying activity had been unlawful or D'Amato had had knowledge that the marketing vice-president lacked authority for what he had done.[39]

---

36. Unauthorized use of such information for personal gain violates federal fraud statutes whenever the mail, a telephone or any other electronic transmission is used in the scheme. See, e.g., United States v. Grossman, 843 F.2d 78 (2d Cir.1988). Moreover, lawyers often represent clients who themselves possess confidential information. If a lawyer knows a client is using such information for personal gain, and mail or some form of electronic transmission is employed, the lawyer risks prosecution as an aider and abettor whenever the lawyer provides substantial assistance to the client's plan. See United States v. Bronston, 658 F.2d 920 (2d Cir.1981) (law-

yer deprived his firm's client of honest services by representing another client whose interests directly conflicted).

37. United States v. D'Amato, 39 F.3d 1249 (2d Cir.1994).

38. 39 F.3d at 1261–62.

39. A number of bar and civil liberties groups filed or joined in amicus briefs to the court of appeals urging reversal of D'Amato's conviction. The amici worried that upholding the conviction would criminalize common billing practices that agents of a company had directed a lawyer to follow and trench on constitutionally protected political activities. See Richard

Conspiracy

Conspiracy—an *agreement* to do something unlawful (or something lawful through unlawful means)—often goes hand in hand with an unlawful act and forms a separate criminal offense. Thus, in addition to substantive offenses, Benjamin was convicted of conspiracy to commit the substantive offenses. The agreement that forms the core of any conspiracy charge need not be proved through direct evidence, nor must the agreement be explicit: A tacit understanding to do something illegal in concert with others will suffice, and a tacit agreement may be proved by showing that two or more people acted in a way that permits the inference they had some form of agreement.[40] Successful withdrawal from a conspiracy requires an "affirmative act bringing home the fact of [one's] withdrawal to [one's] confederates."[41] Disclosing the conspiracy to authorities is obviously the most effective affirmative act.

Conspiracy may also constitute an intentional tort, usually referred to as "acting in concert." For example, one court held a lawyer liable for civil conspiracy when the lawyer: (1) prepared materially misleading documents to secure a bank loan for a partnership in which the lawyer was a member, (2) knew that the misleading information was being used to secure new loans and (3) benefitted from the money fraudulently obtained, which was used to pay a debt of the partnership.[42]

RICO

The Racketeer Influenced and Corrupt Organizations Act (RICO)[43] defines "racketeering" acts to include not only murder and kidnapping but mail, wire and securities fraud. The inclusion of these latter "white-collar" crimes gives the statute a reach far beyond its original target, the "mob," and makes lawyers vulnerable to RICO charges.[44] The wide reach of RICO has engendered much criticism by many groups, including lawyers,[45] but

Painter, If This Is Mail Fraud, Then Most Lawyers Are Guilty, Wall St. J., May 4, 1994, at A15.

40. Direct Sales Co. v. United States, 319 U.S. 703 (1943). On conspiracy see generally LaFave and Scott, supra, at §§ 6.4–6.5.

41. Loser v. Superior Court, 177 P.2d 320 (Cal.App.1947).

42. Hartford Accident and Indemnity Co. v. Sullivan, 846 F.2d 377 (7th Cir.1988).

43. 18 U.S.C. §§ 1961–68 (1982 & Supp. III 1985).

44. "Only 9% of all civil RICO cases have involved allegations of criminal activity normally associated with professional criminals. The central purpose that Congress sought to promote through civil RICO is

now a mere footnote." Sedima, S.P.R.L. v. Imrex Co., 473 U.S. 479, 506 (1985) (Marshall, J., dissenting).

45. "In practice, [civil RICO] frequently has been invoked against legitimate businesses in ordinary commercial settings.... [T]he ABA Task Force that studied civil RICO found that 40% of the reported cases involved securities fraud, 37% involved common-law fraud in a commercial or business setting. Many a prudent defendant, facing ruinous exposure, will decide to settle even a case with no merit. It is thus not surprising that civil RICO has been used for extortive purposes, giving rise to the very evils that it was designed to combat." Report of the Ad Hoc Civil RICO Task Force of the ABA Section of Corporation, Banking and Business Law 69 (1985).

efforts to persuade Congress to limit RICO's reach have thus far failed.[46] A 1993 decision, however, provides protection for outside lawyers who merely advise an organization subject to a racketeering claim.[47]

RICO prohibits, in any enterprise affecting interstate commerce, the following: (1) investing income derived from a pattern of racketeering, (2) acquiring or maintaining an interest through a pattern of racketeering, (3) participating in the enterprise's affairs through a pattern of racketeering and (4) conspiring to engage in any of these activities. Two acts of racketeering and the threat of continuing racketeering activity suffice to establish a "pattern" of racketeering. Thus, given the definition of racketeering acts, two instances of mail or wire fraud would satisfy the "two-act" requirement.

RICO authorizes civil remedies as well as criminal sanctions. Moreover, the Supreme Court has refused to interpret RICO as requiring a criminal conviction to support civil RICO liability:[48] " 'Proof of two acts ... without more does not establish a pattern.... [C]ontinuity plus relationship [are what] produce a pattern.' "[49] A private party who prevails on the merits in a RICO action is entitled to treble damages and litigation expenses, including attorneys' fees.

In United States v. Teitler[50] the Second Circuit affirmed the conviction of two lawyers for engaging in mail fraud, conspiring to conduct the affairs of an enterprise through a pattern of racketeering and conducting the affairs of an enterprise through racketeering. The enterprise in question was their law firm:

> [T]he method of operation employed by the enterprise included the creation of false documents and the encouragement of perjury by the firm's clients in order to inflate their injuries and expenses so as to obtain better settlements in negligence lawsuits brought by the firm.... [T]he fraud took several forms: creation of false medical bills; submission of false affidavits to document housekeeping services that were never rendered and lost wages that were never earned; referral of clients to doctors who provided backdated bills and exaggerated medical reports; and procurement of false testimony at trials and examinations before trial.... Further, when a grand jury investigation was underway, defendants Norman Teitler, head of the firm, and Maureen

---

46. For criticism of RICO liability, see Dennis O. Lynch, RICO: The Crime of Being a Criminal, Parts I & II, 87 Colum.L.Rev. 661; Parts III & IV, 87 Colum.L.Rev. 920 (1987); Note, Civil RICO is a Misnomer ..., 100 Harv.L.Rev. 1288 (1987). But see Michael Goldsmith, Civil RICO Reform: The Basis for a Compromise, 71 Minn. L.Rev. 827 (1987) (describing the criticism of RICO as overstated and proposing a moderate revision).

47. Reves v. Ernst & Young, 507 U.S. 170 (1993) (an outside accounting firm to an organization experiencing financial difficulty did not "participate" in the "conduct" of the organization by failing to inform its board of directors that if a major asset was given a market rather than book value the organization would probably be insolvent).

48. Sedima, S.P.R.L. v. Imrex Co., 473 U.S. 479 (1985).

49. 473 U.S. at 496 n. 14.

50. 802 F.2d 606 (2d Cir.1986).

Murphy, an employee, allegedly tried to induce false testimony before the grand jury.[51]

3.   PAYING LAWYERS WITH PROCEEDS OF CRIME

In the 1980s a series of legislative enactments aimed at organized crime and drug trafficking, coupled with more vigorous law enforcement, led to extensive litigation in which prosecutors sought to obtain information from lawyers concerning amount of fees paid, form of payment and identity of the payor. Federal racketeering and drug laws require forfeiture of assets acquired directly or indirectly through specified criminal activity. The Internal Revenue Code requires every person who receives more than $10,000 in cash in connection with a trade or business to report information concerning the transaction with the Internal Revenue Service.

If the lawyer knows that the amounts paid to her are the proceeds of ongoing criminal activity, the lawyer's action in accepting the payment is illegal because the money is either contraband or stolen property. In the typical case, however, the government does not claim that the lawyer has the requisite knowledge or mental state to establish the lawyer's criminal liability. Thus, the primary issue presented by prosecutorial efforts to discover fee arrangements and client identity and to forfeit fees is one of confidentiality: Whether the lawyer is required to divulge information concerning fee arrangements and client identity. The issues raised by these provisions are discussed below in the Koniak excerpt at p. 129 and in Chapter 4 at p. 257.

B.   TORT LAW

1.   NEGLIGENT MISREPRESENTATION

Greycas, Inc. v. Proud

United States Court of Appeals, Seventh Circuit, 1987.
826 F.2d 1560.

■ Before BAUER, CHIEF JUDGE, and CUMMINGS and POSNER, CIRCUIT JUDGES.

■ POSNER, CIRCUIT JUDGE.

Theodore S. Proud, Jr., a member of the Illinois bar who practices law in a suburb of Chicago, appeals from a judgment against him for $833,760, entered after a bench trial. The tale of malpractice and misrepresentation that led to the judgment begins with Proud's brother-in-law, Wayne Crawford, like Proud a lawyer but one who devoted most of his attention to a large farm that he owned in downstate Illinois. The farm fell on hard times

---

51. 808 F.2d at 609. Criminal and civil RICO cases against personal injury lawyers for assertion of fraudulent claims against liability insurers have become quite frequent.

and by 1981 Crawford was in dire financial straits. He had pledged most of his farm machinery to lenders, yet now desperately needed more money. He approached Greycas, Inc., the plaintiff in this case, a large financial company headquartered in Arizona, seeking a large loan that he offered to secure with the farm machinery. He did not tell Greycas about his financial difficulties or that he had pledged the machinery to other lenders, but he did make clear that he needed the loan in a hurry. Greycas obtained several appraisals of Crawford's farm machinery but did not investigate Crawford's financial position or discover that he had pledged the collateral to other lenders, who had perfected their liens in the collateral. Greycas agreed to lend Crawford $1,367,966.50, which was less than the appraised value of the machinery.

The loan was subject, however, to an important condition, which is at the heart of this case: Crawford was required to submit a letter to Greycas, from counsel whom he would retain, assuring Greycas that there were no prior liens on the machinery that was to secure the loan. Crawford asked Proud to prepare the letter, and he did so, and mailed it to Greycas, and within 20 days of the first contact between Crawford and Greycas the loan closed and the money was disbursed. A year later Crawford defaulted on the loan; shortly afterward he committed suicide. Greycas then learned that most of the farm machinery that Crawford had pledged to it had previously been pledged to other lenders.

The machinery was sold at auction. The Illinois state court that determined the creditors' priorities in the proceeds of the sale held that Greycas did not have a first priority on most of the machinery that secured its loan; as a result Greycas has been able to recover only a small part of the loan. The judgment it obtained in the present suit is the district judge's estimate of the value that it would have realized on its collateral had there been no prior liens, as Proud represented in his letter.

That letter is the centerpiece of the litigation. Typed on the stationery of Proud's firm and addressed to Greycas, it identifies Proud as Crawford's lawyer and states that, "in such capacity, I have been asked to render my opinion in connection with" the proposed loan to Crawford. It also states that "this opinion is being delivered in accordance with the requirements of the Loan Agreement" and that

> I have conducted a U.C.C., tax, and judgment search with respect to the Company [i.e., Crawford's farm] as of March 19, 1981, and except as hereinafter noted all units listed on the attached Exhibit A ("Equipment") are free and clear of all liens or encumbrances other than Lender's perfected security interest therein which was recorded March 19, 1981 at the Office of the Recorder of Deeds of Fayette County, Illinois.

The reference to the lender's security interest is to Greycas's interest; Crawford, pursuant to the loan agreement, had filed a notice of that interest with the recorder. The excepted units to which the letter refers are four vehicles. Exhibit A is a long list of farm machinery—the collateral that

Greycas thought it was getting to secure the loan, free of any other liens. . . .

Proud never conducted a search for prior liens on the machinery listed in Exhibit A. His brother-in-law gave him the list and told him there were no liens other than the one that Crawford had just filed for Greycas. Proud made no effort to verify Crawford's statement. The theory of the complaint is that Proud was negligent in representing that there were no prior liens, merely on his brother-in-law's say-so. No doubt Proud *was* negligent in failing to conduct a search, but we are not clear why the *misrepresentation* is alleged to be negligent rather than deliberate and hence fraudulent, in which event Greycas's alleged contributory negligence would not be an issue (as it is, we shall see), since there is no defense of contributory or comparative negligence to a deliberate tort, such as fraud. Proud did not merely say, "There are no liens"; he said, "I have conducted a U.C.C., tax, and judgment search"; and not only is this statement, too, a false one, but its falsehood cannot have been inadvertent, for Proud knew he had not conducted such a search. The concealment of his relationship with Crawford might also support a charge of fraud. But Greycas decided, for whatever reason, to argue negligent misrepresentation rather than fraud. It may have feared that Proud's insurance policy for professional malpractice excluded deliberate wrongdoing from its coverage, or may not have wanted to bear the higher burden of proving fraud, or may have feared that an accusation of fraud would make it harder to settle the case—for most cases, of course, are settled, though this one has not been. In any event, Proud does not argue that either he is liable for fraud or he is liable for nothing.

He also does not, and could not, deny or justify the misrepresentation; but he argues that it is not actionable under the tort law of Illinois, because he had no duty of care to Greycas. (This is a diversity case and the parties agree that Illinois tort law governs the substantive issues.) He argues that Greycas had an adversarial relationship with Proud's client, Crawford, and that a lawyer has no duty of straight dealing to an adversary, at least none enforceable by a tort suit. In so arguing, Proud is characterizing Greycas's suit as one for professional malpractice rather than negligent misrepresentation, yet elsewhere in his briefs he insists that the suit was solely for negligent misrepresentation—while Greycas insists that its suit charges both torts. Legal malpractice based on a false representation, and negligent misrepresentation by a lawyer, are such similar legal concepts, however, that we have great difficulty both in holding them apart in our minds and in understanding why the parties are quarreling over the exact characterization; no one suggests, for example, that the statute of limitations might have run on one but not the other tort. So we shall discuss both.

Proud is undoubtedly correct in arguing that a lawyer has no general duty of care toward his adversary's client; it would be a considerable and, as it seems to us, an undesirable novelty to hold that every bit of sharp dealing by a lawyer gives rise to prima facie tort liability to the opposing party in the lawsuit or negotiation. The tort of malpractice normally refers to a lawyer's careless or otherwise wrongful conduct toward his own client.

Proud argues that Crawford rather than Greycas was his client, and although this is not so clear as Proud supposes—another characterization of the transaction is that Crawford undertook to obtain a lawyer for Greycas in the loan transaction—we shall assume for purposes of discussion that Greycas was not Proud's client.

Therefore if malpractice just meant carelessness or other misconduct toward one's own client, Proud would not be liable for malpractice to Greycas. But in Pelham v. Griesheimer, 440 N.E.2d 96 (Ill.1982), the Supreme Court of Illinois discarded the old common law requirement of privity of contract for professional malpractice; so now it is possible for someone who is not the lawyer's (or other professional's) client to sue him for malpractice. The court in *Pelham* was worried, though, about the possibility of a lawyer's being held liable "to an unlimited and unknown number of potential plaintiffs," . . . so it added that "for a nonclient to succeed in a negligence action against an attorney, he must prove that the primary purpose and intent of the attorney-client relationship itself was to benefit or influence the third party," . . . . That, however, describes this case exactly. Crawford hired Proud not only for the primary purpose, but for the sole purpose, of influencing Greycas to make Crawford a loan. The case is much like Brumley v. Touche, Ross & Co., 487 N.E.2d 641, 644–45 (Ill.App.1985), where a complaint that an accounting firm had negligently prepared an audit report that the firm knew would be shown to an investor in the audited corporation and relied on by that investor was held to state a claim for professional malpractice. In Conroy v. Andeck Resources '81 Year–End Ltd., 484 N.E.2d 525, 536–37 (Ill.App.1985), in contrast, a law firm that represented an offeror of securities was held not to have any duty of care to investors. The representation was not intended for the benefit of investors. Their reliance on the law firm's using due care in the services it provided in connection with the offer was not invited. Cf. Barker v. Henderson, Franklin, Starnes & Holt, 797 F.2d 490, 497 (7th Cir.1986).

All this assumes that *Pelham* governs this case, but arguably it does not, for Greycas, as we noted, may have decided to bring this as a suit for negligent misrepresentation rather than professional malpractice. We know of no obstacle to such an election; nothing is more common in American jurisprudence than overlapping torts.

The claim of negligent misrepresentation might seem utterly straightforward. It might seem that by addressing a letter to Greycas intended (as Proud's counsel admitted at argument) to induce reliance on the statements in it, Proud made himself prima facie liable for any material misrepresentations, careless or deliberate, in the letter, whether or not Proud was Crawford's lawyer or for that matter anyone's lawyer. Knowing that Greycas was relying on him to determine whether the collateral for the loan was encumbered and to advise Greycas of the results of his determination, Proud negligently misrepresented the situation, to Greycas's detriment. But merely labeling a suit as one for negligent misrepresentation rather than professional malpractice will not make the problem of indefinite and perhaps excessive liability, which induced the court in

Pelham to place limitations on the duty of care, go away. So one is not surprised to find that courts have placed similar limitations on suits for negligent misrepresentation—so similar that we are led to question whether ... these really are different torts, at least when both grow out of negligent misrepresentations by lawyers. For example, the *Brumley* case, which we cited earlier, is a professional-malpractice case, yet it has essentially the same facts as Ultramares Corp. v. Touche, Niven & Co., 174 N.E. 441 (N.Y.1931), where the New York Court of Appeals, in a famous opinion by Judge Cardozo, held that an accountant's negligent misrepresentation was not actionable at the suit of a lender who had relied on the accountant's certified audit of the borrower.

The absence of a contract between the lender and the accountant defeated the suit in *Ultramares*—yet why should privity of contract have been required for liability just because the negligence lay in disseminating information rather than in designing or manufacturing a product? The privity limitation in products cases had been rejected, in another famous Cardozo opinion, years earlier. See MacPherson v. Buick Motor Co., 111 N.E. 1050 (N.Y.1916). Professor Bishop suggests that courts were worried that imposing heavy liabilities on producers of information might cause socially valuable information to be underproduced. See Negligent Misrepresentation Through Economists' Eyes, 96 L.Q.Rev. 360 (1980). Many producers of information have difficulty appropriating its benefits to society. The property-rights system in information is incomplete; someone who comes up with a new idea that the law of intellectual property does not protect cannot prevent others from using the idea without reimbursing his costs of invention or discovery. So the law must be careful not to weigh these producers down too heavily with tort liabilities. For example, information produced by securities analysts, the news media, academicians, and so forth is socially valuable, but as its producers can't capture the full value of the information in their fees and other remuneration the information may be underproduced. Maybe it is right, therefore—or at least efficient— that none of these producers should have to bear the full costs.... At least that was once the view; and while *Ultramares* has now been rejected, in Illinois as elsewhere—maybe because providers of information are deemed more robust today than they once were or maybe because it is now believed that auditors, surveyors, and other providers of professional services were always able to capture the social value of even the information component of those services in the fees they charged their clients—a residuum of concern remains. So when in Rozny v. Marnul, 250 N.E.2d 656 (Ill.1969), the Supreme Court of Illinois, joining the march away from *Ultramares*, held for the first time that negligent misrepresentation was actionable despite the absence of a contract, and thus cast aside the same "privity of contract" limitation later overruled with regard to professional malpractice in *Pelham*, the court was careful to emphasize facts in the particular case before it that limited the scope of its holding—facts such as that the defendant, a surveyor, had placed his "absolute guarantee for accuracy" on the plat and that only a few persons would receive and rely on it, thus limiting the potential scope of liability....

Later Illinois cases, however, influenced by section 552 of the Second Restatement of Torts (1977), state the limitation on liability for negligent misrepresentation in more compact terms—as well as in narrower scope— than *Rozny*. These are cases in the intermediate appellate court, but, as we have no reason to think the Supreme Court of Illinois would reject them, we are bound to follow them.... They hold that "one who in the course of his business or profession supplies information for the guidance of others in their business transactions" is liable for negligent misrepresentations that induce detrimental reliance.... Whether there is a practical as distinct from a merely semantic difference between this formulation of the duty limitation and that of *Pelham* may be doubted but cannot change the outcome of this case. Proud, in the practice of his profession, supplied information (or rather misinformation) to Greycas that was intended to guide Greycas in commercial dealings with Crawford. Proud therefore had a duty to use due care to see that the information was correct. He used no care.

Proud must lose on the issue of liability even if the narrower, ad hoc approach of *Rozny* is used instead of the approach of section 552 of the Restatement. Information about the existence of previous liens on particular items of property is of limited social as distinct from private value, by which we mean simply that the information is not likely to be disseminated widely. There is consequently no reason to give it special encouragement by overlooking carelessness in its collection and expression. Where as in this case the defendant makes the negligent misrepresentation directly to the plaintiff in the course of the defendant's business or profession, the courts have little difficulty in finding a duty of care. Prosser and Keeton on the Law of Torts ... § 107, at p. 747.

There is no serious doubt about the existence of a causal relationship between the misrepresentation and the loan. Greycas would not have made the loan without Proud's letter. Nor would it have made the loan had Proud advised it that the collateral was so heavily encumbered that the loan was as if unsecured, for then Greycas would have known that the probability of repayment was slight. Merely to charge a higher interest rate would not have been an attractive alternative to security; it would have made default virtually inevitable by saddling Crawford with a huge fixed debt....

Proud argues, however, that his damages should be reduced in recognition of Greycas's own contributory negligence, which, though no longer a complete defense in Illinois, is a partial defense, renamed "comparative negligence." ... It is as much a defense to negligent misrepresentation as to any other tort of negligence.... On the issue of comparative negligence the district court said only that "defendant may have proved negligence upon the part of plaintiff but that negligence, if any, had no causal relationship to the malpractice of the defendant or the damages to the plaintiff." This comment is not easy to fathom. If Greycas was careless in deciding whether to make the loan, this implies that a reasonable investigation by Greycas would have shown that the collateral for the loan was already heavily encumbered; knowing this, Greycas would not have made the loan and therefore would not have suffered any damages.

But we think it too clear to require a remand for further proceedings that Proud failed to prove a want of due care by Greycas. Due care is the care that is optimal given that the other party is exercising due care.... It is not the higher level of care that would be optimal if potential tort victims were required to assume that the rest of the world was negligent. A pedestrian is not required to exercise a level of care (e.g., wearing a helmet or a shin guard) that would be optimal if there were no sanctions against reckless driving. Otherwise drivers would be encouraged to drive recklessly, and knowing this pedestrians would be encouraged to wear helmets and shin guards. The result would be a shift from a superior method of accident avoidance (not driving recklessly) to an inferior one (pedestrian armor).

So we must ask whether Greycas would have been careless not to conduct its own UCC search had Proud done what he had said he did— conduct his own UCC search. The answer is no. The law normally does not require duplicative precautions unless one is likely to fail or the consequences of failure (slight though the likelihood may be) would be catastrophic. One UCC search is enough to disclose prior liens, and Greycas acted reasonably in relying on Proud to conduct it. Although Greycas had much warning that Crawford was in financial trouble and that the loan might not be repaid, that was a reason for charging a hefty interest rate and insisting that the loan be secured; it was not a reason for duplicating Proud's work. It is not hard to conduct a UCC lien search; it just requires checking the records in the recorder's office for the county where the debtor lives. See Ill.Rev.Stat. ch. 26, ¶ 9–401. So the only reason to backstop Proud was if Greycas should have assumed he was careless or dishonest; and we have just said that the duty of care does not require such an assumption. Had Proud disclosed that he was Crawford's brother-in-law this might have been a warning signal that Greycas could ignore only at its peril. To go forward in the face of a known danger is to assume the risk.... But Proud did not disclose his relationship to Crawford.

The last issue concerns the amount of damages awarded Greycas....

. . .

... [T]he judge was, if anything, unduly generous to Proud, in giving Greycas only the value of the collateral on the date of default, rather than the unpaid principal of the loan. But for Proud's misrepresentations, Greycas would not have made the loan, so its damages are not just the collateral but the entire uncollectable portion of the loan together with the interest that the money would have earned in an alternative use ... We therefore conclude that the realizable value of Greycas's collateral on the date of Crawford's default was a real loss.

A final point. The record of this case reveals serious misconduct by an Illinois attorney. We are therefore sending a copy of this opinion to the Attorney Registration and Disciplinary Commission of the Supreme Court of Illinois for such disciplinary action as may be deemed appropriate in the circumstances.[1]

Affirmed.

■ BAUER, CHIEF JUDGE, concurring.

I am in agreement with the majority opinion. I believe that Proud would be liable without reference to legal malpractice or negligent misrepresentation. The evidence in this case indicates that he is guilty of fraud or intentional misrepresentation. He was lying when he represented that he had made U.C.C., tax and judgment searches on his brother-in-law's farm. He intended the misrepresentation to induce Greycas to make a loan to his brother-in-law; Greycas justifiably relied upon the misrepresentation in making the loan and was injured as a result. Under these facts, Proud's misrepresentation was indefensible.

Liability to Non–Clients

Why did Greycas sue lawyer Proud for negligence rather than for intentional tort? How does the court justify holding a lawyer liable in negligence to a non-client?

In discussing comparative negligence the court points out that "[a] pedestrian is not required to exercise a level of care (e.g., wearing a helmet) that would be optimal if there were no sanctions against reckless driving." Yet later the court suggests that if Proud had disclosed to Greycas that he was Crawford's brother-in-law, "this might have been a warning signal that Greycas could ignore only at its peril. To go forward in the face of a known danger is to assume the risk." Making false statements is unethical whether or not they are made on behalf of one's brother-in-law. If made with intent to defraud, they are fraudulent regardless of the relationship between the maker and the party he is "helping." Why then should a third party be required to see the relationship as a warning signal?

Negligent Misrepresentation Cases

In Greyhound Leasing & Financial Corp. v. Norwest Bank of Jamestown,[2] as in *Greycas*, a lender, Greyhound, required a lawyer's opinion letter stating that farm equipment securing a proposed loan was unencumbered. Greyhound wanted a lawyer from the farmer's locality to write the letter because a local lawyer would be more likely to be familiar with the farmer's business activities. The farmer told the lawyer that all the equipment was brand new and not yet "owned or possessed by him." Greyhound, although it knew that some of the equipment was used, sent the lawyer documents asserting that the equipment was new, making the

1. [Editors' note:] After a disciplinary hearing in 1990, Proud was suspended for one year in Illinois.

2. 854 F.2d 1122 (8th Cir.1988).

transaction eligible for federal credits. Relying on the word of his client and the documents sent by Greyhound, the lawyer did not conduct a lien search because in North Dakota one cannot create a valid lien on farm equipment until it is "owned or possessed." The lawyer wrote a letter stating that he was "not aware of any liens or encumbrances . . . created or suffered by the lessee nor have they [sic] granted or conveyed any liens or encumbrances of any nature with respect thereto." In fact, the equipment was not new and almost all was encumbered by at least one lien. Shortly after Greyhound disbursed the loan money, the farmer filed for bankruptcy. Finding itself with virtually no collateral and a bankrupt debtor, Greyhound filed suit against the lawyer.

The Eighth Circuit upheld a judgment for the lawyer. Assuming arguendo that the letter was a negligent misrepresentation, the court of appeals held that Greyhound was barred under North Dakota's doctrine of comparative negligence because its negligence exceeded the lawyer's. First, knowing the equipment was not new, Greyhound negligently prepared documents that stated otherwise in order to gain a tax benefit. Second, Greyhound negligently failed to make its own independent investigation of the lien situation.

Greyhound claims to have paid out $1 million in reliance on the opinion of a lawyer whom it never contacted or instructed and to whom it arranged the transmittal of seriously inaccurate documents. It devised for the lawyer to sign a most equivocal form of opinion letter which does not clearly set forth the representation which Greyhound now says it thought it was getting from the lawyer, and relied upon it. It seems to us eminently reasonable to hold, as the trial judge did, that under the circumstances, Greyhound had an independent obligation to investigate the existence of liens.[3]

Is *Greyhound*'s analysis consistent with the reasoning in *Greycas*?

In Roberts v. Ball, Hunt, Hart, Brown & Baerwitz,[4] a law firm's client needed a loan and asked the firm to prepare an opinion letter that the client, a partnership, could show to its potential creditor. Knowing the intended use, the firm prepared a letter stating that the fourteen partners of the client-partnership were all general partners. The creditor, Roberts, considered this assurance critical because general partners are liable for the debts of the partnership in the event of default. The client gave the letter to Roberts, who, relying on the letter, made the loan. When the partnership defaulted and Roberts sought to collect from the partners, thirteen of the fourteen partners defended by claiming to be only limited partners. Roberts then sued the law firm for fraud and negligent misrepresentation, claiming that at the time the firm drafted the letter it knew that most of the partners believed they were limited and not general partners and were asserting that position in partnership meetings. According to Roberts, the firm had a duty to disclose these material facts in the opinion letter.

3. Id. at 1125.   4.   128 Cal.Rptr. 901 (Cal.App.1976).

The firm defended by saying it had no intent to deceive and thus was not liable for fraud. The court agreed that the complaint failed to state a cause of action for fraud because there was no allegation of intent to deceive, but held that the firm might be liable for negligent misrepresentation. California, the court stated, rejects the "traditional view ... that an attorney may not ... be held liable to third persons [for negligence] because he is not in privity with them, and owes them no duty to act with care."[5]

Some cases in which a lawyer assists an offeror in the sale of securities require that the lawyer exercise due diligence in checking the client's factual representations.[6] In other cases, however, adversarial negotiations with a purchaser or small group of purchasers lead to a different result: A seller's lawyer engaged in adversarial contract negotiations in connection with a sale of stock is not liable to purchasers who rely on the lawyer's negligent misrepresentations if "the duties involved, including negotiations and drafting of contractual agreements ... [are] clearly adversarial in nature" and were not intended to benefit the purchasers directly.[7]

Relaxation of Privity Requirement[8]

The privity-of-contract doctrine is discussed in Judge Posner's opinion in the *Greycas* case.[9] Traditionally, a lawyer is liable for negligence only to those in privity of contract with the lawyer (typically clients).[10] Although

5. 128 Cal.Rptr. at 905, citing Lucas v. Hamm, 364 P.2d 685, 687 (Cal.1961) (testator's lawyer owed duty of care to will beneficiaries).

6. See, e.g., Felts v. National Account Systems Association, 469 F.Supp. 54, 68 (N.D.Miss.1978) (offeror's lawyer liable to purchasers of unregistered securities for negligent failure to verify or investigate underlying material facts: "law and public policy require that the attorney exercise his position of trust and superior knowledge responsibly so as not to adversely affect persons whose rights and interests are certain and foreseeable").

7. Astor Chauffeured Limousine Co. v. Runnfeldt Investment Corp., 1988 WL 101267 (N.D.Ill.), vacated and remanded for recomputation of damages, 910 F.2d 1540 (7th Cir.1990) (applying Illinois law). See the discussion of "adversarial" relationships in *Greycas*.

8. Lawyer's liability to third parties for professional malpractice is discussed in Chapter 3 and in the client fraud section of Chapter 4. See also John A. Siliciano, Negligent Accounting and the Limits of Instrumental Tort Reform, 86 Mich.L.Rev. 1929 (1988); Victor P. Goldberg, Accountable Ac-

countants: Is Third–Party Liability Necessary?, 17 J.Legal Stud. 295 (1988); and Bily v. Arthur Young and Co., 834 P.2d 745 (Cal.1992) (auditor owes no general duty of care regarding the conduct of an audit to persons other than the client, but is liable for negligent misrepresentation when an audit report is made to influence a transaction with a non-client who relied on a negligent misrepresentation).

9. For discussion of the current status of the privity doctrine as applied to the liability of lawyers to non-clients, see Symposium, The Lawyer's Duties and Liabilities to Third Parties, 37 S.Tex.L.Rev. 957–1313 (1996) (especially articles by Geoffrey Hazard, John Bauman, John Sutton, John Price and Edward Carr).

10. An English case, Robertson v. Fleming, 4 Macq.H. of L.Cas. 167 (House of Lords, Scottish Appeals, 1861), first enunciated the privity rule; Fish v. Kelly, 17 C.B. (N.S.) 194 (Common Bench 1864), restated the rule. In the United States, the most authoritative early pronouncement came in 1880 on facts strikingly similar to those in *Greycas*. National Savings Bank v. Ward, 100 U.S. 195 (1880), involved a lawyer who

the privity doctrine has been abolished in negligence cases involving physical harm (*MacPherson v. Buick* and all that), it retains some but diminishing vigor in negligence suits claiming purely economic harm, such as a legal malpractice or negligent misrepresentation claim brought against a lawyer by a non-client. California was the first state to abandon the privity requirement in third-party claims against lawyers. The California court did so with a balance of factors test which it has employed in a number of negligence contexts.[11] Some other jurisdictions have adopted this approach, which tends to turn on whether it is reasonably foreseeable that a lawyer's absence of due care will directly harm a third person. A few states, viewing the multi-factor approach as too uncertain in application, have used a third-party beneficiary contract approach in holding that a lawyer in some situations owes a duty of care to a non-client.[12]

The two Illinois tort approaches summarized in Judge Posner's opinion in *Greycas* also have a following in a number of states: (1) was the purpose of the lawyer-client relationship to benefit or influence a third person? or (2), alternatively, following the Restatement of Torts (Second) § 552, has someone in the business of supplying information "supplie[d] information for the guidance of others [on which they have reasonable relied] in their business transactions?" In jurisdictions that have created exceptions to privity, the duty of care is generally limited to situations in which the lawyer, in handling a transaction for a client, is dealing directly with the injured third person or the representation seeks to benefit that person.[13] Few if any decisions hold that a lawyer in adversarial litigation has a duty of care to opposing parties.[14]

negligently conducted a title search, failing to find a prior conveyance; a bank loaned money to the lawyer's client relying on the lawyer's opinion letter, which asserted a clear title. The Supreme Court refused to find the lawyer liable to the bank because the bank was not in privity with the lawyer.

11.   See Biakanja v. Irving, 320 P.2d 16 (Cal. 1958). The six factors are: (1) the extent to which the transaction was intended to affect the plaintiff; (2) the foreseeability of harm to the plaintiff; (3) the degree of certainty that the plaintiff suffered injury; (4) the closeness of the connection between the lawyer's conduct and the injury suffered by the plaintiff; (5) the moral blame attached to the lawyer's conduct; and (6) the policy of preventing future harm. This test is also employed by some other states; see Trask v. Butler, 872 P.2d 1080, 1083–84 (Wash.1994) (determining that a lawyer hired by the personal representative of an estate did not owe a duty to the estate or its beneficiaries).

12.   See, e.g., Guy v. Liederbach, 459 A.2d 744, 752 (Pa.1983) (lawyer who drafts a will owes a duty of care to intended beneficiaries). The third-party beneficiary position resembles Posner's suggestion that perhaps Proud was Greycas's lawyer.

13.   See Home Budget Loans, Inc. v. Jacoby & Meyers Law Offices, 255 Cal.Rptr. 483 (Cal.App.1989) (mortgage broker, who insisted that debtor retain a lawyer to review mortgage documents and verify to broker that he had done so, liable to broker for negligence).

14.   See, e.g., Garcia v. Rodey, Dickason, Sloan, Akin & Robb, 750 P.2d 118 (N.M. 1988) (plaintiff could not recover for constructive fraud against defendant's lawyers, who had stated before trial that they would not raise a defense and then successfully did so on appeal). Cases involving a litigation context often turn on failure to prove justifiable reliance: a litigant cannot reasonably rely on a statement by an opposing party's lawyer.

Restatement § 73 recognizes exceptions in three of the common situations in which the privity question frequently arises:[15]

Inviting reliance of non-clients. The first exception is the common situation in which "the lawyer or (with the lawyer's acquiescence) the lawyer's client invites the non-client to rely on the lawyer's opinion or provision of other legal services, and the non-client so relies." Section 73(2)(a). The most common scenario is that involved in *Greycas:* a lawyer's opinion is directed to a third person to facilitate a transaction with the client. The vast majority of states impose a duty of care on the lawyer in this situation, even those that, like New York, generally adhere to the privity doctrine in other contexts.[16] The knowledge of the attorney that her work will be used by the client and will be relied on by a specific person or identifiable group of recipients is considered a relationship, assumed by the lawyer, that operates as a proxy for privity of contract.

Petrillo v. Bachenberg[17] is a case pushing the "inviting reliance" exception to the margins. Lawyer Hellrigel's client, a contractor, desiring to sell a parcel of real estate, hired an engineering firm to perform percolation tests to determine whether the site could support the required septic system. The township required two successful tests for approval of a septic system. Thirty tests were necessary before two successful ones were recorded. Hellrigel created a composite report composed of one page from each of two reports; this "composite report" made it appear that the property had passed two of seven tests rather than two of thirty. Hellrigel sent the report to Bachenberg, the client's broker, where it became part of the sales packet on the property. The broker eventually purchased the property on his own account and continued to offer it for sale. It was subsequently purchased for use as a day care center by Petrillo, who was given the composite report by Bachenberg. Petrillo then incurred substantial engineering and other expenses before discovering that the land would not support the required septic system. Petrillo's subsequent suit charged Hellrigel, who had also assisted Bachenberg in the Petrillo sale, with knowingly providing misleading information to her.

The opinion in *Petrillo,* relying on Restatement § 73, concludes that "attorneys may owe a duty of care to non-clients when the attorneys know, or should know, that non-clients will rely on the attorney's representations and that the non-clients are not too remote from the attorneys to warrant protection."[18]

> By providing the composite report to Bachenberg and subsequently assisting him in the sale, Herrigel assumed a duty to Petrillo to provide

---

15. The Restatement provisions quoted in the text contain qualifications that, for purposes of simplicity, have not been included. The interested reader should refer to the full text and its comments.

16. Prudential Ins. Co. v. Dewey, Ballantine, Bushby, Palmer & Wood, 605 N.E.2d 318, 320–22 (N.Y.1992) (lawyer may be liable to a non-client when "a relationship so close as to approach that of privity" exists, such as when a lawyer prepares a legal opinion intended to induce reliance by a third party).

17. 655 A.2d 1354 (N.J.1995).

18. 655 A.2d at 1359.

reliable information regarding the percolation tests. Hellrigel controlled the risk that the composite report would mislead a purchaser. [He could have supplied the complete reports.] Fairness suggests that he should bear the risk of loss resulting from the delivery of a misleading report. . . . Hellrigel should have foreseen that a prospective purchaser would rely on the composite report in deciding whether to sign the contract and proceed with engineering and site work.[19]

Non-client enforcing duties to client. The second situation in which a duty of care arises is when "the lawyer knows a client intends as one of the primary objectives of the representation that the lawyer's services benefit the non-client. . . ." Section 73(3(a). The negligently-drafted will or other testamentary instrument is the most common example. In these situations, the testator (or settlor of a testamentary trust) is usually dead when the question of the instrument's validity or meaning later arises. If the intended beneficiaries of the lawyer's work cannot enforce the duty of care the lawyer owed to the testator-settlor, no one can. Lawyers engaged in some types of estate planning work are effectively immunized from malpractice liability if the privity rule is applied. Most jurisdictions, but with New York, Ohio and Texas as holdouts, view the derivative enforcement by the beneficiary of the lawyer's duties to the client as a relationship equivalent to privity of contract.[20]

Breach of fiduciary duty owed by a client-fiduciary to a beneficiary. The third exception to privity applies when "the lawyer's client is a trustee, guardian, executor or other fiduciary acting primarily to perform similar functions for the non-client" and "circumstances known to the lawyer make it clear that appropriate action by the lawyer is necessary . . . to prevent or rectify the breach of a fiduciary duty owned by the client to the non-client, where (i) the breach is a crime or fraud or (ii) the lawyer has assisted or is assisting the breach. . . ." This situation will be considered in Chapter 8, below, in connection with Fickett v. Superior Court.[21]

A few jurisdictions, of which Texas is one, adhere strictly to the privity doctrine in these and other situations.[22] Non-clients who are dealing with a

---

19. 655 A.2d at 1361. A vigorous dissent argued that Hellrigel's connection with the ultimate purchaser, Petrillo, was too remote: Petrillo had relied only on Bachenberg and Hellrigel had no knowledge of what Bachenberg had told Petrillo.

20. In addition to Lucas v. Hamm, 364 P.2d 685 (Cal.1961), see Hale v. Groce, 744 P.2d 1289 (Ore.1987); and Schreiner v. Scoville, 410 N.W.2d 679 (Iowa 1987); contra, Barcelo v. Elliott, 923 S.W.2d 575 (Tex.1996). See John R. Price, Duties of Estate Planners to Nonclients: Identifying, Anticipating and Avoiding the Problems, 37 S.Tex. L. Rev. 1063 (1996).

21. 558 P.2d 988 (Ariz.App.1976) (lawyer for conservator liable to ward for failure to use care in preventing conservator's misappropriation of assets of incompetent ward).

22. See Barcelo v. Elliott, 923 S.W.2d 575, 579 (Tex.1996) (lawyer drafting a trust instrument owes no duty of care to trust beneficiaries). Until 1999 Texas was apparently the only state in which a lawyer had no duty of care to a person to whom the lawyer has given an opinion at the direction of the client to facilitate a client transaction with that person. See McCamish, Martin, Brown & Loeffler v. F.E. Appling Interests, 991 S.W.2d 787 (Tex.1999) (holding that lawyers may be sued by non-clients for negligent misrepresentation, although reaffirming the requirement of privity in suits for malpractice, including

lawyer, through that lawyer's client, can protect themselves only by contract.[23] It is conceivable that a large lending institution like Greycas might seek and get a privity waiver from the lawyer providing the opinion. But will unrepresented parties in business transactions anticipate and raise this question? Will clients who retain a lawyer to draft an estate plan insist that the lawyer waive privity? Should a lawyer be required to inform the client of the absence of third-party liability unless the lawyer waives privity?

2.   INTENTIONAL TORTS

As both the majority and concurrence in *Greycas* point out, Greycas could have sued Proud for fraud instead of negligent misrepresentation and malpractice. Proud said he conducted a U.C.C., tax and judgment search when he had not, and he lied with the intent of separating Greycas from its money. Doesn't this constitute the intentional tort of fraud?[24]

Generally, the law grants a lawyer no privilege to commit intentional torts against third parties in the course of representing a client or to assist a client in committing intentional torts against third parties. The most notable exception to this rule is the lawyer's virtually absolute privilege to make defamatory statements orally or in writing in court or which are reasonably related to a pending or contemplated litigation.[25] In addition, as with all fiduciaries, a lawyer has a qualified privilege to make statements intended to protect the interests of others.[26]

To prove the intentional torts of fraud and misrepresentation, the plaintiff must show that a lawyer intended to deceive and that the plaintiff belonged to a class of people that the lawyer might reasonably have foreseen being deceived. No special duty or relationship is necessary. If the lawyer honestly believed that the communication was truthful, she lacked the intent necessary for fraud unless her belief was reckless.

Fraudulent intent may be shown by a reckless disregard for the truth or falsity of the proposition asserted. For example, in In re Flight Transpor-

---

suits by heirs of intestate-client); Edward A. Carr, Attorney Opinion Letters: Model Rule 2.3 and the Texas Experience, 37 S.Tex.L.Rev. 1127, 1138–43 (1996).

23. The contract approach is supported, and tort approaches criticized, by John H. Bauman, A Sense of Duty: Regulation of Lawyer Responsibility to Third Parties, 37 S.Tex.L.Rev. 995 (1996).

24. The basic elements of the intentional tort of misrepresentation (fraud) are: (1) a material false statement, (2) made with an intent to deceive, (3) which is reasonably relied on by a person to whom it is made (4) to that person's detriment.

25. The absolute privilege for judicial proceedings is not limited to lawyers but applies to judges, parties, witnesses and other participants. The purpose of the privilege is to ensure that adjudication is not hampered by fears of tort liability. Statements preliminary to a proceeding or given to a newspaper are only conditionally protected, if protected at all. See W. Prosser and P. Keeton, Prosser on Torts § 114 (5th ed.1984).

26. See, e.g., Pelagatti v. Cohen, 536 A.2d 1337 (Pa.Super.1987) (discussing both the absolute and qualified privilege); and Dano v. Royal Globe Ins. Co., 451 N.E.2d 488 (N.Y.1983). See Chapter 5 infra, discussing lawyer's tort liability for conduct connected to litigation along with other legal limits on the advocate's conduct in litigation.

tation Corporation Securities Litigation,[27] the court held that the purchasers of securities stated a cause of action for common law fraud against the law firm that had represented the securities' underwriters by alleging (1) that the firm, knowingly or in reckless disregard of the facts, either had made or had aided others in making untrue statements of material facts and had omitted to state other material facts necessary in order to make the statements made not misleading; (2) that the purchasers had relied on the untrue statements; and (3) that the firm by preparing the allegedly fraudulent prospectuses had assumed a duty to prospective purchasers.

May a lawyer safely rely on her client's assertions without some independent verification of the facts?

> It is claimed that a lawyer is entitled to rely on the statements of his client and that to require him to verify their accuracy would set an unreasonably high standard. This is too broad a generalization. It is all a matter of degree. To require an audit would obviously be unreasonable. On the other hand, to require a check of matters easily verifiable is not unreasonable. Even honest clients can make mistakes.[28]

In Newburger, Loeb & Co., Inc. v. Gross,[29] the Finley, Kumble law firm, through its partner Robert Persky, represented several general partners of a failing brokerage firm. Those general partners wanted to transfer the brokerage firm's assets to a newly formed corporation. New York law, however, requires that all partners consent to such a transfer unless the partnership agreement expressly provides otherwise, and some of the brokerage firm's other partners opposed the transfer. Persky reasoned that provisions in the partnership agreement granting the general partners the power to terminate the partnership included the power to transfer assets. He thus issued an opinion letter—necessary for the transfer—stating that the brokerage partnership had authority to make the transfer. Another law firm had declined to issue such an opinion.

Finding "simply no language in the partnership agreement" that could legitimately be construed as Persky concluded, the appellate court held the transfer to be a conversion and the Finley Kumble lawyers liable for assisting their clients in intentionally tortious conduct. Finley Kumble claimed that because it had acted in its professional capacity, it was immune from suit by third parties for having given its clients bad advice. The court rejected this defense: " ... while an attorney is privileged to give honest advice, even if erroneous, and generally is not responsible for the motives of his clients, admission to the bar does not create a license to act

---

27.   593 F.Supp. 612 (D.Minn.1984).

28.   Seidel v. Public Service Co. of New Hampshire, 616 F.Supp. 1342, 1362 (D.N.H.1985), quoting Escott v. BarChris Constr. Corp., 283 F.Supp. 643, 690 (S.D.N.Y.1968). See also Stokes v. Lokken, 644 F.2d 779 (8th Cir.1981) (lawyer who

recklessly relies on information provided by client may be liable for fraud); and Ames

Ames Bank v. Hahn, 287 N.W.2d 687 (Neb. 1980) (lawyer may be liable for misrepresentation for making statement without any knowledge as to whether it is true).

29.   563 F.2d 1057 (2d Cir.1977).

maliciously, fraudulently, or knowingly to tread upon the legal rights of others."[30]

If, however, a lawyer does not know and has no reason to know that her client is using her advice to engage in activity constituting an intentional tort, the courts hold that the lawyer is not liable. A lawyer is not liable merely for giving good faith advice.[31] Nor is a lawyer liable merely for being near the scene of a client's tortious conduct. In Worldwide Marine Trading Corp. v. Marine Transport Service Inc.,[32] the court held that a lawyer's activities did not amount to culpable participation either in his client's tortious interference with contract or in violation of the antitrust laws. The court said that, unless the lawyer was a "stakeholder" in the alleged conspiracy, the lawyer "must [have done] more than be present at the scene, and indeed must [have done] more than merely advise":

> There is an important societal interest in protecting the lawyer from third-party lawsuits, and thus in requiring a showing of a knowingly fraudulent or tortious action by the lawyer before permitting third-party recovery from the lawyer.... A lawyer must be able to act decisively on behalf of his client, without fearing that he will provide "the deep pocket" in subsequent litigation....[33]

Lawyers are also held liable for assisting in the intentional breach of fiduciary duties.[34] The special responsibilities of lawyers who represent fiduciaries are addressed in Chapter 8 below.

3.   ASSISTING A CLIENT IN TORTIOUS OR ILLEGAL CONDUCT

Geoffrey C. Hazard, Jr. "How Far May a Lawyer Go in Assisting a Client in Unlawful Conduct?"

35 U. of Miami L.Rev. 669 (1981).[35]

The general question to be considered is: How far may a lawyer lawfully go in providing assistance to a client that might enable the client to carry out an act that is to some degree illegal?

. . .

The services that a lawyer can provide cover a wide spectrum, regardless of the client purposes that may be involved. At one end of the spectrum is simply advice as to what the law "is," without specific aid or encouragement to the client. It is not easy to provide advice that is neutral with

---

30.   563 F.2d at 1080.

31.   See Yoggerst v. Stewart, 623 F.2d 35 (7th Cir.1980), distinguishing *Newburger* and holding that "an attorney, offering advice in good faith, is not liable for the torts of a client."

32.   527 F.Supp. 581 (E.D.Pa.1981).

33.   Id. at 586.

34.   See Whitfield v. Lindemann, 853 F.2d 1298 (5th Cir.1988) (liability of lawyer is not limited to amount of personal gain).

35.   Copyright © 1981 by the University of Miami Law Review. Reprinted with permission.

respect to the purposes implicit in the request for advice. Nevertheless, it is possible to give unsuggestive advice, and doing so is the least instrumental form of assistance that a lawyer can provide a client. At the other end of the spectrum of lawyer assistance is pure instrumentalism—lawyer's physical execution of a purpose that the client would like to realize but cannot or will not actually execute himself. One example would be a lawyer who serves as "bagman" in an illegal payoff for a client who wishes to remain behind the scenes.

At the least instrumental end of the spectrum, the lawyer merely provides the client with an expert definition of the limits of the law, leaving it to the client to consider whether those limits should be transgressed. At the other end of the spectrum, the lawyer personally provides the means without which the client could not achieve the illicit purpose. The law clearly [permits] providing assistance at the least instrumental end of this spectrum. The law clearly prohibits conduct at the other end. But what about forms of conduct that fall within these extremes? ... The questions raised by conduct falling in the middle of the spectrum ... are difficult, and the answers are usually qualified. What advice should the lawyer give about the limits of the law of fraud or breach of fiduciary duty to a client who has fiduciary obligations but shows signs of being self-interested? What about a client who requests his attorney to prepare documents for a transaction whose factual particulars the client refuses to disclose but the lawyer has reason to suspect? What about a client who asks his lawyer to make frequent, but unscheduled, deposits of very large sums of cash in bank accounts bearing fictitious names? In the latter case, what if the city is Miami in 1981, and the client is twenty-four years of age?

. . .

It is rare that the lawyer fully knows a client's purposes or fully anticipates the ways in which the client might make use of the lawyer's services. Indeed, the client himself often does not fully realize his purposes until the moment of choice has come and gone. Furthermore, a lawyer does not learn of a client's purposes in a continuous narrative. Rather, revelation comes in fragments, often beginning in the historical middle rather than at the historical beginning. As the matter unfolds, it may appear to the lawyer that the portents of abuse are strong or weak, clear or ambiguous, firm or wavering. When are these portents sufficiently certain so that the lawyer "knows" that the client intends an illegal objective and is bent on its accomplishment?

It is sometimes suggested that the dilemma is false, because surely a lawyer cannot "know" what a client intends. This suggestion is either disingenuous or absurd. Of course, speaking in terms of radical epistemology, it is true that a lawyer cannot "know" what a client—or anyone else— intends. In these terms it is impossible for a lawyer to "know" anything. Yet the practice of law is based on practical knowledge, that is, practical assessments leading to empirical conclusions which form the basis for irrevocable action. Lawyers certainly possess such practical knowledge. If a lawyer can have practical knowledge of how the purposes of others may affect his client, he can have the same knowledge of how his client's purposes may affect others. It is in that sense that the lawyer can "know" when a client's purpose is illegal....

The general category embraced by the term "illegality" also includes, beyond the criminal law, various torts. Certain kinds of torts are readily subsumed under the rubric of "illegality." These torts include the civil counterparts of criminal offenses that are *mala in se*: wrongful death by willful unexcused act, physically harmful battery, knowing conversion, and some forms of abuse of process. Other intentional torts, such as piracy of trade secrets or invasion of privacy, can also be included.

On the other hand, it is less apparent why negligence should be regarded as "illegal" conduct even if it results in tort liability. Yet negligence is a violation of the legal standard of reasonable care and is in this sense a violation of law. Suppose, for example, a client asks his lawyer whether compliance with old safety regulations is sufficient, and the lawyer indicates that such compliance would be sufficient because a tenuous argument can be made that new and stricter safety regulations are constitutionally invalid. If someone is injured as a result of the client's noncompliance with the new regulations, is the lawyer chargeable with having materially assisted the client in "illegal conduct"? How would the outcome be affected if that violation also entails criminal sanctions?

... We may feel confident about including [torts that are counterparts of serious criminal offenses], but as we move away from this core meaning, the boundaries become increasingly doubtful.

We can also approach the question from a different direction. There is a wide range of client conduct that gives rise to civil liability, but which we would not readily call "illegal" in the present context. Consider, for example, the deliberate default in performance of a contract obligation, the deliberate exercise of dominion and control over property of which another person claims ownership, or the deliberate decision to make a search and seizure of doubtful legality. Should any of these forms of conduct be categorized as "illegal" for the purpose of limiting the client endeavors that a lawyer may further?

The term "illegality" in ordinary legal parlance does not embrace breach of contract or invasion of a property interest [unless tortious conduct is involved]. Yet there are breaches of contract and invasions of personal and property interests that are more flagrant and more harmful than many torts, and indeed more harmful than many regulatory offenses.

.   .   .

The law of legal ethics ... specially presupposes the law of torts and of agency. A lawyer in the service of a client is typically an agent. But legal representation is a special kind of agency, involving legally conferred special powers that provide the lawyer with some autonomy from the client in carrying out the agency....

In general, the law of agency imposes limits on what an agent may, with legal impunity, do for a principal. Section 343 of the Restatement (Second) of Agency states: "An agent who does an act otherwise a tort is not relieved from liability by the fact that he acted ... on account of the principal, except where he is exercising ... a privilege held by him for the protection of the principal's interests...."[15] As explained in Comment b to this section, an agent's act is privileged if "a reasonable belief in the existence of facts causes an act to be privileged, and a command by the principal gives the agent reason to believe in the existence of such facts." Thus, if a client directs his lawyer to commence criminal proceedings against another, and if the lawyer "has reasonable grounds for believing the other guilty of the crime, the [lawyer] is not guilty of malicious prosecution."

Section 348 of the Restatement is also pertinent to the kinds of transactions in which lawyers can be involved. That section provides that "[a]n agent who fraudulently makes representations, uses duress, or knowingly assists in the commission of tortious fraud or duress by his principal or by others is subject to liability in tort to the injured person...." The comments following section 348 make it clear that if a lawyer acts for a client in a transaction that the lawyer knows is founded on misrepresentations, the lawyer acts tortiously.[19]

. . .

The vital circumstance under the law of agency is therefore not the fact that the actor is an agent, but the existence of facts that render his actions privileged. Applying the law of agency to lawyers, the vital question is what the lawyer knows about the client's endeavor. Using defamation and false arrest as illustrations, Comment b to section 343 of the Restatement (Second) of Agency observes that if "a reasonable belief in the existence of facts causes an act to be privileged," and if what the agent (lawyer) is told by the principal (client) "gives the agent reason to believe in the existence of such facts," then the agent (lawyer) has the privilege that is conferred on innocent actors.

But what if the client's endeavor is *not* one that a "reasonable belief in the existence of facts" will cause to be privileged? For example, in the tort of conversion it is not a defense that the agent reasonably believes that the property was his principal's. This problem is explicitly addressed in section 349 of the Restatement (Second) of Agency: An agent whose acts "would

---

15. Restatement (Second) of Agency § 343 (1957).

19. Comment a, for example, states: "[A]n agent who enters into transactions with a buyer knowing that the buyer is relying upon the previous misrepresentations by the principal or other agent is liable to the same extent as if he had made the previous misrepresentations." Id. Comment a. Comment c adds: "[I]f an agent who has been given misinformation by a principal, on the strength of which he makes statements to a third person, later discovers the untruth and refrains from taking steps to inform the other party, the agent is subject to liability if subsequently the other party completes the transaction with the principal or another agent, relying in part upon the statements of the first agent."

otherwise constitute trespass to or conversion of a chattel is not relieved from liability by the fact that he acts on account of his principal and reasonably, although mistakenly, believes that the principal is entitled to possession of the chattels." Under this rule, what is the situation of a lawyer who advises a client to seize property in possession of a debtor?[24]

The lawyer's knowledge is again the vital question in cases involving misrepresentations in a contract transaction. Under section 348 of the Restatement (Second) of Agency, for example, a lawyer faces liability if he "knowingly assists in the commission of tortious fraud" by his client. If the lawyer proceeds "knowing that the buyer is relying upon the previous misrepresentations by the [client]," then the lawyer is "liable to the same extent as if he had made the previous misrepresentations." [Comment a.] Moreover, if the lawyer "has been given misinformation by a [client], on the strength of which he makes statements to a third person, [and] later discovers the untruth and refrains from taking steps to inform the other party, the [lawyer] is subject to liability if subsequently the other party completes the transaction ... relying in part upon the statements of the [lawyer]." [Comment c.] Under these rules, then, a lawyer would be liable if he discovered on the eve of a closing that the other party had relied on statements by the client that the lawyer knew were false or fraudulently misleading.[28] Such conduct also would seem to be "illegal" within the meaning of DR 7–102(A)(7).

The rules of tort law are similar to the rules of agency, but are cast in terms of "persons acting in concert." That agents and principals act "in concert" is clear as a matter of ordinary usage. Section 343, Comment d of the Restatement (Second) of Agency expressly refers to section 876 of the Restatement (Second) of Torts, which is entitled "Persons Acting in Concert." Section 876 provides:

> For harm resulting to a third person from the tortious conduct of another, one is subject to liability if he (a) does a tortious act in concert with the other or pursuant to a common design with him, or (b) knows that the other's conduct constitutes a breach of duty and gives substantial assistance or encouragement to the other so to conduct himself. . . . [30]

24. Flagg Bros., Inc. v. Brooks, 436 U.S. 149 (1978) addresses the situation of a lawyer who advises a client about seizing property in the possession of a debtor. It would seem that if the lawyer "assists" the client, and if the seizure turns out not to be legally privileged, then the lawyer, as well as the client, is prima facie legally responsible. Restatement (Second) of Agency § 343, Comment d, says that "[T]he act of the agent may play too small a part to render him legally responsible for the result, or

the agent's innocence and purpose may create a privilege for him to act." It is hard to see how the lawyer's role in such a situation is "too small" to count. The comment does not indicate the scope of the privilege that could result in immunity.

28. ...[See] SEC v. National Student Marketing Corp., 457 F.Supp. 682 (D.D.C.1978) [reprinted below at p. 104]....

30. Restatement (Second) of Torts § 876 (1977).

Advice to a tortfeasor is equivalent to active participation in the tort if the advisor knows that the contemplated act is tortious, and if the advice is a "substantial factor in causing the resulting tort."

. . .

Finally, one can look to the principles of complicity expressed in the criminal law for guidance. Section 2.06(1) of the Model Penal Code provides that "[a] person is guilty of an offense if it is committed by his own conduct or by the conduct of another person for which he is legally accountable...."[36] Section 2.06(2)(c) of the Code provides that a person is legally accountable for the conduct of another person if he is an "accomplice of such other person." And section 2.06(3)(a)(ii) provides that an accomplice is one who "aids ... in planning or committing" the offense "with the purpose of promoting or facilitating the commission of the offense." Restating these provisions, a lawyer is guilty of an offense if he aids a client in facilitating conduct that is an offense.[39]

The case law on the question is sparse.... In most of the cases, the lawyer has overtly assisted his client in accomplishing manifestly illegal purposes. Thus, courts have held that it is improper for a lawyer to give advice as to how to commit a crime or fraud[41] or how to conceal criminal or fraudulent acts.[42] These cases beget law that is not hard to formulate. There is less guidance when the conduct is less blatant, but there is enough to point the way. One case, for example, states the test ... as whether "the lawyer conveyed to the client the idea that by adopting a particular course of action [the client] may successfully [accomplish the illegal purpose]?"[43] As to the mode of assistance, courts have held that it is unlawful for a lawyer to negotiate for his client in pursuance of an illegal purpose[44] or to prepare documents to effectuate it.[45] As to the extent of knowledge that will result in complicity, the cases say not only that liability results from actual knowledge of the client's illegal purpose, but also that it results from knowledge of facts that reasonably should excite suspicion.[46]

---

36. Model Penal Code § 2.06(1) (Proposed Official Draft, 1962).

39. There is very little authority on the degree of lawyer involvement in a client's criminal endeavor that would constitute "aiding." See Johnson v. Youden, [1950] 1 K.B. 544, involving a criminal prosecution against a solicitor who effected the conveyance of real property at a price in excess of that permitted by applicable price control regulations. The action was dismissed because there was no showing that the solicitor knew about the calculation of the price such that, given his assumed knowledge of the law, he knew that the price violated the law.

41. E.g., In re Feltman, 237 A.2d 473 (N.J. 1968).

42. E.g., Townsend v. State Bar, 197 P.2d 326 (Cal.1948); In re Giordano, 229 A.2d 524 (N.J.1967).

43. In re Bullowa, 229 N.Y.S. 145, 154 (1928). See also Attorney Grievance Comm'n v. Kerpelman, 420 A.2d 940 (Md. 1980).

44. E.g., In re La Duca, 299 A.2d 405 (N.J. 1973).

45. E.g., Galbraith v. State Bar, 23 P.2d 291 (Cal.1933).

46. E.g., In re Wines, 370 S.W.2d 328 (Mo. 1963); State ex rel. Nebraska State Bar Ass'n v. Holscher, 230 N.W.2d 75 (Neb. 1975); In re Blatt, 324 A.2d 15 (N.J.1974).

This analysis indicates the dimensions of the lawyer's duty under criminal and civil law to refrain from "assisting" a client in conduct that is "illegal." A lawyer violates that duty if:

(1) The client is engaged in a course of conduct that violates the criminal law or is an intentional violation of a civil obligation, other than failure to perform a contract or failure to sustain a good faith claim to property;

(2) The lawyer has knowledge of the facts sufficient to reasonably discern that the client's course of conduct is such a violation; and

(3) The lawyer facilitates the client's course of conduct either by giving advice that encourages the client to pursue the conduct or indicates how to reduce the risks of detection, or by performing an act that substantially furthers the course of conduct.

When Does a Lawyer Cross the Line into Illegality?

Is a lawyer who advises a client that breaching a contract may be less costly than carrying it out liable for damages to the non-client party if the client follows the lawyer's advice? Will your answer be different if the lawyer assists a client in persuading a non-client to break a contract with a third person? When does legal advice given in connection with a client's property dispute with a third person become the intentional tort of conversion? May a lawyer advise (and defend in further litigation that may arise) a product manufacturer who is continuing to distribute a product that some juries, but not the manufacturer, believe is so unsafe as to be a "defective product?"[73] What if the product violates current state or federal safety regulations? Finally, is the lawyer liable to a non-client who is injured by improper "hardball" tactics in the courtroom that include malicious and false statements about the claimant?

Does a lawyer commit a federal civil rights violation by invoking summary procedures that have now been declared unconstitutional? In Wyatt v. Cole,[74] the lawyer for one partner in a soured business venture brought a replevin proceeding in Mississippi to obtain summary possession of property his client claimed. The other partner brought a federal civil

---

73. Ford sought to justify its placement of the gas tank in Pinto cars on the ground that "the $11 increased cost on 12.5 million cars and light trucks would be almost three times greater than the estimated injury costs" (180 deaths and a similar number of serious burn injuries). This decision was revisited in a criminal trial against Ford for reckless homicide in Indiana and a California damage award of $125 million (later reduced to $6.6 million by a judge). See David Luban, Lawyers and Justice 206–34 (1989) (discussing the *Pinto* case). Dow Corning decided to take a more conciliatory approach in the 1992 breast implant controversy.

74. 504 U.S. 158 (1992). The Court left open the question whether an affirmative defense of good faith or probable cause to invoke the state procedure is available to private defendants.

rights action under 42 U.S.C. § 1983 against the first partner and his lawyer for employing an unconstitutional summary remedy to seize property. The Court held that private individuals who use unconstitutional state procedures do not have the qualified tort immunity available to public officials.

C. SECURITIES AND REGULATORY LAW

1. LAWYER'S OPINION FUNCTION

Parties to business transactions often seek legal reassurance on certain issues from opposing parties' counsel. This reassurance, known as a third-party legal opinion (or comfort letter), may be either written or oral but typically takes the form of a formal letter, the contents of which counsel haggle over as much as any other transactional point. Opinions often deal with such matters as legal authority to act, valid incorporation and compliance with particular laws, such as applicable federal and state securities laws. Some of the professional concerns connected with the opinion function are ably summarized in a well-known article by James J. Fuld.[1]

Conscientious lawyers, Fuld reports, are concerned at the risks created for lawyers by increasing requests for legal opinions of broad scope that are relied on by persons with whom the client is dealing. Lawyers who have two sets of draft opinions for each transaction, depending upon which party they represent, stimulate haggling about opinion terms and sometimes impose their will in situations in which their client has a superior bargaining position. Lawyers should be reluctant, Fuld argues, to request or provide opinions that purport to certify matters on which no lawyer can feel fully confident, such as an opinion that a corporate client is complying with all applicable federal, state and local laws. Opinions that contain factual detail about the client also imperil the client's attorney-client privilege. Nor is it responsible for a lawyer to give an opinion involving the law of another jurisdiction without involving local counsel.[2]

To whom does the opining lawyer owe duties? Fuld states:

> . . . It is clear that he has an obligation to his client, and if the lawyer addresses his opinion to a third party, he has duties to the third party. I believe, however, that the duties may not be exactly the same. To his client the lawyer owes a duty to deliver an opinion which is appropriate for the client and which the client can understand and act upon; there is no one else who can help the client to understand the opinion and if

1. James J. Fuld, Lawyers' Standards and Responsibilities in Rendering in Rendering Opinions, 33 Bus.Lawyer 1295 (1978).

2. Two qualifications to this established general rule should be noted: a lawyer admitted in any state may opine on federal law; and experienced corporate lawyers often treat Delaware corporation law, because of its flagship role, as a species of national law.

necessary obtain a different opinion. But a third-party recipient is usually represented by his own lawyer, who is uniquely familiar with the third-party's particular legal and tax problems, and the opining lawyer's duties are therefore merely to give his careful opinion on the matters requested.

. . .

Whatever the law may ultimately be held to be, I would recommend that a lawyer assume that his opinion, or a summary of, or reference to, it, will be seen by persons other than the original recipient, and that the lawyer may be charged with legal responsibility for their reliance. Such an opinion should, therefore, not only attempt to limit the class of persons who may rely on the opinion, but perhaps more importantly, include all qualifications, conditions, assumptions and references to other documents in order to alert subsequent users of the opinion regarding any uncertainties involved. Anyone other than the intended recipient should be told to consult his own advisor. And, if this is understood in advance with the client, the opinion should further state that no summary of, or reference to, the opinion is to be made without the lawyer's written consent. Even all these steps may not be sufficient.... [3]

Third–Party Legal Opinions

Increasing concern over a lawyer's civil liability for third-party legal opinions has prompted bar associations across the United States to draft opinion guidelines and standards.[4] Widespread acceptance of such standards not only mitigates the risk of misunderstanding of opinion language, but also provides support to a lawyer unwilling to give a risky opinion desired by an opposing party. Agreement on standards also provides a common starting point for negotiations, perhaps reducing the "two files of opinions" phenomenon discussed by Fuld.[5]

The most significant, and potentially most far-reaching in effect, of the various third-party opinion standards efforts is the Third–Party Legal Opinion Report of the ABA's Section on Business Law.[6] The avowed purpose of the project was to serve as "the first step toward the establishment of a national consensus as to the purpose, format and coverage of a

---

3. Id. at 1309–10.

4. In addition to the ABA report described in the text, see Special Report by the Tri-Bar Opinion Committee, The Remedies Opinion, 46 Bus.Law. 959 (1991) (a joint effort of three major New York bar associations).

5. See also Norman Redlich, Lawyers' Standards and Responsibilities in Rendering Opinions, 33 Bus.Law. 1317 (1978).

6. ABA Section on Business Law, Third–Party Legal Opinion Report, 47 Bus.Law. (Nov. 1991). The report originated in a 1989 conference at which 71 practitioners presented papers. In its final form it reflects the comments of more than 24 bar groups. The resulting "Accord," as it is referred to, contains many pages of densely written fine print and includes guidelines for negotiating a legal opinion.

third-party legal opinion, the precise meaning of its language and the recognition of certain guidelines for its negotiation."

Opinion Letters and M.R. 2.3

The Model Code did not address evaluations of the client's affairs for use by third parties. Model Rule 2.3, however, provides that a lawyer may undertake such an evaluation as long as (1) it is reasonable to believe that making the evaluation is compatible with the lawyer's other duties to the client, and (2) the client consents after consultation.[7] As to the confidentiality of information learned in the course of making the evaluation, M.R. 2.3(b) states:

> Except as disclosure is required in connection with a report of an evaluation, information relating to the evaluation is otherwise protected by Rule 1.6 [the rule on confidentiality].

Comment [5] to 2.3 states:

> The quality of an evaluation depends on the freedom and extent of the investigation upon which it is based. Ordinarily a lawyer should have whatever latitude of investigation seems necessary as a matter of professional judgment. Under some circumstances, however, the terms of the evaluation may be limited. For example, certain issues or sources may be categorically excluded, or the scope of search may be limited by time constraints or the noncooperation of persons having relevant information. Any such limitations which are material to the evaluation should be described in the report. If after a lawyer has commenced an evaluation, the client refuses to comply with the terms upon which it was understood the evaluation was to have been made, the lawyer's obligations are determined by law, having reference to the terms of the client's agreement and the surrounding circumstances.

Notice that the Comment refers to law outside the Rules in determining whether disclosure of adverse information may be necessary. Whether the lawyer may withdraw and whether disclosure is necessary to avoid assisting a fraud also are answered by reference to criminal, tort and relevant statutory law.

Read Model Rule 4.1. How is it related to M.R. 2.3? M.R. 4.1 uses the word "knowingly." Read the definition of "knowingly" in the Terminology section of the Model Rules. Should a different word or phrase have been substituted for "knowingly" in M.R. 4.1? What would M.R. 2.3 and 4.1 have required of the lawyer doing the lien search in *Greycas*? M.R. 4.1 is considered further in connection with the disclosure of client fraud in Chapter 4 at p. 282.

---

7. See Edward A. Carr, Attorney Opinion Letters: Model Rule 2.3 and the Texas Experience, 37 S. Tex. L.Rev. 1127, 1131–38 (1996) (exploring practical considerations that should be given before giving a legal opinion to a third person at the request of the client).

2. AIDING AND ABETTING A SECURITIES LAW VIOLATION

SEC v. National Student Marketing Corp.

United States District Court for the District of Columbia, 1978.
457 F.Supp. 682.

■ Before BARRINGTON PARKER, DISTRICT JUDGE.

[This was a a civil enforcement action brought by the SEC seeking injunctive and declaratory relief against two law firms, White & Case and Lord, Bissell & Brook (LBB), for their role in the 1969 merger of National Student Marketing Corporation (NSMC) and Interstate National Corporation (Interstate); the two companies and some of their principal officers were also defendants. NSMC, which marketed products for high school and college students, was a prosperous company in 1969, or so the financial community thought. In that year NSMC expressed an interest in acquiring Interstate National Corporation, an insurance holding company.

[On June 10, 1969, NSMC's president and one of its senior vice-presidents made a presentation to the Interstate directors concerning the proposed merger. They provided the Interstate directors with NSMC's 1968 annual report, its financial report for the first half of 1969, and financial projections of earnings for the fiscal year ending on August 31, 1969. They sweetened their initial offer (1) from one share of NSMC common stock for every two shares of Interstate to two shares of NSMC stock for every three shares of Interstate; and (2) by promising the Interstate directors that they would be permitted to sell up to 25% of the NSMC shares they would acquire in a registered public offering planned for the fall of 1969.

[This resulted in an agreement in principle for the merger. NSMC and Interstate issued press releases, which included information about NSMC's earnings for the first half of fiscal year 1969.

[On August 12, 1969, the Interstate directors met to review the final version of the merger agreement. The agreement provided: (1) that both corporations warranted that the information in their Proxy statements would "be accurate and correct and [would] not omit to state a material fact necessary to make such information not misleading"; and (2) that the financial statements included "are true and correct and have been prepared in accordance with generally accepted accounting principles". It also included NSMC's specific assurance that its 1968 year-end and May 31, 1969, nine-month financial statements:

> fairly present the results of the operation of NSMC ... for the periods indicated, subject in the case of the nine-month statements to year-end audit adjustments.

[The agreement also provided that the merger was conditioned on the prior receipt by each corporation of (1) an opinion letter from the other corporation's lawyers that all transactions in connection with the merger had been taken in full compliance with applicable law; and (2) a satisfactory "comfort letter" from the other corporation's independent public accountants. Each comfort letter was to state that the accountants had no reason to believe that any material adjustments in the interim financials were required in order fairly to present the results of the operations of the company. The agreement could be terminated by mutual consent of the two corporations' boards of directors at any time prior to completion of the merger. It also gave each party the right to waive any of the conditions to that party's obligations. Finally, the agreement specified that the merger be consummated on or before November 28, 1969.

[Both corporations used proxy statements and notices of special stockholder meetings to secure stockholder approval of the proposed merger. The material sent by Interstate to its shareholders included a copy of the merger agreement, NSMC's proxy statement and NSMC's financial statement for August 31, 1968 and the nine-month interim financial statement, ending on May 31, 1969. The nine-month interim statement showed an NSMC profit of approximately $700,000. The shareholders of both companies seemed enthusiastic about the merger, approving it by large majorities.

[In mid-October Peat Marwick—the independent accountant as it happened for both Interstate and NSMC—began working on the comfort letter on NSMC's financial condition. It soon determined that NSMC's nine-month interim financials had to be adjusted so that, instead of showing a $700,000 profit for these nine months, NSMC would show a loss of almost $200,000. Peat Marwick discussed the proposed adjustments with representatives of NSMC, but neither the accountants nor NSMC told Interstate of the proposed change. Peat Marwick completed a draft of the comfort letter on the morning of the closing.

[The closing was scheduled for 2:00 p.m. on Friday, October 31, at the New York offices of the law firm of White & Case. White & Case represented NSMC, with Epley as the partner in charge of the firm's representation. Epley and several White & Case associates were at the meeting in behalf of NSMC, along with NSMC's president, Randell, and general counsel, Davies. The law firm of Lord Bissell & Brook, through its partners Meyer and Schauer, represented Interstate. Meyer was also a director and shareholder of Interstate. Interstate's president, Brown, and three other members of the Interstate board of directors and executive committee were also at the meeting in Interstate's behalf.]

Although Schauer had had an opportunity to review most of the merger documents at White & Case on the previous day, the comfort letter had not been delivered. When he arrived at White & Case on the morning of the merger, the letter was still not available, but he was informed by a representative of the firm that it was expected to arrive at any moment.

The meeting proceeded. When the letter had not arrived by approximately 2:15 p.m., Epley telephoned Peat Marwick's Washington office to inquire about it. Anthony M. Natelli, the partner in charge, thereupon dictated to Epley's secretary a letter which provided in part:

[N]othing has come to our attention which caused us to believe that:

1. The National Student Marketing Corporation's unaudited consolidated financial statements as of and for the nine months ended May 31, 1969:

  a. Were not prepared in accordance with accounting principles ... followed in the preparation [of previous financial statements];

  b. Would require any material adjustments for a fair and reasonable presentation of the information shown except with respect to [NSMC's nine month interim financial statement covering the period ending on] ... May 31, 1969 ... our examination ... disclosed the following significant adjustments which in our opinion should be reflected retroactive to May 31, 1969:

    1. In adjusting the amortization of deferred costs at May 31, 1969 ... an adjustment of $500,000 was required....

    2. In August 1969 management wrote off receivables in amounts of $300,000. It appears that the uncollectibility of these receivables could have been determined at May 31, 1969 and such charge off should have been reflected as of that date

    3. Acquisition costs in the amount of $84,000 for proposed acquisitions which the Company decided not to pursue were transferred from additional paid-in capital to general and administrative expenses. In our opinion, these should have been so transferred as of May 31, 1969

· · ·

Epley delivered one copy of the typed letter to the conference room where the closing was taking place. Epley then returned to his office.

Schauer was the first to read the unsigned letter. He then handed it to Cameron Brown, advising him to read it.... [Meyer also read it.] They asked Randell and Joy a number of questions relating to the nature and effect of the adjustments. The NSMC officers gave assurances that the adjustments would have no significant effect on the predicted year-end earnings of NSMC and that a substantial portion of the $500,000 adjustments to deferred costs would be recovered. Moreover, they indicated that NSMC's year-end audit for fiscal 1969 had been completed by Peat Marwick, would be published in a couple of weeks, and would demonstrate that NSMC itself had made each of the adjustments for its fourth quarter. The comfort letter, they explained, simply determined that those adjustments should be reflected in the third quarter ended May 31, 1969, rather than the final quarter of NSMC's fiscal year. Randell and Joy indicated that while NSMC disagreed with what they felt was a tightening up of its accounting practices, everything requested by Peat Marwick to "clean up" its books had been undertaken.

At the conclusion of this discussion, certain of the Interstate representatives, including at least Brown, Schauer and Meyer, conferred privately to consider their alternatives in light of the apparent nonconformity of the comfort letter with the requirements of the Merger Agreement. Although

they considered the letter a serious matter and the adjustments as significant and important, they were nonetheless under some pressure to determine a course of action promptly since there was a 4 p.m. filing deadline if
the closing were to be consummated as scheduled on October 31.[20] Among
the alternatives considered were: (1) delaying or postponing the closing,
either to secure more information or to resolicit the shareholders with
corrected financials; (2) closing the merger; or (3) calling it off completely.

The consensus of the directors was that there was no need to delay the
closing. The comfort letter contained all relevant information and in light
of the explanations given by Randell and Joy, they already had sufficient
information upon which to make a decision. Any delay for the purpose of
resoliciting the shareholders was considered impractical because it would
require the use of year-end figures instead of the stale nine-month interim
financials. Such a requirement would make it impossible to resolicit shareholder approval before the merger upset date of November 28, 1969, and
would cause either the complete abandonment of the merger or its renegotiation on terms possibly far less favorable to Interstate. The directors also
recognized that delay or abandonment of the merger would result in a
decline in the stock of both companies, thereby harming the shareholders
and possibly subjecting the directors to lawsuits based on their failure to
close the merger. The Interstate representatives decided to proceed with
the closing. They did, however, solicit and receive further assurances from
the NSMC representatives that the stated adjustments were the only ones
to be made to the company's financial statements and that 1969 earnings
would be as predicted. When asked by Brown whether the closing could
proceed on the basis of an unsigned comfort letter, Meyer responded that if
a White & Case partner assured them that this was in fact the comfort
letter and that a signed copy would be forthcoming from Peat Marwick,
they could close. Epley gave this assurance. Meyer then announced that
Interstate was prepared to proceed, the closing was consummated, and a
previously arranged telephone call was made which resulted in the filing of
the Articles of Merger at the Office of the Recorder of Deeds of the District
of Columbia. Large packets of merger documents, including the required
counsel opinion letters, were exchanged.[22] The closing was solemnized with
a toast of warm champagne.

. . .

20. The pressure to close on October 31
derived from a public announcement to
that effect; it was therefore likely that any
delay would have had an adverse impact on
the stock of both companies. The 4 p.m.
deadline was the closing time of the District of Columbia office where the merger
documents were to be filed.

22. The LBB opinion letter, delivered to
NSMC at the closing, reads in pertinent
part:

Gentlemen:

We have acted as counsel to Interstate in connection with the merger of
Interstate into NSMC pursuant to the
Plan. In such capacity, we have examined the Plan together with Exhibits A,
B and C thereto; the charters, by-laws
and minutes of Interstate and its Subsidiaries (as defined in the Plan), corporate
records, certificates of public officials and
of officers and representatives of Interstate and such other documents deemed

Comfort Letter
eventually
would show/ a
loss

Unknown to the Interstate group, several telephone conversations relating to the substance of the comfort letter occurred on the afternoon of the closing between Peat Marwick representatives and Epley.... Epley was told that an additional paragraph would be added in order to characterize the adjustments. The paragraph recited that with the noted adjustments properly made, NSMC's unaudited consolidated statement for the nine-month period would not reflect a profit as had been indicated but rather a net loss, and the consolidated operations of NSMC as they existed on May 31, 1969, would show a break-even as to net earnings for the year ended August 31, 1969. Epley had the additional paragraph typed out, but failed to inform or disclose this change to Interstate. In a second conversation, after the closing was completed and the Interstate representatives had departed, Epley was informed of still another proposed addition, namely, a paragraph urging resolicitation of both companies' shareholders and disclosure of NSMC's corrected nine-month financials prior to closing. To this, he responded that the deal was closed and the letter was not needed. Peat Marwick nonetheless advised Epley that the letter would be delivered and that its counsel was considering whether further action should be taken by the firm.

The final written draft of the comfort letter arrived at White & Case late that afternoon. Peat Marwick believed that Interstate had been informed and was aware of the conversations between its representatives and Epley and of its concern about the adjustments. Because of this belief and especially since the merger had been closed without benefit of the completed letter, Peat Marwick's counsel perceived no obligation to do anything further about the merger. Nonetheless, a signed copy of the final letter was sent to each board member of the two companies, presumably in an effort to underline the accountants' concern about consummation of the merger without shareholder resolicitation.

The signed comfort letter was delivered to the Interstate offices on Monday, November 3. It was first seen and read by Donald Jeffers, Interstate's chief financial officer. He had not been present at the October 31 closing or informed of the adjustments to the interim financials. Concerned, he contacted Brown immediately and read the letter to him. Since a

necessary to enable us to give the opinion hereinafter expressed.

Based on the foregoing and having due regard to legal considerations we deem relevant, we are of the opinion that: . . .

7. The Plan has been duly executed and delivered by Interstate and is a valid and binding obligation in accordance with its terms and any corporate action by Interstate required in order to authorize the transactions therein contemplated has been taken.

8. To our knowledge, neither Interstate nor any Subsidiary is engaged in or threatened with any legal action or other proceeding, or has incurred or been charged with any presently pending violation of any Federal, state or local law or administrative regulation, which would materially adversely affect or impair the financial condition, business, operations, prospects, properties or assets of Interstate.

meeting with other Interstate principals was scheduled for the next morning the letter was added to the other matters to be discussed.

The signed letter was virtually identical to the unsigned version delivered at the closing, except for the addition of the following two paragraphs:

> Your attention is called, however, to the fact that if the aforementioned adjustments had been made at May 31, 1969 the unaudited consolidated statement of earnings of National Student Marketing Corporation would have shown a net loss of approximately $80,000. It is presently estimated that the consolidated operations of the company as it existed at May 31, 1969 will be approximately a break-even as to net earnings for the year ended August 31, 1969.

> In view of the above mentioned facts, we believe the companies should consider submitting corrected interim unaudited financial information to the shareholders prior to proceeding with the closing.

The only other change was the reduction in the write-off to receivables from $300,000 to $200,000, making total negative adjustments to NSMC's nine-month financials in the amount of $784,000.

At the meeting the following day, the matter was fully discussed by the former Interstate principals. Of particular concern were the additional "break-even" and "resolicitation" paragraphs.[25] Brown explained what had occurred at the closing and the reasons for the decision to consummate the merger. He called Meyer at LBB, who by that time was also aware of the letter. After some discussion, it was decided that more information was needed. Brown and Jeffers agreed to contact Peat Marwick and Meyer agreed that his firm would contact Epley at White & Case.

On that afternoon, Schauer contacted Epley by telephone. Epley stated that he had not known of the additional paragraphs until after the closing. He added that in any case the additions did not expand upon the contents of the earlier unsigned letter; the "break-even" paragraph simply reflected the results of an arithmetic computation of the effects of the adjustments, and the "resolicitation" paragraph was gratuitous and a matter for lawyers, not accountants. While Schauer disagreed, Epley again responded that the additional paragraphs made no difference and that NSMC regarded the deal as closed.

... Meanwhile, the market value of NSMC stock continued to increase, and the directors noted that any action on their part to undo the merger would most likely adversely affect its price. By the end of the week, the

---

25. A significant cause of their concern was a statement contained in a copy of a letter from Peat Marwick to Epley which accompanied the signed comfort letter; that letter suggested that Epley was aware of the additional paragraphs on the day of the closing. SEC Exhibit 57, Letter dated October 31, 1969, from Peat Marwick to Mr. Eplee (sic). Jeffers, however, was concerned with the adjustments in general, stating that it was very unusual for them to be included in a comfort letter, that he was surprised the Interstate representatives had closed without a signed comfort letter, and that the deferred cost adjustment of $500,000 was "a hell of a big adjustment".

decision was made to abstain from any action. Thereafter, Brown issued a memorandum to all Interstate employees announcing completion of the merger. No effort was ever made by any of the defendants to disclose the contents of the comfort letter to the former shareholders of Interstate, the SEC or to the public in general.

D. The Stock Sales

Early in the negotiations the principal Interstate shareholders understood that they would be able to sell a portion of the NSMC stock received in the merger through a public offering planned for the fall of 1969. Various shareholders, including Brown, Tate, Allison, Bach and Meyer, intended to profit by this opportunity and sell up to 25 percent of their newly acquired stock. . . .

White Weld [the brokerage firm handling the sales] began processing the sales on the afternoon of October 31. It subsequently sold a total of 59,500 shares of NSMC stock. The gross received was slightly less than $3 million. Brown received approximately $500,000 for his shares and Meyer received approximately $86,000 for the shares he held. . . . White Weld was never informed of the comfort letter adjustments before it undertook the sale as agents for the Interstate principals.

. . .

E. Subsequent Events

Following the acquisition of Interstate and several other companies NSMC stock rose steadily in price, reaching a peak in mid-December. However, in early 1970, after several newspaper and magazine articles appeared questioning NSMC's financial health, the value of the stock decreased drastically. Several private lawsuits were filed and the SEC initiated a wide-ranging investigation which led to the filing of this action.

II. THE PRESENT ACTION

[This was a civil proceeding brought by the Securities and Exchange Commission, seeking injunctive sanctions against NSMC, the NSMC representatives and the Interstate representatives for their participation in alleged securities law violations in the merger of the two companies. While the suit was in the discovery stage, NSMC and its representatives, including Peat Marwick, the Peat Marwick partner who dictated the "comfort letter" and Epley, consented to the entry of judgments of permanent injunctions against them. Epley was suspended from securities practice for 180 days. White & Case, also a defendant, entered into a settlement with the SEC. The firm agreed to follow specified procedures in handling future securities matters. Thus, the only defendants that remained before the court in this case were those who had represented Interstate: the law firm of Lord, Bissell & Brook and its two partners, Meyer and Schauer, and Brown, the former president of Interstate.][a]

a. [Editors' note:] Before reading on think   about what, if anything, the lawyers for

... [T]he Commission alleges that the defendants, both as principals and as aiders and abettors, violated § 10(b) of the 1934 Act,[37] Rule 10b–5 promulgated thereunder,[38] and § 17(a) of the 1933 Act,[39] through their participation in the Interstate/NSMC merger and subsequent stock sales by Interstate principals, in each instance without disclosing the material information revealed by the Peat Marwick comfort letter.

Numerous charges, all of which appear to allege secondary liability, are leveled against the attorney defendants. Schauer is charged with "participating in the merger between Interstate and NSMC," apparently referring to his failure to interfere with the closing of the merger after receipt of the comfort letter. Such inaction, when alleged to facilitate a transaction, falls under the rubric of aiding and abetting. See Kerbs v. Fall River Industries, Inc., 502 F.2d 731, 739–40 (10th Cir.1974). Both Schauer and Meyer are charged with issuing false opinions in connection with the merger and stock sales, thereby facilitating each transaction, and with acquiescence in the merger after learning the contents of the signed comfort letter. The Commission contends that the attorneys should have refused to issue the opinions in view of the adjustments revealed by the unsigned comfort letter, and after receipt of the signed version, they should have withdrawn

SEC believe what the attorney's should have done

Interstate did wrong. What, if anything, should they have done differently before the closing meeting? At the closing meeting? After the closing meeting?

37. Section 10(b), 15 U.S.C. § 78j(b), reads as follows:

It shall be unlawful for any person, directly or indirectly, by the use of any means or instrumentality of interstate commerce or of the mails, or of any facility of any national securities exchange ... (b) To use or employ, in connection with the purchase or sale of any security registered on a national securities exchange or any security not so registered, any manipulative or deceptive device or contrivance in contravention of such rules and regulations as the Commission may prescribe as necessary or appropriate in the public interest or for the protection of investors.

38. Rule 10b–5, 17 C.F.R. § 240.10b–5, provides:

It shall be unlawful for any person, directly or indirectly, by the use of any means or instrumentality of interstate commerce, or of the mails or of any facility of any national securities exchange,

(a) To employ any device, scheme, or artifice to defraud,

(b) To make any untrue statement of a material fact or to omit to state a material fact necessary in order to make

the statements made, in the light of the circumstances under which they were made, not misleading, or

(c) To engage in any act, practice, or course of business which operates or would operate as a fraud or deceit upon any person, in connection with the purchase or sale of any security.

39. Section 17(a), 15 U.S.C. § 77q(a), provides:

It shall be unlawful for any person in the offer or sale of any securities by the use of any means or instruments of transportation or communication in interstate commerce or by the use of the mails, directly or indirectly—

(1) to employ any device, scheme, or artifice to defraud, or

(2) to obtain money or property by means of any untrue statement of a material fact or any omission to state a material fact necessary in order to make the statements made, in the light of the circumstances under which they were made, not misleading, or

(3) to engage in any transaction, practice, or course of business which operates or would operate as a fraud or deceit upon the purchaser.

their opinion with regard to the merger and demanded resolicitation of the Interstate shareholders. If the Interstate directors refused, the attorneys should have withdrawn from the representation and informed the shareholders or the Commission....

Since any liability of the alleged aiders and abettors depends on a finding of a primary violation of the antifraud provisions, the Court will first address the issues relating to the Commission's charges against the principals....

A. Nexus With a Sale

For the SEC to prove a violation of the antifraud provisions, it must demonstrate that the alleged misconduct was "in the offer or sale" of a security under § 17(a) or "in connection with the purchase or sale" of a security under § 10(b) and Rule 10b–5. The Commission has made the requisite showing for each of the provisions with respect to the defendants' activities leading to the closing of the merger....

B. Materiality

Also essential to an alleged violation of the antifraud provisions is that the omission or misstatement be material....

Initially, the sheer magnitude of the adjustments supports a finding that they were material. The interim financials issued by NSMC reflected a profit of $702,270 for the nine-month period end[ing] May 31, 1969.... The aggregate adjustments amounted to $884,000, thereby reducing the reported profit by 125 percent and resulting in a net loss for the nine-month period of approximately $180,000. Viewing these figures alone, it is difficult to imagine how the adjustments could not be material.

. . .

C. Scienter

Finally, there must be proof that Brown and Meyer acted with the requisite degree of culpability. Unfortunately, the level of culpability required in an SEC injunctive action is far from certain....

Though these are important issues, the resolution of which would be welcome to the securities bar, the Court concludes that they need not be decided at this time, because the conduct of Brown and Meyer in this case meets the prevailing standard for scienter.

After receiving the unsigned comfort letter at the closing, the Interstate representatives immediately expressed concern over the new information; they caucused privately and sought and received various oral assurances from the NSMC representatives. Moreover, the new information included adjustments which were far from insubstantial; they reduced the reported profit of NSMC by several hundreds of thousands of dollars and converted what had been a sizable profit into a net loss. Despite the obvious materiality of this information, especially as demonstrated by their conduct, they made a conscious decision not to disclose it. Such conduct has been found sufficient to meet the scienter requirement. McLean v. Alexander, 420 F.Supp. 1057, 1080–82 (D.Del.1976); see Nassar & Co., Inc. v. SEC, 185 U.S.App.D.C. 125, 130 n. 3, 566 F.2d 790, 795 n. 3 (1977) (Leventhal, J., concurring); Lanza v. Drexel & Co., 479 F.2d 1277, 1305 (2d Cir.1973).

. . .

... Brown and Meyer expected to profit handsomely from the merger and the subsequent stock sales. They were in no haste to disseminate the comfort letter information, and in fact they never revealed the adjustments, even after NSMC's year-end audit had been released....

In any event, to the extent an inference of *actual* intent to deceive, manipulate, or defraud may be inappropriate, the defendants' actions here clearly constitute "the kind of recklessness that is equivalent to wilful fraud," SEC v. Texas Gulf Sulphur Co., 401 F.2d at 868 (concurring opinion), and which also satisfies the scienter requirement....

IV. AIDING AND ABETTING

The Court must now turn to the Commission's charges that the defendants aided and abetted these two violations of the antifraud provisions. The violations themselves establish the first element of aiding and abetting liability, namely that another person has committed a securities law violation.... The remaining elements, though not set forth with any uniformity, are essentially that the alleged aider and abettor had a "general awareness that his role was part of an overall activity that is improper, and [that he] knowingly and substantially assisted the violation." SEC v. Coffey [493 F.2d 1304, 1316 (6th Cir.1974) cert. denied, 420 U.S. 908 (1975)].

The Commission's allegations of aiding and abetting by the defendants, seem to fall into four basic categories: (1) the failure of the attorney defendants to take any action to interfere in the consummation of the merger; (2) the issuance by the attorneys of an opinion with respect to the merger; (3) the attorneys' subsequent failure to withdraw that opinion and inform the Interstate shareholders or the SEC of the inaccuracy of the nine-month financials; and (4) the issuance by the attorneys and Brown of an opinion and letter, respectively, concerning the validity of the stock sales under Rule 133.[b] The SEC's position is that the defendants acted or failed to act with an awareness of the fraudulent conduct by the principals, and thereby substantially assisted the two violations. The Court concurs with regard to the attorneys' failure to interfere with the closing, but must conclude that the remaining actions or inaction alleged to constitute aiding and abetting did not substantially facilitate either the merger or the stock sales.

As noted, the first element of aiding and abetting liability has been established by the finding that Brown and Meyer committed primary

b. [Editors' note:] This refers to the legality under SEC Rule 133 of sales of stock by the Interstate principals as "insiders," following the merger.

violations of the securities laws. Support for the second element, that the defendants were generally aware of the fraudulent activity, is provided by the previous discussion concerning scienter. . . . Despite the obvious materiality of the information, see section III–B supra, each knew that it had not been disclosed prior to the merger and stock sale transactions. Thus, this is not a situation where the aider and abettor merely failed to discover the fraud, see Rolf v. Blyth, Eastman Dillon & Co., 570 F.2d at 52 (Mansfield, J., dissenting), or reasonably believed that the victims were already aware of the withheld information, Hirsch v. du Pont, 553 F.2d 750, 759 (2d Cir.1977). . . .

The final requirement for aiding and abetting liability is that the conduct provide knowing, substantial assistance to the violation. In addressing this issue, the Court will consider each of the SEC's allegations separately. The major problem arising with regard to the Commission's contention that the attorneys failed to interfere in the closing of the merger is whether inaction or silence constitutes substantial assistance. While there is no definitive answer to this question, courts have been willing to consider inaction as a form of substantial assistance when the accused aider and abettor had a duty to disclose. . . .

Upon receipt of the unsigned comfort letter, it became clear that the merger had been approved by the Interstate shareholders on the basis of materially misleading information. In view of the obvious materiality of the information, especially to attorneys learned in securities law, the attorneys' responsibilities to their corporate client required them to take steps to ensure that the information would be disclosed to the shareholders. However, it is unnecessary to determine the precise extent of their obligations here, since it is undisputed that they took no steps whatsoever to delay the closing pending disclosure to and resolicitation of the Interstate shareholders. But, at the very least, they were required to speak out at the closing concerning the obvious materiality of the information and the concomitant requirement that the merger not be closed until the adjustments were disclosed and approval of the merger was again obtained from the Interstate shareholders. Their silence was not only a breach of this duty to speak, but in addition lent the appearance of legitimacy to the closing, ... Contrary to the attorney defendants' contention, imposition of such a duty will not require lawyers to go beyond their accepted role in securities transactions, nor will it compel them to "err on the side of conservatism, . . . thereby inhibiting clients' business judgments and candid attorney-client communications." Courts will not lightly overrule an attorney's determination of materiality and the need for disclosure. However, where, as here, the significance of the information clearly removes any doubt concerning the materiality of the information, attorneys cannot rest on asserted "business judgments" as justification for their failure to make a legal decision pursuant to their fiduciary responsibilities to client shareholders.

The Commission also asserts that the attorneys substantially assisted the merger violation through the issuance of an opinion that was false and misleading due to its omission of the receipt of the comfort letter and of the completion of the merger on the basis of the false and misleading nine-month financials. The defendants contend that a technical reading of the opinion demonstrates that it is not false and misleading, and that it provides accurate opinions as to Interstate's compliance with certain corporate formalities. Of concern to the Court, however, is not the truth or falsity of the opinion, but whether it substantially assisted the violation. Upon consideration of all the circumstances . . ., the Court concludes that it did not.

Contrary to the implication made by the SEC, the opinion issued by the attorneys at the closing did not play a large part in the consummation of the merger. Instead, it was simply one of many conditions to the obligation of NSMC to complete the merger. It addressed a number of corporate formalities required of Interstate by the Merger Agreement, only a few of which could possibly involve compliance with the antifraud provisions of the securities laws. Moreover, the opinion was explicitly for the benefit of NSMC, which was already well aware of the adjustments contained in the comfort letter. Thus, this is not a case where an opinion of counsel addresses a specific issue and is undeniably relied on in completing the transaction. Compare SEC v. Coven, 581 F.2d 1020, at 1028; SEC v. Spectrum, Ltd., 489 F.2d 535 (2d Cir.1973). Under these circumstances, it is unreasonable to suggest that the opinion provided substantial assistance to the merger.

The SEC's contention with regard to counsel's alleged acquiescence in the merger transaction raises significant questions concerning the responsibility of counsel. The basis for the charge appears to be counsel's failure, after the merger, to withdraw their opinion, to demand resolicitation of the shareholders, to advise their clients concerning rights of rescission of the merger, and ultimately, to inform the Interstate shareholders or the SEC of the completion of the merger based on materially false and misleading financial statements. The defendants counter with the argument that their actions following the merger are not subject to the coverage of the securities laws.

The filing of the complaint in this proceeding generated significant interest and an almost overwhelming amount of comment within the legal profession on the scope of a securities lawyer's obligations to his client and to the investing public. The very initiation of this action, therefore, has provided a necessary and worthwhile impetus for the profession's recognition and assessment of its responsibilities in this area. The Court's examination, however, must be more limited. Although the complaint alleges varying instances of misconduct on the part of several attorneys and firms, the Court must narrow its focus to the present defendants and the charges against them.

Meyer, Schauer and Lord, Bissell & Brook are, in essence, here charged with failing to take any action to "undo" the merger. The Court has already concluded that counsel had a duty to the Interstate shareholders to delay the closing of the merger pending disclosure and resolicitation with corrected financials, and that the breach of that duty constituted a violation of the antifraud provisions through aiding and abetting the merger transaction. The Commission's charge, however, concerns the period following that transaction. Even if the attorneys' fiduciary responsibilities to the Interstate shareholders continued beyond the merger, the breach of such a duty would not have the requisite relationship to a securities transaction, since the merger had already been completed. It is equally obvious that such subsequent action or inaction by the attorneys could not substantially assist the merger.

The final contention of the SEC concerns the issuance by the attorneys and Brown of the Rule 133 opinion and letter, respectively. [These documents asserted that the Interstate directors could sell their shares without violating Rule 133.] Little discussion is necessary with respect to this charge, for the Commission has clearly failed to show that these documents substantially assisted the stock sales. Neither of the documents were required by the Merger Agreement, but were requested by NSMC at the closing of the merger. The documents were not intended for the investing public, but for the sole use of NSMC and its counsel in preparing a formal, independent opinion concerning the validity of the sales under Rule 133. Further, the documents were limited to primarily factual issues relevant to the requirements of the Rule, and in no way indicated that they could be relied upon with regard to compliance with the antifraud provisions. Under the circumstances, the Court concludes that the Rule 133 documents issued by the attorneys and Brown did not substantially assist the stock sales by Interstate principals, specifically Brown and Meyer.

Thus, the Court finds that the attorney defendants aided and abetted the violation of § 10(b), Rule 10b–5, and § 17(a) through their participation in the closing of the merger.

V.   APPROPRIATENESS OF INJUNCTIVE RELIEF

Although the Commission has proved past violations by the defendants, that does not end the Court's inquiry. Proof of a past violation is not a prerequisite to the grant of injunctive relief ... but it may, in combination with other factors, warrant an inference of future misconduct by the charged party, SEC v. Manor Nursing Centers, Inc., 458 F.2d 1082, 1100 (2d Cir.1972). The crucial question, though, remains not whether a violation has occurred, but whether there exists a reasonable likelihood of future illegal conduct by the defendant. . . .

The Commission has not demonstrated that the defendants engaged in the type of repeated and persistent misconduct which usually justifies the issuance of injunctive relief. . . . Instead, it has shown violations which principally occurred within a period of a few hours at the closing of the merger in 1969. The Commission has not charged, or even suggested, that the defendants were involved in similar misconduct either before or after the events involved in this proceeding. Thus, the violations proved by the SEC appear to be part of an isolated incident, unlikely to recur and insufficient to warrant an injunction. . . .

Finally, the Commission asserts that an injunction is necessary because the professional occupations of the defendants provide significant opportunities for further involvement in securities transactions. It notes that ... Meyer, Schauer and LBB continue to be involved in various corporate activities, including securities transactions, as part of their legal practice....[c] [T]hat fact is countered somewhat by their professional responsibilities as attorneys and officers of the court to conform their conduct to the dictates of the law. The Court is confident that they will take appropriate steps to ensure that their professional conduct in the future comports with the law.[d]

National Student Marketing: A Legal Ethics Landmark

What is the test for aiding and abetting a client's fraud stated by the court? Did Interstate's officers violate the securities laws? Did Interstate's lawyers assist in the violation? What, if anything, should the lawyers for NSMC and Interstate have done differently during the merger negotiations? Before the closing meeting? At the meeting? Why was the exchange of legal opinions not considered substantial assistance? Why did the court refuse to impose injunctive relief on the lawyers and their law firms? The Koniak excerpt, infra, p. 133, criticizes the decision on this ground; is she correct? The material in note c, supra, provides information that may be relevant. Why is the organized bar so hostile to the idea that lawyers should serve as "gatekeepers" who screen out fraudulent transactions?

According to the court, what should the Lord Bissell lawyers have done at the closing? Suppose Meyer and Schauer had advised the Interstate officers not to close the merger and the officers had rejected the advice? What then? How is it possible that a lawyer can be liable for silence or inaction (i.e., not taking some steps to prevent completion of the transaction)? Would the ethics rules of New York (where the transaction was closed), District of Columbia (place of incorporation of NSMC) or Illinois (home of Interstate) permit Meyer or Schauer to disclose their concerns to shareholders of Interstate? To the SEC? In 1969 DR 7–102(B)(1) was in effect in all three jurisdictions, minus the "except" clause at the end that was adopted by the ABA in 1974. Read Model Rule 1.13(b) and the

---

c. [Editors' note:] Some years after *National Student Marketing*, Lord, Bissell & Brook was charged with assisting another client's securities violation. In that case, which the firm settled for $24 million, the firm's managing partner testified that:

> Judge Parker's opinion in the National Student Marketing case was never circulated to the partners, that there was no partnership meeting about the ruling, that no policies were established to guard against a recurrence, and the partner himself did not remember having read the opinion.

Tim O'Brien, Some Firms Never Learn: Lord Bissell's Second Escape from Fraud Changes Cost $24 Million—And It Could Happen Again, Am. Lawyer, Oct. 1989.

d. [Editors' note:] The SEC appealed the district court's denial of sanctions against Lord, Bissell and Brook and its two partners and they appealed from the court's holding of substantive violations. The appeal was dismissed when the district court approved a $1.3 million settlement of related private suits against the lawyers. See Stan Crock, SEC Agrees to Settle a Landmark Case Involving National Student Marketing, Wall St.J., Jan. 2, 1982, p. 8.

Comment thereto. If it had been in effect when National Student Marketing was decided, would it have helped the lawyers avoid liability?

National Student Marketing Corp. (NSMC), a conglomerate established to sell to college students everything from coffee mugs to computer-matched dates, was one of a number of short-lived glamour stocks in the late 1960s.[1] NSMC stock went from $1 per share in 1968 to a high of $69 per share shortly after the merger. In December 1969 Barron's published a negative article on NSMC, and the company reported it would post a major loss in the first quarter of 1970. Those developments exposed a mess of inflated assets, misleading statements and hidden losses. NSMC's stock plummeted, and estimates of investors' losses reached as high as $100 million. Some NSMC principals and a Peat Marwick accountant were convicted of securities law violations and served prison sentences. The SEC's effort to reach the lawyers involved in the merger transaction created a tremendous stir in the corporate and securities bar and resulted in a rushed amendment to the ABA Code of Professional Responsibility.[2] The long, drawn-out litigation took nearly ten years: White & Case and Epley entered consent decrees that obligated them to follow set procedures if they suspected any foul play in securities cases; and the remaining defendants (mostly Interstate officers and their lawyers) defended on the merits, resulting in the reprinted decision.

Meanwhile, private securities fraud actions had been brought against the same parties. In 1982 nearly all of these suits were settled. The settlement provided $30 million for NSMC investors. White & Case contributed $1.95 million to the fund, and Lord, Bissell & Brook $1.3 million.[3]

Liability of Lawyers as Principals (Primary Liability)

As *Benjamin* indicates, lawyers who take an active role as entrepreneur investors, directors, officers or signatories of prospectuses may be liable as principals under the securities laws provisions that impose liability without proof of wrongful intent.[4] Lawyers and accountants who merely advise an offeror, however, may escape liability as principals under § 12(1)

---

1. See Burt Schorr, White & Case on Trial, 7 Juris Dr. 15 (March 1977). See also Wall St.J., Dec. 6, 1976, at p. 1.

2. Then–SEC Commissioner Sommer stated in 1974 that "in securities matters (other than those where advocacy is clearly proper) the attorney will have to function in a manner more akin to that of the auditor than to that of the advocate." Sommer, Emerging Responsibilities of the Securities Lawyer, [1973–74 Transfer Binder] Fed. Sec. L. Rep. (CCH) ¶ 79,631 (Jan. 1974). The ABA reacted by amending DR 7–102(B)(1) of the Model Code to eliminate, as a practical matter, the lawyer's duty to reveal a client's fraud in which the lawyer's services had been used. See, e.g., Junius Hoffman, On Learning of a Corporate Client's Crime of Fraud, 33 Bus.Law. 1389, 1405–07 (1978) (the amendment was designed to resolve the "conflict" raised between the SEC position and the bar's conception of its primary loyalty to clients).

3. See David Lauter, Two Law Firms Pay $3M To Settle Stock Scandal, Nat'l L. J., Sept. 20, 1982, at pp. 4, 25.

4. See, e.g., *Benjamin,* supra; S.E.C. v. Manor Nursing Centers, Inc., 458 F.2d 1082 (2d Cir.1972); S.E.C. v. Coven, 581 F.2d 1020 (2d Cir.1978).

of the 1933 Act.[5] If a lawyer provides substantial assistance in preparing or reviewing the offering materials, but does not sign the prospectus or make affirmative representations to investors, the lawyer may be liable only as an accessory, requiring proof of wrongful intent.[6] See later developments described below.

Liability of Lawyers for Aiding and Abetting a Securities Violation (Secondary Liability)

The SEC's effort to enlist securities lawyers in the prevention of securities fraud has led to a small number of other enforcement proceedings under Rule 2(e) of the Commission's rules of practice. See In re Carter and Johnson, infra p. 739, and notes following it.

The civil liability of lawyers and other advisors for aiding and abetting a securities law violation was curtailed in Central Bank of Denver v. First Interstate Bank of Denver.[7] Five members of the Court, in an opinion by Justice Kennedy, held that the language of the statute did not create a federal cause of action for aiding and abetting securities violations. The issue, Justice Kennedy said, is "not whether imposing private civil liability on aiders and abettors is good policy but whether aiding and abetting is covered by the statute." "Policy considerations cannot override our interpretation of the text and structure of the act." Four dissenting justices, in an opinion by Justice Stevens, argued that the settled interpretation of the statute, enforced in all federal circuits for many years and left untouched by the 1975 legislative revision of the Act, should not be disturbed unless and until Congress so decides. The case was also unusual because the question it decided was not the question raised in the certiorari petition, but was added by initiative of the Court.

The *Central Bank* decision was greeted with approval by securities lawyers and others who advise and assist issuers of securities and featured in two subsequent federal statutes dealing with remedies for securities fraud. The overall consequences may be summarized as follows:

First, § 15 of the Private Securities Litigation Reform Act of 1995[8] confers authority on the SEC to bring civil enforcement actions against aiders and abetters, including lawyers and accountants. Thus the SEC action in *National Student Marketing*, if it occurred today, would be unaffected by *Central Bank*.[9] *Second*, the liability of principals under the

---

5. See Pinter v. Dahl, 486 U.S. 622, 647 (1988) (section 12(1) contemplates a contractual relationship akin to that of seller and buyer of securities, but does not extend to those "whose motivation [in soliciting the sale is] solely to benefit the buyer."

6. See, e.g., Westlake v. Abrams, 565 F.Supp. 1330, 1350 (N.D.Ga.1983): "[a lawyer] cannot be held to be a controlling person merely because he renders advice in pursuing litigation on behalf of his client."

But cf. Klein v. Boyd, considered below at p. 289.

7. 511 U.S. 164 (1994).

8. Pub. L. No. 104–67, 109 Stat. 737 (1995) (codified as amended in scattered sections of 15 U.S.C.).

9. Only the private civil cause of action is affected by the *Central Bank* decision and the new securities legislation; federal criminal law contains explicit language imposing criminal liability on those who aid and abet

Act extends to those who "directly or indirectly" engage in proscribed activity. Many of the claims that have been litigated on an aiding-and-abetting theory are now being brought on the theory that the lawyers are liable as principals. For example, a materially misleading legal opinion, or one that contains material omissions, may give rise to primary liability if investors rely on it in making an investment decision.[10] *Finally*, claims under state securities and tort law are unaffected by the *Central Bank* decision, except as they are preempted by the Securities Litigation Uniform Standards Act of 1998,[11] which requires that certain categories of class actions for securities violations be brought only in federal courts. In general, by providing a uniform national standard for most securities fraud class actions, the 1998 act drastically reduces lawyers' exposure to liability under state law for securities or common law fraud.[12]

3. CULPABLE INTENT

In Barker v. Henderson, Franklin, Starnes & Holt,[13] a claim that a lawyer unlawfully assisted a fraudulent securities transaction was dismissed on summary judgment because the lawyer's participation was too insubstantial. A general practitioner had assisted an organization in corporate and property matters involved in creating the project in which interests were later sold to private investors. Although the lawyer received the selling materials, he did not review or approve them and his name was not on them. The client, pursuant to the lawyer's advice, engaged a large Detroit firm to handle securities law matters; that firm settled the case against it for assisting client fraud for $612,500.

Judge Easterbrook, speaking for the court in *Barker*, used language that has been relied on by professional firms defending aiding and abetting claims:

> ... A plaintiff's case against an aider, abetter, or conspirator may not rest on a bare inference that the defendant "must have had" knowledge of the facts. The plaintiff must support the inference with some

criminal conduct that constitutes fraud under the securities laws.

10. See, e.g., Kline v. First Western Government Securities, Inc., 24 F.3d 480 (3d Cir. 1994) (lawyer providing a tax opinion in connection with the private syndication of a tax shelter offering can be liable under Rule 10b–5, even though all the facts in the opinion are stated as assumptions based upon representations of management, if the lawyer knows that management has withheld or misstated material information).

11. Pub. L. No. 105–353, 112 Stat. 3227 (1998) (codified in scattered sections of 15 U.S.C.).

12. For guidance through the complexities, see David M. Levine & Adam C. Pritchard, The Securities Litigation Uniform Standards Acts of 1998: The Sun Sets on California's Blue Sky Laws, 54 Bus.L. 1 (1998); Richard W. Painter, Responding to a False Alarm: Federal Preemption of State Securities Fraud Causes of Action, 84 Cornell L.Rev. 1 (1998). State claims of up to 50 claimants may proceed separately in a state's courts; derivative actions are unaffected as are certain change-of-control class actions and claims brought by local or state governments; otherwise, class actions for securities fraud can only be brought in federal courts.

13. 797 F.2d 490 (7th Cir.1986).

reason to conclude that the defendant has thrown in his lot with the primary violators.

Law firms and accountants may act or remain silent for good reasons as well as bad ones, and allowing scienter or conspiracy to defraud to be inferred from the silence of a professional firm may expand the scope of liability far beyond that authorized in [controlling Supreme Court decisions]. If the plaintiff does not have direct evidence of scienter, the court should ask whether the fraud (or cover-up) was in the interest of the defendants. Did they gain by bilking the buyers of the securities? Cf. Dirks, 463 U.S. at 662–64. In this case the Firms did not gain [an accounting firm was also involved]. They received none of the proceeds from the sales. They did not receive fees for rendering advice in connection with the sales to the plaintiffs. Both Firms billed so little time to the Foundation between 1974 and 1976 (and none after October 1976) that it is inconceivable that they joined a venture to feather their nests by defrauding investors. They had nothing to gain and everything to lose. There is no sound basis, therefore, on which a jury could infer that the Firms joined common cause with other offenders or aided and abetted a scheme with the necessary state of mind.[14]

Is the problem in *Barker* absence of both direct evidence of wrongful intent and positive activity to facilitate the fraud? Would the result be the same if the lawyer in *Barker* had handled the securities aspect of the transaction?[15]

The court in *Barker* also stated that "an award of damages under the securities laws is not the way to blaze the trail toward improved ethical standards in the legal ... profession.... The securities law ... must lag behind changes in ethical and fiduciary standards."[16] Should ethical rules dictate who is liable under the securities laws or other regulatory law?

Is Silence or Inaction a Safe Course?

National Student Marketing and subsequent decisions, some arising from the fallout of the savings and loan debacle of the late 1980's, hold that a lawyer must take some preventive action when the lawyer issues legal opinions and facilitates a sale of securities knowing that the client has made knowingly false representations in the selling materials. The case law is more confused when the lawyer, without issuing a legal opinion relied on by third persons, assists a client in closing a transaction knowing that the client has made material misrepresentations to those with whom the client is dealing. The issues are more fully developed in Chapter 4, infra p. 282, in connection with the materials dealing with lawyer disclosure of on ongoing or prospective client fraud on third persons. See also the discussion in

14. 797 F.2d at 497.

15. See Roberts v. Peat, Marwick, Mitchell & Co., 857 F.2d 646 (9th Cir.1988), distinguishing *Barker* on the ground that the lawyers in *Barker*, unlike the accountants in *Roberts*, had not reviewed the selling documents before their distribution and had not put their names on the prospectus.

16. 797 F.2d at 497.

Chapter 8, p. 743, of issues raised by cases against the legal advisers of thrifts who became insolvent in the savings and loan crisis.

4.   CONFLICTING VISIONS OF THE LAW GOVERNING LAWYERS

Susan P. Koniak "The Law Between the Bar and the State"

70 North Carolina Law Review 1389 (1992).[1]

The state and the profession have different understandings of the law governing lawyers—they have in effect different "law."[2] The law of lawyering is not inherently more amorphous, contradictory or obtuse than other law. It is not radically uncertain; it is essentially contested. There is a continuing struggle between the profession and the state over whether the profession's vision of law or the state's will reign.

> II.   The Inadequacy of the Traditional Understanding of the Relationship Between Law and Professional Ethics

As traditionally conceived, the domain of professional ethics begins where the law of the state leaves off.[3] By this I mean that ethics is generally understood to be about obligations above and beyond the requirements of law.[4]

Professional ethics thus conceived does not compete with state law, nor could it possibly conflict with it. Professional ethics merely supplements state law, supplying norms to govern conduct that the society at large lacks the necessary expertise to regulate[5] or for which the state's standards are

1. Copyright © University of North Carolina Law Review. Reprinted with permission. [Editors' note:] The footnotes in this condensation of the article have been renumbered. Some other changes in the original text, primarily updating, have been made. Changes and omissions from the original are not indicated.

2. This article uses Robert Cover's rich and original vision of law, which he articulated most fully in Robert M. Cover, The Supreme Court, 1982 Term—Foreword, Nomos and Narrative, 97 Harv.L.Rev. 4 (1983) [hereinafter Cover, Nomos].

3. See, e.g., William J. Goode, Community within a Community: The Professions, 22 Am.Soc.Rev. 194, 195 (1957) ("Although the occupational behavior of members is regulated by law, the professional community exacts a higher standard of behavior than does the law.").

4. The view that ethics should be about something other than and more than law is

exemplified by Professor Stephen Gillers in What We Talked About When We Talked About Ethics: A Critical View of the Model Rules, 46 Ohio St.L.J. 243, 247–48 (1985), an article criticizing the Model Rules of Professional Conduct because, among other things, much of it merely repeats the injunctions of civil and criminal law. "The more [the document traces the commands of civil or criminal law] . . ., the less it can be considered a code of ethics." Id. at 246. "It is [the] extralegal realm that defines ethics." Id. at 248.

5. The classic sociological understanding of the professions is that society and individual consumers are too lacking in expertise to control or monitor adequately the performance of professionals. At the same time the larger society and individual consumers are intensely interested in controlling the conduct of professionals because of the high stakes involved in the tasks committed to professionals—high stakes both for

insufficiently exacting. But the traditional understanding of the relationship between professional ethics and law—at least among professionals
themselves—goes further than the mere statement that ethics begins
where law leaves off; it also includes the notion that it is appropriate for
the state to leave substantial areas of conduct in which the profession's
own norms govern, i.e., that state law should "leave off" sooner rather
than later. The rhetoric of the professions is filled with talk of the "right"
of self-regulation, of the "encroachments" by the state into areas of
professional control, and of the need to ward off increased state regulation
by toughening internal controls.

In so far as the traditional understanding of the relationship between
law and ethics includes an ongoing debate over the extent and nature of the
"right" of self-regulation, it exposes the competition between state and
group over normative space. But the nature and force of that competition is
masked because the traditional understanding asserts that the domain of
professional ethics does leave off where state law begins. The traditional
understanding thus suggests that a consensus exists on the authoritative
position of state law where state law exists. It suggests that, if the
professions and the state agree on when the state has spoken and on what
the state has said, the effect of the state pronouncement is to invalidate as
a basis of action group norms that are in conflict with state law. These
assumptions, however, are based on a naive positivism about state law;
they minimize the richness and power of the group's normative vision; and
they conceal the dynamic interplay between state and group norms.

Consider the following example:

By 1985, the number of criminal defense lawyers being subpoenaed
before grand juries had risen dramatically,[6] and opposition to this practice
by individual lawyers and the organized bar was increasing apace.[7] The

---

the individual client and for the larger society because professional work implicates
central social values like justice and the
physical well-being of societal members.
The professions and society thus "strike a
bargain:" in exchange for high status, high
remuneration, protection from lay competition and a significant degree of autonomy
from state control, the professions adopt
norms designed to protect individual consumers and the public at large, seek to
educate members so they will internalize
these norms and monitor compliance with
and sanction deviations from such norms.
See Dietrich Rueschemeyer, Lawyers and
their Society 13–14 (1973) for a statement
of this classic sociological explanation of
professional ethics. For a similar explanation of professional ethics from an economist, see Kenneth Arrow, The Limits of
Organization 36–37 (1974).

6. This increase was in large part due to the
broad forfeiture provisions of the Racketeer
Influenced and Corrupt Organizations Act
(RICO), 18 U.S.C. §§ 1961–68 (1982 &
Supp. III, 1985) (see particularly
§ 1963(c)); and the Continuing Criminal
Enterprise Statute (CCE), 21 U.S.C.
§ 853(c), which prosecutors interpreted as
applying to attorney's fees. See the note
above on p. 73.

7. See, e.g., Merkle & Moscarino, At Issue:
Are Prosecutors Invading the Attorney–
Client Relationship?, 71 A.B.A.J. 38 (1985);
Pierce & Colamarino, Defense Counsel as a
Witness for the Prosecution: Curbing the
Practice of Issuing Grand Jury Subpoenas
to Counsel for Targets of Investigations, 36
Hastings L.J. 821 (1985); and Zwerling,
Federal Grand Juries v. Attorney Indepen-
dence and the Attorney–Client Privilege,
27 Hastings L.J. 1263 (1976). In In re

state was largely unresponsive to the bar's opposition. The courts that had considered the question had rejected the lawyers' claims that client and fee identity were generally privileged from disclosure and that special procedures, such as prior judicial approval, should be required before the government is allowed to subpoena a criminal defense lawyer.[8] And while the Justice Department issued guidelines on this subject in 1985, these guidelines provided that such subpoenas could be issued upon a rather modest showing of need by the U.S. Attorney's office involved, and more important, they provided that the showing of need be made to the Department of Justice itself, not to a court.[9]

The Massachusetts bar then proposed an ethics rule making it unethical for a prosecutor to call a lawyer before a grand jury to testify about a client without prior judicial approval. The Supreme Judicial Court of Massachusetts adopted the rule in 1986, and the United States District Court for the District of Massachusetts refused to enjoin its operation.[10] The federal government challenged the district court decision arguing, among other things, that ethics rules should not be used to change grand jury procedures, an area governed by the Federal Rules of Criminal Procedure.[11] In United States v. Klubock,[12] the United States Court of Appeals for the First Circuit split four-four, leaving in place the district court opinion upholding the rule. In the meantime, courts have continued to hold that special procedures are neither required nor advisable under the Constitution or other law,[13] while state bars, following Massachusetts' lead, have proposed ethics rules that would require such procedures.[14]

Grand Jury Subpoena (Slotnick), 781 F.2d 238 (2d Cir.1986) (en banc), amicus briefs opposing the government's use of such subpoenas and arguing for special procedures to limit the practice were filed by Association of The Bar of the City of New York, New York County Lawyers Association, New York Criminal Bar Association, National Association of Criminal Defense Lawyers and New Jersey Association of Criminal Defense Lawyers.

8. See, e.g., In re Grand Jury Proceedings (Freeman), 708 F.2d 1571, 1575 (11th Cir. 1983); In re Grand Jury Proceeding (Schofield), 721 F.2d 1221, 1222–23 (9th Cir. 1983); In re Klein, 776 F.2d 628, 632–33 (7th Cir.1985); In re Grand Jury Subpoena (Slotnick), 781 F.2d 238, 247–50 (2d Cir. 1986) (en banc).

9. The text of the guidelines is reprinted in In re Grand Jury Subpoena to Attorney (Under Seal), 679 F.Supp. 1403, 1408 n. 15 (N.D.W.Va.1988).

10. United States v. Klubock, 639 F.Supp. 117 (D.Mass.1986). The district court declined, however, to rule on whether the rule had been incorporated into the federal

court rules for the district by virtue of the state court adoption. Id. at 121.

11. United States v. Klubock, 832 F.2d 664, 665 (1st Cir.1987) (en banc). The government made three arguments: (1) the rule was invalid under the Supremacy Clause of the Constitution because it was an attempt by state authorities to control federal prosecutors; (2) the district court lacked the power to promulgate the rule because it effected a substantial change in grand jury procedures, which should be made by amending the Federal Rules of Criminal Procedure or by separate congressional enactment; and (3) the court of appeals should exercise its supervisory powers to invalidate the law because the rule was so unwise.

12. 832 F.2d 664 (1st Cir.1987) (en banc).

13. See, e.g., United States v. Perry, 857 F.2d 1346, 1348 (9th Cir.1988); In re Nackson, 114 N.J. 527, 537, 555 A.2d 1101, 1107 (1989).

14. As of 1993, apparently six state supreme courts have adopted subpoena rules proposed by bar associations: Massachu-

In 1988, the American Bar Association passed its second resolution on this issue, and it called for even tighter limitations on the government's power to subpoena lawyers to testify before grand juries than those the ABA had originally proposed.[15] The courts, prosecutors and legislatures have remained largely unresponsive to the bar's position.[16] In 1990, the ABA amended the Model Rules of Professional Conduct to require prosecutors to obtain prior judicial approval before seeking to subpoena a lawyer about her client's affairs and making it unethical for a prosecutor to seek judicial approval unless the information sought is not privileged, it is essential to the investigation and there is no feasible alternative means of obtaining it.[17]

In Baylson v. Disciplinary Board of Supreme Court of Pennsylvania,[18] however, the Third Circuit held that the Pennsylvania subpoena rule, which had become a local rule of federal district courts by automatic incorporation, could not be enforced against federal prosecutors because its adoption as federal law falls outside the rule-making authority of the district courts and its enforcement as state law violates the Supremacy Clause of the Constitution.[19]

This example suggests a far more active competition between state and group norms than the traditional understanding suggests, and it is far from an isolated example of this struggle over law.

setts, New Hampshire, Pennsylvania, Rhode Island, Tennessee and Virginia. The high courts of at least four jurisdictions have rejected a proposed subpoena rule: District of Columbia, Florida, New Jersey and New York.

15. The February 1988 resolution calls for an adversarial hearing as a prerequisite to judicial approval, whereas the 1986 resolution called for an ex parte proceeding. It also would require the prosecutor to show that the information sought is "essential" to an ongoing investigation, whereas the 1986 resolution required only a showing of "relevance."

16. For example, despite strong lobbying efforts on the part of the ABA and the National Association of Criminal Defense Lawyers (NACDL) among other bar groups, Congress has not enacted any legislative restrictions on the use of attorney subpoenas, although bills to accomplish this have been introduced. Courts have similarly rejected pleas for special procedures and pleas to expand the protection for client identity or fee information under the attorney-client privilege. See, e.g., In re Grand Jury Subpoenas ex rel. United States v. Anderson, 906 F.2d 1485, 1499

(10th Cir.1990). Moreover, while several state supreme courts have adopted bar-proposed ethics rules requiring special procedures, other state courts have rejected such proposals and no federal court has officially adopted the rule.

17. Model Rule 3.8(f) (as amended February 1990).

18. 975 F.2d 102 (3d Cir.1992).

19. The court said, 975 F.2d at 112,

... Pennsylvania does have an important interest in regulating the conduct of attorneys licensed to practice in the state. But " 'the law of the state, though enacted in the exercise of powers not controverted, must yield' when incompatible with federal legislation." Sperry, 373 U.S. at 384, quoting Gibbons v. Ogden, 9 Wheat. 1, 211 (1824). Rule 3.10, as written, is simply incompatible with federal grand jury law....

For discussion of the subpoena controversy, see Roger C. Cramton & Lisa K. Udell, State Ethics Rules and Federal Prosecutors: The Controversies Over the Anti–Contact and Subpoena Rules, 53 U.Pitt. L.Rev. 291, 359–85 (1992).

III.   The Profession's Ethos as Law

Law is more than a collection of rules. Rules demand explanation to have meaning. Stories must be told to create even the semblance of a shared understanding of what the rules require. Stories, in turn, demand explanation in the form of a rule—the "point" of the story. But law is not just rules and stories. Rules and stories alone (literature, history), while essential to normative discourse, are to be distinguished from law because they do not license transformations of reality through the use of force.[20] Law does. Law is rules and stories and a commitment of human will to change the world that is into the world that our rules and stories tell us ought to be. This commitment to realize the "ought" distinguishes law from utopian vision, literature and history.

Law understood as rules, the stories told about the rules and the commitment to act in accordance with those rules and stories requires no state.[21] A community and the state may share an understanding of what constitutes the operative rule, but if they have radically different understandings of what that rule means (different stories) and each is committed to action based on its understanding, we have two distinct laws.

Why insist on calling each "law?" There are two reasons. First, by calling the bar's understanding of its responsibilities and obligations "law" I am taking a normative position. The word "law" has a rich history. It has long been used to describe normative systems other than those officially endorsed by the state: natural law, religious law, the law of the market-place, etc. The continuing triumph of positivism can best be gauged by how the word "law" has come to be restricted in its meaning: "Law" is only that which the state speaks. Today those who dare dignify non-official norms with the name of "law" must defend their choice, while any state pronouncement is automatically dignified and implicitly legitimated with the word "law." I reject this triumph of positivism.

The second reason is practical. By reserving the label "law" for official state pronouncements and relegating the normative visions of communities to the status of "non-law" or, at best, advocacy about law, we may miss the force and effect that committed communities with their own vision of law have on state law. State law inevitably changes in the face of action taken in the name of alternative normative visions. In other words, the state must decide whether and to what extent the state and the group will be reshaped in the struggle.

---

20. Cover, Nomos, supra at 9. "The creation of legal meaning cannot take place in silence. But neither can it take place without the committed action that distinguishes law from literature." Id. at 49.

21. Cover, Nomos, supra at 11 and n. 30. Professor Cover explains:

The state becomes central in the process not because it is well suited to jurisgenesis [the creation of legal meaning] nor

because the cultural processes of giving meaning to normative activity cease in the presence of the state. The state becomes central only because . . . an act of commitment is a central aspect of legal meaning. And violence [as to which the state has an imperfect but important monopoly] is one extremely powerful measure and test of commitment.

Let's take an example from legal ethics. The Tax Reform Act of 1984[22] requires people to report cash payments of $10,000 or more received in their trade or business. The person who received the money must fill in a reporting form, IRS Form 8300, which asks for the paying party's name, address, social security number, and occupation and, when applicable, for the name of the person on whose behalf the transaction was conducted. In October 1989, the IRS sent letters to 956 lawyers demanding that they fully complete these forms.[23] The lawyers had submitted incomplete forms, claiming much of the information could not be provided because it was protected by the attorney-client privilege.[24] The vast majority of lawyers receiving the IRS demand letter refused to comply.[25] The IRS then issued ninety summonses to non-complying lawyers who had reported unusually large cash payments or who had declared multiple instances of cash payments over $10,000. Many, if not most, of the ninety lawyers refused to comply. The government brought a test case in the Southern District of New York to force compliance. The district court ordered the lawyers to comply, holding that nothing in the case justified departing from the general rule that client identity and fee information are not privileged.[26] After the district court ruling and with organized bar support,[27] many of the other ninety lawyers who had received summonses and the other 771 lawyers who did not respond to the IRS demand letter continued to resist.[28]

22. Tax Reform Act of 1984, 26 U.S.C. § 6050I.

23. Fred Strasser, Lawyers Must Name Names, Nat'l L.J., June 24, 1991, p. 18.

24. Id. This claim of privilege was asserted despite the fact that courts unanimously have held, in other contexts, that client identity and fee information are generally not protected by the privilege. See, e.g., United States v. Hodge and Zweig, 548 F.2d 1347, 1355 (9th Cir. 977) [discussed below at p. 245]. The circumstances under which client identity and fee information might be privileged are uniformly described by the courts as quite rare. See, e.g., In re Grand Jury Subpoenas (Hirsch), 803 F.2d 493, 497 (9th Cir.1986).

25. Alexander Stille, A Strategic Retreat for the IRS on Disclosure of Attorney Fees, Nat'l L. J., May 14, 1990, p. 3 ("Only 95 lawyers answered the letters by providing client information, according to Elle Murphy, director of public information at the IRS").

26. United States v. Fischetti Pomerantz & Russo, No. N–18–304 (VLB), slip op. at 53–4 (S.D.N.Y. Mar. 13, 1990).

27. The organized bar demonstrated its support of these lawyers in various ways.

The Association of the Bar of the City of New York, the National Association of Criminal Defense Lawyers and the New York Council of Defense Lawyers filed amicus briefs on behalf of the lawyers in *Fischetti*. The American Bar Association communicated to the Justice Department that wholesale enforcement of the federal law would have a devastating impact on the attorney-client relationship. Perhaps most important for my purposes, several bars have issued ethics opinions stating or strongly suggesting that compliance with the IRS or similar state revenue agency demands is unethical, at least in the absence of a court order, and that even when a court orders exists, the lawyer may ethically choose not to comply. See, e.g., State Bar of Georgia, Advisory Op. 41 (Sept. 21, 1984); Florida Bar Staff Op. TEO88203 (1988); Nat'l Ass'n Crim. Defense Lawyers Ethical Advisory Comm. Op. 89–1 (Nov. 22, 1989); Chicago Bar Ass'n Op. 86–2 (May 11, 1988); and New Mexico Bar Op. 1989–2 (1989).

28. Steve Albert, Courting a Showdown: More Lawyers Defy IRS Demands for Client Data, Legal Times, Apr. 30, 1990, p. 2.

These lawyers and bar groups claimed that complying with state law (as manifested by the federal statute, the IRS regulations, the IRS activities in applying these rules to lawyers, the long-line of court precedents suggesting there is no valid claim of privilege as to client identity and fee, and the district court opinion) would violate the ethical responsibilities of the lawyers involved. For example, the president of the Criminal Trial Lawyers Association of Northern California, urging other lawyers to resist, stated: "There are ethical responsibilities we have as lawyers that foreclose giving information which may put our clients in jeopardy."[29] On appeal, the Second Circuit upheld the district court, dismissing as "without merit" the contention that the reporting requirement conflicts with the attorney-client privilege.[30] After this decision, when asked what advice he would give to lawyers in the circuit, the head of the National Association of Criminal Defense Lawyers' "8300 Task Force" commented: "I would say many people subscribe to the notion that you don't violate a confidence until you are ordered to do so by a court."[31] From the context, it is obvious he means personally ordered.

IV.   Two Laws Masquerading as One

A.   What We Might Expect to Find

The legal profession is, by definition, inextricably connected to the state and its laws. The state has the last say over such central matters of group definition as who may be admitted to group membership and who may be excluded. Moreover, the central privilege of membership in the profession is the right to speak to the state on behalf of another in the state's courts. Thus, the profession is dependent on the state for boundary and functional definition, central matters in the normative vision of any community. But the state's *nomos* is similarly dependent on the profession. To be a lawyer is to have a right to participate in the creation and maintenance of the state's *nomos* that is denied to other persons in the society.

As an expression of the real interdependence of the two normative worlds, we would expect to find significant areas in which the two normative worlds coincide. Further, the intensity and particular nature of the interdependence of bar and state increases the need of all involved to

---

29. William Carlson, Drug War's Fallout on Defense Lawyers, S.F. Chron., Jan. 15, 1990, at A1. Consider also the argument of counsel in *Fischetti*: "[W]e are here because we have no choice but to be here. We are not here as willing gladiators, we are here because the government began this proceeding. We are ethically counseled, in a number of opinions that we have cited, not to disclose client identity without testing the enforceability of the statute in a court." *Fischetti*, slip. op. at 26.

30. United States v. Goldberger & Dubin, 935 F.2d 501, 504 (2d Cir.1991) (*Fischetti* on appeal). The court held that the lawyers had to await government enforcement before challenging the summonses. "[T]he [privilege] protects only those disclosures that are necessary to obtain informed legal advice and that would not be made without the privilege." See also United States v. Leventhal, 961 F.2d 936 (11th Cir.1992) (following *Goldberger & Dubin*).

31. Strasser, supra (quoting Gerald B. Lefcourt, head of the "8300 Task Force").

maintain the myth of a unitary normative system. The idea that the ministers of the state law are somehow less than faithful to that law is simply too powerful a suggestion to be incorporated easily into either the state's or the bar's normative system. Thus, we would expect to find that each normative world has developed means of masking the existence of the profession's conflicting norms.

B. The Hierarchy of Norms

For the most part, the bar and the state agree on the precepts that are relevant to the law governing lawyers: precepts contained in the Constitution of the United States; the ethics rules as embodied in various codes promulgated by the bar; the common law of lawyering, particularly the attorney-client privilege and precepts embodied in "other law," including the law of torts, criminal law, securities law and the law of procedure. I say "for the most part" for two reasons. First, the state treats ethics rules as "law" only to the extent that they are (and in the form in which they are) adopted by the state. On the other hand, the bar may treat as law ethics rules adopted by the ABA or a state bar organization but not adopted by the state. Second, the extent to which the bar accepts that precepts of "other law" govern the conduct of lawyers is not clear. Sometimes lawyers and bar groups speak as if lawyers enjoy some form of immunity from the precepts of other law. But, even if we put aside for the moment these two areas of potential disagreement on precepts and assume that the bar and the state are in total agreement on the relevant precepts, the existence of shared precepts indicates a unitary normative system only if the precepts are ordered and interpreted by each group (the bar and the state) in the same way. They are not. In the bar's *nomos* ethics rules[32] are presumed to control when they conflict with other law, while in the state's *nomos* other law is presumed to control when it conflicts with the ethics rules.

In the state's hierarchy of norms—as it exists in theory—ethics rules occupy a relatively lowly status. Ethics rules are generally court rules not legislation, and they are more often state law, not federal law. Those two facts relegate ethics rules to a lowly status in the state's hierarchy of precepts.[33] Moreover, federal and state courts often state that the only instances in which they are bound to treat the ethics rules as binding

---

32. This is not to say that in the bar's *nomos* each precept in the ethics rules carries equal power to trump other law. The bar is so weakly committed to some rules that they may be said to have taken on the status of "non-law" for the bar, and thus they lack the power to trump other law.

33. First, Constitutional requirements, including those on procedure, trump all other law. Second, federal law trumps state law. Third, on matters of substantive law, legislation trumps rules adopted by courts. Fourth, on matters of procedure, federal legislation trumps rules adopted by federal courts, and federal rules of procedure adopted pursuant to congressional authorization, such as the Federal Rules of Civil Procedure, trump rules adopted by federal courts, which include ethics rules. And while in many states rules of procedure adopted by a court pursuant to the court's inherent powers, which is how ethics rules are adopted, trump conflicting state legislative pronouncements on procedure, this may be truer in theory than in practice.

precepts are in disciplinary proceedings against lawyers.[34] Thus, even when the ethics rules purport to speak directly on a matter and are the only existing source of precept on the question, they may be ignored with relative ease so long as the case is not a disciplinary proceeding.

The strongest evidence that the bar's hierarchy of norms differs from the state's is found in the bar narratives that explicate the rules—ethics opinions. Just as court opinions provide a body of narratives and precepts that are intended to be realized in action, ethics opinions perform a similar function in the bar's *nomos*. Ethics opinions are also a particular strong source of evidence on the content of the bar's *nomos* because they are generally not subject to prior state control. They therefore express law to which the bar, but not necessarily the state, is committed.

What do the ethics opinions tell us about the bar's ordering of norms? Some ethics opinions actively and openly encourage disobedience of other law.[35] They provide the strongest evidence that the bar's hierarchy of norms places ethics rules above other state precepts. Such opinions are, however, relatively rare.[36] What is surprising is that they exist at all.

Much more common are ethics opinions stating that the ethics rules permit, but do not require, compliance with other law.[37] While less dramat-

---

34. See, e.g., W.T. Grant Co. v. Haines, 531 F.2d 671, 676–77 (2d Cir.1976) (holding that lawyer's violation of ethics rule against advising unrepresented party is insufficient basis upon which to dismiss client's lawsuit or disqualify the law firm). Courts typically consult the ethics rules in non-disciplinary cases involving a lawyer's conduct, but they treat the rules as a source of guidance rather than as binding precept. See the note on the role of ethics rules in determining a lawyer's duty of care in legal malpractice, infra at p. 171.

35. State Bar of New Mexico Advisory Op. 1989–2 states:

> [T]he intent of the New Mexico Rules of Professional Conduct is that attorney should not reveal exactly what the federal [requirement that a lawyer report the source of a cash payment of $10,000 or more] requires [an] attorney to reveal. Thus, there is a conflict between [the two]. Our Committee does not resolve the conflict, but we [recommend that a lawyer] consistent with the highest ideals of the profession ... may, with the client's consent, agree to "make a good faith effort to determine the validity, scope, meaning or application" of the law at issue [citing a state-court-adopted ethics rule requiring confidentiality] ....

36. Other examples of openly defiant ethics opinions include: State Bar Wis. Formal Op. 3–90–3 (Apr. 2, 1990) (lawyer should not make disclosure when faced with an IRS summons unless and until a court, preferably an appellate court, considers the validity of the summons and any judicial enforcement orders in this area and that court's ruling requires such disclosure."); Nat'l Ass'n Crim. Defense Lawyers Ethical Advisory Comm. Op. 89–1 (Nov. 22, 1989) (same); Chicago Bar Ass'n Op. 86–2 (May 11, 1988) (lawyer would not be condemned for filing a completed IRS form; "however, the better course ... is to file an IRS form that asserts the attorney-client privilege and gives notice ... that information has been withheld ..."); State Bar of Georgia, Advisory Op. No, 41 (Sept. 21, 1984) (a lawyer should pursue all reasonable avenues of appeal before complying with requests from state agency). Openly defiant ethics opinions are much more likely to involve certain precepts, like the rule on confidentiality, than others.

37. See, e.g., Ass'n of the Bar of New York Op. 1990–2 (Feb. 27, 1990) (lawyer may comply with Fed.R.Civ.Pro. 26(e)); Chicago Bar Ass'n. Op. 86–4 (undated) (lawyer is permitted but not required to disclose to IRS its overpayment to client if he is under a legal obligation pursuant to statute or

ic, these opinions also provide evidence that the bar's hierarchy of norms presumes that ethics rules trump other norms. How else can one understand the question: Do the ethics rules permit compliance with other law? Or the answer, that compliance is permitted?

The bar's understanding that ethics rules trump other law (or qualify it or render it ambiguous) is also evident in its efforts to pass ethics rules or interpret existing rules to stop state action that the courts have held is permitted under other law. Ethics rules that would require prosecutors to get prior judicial approval and demonstrate extreme need before subpoenaing lawyers to testify before grand juries about their clients' affairs are just one example of this. Other examples include ethics rules and ethics opinions prohibiting the disclosure of client fraud in connection with the sale or purchase of securities to the Securities and Exchange Commission, purchasers, or stockholders;[38] prohibiting the simultaneous negotiation of attorneys' fees in civil rights cases;[39] and prohibiting disclosure of information to the Legal Services Corporation.[40]

V. The Centrality of Confidentiality in the Bar's Nomos

Introduction

The bar texts discussed above show that it is confidentiality, and particularly the duty to keep client confidences from the state, more often than any other norm, which triggers the obligation to resist competing

regulation to disclose such information); ABA Comm. on Ethics and Prof. Resp., Informal Op. 1349 (1975) ("[W]e do not decide whether local criminal law makes it unlawful for S to fail to reveal the information.... If disclosure is required by such law, S may, but is not required under DR 4–101(C)(2), to make disclosure.").

38. In 1974 the ABA adopted an amendment to DR 7–102(B)(1) of the 1969 Model Code which all but eliminated the lawyer's duty to reveal a client's fraud in which the lawyer's services had been used. This amendment was a response to a several court decisions that had alarmed the securities bar, including *National Student Marketing*. See, e.g., Hoffman, On Learning of a Corporate Client's Crime or Fraud, 33 Bus.Law. 1389, 1405–07 (1978) (explaining that the amendment was one of a series of attempts by bar groups to resolve the "conflict" raised between the state's position and the securities' lawyers' ethical obligations). In the 1980s, this struggle over the law governing securities lawyers was played out in the ABA's adoption in 1983 of Model Rules 1.13 and 1.6. Rule 1.13, as adopted, eliminated the lawyer's discretion to disclose criminal or fraudulent corporate activity to stockholders, government agencies or those defrauded by the corporation's activities—discretion that had been included in the draft presented to the House of Delegates. Rule 1.6 eliminated the lawyer's discretion to reveal client fraud—discretion that had been included in the Kutak draft.

39. See Evans v. Jeff D., 475 U.S. 717 (1986), discussed below at p. 529 (upholding fee waivers despite ethics opinions concluding that simultaneous negotiation of a fee award and an award on the merits is unethical). In his dissent in *Evans*, Justice Brennan invited the bar to use ethics opinions to try and outlaw simultaneous negotiations. 475 U.S. at 765 (1986). This invitation for the bar to continue its own normative understanding is consistent with Brennan's general approach of inviting alternate normative understandings to counteract Court decisions with which he disagrees.

40. See, e.g., N.H. Bar Ass'n Formal Op. No. 1988–9/13 (Feb. 9, 1989); ABA Comm. on Ethics and Prof.Resp. Informal Op. 1394 (1977); ABA Comm. on Ethics and Prof.Resp. Informal Op. 1287 (1974).

state norms, and which justifies the passage of ethics rules to "undo" state pronouncements. That the bar deems individual acts of resistance and group efforts to repeal state pronouncements as appropriate responses to state efforts to secure client confidences reveals the bar's interpretation of the norm, i.e., that it is absolute or nearly-so.

Confidentiality is a constitutional norm in the bar's *nomos*. By constitutional norm, I mean a norm so central to group definition (to that which constitutes a group) that perceived threats to the norm are understood by the group as threats against the group itself—against the group's very existence; that proposals to change the norm are seen by the group as proposals to change the essence/character/function of the group itself; and consequently that extreme action is thought to be justified in defense of the norm.

The special importance of the norm of confidentiality in the bar's *nomos* is not apparent on the face of the ethics codes as adopted by the states, nor is it readily apparent on the face of the ethics rules as drafted by the ABA. Confidentiality is not the first norm stated in the professional codes. Moreover, the language describing confidentiality in all three documents is relatively dry and straightforward, and each document contains exceptions to the duty to keep client confidences.

The ethics codes may mask the power of the norm of confidentiality, but the ethics opinions interpreting the codes make it plain. A pattern emerges in these opinions: rules affirming a duty or the discretion to disclose are either narrowed to the point of near-irrelevance or held to be overridden by rules requiring silence.[41]

VII.   Commitment

Because the *nomos* is but the process of human action stretched between vision and reality, a legal interpretation cannot be valid if no one is prepared to live by it.[42]

We call the state's normative vision "law" because we know that the state means it. It is committed to its interpretation. It is prepared to act, using all the resources of violence at its disposal, if necessary, to enforce its interpretations. Earlier, to justify my use of the word "law" to describe the profession's normative vision, I argued that the profession means it too, that it too is committed to its interpretations. If, however, the profession's law diverges from that of the state, how can the profession maintain its commitment given the state's imperfect monopoly over violence?[43] The

---

41. See discussion in Chapter 4 below, p. 282.

42. Cover, Nomos, supra at 44.

43. To appreciate the importance of the question posed in the text, consider the following quote:

> Certain efforts to [maintain a separate *nomos*] have an almost doomed charac-

ter. The state's claims over legal meaning are at bottom, so closely tied to the state's imperfect monopoly over the domain of violence that the claim of a community to an autonomous meaning must be linked to the community's willingness to live out its meaning in defiance. Outright defiance, guerrilla warfare, and terrorism are, of course, the most direct

answer lies in understanding that commitment is not an all or nothing proposition for either the state or the community.[44] As we shall see, judges are particularly unlikely to assert their interpretive power or back their interpretations with violence in cases in which their understanding of law diverges from the bar's. The state's commitment is weak. On the other hand, the bar's commitment is relatively strong.

A. The Weakness of the State's Commitment

In cases involving the law governing lawyers, the courts show a weak commitment to state law—to the maintenance of a state *nomos*—in two basic ways. First, [the courts] are reluctant to create legal meaning and as a consequence create little. Second, they show little inclination to back with violence the legal meaning they do create. Consider the court's decision in SEC v. National Student Marketing.[45]

In *National Student Marketing* the SEC sought to enjoin several lawyers and their law firms, claiming that they had closed a merger deal knowing that shareholder approval had been obtained on the basis of materially misleading documents. The SEC had a complete vision of law— norm, narrative and commitment—and one at odds with the bar's *nomos*. The court's decision showed commitment neither to the law it articulated nor to the court's role as interpreter of law.

The court agreed with the SEC that the lawyers had violated the securities laws by knowingly and substantially assisting their clients to commit fraud. Having articulated precepts that it is wrong to remain silent and do nothing while assisting clients in a fraudulent securities transaction, however, the court failed to connect them to the lawyers' actions in this case:

> [I]t is unnecessary to determine the precise extent of their obligations here, since ... they took no steps whatsoever to delay the closing.... But, at the very least, they were required to speak out [to their clients] at the closing.... [46]

In failing to provide a narrative, in failing to connect norms to the actions of the past, the court showed a weak commitment to its role as creator of legal meaning. The court refused to explain what parts of the world as it exists (represented in this case by the actions of the lawyers) are to be changed by its norms. It thus created little law to project into the future. Was it wrong under state law that the lawyers failed to resign? That they failed to inform officers of the corporate client not present at the meeting? That they failed to inform shareholders or the SEC? Does the law

---

responses. They are responses, however, that may—as in the United States—be unjustifiable and doomed to failure.

Cover, Nomos, supra at 52.

44. "Some interpretations are writ in blood and run with a warranty of blood as part of

their validating force. Other interpretations carry more conventional limits to what will be hazarded on their behalf." Id. at 46.

45. 457 F.Supp. 682 (D.D.C.1978), reprinted above at p. 104.

46. 475 F.Supp. at 713.

demand that lawyers in the future do any of these things? With the words "at the very least," the court admits that the narrative is incomplete, that state law has more meaning, but it does not assert its power to control that meaning. Instead, it invites the bar to provide that meaning:

> The very initiation of this action ... has provided a necessary and worthwhile impetus for the profession's recognition and assessment of its responsibilities in this area.[47]

By telling a community that it should reconsider its behavior and beliefs in light of state power whether or not the use of that power is legitimate, a court abandons its commitment to a state built on the meaning of shared principles and helps constitute a state built instead on obedience to authority.

The court explained its failure to create law by stating that further explication would be "unnecessary [to resolve the case before it]" and that it "must narrow its focus to the present defendants and the charges against them." These statements are allusions to the rule against rendering advisory opinions. The case was before the court to determine whether an injunction was warranted against the defendants. What exactly the lawyers did wrong and the degree to which it was wrong were issues thus directly before the court. The court had to reach for the advisory opinion rule to avoid discussing these issues. This stretch demonstrates the court's weak commitment. The court uses the advisory opinion rule in a case where it does not naturally apply as an excuse not to make law. Moreover, the advisory opinion rule assumes "an ironic cast"[48] in this case: the court's refusal to grant any relief against the defendants, a matter to which we turn next, renders the entire opinion no more than advice.

The court refused to enjoin the lawyers from further violations of the securities laws; it granted the SEC no relief against the defendants. By denying relief, the court showed a weak commitment to the little law it did create and to whatever more the securities laws might mean as applied to lawyers whose clients are engaged in fraud. It refused to back its interpretation with force, and more striking, it explained that force was unnecessary, in part, because the defendants were lawyers. The court expressed its confidence that the defendants' "professional responsibilities as attorneys and officers of the court" will lead them to honor the court's interpretation without force.[49] In other words, state law will depend on the bar's *nomos*

---

47. 457 F.Supp. at 715.

48. Professor Cover used this phrase to describe the thickness of legal meaning. In his example, it was the Due Process Clause's reference to "life" that had taken on an ironic cast both for opponents of the death penalty and opponents of abortion. Cover, Nomos, supra at 7. When a precept takes on an ironic cast for a community or for the society at large, those who perceive the irony will view any invocation of the precept by the state with suspicion.

49. Subsequent events suggest that weak commitment to law by a court helps the bar maintain its divergent understanding of law:

> According to the allegations contained in two lawsuits that Lord, Bissell [and Brook] recently settled for twenty four million dollars, shortly after the decision in *National Student Marketing*, the firm began aggressively representing National Mortgage Equity Corporation, a controversial venture designed to capitalize on

for vindication. The court thus speaks as if the bar's law were somehow stronger and more binding on group members than state law. The power of the bar's law does not trouble the court because in the court's vision the paramount precept for lawyers must be (and therefore for the court is) the obligation to comply with state law. This understanding of the hierarchy of norms contained in the ethics rules is, however, a state understanding. In the bar's *nomos* the duty to comply with other law does not, as we have seen, trump all other norms.

The evidence of weak commitment found in *National Student Marketing* is common in cases involving the law governing lawyers. The *Stenhach* case reprinted in Chapter 1 provides another example. Moreover, there are numerous other examples of the courts' weak commitment in cases involving the law governing lawyers: cases in which the court refuses to use force to back its interpretation;[50] cases in which the court refuses to create legal meaning;[51] cases using temporary or inherently weak boundary rules;[52] and cases in which the court suggests that the bar's understanding of law controls the court's interpretation.[53] There are, of course, counter examples.[54]

the newly emerging market in second mortgages.... [A]ccording to the deposition testimony of the firm's managing partner, the firm changed virtually none of its practices as a result of the SEC's prosecutions in *National Student Marketing*.

David B. Wilkins, Who Should Regulate Lawyers?, 105 Harv. L. Rev. 799, 870–871 (1992) (citing Tim O'Brien, Some Firms Never Learn: Lord Bissell's Second Escape from Fraud Charges Cost $24 Million—And It Could Happen Again, Am. Law., Oct. 1989, at 63, 64)....

50. See, e.g., In re Thompson, 416 F.Supp. 991, 996 (S.D.Tex.1976) (refusing to hold lawyer in contempt of court's order of discharge in bankruptcy, although his threats against discharged bankrupt on behalf of unsecured creditor were "inexcusable and in obvious disregard of the purposes" of the "bankruptcy act"); In re Corboy, 528 N.E.2d 694, 701 (Ill.1988) (imposing no sanction because the lawyers "acted without guidance of precedent or settled opinion, and there was, apparently, considerable belief among members of the bar that they had acted properly"); Mozzochi v. Beck, 529 A.2d 171, 174 (Conn.1987) (holding lawyers who breach their duty "to their clients and to the judicial system" by filing suit after learning that the allegations are wholly without merit are not liable for abuse of process because "[a]ny other rule would ineluctably interfere with the attor-

ney's primary duty of robust representation."). See also In re Carter and Johnson, discussed at p. 739 below.

51. See Barker v. Henderson, 797 F.2d 490, 497 (7th Cir.1986) (refusing to discuss "the extent to which lawyers ... should reveal their clients' wrongdoing—and to whom they should reveal," noting that "[t]he professions and the regulatory agencies will debate questions raised by cases such as this one for years to come").

52. See, e.g., Financial General Bankshares, Inc. v. Metzger, 680 F.2d 768, 775 (D.C.Cir. 1982) ("the unsettled nature of District of Columbia law regarding the fiduciary duties of an attorney to a client" rendered it an abuse of discretion by the district court to decide that pendent jurisdiction claim).

53. See, e.g., United States v. Klubock, 832 F.2d 649, 654 (1st Cir.1987) (en banc) (bar's understanding of when and how lawyers are to be called before grand juries governs because the "fundamental underlying problem ... is an ethical one"); Barker v. Henderson, 797 F.2d 490, 497 (7th Cir.1986) ("[A]n award of damages under the securities laws is not the way to blaze the trail toward improved ethical standards in the legal and accounting professions.... The securities law ... must lag behind changes in ethical and fiduciary standards").

54. See, e.g., United States v. Cintolo, 818 F.2d 980 (1st Cir.1987), discussed above at

Detecting trends in something as complex as the degree of state commitment is a difficult business. There are, however, many indications that the commitment is increasing.[55] On the other hand, given how pervasive and longstanding the practice of low commitment has been and how sympathetic to the bar's vision many judges are, I would not predict a complete about face in the immediate future.

The Bar's Commitment: Texts of Resistance

> Whenever a community resists ... some ... law of the state, it necessarily enters into a secondary hermeneutic—the interpretation of the texts of resistance.[56]

As we have seen, the bar's sacred stories predict a crisis between a lawyer's obligations to her client and the demands of state law put forth by prosecutors, judges and other state actors.[57]

It is in the bar's texts of resistance that we find the bar's understanding of its obligation to the state and its law. The texts do not deny the obligation; they interpret it.

In the bar's texts of resistance, after deciding that something the state calls "law" conflicts with bar law the question becomes: Is that troublesome thing, which the state calls law, law for purposes of the lawyer's obligation to obey? The first interpretive move is that legislation and regulation that conflict with bar law are not "law" for purposes of this norm. The comment to Rule 1.6 itself suggests this move by omitting reference to legislation and regulation. It reads: "The lawyer must comply

p. 73; In re Grand Jury Subpoenas, ex rel. United States v. Anderson, 906 F.2d 1485, 1499 (10th Cir.1990) (upholding district court order jailing lawyers for contempt for refusing to reveal the source of their fees to the grand jury and rejecting lawyers argument that their refusal was justified by their ethical obligations); In re Solerwitz, 848 F.2d 1573 (Fed.Cir.1988) (suspending a lawyer for filing and maintaining frivolous appeals even though three ethics experts testified the lawyer's conduct was proper).

55. Goldfarb v. Virginia State Bar, 421 U.S. 773, 793 (1975), holding that activities of a mandatory bar association are not exempt from the antitrust laws, is an early and significant sign of an increased commitment to the role of state law vis a vis the profession. Another important sign is the significant erosion in the traditional rule that a lack of privity prevents third parties from suing lawyers for negligence. See, Greycas v. Proud, 826 F.2d 1560 (7th Cir.

1987). The amendment of Fed.R.Civ.P. Rule 11 in 1983 (holding lawyers to a greater level of candor in pleadings and other court papers) and the adoption of similar rules in the states may be another sign of the courts' increased commitment to its vision of lawyering. Rule 11 is discussed at p. 404 below.

56. Cover, Nomos, supra, at 49.

57. Consider William Kunstler's response when sanctioned under Rule 11 for his conduct in suing state prosecutors for harassing Native American activists. In re Kunstler (Robinson Defense Comm. v. Britt), 914 F.2d 505, 525 (4th Cir.1990). Kunstler said: "I'll tell you this: I'm not going to pay any fine. I'm going to rot in jail if that's what I have to do to dramatize this thing. I think I could do no better thing for my country." Don J. DeBenedictis, Rule 11 Snags Lawyers, 77 A.B.A.J. 16, 17 (1991).

with the final orders of a court or other tribunal of competent jurisdiction requiring the lawyer to give information about the client." It may be that the bar treats judicial decisions as a higher form of law, in part, because it regards judges as semi-brothers and hence mediators between the state and the bar. The point here is that what counts as law is limited by this first interpretive move.

While neither legislation nor regulation are law that require obedience, bar texts emphasize that their non-law status is strictly limited to the extent that they conflict with bar law and no further. For example, while client confidentiality, according to the bar, precludes a lawyer from complying with tax law and regulations that require the lawyer to provide the client's name and other identifying information, "confidentiality ... do[es] not relieve the lawyer of the statutory duty to file the required form."[58] It "must still be filed, but the lawyer should insert ... in place of the client's name ... a statement that the lawyer and the client are asserting client confidentiality, the attorney-client privilege and, if applicable, the Fifth and Sixth Amendment privileges."[59] Resistance is to be tailored to contest the "invalid" portion of the legislation or regulation and should not otherwise show disrespect to the state's legislation or regulation.

Moreover, while for the bar neither legislation nor regulation are "law" for purposes of the duty to obey (when they conflict with bar law), bar texts typically distinguish between the two: the obligation to resist regulation is generally greater than the obligation to resist legislation. For example, the Statement of Policy adopted by the ABA House of Delegates on the duties of lawyers to comply with the securities laws states:

> [A]ny principle of law which, except as permitted or required by the [Code of Professional Responsibility], permits or obliges a lawyer to disclose to the S.E.C. otherwise confidential information should be established *only by statute* after full and careful consideration of the public interests involved and should be resisted unless clearly mandated by law.[60]

Implicitly, this suggests greater resistance is owed SEC regulations inconsistent with bar law than legislation, which must be resisted too, but not if "clearly mandated by law." How one decides whether legislation is "clearly mandated by law" is not fully described by this ABA Statement, although a reference to "a questionable lower court decision" carries the inference that an interpretation of legislation that conflicts with the bar's law and that is supported by only a lower court decision is not "clearly mandated by law."

---

58. Ethics Advisory Comm. of Nat'l Ass'n of Crim. Defense Lawyers, Formal Op. 89–1 (Nov. 22, 1989); see also, State Bar Wis. Formal Op. E–90–3 (Apr. 2, 1990) (approving and incorporating NACDL Op. 89–1).

59. Id.

60. See ABA's Section of Corporation, Banking, and Business Law, Statement of Policy Adopted by the American Bar Association Regarding Responsibilities and Liabilities of Lawyers in Advising with Respect to the Compliance by Clients with Laws Administered by the Securities and Exchange Commission, 61 A.B.A. J. 1085 (1975) (emphasis added).

This brings us to the bar's next interpretive problem, whether court orders and decisions are law that must be obeyed. It is at this point that we may gauge the true nature of the bar's commitment. For at this point the state's use of force may be imminent. The comment to Rule 1.6 states that lawyers "must comply with the final orders of a court or other tribunal of competent jurisdiction." The qualifications in this sentence—"final orders" and "competent jurisdiction"—are, however, important indicators of the bar's understanding. Generally, bar texts of resistance allow a lawyer to comply with court orders, but do not require that she do so.[61] For example, the ABA has explained its understanding of the ethics rules as follows:

> If the motion to quash is denied, the lawyer must either testify or run the risk of being held in contempt. . . . The lawyer has an ethical duty to preserve client confidences and to test any interference with that duty in court. . . . If a contempt citation is upheld on appeal, however, the lawyer has little choice but to testify or go to jail. Both the Model Rules and the Model Code recognize that a lawyer's ethical duty to preserve client confidences gives way to final court orders.[62]

While this quote carefully avoids explicitly requiring resistance, the message is clear that a lawyer should resist a lower court order: ethical duty "gives way" according to the text only after a final court order, and "final court orders" are, according to the quote, orders of an appellate court. Even more telling of the bar's commitment to its law than the strong encouragement to resist lower court orders is the suggestion that bar law "gives way" to appellate orders not because they are legitimate and authoritative interpretations but because the state at this point is extremely likely to use force: "the lawyer may have little choice but to testify or go to jail." It is accommodation pure and simple that is being expressed not concession to the appellate court's role as authoritative interpreter of its law.

The view that it is the state's force and not its interpretation or its right to interpret that relieves a lawyer of the obligation to resist appellate orders is also expressed by the bar's understanding of the reach of such orders. Bar texts do not contain any suggestion of an obligation to check controlling precedent in the relevant jurisdiction before deciding whether to comply. Moreover, given the weight of authority on such issues as whether a client's identity or fees paid an attorney are privileged, it is clearly the message of these bar texts that court decisions contrary to bar law are to be understood as having decided the question before them and no more. As the NACDL put it in testifying before Congress: "Our members will litigate these issues at every turn . . . ."[63]

---

61. See, e.g., Ala. Formal Op. 88–76 (Sept. 1, 1988) ("If ordered to testify by the court, the lawyer may either do so or may seek appellate relief"); and Va. Bar Formal Op. 787 (Apr. 4, 1986) (similar).

62. 83 ABA/BNA Lawyers' Man.Prof.Conduct 5, 11 (1989) (emphasis added) (citations omitted). . . .

63. Statement of Alan Ellis, President–Elect, and Scott Wallace, Legislative Director, on Behalf of the Nat'l Ass'n Crim. Defense Lawyers Before the Subcommittee on Government Information, Justice and Agriculture, House Committee on Government Operations, May 10, 1990 at 12 (on file with author).

This posture "is an attempt to separate completely the projection of understanding from the decree that is the direct exercise of court power. Such separation allows one to 'acquiesce' by refraining from resistance while simultaneously refusing to extend the social range of the Court's hermeneutic."[64] The efficacy of this move is dependent on the level of the courts' commitment. Courts, after all, have the means to insist that their interpretations are projected into the future: injunctions. But the likelihood of the courts using such a tool against lawyers is remote, given how weakly committed they are to their role when they find themselves at odds with the bar. The bar's commitment, on the other hand, is, as we have just seen, strong. It is the interaction of these two levels of commitment that allows the divergence in normative understanding to continue.

———

Divergent Professional Norms

Do you agree with the Cover–Koniak view that private groups, such as the ABA or a state bar association, contribute to the creation and explanation of "law"? That the organized bar's conception of the legal obligations of lawyers is at odds at some critical points with that of official lawmakers (legislatures and courts)?

Consider the persistent refusal of criminal defense lawyers to comply with IRS requests for client identity, requests that are founded in statutory requirements the courts have repeatedly upheld. Does that story indicate the importance of commitment in shaping the law? The centrality of the principle of confidentiality in the profession's normative priorities?

D. Tax Law

INTRODUCTORY NOTE

Lawyers representing taxpayers must decide whether legal advice or assistance constitutes prohibited assistance. Consider the following hypothetical:

64. Cover, Nomos, supra, at 54 n.146. Professor Cover is discussing Lincoln's famous remarks on the *Dred Scott* decision, Scott v. Sanford, 60 U.S. (19 How.) 393 (1857):

> I do not resist [*Dred Scott*]. If I wanted to take Dred Scott from his master, I would be interfering with property.... But I am doing no such thing as that, but all that I am doing is refusing to obey it as a political rule. If I were in Congress, and a vote should come up on a question whether slavery should be prohibited in a new territory, in spite of that Dred Scott decision. I would vote that it should.

Id. (quoting Speech by Abraham Lincoln at Chicago, Illinois, July 10, 1858). Professor Cover explains that what Lincoln is saying is that "[o]ur future actions are to be governed by our own understanding, not the Court's." Id. at 54.

After a successful sex discrimination suit under Title VII of the Civil Rights Act of 1964, a client receives damages equal to the back wages she would have received but for the discrimination. She does not want to report the damages as taxable income. Wages, of course, are reportable income but a tort recovery for personal injuries is not. Her lawyer determines that taxability in this case depends upon whether the damages may be characterized as a substitute for back wages or analogized to a tort recovery for personal injuries (Internal Revenue Code § 104(a)(2) excludes from taxable income damages derived from "personal injuries or sickness"). The Internal Revenue Service originally characterized back-pay awards under Title VII as wages reportable as income, and the courts accepted this view.[1] The rulings and decisions were consistent until 1986 when the Tax Court accepted the tort analogy in one case. By the end of 1991, the Third and Sixth Circuits had also found Title VII damages excludable from income.[2] Other federal courts continued to treat such damages as taxable income.[3] In 1992 the U.S. Supreme Court resolved the conflict of circuits by holding that back-pay awards in settlement of Title VII claims are not excludable from a taxpayer's gross income.[4]

How should a lawyer advising this client in 1979 have counseled her to treat the damages? Would it have mattered if the lawyer believed the tort analogy to be the best characterization despite the contrary case law? What about in 1986 after the Tax Court broke with the accepted view and found Title VII damages excludable? In early 1992 when a clear conflict between circuits existed and the Supreme Court was considering the issue? Even if the lawyer decided that the damages were excludable, should the amount nonetheless be reported to flag the IRS as to the existence of the damages and the possible question of income? How would these questions be answered if ABA Formal Opinion 85–352, reprinted below, had been in effect?

ABA Formal Opinion 85–352

American Bar Association Standing Committee on Professional Ethics.
July 7, 1985.

The Committee has been requested by the Section of Taxation of the American Bar Association to reconsider the "reasonable basis" standard in the Committee's Formal Opinion 314 governing the position a lawyer may advise a client to take on a tax return.

1. See, e.g., Rev.Rul. 72–341, 1972–2 C.B. 32; and Hodge v. Commissioner, 64 T.C. 616 (1975).

2. See Threlkeld v. Commissioner, 87 T.C. 1294 (1986), aff'd, 848 F.2d 81 (6th Cir. 1988); and Metzger v. Commissioner, 88 T.C. 834 (1987), aff'd without published opinion, 845 F.2d 1013 (3d Cir.1988).

3. See Thompson v. Commissioner, 866 F.2d 709 (4th Cir.1989); Johnston v. Harris County Flood Control Dist., 869 F.2d 1565 (5th Cir.1989), cert. denied, 493 U.S. 1019 (1990); Watkins v. United States, 223 Ct. Cl. 731 (1980); and Sparrow v. Commissioner, 949 F.2d 434 (D.C.Cir.1991).

4. United States v. Burke, 504 U.S. 229 (1992), reversing 929 F.2d 1119 (6th Cir.).

Opinion 314 (April 27, 1965) was issued in response to a number of specific inquiries regarding the ethical relationship between the Internal Revenue Service and lawyers practicing before it. The opinion formulated general principles governing this relationship, including the following: "[A] lawyer who is asked to advise his client in the course of the preparation of the client's tax returns may freely urge the statement of positions most favorable to the client just as long as there is a reasonable basis for this position."

The Committee is informed that the standard of "reasonable basis" has been construed by many lawyers to support the use of any colorable claim on a tax return to justify exploitation of the lottery of the tax return audit selection process. . . .

. . . [A]s a result of serious controversy over this standard and its persistent criticism by distinguished members of the tax bar, IRS officials and members of Congress, sufficient doubt has been created regarding the validity of the standard so as to erode its effectiveness as an ethical guideline. For this reason, the Committee has concluded that it should be restated. Another reason for restating the standard is that since publication of Opinion 314, the ABA has adopted in succession the Model Code of Professional Responsibility (1969; revised 1980) and the Model Rules of Professional Conduct (1983). Both the Model Code and the Model Rules directly address the duty of a lawyer in presenting or arguing positions for a client in language that does not refer to "reasonable basis." It is therefore appropriate to conform the standard of Opinion 314 to the language of the new rules.

This opinion reconsiders and revises only that part of Opinion 314 that relates to the lawyer's duty in advising a client of positions that can be taken on a tax return. It does not deal with a lawyer's opinion on tax shelter investment offering, which is specifically addressed by this Committee's Formal Opinion 346 (Revised), and which involves very different considerations, including third party reliance.

The ethical standards governing the conduct of a lawyer in advising a client on positions that can be taken in a tax return are no different from those governing a lawyer's conduct in advising or taking positions for a client in other civil matters. Although the Model Rules distinguish between the roles of advisor and advocate (see, for example, Model Rules 2.1 and 3.1), both roles are involved here, and the ethical standards applicable to them provide relevant guidance. In many cases a lawyer must realistically anticipate that the filing of the tax return may be the first step in a process that may result in an adversary relationship between the client and the IRS. This normally occurs in situations when a lawyer advises an aggressive position on a tax return, not when the position taken is a safe or conservative one that is unlikely to be challenged by the IRS.

[The opinion then quoted Model Rules 3.1 and 1.2(d).]

On the basis of these rules and analogous provisions of the Model Code, a lawyer, in representing a client in the course of the preparation of the client's tax return, may advise the statement of positions most favorable to the client if the lawyer has a good faith belief that those positions are warranted in existing law or can be supported by a good faith argument for an extension, modification or reversal of existing law. A lawyer can have a good faith belief in this context even if the lawyer believes the client's position probably will not prevail. (Comment to Rule 3.1; see also Model Code EC 7–4.) However, good faith requires that there be some realistic possibility of success if the matter is litigated.

This formulation of the lawyer's duty in the situation addressed by this opinion is consistent with the basic duty of the lawyer to a client, recognized in ethical standards since the ABA Canons of Professional Ethics, and in the opinions of this Committee: zealously and loyally to represent the interests of the client within the bounds of the law.

Thus, where a lawyer has a good faith belief in the validity of a position in accordance with the standard stated above that a particular transaction does not result in taxable income or that certain expenditures are properly deductible as expenses, the lawyer has no duty to require as a condition of his or her continued representation that riders be attached to the client's tax return explaining the circumstances surrounding the transaction or the expenditures.

In the role of advisor, the lawyer should counsel the client as to whether the position is likely to be sustained by a court if challenged by the IRS, as well as of the potential penalty consequences to the client if the position is taken on the tax return without disclosure. Section 6661 of the Internal Revenue Code imposes a penalty for substantial understatement of tax liability which can be avoided if the facts are adequately disclosed or if there is or was substantial authority for the position taken by the taxpayer. Competent representation of the client would require the lawyer to advise the client fully as to whether there is or was substantial authority for the position taken in the tax return. If the lawyer is unable to conclude that the position is supported by substantial authority, the lawyer should advise the client of the penalty the client may suffer and of the opportunity to avoid such penalty by adequately disclosing the facts in the return or in a statement attached to the return. If after receiving such advice the client decides to risk the penalty by making no disclosure and to take the position initially advised by the lawyer in accordance with the standard stated above, the lawyer has met his or her ethical responsibility with respect to the advice.

In all cases, however, with regard both to the preparation of returns and negotiating administrative settlements, the lawyer is under a duty not to mislead the Internal Revenue Service deliberately, either by misstatements or by silence or by permitting the client to mislead. Rules 4.1 and 8.4(c); DRs 1–102(A)(4), 7–102(A)(3) and (5).

In summary, a lawyer may advise reporting a position on a return even where the lawyer believes the position probably will not prevail, there is no "substantial authority" in support of the position, and there will be no disclosure of the position in the return. However, the position to be asserted must be one which the lawyer in good faith believes is warranted in existing law or can be supported by a good faith argument for an extension, modification or reversal of existing law. This requires that there is some realistic possibility of success if the matter is litigated. In addition, in his role as advisor, the lawyer should refer to potential penalties and other legal consequences should the client take the position advised.

———

Tax Law and Prohibited Assistance[5]

The lawyer providing tax advice or preparing a client's tax return must balance client desires against the often murky requirements of the tax code. Determining the appropriate balance is simple only in the extreme cases. For example, the lawyer may not aid a client in tax evasion, such as by failing to report clearly taxable income or by claiming deductions based on fictitious events or transactions. To assist a client in such behavior constitutes the crime of aiding and abetting tax evasion.[6] Such assistance also violates the ethical rule that a lawyer may not assist a client in crime or fraud. See M.R. 1.2(d) and DR 7–102(A)(7). On the other hand, any taxpayer may claim every "legitimate" exemption or deduction even if a plausible legal argument might be made against the claim. A lawyer violates no laws or ethical duties by aiding a client in determining what counts as "legitimate."

Between the two extremes lies a spectrum of possible balancing points, and debate over the appropriate balance has continued for at least 40 years.[7] At a minimum, for a lawyer to recommend a position, that position must not be frivolous.[8] Requiring a reasonable basis for success, as did ABA Formal Opinion 314, discussed above, demands only slightly more than the non-frivolous standard. Even the current ethical standard expressed in ABA Opinion 85–352 mandates only a realistic possibility of success, which some IRS sources have treated as about a 33 percent likelihood of success for the taxpayer should the position be litigated.[9]

Aside from meeting ethical requirements in advocating a position, a lawyer actually preparing a tax return faces a practical dilemma in deter-

---

5. Ethical issues in tax practice are discussed in Bernard Wolfman & James P. Holden, Ethical Problems in Modern Tax Practice (2d ed. 1985). See also Bernard Wolfman, James P. Holden, & Kenneth L. Harris, Standards of Tax Practice: Professional Responsibility and Ethics (CCH 1991); George Cooper, The Avoidance Dynamic: A Tale of Tax Planning, Tax Ethics, and Tax Reform, 80 Colum.L.Rev. 1553 (1980).

6. See, e.g., United States v. Feaster, 843 F.2d 1392 (6th Cir.1988) (unreported opinion, text available on WESTLAW).

7. See Randolph Paul, The Responsibilities of the Tax Adviser, 63 Harv.L.Rev. 377 (1950).

8. See M.R. 3.1: "A lawyer shall not ... assert or controvert an issue ... unless there is a basis for doing so that is not frivolous, which includes a good faith argument for an extension, modification or reversal of existing law...." See also DR 7–102(A)(1).

9. See Wolfman, Holden & Harris, supra, at 69.

mining whether to indicate on the return that claims for exemptions of income from tax, or for deductions from otherwise taxable income, are legally debatable. Such an indication may "flag" the return for special attention of the Internal Revenue Service, and that special attention in turn may result in a disallowance that otherwise would not have been imposed and consequently higher tax for the client. Given that the IRS does not audit all returns but only a small fraction of them, to the extent that the lawyer or other professional assisting the taxpayer does "flag" a client's return, the client may be worse off than if he had had no professional assistance.

Further complicating the situation is the fact that taxpayers have reporting responsibilities of their own under the Internal Revenue Code, with penalties for understatement of tax liabilities; and these duties do not parallel the ethical duties imposed on lawyers. In general, taxpayers can avoid an understatement penalty if either they disclose the debatable point on their tax return or there is substantial authority for their position.[10] The Catch–22 raised by disclosure has already been noted, and the substantial authority standard is not precisely defined relative to the lawyers' realistic possibility of success guideline. The lawyer thus must reconcile the two sets of standards.

Michael Durst shows the anomaly in trying to require the lawyer to advise the taxpayer to adhere to a higher standard of reporting than is required by the penalty provisions of the tax law.[11] Put differently, the way to induce tax lawyers to give advice conforming to a certain standard is to impose that standard directly on the taxpayer.

One approach to resolving the ethical questions peculiar to tax practice involves analogizing the process of filing a tax return to some other legal transaction. ABA Formal Opinion 85–352 analogizes the tax return process to a pleading in litigation, wherein assertions short of frivolousness may be predicated on interpretation of law and fact most favorable to the proponent. Critics point out that pleadings are filed between parties with a ripened legal dispute, whereas a tax return is a submission of information that, in principle, is not in dispute. Another analogy might be to a securities disclosure document, such as was involved in *National Student Marketing*. Such a comparison would suggest that a tax return should disclose any fact or circumstance that a reasonable tax collector would think material in determining the amount of tax due under the return. Needless to say, the bar has not encouraged this analogy, but its very

10. Current tax law does not require that a tax return conform to the standards of disclosure that apply under the securities laws. However, § 6661(b)(2)(B) of the Internal Revenue Code, 26 U.S.C. § 6661(b)(2)(B), provides for a ten percent addition to the amount of an underpaid tax if the amount of understatement exceeds ten percent of the tax due or $5,000, but the amount of understatement is reduced if "there was substantial support of [the tax treatment of an item]" or the "facts affecting the item's tax treatment are adequately disclosed in the return or in a statement attached to the return."

11. Michael Durst, The Tax Lawyer's Professional Responsibility, 39 U.Fla.L.Rev. 1027 (1987).

advancement does reflect the breadth of disagreement that exists as to the appropriate standard to govern a lawyer advising a client in preparing a return.

Did the ABA opinion take adequate account of the standards of candor and disclosure that govern pleadings and representations to a court? See Model Rules 3.1 and 3.3; DR 7–102(A)(2), (3) and (6). Does Model Rule 3.3(d), dealing with ex parte submissions to a tribunal, have any application? M.R. 3.3(d) provides: "In an ex parte proceeding, a lawyer shall inform the tribunal of all material facts known to the lawyer which will enable the tribunal to make an informed decision, whether or not the facts are adverse."

E.   PROCEDURAL LAW

Of the bodies of law external to the rules of professional conduct that are important for lawyers, none is more significant than the law of procedure. For the lawyer, the law of procedure is a set of legal empowerments accompanied by limitations and obligations. The very term "attorney" denotes one who is an agent in legal matters, particularly litigation. Agency is itself a relationship involving powers, limitations and obligations.[12] Agency law governs lawyers in many contexts in which the rules of professional conduct are silent or incomplete. Moreover, legal regulation allows only lawyers to undertake agent relationships that involve "practice of law."[13] The term "practice of law" is indeterminate at the margin of meaning but certainly includes advocacy in criminal and civil litigation. Hence, the law of procedure has special significance for lawyers because only they may be employed as advocates.

The function of advocacy is governed by and takes its form from the law of criminal and civil procedure. The rules of procedure, although they generally address the "parties," contemplate that litigation ordinarily will be conducted by lawyers.

1.   EMPOWERMENTS IN PROCEDURAL LAW

The law of procedure is largely a set of legal empowerments. For example, Rule 4(a) of the Federal Rules of Civil Procedure begins as follows:

> Upon the filing of the complaint the clerk shall forthwith issue a summons to the plaintiff or the plaintiff's attorney. . . .

Rule 4(a) does not say so, but rather presupposes that the attorney for the plaintiff will have drafted the complaint in conformity with the pleading rules stated in Fed.R.Civ.P. 8–12 and other provisions of the Federal

---

12. See generally Restatement (Second) of Agency.

13. See, e.g., Florida Bar v. Brumbaugh, 355 So.2d 1186 (Fla.1978), discussed infra at p. 1004.

Rules. Rule 4(a) similarly presupposes that the plaintiff's attorney will also have prepared the summons itself, in contemplation that the clerk will simply stamp the document, record that fact and then hand the summons back to the lawyer, who will arrange service on the defendant. Similarly, Fed.R.Civ.P. 26(a) provides that "parties may obtain discovery ... upon oral examination or written questions ...," but contemplates that attorneys will conduct discovery on behalf of parties.

Criminal procedure involves similar presuppositions. For example 18 U.S.C. § 3041 provides:

> For any offense against the United States, the offender may, by any ... judge of the United States, ... be arrested and imprisoned or released as provided in chapter 207 of this title....

Section 3041 does not say so, but it presupposes that ordinarily a judge will order such arrest only on application of the U.S. district attorney, a lawyer for the Department of Justice or some other lawyer for the government.

Such rules and presuppositions reflect the fact that commencing criminal or civil litigation, with potentially momentous effect on the lives of the parties involved, for most practical purposes lies exclusively within the authority of people who are lawyers. The same holds for all subsequent stages of litigation. Litigation is an exercise of the power of the state over which lawyers have important control.

2.   LIMITATIONS IN PROCEDURAL LAW

The powers that lawyers exercise in conducting litigation are subject to all kinds of limitations. These limits are the focus of Chapter 5 below. For example, Fed.R.Civ.P. 11, as amended in 1983, provides:

> The signature of an attorney ... constitutes a certificate by the signer that the signer has read the pleading, motion, or other paper; that to the best of the signer's knowledge, information, and belief formed after reasonable inquiry it is well grounded in fact and is warranted by existing law or a good faith argument for the extension, modification, or reversal of existing law, and that it is not interposed for any improper purpose, such as to harass or to cause unnecessary delay or needless increase in the cost of litigation.

Another set of explicit limits appears in Fed.R.Civ.P. 37, governing discovery.

The sanction of contempt of court cuts across all activities directly involving the courts. The contempt power is founded both in common law and in statute, e.g., 18 U.S.C. § 401, which provides as regards criminal contempt:

> A court of the United States shall have power to punish by fine or imprisonment ... such contempt of its authority ... as ... misbehavior of any person in its presence or so near thereto as to obstruct the administration of justice....

Another set of limits, pervasive in the law of procedure, involves the requirement that procedural options be exercised in timely fashion or otherwise be forfeited. Statutes of limitations, governing the time within which litigation must be commenced following the occurrence of a legal grievance, are an obvious example.[14] But virtually every procedural empowerment carries with it a limitation on the time within which it may be invoked.[15]

Yet another restriction on lawyer powers appears in requirements of court permission for procedural steps to be taken. For example, Fed. R.Civ.P. 23, which permits an action to proceed as a class action only upon the court's authorization, provides in part:

> As soon as practicable after the commencement of an action brought as a class action, the *court* shall determine by order *whether* it is to be so maintained.[16] (Emphasis supplied.)

Similarly, Fed.R.Civ.P. 26(c) confers broad power upon the court to regulate discovery, including power to direct that "discovery not be had."[17] More generally, the courts have broad "inherent power," often expressed in capacious terms:

> A court set up by the Constitution has within it the power of self-preservation, indeed, the power to remove all obstructions to its successful and convenient operation.[18]

3. OBLIGATIONS IN PROCEDURAL LAW

A power conferred on a lawyer by the law of procedure also carries obligations concerning how the power is exercised. Broadly speaking, a lawyer has an obligation to a client to employ litigation powers to maximize the client's interest. Model Rules 1.1 and 1.2(a). At the same time, the lawyer has an obligation not to employ those powers in a way that is illegal, fraudulent or merely for harassment. See Fed.R.Civ.P. 11, quoted above; Rule 16 (governing pretrial conferences and giving the court authority to "discourag[e] wasteful pretrial activities"); and Rule 37, referred to above. Moreover, the concept that a lawyer is an "officer of the court" implies a general obligation to conduct litigation within the limits of accepted conventions. As stated in Cohen v. Hurley:

> It is no less true than trite that lawyers must operate in a three-fold capacity, as self-employed businessmen as it were, as trusted agents of their clients, and as assistants to the court in search of a just solution of disputes.[19]

---

14. The failure of a lawyer to bring suit within the limitations period is the most obvious form of legal malpractice. See Ronald E. Mallen & Jeffrey M. Smith, Legal Malpractice, § 24.13 (3d ed. 1989).

15. See, e.g., Fed.R.Civ.P. 6, "Time"; Rule 60(b) (time limitations on a motion to set aside a judgment on the ground of its procurement by mistake or fraud).

16. Fed.R.Civ.P. Rule 23(c)(1).

17. Fed.R.Civ.P. 26(c)(1).

18. Millholen v. Riley, 293 P. 69, 71 (Cal. 1930).

19. 366 U.S. 117, 122 (1961).

A lawyer's obligations to the court and to opposing parties in connection with litigation are codified in M.R. 3.1 through 3.8. See also M.R. 3.9, dealing with obligations in non-adjudicative proceedings. Those Rules refer to the law of procedure both expressly and impliedly. For example, a key formula in M.R. 3.1 corresponds to that in Fed.R.Civ.P. 11, quoted above. M.R. 3.1 provides:

> A lawyer shall not bring or defend a proceeding, or assert or controvert an issue therein, unless there is a basis for doing so that is not frivolous, which includes a good faith argument for an extension, modification or reversal of existing law. . . .

Another example of an ethical rule's reference to the law of procedure is M.R. 3.4(a), which provides:

> A lawyer shall not *unlawfully* obstruct another party's access to evidence or *unlawfully* alter, destroy or conceal a document or other material having potential evidentiary value. . . . (Emphasis supplied.)

More generally, M.R. 3.4(c) provides:

> A lawyer shall not knowingly disobey an obligation under the *rules of a tribunal* except for an open refusal based on an assertion that no valid obligation exists. . . . (Emphasis supplied.)

A question of proper professional conduct in litigation therefore usually depends, wholly or in part, on the law of procedure. The law of procedure, however, is itself a distillate of professional practice. After all, the modern codified version of procedural law originated in common law, which in turn reflects the historic practice of law.[20] Moreover, the law of procedure embodies the understandings of the community of practicing lawyers; procedure is understood in terms of the bar's concepts, norms and expectations about appropriate behavior in conducting litigation. Because the community of practicing lawyers differs in experience, interest, political position and ethical concepts, controversies inevitably arise over what the law of procedure permits and requires of lawyers. See generally Chapter 1 above.

---

20. See generally, e.g., F. James & G. Hazard, Civil Procedure, § 1.3 et seq. (3d ed. 1984).

CHAPTER 3

COMPETENCE

I find no pleasure in saying to you that the majority of lawyers who appear in court are so poorly trained that they are not properly performing their job....

From more than twenty years of active practice ... and from more than ten years on the bench, I think I have gained a fairly reasonable ... view of what goes on in courtrooms.... [M]y appraisal of courtroom performance was so low that I began to check it with lawyers and judges in various parts of the country to see whether I misjudged....

On the most favorable view expressed, seventy-five percent of the lawyers appearing in the courtroom were deficient by reason of poor preparation, lack of ability to conduct a proper cross-examination, lack of ability to present expert testimony, ... lack of ability to frame objections ..., [and] lack of basic analytic ability in the framing of issues....[1]

Warren E. Burger

HOW WIDESPREAD IS INCOMPETENCE?

Warren Burger, as an appellate judge and as Chief Justice of the United States, focused the attention of the legal profession and the public on lawyer competency with his provocative assertion in 1967 that a large majority of trial lawyers were incompetent. In subsequent speeches, Burger continued to assert his belief that 75 percent might be an accurate figure, but accepted as a "working hypothesis" a lower number: "that from one-third to one-half of the lawyers who appear in serious cases are not really qualified to render fully adequate representation."[2] The resulting controversy generated much heat, some proposals for reform—usually the imposition of further educational or apprenticeship requirements on new lawyers—and a modest collection of empirical studies of lawyer behavior and attitudes.

Documenting the level of competence in the practice of law is virtually impossible. Surveys that ask lawyers or judges to estimate the frequency of incompetence are notoriously unreliable, and varying results are reported.[3] The most careful study, by the Federal Judicial Center, revealed that when

1. Warren E. Burger, A Sick Profession?, 5 Tulsa L.J. 1 (1968) (remarks at the Winter Convention of the American College of Trial Lawyers, April 11, 1967).

2. Warren E. Burger, The Special Skills of Advocacy: Are Specialized Training and Certification of Advocates Essential to Our System of Justice?, 42 Fordham L.Rev. 227, 234 (1978).

3. See Roger C. Cramton & Erik M. Jensen, The State of Trial Advocacy and Legal Education: Three New Studies, 30 J.Leg.Ed. 253 (1979) (reviewing the literature and criticizing Burger's figures as unscientific, anecdotal and overstated).

asked to rate actual levels of trial "performance" rather than to give a general impression of the frequency of incompetence, federal judges reported 8.6 percent of trial lawyer performances as incompetent and another 16.8 percent as barely adequate.[4] Surveys asking judges what proportion of trial lawyers are incompetent tend to yield somewhat larger percentages.[5] What is one to make of such figures, given the absence of reliable measures and agreement on standards of competence? Some prominent commentators have asserted that lawyers are less competent today than in the past and have attributed the decline in part to the large number of new lawyers entering the profession. What evidence would be sufficient to support or refute this assertion?

Defining "competence" is a difficult matter. The word connotes performance rather than capacity. Model Rule 1.1 defines competence with a list: "legal knowledge, skill, thoroughness and preparation reasonably necessary for the representation." Presumably the standard, like that in malpractice, is one of prudent norms of professional performance, not of client expectations. Studies of the quality of professional care suggest that, given a certain level of intelligence, education and experience, the delivery of quality professional care depends more on intangible aspirations than anything else: caring about law, caring about clients and caring about one's image of oneself as a good professional who keeps up to date and takes pride in providing quality professional services.[6]

The lawyer competency controversy triggered consideration of numerous proposals to change legal education or impose apprenticeship requirements on new entrants. The growth of clinical legal education during the 1970s and 1980s was furthered by this debate, but the apprenticeship proposals encountered academic and professional opposition. Many commentators urged caution in considering proposals to amend law school curricula as a means of reducing incompetent trial performance given how sketchy our understanding is of the relationship between competence and law school study.[7]

4. Id. at 257, citing and discussing the Federal Judicial Center study reported by Anthony Partridge and Gordon Bermant, The Quality of Advocacy in the Federal Courts (1978).

5. See Eleanor Maddi, Trial Advocacy Competence: The Judicial Perspective, 1978 Am.Bar Found.Research J. 105 (reporting a survey of 40 judges in the Second Circuit, which revealed that these judges considered 10 to 12 percent of the lawyers they observed in civil and criminal cases to be incompetent; and a national survey of more than one thousand federal and state trial judges, who estimated that 20 percent of trial lawyers were incompetent, but that dropped to 13 percent when they were asked about the lawyers in the last five

trials over which they had presided). See also LawPoll, 64 A.B.A.J. 832 (1978) (nationwide survey of lawyers showing that 41 percent of those responding, and 72 percent of the litigators, agreed with Burger's "working hypothesis" of one-third to one-half incompetent).

6. See Roger C. Cramton, Lawyer Competence and the Law Schools, 4 U.Ark.Little Rock L.J. 1 (1981); see also Douglas E. Rosenthal, Evaluating the Competence of Lawyers, 11 Law & Soc'y Rev. 257 (1976).

7. See, e.g., Cramton & Jensen, supra; Christen R. Blair, Trial Lawyer Incompetence: What the Studies Suggest About the Problem, the Causes and the Cure, 11 Cap.U.L.Rev. 419 (1982); and H. Russell Cort and Jack L. Sammons, The Search for

A. Checks on Incompetence

Preventive measures designed to ensure that clients receive competent legal services begin with bar admission requirements. In general, seven years of higher education, including graduation from one of the 179 law schools approved by the ABA, are required in order to qualify for admission to the bar in American states. In addition, the bar admission process seeks to exclude those who are deficient in character or fitness. Bar examinations are designed to test legal ability and knowledge. Admission standards for law school and requirements for admission to the bar are discussed in Chapter 9 infra at p. 869.

Reactive measures, which are also intended to have a deterrent effect, include professional discipline, civil liability for negligence (legal malpractice) and sanctions administered by a tribunal in which a lawyer is litigating. May ordinary Americans safely rely on this array of measures as assuring competent legal assistance at a reasonable cost?

1. Ethics Rules on Competence

The Canons of Ethics did not contain a provision on competence. Canon 6 of the Model Code recognized the importance of competence: "A Lawyer Should Represent a Client Competently." Despite grandiloquent language in the Canon's ethical considerations, the disciplinary rule on competence is not stringent. DR 6–101(A)(1) states that a lawyer shall not "handle a legal matter which he knows or should know that he is not competent to handle, without associating with . . . a lawyer who is competent to handle it." EC 6–3 explains that this does not prevent a novice in an area of law from accepting employment in that area "if in good faith he expects to become qualified through study and investigation, as long as such preparation would not result in unreasonable delay or expense to the client." Once the representation has been accepted, DR 6–102(A)(2) provides that a lawyer shall not "handle a matter without preparation adequate in the circumstances," and DR 6–102(A)(3) prohibits the lawyer from "neglect[ing] a legal matter entrusted to him."

Model Rule 1.1 provides:

A lawyer shall provide competent representation to a client. Competent representation requires the legal knowledge, skill, thoroughness and preparation reasonably necessary for the representation.

Comment [1] to M.R. 1.1 states that while "[i]n many instances, the required proficiency is that of the general practitioner," nonetheless "[e]xpertise in a particular field of law may be required in some circumstances." However, Comment [2] contains language similar to EC 6–3 to the effect

"Good Lawyering": A Concept and Model of Lawyering Competencies, 29 Clev. St.L.Rev. 397 (1980); Marvin E. Frankel, Curing Lawyers' Incompetence: Primum non Nocere, 10 Creighton L.Rev. 613 (1977).

that a novice can provide adequate representation if she engages in necessary study or associates with someone of established competence in the field.

M.R. 1.3 requires that a lawyer act with reasonable diligence, and M.R. 1.4(a) requires that a lawyer "keep a client reasonably informed of the status of the representation and promptly comply with reasonable requests for information."

Discipline for incompetence has been relatively rare.[8] Most cases have involved either egregious, repeated instances of incompetence or incompetence combined with other misconduct.[9] Court decisions and ethics opinions often state that it is inappropriate to impose discipline for conduct that amounts "only" to negligent malpractice.[10] Is this position justified?

Some states have adopted a standard of competence that states clearly the limited application of professional discipline to individual instances of negligent lawyering. For example, California Rule of Prof. Conduct 3–110(A) provides that a lawyer "shall not intentionally, recklessly, or repeatedly fail to perform legal services with competence." This standard more closely reflects the actual conduct of state disciplinary bodies. Rule 3–110(B) defines competence as "(1) diligence, (2) learning and skill, and (3) mental, emotional, and physical ability reasonably necessary for the performance of [legal] service."

2.   CONTINUING LEGAL EDUCATION[11]

Continuing legal education (CLE) is a major part of a modern lawyer's professional life. CLE is a large and highly competitive industry. Virtually all bar associations, national, state and local, and a number of law schools, provide a variety of CLE programs: lectures, panels, video and audio tapes, pamphlets, checklists, books and articles. Many private entrepreneurs also

8. See Susan R. Martyn, Lawyer Competence and Lawyer Discipline: Beyond the Bar? 71 Geo.L.J. 705 (1981).

9. See, e.g., Attorney Grievance Com'n v. Werner, 553 A.2d 722 (Md.1989) (gross neglect, multiple misrepresentations and failure to cooperate with bar authorities); Office of Disciplinary Counsel v. Henry, 664 S.W.2d 62 (Tenn.1983) (gross incompetence in four cases); In re Albert, 212 N.W.2d 17 (Mich.1973) (neglect of the claims of a number of clients and failure to keep clients informed of the status of their cases); In re Kennedy, 176 S.E.2d 125 (S.C. 1970) (repeated instances of incompetence).

10. See, e.g., Florida Bar v. Neale, 384 So.2d 1264, 1265 (Fla.1980) (professional discipline for neglect should not be used "as a substitute for what is essentially a malpractice action"); Committee on Legal Ethics v. Mullins, 226 S.E.2d 427 (W.Va.

1976). Also see ABA Informal Op. 1273 (1973) (neglect "involves more than a single act or omission"); ABA Comm. on Ethics and Prof. Resp. Formal Op. 335 n.1 (1974) (discipline for "neglect" under the Model Code requires "indifference and a consistent failure to carry out the obligations [the lawyer had] assumed to his client or a conscious disregard for the responsibility owed to his client").

11. For discussion of continuing legal education, see ALI–ABA Committee on Continuing Legal Education, CLE and the Lawyer's Responsibilities in an Evolving Profession (Arden House, 1988); Study of the Quality of Continuing Legal Education (1980); and A Model for Continuing Legal Education: Structure, Methods, and Curriculum (1980).

provide offerings. When CLE is voluntary, some lawyers regularly take courses while others never or rarely attend. Because of fear that those who need it most take it least, CLE has been made mandatory in most states.[12] How much CLE training is sufficient? How does a lawyer gauge whether her level of knowledge of a subject is at least average other than by going to courses to hear what other lawyers know on the subject? Is conveying such awareness a sufficient justification for mandatory CLE?

Lawyers have challenged "mandatory CLE," as it is called, on free speech, due process and other constitutional grounds, but such challenges have failed.[13]

3. PEER REVIEW

The theory behind peer review is that lawyers may maintain and improve their competence by submitting their practice methods to the scrutiny of knowledgeable colleagues for comment and constructive criticism.[14] ALI–ABA has studied and supported experimental peer review programs in several states. However, peer review has had difficulty gaining general acceptance. Peer review procedures are invoked if a lawyer's practice is found substandard, for example, in connection with a grievance inquiry. For obvious reasons, lawyers do not wish their practice to be so designated. Also, the psychology of education suggests that it is not easy to teach someone after having called her incompetent. On the other hand, making peer review compulsory for all would be an expensive form of mandatory CLE.

Informal peer review, of course, goes on all the time. Weren't Chief Justice Burger's remarks about the competence of trial lawyers, quoted at the beginning of this chapter, essentially peer review? Isn't peer review involved in evaluating an associate in a law firm for partnership or in establishing the shares of partners in the profits of a firm's practice? One

12. As of June 1999, most states have adopted mandatory CLE requirements. The California requirement of 36 hours every three years requires that at least four hours be on the subject of legal ethics and that one hour each be devoted to substance abuse and the elimination of bias. Katherine Bishop, California Lawyers Must Take Refresher Courses, N.Y. Times, Aug. 9, 1991, at p. B7. In New York, four of the required 24 hours over two years must be on "ethics and professionalism."

13. See, e.g., Verner v. Colorado, 716 F.2d 1352 (10th Cir.1983) (mandatory CLE does not violate lawyers' constitutional rights to due process, free speech or assembly, equal protection of the law, the 8th Amendment's prohibition against cruel and unusual punishment, or the 13th Amendment's prohibition against involun-

tary servitude; the state may require lawyers to take CLE courses as a condition of maintaining their licenses); see also Brown v. McGarr, 774 F.2d 777 (7th Cir.1985) (practice requirements for federal "trial bar" do not deprive lawyers of property without due process of law). Discipline may be imposed for violation of CLE attendance requirements. See, e.g., In re Smith, 939 P.2d 422 (Ariz.1997) (lawyer suspended for non-attendance).

14. See ALI–ABA Committee on Continuing Professional Education, A Model Peer Review System (1980); ALI–ABA Committee on Continuing Professional Education, Law Practice Quality Evaluation: An Appraisal of Peer Review and Other Measures To Enhance Professional Performance (1987).

reason law firms experience lower rates of malpractice claims than sole practitioners is that the members of a firm undergo continuous peer review in the ordinary course of the firm's practice.

4. REPUTATION AND THE MARKET

Traditionally, a lawyer's reputation reflected his proficiency. Reputation is established partly through the opinion of clients, but at least equally through the opinion of other lawyers. To this extent, a lawyer's reputation is the distillate of peer review. Today, reputation remains important within the circle of a lawyer's professional acquaintance. A nonspecialist practitioner located in a metropolitan area rather than a small face-to-face community, however, has a largely disconnected circle of acquaintance. Apart from well-developed legal specializations, the impersonal nature of modern law practice in urban areas means that the informal peer review expressed in professional reputation is relatively weak. Are mandatory CLE and peer review adequate to replace reputational controls in protecting against incompetence?

Why not trust the market to differentiate between competent and incompetent lawyers? The market probably operates quite well as a competence filter with regard to specialized types of legal services provided to sophisticated clients such as large business corporations.[15] However, available evidence indicates that most individuals use a lawyer's services on only two or three occasions in a lifetime.[16] Such limited experience as a client, usually on very different types of matters handled by different types of lawyers, does not provide much basis for making market comparisons. Should current and prospective clients be able to pool their experience by joining together to purchase legal services? That is what prepaid and legal services plans involve. See Chapter 10 below, discussing group legal services beginning at p. 1039.

B. MALPRACTICE

INTRODUCTORY NOTE

Despite the many limitations of the malpractice remedy, the threat or actuality of legal malpractice liability is viewed by many scholars of the legal profession as probably the most significant regulator of lawyer behavior.[17] Although accurate data is hard to come by—most malpractice insur-

---

15. Consider, for example, the search made for the lawyer in Brobeck, Phleger & Harrison v. Telex Corp., 602 F.2d 866 (9th Cir.1979), p. 495 below.

16. See Barbara A. Curran, The Legal Needs of the Public: The Final Report of a National Survey (1977).

17. See, e.g., Roger C. Cramton, Delivery of Legal Services to Ordinary Americans, 44 Case W.Res.L.Rev. 531, 549 (1994) ("legal malpractice liability has emerged as a form of accountability that polices the profession and protects consumers"); Geoffrey C. Hazard, Jr., The Future of Legal Ethics,

ers do not report their data, most settlements are confidential and the ABA's studies are influenced by the profession's self interest—reliable estimates place the annual cost of legal malpractice at more than $4 billion, a figure roughly equivalent to the overall cost of medical malpractice.[18] Unlike the health care field, where nearly all providers are covered by malpractice insurance, an astonishing percentage of lawyers—varying from 30–60 percent from state to state—carry no insurance coverage.[19] Since those who lack malpractice insurance are also likely to have limited personal assets, the cost of malpractice, when the victim brings suit or obtains an award, falls on those lawyers who are insured. Although Canadian provinces and other countries require malpractice insurance of lawyers, the legal profession in the U.S. has strongly resisted such a requirement and only one state, Oregon, mandates liability insurance.

Everyone agrees that legal malpractice cases have increased enormously in number and cost in recent decades. This development has been augmented by the expansion of the number of situations in which a lawyer owes a duty of care to non-client third parties, in addition to the traditional duties to client. But much else about the incidence and details of malpractice liability is unknown or in dispute. Manuel Ramos, in a number of recent studies,[20] finds, contrary to ABA reports, that malpractice liability is not disproportionately a problem of solo or small-firm practitioners rather than those in mid-sized or large law firms; and that malpractice is not confined to low-income lawyers from less prestigious law schools or to rural more than urban lawyers or to younger or older lawyers; etc. Ramos concludes that there is no identifiable group of "bad" lawyers who account for a disproportionate number of malpractice claims. As in other fields involving highly contested torts, less than one-half of the available insurance amounts go to successful plaintiffs.[21]

100 Yale L.J. 1239, 1279 (1991) ("The bar has become too large, diverse, and balkanized in its practice specialties for the old informal system [of peer review and professional discipline] to be effective as an institution of governance.... [T]he courts will continue to be an indispensable instrument for ordering and clarifying norms...."); and Deborah L. Rhode, quoted in Stephanie B. Goldberg, The Profession: Identity Crisis, ABA J., Dec.1994, at 74, 76 ("the lax standards and enforcement structure [of professional discipline] that the profession has set for itself are being increasingly displaced by civil liability claims and by administrative agency oversight").

18. See Manuel R. Ramos, Legal Malpractice: Reforming Lawyers and Law Professors, 70 Tulane L.Rev. 2583, 2586 (1996).

19. Data cited by Manuel R. Ramos indicates that 55 percent of California lawyers were uninsured in 1991; 90 percent of solo practitioners in Houston; and 35 percent of Oregon lawyers were uninsured when its mandatory insurance program was put in place in 1978. Id. at 2610–13 (1996).

20. Manuel R. Ramos, Legal Malpractice: No Lawyer or Client Is Safe, 47 Fla. L. Rev. 1 (1995) (reporting a detailed study of Florida lawyers, who are required to report malpractice claims against them, and correlating this data with many other indicators); and Ramos, Legal Malpractice: Reforming Lawyers and Law Professors, 70 Tulane L.Rev. 2583, 2609 (1996) (discussing Oregon's mandatory malpractice insurance program and concluding that similar legislation is required to "more fairly compensate aggrieved clients and nonclients" and to "efficiently and economically handle legal malpractice claims").

21. Id. at 2600.

1. OVERVIEW OF TORT OF MALPRACTICE

The elements of a legal malpractice claim are:

1. Duty. A duty of care arising from an attorney-client relationship[22] or, in those jurisdictions that have created exceptions to privity of contract, some other showing that there was a duty to the plaintiff, e.g., that a substantial purpose of the attorney-client relationship was to influence or benefit the plaintiff.

2. Breach of duty. A failure by the lawyer to exercise the care that reasonably competent lawyers exercise under similar circumstances. The duty of care is usually expressed in a formula that includes knowledge, skill, prudence and diligence. The reference to the custom of other lawyers means that ordinarily the plaintiff must obtain the testimony of expert lawyers concerning the standard applicable in the particular situation.

3. Causation. Cause-in-fact and proximate cause must be shown, i.e., evidence that the lawyer's failure was the actual and proximate cause of the plaintiff's injury.

4. Harm. Legally cognizable harm must have been caused by the lawyer's act or omission. Legal malpractice usually seeks a recovery for purely economic harm: e.g., a showing that the plaintiff would have achieved a different and more advantageous result in the transaction or litigation but for the lawyer's conduct. The availability of damages for emotional or psychic harm is a topic of continuing controversy and disagreement.[23]

The law of legal malpractice is a subject in itself. In the notes that follow, we touch on only a few of the many questions in this area.[24] There is a substantial literature on subsidiary problems such as use of expert testimony,[25] accrual of the cause of action and tolling of the statute of limitations through continuation of the lawyer-client relationship[26] and

---

22. See Togstad v. Vesely, Otto, Miller & Keefe, 291 N.W.2d 686 (Minn.1980), printed in Chapter 6 infra at p. 457, and the notes following it for a discussion of when, for purposes of a legal malpractice claim, an attorney-client relationship will be found to exist.

23. See Note, An Attorney's Liability for the Negligent Infliction of Emotional Distress, 58 Fordham L.Rev.1309 (1990) (damages for emotional distress generally are limited to cases in which the client suffered a physical injury or the attorney acted egregiously, but some recent cases permit such damages without regard to the degree of lawyer negligence). See, e.g., Pinkham v. Burgess, 933 F.2d 1066 (1st Cir.1991) (affirming an award of $186,500 for emotional

distress caused to a client by lawyer's negligent representation in a civil rights case).

24. For more elaborate treatment of this subject, see Ronald E. Mallen and Jeffrey M. Smith, Legal Malpractice (3d ed.1989); Wolfram, Modern Legal Ethics § 5.6 et seq. (1986); William L. Prosser and W. Page Keeton, Prosser and Keeton on Torts 185 et seq. (5th ed.1984).

25. See, e.g., Charles M. Liebson, Legal Malpractice Cases: Special Problems in Identifying Issues of Law and Fact and in the Use of Expert Testimony, 75 Ky.L.J. 1 (1986–87).

26. Joseph H. Koffler, Legal Malpractice Statutes of Limitations: A Critical Analysis of a Burgeoning Crisis, 20 Akron L.Rev. 209 (1986).

liability for particular types of mistakes.[27]

Lucas v. Hamm

Supreme Court of California, 1961.
56 Cal.2d 583, 15 Cal.Rptr. 821, 364 P.2d 685.

■ GIBSON, CHIEF JUSTICE.

[Attorney Hamm was retained to draft a will. The testator's instructions called for creation of a trust of the residue for the benefit of the plaintiffs. Hamm prepared and the client executed a will providing that this trust of the residue would terminate "at 12 o'clock noon on a day five years after" termination of the testator's estate. After the testator's death, Hamm, as the lawyer for the testator's estate, advised plaintiffs that the trust provision was invalid under the California rule against perpetuities, which prohibits any restraint on alienation "for a period longer than 21 years after some life in being at the creation of the interest...." As a result, plaintiffs entered into a settlement with intestate heirs, receiving $75,000 less than they would have received if the instructions given by the testator had been effectuated. The plaintiffs sued Hamm, alleging that his negligence in drafting the will had caused their loss. The trial court dismissed the complaint for failing to state a cause of action and the plaintiffs appealed.]

... We are of the view that the extension of [a lawyer's] liability to beneficiaries injured by a negligently drawn will does not place an undue burden on the profession, particularly when we take into consideration that a contrary conclusion would cause the innocent beneficiary to bear the loss. [The court applied a balancing-of-factors approach in holding that it was reasonably foreseeable to Hamm, when he drafted the will, that absence of due care would result in harm to the intended will beneficiaries.]

It follows that the lack of privity between plaintiffs and defendant does not preclude plaintiffs from maintaining an action in tort against defendant.

. . .

The general rule with respect to the liability of an attorney for failure to properly perform his duties to his client is that the attorney, by accepting employment to give legal advice or to render other legal services, impliedly agrees to use such skill, prudence, and diligence as lawyers of ordinary skill and capacity commonly possess and exercise in the performance of the tasks which they undertake.... The attorney is not liable for every mistake he may make in his practice; he is not, in the absence of an express agreement, an insurer of the soundness of his opinions or of the validity of an instrument that he is engaged to draft; and he is not liable for

---

27. See, e.g., Note, Liability of Attorneys for Legal Opinions Under the Federal Securities Laws, 27 B.C.L.Rev. 325 (1986).

being in error as to a question of law on which reasonable doubt may be entertained by well-informed lawyers....

The complaint, as we have seen, alleges that defendant drafted the will in such a manner that the trust was invalid because it violated the rules relating to perpetuities and restraints on alienation. These closely akin subjects have long perplexed the courts and the bar. Professor Gray, a leading authority in the field, stated: "There is something in the subject which seems to facilitate error. Perhaps it is because the mode of reasoning is unlike that with which lawyers are most familiar.... A long list might be formed of the demonstrable blunders with regard to its questions made by eminent men, blunders which they themselves have been sometimes the first to acknowledge; and there are few lawyers of any practice in drawing wills and settlements who have not at some time either fallen into the net which the Rule spreads for the unwary, or at least shuddered to think how narrowly they have escaped it." Gray, The Rule Against Perpetuities (4th ed. 1942) p. xi; see also Leach, Perpetuities Legislation (1954) 67 Harv. L.Rev. 1349 (describing the rule as a "technicality-ridden legal nightmare" and a "dangerous instrumentality in the hands of most members of the bar"). Of the California law on perpetuities and restraints it has been said that few, if any, areas of the law have been fraught with more confusion or concealed more traps for the unwary draftsman; that members of the bar, probate courts, and title insurance companies make errors in these matters; that the code provisions adopted in 1872 created a situation worse than if the matter had been left to the common law; and that the legislation adopted in 1951 (under which the will involved here was drawn), despite the best of intentions, added further complexities. (See 38 Cal. Jur.2d 443; Coil, Perpetuities and Restraints; A Needed Reform (1955) 30 State Bar J. 87, 88–90.)

In view of the state of the law relating to perpetuities and restraints on alienation and the nature of the error, if any, assertedly made by defendant in preparing the instrument, it would not be proper to hold that defendant failed to use such skill, prudence, and diligence as lawyers of ordinary skill and capacity commonly exercise. The provision of the will quoted in the complaint, namely, that the trust was to terminate five years after the order of the probate court distributing the property to the trustee, could cause the trust to be invalid only because of the remote possibility that the order of distribution would be delayed for a period longer than a life in being at the creation of the interest plus 16 years (the 21–year statutory period less the five years specified in the will). Although it has been held that a possibility of this type could result in invalidity of a bequest (Estate of Johnston, 47 Cal.2d 265, 269–270, 303 P.2d 1; Estate of Campbell, 28 Cal.App.2d 102, 103 et seq., 82 P.2d 22), the possible occurrence of such a delay was so remote and unlikely that an attorney of ordinary skill acting under the same circumstances might well have "fallen into the net which the Rule spreads for the unwary" and failed to recognize the danger....

[The court affirmed the trial court's dismissal of the complaint. The opinion also considered and rejected a count of the complaint that alleged negligence by Hamm as lawyer for the estate in negotiating the settlement with the intestate heirs.]

Malpractice Liability to Non–Clients

The decision in *Lucas* suggests that judges as well as lawyers have trouble understanding the rule against perpetuities. If a reasonably competent lawyer may not be expected to understand the rule against perpetuities, is it equitable that courts apply the rule to disinherit people? What about complicated tax and securities problems? Complicated issues of constitutional criminal procedure? Is the following a fair statement of the position taken by the California Supreme Court in *Lucas?*: "California law is so confused and uncertain that citizens have to rely on lawyers; but, because the law is a mess, lawyers cannot be held responsible for giving incompetent advice."[28] Who is in the best position to reform or simplify the California rule against perpetuities?

Would the result in *Lucas* be the same if lawyer Hamm had held himself out as limiting his practice to trusts and estates law?[29]

The impoverished standard of care set forth in *Lucas* may be related to the boldness of the court's other holding. *Lucas* was the initial decision holding that a lawyer may owe a duty of care to a non-client. Sometimes when courts stretch their muscles in a way that threatens an important interest, they qualify it with a statement that says, in effect, "this won't be so bad."

The traditional rule is that absent fraud, collusion, or privity of contract, an attorney is not liable to a non-client third person for professional malpractice.[30] But a growing number of jurisdictions have created exceptions to the privity requirement on one or another theory connecting the lawyer's conduct with the plaintiff's harm.[31]

---

28.   An English commentator, R. E. Megarry, criticized the *Lucas* decision as "a slur on the profession which, like the mule, will display neither pride of ancestry nor hope of posterity." Megarry, 81 L.Q.Rev. 478, 481 (1965). "The standard of competence in California thus seems to be that it is not negligent for lawyers to draft wills knowing little or nothing of the rule against perpetuities, and without consulting anyone skilled in the rule...." See also Gerald P. Johnston, Legal Malpractice in Estate Planning—Perilous Times Ahead for the Practitioner, 67 Iowa L. Rev. 629 (1982).

29.   See Horne v. Peckham, 158 Cal.Rptr. 714 (1979) (inexperienced practitioner drafting a "Clifford trust" without consult-

ing a tax or estate planning specialist), discussed later in this section.

30.   National Savings Bank v. Ward, 100 U.S. 195 (1880).

31.   See the *Greycas* case and the notes that follow it in Chapter 2 above at p. 79. California's balancing-of-factors approach lists seven factors relevant to the question whether an actor has a duty of care to a third person in the absence of privity of contract. This approach, which originated in Biakanja v. Irving, 320 P.2d 16 (Cal. 1958) (notary public liable to intended beneficiary of a will that was denied probate because it lacked proper attestation), was extended to lawyers in *Lucas*.

A number of state courts follow the holding in Lucas v. Hamm, allowing a claim for malpractice by the intended beneficiaries of a will.[32] In Lorraine v. Grover, Ciment, Weinstein & Stauber,[33] the Florida court reaffirmed the traditional rule that privity is required but recognized an exception for the beneficiaries of a will to whom lawyers have a "direct duty."[34] Pennsylvania reached the same result but refused to do so under tort law.[35] Rejecting California's balancing-of-factors approach as unworkable, the Pennsylvania court settled instead on liability to the intended beneficiary under a third-party-beneficiary contract approach.[36] New York courts, however, have rejected negligence claims brought against lawyers by the intended beneficiaries of wills,[37] although they impose a duty of care on a lawyer who gives a legal opinion to a third party to facilitate a transaction with the lawyer's client.[38]

In Metzker v. Slocum,[39] a couple hired a lawyer to carry out an adoption, but the adoption was never perfected as a result of the lawyer's negligence. The parents subsequently divorced, and the minor child was left without support. The child sued the lawyer for negligence. The Oregon court held that the lawyer was not liable to the child, a third party to the original transaction. The court said that even applying the liberal California balancing-of-factors test for third-party liability there would be no liability because the relationship between the negligence and the harm was too tenuous and the foreseeability of harm to the child was minimal. Aren't both propositions dubious, at best?

2.   CAUSATION AND STANDARD OF CARE

Smith v. Lewis

Supreme Court of California, 1975.
530 P.2d 589.

■ MOSK, JUSTICE.

Defendant Jerome R. Lewis, an attorney, appeals from a judgment [for $100,000] entered upon a jury verdict for plaintiff Rosemary E. Smith in an

32. See, e.g., Schreiner v. Scoville, 410 N.W.2d 679 (Iowa 1987); and Auric v. Continental Cas. Co., 331 N.W.2d 325 (Wis. 1983).

33. 467 So.2d 315 (Fla.App.1985).

34. For a similar approach see Needham v. Hamilton, 459 A.2d 1060 (D.C.App.1983).

35. Guy v. Liederbach, 459 A.2d 744 (Pa. 1983).

36. Restatement (Second) Contracts § 302(1) (1981) (intended beneficiaries of a contract may recover on the contract when necessary to effectuate the intention of the parties to the contract). See also Hale v. Groce, 744 P.2d 1289 (Ore.1987) (intended beneficiary's tort action barred by statute of limitations but may proceed under contract theory); and Stowe v. Smith, 441 A.2d 81 (Conn.1981) (contract approach).

37. See, e.g., Victor v. Goldman, 344 N.Y.S.2d 672 (1973), aff'd, 351 N.Y.S.2d 956 (2d Dept.1974).

38. See, e.g., Prudential Ins. Co. v. Dewey, Ballantine, Bushby, Palmer & Wood, 605 N.E.2d 318, 320–22 (N.Y.1992) (duty of care required in preparation of legal opinion intended to induce reliance by third party).

39. 537 P.2d 74 (Ore.1975).

action for legal malpractice. The action arises as a result of legal services rendered by defendant to plaintiff in a prior divorce proceeding. The gist of plaintiff's complaint is that defendant negligently failed in the divorce action to assert her community interest in the retirement benefits of her husband.

Defendant principally contends, inter alia, that the law with regard to the characterization of retirement benefits was so unclear at the time he represented plaintiff as to insulate him from liability for failing to assert a claim therefor on behalf of his client. We conclude defendant's appeal is without merit, and therefore affirm the judgment.

In 1943 plaintiff married General Clarence D. Smith. Between 1945 and his retirement in 1966 General Smith was employed by the California National Guard. As plaintiff testified, she informed defendant her husband "was paid by the state . . . it was a job just like anyone else goes to." For the first 16 years of that period the husband belonged to the State Employees' Retirement System, a contributory plan. Between 1961 and the date of his retirement he belonged to the California National Guard retirement program, a noncontributory plan. In addition, by attending National Guard reserve drills he qualified for separate retirement benefits from the federal government, also through a noncontributory plan. The state and federal retirement programs each provide lifetime monthly benefits which terminate upon the death of the retiree. The programs make no allowance for the retiree's widow.

On January 1, 1967, the State of California began to pay General Smith gross retirement benefits of $796.26 per month. Payments under the federal program, however, will not begin until 1983, i.e., 17 years after his actual retirement, when General Smith reaches the age of 60. All benefits which General Smith is entitled to receive were earned during the time he was married to plaintiff.

On February 17, 1967, plaintiff retained defendant to represent her in a divorce action against General Smith. According to plaintiff's testimony, defendant advised her that her husband's retirement benefits were not community property. Three days later defendant filed plaintiff's complaint for divorce. General Smith's retirement benefits were not pleaded as items of community property, and therefore were not considered in the litigation or apportioned by the trial court. The divorce was uncontested and the interlocutory decree divided the minimal described community property and awarded Mrs. Smith $400 per month in alimony and child support. The final decree was entered on February 17, 1968.

On July 17, 1968, pursuant to a request by plaintiff, defendant filed on her behalf a motion to amend the decree, alleging under oath that because of his mistake, inadvertence, and excusable neglect (Code Civ. Proc., § 473) the retirement benefits of General Smith had been omitted from the list of community assets owned by the parties, and that such benefits were in fact community property. The motion was denied on the ground of untimeliness. Plaintiff consulted other counsel, and shortly thereafter filed this malpractice action against defendant.

Defendant admits in his testimony that he assumed General Smith's retirement benefits were separate property when he assessed plaintiff's community property rights. It is his position that as a matter of law an attorney is not liable for mistaken advice when well informed lawyers in the community entertain reasonable doubt as to the proper resolution of the particular legal question involved. Because, he asserts, the law defining the character of retirement benefits was uncertain at the time of his legal services to plaintiff, defendant contends the trial court committed error in refusing to grant his motions for nonsuit and judgment notwithstanding the verdict and in submitting the issue of negligence to the jury under appropriate instructions.[3]

The law is now settled in California that "retirement benefits which flow from the employment relationship, to the extent they have vested, are community property subject to equal division between the spouses in the event the marriage is dissolved." [Six California cases were cited.] Because such benefits are part of the consideration earned by the employee, they are accorded community treatment regardless of whether they derive from a state, federal, or private source, or from a contributory or noncontributory plan. In light of these principles, it becomes apparent that General Smith's retirement pay must properly be characterized as community property.

We cannot, however, evaluate the quality of defendant's professional services on the basis of the law as it appears today. In determining whether defendant exhibited the requisite degree of competence in his handling of plaintiff's divorce action, the crucial inquiry is whether his advice was so legally deficient when it was given that he may be found to have failed to use "such skill, prudence, and diligence as lawyers of ordinary skill and capacity commonly possess and exercise in the performance of the tasks which they undertake." (Lucas v. Hamm (1961) 56 Cal.2d 583, 591, 15 Cal.Rptr. 821, 825, 364 P.2d 685, 689.) We must, therefore examine the indicia of the law which were readily available to defendant at the time he performed the legal services in question.

The major authoritative reference works which attorneys routinely consult for a brief and reliable exposition of the law relevant to a specific problem uniformly indicated in 1967 that vested retirement benefits earned

---

3. The jury was instructed as follows:

"In performing legal services for a client in a divorce action an attorney has the duty to have that degree of learning and skill ordinarily possessed by attorneys of good standing, practicing in the same or similar locality and under similar circumstances.

"[An attorney is also required] to use reasonable diligence and his best judgment in the exercise of his skill and the accomplishment of his learning, in an effort to accomplish the best possible result for his client."

"An attorney is not liable for every mistake he may make in his practice; he is not in the absence of an express agreement, an insurer of the soundness of his opinions."

during marriage were generally subject to community treatment.[5] (See, e.g., Note, Pensions, and Reserve or Retired Pay, as Community Property, 134 A.L.R. 368; 15 Am.Jur.2d Community Property, § 46, p. 859; 38 Cal.Jur.2d, Pensions, § 12, p. 325; 10 Cal.Jur.2d, Community Property, § 25, p. 692; 1 Cal.Family Lawyer (Cont.Ed.Bar 1962) p. 111; 4 Witkin, Summary of Cal.Law (1960) pp. 2723–2724; cf. 41 C.J.S. Husband and Wife § 475, p. 1010 & fn. 69 and 1967 Supp. p. 1011.) A typical statement appeared in the California Family Lawyer, a work with which defendant admitted general familiarity: "Of increasing importance is the fact that pension or retirement benefits are community property, even though they are not paid or payable until after termination of the marriage by death or divorce." (1 Cal.Family Lawyer, supra, at p. 111.)

Although it is true this court had not foreclosed all conflicts on some aspects of the issue at that time, the community character of retirement benefits had been reported in a number of appellate opinions often cited in the literature and readily accessible to defendant. In Benson v. City of Los Angeles (1963), 60 Cal.2d 355, 33 Cal.Rptr. 257, 384 P.2d 649 decided four years before defendant was retained herein, we stated directly that "pension rights which are earned during the course of a marriage are the community property of the employee and his wife." ... In *French*, decided two decades earlier, we indicated that "retire[ment] pay is community property because it is compensation for services rendered in the past." (17 Cal.2d at p. 778, 112 P.2d at p. 236.) The other cases contain equally unequivocal dicta.

We are aware, moreover, of no significant authority existing in 1967 which proposed a result contrary to that suggested by the cases and the literature, or which purported to rebut the general statutory presumption, as it applies to retirement benefits, that all property acquired by either spouse during marriage belongs to the community....

On the other hand, substantial uncertainty may have existed in 1967 with regard to the community character of General Smith's federal pension. The above-discussed treaties reveal a debate which lingered among members of the legal community at that time concerning the point at which retirement benefits actually vest. [Citations to law review literature omitted.] Because the federal payments were contingent upon General Smith's survival to age 60, 17 years subsequent to the divorce, it could have been argued with some force that plaintiff and General Smith shared a mere expectancy interest in the future benefits. Alternatively, a reasonable contention could have been advanced in 1967 that federal retirement benefits were the personal entitlement of the employee spouse and were not subject to community division upon divorce in the absence of express congressional approval.... Although we [subsequently rejected this analysis in a 1974 case], the issue was clearly an arguable one upon which reasonable lawyers could differ....

---

5. In evaluating the competence of an attorney's services, we may justifiably consider his failure to consult familiar encyclopedias of the law. People v. Ibarra (1963) 60 Cal.2d 460, 465, 34 Cal.Rptr. 863, 386 P.2d 487.

Of course, the fact that in 1967 a reasonable argument could have been offered to support the characterization of General Smith's federal benefits as separate property does not indicate the trial court erred in submitting the issue of defendant's malpractice to the jury. The state benefits, the large majority of the payments at issue, were unquestionably community property according to all available authority and should have been claimed as such. As for the federal benefits, the record documents defendant's failure to conduct any reasonable research into their proper characterization under community property law.[7] Instead, he dogmatically asserted his theory, which he was unable to support with authority and later recanted, that all noncontributory military retirement benefits, whether state or federal, were immune from community treatment upon divorce. The jury could well have found defendant's refusal to educate himself to the applicable principles of law constituted negligence which prevented him from exercising informed discretion with regard to his client's rights.

As the jury was correctly instructed, an attorney does not ordinarily guarantee the soundness of his opinions and, accordingly, is not liable for every mistake he may make in his practice. He is expected, however, to possess knowledge of those plain and elementary principles of law which are commonly known by well informed attorneys, and to discover those additional rules of law which, although not commonly known, may readily be found by standard research techniques. . . . If the law on a particular subject is doubtful or debatable, an attorney will not be held responsible for failing to anticipate the manner in which the uncertainty will be resolved. . . . But even with respect to an unsettled area of the law, we believe an attorney assumes an obligation to his client to undertake reasonable research in an effort to ascertain relevant legal principles and to make an informed decision as to a course of conduct based upon an intelligent assessment of the problem. In the instant case, ample evidence was introduced to support a jury finding that defendant failed to perform such adequate research into the question of the community character of retirement benefits and thus was unable to exercise the informed judgment to which his client was entitled. (See fn. 7, ante.)

We recognize, of course, that an attorney engaging in litigation may have occasion to choose among various alternative strategies available to his client, one of which may be to refrain from pressing a debatable point because potential benefit may not equal detriment in terms of expenditure at time and resources or because of calculated tactics to the advantage of

---

7. At trial defendant testified that prior to the division of property in the divorce action, he had assumed the retirement benefits were not subject to community treatment, despite the fact General Smith had already begun to receive payments from the state; that he did not at that time undertake any research on the point nor did he discuss the matter with plaintiff; that subsequent to the divorce plaintiff asked defendant to research the question whereupon defendant discovered the *French* case which contained dictum in support of plaintiff's position; that the *French* decision caused him to change his opinion and conclude "that the Supreme Court, when it was confronted with this [the language in *French*] may hold that it [vested military retirement pay] is community property." . . .

his client. But, as the Ninth Circuit put it somewhat brutally in Pineda v. Craven (9th Cir.1970) 424 F.2d 369, 372: "There is nothing strategic or tactical about ignorance. . . ." In the case before us it is difficult to conceive of tactical advantage which could have been served by neglecting to advance a claim so clearly in plaintiff's best interest, nor does defendant suggest any. The decision to forego litigation on the issue of plaintiff's community property right to a share of General Smith's retirement benefits was apparently the product of a culpable misconception of the relevant principles of law, and the jury could have so found.

Furthermore, no lawyer would suggest the property characterization of General Smith's retirement benefits to be so esoteric an issue that defendant could not reasonably have been expected to be aware of it or its probable resolution. (Lucas v. Hamm (1961) supra, 56 Cal.2d 583, 15 Cal.Rptr. 821, 364 P.2d 685.) In *Lucas* we held that the rule against perpetuities poses such complex and difficult problems for the draftsman that even careful and competent attorneys occasionally fall prey to its traps. The situation before us is not analogous. Certainly one of the central issues in any divorce proceeding is the extent and division of the community property. In this case the question reached monumental proportions, since General Smith's retirement benefits constituted the only significant asset available to the community.[8] In undertaking professional representation of plaintiff, defendant assumed the duty to familiarize himself with the law defining the character of retirement benefits; instead, he rendered erroneous advice contrary to the best interests of his client without the guidance through research of readily available authority.

. . .

. . . Even as to doubtful matters, an attorney is expected to perform sufficient research to enable him to make an informed and intelligent judgment on behalf of his client.[9]

[The court rejected defendant's further argument that the $100,000 verdict was excessive. Plaintiff's expert had testified that the combined value of the two pensions was $322,032.]

The judgment is affirmed.

---

8. It is undisputed that the only assets the parties had to show as community property after 24 years of marriage, aside from General Smith's retirement benefits, were an equity of $1,800 in a house, some furniture, shares of stock worth $2,300, and two automobiles on which money was owing.

9. The principal thrust of the dissent is its conclusion that "even assuming that defendant was negligent in failing to research the pension questions, the record does not furnish a balance of probabilities that his negligence—rather than the uncertain status of the law and the availability of uncontested alimony—caused plaintiff to lose a $100,000 pension award." Whether defendant's negligence was a cause in fact of plaintiff's damage—an element of proximate cause—is a factual question for the jury to resolve. . . . Here the jury was correctly instructed that plaintiff had the burden of proving, inter alia, that defendant's negligence was a proximate cause of the damage suffered, and proximate cause was defined as "a cause which, natural and continuous sequence, produces the damage, and without which the damage would not have occurred." . . .

■ CLARK, JUSTICE (dissenting).

[The dissent argued at length that the law confronting the defendant in 1967 was not nearly as clear as the majority contended; that the legal complexity of military pensions as community property fell within the protection afforded by the *Lucas* case; and that, as a tactical matter, the defendant better served his client by securing alimony than by litigating the community property point. The dissent concluded:]

Given the uncertain status of the law, the circumstances of the parties, and the close relationship between property division and alimony payment, an ethical, diligent and careful lawyer would have avoided litigation over pension rights and instead would have sought a compensating alimony award for any inequity.... So far as appears, defendant secured such compensating award.

Accordingly, even assuming that defendant was negligent in failing to research the pension questions, the record does not furnish a balance of probabilities that his negligence—rather than the uncertain status of the law and the availability of uncontested alimony—caused plaintiff to lose a $100,000 pension award.

Causation of Harm

The dissent in Smith v. Lewis rests primarily on a causation argument: Was the harm caused by the failure of lawyer Lewis to conduct research or by the uncertainty of state and federal law dealing with community property interests in retirement pensions? Note that the majority treats this causation question as a question of fact for the jury (see the court's footnote 9), while the dissent would have resolved it as a matter of law. Does the decision require a lawyer to communicate legal uncertainty to her client so that the client can make decisions accordingly?[37]

Causation issues in malpractice cases are frequent and often difficult. If a lawyer's breach of duty to a client occurs in the handling of litigation and the harm suffered is the loss of a recoverable claim, the client will usually be required to prove that the underlying case would have succeeded if it had been properly brought or litigated. A failure, for example, to file a client's medical malpractice case before the limitations period expired requires proof by the client that a recovery of a specified amount would have been obtained but for the failure. This trial of a "case within a case" puts the lawyer charged with legal malpractice in the awkward position of

37. In Procanik v. Cillo, 543 A.2d 985 (N.J.Super.1988), a New Jersey lawyer declined to undertake a woman's claim that her attending physician had failed to inform her that the fetus had a birth defect in time for her to obtain an abortion. At the time New Jersey tort law was unclear as to whether a cause of action for "wrong-ful life" would be recognized. The court held that a legal malpractice claim was not stated against the lawyer because he failed to state the law's uncertainty in his letter declining to take the case; his failure to inform the client that New Jersey law was in the process of change was not malpractice.

defending the physician charged with medical malpractice (the opposing party in the case in which the lawyer's negligence occurred).

Suppose a lawyer fails to communicate a settlement offer to his client, believing that a larger recovery will be obtained at trial. The trial is lost. Does the client have a malpractice claim against the lawyer? What are the damages?

Suppose a lawyer is negligent in a number of respects in handling the defense of a client accused of crime. The client is convicted and later brings a malpractice action against her lawyer. Should the client, in order to establish that the conviction resulted from the lawyer's negligence, have to prove that he was innocent of the crime charged?[38] Or only that he would have been acquitted?[39]

Standard of Care

As set forth in *Smith,* the duty to conduct a reasonable investigation of applicable law holds lawyers to a higher standard than suggested by *Lucas.* What is left of *Lucas* after *Smith?*[40] *Smith* has been cited and followed in other states; *Lucas,* insofar as it creates a lower standard of care for perpetuities matters, is not followed outside California.

What is a lawyer's duty when the law is unsettled, as it was in California and elsewhere concerning the treatment of a spouse's retirement interest in a federal pension? Some cases give a lawyer large latitude when law is uncertain (sometimes referred to as "judgmental immunity"), but others follow *Smith* is requiring the lawyer to advice the client that the issue is unsettled.[41]

Should attorney Lewis have been disciplined in California? Would he be? Would the result have been different if Lewis had taken the case as a favor at no fee or a minimal fee? If his client had agreed in advance to a limited representation?

38. See, e.g., Carmel v. Lunney, 511 N.E.2d 1126 (N.Y.1987) (failure to allege innocence of the underlying offense defeats a malpractice claim against the defense lawyer as a matter of law).

39. See, e.g., Hines v. Davidson, 489 So.2d 572 (Ala.1986).

40. Wright v. Williams, 121 Cal.Rptr. 194, 199 n. 2 (1975), expressed doubts whether *Lucas v. Hamm* was still good law in California. But see Aloy v. Mash, 696 P.2d 656 (Cal.1985) (employing the reasonable investigation standard of *Smith* and repeating in dicta the distinction between less difficult areas of law and the rule against perpetuities).]; and Meighan v. Shore, 34 Cal. App.4th 1025, 1035 (1995) (dictum that lawyer is not culpable for "running afoul of the hypertechnical rules against perpetuities and restraints on alienation").

41. *Compare* Crosby v. Jones, 705 So.2d 1356 (Fla.1998) (lawyer need not advise client concerning "a fairly debateable point of law"), *with* Wood v. McGrath, North, Mullin & Kratz, 589 N.W.2d 103 (Neb. 1999) (lawyer's failure to advise client on unsettled law relating to status of marital property was guilty of malpractice). See also, Jordache Enterprises Inc. v. Brobeck, Phleger & Harrison, 958 P.2d 1062 (Cal. 1998) (failure to advise a client about insurance coverage may constitute malpractice).

Duty When Negotiating a Settlement

May a lawyer be liable to a client who has agreed to a settlement negotiated and proposed by the lawyer? Some courts view settlements as a black box that should be protected by finality in the absence of fraud, duress or coercion. But twelve jurisdictions have now held that allegations by the former client that the lawyer provided incomplete and inaccurate information, relied on by the client, concerning the value of the claims (or other failures of communication) are enough to get the case to a jury.[42]

Professional Custom Sets the Standard

Professional malpractice differs from ordinary negligence in that the standard of care is determined by the skill, knowledge, prudence and diligence brought to bear on similar matters by a lawyer of ordinary competence. In ordinary negligence cases, evidence of the custom of a trade or industry is relevant and admissible either to show departure from or compliance with customary care, but custom is not dispositive. As Judge Learned Hand wrote:

> [I]n most cases reasonable prudence is in fact common prudence; but strictly it is never its measure; a whole calling may have unduly lagged in the adoption of new and available devices. It never may set its own tests, however persuasive be its usages. Courts must in the end say what is required; there are precautions so imperative that even their universal disregard will not excuse their omission.[43]

With respect to professions, standards of practice (customary care) are given greater, usually exclusive, deference. The legal standard is stated in terms of the care provided by the ordinary practitioner, and expert testimony of practice standards is ordinarily required as part of the plaintiff's prima facie case.[44] Yet a scattering of decisions have relied on Hand's dictum in holding that what expert witnesses stated as the general practice of physicians was negligent.[45] In Gleason v. Title Guarantee Co.,[46] a lawyer, instead of checking titles, relied on telephone conversations with the title

---

42. *Compare* Muhammad v. Strassburger, McKenna, Messer, Shilobod & Gutnick, 587 A.2d 1346 (Pa.1991) (dissatisfied litigant who accepted a settlement may not recover from his attorney in absence of fraud), *with* Ziegelheim v. Apollo, 607 A.2d 1298 (N.J.1992) (lawyer's duty of care includes giving reasonable advice about the prospects and value of a claim). See Steve France, Giving Up the Fight, ABA J., Feb. 1999, at 28 (reporting that a dozen states follow *Ziegelheim.*

43. The T.J. Hooper, 60 F.2d 737, 740 (2d Cir.1932). In *The T.J. Hooper* the court found the defendant negligent for not having a working radio set aboard its tug boat. It is interesting to note that, contrary to

what Hand's language suggests, most tugs did have radios at the time. See The T.J. Hooper, 53 F.2d 107, 111 (S.D.N.Y.1931).

44. For discussion of the standard of care in legal malpractice, see Wolfram, Modern Legal Ethics § 5.6 (1986).

45. The leading case is Helling v. Carey, 519 P.2d 981 (Wash.1974) (failure of ophthalmologist routinely to administer glaucoma test to patient under 40 years of age). See also Truhitte v. French Hospital, 180 Cal.Rptr. 152 (1982) (surgical practice of delegating to a nurse the job of keeping track of the sponges during an operation found to be negligent).

46. 300 F.2d 813 (5th Cir.1962).

company, which was the customary practice of lawyers in that area of Florida. The court, citing *The T.J. Hooper*, said that custom provides no defense if the custom is itself negligent. Following this logic, even if most lawyers misunderstand the rule against perpetuities, should it be negligent for a lawyer to draft a will with future interest provisions if she does not understand the rule?

Expert Testimony

The plaintiff in a malpractice action generally must produce expert testimony to establish both the level of care owed by the attorney under the circumstances and the failure to conform to that level of care.[47] In Waldman v. Levine,[48] for example, the lawyers, without consulting a medical expert in obstetrical matters, advised the client to settle a medical malpractice claim for little more than $2,000; the client's claim was that her daughter's death after childbirth was due to obstetric malpractice. The expert in the malpractice case against the lawyers testified that failing to consult an obstetrical expert in such a case was "conduct ... below the minimum standard of care for attorneys in medical malpractice cases."[49] The court affirmed the jury's verdict against the lawyers and the award of $600,000 in damages.

Expert testimony is generally unnecessary "when the attorney's lack of care and skill is so obvious that the trier of fact can find negligence as a matter of common knowledge."[50] In Wagenmann v. Adams,[51] the lawyer, representing a client who had been arrested for disturbing the peace, told the client that his only alternatives were to leave town immediately or commit himself to a mental hospital; the lawyer took no action to secure the client's release when the client was involuntarily committed. On those facts, the court held expert testimony unnecessary to establish that the lawyer committed malpractice. Examples of other cases where courts held expert testimony to be unnecessary include: failure to take any action with regard to estate matters;[52] failure to obey client's instructions;[53] and failure to sue before expiration of limitations period.[54]

Not long ago it was extremely difficult to get one lawyer to testify against another in a malpractice action. Today, it is much easier although difficulty persists in some areas, especially in communities with relatively

---

47. See Wagenmann v. Adams, 829 F.2d 196, 218 (1st Cir.1987); Progressive Sales v. Williams, Willeford, Boger, Grady & Davis, 356 S.E.2d 372 (N.C.App.1987).

48. 544 A.2d 683 (D.C.App.1988).

49. 544 A.2d at 687.

50. O'Neil v. Bergan, 452 A.2d 337, 341 (D.C.App.1982).

51. 829 F.2d 196, 220 (1st Cir.1987) (affirming a judgment against the lawyer of $50,000).

52. Sorenson v. Fio Rito, 413 N.E.2d 47, 53 (Ill.App.1980).

53. Olfe v. Gordon, 286 N.W.2d 573, 578 (Wis.1980) (expert testimony not required when lawyer violated instructions of client that property transaction not be encumbered by a security interest superior to client's).

54. George v. Caton, 600 P.2d 822, 829 (N.M.App.1979).

few lawyers. In Patterson v. Atlanta Bar Ass'n,[55] the plaintiffs claimed, inter alia, that individual members of the bar and various bar associations were engaged in a conspiracy to prevent lawyers from testifying as expert witnesses in malpractice cases. The court found that the plaintiffs had presented no evidence of conspiracy. Nevertheless, the filing of such a suit lends some support to the proposition that finding a lawyer to testify against another lawyer remains problematic.

National or Local Standard

Should the performance of the lawyer charged with malpractice be compared with that of the profession at large, only with that of lawyers practicing in the same jurisdiction,[56] or, most narrowly, only with that of lawyers practicing in the same or a similar locality? A national standard forces the upgrading of local performance and makes it easier for a plaintiff to obtain expert witnesses. On the other hand, the predicament of lawyers who practice more informally (and more cheaply) in small communities should not be entirely ignored.[57]

A related issue concerns whether a lawyer venturing into a field replete with specialists is or should be judged by the standards of specialized practice. For example, if a general practitioner undertakes a trademark search, will she be liable for professional negligence under the standards of trademark specialists?[58] Should the lawyer be liable for accepting the representation? Should liability depend on what the lawyer communicates to the client concerning experience and ability and what the client agrees to?[59]

In Horne v. Peckham,[60] the lawyer, after consulting "the client's accountant ..., a two volume set of American Jurisprudence" and a tax "expert" who, unknown to the lawyer, had been admitted to the bar only one year earlier, drew up a trust to shelter the client's money from federal taxes. Not surprisingly, the lawyer botched it, and the trust failed to accomplish its purpose. The lawyer testified that he told the client he had "no expertise in tax matters." The court affirmed the jury verdict against the lawyer for malpractice and approved a jury instruction that it "is the duty of an attorney who is a general practitioner to refer his client to a specialist or recommend the assistance of a specialist if under the circumstances a reasonably careful and skillful practitioner would do so."[61] If the

55. 373 S.E.2d 514 (Ga.1988).

56. Kellos v. Sawilowsky, 322 S.E.2d 897 (Ga.App.1984), held that the standard to be applied was that of lawyers practicing in the state of Georgia but noted that in practice it would make little difference whether one applied a national or local standard.

57. See Wolfram, Modern Legal Ethics 213 (1986).

58. See, e.g., Mayo v. Engel, 733 F.2d 807 (11th Cir.1984) (lawyer held not liable for professional negligence in a trademark

search where the firm never held itself out to be expert in trademark work).

59. See, e.g., Walker v. Bangs, 601 P.2d 1279 (Wash.1979) (if a lawyer holds himself out as specializing in a particular field, he "will be held to the standard of performance of those who hold themselves out as specialists in the area").

60. 158 Cal.Rptr. 714 (1979).

61. 158 Cal.Rptr. at 720.

lawyer fails to consult an expert, the courts will hold the lawyer to the standard of a specialist in the field.

3.   OTHER ISSUES

Violation of Ethical Rules as a Basis for Malpractice

Generally, courts treat the violation of a relevant statute or regulation setting a standard of performance as negligence per se in tort cases based on negligence. Should violation of an ethics rule imposed on lawyers be similarly treated when the violation causes a client harm?[62]

The Preliminary Statement to the Model Code of Professional Responsibility states that the Code "does not undertake to define standards for civil liability of lawyers for professional conduct." The Scope Section of the Model Rules states: "Violation of a Rule should not give rise to a cause of action nor should it create any presumption that a legal duty has been breached." Why not? Does this mean that reasonably careful lawyers breach the Rules on occasion? Should the ABA's attempt to confine the Rules to professional discipline be viewed as special pleading or wishful thinking?

The profession's effort to prevent plaintiffs from predicating civil liability on a violation of ethics rules has been only partially successful.[63] Courts generally state that the violation of an ethics rule does not create a civil cause of action or constitute negligence per se.[64] On the other hand, most courts view ethics rules as relevant and admissible evidence and occasionally as creating a rebuttable presumption of negligence.[65] Expert witnesses in malpractice actions rely on the ethics rules and courts cite them in malpractice decisions.[66]

---

62.   See David Luban, Ethics and Malpractice, 12 Miss.Coll.L.Rev. 151 (1991) (arguing that ethical codes should be used as standards for civil liability whenever the alleged misconduct would warrant professional discipline); Charles W. Wolfram, The Code of Professional Responsibility as a Measure of Attorney Liability in Civil Litigation, 30 S.C.L. Rev. 281 (1979) (ethical code "should serve as a measure both of professional discipline and of civil liability sanctions"); and Robert Dalhquist, The Code of Professional Responsibility, 9 Ohio. No.U.L.Rev. 1 (1982) (responding to Wolfram).

63.   For a review of the decisions and conflicting arguments, see Note, The Evidentiary use of the Ethics Codes in Legal Malpractice: Erasing a Double Standard, 109 Harv.L.Rev. 1102 (1996).

64.   Miami International Realty Co. v. Paynter, 841 F.2d 348, 352 (10th Cir.1988)

("Colorado courts have not decided how its Code of Professional Responsibility is to be treated as an element of proof in a malpractice case" although it appears clear that under Colorado case law the Code does not create a private cause of action).

65.   See Lipton v. Boesky, 313 N.W.2d 163, 166–67 (Mich.App.1981): "The Code of Professional Responsibility is a standard of practice for attorneys which expresses in general terms the standards of professional conduct expected of lawyers in their relationships with the public, the legal system and the profession. Holding a specific client unable to rely on the same standards in his professional relations with his own attorney would be patently unfair. We hold that, as with statutes, a violation of the Code is rebuttable evidence of malpractice."

66.   See Charles W. Wolfram, The Code of Professional Responsibility as a Measure of Attorney Liability in Civil Litigation, 30

Limiting Malpractice Liability by Agreement

Model Rule 1.8(h) provides that a lawyer may prospectively limit her malpractice liability to the client, but only if permitted under applicable state law and the client is independently represented on the limitation.[67] Further, M.R. 1.8(h) prohibits a lawyer from settling a malpractice claim with a client or former client who is not represented by independent counsel unless the lawyer first advises the client in writing that independent representation would be appropriate. There is no similar provision in the Code.

An agreement settling a client's malpractice claim will be enforceable and the lawyer not subject to discipline only if made in full conformity with M.R. 1.8(h). In addition to full disclosure of the facts constituting malpractice, the lawyer must encourage the client in writing to seek independent counsel and leave the client a reasonable period of time to consider the matter and consult counsel prior to negotiation or release of malpractice liability.[68]

In In re Tallon,[69] the court disciplined a lawyer for having his client sign a general release of all malpractice claims against him without first notifying the client of the nature of her potential claims, withdrawing from the representation and advising her of her right to retain independent representation in the matter.[70] Does *Tallon* mean that it is malpractice for a lawyer not to inform a client of the lawyer's prior malpractice in handling the client's matter?

Malpractice Insurance

Steady increases in the costs of malpractice awards and the defense of malpractice claims have caused a steep rise in malpractice insurance premiums charged U.S. law firms.[71] The average annual cost of legal malpractice insurance rose 63% from 1986–1994 to an average of $4,601

S.C.L.Rev. 281 (1979); and Wolfram, Modern Legal Ethics § 2.6.1 (1986). Washington bans specific mention of the ethics rules in expert testimony or jury instructions, although the rules may provide the substantive content of both expert testimony and jury instructions. Hizey v. Carpenter, 830 P.2d 646 (Wash.1992) (expert opinion may be based on a lawyer's failure to conform to an ethics rule but testimony must address the breach of legal duty and not a supposed breach of the ethics rules).

67. DR 6–102 of the Model Code contains a broader provision prohibiting a lawyer from contracting with the client to limit the lawyer's malpractice liability.

68. See Joanne Pitulla, Please Release Me, ABA J., Aug.1996, at 92 (discussing D.C. Op. 260 (1996)).

69. 86 A.D.2d 897, 447 N.Y.S.2d 50 (1982).

70. See also In re Weiblen, 439 N.W.2d 7 (Minn.1989) (lawyer attempted to obtain complete release from liability for any malpractice); Committee on Legal Ethics v. Hazlett, 179 W.Va. 303, 367 S.E.2d 772 (1988) (request for malpractice release as a condition of turning over client's files). Generally see Leonard E. Gross, Contractual Limitations on Attorney Malpractice Liability: An Economic Approach, 75 Kentucky L.J. 793 (1986–87).

71. See Manuel Ramos, Legal Malpractice: Reforming Lawyers and Law Professors, 70 Tulane L. Rev. 2583, 2629 (1996).

per lawyer. Large law firms were affected even more as dozens of them were hit by awards ranging from $10 million to over $50 million. ALAS, the insurer of 375 large law firms, increased its premiums a total of 72 percent from 1991 to 1993. Some commentators blamed the increase on the spate of savings-and-loan awards. By 1998, the number of malpractice awards leveled off and the percentage of successful suits declined, but average awards continued to increase in amount.[72]

Should lawyers be required to carry malpractice insurance as a condition of practice?[73] Oregon, which requires all Oregon-based lawyers to purchase primary malpractice insurance from the state bar, is the only state requiring lawyers to have insurance.[74]

Malpractice insurance comes in two major forms: (1) *Occurrence insurance* covers the lawyer for acts or omissions during the policy term, regardless of when the claim is asserted; and (2) *claims made insurance* covers only claims made during the policy term, regardless of when the act or omission took place. Because occurrence coverage is more expensive, claims made coverage is more common. But cheaper may not be better: If a lawyer retires or becomes a judge and a claims made policy expires, no coverage exists for a later claim involving acts or omissions that occurred during the policy year.

Policies for legal malpractice insurance typically exclude from coverage: (1) claims arising out of criminal acts of the lawyer; (2) claims arising out of "any dishonest, fraudulent or malicious act, error or omission" of the lawyer; and (3) "punitive or exemplary damages, fines, sanctions or penalties." In Perl v. St. Paul Fire & Marine Insurance Co.,[75] the lawyers had failed to disclose to the client that the insurance adjuster with whom the firm negotiated on the client's behalf worked for the law firm as an investigator. The court awarded the client as damages a full refund of the fees she had paid the lawyers. The lawyer's insurance company refused to pay, claiming that the policy's terms excluded such damages and that, if the damages were not excluded, the policy was void as against public policy. The court held that the policy did cover the damages: (1) The exclusion for fraudulent acts did not exclude breach of a fiduciary duty, which is "constructive" not "actual" fraud; and (2) reimbursement of attorney's fees was not the equivalent of "exemplary or punitive damages," which the policy excluded from coverage. However, the court held that a policy that insures lawyers against loss of attorney's fees upon breach of their fiduciary duties is void as against public policy. Despite the latter holding, the

---

72. See, e.g., Gail Cox, Malpractice Epidemic Is Receding, Nat'l L.J., Mar. 16, 1998, p. A1; and John Gibeaut, Good News, Bad News on Malpractice, ABA Journal 100 (Mar. 1997).

73. See Theodore J. Schneyer, Mandatory Malpractice Insurance for Lawyers in Wisconsin and Elsewhere, 1979 Wis.L.Rev. 1019 (a study on the need for mandatory insurance); and Wolfram, Modern Legal Ethics § 5.6.8 (1986) (arguing that mandatory insurance may not be efficient).

74. See Or.Rev.Stat. § 9.080; and Hass v. Oregon State Bar, 883 F.2d 1453 (9th Cir. 1989) (upholding the insurance requirement against antitrust and Commerce Clause challenges).

75. 345 N.W.2d 209 (Minn.1984).

court's final decision stated that the policy was not void to the extent that it insured the firm as opposed to the individual lawyer who committed the breach. Which of the court's conflicting messages is the right one?

Vicarious Liability of Partners

The enormous settlement awards in a number of recent cases have given rise to concerns that large verdicts or settlements will bankrupt every partner in a firm.[76] Spurred by this threat, virtually every state bar association, allied with accountants' groups and those of other professionals, urged state legislatures and high courts to enact statutes, court rules or both to eliminate the vicarious liability of law firm partners for the negligent acts of another firm lawyer. In response, most jurisdictions have enacted so-called "LLP statutes" providing for limited liability partnerships.[77]

Under these statutes, in general, a prevailing malpractice plaintiff may satisfy an award out of the assets of the partnership, including its liability insurance coverage. In addition, the personal assets of two groups of firm lawyers remain at risk of personal liability: (1) any firm lawyer whose negligent acts gave rise to the liability, and (2) partners with supervisory responsibility on the matter. But the statutes and/or court rules immunize from liability the partners who did not participate in or supervise the negligent conduct. In a smaller number of states, existing professional corporation laws are being amended or interpreted to much the same effect.

Those opposing the enactments or interpretations argued unsuccessfully that the traditional practice of partners being liable for the wrongful acts of their partners and associates provides a desirable incentive for quality control.[78] In addition to this prevention and deterrence argument, firm assets are often insufficient to satisfy a judgment: partnership assets are very limited in many law firms, which have little working capital and substantial debt financing. Moreover, many law firms have only limited malpractice insurance coverage and some are totally uninsured; LLP statutes may be a further incentive not to carry malpractice insurance. These arguments failed to defeat the enactment of LLP statutes, but were

76. See, e.g., the *Jones, Day* case (settlement awards of $24 million to bondholders and $51 million to the RTC, see p. 745 infra) and *Kaye, Scholer* case ($41 million to OTS, see p. 756 infra). See also Thom Weidlich, Limiting Lawyers' Liability, Nat'l L.J., Feb.7, 1994, at 1, 38.

77. See Susan Saab Fortney, Seeking Shelter in the Minefield of Unintended Consequences: The Traps of Limited Liability Law Firms, 54 Wash. & Lee L. Rev. 717 (1997).

78. See Walter W. Steele, Jr., How Lawyers Protect the Family Jewels ... The Invention of Limited Liability Partnerships, 39 S.Tex.L.Rev. 621, 627–28 (1998): "[A] concept that allows partners to share the economic and professional benefits without sharing liability in order to save partners' economic hides is more than a contradiction—it is a hypocrisy. The words of one of America's first scholars of partnership law seem as profound as when they were published in 1889: 'The liability for each other is the ground-work of partnership. Take away the solidarity, and no partnership exists.... Isn't that the office of a partner? To bear the sins of his co-partner, rather than visit them upon innocent strangers?' "

influential in leading a number of states to narrow the immunity and to require LLPs to obtain specified amounts of malpractice insurance coverage.[79] In fighting for the abolition of vicarious liability for law firm members, did the organized bar put pocket-book interests ahead of the interests of those harmed by negligent conduct and the public interest in law firms being legally accountable for their actions?

Role of Malpractice Insurers in Loss Prevention

As to preventive measures, malpractice insurers have the incentive and are well positioned to play an important role.[80] Here is a summary of George Cohen's views: Loss prevention activity by legal malpractice insurers has increased in recent years. Although one might dismiss this activity as mere window-dressing and cheap advertising by insurers, some recent evidence suggests that such loss prevention efforts do have an impact. But why would legal malpractice insurers offer loss prevention services? And why would lawyers be interested in such services? After all, many insurers do not provide any significant loss prevention services, even in closely related areas such as medical malpractice. In fact, we have gotten accustomed to thinking of insurance as *reducing* incentives for preventive behavior—the so-called "moral hazard" problem—rather than improving those incentives. Moreover, it seems strange that lawyers would look to insurers rather than other lawyers to provide them with information on how to avoid legal liability. We would be surprised, for example, if manufacturers of fire safety equipment sought loss prevention services from their fire insurer.

It is easy to understand why lawyers would want to spend more on loss prevention services: the risk of malpractice liability—both the likelihood and the severity—has significantly increased. And if legal malpractice insurers can offer loss prevention services more cheaply and effectively than other institutions, they can in fact reduce moral hazard rather than increase it. But what advantage might legal malpractice insurers have over lawyers in providing loss prevention services? First, they may have superior information about loss prevention owing to: economies of scale in collecting data on customary and cost-effective practices, rapid changes in the nature of legal malpractice liability, the types of precautions that are effective against malpractice, or cognitive dissonance by insured lawyers. Second, law firms may be less able or willing to police misconduct by their own members, given the growth of firms and increased specialization, which make monitoring fellow lawyers difficult, increased competition, which makes it harder for lawyers to resist client demands, and the rise of limited liability entities, which somewhat dampen the incentives of lawyers in firms to monitor each other. Insurers, particularly mutual insurers such as ALAS, may have the bargaining leverage to enforce loss prevention against

79. See, e.g., Wisconsin Supreme Court Rule 20:5.7.

80. See George M. Cohen, Legal Malpractice Insurance and Loss Prevention: A Comparative Analysis of Economic Institutions, 4 Conn.Ins.L.J. 305 (1997).

overly aggressive lawyers that large law firms lack. Whether the advantages currently enjoyed by legal malpractice insurers will increase or recede over time is difficult to predict.

C. EFFECTIVE ASSISTANCE OF COUNSEL UNDER THE SIXTH AMENDMENT

INTRODUCTORY NOTE

The Sixth Amendment to the United States Constitution provides that "[i]n all criminal prosecutions, the accused shall enjoy the right . . . to have the Assistance of Counsel for his defense." This provision was a clear departure from 18th century English criminal law, which did not permit a felony defendant to be represented by counsel. Until 1932, however, the Sixth Amendment provided a right to be represented only if the defendant could afford a retained lawyer or the court chose to appoint one. In Powell v. Alabama[1] the Supreme Court required Alabama to appoint counsel for the Scottsboro Boys, who had been sentenced to death in a highly controversial interracial rape case. This holding evolved first into a constitutional requirement that state courts appoint counsel if fundamental unfairness would otherwise result.[2] In 1963 Gideon v. Wainright[3] extended the right to appointed counsel to every felony case in which the defendant could not afford representation. The current rule is that counsel must be appointed in every criminal case, including misdemeanors, in which a prison sentence is imposed,[4] unless the defendant exercises the right of self-representation.[5]

A complicated body of law deals with the stage at which an individual under investigation becomes an "accused" in a "criminal prosecution" who has a right to appointed counsel. In demarcating the critical stages of a criminal prosecution at which there is a right to appointed counsel, the Court has sought to avoid impairing the investigatory activity essential for effective law enforcement. Thus, a defendant has a right to appointed counsel at a preliminary hearing at which probable cause to proceed is determined,[6] at a post-arrest lineup,[7] at trial and sentencing, and through a

1. 287 U.S. 45, 60 (1932) (failure to appoint defense counsel for the Scottsboro Boys, who were charged and convicted of raping a white woman, was fundamentally unfair and a violation of due process). See Dan T. Carter, Scottsboro: A Tragedy of the American South (1979).

2. Betts v. Brady, 316 U.S. 455, 466 (1942). Johnson v. Zerbst, 304 U.S. 458 (1938), required the appointment of defense counsel in federal felony trials. Many states gradually adopted the same position.

3. 372 U.S. 335 (1963). See Anthony Lewis, Gideon's Trumpet (1964) for a detailed history of the case.

4. Scott v. Illinois, 440 U.S. 367 (1979) (appointed counsel not required in a misdemeanor case in which imprisonment might have been, but was not, imposed). See Lawrence Herman and Charles A. Thompson, Scott v. Illinois and the Right to Counsel: A Decision in Search of a Doctrine?, 17 Am. Crim.L.Rev. 71 (1979–80).

5. Faretta v. California, 422 U.S. 806 (1975).

6. Coleman v. Alabama, 399 U.S. 1 (1970).

first appeal;[8] but the right does not extend to discretionary appeals, habeas corpus proceedings, or other post-conviction remedies.[9] Some showing of indigency must be made for a defendant to qualify for appointed counsel. Some jurisdictions use a court-appointment system in which the court appoints a defense lawyer from a roster of eligible lawyers. Others employ a public defender system.

When a Sixth Amendment right to counsel attaches, what level of competence is required? In McMann v. Richardson,[10] the Court required that defense counsel's assistance fall "within the range of competence demanded of attorneys in criminal cases."[11] Older cases requiring a showing that defense counsel's failings constituted a "farce and mockery of justice" were gradually replaced by various tests turning on whether the lawyer's conduct was reasonable under the circumstances.[12] In the *Strickland* case, reproduced below, the Court addressed for the first time the specifics of ineffective assistance under the Sixth Amendment.[13]

1. INEFFECTIVE ASSISTANCE: THE CONSTITUTIONAL STANDARD

Strickland v. Washington

Supreme Court of the United States, 1984.
466 U.S. 668.

■ JUSTICE O'CONNOR delivered the opinion of the Court.

This case requires us to consider the proper standards for judging a criminal defendant's contention that the Constitution requires a conviction

---

7. United States v. Wade, 388 U.S. 218 (1967).

8. Evitts v. Lucey, 469 U.S. 387 (1985).

9. Pennsylvania v. Finley, 481 U.S. 551 (1987) (state post-conviction remedy); Ross v. Moffitt, 417 U.S. 600 (1974) (discretionary further appeal); Williams v. Missouri, 640 F.2d 140, 144 (8th Cir.1981) (federal habeas corpus); United States v. Degand, 614 F.2d 176, 179 (8th Cir.1980) (federal post-conviction attack). But see Anti–Drug Abuse Act of 1988, Pub.L. 100–690, 102 Stat. 4181 (providing for appointed counsel in federal habeas corpus actions involving challenges to the death penalty); many states have similar laws for death penalty challenges, but not all. See Murray v. Giarratano, 492 U.S. 1 (1989) (describing and upholding as constitutional Virginia's system in which death row inmates seeking habeas review are provided law books not lawyers).

10. 397 U.S. 759 (1970) (defendant who had pleaded guilty after giving an allegedly coerced confession could not attack his conviction unless his lawyer's advice concerning the confession constituted ineffective assistance of counsel).

11. 397 U.S. at 770–71.

12. See Trapnell v. United States, 725 F.2d 149, 151–155 (2d Cir.1983) (abandoning the "farce and mockery" rule and summarizing the developments in other federal circuits). For an example of a pre-*Strickland* effort to develop objective standards, see Judge David Bazelon's article, The Realities of *Gideon* and *Argersinger*, 64 Geo.L.J. 811, 837–838 (1976).

13. See Vivian O. Berger, The Supreme Court and Defense Counsel: Old Roads, New Paths—A Dead End?, 86 Colum.L.Rev. 9 (1986), for a thoughtful and thorough review of the Supreme Court cases on ineffective assistance of counsel.

or death sentence to be set aside because counsel's assistance at the trial or sentencing was ineffective.

I

A

During a 10–day period in September 1976, respondent [David Washington] planned and committed three groups of crimes, which included three brutal stabbing murders, torture, kidnaping, severe assaults, attempted murders, attempted extortion, and theft. After his two accomplices were arrested, respondent surrendered to police and voluntarily gave a lengthy statement confessing to the third of the criminal episodes. The State of Florida indicted respondent for kidnaping and murder and appointed an experienced criminal lawyer [William R. Tunkey of Miami] to represent him.

Counsel actively pursued pretrial motions and discovery. He cut his efforts short, however, and he experienced a sense of hopelessness about the case, when he learned that, against his specific advice, respondent had also confessed to the first two murders. By the date set for trial, respondent was subject to indictment for three counts of first-degree murder and multiple counts of robbery, kidnaping for ransom, breaking and entering and assault, attempted murder, and conspiracy to commit robbery. Respondent waived his right to a jury trial, again acting against counsel's advice, and pleaded guilty to all charges, including the three capital murder charges.

In the plea colloquy, respondent told the trial judge that, although he had committed a string of burglaries, he had no significant prior criminal record and that at the time of his criminal spree he was under extreme stress caused by his inability to support his family. . . . He also stated, however, that he accepted responsibility for the crimes. . . . The trial judge told respondent that he had "a great deal of respect for people who are willing to step forward and admit their responsibility" but that he was making no statement at all about his likely sentencing decision.

Counsel advised respondent to invoke his right under Florida law to an advisory jury at his capital sentencing hearing. Respondent rejected the advice and waived the right. He chose instead to be sentenced by the trial judge without a jury recommendation.

In preparing for the sentencing hearing, counsel spoke with respondent about his background. He also spoke on the telephone with respondent's wife and mother, though he did not follow up on the one unsuccessful effort to meet with them. He did not otherwise seek out character witnesses for respondent. . . . Nor did he request a psychiatric examination, since his conversations with his client gave no indication that respondent had psychological problems. . . .

Counsel decided not to present and hence not to look further for evidence concerning respondent's character and emotional state. That decision reflected trial counsel's sense of hopelessness about overcoming the evidentiary effect of respondent's confessions to the gruesome crimes. It also reflected the judgment that it was advisable to rely on the plea colloquy for evidence about respondent's background and about his claim of emotional stress: the plea colloquy communicated sufficient information about these subjects, and by forgoing the opportunity to present new evidence on these subjects, counsel prevented the State from cross-examining respondent on his claim and from putting on psychiatric evidence of its own....

Counsel also excluded from the sentencing hearing other evidence he thought was potentially damaging. He successfully moved to exclude respondent's "rap sheet." ... Because he judged that a presentence report might prove more detrimental than helpful, as it would have included respondent's criminal history and thereby would have undermined the claim of no significant history of criminal activity, he did not request that one be prepared....

At the sentencing hearing, counsel's strategy was based primarily on the trial judge's remarks at the plea colloquy as well as on his reputation as a sentencing judge who thought it important for a convicted defendant to own up to his crime. Counsel argued that respondent's remorse and acceptance of responsibility justified sparing him from the death penalty.... Counsel also argued that respondent had no history of criminal activity and that respondent committed the crimes under extreme mental or emotional disturbance, thus coming within the statutory list of mitigating circumstances. He further argued that respondent should be spared death because he had surrendered, confessed, and offered to testify against a codefendant and because respondent was fundamentally a good person who had briefly gone badly wrong in extremely stressful circumstances. The State put on evidence and witnesses largely for the purpose of describing the details of the crimes. Counsel did not cross-examine the medical experts who testified about the manner of death of respondent's victims.

The trial judge found several aggravating circumstances with respect to each of the three murders. He found that all three murders were especially heinous, atrocious, and cruel, all involving repeated stabbings. All three murders were committed in the course of at least one other dangerous and violent felony, and since all involved robbery, the murders were for pecuniary gain. All three murders were committed to avoid arrest for the accompanying crimes and to hinder law enforcement. In the course of one of the murders, respondent knowingly subjected numerous persons to a grave risk of death by deliberately stabbing and shooting the murder victim's sisters-in-law, who sustained severe—in one case, ultimately fatal—injuries.

With respect to mitigating circumstances, the trial judge made the same findings for all three capital murders. First, although there was no admitted evidence of prior convictions, respondent had stated that he had engaged in a course of stealing. In any case, even if respondent had no significant history of criminal activity, the aggravating circumstances "would still clearly far outweigh" that mitigating factor. Second, the judge found that, during all three crimes, respondent was not suffering from extreme mental or emotional disturbance and could appreciate the criminality of his acts. Third, none of the victims was a participant in, or consented to, respondent's conduct. Fourth, respondent's participation in the crimes was neither minor nor the result of duress or domination by an accomplice. Finally, respondent's age (26) could not be considered a factor in mitigation, especially when viewed in light of respondent's planning of the crimes and disposition of the proceeds of the various accompanying thefts.

In short, the trial judge found numerous aggravating circumstances and no (or a single comparatively insignificant) mitigating circumstance. With respect to each of the three convictions for capital murder, the trial judge concluded: "A careful consideration of all matters presented to the court impels the conclusion that there are insufficient mitigating circumstances ... to outweigh the aggravating circumstances." See Washington v. State, 362 So.2d 658, 663–664 (Fla.1978), (quoting trial court findings), cert. denied, 441 U.S. 937 (1979). He therefore sentenced respondent to death on each of the three counts of murder and to prison terms for the other crimes. The Florida Supreme Court upheld the convictions and sentences on direct appeal.

B

Respondent subsequently sought collateral relief in state court on numerous grounds, among them that counsel had rendered ineffective assistance at the sentencing proceeding. Respondent challenged counsel's assistance in six respects. He asserted that counsel was ineffective because he failed to move for a continuance to prepare for sentencing, to request a psychiatric report, to investigate and present character witnesses, to seek a presentence investigation report, to present meaningful arguments to the sentencing judge, and to investigate the medical examiner's reports or cross-examine the medical experts. In support of the claim, respondent submitted 14 affidavits from friends, neighbors, and relatives stating that they would have testified if asked to do so. He also submitted one psychiatric report and one psychological report stating that respondent, though not under the influence of extreme mental or emotional disturbance, was "chronically frustrated and depressed because of his economic dilemma" at the time of his crimes....

The trial court denied relief without an evidentiary hearing, finding that the record evidence conclusively showed that the ineffectiveness claim was meritless.... Four of the assertedly prejudicial errors required little discussion. [The trial court dealt with two of the asserted errors at greater length: the failure to investigate and present character witnesses. As to both of these grounds, the court concluded under] the standard for ineffectiveness claims articulated by the Florida Supreme Court in Knight v. State, 394 So.2d 997 (1981), that respondent had not shown that counsel's assistance reflected any substantial and serious deficiency measurably below that of competent counsel that was likely to have affected the outcome of the sentencing proceeding. The court specifically found: "[A]s a matter of law, the record affirmatively demonstrates beyond any doubt that even if [counsel] had done each of the ... things [that respondent alleged counsel had failed to do] at the time of sentencing, there is not even the remotest chance that the outcome would have been any different. The plain fact is that the aggravating circumstances proved in this case were completely *overwhelming* . . . ."

C

Respondent next filed a petition for a writ of habeas corpus in the United States District Court for the Southern District of Florida. . . .

... On the legal issue of ineffectiveness, the District Court concluded that, although trial counsel made errors in judgment in failing to investigate nonstatutory mitigating evidence further than he did, no prejudice to respondent's sentence resulted from any such error in judgment. . . .

On appeal, a panel of the United States Court of Appeals for the Fifth Circuit affirmed in part, vacated in part, and remanded with instructions to apply to the particular facts the framework for analyzing ineffectiveness claims that it developed in its opinion. . . . The panel decision was itself vacated when ... the Eleventh Circuit ... decided to rehear the case en banc. The full Court of Appeals developed its own framework for analyzing ineffective assistance claims and reversed the judgment of the District Court and remanded the case for new factfinding under the newly announced standards.

. . .

Turning to the merits, the Court of Appeals stated that the Sixth Amendment right to assistance of counsel accorded criminal defendants a right to "counsel reasonably likely to render and rendering reasonably effective assistance given the totality of the circumstances." The court remarked in passing that no special standard applies in capital cases such as the one before it: the punishment that a defendant faces is merely one of the circumstances to be considered in determining whether counsel was reasonably effective. . . .

[W]e granted certiorari to consider the standards by which to judge a contention that the Constitution requires that a criminal judgment be overturned because of the actual ineffective assistance of counsel.

II

In a long line of cases ... this Court has recognized that the Sixth Amendment right to counsel exists, and is needed, in order to protect the fundamental right to a fair trial. . . .

For that reason, the Court has recognized that "the right to counsel is the right to the effective assistance of counsel." . . .

The Court has not elaborated on the meaning of the constitutional requirement of effective assistance in cases—presenting claims of "actual ineffectiveness." In giving meaning to the requirement, however, we must take its purpose—to ensure a fair trial—as the guide. The benchmark for judging any claim of ineffectiveness must be whether counsel's conduct so undermined the proper functioning of the adversarial process that the trial cannot be relied on as having produced a just result.

The same principle applies to a capital sentencing proceeding such as that provided by Florida law....

III

A convicted defendant's claim that counsel's assistance was so defective as to require reversal of a conviction or death sentence has two components. First, the defendant must show that counsel's performance was deficient. This requires showing that counsel made errors so serious that counsel was not functioning as the "counsel" guaranteed the defendant by the Sixth Amendment. Second, the defendant must show that the deficient performance prejudiced the defense. This requires showing that counsel's errors were so serious as to deprive the defendant of a fair trial, a trial whose result is reliable. Unless a defendant makes both showings, it cannot be said that the conviction or death sentence resulted from a breakdown in the adversary process that renders the result unreliable.

A

As all the Federal Courts of Appeals have now held, the proper standard for attorney performance is that of reasonably effective assistance.... The Court indirectly recognized as much when it stated in McMann v. Richardson, 397 U.S. [759], 770, 771, that a guilty plea cannot be attacked as based on inadequate legal advice unless counsel was not "a reasonably competent attorney" and the advice was not "within the range of competence demanded of attorneys in criminal cases." See also Cuyler v. Sullivan, 446 U.S. [335], 344. When a convicted defendant complains of the ineffectiveness of counsel's assistance, the defendant must show that counsel's representation fell below an objective standard of reasonableness.

More specific guidelines are not appropriate. The Sixth Amendment refers simply to "counsel," not specifying particular requirements of effective assistance. It relies instead on the legal profession's maintenance of standards sufficient to justify the law's presumption that counsel will fulfill the role in the adversary process that the Amendment envisions.... The proper measure of attorney performance remains simply reasonableness under prevailing professional norms.

Representation of a criminal defendant entails certain basic duties. Counsel's function is to assist the defendant, and hence counsel owes the client a duty of loyalty, a duty to avoid conflicts of interest.... From counsel's function as assistant to the defendant derives the overarching duty to advocate the defendant's cause and the more particular duties to consult with the defendant on important decisions and to keep the defendant informed of important developments in the course of the prosecution. Counsel also has a duty to bring to bear such skill and knowledge as will render the trial a reliable adversarial testing process. . . .

These basic duties neither exhaustively define the obligations of counsel nor form a checklist for judicial evaluation of attorney performance. In any case presenting an ineffectiveness claim, the performance inquiry must be whether counsel's assistance was reasonable considering all the circumstances. Prevailing norms of practice as reflected in American Bar Association standards and the like . . . are guides to determining what is reasonable, but they are only guides. No particular set of detailed rules for counsel's conduct can satisfactorily take account of the variety of circumstances faced by defense counsel or the range of legitimate decisions regarding how best to represent a criminal defendant. Any such set of rules would interfere with the constitutionally protected independence of counsel and restrict the wide latitude counsel must have in making tactical decisions. . . . Indeed, the existence of detailed guidelines for representation could distract counsel from the overriding mission of vigorous advocacy of the defendant's cause. Moreover, the purpose of the effective assistance guarantee of the Sixth Amendment is not to improve the quality of legal representation, although that is a goal of considerable importance to the legal system. The purpose is simply to ensure that criminal defendants receive a fair trial.

Judicial scrutiny of counsel's performance must be highly deferential. It is all too tempting for a defendant to second-guess counsel's assistance after conviction or adverse sentence, and it is all too easy for a court, examining counsel's defense after it has proved unsuccessful, to conclude that a particular act or omission of counsel was unreasonable. . . . A fair assessment of attorney performance requires that every effort be made to eliminate the distorting effects of hindsight, to reconstruct the circumstances of counsel's challenged conduct, and to evaluate the conduct from counsel's perspective at the time. Because of the difficulties inherent in making the evaluation, a court must indulge a strong presumption that counsel's conduct falls within the wide range of reasonable professional assistance; that is, the defendant must overcome the presumption that, under the circumstances, the challenged action "might be considered sound trial strategy." See Michel v. Louisiana, 350 U.S. [91], 101. There are countless ways to provide effective assistance in any given case. Even the best criminal defense attorneys would not defend a particular client in the same way. . . .

The availability of intrusive post-trial inquiry into attorney performance or of detailed guidelines for its evaluation would encourage the proliferation of ineffectiveness challenges. Criminal trials resolved unfavorably to the defendant would increasingly come to be followed by a second trial, this one of counsel's unsuccessful defense. Counsel's performance and even willingness to serve could be adversely affected. Intensive scrutiny of counsel and rigid requirements for acceptable assistance could dampen the ardor and impair the independence of defense counsel, discourage the acceptance of assigned cases, and undermine the trust between attorney and client.

Thus, a court deciding an actual ineffectiveness claim must judge the reasonableness of counsel's challenged conduct on the facts of the particular case, viewed as of the time of counsel's conduct. A convicted defendant making a claim of ineffective assistance must identify the acts or omissions of counsel that are alleged not to have been the result of reasonable professional judgment. The court must then determine whether, in light of all the circumstances, the identified acts or omissions were outside the wide range of professionally competent assistance. In making that determination, the court should keep in mind that counsel's function, as elaborated in prevailing professional norms, is to make the adversarial testing process work in the particular case. At the same time, the court should recognize that counsel is strongly presumed to have rendered adequate assistance and made all significant decisions in the exercise of reasonable professional judgment.

These standards require no special amplification in order to define counsel's duty to investigate, the duty at issue in this case. As the Court of Appeals concluded, strategic choices made after thorough investigation of law and facts relevant to plausible options are virtually unchallengeable; and strategic choices made after less than complete investigation are reasonable precisely to the extent that reasonable professional judgments support the limitations on investigation. In other words, counsel has a duty to make reasonable investigations or to make a reasonable decision that makes particular investigations unnecessary. In any ineffectiveness case, a particular decision not to investigate must be directly assessed for reasonableness in all the circumstances, applying a heavy measure of deference to counsel's judgments.

The reasonableness of counsel's actions may be determined or substantially influenced by the defendant's own statements or actions. Counsel's actions are usually based, quite properly, on informed strategic choices made by the defendant and on information supplied by the defendant. In particular, what investigation decisions are reasonable depends critically on such information. For example, when the facts that support a certain potential line of defense are generally known to counsel because of what the defendant has said, the need for further investigation may be considerably diminished or eliminated altogether. And when a defendant has given counsel reason to believe that pursuing certain investigations would be fruitless or even harmful, counsel's failure to pursue those investigations may not later be challenged as unreasonable. In short, inquiry into counsel's conversations with the defendant may be critical to a proper assessment of counsel's investigation decisions, just as it may be critical to a proper assessment of counsel's other litigation decisions. . . .

B

An error by counsel, even if professionally unreasonable, does not warrant setting aside the judgment of a criminal proceeding if the error had no effect on the judgment.... The purpose of the Sixth Amendment guarantee of counsel is to ensure that a defendant has the assistance necessary to justify reliance on the outcome of the proceeding. Accordingly, any deficiencies in counsel's performance must be prejudicial to the defense in order to constitute ineffective assistance under the Constitution.

In certain Sixth Amendment contexts, prejudice is presumed. Actual or constructive denial of the assistance of counsel altogether is legally presumed to result in prejudice. So are various kinds of state interference with counsel's assistance.... Prejudice in these circumstances is so likely that case-by-case inquiry into prejudice is not worth the cost.... Moreover, such circumstances involve impairments of the Sixth Amendment right that are easy to identify and, for that reason and because the prosecution is directly responsible, easy for the government to prevent.

One type of actual ineffectiveness claim warrants a similar, though more limited, presumption of prejudice. In Cuyler v. Sullivan, 446 U.S., at 345–350, the Court held that prejudice is presumed when counsel is burdened by an actual conflict of interest. In those circumstances, counsel breaches the duty of loyalty, perhaps the most basic of counsel's duties. Moreover, it is difficult to measure the precise effect on the defense of representation corrupted by conflicting interests. Given the obligation of counsel to avoid conflicts of interest and the ability of trial courts to make early inquiry in certain situations likely to give rise to conflicts, see, e.g., Fed.Rule Crim.Proc. 44(c), it is reasonable for the criminal justice system to maintain a fairly rigid rule of presumed prejudice for conflicts of interest. Even so, the rule is not quite the per se rule of prejudice that exists for the Sixth Amendment claims mentioned above. Prejudice is presumed only if the defendant demonstrates that counsel "actively represented conflicting interests" and that "an actual conflict of interest adversely affected his lawyer's performance." Cuyler v. Sullivan, *supra*, 446 U.S., at 350, 348.

Conflict of interest claims aside, actual ineffectiveness claims alleging a deficiency in attorney performance are subject to a general requirement that the defendant affirmatively prove prejudice. The government is not responsible for, and hence not able to prevent, attorney errors that will result in reversal of a conviction or sentence. Attorney errors come in an infinite variety and are as likely to be utterly harmless in a particular case as they are to be prejudicial. They cannot be classified according to likelihood of causing prejudice. Nor can they be defined with sufficient precision to inform defense attorneys correctly just what conduct to avoid. Representation is an art, and an act or omission that is unprofessional in one case may be sound or even brilliant in another. Even if a defendant shows that particular errors of counsel were unreasonable, therefore, the defendant must show that they actually had an adverse effect on the defense.

It is not enough for the defendant to show that the errors had some conceivable effect on the outcome of the proceeding. Virtually every act or omission of counsel would meet that test, ... and not every error that conceivably could have influenced the outcome undermines the reliability of the result of the proceeding. Respondent suggests requiring a showing that the errors "impaired the presentation of the defense." That standard, however, provides no workable principle. Since any error, if it is indeed an error, "impairs" the presentation of the defense, the proposed standard is inadequate because it provides no way of deciding what impairments are sufficiently serious to warrant setting aside the outcome of the proceeding.

On the other hand, we believe that a defendant need not show that counsel's deficient conduct more likely than not altered the outcome in the case. This outcome-determinative standard has several strengths. It defines the relevant inquiry in a way familiar to courts, though the inquiry, as is inevitable, is anything but precise. The standard also reflects the profound importance of finality in criminal proceedings. Moreover, it comports with the widely used standard for assessing motions for new trial based on newly discovered evidence.... Nevertheless, the standard is not quite appropriate.

... The high standard for newly discovered evidence claims presupposes that all the essential elements of a presumptively accurate and fair proceeding were present in the proceeding whose result is challenged.... An ineffective assistance claim asserts the absence of one of the crucial assurances that the result of the proceeding is reliable, so finality concerns are somewhat weaker and the appropriate standard of prejudice should be somewhat lower. The result of a proceeding can be rendered unreliable, and hence the proceeding itself unfair, even if the errors of counsel cannot be shown by a preponderance of the evidence to have determined the outcome.

Accordingly, the appropriate test for prejudice finds its roots in the test for materiality of exculpatory information not disclosed to the defense by the prosecution, ... and in the test for materiality of testimony made unavailable to the defense by Government deportation of a witness.... The defendant must show that there is a reasonable probability that, but for counsel's unprofessional errors, the result of the proceeding would have been different. A reasonable probability is a probability sufficient to undermine confidence in the outcome.

In making the determination whether the specified errors resulted in the required prejudice, a court should presume, absent challenge to the judgment on grounds of evidentiary insufficiency, that the judge or jury acted according to law. An assessment of the likelihood of a result more favorable to the defendant must exclude the possibility of arbitrariness, whimsy, caprice, "nullification," and the like. A defendant has no entitlement to the luck of a lawless decisionmaker, even if a lawless decision cannot be reviewed. The assessment of prejudice should proceed on the assumption that the decisionmaker is reasonably, conscientiously, and impartially applying the standards that govern the decision. It should not depend on the idiosyncracies of the particular decisionmaker, such as unusual propensities toward harshness or leniency. Although these factors may actually have entered into counsel's selection of strategies and, to that limited extent, may thus affect the performance inquiry, they are irrelevant to the prejudice inquiry. Thus, evidence about the actual process of decision, if not part of the record of the proceeding under review, and evidence about, for example, a particular judge's sentencing practices, should not be considered in the prejudice determination.

The governing legal standard plays a critical role in defining the question to be asked in assessing the prejudice from counsel's errors. When a defendant challenges a conviction, the question is whether there is a reasonable probability that, absent the errors, the factfinder would have had a reasonable doubt respecting guilt. When a defendant challenges a death sentence such as the one at issue in this case, the question is whether there is a reasonable probability that, absent the errors, the sentencer— including an appellate court, to the extent it independently reweighs the evidence—would have concluded that the balance of aggravating and mitigating circumstances did not warrant death.

In making this determination, a court hearing an ineffectiveness claim must consider the totality of the evidence before the judge or jury. Some of the factual findings will have been unaffected by the errors, and factual findings that were affected will have been affected in different ways. Some errors will have had a pervasive effect on the inferences to be drawn from the evidence, altering the entire evidentiary picture, and some will have had an isolated, trivial effect. Moreover, a verdict or conclusion only weakly supported by the record is more likely to have been affected by errors than one with overwhelming record support. Taking the unaffected findings as a given, and taking due account of the effect of the errors on the remaining findings, a court making the prejudice inquiry must ask if the defendant has met the burden of showing that the decision reached would reasonably likely have been different absent the errors.

IV

A number of practical considerations are important for the application of the standards we have outlined. Most important, in adjudicating a claim of actual ineffectiveness of counsel, a court should keep in mind that the principles we have stated do not establish mechanical rules. Although those principles should guide the process of decision, the ultimate focus of inquiry must be on the fundamental fairness of the proceeding whose result is being challenged. In every case the court should be concerned with whether, despite the strong presumption of reliability, the result of the particular proceeding is unreliable because of a breakdown in the adversarial process that our system counts on to produce just results.

To the extent that this has already been the guiding inquiry in the lower courts, the standards articulated today do not require reconsideration of ineffectiveness claims rejected under different standards. . . . In particular, the minor differences in the lower courts' precise formulations of the performance standard are insignificant: the different formulations are mere variations of the overarching reasonableness standard. With regard to the prejudice inquiry, only the strict outcome-determinative test, among the standards articulated in the lower courts, imposes a heavier burden on defendants than the tests laid down today. The difference, however, should alter the merit of an ineffectiveness claim only in the rarest case.

Although we have discussed the performance component of an ineffectiveness claim prior to the prejudice component, there is no reason for a court deciding an ineffective assistance claim to approach the inquiry in the same order or even to address both components of the inquiry if the defendant makes an insufficient showing on one. In particular, a court need not determine whether counsel's performance was deficient before examining the prejudice suffered by the defendant as a result of the alleged deficiencies. The object of an ineffectiveness claim is not to grade counsel's performance. If it is easier to dispose of an ineffectiveness claim on the ground of lack of sufficient prejudice, which we expect will often be so, that course should be followed. Courts should strive to ensure that ineffectiveness claims not become so burdensome to defense counsel that the entire criminal justice system suffers as a result.

The principles governing ineffectiveness claims should apply in federal collateral proceedings as they do on direct appeal or in motions for a new trial. . . . Since fundamental fairness is the central concern of the writ of habeas corpus, . . . no special standards ought to apply to ineffectiveness claims made in habeas proceedings.

Finally, in a federal habeas challenge to a state criminal judgment, a state court conclusion that counsel rendered effective assistance is not a finding of fact binding on the federal court to the extent stated by 28 U.S.C. § 2254(d). . . . Although state court findings of fact made in the course of deciding an ineffectiveness claim are subject to the deference requirement of § 2254(d), and although district court findings are subject to the clearly erroneous standard of Federal Rule of Civil Procedure 52(a), both the performance and prejudice components of the ineffectiveness inquiry are mixed questions of law and fact.

V

Having articulated general standards for judging ineffectiveness claims, we think it useful to apply those standards to the facts of this case in order to illustrate the meaning of the general principles. The record makes it possible to do so. There are no conflicts between the state and federal courts over findings of fact, and the principles we have articulated are sufficiently close to the principles applied both in the Florida courts and in the District Court that it is clear that the factfinding was not affected by erroneous legal principles. . . .

Application of the governing principles is not difficult in this case. The facts as described above, make clear that the conduct of respondent's counsel at and before respondent's sentencing proceeding cannot be found unreasonable. They also make clear that, even assuming the challenged conduct of counsel was unreasonable, respondent suffered insufficient prejudice to warrant setting aside his death sentence.

With respect to the performance component, the record shows that respondent's counsel made a strategic choice to argue for the extreme emotional distress mitigating circumstance and to rely as fully as possible on respondent's acceptance of responsibility for his crimes. Although counsel understandably felt hopeless about respondent's prospects, nothing in the record indicates, as one possible reading of the District Court's opinion suggests, that counsel's sense of hopelessness distorted his professional judgment. Counsel's strategy choice was well within the range of professionally reasonable judgments, and the decision not to seek more character or psychological evidence than was already in hand was likewise reasonable.

The trial judge's views on the importance of owning up to one's crimes were well known to counsel. The aggravating circumstances were utterly overwhelming. Trial counsel could reasonably surmise from his conversations with respondent that character and psychological evidence would be of little help. Respondent had already been able to mention at the plea colloquy the substance of what there was to know about his financial and emotional troubles. Restricting testimony on respondent's character to what had come in at the plea colloquy ensured that contrary character and psychological evidence and respondent's criminal history, which counsel had successfully moved to exclude, would not come in. On these facts, there can be little question, even without application of the presumption of adequate performance, that trial counsel's defense, though unsuccessful, was the result of reasonable professional judgment.

With respect to the prejudice component, the lack of merit of respondent's claim is even more stark. The evidence that respondent says his trial counsel should have offered at the sentencing hearing would barely have altered the sentencing profile presented to the sentencing judge. As the state courts and District Court found, at most this evidence shows that numerous people who knew respondent thought he was generally a good person and that a psychiatrist and a psychologist believed he was under considerable emotional stress that did not rise to the level of extreme disturbance. Given the overwhelming aggravating factors, there is no reasonable probability that the omitted evidence would have changed the conclusion that the aggravating circumstances outweighed the mitigating circumstances and, hence, the sentence imposed. Indeed, admission of the evidence respondent now offers might even have been harmful to his case: his "rap sheet" would probably have been admitted into evidence, and the psychological reports would have directly contradicted respondent's claim that the mitigating circumstance of extreme emotional disturbance applied to his case.

Our conclusions on both the prejudice and performance components of the ineffectiveness inquiry do not depend on the trial judge's testimony at the District Court hearing. We therefore need not consider the general admissibility of that testimony, although, that testimony is irrelevant to the prejudice inquiry. Moreover, the prejudice question is resolvable, and hence the ineffectiveness claim can be rejected, without regard to the evidence presented at the District Court hearing. The state courts properly concluded that the ineffectiveness claim was meritless without holding an evidentiary hearing.

Failure to make the required showing of either deficient performance or sufficient prejudice defeats the ineffectiveness claim. Here there is a double failure. More generally, respondent has made no showing that the justice of his sentence was rendered unreliable by a breakdown in the adversary process caused by deficiencies in counsel's assistance. Respondent's sentencing proceeding was not fundamentally unfair.

We conclude, therefore, that the District Court properly declined to issue a writ of habeas corpus. The judgment of the Court of Appeals is accordingly

Reversed.[14]

■ [JUSTICE BRENNAN joined in the Court's opinion, but dissented from the judgment on the ground that capital punishment was violative of the Eighth Amendment.]

■ [JUSTICE MARSHALL, dissenting, first attacked the refusal of the Court to adopt more specific standards to govern the performance of defense counsel. He argued that to tell the lower courts that counsel in a criminal case must act like " 'a reasonably competent attorney' is to tell them nothing" and that the Court should not have disapproved of the admirable job that lower courts had been doing in creating workable objective standards of reasonableness. Second, he expressed strong disagreement with the "prejudice" standard adopted by the Court. He argued that prejudice could not be determined after the fact and should be presumed if incompetence of defense counsel had been established. A more fundamental problem with the prejudice standard, he argued, was that it treated the Sixth Amendment's guarantee of effective assistance of counsel as if its only purpose was to ensure that the innocent were not convicted:]

> ... In my view, the guarantee also functions to ensure that convictions are obtained only through fundamentally fair procedures. The majority contends that the Sixth Amendment is not violated when a manifestly guilty defendant is convicted after a trial in which he was represented by a manifestly ineffective attorney. I cannot agree. Every defendant is entitled to a trial in which his interests are vigorously and conscientiously advocated by an able lawyer. A proceeding in which the defendant does not receive meaningful assistance in meeting the forces of the State does not, in my opinion, constitute due process. [466 U.S. at 711.]

[Justice Marshall also criticized the majority's repeated emphasis on the heavy presumption in favor of competence that the lower courts were admonished to apply. Finally, he argued that a separate and higher standard for effective assistance of counsel should be applied in capital cases.

---

14. [Editors' note:] David Washington was executed in Florida on July 13, 1984.

Applying these considerations to the facts of the case, Justice Marshall concluded:]

If counsel had investigated the availability of mitigating evidence, he might well have decided to present some such material at the hearing. If he had done so, there is a significant chance that respondent would have been given a life sentence. In my view, those possibilities, conjoined with the unreasonableness of counsel's failure to investigate, are more than sufficient to establish a violation of the Sixth Amendment and to entitle respondent to a new sentencing proceeding. [466 U.S. at 719.]

Deficient Professional Performance

What did Washington's defense lawyer do or not do that was said to constitute ineffective assistance? Would his conduct have subjected him to professional discipline under the Model Rules or the Model Code? What is the relevance of ABA Standards Relating to the Administration of Criminal Justice, especially Standard 4–4.1 dealing with the duty to investigate, to professional discipline or the constitutional claim of ineffective assistance of counsel?[15] Would Washington's lawyer have been liable to Washington for malpractice?

William Genego argues that Washington's lawyer could not have made a "tactical" or "strategic" decision not to use psychiatric evidence or character evidence when he had made no inquiry as to what such evidence might show.[16] A lawyer cannot know whether evidence will be helpful until the lawyer obtains it; if the evidence is unfavorable or its introduction will permit the prosecutor to pursue harmful paths otherwise unavailable, a tactical decision not to offer the evidence can then be made. Pursuing any available evidence, Genego argues, should be required, especially when someone's life is at stake, as in Washington's sentencing hearing. Should the courts hold counsel to a higher standard in death penalty cases?[17] The ABA has proposed special standards for capital cases.[18]

15. The Standards, first approved in 1968 and revised in 1979 and 1991, are reproduced in Thomas D. Morgan and Ronald D. Rotunda, 1999 Selected Standards on Professional Responsibility (1999).

16. William J. Genego, The Future of Effective Assistance of Counsel: Performance Standards and Competent Representation, 22 Amer.Crim.L.Rev. 181, 196–97 (1984) (arguing that a psychiatric examination of Washington and exploration of character evidence might have supported mitigating factors under the Florida death penalty statute or, at a minimum, permitted Washington's claim of mental stress to be "presented in a more favorable light").

17. See State v. Davis, 116 N.J. 341, 561 A.2d 1082, 1089 (1989) (refusing to interpret the state constitution as requiring a more stringent test of competency in death penalty cases than the test in *Strickland*). Arguments for a higher standard are developed by Margaret J. Radin, Cruel Punishment and Respect for Persons: Super Due Process for Death, 53 S.Cal.L.Rev. 1143 (1980); and Charles L. Black, Capital Punishment: The Inevitability of Caprice and Mistake (2d ed. 1981).

18. ABA, Toward a More Just and Effective System of Review in State Death Penalty Cases (Ira P. Robbins, Reporter, August 1990).

The Court's deference to professional standards, combined with the repeated assertion of a strong presumption of competency, suggests that the Court believes substandard performance by defense counsel is extremely rare. Is this confidence misplaced? Vivian Berger argues that it flies in the face of evidence that "counsel inadequacy poses a very severe, if difficult to measure, problem."[19] She cites a number of factors that suggest a "grave" problem: (1) the observations of informed observers (recall the statements of former Chief Justice Burger on p. 149 supra); (2) studies of the prevalent conditions under which defense services are made available that report "the crushing caseloads of public defenders and the cut-rate fees for appointed counsel," circumstances that "stamp a 'stigma of inferiority' on the in forma pauperis bar" and "promote lackluster performance by discouraging careful investigation";[20] and (3) the modern revolution in constitutional criminal procedure that has made criminal defense a much more complex and demanding field of practice. Perhaps a familiarity with these conditions has led the courts' grappling with ineffective assistance issues to take the approach of "legitimating 'necessary evils' ".[21] If so, why isn't the Court more candid and honest about current conditions?

A detailed study of the representation of indigent defendants in New York City provided shocking statistics: defense counsel in homicide cases submitted no vouchers for investigative expenses in 73 percent of the cases; and filed no legal motions in 73 percent of the cases (the figures are higher in other felony cases).[22] Defendants charged with felonies were given only a short period of time (sometimes as little as 15 seconds) to decide whether to accept plea agreements offered by calendar judges. The public was upset by the view of the criminal justice system conveyed by the O. J. Simpson trial, on which the Los Angeles taxpayers spent $8 million. Would the public prefer to evaluate the justice system on the basis of a typical case in New York City?[23]

19. Vivian O. Berger, The Supreme Court and Defense Counsel: Old Roads, New Paths—A Dead End?, 86 Colum.L.Rev. 9, 64 (1986).

20. Id. at 60–61. The institutional arrangements for the selection and compensation of appointed counsel also result in many defendants being represented either by young and inexperienced defense counsel, who are learning by trial and error, or by senior counsel who are burned out and cynical. Id. at 62.

21. See Genego, supra note 16, at 201:

Inadequate representation is a major institutional problem. By all accounts there are far too many defendants who are represented by inadequate counsel; the courts cannot, in the limited context of granting postconviction relief, adequately

respond to the problem. When confronted with such fundamental issues in the criminal justice system, courts have tended to respond by legitimating "necessary evils," such as when the Supreme Court upheld the constitutionality of plea bargaining.

G.K. Chesterton once suggested that abuses in the legal system arose not because police or judges were "wicked" or "stupid" but simply because they had "gotten used to it." G. K. Chesterton, The Twelve Men, in Tremendous Trifles 57–58 (1955).

22. See Michael McConville & Chester L. Mirsky, Criminal Defense of the Poor in New York City, 15 NYU Rev. L. & Soc. Change 581 (1987).

23. See Albert W. Alschuler, 41 U.Chi.Law Record 7 (Fall 1995).

Is the Sixth Amendment violated when the appointed defense counsel in a complex federal mail fraud case is a real estate lawyer who has never tried a jury case? In United States v. Cronic,[24] decided the same day as *Strickland*, the Court held that it is not enough to show that the lawyer was not an experienced criminal lawyer; the defendant must show specific errors.[25] May a lawyer under such circumstances decline to serve? United States v. Wendy[26] held it improper to hold appointed counsel in contempt of court for refusing to proceed to trial because he was a tax lawyer who had never tried a case before.[27]

Required Showing of Prejudice

Except in certain limited circumstances, discussed below, the convicted defendant must show a "reasonable probability" that, but for counsel's unprofessional errors, the result would have been different. Doesn't the Court's test collapse two questions into one? (Was a right violated? What remedy, if any, should be accorded?) Is this tort-like standard, requiring proof of harm in order to establish the invasion of a right, appropriate? Contrast Justice Marshall's view that automatic reversal should flow from a demonstration that counsel's performance was seriously inadequate. Does the Court's statement that lower courts need not consider counsel's performance "[i]f it is *easier* to dispose of an ineffectiveness claim on the ground of lack of sufficient prejudice, *which we expect will often be so*," invite lower courts "to avoid refining more detailed criteria for lawyer conduct" and suggest "that virtually all challenges to counsel can be readily rejected"?[28]

Effect of *Strickland*

A 1988 law review survey of the case law, reporting nearly five years' experience under *Strickland*, showed that ineffectiveness claims were sustained in a minuscule 4 percent of cases (30 of 702 cases).[29] In six of the twelve federal circuits, accounting for 165 of the 702 cases, no defendant had prevailed in a claim of ineffective assistance of counsel. Moreover, most of the cases rejecting the defendant's claim (43.3 percent) did so on the ground that prejudice had not been shown. In other words, in almost half

---

24. 466 U.S. 648 (1984).

25. See also People v. Perez, 594 P.2d 1 (Cal.1979) (en banc) (upholding the representation of indigent defendants with their consent by "certified" law students supervised by an attorney).

26. 575 F.2d 1025 (2d Cir.1978).

27. See also State v. Gasen, 356 N.E.2d 505 (Ohio App.1976) (reversing a contempt citation of a public defender who refused to proceed with a preliminary hearing because the court had not given him time to read the file on the case or consult with the defendants); and Easley v. State, 334 So.2d 630 (Fla.App.1976) (lawyer not in contempt because he had an obligation to tell defendant that he lacked competence to proceed).

28. Berger, supra note 19, at 86–87 (emphasis added). The Court refers to ineffectiveness claims as entailing an "intrusive post-trial inquiry," the availability of which needs to be restricted so as not to "encourage the proliferation of ineffectiveness challenges."

29. Note, How To Thread the Needle: Toward a Checklist–Based Standard for Evaluating Ineffective Assistance of Counsel Claims, 77 Geo.L.J. 413, 458–461 (1988).

of the cases, the defendant's allegations of bungling by the lawyer were "relegated to [the] 'guilty anyway' category."[30] Compare these figures to the estimates of trial lawyer incompetence reported by knowledgeable observers and available survey research;[31] do they indicate that criminal defendants receive competent representation? The data suggest that, although *Strickland* said it was not adopting an outcome-determinative test, lowers courts are applying *Strickland* as if it had.

Examples of "Competent" Representation After *Strickland*

In Mitchell v. Kemp,[32] Mitchell pleaded guilty to killing a 14–year–old boy and seriously wounding the boy's mother during an armed robbery of a convenience store. Mitchell made two confessions shortly after being taken into custody. Mitchell's defense lawyer interviewed some of the police officers involved in taking the confessions, but did not interview the one who had signed the Miranda form because he did not like that officer and believed the others had spoken truthfully. He made no attempt to interview any witnesses to obtain mitigating character evidence because Mitchell's father had been uncooperative in two phone calls and Mitchell had said he did not want his family involved. The court of appeals affirmed the district court's rejection of the claims of ineffective assistance of counsel. The failure to investigate the voluntariness of the confessions by talking with each police officer was not prejudicial because of the guilty plea and the state's proof of the crimes. The failure to produce character evidence raised a "difficult question," but was affirmed on the ground that it was the result of strategic choices.

Justice Marshall, joined by Justices Brennan and Blackmun, dissented from the denial of certiorari. Justice Marshall concluded that permitting these failures interpreted the Sixth Amendment guarantee to require "no more than that 'a person who happens to be a lawyer is present at trial alongside the accused.'"

> Counsel's failure to investigate mitigating circumstances left him ignorant of the abundant information that was available to an attorney exercising minimal diligence in fighting for Billy Mitchell's life. The affidavits of individuals who would have testified on petitioner's behalf fill 170 pages of the record in the District Court....
>
> Had defense counsel tapped these resources, he would have been able to present the sentencing judge with a picture of a youth who, despite growing up in "the most poverty-stricken and crime-ridden

30. Id. at 433. In most of these cases, the courts never addressed the adequacy of the defense lawyer's performance, but 5 percent of the "no prejudice" cases indicated that counsel's performance was less than adequate.

31. Former Chief Justice Burger's "working hypothesis" that at least one-third to one-half of trial lawyers are incompetent, see p. 149 above, may be an overstatement. But the more modest estimates provided by the judges in the Maddi or Partridge and Bermant studies (see p. 150 above) suggest that 9–12 percent of trial lawyer performances are inadequate.

32. 762 F.2d 886 (11th Cir.1985), cert. denied, 483 U.S. 1026 (1987).

section of Jacksonville, Florida," had impressed his community as a person of exceptional character. He had been captain of the football team; leader of the prayer before each game; an above-average student; an active member of the student council, school choir, church choir, glee club, math club, and track team; a boy scout; captain of the patrol boys; and an attendant to the junior high school queen.

. . .

An account of what happened to this well-adjusted young person was also readily available to anyone who took the time to ask. When petitioner was 16 years old, his parents were divorced, and soon thereafter petitioner . . . and two friends were arrested for attempted robbery. Petitioner professed his innocence, but was persuaded by his father to plead guilty, because "things would go easier for him." The charges against the two friends were dropped. Petitioner was sentenced to six months in prison, where he was subjected to repeated violent homosexual attacks, experienced severe depression, and lost 30 pounds. When he was released, he continued to be highly depressed, and eventually committed the crime for which he received a sentence of death.

Counsel's explanation for his total lack of preparation for the sentencing hearing is that he carried an "ace in the hole." His sole strategy for representing his client's interests rested on his belief that, under Georgia law, the State would not be permitted to introduce any evidence of aggravating circumstances of which the defense had not been notified in writing. Prior to sentencing, the State had provided petitioner's counsel with oral notice of the aggravating circumstances upon which it would rely, but had not furnished written notice. Although the state statute upon which counsel's theory relied did not mention written notice, and no court decision had ever required that such notice be in writing, counsel was content to rest his entire defense, and the fate of his client, on an untried legal theory. At sentencing, counsel took the first opportunity to object to the admission of aggravating evidence of which he had not received prior written notice; the court promptly overruled his objection, and the "ace in the hole" was gone. . . .

. . . [P]etitioner's attorney also claimed that he had not wished to present any mitigating character evidence because that would have opened the door to the State's introduction of petitioner's prior conviction. . . . In this case, [such a decision] was patently unreasonable. . . . Moreover, under state law, the prior conviction would have been admissible even though the defense put on no evidence. If counsel in this case made any decisions at all, they were barren of even minimal supporting information or knowledge.

. . .

As a result of counsel's nonfeasance, no one argued to the sentencing judge that petitioner should not die. The judge heard only a technical argument regarding the admissibility of aggravating circumstances without prior written notice, which he consistently rejected, in addition to a reference to petitioner's youth.... Prejudice to the defendant's case is obvious when not even a suggestion that petitioner's life had some value, that his crime was aberrational, or that he was suffering from severe depression reached the ears and the conscience of the sentencing judge.... The judge heard not even a plea for mercy.[33]

Can a failure to investigate ever suffice to establish ineffective assistance of counsel? In Kimmelman v. Morrison,[34] the Supreme Court held counsel ineffective when his failure to conduct pretrial discovery resulted in a failure to raise an objection under the Fourth Amendment to illegally seized evidence.[35] Nonetheless, in the vast majority of cases even a complete failure to investigate does not lead to reversal.[36]

The *Strickland* standard may seem to guarantee precious little protection for a criminal defendant at trial, but one should keep in mind that not even this standard protects a convicted defendant from the consequences of her attorney's incompetence in a habeas proceeding. Because there is no right to counsel in habeas proceedings, the Court has held that *Strickland* does not apply.[37] The severity of this holding is apparent once one understands that in almost all instances a lawyer's procedural mistake in a habeas proceeding results in forfeiture of the client's claim to a new trial.[38]

Constitutional Role of Defense Counsel

According to *Strickland*, the purpose of the Sixth Amendment guarantee of effective assistance of counsel is "to ensure that the adversarial testing process works to produce a *just* result," "a fair trial whose result is *reliable*." Assuming this standard vision of counsel's role is appropriate, does the *Strickland* standard as applied guarantee this? Consider *Mitchell*

---

33. 483 U.S. at 1027–31. Billy Mitchell was executed on September 1, 1987.

34. 477 U.S. 365, 366 (1986).

35. See also Sullivan v. Fairman, 819 F.2d 1382, 1391–3 (7th Cir.1987) (failure to contact witnesses whose testimony contradicted that of government's witnesses was ineffective and prejudicial); Grooms v. Solem, 923 F.2d 88 (8th Cir.1991) (ineffective assistance where lawyer failed to investigate defendant's potential alibi); and Capps v. Sullivan, 921 F.2d 260 (10th Cir.1990) (ineffective assistance where lawyer failed to investigate witnesses who could have provided defendant with an entrapment defense).

36. See, e.g., Burger v. Kemp, 483 U.S. 776 (1987) (no investigation of mitigating evidence for presentation at defendant's capital sentencing hearing held not unreasonable); Ballou v. Booker, 777 F.2d 910, 914

(4th Cir.1985) (failure to interview rape victim or examining physicians not unreasonable when counsel already "knew" what happened); Aldrich v. Wainwright, 777 F.2d 630, 633 (11th Cir.1985) (failure to interview state's witnesses or otherwise investigate, along with counsel's admission that he was "totally unprepared," demonstrated unreasonable performance, but not prejudicial); Hoots v. Allsbrook, 785 F.2d 1214, 1221 (4th Cir.1986) (failure to investigate unreasonable but not prejudicial).

37. Coleman v. Thompson, 501 U.S. 722 (1991).

38. Id. (applying the habeas procedural default rule of Wainwright v. Sykes, 433 U.S. 72 (1977), and holding that incompetence of counsel does not fulfill the "cause and prejudice" exception to the default rule).

v. Kemp, supra. Was the sentencing result there reliable? What does it mean to say a sentencing result was reliable?

The next question to consider is whether the Court's version of counsel's role is appropriate. William Genego argues that *Strickland*'s hindsight evaluation of fairness in terms of effects neglects process concerns relating to counsel's role in the adversary system:[39]

> The role of an attorney for a defendant facing criminal prosecution is not, however, to see that his or her client received a fair trial and that a just outcome resulted. The attorney's role is to do everything ethically proper to see that the client receives the most favorable outcome possible—whether or not it produces an outcome which society considers just. [Citing EC 7–1: "The duty of a lawyer, both to his client and the legal system, is to represent his client zealously within the bounds of the law."] Society relies on the adversary system to produce just results from partisan advocacy. The guiding principle in determining whether an attorney has provided effective representation must then be whether he or she discharged the role of partisan advocate faithfully and zealously, not whether the performance yielded what a court views as a just result.[38]

Does the Constitution require a state to require its defense lawyers to conform to a "total commitment to client" model of lawyering? Does it provide a federal remedy for every departure from that model? What weight should be given to the three "f-words" impliedly emphasized by the Court: federalism (respect for state court adjudications of fact and law); efficiency (the social cost of reversing every conviction that might have been affected by deficient professional performance); and finality (reducing incentives for endless and repeated federal challenges to criminal convictions that have survived at least two prior reviews)? Isn't there a great danger that the Court's approach, as Justice Marshall argued, limits the success of ineffectiveness claims to defendants who can prove they were innocent?

Under Genego's approach, does defense counsel have an incentive to seed error into a criminal case that is a clear loser by failing to do a competent job?[39] Like all rules, the ineffectiveness rule itself may be put to tactical use by counsel more concerned with "winning for client" than with either just results or the integrity of the adjudicatory process. How likely is such behavior? What controls would minimize the risk?

Vivian Berger contrasts the Court's many decisions that enhance the dependence of client on defense counsel by binding the client by counsel's actions,[40] with *Strickland*, which provides very limited protection against

---

39. See Berger, supra note 19, at 93–96, and Genego, supra note 16, at 198–202.

38. Genego, supra note 16, at 200.

39. This issue was raised by Justice Rehnquist in Wainwright v. Sykes, 433 U.S. 72, 89 (1977), and responded to in that case by

Justices Brennan and Marshall, dissenting, 433 U.S. at 102 and note 4.

40. Numerous decisions dealing with collateral attack on guilty pleas and availability of the federal habeas remedy bind a convicted defendant by her lawyer's advertent

incompetent lawyering to the ignorant and vulnerable client. The Court, in simultaneously maximizing the defendant's need for competent representation and minimizing the Constitution's competence safeguard, has made the lawyer—with her broad power to decide matters contrary to the client's wishes—not simply another "indignity" the indigent defendant must bear, but also potentially the client's greatest enemy.[41]

When Prejudice Is Presumed

In *Strickland* the Court stated that prejudice will be presumed in certain limited circumstances: when there has been an "actual or constructive denial of the assistance of counsel altogether," or when the government interferes with counsel's assistance in such a way that "prejudice ... is so likely that case-by-case inquiry into prejudice is not worth the cost." The Court also made it clear that a defendant need not show prejudice when his trial was conducted without counsel despite her desire for representation or when counsel in a criminal case was under an actual conflict of interest.[42]

Since *Strickland*, the Court has affirmed that prejudice also is not required in the following two situations. The first is failure to file an *Anders* brief. Anders v. California[43] requires appellate counsel in criminal cases who seek leave to withdraw based on their judgment that an appeal is meritless to file a brief referring to anything in the record that might arguably support the appeal. Such a brief is called an *Anders* brief. Failure to file an *Anders* brief requires reversal; no showing of prejudice is required, nor may such conduct be labeled harmless error.[44] The second situation is when the defendant is prevented from conferring with her counsel for any significant period of time.[45]

Apart from these situations, the courts have dispensed with the requirement of demonstrating prejudice in relatively few instances. The category of "actual or constructive denial" of the assistance of counsel is interpreted quite narrowly, not reaching cases in which defense counsel

or inadvertent actions in raising or not raising particular issues. See Berger at 17–25 (discussing habeas and guilty plea decisions). Other decisions permit defense counsel to decide important matters either without consulting the defendant or against the defendant's expressed desires. See, e.g., Jones v. Barnes, 463 U.S. 745 (1983) (lawyer, not client, decides what arguments are presented in an appellate brief), considered infra at 480. These constitutional decisions make the criminal defendant very dependent on the competence of defense counsel.

41. Berger, supra note 19, at 11.

42. See Cuyler v. Sullivan, reprinted in Chapter 7 infra at p. 608.

43. 386 U.S. 738 (1967).

44. Penson v. Ohio, 488 U.S. 75 (1988).

45. See Geders v. United States, 425 U.S. 80 (1976) (defendant not allowed to confer with counsel during overnight trial recess). In Perry v. Leeke, 488 U.S. 272 (1989), the Court reaffirmed that a violation of *Geders* was not subject to the requirement that prejudice be shown, but held that *Geders* was not violated when the defendant was prevented from conferring with counsel during a 15–minute trial recess, that prejudice therefore had to be shown and that it was not.

had mental problems during the trial[46] or suffered from drug addiction.[47] Where a denial has been found, the courts have sometimes used the doctrine of harmless error to avoid reversal.[48]

Government interference with the right to counsel must be egregious before prejudice will be presumed. "Not all government interference triggers the per se [prejudice] rule. The common thread in cases where the government's conduct was found to be 'egregious' is conduct which jeopardizes the integrity of the legal process."[49]

Are there specific blunders by counsel that are so blatantly incompetent that no separate showing of prejudice should be required? What about failing to remove for cause an obviously biased juror?[50]

Effective Assistance of Counsel Under State Constitutions

The state courts—the laboratories of our federal judicial system—are free to develop more rigorous standards for judging effective assistance of counsel under state constitutional provisions. However, almost all follow *Strickland*.[51] Some states employ somewhat different verbal formulation but it is not clear that the differences result in different outcomes.[52]

Perhaps the most serious problem in day-to-day administration is the inadequate compensation provided for court-appointed lawyers who represent indigent defendants in serious criminal cases.[53] In most states compen-

---

46. In Smith v. Ylst, 826 F.2d 872 (9th Cir.1987), psychiatric reports showed that the defendant's lawyer suffered "paranoid psychotic reactions" during the trial, but the court upheld the conviction because the defendant failed to show prejudice.

47. See Berry v. King, 765 F.2d 451, 454 (5th Cir.1985) (no presumption of prejudice on showing that defense counsel was addicted to drugs, and prejudice not shown by counsel's stipulation to virtually all elements of the crime when state could easily have proved the elements).

48. See, e.g., Thomas v. Kemp, 796 F.2d 1322, 1326–27 (11th Cir.1986) (defendant, facing capital charge, was denied presence of a lawyer at preliminary hearing; no reversal because harmless error); Siverson v. O'Leary, 764 F.2d 1208 (7th Cir.1985) (defense counsel's absence during jury deliberations and when jury returned verdict presumed prejudicial, but error harmless).

49. United States v. Perry, 857 F.2d 1346, 1349 (9th Cir.1988) (giving examples).

50. Compare Presley v. State, 750 S.W.2d 602 (Mo.App.1988) (holding that prejudice is presumed in this situation), with Wicker v. McCotter, 783 F.2d 487 (5th Cir.1986)

(holding such conduct was a strategic choice).

51. See, e.g., State v. Nash, 694 P.2d 222 (Ariz.1985); People v. Ledesma, 729 P.2d 839 (Cal.1987); People v. Albanese, 473 N.E.2d 1246 (Ill.1984); State v. Davis, 561 A.2d 1082 (N.J.1989). South Carolina has adopted a somewhat different prejudice test. See Frett v. State, 378 S.E.2d 249 (S.C.1988) (prejudice established if defendant shows that conduct of trial, not necessarily its outcome, would have altered his position in a beneficial way).

52. See, e.g., Commonwealth v. Buehl, 508 A.2d 1167 (Pa.1986), holding that the Pennsylvania Constitution requires the same showing of prejudice as in *Strickland* but a different inquiry as to counsel's performance: The court asks whether the course the defendant suggests counsel should have pursued is frivolous; if not, then the court asks whether the course counsel chose "had some reasonable basis designed to serve the interests of [the] client." 508 A.2d at 1174.

53. The Federal Criminal Justice Act, 18 U.S.C. § 3006A(d), provides for compensation at hourly rates of $60 per hour in

sation provisions for court-appointed counsel are substantially less than the prevailing rates for privately retained lawyers.[54] Rates of compensation are as low as $15 an hour. Statutory provisions generally limit compensation to a maximum allowance ranging from $100 to $5,000, with most states imposing a limitation on felony cases between $1,000 and $3,000. Would the issues presented by *Strickland* be so troublesome if state courts did it right the first time by providing defendants with competent lawyers receiving adequate compensation and supported with adequate investigative resources?

A Preventive Approach?

Professional discipline, civil malpractice liability and after-the-fact review of ineffective assistance claims share the common characteristic that they come along after the damage, if any, is done. Would preventive measures be more effective? Judge Bazelon sought unsuccessfully to commit the Court of Appeals for the District of Columbia to a prophylactic approach involving a more active role on the part of the trial judge.[55] For example, the trial judge would require the defense lawyer to submit a checklist and report indicating that "a complete investigation" has been performed and "reviewing the steps he has taken in pretrial preparation, including what records were obtained, which witnesses were interviewed, when the defendant was consulted, and what motions were filed."[56] Justice O'Connor's opinion in *Strickland* rejected this approach, arguing that a "set of rules" for defense counsel "would interfere with the constitutionally protected independence of counsel and restrict the wide latitude counsel must have in making tactical decisions." How would requiring defense counsel, for example, to take certain investigatory steps interfere with the defendant's rights?

If monitoring by trial judges "poses risks of violating defendants' rights by the very process designed to protect them,"[57] what alternatives are desirable? Some possible types of systemic reform are continuing legal education, professional certification or specialization requirements for practice in certain courts or subjects, more clinically oriented law school training, higher pay and greater auxiliary resources for assigned counsel and structural changes in the delivery of defense services. How likely are these changes? How effective would they be? Professor Berger urges the

court and $40 per hour for office and investigative work, unless the Judicial Conference determines that a higher rate not to exceed $75 per hour is justified for a circuit or a particular district; the maximum amount for handling a felony case is $3,500 for each attorney; and larger payments may be made "for extended or complex representation" with judicial approval. See Costs Mount for Indigent Defense, Nat'l L.J., Aug. 7, 1995, at A18.

54. See Note, The Breath of the Unfee'd Lawyer: Statutory Fee Limitations and In-

effective Assistance of Counsel in Capital Litigation, 90 Mich.L.Rev. 626, 627 (1991) (arguing that fee limitations deprive indigent defendants of their right to effective assistance of counsel).

55. United States v. Decoster, 624 F.2d 196, 215 (D.C.Cir.1976) (en banc, Bazelon and Wright, dissenting).

56. 624 F.2d at 297.

57. Berger, supra note 19, at 114, note 528.

Court to play an educative role in defining ineffective assistance, but concludes that constitutionalizing lawyer behavior (except at the extremes) is neither appropriate nor wise: "[O]ther institutions [will] have to carry the lion's share of the remedial burden."[58]

2. MALPRACTICE CLAIMS AGAINST CRIMINAL DEFENSE LAWYERS

In many states criminal defense lawyers are not accountable to their clients in malpractice actions. First, a number of jurisdictions hold public defenders immune from malpractice suits. Second, many states require the convicted criminal defendant, as part of the required proof of causation of harm, to be successful in having the conviction either set aside by direct appeal or by collateral attack, the latter involving a determination that the lawyer violated the constitutional requirement of effective assistance of counsel.[59] In Zeidwig v. Ward[60] the court reasoned:

> If we were to allow a claim in this instance, we would be approving a policy that would approve the imprisonment of a defendant for a criminal offense ... but which would allow the same defendant to collect from his counsel damages ... because he was improperly imprisoned.[61]

Third, an increasing number of jurisdictions also require that the convicted client prove actual innocence of the offense charged.[62] The cumulative effect of these requirements drastically reduces the accountability of criminal defense lawyers to their clients.[63]

Do these limitations result in criminal defense lawyers being held to a lesser standard in malpractice cases than lawyers trying civil cases? In Levine v. Kling,[64] Judge Posner argued that since a defendant who is legally guilty has no legal right to be found not guilty, the defendant should not collect damages because his lawyer could not avoid a just result. However, if the defendant had a valid legal defense, such as double jeopardy, but was factually guilty, the failure to assert the defense should give rise to a malpractice action. Do you agree?

---

58. Id. at 115.

59. See, e.g., Knoblauch v. Kenyon, 415 N.W.2d 286 (Mich.App.1987) (denial of ineffective assistance claim precludes subsequent malpractice action); Johnson v. Raban, 702 S.W.2d 134 (Mo.App.1985) (same).

60. 548 So.2d 209 (Fla.1989).

61. Id. at 214.

62. See, e.g., Wiley v. County of San Diego, 966 P.2d 983 (Cal.1998); Carmel v. Lunney, 511 N.E.2d 1126 (N.Y.1987) ("the undisturbed determination of the client's guilt in the subsequent criminal prosecution precludes him, as a matter of law, from recovering for civil damages flowing from the allegedly negligent representation"); com-

pare Hines v. Davidson, 489 So.2d 572 (Ala.1986) (criminal defendant required to show that he would have been acquitted but for the lawyer's negligence).

63. For a critique of limitations on malpractice actions brought by criminal defendants, see Susan P. Koniak, Through the Looking Glass of Ethics and The Wrong with Rights We Find There, 9 Geo. J. Leg. Ethics 1, 5–12 (1995).

64. 123 F.3d 580 (7th Cir.1997). The Restatement § 75, comment *d,* adopts the majority rule that obtaining successful post-conviction relief is a precondition to a malpractice action.

In Ferri v. Ackerman[65] the Supreme Court held that counsel appointed in federal criminal cases under the Criminal Justice Act of 1964 enjoy no inherent immunity from malpractice claims. In Polk County v. Dodson,[66] the Supreme Court held that a public defender "when performing a lawyer's traditional functions as counsel to a defendant in a criminal proceeding" does not act "under color of state law" within the meaning of 42 U.S.C. § 1983. The plaintiff had sued under § 1983, claiming that his rights to counsel and to due process were violated when his counsel moved to withdraw on the ground that he thought plaintiff's appeal was frivolous. In Tower v. Glover,[67] the Court held that § 1983 applies when a plaintiff alleges that the public defender conspired with state officials to ensure the plaintiff's conviction.

65. 444 U.S. 193 (1979).

66. 454 U.S. 312, 325 (1981). State prosecutors are absolutely immune from liability under § 1983 for conduct in initiating and trying criminal cases, but not for giving legal advice to police prior to an application for a search warrant. Burns v. Reed, 500 U.S. 478 (1991).

67. 467 U.S. 914 (1984).

CHAPTER 4

CONFIDENTIALITY

[handwritten: ACP → Agency Law + Law of Evidence]

INTRODUCTORY NOTE

The law governing client confidences has two sources: agency law and the law of evidence. Lawyers, like all agents, have a duty to treat information from and about their principals as confidential to the extent that the principal so intends and a duty not to use information about the principal against the principal or for the personal gain of the agent.[1] These duties continue after the agency ends. The professional duty of confidentiality in the ethics codes, discussed later in this chapter, expands the agency duty. The professional duty governs the lawyer in all activities and at all times: in the law office, in public settings, in private social gatherings. Breach of confidentiality may lead to one or more of a number of remedies.[2] *[handwritten: 2] [handwritten: 1]*

The professional duty of confidentiality is also broader than the attorney-client privilege of evidence law: The professional duty protects information about the client that the lawyer learns from third parties; the privilege extends only to information transmitted directly between client and lawyer. Neither the professional duty of confidentiality nor its agency counterpart, however, allow the lawyer-agent to refuse to testify or produce evidence about confidential matters in court or before other government bodies that have the power to compel testimony, such as administrative agencies or legislative committees. This is where the attorney-client privilege comes into play. *[handwritten: 3] [handwritten: ↑ info about client told to lawyer from 3rd parties is protected]*

The law of evidence excludes some evidence as presumptively unreliable, e.g., evidence that violates the hearsay rule. It excludes other evidence to protect an interest or relationship, e.g., the marital relationship, deemed of sufficient importance that the law tolerates the loss of reliable evidence to protect that interest. Exclusionary rules of the latter type are known as privileges. Because recognizing a privilege impairs a tribunal's pursuit of truth, courts interpret privileges narrowly and place the burden on the proponent of privilege to prove that its elements have been met. *[handwritten: 4]*

---

1. Agency law requires an agent "not to use or to communicate information confidentially given him by the principal or acquired by him during the course of or on account of his agency," subject to a power of the agent to reveal information when necessary to protect the superior interest of a third person. Restatement (Second) of Agency § 395, cmt. *f* (1958).

2. A lawyer's breach of confidentiality may lead to professional discipline or malpractice liability or both. In addition, agency law provides the basis for other remedies, such as tort or contract damages and injunctive relief.

Because the attorney-client privilege prevents testimonial disclosure of a client's communications, commentators over the years have attacked the privilege as a device by which lawyers assist wrongdoers in concealing their wrongs "in the face of a specific demand for its disclosure by the very person suffering the wrong."[3] In the early 1800s Jeremy Bentham put this objection forcefully, urging the elimination of the privilege: "What, then, would be the consequence? That a guilty person will not in general be able to derive so much assistance from his law advisor, in the way of concerting a false defense, as he may do at present."[4] Bentham's single-minded devotion to the truth-seeking aspect of adjudication has not prevailed in the courts, which have accorded greater weight to a client's interest in freedom of consultation with a legal advisor. What reasons support the privilege? Are these reasons inconsistent with a modification of the privilege so as to make it inapplicable if a strong need for the privileged matter arises in a trial?[5]

The modern rationale for the attorney-client privilege is that the privilege encourages open communication between clients and their lawyers, serving both the interests of clients who need effective legal representation and society's interests in having clients advised about the legality of proposed actions and effectively represented in the adversary process.

The attorney-client privilege is recognized in every jurisdiction either by statute or common law. In federal courts the contours of the privilege are determined by federal law on issues of federal law and by state law on state law matters.[6]

English common law recognized the privilege as early as the 16th century, although English courts did not fully accept the privilege until after 1800.[7] The privilege has developed in the United States through common law decisions and statutory enactments and not as a matter of constitutional right. Federal and state constitutions, however, recognize rights supported by the attorney-client privilege, namely the privilege against self-incrimination and the right to counsel. The relationship between the Fifth Amendment privilege against self-incrimination and the attorney-client privilege is considered in the *Fisher* case below.

3. See Geoffrey C. Hazard, Jr., An Historical Perspective on the Attorney–Client Privilege, 66 Calif.L.Rev. 1061, 1062 (1978) (discussing attacks on the privilege).

4. Jeremy Bentham, Rationale of Judicial Evidence (1827), quoted in John H. Wigmore, 7 Evidence 569 (McNaughton ed., 1961).

5. See Note, The Attorney–Client Privilege: Fixed Rules, Balancing, and Constitutional Entitlement, 91 Harv.L.Rev. 464 (1977).

6. As adopted in 1975, Fed.Evid.Rule 501 requires federal courts to follow state privi-lege law in all cases in which "state law supplies the rule of decision." In cases in which federal substantive law applies, Rule 501 provides that privilege claims are to be decided by "the common law, interpreted in the light of reason and experience."

7. Geoffrey C. Hazard, Jr., An Historical Perspective on the Attorney–Client Privilege, 66 Calif.L.Rev. 1061, 1070 (1978) (discussing the history of the privilege). See also Max Radin, The Privilege of Confidential Communication Between Lawyer and Client, 16 Calif.L.Rev. 487 (1928).

The relationship between the Sixth Amendment's right to counsel and the attorney-client privilege has uncertain contours.[8] The federal court decisions agree that *government use* of information protected by the attorney-client privilege may infringe the defendant's Sixth Amendment right to counsel, though they differ on what is material infringement.[9] These decisions assume the existence of a state privilege and implicitly acknowledge its importance to the Sixth Amendment's right to counsel in criminal trials. They strongly suggest that, should a state legislature abolish the attorney-client privilege, the courts would hold the statute unconstitutional. This point remains a theoretical one because no state is likely to abolish the privilege. The more important and more difficult question is whether the courts would hold that a narrowing of the privilege violates a criminal defendant's right to counsel. Thus far the courts have shown no inclination to require any particular scope for the privilege under the Sixth Amendment. On the other hand, no state has sought to restrict the privilege significantly.

Look for dissimer of a narrow interpretation of privilege

118, 119, 120)

A. ATTORNEY-CLIENT PRIVILEGE

The scope of the attorney-client privilege is a complicated subject. The materials that follow provide only an overview.[10]

The precise formulation of the attorney-client privilege varies from jurisdiction to jurisdiction.[11] The Restatement of Law Governing Lawyers § 118 defines the attorney-client privilege as protecting:

(1) *a communication* [defined in § 119 as "any expression through which a privileged person ... undertakes to convey information to another privileged person and any document or other record revealing such expression"]

(2) *made between privileged persons* [defined in § 120 as "the client (including a prospective client), the client's lawyer, agents of

---

8. See Marano v. Holland, 366 S.E.2d 117 (W.Va.1988) (citing cases suggesting but not holding that the Sixth Amendment right to counsel includes some form of attorney-client privilege). On the connection between the Sixth Amendment and the privilege, see David E. Seidelson, The Attorney–Client Privilege and Clients' Constitutional Rights, 6 Hofstra L.Rev. 693 (1978).

9. See United States v. Mastroianni, 749 F.2d 900 (1st Cir.1984) (describing the differences among the circuit courts).

10. Generally see John W. Strong et al., McCormick on Evidence c. 10 (4th ed. 1992); Wolfram, Modern Legal Ethics § 6.3 et seq. (1986); 8 John H. Wigmore, Evi-

dence § 2291 (J. McNaughton rev. ed. 1961); and Developments in the Law—Privileged Communications, 98 Harv. L.Rev. 1450, 1501 et seq. (1985). Proposed Federal Rule of Evidence 503 (1972), although not adopted by Congress, is viewed by courts and commentators as an authoritative summary of the common law of the attorney-client privilege.

11. See Wolfram, Modern Legal Ethics 250–68 (1986), for a modern discussion of the privilege. Sections 118–34 of the Restatement address the attorney-client privilege; the comments and reporter's notes provide an excellent treatment of the subject.

either who facilitate communications between them, and agents of the lawyer who facilitate the representation"]

(3) *in confidence* [§ 121 states in part that "a communication is in confidence . . . if, at the time and in the circumstances of the communication, the communicating person reasonably believes that no one will learn the contents of the communication except a privileged person. . . ."

(4) *for the purpose of obtaining or providing legal assistance for the client* [§ 122 defines this term to include any communication "made to or to assist a person (1) who is a lawyer or who the client or prospective client reasonably believes to be a lawyer; and (2) whom the client or prospective client consults for the purpose of obtaining legal assistance"].[12]

1. ASPECTS OF THE PRIVILEGE

A "Client" Seeking "Legal Advice" From a "Lawyer"

The attorney-client privilege does not protect privacy per se; the rule protects privacy only in the context and for the purpose of encouraging full disclosure to a legal advisor by one seeking legal services. A "client" is a person who consults with a lawyer to obtain legal advice including, of course, a prospective client and a lawyer who seeks legal advice from another lawyer.[13] A "lawyer" is a person whom the client reasonably believes is a lawyer; "legal advice" turns on the intent of the client in making the communication. For example, the privilege does not cover a person who seeks business advice or who speaks to a lawyer merely as a friend. Payment of a fee, however, is not required; and preliminary conversations for the purpose of obtaining representation are privileged even if the lawyer subsequently declines the representation. Termination of the attorney-client relationship does not end the privilege; protection continues indefinitely.[14]

Privileged Communications

12. The most quoted statement of the privilege is Wigmore's classic formulation: "[1] Where legal advice of any kind is sought [2] from a professional legal adviser in his capacity as such, [3] the communications relating to that purpose, [4] made in confidence [5] by the client, [6] are at his instance permanently protected [7] from disclosure by himself or by the legal adviser, [8] except the protection be waived." Wigmore on Evidence § 2292 (McNaughton ed.1961).

13. See, e.g., United States v. Rowe, 96 F.3d 1294 (9th Cir.1996) (when a law firm's managing partner asked two associates of the firm to investigate whether a partner had mishandled client funds, the associates' conversations with the managing partner about the investigation were privileged).

14. See Swidler & Berlin v. United States, 524 U.S. 399 (1998) (lawyer's notes made just prior to client's suicide protected against request by federal grand jury); and Matter of Doe (Stuart), 562 N.E.2d 69 (Mass. 1990) (murder suspect's conversations with his lawyer continued to be privileged after the suspect's death by suicide; a balancing-of-interests test held inappropriate).

Client communications to a lawyer—whether oral, written, or non-verbal (e.g., rolling up a sleeve to reveal a tattoo)—are privileged if relevant to the legal subject matter on which the client seeks legal assistance. Observations or things that are evidence of events and occurrences are not privileged, except in the form in which a client communicates them to a lawyer. Thus a client may be compelled to testify about events involving the client if no other privilege, such as the Fifth Amendment privilege against self-incrimination, prevents disclosure. And the client's lawyer may be compelled to testify to facts about the client's appearance (e.g., a cut or bruise the lawyer observes on the client's face); the lawyer's observations are not client communications.

The privilege protects documents if prepared for the purpose of seeking a lawyer's advice but not preexisting documents or those prepared for another purpose (e.g., tax working papers) even if turned over to a lawyer.[15] Physical evidence of a crime also falls outside of the privilege.[16] The client's name, the fact that the client has retained the lawyer, details of the retainer or fee and who paid it and the client's whereabouts are generally not privileged.[17] A major exception to the privilege, known as the crime-fraud exception, is considered separately later in this chapter.

It is worth repeating that underlying facts or evidence are not protected by the privilege but only a client's communications to a lawyer made for the purpose of obtaining legal advice.[18] Thus a lawyer's client may be required to testify concerning any fact unless the information is protected by some other privilege, such as the Fifth Amendment privilege against self-incrimination. The attorney-client privilege, which applies only to what the client has told the lawyer and vice versa, "is not intended to enable a client to keep secret all information that might prove to be damaging," but only to insure "that clients do not suffer as a result of consulting lawyers and confiding in them." The privilege "is not intended to give the client

---

15. See Fisher v. United States, 425 U.S. 391 (1976), reprinted below at p. 227.

16. See Commonwealth v. Stenhach, 514 A.2d 114 (Pa.Super.1986), reprinted supra at p. 41.

17. See the extensive discussion of these issues below at p. 254.

18. An example may clarify the point. Suppose C, a client, who has been involved in an accident, goes to a lawyer, L, for legal advice concerning her potential rights and liabilities. She speaks fully and frankly about the incident to L, who assures her that everything she says is confidential and will not be disclosed. Her communications include the information that T, a third person, was a witness to the incident. L's later investigation discovers that W also

has relevant evidence. Will the privilege prevent the opposing party from offering the evidence of T, C or W ? Clearly not. Although C or L cannot be required to testify without C's consent as to any information that C has communicated to L, the privilege does not deny the opposing party access to T's testimony or even to C's knowledge of T's existence as a witness. Under modern procedural systems, C may be compelled by proper discovery to disclose T's existence and T may be deposed or called as a witness. Nor does the privilege extend to what T or W or other third persons communicate to L (although this will be protected information under the professional codes and will receive limited protection under the work-product immunity doctrine).

exclusive property rights in all information discovered by counsel while acting on the client's behalf."[19]

A "Communication" "Made in Confidence"

Because the purpose of the privilege is to facilitate effective legal assistance, the privilege is lost if the communication is not made in secrecy. The presence of third persons (other than agents of the lawyer or client who are necessary to protect the interests of the client) destroys the privilege.[20] Lawyers cannot provide legal advice without the assistance of secretaries, investigators and paralegals; their presence does not affect the privilege. Communications made for public consumption or intended for a non-lawyer are not privileged (e.g., a suicide note addressed to a relative but turned over to a lawyer). Also, a client waives the privilege if, after communicating privileged information to a lawyer, the client disseminates the information to third persons.

Communications From Lawyer to Client

The classic formulation of the privilege by Wigmore limits it to communications made by a client to a lawyer. What about the lawyer's advice to the client? Some courts hold that all communications from lawyer to client are privileged, even when initiated by the lawyer. This approach relies in part on the lawyer's duty to keep the client informed and assumes that any statement by the lawyer would reveal a confidence previously entrusted to her by the client.[21] The other approach extends the privilege to lawyer statements only when the court finds that the statements in fact reveal the substance of a client confidence.

Joint Clients and Cooperating Parties

If two or more persons jointly retain a lawyer to represent them in a matter, communications made by any of the clients to the lawyer on the subject of the joint representation are not privileged against use by one joint client against another.[22] This rule, referred to as the "co-client rule," is an exception to the general rule that disclosure to third persons waives the privilege. The issue arises most often when one co-client feels her interests have been inadequately represented and sues another co-client or the lawyer.[23] The theory behind abrogation of the privilege in such cases is that the joint clients intend their communications to be secret from the rest

---

19. Stephen A. Saltzburg, Communications Falling Within the Attorney–Client Privilege, 66 Iowa L.Rev. 811, 816 (1981).

20. See, e.g., In re Himmel, 533 N.E.2d 790 (Ill.1988) (communication in front of mother and fiancé not privileged); Bolyea v. First Presbyterian Church of Wilton, 196 N.W.2d 149 (N.D.1972) (communication in front of others not privileged because not necessary to the preparation of a deed).

21. See, e.g., In re LTV Securities Litigation, 89 F.R.D. 595, 602 (N.D.Tex.1981).

22. For discussion of the co-client rule see Restatement § 125 and Wolfram, Modern Legal Ethics § 6.4.8 (1986).

23. See, e.g., Brennan's, Inc. v. Brennan's Restaurants, Inc., 590 F.2d 168 (5th Cir. 1979), reprinted at p. 642 infra.

of the world but not from one another.[24] Courts generally do not allow one joint client to waive the privilege for use against (or by) a third party except that a joint client may waive the privilege as to her own statements.

A lawyer should consider and discuss with clients the limited scope of the privilege in joint client relationships before entering into a representation of multiple clients. See M.R. 2.2(a)(1) (lawyer who acts as an intermediary between clients must consult with each client on, inter alia, "the effect on the attorney-client privilege"). The conflict of interest ramifications of a lawyer simultaneously representing more than one person engaged in a joint endeavor in which there are both common and differing interests are considered in Chapter 7 below at p. 618.

The common interest privilege (sometimes referred to as "pooled information" or "joint defense") is another exception to the general rule that disclosure to third parties waives the attorney-client privilege. A common interest arrangement permits persons who have common interests to coordinate their positions without destroying the privileged status of their communications.[25] This doctrine, which facilitates cooperation in litigation and transactions, protects communications only if and so long as a community of interest on one or more issues exists between the parties and only with respect to communications that serve the purpose of advancing the common interests. As with co-clients, a falling out between cooperating persons leads to loss of privilege in a subsequent adverse proceeding between them.

Exceptions to Attorney–Client Privilege

Five well-established exceptions to the attorney-client privilege are restated in §§ 131–134B of the Restatement: The exceptions concern: (1) a dispute concerning a decedent's disposition of property (§ 131); client crime or fraud (§ 132), considered in detail at p. 282 infra.; (3) lawyer self-protection (§ 133), considered at p. 272 infra; (4) disputes in which a trustee or other fiduciary is charged with a breach of fiduciary duty by a beneficiary (§ 134A); and (5) disputes between representatives of an organizational client and constituents of the organization (the *Garner* doctrine, discussed at p. 768 infra) (§ 134B).

2. CORPORATIONS AND THE ATTORNEY-CLIENT PRIVILEGE

Upjohn v. United States
Supreme Court of the United States, 1981.
449 U.S. 383.

■ JUSTICE REHNQUIST delivered the opinion of the Court.

We granted certiorari in this case to address important questions concerning the scope of the attorney-client privilege in the corporate

---

24. But see Ogden v. Groves, 241 So.2d 756 (Fla.App.1970) (attorney could testify only to statements by joint clients made in one another's presence, not to private statements by any of the joint clients to the lawyer).

25. See Restatement § 126; see also Proposed Fed.R.Evid. 503(b)(3), providing that the privilege extends to communications between a client "or his lawyer to a lawyer representing another in a matter of common interest."

context and the applicability of the work-product doctrine in proceedings to enforce tax summonses. . . .

I

Petitioner Upjohn Co. manufactures and sells pharmaceuticals here and abroad. In January 1976 independent accountants conducting an audit of one of Upjohn's foreign subsidiaries discovered that the subsidiary made payments to or for the benefit of foreign government officials in order to secure government business. The accountants so informed petitioner, Mr. Gerard Thomas, Upjohn's Vice President, Secretary, and General Counsel. Thomas is a member of the Michigan and New York Bars, and has been Upjohn's General Counsel for 20 years. He consulted with outside counsel and R.T. Parfet, Jr., Upjohn's Chairman of the Board. It was decided that the company would conduct an internal investigation of what were termed "questionable payments." As part of this investigation the attorneys prepared a letter containing a questionnaire which was sent to "All Foreign General and Area Managers" over the Chairman's signature. The letter began by noting recent disclosures that several American companies made "possibly illegal" payments to foreign government officials and emphasized that the management needed full information concerning any such payments made by Upjohn. The letter indicated that the Chairman had asked Thomas, identified as "the company's General Counsel," "to conduct an investigation for the purpose of determining the nature and magnitude of any payments made by the Upjohn Company or any of its subsidiaries to any employee or official of a foreign government." The questionnaire sought detailed information concerning such payments. Managers were instructed to treat the investigation as "highly confidential" and not to discuss it with anyone other than Upjohn employees who might be helpful in providing the requested information. Responses were to be sent directly to Thomas. Thomas and outside counsel also interviewed the recipients of the questionnaire and some 33 other Upjohn officers or employees as part of the investigation.

On March 26, 1976, the company voluntarily submitted a preliminary report to the Securities and Exchange Commission on Form 8–K disclosing certain questionable payments. A copy of the report was simultaneously submitted to the Internal Revenue Service, which immediately began an investigation to determine the tax consequences of the payments. Special agents conducting the investigation were given lists by Upjohn of all those interviewed and all who had responded to the questionnaire. On November 23, 1976, the Service issued a summons pursuant to 26 U.S.C. § 7602 demanding production of:

"All files relative to the investigation conducted under the supervision of Gerard Thomas to identify payments to employees of foreign governments and any political contributions made by the Upjohn Company or any of its affiliates since January 1, 1971 and to determine whether any funds of the Upjohn Company had been improperly accounted for on the corporate books during the same period.

"The records should include but not be limited to written questionnaires sent to managers of the Upjohn Company's foreign affiliates, and memorandums or notes of the interviews conducted in the United States and abroad with officers and employees of the Upjohn Company and its subsidiaries."

The company declined to produce the documents specified in the second paragraph on the grounds that they were protected from disclosure by the attorney-client privilege and constituted the work product of attorneys prepared in anticipation of litigation. On August 31, 1977, the United States filed a petition seeking enforcement of the summons under 26 U.S.C. §§ 7402(b) and 7604(a) in the United States District Court for the Western District of Michigan. . . .

II

Federal Rule of Evidence 501 provides that "the privilege of a witness . . . shall be governed by the principles of the common law as they may be interpreted by the courts of the United States in light of reason and experience." The attorney-client privilege is the oldest of the privileges for confidential communications known to the common law. 8 J. Wigmore, Evidence § 2290 (McNaughton rev. 1961). Its purpose is to encourage full and frank communication between attorneys and their clients and thereby promote broader public interests in the observance of law and administration of justice. The privilege recognizes that sound legal advice or advocacy serves public ends and that such advice or advocacy depends upon the lawyer's being fully informed by the client. As we stated last Term in Trammel v. United States, 445 U.S. 40, 51 (1980): "The lawyer-client privilege rests on the need for the advocate and counselor to know all that relates to the client's reasons for seeking representation if the professional mission is to be carried out." And in Fisher v. United States, 425 U.S. 391, 403 (1976), we recognized the purpose of the privilege to be "to encourage clients to make full disclosure to their attorneys." This rationale for the privilege has long been recognized by the Court, see Hunt v. Blackburn, 128 U.S. 464, 470 (1888). . . . Admittedly complications in the application of the privilege arise when the client is a corporation, which in theory is an artificial creature of the law, and not an individual; but this Court has assumed that the privilege applies when the client is a corporation, United States v. Louisville & Nashville R. Co., 236 U.S. 318, 336 (1915), and the Government does not contest the general proposition.

The Court of Appeals, however, considered the application of the privilege in the corporate context to present a "different problem," since the client was an inanimate entity and "only the senior management, guiding and integrating the several operations, . . . can be said to possess an identity analogous to the corporation as a whole." The first case to articulate the so-called "control group test" adopted by the court below, Philadelphia v. Westinghouse Electric Corp., 210 F.Supp. 483, 485

(E.D.Pa.), petition for mandamus and prohibition denied sub nom. General Electric Co. v. Kirkpatrick, 312 F.2d 742 (C.A.3 1962), reflected a similar conceptual approach:

> "Keeping in mind that the question is, Is it the corporation which is seeking the lawyer's advice when the asserted privileged communication is made?, the most satisfactory solution, I think, is that if the employee making the communication, of whatever rank he may be, is in a position to control or even to take a substantial part in a decision about any action which the corporation may take upon the advice of the attorney, ... then, in effect, *he is (or personifies) the corporation* when he makes his disclosure to the lawyer and the privilege would apply." (Emphasis supplied.)

Such a view, we think, overlooks the fact that the privilege exists to protect not only the giving of professional advice to those who can act on it but also the giving of information to the lawyer to enable him to give sound and informed advice.... The first step in the resolution of any legal problem is ascertaining the factual background and sifting through the facts with an eye to the legally relevant. See ABA Code of Professional Responsibility, Ethical Consideration 4–1:

> "A lawyer should be fully informed of all the facts of the matter he is handling in order for his client to obtain the full advantage of our legal system. It is for the lawyer in the exercise of his independent professional judgment to separate the relevant and important from the irrelevant and unimportant. The observance of the ethical obligation of a lawyer to hold inviolate the confidences and secrets of his client not only facilitates the full development of facts essential to proper representation of the client but also encourages laymen to seek early legal assistance."

See also Hickman v. Taylor, 329 U.S. 495, 511 (1947).

In the case of the individual client the provider of information and the person who acts on the lawyer's advice are one and the same. In the corporate context, however, it will frequently be employees beyond the control group as defined by the court below—"officers and agents ... responsible for directing [the company's] actions in response to legal advice"—who will possess the information needed by the corporation's lawyers. Middle-level—and indeed lower-level—employees can, by actions within the scope of their employment, embroil the corporation in serious legal difficulties, and it is only natural that these employees would have the relevant information needed by corporate counsel if he is adequately to advise the client with respect to such actual or potential difficulties. This fact was noted in Diversified Industries, Inc. v. Meredith, 572 F.2d 596 (C.A.8 1977) (en banc):

> "In a corporation, it may be necessary to glean information relevant to a legal problem from middle management or non-management personnel as well as from top executives. The attorney dealing with a complex legal problem 'is thus faced with a "Hobson's choice".

If he interviews employees not having "the very highest authority", their communications to him will not be privileged. If, on the other hand, he interviews *only* those employees with the "very highest authority", he may find it extremely difficult, if not impossible, to determine what happened.' " Id., at 608–609 (quoting Weinschel, Corporate Employee Interviews and the Attorney–Client Privilege, 12 B.C.Ind. & Com.L.Rev. 873, 876 (1971)).

The control group test adopted by the court below thus frustrates the very purpose of the privilege by discouraging the communication of relevant information by employees of the client to attorneys seeking to render legal advice to the client corporation. The attorney's advice will also frequently be more significant to noncontrol group members than to those who officially sanction the advice, and the control group test makes it more difficult to convey full and frank legal advice to the employees who will put into effect the client corporation's policy. See, e.g., Duplan Corp. v. Deering Milliken, Inc., 397 F.Supp. 1146, 1164 (D.S.C.1974) ("After the lawyer forms his or her opinion, it is of no immediate benefit to the Chairman of the Board or the President. It must be given to the corporate personnel who will apply it").

The narrow scope given the attorney-client privilege by the court below not only makes it difficult for corporate attorneys to formulate sound advice when their client is faced with a specific legal problem but also threatens to limit the valuable efforts of corporate counsel to ensure their client's compliance with the law. In light of the vast and complicated array of regulatory legislation confronting the modern corporation, corporations, unlike most individuals, "constantly go to lawyers to find out how to obey the law," Burnham, The Attorney–Client Privilege in the Corporate Arena, 24 Bus.Law. 901, 913 (1969), particularly since compliance with the law in this area is hardly an instinctive matter, see, e.g., United States v. United States Gypsum Co., 438 U.S. 422, 440–441 (1978) ("the behavior proscribed by the [Sherman] Act is often difficult to distinguish from the gray zone of socially acceptable and economically justifiable business conduct"). The test adopted by the court below is difficult to apply in practice, though no abstractly formulated and unvarying "test" will necessarily enable courts to decide questions such as this with mathematical precision. But if the purpose of the attorney-client privilege is to be served, the attorney and client must be able to predict with some degree of certainty whether particular discussions will be protected. An uncertain privilege, or one which purports to be certain but results in widely varying applications by the courts, is little better than no privilege at all. The very terms of the test adopted by the court below suggest the unpredictability of its application. The test restricts the availability of the privilege to those officers who play a "substantial role" in deciding and directing a corporation's legal response. Disparate decisions in cases applying this test illustrate its unpredictability. Compare, e.g., Hogan v. Zletz, 43 F.R.D. 308, 315–316 (N.D.Okl. 1967), aff'd in part sub nom. Natta v. Hogan, 392 F.2d 686 (C.A.10 1968) (control group includes managers and assistant managers of patent division and research and development department), with Congoleum Industries,

Inc. v. GAF Corp., 49 F.R.D. 82, 83–85 (E.D.Pa.1969), aff'd, 478 F.2d 1398 (C.A.3 1973) (control group includes only division and corporate vice presidents, and not two directors of research and vice president for production and research).

The communications at issue were made by Upjohn employees to counsel for Upjohn acting as such, at the direction of corporate superiors in order to secure legal advice from counsel. As the Magistrate found, "Mr. Thomas consulted with the Chairman of the Board and outside counsel and thereafter conducted a factual investigation to determine the nature and extent of the questionable payments *and to be in a position to give legal advice to the company with respect to the payments.*" (Emphasis supplied.) Information, not available from upper-echelon management, was needed to supply a basis for legal advice concerning compliance with securities and tax laws, foreign laws, currency regulations, duties to shareholders, and potential litigation in each of these areas. The communications concerned matters within the scope of the employees' corporate duties, and the employees themselves were sufficiently aware that they were being questioned in order that the corporation could obtain legal advice. The questionnaire identified Thomas as "the company's General Counsel" and referred in its opening sentence to the possible illegality of payments such as the ones on which information was sought. App. 40a. A statement of policy accompanying the questionnaire clearly indicated the legal implications of the investigation. The policy statement was issued "in order that there be no uncertainty in the future as to the policy with respect to the practices which are the subject of this investigation." It began "Upjohn will comply with all laws and regulations," and stated that commissions or payments "will not be used as a subterfuge for bribes or illegal payments" and that all payments must be "proper and legal." Any future agreements with foreign distributors or agents were to be approved "by a company attorney" and any questions concerning the policy were to be referred "to the company's General Counsel." This statement was issued to Upjohn employees worldwide, so that even those interviewees not receiving a questionnaire were aware of the legal implications of the interviews. Pursuant to explicit instructions from the Chairman of the Board, the communications were considered "highly confidential" when made, and have been kept confidential by the company. Consistent with the underlying purposes of the attorney-client privilege, these communications must be protected against compelled disclosure.

The Court of Appeals declined to extend the attorney-client privilege beyond the limits of the control group test for fear that doing so would entail severe burdens on discovery and create a broad "zone of silence" over corporate affairs. Application of the attorney-client privilege to communications such as those involved here, however, puts the adversary in no worse position than if the communications had never taken place. The privilege only protects disclosure of communications; it does not protect disclosure of the underlying facts by those who communicated with the attorney:

"[T]he protection of the privilege extends only to *communications* and not to facts. A fact is one thing and a communication concerning that fact is an entirely different thing. The client cannot be compelled to answer the question, 'What did you say or write to the attorney?' but may not refuse to disclose any relevant fact within his knowledge merely because he incorporated a statement of such fact into his communication to his attorney." Philadelphia v. Westinghouse Electric Corp., 205 F.Supp. 830, 831 (E.D.Pa.1962).

See also Diversified Industries, 572 F.2d, at 611; State ex rel. Dudek v. Circuit Court, 34 Wis.2d 559, 580, 150 N.W.2d 387, 399 (1967) ("the courts have noted that a party cannot conceal a fact merely by revealing it to his lawyer"). Here the Government was free to question the employees who communicated with Thomas and outside counsel. Upjohn has provided the IRS with a list of such employees, and the IRS has already interviewed some 25 of them. While it would probably be more convenient for the Government to secure the results of petitioner's internal investigation by simply subpoenaing the questionnaires and notes taken by petitioner's attorneys, such considerations of convenience do not overcome the policies served by the attorney-client privilege. As Justice Jackson noted in his concurring opinion in Hickman v. Taylor, 329 U.S., at 516: "Discovery was hardly intended to enable a learned profession to perform its functions ... on wits borrowed from the adversary."

Needless to say, we decide only the case before us, and do not undertake to draft a set of rules which should govern challenges to investigatory subpoenas. Any such approach would violate the spirit of Federal Rule of Evidence 501.... While such a "case-by-case" basis may to some slight extent undermine desirable certainty in the boundaries of the attorney-client privilege, it obeys the spirit of the Rules. At the same time we conclude that the narrow "control group test" sanctioned by the Court of Appeals in this case cannot, consistent with "the principles of the common law as ... interpreted ... in the light of reason and experience," Fed.Rule Evid. 501, govern the development of the law in this area.

III

Our decision that the communications by Upjohn employees to counsel are covered by the attorney-client privilege disposes of the case so far as the responses to the questionnaires and any notes reflecting responses to interview questions are concerned. The summons reaches further, however, and Thomas has testified that his notes and memoranda of interviews go beyond recording responses to his questions. To the extent that the material subject to the summons is not protected by the attorney-client privilege as disclosing communications between an employee and counsel, we must reach the ruling by the Court of Appeals that the work-product doctrine does not apply to summonses issued under 26 U.S.C. § 7602.[6]

---

6. The following discussion will also be relevant to counsel's notes and memoranda of interviews with the seven former employ-

The Government concedes, wisely, that the Court of Appeals erred and that the work-product doctrine does apply to IRS summonses. . . .

As we stated last Term, the obligation imposed by a tax summons remains "subject to the traditional privileges and limitations." United States v. Euge, 444 U.S. 707, 714 (1980). Nothing in the language of the IRS summons provisions or their legislative history suggests an intent on the part of Congress to preclude application of the work-product doctrine. Rule 26(b)(3) codifies the work-product doctrine, and the Federal Rules of Civil Procedure are made applicable to summons enforcement proceedings by Rule 81(a)(3). . . . While conceding the applicability of the work-product doctrine, the Government asserts that it has made a sufficient showing of necessity to overcome its protections. The Magistrate apparently so found. The Government relies on the following language in *Hickman* :

> "We do not mean to say that all written materials obtained or prepared by an adversary's counsel with an eye toward litigation are necessarily free from discovery in all cases. Where relevant and non-privileged facts remain hidden in an attorney's file and where production of those facts is essential to the preparation of one's case, discovery may properly be had. . . . And production might be justified where the witnesses are no longer available or can be reached only with difficulty." 329 U.S., at 511.

The Government stresses that interviewees are scattered across the globe and that Upjohn has forbidden its employees to answer questions it considers irrelevant. The above-quoted language from *Hickman*, however, did not apply to "oral statements made by witnesses . . . whether presently in the form of [the attorney's] mental impressions or memoranda." Id., at 512, 67 S.Ct., at 394. As to such material the Court did "not believe that any showing of necessity can be made under the circumstances of this case so as to justify production. . . . If there should be a rare situation justifying production of these matters petitioner's case is not of that type." Id., at 512–513. . . . Forcing an attorney to disclose notes and memoranda of witnesses' oral statements is particularly disfavored because it tends to reveal the attorney's mental processes, 329 U.S., at 513 ("what he saw fit to write down regarding witnesses' remarks"); id., at 516–517 ("the statement would be his [the attorney's] language, permeated with his inferences") (Jackson, J., concurring).[8]

Rule 26 accords special protection to work product revealing the attorney's mental processes. The Rule permits disclosure of documents and tangible things constituting attorney work product upon a showing of substantial need and inability to obtain the equivalent without undue

---

ees should it be determined that the attorney-client privilege does not apply to them.

8. Thomas described his notes of the interviews as containing "what I considered to be the important questions, the substance of the responses to them, my beliefs as to the importance of these, my beliefs as to how they related to the inquiry, my thoughts as to how they related to other questions. In some instances they might even suggest other questions that I would have to ask or things that I needed to find elsewhere."

hardship. This was the standard applied by the Magistrate. Rule 26 goes on, however, to state that "[i]n ordering discovery of such materials when the required showing has been made, the court shall protect against disclosure of the mental impressions, conclusions, opinions or legal theories of an attorney or other representative of a party concerning the litigation." Although this language does not specifically refer to memoranda based on oral statements of witnesses, the *Hickman* court stressed the danger that compelled disclosure of such memoranda would reveal the attorney's mental processes. It is clear that this is the sort of material the draftsmen of the Rule had in mind as deserving special protection. See Notes of Advisory Committee on 1970 Amendment to Rules, 28 U.S.C.App., p. 442.

Based on the foregoing, some courts have concluded that *no* showing of necessity can overcome protection of work product which is based on oral statements from witnesses. See, e.g., In re Grand Jury Proceedings, 473 F.2d 840, 848 (C.A.8 1973) (personal recollections, notes, and memoranda pertaining to conversation with witnesses); In re Grand Jury Investigation, 412 F.Supp. 943, 949 (E.D.Pa.1976) (notes of conversation with witness "are so much a product of the lawyer's thinking and so little probative of the witness's actual words that they are absolutely protected from disclosure"). Those courts declining to adopt an absolute rule have nonetheless recognized that such material is entitled to special protection. See, e.g., In re Grand Jury Investigation, 599 F.2d 1224, 1231 (C.A.3 1979) ("special considerations ... must shape any ruling on the discoverability of interview memoranda ...; such documents will be discoverable only in a 'rare situation' "); Cf. In re Grand Jury Subpoena, 599 F.2d 504, 511–512 (C.A.2 1979).

We do not decide the issue at this time. It is clear that the Magistrate applied the wrong standard when he concluded that the Government had made a sufficient showing of necessity to overcome the protections of the work-product doctrine. The Magistrate applied the "substantial need" and "without undue hardship" standard articulated in the first part of Rule 26(b)(3). The notes and memoranda sought by the Government here, however, are work product based on oral statements. If they reveal communications, they are, in this case, protected by the attorney-client privilege. To the extent they do not reveal communications, they reveal the attorneys' mental processes in evaluating the communications. As Rule 26 and *Hickman* make clear, such work product cannot be disclosed simply on a showing of substantial need and inability to obtain the equivalent without undue hardship.

While we are not prepared at this juncture to say that such material is always protected by the work-product rule, we think a far stronger showing of necessity and unavailability by other means than was made by the Government or applied by the Magistrate in this case would be necessary to compel disclosure....

■ CHIEF JUSTICE BURGER, concurring in part and concurring in the judgment.

... I agree fully with the Court's rejection of the so-called "control group" test, its reasons for doing so, and its ultimate holding that the communications at issue are privileged. As the Court states, however, "if the purpose of the attorney-client privilege is to be served, the attorney and client must be able to predict with some degree of certainty whether particular discussions will be protected." For this very reason, I believe that we should articulate a standard that will govern similar cases and afford guidance to corporations, counsel advising them, and federal courts.

... [T]he Court should make clear now that, as a general rule, a communication is privileged at least when, as here, an employee or former employee speaks at the direction of the management with an attorney regarding conduct or proposed conduct within the scope of employment. The attorney must be one authorized by the management to inquire into the subject and must be seeking information to assist counsel in performing any of the following functions: (a) evaluating whether the employee's conduct has bound or would bind the corporation; (b) assessing the legal consequences, if any, of that conduct; or (c) formulating appropriate legal responses to actions that have been or may be taken by others with regard to that conduct....

Scope of the Corporate Privilege

What test does *Upjohn* provide for determining the scope of the corporate privilege? Does it make privileged every communication between a corporation's lawyers and any of its employees?

The strongest argument for the "control group" test is that the test prevents too broad a "zone of silence" over corporate affairs. After *Upjohn* might a corporation route all corporate documents through its general counsel's office ostensibly to keep its lawyer informed but actually to set up a later claim of privilege? Would such a plan work?

Under *Upjohn* may the IRS use compulsory process to obtain the following: (1) The accounting report prepared by the outside accounting firm that first raised the subject of "questionable payments?" (2) A memorandum, prepared by the manager of Upjohn's Turkish operations on his own initiative, detailing illegal payments to Turkish officials and reports of similar payments made by other Upjohn employees in Greece and Italy? Does it make a difference whether the report or memorandum is addressed to Upjohn's chairman, Parfet, or to its general counsel, Thomas? Is the privilege inapplicable to either document because it was not made "at the direction of corporate superiors in order to secure legal advice from counsel"?[1] Is the privilege inapplicable because the document comes from a non-employee or the information it contains does not relate to the employ-

1. See John E. Sexton, A Post–Upjohn Consideration of the Corporate Attorney–Client Privilege, 57 N.Y.U.L.Rev. 443, 508–10 (1982); Note, The Attorney–Client Privi- lege and the Corporate Client: Where Do We Go After Upjohn?, 81 Mich.L.Rev. 665 (1983).

ee's duties for the corporation? Does Chief Justice Burger's formulation of the privilege answer these hypothetical situations?[2]

Suppose Upjohn executives decide to offer government agencies an airtight case against the Turkish manager on condition that claims involving other "questionable payments" are dropped. Can the manager prevent Upjohn from delivering his questionnaire and interview responses to the government? What about the report that Upjohn has made to the IRS and the SEC? May Upjohn shareholders or other claimants discover that document in an action against Upjohn?

The Restatement formulates the scope of the privilege of an organizational client with a "need to know" test: Section 123 provides that a communication between any agent of the organization and the organization's lawyer, "concern[ing] a legal matter of interest to the organization" is privileged if "disclosed only to: (a) privileged persons . . .; and (b) other agents of the organization who reasonably need to know of the communication in order to act for the organization." The terms employed—"a legal matter of interest to the organization" and "agent"—are of great breadth. Moreover, the comments to § 123 broaden the scope of the corporate privilege by eliminating the qualifying factors mentioned in the Rehnquist opinion and the Burger concurrence in *Upjohn*: communications by former employees of an organization are covered if "the former agent has a continuing legal obligation to the principal-organization to furnish the information to the organization's lawyer [cmt. *e*]; a communication need not be directed by a organizational superior to be privileged [cmt. *h*]; and the communication need not be within the scope of employment of the communicating employee [cmt. *e*].[3] The breadth of the Restatement provision makes it easier to apply than the uncertainties of the subject-matter "test" adopted by *Upjohn*, since virtually all communications with a corporate lawyer by any current or former employee turn out to be privileged. Is this result achieved by casting too wide a veil of secrecy over organizational affairs?

Why a Corporate Privilege?

The *Upjohn* case appears to have quieted concerns emanating from lower court decisions about the application of the attorney-client privilege to corporations. In its extreme form, the question was whether an artificial entity such as a corporation qualifies as a "client" for purposes of the privilege. Considerations of individual dignity and autonomy that undergird the Fifth Amendment privilege against self-incrimination and the Sixth Amendment right to counsel are limited to natural persons. If the attorney-client privilege rests on similar considerations, should artificial legal entities be confined to the work-product immunity?[4]

2. See Robert Stern, Attorney–Client Privilege: Supreme Court Repudiates the Control Group Test, 67 A.B.A.J. 1142, 1146 (1981).

3. See Sherman L. Cohn, The Organizational Client: Attorney–Client Privilege and the No–Contact Rule, 10 Geo.J.Legal Ethics 739, 760–70 (1997).

4. An individual's attorney-client privilege extends only to information supplied by that person to his lawyer. Communications relating to the client from third persons,

A federal district judge startled the corporate bar in 1962 by holding that only natural persons, not corporations, were "clients."[5] Although subsequent decisions rejected this position, the Third Circuit evolved the "control group test" as a limitation on the corporate privilege.[6] Does *Upjohn* settle the question of the applicability of the attorney-client privilege to corporations? Note that state courts are not bound by federal evidence law; even in federal courts, state law governs testimonial privileges insofar as state-created claims and defenses are involved.[7] Federal and state decisions also apply the privilege to other artificial entities, such as partnerships, unincorporated associations and governmental bodies.

Who May Claim the Privilege on Behalf of a Corporation?

The current management of a corporation controls the privilege on behalf of the corporation. When management is replaced, the successor controls the privilege. This may result in decisions to waive the privilege that may be embarrassing to members of the prior management.[8] Moreover, shareholders in a derivative suit may successfully challenge management's decision to invoke the privilege and thereby gain access to otherwise confidential corporate communications.[9]

Speaking With Corporate Employees or Advising Them Not to Speak With Opposing Counsel

The Court in *Upjohn* states that the IRS may question the employees from whom Upjohn's general counsel obtained information. Would such questioning violate professional constraints against direct contact with another lawyer's clients? See Model Rule 4.2 and DR 7-104(A)(1). If the employees refuse to cooperate informally, will a subpoena be effective? What if an employee refuses to respond on grounds that his answers may incriminate him? Whether an opposing party may contact employees of an organization directly without notifying the organization's lawyer is considered in Chapter 6 below at p. 533.

---

however closely related to the individual client, are not privileged. Yet *Upjohn* extends the corporate attorney-client privilege to information from anyone related to the corporation. Does this make the corporate attorney-client privilege broader than that available to individuals?

5. Radiant Burners, Inc. v. American Gas Ass'n, 207 F.Supp. 771, 209 F.Supp. 321 (N.D.Ill.1962), rev'd, 320 F.2d 314 (7th Cir. 1963).

6. City of Philadelphia v. Westinghouse Elec. Corp., 210 F.Supp. 483 (E.D.Pa.1962), left standing on appeal, 312 F.2d 742 (3d Cir.1962).

7. *Upjohn* is not controlling in state courts or in federal diversity cases. See, e.g., Consolidation Coal Co. v. Bucyrus–Erie Co., 432 N.E.2d 250 (Ill.1982) (*Upjohn* rejected; control group test applied). However, most states reach the same result as *Upjohn*.

8. See Commodity Futures Trading Commission v. Weintraub, 471 U.S. 343 (1985) (court-appointed successor may waive the corporation's privilege).

9. See Garner v. Wolfinbarger, 430 F.2d 1093 (5th Cir.1970) (setting out factors to be considered in whether to grant shareholders access to otherwise privileged information), discussed in Chapter 8 infra at p. 768.

In *Upjohn* corporate employees were "forbidden ... to answer questions" that were posed by government lawyers which the company considered irrelevant. Could Upjohn also insist that one of its lawyers be present when the IRS interviews an employee? Model Rule 3.4(f) provides:

> A lawyer shall not ... request a person other than a client to refrain from voluntarily giving relevant information to another party unless: (1) the person is a relative or an employee or other agent of a client; and (2) the lawyer reasonably believes that the person's interests will not be adversely affected by refraining from giving such information.

Recall that urging some one not to give evidence may sometimes constitute the crime of "obstruction of justice." Is there a clear line between protecting a client by urging employees not to cooperate with an adversary and obstructing another party's access to evidence?

Governmental Clients and Attorney–Client Privilege

The scope of the attorney-client privilege as applied to governmental clients has been less well explored than the scope of the privilege in general. Professor Wolfram argues that the privilege should be given a narrow reading in this context because of the countervailing policies of open government. Freedom of information statutes contain specified exceptions and the lawyer work-product doctrine provides more limited but essential protection in litigation contexts.[10]

3. WORK–PRODUCT DOCTRINE

The work-product doctrine is connected to, but different from, the attorney-client privilege.[11] As *Upjohn* demonstrates, the work-product rule governs documents prepared by lawyers in anticipation of litigation that do not include communications protected by the privilege.

The leading case on the work-product doctrine is *Hickman v. Taylor*.[12] In *Hickman* the Court recognized a qualified immunity for the work product of lawyers, holding that such material was discoverable only upon a substantial showing of "necessity or justification." *Hickman* has been codified in Federal Rule of Civil Procedure 26(b)(3), which provides in part:

> [A] party may obtain discovery of [material] ... otherwise discoverable under ... this rule and prepared in anticipation of litigation ... only upon showing that the party seeking discovery has substantial need of the materials in the preparation of his case and that he is unable without undue hardship to obtain the substantial equivalent of the materials by other means. In ordering discovery of such materials when the required showing has been made, the court shall protect against disclosure of the mental impressions, conclusions, opinions, or legal theories of an attorney ... concerning the litigation.

---

10. See Restatement § 124; Wolfram, Modern Legal Ethics § 6.5.6 (1986).

11. On the work-product doctrine see generally Restatement §§ 136–43; and Special

Project: The Work Product Doctrine, 68 Cornell L.Rev. 760 (1983).

12. 329 U.S. 495 (1947).

Material other than a lawyer's mental impressions, theories and opinions is called "ordinary work product." Ordinary or fact work product has been held discoverable for impeachment purposes,[13] because a witness is unavailable or hostile,[14] because of the delay or expense that would be incurred if the opposing party were not given access to the material[15] and where the passage of time makes the material otherwise inaccessible.[16] Does *Upjohn* raise the level of hardship required to obtain fact work product?

Lawyer's Mental Impressions and Theories

The language in Fed.R.Civ.Proc. Rule 26(b)(3) and in corresponding state formulations of the work-product doctrine accords the mental impressions, opinions and theories of the lawyer special protection. *Upjohn* left open the issue of whether mental impressions and the like are absolutely protected from discovery. What showing of need did the IRS make in *Upjohn*? After *Upjohn*, what showing is required to overcome work-product protection?

Most state courts follow the lead of *Upjohn*, holding that absent some extreme necessity the mental impressions of lawyers are not discoverable.[17] Others hold that under no circumstances are mental impressions discoverable.[18]

Material "Prepared in Anticipation of Litigation"

As formulated in *Hickman* and codified in Rule 26(b)(3), the work-product rule protects only material "prepared in anticipation of litigation." *Upjohn* demonstrates, without discussing what the phrase means, that this may include reports prepared prior to the commencement of a proceeding. On the other hand, "the work product rule does not come into play merely because there is a remote prospect of future litigation."[19] The scope of the phrase "prepared in anticipation of litigation" thus is uncertain:[20]

In United States v. Adlman,[21] the lawyer for a corporation asked an outside accountant to evaluate the tax implications of a merger of two wholly-owned subsidiaries. The result was a 58–page analysis of likely IRS challenges to the reorganization and to an expected corporate claim for a

13. Brennan v. Engineered Products, 506 F.2d 299 (8th Cir.1974).

14. Xerox v. IBM, 64 F.R.D. 367 (S.D.N.Y. 1974) (witness lost memory); Fidelity & Deposit Co. v. S. Stefan Strauss, Inc., 52 F.R.D. 536 (E.D.Pa.1971) (witness employee of adversary); Almaguer v. Chicago, R.I. & P.R., 55 F.R.D. 147 (D.Neb.1972) (witness hostile).

15. Arney v. Geo. A. Hormel & Co., 53 F.R.D. 179 (D.Minn.1971).

16. Hamilton v. Canal Barge Co., 395 F.Supp. 975 (D.La.1974).

17. See, e.g., Klaiber v. Orzel, 714 P.2d 813 (Ariz.1986); and Consolidation Coal Co. v. Bucyrus–Erie Co., 432 N.E.2d 250 (Ill. 1982).

18. See, e.g., Broussard v. State Farm Mutual, 519 So.2d 136 (La.1988); Dennie v. Metropolitan Medical Center, 387 N.W.2d 401 (Minn.1986).

19. Diversified Industries, Inc. v. Meredith, 572 F.2d 596, 604 (8th Cir.1977).

20. Note, Work Product Discovery: A Multifactor Approach to the Anticipation of Litigation Requirement in Federal Rule of Civil Procedure 26(b)(3), 66 Iowa L.Rev. 1277, 1277–78 (1981).

21. 68 F.3d 1495 (2d Cir.1995).

$35 million tax refund. The memo included proposed defensive strategies, structuring methods and predictions about expected litigation. After the merger, the IRS sought to compel production of the report. The district court had held that the report was not covered by the work product doctrine because "neither the litigation nor the events giving rise to it (the proposed merger) had yet occurred."[22] Rejecting this reasoning, the Second Circuit said: "Although the non-occurrence of the events giving rise to the anticipated litigation is a factor that can argue against application of the work product doctrine, especially when the expected litigation is merely a vague abstract possibility without precise form, ... there is no rule that bars application of work product protection to documents created prior to the event giving rise to litigation. Nor do we see any reason for such a limitation."

On remand, the district court ruled that the documents were not protected, and the court of appeals again reversed. The court stated: "[D]ocuments should be deemed prepared 'in anticipation of litigation,' and thus [protected], if 'in light of the nature of the document and the factual situation in the particular case, the document can fairly be said to have been prepared or obtained because of the prospect of litigation.' "[23] Judge Kearse, dissenting, argued that the work-product privilege does not extend to materials, such as the report in question, prepared to guide a business decision at a stage well before any "anticipation" of a lawsuit.[24]

Whether material was prepared in anticipation of litigation is an important question for insurance companies. Are all claims investigations "in anticipation of litigation"? Two positions have emerged. Most courts say that litigation is not "anticipated" until an attorney has become involved and has either prepared the documents herself or requested their preparation.[25] Under this rule, unless the insurer's investigation has been performed at the request or under the direction of an attorney, the materials resulting from the investigation are "conclusively presumed to have been made in the ordinary course of business and not in anticipation of litigation."[26] One court has given the following rationale for this approach:

> Because a substantial part of an insurance company's business is to investigate claims made by an insured against the company or by some other party against an insured, it must be presumed that such investigations are part of the normal business activity of the company and that reports and witness' statements compiled by or on behalf of the insurer in the course of such investigations are ordinary business records as distinguished from trial preparation materials.[27]

---

22. Id. at 1501.

23. United States v. Adlman, 134 F.3d 1194, 1201 (2d Cir.1998).

24. Id. at 1205.

25. See, e.g., McDougall v. Dunn, 468 F.2d 468, 474–75 (4th Cir.1972).

26. Henry Enterprises v. Smith, 592 P.2d 915, 920 (Kan.1979).

27. Hawkins v. District Court, 638 P.2d 1372, 1378 (Colo.1982) (en banc, quoting Thomas Organ Co. v. Jadranska Slobodna Plovidba, 54 F.R.D. 367, 373 (N.D.Ill. 1972)).

The alternative position treats virtually all insurance investigations as made in anticipation of litigation.[28] Liability insurers who investigate claims do anticipate litigation, but should work-product protection be provided for the work of claims investigators who are nominally supervised by a lawyer? What degree of attorney involvement in a claims investigation should be required to satisfy the "anticipation of litigation" requirement?[29]

The work-product rule does not cover material prepared as part of a future or ongoing crime or fraud, whether or not in anticipation of litigation.[30]

Who May Invoke Attorney–Client and Work–Product Protection?

The client, not the lawyer, "owns" the attorney-client privilege, which means that a lawyer cannot successfully invoke the privilege if the client has waived it. As to work-product protection, courts disagree as to whether the protection is the client's, the lawyer's or belongs to both. Restatement § 139 states the majority rule that "work product immunity may be invoked by or for [a person] on whose behalf it was prepared." Some courts hold that the lawyer as well as the client must consent to disclosure.[31] A few decisions hold that a lawyer in some situations may resist disclosure of work product in the face of a client's request for it.[32]

Although some decisions hold that work product protection terminates at the end of the litigation for which the material was prepared, the dominant position is that, if litigation was reasonably anticipated, the immunity applies even if litigation occurs in an unexpected way.[33] What, if anything, in the rationale for the work-product rule suggests that its duration be limited?

28. See Ashmead v. Harris, 336 N.W.2d 197, 201 (Iowa 1983).

29. See National Farmers Union Property and Casualty Co. v. District Court, 718 P.2d 1044 (Colo.1986) (memoranda prepared by lawyers for insurance company not protected by work product rule because lawyers were performing same function as claims adjuster, and resulting report is a discoverable business record). Compare Shelton v. American Motors Corp., 805 F.2d 1323, 1329 (8th Cir.1986) ("selection and compilation of documents [by lawyer] ... reflects legal theories and thought processes which are protected as work product").

30. See, e.g., In re Doe, 662 F.2d 1073, 1079–80 (4th Cir.1981); see also discussion of the crime-fraud exception at p. 282 infra.

31. See, e.g., In re Special September 1978 Grand Jury, 640 F.2d 49 (7th Cir.1980).

32. In Lasky, Haas, Cohler & Munter v. Superior Court, 218 Cal.Rptr. 205 (1985) (so holding, but the client's request apparently was under legal coercion from a third party; the court stated that a client could obtain material relevant to a legal malpractice case).

33. Restatement § 137, cmt. *j*; In re Grand Jury Proceedings, 43 F.3d 966, 971 (5th Cir.1994) (protection extends to all future litigation); and Research Inst. for Medicine & Chemistry, Inc. v. Wisconsin Alumni Research Found., 114 F.R.D. 672, 680 (W.D.Wis.1987) (protection applies only in litigation for which materials are prepared).

Accountants Versus Lawyers

Federal securities laws require publicly held corporations to file financial statements that include an independent audit. The accountant must determine whether a corporation has sufficient reserve funds to handle any additional taxes that might arise. Typically, the outside auditor prepares work sheets reviewing the company's own evaluation of its tax liability and outlining the corporation's other possible areas of tax vulnerability. Arthur Young & Co. performed this function for one of its clients, Amerada Hess Corp. The IRS, during an investigation of Amerada's taxes, asked for the work sheets for particular tax years; when Amerada instructed Arthur Young not to produce them, the IRS sought court enforcement of its summons. The Court unanimously held that "tax accrual workpapers prepared by a corporation's independent certified public accountant in the course of regular financial audits are [subject to] disclosure in response to an Internal Revenue Service summons."[34]

The decision reflected the broad statutory authority of the IRS to compel production of taxpayer records and the desirability, in a tax system that relies on voluntary reporting, of assuring government access. But the contrasting treatment given to IRS summonses in *Upjohn* and *Arthur Young* did not go unnoticed. Reliable audits depend upon candor and full disclosure in the provision of information. Accounting firms asserted that failure to protect an auditor's working papers would reduce the flow of information from corporate clients, reducing the reliability of independent audits.[35]

Chief Justice Burger, writing for the Court in *Arthur Young*, rejected the argument that "a work-product immunity for accountants' tax accrual workpapers is a fitting analogue to the attorney work-product doctrine established in Hickman v. Taylor."

> ... The *Hickman* work-product doctrine was founded upon the private attorney's role as the client's confidential advisor and advocate, a loyal representative whose duty it is to present the client's case in the most favorable possible light. An independent certified public accountant performs a different role. By certifying the public reports that collectively depict a corporation's financial status, the independent auditor assumes a *public* responsibility transcending any employment relationship with the client. The independent public accountant performing this special function owes ultimate allegiance to the corporation's creditors and stockholders, as well as to [the] investing public. This "public watchdog" function demands that the accountant maintain total independence from the client at all times and requires complete fidelity to the public trust. To insulate from disclosure a certified public accountant's interpretations of the client's financial statements would be to ignore the significance of the accountant's role as a disinterested analyst charged with public obligation.

34. United States v. Arthur Young & Co., 465 U.S. 805 (1984).

35. See Stephen Wermiel, Justices Allow Review by IRS of Audit Papers, Wall St.J., Mar. 22, 1984, p. 2.

We cannot accept the view that [without the protection of confidentiality] a corporation might be tempted to withhold from its auditor certain information relevant and material to a proper evaluation of its financial statements.... [T]he independent certified public accountant cannot be content with the corporation's representations that its tax accrual reserves are adequate; the auditor is ethically and professionally obligated to ascertain for himself as far as possible whether the corporation's contingent tax liabilities have been accurately stated. If the auditor were convinced that the scope of the examination had been limited by management's reluctance to disclose matters relating to the tax accrual reserves, the auditor would be ... required to issue a qualified opinion, an adverse opinion, or a disclaimer of opinion, thereby notifying the investing public of possible potential problems inherent in the corporation's financial reports.... Thus, the independent auditor's obligation to serve the public interest assures that the integrity of the securities markets will be preserved, without the need for a work-product immunity for accountants' tax accrual workpapers.[36]

Are you satisfied that the arguments for lawyer confidentiality are better than those for accountant confidentiality? Are lawyers always acting as "advocates" and accountants always as "auditors?" In a world in which different service professions compete for business, *Upjohn* and *Arthur Young* give lawyers something to sell that accountants and others do not— a large but uncertain degree of protection against compelled disclosure. Does the attorney-client privilege, as applied in *Upjohn*, provide an artificial stimulus for large organizations to hire lawyers whenever trouble is afoot in an effort to shield dirty linen from public scrutiny and response?

In 1995 accountants, supported by consumer and business groups, achieved a victory they had been unable to accomplish by judicial interpretation in *Arthur Young*. Section 7525 of the IRS Restructuring and Reform Act of 1998 extended "[w]ith respect to tax advice, the same common law protections of confidentiality which apply to a communication between a taxpayer and an attorney" to "a communication between a taxpayer and any federally authorized tax practitioner...."[37] The newly created statutory privilege applies to any "tax advice" by an accountant-tax practitioner "with respect to a matter which is within the scope of the individual's [tax practice] authority...." Two exceptions are stated in the provision: the privilege (1) may not be asserted in a criminal tax matter before the IRS or a federal court; and (2) does not apply to any written communication between a tax practitioner and a promoter of a tax shelter. These exceptions raise troublesome questions that may mislead consumers. If tax advice, for example, ultimately leads to a criminal inquiry or proceeding, the privilege evaporates and the accountant, unlike the lawyer, must testify wholly apart from the crime-fraud exception. The legislation presumably

36. 465 U.S. at 817–19.

37. See CCH, 1998 Tax Legislation: IRS Restructuring and Reform ¶ 1141 (June 1998).

does not cover advice about state taxes, which are unprotected except in the small number of states with an accountant's privilege. Many other uncertainties remain, such as whether the statute by implication creates the work-product immunity sought in the *Arthur Young* case. The legislative history also states that the privilege does not apply to "the communications and documents generated in the course of preparing [a] tax return." The committee reports appear to assume that when lawyers prepare tax returns they are engaged in business, as opposed to the practice of law, and that therefore the attorney-client privilege would not attach. That conclusion is probably correct with respect to preparation of routine tax returns by lawyers as a sideline, but surely does not apply to the legal advice given in connection with complex returns. The courts will have to struggle with this and the other uncertainties created by this statute. The answers the courts provide are likely to give rise to particulars of federal privilege law that will probably apply to lawyers as well as accountants.

4.   DOCUMENTS, ATTORNEY–CLIENT PRIVILEGE AND THE BILL OF RIGHTS

Fisher v. United States

Supreme Court of the United States, 1976.
425 U.S. 391.

■ MR. JUSTICE WHITE delivered the opinion of the Court.

In these two cases we are called upon to decide whether a summons directing an attorney to produce documents delivered to him by his client in connection with the attorney-client relationship is enforceable over claims that the documents were constitutionally immune from summons in the hands of the client and retained that immunity in the hands of the attorney.

... In our view the documents were not privileged either in the hands of the lawyers or of their clients...

[In one of the two cases, United States v. Kasmir, 499 F.2d 444 (5th Cir.1974), two special agents of the Internal Revenue Service visited Dr. E.J. Mason's medical office, informed him that his tax returns for 1969, 1970, and 1971 were under investigation, and gave him Miranda warnings. When the agents asked to see Mason's books and records, Mason called his accountant, Candy, who advised him to say nothing and not to produce his records. Candy then called Kasmir, a lawyer, whom Mason retained as his attorney later the same day. Early the next morning, at Mason's direction, Candy delivered various records and documents to Mason, who then turned them over to Kasmir as his attorney. The next day the IRS served a summons on Kasmir directing him to produce "the following records of Tannebaum Bindler & Lewis [the accounting firm].

"1.   Accountant's workpapers pertaining to Dr. E.J. Mason's books and records of 1969, 1970 and 1971.

"2. Retained copies of E.J. Mason's income tax returns for 1969, 1970 and 1971.

"3. Retained copies of reports and other correspondence between Tannenbaum Bindler & Lewis and Dr. E.J. Mason during 1969, 1970 and 1971."

[When Kasmir refused to comply with the summons, the government sought enforcement. The district court granted enforcement, but the court of appeals reversed. United States v. Kasmir, 499 F.2d 444 (5th Cir.1974). The second case, United States v. Fisher, 500 F.2d 683 (3d Cir.1974), reached a result contrary to *Kasmir*. In *Fisher* the IRS sought analyses by the taxpayers' accountant of income and expenses, which had been prepared from canceled checks and deposit receipts of the taxpayers' businesses, and later turned over to their lawyer. In *Fisher* as in *Kasmir*, the attorney claimed that enforcement would involve compulsory self-incrimination of the taxpayers in violation of their Fifth Amendment privilege, would involve a seizure of the papers without necessary compliance with the Fourth Amendment and would violate the taxpayers' right to communicate in confidence with their attorneys.]

II

All of the parties in these cases and the Court of Appeals for the Fifth Circuit have concurred in the proposition that if the Fifth Amendment would have excused a *taxpayer* from turning over the accountant's papers had he possessed them, the *attorney* to whom they are delivered for the purpose of obtaining legal advice should also be immune from subpoena. Although we agree with this proposition for the reasons set forth in Part III, infra, we are convinced that, under our decision in Couch v. United States, 409 U.S. 322 (1973), it is not the taxpayer's Fifth Amendment privilege that would excuse the *attorney* from production.

The relevant part of that Amendment provides:

"No person ... shall be *compelled* in any criminal case to be a *witness against himself*." (Emphasis added.)

The taxpayer's privilege under this Amendment is not violated by enforcement of the summonses involved in these cases because enforcement against a taxpayer's lawyer would not "compel" the taxpayer to do anything—and certainly would not compel him to be a "witness" against himself. The Court has held repeatedly that the Fifth Amendment is limited to prohibiting the use of "physical or moral compulsion" exerted on the person asserting the privilege.... In Couch v. United States, supra, we recently ruled that the Fifth Amendment rights of a taxpayer were not violated by the enforcement of a documentary summons directed to her accountant and requiring production of the taxpayer's own records in the possession of the accountant. We did so on the ground that in such a case "the ingredient of personal compulsion against an accused is lacking." 409 U.S., at 329....

Here, the taxpayers are compelled to do no more than was the taxpayer in *Couch*. The taxpayers' Fifth Amendment privilege is therefore not violated by enforcement of the summonses directed toward their attorneys. This is true whether or not the Amendment would have barred a subpoena directing the taxpayer to produce the documents while they were in his hands.

The fact that the attorneys are agents of the taxpayers does not change this result. *Couch* held as much, since the accountant there was also the taxpayer's agent, and in this respect reflected a longstanding view. In *Hale v. Henkel*, 201 U.S. 43, 69–70 (1906), the Court said that the privilege "was never intended to permit [a person] to plead the fact that some third person might be incriminated by his testimony, even though he were the agent of such person.... [T]he Amendment is limited to a person who shall be compelled in any criminal case to be a witness against *himself*." (Emphasis in original.) "It is extortion of information from the accused himself that offends our sense of justice." *Couch v. United States, supra*, 409 U.S., at 328.... Agent or no, the lawyer is not the taxpayer. The taxpayer is the "accused," and nothing is being extorted from him.

. . .

... Here, the taxpayers retained any privilege they ever had not to be compelled to testify against themselves and not to be compelled themselves to produce private papers in their possession. *This* personal privilege was in no way decreased by the transfer. It is simply that by reason of the transfer of the documents to the attorneys, those papers may be subpoenaed without compulsion on the taxpayer. The protection of the Fifth Amendment is therefore not available. "A party is privileged from producing evidence but not from its production [by others]." *Johnson v. United States*, 228 U.S., at 458....

The Court of Appeals for the Fifth Circuit suggested that because legally and ethically the attorney was required to respect the confidences of his client, the latter had a reasonable expectation of privacy for the records in the hands of the attorney and therefore did not forfeit his Fifth Amendment privilege with respect to the records by transferring them in order to obtain legal advice. It is true that the Court has often stated that one of the several purposes served by the constitutional privilege against compelled testimonial self-incrimination is that of protecting personal privacy. But the Court has never suggested that every invasion of privacy violates the privilege. Within the limits imposed by the language of the Fifth Amendment, which we necessarily observe, the privilege truly serves privacy interests; but the Court has never on any ground, personal privacy included, applied the Fifth Amendment to prevent the otherwise proper acquisition or use of evidence which, in the Court's view, did not involve compelled testimonial self-incrimination of some sort.[5]

---

5. There is a line of cases in which the Court stated that the Fifth Amendment was offended by the use in evidence of documents or property seized in violation of the Fourth Amendment. *Gouled v. United States*, 255 U.S. 298, 306 (1921); *Agnel-*

The proposition that the Fifth Amendment protects private information obtained without compelling self-incriminating testimony is contrary
to the clear statements of this Court that under appropriate safeguards
private incriminating statements of an accused may be overheard and used
in evidence, if they are not compelled at the time they were uttered. Katz v.
United States, 389 U.S. 347, 354 (1967); Osborn v. United States, 385 U.S.
323, 329–330 (1966); and Berger v. New York, 388 U.S. 41, 57 (1967); cf.
Hoffa v. United States, 385 U.S. 293, 304 (1966); and that disclosure of
private information may be compelled if immunity removes the risk of
incrimination. Kastigar v. United States, 406 U.S. 441 (1972). If the Fifth
Amendment protected generally against the obtaining of private information from a man's mouth or pen or house, its protections would presumably
not be lifted by probable cause and a warrant or by immunity. The privacy
invasion is not mitigated by immunity; and the Fifth Amendment's strictures, unlike the Fourth's, are not removed by showing reasonableness.
The Framers addressed the subject of personal privacy directly in the
Fourth Amendment. They struck a balance so that when the State's reason
to believe incriminating evidence will be found becomes sufficiently great,
the invasion of privacy becomes justified and a warrant to search and seize
will issue. They did not seek in still another Amendment—the Fifth—to
achieve a general protection of privacy but to deal with the more specific
issue of compelled self-incrimination.

We cannot cut the Fifth Amendment completely loose from the moor-
ings of its language, and make it serve as a general protector of privacy—a
word not mentioned in its text and a concept directly addressed in the
Fourth Amendment. We adhere to the view that the Fifth Amendment
protects against "compelled self-incrimination, not [the disclosure of] private information." United States v. Nobles, 422 U.S. 225, 233 n. 7 (1975).

Insofar as private information not obtained through compelled self-
incriminating testimony is legally protected, its protection stems from other
sources[6]—the Fourth Amendment's protection against seizures without
warrant or probable cause and against subpoenas which suffer from "too
much indefiniteness or breadth in the things required to be 'particularly

---

lo v. United States, 269 U.S. 20, 33–34
(1925); United States v. Lefkowitz, 285
U.S. 452, 466–467 (1932); Mapp v. Ohio,
367 U.S. 643, 661 (1961) (Black, J., concurring). But the Court purported to find elements of compulsion in such situations.
"In either case he is the unwilling source
of the evidence, and the Fifth Amendment
forbids that he shall be compelled to be a
witness against himself in a criminal case."
Gouled v. United States, supra, 255 U.S.,
at 306. . . . In any event the predicate for
those cases, lacking here, was a violation of
the Fourth Amendment. Cf. Burdeau v.
McDowell, supra, 256 U.S. 465, 475–476
(1921).

6. In Couch v. United States, 409 U.S. 322
(1973), on which taxpayers rely for their
claim that the Fifth Amendment protects
their "legitimate expectation of privacy,"
the Court differentiated between the things
protected by the Fourth and Fifth Amendments. "We hold today that no Fourth or
Fifth Amendment claim can prevail where,
as in this case, there exists no legitimate
expectation of privacy and no semblance of
governmental compulsion against the person of the accused." Id., 409 U.S., at
336. . . .

described,' " Oklahoma Press Pub. Co. v. Walling, 327 U.S. 186, 208 (1946); In re Horowitz, 482 F.2d 72, 75–80 (C.A.2 1973) (Friendly, J.); the First Amendment, see NAACP v. Alabama, 357 U.S. 449, 462 (1958); or evidentiary privileges such as the attorney–client privilege.[7]

III

... The taxpayers in these cases, however, have from the outset consistently urged that they should not be forced to expose otherwise protected documents to summons simply because they have sought legal advice and turned the papers over to their attorneys. . . .

Confidential disclosures by a client to an attorney made in order to obtain legal assistance are privileged. 8 J. Wigmore, Evidence, § 2292 (McNaughton rev. 1961) (hereinafter Wigmore); McCormick § 87, p. 175. The purpose of the privilege is to encourage clients to make full disclosure to their attorneys. 8 Wigmore § 2291, and § 2306, p. 590; McCormick § 87, p. 175, § 92, p. 192. . . . As a practical matter, if the client knows that damaging information could more readily be obtained from the attorney following disclosure than from himself in the absence of disclosure, the client would be reluctant to confide in his lawyer and it would be difficult to obtain fully informed legal advice. However, since the privilege has the effect of withholding relevant information from the factfinder, it applies only where necessary to achieve its purpose. Accordingly it protects only those disclosures—necessary to obtain informed legal advice—which might not have been made absent the privilege. In re Horowitz, supra, 482 F.2d 72, at 81 (Friendly, J.); United States v. Goldfarb, supra, 328 F.2d 280; 8 Wigmore, § 2291, p. 554; McCormick, § 89, p. 185. This Court and the lower courts have thus uniformly held that pre-existing documents which could have been obtained by court process from the client when he was in possession may also be obtained from the attorney by similar process following transfer by the client in order to obtain more informed legal advice. Grant v. United States, 227 U.S. 74, 79–80 (1913); 8 Wigmore § 2307 and cases there cited; McCormick § 90, p. 185. . . . State ex rel. Sowers v. Olwell, 64 Wash.2d 828, 394 P.2d 681 (1964). The purpose of the privilege requires no broader rule. Pre-existing documents obtainable from the client are not appreciably easier to obtain from the attorney after transfer to him. Thus, even absent the attorney-client privilege, clients will not be discouraged from disclosing the documents to the attorney, and their ability to obtain informed legal advice will remain unfettered. It is otherwise if the documents are not obtainable by subpoena duces tecum or summons while in the exclusive possession of the client, for the client will then be reluctant to transfer possession to the lawyer unless the documents

---

7. The taxpayers and their attorneys have not raised arguments of a Fourth Amendment nature before this Court and could not be successful if they had. The summonses are narrowly drawn and seek only documents of unquestionable relevance to the tax investigation. Special problems of privacy which might be presented by subpoena of a personal diary, United States v. Bennett, 409 F.2d 888, 897 (C.A.2 1969) (Friendly, J.), are not involved here.

First Amendment values are also plainly not implicated in these cases.

are also privileged in the latter's hands. . . . We accordingly proceed to the question whether the documents could have been obtained by summons addressed to the taxpayer while the documents were in his possession. The only bar to enforcement of such summons asserted by the parties or the courts below is the Fifth Amendment's privilege against self-incrimination. . . .

IV

The proposition that the Fifth Amendment prevents compelled production of documents over objection that such production might incriminate stems from Boyd v. United States, 116 U.S. 616 (1886). *Boyd* involved a civil forfeiture proceeding brought by the Government against two partners for fraudulently attempting to import 35 cases of glass without paying the prescribed duty. The partnership had contracted with the Government to furnish the glass needed in the construction of a Government building. The glass specified was foreign glass, it being understood that if part or all of the glass was furnished from the partnership's existing duty-paid inventory, it could be replaced by duty-free imports. Pursuant to this arrangement, 29 cases of glass were imported by the partnership duty free. The partners then represented that they were entitled to duty-free entry of an additional 35 cases which were soon to arrive. The forfeiture action concerned these 35 cases. The Government's position was that the partnership had replaced all of the glass used in construction of the Government building when it imported the 29 cases. At trial, the Government obtained a court order directing the partners to produce an invoice the partnership had received from the shipper covering the previous 29–case shipment. The invoice was disclosed, offered in evidence, and used, over the Fifth Amendment objection of the partners, to establish that the partners were fraudulently claiming a greater exemption from duty than they were entitled to under the contract. This Court held that the invoice was inadmissible and reversed the judgment in favor of the Government. The Court ruled that the Fourth Amendment applied to court orders in the nature of subpoenas duces tecum in the same manner in which it applies to search warrants, id., at 622, . . . and that the Government may not, consistent with the Fourth Amendment, seize a person's documents or other property as evidence unless it can claim a proprietary interest in the property superior to that of the person from whom the property is obtained. Id., at 623–624. . . . The invoice in question was thus held to have been obtained in violation of the Fourth Amendment. The Court went on to hold that the accused in a criminal case or the defendant in a forfeiture action could not be forced to produce evidentiary items without violating the Fifth Amendment as well as the Fourth. More specifically, the Court declared, "a compulsory production of the private books and papers of the owner of goods sought to be forfeited . . . is compelling him to be a witness against himself, within the meaning of the Fifth Amendment to the Constitution." Id., at 634–635. . . . Admitting the partnership invoice into evidence had violated both the Fifth and Fourth Amendments.

Among its several pronouncements, *Boyd* was understood to declare that the seizure, under warrant or otherwise, of any purely evidentiary materials violated the Fourth Amendment and that the Fifth Amendment rendered these seized materials inadmissible. Gouled v. United States, 255 U.S. 298 (1921).... That rule applied to documents as well as to other evidentiary items—"[t]here is no special sanctity in papers, as distinguished from other forms of property, to render them immune from search and seizure, if only they fall within the scope of the principles of the cases in which other property may be seized...." Gouled v. United States, supra, 255 U.S., at 309.... Private papers taken from the taxpayer, like other "mere evidence," could not be used against the accused over his Fourth and Fifth Amendment objections.

Several of *Boyd's* express or implicit declarations have not stood the test of time....

[T]he Fifth Amendment does not independently proscribe the compelled production of every sort of incriminating evidence but applies only when the accused is compelled to make a *testimonial* communication that is incriminating. We have, accordingly, declined to extend the protection of the privilege to the giving of blood samples, Schmerber v. California, 384 U.S. 757, 763–764, (1966); to the giving of handwriting exemplars, Gilbert v. California, 388 U.S. 263, 265–267 (1967); voice exemplars, United States v. Wade, 388 U.S. 218, 222–223 (1967); or the donning of a blouse worn by the perpetrator, Holt v. United States, 218 U.S. 245 (1910). Furthermore, despite *Boyd*, neither a partnership nor the individual partners are shielded from compelled production of partnership records on self-incrimination grounds. Bellis v. United States, 417 U.S. 85 (1974). It would appear that under that case the precise claim sustained in *Boyd* would now be rejected for reasons not there considered.

. . .

A subpoena served on a taxpayer requiring him to produce an accountant's workpapers in his possession without doubt involves substantial compulsion. But it does not compel oral testimony; nor would it ordinarily compel the taxpayer to restate, repeat, or affirm the truth of the contents of the documents sought. Therefore, the Fifth Amendment would not be violated by the fact alone that the papers on their face might incriminate the taxpayer, for the privilege protects a person only against being incriminated by his own compelled testimonial communications. Schmerber v. California, supra; United States v. Wade, supra, and Gilbert v. California, supra. The accountant's workpapers are not the taxpayer's. They were not prepared by the taxpayer, and they contain no testimonial declarations by him. Furthermore, as far as this record demonstrates, the preparation of all of the papers sought in these cases was wholly voluntary, and they cannot be said to contain compelled testimonial evidence, either of the taxpayers or of anyone else.[11] The taxpayer cannot avoid compliance with the subpoena

---

11.   The fact that the documents may have been written by the person asserting the privilege is insufficient to trigger the privilege, Wilson v. United States, 221 U.S. 361,

merely by asserting that the item of evidence which he is required to produce contains incriminating writing, whether his own or that of someone else.

The act of producing evidence in response to a subpoena nevertheless has communicative aspects of its own, wholly aside from the contents of the papers produced. Compliance with the subpoena tacitly concedes the existence of the papers demanded and their possession or control by the taxpayer. It also would indicate the taxpayer's belief that the papers are those described in the subpoena. Curcio v. United States, 354 U.S. 118, 125 (1957). The elements of compulsion are clearly present, but the more difficult issues are whether the tacit averments of the taxpayer are both "testimonial" and "incriminating" for purposes of applying the Fifth Amendment. These questions perhaps do not lend themselves to categorical answers; their resolution may instead depend on the facts and circumstances of particular cases or classes thereof. In light of the records now before us, we are confident that however incriminating the contents of the accountant's workpapers might be, the act of producing them—the only thing which the taxpayer is compelled to do—would not itself involve testimonial self-incrimination.

It is doubtful that implicitly admitting the existence and possession of the papers rises to the level of testimony within the protection of the Fifth Amendment. The papers belong to the accountant, were prepared by him, and are the kind usually prepared by an accountant working on the tax returns of his client. Surely the Government is in no way relying on the "truth-telling" of the taxpayer to prove the existence of or his access to the documents. 8 Wigmore § 2264, p. 380. The existence and location of the papers are a foregone conclusion and the taxpayer adds little or nothing to the sum total of the Government's information by conceding that he in fact has the papers. Under these circumstances by enforcement of the summons "no constitutional rights are touched. The question is not of testimony but of surrender." In re Harris, 221 U.S. 274, 279 (1911).

When an accused is required to submit a handwriting exemplar he admits his ability to write and impliedly asserts that the exemplar is his writing. But in common experience, the first would be a near truism and the latter self-evident. In any event, although the exemplar may be incriminating to the accused and although he is compelled to furnish it, his Fifth Amendment privilege is not violated because nothing he has said or done is

378 (1911). And, unless the Government has compelled the subpoenaed person to write the document, cf. Marchetti v. United States, 390 U.S. 39 (1968); Grosso v. United States, 390 U.S. 62 (1968), the fact that it was written by him is not controlling with respect to the Fifth Amendment issue. Conversations may be seized and introduced in evidence under proper safeguards, Katz v. United States, 389 U.S. 347 (1967); Osborn v. United States, 385 U.S. 323 (1966); Berger v. New York, 388 U.S. 41 (1967); United States v. Bennett, 409 F.2d, at 897 n. 9, if not compelled. In the case of a documentary subpoena the only thing compelled is the act of producing the document and the compelled act is the same as the one performed when a chattel or document not authored by the producer is demanded. McCormick § 128, p. 261.

deemed to be sufficiently testimonial for purposes of the privilege. This Court has also time and again allowed subpoenas against the custodian of corporate documents or those belonging to other collective entities such as unions and partnerships and those of bankrupt businesses over claims that the documents will incriminate the custodian despite the fact that producing the documents tacitly admits their existence and their location in the hands of their possessor. E.g., Wilson v. United States, 221 U.S. 361 (1911); Dreier v. United States, 221 U.S. 394 (1911); United States v. White, 322 U.S. 694 (1944); Bellis v. United States, 417 U.S. 85 (1974); *In re Harris*, supra. The existence and possession or control of the subpoenaed documents being no more in issue here than in the above cases, the summons is equally enforceable.

Moreover, assuming that these aspects of producing the accountant's papers have some minimal testimonial significance, surely it is not illegal to seek accounting help in connection with one's tax returns or for the accountant to prepare workpapers and deliver them to the taxpayer. At this juncture, we are quite unprepared to hold that either the fact of existence of the papers or of their possession by the taxpayer poses any realistic threat of incrimination to the taxpayer.

As for the possibility that responding to the subpoena would authenticate[12] the workpapers, production would express nothing more than the taxpayer's belief that the papers are those described in the subpoena. The taxpayer would be no more competent to authenticate the accountant's workpapers or reports[13] by producing them than he would be to authenticate them if testifying orally. The taxpayer did not prepare the papers and could not vouch for their accuracy. The documents would not be admissible in evidence against the taxpayer without authenticating testimony. Without more, responding to the subpoena in the circumstances before us would not appear to represent a substantial threat of self-incrimination. Moreover, in Wilson v. United States, supra; Dreier v. United States, supra; United States v. White, supra; Bellis v. United States, supra; and *In re Harris*, supra, the custodian of corporate, union, or partnership books or those of a bankrupt business was ordered to respond to a subpoena for the business' books even though doing so involved a "representation that the documents

---

12. The "implicit authentication" rationale appears to be the prevailing justification for the Fifth Amendment's application to documentary subpoenas. Schmerber v. California, 384 U.S., at 763–764 . . . ("the privilege reaches . . . the compulsion of responses which are also communications, for example, compliance with a subpoena to produce one's papers. Boyd v. United States, 116 U.S. 616"); Couch v. United States, 409 U.S., at 344, 346 . . . (Marshall, J., dissenting) (the person complying with the subpoena "implicitly testifies that the evidence he brings forth is in fact the evidence demanded"); United States v. Beat-

tie, 522 F.2d 267, 270 (C.A.2 1975) (Friendly, J.) ("[a] subpoena demanding that an accused produce his own records is . . . the equivalent of requiring him to take the stand and admit their genuineness"), cert. pending, Nos. 75–407, 75–700. . . .

13. In seeking the accountant's "retained copies" of correspondence with the taxpayer in No. 74–611, we assume that the summons sought only "copies" of original letters sent from the accountant to the taxpayer—the truth of the contents of which could be testified to only by the accountant.

produced are those demanded by the subpoena," Curcio v. United States, 354 U.S., at 125 . . . . [14]

Whether the Fifth Amendment would shield the taxpayer from producing his own tax records in his possession is a question not involved here; for the papers demanded here are not his "private papers," see Boyd v. United States, supra, 116 U.S., at 634–635. . . . We do hold that compliance with a summons directing the taxpayer to produce the accountant's documents involved in these cases would involve no incriminating testimony within the protection of the Fifth Amendment.

. . .

■ MR. JUSTICE STEVENS took no part in the consideration or disposition of these cases.

■ MR. JUSTICE BRENNAN, concurring in the judgment.

I concur in the judgment. Given the prior access by accountants retained by the taxpayers to the papers involved in these cases and the wholly business rather than personal nature of the papers, I agree that the privilege against compelled self-incrimination did not in either of these cases protect the papers from production in response to the summonses. See Couch v. United States, 409 U.S. 322, 335–336 (1973); id., at 337 (Brennan, J., concurring). I do not join the Court's opinion, however, because of the portent of much of what is said of a serious crippling of the protection secured by the privilege against compelled production of one's private books and papers. . . .

———

Documents Given to a Lawyer by a Client[1]

If the client had created the subpoenaed documents solely to assist the lawyer in preparing a defense, would the result in *Fisher* have been different? What if the lawyer had prepared the documents in anticipation of the IRS's bringing suit against the lawyer's client?

The *Fisher* Court held that under the attorney-client privilege pre-existing documents in the hands of the lawyer are exempt from subpoena only if under the Fifth Amendment the documents would be exempt from subpoena in the hands of the client. The question then became whether the Fifth Amendment would protect the client from having to produce the documents. On this question the Court held that compelled production does

---

14. In these cases compliance with the subpoena is required even though the books have been kept by the person subpoenaed and his producing them would itself be sufficient authentication to permit their introduction against him.

1. On the issues raised by *Fisher* and *Doe I*, see Robert H. Heidt, The Fifth Amendment

Privilege and Documents—Cutting Fisher's Tangled Line, 49 Mo.L.Rev. 439 (1984); Robert P. Mosteller, Simplifying Subpoena Law: Taking the Fifth Amendment Seriously, 73 Va.L.Rev. 1 (1987); and Note, Fifth Amendment Privilege for Producing Corporate Documents, 84 Mich.L.Rev. 1544 (1986).

not violate the Fifth Amendment unless the compulsion is both "testimonial" and "incriminating." The contents of the documents apparently were incriminating. Why was the act of producing them not "incriminating" and "testimonial?"

The Court went to considerable pains to differentiate a lawyer's direct reliance on the client's Fifth Amendment rights and the derivative use of the attorney-client privilege by the lawyer to raise the Fifth Amendment question. In doing so, did not the Court expand the normal contours of the attorney-client privilege? What is the "confidential communication made for purposes of obtaining legal advice" when the client delivers his accountant's files concerning him to his lawyer?

Extending the attorney-client privilege to include material that would have been privileged on other grounds, such as the Fifth Amendment, had the material remained in the client's hands makes a great deal of sense because such an extension avoids putting a client in a worse position than he would have been in if he had not consulted a lawyer. On the other hand, requiring that the material be otherwise privileged prevents a client from obtaining a better position in terms of non-production of evidentiary material just because he has delivered it to a lawyer. If delivery to a lawyer alone rendered material immune from production, lawyers would be engaged in the warehouse business; and a race to discover and transmit papers would accompany suspicion of an impending government investigation.

Would the result in *Fisher* have differed if the papers involved had been the books and records of Dr. Mason's medical practice rather than those of his accountant? In United States v. Doe [*Doe I*],[2] the government subpoenaed business records from the sole proprietor of a restaurant. The Court held that the documents were not themselves privileged under the Fifth Amendment, clearing up any doubt remaining after *Fisher* as to whether an individual's business records enjoyed some special Fifth Amendment privilege not accorded to the records of a partnership or corporation. The Court held, however, that the act of producing the documents was sufficiently "testimonial" to give the defendant a Fifth Amendment right to refuse absent a grant of use immunity.

In a subsequent unrelated case with the same title, *Doe II*,[3] the Court upheld a lower court order obtained by the government requiring a suspect to sign a form stating that he consented to the surrender by a foreign bank to prosecutors of the records of any accounts that he might have. Justice Blackmun's opinion for the majority of five said the compelled signature was "not testimonial in nature" because the government-drafted form was worded hypothetically and did not require the suspect to admit whether or not he in fact had a foreign bank account. The opinion relied on decisions requiring a suspect to provide blood, handwriting and voice samples.

2. 465 U.S. 605 (1984).

3. Doe v. United States [*Doe II*], 487 U.S. 201 (1988).

Whither *Boyd*?

The argument, partially rejected in *Doe I*, that some special protection under the Fifth Amendment should be accorded an individual's business records comes from Boyd v. United States,[4] one of the earliest Fourth and Fifth Amendment cases to be decided by the Supreme Court. In sweeping language, *Boyd* suggested that the Fifth and Fourth Amendments protected the private papers of an individual, "his dearest property."[5] Subsequent cases replaced *Boyd*'s "property-oriented" view of the Fifth Amendment with an analysis concerned only with whether the act of producing the documents was itself testimonial and incriminatory.[6] After *Doe I*, special protection for papers may exist only for non-business papers of an individual.[7]

Other doctrinal developments have continued to narrow the application of any vestiges of the *Boyd* doctrine.[8] One line of cases has developed the "entity exception": The self-incrimination privilege is not available to a corporation, union, partnership, or other structured organization operating as a joint entity.[9] Moreover, the custodian of entity records may not rely on a personal privilege to refuse to produce the records even though the records are highly incriminating to the custodian.[10] Finally, the "required records" doctrine holds that requiring a person to keep records of certain business activities and to make those records available for government inspection does not violate the self-incrimination clause.[11] Consider the

4. 116 U.S. 616 (1886).

5. 116 U.S. at 628.

6. See Wayne R. LaFave & Jerold H. Israel, Criminal Procedure 398–407 (1985) for discussion of the case law dealing with self-incrimination and the production of documents.

7. *Compare* Smith v. Richert, 35 F.3d 300 (7th Cir.1994) (production of taxpayer records may be sufficiently testimonial to give Fifth Amendment protection) and Butcher v. Bailey, 753 F.2d 465 (6th Cir.1985) (there may be protection for personal private papers); *with* In re Grand Jury Proceedings on February 4, 1982, 759 F.2d 1418 (9th Cir.1985) (no protection for personal papers).

8. In *Doe I*, Justice O'Connor's concurring opinion asserted

that the Fifth Amendment provides absolutely no protection for the contents of private papers of any kind. The notion that the Fifth Amendment protects the privacy of papers originated in *Boyd v. United States*, but our decision in *Fisher v. United States* sounded the death-knell for *Boyd*. ... Today's decision puts a long-overdue end to that fruitless search.

465 U.S. at 618. Justices Brennan and Marshall, dissenting in *Doe*, took issue with Justice O'Connor's burial of *Boyd*, an obituary not explicitly endorsed by the majority opinion. Why is the Court so reluctant to explicitly overrule *Boyd*, a decision whose holdings have been contradicted by subsequent decisions? Although the Court is unlikely to use *Boyd* to protect an individual's privacy interest in material objects, the Court apparently finds it difficult to dismiss as "wrong" a case it has found worthy of struggling with for so long.

9. See, e.g., Hale v. Henkel, 201 U.S. 43 (1906) (corporation); United States v. White, 322 U.S. 694 (1944) (union); Bellis v. United States, 417 U.S. 85 (1974) (law partnership consisting of three partners and six employees).

10. Braswell v. United States, 487 U.S. 99 (1988) (individual custodian of records of his closely held corporation compelled to produce those records even if the very act of handing them over would incriminate him).

11. Shapiro v. United States, 335 U.S. 1 (1948) (sales records required to be kept by Emergency Price Control Act); California v.

application of the required records doctrine to a state rule requiring lawyers to keep records of client trust accounts and to make them available for random audits by state bar auditors.

In Smith v. Richert,[12] the Seventh Circuit distinguished the situation of an ordinary taxpayer from a regulated business. When someone enters a regulated endeavor, the required records must be made available for inspection. "The decision to become a taxpayer," however, "cannot be thought voluntary in the same sense. Almost anyone who works is a taxpayer, along with many who do not." The court held that an Indiana statute requiring "any person subject to an Indiana tax" to keep required records and provide them for inspection would violate the taxpayer's Fifth Amendment privilege against self-incrimination if the taxpayer was required to produce W–2 and 1099 forms since doing so would foreclose any defense of nonwillfulness.

Searches of Law Offices

Fisher dealt with a subpoena and not a search warrant. Even where a person under investigation has a Fifth Amendment right to refuse to *produce* documents in compliance with a subpoena, that person has no Fifth Amendment right to refuse to allow the police to conduct a search pursuant to a valid search warrant or a search otherwise constitutional under the Fourth Amendment. Therefore, if the government seeks to search a lawyer's office for incriminating documents, the lawyer's objections must be grounded in the Fourth Amendment or the attorney-client privilege. If the search is not unreasonable under the Fourth Amendment and the documents are not covered by the attorney-client privilege (because, for example, they were not created to communicate with the lawyer), the courts will uphold the validity of the search.[13] A federal statute, however, requires prosecutorial guidelines for searches of offices of lawyers and others.[14] For discussion of the short-lived amendment to Model Rule 3.8(f), providing for procedural prerequisites before a court issued subpoenas to a lawyer, see p. 258 infra.

Cases dealing with law office searches generally involve lawyers who themselves are the target of the search. In *Impounded I*,[15] the affidavit

Byers, 402 U.S. 424 (1971) (upholding against Fifth Amendment objections "hit and run" statute requiring a driver involved in a motor vehicle accident to stop and report the accident); cf. Grosso v. United States, 390 U.S. 62 (1968) (privilege against self-incrimination is a defense to criminal prosecutions for violation of registration and taxing provisions of the federal wagering statutes).

12.   35 F.3d 300 (7th Cir.1994).

13.   See, e.g., Andresen v. Maryland, 427 U.S. 463 (1976) (a warrant-authorized search and seizure of business records constitutes a taking by the government, not

testimonial compulsion protected by the Fifth Amendment).

14.   See 42 U.S.C. §§ 2000aa–11, which requires the Attorney General to issue guidelines for searches of lawyer's offices and the offices of other professionals whose relationships with their clients are protected by privileges, e.g., doctors and clergy. The resulting guidelines for searches of lawyer's offices appear at 37 Crim.L.Rep. (BNA) 2479.

15.   In re Impounded Case (Law Firm) [Impounded I], 840 F.2d 196 (3d Cir.1988). See Koniak excerpt, p. 122 supra, and the note on this topic at p. 258 infra.

supporting the search warrant asserted probable cause to believe that the law firm and some of its lawyers were engaged in tax evasion and mail fraud. The alleged scheme involved the firm's failure to report accurately its share of personal injury awards. The government seized approximately 420 complete files from the office and documents from other closed personal injury files. The district court held the search unconstitutional because the warrant was overbroad in that it allowed the search and seizure of client files without particular allegations of under-reporting of settlements in those particular cases. The court of appeals upheld the search. It noted that searches of law offices were not per se unreasonable under the Fourth Amendment and that the proper role of the court was "to 'scrutinize carefully the particularity and breadth of the warrant authorizing the search, the nature and scope of the search, and any resulting seizure.' "[16] The breadth of the alleged scheme—a broad and ongoing effort by the firm and many of its lawyers to defraud the government—kept the search from being overbroad. Privileged information, the court held, could be protected by requiring the government to obtain leave of the court before examining any of the seized items.[17]

5. THE CRIME-FRAUD EXCEPTION

In Re Sealed Case (Lewinsky)

United States Court of Appeals for the District of Columbia Circuit, 1998.
162 F.3d 670.

■ Before GINSBURG, RANDOLPH, and TATEL, CIRCUIT JUDGES.

RANDOLPH, CIRCUIT JUDGE

In 1997, Monica S. Lewinsky, a former White House intern, received a subpoena to produce items and to testify in Paula Jones v. William Jefferson Clinton, a civil matter then pending in the United States District Court for the Eastern District of Arkansas. The subpoena requested, among other things, documents relating to an alleged relationship between President Clinton and Lewinsky and any gifts the President may have given her. Lewinsky retained Francis D. Carter, Esq., to represent her regarding the subpoena.

Carter drafted an affidavit for Lewinsky, which she signed under penalty of perjury. The affidavit, submitted to the Arkansas district court as an exhibit to Lewinsky's motion to quash the subpoena, states in relevant part:

---

16. 840 F.2d at 200, quoting Klitzman, Klitzman & Gallagher v. Krut, 744 F.2d 955, 959 (3d Cir.1984) (when only one lawyer was the target, search was overbroad because the warrant authorized a whole-sale search and seizure of the firm's business records).

17. A later stage of the same case turned on the client-fraud exception to the attorney-client privilege. In re Impounded Case (Law Firm) [Impounded II], 879 F.2d 1211 (3d Cir.1989).

I have never had a sexual relationship with the President, [and] he did not propose that we have a sexual relationship.... The occasions that I saw the President after I left my employment at the White House in April, 1996, were official receptions, formal functions or events related to the U.S. Department of Defense, where I was working at the time. There were other people present on those occasions.

On January 16, 1998, at the request of the Attorney General, a Special Division of this Court expanded the jurisdiction of the Office of Independent Counsel to include "authority to investigate ... whether Monica Lewinsky or others suborned perjury, obstructed justice, intimidated witnesses, or otherwise violated federal law ... in dealing with witnesses, potential witnesses, attorneys, or others concerning the civil case Jones v. Clinton." Order of the Special Division, Jan. 16, 1998. On February 2 and 9, 1998, as part of that investigation, a grand jury issued subpoenas to Carter, the first for documents and other items, the second for his testimony. Carter moved to quash the subpoenas, contending, inter alia, that the documents, testimony, and other items sought were protected from disclosure by the attorney-client privilege, the work-product privilege, and Lewinsky's Fifth Amendment privilege against self-incrimination. Lewinsky, as the real-party-in-interest, filed a response in support of Carter's motion. The United States opposed the motion, arguing among other things that the crime-fraud exception vitiated any claims of attorney-client or work-product privilege and that the Fifth Amendment did not bar production of the requested materials. The district court ordered Carter to comply with the two grand jury subpoenas except to the extent that compliance would "call for him to disclose materials in his possession that may not be revealed without violating Monica S. Lewinsky's Fifth Amendment rights."

Carter and Lewinsky argue in separate appeals that the district court erred in rejecting their motions to quash the grand jury subpoenas in their entirety. In its cross-appeal, the United States, through the Office of Independent Counsel, claims that the Fifth Amendment does not bar production of any of the materials the grand jury subpoenaed from Carter.

We dismiss Carter's appeal for want of jurisdiction. Well-settled law dictates that "one to whom a subpoena is directed may not appeal the denial of a motion to quash that subpoena but must either obey its commands or refuse to do so and contest the validity of the subpoena if he is subsequently cited for contempt on account of his failure to obey." United States v. Ryan, 402 U.S. 530, 532 (1971); see Cobbledick v. United States, 309 U.S. 323, 328 (1940); In re Sealed Case, 107 F.3d 46, 48 n. 1 (D.C.Cir.1997). Rather than risking contempt, Carter has sworn that he will comply with the subpoenas if ordered to do so.

Our jurisdiction over Lewinsky's appeal is another matter. Lewinsky is the holder of the privilege. Given Carter's sworn declaration that he will give testimony if ordered, she is entitled to appeal the district court's ruling rejecting Carter's assertion of the privilege. See In re Sealed Case, 107 F.3d at 48 n.1.

The district court held that the crime-fraud exception to the attorney-client privilege applied. After reviewing the government's in camera submission, the court found that "Ms. Lewinsky consulted Mr. Carter for the purpose of committing perjury and obstructing justice and used the material he prepared for her for the purpose of committing perjury and obstructing justice."[2] Lewinsky tells us she could not have committed either crime: the government could not establish perjury because her denial of having had a "sexual relationship" with President Clinton was not "material" to the Arkansas proceedings within the meaning of 18 U.S.C. § 1623(a); and her affidavit containing this denial could not have constituted a "corrupt[ ] ... endeavor[ ] to influence" the Arkansas district court within the meaning of 18 U.S.C. § 1503. Both of Lewinsky's propositions rely on the Arkansas district court's ruling on January 30, 1998, after Lewinsky had filed her affidavit, that although evidence concerning Lewinsky might be relevant, it would be excluded from the civil case under Fed. R. Evid. 403 as unduly prejudicial, "not essential to the core issues in the case," and to prevent undue delay resulting from the Independent Counsel's investigation.[3]

A statement is "material" if it "has a natural tendency to influence, or was capable of influencing, the decision of the tribunal in making a [particular] determination." United States v. Barrett, 111 F.3d 947, 953 (D.C.Cir.), cert. denied, 118 S. Ct. 176 (1997). The "central object" of any materiality inquiry is "whether the misrepresentation or concealment was predictably capable of affecting, i.e., had a natural tendency to affect, the official decision." Kungys v. United States, 485 U.S. 759, 771 (1988). Lewinsky used the statement in her affidavit, quoted above, to support her motion to quash the subpoena issued in the discovery phase of the Arkansas litigation. District courts faced with such motions must decide whether the testimony or material sought is reasonably calculated to lead to admissible evidence and, if so, whether the need for the testimony, its probative value, the nature and importance of the litigation, and similar factors outweigh any burden enforcement of the subpoena might impose. See Fed. R. Civ. P. 26(b)(1), 45(c)(3)(A)(iv); Linder v. Department of Defense, 328 U.S. App. D.C. 154, 133 F.3d 17, 24 (D.C.Cir.1998); see generally 9A§ 2459 (2d ed. 1995). There can be no doubt that Lewinsky's statements in her affidavit were—in the words of Kungys v. United States—"predictably capable of affecting" this decision. She executed and filed her affidavit for this very purpose.

As to obstruction of justice, 18 U.S.C.§ 1503 is satisfied whenever a person, with the "intent to influence judicial or grand jury proceedings," takes actions having the "natural and probable effect" of doing so. United

---

2. The district court did not find, nor did the Independent Counsel suggest, any impropriety by Carter.

3. Lewinsky does not appear to contest directly the district court's finding that she made one or more false statements in her sworn affidavit. Even so, we have independently reviewed the in camera materials considered by the district court and conclude that sufficient evidence existed to support the court's finding.

States v. Aguilar, 515 U.S. 593, 600 (1995) (citations and quotation marks omitted); see United States v. Russo, 104 F.3d 431, 435–36 (D.C.Cir.1997). Our review of the in camera materials on which the district court based its decision convinces us that the government sufficiently established the elements of a violation of § 1503. That is, the government offered "evidence that if believed by the trier of fact would establish the elements of" the crime of obstruction of justice. In re Sealed Case, 107 F.3d at 50; see In re Sealed Case, 754 F.2d 395, 399–400 (D.C.Cir.1985) (same).

Lewinsky maintains that the district court erred in treating, as admissible for in camera review, transcripts of taped conversations between Lewinsky and Linda Tripp. She relies on the following statement in United States v. Zolin, 491 U.S. 554, 575 (1989): "the threshold showing to obtain in camera review may be met by using any relevant evidence, lawfully obtained, that has not been adjudicated to be privileged." *Zolin*, and the statement just quoted, dealt with a rather different problem than the one presented here. Sometimes a party seeking to overcome the privilege by invoking the crime-fraud exception asks the district court to examine in camera the privileged material to determine whether it provides evidence of a crime. The issue *Zolin* addressed is under what circumstances a district court should undertake such in camera review. *Zolin*'s answer, as the quotation indicates, was that the court should do so only when there has been a threshold showing through evidence lawfully obtained. See In re Grand Jury Proceedings, 33 F.3d 342, 350 (4th Cir.1994). In this case, the district court reviewed in camera not the allegedly privileged material, but other evidence intended to establish that the crime-fraud exception applied. In any event, even if *Zolin* applied, Lewinsky gains nothing from the decision. She maintains that the Tripp tapes were not "lawfully obtained" and therefore should not have been considered in camera. But the government satisfied its burden wholly apart from the Tripp tapes. Other government evidence—consisting of grand jury testimony and documents—established that the crime-fraud exception applied. Because that other evidence, if believed by the trier of fact, combined with the circumstances under which Lewinsky retained Carter, would establish the elements of the crime-fraud exception, there is no reason for us to consider her arguments about the tapes.[4]

Lewinsky raises other objections to the district court's decision, including the argument that production of the subpoenaed materials would violate her Fifth Amendment privilege against self-incrimination. Our resolution of the cross-appeal, discussed next, disposes of that claim. As to

---

4. Lewinsky's brief suggests, in a short passage, that other evidence obtained by the grand jury is tainted by the alleged illegality of the Tripp tapes. United States v. Calandra 414 U.S. 338, (1974), refused to extend the exclusionary rule—and hence doctrines such as the fruit-of-the-poisonous-tree—to grand jury proceedings. No grand jury witness may refuse to answer questions on the ground that the questions are based on illegally obtained evidence. See 414 U.S. at 353–55. It follows that regardless of the legality of the Tripp tapes, the grand jury did not unlawfully obtain the other evidence presented to the district court in camera.

the remainder of Lewinsky's arguments, we have accorded each of them full consideration and conclude that none has merit.

This brings us to the Independent Counsel's cross-appeal. The district court ruled that compelling Carter to produce materials his client gave him would violate Lewinsky's Fifth Amendment privilege because it would compel her to admit the materials exist and had been in her possession. The Supreme Court foreclosed that line of reasoning in Fisher v. United States, 425 U.S. 391 (1976). Documents transferred from the accused to his attorney are "obtainable without personal compulsion on the accused," and hence the accused's "Fifth Amendment privilege is ... not violated by enforcement of the [subpoena] directed toward [his] attorneys. This is true whether or not the Amendment would have barred a subpoena directing the [accused] to produce the documents while they were in his hands." Id. at 398, 397; see also Couch v. United States, 409 U.S. 322, 328 (1973).

Regardless whether Lewinsky herself would have been able to invoke her Fifth Amendment privilege, but see Andresen v. Maryland, 427 U.S. 463, 473–74 (1976), the district court's refusal to order full compliance with the subpoenas could be sustained only if the materials sought fell under a valid claim of attorney-client privilege. See *Fisher*, 425 U.S. at 403–05; see also In re Feldberg, 862 F.2d 622, 629 (7th Cir.1988). But the district court held, correctly, that no valid attorney-client privilege existed. Under *Fisher*, the district court therefore should have denied the motions to quash in their entirety.

Accordingly, we affirm in part and reverse in part the order of the district court and remand the case for proceedings consistent with this opinion. . . .

———

Establishing the Crime–Fraud Exception

As Justice Cardozo said:

> The privilege takes flight if the relation is abused. A client who consults an attorney for advice that will serve him in the commission of a fraud will have no help from the law.[1]

The crime-fraud exception is a corollary to the prohibition against assisting a client to commit a fraud or crime (see Rule 1.2(d)). The crime-fraud exception applies to ongoing criminal activity as well as to future criminal activity, but does not apply to past crimes about which the law encourages the seeking of legal counsel. The distinction between past crimes and ongoing ones is clear in principle. However, many a lawyer has

---

1. Clark v. United States, 289 U.S. 1, 15 (1933). On the crime-fraud exception and its relation to confidentiality, see Geoffrey C. Hazard, Jr., An Historical Perspective on the Attorney–Client Privilege, 66 Cal. L.Rev. 1061 (1978), with which compare David Fried, Too High a Price for the Truth: The Exception to the Attorney–Client Privilege for Contemplated Crimes and Frauds, 64 N.C.L.Rev. 443 (1986) (arguing that the exception is interpreted too broadly).

fallen into difficulty by treating an ongoing fraud as a past crime. See the discussion of the *O.P.M.* case infra at p. 304. An undiscovered fraud that has not been rectified may be considered as ongoing, not past, so long as the consequences of the fraud continue.

In United States v. Hodge & Zweig,[2] then Circuit Judge, now Justice, Kennedy summarized the application of the crime-fraud exception to the attorney-client privilege:

> Because the attorney-client privilege is not to be used as a cloak for illegal or fraudulent behavior, it is well established that the privilege does not apply where legal representation was secured in furtherance of intended, or present, continuing illegality. The crime-fraud exception applies even when the attorney is completely unaware that his advice is sought in furtherance of such an improper purpose. To invoke the exception successfully, the party seeking disclosure ... must make out a prima facie case that the attorney was retained in order to promote intended or continuing criminal or fraudulent activity.

The Eleventh Circuit has a more detailed statement of the required showing:

> First, there must be a prima facie showing that the client was engaged in criminal or fraudulent conduct when he sought the advice of counsel, that he was planning such conduct when he sought the advice of counsel, or that he committed a crime or fraud subsequent to receiving the benefit of counsel's advice. Second, there must be a showing that the attorney's assistance was obtained in furtherance of the criminal or fraudulent activity or was closely related to it."[3]

In many cases a further step is involved. After a preliminary " 'showing of a factual basis adequate to support a good faith belief by a reasonable person ...' that in camera review ... may reveal evidence to establish the claim that the crime-fraud exception applies," the trial court may examine material claimed to be privileged to determine whether the privilege applies.[4] This threshold showing requires less than is required to make the prima facie case to prove the application of the crime-fraud exception. In the *Lewinsky* case, the trial court first examined confidential grand jury testimony and documents in making the threshold decision of a reasonable belief that an examination of the allegedly privileged material would establish the crime-fraud exception. The trial court then made an examination in camera of further grand jury documents offered by the government before concluding that the prima facie case of client crime had been made. The dual inquiry, repeated by the appellate court, resulted in a determination that Lewinsky consulted attorney Carter in furtherance of planned perjury and obstruction of justice in the Paula Jones case.

2. 548 F.2d 1347, 1354 (9th Cir.1977).

3. In re Grand Jury Investigation (Schroeder), 842 F.2d 1223, 1226 (11th Cir.1987).

4. United States v. Zolin, 491 U.S. 554, 572 (1989) (quoting Caldwell v. District Court, 644 P.2d 26, 33 (Colo.1982)).

In federal courts and those of many states the content of the communication revealed in the in camera inspection may be used in determining whether a crime or fraud was involved. The rule is otherwise in a number of states.[5] What opportunity should be afforded the person asserting the privilege to rebut the evidence that the exception applies?[6]

While most civil frauds are criminal as well, the exception applies whether or not the fraud involves criminal liability.[7] Should the crime-fraud exception extend to the client's intent to commit any intentional tort? Charles Wolfram suggests that "fraud" is and should be read as a catch-all phrase to include any intentional wrong "involving a client acting with bad faith...."[8] The relationship between antitrust law, the First Amendment and the attorney-client privilege is considered in a number of cases.[9]

Crime-Fraud Exception: The Client's Motive

Client communications to a lawyer *"in furtherance of* the criminal or fraudulent activity or *closely related* to it"* are not privileged. Courts in crime-fraud exception cases usually assume, as the court did in *Lewinsky*, that the legal advisor is unaware of, and did not assist, the client's criminal or fraudulent intent. This focus on the client's state of mind flows from the client's right to advice concerning the boundaries of law, but not to help when the client doesn't care where the boundary is. The inquiry into the client's state of mind involves drawing fine distinctions between legitimate advice on matters of uncertain legality, on the one hand, and counseling a criminal course of conduct, on the other. In *Ohio–Sealy*,[10] a lawyer was engaged in an effort to restructure a restrictive trade agreement that had been held to violate antitrust law; the client wanted to achieve much the same effect without running afoul of precedent. Despite documents revealing the client's belief that its activities would ultimately be found illegal, the court declined to find the lack of good faith on the client's part that

---

5. State law may differ from *Zolin*. For example, under Cal.Evid.Code § 915(a) the content of the communication may not be used to determine whether an exception to the privilege applies. See also Burton v. R. J. Reynolds Tobacco Co., 167 F.R.D. 134, 141 (D.C.Kan.1996) (applying the Kansas standard, rather than the more relaxed *Zolin* standard: documents examined in camera cannot be used to prove the prima facie case of crime-fraud).

6. See Company X v. United States, 857 F.2d 710 (10th Cir.1988) (determination that exception applies may be made upon ex parte showing and judge need not first examine all documents in camera).

7. See In re Burlington Northern, Inc., 822 F.2d 518 (5th Cir.1987) (civil violation of the antitrust laws is a "fraud" sufficient to trigger the exception to the attorney-client

privilege); Natta v. Zletz, 418 F.2d 633 (7th Cir.1969) (fraud upon the Patent and Trademark Office triggers the exception).

8. Wolfram, Modern Legal Ethics § 6.4.10 (1986).

9. See, e.g., In re Burlington Northern, Inc., 822 F.2d 518 (5th Cir.1987) (petitioning of the government, which includes suing and in some cases defending a suit, is exempt from the antitrust laws unless the petitioning is a mere sham to cover violation of the antitrust laws; plaintiffs sought access to conversations between defendants and their lawyers to prove claim of a sham defense). For the *Noerr–Pennington* doctrine, see United Mine Workers v. Pennington, 381 U.S. 657 (1965).

10. Ohio–Sealey Mattress Mfg. Co. v. Kaplan, 90 F.R.D. 21 (N.D.Ill.1980).

triggers the crime-fraud exception. The client's belief was read as an evaluation of the weakness of their position, not as an awareness of wrongdoing.[11] But another fact-finder might have reached the opposite conclusion on the same record.

But when does a client have the requisite intent? In *Lewinsky* the court could compare the affidavit Carter prepared for Lewinsky with the grand jury testimony of other witnesses that indicated her affidavit was false. In other cases determining the client's motive requires a court to draw inferences from ambiguous facts.

In United States v. Bauer,[12] for example, the client, Bauer, consulted his lawyer, Rivera, on a number of occasions concerning his impending bankruptcy. During the 12–month period prior to filing a bankruptcy petition, Bauer transferred substantial assets to his spouse and other family members. He was indicted and convicted for making false statements on his bankruptcy petition. At the trial Bauer admitted the transfers and that his statement on the petition was false; his defense was that he did not possess the requisite criminal intent because he was the victim of his own ignorance, mistake or stupidity. Over Bauer's objections, Rivera was required to testify that the legal advice he had given Bauer included a warning that a bankruptcy petition was filed under oath and required the disclosure of all property. The Ninth Circuit, reversing Bauer's conviction, first held that Rivera's legal advice was protected by the attorney-client privilege.[13] It then rejected the government's argument that Bauer's communications were made in furtherance of a criminal plan. The court stated:

> Rivera advised Bauer to disclose all of his assets and avoid lying on his bankruptcy petition. Bauer in fact did precisely the opposite. It is impossible to discern a causal connection or functional relationship between the advice given by Rivera and the actions taken by Bauer. Therefore, the crime-fraud exception to the attorney-client privilege does not apply.[14]

Finally, the court concluded that the government's evidence of Bauer's corrupt intent was inconclusive and, therefore, the government's use and reliance on his lawyer's testimony, in violation of his attorney-client privilege, was not harmless error.

Is the court's view of Bauer's motive in consulting a lawyer plausible or convincing? Bauer presumably consulted lawyer Rivera to be instructed what to do and not to do in filing a bankruptcy petition. Bauer then ignored Rivera's advice about the illegality of transfers within the twelve-

---

11. *Ohio–Sealy* also holds that the crime-fraud rule obliges the lawyer to advise the client to stop any unlawful activity in which the lawyer discovers the client is engaged.

12. 132 F.3d 504 (9th Cir.1997).

13. The court rejected the government's argument that Riviera was merely a conduit for communicating the warning on the pe-

tition form, distinguishing other cases in which a lawyer's notice to a client of the date of a forthcoming hearing or similar matters is not privileged because the lawyer is merely a messenger of public information.

14. 132 F.3d at 510.

month period prior to the filing of the bankruptcy petition. When a client goes to a lawyer with a legal uncertainty, and the lawyer says "do X, but don't do Y," and the client immediately does Y, why isn't the lawyer's advice closely related to the client's communications seeking advice? Why doesn't the trial court's exposure to the parties and witnesses give it a more reliable sense of Bauer's motive than the appellate court can derive from the written record?

Purcell v. District Attorney[15] is another puzzling case, but with a different twist. Tyree, who had been fired as custodian of an apartment building and asked to vacate his apartment in the building, consulted a legal services lawyer, Purcell. In the course of seeking advice concerning his prospective eviction, Tyree told Purcell that he planned to set fire to the apartment building and had already put in place flammable materials for that purpose. Purcell apparently attempted to dissuade Tyree but was left unconfident that he had succeeded. Consequently, he informed the police of Tyree's threats. Tyree was arrested and charged with attempted arson. In the subsequent trial, the prosecution sought to compel Purcell to testify concerning his client's threats. The Massachusetts high court leaned over backwards to conclude that the client's threats were protected by the attorney-client privilege, that is, that they were made for the purpose of obtaining legal advice, and yet the client's threats were not viewed as communications seeking assistance in furtherance of ongoing or future criminal conduct.[16] Perhaps the explanation lies in the fact that *Purcell*, unlike nearly all crime-fraud cases, involves an interplay between evidentiary law (the attorney-client privilege and its crime-fraud exception) *and* the professional duty of confidentiality. The court in *Purcell* was moved by policy considerations relating to the lawyer's effort to dissuade his client from wrongdoing and, that failing, exercising the permission given by the Massachusetts ethics code to prevent the threatened harm by disclosing the client's plausible threats:

> [T]he attorney-client privilege should apply to communications concerning possible future, as well as past, criminal conduct, because an informed lawyer may be able to dissuade the client from improper future conduct and, if not, under the ethical rules may elect in the public interest to make a limited disclosure of the client's threatened conduct.[17]

This make sense when the client follows the attorney's advice and chooses a lawful path; but should it apply, as in *Bauer* and *Purcell*, when the client ignores the lawyer's advice? Or is *Purcell* different because it is unclear at the time of the client's arrest whether or not the client had abandoned the arson plan?[18]

15.   676 N.E.2d 436 (Mass.1997).

16.   The decision is somewhat opaque on this point. On remand, the trial court read the opinion as holding that the threats were not made in furtherance of the client's proposed crime and were protected by the attorney-client privilege. Lawyer Purcell was not required to help convict his former client.

17.   *Purcell*, 676 N.E.2d at 441.

18.   Cf. United States v. Ballard, 779 F.2d 287 (5th Cir.1986) (when client used second lawyer to file a bankruptcy petition

Should the crime-fraud exception apply when the client is unaware that the intended purpose is illegal? In In re Impounded Case (Law Firm) [*Impounded II*],[19] the law firm, asserting the privilege on behalf of its innocent clients, claimed that the crime-fraud exception did not apply when the alleged criminality was solely that of the law firm. The court rejected this argument, holding that the privilege would have to yield to the societal interest of bringing to justice lawyers engaged in criminal activities.[20]

Professional Attitudes Toward the Privilege and Its Exceptions

Judicial decisions involving the scope of the attorney-client privilege or the application of its crime-fraud exception are influenced by professional narratives and ideology. In the *Bauer* case, sustaining the claim of privilege against the crime-fraud exception, the court, quoting from a number of leading cases, spoke eloquently about the public and private benefits of the "seal of secrecy" of this "most revered" and "most sacred" privilege. Contrast that language with the opposing principle stated in a legion of decisions: The privilege should be construed strictly because it suppresses evidence that is essential to truthful outcomes and contravenes the fundamental principle that the public has a right to receive every person's evidence.[21]

Criminal defense lawyers and other litigators who view the attorney-client privilege as the most sacred of a lawyer's obligations are inspired by narratives in which some of their number have had the courage of their convictions. Linda Backiel, for example, was willing to go to jail rather than obey a court order to reveal information that would hurt her client, Elizabeth Ann Duke.[22] Duke, a member of a revolutionary group that had stored arms and explosives in a shed in a Philadelphia suburb, was arrested in 1985 and Ms. Backiel helped Duke to gain release on bail. When Duke was released, she conferred with Ms. Backiel and gave Backiel a note stating her reasons for fleeing. Shortly thereafter, Duke disappeared. In a federal investigation of Duke's bail-jumping in 1991, Backiel was called to testify and asked to produce the note. When Backiel refused, she was, after lengthy hearings and appeals, committed for contempt. Backiel, who spent six months in prison before being released, stated: "I can't be turned into a witness for the prosecution," and added, "everyone who goes to law school should spend a week in jail; ... they'd get a sense of the arbitrariness and

omitting proceeds of a sale of real estate, after first lawyer, who had earlier assisted client in the real estate transaction, had advised client that proceeds of sale would have to be included in bankruptcy petition, testimony of first lawyer's advice was not privileged).

19. 879 F.2d 1211 (3d Cir.1989).

20. But see State v. Green, 493 So.2d 1178, 1182 (La.1986) (lawyer's criminal intent of which client was unaware will not trigger crime-fraud exception).

21. See, e.g., Trammel v. United States, 445 U.S. 40, 50–51(1980); Fisher v. United States, 425 U.S. 391, 403 (1976); United States v. (Under Seal), 748 F.2d 871, 875 (4th Cir.1984) (stating that because of its social costs the privilege should be strictly construed and citing Wigmore).

22. "Defense Lawyer Is Jailed over Client Confidentiality," N.Y.Times, p. A3 (Feb. 15, 1991).

power of the law. I think they'd understand the importance of having an advocate."[23] Is Backiel a lawyer hero or a foolish revolutionary?

Big Tobacco and Its Lawyers[24]

Efforts by plaintiffs' trial lawyers to hold tobacco companies liable for cancer and other smoking harms were unsuccessful until 1992, when the Budd Larner firm won a Pyrrhic victory in the famous *Cipollone* case.[25] After decades of pretrial maneuvers, numerous appeals, a trip to the U.S. Supreme Court and a lengthy trial, the plaintiff won a $400,000 verdict. Budd Larner's expenses in litigating this and several companion cases were more than $5 million. Financially exhausted, the firm petitioned the district court for permission to withdraw from representation in the *Haines* case[26] and those of other victims, claiming that continuing would impose an "unreasonable financial burden" on the firm under M.R. 1.16(b)(5).[27] Although Budd Larner was forced to its knees by its expenses in the *Cipollone* and *Haines* cases, the firm's exposure of industry documents in those cases ultimately led to a weakness in the industry's defensive armor that by 1998 threatened catastrophic liability losses. The subsequent developments also raised serious crime-fraud questions concerning the conduct of tobacco company lawyers as well as their clients.

The *Haines* case had involved a fierce fight concerning the discovery of certain documents that the defendants claimed were protected under the attorney-client privilege. The plaintiffs claimed that the tobacco industry had engaged in fraudulent conduct by concealing its knowledge of health risks associated with smoking. They focused on the role of the Council for Tobacco Research (CTR), which, although it presented itself as an indepen-

23. Id.

24. This discussion draws on Ralph Nader & Wesley J. Smith, No Contest: Corporate Lawyers and the Perversion of Justice in America 18–19, 21–24, 30 (1996) (hereafter Nader & Smith).

25. Cipollone v. Liggett Group, Inc., 893 F.2d 541 (3d Cir.1990), aff'd in part and rev'd in part, 505 U.S. 504 (1992).

26. See Haines v. Liggett Group, Inc., 975 F.2d 81 (3d Cir.1992), rev'g and remanding,140 F.R.D. 681 (D.N.J.1992).

27. See Smith v. R. J. Reynolds Tobacco Co., 630 A.2d 820, 826 (N.J.Super.1993) (denying withdrawal on the part of the Budd Larner firm without a further showing). In its effort to withdraw, the firm argued that "[t]he tobacco industry's defense strategy is to resist discovery, appeal virtually every adverse decision and avoid settlement. The industry does everything it can to cause plaintiff's attorneys to spend a great deal of money." Id. The brief quoted a talk by an R. J. Reynolds lawyer in which he boasted to an audience about his success in forcing ten California smoking victims to dismiss their cases voluntarily:

> [T]he aggressive posture we have taken regarding depositions and discovery in general continues to make these cases extremely burdensome and expensive for plaintiffs' lawyers, particularly sole practitioners. To paraphrase General Patton, the way we won these cases was not by spending all of Reynolds' money, but by making the other son of a bitch spend all of his.

Brief on appeal in Cipollone v. Liggett Group, Inc., 799 F.Supp. 466 (D.N.J.1992), quoted in Nader & Smith, at 27. For further discussion of tobacco companies' litigation strategies, see Patricia Bellew Gray, Tobacco Firms Defend Smoker Liability Suits with Heavy Artillery, Wall St. J., Apr. 29, 1987; and Alison Frankel, Was Budd Larner Another Smoking Victim?, N.J. L.J., July 12, 1993.

dent research institute, was created and funded by tobacco interests. While the tobacco industry claimed that "tobacco lawyers in the past had influenced decisions as to which CTR research efforts should be funded by industry contributions" (and thus the attorney-client privilege applied to certain CTR documents), Haines asserted "that, in fact, the CTR had only one goal: to cover up the truth about the harmful effects of tobacco use."[28] Thus, the plaintiffs claimed that the crime-fraud exception to the attorney-client privilege applied:

> Specifically, they contended that the documents would show that CTR established a "special projects" section, directed by industry lawyers rather than scientists, where data considered to be harmful to tobacco interests would be placed and protected from public disclosure through claims of "attorney-client privilege".... [Haines' attorneys] claimed that in this case the industry abused the privilege by bringing in lawyers to "special project" efforts solely to take advantage of the doctrine and keep records sealed. They claimed, in effect, that the tobacco industry, in its careful structuring of CTR, wanted to have it both ways: For purposes of publicly releasing credible studies on smoking and health, it was an independent, scientific research organization. For purposes of keeping unfavorable research results and communications secret, it was, instead, a law firm, bound by privilege to avoid disclosure.[29]

The magistrate judge appointed to resolve the issue concluded, after an in camera review of the documents at issue, that the crime-fraud exception did not apply, and Haines appealed to the district court. Upon reviewing a number of the documents at issue, Judge H. Lee Sarokin, who had also presided over the *Cipollone* case, determined that the crime-fraud exception applied to at least five CTR-related documents. He reasoned that the tobacco industry had committed fraud in its claims that CTR was an independent organization, all the while intending to assert the attorney-client privilege to prevent the discovery of harmful documents. Judge Sarokin stated that he was appointing a new special master to determine the applicability of the exception to additional CTR documents.

Judge Sarokin's decision quoted some of the CTR documents he had reviewed, including the minutes of a CTR meeting of the Committee of General Counsel that quoted one participant as stating:

> When we started the CTR Special Projects, the idea was that the scientific director of CTR would review a project. If he liked it, it was a CTR special project. If he did not like it, then it became a lawyers' special project.... We wanted to protect it under the lawyers. We did not want it out in the open.[30]

Judge Sarokin also quoted a memorandum recounting a 1978 presentation:

---

28. Nader & Smith, at 18.

29. Id. at 18–19.

30. Haines v. Liggett Group, Inc., 140 F.R.D. 681, 695 (D.N.J.1992), rev'd, 975 F.2d 81 (3d Cir.1992).

CTR began as an organization called Tobacco Industry Research Council (TIRC). *It was set up as an industry "shield" in 1954.* That was the year statistical accusations relating to smoking to diseases were leveled at the industry [and] litigation began.... *CTR has helped our legal counsel by giving advise and technical information, which was needed in court trials. CTR has provided spokesmen for the industry at Congressional hearings. The monies spent on CTR provides a base for introduction of witnesses....*

On these projects, CTR has acted as a front; however, there are times when CTR has been reluctant to serve in that capacity.... [31]

Judge Sarokin concluded that a jury could find that the tobacco industry's allegedly independent CTR studies regarding "the dangers of smoking and its promise to disclose its findings was nothing but a public relations ploy—a fraud—to deflect the growing evidence against the industry, to encourage smokers to continue and non-smokers to begin, and to reassure the public that adverse information would be disclosed."[32] On review by mandumus, however, the Third Circuit overruled Judge Sarokin, determining that he had improperly relied on *Cipollone* case documents in making his decision. The court also removed Judge Sarokin from the case because a few statements in his opinion had destroyed the "appearance of impartiality" and assigned the matter to a new judge for reconsideration of the crime-fraud issue.[33] The reconsideration never took place because the Budd Larner firm, financially exhausted by its foray into tobacco litigation, abandoned the case. The firm's efforts, however, had strongly suggested that tobacco companies had hidden evidence of health risks while seeking to promote the sale of their products.

In 1997 and 1998 a succession of tobacco cases held that documents hitherto protected by attorney-client privilege were admissible under the crime-fraud exception.[34] Company lawyers had been deciding whether industry-supported studies should be published or suppressed. The studies in question dealt primarily with the effects of nicotine (was it addictive? could its addictive quality be enhanced by manipulation of the amount of nicotine or adding other substances?) and the role of smoking tars in causing various forms of cancer. Thousands of documents from tobacco maker Brown & Williamson, for example, suggested "repeated efforts to shield from disclosure damaging internal studies about the health effects of smoking. The preferred means: a familiar one—get the lawyers involved, and thereby be in a position to invoke attorney-client privilege if the files

31. Id. at 696.

32. Id. at 684.

33. Haines v. Liggett Group, Inc., 975 F.2d 81 (3d Cir.1992), reversing and remanding, 140 F.R.D. 681 (D.N.J.1992). The Third Circuit noted, however, that Judge Sarokin was not "incapable of discharging judicial duties free from bias or prejudice." Id.

34. See, e.g., Burton v. R.J. Reynolds Tobacco Co., 177 F.R.D. 491 (D.Kan.1997); American Tobacco Co. v. State of Florida, 697 So.2d 1249 (Fla.App.1997); and Minnesota v. Philip Morris Inc., 1998 WL 257214 (Minn.Dist.Ct.1998).

are ever demanded in litigation or by government authorities.''[35] A 1998–99 grand jury investigation by the Department of Justice is said to be considering the conduct of company lawyers; and several lawsuits have named company lawyers as co-defendants.[36]

Tobacco lawyers claim that they were doing what lawyers are expected to do for their clients: to give legal advice about past conduct (e.g., whether a particular study the industry had supported would adversely affect results in pending or future litigation) and to advise the client about legal uncertainties of future liability exposure (e.g., would a particular study of nicotine's effects or smoking's causation of cancer hurt the company in future litigation?). A lawyer who crosses the line between giving neutral advice and actively helping to commit or conceal a continuing crime or fraud is subject to discipline (see Rules 1.2(d) and 8.4(c)) and may be sued for civil damages or prosecuted.

Did tobacco companies and their lawyers abuse the attorney-client privilege by successfully using it for many years to shield corporate research on the health risks of smoking while making public relations decisions on whether to publish, conduct or continue "scientific" studies of nicotine and smoking? Did the lawyers, by structuring and maintaining the attorney-client privilege shield, cross the line between giving legitimate counsel and providing illegal assistance? By helping the industry to defraud the public by disseminating misleading information on the work and purpose of the CTR? By failing to withdraw? On the other hand, is there a danger that the current desire to punish the tobacco industry may result in decisions that impair the ability of corporate lawyers to consult confidentially with their clients?

Procedures for Invoking the Privilege

To assert the privilege, most courts hold that the witness must appear, testify and invoke the privilege in response to a particular question.[37] The burden is then on the witness to prove that all the elements of the privilege are present.[38] In determining whether the lawyer has asserted a valid claim of privilege, the district court may use an *in camera* proceeding to prevent the release of information which the assertion of privilege is designed to prevent. See United States v. Zolin, supra, on the review of allegedly privileged material in camera.

The lawyer generally has a duty to invoke the privilege when called to testify about privileged matters; the client need not specially request that

35. Nader & Smith, at 30.

36. See Milo Geyelin & Ann Davis, Tobacco Foes Target Role of Lawyers, Wall St. J., Apr. 23, 1998, p. B6; Diana Henriques, Tobacco Lawyers' Role Is Questioned, N.Y. Times, Apr. 23, 1998, p. A18; and Geoffrey C. Hazard, Tobacco Lawyers Shame the Entire Profession, Nat'l L.J., May 18, 1998, p. A22.

37. In re Certain Complaints Under Investigation, 783 F.2d 1488, 1518 (11th Cir.1986) (collecting cases).

38. In re Grand Jury Empanelled February 14, 1978 (Markowitz), 603 F.2d 469 (3d Cir.1979).

the lawyer do so.[39] If the court finds that the matter is not privileged, the lawyer is not obliged to continue to refuse to testify in order to appeal the ruling. A lawyer's refusal to comply with a court ruling that the privilege is inapplicable involves some risk because a contempt citation may result in immediate imprisonment and continuing sanctions.[40]

6.   CLIENT IDENTITY, FEE ARRANGEMENTS AND SIMILAR MATTERS

Client Identity

Courts frequently state that client identity and fee arrangements are not privileged.[41] This general rule reflects the usual situation in which the client's identity is not at issue and the client's communications are unrelated to identity. *Baird v. Koerner*[42] is a frequently-cited case in which the client's identity is part of the client confidential communication to his lawyer. The client in *Baird* had substantially under-reported his income to the IRS and feared the imposition of penalties. At the client's direction, his lawyer sent a check to the IRS, withholding the client's name and explaining why. The Ninth Circuit upheld the lawyer's refusal to reveal his client's name, stating that "it may well be the link that could form a chain of testimony necessary to convict an individual of a federal crime."[43]

While courts frequently cite the *Baird* case, the "last-link" rationale for protecting client identity is incoherent and has been rarely applied.[44] In In re Grand Jury Subpoenas (Hirsch),[45] for example, the Ninth Circuit explicitly stated that "it is not the law that the requisites of the attorney-client privilege are met whenever evidence regarding the fees paid the attorney would implicate the client in a criminal offense regarding which the client sought legal advice." According to the *Hirsch* court, *Baird* involved "a unique factual situation": "[U]nder the facts of that case, the client's identity was in substance [itself] a confidential communication."[46] In other words, the court read *Baird* as protecting fee and identity information that would implicate the client in criminal activity only when the client communicated that information to the lawyer as part of seeking

---

39. EC 4–4; Comment [20] to Model Rule 1.6.

40. See Maness v. Meyers, 419 U.S. 449, 458–459 (1975). For an extreme case see Dike v. Dike, 448 P.2d 490 (Wash.1968) (trial judge had lawyer booked and held in jail until bail was paid; the court upheld the trial court's ruling on the privilege, but vacated its contempt order).

41. Restatement § 119, cmt. *g* and reporter's note (citing cases and authorities).

42. 279 F.2d 623 (9th Cir.1960).

43. 279 F.2d at 633.

44. See, e.g., In re Slaughter, 694 F.2d 1258 (11th Cir.1982), and In re Grand Jury Pro-ceedings, 680 F.2d 1026 (5th Cir.1982) (en banc) (both holding the exception is limited and narrow). See also In re Grand Jury Proceedings Subpoena (Wine), 841 F.2d 230 (8th Cir.1988) (finding *Baird* inapplicable and noting the Ninth Circuit's limitation of *Baird* to its facts).

45. 803 F.2d 493 (9th Cir.1986).

46. Id. at 497. See also In re Grand Jury Matter (French), 969 F.2d 995 (11th Cir. 1992) (lawyer must identify clients who may have paid him with counterfeit money; the *Baird* exception does not protect testimony which may incriminate client but only communications made for purposes of legal advice).

legal advice and not merely as a necessary corollary to advice-getting. Is this a sensible distinction? When the court calls *Baird*'s facts unique, might it be referring to the fact that the lawyer and client were acting to rectify the client's prior fraud?[47]

The Restatement summarizes current law:

Testimony about such matters [as the identity of a client or a non-client who paid the fee, the amount of the fee or the details of the retainer agreement, and the client's whereabouts] normally does not reveal the content of communications from the client. However, admissibility of such testimony should be based on the extent to which it reveals the content of a privileged communication. The privilege applies if the testimony directly or by reasonable inference would reveal the content of a confidential communication. But the privilege does not protect clients or lawyers against revealing a lawyer's knowledge about a client solely on the ground that doing so would incriminate the client or otherwise prejudice the client's interest.[48]

The Hit-and-Run Driver

The *Baltes* case in 1988 attracted substantial media attention.[49] The client showed up at lawyer Krischer's office, stated his name and said that he was responsible for a hit-and-run auto incident in which a pedestrian had been killed. He asked Krischer to negotiate a resolution of the matter with the authorities but not to reveal his identity. Without identifying the client, Krischer asked another lawyer to negotiate with the state's attorney. Baltes, the plaintiff in this civil suit against the nameless client, sought to compel Krischer to divulge the client's identity. The court held that the Florida statutory attorney-client privilege protected identity. Leaving the scene of an accident, without providing statutorily required information to the police or others involved in the accident, was not an ongoing crime. The *Baltes* case is one of a number dealing with a hit-and-run driver's identity. Nearly all of the decisions, viewing the criminal statute as having been violated once and for all when the driver leaves the scene of the accident without assisting and reporting, hold that the client's identity in this situation is part of the privileged communication. In such cases, the crime is a past one and the identity of the client is inextricably linked with the client's effort to obtain legal advice.[50]

---

47. May a lawyer assist a client in returning stolen property without revealing the client's identity? The cases go both ways. See Dean v. Dean, 607 So.2d 494 (Fla.Dist. Ct.App. 4th Dist.1992) (holding that a client's identity is privileged; dissent discusses cases holding that acting as a conduit for return of stolen property is not "legal advice").

48. Restatement § 119, cmt. g.

49. Baltes v. Doe (Fla.Cir.Ct.1988) is not reported. The case is summarized in Dean v. Dean, 607 So.2d 494, 495–96 (Fla.Dist. Ct.App. 4th Dist.1992). For discussion of *Baltes,* see Charles W. Wolfram, Hide and Secrets: The Boundaries of Privilege, Legal Times, Apr. 3, 1989, p. 23.

50. See, e.g., D'Alessio v. Gilberg, 617 N.Y.S.2d 484 (N.Y.App.Div., 1994); Miller v. Begley, 639 N.E.2d 139 (Ohio.App.1994).

Suppose the hit-and-run statute imposes a continuing duty to report, with penalties cumulating until a report is made? When the criminal violation is a continuing one, the decisions are virtually unanimous in concluding that the lawyer's testimony can be required. The most common situations are those of a client who has jumped bail and remains a fugitive and that of the spouse or relative who, in violation of a custody order, has fled with a child.[51]

Client's Physical Characteristics

The attorney-client privilege protects only "communications" that are intended to be "confidential." Thus, the physical characteristics of a client, such as complexion, demeanor and dress, are not generally considered privileged because they are neither "communications" nor matters which in the usual case a client considers confidential.[52] Should a lawyer be permitted to testify over a client's objection on observations of the client's demeanor that speak to the client's competence?[53]

Client Whereabouts

Communications about a client's whereabouts generally are not privileged and the lawyer's testimony can be compelled.[54] Whether, consistent with the professional duty of confidentiality, a lawyer may voluntarily disclose a client's whereabouts is a more difficult issue. See the notes preceding the *Hawkins* case below at p. 324 infra.

Lawyer Resistance to Reporting Cash Receipts

Case law on fee arrangements and client identity notwithstanding, many lawyers continue to act on the belief and assert the position that fees and identity are generally privileged. One illuminating example is the controversy between the bar and the federal government over reporting cash receipts. The Tax Reform Act of 1984[55] and regulations implementing

51. See United States v. Freeman, 519 F.2d 67, 68 (9th Cir.1975) (date and time of a bail hearing is not privileged in the subsequent bail-jumping prosecution of the client); Bersani v. Bersani, 565 A.2d 1368 (Conn.Super.Ct.1989) (mother's conduct in leaving the country with two children, after custody awarded to her ex-husband, was fraud on court that made client-fraud exception applicable); Commonwealth v. Maguigan, 511 A.2d 1327, 1333–37 (Pa.1986) (whereabouts of client who was fugitive from justice not privileged).

52. United States v. Kendrick, 331 F.2d 110 (4th Cir.1964).

53. See *Kendrick* (yes); Gunther v. United States, 230 F.2d 222 (D.C.Cir.1956) (no).

54. See, e.g., Burden v. Church of Scientology, 526 F.Supp. 44 (M.D.Fla.1981) (infor-

mation on whereabouts needed to serve complaint); Commonwealth v. Maguigan, 511 A.2d 1327 (Pa.1986) (whereabouts of fugitive client not privileged). Cf. In re Grand Jury Subpoenas (Field), 408 F.Supp. 1169 (S.D.N.Y.1976) (client's new address privileged, despite general rule, because it was communicated to lawyer as part of obtaining legal advice about moving); and In the Matter of Nackson, 534 A.2d 65 (N.J.Super.1987) (lawyer could not be compelled to disclose where other means available for obtaining information on fugitive client).

55. Tax Reform Act of 1984, Pub. L. No. 98–369, 98 Stat. 494 (1984) (codified as amended in 26 U.S.C.).

it require anyone who receives a cash payment of more than $10,000 in a trade or business to report to the IRS the paying party's name, address, social security number, occupation and, when applicable, the name of the person on whose behalf the transaction was conducted.[56]

The organized resistance of lawyers and bar associations to this reporting requirement is discussed in the Koniak article at p. 127 supra. Although lawyers have not succeeded in efforts to exempt themselves by statute, regulation, interpretation or constitutional challenge,[57] the refusal of many criminal defense lawyers to identify clients has stymied the IRS, requiring it to bring enforcement proceedings to obtain a court order directing a particular lawyer to provide the identity of the payer. Gerald Lefcourt, who headed the National Association of Criminal Defense Lawyer's "8300 Task Force" has led this opposition. After the *Goldberger & Dubin* case,[58] Lefcourt advised lawyers not to "violate a confidence until you are ordered to do so by a court." In response the IRS stiffened its enforcement strategy, warning lawyers that enforcement of the reporting requirements would now involve civil penalties of up to $25,000 for "intentional disregard" of the statutory requirement. When Lefcourt continued his refusal to include the payer's name in his reports of cash receipts of more than $10,000, the IRS assessed a penalty of $25,000 which Lefcourt then challenged in a refund action.[59] The Second Circuit upheld the penalty: Lefcourt acted voluntarily and deliberately in failing to report the client's name, and the possible or even likely incrimination of the client does not constitute a special circumstance justifying non-disclosure.[60] Is continued lawyer resistance to this statutory and judicial law justified?

7. THE ATTORNEY-CLIENT PRIVILEGE AND THE "WAR ON CRIME"

Federal and state efforts to crack down on drug conspiracies and organized crime activities have led in recent decades to a number of measures that have deeply concerned criminal defense lawyers, bar associa-

---

56. 26 U.S.C. § 6050I (1991).

57. In the test case challenging the report requirement, the Second Circuit dismissed as "without merit" the contention that the reporting requirement conflicts with the attorney-client privilege: "[T]he identification in Form 8300 of respondents' clients who make substantial cash fee payments is not a disclosure of privileged information ... even though it might incriminate the client." United States v. Goldberger & Dubin, 935 F.2d 501, 504 (2d Cir.1991): "[T]he [privilege] protects only those disclosures that are necessary to obtain informed legal advice and that would not be made without the privilege." No Sixth Amendment issue was presented because the client or lawyer could always avoid the report requirement by making non-cash fee

payments. Other circuits have followed *Goldberger & Dubin*, but several decisions have recognized exceptions in particular situations. See, e.g., United States v. Sindel, 53 F.3d 874 (8th Cir.1995) (identity of one client, but not others, was privileged when "there is a strong probability that disclosure would implicate the client in the very criminal activity for which legal advice was sought").

58. 935 F.2d 501, 504 (2d Cir.1991).

59. Lefcourt v. United States, 125 F.3d 79 (2d Cir.1997).

60. See also, Office of Disciplinary Counsel v. Massey, 687 N.E.2d 734 (Ohio 1998) (six months' disciplinary suspension for having client pay a series of amounts under $10,-000 in effort to evade the requirement).

tions and a number of scholars and judges. In the eyes of some, these measures are an assault on the lawyer's "sacred trust" to maintain client confidences; the assault, many lawyers believe, simultaneously undermines the attorney-client privilege and threatens a criminal defendant's Sixth Amendment right to counsel. Government intrusion into the attorney-client relation is said to create conflicts of interest between lawyer and client and damage a lawyer's ability to provide effective representation.

Subpoenas to Lawyers

One concern involves an increasing use by prosecutors of subpoenas requesting lawyers to testify before grand juries on matters relating to client identity, fee arrangements or client affairs (see discussion in Koniak excerpt, p. 123 supra).[61] Efforts by defense lawyers and bar associations to shape grand jury law to provide for a court hearing prior to issuance of subpoenas to lawyers were rejected by the courts. In 1990, the ABA, seeking to achieve the same objective through an amendment of Model Rule 3.8, adopted a provision requiring prosecutors to obtain "prior judicial approval after an opportunity for an adversarial hearing" before serving a subpoena on a lawyer in a grand jury or other criminal proceeding to seek evidence about the lawyer's past or present clients. Federal prosecutors then challenged the application of the rule to federal grand jury subpoenas in the half-dozen states that had adopted the ABA recommended rule or a similar one.[62] In 1995, withdrawing the 1990 language, the ABA amended Rule 3.8 by deleting subparagraph (f)(2). The accompanying report stated that the requirement was more properly a matter of criminal procedure, affecting the operation of courts and grand juries, than it was a regulation of prosecutorial ethics. See current Rule 3.8(f) for the remaining requirements concerning subpoenas to lawyers.

The controversy over the subpoena rule demonstrates the bar's use of the ethics rules as a competing source of norms to the courts' interpretation of the law. Having failed in efforts to persuade Congress or the courts to adopt its interpretation of the Sixth Amendment, the attorney-client privilege and grand jury law, the bar sought to achieve its objectives by

61. For discussion of law and controversy bearing on increased use of lawyer subpoenas, see Susan P. Koniak, The Law Between the Bar and the State, 70 N.C.L.Rev. 1389 (1992), above at p. 123; Roger C. Cramton and Lisa K. Udell, State Ethics Rules and Federal Prosecutors: The Controversies Over the Anti–Contact and Subpoena Rules, 53 U.Pitt.L.Rev. 291, 359–85 (1992); and Fred C. Zacharias, A Critical Look at Rules Governing Grand Jury Subpoenas of Attorneys, 76 Minn.L.Rev. 917 (1992).

62. See Baylson v. Disciplinary Board of Supreme Court of Pennsylvania, 975 F.2d 102 (3d Cir.1992) (Pennsylvania subpoena rule cannot be applied to federal prosecutors because its adoption as federal law falls outside the rule-making authority of a federal district court and its enforcement as state law violates the Supremacy Clause); cf. United States v. Klubock, 832 F.2d 664 (1st Cir.1987) (en banc affirmance of Massachusetts subpoena rule, also adopted as a rule of the federal court, by an equally divided court).

shifting the focus to a lawmaking arena—ethics rules—in which the bar has a more influential role.[63] Is that appropriate?

Forfeiture of Crime Proceeds

Fee forfeiture statutes are the second measure giving rise to concern. Their existence is one reason prosecutors seek information from lawyers by subpoena. Under a battery of federal statutes—RICO, CCE and the Comprehensive Crime Control Act of 1984[64]—fees paid to a lawyer for a criminal defense are subject to forfeiture if the money was realized from illegal activity. Moreover, the government may seek forfeiture not only at the inception of the representation but after the criminal proceeding that results in conviction. Thus a private criminal defense lawyer is taking substantial financial risks when she takes a case where the fee money may be subject to forfeiture, as it may be in any narcotics case and many RICO cases.[65]

In 1989, the Supreme Court in two 5–4 decisions held that the forfeiture provisions did not exempt assets used to pay an attorney. The defendant's assets may be frozen before conviction based on a finding of probable cause to believe that the assets are forfeitable;[66] and forfeiture of attorney's fees does not violate the defendant's Sixth Amendment right to counsel or Fifth Amendment right to due process.[67] The Court rejected "the drug merchant['s] claims that his possession of huge sums of money ... entitles him to something more [than appointed counsel]." There is no "constitutional right to use the proceeds of crime to finance an expensive defense":

> A defendant has no Sixth Amendment right to spend another person's money for services rendered by an attorney, even if those funds are the only way that that defendant will be able to retain the attorney of his choice. A robbery suspect, for example, has no Sixth Amendment right to use funds he has stolen from a bank to retain an attorney to defend him if he is apprehended. The money, though in his possession, is not rightfully his; the government does not violate the Sixth Amendment if it seizes the robbery proceeds, and refuses to permit the defendant to use them to pay for his defense. "[N]o lawyer, in any case, ... has the

63. See Roger C. Cramton & Lisa K. Udell, State Ethics Rules and Federal Prosecutors: The Controversies Over the Anti–Contact and Subpoena Rules, 53 U.Pitt. L.Rev. 291, 359–85 (1992).

64. The Racketeer Influenced and Corrupt Organizations Act (RICO), 18 U.S.C. §§ 1961–68) and Continuing Criminal Enterprise Statute (CCE), 21 U.S.C. § 848, are supplemented by the Comprehensive Crime Control Act of 1984, 18 U.S.C. § 1963(c) and 21 U.S.C. § 853(c). See the

discussion of these statutes in chapter 2 at p. 77 above.

65. See generally Ass'n Bar City of New York Committee on Criminal Advocacy, The Forfeiture of Attorney Fees in Criminal Cases: A Call for Immediate Remedial Action, 41 The Record 469 (1986); A. Morgan Cloud, Forfeiting Defense Attorneys' Fees, 1987 Wis.L.Rev. 1.

66. United States v. Monsanto, 491 U.S. 600 (1989).

67. Caplin & Drysdale v. United States, 491 U.S. 617 (1989).

right to accept stolen property, or ... ransom money, in payment of a fee.... The privilege to practice law is not a license to steal."[68]

Justice Blackmun's dissent in *Caplin & Drysdale* argued that

[t]he right to retain private counsel serves to foster the trust between attorney and client that is necessary for the attorney to be a truly effective advocate.... When the Government insists upon the right to choose the defendant's counsel for him, that relationship of trust is undermined: counsel is too readily perceived as the Government's agent rather than his own....

The right to retain private counsel also serves to assure some modicum of equality between the Government and those it chooses to prosecute.... [W]hen the Government provides for appointed counsel, there is no guarantee that levels of compensation and staffing will be even average.... Without the defendant's right to retain private counsel, the Government too readily could defeat its adversaries simply by outspending them.[69]

Underlying *Caplin & Drysdale* is the fact that the wealthy are more likely to receive better representation than the poor and that one's liberty, property or other important interests may depend on how good a lawyer one has. Does the majority grapple with this truth? Does the dissent grapple with the problem any more honestly than the majority?[70]

Reporting of Cash Receipts

The third measure giving rise to concern is the reporting requirement of section 6050I of the Internal Revenue Code, discussed supra. This provision requires any person who receives more than $10,000 in cash in connection with a trade or business to file a report with the IRS. The implementing regulations leave no doubt that lawyers are engaged in a trade or business for purposes of the reporting requirement. The IRS provision is reinforced by the federal money laundering statute, which makes it a crime knowingly to engage in a monetary transaction with a financial institution if the amount of the transaction exceeds $10,000 and the funds are derived from specified criminal activity. If a lawyer knows that a client's fee comes from illegal activity, she cannot deposit a fee of more than $10,000 without committing a crime.[71]

---

68. Id. at 626.

69. Id. at 646–47.

70. The dissent alludes to the low pay rates and meager resources of public defender and appointed counsel programs. Is this "problem" significant only in "complex" cases of the sort brought under RICO? Many non-forfeiture cases involve higher stakes—the life of the defendant, for example. Perhaps so many of those cases appear "simple" because appointed counsel does not have the resources to explore (or cre-

ate) complexities. By appearing to concede that the generally inadequate resources of appointed counsel programs are only of constitutional significance in forfeiture cases, does the dissent, like the majority, perpetuate a myth that as a general matter poor defendants are accorded equal justice?

71. See Kathleen F. Brickey, Tainted Assets and the Right to Counsel—The Money Laundering Conundrum, 66 Wash.U.L.Q. 47, 47–49 (1988) (discussing the federal fee forfeiture and money laundering statutes).

8. WAIVER OF ATTORNEY–CLIENT PRIVILEGE[1]

Once a privileged communication has been made, the privilege continues indefinitely unless action or inaction of the client terminates the confidential status of the communication. The fact that the privilege survives the termination of the lawyer-client relationship and even the death of the client presents interesting questions concerning the availability to future generations of historical materials reposing in lawyer files. If, for example, John Wilkes Booth had consulted a Virginia lawyer after shooting President Lincoln, may the successor firm make those records available many years later, or is the consent of Booth's descendants required?[2]

The Supreme Court, interpreting the federal common law governing the attorney-client privilege, held that notes taken by a private attorney consulted by deputy White House counsel Vincent Foster nine days before Foster committed suicide were protected after Foster's death against a request by a federal grand jury.[3] Independent counsel Kenneth Starr sought three pages of handwritten notes by Foster's private lawyer. Starr argued for a balancing test in which compelling law enforcement needs should override the privilege when the evidence is not available from other sources. A 6–3 majority, in an opinion by Chief Justice Rehnquist, held that Starr had "not made a sufficient showing to overturn the common law rule" that the privilege does not end at the client's death. "Knowing that communications will remain confidential even after death encourages the client to communicate fully and frankly with counsel." Justice O'Connor's dissenting opinion argued that the attorney-client privilege should yield in the rare situations when the protected information is needed to exonerate an innocent defendant or when there is a compelling need by law enforcement officials. She mentioned the fact situation in State v. Macumber,[4] in which a client confessed to his lawyer before he died that he committed a murder for which another person was on trial. Who is right? Should an innocent person be executed because a lawyer cannot be compelled (attorney-client privilege) or permitted (professional duty of confidentiality) to provide exonerating testimony? Should the compelling needs of law enforcement trump the privilege of dead clients? Live clients too?

A client loses the privilege with respect to a particular communication either by consent or by conduct inconsistent with maintaining the privilege. Consent usually takes the form of disclosure of a privileged communication

---

1. See generally George A. Davidson & William H. Voth, Waiver of the Attorney–Client Privilege, 64 Or.L.Rev. 637 (1986); Richard L. Marcus, The Perils of Privilege: Waiver and the Litigator, 84 Mich.L.Rev. 1605 (1986).

2. There is very little law on the subject. Restatement § 112, cmt. *h* states that "a lawyer may cooperate with reasonable efforts to obtain information about clients and law practice for public purposes, such as historical research, when no material risk to a client is entailed, such as financial or reputational harm." See also David A. Kaplan, Does Attorney–Client Privilege Outweigh Demands of History?, Nat'l L. J., July 4, 1988, p. 36.

3. Swidler & Berlin v. United States, 524 U.S. 399 (1998).

4. 544 P.2d 1084 (Ariz.1976).

in an unprivileged setting; conduct inconsistent with maintaining the privilege includes a failure to object to an attempt by another to obtain or provide evidence of a privileged communication. Only the client may waive the privilege; but, because lawyers have implied authority to waive a client's confidentiality rights in the course of representation, waiver may flow from a lawyer's action even though the client was not consulted.[5] Whether a lawyer's disclosure constitutes an exercise of that implied authority is a question of agency law, which looks to whether the disclosure was within the course of representation and not to whether the disclosure was prudent.

Waiver by Putting–In–Issue

State v. von Bulow [*von Bulow I*],[6] arose out of the near death and permanent incapacitation of Martha von Bulow, a wealthy heiress. Family members, suspecting that her husband, Claus von Bulow, may have poisoned her, retained a former prosecutor, Richard Kuh, to investigate the events. Kuh's investigation produced physical evidence, witness statements and other materials that the family members then turned over to the police. At a pretrial hearing of subsequent charges against him for attempted murder, von Bulow sought disclosure of additional material that had not been supplied to public officials. The trial court ruled that all the documents withheld were protected by the attorney-client privilege or the work-product doctrine. von Bulow, after being found guilty of twice attempting to murder his wife by injecting her with doses of insulin, attacked this ruling on appeal. The Rhode Island Supreme Court held that the attorney-client privilege and work-product immunity had been waived by the partial revelation of protected material. von Bulow's conviction was reversed on this and other grounds and the case remanded for a new trial.

The court stated:

> An essential element that must be proved in establishing the existence of the privilege is that it has not been waived. Absent such a waiver, the [unrevealed] communications would be protected from disclosure since the privilege normally protects a client from having to disclose even the subject matter of confidential communications with his attorney. United States v. Aronoff, 466 F.Supp. 855, 861 (S.D.N.Y. 1979). The privilege may be waived, however, when there has been disclosure of a confidential communication to a third party. Id. at 862.
>
> . . .
>
> . . . [T]he extent to which disclosures relating to the subject matter of the attorney-client relationship were made was sufficient to waive the privilege. As the court stated in United States v. Aronoff, 466 F.Supp. at 862, this principle has been referred to as "waiver by implication" and it is based on considerations of fairness.

5. See Restatement § 128 (waiver by agreement, disclaimer, or failure to object).

6. 475 A.2d 995 (R.I.1984).

"[W]hen [the client's] conduct touches a certain point of disclosure, fairness requires that his privilege shall cease whether he intended that result or not. He cannot be allowed, after disclosing as much as he pleases, to withhold the remainder. He may elect to withhold or to disclose, but after a certain point his election must remain final. 8 Wigmore, supra § 2327, at 636. See also McCormick on Evidence § 93, at 194 (2d ed. 1972)." Id.

Consistent with these principles of fairness, it has been held that the attorney-client privilege properly serves as a shield and not as an offensive tool of litigation. The court in *Aronoff* recognized that "[w]here a privilege-holder has made assertions about privileged communications, but has attempted to bar other evidence of those communications, there is a serious danger that his assertions are false or misleading." United States v. Aronoff, 466 F.Supp. at 862. "A party may not, therefore, insist upon protection of the privilege for damaging communications while disclosing those which it considers to be favorable to its position.". . . .

The facts of the present case are a classic example of the impermissible selective use of privileged information. While maintaining that communications were intended to be confidential, Alex and his attorney, at Alex's direction, disclosed information sufficient to trigger an investigation by the state and an indictment. These same parties later refused to disclose other evidence of the same communications. The inequity of allowing the privilege holder in this case to disclose as much as he pleased while withholding the remainder is heightened by the fact that defendant was on trial for attempted murder. The effect of excluding such evidence was therefore to deny defendant access to information that he was entitled to examine in the preparation of his defense.[7]

Was the Rhode Island court in *von Bulow I* justified in penetrating the confidentiality interests of family members in information communicated to their lawyer? Is it relevant that some of the information gathered by attorney Kuh came from third persons and included physical evidence of crime? Both family members and the prosecutor were aligned in interest against von Bulow. Did the court overlook the common interest application of the privilege?[8]

Generally, client disclosure of privileged information to third parties (or lawyer disclosure authorized by the client) destroys the privilege.[9] Even partial disclosure may destroy the privilege in some cases: When a client during litigation puts in issue a privileged communication, the client

---

7.   475 A.2d at 1006–08.

8.   See the discussion of the common interest application of the attorney-client privilege at p. 209 supra.

9.   See, e.g., Clady v. County of Los Angeles, 770 F.2d 1421 (9th Cir.1985) (general rule); and Weil v. Investment/Indicators, Research & Management, Inc., 647 F.2d 18, 23–25 (9th Cir.1981) (out-of-court waiver).

impliedly waives the privilege. The extent of the waiver may exceed the dimensions of the initial disclosure.

The implied waiver that results from a client's putting privileged information in issue is an evidence rule of forensic fairness: opening one part of a topic opens the whole topic. A familiar application of this principle is that a criminal defendant who takes the stand waives the privilege against self-incrimination, and hence must respond to cross-examination on all relevant matters, not merely those covered in the defendant's direct testimony.[10] When the client attacks the lawyer's conduct, whether in a malpractice suit, a disciplinary charge or other setting, fairness requires that the lawyer be able to use client communications in defense.[11] By challenging a conviction based on ineffective assistance of counsel, for example, a petitioner waives the privilege to the extent necessary to resolve the claim.[12]

Waiver may also result from assertion of a claim of good faith reliance on a lawyer's advice. In United States v. Bilzerian,[13] the defendant failed to take the stand to assert his good faith reliance because the trial court had ruled that he could not do so without waiving the attorney-client privilege. The Second Circuit affirmed the subsequent conviction, holding that "the privilege may be implicitly waived when defendant asserts a claim that in fairness requires examination of protected communications":[14]

> ... Bilzerian's testimony that he thought his actions were legal would have put his knowledge of the law and the basis for his understanding of what the law required in issue. His conversations with counsel regarding the legality of his schemes would have been directly relevant in determining the extent of his knowledge and, as a result, his intent.[15]

For a discussion of the "self-defense" exception to the attorney-client privilege, which allows lawyers to reveal privileged information when their actions are at issue, see *Meyerhofer* and the notes following it, p. 274 below.

Some courts have held that disclosures made in a voluntary effort to cooperate with the government waive the privilege only as to the government—a form of limited waiver; the goal of such rulings is to encourage voluntary cooperation with the government.[16] Most courts, however, hold

---

10. See United States ex rel. Edney v. Smith, 425 F.Supp. 1038 (E.D.N.Y.1976), aff'd, 556 F.2d 556 (2d Cir.1977) (implied waiver by own testimony).

11. It makes little difference whether lawyer self-defense is viewed as waiver under the fairness doctrine or as an exception to the privilege. The attorney-client privilege, it is said, does not apply "as to a communication relevant to an issue of breach of duty by the lawyer to his client or by the client to his lawyer." See Proposed Fed. R.Evid. 503(d)(3).

12. See, e.g., United States v. Woodall, 438 F.2d 1317 (5th Cir.1970) (en banc).

13. 926 F.2d 1285 (2d Cir.1991). See also United States v. Miller, 600 F.2d 498, 501–02 (5th Cir.1979) (defendant waived privilege by raising defense of good faith reliance on attorney's advice).

14. Id. at 1292.

15. Id.

16. See, e.g., Diversified Industries, Inc. v. Meredith, 572 F.2d 596, 611 (8th Cir.1977) (en banc).

that disclosure to any potential adversary, including the government, constitutes a waiver as to all others.[17] A substantial case law also deals with the work-product doctrine as applied to documents voluntarily disclosed to the government.[18]

Waiver by Subsequent Disclosure: *von Bulow II*

In In re von Bulow [*von Bulow II*],[19] two children of Martha von Bulow brought a civil damage action in federal court against their foster father, Claus von Bulow, for attempting to kill their mother. In a Rhode Island state court, von Bulow had been acquitted of criminal charges alleging the same conduct after an initial conviction, appellate court reversal and retrial. After von Bulow's acquittal on retrial, Alan Dershowitz, who had handled the appeal from the initial conviction, published *Reversal of Fortune*, a book detailing his successful exploits on von Bulow's behalf. The book, subsequently made into a movie, partially disclosed the content of a number of communications between von Bulow and his lawyer, Dershowitz. The plaintiffs in *von Bulow II*, viewing the partial disclosures in *Reversal of Fortune* as a waiver of von Bulow's attorney-client privilege, sought disclosure of the remainder of the conversations. The district court ruled broadly in favor of waiver, but von Bulow sought and obtained relief by mandamus from the Second Circuit.

The Second Circuit, after holding that the situation warranted the exercise of mandamus jurisdiction, held that von Bulow, by encouraging the publication of the book and actively promoting its sale, waived the privilege by consent with respect to information actually disclosed in the book. More importantly, however, the court held that the extrajudicial dissemination to the general public of certain privileged information did not waive the privilege as to any portions of conversations not revealed. The court distinguished the forensic rule, discussed above, which allows an opposing party to inquire into the remainder of a privileged communication after the party offers evidence of a portion of a privileged communication:

> [W]here, as here, disclosures of privileged information are made extra-judicially and without prejudice to the opposing party, there exists no reason in logic or equity to broaden the waiver beyond those matters actually revealed. Matters actually disclosed in public lose their privileged status because they obviously are no longer confidential. The cat is let out of the bag, so to speak. But related matters not so disclosed remain confidential. Although it is true that disclosures in the public

17. In In re Subpoenas Duces Tecum, 738 F.2d 1367 (D.C.Cir.1984), Tesoro Petroleum provided the Securities and Exchange Commission with information on illegal foreign bribes in exchange for more lenient treatment from the SEC. In a derivative suit against the corporation, shareholders sought the documents Tesoro had provided to the SEC. Held, the privilege was waived as to those documents, rejecting the argument that the waiver doctrine should yield to the public policy in favor of encouraging voluntary cooperation with the government. See also In re Martin Marietta, 856 F.2d 619 (4th Cir.1988).

18. See, e.g., Chubb Integrated Systems v. National Bank of Washington, 103 F.R.D. 52, 67 (D.D.C.1984).

19. 828 F.2d 94 (2d Cir.1987).

arena may be "one-sided" or "misleading", so long as such disclosures are and remain extrajudicial, there is no *legal* prejudice that warrants a broad court-imposed subject matter waiver. The reason is that disclosures made in public rather than in court—even if selective— create no risk of *legal* prejudice until put at issue in the litigation by the privilege-holder. Therefore, insofar as the district court broadened petitioner's waiver to include related conversations on the same subject it was in error.[20]

Is *von Bulow II* correct in distinguishing so sharply between the forensic rule of implied waiver by putting a matter in issue and that of waiver by subsequent extrajudicial disclosure?[21] Should von Bulow's disclosure of some secret information result in forfeiture of other secret information? Should the purpose of the extrajudicial disclosures affect the extent of waiver? For example, should disclosures in a book intended to establish the innocence of a defendant, whether or not intended to mislead or prejudice, trigger a broader forfeiture than disclosures made to a government agency for purposes of assisting an ongoing investigation?[22] Should the party alleging waiver have to show that the disclosure was actually misleading, or should it be enough that the disclosure was intended to prejudice the proceedings?

Privileged Subsequent Disclosure

If a disclosure is itself privileged, as with disclosure to other lawyers who are assisting with a case,[23] it does not waive the privilege. Similarly, statements made in the course of settlement negotiations or plea bargaining are inadmissible to prove liability in subsequent litigation between the negotiating parties.[24] Supplementing the protections provided by those rules, many cautious lawyers preface any damaging disclosure in negotiations or plea bargaining by stating that the statement is made "without prejudice" or make the admission in hypothetical conditional form.

---

20. Id. at 102–03. The civil suit was later settled by an agreement by which von Bulow gave up all claim to his wife's estate, agreed to divorce her and relinquished all rights to write books or earn money by publicizing the case. In return, von Bulow's daughter was restored to a one-third share in her grandmother's estate and the plaintiffs agreed to drop their lawsuit. N.Y. Times, Dec. 24, 1987, at p. B1.

21. See generally Note, Fairness and the Doctrine of Subject Matter Waiver of the Attorney–Client Privilege in Extrajudicial Disclosure Situations, 1988 U.Ill.L.Rev. 999. The case law is divided on the scope of non-litigation partial waivers and Restatement § 129, cmt. *f* takes no position on the issue.

22. In a footnote the court in *von Bulow II* left open the possibility that plaintiffs could demonstrate that "von Bulow's assertion of his attorney-client privilege is misleading or otherwise prejudicial": "assertions before trial may mislead or prejudice an adversary at trial and thereby impede the proper functioning of the judicial system." 828 F.2d at 102 n. 1.

23. See, e.g., Transmirra Prods. Corp. v. Monsanto Chemical Co., 26 F.R.D. 572, 576–77 (S.D.N.Y.1960); and the note above on the privilege between joint clients and cooperating parties.

24. See, e.g., Fed.R.Evid. 408 (statements in settlement negotiations); and Fed.R.Evid. 410(4) (statements in plea bargaining).

Inadvertent Disclosure

The traditional rule has been that inadvertent disclosure waives the privilege as effectively as intentional disclosure, apparently on the theory that inadvertent disclosure is inconsistent with an intention to preserve confidentiality.[25] The reality of modern discovery, however, has made the inadvertent disclosure of privileged documents an increasing problem and the case law on this subject is changing.[26] Some courts have rejected the traditional rule entirely,[27] others adhere to it,[28] and a growing number take a middle-ground approach, preserving the privilege unless, in effect, the disclosure resulted from the palpable negligence of either the client or her lawyer.[29]

Restatement § 129, comment *b*, provides that "[a] subsequent disclosure through a voluntary act constitutes a waiver even though not intended to have that effect. Waiver does not result if the client of other disclosing person took precautions reasonable in the circumstances to guard against such [inadvertent] disclosure [and then lists five relevant factors for determining 'reasonableness']."

B. PROFESSIONAL DUTY OF CONFIDENTIALITY

INTRODUCTORY NOTE

Agency law provides that "an agent [has] a duty to the principal not to use or to communicate information confidentially given him by the principal or acquired by him during the course of or on account of his agency."[1] "Client confidential information" is a broad category including all information about the client that the lawyer has a duty to keep secret. It includes information about the client learned from other sources.

In addition to evidence and agency law, state lawyer codes prescribe a duty of confidentiality, usually based to some extent on the provisions in

25. See 8 Wigmore, Evidence § 2325 at 633 (McNaughton rev. 1961).

26. See Transamerica Computer Co. v. IBM Corp., 573 F.2d 646 (9th Cir.1978).

27. Some courts seem to have abandoned the traditional rule, holding that an inadvertent disclosure does not result in waiver. See, e.g., Mendenhall v. Barber–Greene Co., 531 F.Supp. 951, 954–55 (N.D.Ill. 1982).

28. Cases adhering to the traditional rule include International Digital Systems Corp. v. Digital Equipment Corp., 120 F.R.D. 445, 450 (D.Mass.1988) (stating that the strict rule "would probably do more than anything else to instill in attorneys the need for effective precautions against such disclosure").

29. See, e.g., Lois Sportswear, U.S.A., Inc. v. Levi Strauss & Co., 104 F.R.D. 103 (S.D.N.Y.1985) (listing several factors in deciding whether the inadvertent disclosure waived the privilege: "(1) the reasonableness of the precautions to prevent inadvertent disclosure; (2) the time taken to rectify the error; (3) the scope of the discovery; (4) the extent of the disclosure; and (5) the 'overriding issue of fairness' ").

1. See Restatement (Second) of Agency §§ 395–96 (1958) § 395. See also 2 Floyd R. Mechem, Treatise on the Law of Agency § 2150 (2d ed.1914).

the ABA Model Code or Model Rules.[2] These provisions, while reflecting evidence and agency law, do not fully correspond in breadth and limits to the rules of confidentiality under that law. They might better be described as codifications of the profession's lore of confidentiality. The breadth of the exceptions to confidentiality acknowledged by the law of agency conflicts with the profession's understanding of its duty to preserve confidences. Under agency law, for example, the agent's duty of confidentiality is qualified by the agent's power to reveal confidences when necessary to protect a third party with a superior interest to the principal's interest in confidentiality.[3] Contrast the narrower exceptions in Model Rule 1.6(b).

We first consider the scope of confidentiality under the Model Code of Professional Responsibility and the Model Rules of Professional Conduct.[4] Next, we examine the exceptions.

In examining the exceptions to confidentiality, two pervasive themes emerge:

(1) What relationship do the confidentiality rules envision between a lawyer and a client who is engaged in criminal or fraudulent conduct? Do the rules allow sufficient room for a lawyer to protect herself from civil and criminal liability for the client's illegal conduct? Do they adequately reinforce the prohibition against assisting a client in illegal conduct?

(2) Do the confidentiality rules properly balance the interests of clients and other societal and individual interests, such as protecting innocent third parties from harm?

The justification for the principle of client confidentiality is encouragement of clients to communicate fully with the lawyer and to seek early legal assistance even about embarrassing matters. See Comments [1]—[4] to M.R. 1.6 and EC 4–1. Is the exception in the law of agency, allowing disclosure to protect a "superior interest" of a third party, inadequate to serve the purposes of lawyer-client confidentiality?

Another interest served by confidentiality is more closely aligned with the law of agency. To encourage people to rely on others, they must be able

---

2. California is apparently the only state that does not have a provision in its lawyer code dealing with confidentiality. A statutory version of the "Lawyer's Oath" states the default rule of confidentiality, Cal. Bus. & Prof. Code § 6068(e), leading some California bar leaders to argue (mistakenly) that the professional duty of confidentiality is an absolute duty, i.e., without any exceptions. California case law, however, creates many of the typical exceptions to confidentiality and a recent case, General Dynamics Corp. v. Superior Court, 876 P.2d 487, 503 (Cal.1994), suggests that the exceptions to California's statutory attorney-client privilege are also exceptions to the professional duty of confidentiality. See Roger C. Cram-

ton, Proposed Legislation Concerning a Lawyer's Duty of Confidentiality, 22 Pepperdine L. Rev. 1467 (1995).

3. See § 395, cmt. f; 2 Mechem, Agency § 2404 (2d ed.1914).

4. See Fred C. Zacharias, Rethinking Confidentiality, 74 Iowa L.Rev. 351 (1989) (reviewing the law of confidentiality and reporting an empirical study of client and lawyer impressions of the confidentiality rule); and Nancy J. Moore, Limits to Attorney–Client Confidentiality: A "Philosophically Informed" and Comparative Approach to Legal and Medical Ethics, 36 Case W.Res.L.Rev. 177 (1986).

to trust those in whose hands they place their affairs. The duty of confidentiality is a corollary of the more general duty of loyalty. This suggests a greater duty of loyalty, and a correspondingly greater duty of confidentiality, from those in whom a greater degree of trust is placed than in ordinary agents. Lawyers are not ordinary agents. Lawyers, however, are not the only professionals who are entrusted with matters of great importance. Yet the information they acquire concerning a client's matter receives greater protection than that afforded other professionals, for example, physicians.[5] In any case, why should this duty of loyalty extend to confidences about contemplated and ongoing illegal activity?

1.   Scope of Duty of Confidentiality

Model Code of Professional Responsibility

DR 4–101 of the Model Code of Professional Responsibility is the Code's principal confidentiality provision. DR 4–101(A) defines the information to be protected. DR 4–101(B) defines the scope of the duty. DR 4–101(C) sets out exceptions. The question of client fraud is treated in a separate provision, DR 7–102(B)(1). DR 4–101(D) deals with disclosure and use of confidential information by the lawyer's agents.

DR 4–101(A) defines two types of confidential information, "confidences" and "secrets." All subsequent provisions of the Code apply to both categories. "Confidences" refers to information protected by the attorney-client privilege under applicable law, and "secrets" refers to other information gained in the professional relationship that the client has requested be held inviolate or the disclosure of which would be embarrassing or likely to be detrimental to the client.

The definition of "confidences" thus is a source external to the Code; it is defined by the law of evidence. The definition of "secrets" covers non-privileged information gained in the relationship, but does not cover information gained before or after the relationship. Should it? The attorney-client privilege is limited to information received from the client *during* the representation, but the agent's duty is broader, covering information "acquired ... on account of [the] agency." Recall that the law of agency applies to lawyers. Is the agency definition better than that in the Code provision? Is the agency definition broad enough?

"Secrets" does not cover all information gained in the course of the representation, only that which the client requests be secret or which would harm or embarrass the client if disclosed. Should the lawyer be left to decide whether information would harm or embarrass the client when the client has not requested secrecy?

---

5. Compare the *Hawkins* case printed below   at p. 329.
at p. 325 with *Tarasoff*, which is discussed

The distinction between "confidences" and "secrets" became a source of controversy in interpreting an ABA amendment to DR 7–102(B)(1).[6] The distinction, however, has never assumed practical importance in determining whether there is a duty of confidentiality and was abandoned in the Model Rules, see M.R. 1.6.

DR 4–101(B) provides:

Except when permitted under DR 4–101(C), a lawyer shall not knowingly:

> (1) Reveal a confidence or secret of his client.

> (2) Use a confidence or secret of his client to the disadvantage of the client.

> (3) Use a confidence or secret of his client for the advantage of himself or of a third person, unless the client consents after full disclosure.

The Model Code specifies that "knowing" use or disclosure is a violation, apparently excluding inadvertent non-negligent disclosure. However DR 4–101(D) requires exercise of reasonable care in supervising agents who possess confidential client information, suggesting that negligent disclosure by the lawyer would violate DR 4–101(B).

Model Rules of Professional Conduct

Model Rule 1.6 is the key provision on confidentiality. It was the most hotly debated of the rules during the drafting process of the Kutak Commission and on the floor of the ABA House of Delegates.[7] In the process of being adopted by the states, M.R. 1.6 has also been more significantly redrafted than any of the other model rules. The heart of the controversy involves the scope of the exceptions, discussed below.

M.R. 1.6(a) is broader than DR 4–101. First, it protects all information "relating to the representation" whether the lawyer learned the information before, during or after the representation. Second, the rule applies whether or not disclosure would harm or embarrass the client. It also eliminates the word "knowingly" from its prohibition, stating flatly "a lawyer shall not." Restatement § 111 follows the Model Rules in broadly defining "confidential client information" as all "information relating to that client, acquired by a lawyer or agent of the lawyer in the course of or as the result of representing the client," but adds a qualification not contained in Rule 1.6: "other than information that is generally known."

Using as Opposed to Revealing Client Information

Use of confidential information is governed by the rules on conflict of interest. M.R. 1.8(b) prohibits using confidential information concerning a

---

6. See the discussion at p. 284 infra, describing the controversy and the ABA's resolution of it in Formal Op. 341.

7. The Kutak Commission was the ABA body that drafted the Model Rules for consideration by the ABA House of Delegates.

For a good summary of the controversy, see Ted Schneyer, Professionalism as Bar Politics: The Making of the Model Rules of Professional Conduct, 1989 J. Law & Soc. Inquiry 677.

present client to the disadvantage of that client without the client's consent given after consultation, except as M.R. 1.6 or 3.3 permit; and M.R. 1.9(c)(1) prohibits using confidential information of a former client to that client's disadvantage except as M.R. 1.6 and 3.3 permit *or* until the information has become generally known. Neither M.R. 1.6, 1.8(b) nor 1.9(c)(1) prohibit the use of confidential information to benefit the lawyer when the client will not be harmed by the use. Should a lawyer be prohibited from benefiting from a client confidence in a way that does not harm the client?

Such self-dealing is prohibited by the law of agency.[8] Under some circumstances it may also constitute mail fraud.[9] Use of confidential information to benefit the lawyer may also violate federal or state laws prohibiting insider trading.

Publicly Available Information as Confidential Information

Under the Model Rules as under the Model Code, the lawyer's obligation not to *reveal* confidential information applies whether or not the information is publicly known. See M.R. 1.9(c)(2). However, M.R. 1.9(c)(1), unlike the Code, allows the *use* of generally known information against a *former* client.[10] The Restatement, as indicated earlier, applies this same permission more generally by including an exception for "information that is generally known" in its definition of information protected by the professional duty of confidentiality. Restatement § 111.

What interests are sacrificed by allowing a lawyer to use generally known information to the detriment of a former client? Why does Model Rule 1.8(b) not have an exception for generally known information similar to the one in M.R. 1.9(c)(1)? The law of agency allows agents to use confidential information to the disadvantage of a former principal when that information is available from public sources.[11] M.R. 1.9(c)(1)'s exception seems narrower than that of agency law in that the information must be "generally known."

Client Consent and Implied Authority to Reveal

Model Rule 1.6(a) and DR 4–101(C)(1) allow for disclosure of any client confidence if the client consents after consultation with the lawyer as to the consequences of such a decision. See also M.R. 1.8(b).

---

8. See Restatement (Second) of Agency § 395 (1958) and the comment to § 388.

9. See United States v. O'Hagan, 521 U.S. 642 (1997) (lawyer) and Carpenter v. United States, 484 U.S. 19 (1987) (journalist), discussed at p. 75 supra, applying the mail fraud statute to agents who use a principal's information for their own gain.

10. For cases on whether public information is confidential, see, e.g., City of Wichita v. Chapman, 521 P.2d 589, 596 (Kan. 1974) (public information not a confidence); NCK Org. Ltd. v. Bregman, 542 F.2d 128, 133 (2d Cir.1976) (public information a confidence).

11. See Restatement (Second) of Agency § 395 (1958).

Lawyers, however, would be unable to do their job, which is to represent people, if they had to have express consent before speaking about anything that involves a confidence. Comment [7] to M.R. 1.6 explains:

> A lawyer is impliedly authorized to make disclosures about a client when appropriate in carrying out the representation, except to the extent that the client's instructions or special circumstances limit that authority. In litigation, for example, a lawyer may disclose information by admitting a fact that cannot properly be disputed, or in negotiation by making a disclosure that facilitates a satisfactory conclusion.

The Model Code has no similar provision on implied authority. However, the Code's definition of "secrets" as information that would embarrass or harm the client if revealed yields a similar result.

Consequences of Breaching the Duty of Confidentiality

A variety of sanctions are visited on lawyers who breach confidentiality. A violation of Rule 1.6(b), for example, may result in professional discipline. In In re Pressly,[12] for example, a mother informed her lawyer that she suspected her former husband was abusing their daughter during visitations; the lawyer was disciplined for revealing the client's suspicions to her former husband's lawyer, against her instructions. In another case a lawyer was disqualified from a complex intellectual property case and ordered to pay substantial attorney fees for sharing his client's confidential information with one of its competitors.[13] In Perez v. Kirk & Carrigan,[14] a truck driver for a bottling company was held to have stated a claim for civil damages when the company's lawyers, after stating that they also represented him, turned over to the prosecutor his statement to them concerning a collision with a school bus in which 21 children were killed, an action that led to the driver's indictment for involuntary manslaughter. Finally, in some situations breach of confidentiality is a crime. Recall United States v. O'Hagan,[15] in which a lawyer used information that his firm's client was planning a hostile tender offer of a major company to profit from trading in the target's stock. The Court upheld convictions for securities and mail fraud violations.

2. SELF-DEFENSE EXCEPTION

Exceptions to the professional duty of confidentiality may be classified into three broad areas: (1) protection of lawyers threatened by a claim or charge brought by the client or a third person (the self-defense exception); (2) protection of innocent third parties who are being or may be victimized by the client; and (3) prevention or rectification of fraud on the tribunal. The first two of these areas, self-defense and the defense of third parties, are discussed in this chapter. The third category, fraud on the court, is considered in Chapter 5.

---

12. 628 A.2d 927 (Vt.1993).

13. See "Attorney Booted from IP Case," Nat'l L.J. p. 4B, Oct. 19, 1998.

14. 822 S.W.2d 261 (Tex.Ct.App.1991).

15. 521 U.S. 642 (1997).

The self-defense exception arises primarily in three types of cases: (1) when a client charges a lawyer with wrongdoing in the course of representation; (2) when a lawyer sues the client to enforce some duty owed the lawyer, such as payment of a fee; and (3) when a third person accuses a lawyer of wrongdoing in the course of representing a client, perhaps in complicity with the client.

The first situation, in which the client attacks the lawyer by filing a malpractice action, a disciplinary complaint or other formal charge, raises the fewest problems. The client has waived the attorney-client privilege by putting the lawyer's representation in issue. Fairness, even due process, requires that the lawyer be permitted to use confidential information to respond to what may be false charges. The self-defense exception to the professional duty of confidentiality is an obvious corollary of this principle.

The second situation, in which the lawyer seeks to enforce a duty owed to her by her client, appears more problematic, but has strong support in agency law. It is unfair for the beneficiary of a fiduciary's services to receive those services and not perform duties owed to the fiduciary. When the lawyer sues a client to collect a fee, moreover, the claim itself involves very limited or no disclosure of client confidences, since fee arrangements are not ordinarily privileged. Confidential information will come out only if the client defends the fee action by attacking the amount charged or the lawyer's representation. Thus the client has some control of the scope of the waiver. On the other hand, the cost of maintaining confidentiality may be paying what the lawyer claims is owed, whether it is or not.

The third situation, involved in *Meyerhofer* below, is the most troublesome, since the client has no control of loss of confidentiality when disclosure flows from a third person's claim against the client's lawyer. On the other hand, when the third party's claim against the lawyer is based on wrongful conduct in which the client participated, the client may be said to bear some responsibility for the loss of secrecy.

Almost without objection the bar has agreed that the principle of confidentiality must yield to a self-defense exception for lawyers.[16] Even ATLA's competing professional code, which was in large part a response to the perceived attack on confidentiality embodied in the Kutak Commission draft of the Model Rules,[17] contains a fairly broad self-defense exception to confidentiality.[18]

16. For a general discussion and critique of the self-defense exception, see Henry D. Levine, Self–Interest or Self–Defense: Lawyer Disregard of the Attorney–Client Privilege for Profit and Protection, 5 Hofstra L.Rev. 783 (1977).

17. See the Preface to the American Lawyers Code of Conduct (ALCC), reprinted in Morgan & Rotunda, 1999 Selected Standards on Professional Responsibility at 251: "This code is quite frankly presented as an alternative ... to the new Rules of Professional Conduct that the ABA is apparently about to hawk as the latest thing in legal ethics." Published in 1982, the ALCC was a product of a special commission under the auspices of the research arm of the American Trial Lawyers Association (ATLA), composed primarily of plaintiffs' trial lawyers.

18. ALCC Rule 1.5 permits disclosure of client confidences in the lawyer's self-defense.

The Model Rules, like its predecessor,[19] makes no distinction between accusations against the lawyer made by a third party and those made by the client. Model Rule 1.6(b)(2) provides:

> A lawyer may reveal [confidential] information to the extent the lawyer reasonably believes necessary ... to establish a claim or defense on behalf of the lawyer in a controversy between the lawyer and the client, to establish a defense to a criminal charge or civil claim against the lawyer based upon conduct in which the client was involved, or to respond to allegations in any proceeding concerning the lawyer's representation of the client.

Comment [18] to M.R. 1.6 emphasizes a broad reading of this exception:

> The lawyer's right to respond arises when an assertion of such complicity has been made. Paragraph (b)(2) does not require the lawyer to await the commencement of an action or proceeding that charges such complicity, so that a defense may be established by responding directly to a third party who has made such an assertion.

Several bar ethics opinions take the position that the lawyer may be forthcoming with the prosecutor when she learns that she has been accused by someone, even though the prosecutor has not yet threatened prosecution.[20]

Meyerhofer v. Empire Fire and Marine Ins. Co.

United States Court of Appeals, Second Circuit, 1974.
497 F.2d 1190.

■ Before Moore, Friendly and Anderson, Circuit Judges.

■ Moore, Circuit Judge:

[The plaintiffs appealed from an order of the trial court disqualifying the law firm representing them.]

The full import of the problems and issues presented on this appeal cannot be appreciated and analyzed without an initial statement of the facts out of which they arise.

Empire Fire and Marine Insurance Company on May 31, 1972, made a public offering of 500,000 shares of its stock, pursuant to a registration statement filed with the Securities and Exchange Commission (SEC) on March 28, 1972. The stock was offered at $16 a share. Empire's attorney on the issue was the firm of Sitomer, Sitomer & Porges. Stuart Charles Goldberg was an attorney in the firm and had done some work on the issue.

---

19. DR 4–101(C)(4) permits the lawyer to disclose "[c]onfidences or secrets necessary to establish or collect his fee or to defend himself or his employees, or associates against an accusation of wrongful conduct."

20. See Ass'n Bar City of New York Op. 1986–7; Mich.Op. CI–900 (1983); Maine Op. 55 (1985).

Plaintiff Meyerhofer, on or about January 11, 1973, purchased 100 shares of Empire stock at $17 a share. He alleges that as of June 5, 1973, the market price of his stock was only $7 a share—hence, he has sustained an unrealized loss of $1,000.... Plaintiff Federman, on or about May 31, 1972, purchased 200 shares at $16 a share, 100 of which he sold for $1,363, sustaining a loss of some $237 on the stock sold and an unrealized loss of $900 on the stock retained.

On May 2, 1973, plaintiffs, represented by the firm of Bernson, Hoeniger, Freitag & Abbey (the Bernson firm), on behalf of themselves and all other purchasers of Empire common stock, brought this action alleging that the registration statement and the prospectus under which the Empire stock had been issued were materially false and misleading. Thereafter, an amended complaint, dated June 5, 1973, was served. The legal theories in both were identical, namely, violations of various sections of the Securities Exchange Act of 1933, the Securities Exchange Act of 1934, Rule 10b–5, and common law negligence, fraud and deceit. Damages for all members of the class or rescission were alternatively sought.

The lawsuit was apparently inspired by a Form 10–K which Empire filed with the SEC on or about April 12, 1973. This Form revealed that "The Registration Statement under the Securities Act of 1933 with respect to the public offering of the 500,000 shares of Common Stock did not disclose the proposed $200,000 payment to the law firm as well as certain other features of the compensation arrangements between the Company [Empire] and such law firm [defendant Sitomer, Sitomer and Porges]." Later that month Empire disseminated to its shareholders a proxy statement and annual report making similar disclosures.

The defendants named were Empire, officers and directors of Empire, the Sitomer firm and its three partners, A.L. Sitomer, S.J. Sitomer and R.E. Porges, Faulkner, Dawkins & Sullivan Securities Corp., the managing underwriter, Stuart Charles Goldberg, originally alleged to have been a partner of the Sitomer firm, and certain selling stockholders of Empire shares.

On May 2, 1973, the complaint was served on the Sitomer defendants and Faulkner. No service was made on Goldberg who was then no longer associated with the Sitomer firm. However, he was advised by telephone that he had been made a defendant. Goldberg inquired of the Bernson firm as to the nature of the charges against him and was informed generally as to the substance of the complaint and in particular the lack of disclosure of the finder's fee arrangement. Thus informed, Goldberg requested an opportunity to prove his non-involvement in any such arrangement and his lack of knowledge thereof. At this stage there was unfolded the series of events which ultimately resulted in the motion and order thereon now before us on appeal.

Goldberg, after his graduation from [Cornell] Law School in 1966, had rather specialized experience in the securities field and had published various books and treatises on related subjects. He became associated with the Sitomer firm in November 1971. While there Goldberg worked on phases of various registration statements including Empire, although another associate was responsible for the Empire registration statement and prospectus. However, Goldberg expressed concern over what he regarded as excessive fees, the nondisclosure or inadequate disclosure thereof, and the extent to which they might include a "finder's fee," both as to Empire and other issues.

The Empire registration became effective on May 31, 1972. The excessive fee question had not been put to rest in Goldberg's mind because in middle January 1973 it arose in connection with another registration (referred to as "Glacier"). Goldberg had worked on Glacier. Little purpose will be served by detailing the events during the critical period January 18 to 22, 1973, in which Goldberg and the Sitomer partners were debating the fee disclosure problem. In summary Goldberg insisted on a full and complete disclosure of fees in the Empire and Glacier offerings. The Sitomer partners apparently disagreed and Goldberg resigned from the firm on January 22, 1973.

On January 22, 1973, Goldberg appeared before the SEC and placed before it information subsequently embodied in his affidavit dated January 26, 1973, which becomes crucial to the issues now to be considered.

Some three months later, upon being informed that he was to be included as a defendant in the impending action, Goldberg asked the Bernson firm for an opportunity to demonstrate that he had been unaware of the finder's fee arrangement which, he said, Empire and the Sitomer firm had concealed from him all along. Goldberg met with members of the Bernson firm on at least two occasions. After consulting his own attorney, as well as William P. Sullivan, Special Counsel with the Securities and Exchange Commission, Division of Enforcement, Goldberg gave plaintiffs' counsel a copy of the January 26th affidavit which he had authored more than three months earlier. He hoped that it would verify his nonparticipation in the finder's fee omission and convince the Bernson firm that he should not be a defendant. The Bernson firm was satisfied with Goldberg's explanations and, upon their motion, granted by the court, he was dropped as a defendant. After receiving Goldberg's affidavit, the Bernson firm amended plaintiff's complaint. The amendments added more specific facts but did not change the theory or substance of the original complaint.

By motion dated June 7, 1973, the remaining defendants moved "pursuant to Canons 4 and 9 of the Code of Professional Responsibility, the Disciplinary Rules and Ethical Considerations applicable thereto, and the supervisory power of this Court" for the order of disqualification now on appeal.

By memorandum decision and order, the District Court ordered that the Bernson firm and Goldberg be barred from acting as counsel or participating with counsel for plaintiffs in this or any future action against Empire involving the transactions placed in issue in this lawsuit and from disclosing confidential information to others.

The complaint was dismissed without prejudice. The basis for the Court's decision is the premise that Goldberg had obtained confidential information from his client Empire which, in breach of relevant ethical canons, he revealed to plaintiffs' attorneys in their suit against Empire. The Court said its decision was compelled by "the broader obligations of Canons 4 and 9." [In a footnote the court quoted ECs 4–1 and 4–4 through 4–6, DR 4–101, and ECs 9–1 and 9–6.]

There is no proof—not even a suggestion—that Goldberg had revealed any information, confidential or otherwise, that might have caused the instigation of the suit. To the contrary, it was not until after the suit was commenced that Goldberg learned that he was in jeopardy. The District Court recognized that the complaint had been based on Empire's—not Goldberg's—disclosures, but concluded because of this that Goldberg was under no further obligation "to reveal the information or to discuss the matter with plaintiffs' counsel."

Despite the breadth of paragraphs EC 4–4 and DR 4–101(B), DR 4–101(C) recognizes that a lawyer may reveal confidences or secrets necessary to defend himself against "an accusation of wrongful conduct." This is exactly what Goldberg had to face when, in their original complaint, plaintiffs named him as a defendant who wilfully violated the securities laws.

The charge, of knowing participation in the filing of a false and misleading registration statement, was a serious one. The complaint alleged violation of criminal statutes and civil liability computable at over four million dollars. The cost in money of simply defending such an action might be very substantial. The damage to his professional reputation which might be occasioned by the mere pendency of such a charge was an even greater cause for concern.

Under these circumstances Goldberg had the right to make an appropriate disclosure with respect to his role in the public offering. Concomitantly, he had the right to support his version of the facts with suitable evidence.

The problem arises from the fact that the method Goldberg used to accomplish this was to deliver to Mr. Abbey, a member of the Bernson firm, the thirty page affidavit, accompanied by sixteen exhibits, which he had submitted to the SEC. This document not only went into extensive detail concerning Goldberg's efforts to cause the Sitomer firm to rectify the nondisclosure with respect to Empire but even more extensive detail concerning how these efforts had been precipitated by counsel for the underwriters having come upon evidence showing that a similar nondisclosure was contemplated with respect to Glacier and their insistence that full corrective measures should be taken. Although Goldberg's description reflected seriously on his employer, the Sitomer firm and, also, in at least some degree, on Glacier, he was clearly in a situation of some urgency. Moreover, before he turned over the affidavit, he consulted both his own attorney and a distinguished practitioner of securities law, and he and Abbey made a joint telephone call to Mr. Sullivan of the SEC. Moreover, it is not clear that, in the context of this case, Canon 4 applies to anything except information gained from Empire. Finally, because of Goldberg's apparent intimacy with the offering, the most effective way for him to substantiate his story was for him to disclose the SEC affidavit. It was the fact that he had written such an affidavit at an earlier date which demonstrated that his story was not simply fabricated in response to plaintiff's complaint.

The District Court held: "All that need be shown ... is that during the attorney-client relationship Goldberg had access to his client's information relevant to the issues here." See Emle Industries, Inc. v. Patentex, Inc., 478 F.2d 562 (2d Cir.1973). However, the irrebuttable presumption of *Emle Industries* has no application to the instant circumstances because Goldberg never sought to "prosecute litigation," either as a party, compare Richardson v. Hamilton International Corp., 62 F.R.D. 413 (E.D.Pa.1974), or as counsel for a plaintiff party. Compare T.C. Theatre Corporation v. Warner Brothers Pictures, 113 F.Supp. 265 (S.D.N.Y.1953). At most the record discloses that Goldberg might be called as a witness for the plaintiffs but that role does not invest him with the intimacy with the prosecution of the litigation which must exist for the *Emle* presumption to attach.

In addition to finding that Goldberg had violated Canon 4, the District Court found that the relationship between Goldberg and the Bernson firm violated Canon 9 of the Code of Professional Responsibility which provides that:

> EC 9–6 Every lawyer [must] strive to avoid not only professional impropriety but also the appearance of impropriety.

The District Court reasoned that even though there was no evidence of bad faith on the part of either Goldberg or the Bernson firm, a shallow reading of the facts might lead a casual observer to conclude that there was an aura of complicity about their relationship. However, this provision should not be read so broadly as to eviscerate the right of self-defense conferred by DR 4–101(C)(4).

Nevertheless, Emle Industries, Inc. v. Patentex, Inc., supra, requires that a strict prophylactic rule be applied in these cases to ensure that a lawyer avoids representation of a party in a suit against a former client where there may be the appearance of a possible violation of confidence. To the extent that the District Court's order prohibits Goldberg from *representing* the interests of these or any other plaintiffs in this or similar actions, we affirm that order. We also affirm so much of the District Court's order as enjoins Goldberg from disclosing material information except on discovery or at trial.

The burden of the District Court's order did not fall most harshly on Goldberg; rather its greatest impact has been felt by Bernson, Hoeniger, Freitag & Abbey, plaintiffs' counsel, which was disqualified from participation in the case. The District Court based its holding, not on the fact that the Bernson firm showed bad faith when it received Goldberg's affidavit, but rather on the fact that it was involved in a tainted association with Goldberg because his disclosures to them inadvertently violated Canons 4 and 9 of the Code of Professional Responsibility. Because there are no violations of either of these Canons in this case, we can find no basis to hold that the relationship between Goldberg and the Bernson firm was tainted. The District Court was apparently unpersuaded by appellees' salvo of innuendo to the effect that Goldberg "struck a deal" with the Bernson firm or tried to do more than prove his innocence to them. Since its relationship with Goldberg was not tainted by violations of the Code of Professional Responsibility, there appears to be no warrant for its disqualification from participation in either this or similar actions. *A fortiori* there was no sound basis for disqualifying plaintiffs or dismissing the complaint.

Order dismissing action without prejudice and enjoining Bernson, Hoeniger, Freitag & Abbey from acting as counsel for plaintiffs herein reversed.... To the extent that the orders appealed from prohibit Goldberg from acting as a party or as an attorney for a party in any action arising out of the facts herein alleged, or from disclosing material information except on discovery or at trial, they are affirmed.

Third–Party Charges Against a Lawyer

Is *Meyerhofer* a "confidentiality" or a "privilege" case? Why?

Was Goldberg justified in making his disclosure to the plaintiffs who were suing his former client? Why should the client's confidences be at the mercy of the actions of non-clients?[21]

Is it possible that Empire did not know of the obligation to disclose the fee arrangement in the prospectus? Could the fraud, if such it was, have been the firm's and not the client's? If so, does that suggest that Goldberg's initial disclosure should have been to the client rather than to the SEC?

Model Rule 1.13 speaks of a lawyer's duties to an organizational client. It prescribes a course of conduct to be followed when a lawyer knows that an agent of the organizational client is violating a legal obligation to the client or violating the law in a manner that might be imputed to the organization[22] Under M.R. 1.13, should Goldberg have discussed the matter directly with Empire officers before going to the SEC? Would he have a duty to do so before disclosing in self-defense? Comment [18] to Model Rule 1.6(b)(2), the self-defense exception to confidentiality, states: "Where practicable and not prejudicial to the lawyer's ability to establish the defense,

---

21. The Model Code and Model Rules reject a distinction between an accusation made by a client and one made by a third person, see DR 4–101(C)(4) and M.R. 1.6(b)(2). ALCC Rule 1.5, on the other hand, distinguishes between the two situations: When the charge is made by a third party, disclosure of client confidences is permitted only *after charges are formally instituted;* when the charge is made by the client, disclosure may be made prior to formal proceedings. Does an exception for charges made by third parties encourage third parties to sue lawyers in an attempt to gain access to confidential information?

22. See the discussion of M.R. 1.13 in Chapter 8 infra at p. 737.

the lawyer should advise the client of the third party's assertions and request that the client respond appropriately."[23]

If the Bernson firm had had access to and had used Goldberg's affidavit to file suit against Empire, what result? In Beiny v. Wynyard[24] a prominent Wall Street firm procured attorney-client privileged documents through deception. It was held that the evidence so procured should be suppressed and the firm disqualified. A number of cases disqualify a law firm that has gained improper access to the opposing party's evidence.[25] Lawyers may also be disciplined for abuse of the self-defense exception.[26]

Although the court's decision deals only with Goldberg's disclosure to the plaintiffs, the earlier disclosure to the SEC raises serious questions. Goldberg, relying on the SEC position in the then-pending *National Student Marketing* case, supra p. 104, may have believed he had an affirmative duty under federal law to prevent a securities law violation. If Goldberg did have such a duty, and if the client refused to make the required disclosure, DR 4–101(C)(3), then in effect in New York, would permit a New York lawyer to reveal the client's intention to commit a criminal fraud. But what if the fraud is that of Goldberg's firm, which has not communicated the legal problem to its client?

Does the self-defense exception of M.R. 1.6(b)(2) or DR 4–101(C)(4) permit a lawyer to disclose prior to an "accusation" when the lawyer believes one may be forthcoming? Is this what Goldberg did when he went to the SEC? Assuming Goldberg had gone to Empire and it had refused to disclose the fee arrangements in the prospectus, would Goldberg then have been justified in going to the SEC prior to an "accusation" of wrongdoing? Even if so, was what he did "self-defense" given the proactive nature of his conduct? The more natural classification is disclosure to stop ongoing fraud rather than disclosure in self-defense, but the Model Rules treatment of client fraud disclosures makes resort to the self-defense exception necessary. See Model Rule 1.6(b)(1) (making no provision for disclosure of ongoing client fraud). This issue will be more fully explored when we take up client fraud below.

The disclosures permitted by M.R. 1.6(b)(2) are limited by the requirement that the lawyer reasonably believe they are necessary. Comment [18] adds: "disclosure should be no greater than the lawyer reasonably believes is necessary to vindicate innocence, the disclosure should be made in a

---

23. See also Canon 41 and DR 7–102(B), provisions dealing with client fraud, which require the lawyer to ask the client to rectify before the lawyer discloses the fraud.

24. 129 A.D.2d 126, 517 N.Y.S.2d 474 (1987).

25. See, e.g., MMR/Wallace Power & Ind., Inc. v. Thames Associates, 764 F.Supp. 712 (D.Conn.1991) (disqualification of lawyer for obtaining privileged information from former employee of opposing party who

was a member of that party's litigation team).

26. See Dixon v. California State Bar, 653 P.2d 321 (Cal.1982) (discipline imposed for using confidences in a suit brought by client to enjoin the lawyer from harassing client); Florida Bar v. Ball, 406 So.2d 459 (Fla.1981) (lawyer suspended for disclosing to adoption agency that clients did not pay the lawyer's fee and therefore might be a financial risk).

manner which limits access to the information to the tribunal or other persons having a need to know it, and appropriate protective orders or other arrangements should be made by the lawyer to the fullest extent practicable."[27] How do Goldberg's actions match up against these standards?

Should judicial approval be required before the lawyer reveals confidences?[28] In the *First Federal* case,[29] the court adopted procedural safeguards to protect confidentiality interests. The court ordered the lawyer to submit all proposed disclosures to the court for review in camera along with an affidavit explaining the necessity for each proposed disclosure. The client was then given the opportunity to respond to the lawyer's showing. In deciding what disclosures to allow, the court used the "reasonable necessity" standard of M.R. 1.6.

Self–Defense Exception to Attorney–Client Privilege

In an action to collect a fee, a lawyer may disclose otherwise privileged communications to establish the claim.[30] The privilege also yields to the lawyer's need to defend herself in a malpractice suit brought against her by the client.[31] If the client attacks the lawyer's work in a proceeding to which the lawyer is not a party, the privilege also yields.[32] A common example is a habeas corpus proceeding brought by a convicted person in which the claim is ineffective assistance of counsel.[33]

Statutory definitions of the attorney-client privilege include a self-defense exception. Proposed Federal Rule of Evidence 503(d)(3), for example, would have allowed disclosure of a "communication relevant to an issue of breach of duty by the lawyer to his client or by the client to his lawyer."[34] This formulation, however, arguably provides no exception where the lawyer is accused of wrongdoing in complicity with the client, such as charged against Goldberg in the *Meyerhofer* case.

Although the court in *Meyerhofer* deals only with confidentiality and not the attorney-client privilege, the case has been read as supporting an

---

27. See also the Comment's statement that the lawyer should, where practicable, inform the client and request that the client itself respond to the charges.

28. See Henry D. Levine, Self–Interest or Self–Defense: Lawyer Disregard of the Attorney–Client Privilege for Profit and Protection, 5 Hofstra L.Rev. 783, 825–26 (1977) (prior judicial approval should be required).

29. First Federal Savings & Loan Ass'n of Pittsburgh v. Oppenheim, Appel, Dixon & Co., 110 F.R.D. 557 (S.D.N.Y.1986).

30. See, e.g., Cannon v. U.S. Acoustics Corp., 532 F.2d 1118 (7th Cir.1976).

31. See, e.g., Nave v. Baird, 12 Ind. 318, 319 (1859).

32. See, e.g., Flood v. Commissioner, 468 F.2d 904, 905 (9th Cir.1972) (lawyer could testify to establish that settlement of former client's case was within lawyer's authority).

33. See the cases cited supra in the note on p. 193.

34. See West's Ann.Cal.Evid.Code § 958 (1966) ("no privilege . . . as to a communication relevant to an issue of breach, by the lawyer or by the client, of a duty arising out of the lawyer-client relationship").

exception to the *privilege* where lawyers are accused of wrongdoing in complicity with a client.[35]

C. CLIENT FRAUD

INTRODUCTION

Perhaps no other subject in professional ethics has generated more heated debate than that of a lawyer's proper course of action upon discovery of client fraud. A historical review of the rules and ethics opinions on the subject reveals a longstanding morass of conflicting precepts: Rules imposing a duty to disclose are followed by ethics opinions interpreting those rules as requiring non-disclosure.[1] A later rule appearing to require non-disclosure, M.R. 1.6, has a commentary that allows disclosure as long as it is done through signals instead of words. In general, rules adopted by state courts provide for disclosure of client fraud while bar interpretations call for non-disclosure. Judicial decisions involving a lawyer's liability for failing to prevent a client's fraud in which the lawyer's services were involved have very little relationship to the ethics rules dealing with the same conduct. In short, the law on this subject is confusing and inconsistent.

1. ETHICS CODES AND CLIENT FRAUD

The professional duty of confidentiality builds on and supports the client's attorney-client privilege. The functions and purposes of the privilege determine its limits and are relevant to any consideration of the professional duty of confidentiality. The privilege is intended to further *lawful* advice and conduct.[2] When the client, concealing his illegal intent and objective, consults a lawyer to commit a crime or fraud, the privilege evaporates. The crime-fraud exception to the attorney-client privilege, recognized in every jurisdiction, is supported by two fundamental propositions of the profession's historic tradition of public responsibility. First, in all jurisdictions a lawyer is prohibited from counseling or assisting a client in unlawful conduct.[3] Second, in the vast majority of jurisdictions a lawyer

---

35. See In re National Mortgage Equity Corp., 120 F.R.D. 687 (C.D.Cal.) (a law firm, which had unknowingly assisted a client in a fraudulent private-placement securities issue, could disclose otherwise privileged information to show that it was not a party to the client's fraudulent conduct), appeal dismissed, 857 F.2d 1238 (9th Cir. 1988). The case recognizes a self-defense exception to the attorney-client privilege, essentially parallel to *Meyerhofer*.

1. Compare Canon 41 with ABA Formal Op. 287 (1953), and DR 7–102(B)(7) with ABA Formal Op. 341 (1975).

2. The rationale for the privilege expressed in the *Upjohn* case, supra p. 209, emphasizes the role of the privilege is furthering the public values of "lawful advice" and "sound administration of justice." Upjohn v. United States, 449 U.S. 383, 389 (1981).

3. See M.R. 1.2(d) and its predecessor, DR 7–102(A)(7). One or the other of these provisions is included in the professional code of every state except California, which has its own comparable provision. Calif. R. Prof. Conduct 3–210 (lawyer may not advise the violation of law).

is permitted to disclose confidential information to prevent the client from committing or continuing a crime or fraud.[4]

The Canons and the Model Code

The ABA Canons of Professional Ethics provided ethical guidelines for lawyers until replaced by the ABA Model Code of Professional Responsibility in 1970. The Canons included several prominent exceptions to the general requirement of lawyer secrecy. Canon 37, after stating the default rule of confidentiality, permitted disclosure to prevent "[t]he announced intention of a client to commit a crime." Canon 29 required disclosure by a trial lawyer of perjury committed in a case handled by the lawyer. Canon 41 required a lawyer, when the client refused to act, "to rectify ... some [client] fraud or deception ... unjustly imposed on the court or a party" by "promptly informing the injured person or his counsel, so that they may take appropriate steps."

Ethics opinions interpreting Canons 37 and 41 confounded the apparent clarity of the three canons. For example, ABA Formal Opinion 268 (1945) stated that a lawyer, who withdrew from representation upon learning that his client intended to commit perjury, had no discretion to reveal the intended perjury to successor counsel employed to present the false evidence. Whither Canon 37? Similarly, ABA Formal Opinion 287 (1953) barred a lawyer who discovered his client had committed perjury in a civil case from disclosing the perjury because that would violate the duty to keep confidences. Whither Canons 29 and 41?

Despite the ethics opinions just mentioned, the Canons' exceptions to confidentiality were continued in the 1969 Model Code. As initially promulgated in 1969 and as adopted in nearly all states, the Model Code appeared to reaffirm the explicit provisions of the Canons and overturn the contrary interpretations of the ethics opinions. DR 4–101(C)(3) permitted a lawyer to reveal "[t]he intention of his client to commit a crime and the information necessary to prevent the crime." Like Canon 37, DR 4–101(C)(3) applied to all future crimes and was discretionary.

Again like the Canons, the Model Code dealt with the discovery of past fraud in a separate provision. DR 7–102(B)(1) as originally adopted provided:

> A lawyer who receives information clearly establishing that: (1) His client has, in the course of the representation, perpetrated a fraud upon a person or tribunal shall promptly call upon his client to rectify

---

4. In 1998, according to Attorneys' Assurance Liability Society, Ethics Rules on Client Confidences, reprinted in Morgan & Rotunda, 1999 Selected Standards of Professional Responsibility 133, 30 jurisdictions either permit or require a lawyer to disclose a client's intention to commit any future crime; and at least 41 jurisdictions permit or require a lawyer to disclose the client's intention to commit a criminal fraud likely to result in financial injury to another person.

the same, and if his client refuses or is unable to do so, he shall reveal the fraud to the affected person or tribunal.[5]

In the 1970s the organized bar became concerned that these provisions might mean what they said. SEC charges against two law firms for failing to prevent a client fraud was the principal precipitating event.[6] In reaction, the ABA partially abandoned its formal position that a lawyer was required to disclose information to rectify a fraud on a person or tribunal when the lawyer's services had been used to perpetrate the fraud. The 1974 amendment added the following italicized "except" clause to DR 7–102(B)(1) so that it read as follows:

> [to rectify a fraud upon a person or tribunal when the client has refused to do so, a lawyer] shall reveal the fraud to the affected person or tribunal, *except when the information is protected as a privileged communication.*

As interpreted in 1975 by ABA Formal Opinion 341, a lawyer has a duty to disclose client fraud only when fortuitously informed by a person, who is unaware that the lawyer is representing the client implicated, that the client committed fraud in the course of the representation.[7] To effectively repeal the duty to rectify fraud, while nominally preserving it, is surely disingenuous.

The 1974 amendment, however, was adopted by only 14 states[8] and even where adopted a lawyer remained free under DR 4–101(C)(3) to disclose information to prevent a client's criminal fraud. The ethics codes in most states continued to require a lawyer to rectify a client fraud. With

5. DR 7–102(B)(1) did not expressly indicate that the duty to disclose fraud was an exception to the confidentiality rule, but logic compels the conclusion that an exception was intended. How else could a lawyer "reveal fraud to the affected person," as required by DR 7–102(B)(1), while at the same time obeying the injunction of DR 4–101(B) that "a lawyer shall not reveal a confidence or secret of his client"? Also, a footnote to DR 7–102(B)(1) refers to DR 4–101(C)(2), which allows disclosure "when permitted under Disciplinary Rules...."

6. In *National Student Marketing*, supra p. 104, the SEC charged that White & Case and Lord, Bissell & Brook had aided and abetted their clients' securities fraud by failing to prevent the closing of a merger on the basis of misleading proxy solicitations to the shareholders of the two companies.

7. The ABA may have intended the amendment to cancel the duty to reveal fraud when doing so would require revealing information prejudicial to the client (i.e., "se-

crets"). But a natural reading of the term "privileged communications" suggests a narrower meaning: Client fraud must be disclosed only if a lawyer's knowledge of the fraud came from information not protected as a "confidence" by the attorney-client privilege. The narrower reading also gains support from the argument that otherwise the amendment effectively repeals DR 7–101(B)(1). If "secrets" as well as "confidences" qualify as privileged communications, the amendment would cancel a lawyer's duty under DR 7–102(B)(1) to rectify client fraud in virtually all circumstances in which the duty could arise: In what situation could a lawyer reveal a client's fraud, the client having refused to do so, without revealing a client "secret" as that term is defined in the Code?

8. Only a few of the 14 states adopting the "except" clause amendment took a formal position on the question dealt with in Opinion 341. New York, however, did adopt the amendment in a form that protected both confidences and secrets.

or without the 1974 amendment, however, the ABA position on client fraud became incoherent.

Model Rules of Professional Conduct

The ABA special commission that drafted the Model Rules, known as the Kutak Commission, was well aware of the difficulties with the Code's approach to client fraud.[9] The Commission's proposed final draft attempted to reconcile the profession's hostility to policing and "betraying" clients with the substantive law dealing both with a lawyer's liability for aiding client fraud and the crime-fraud exception to the attorney-client privilege. The proposal concerning client fraud read:

> A lawyer may reveal [confidential] information to the extent the lawyer reasonably believes necessary:
>
> > (1) to prevent the client from committing a criminal or fraudulent act that the lawyer reasonably believes is likely to result in ... substantial injury to the financial interests or property of another; [or] (2) to rectify the consequences of a client's criminal or fraudulent act in the furtherance of which the lawyer's services had been used.... [10]

Proposed Rule 1.6(b) covered prevention of a fraud, whether or not the lawyer's services had been involved, and rectification of a fraud where the lawyer's services had been used, both courses of action being discretionary and neither requiring a warning to the client.

Although the Kutak Commission viewed its proposal as a fair restatement of existing law, critics from within the profession bitterly attacked the proposed rule.[11] Those attackers repeatedly charged that permitting disclosure of client fraud in some situations constituted a "radical" change from existing law, a change that would undermine confidentiality by making clients less candid and by reducing lawyers' opportunities to channel client

---

9. For an account of the six-year process by which the ABA developed the Model Rules, see Ted Schneyer, Professionalism as Bar Politics: The Making of the Model Rules of Professional Conduct, 1989 Law & Soc.Inquiry 677 (evaluating the rule-making process as a species of de facto lawmaking by a private group and identifying common themes in the way lawyers think about legal ethics as "professionalism-in-fact"). Schneyer argues that the elite corporate defense bar (the American College of Trial Lawyers) that led the assault on the crime-fraud exception shifted its position on client fraud because it feared, in light of the *National Student Marketing* case, that the Kutak proposals would have "real legal bite." Id. at 718–23. It is ironic that the American College's own Code of Trial Conduct (1972) repeated the traditional permission to disclose to prevent a client crime and stated that a lawyer "should [disclose] if injury to person or property is likely to ensue." Id. at 720.

10. Model Rules of Professional Conduct Rule 1.6(b) (Proposed Final Draft 1981).

11. See, e.g., Monroe H. Freedman, Lawyer–Client Confidence: The Model Rules' Radical Assault on the Traditional Role of the Lawyer, 68 A.B.A.J. 428 (1982). The attack on the confidentiality provisions of the proposed Model Rules was led by two organizations of trial lawyers: the American College of Trial Lawyers [ACTL] (primarily litigators for large corporations) and the American Trial Lawyers Association [ATLA] (primarily plaintiffs' trial lawyers).

behavior along legal lines. Critics also argued that permitting disclosure would serve as a basis for expanded civil liability for lawyers who failed to disclose. After heated debate, the ABA House of Delegates in 1983 amended proposed Rule 1.6 to prohibit any disclosure of client fraud.[12] Model Rule 1.6(b) as adopted is a comprehensive and unqualified prohibition of disclosure of any client information, subject only to the homicide/bodily injury exception, the "self-defense" exception and the uncontroversial exception regarding disclosures "impliedly authorized" to carry out the representation.[13]

What does a lawyer do to protect herself in a situation where she has unwittingly been made the instrument of client fraud but cannot yet invoke the self-defense exception because no accusation has been made? The proponents of non-disclosure argued that the lawyer should resign, an action that would signal the lawyer's innocence and provide warning to other participants in a transaction that has not yet been consummated. Resignation will not provide a warning signal, however, if the fraudulent transaction has already been closed or if unsophisticated participants do not comprehend the significance of the lawyer's withdrawal. The morally conscientious lawyer, as well as the lawyer interested only in self-protection, would remain at risk in those situations.

The ABA House of Delegates in February 1983 adopted the black-letter text of amended Model Rule 1.6(b), with consideration of the Comment deferred to the August 1983 meeting. During the interim, negotiations between the opposing factions resulted in agreement on the addition of the following sentence to Comment [16]:

> Neither this Rule nor Rule 1.8(b) nor Rule 1.16(d) prevents the lawyer from giving notice of the fact of withdrawal, and the lawyer may also withdraw or disaffirm any opinion, document, affirmation, or the like.

The proponents of the amended rule took the position that waving a red flag at the time of withdrawal did not involve a disclosure of confidential client information because the permitted actions, such as withdrawing a legal opinion, do not reveal a lawyer's knowledge of the details of the client's fraud. This view reconciles the "noisy withdrawal" permitted by the Comment with the black-letter text of the rule. A number of academic commentators have disagreed with this view, however, arguing that the intended warning is, in effect, the revelation of a confidence. Is the "noisy withdrawal" permitted by Comment [16] consistent with the authoritative black-letter text?[14]

12. See "Lawyers Vote Against Disclosure of Fraudulent Activity by Clients," N.Y. Times, Feb. 8, 1983, p. 1.

13. Note that while the Canons and Model Code dealt with client fraud on the tribunal in the same manner in which they dealt with client fraud on private parties, the Model Rules take a sharply different approach to the two problems. Although the Model Rules as adopted make no provision for disclosure of client fraud on third parties, they *mandate* disclosure of client fraud on the court. See M.R. 3.3(a)(4). The question of fraud on the tribunal is considered in Chapter 5 infra.

14. The Preamble to the Model Rules states that "the text of each rule is authoritative"

At one level the revised Comment can be understood as allowing what M.R. 1.6 itself appears to forbid: disclosure of unrectified client fraud in which the lawyer's services were used. Performance of a ritual that is intended as a signal is likely to be understood as a signal, thus revealing the information that the signal denotes. Although an effective signal may be equivalent to outright disclosure from the client's perspective, it may be materially different from the lawyer's perspective. Communicating in such an unnatural manner—avoiding direct communication—allows the bar to reaffirm the power of the norm of confidentiality even as it provides escapes from it. Moreover, banishing the "exception" to the Comment casts doubt on its existence and suggests that it should be relied on as the basis of action in only the most urgent cases. Comments, after all, are "intended as guides to interpretation, but the text of each Rule is authoritative."[15]

The 1983 debate on client fraud was replayed at the 1991 meeting of the ABA House of Delegates.[16] The ABA's Committee on Ethics and Professional Responsibility recommended that language very similar to that deleted in 1983 be added to M.R. 1.6(b). The committee had found the 1983 version of the rule "unworkable" in the absence of a provision allowing disclosure of "the consequences of a client's criminal or fraudulent act in the commission of which the lawyer's services had been used." The committee's report stated:

> [W]e have had called to our attention situations with respect to which a literal application of the existing provisions ... dictates results which we believe to be unjust and inconsistent and which threaten to unfairly subject lawyers to potential civil liability and criminal prosecution.[17]

The House of Delegates rejected the committee's proposal, 251–158.[18]

The internal professional debate over disclosure to prevent or rectify client fraud was revisited in a 1992 ABA ethics opinion.[19] The majority concluded that a lawyer, whose services had been used to obtain a bank loan on client representations that turned out to be fraudulent, must withdraw from further representation involving client transactions with the same bank; in making this mandatory withdrawal, the lawyer might withdraw "noisily" by notifying the bank that she no longer stands behind the opinion letter given at the time the loan was made. The majority relied less on Comment [16] to Rule 1.6 than on the implications of Rules 1.2(d) (lawyer cannot assist a client in criminal or fraudulent conduct) and 1.16(a)

---

and that "[t]he Comments are intended as guides to interpretation."

15.   Scope note to Model Rules.

16.   7 Law.Man.Prof.Conduct 256, 258 (Aug. 28, 1991).

17.   Id. at 173 (June 19, 1991).

18.   Id. at 258 (Aug. 28, 1991). John Elam, representing the American College of Trial Lawyers, argued that discretionary rectification "will become a mandate" if lawyers have "the discretion to blow the whistle"

on clients. Other opponents argued that the rectification rule would subject lawyers to liability if they failed to disclose something that they had discretion to disclose. A trial lawyer posed the issue as: "Is the lawyer the policeman of the client's conduct or the repository of the client's confidences?" Id. at 258–59.

19.   ABA Comm. on Ethics and Prof.Resp. Formal Op. 92–366, 8 Law.Man.Prof.Conduct 394 (Dec. 16, 1992).

(requiring withdrawal when a continued "representation will result in violation of the rules or other law." Three dissenters argued that, because the lawyer's work on the loan was over, the lawyer was not required to withdraw from future loan transactions, even with the same lender, and, if the lawyer chose to withdraw, could not breach confidentiality by waving a red flag while doing so. The dissenters pointed out that the ABA House of Delegates had twice rejected proposals to amend Rule 1.6(b) to permit disclosure to prevent or rectify client fraud. A new exception to the Rule, they reasoned, must come from action by the House of Delegates.

Since 1983, nearly all states have adopted a version of the Model Rules or have revised their lawyer code. Client fraud has been given extensive consideration. Only a handful of the 42 jurisdictions that have adopted some version of the Model Rules have followed M.R. 1.6 in its entirety.

The Restatement on Prevention and Rectification of Client Fraud

Section 117B of the Restatement follows the majority approach of the states in permitting disclosure to prevent client fraud, but adopts the minority position in also permitting disclosure to rectify past client fraud:

(1) A lawyer may use or disclose confidential client information when and to the extent that the lawyer reasonably believes such use or disclosure is necessary to prevent a crime or fraud, and:

(a) the crime or fraud threatens substantial financial loss to a person;

(b) the loss has not yet occurred;

(c) the lawyer's client intends to commit the crime or fraud either directly or through a third person;

(d) the client has employed or is employing the lawyer's services in committing the crime or fraud.

(2) In the situation of a loss otherwise described in Subsection (1) but that has already occurred, a lawyer may use or disclose confidential client information when and to the extent that the lawyer reasonably believes such use or disclosure is necessary to rectify or mitigate the loss.[20]

Given that fraud is generally considered an ongoing crime or wrong, is the Restatement's distinction meaningful? To put this another way, when is disclosure of a past fraud not necessary to rectify it? Obviously, when the fraud and the fraud's perpetrators have already been discovered. When else? Should the lawyer's discretion to disclose past fraud or crimes be limited to those frauds and crimes in which the lawyer's services have been used? Why? If it isn't so limited, does inviting lawyers to reveal past crimes to "mitigate the loss" threaten the paradigm of "privileged" or "confiden-

---

20. Subparagraph (3) of Restatement § 117B requires the lawyer, "if feasible," to remonstrate with the client before warn-ing the victim or taking other action to prevent the harm.

tial" communications—the client's confession of a past crime to her lawyer?

2.   LIABILITY OF A LAWYER WHO FACILITATES A FRAUDULENT TRANSACTION

Klein v. Boyd

United States Court of Appeals for the Third Circuit, 1998.
Fed.Sec.L.Rep. ¶ 90,136, Vacated on Grant of Rehearing en Banc (Mar. 9, 1998).

■ Before: MANSMANN and NYGAARD, Circuit Judges, and BLOCH, U.S. District Court Judge for the Western District of Pennsylvania, sitting by designation.

■ Opinion of MANSMANN, Circuit Judge.

After a limited partnership failed, four investors in the partnership brought suit against ... the law firm that represented the partnership. The investors asserted causes of action under section 10(b) of the Securities Exchange Act of 1934, 15 U.S.C. § 78j(b), and companion Rule 10b–5, 17 C.F.R. § 240.10b–5, section 1962 of the Racketeer Influenced and Corrupt Organizations Act (RICO), 18 U.S.C. § 1962, and common law fraud. ...

. . .

The investors appealed from the district court's final order granting the law firm's motion for summary judgment.... [W]e disagree with the district court's disposition of the federal securities claim and conclude that the investors have proffered sufficient evidence to establish a genuine issue of material fact as to (1) whether the law firm made a statement containing a material omission upon which the investors relied, and (2) whether the law firm acted with scienter. In so concluding, we hold that a lawyer who can fairly be characterized as an author or a co-author of a client's fraudulent document may be held primarily liable to a third-party investor under the federal securities laws for the material misstatements or omissions contained in the document, even when the lawyer did not sign or endorse the document and the investor is therefore unaware of the lawyer's role in the fraud. We will reverse the judgment of the district court insofar as it granted the law firm's motion for summary judgment on the federal securities claim as to three of the four investors. Similarly, we will reverse the judgment of the district court on the investors' common law fraud claim, which claim was timely as to all four investors.

As to the investors' RICO claims, we conclude that the law firm did not participate in the operation or management of the purported enterprise and cannot, therefore, be liable under 18 U.S.C. § 1962(c). Consequently, the law firm cannot be liable, under 18 U.S.C. § 1962(d), for conspiracy to violate section 1962(c). We hold that there is no private cause of action for aiding and abetting a RICO violation. We will, therefore, affirm the judgment of the district court insofar as it granted the law firm's motion for summary judgment on the investors' RICO claims. . . .

I.

[In 1992, William Coleman, who had a long history of securities fraud, regulatory sanction and customer claims of fraudulent conduct, joined with Tarantino to purchase a securities broker business. They hired Drinker Biddle & Reath ("Drinker"), a Philadelphia law firm, to provide legal services for the new business entity. Robert Strouse, a partner at Drinker, assumed responsibility for the matter; he was assisted by Paula Calhoun, a junior associate. A new entity, Mercer LP, a limited partnership, was to purchase the brokerage business with an existing corporation, Mercer, Inc., to serve as corporate general partner. Coleman was the primary owner of Mercer LP. Strouse learned at this initial meeting that the Kastners, a married couple for whom Coleman had performed brokerage services, had become investors in Mercer LP, along with their daughter, Klein, each of the three contributing $50,000. In fact, Coleman and Tarantino had begun business as Mercer LP prior to the creation of the necessary partnership and subscription agreements. Strouse advised that the paper work be completed as soon as possible and, in addition, that the investors be provided a disclosure document and given an opportunity to reaffirm or rescind their investments.

[Strouse learned of Coleman's history of securities violations and customer complaints in November or December, 1992. In February 1993, Drinker completed the partnership agreement, a subscription agreement, and a disclosure letter that reflected the compliance history of Coleman and another officer of Mercer, Inc., including documents describing the various state supervisory orders and judgments entered against Coleman and the fact that NASD had substantially restricted Coleman's conduct as a broker. This disclosure document is referred to by the parties and the court as "the February Disclosure Package." Strouse and Calhoun gave the disclosure package to Coleman and Tarantino on February 5, 1993, and instructed them to deliver it to the investors and obtain necessary signatures.

[In May 1993 Strouse learned that the February Disclosure Package had not been delivered to the investors. Strouse advised that the package should be delivered and all necessary signatures obtained. Coleman and Tarantino balked at Strouse's advice and the package was never delivered. Further state orders and restrictions on Coleman were entered in 1993. Strouse learned of these orders no later than August 1993. Yet Drinker continued to perform legal services for Mercer LP, including a renewal in August 1993 of the 1992 investments of Klein and the Kastners. At the same time, Coleman persuaded Klein, who may have been in Massachusetts at the time, to invest an additional $200,000 in Mercer LP. At that time, when it became clear that Mercer LP would not be permitted to register to do business as a broker-dealer in certain states while Coleman was a part owner, Coleman sold his interest in Mercer LP to his mother.

[In November 1993, as part of the renewal of the investments of Klein and the Kastners, Drinker prepared a disclosure package for them. This so-called "November Disclosure Package" did not contain any information about Coleman's checkered compliance history and current restrictions. After the investors had signed and returned the documents, Calhoun sent them a complete set of the executed partnership documents with a one-line cover memo stating, "Enclosed for your records is an original set of partnership documents." This is the only direct communication from Drinker to the investors.

[In late 1993 and thereafter, Mercer LP fell into financial difficulties. In May 1994, a new investor, Warren, contributed a $100,000 investment on terms similar to those of the other investors and without disclosure of Coleman's history or the partnership's recent financial problems. In June 1994, Klein, concerned about her investments with Mercer LP, consulted an attorney in an attempt to recover her funds. As a result of the attorney's inquiries, Klein learned of Coleman's compliance history no later than fall 1994. After a Mercer LP official, Schappell, was killed by a bus, it was discovered that he had fraudulently mishandled some of his customers' accounts. Strouse advised the Mercer, Inc. board not to discuss this matter with anyone, and another Mercer LP officer sent the investors letters stating that Mercer LP faced problems because of Schappell's "untimely" death; the letters did not indicate the fraudulent conduct in which he had engaged. In February 1995, Mercer LP failed. The three investors lost their entire $400,000 investment ($200,000 from Klein, $100,000 from the Kastners, and $100,000 from Warren).]

On August 23, 1995, the investors sued Mercer, Inc., Mercer LP, Boyd and Coleman. During discovery, the investors served subpoenas on Drinker and Tarantino. Among the documents produced in response to these subpoenas was the February Disclosure Package. This was the first time the investors had ever been aware of the package. On December 4, 1995, the investors filed their first amended complaint which asserted claims against Drinker....

. . .

The district court granted Drinker's motion for summary judgment on all counts. Subsequently, the investors settled with the remaining defendants. The investors appealed from the final order of the district court granting Drinker's motion for summary judgment on the securities act claim, the RICO claim, and the common law fraud claim. ....

II.

Section 10(b) of the Securities Exchange Act of 1934, 15 U.S.C. § 78j(b), forbids "manipulative or deceptive acts in connection with the purchase or sale of securities." Central Bank of Denver, N.A. v. First Interstate Bank of Denver, N.A., 511 U.S. 164, 173 (1994); Santa Fe Indus., Inc. v. Green, 430 U.S. 462, 473–74 (1977). Rule 10b–5, promulgated by the Securities and Exchange Commission under section 10(b), makes it unlawful for "any person, directly or indirectly ... [t]o make any untrue statement of a material fact or to omit to state a material fact necessary in order to make the statements made, in the light of the circumstances under which they were made, not misleading." 17 C.F.R. § 240.10b–5(b). Although section 10(b) and Rule 10b–5 do not explicitly provide a private right of action, the courts have inferred one. Scattergood v. Perelman, 945 F.2d 618, 622 (3d Cir.1991); see also Central Bank of Denver, 511 U.S. at 166, 171.

To state a claim under section 10(b) and Rule 10b–5, a private plaintiff must allege that the defendant (1) with scienter (2) made misleading statements or omissions (3) of material fact (4) in connection with the purchase or sale of securities (5) upon which the plaintiff relied in entering the transaction and (6) that the plaintiff suffered economic loss as a proximate result. ...

[The court held that the federal securities claims of one investor, Klein, were barred by statute of limitations because not commenced "within one year after the discovery of facts constituting the violation ...".]

The district court also concluded that Drinker could not be liable to any of the investors under section 10(b) and Rule 10b–5 for the alleged omissions because Drinker never signed the documents it prepared regarding the investments and its name did not appear on any of the relevant Mercer LP documents. Since the investors were not aware of Drinker's involvement in the preparation of the disclosure documents, the district court reasoned, Drinker did not make any statements upon which the investors relied.

The district court explained that a duty to disclose under section 10(b) and Rule 10b–5 arises from the existence of a fiduciary relationship. ....Reasoning that the investors were not in a fiduciary relationship with Drinker, the district court concluded that Drinker did not have a duty to disclose information to the investors. Absent a duty to disclose, the court reasoned, there can be no liability for failure to disclose a material fact.

In *Central Bank of Denver*, the Supreme Court held that ... a private plaintiff may not maintain an aiding and abetting action under section 10(b). 511 U.S. at 177, 191.... Although refusing to recognize a private cause of action for aiding and abetting liability, the Court acknowledged that secondary actors in the securities markets may still be liable under the securities acts.... [21]

. . .

After *Central Bank of Denver*, it is reasonably clear that secondary actors such as lawyers can be held primarily liable for the misrepresentations and omissions contained in disclosure documents and other statements released to investors under the secondary actors' own names, assum-

---

21. [Editors' note:] For further discussion of developments affecting remedies for se-   curities violations, see p. 119 supra.

ing the other requirements for liability are met. For example, in *Kline v. First Western Gov't Sec., Inc.*, 24 F.3d 480 (3d Cir.1994), a law firm issued three opinion letters concerning the tax consequences of an investment in forward contracts through First Western. Although the letters stated that they were for the exclusive use of First Western, the law firm was aware that its opinion letters had reached potential investors. Id. at 483. The investors alleged that the opinion letters, upon which they relied in deciding to invest, omitted material facts concerning the structure of the First Western transactions. . . .

We reversed [the district court's summary judgment for the law firm]. We noted: "We are dealing here with a situation in which [the law firm], by authoring its opinion letters, has elected to speak regarding the transactions at issue. Plaintiffs allege that this speech was misleading because [the law firm] failed to include in its opinion letters information that, if included, would have undermined the conclusions reached in those letters." Id. We concluded that once a law firm has chosen to speak, it may not omit facts material to its non-confidential opinions. Id. at 490–91.

We reasoned that the law firm's duty to not omit material facts did not arise from a fiduciary duty owed to the investors; rather, the duty arose when the law firm undertook the affirmative act of communicating with the investors:

> [W]hen a professional undertakes the affirmative act of communicating or disseminating information, there is a general obligation or 'duty' to speak truthfully. . . . And encompassed within that general obligation is also an obligation or 'duty' to communicate any additional or qualifying information, then known, the absence of which would render misleading that which was communicated. . . . [This duty] is simply one facet of the general obligation to speak truthfully, arising out of and because of an affirmative act by the defendant in communicating.

Id. at 491 (quotations omitted). Summary judgment was inappropriate even though the law firm never communicated directly with the investors, but merely prepared opinion letters with knowledge that First Western was distributing those letters to potential investors.

In *Ackerman v. Schwartz*, 947 F.2d 841 (7th Cir.1991), attorney Howard Schwartz wrote an opinion letter which allegedly recited untrue "facts." The court of appeals held: "Although the lack of duty to investors means that Schwartz had no obligation to blow the whistle, and none to correct a letter he had not authorized to be circulated in the first place . . . , Schwartz cannot evade responsibility to the extent he permitted the promoters to release his letter." Id. at 848. The court concluded that, if Schwartz authorized the inclusion of his letter with the offering documents, Schwartz could be liable as a principal, and not merely as an aider and abettor. Id. According to the court: "In order to recover from a professional for a report rendered to his client, the third party must establish that the professional was aware that the report would be used for a particular purpose, in furtherance of which a known person would rely, and the professional must show an understanding of this impending reliance." Id. at 846.

If Drinker had prepared signed opinion letters, or other documents acknowledging Drinker's preparation and/or endorsement of the documents, for distribution to the investors that were materially misleading, we would have little difficulty acknowledging Drinker's liability for a primary violation of section 10(b) and Rule 10b–5, assuming the other requirements of liability were met. With one exception which we do not deem material to the outcome of this case, however, Drinker did not sign any documents for distribution to the investors. Indeed, the investors concede that they did not know about Drinker's involvement with Mercer LP until after they invested. We are thus faced with a question far more difficult than the one we answered in *Kline*: Whether a lawyer who participated in the drafting of a client's fraudulent document may be held primarily liable to a third-party investor under the federal securities laws for the material misstatements or omissions contained in the document, when the lawyer did not sign or endorse the document and the investor is therefore unaware of the lawyer's role in the fraud.

We conclude that lawyers and other secondary actors who significantly participate in the creation of their client's misrepresentations, to such a degree that they may fairly be deemed authors or co-authors of those misrepresentations, should be held accountable as primary violators under section 10(b) and Rule 10b–5 even when the lawyers or other secondary actors are not identified to the investor, assuming the other requirements of primary liability are met. To obtain relief under section 10(b) and Rule 10b–5, a private plaintiff must show, inter alia, that he or she relied on a misleading statement of the defendant and suffered an economic loss as a proximate result. Scattergood, 945 F.2d at 622. Section 10(b) and Rule 10b–5 require the plaintiff to demonstrate reliance on the misleading *statement*; they do not require the plaintiff to demonstrate that he or she relied on the *defendant's role* in the preparation or dissemination of the statement. When an investor reasonably relies on a materially misleading statement in connection with the purchase or sale of a security, the author of the statement should not be allowed to escape liability under the federal securities laws merely because the author is unknown to the investor.

In *In re ZZZZ Best Sec. Litig.*, 864 F.Supp. 960 (C.D.Cal.1994), investors alleged that ZZZZ Best perpetrated a fraud in connection with the sale of ZZZZ Best securities. The plaintiffs also alleged that Ernst & Young was liable for its involvement in the creation, review and issuance of approximately thirteen publicly released statements related to the scheme. None of the statements attributed its existence to Ernst & Young or even hinted that the firm might have been involved in the issuance of any of the statements. Id. at 965. Ernst & Young argued that those statements released to the public by ZZZZ Best and attributable only to ZZZZ Best or others, even if reviewed, edited or approved by Ernst & Young, were not actionable against Ernst & Young as violations of section 10(b) and Rule 10b–5.

The investors countered that if a "secondary actor" such as Ernst & Young actively participates in the creation of a materially misleading statement issued by a "primary actor" such as ZZZZ Best, then the so-called secondary actor has committed a primary violation of section 10(b). According to the plaintiffs, since Ernst & Young was actively involved in the writing and reviewing of the financial reports and press releases provided to the public by ZZZZ Best, and since Ernst & Young knowingly included information which was misleading in the documents, Ernst & Young committed a primary violation of section 10(b) and Rule 10b–5.

The court agreed with the investors. Id. at 970. Acknowledging that the investors might not have been able to attribute the misstatements and omissions directly to Ernst & Young, the court reasoned that the investors still relied on the statements. According to the court, "anyone intricately involved in their creation and the resulting deception should be liable under Section 10(b)/Rule 10b–5." Id.

Ernst & Young specifically challenged the investors' omissions-based claim on the ground that an alleged failure to act cannot give rise to a section 10(b) claim unless the investors establish a relationship with the defendant which gives rise to a duty to disclose. While agreeing with this general proposition, the court noted that "a general duty does exist to communicate any additional information, which in its absence would render misleading that which was already communicated." Id. at 971. If Ernst & Young was found to have sufficiently participated in the preparation of the misrepresentations and omissions such that they were attributable to the firm, the court reasoned, then Ernst & Young would have a duty to disclose or correct these previously released misrepresentations. Id. We find the reasoning of the court in *ZZZZ Best* to be persuasive.[22]

Drinker contends that it did not have a duty to "blow the whistle" on Mercer LP. It is reasonably clear that mere silence, absent a duty to speak, is not actionable under section 10(b) or Rule 10b–5. Chiarella v. United States, 445 U.S. 222, 235 (1980). Drinker also contends that it did not owe a fiduciary duty to the investors. We do not disagree. Our analysis does not end there, however. The investors contend, and we agree, that a duty to disclose may arise *either* from a fiduciary relationship *or* from affirmative representations that omit a material fact such that the representations made are misleading.

We need not address the issue of whether a lawyer has an absolute duty to "blow the whistle" on his client. Instead, we are convinced that, as with the facts alleged here, when a lawyer elects to speak, the lawyer does have a duty to speak truthfully. *See* 17 C.F.R. § 240.10b–5 (making it unlawful to "omit to state a material fact necessary in order to make the statements made, in the light of the circumstances under which they were made, not misleading"); see also *Kline*, 24 F.3d at 491 (when law firm

22. [Editors' note:] The law firm representing ZZZZ Best was also charged with securities fraud by investors. In 1994 the law firm and its liability insurer settled these claims for $29 million.

elects to speak, it assumes the duty to communicate any additional or qualifying information, then known, the absence of which would render misleading that which was communicated). The fact that the lawyer is speaking "behind the scenes" does not absolve the lawyer of this duty. When a lawyer prepares a document with knowledge that the document will be distributed to investors, the lawyer has elected to speak to the investors, even though the document may not be facially attributed to the lawyer. While Drinker did not owe a fiduciary duty to the investors to "blow the whistle" on Mercer LP, Drinker did have a duty to correct material omissions contained in *its* statements.

We do not suggest that a lawyer who merely provides "substantial assistance" to a client may be liable under section 10(b) and Rule 10b–5. Such a holding would be inconsistent with the Supreme Court's rejection of a private cause of action for aiding and abetting. See Central Bank of Denver, 511 U.S. at 168 (listing "substantial assistance given to primary violator" as one element of rejected aiding and abetting cause of action). Rather, we believe that a person may be liable for a primary violation of section 10(b) and Rule 10b–5 when the person's participation in the creation of a statement containing a misrepresentation or omission of material fact is sufficiently significant that the statement can properly be attributed to the person as its author or co-author. At that point, the person has done more than provide mere substantial assistance; the person has become a primary violator of section 10(b) and Rule 10b–5, assuming that the other requirements of section 10(b) and Rule 10b–5 are satisfied. This is true even if the investor is unable to attribute the statement to the person at the time of the transaction.

We hold that when a person participates in the creation of a statement for distribution to investors that is misleading due to a material misstatement or omission, but the person is not identified to the investors, the person may still be liable as a primary violator of section 10(b) and rule 10b–5 so long as (1) the person knows (or is reckless in not knowing) that the statement will be relied upon by investors, (2) the person is aware (or is reckless in not being aware) of the material misstatement or omission, (3) the person played such a substantial role in the creation of the statement that the person could fairly be said to be the "author" or "co-author" of the statement, and (4) the other requirements of primary liability are satisfied.

Our holding is not without precedent. [The court summarized and relied on In re Software Toolworks Inc. Sec. Litig., 50 F.3d 615 (9th Cir.1994), in which an accounting firm was held subject to liability to investors for allegedly drafting a letter sent by the client under the client's name to investors when, "as members of the drafting group," the accounting firm had access to information indicating that statements in the letter were misleading because material facts were omitted.]

. . .

Viewing the facts of this case in a manner most favorable to the investors, we conclude that plaintiffs have adduced sufficient evidence to create an issue of material fact as to whether (1) Drinker was an author or co-author of the disclosure documents; (2) Drinker knew that those documents would be relied upon by the investors; and (3) Drinker knew that material information was omitted from those documents. As a result, Drinker had a duty to ensure that the statements it made in the November Disclosure Package and May Disclosure Letter did not contain misstatements or omissions of material fact. The investors have proffered sufficient evidence at this stage to demonstrate that Drinker did not fulfill its duty.

C.

The district court also concluded that the investors failed to demonstrate a genuine issue of material fact on the issue of scienter. Scienter is a necessary element of a cause of action under section 10(b) and Rule 10b–5. In re Phillips Petroleum Sec. Litig., 881 F.2d 1236, 1242 (3d Cir.1989). Scienter is defined as "a mental state embracing intent to deceive, manipulate, or defraud." Scienter may be found "only where there is intentional or willful conduct designed to deceive or defraud investors by controlling or artificially affecting the price of securities." It is insufficient to show mere negligent conduct. Scienter must be proven by showing that "the defendant lacked a genuine belief that the information disclosed was accurate and complete in all material respects." Phillips Petroleum, 881 F.2d at 1244 (quotations omitted).

A showing of recklessness on the part of the defendant is sufficient to establish scienter for a claim under section 10(b) and Rule 10b–5. Id. Recklessness is defined as "an extreme departure from the standards of ordinary care ... which presents a danger of misleading ... that is either known to the defendant or is so obvious that the actor must be aware of it." Id. (quotation omitted). [C]ircumstantial evidence may often be the principal, if not the only, means of proving scienter.

We conclude that the investors have demonstrated the existence of a genuine issue of material fact on the issue of scienter. Viewing the facts in the light most favorable to the investors, a trier of fact could reasonably find the following: (1) Strouse knew that Mercer LP, through Coleman, improperly solicited the investors' original investments without making the necessary disclosures; (2) Strouse knew in May 1993 that the investors never received the February Disclosure Package and therefore never had an opportunity to rescind their original investments; (3) although Strouse encouraged Mercer LP to distribute the package in May 1993, he never attempted to determine whether the package was subsequently delivered; (4) Strouse knew that Mercer LP and Coleman faced numerous regulatory difficulties throughout 1993 that presented severe difficulties for Mercer LP's financial future; (5) in September or October 1993, Strouse knew that Mercer LP, possibly through Coleman, had once again solicited substantial investments from the investors without distributing necessary disclosures; and (6) Strouse prepared the November Disclosure Package and May

Disclosure Letter without including the material information that was contained in the undelivered February Disclosure Package and without including material information about his client's 1993 difficulties.

From the above facts, it would be reasonable for a trier of fact to infer that Strouse, who knew that Mercer LP and the investors' investments were in serious trouble, was concerned about his representation of Mercer LP and the behavior of his client. Although Strouse was not necessarily in a position to prevent Mercer LP from engaging in various misdeeds throughout its existence, a trier of fact could reasonably infer that Strouse did not do all that he should have done to ensure that his clients complied with the law and distributed the February Disclosure Package.... In sum, a trier of fact might reasonably infer that Drinker intentionally concealed material information from the November and May disclosure documents, and that it was motivated by a desire to avoid the financial and reputational repercussions that could follow from the investors' anticipated decision to rescind their investments. In other words, a trier of fact might reasonably conclude that Drinker acted with scienter.

Or it might not. Drinker offers several explanations for its decision not to include the information about Coleman and Mercer LP in the November Disclosure Package and the May Disclosure Letter. We need not decide whether Drinker in fact acted with scienter when it decided to exclude certain information from the November and May disclosure documents. It is sufficient that we decide that a trier of fact could so conclude.

[In parts III and IV of its opinion, the court held, first, that the investors' claims based on state common law of fraud (intentional misrepresentation) were improperly dismissed for much the same reasons as those applicable to the federal securities claims; and second, that the RICO claims, however, were properly dismissed.]

[Subsequently, a petition for rehearing *en banc* was granted by the active judges in the Third Circuit. Shortly prior to oral argument, the parties settled the case and the panel decision was vacated. Although the vacated opinion is not "authority," it contains a good summary of a number of cases that can be cited as precedent.]

———

SCHATZ v. ROSENBERG.[22] In this case, the plaintiffs appealed from the trial court's order dismissing claims that a law firm, knowing that its client was making false representations of financial worth, provided this information to the plaintiffs along with the the closing documents the firm had prepared. The documents included an updated letter from the client, prepared by the firm and delivered to the plaintiffs, stating that the client's

---

22. 943 F.2d 485 (4th Cir.1991), cert. denied, 503 U.S. 936 (1992). Although *Schatz* had been cited 270 times prior to April 1999, the decision has been ignored by most courts and distinguished or rejected by a few. See, e.g., In re Rospatch Securities Litigation, 1992 WL 226912 (W.D.Mich.1992) (declining to follow *Schatz*).

financial situation had not changed. The underlying transaction was the sale of two bed manufacturing companies largely owned by Mr. & Mrs. Schatz to defendant Mark Rosenberg. Rosenberg was represented by the law firm of Weinberg & Green throughout the transaction, in which the Schatzes received $1.5 million in promissory notes for their controlling interest in the two companies, notes which Rosenberg personally guaranteed. The plaintiffs relied on a financial statement dated March 31, 1986 and an update letter delivered at the closing on December 31, 1986, which represented that Rosenberg's net worth exceeded $7 million. Between April and December 1986 Rosenberg's financial empire had crumbled; and the financial documents misrepresented his financial condition. After the transaction was completed, Rosenberg siphoned off the assets of the companies he had bought in a vain effort to prop up the financial condition of his own enterprises. When he filed for bankruptcy the companies were essentially worthless and the Schatzes suffered financial loss.

The Fourth Circuit panel affirmed the dismissal of the counts charging the firm with liability as a principal or aider and abettor under federal securities laws and under Maryland tort law. With respect to § 10(b) of the federal securities act, the court held that "lawyers have no duty to disclose information about clients to third party purchasers or investors in the absence of a confidential relationship between the attorney and the third party," relying on the *Barker* case, supra p. 120.[23] The court distinguished cases in which a lawyer issued a misleading legal opinion to the person entering into a transaction with the client. Because Weinberg & Green only passed along Rosenberg's representations and did not make any of its own, the firm was not liable for his representations. On this point the court conceded that agency law was to the contrary,[24] but it held that the greater confidentiality of the lawyer's role led to a lesser standard for lawyers:

> We hold ... that a lawyer or law firm cannot be liable for the representations of a client, even if the lawyer incorporates the client's misrepresentations into legal documents or agreements necessary for closing the transaction. In this case, Weinberg & Green merely "papered the deal," that is, put into writing the terms on which the Schatzes and Rosenberg agreed and prepared the documents necessary for closing the transactions. Thus, Weinberg & Green performed the role of a scrivener. Under these circumstances, a law firm cannot be held liable for misrepresentations made by a client in a financial disclosure statement.[25]

---

23. The aiding and abetting count, which would not have survived the *Central Bank* case, was rejected on the ground that the firm's legal work in closing the transaction did not meet the "substantial assistance" threshold.

24. See Restatement (Second) of Agency § 348: "An agent who fraudulently makes representations, ... or knowingly assists in the commission of tortious fraud ... by his principal ... is subject to liability in tort to the injured person although the fraud ... occurs in a transaction on behalf of the principal."

25. 943 F.2d at 495–96.

The court also rejected the claims based on Maryland law. Under the Maryland Rules of Professional Conduct, Weinberg had a clear ethical duty either to withdraw from the representation (i.e., not close the transaction) or disclose the misrepresentations to the Schatzes. Maryland tort law, however, applies the privity rule in this context, allowing a non-client to sue a lawyer only when the non-client is a third-party beneficiary of the lawyer-client relationship. Public policy, the court concluded

> counsels against imposing such a duty. Attorney liability to third parties should not be expanded beyond conflicts of interest. . . . Any other result may prevent a client from reposing complete trust in his lawyer for fear that he might reveal a fact which would trigger the lawyer's duty to the third party. Similarly, if attorneys had a duty to disclose information to third parties, attorneys would have an incentive not to press clients for information . . . [leading to more rather than less fraud].[26]

Lawyer Liability for Facilitating Client Transactions that Defraud Third Persons

Is *Schatz* directly contrary to *Klein*? If not, how can the two cases be distinguished? Does the disagreement involve substantive issues of federal securities law? Of state fraud law? The rejection of the privity doctrine in some states but not in others? Differences in the professional duty of confidentiality in various states (some requiring or permitting disclosure of client fraud by the lawyer and others prohibiting it)? Since many transactions cross state lines and federal and state fraud law overlap, isn't it important that a national standard be applicable? If so, what should it be?

Consider the spectrum of lawyer action or non-action in cases in which a person entering into a transaction with the lawyer's client has relied on material false representations. At one extreme, when the lawyer makes a material false representation to the third person, which that person reasonably relies on to his detriment, judicial decisions hold the lawyer liable for intentional fraud or negligent misrepresentation.[27]

At the other extreme, represented by the *Barker* case, p. 120 supra, a lawyer cannot be held primarily or secondarily liable when the lawyer's limited work in connection with a transaction did not involve the prepara-

---

26.   943 F.2d at 493.

27.   See Rubin & Cohen v. Schottenstein, Zox & Dunn, 143 F.4d 263 (6th Cir. 1998) (en banc), in which a group of potential investors lost their investment after being referred by the company to its lawyers, who told them all was well and that there was no need to call the bank as part of the investors' due diligence. A panel decision that the lawyers had no duty to persons not their clients was reversed by the Sixth Circuit acting en banc. The court held that, under both the securities laws and the common law, while the lawyers did not have an obligation to volunteer information, when they undertook to provide information to persons dealing with their client, the persons with whom they dealt had a right to rely on the accuracy of the representations. See also Fire Insurance Exchange v. Bell, 643 N.E.2d 310 (Ind.1994) (lawyer who falsely stated in a personal injury settlement negotiation that his client's liability insurance policy had a $100,000 limit is liable to the opposing party for fraud).

tion of the materials containing the material misrepresentations. The required mental state ("willfulness" under the federal securities fraud statutes) does not exist; and aiding and abetting liability also cannot be sustained because one element—the lawyer's facilitation of the client's fraud—is either lacking or insufficient.

Klein and *Schatz* fall into the middle ground:[28] The law firm in each case prepared documents for the client to facilitate a transaction that turned out to be fraudulent. In *Schatz* the lawyer, allegedly knowing of the client's misrepresentation, passed along the client's false statements of his net worth to the opposing party in the transaction and dealt face-to-face with that party's lawyer. In *Klein* the lawyer advised his client, a brokerage firm seeking investment capital, to disclose material facts to potential investors; when the client refused to do so, the lawyer continued to facilitate a series of loan transactions with the investors. Are these factual differences ones that should make a difference? Which case is easier to decide for the plaintiffs?

Suppose the fraudulent actor in both cases had been assisted by an ordinary commercial agent, a nonlawyer. An agent who "fraudulently makes representations ... or knowingly assists in the commission of tortious fraud ... is subject to liability in tort to the injured person although the fraud ... occurs in a transaction on behalf of the principal." If the agent fails to disclose misrepresentations of the principal that are known or should have been known to the agent, the agent is liable to the person harmed.[29] Why should a lesser standard apply to lawyers? Doesn't the opposing party to a transaction rely on the other side's lawyer not to close a transaction in which the lawyer knows that the client is misleading, and probably defrauding, a third person?

The court in *Schatz*, at the end of its opinion, quoted Judge Easterbrook's comment in the *Barker* case that "an award of damages under the securities law is not the way to blaze the trail toward improved ethical standards in the legal ... profession.... The securities law ... must lag behind changes in ethical and fiduciary standards." Isn't this comment inconsistent with the court's prior conclusion that the Maryland ethics rules, requiring Weinberg & Green to disclose the misrepresented facts to Schatz, does not define a lawyer's standard of care? If the lawyer knows her client's statements orally or in writing are both material and false, shouldn't the lawyer be liable if, in violation of the universal ethics rule prohibiting unlawful assistance and the further one requiring withdrawal

---

28. *Petrillo*, summarized above at p. 90, also falls in the middle ground. In *Petrillo* the lawyer provided a misleading report to his client's broker, who later acquired the property in his own right and ultimately resold it to the plaintiff. The lawyer was held liable to the ultimate purchaser.

29. Restatement (Second) of Agency § 348, cmt. b (1958). The agent does not have a due diligence duty to inquiry, but will be liable if "he knows or should know" of the principal's misrepresentations "before the consummation of the fraudulent transaction," but not if the knowledge came subsequently. Id., cmt. c.

under these circumstances, the lawyer goes ahead and closes the transaction?[30]

Why are the rules governing the conduct of lawyers given so little attention in cases involving lawyer liability to non-clients? One explanation is that the courts are taking too naively or unthinkingly the statement that the ethics rules "are not designed to be a basis for civil liability" (see Comment [18] of the Scope preamble to the Model Rules).[31] The puzzling fact remains that lawyer liability decisions in many states bear little or no relationship to whether the jurisdiction prohibits, permits or requires disclosure in the particular situation. Disciplinary exposure and tort liability seem to be developing on separate tracks, giving a lawyer inconsistent directives, such as when the ethics rule prohibits disclosure but the tort rule imposes liability for failing to prevent a client fraud, or vice versa. Is this inconsistency unfair to lawyers? Should the ethics rules be relevant to or controlling in a court's determination of whether or not the lawyer owes a duty of care to third persons?

The "Hindsight Bias"

One of the best-established findings of cognitive psychology is the "hindsight bias:" the tendency of all human beings to exaggerate the extent to which an event that they know has happened could be anticipated in advance.[32] "People believe that others should have been able to anticipate events [that occurred] much better that was actually the case."[33] The result is "[t]he defendant's level of care will be reviewed by a judge or jury who already knows that it proved inadequate to avoid the plaintiff's injury. . . . The bias, in general, makes defendants appear more culpable than they really are."[34] This fact of human psychology has implications for a lawyer who facilitated a client transaction that turns out to have been fraudulent.

---

30. In FDIC v. O'Melveny & Meyers, 969 F.2d 744 (9th Cir.1992), discussed p. 758 infra, the successor in interest to the client sued a law firm for failing to discover that two controlling shareholders were looting the regulated entity. The client's usual law and accounting firms had resigned or been fired before O'Melveny was retained to facilitate the client's solicitation of investors in private placement real estate deals. O'Melveny handled the transactions not knowing that the client was essentially insolvent. Because the investors had been reimbursed for their loss by the federal conservator, no third-party action was brought. If the client had been a private company that become insolvent, the investors might have sued the law firm. Secondary actors, such as a law firm, generally have no duty to investigate facts supplied by the client unless circumstances suggest that some material facts may be false. How extensive an investigation and paid for by whom? But in the circumstances of *O'Melveny*, should the law firm ask the client to consent to conversations with the former law firm and accounting firm concerning the reasons for their resignations?

31. Cf. *O'Melveny*, 969 F.2d at 748 n. 4, in which the court said:

> While professional standards are not meant to give rise to civil liability, we find that "[t]he attempt to deny that there is anything in these codes of conduct that is relevant to the legal duty owed by a lawyer to his client is simply breathtaking. It is also quite wrong."

32. See Jeffrey J. Rachlinski, A Positive Psychological Theory of Judging in Hindsight, 65 U.Chi.L.Rev. 571 (1998).

33. Baruch Fischoff, quoted in Rachlinski, supra, at 572.

34. Id.

The fact-finder, knowing that the fraud took place, will be inclined to exaggerate the degree to which the lawyer was aware of the client's fraudulent purpose or knowingly assisted in its accomplishment.

Making False Statements to Others: Model Rule 4.1

Model Rule 4.1, Truthfulness in Statements to Others, provides:

In the course of representing a client a lawyer shall not knowingly:

(a) make a false statement of material fact or law to a third person; or

(b) fail to disclose a material fact to a third person when disclosure is necessary to avoid assisting a criminal or fraudulent act by a client, unless disclosure is prohibited by Rule 1.6.

Read the definition of "knowingly" in the Terminology section of the Model Rules. Should M.R. 4.1 say "knowingly or recklessly"? The relationship between M.R. 4.1(b) and M.R. 1.6(b) makes the scope of the exceptions to confidentiality in the latter rule especially important. If a lawyer is prohibited under Rule 1.6(b) from disclosing a future or ongoing client fraud on a third person, the lawyer is also prohibited from disclosure under Rule 4.1(b). On the other hand, if the jurisdiction's version of Rule 1.6(b) *permits* disclosure to prevent or rectify client fraud, Rule 4.1(b) has the effect in most fraud situations of *requiring* disclosure.

The proviso to M.R. 4.1(b), by permitting disclosure only when not prohibited by M.R. 1.6, invites lawyers to keep silent about a client's material omissions even when disclosure "is necessary to avoid assisting a criminal or fraudulent act by the client." Lawyers who read M.R. 4.1(b) this way must believe either that the ethics rules require them to risk imprisonment and civil penalties when the only alternative is to "turn in" their fraud-doing clients or that the Rules provide some sort of defense to conduct that would otherwise be criminal or civil fraud.

One possible reconciliation of M.R. 4.1(b) and the law of fraud relies on an expansive reading of the self-defense exception of M.R. 1.6(b)(2) to permit disclosure of client fraud when non-disclosure would expose a lawyer to potential civil or criminal liability. Since disclosure then would be permitted under M.R. 1.6, it would be required under M.R. 4.1(b) if "necessary to avoid assisting a criminal or fraudulent act by a client." Another possible reconciliation rests on an assumption that lawyers will understand that civil and criminal law dealing with fraud "trumps" the ethics rule, which deals only with professional discipline. Perhaps the ABA decided against discipline for lawyers who tacitly assist fraud by omitting material facts, returning the problem to the civil and criminal law. But there is no hint of these subtleties in the text of or Comment to M.R. 4.1. Will lawyers who resort to the Rule for guidance understand these subtleties?

3.   O.P.M.: A CASE STUDY AND ITS LESSONS

THE O.P.M. FRAUD[35]

Just as the *National Student Marketing Case*, p. 104 supra, was *the* legal ethics case of the 1970s and *Kaye Scholer*, p. 756 infra, was the most discussed case of the 1990s, the *O.P.M. Case* had the same distinction in the 1980s. At its time, the $210 million O.P.M. fraud was the largest in American history, but its notoriety is attributable largely to the coincidence that the public revelation of the lawyers' role in the fraud coincided with professional and public debate in the early 1980s on the tension between loyalty to one's client, including the obligation to keep client secrets, and protecting others from harm at the client's hands—a debate fueled by the ABA's then ongoing effort to revise the Model Code, the effort which ultimately gave rise to the Model Rules. Reports exposing the breadth and depth of the OPM scam, which included detailed accounts of how OPM's lawyers fiddled (and collected their fees) while their client had, through fraud, burned an impressive list of financial institutions, became public just as the ABA was debating the client fraud issue in its final consideration of the Model Rules. By voting for the black-letter text of Rule 1.6—text that prohibits a lawyer from disclosing a client's ongoing or prospective fraud—the ABA effectively blessed what the OPM lawyers had done. A dark day in the profession's history, in our opinion.

O.P.M., an acronym for "other people's money," was created in 1970 by Myron Goodman and Mordy Weissman to purchase main-frame computers from vendors such as I.B.M. and lease them to businesses such as A.T. & T. and Rockwell. Banks, insurance companies and other financial institutions would lend O.P.M. the money to purchase computers, receiving in return a security interest in the equipment and the right to be repaid by periodic payments from the companies that were leasing and using the computers. Most, if not all, of the lenders were recruited by Lehman Brothers, O.P.M.'s investment banker.

During the 1970s O.P.M. became one of the largest computer-leasing companies. The company won its market share by slashing its prices, but as a result the lease payments it was due were too low to meet O.P.M.'s operating costs, which included the purchase price of the computers it leased and the price of maintaining the high standard of living to which the O.P.M. owners, Goodman and Weissman, had quickly become accustomed. O.P.M. retained the appearance of solvency because Goodman and Weissman resorted to fraud. As Stuart Taylor put it:

> Almost from the start, the enterprise was basically insolvent and survived by means of fraud and bribery. A single computer would be used as collateral for two or three loans with different banks; the value of a given piece of equipment would be inflated to obtain larger loans. (Judge Haight, at the time of [their subsequent] sentencing, told how

---

35. This description is drawn largely from Stuart Taylor, Jr., Ethics and the Law: A Case History, N.Y. Times Magazine, p. 31 et seq. (Jan. 9, 1983); and Report of the Trustee, In re O.P.M. (S.D.N.Y. 1983).

"Mr. Goodman would crouch under a glass table with a flashlight and Mr. Weissman would trace the forged signatures.")

The fraud was a classic "pyramid" or "Ponzi" scheme: every new loan O.P.M. obtained by lying to a lender about the size of the lease payments that would be due on particular computers, about the existence of the computer that was to generate the lease payments, about the existence of a lease contract for a particular computer, or about some combination of the above or some other matter, would be used by O.P.M. to pay off some previous fraudulent loan or some previous legitimate loan that had been backed by a lease that was insufficient because of some discount price provision or an early termination clause that had been used to entice reluctant lessees. But, inevitably, the new loans also had to be repaid. Consequently, O.P.M. had to resort to ever more fraudulent transactions to produce loan receipts that could be used to make payments on its last (fraudulently or legitimately obtained) loans.

Throughout the decade of fraud, the law firm of Singer Hutner handled the company's legal work. The firm documented and closed lease transactions and provided legal opinions to the lenders concerning the existence and soundness of the security for the loans: lease contracts for O.P.M.'s computers. By 1980, the law firm, growing with its client, employed 29 lawyers and collected about $3.2 million in fees and expenses (60% of its total income) from O.P.M.

By early 1979, according to the report later filed by O.P.M.'s bankruptcy trustee, "Singer Hutner had received indications that Goodman and Weissman were capable of serious illegality." The firm knew that Goodman and Weissman had purchased a Louisiana bank and shortly thereafter were charged with check-kiting; the firm helped to arrange a guilty plea: a $110,000 fine and no jail time. The firm also knew that O.P.M. was suffering severe cash shortages.

During 1979 and 1980, Singer Hutner closed an increasing number of lease transactions involving Rockwell, a large defense contractor. As the trustee's report explained, the Rockwell closings by Singer Hutner differed in many particulars from previous O.P.M. lease closings:

> Among other things, Goodman ... directed Singer Hutner to send Rockwell's copies of financing documents to O.P.M. after the closings and instructed the lawyers not to contact Rockwell without Goodman's prior permission. ...IBM mass storage units began to appear on purported leases to Rockwell in numbers far greater than Rockwell could possibly need. Insurance for Rockwell equipment came from O.P.M.'s insurer, despite Rockwell's contractual obligation to maintain the insurance. A number of inconsistencies and pecularities appeared in title documents presented by [O.P.M.'s] fraud team for Rockwell closings.

And the firm was aware that, on some leases, O.P.M. was making the rental payments to the financing institution, although the lease specifically called for the lessee to pay its rent directly to the lender rather than the lessee.

On June 12, 1980, the law firm received a letter from John A. Clifton, who had just resigned as O.P.M.'s financial officer. Clifton had discovered evidence that the Rockwell leases, which O.P.M. had used to obtain substantial loans, were fraudulent. After consulting his own lawyer, Clifton wrote to Singer Hutner, explaining what he had discovered about its client. This letter was delivered on June 12, 1980 to the desk of Andrew Reinhard, a Singer Hutner partner and someone Goodman called his "closest friend aside from Weissman."

Goodman, however, arrived at the firm along with Clifton's letter and somehow managed to get his hands on the letter. According to Stuart Taylor, accounts of how Goodman got the letter differed.

> The lawyers say that Goodman snatched the letter unopened from Reinhard's hand or seized it from the top of his desk. Goodman says this was a "cover story" agreed upon between him and Reinhard—that in fact he found Reinhard reading the letter as he passed his office. By all accounts, Goodman took the Clifton letter with him when he left [the firm.]

Before leaving the firm, however, Goodman told Joseph Hutner, the senior partner in the firm, that he was responsible for a wrong that he could not set right because it involved millions more than he could raise.

Subsequently, Hutner met with Clifton's lawyer, but did not request Clifton's letter or seek the details of the fraud. Hutner was told, however, that "Clifton had evidence of a multimillion-dollar fraud, that the firm's opinion letters were based upon false documents, and that O.P.M." to survive, would probably have to continue the same type of "wrongful activity." Clifton's lawyer's impression was that Hutner knew more than he was letting on, that he was working hard at preserving a "screen of deniability," speaking, for example, through the use of hypotheticals. Clifton's lawyer later said of this meeting: "I had visions of [Hutner] ... clamping his hands over his ears and running out of the office."

Faced with the warning that it had closed fraudulent transactions for O.P.M., Singer Hutner hired two ethics consultants (Joseph M. McLaughlin, an evidence specialist, is now a federal judge and the other consultant, Henry Putzel, a former prosecutor, is a white collar criminal defense lawyer). The firm told them that it wanted to do what was proper, but that it also desired, if possible, to continue to represent O.P.M., its principal client. The consultants told the firm what it wanted to hear. The consultants' advice boiled down to this: First, because Goodman had stated that the frauds were in the past, the New York Code of Professional Responsibility prohibited Singer Hutner from disclosing the past fraud. (See DR 4–101(C)(3), permitting disclosure of a client's "intention ... to commit a [future] crime;" and the New York version of DR 7–102(B)(1), which prohibited rectification of a client's past fraud on a third person when the lawyer's "information is protected as a confidence or secret.") Second,

Singer Hutner could continue closing O.P.M. lease transactions, while seeking to obtain details of past wrongdoing, if Goodman provided the firm with a certificate in writing verifying the legitimacy of each new transaction. Third, because Singer Hutner had no direct knowledge that O.P.M. managers would continue the frauds, the firm did not need to withdraw from the representation or disaffirm its prior opinions.

Ethics advice in hand, the firm continued to close O.P.M. lease transactions during the summer of 1980, including $39 million of additional fraudulent loans in July and August alone. Goodman, of course, cheerfully provided false verifications in writing of transaction essentials. Apparently, Singer Hutner thought those verifications enough to eliminate any need to inquire further into or worry much about the suspicious incidents that continued to plague O.P.M. closings, e.g., identical equipment descriptions on two leases, which O.P.M. said was a typographical error.

In September 1980, Goodman finally disclosed the magnitude of the prior fraud (estimating it at $90 million) and the firm decided to withdraw gradually while requiring O.P.M. to pay its fees in advance. But the firm remained silent even after learning from Goodman in late September that the fraud had continued throughout the summer. As part of its slow withdrawal strategy—a strategy devised by one of the firm's ethics consultant who warned Singer Hutner to withdraw in a manner that did not harm the client—Singer Hutner continued to close lease transactions for O.P.M. in the fall of 1980. The firm responded to inquiries about its resignation as O.P.M.'s counsel from lenders and others by saying that Singer Hutner and O.P.M. had "agreed" to part ways. When Kaye Scholer was retained as successor counsel by O.P.M., Peter Fishbein, a Kaye Scholer partner, called his old friend, Hutner, and asked whether there was anything Fishbein should know before undertaking the representation, Hutner responded that "the decision to terminate was mutual and that there was mutual agreement that the circumstances of termination would not be discussed." In the subsequent bankruptcy hearing, Hutner testified that this conversation "caused me more personal pain than anything" else that had happened. Kaye Scholer closed $15 million more in fraudulent O.P.M. transactions before the house of cards collapsed.

If O.P.M.'s scam was dependent on lawyers paying as little attention as possible (and then some) to what was going on in front of their noses, it should come as no surprise that the scheme collapsed because one lawyer was doing what lawyers are supposed to do, worrying about all the annoying details. In 1981, a lawyer for a St. Paul lender noticed that insurance on a leased computer was being paid by O.P.M. even though the documents provided that Rockwell would pay them. He called Rockwell's legal counsel, not because he divined that this inconsistency meant a fraud was afoot, but because a detail in the contract no longer conformed to the parties' practice and thus should be changed. Upon receiving this call, Rockwell's counsel went to pull the contract and found there was no contract, no lease, no computers of O.P.M.'s at Rockwell matching those described in the contract. And that was the beginning of the end. A report to the U.S. Attorney's office in New York City led in a few days to the arrest of Goodman and Weissman and the seizure of O.P.M.

The bankruptcy trustee, after an extensive investigation, wrote that Singer Hutner could have followed other courses, consistent with their ethical responsibilities, that would have stopped the fraud. Instead, after receiving notice that it was dealing with a crook, it acted in a way that helped [O.P.M.] continue the fraud for eight additional months during which financial institutions were bilked out of more than $85 million.

Singer Hutner dissolved as a result of the O.P.M. case; the reputations and careers of lawyers in the firm were adversely affected; prosecutors, grand juries and disciplinary authorities scrutinized the conduct of individual lawyers. Although none of the lawyers was prosecuted or publicly disciplined, it should be noted that Goodman was the chief witness against Reinhard, his principal lawyer and near "closest friend," whom Goodman claimed was a knowing participant in the fraud almost from the start. The law, accounting and investment banking firms involved in handling O.P.M. transactions settled liability claims by fraud victims for $65 million. Singer Hutner's share in these settlements was $10 million, the maximum coverage of its malpractice insurance.

Do the rules of professional conduct *require* a lawyer to act in a manner that involves such dire consequences? What other courses of action might the Singer Hutner lawyers have taken? Were the ethics consultants correct in concluding in June 1980 that only a past fraud was involved? Is it a continuing fraud if the consequences of past misrepresentations are still unfolding and the fraud has not been rectified? Consider the O.P.M. financial statements that would be sent to each lender in connection with a proposed lease transaction; didn't Singer Hutner have knowledge, after June 12, 1980, that these statements grossly misrepresented O.P.M.'s financial position? What would have been the firm's options if the Model Rules, as proposed by the ABA, had been applicable? What options would have been available in the vast majority of states today, 38 of which permit a lawyer to disclose information to prevent a continuing criminal fraud and 4 of which require a lawyer to disclose? Why would Hutner say that his misleading another lawyer, Fishbein, caused him "more personal pain" than "anything else?" If he believed, as his ethics advisors apparently told him, that the ethics rules required him to mislead Fishbein and allowed, although presumably did not require, him to help O.P.M. commit fraud, why was harming another lawyer in the name of ethical "duty" more painful than defrauding innocent third parties in the name of ethical "license?"

Lessons of *O.P.M.* and Other Client Fraud Cases

1. Rely on your instincts, feelings and the known (or easily discoverable facts) about people in deciding whether to accept or continue representation. In representing a client in business transactions with third person, do not represent clients whom you don't like or trust. Act promptly on early warnings that the client is a crook, such as the kite-checking scam in

O.P.M. Were there early warning signals in the *Klein* and *Schatz* cases that should have led the lawyers to withdraw or to make further inquiries before proceeding? Think about the embarrassment, reputational losses and monetary and other costs of the failure to act on these warning signals. Even if you and your firm escape civil liability, as happened in *Schatz*, those other consequences are large and harmful.

2.   *Don't pretend you or your firm are invulnerable.* Every major law firm in the land and many of its most celebrated lawyers (e.g., the legendary Clark Clifford, whose reputation was tarnished by the BCCI fraud) have been victimized by a crooked client. If it can happen to them, it can happen to you.

3.   *It pays to be fussy about the details of transactions.* Note that the O.P.M. fraud was brought to an end not by the lawyers, accountants and investment bankers who worked extensively on O.P.M. matters and were paid huge fees, but by a distant and picky lawyer bothered by the details of a single transaction.

4.   *Take disclaimers in opinion letters, prospectuses, etc., very seriously.* In the O.P.M. case, documents provided by Lehman Bros. to O.P.M.'s prospective lenders and lessees routinely included a disclaimer that stated that the investment banker was not vouching for anything about the deal it was brokering or the parties to that deal. While these disclaimers did not prevent Lehman Bros. from paying out a substantial amount to settle its potential liability for negligence in connection with the O.P.M. fraud, those on the other end of those disclaimers should have paid attention and pushed Lehman Bros. to disclose anything adverse that might be material to the lender. As it turns out, Lehman Bros. had knowledge of some material adverse facts. If the disclaimers state that essential facts have not been independently verified but are supplied by an interested participant in the transaction, you may have to make inquiries about those facts to protect yourself and your client.

5.   *Look at all of the law that governs lawyers, not just the lawyer codes in isolation.* When a problem arises, consult a lawyer who is knowledgeable about *both* the practice context as well as the law of lawyering. The ethics consultants in the *O.P.M.* case apparently knew little or nothing (and did nothing to find out) about lawyer exposure to civil liability for facilitating fraudulent transactions; it seems never to have occurred to them that unrectified fraud was not solely past conduct; or that new misrepresentations were being made whenever O.P.M.'s financial statement was sent to a lender in connection with a new lease transaction.

6.   *Learn about a major client's business and ask about sudden changes in practice.* In *O.P.M.*, for example, Singer Hutner failed to recognize that its client's computer leases with Rockwell were so numerous that, if they had existed, they would have comprised 20 percent of the world's main-frame computer capacity. Nor did they ask why the Rockwell leases departed from the usual lease practices of the industry. Nor did they pursue these or other questions by direct inquiry of lawyers at Rockwell.

7. *Inquire closely into a client's termination of any long-term advisors,* such as the accounting firm that has been auditing its books. When O.P.M. suddenly switched from one accounting firm to another, it began to show profits for the first time. The trustee's later report found that the initial firm had been discharged because it did not "bend" under O.P.M.'s pressure to report a positive net worth; the successor firm, which did so, "departed from generally accepted accounting principles" and certified "materially false and misleading" O.P.M. financial statements. Moreover, don't agree to represent a client who has parted company with another lawyer without obtaining permission to talk with that lawyer. If Kaye Scholer's Peter Fishbein had read the tea leaves of his phone conversation with Joseph Hutner correctly, he would have insisted, before becoming successor counsel, that O.P.M. waive confidentiality so that he could explore the circumstances of Singer Hutner's resignation.

8. *If possible, avoid becoming dependent on a single client unless you have great confidence in the integrity and soundness of its owners and managers.* This inquiry is even more pressing if you are employed full-time by an organization. Working in a law firm spreads and reduces the risks to the individual lawyer and the firm. If no single client constitutes a substantial percentage of the firm's fee receipts, the firm is in a much better position to make the tough judgment that it should fire a client it does not trust. In the *Klein* case, supra, why did the Drinker firm, a prestigious firm with a diverse client base, continue the representation of a client with a shady past who rejected the firm's advice concerning required disclosures to investors? Was it that one partner had too much discretion about which clients to maintain or too little obligation to share suspicious facts about clients with his fellow partners?

9. *Don't assume the attorney-client privilege or the work-product immunity will protect legal files or lawyer-client communications.* Any transaction can go sour and, if it does, it is likely to be subject to after-the-fact scrutiny. A successor in bankruptcy, as in *O.P.M.*, will waive the privilege and confidentiality in an effort to recover assets from the managers who looted the enterprise and the lawyers and accountants who assisted them. In other cases, the fraud victims will be successful in using the crime-fraud exception to penetrate the privilege. If victimized shareholders are the claimants, they will invoke the *Garner* doctrine to circumvent privilege, see p. 768 infra.

———

D.   CONFIDENTIALITY WHEN BODILY HARM OR DEATH MAY RESULT

INTRODUCTORY NOTE

The ultimate test of one's commitment to principle comes in those situations when life is threatened. Are we willing to go to war to protect a principle? Are we willing to kill or be killed? To sacrifice others? Should the press be enjoined from printing troop movements if publication would threaten soldiers' lives? In the area of client confidentiality, decisions where life hangs in the balance are extremely rare—in contrast to the frequency in which substantial economic harm is threatened by client fraud. Nevertheless, examining confidentiality in those extreme situations in which life is threatened illuminates the principle at stake, our commitment to it and our compassion for the suffering of others.

Robert Cover's study of the response of judges, particularly antislavery judges, to cases involving enforcement of the slave laws supplies a helpful perspective on the dramatic situations in this section.[1] In discussing the few cases that directly raised the question of the right of slaves to revolt, Cover says:

> Moralists have often sought to strip ethical issues of the complicating layers of fact and competing interests that seem to always characterize choice in society. Indeed the common association of natural right with a preexisting state of nature is itself an example of such an attempt. The tendency remains strong today as it was thousands of years ago. We have the relatively recent attempt of Professor Fuller to plumb the depths of the scope of responsibility for the taking of human life, the famous case of the speluncean explorers,[2] which itself is but an elaboration of the hypothetical of Rabbi Akiva, now two millennia old, of two men lost in the desert with enough water for one.[3] What is of interest to us is not only that philosophers should create such hypotheticals, but that where life imitated art, where events have occurred that seem in part to mirror the choices presented by these hypotheticals, jurists have seized on the cases as presenting fundamental problems about the nature of law. Thus, cases like United States v. Holmes and Regina v. Dudley and Stephens have received extended attention from jurists. [Regina v. Dudley and Stephens, 14 Q.B.D. 273 (1884) involved the killing of a boy by shipwrecked sailors in the good-faith belief that without cannibalism all would die. The boy was not consulted. In United States v. Holmes, 26 Fed.Cas. 360 (No. 15,383) (C.C.D.Pa.1842), a mate directed seamen to throw passengers overboard from a lifeboat after a shipwreck. The mate reasonably believed that if all had stayed aboard, the lifeboat would have gone down.]

The same inclination to seize on dramatic and rare instances of stark moral choice and to analyze them stripped of context can be discerned in the field of legal ethics. Law teachers often illustrate the conflict between confidentiality and protection of life with the example of a client who confesses to her lawyer that she has committed a crime for which another is scheduled to be executed on the morrow. Andrew Kaufman provides a real occurrence of the "execution" problem from the infamous Leo Frank

---

1. Robert M. Cover, Justice Accused 108 (1975).

2. L. Fuller, The Case of the Speluncean Explorers, 62 Harv.L.Rev. 616 (1949).

3. Babylonian Talmud, Tractate Baba Mezia, 62a.

case: "After the conviction of Frank had been affirmed, a client told [Judge Arthur] Powell, then a practicing attorney, that he, not Frank, had committed the murder. Powell reports that his decision not to reveal the confidential communication was eased by the commutation of Frank's sentence to life imprisonment. Shortly thereafter, Frank was lynched by a mob."[4]

The danger of such extreme examples is that, by focusing our attention on the rare and exceptional, they may train us to see moral choice only when it is presented in stark terms, allowing us to ignore the important lesson that in searching for an "ethical" or "moral" course of action in more mundane situations the choices are apparent only after a deeper examination of context. See the Gilligan excerpt in Chapter 1 at p. 36. The hard ethical questions in life arise not only in those rare instances that mirror the moralist's stark hypotheticals, but also in the vaguer, infinitely more complex arena of ordinary life.

1.   PROFESSIONAL RULES

As explained above, both the Canons of Professional Ethics and the Model Code of Professional Responsibility permitted disclosure of any crime, no matter how trivial, that a client intends to commit. See Canon 37 and DR 4–101(C)(3). The Model Rules restrict this permission. M.R. 1.6(b)(1) provides: "A lawyer *may* reveal information to the extent the lawyer *reasonably believes* necessary: (1) to prevent the client from committing a *criminal* act that the lawyer *believes* is likely to result in *imminent death or substantial bodily harm*." (Emphasis added.)

M.R. 1.6(b)(1) makes disclosure permissive rather than mandatory and judges scope of disclosure by an objective standard of reasonable belief. But a lawyer's honest, even if unreasonable, belief that imminent death or substantial bodily harm will result protects a lawyer who has reasonably concluded that disclosure is necessary to prevent a client's life-threatening criminal act. The ABA House of Delegates added the word "imminent" to the Rule during discussion on the floor. Why? Does "imminent" also modify "bodily harm"? And why the word "substantial"? Should not any bodily harm suffice to trigger permissive disclosure?

Recall Spaulding v. Zimmerman, printed in Chapter 1 at p. 5. Would Model Rule 1.6 have permitted the defense lawyers, assuming their clients did not consent, to inform David Spaulding that he had a life-threatening aneurysm? Compare proposed ALCC Rule 1.6: "A lawyer may reveal a client's confidence when and to the extent that the lawyer reasonably believes that divulgence is necessary to prevent imminent danger to human life. The lawyer shall use all reasonable means to protect the client's

---

4.   See, e.g., Andrew L. Kaufman, Problems in Professional Responsibility 212–14, 216–218 (2d ed.1984), citing Arthur Powell, I Can Go Home Again 287–292 (1943) and Powell, Privilege of Counsel and Confidential Communications, 6 Ga.Bar J. 333 (1944). Kaufman also points out that such examples are rare in practice and "are designed to test the limits of our belief in the principle of confidentiality." See Frank v. Mangum, 237 U.S. 309 (1915).

interests that are consistent with preventing loss of life." The ATLA commission, which put forth the ALCC, did not approve the proposed rule. The ALCC as adopted included no exception to the duty of confidentiality for disclosure either of client fraud on third parties or of the threat of death or bodily harm.

Consider the effect of the restrictions in M.R. 1.6(b)(1) on the execution hypothetical described above. If client perjury had secured the conviction of an innocent person who was about to be executed, the lawyer might view the unrectified fraud as one in which the lawyer had offered false evidence on behalf of the client. Under M.R. 3.3(a)(4), disclosure would be required by a lawyer who offered the false evidence and permitted on the part of a subsequent lawyer in the majority of states in which a lawyer may disclose information to prevent a client's future crime. Disclosure would be prohibited in the smaller number of states which adopted Rule 1.6(b) in the form recommended by the ABA. But what if the client had not participated in fraud to secure the conviction?

The leading case dealing with the reality of the execution hypothetical is State v. Macumber.[5] In *Macumber* a lawyer reported to public officials that his client, now deceased, had confessed to a crime for which another person had been prosecuted and convicted. The disclosure was ethically permissible (i.e., not in violation of the lawyer's duty of confidentiality) on the basis of a state ethics opinion given with the particular situation in mind; but the prosecutors did not credit the lawyer's report, believing that they had overwhelming evidence of the guilt of the person charged. Under these circumstances, the deceased client's communication was ruled inadmissible in a subsequent hearing challenging the allegedly wrongful conviction; the client's attorney-client privilege survived his death.[6]

Suppose a client had engaged in fraud to secure the conviction of an innocent person for a crime committed by the client, the punishment for which was a two-year prison term. Could the lawyer disclose under M.R. 1.6? Does imprisonment amount to "substantial bodily harm?" Does M.R. 3.3 help? Earlier drafts of the Model Rules imposed a mandatory duty to disclose information necessary "to prevent the client from committing an act that would seriously endanger the life or safety of a person, result in wrongful detention or incarceration of a person. . . ."[7] Putting aside for the moment the change from mandatory to permissive disclosure, what is to be made of the elimination of: (1) any explicit mention of wrongful imprisonment as a ground for disclosure and (2) the right to disclose noncriminal acts of a client that would result in death or wrongful imprisonment? Do

5.   544 P.2d 1084 (Ariz.1976) (reversing conviction and remanding for new trial); and State v. Macumber, 582 P.2d 162 (Ariz. 1978) (affirming conviction after second trial).

6.   See *Macumber*, 544 P.2d at 1087 (holding that lawyer's permissible disclosure did not waive the deceased client's attorney-client privilege). For discussion of *Macumber*, see

W. William Hodes, Introduction: What Ought to Be Done—What Can Be Done—When the Wrong Person Is in Jail or About to Be Executed?, 29 Loy.L.A.L.Rev. 1547 (1996).

7.   Unofficial Drafts of Aug. 20, 1979 and Sept. 21, 1979, Rule 1.5(b)(1).

you think the bar's position reflects the fact that most lawyers would not disclose to prevent wrongful imprisonment or execution?

Section 117A of the Restatement provides for broader disclosure when threats to life and bodily harm are at stake than is provided in any U.S. jurisdiction. Section 117A(1) provides: "(1) A lawyer may use or disclose confidential client information when and to the extent that the lawyer reasonably believes such use or disclosure is necessary to prevent reasonably certain death or serious bodily harm to a person." This provision eliminates several preconditions that Model Rule 1.6(b) requires for disclosure when life or bodily harm is threatened. First, it need not be the client's actions that threaten the life or body of another; the lawyer may disclose a confidential communication that led the lawyer to believe that one other than the client, such as the client's friend or spouse, might harm someone or that a natural event reported to the lawyer by the client was about to occur, such as collapse of a building. Second, no future criminal conduct of anyone need be involved. Third, the words "reasonably certain" are substituted for "imminent," moving away from the temporal idea of immediate harm. Thus the Restatement language would reach the facts of the *Spaulding* case, p. 5 supra, in which defense lawyers learned of a life-threatening condition of the plaintiff of which he was unaware.[8]

2.   LIMITS OF CONFIDENTIALITY

People v. Fentress

Dutchess County Court, 1980.
103 Misc.2d 179, 425 N.Y.S.2d 485.

■ ALBERT M. ROSENBLATT, JUDGE.

The defendant stands indicted for intentional murder [Penal Law 125.25[1]]. While the facts adduced before the grand jury are sufficient to establish the crime, the defendant avers that the indictment must be dismissed because it is the product of tainted and inadmissible evidence, presented in violation of the attorney-client privilege, as codified in CPLR 4503. . . .

[New York CPLR 4503 provides that "evidence of a confidential communication made between the attorney or his employee and the client in the course of professional employment . . . and *evidence resulting therefrom*, shall not be disclosed (by any governmental agency in any proceeding)." (Emphasis added.) A preliminary hearing was held to determine whether the statute had been violated; the prosecution agreed that testimony concerning possible confidences at this preliminary hearing would not be viewed as a waiver of privilege in any subsequent trial.]

. . .

---

8. For discussion of the desirability of broadening exceptions to confidentiality in this and other ways, see Roger C. Cramton & Lori P. Knowles, Professional Secrecy and Its Exceptions, 83 Minn.L.Rev. 63, 106–27 (1998).

Albert Fentress was a schoolteacher in the City of Poughkeepsie School System.

Among his colleagues there for more than a decade was Enid Schwartz, a fellow teacher and personal friend, whom Fentress visited at her home once or twice yearly. Her friendship with Fentress was substantial, and was based on his having taught two of her children, as well as on the independent basis of their relationships as colleagues over the years.

One of these sons, Wallace, had been taught by Fentress in the ninth grade, and through the years had developed an independent personal friendship with him. After graduating, Wallace Schwartz and Fentress visited at each others' homes and had engaged in sports together.

After Wallace graduated from law school, and joined a civil firm in New York City, he gave Fentress his card and told him that he could call him at any time. On August 20, 1979, the Court finds the following to have occurred:

2:12 a.m. Fentress, from his home at 216 Grand Avenue in Poughkeepsie, called Wallace Schwartz at the latter's home in Hartsdale, Westchester County. The first thing that Fentress said was that he was about to kill himself. Fentress spoke in a low monotone, and was distraught, but coherent. He told Schwartz that he had just killed someone, that a terrible thing had happened, which he could not square with God, and that he was going to kill himself.

Incredulous, Wallace Schwartz said it must have been an accident, but was told it was not, and that there had been a sexual mutilation as well.

In continuing attempts to dissuade his valued friend from suicide, Wallace Schwartz told Fentress that suicide would not square anything with God, and that whatever had happened, Fentress could get help. Wallace Schwartz invited Fentress to his house, and offered to go to Fentress' house, but Fentress refused.

Wallace Schwartz then suggested various persons who might be able to call and stay with Fentress, all of whom were rejected. However, later in the conversation Fentress said he would like the local rabbi, Rabbi Zimet, to come to his house and asked Wallace Schwartz to call the rabbi for him, which Wallace Schwartz agreed to do immediately. Fentress said he would leave the door open, and wait for the rabbi. It was also agreed that the police be summoned. . . .

Schwartz testified that it was his "legal" advice to Fentress that the police be called.

Fentress agreed, and stated that he would like to have both *Wallace Schwartz and the rabbi* present when the police arrived. . . .

At this point, of course, Schwartz did not have firsthand knowledge of the facts, but, recognizing the urgent need for immediate action (he could not fully conclude that any victim was actually dead) and because he was some fifty miles away, he immediately attempted to arrange to contact the rabbi.[1]

2:40 a.m. Wallace Schwartz called his mother, Enid Schwartz, who lived in Poughkeepsie, to enlist her aid in calling the rabbi and arranging for him to go to Fentress' house.

Wallace Schwartz told Enid of the call he had just received, and of his extreme anxiety about Fentress having said that there had been a killing, or that he had killed someone, and that he was going to kill himself, and wanted Rabbi Zimet to come to see him. Enid, herself a close friend of Fentress, agreed to call the rabbi but said she was going to call Albert Fentress first to verify that there was a real problem there.

2:45 a.m. As soon as Enid hung up, she called and asked Fentress *what had happened*. He told her either that he had killed someone, or that there had been a killing.

Notably, she never told Fentress that Wallace Schwartz had revealed to her any of the substance of the conversation between Fentress and Wallace Schwartz.

When Enid telephoned Fentress she did not state or imply, nor could she have concluded, that Fentress had committed a crime. She knew, from Wallace, that Fentress may have killed *someone*, but she could not have concluded whether it was self-defense or the justifiable killing of an intruder, or willful murder. Her overriding concern was for the preservation of the life of her friend, Albert Fentress. When she began the conversation by asking Fentress what happened, Fentress stated that there had been a killing.

During the 2:45 a.m. conversation, Enid told Fentress that the police must be called, saying either "You must call the police" or "I am going to call the police." Fentress' response was that he would like Rabbi Zimet there waiting until the police came. She got the understanding that Albert Fentress acknowledged that it was proper for the police to come....

Notably, Fentress did not state that he wanted his attorney there, only the rabbi. This is important, in that Fentress recognized that the presence of an attorney in the case would not (or should not) stem the arrival of the police. The Court thus finds that Fentress agreed that the police be called, and further, that he did not attempt to place any condition, as to the presence of an attorney, on their being called. His wish for a rabbi, while understandable for purposes of spiritual comfort, has no legal implications whatever.

---

1. It should be noted, at this point, that Fentress was not and is not Jewish. While there was some peripheral discussion at the hearing about the possible clergyman-penitent relationship, the court finds it lacking. Rabbi Zimet, as it turned out, could not be reached, and through no one's fault never appeared at defendant's house or spoke to the defendant. The only connection between the defendant and the rabbi is that they both were at Wallace Schwartz' wedding where, one may speculate, they may have met.

2:50 a.m. After Enid spoke to Fentress, she immediately called Rabbi Zimet but there was no answer.

While Fentress had asked her to let him know if she reached the rabbi, she was fearful that if she informed him of her failure, he might carry out his suicide threat.

It was because she could not reach the rabbi that she decided to call the police, to protect Fentress from harming himself.

2:59 a.m. Enid Schwartz called her son Wallace, to tell him of her unsuccessful attempts to reach the rabbi, and her intention to call the police. The Court finds that the decision to call the police was made by Enid alone, although Wallace Schwartz concurred in it, principally because they both wished to prevent the defendant's suicide. Because of Wallace Schwartz' concern for Fentress' (legal) position, he cautioned his mother to be discreet in what she told the police, and to limit her remarks to the effect that there may have been a shooting at Fentress's house, and that there was fear that Fentress might commit suicide.

3:05 a.m. Enid called the police and told Officer Thomas Ghee that it was reported to her by her son, and then by Fentress, that there had been a shooting or killing at his home. She warned the police that because of Fentress' alleged suicidal intentions, it would be unwise to approach with sirens.

3:15 a.m. The police, dispatched by Sgt. Krauer, arrived at defendant's house. The lights were on and the door open. Fentress was seated next to an open window, and beckoned: "Officer, please come in and take the gun."

3:19 a.m. The defendant was given his *Miranda* warnings, according to Officer Perkins. The defendant declined to speak, stating that he was "waiting for his attorney," whom "he had already contacted," and whom he was expecting shortly. The police desisted questioning.

3:30 a.m. Fentress was driven to the police station, and told the police that his attorney was Wallace Schwartz. After arriving at the police station, Fentress, on three or four occasions, asked for "his attorney, Wallace Schwartz."

5:09 a.m. Wallace Schwartz arrived in Poughkeepsie, and advised the police that he was not a criminal lawyer and would not be able to properly represent the defendant. By that time Wallace Schwartz had decided to recommend Peter L. Maroulis to the defendant.

Peter L. Maroulis telephoned the police, and instructed them not to question the defendant. They had not; they did not.

. . .

The primary issues to be decided are, therefore, whether the requisites for confidentiality were established, and if so, whether they were waived by Fentress.

Wigmore, as usual, is an apt starting place, and provides the most orderly formulation of the rule. [The court quoted Wigmore's statement of the attorney-client privilege, reprinted above at p. 206, n. 12.]

If Wallace Schwartz was not being consulted in a professional capacity for legal advice, the inquiry is at an end.... The district attorney argues that Wallace Schwartz was predominantly a friend, who never handled a criminal case, and was neither retained nor gave any appreciable amount of legal advice to the defendant. To be sure, he "withdrew" in favor of Mr. Maroulis at the earliest time, and made no secret of his discomfort in the unfamiliar surroundings of the criminal law.

It is well settled, however, that the professional relationship may exist in a financial vacuum, and that the absence of a fee or retainer does not alone destroy it (People v. Arroyave, 401 N.E.2d 393 (1980); Bacon v. Frisbie, 80 N.Y. 394; Gage v. Gage, 13 App.Div. 565, 43 N.Y.S. 810).

Under any view, the defendant and Wallace Schwartz were friends. And while there would be no privilege if Wallace Schwartz was acting solely as a friend, abjuring professional involvement (Kitz v. Buckmaster, 61 N.Y.S. 64, mot. for lv. to app. den. 62 N.Y.S. 1140), it may be inferred that the defendant communicated with Wallace Schwartz because he was not only a friend but an attorney, from whom he was seeking support, advice, and guidance. That Wallace Schwartz was in effect called upon to serve as psychologist, therapist, counselor, and friend, does not derogate from his role as lawyer (Privileged Communications, 71 Yale L.J. 1226 at 1252).

Fentress told the police on several occasions that he had an attorney, Wallace Schwartz, and was eagerly awaiting his arrival. It is indicative of his own subjective and articulated belief that he contacted his friend, Wallace Schwartz, *qua attorney* (Nichols v. Village Voice, Inc., 417 N.Y.S.2d 415), but did not, and could not, have concluded that their conversation was to be kept confidential in all respects.

Fentress urges, as he must to fit within Section 4503, that his call was for "legal advice." Ironically, the only "legal advice" which he can identify—and the Court adopts it as such—is the advice that the police must be called, the very advice which Fentress is now trying to disown. He cannot have it both ways.

Wallace Schwartz's advice was not the least bit unprofessional. Even the most seasoned criminal lawyers often "legally advise" their clients to turn themselves in for reasons which are strategic, if not moral. An experienced criminal practitioner might, of course, refrain from making that suggestion and still be on arguably stable grounds (both legally and ethically, despite the existence of an undetected body),[3] but he would have to weigh the risk of its ultimate discovery, and the disdain of a jury for any defense interposed by someone who had the cunning to suppress the corpus

---

3. People v. Belge, 372 N.Y.S.2d 798, aff'd 376 N.Y.S.2d 771, aff'd 359 N.E.2d 377; N.Y.State Bar Op. 479 (1978). [Editors' note:] See the discussion of *Belge* (*Dead Bodies Case*) in Chapter 1 at p. 57.

delicti. Duplicity is not tactically sound "legal advice." What other "legal advice" could Wallace Schwartz have given?

Had Schwartz affirmatively advised Fentress to conceal or dispose of the body, he would have been counselling the commission of a crime (Penal Law 215.40(2), impeding the discovery of evidence; People v. DeFelice, 125 N.Y.S.2d 80) which involves professional actions beyond those found endurable in *Belge*. They are violative of Code of Professional Responsibility DR 1–102A(4)(5), and may thus demolish the attorney-client privilege itself.[4] According to the Code of Professional Responsibility EC 7–5, "A lawyer should never encourage or aid his client to commit criminal acts or counsel his client on how to violate the law and avoid punishment therefor."

Not every communication made to a lawyer in his professional capacity is confidential or intended to be so. As a general rule the question of privileged confidentiality depends on the circumstances.... Fentress' intentions and his reasonable expectations of confidentiality or disclosure, as expressed and inferred from his conversations are of critical importance. (See 24 Ohio State L.J., supra, at 26) Fentress, when he spoke to Wallace Schwartz at 2:12 a.m., imparted the killing, and his suicidal intentions. Wallace Schwartz told him, and he agreed, that the police would have to be called. According to testimony of Wallace Schwartz:

> "Al (Fentress) indicated that he would leave the door open for the rabbi, that the rabbi can come over, and that he would wait for the rabbi, and that at that time I, meaning me, could call the police.... *I wanted to make sure that Al understood what I intended to do.*"

> "Towards the end of the conversation the police were (again) mentioned in relation to his waiting for me with the rabbi. I believe at that time it was Al that mentioned that I could call the police at that time."

The conclusion is inescapable, and the Court has found as a fact, that Fentress did not intend to keep the corpus of the crime from the police. His renunciation of confidentiality (as to the fact of the homicide) appeared again when Enid suggested that the police be called, and Fentress again specifically disavowed any expectation of keeping the fact of the homicide from the police. Enid's testimony confirms it, and the Court has adopted as a fact, the defendant's expectations of non-confidentiality regarding the corpus:

Q: He expected the police to come?

A: I don't know what he expected. That's what he *said to me....*

When Fentress concurred in the decision to call the police, he waived confidentiality of the *corpus*. Both to Wallace Schwartz and Enid Schwartz,

---

4. The privilege may not be asserted when the communication relates to the commission of a future crime, or to advise the client to suppress or destroy evidence ... or to conceal wrong doing.... The same result would follow, of course, if the attor-ney were to aid in impeding discovery of evidence.... Lastly, there is the actual entrustment of evidence to the lawyer. See, The Right of a Criminal Defense Attorney to Withhold Physical Evidence Received From His Client, 38 U.Chi.L.Rev. 211, 213.

he knew that disclosure to the police was inevitable both from his view-point and from the advice he received from his attorney, and later, from his friend, Enid Schwartz. His express eschewal of confidentiality is controlling (Rousseau v. Bleau, 131 N.Y. 177, 183, 30 N.E. 52, 53). "If the communication is made to an attorney with the knowledge and intent that it be disclosed to a third person it is fairly clear that it was not meant to be kept confidential and it is therefore not privileged." . . .

After the 2:12 a.m. conversation between Fentress and Wallace Schwartz, and the 2:40 a.m. conversation between Wallace Schwartz and Enid, Fentress received a telephone call from Enid at 2:45 a.m. She did not tell Fentress that Wallace Schwartz had related to her any admissions that Fentress made to Wallace Schwartz. She began immediately by asking Fentress what happened, and he then told her that there had been a killing. They both then agreed that the police would have to be summoned . . . with Fentress stating that he wanted her to call Rabbi Zimet.

At this point, for reasons which are expanded upon below, the Court finds that the conversation between Fentress and Enid, in which he divulged the killing, was a communication made independently freely by Fentress to Enid, a friend and teaching colleague whom he had known for ten years. He did not make the disclosure on the belief or expectation that Enid was an extension of Wallace Schwartz, qua attorney, or under the impression that she was Wallace Schwartz' agent for *purposes of any attorney-client* confidentiality.

The Court has found as a fact that Fentress's disclosure to her was not prompted on *constraint* of any previous disclosure that he made to Wallace Schwartz, but was independent of it, causally disconnected, and in response to a question by a friend who did not intimate to him that she was privy to any actual facts regarding his actions (United States v. Bayer, 331 U.S. 532, 540; People v. Tanner, 30 N.Y.2d 102, 106, 282 N.E.2d 98, 99; People v. Jennings, 33 N.Y.2d 880, 307 N.E.2d 561). The little that Enid knew—of a highly ambiguous nature—she did not disclose to Fentress and he could not have reasonably believed that she was privy to any *incriminating* facts merely from her inquiry, apprehensive though it was, as to "what happened." When Fentress replied, and told her that he killed someone, no confidentiality existed or was intended by him, and any previous attorney-client privilege which may have been created by the (2:12 a.m.) call between Fentress and Wallace Schwartz had been broken and attenuated. Thus, the evidence before the grand jury was not the "result" of any breach of attorney-client confidentiality within the meaning of CPLR 4503 even if, arguendo, complete confidentiality between Fentress and Wallace Schwartz was intended. This conclusion is confirmed by Fentress's repeated recognition and statements to Enid that the police were to be summoned. Hence, Enid was under no legal or ethical duty to refrain from calling the police. She had not only the defendant's express approval to do so, but her own unilateral and unfettered choice in the matter, just as any person is free to call the police when a friend has confided that he has killed someone and is about to kill himself.

. . .

The advice later given by Wallace Schwartz to his mother, Enid, at 2:59 a.m., that she should be discreet in what she tells the police because there "may" be an attorney-client privilege, did not and does not alter the relationship between Fentress and Enid. To the extent that there was an attorney-client relationship between Fentress and Wallace Schwartz, Enid was no part of it, nor was she in any manner acting as her son's agent, qua attorney. After her conversation with Fentress at 2:40 a.m., she was entirely free to call the police on her own for the reasons given. It is hard to conceive of anyone doing otherwise.

The defendant recognizes that the *presence* of an unnecessary third party will destroy confidentiality.... The waiver doctrine, however, is applied not only when a third non-indispensable person is present, but when such a person is let in on the secret before (Workman v. Boylan Buick, Inc., 36 A.D.2d 978, 321 N.Y.S.2d 983), during or after the attorney-client consultation. Thus, when the client, *after consultation*, reveals the contents of the consultation to someone else a waiver is effectuated (People v. Hitchman, 70 A.D.2d 695, 416 N.Y.S.2d 374). This is not new, and represents the unswerving application of the waiver doctrine on the basis of voluntary disclosures made by clients to third persons after the initial consultation....

Enid was not a person whose participation was necessary for further-ance of the professional relationship. Had she been present during the 2:12 a.m. conversation, her role as a friend could not be transmuted into that of an attorney's agent[7] or be perceived as essential to or in furtherance of the attorney-client conference (Baumann v. Steingester, 213 N.Y. 328, 332, 107 N.E. 578, 579).

. . .

The defendant's announced suicidal intentions pervade the case. Wal-lace Schwartz was burdened with a trilemma. He had just been told of a frightful homicide and an undiscovered victim. Secondly, Fentress said he was about to take a second life, his own. Given the desperation of the call, it would not have been possible for Wallace Schwartz, or anyone else, to determine whether the victim was still alive or beyond all hope. Fentress had mentioned drinking and a sexual mutilation as well. Schwartz could not possibly travel quickly enough to save anyone's life, but he knew that lives were in serious jeopardy at the very least. The implication of Fentress' motion is that Wallace Schwartz somehow broke a confidence by telephon-ing his parents, who lived moments away from Fentress, who was their

7. Naturally, the mere fact that Enid and Wallace Schwartz were related does not itself create agency ..., and the Court finds no other evidence to justify any find-ing of agency.

friend as well, for the express purpose of complying with Fentress' request that Rabbi Zimet be summoned to the scene, and to avert a suicide.

The ethical oath of secrecy must be measured by common sense. . . .

To exalt the oath of silence, in the face of imminent death, would, under these circumstances, be not only morally reprehensible, but ethically unsound. As Professor Monroe Freedman reminds us, "At one extreme, it seems clear that the lawyer should reveal information necessary to save a life." (10 Crim.L.Bull., No. 10, p. 987). If the ethical duty exists primarily to protect the client's interests, what interest can there be superior to the client's life itself?

The issue was addressed in N.Y.State Bar op. 486 (1978) (New York State Bar Journal, August 1978). Posing the question "May a lawyer disclose his client's expressed intention to commit suicide?" the New York State Bar Association, in interpreting EC 4–2 and DR 4–101(C)(3) answered in the affirmative, despite the repeal of suicide as a crime (See, L.1919, ch. 414; Former Penal Law Sec. 2301; Meacham v. NYSMBA, 120 N.Y. 237, 242, 24 N.E. 283, 284).

Thus, even if the defendant flatly forbade Wallace Schwartz from calling the police, the ethical duty of silence would be of dubious operability. We need not decide the legal consequences of such an interdiction, having rejected the defendant's contention that he did not acquiesce in the call to the police, and having found waiver by repetition to Enid Schwartz.

[Fentress was subsequently found not guilty by reason of insanity and committed to a state mental institution. The experienced criminal defense lawyer who replaced Wallace Schwartz video-taped his initial interview with Fentress on the morning after the killing. The tape helped persuade the jury that Fentress had been in a paroxysm of rage or insanity at the time.]

Disclosures to Save Life

Does the New York statute cover only material protected by the attorney-client privilege or does it also cover material protected by the duty of client confidentiality? Is *Fentress* an attorney-client privilege case or one involving the professional duty of confidentiality?

When does talking to a friend, who happens to be a lawyer, become a privileged communication? Do you agree with the court's characterization of Wallace Schwartz's communication as legal advice?

The court says that Fentress waived confidentiality as to the corpus delicti.[9] Do you agree? Why did the court find that Enid Schwartz was not

---

9. Henderson v. State, 962 S.W.2d 544 (Tex. Crim.App.1997), is another corpus delicti case involving the admissibility of physical evidence—a map giving the location of a missing infant that the child's babysitter created for her lawyer after being arrested

acting as the lawyer's agent? Is the court's reasoning persuasive? What difference does it make in terms of admissible evidence at a subsequent criminal trial whether Enid was her son's agent or was acting independently?

Was the discussion of suicide necessary to this opinion? The court asks, "what interest can there be superior to the client's life itself?" and relies on the N.Y. State Bar Association opinion approving disclosure to prevent a client's suicide. Does this reliance suggest that, had Fentress not threatened suicide, the court might not have upheld the lawyer's disclosure? Would this court have approved disclosure in Spaulding v. Zimmerman, printed above at p. 5.

Would the Model Rules permit disclosure in a case like *Fentress*? A 1983 ABA ethics opinion decided that under both the Model Code and the Model Rules a lawyer could disclose his client's intent to commit suicide in a jurisdiction where suicide was no longer a crime.[10] The ethics committee cited with approval several state ethics opinions[11] and relied on EC 7–12 and Model Rule 1.14, which provide that a lawyer has special responsibilities when a client suffers from a disability. Does this imply that suicidal thoughts qualify as a disability?

A New Jersey ethics opinion[12] concluded "that where an attorney for a parent has facts that demonstrate a propensity of that parent to engage in child abuse and hence the continuing unfitness of that parent to raise its [sic] child, ... the information *must* be provided to the [state] Children's Bureau." (Emphasis added.) The ethics committee emphasized that the state's interest in child welfare makes this crime *sui generis*, thus justifying the obligation to report a "propensity" to commit it. Is this opinion wise? Recall that the prosecutor in the *Dead Bodies Case,* discussed above at p. 57, invoked a New York public health statute requiring the reporting of information concerning certain deaths.

Would the lawyers in the *Dead Bodies Case* have been subject to professional discipline if they had revealed the location of the bodies without their client's consent? Would the ethics rules have permitted the lawyers to phone in an anonymous tip providing the authorities with the location of the bodies?

What is the effect of a lawyer's permissible disclosure of confidential information, without the client's consent, on the client's attorney-client

---

on kidnaping charges. The map was not a preexisting document but one prepared for purposes of legal advice. On the dubious assumption that the infant was still alive—he had been missing for more than two weeks and the babysitter had told police she had accidentally killed him—the court enforced a subpoena to the defense lawyer for the map, which then led to the discovery of the infant's body. The court upheld the babysitter's homicide conviction and death sentence.

10. ABA Informal Op. 83–1500 (1983).

11. The cited opinions were the N.Y.S.Bar Ass'n opinion cited in *Fentress* and a similar opinion in Massachusetts, Mass.Bar Ass'n Op. 79–61 (1979).

12. N.J. Op. 280, 97 N.J.L.J. 361 (1974).

privilege concerning the same information? The *Purcell* case, discussed at p. 248 above, holds that the privilege is unaffected: a lawyer who properly disclosed a client's threat to set fire to an apartment building was not required to testify against the client in a subsequent prosecution for attempted arson.[13] This approach reconciles the purposes of disclosure (protecting third persons from serious harm) while preserving the privilege. The conscientious lawyer who reports threatened harm avoids being the instrument of the client's conviction.

Fugitive Clients

Courts usually hold that the whereabouts of a fugitive client or one who has violated a court order is not privileged.[14] But is the information confidential, i.e., may a lawyer disclose absent a court order? After his conviction Garrow, the client in the *Dead Bodies Case,* escaped from the state institution in which he was confined. One of his former lawyers (who no longer represented him) provided the authorities information about Garrow's possible whereabouts based on the lawyer's interviews with, and knowledge of, Garrow. Was this disclosure proper?

A number of ethics opinions have dealt inconsistently with the dilemma confronted by a lawyer who, after a client disappears during a criminal investigation or jumps bail, learns where the client is hiding.[15] If the flight and continuing absence constitute a crime, may or must the lawyer disclose the client's whereabouts, or do the rules prohibit such disclosure? If the client refuses to accept the lawyer's advice to surrender, must the lawyer withdraw from representation? The opinions agree that the lawyer must not assist the client in remaining a fugitive, but go every which way on the other questions.[16] Is a clear rule either requiring or prohibiting disclosure desirable? Or should a lawyer have broad discretion to consider various factors such as the characteristics of the client, the nature of crime, the source of the information, etc.?

13. Purcell v. District Attorney, 676 N.E.2d 436 (Mass.1997). Restatement § 129, cmt. c agrees: "Disclosure by a lawyer that is adverse to the client and not in pursuit of the client's interests does not constitute waiver under this Section. For example, disclosure of a client's life-threatening act (§ 117A) or crime or fraud (§ 117B)...."

14. See cases cited in the note on p. 256 above.

15. ABA Informal Op. 1141 (1970) involves a lawyer contacted by a deserter from the military. The opinion turns on the deserter's purpose in consulting the lawyer: If the deserter contacts the lawyer to discuss his rights, the lawyer should treat the client's whereabouts as privileged. If the deserter wants advice on how best to evade capture, the lawyer must advise him to turn himself in, refuse to represent him if he declines to do so, and advise him that the lawyer will reveal his whereabouts if the client, continuing in his intention to evade capture, contacts the lawyer a second time. (Is the client likely to call back?) The opinion also tries to reconcile the ABA's previous opinions on what a lawyer with a fugitive client should do.

16. Compare ABA Informal Op. 1141 (1970), reviewing some prior inconsistent opinions and concluding that the lawyer should not disclose but must withdraw, with Ass'n Bar City of N.Y. Op. 81–13, 50 U.S.L.W. 2400 (1982), concluding that the lawyer may disclose and need not withdraw.

3. A Duty to Warn?

Hawkins v. King County

Court of Appeals of Washington, Division 1, 1979.
24 Wn.App. 338, 602 P.2d 361.

■ Swanson, Acting Chief Judge.

Michael Hawkins, acting through his guardian ad litem, and his mother Frances M. Hawkins, appeal from a summary judgment dismissing attorney Richard Sanders from an action sounding in tort. Appellants contend Sanders, court-appointed defense attorney for Michael Hawkins, was negligent and committed malpractice by failing to divulge information regarding his client's mental state at a bail hearing. We find no error and affirm.

On July 1, 1975, Michael Hawkins was booked for possession of marijuana. Following his court appointment as Hawkins' defense counsel on July 3, 1975, Richard Sanders conferred with Hawkins for about 45 minutes, at which time Hawkins expressed the desire to be released from jail.

Also on July 3, 1975, Sanders talked with Palmer Smith, an attorney employed by Hawkins' mother Frances Hawkins, to assist in having Hawkins either hospitalized or civilly committed. Smith told Sanders then, and reiterated by letter, that Hawkins was mentally ill and dangerous. On July 8, 1975, Dr. Elwood Jones, a psychiatrist, telephoned and wrote Sanders and averred Hawkins was mentally ill and of danger to himself and others and should not be released from custody. Sanders represented that he intended to comply with his client's request for freedom.

On July 9, 1975, a district judge released Hawkins on a personal surety bond. At the bail hearing, Sanders did not volunteer any information regarding Hawkins' alleged illness or dangerousness, nor were any questions in that vein directed to him either by the judge or the prosecutor. Smith, Jones, and Mrs. Hawkins were informed of Hawkins' release, and all parties later met on two occasions in a counseling environment.

On July 17, 1975, about 8 days after his release, Michael Hawkins assaulted his mother and attempted suicide by jumping off a bridge, causing injuries resulting in the amputation of both legs. The Hawkinses commenced an action for damages against King County, the State of Washington, Community Psychiatric Clinic, Inc., and one of its employees on August 16, 1976, and amended the suit on November 30, 1977, to name Sanders a party defendant. Sanders filed a motion to dismiss for failure to state a claim. . . .

On appeal, the Hawkinses essentially present two arguments: First, that by his failure at the bail hearing to disclose the information he possessed regarding Michael Hawkins' mental state, defense counsel Sanders subjected himself to liability for malpractice, as court rules and the Code of Professional Responsibility mandate such disclosure on ethical and legal grounds. Second, that by the same omission Sanders negligently violated a common law duty to warn foreseeable victims of an individual he knew to be potentially dangerous to himself and others. See Tarasoff v. Regents of University of California, 551 P.2d 334 (Cal.1976).

Sanders asserts the Hawkinses have failed to demonstrate that he breached any duty owed to them and, as an attorney appointed by the court to represent an indigent defendant, that he was a quasi-judicial officer, immune from civil liability.

We defined the elements of a legal malpractice action in Hansen v. Wightman, 538 P.2d 1238, 1246 (Wash.App.1975), as

> the existence of an attorney-client relationship, *the existence of a duty on the part of a lawyer*, failure to perform the duty, and the negligence of the lawyer must have been a proximate cause of damage to the client.

[Footnote and citations omitted. Emphasis added.] The Court, in Cook, Flanagan & Berst v. Clausing, 438 P.2d 865, 867 (Wash.1968) defined the standard care for Washington lawyers:

> [T]he correct standard to which the plaintiff is held in the performance of his professional services is that degree of care, skill, diligence and knowledge commonly possessed and exercised by a reasonable, careful and prudent lawyer in the practice of law in this jurisdiction.

We further note that the Code of Professional Responsibility sets standards of ethics for all members of the Bar of this state.

In considering appellants' argument that Hawkins' defense counsel breached an ethical and legal duty to disclose information to the court, we observe that a lawyer is ethically bound to advocate zealously his client's interests to the fullest extent permitted by law and the disciplinary rules. CPR 7, DR 7–101(A)(1).

Appellants argue that the information Sanders received was particularly relevant to the issues the bail-hearing judge is required to resolve on pretrial release pursuant to CrR 3.[2] In support of this contention, appellants cite DR 7–102(A)(3), which states:

> (A) In his representation of a client, a lawyer shall not: ... (3) Conceal or knowingly fail to disclose that which he is required by law to reveal.

Assuming without deciding that the information received by Sanders from Dr. Jones and Mrs. Hawkins' attorney did not constitute a "confidence or

---

2. The pretrial release hearing was conducted in justice court; therefore, JCrR 2.09 governs; however the provisions of JCrR 2.09 and CrR 3.2 are identical. Both rules identify the relevant factors as follows:

> the length and character of the defendant's residence in the community; his employment status and history and financial condition; his family ties and relationships; his reputation, character and mental condition; his history of response to legal process; his prior criminal record; the willingness of responsible members of the community to vouch for the defendant's reliability and assist him in appearing in court; the nature of the charge; and any other factors indicating the defendant's ties to the community.

secret" which a lawyer generally may not reveal, neither CrR 3.2 nor JCrR 2.09 specifies who has the duty to provide facts for the court's consideration. The quoted rules state only that "the court shall, on the available information, consider the relevant facts ..." JCrR 2.09(b); CrR 3.2(b).[3] Further, the Hawkinses ignore an ethical standard of paramount importance: that an attorney must advocate zealously his client's interests to the fullest extent permissible by law and the disciplinary rules. CPR 7 DR 7–101(A)(1).

While it can be argued that the draftsmen of JCrR 2.09 assumed defense counsel would participate in furnishing information for the court, there is no indication as to the length to which defense counsel should go in revealing information damaging to his client's stated interests. Manifestly, defense counsel has an ethical duty to disclose that which he is required by law to reveal. Appellants, however, have not cited any clear provision of the law which *requires* defense counsel to volunteer information damaging to his client's expressed desire to be released from custody.

We believe that the duty of counsel to be loyal to his client and to represent zealously his client's interest overrides the nebulous and unsupported theory that our rules and ethical code mandate disclosure of information which counsel considers detrimental to his client's stated interest. Because disclosure is not "required by law," appellants' theory of liability on the basis of ethical or court rule violations fails for lack of substance.

Turning then to the Hawkinses' theory of a common law duty to warn or disclose, we note common law support for the precept that attorneys must, upon learning that a client plans an assault or other violent crime, warn foreseeable victims. See Tarasoff v. Regents, supra; State ex rel. Sowers v. Olwell, 394 P.2d 681 (Wash.1964); Dike v. Dike,, 448 P.2d 490 (Wash.1968). *Olwell* and *Dike* make clear our Supreme Court's willingness to limit the attorney's duty of confidentiality when the values protected by that duty are outweighed by other interests necessary to the administration of justice. The difficulty lies in framing a rule that will balance properly "the public interest in safety from violent attack" against the public interest in securing proper resolution of legal disputes without compromising a defendant's right to a loyal and zealous defense. We are persuaded by the position advanced by amicus "that the obligation to warn, when

---

3. The American Bar Association's standards relating to pretrial release include this commentary: "The basic criticism of the administration of bail has been that magistrates were required to make decisions without having sufficient facts.... No agency charged with the specific duty of ascertaining facts relevant to release other than the defendant's criminal record and the nature of the present charge ordinarily exists. Unfortunately counsel, who is present in only a limited number of cases at this stage, seldom makes a special effort to supply the judicial officer with background facts.... Where public defender and other assigned lawyers provide representation on an institutional basis, they are frequently too pressed for time to make a special point of such an inquiry and, most important, to verify the information they may receive in an interview.

"The ideal system would involve the creation of an independent agency answerable directly to the court." ... ABA Standards Relating to Pretrial Release § 4.5 (Approved Draft 1968) commentary at 50.

confidentiality would be compromised to the client's detriment, must be permissive at most, unless it appears beyond a reasonable doubt that the client has formed a firm intention to inflict serious personal injuries on an unknowing third person."

Because appellants rely to a great extent upon *Tarasoff* in arguing a common law duty to disclose, we will demonstrate that the *Tarasoff* decision is inapposite even though the facts are equally atypical and tragic. Tatiana Tarasoff was killed by one Prosenjit Poddar. The victim's parents alleged that 2 months earlier Poddar confided his intention to kill Tatiana to a defendant, Dr. Moore, a psychologist employed by the University of California. After a brief detention of Poddar by the police at Moore's request, Poddar was released pursuant to order of Dr. Moore's superior. No one warned Tatiana of her peril. The plaintiffs claimed the defendant psychologists had a duty to warn foreseeable victims. Defendants denied owing any duty of reasonable care to Tatiana. The trial court sustained a demurrer to the complaint which was reversed on appeal. The Supreme Court of California concluded that the complaint could be amended to state a cause of action against the psychologists by asserting that they had or should have determined Poddar presented a serious danger to Tatiana, pursuant to the standards of their profession, but had failed to exercise reasonable care for her safety.

In *Tarasoff*, the defendant psychologists had first-hand knowledge of Poddar's homicidal intention and knew it to be directed towards Tatiana Tarasoff, who was wholly unaware of her danger. The knowledge of the defendants in *Tarasoff* was gained from statements made to them in the course of treatment and not from statements transmitted by others. Further, the California court in *Tarasoff* did not establish a new duty to warn, but only held that psychologists must exercise such reasonable skill, knowledge, and care possessed and exercised by members of their profession under similar circumstances.

In the instant case Michael Hawkins' potential victims, his mother and sister, knew he might be dangerous and that he had been released from confinement, contrary to Tatiana Tarasoff's ignorance of any risk of harm. Thus, no duty befell Sanders to warn Frances Hawkins of a risk of which she was already fully cognizant. Further, it must not be overlooked that Sanders received no information that Hawkins planned to assault anyone, only that he was mentally ill and likely to be dangerous to himself and others. That Sanders received no information directly from Michael Hawkins is the final distinction between the two cases.

The common law duty to volunteer information about a client to a court considering pretrial release must be limited to situations where information gained convinces counsel that his client intends to commit a crime or inflict injury upon unknowing third persons. Such a duty cannot be extended to the facts before us.

In view of our disposition of this case, we do not reach the question of respondent Sanders' claimed immunity from civil liability.

The decision of the superior court granting summary judgment dismissing the respondents as party defendants is affirmed.

———

Hawkins' Malpractice Claim

Do the Model Rules or the Model Code permit a lawyer to disclose information concerning Hawkins' mental state? Why does the court not discuss DR 4–101(C)(3), in effect in Washington at the time? Does M.R. 1.14 or EC 7–12 help resolve the disclosure question?

Should lawyer Sanders have deferred to the views of Hawkins' mother and psychiatrist concerning his dangerousness? Should he have relied on his own intuitions and observations based on his interview with Hawkins? Two groups of lawyers—criminal defense lawyers and matrimonial lawyers—report that client threats of violence occur quite frequently. Moreover, the threat is often directed at the lawyer herself. A 1997 survey of family lawyers, for example, reported that 64 percent say that they have been threatened with or actually have been the victims of violence, either by their own clients or by those of opposing counsel.[17]

The court points out that no questions on Hawkins' mental state were posed to Sanders in the bail hearing. Would Sanders have had a duty to answer such questions honestly? See M.R. 3.3. If Sanders had lied to or misled the court in response to questions at the bail hearing, would the result on the malpractice claim have been different?

A *Tarasoff* Duty for Lawyers?

Should the law impose civil liability on lawyers who fail to warn of a client's intent to endanger others? If so, what should be the scope of such a duty?

The *Hawkins* court would require lawyers to "volunteer information . . . to the court considering pretrial release where information gained convinces counsel that his client intends to commit a crime or inflict injury upon [specific and] *unknowing* third persons." The court apparently would impose such a duty only in cases of threatened physical injury. Should the court similarly require a lawyer to warn victims of a client's intended fraudulent schemes? Is physical injury so different?

Tarasoff v. Regents of University of California,[18] discussed in *Hawkins*, is the leading case on a psychiatrist's duty to warn or otherwise protect others from patients whom a doctor knows or should know are dangerous. Although often referred to as a case establishing a duty to "warn," *Tarasoff* did not limit the duty described therein to warning:

> The discharge of this duty may require the therapist to take one or more of various steps, depending upon the nature of the case. Thus it

---

17. See Mark Hansen, Lawyers in Harm's Way, ABA J. 93 (March 1998).

18. 551 P.2d 334, 340 (Cal.1976).

may call for him to warn the intended victim or others likely to apprise the victim of the danger, to notify the police, or to take whatever other steps are reasonably necessary under the circumstances.[19]

Does *Hawkins* intimate a duty on the lawyer's part to do anything other than to volunteer information?[20]

Tort law generally accepts the principle that an affirmative duty to act to protect others may be imposed on a person in a special relationship with either a dangerous person or the dangerous person's victim.[21] The doctor-patient relationship, as evidenced by *Tarasoff*, exemplifies such a special relationship. Numerous cases since *Tarasoff* have recognized the liability of psychiatrists and psychologists either for failure to warn of a client's intent to harm others or for failure to take other appropriate steps.[22]

Recall the facts of Spaulding v. Zimmerman, printed in Chapter 1 at p. 5. If David Spaulding had died a year after the settlement, should Zimmerman have been civilly liable for not disclosing the aneurysm to David or the court? Should Zimmerman's lawyers also have been liable for consequences flowing from nondisclosure?

Subsequent California cases to *Tarasoff*, generally followed in other states, limit the therapist's liability to specific identifiable victims on the theory that the scope of potential liability for professionals would be too broad if not so limited.[23] Recall the economic justification for such a limit given in *Greycas*, p. 79 above. Why doesn't Hawkins himself fall into the protected category? His mother?[24]

What standard of knowledge should trigger a duty to warn? Subjective or objective? If objective, should the standard be that the lawyer possessed information that would "convince a reasonable lawyer"? That would "cause a reasonable lawyer to believe"? Do such distinctions matter?

As of early 1999, the authors remain unaware of any decision holding a lawyer civilly liable for damages for failure to warn a victim of the client's intended dangerous conduct. The ALI, in considering a lawyer's civil

---

19. 551 P.2d at 340.

20. See Vanessa Merton, Confidentiality and the "Dangerous" Patient: Implications of Tarasoff for Psychiatrists and Lawyers, 31 Emory L.J. 263 (1982).

21. The special relationship doctrine is a limited exception to the basic principle that tort law does not impose upon one person a duty to prevent another person from harming a third person. See Restatement (Second) of Torts § 314. The Restatement does not define a "special relationship," but § 314A provides examples.

22. See, e.g., Naidu v. Laird, 539 A.2d 1064 (Sup.Ct.Del.1988). The current conflict in this area involves state liability for releasing dangerous parolees or improperly supervising probationers. See, e.g., Division

of Corrections v. Neakok, 721 P.2d 1121 (Alaska 1986).

23. Thompson v. County of Alameda, 614 P.2d 728 (Cal.1980); Brady v. Hopper, 751 F.2d 329 (10th Cir.1984) (suit by James Brady, President Reagan's press secretary, against John Hinckley's psychiatrist). But see Schuster v. Altenberg, 424 N.W.2d 159 (Wis.1988) (under Wisconsin tort law, psychiatrists' duty to warn or protect third parties not limited to cases where victim is readily identifiable).

24. See Jablonski by Pahls v. United States, 712 F.2d 391 (9th Cir.1983) (psychological profile indicating violence against women close to patient sufficiently "targeted").

liability to third persons, explicitly rejected a proposed subparagraph of Restatement § 73 which would have endorsed a *Tarasoff* duty when disclosure was necessary "to prevent the client from committing a crime imminently threatening to cause death or serious bodily injury to an identifiable person who is unaware of the risk and the lawyer's act has facilitated the crime," such as assisting the client in a release from custody. Given the narrowness of that proposed exception to confidentiality, are you surprised it was defeated? Translate the exception into English that a non-lawyer can understand, complete with an illustrating example.[25] (Translating law-talk into normal English is a skill worth developing.) Tell a few non-lawyers that lawyers rejected that duty. What is their reaction?

There is a paradoxical relationship between the ABA view of confidentiality and the courts' view of when liability of a lawyer to a non-client is appropriate. Rule 1.6(b) permits disclosure to protect third-party interests only when the lawyer becomes aware that the client intends to kill or assault a third person. Yet in that situation the courts have refused to impose civil liability. On the other hand, the ABA version of Rule 1.6(b) does not permit a lawyer to take action to prevent a client's criminal fraud on a third person. Yet this is the situation in which many courts find a lawyer civilly liable to a non-client for failing to take action. How can this incongruence between ethical duty and civil liability be explained?

Why Impose a Duty on Therapists and Not Others?

Why impose liability on therapists for failing to warn others about their dangerous clients and not impose similar liability on lawyers and other professionals with special access to a dangerous client's intent? Some therapists deny that they are able to predict dangerousness with any reliability.[26] Does the fact that mental health professionals (and probation boards) routinely make judgments about dangerousness, e.g., in civil commitment hearings, provide a reason for assuming they can predict dangerousness for purposes of tort liability?[27]

---

25. A vivid example is provided by In re Goebel, 703 N.E.2d 1045 (Ind.1998), in which a lawyer was reprimanded for giving, under physical threat, an indicted client information of another firm client suggesting her address, which was then used by the criminal client to track down and kill the second client's husband, who was a prosecution witness against him. The lawyer could have revealed his client's threat to himself and the witness to authorities and to the witness under Indiana's version of M.R. 1.6(b) Instead, he provided under duress a letter to the second client that had been returned marked "No Such Street." The information on the letter, however, permitted the criminal client to find and kill the witness. Should the lawyer be liable on a *Tarasoff* theory for the victim's wrongful death?

26. See Task Force Report, Clinical Aspects of the Violent Individual (American Psychiatric Assn. 1974) at 28 (claiming that psychiatrists are no better than anyone else at predicting dangerousness). But see Daniel J. Givelber et al., *Tarasoff*, Myth and Reality: An Empirical Study of Private Law in Action, 1984 Wis.L.Rev. 443, 456–67 ("The task of assessing dangerousness is not viewed [by those therapists surveyed] as being beyond the competence of individual therapists or as a matter upon which therapists cannot agree.").

27. A prominent psychiatrist believes that psychiatrist-patient confidentiality is subject to more exceptions than that of other

Unlike mental health professionals and probation boards, lawyers are not in the business of predicting dangerousness. Lawyers also believe they have limited capacity to make such predictions. Another argument advanced in favor of distinguishing lawyers from therapists and state correction authorities involves control: Probation boards, at least, may be in a better position than lawyers to control the conduct of a potential tortfeasor. Do therapists also exercise or possess greater control over their patients than lawyers over their clients?[28]

Two studies following *Tarasoff* have found that psychotherapists regard a duty to protect third parties from violent patients as consistent with their ethical obligations.[29] Consider this in light of the medical profession's general confidentiality provision, reprinted below. Another study has found that, contrary to predictions, *Tarasoff* has neither discouraged therapists from treating dangerous patients nor apparently increased the use of involuntary commitment for those patients viewed as dangerous.[30] Do these latter findings suggest that psychotherapists already operate under a self-imposed duty to warn, based on their ethical obligations, and that the *Tarasoff* situation may have been unusual?

Confidentiality Obligations of Physicians

The American Medical Association's provision dealing with confidentiality reads:

> The information disclosed to a physician during the course of the relationship between physician and patient is confidential to the greatest possible degree.... The patient should be able to make [full] disclosure with the knowledge that the physician will respect the confidential communications or information without the express consent of the patient, unless required to do so by law.

> The obligation to safeguard patient confidences is subject to certain exceptions, which are ethically and legally justified because of overriding social considerations. Where a patient threatens to inflict serious bodily harm to another person or to himself or herself and there is a reasonable probability that the patient may carry out the threat, the physician should take reasonable precautions for the protection of the intended victim, including notification of law enforcement authorities. Also, communicable diseases, gunshot wounds, and knife

professional relationships because "psychiatrists have extensive civil authority, e.g., in circumstances involving abortions, personal injury suits, commitment procedures, and not-guilty-by-reason-of-insanity pleas." Dr. Eric A. Plaut, A Perspective on Client Confidentiality, 131 Am.J.Psych. 1021, 1022 (1974). What implications does this have for lawyer confidentiality?

28. See Davis v. Lhim, 124 Mich.App. 291, 335 N.W.2d 481 (1983), which makes control over the patient a key to the psychiatrist's tort liability for subsequent harmful acts.

29. See Daniel J. Givelber et al., supra, 1984 Wis.L.Rev. at 473–76, 486; and Mills, Sullivan & Eth, Protecting Third Parties: A Decade After *Tarasoff*, 144 Am.J.Psych. 68, 69–70 (Jan.1987).

30. Givelber et al., supra.

wounds should be reported as required by applicable statutes or ordinances.[31]

How does this compare with the rules governing lawyers?

The American Medical Association's position on confidentiality of the results of HIV testing for the AID's virus is found in § 2.23:

> The confidentiality of the results of HIV testing must be maintained as much as possible and the limits of a patient's confidentiality should be known to the patient before consent is given.

> Exceptions to confidentiality are appropriate when necessary to protect the public health or when necessary to protect individuals, including health care workers, who are endangered by persons infected with HIV. If a physician knows that a seropositive individual is endangering a third party, the physician should, within the constraints of the law, (1) attempt to persuade the infected patient to cease endangering the third party; (2) if persuasion fails, notify authorities.[32]

Suppose the individual who has tested HIV-positive, worried about possible legal liability, consults a lawyer instead of a doctor, stating that he does not plan to communicate the information to his current sexual partner. Could or should the lawyer inform that person?

4. Underlying Policy Issues

The central issues in drafting exceptions to confidentiality[33] involve, first, defining the interests that justify a possible sacrifice of the client's interest in secrecy; second, determining whether the opportunity to disclose should be permissive or mandatory; third, determining whether limiting language concerning the actor, the victim, or the harm should be included; and fourth, deciding, in connection with client fraud situations, whether disclosure should be limited to prevention[34] and to situations in which the lawyer's services are or have been involved.[35]

---

31. Amer.Med.Ass'n Code of Medical Ethics § 5.05 (1996–97).

32. Id.

33. Portions of this note are adapted, with permission, from Roger C. Cramton & Lori P. Knowles, Professional Secrecy and Its Exceptions: *Spaulding v. Zimmerman* Revisited, 83 Minn.L.Rev. 63, 114–19 (1998) and Geoffrey C. Hazard, Jr., Rectification of Client Fraud: Death and Revival of a Professional Norm, 33 Emory L.J. 271 (1984). On lawyer confidentiality, see also Sissela Bok, Secrets, *passim* (1982); David Luban, Lawyers and Justice: An Ethical Study 177–233 (1984); and Deborah L. Rhode, Ethical Perspectives on Legal Practice, 37 Stan.L.Rev. 589, 612–17 (1985).

34. Prevention is better than after-the-fact rectification, since the intended fraud may simply be an ugly secret between client and lawyer. Interception after the fraud is under way, on the other hand, is likely to result in the client suffering sanctions on the basis of the lawyer's disclosure. There is an unavoidable tension, however, between the proposition that the lawyer should act early, to prevent the fraud, and the requirement that the lawyer should act only on the basis of solid information.

35. Contrast the situation in which representation involves a fraudulent transaction with the situation in which a lawyer, perhaps in defending tax deductions a client has taken, discovers that the client is receiving income from fraud practiced on a

The major argument against broadening exceptions to confidentiality is that clients will be deterred from confiding information to their lawyers.[36] The lack of candor on the part of clients, it is said, will make it difficult for a lawyer to give informed advice. The "sound advice" and "sound administration of justice" thought to result from this highly confidential relationship will not be achieved. Moreover, the fact that the lawyer may disclose client information may diminish client trust and adversely affect the quality of the relationship and the single-mindedness with which the lawyer pursues the client's interests. If and when the lawyer informs the client that disclosure is desirable or contemplated, a serious conflict arises between the lawyer and the client. The client feels betrayed and the relationship ends in bitterness.

The response to these arguments is several fold. First, the principal exceptions to both the professional duty and to the attorney-client privilege are longstanding and have not had the consequences that are feared. The self-defense and client-fraud exceptions involve situations that arise frequently. These historic exceptions have limited lawyer secrecy from the very beginning. There is no evidence that those broad exceptions have had undesirable effects on the candor with which clients communicate to lawyers. A modest broadening of the exceptions in situations that arise relatively rarely is unlikely to have any discernible effect.

A great deal of romanticism often surrounds discussion of "trust" and "candor" in the lawyer-client relationship. Studies indicate that mistrust and suspicion are frequently encountered in the relationship;[37] lawyers frequently state that clients are unwilling to reveal embarrassing or sensitive facts, which need to be dynamited out of them; and factors that restrict client willingness to confide operate in various practice contexts in powerful ways. In the criminal defense field, for example, both lawyer and client may be reluctant to discuss candidly facts relating directly to guilt, since doing so may limit the options available to defense counsel.

Second, arguments that candor will be discouraged by modest rule changes ignore the fact that both lawyers and clients appear to be relatively uninformed concerning the details of exceptions to either the attorney-client privilege or the professional duty of confidentiality and the relationship of the two doctrines to one another.[38] The available empirical evidence,

---

third party, such as embezzlement from an employer. The former situation, unlike the latter, may lead to charges against the lawyer. Moreover, the lawyer's more direct involvement in the client's wrongdoing heightens moral responsibility.

36. See, e.g., Monroe H. Freedman, Understanding Legal Ethics cc. 2, 4 (1990). Freedman's argument for nearly absolute confidentiality also relies on the special constitutional protections afforded criminal defendants.

37. See, e.g., Austin Sarat, Lawyers and Clients: Putting Professional Service on the Agenda of Legal Education, 41 J.Legal Educ. 43 (1991) (summarizing a study of lawyer-client relationship in matrimonial representation); and Robert A. Burt, Conflict and Trust Between Attorney and Client, 69 Geo.L.J. 1015 (1981) (arguing that trust in the relationship would be enhanced by expanding exceptions to confidentiality).

38. See Note, Functional Overlap between Lawyers and Other Professionals: Its Im-

albeit very limited, suggests that most lawyers and clients expect that confidentiality will be breached when important interests of third persons or courts would be impaired.[39] Nor is there any indication that clients are more candid with their lawyers in jurisdictions that have fewer exceptions to confidentiality than they are in jurisdictions with broader exceptions. It must be conceded that there is little solid empirical evidence to support firm conclusions in either direction. When severe harm is threatened that can be prevented by disclosure, the reality of that more certain harm should be preferred to dubious assumptions about effects on client candor.

What types of clients are likely to be informed enough about the details of exceptions to the attorney-client privilege, the work-product immunity and the professional duty of confidentiality so that this knowledge will influence their willingness to confide in a lawyer? This group of informed clients is largely confined to sophisticated repeat-players, usually substantial corporations, who want to use lawyer secrecy to reduce their costs of complying with legal and regulatory requirements. This client group has many advantages in litigation over those with less resources, experience and staying power.[40] The policy issues concerning expectations to confidentiality should be designed with the interests of the general public in mind and not those of narrower groups that have a special interest in a broad sphere of secrecy. The social value of secrecy versus disclosure is less when one is dealing, not with individual citizens encountering law for the first time, but with repeat-player, profit-making organizations that use secrecy to conceal or delay compliance with legal and regulatory requirements.[41]

Third, there is no evidence that exceptions to confidentiality have led

plications for the Privileged Communication Doctrine, 71 Yale L.J. 1226, 1232 (1962) (reporting empirical findings that lawyers are more likely than non-lawyers to believe that the privilege encourages client disclosures and that most non-lawyers are unaware of the privilege or erroneously assume that it extends to communications with a large number of other professionals as well).

39. See Fred C. Zacharias, Rethinking Confidentiality, 74 Iowa L.Rev. 351, 376–96 (1989) (this survey of New York lawyers' and clients' responses to various hypothetical situations found that neither lawyers nor clients were familiar with the details of attorney-client privilege or the professional duty of confidentiality; both lawyers and clients believed that disclosure was permissible in a number of situations, like that in *Spaulding*, in which ethics rules prohibit disclosure; and only a small percentage of clients felt that allowing such disclosure would make them less likely to use a lawyer's services).

40. See, e.g., Marc Galanter, Why the Haves Come Out Ahead, 9 Law & Soc'y Rev. 95 (1974).

41. Daniel Fischel argues that—

Confidentiality rules–the ethical duty of confidentiality, the attorney-client privilege, and the work-product doctrine–benefit lawyers but are of dubious value to clients and society as a whole. Absent some more compelling justification for their existence than has been advanced to date, these doctrines should be abolished.

Daniel R. Fischel, Lawyers and Confidentiality, U. Chicago L.Rev. 1, 33 (1998). We reject this extreme proposal. Nevertheless, Fischel's subordinate argument that confidentiality rules in the corporate context "either have no effect [on law observance] or decrease the level of legal compliance," id., at 28–32, has considerable force and supports our conclusion that broadened exceptions would be in the public interest.

or will lead to frequent whistle-blowing on the part of lawyers.[42] American lawyers are imbued with a professional ideology that gives dominant place to loyalty to client, treats confidentiality as a sacred trust, and abhors lawyer conduct that constitutes a betrayal of client. Lawyers know that harming a client to protect the superior interest of a third party will lead to the ending of the lawyer-client relationship, probable non-payment of fees, client bitterness and recrimination, and possible loss of repute with other lawyers and clients. Experience shows that lawyers are extraordinarily reluctant to risk these consequences. The exceptions to confidentiality should not be drafted so narrowly that this natural risk averseness is reinforced, with the result that loyalty to client, even a client who is abusing the lawyer's services to cause serious harm to third persons, always prevails over the superior interests of others.

Should exceptions to confidentiality be mandated by rule or left to a lawyer's discretion? The arguments for and against discretion are familiar. A blanket command provides more explicit guidance and, if followed by those to whom it is directed, will lead to more uniform and predictable responses. A clear duty helps avoid the problem of a client being subjected, without advance disclosure, to differing responses and risks dependent upon the judgment or conscience of individual lawyers. On the other hand, the situations that arise are often morally complex ones in which practical judgment is influenced by a variety of factors relating to context, personalities, circumstances and relationships. The clarity of the lawyer's knowledge concerning the likelihood of a client's proposed conduct and of its threatened consequences varies enormously from case to case. Wholly apart from the merits, discretionary proposals are more likely to commend themselves to lawyers who fear that mandatory disclosure will lead to civil liability for failure to disclose.[43] For these reasons, we prefer a discretionary approach, but recognize that a strong case can be made for mandating disclosure in some situations.

---

42. Despite the prevalence of whistle-blower statutes applying to state and federal employees, including lawyers, and to agents of government contractors, there are very few, if any, published reports of lawyers acting in this capacity.

43. Emerging case law indicates that a lawyer risks civil liability to a defrauded party if the lawyer makes false or misleading representations in facilitating a client transaction with a third person or if the lawyer learns of the client's fraud but takes no action other than silent withdrawal. It is ironic that in the situation in which all ethics codes provide for disclosure (criminal acts of a client that threaten another's life), there is no reported decision providing for civil liability of the lawyer for failure to disclose (but cf. the dictum in *Hawkins* supra), while in the client fraud situations liability is often imposed even though ABA Model Rule 1.6(b) and the ethics codes of perhaps ten states would prohibit a lawyer from disclosing.

CHAPTER 5

DUTY TO THE COURT

This chapter examines the advocate's special responsibilities to the court and how the legal norms governing the advocate differ from those governing the office lawyer. When a lawyer acts as an advocate rather than as a facilitator of transactions should she have different obligations when confronted with client fraud? Should the responsibilities of a criminal defense lawyer and a civil advocate be the same when the client or a witness proposes to testify falsely?

The civil and criminal law relating to the lawyer's liability for assisting transactional fraud was considered in Chapter 2. This body of law demonstrates that a lawyer who lies to a third party while facilitating a fraudulent transaction may be liable under civil or criminal law for fraud.[1] The lawyer who acts *recklessly* in handling a transaction may also be liable for *civil* fraud, and one who acts carelessly may be liable for negligent misrepresentation.[2]

These hard truths, however, are muddied by the uncertainty and incoherence of the ethics law dealing with prevention or rectification of client fraud. Transactional lawyers who rely on the black-letter text of Model Rule 1.6(b), for example, may be misled into believing that the lawyer's duties to client of loyalty and confidentiality override ordinary substantive fraud law and the law of prohibited assistance insofar as lawyers are concerned.

In studying the following materials, consider whether the tension apparent in transactional fraud between the state's law (the rules announced and enforced by the courts) and the profession's law and lore (the ethics codes and the profession's belief system) carries over to fraud on a tribunal. Does the lawyer as litigator have duties to client that permit action or inaction that impairs the integrity of adjudicatory process?

A. PERJURY

1. PERJURY IN CIVIL CASES

Lying under oath is a crime in every jurisdiction. It matters not whether the lie occurs in a civil or criminal trial or whether the witness lies

---

1. See, e.g., United States v. Benjamin, printed at p. 62 above.

2. See, e.g., Greycas v. Proud, printed at p. 79 above.

on the stand in court or during a sworn deposition.[3]

What should a lawyer do when her client lies under oath? Most discussions of this question begin by assuming that the lying client is a criminal defendant, not a witness in a civil matter, and proceed by insisting that the client might not be lying at all, emphasizing how difficult it is for a lawyer to *know* that the client is lying.

This is unfortunate because most lawyers confront the question of what to do about a lying client in the context of a civil proceeding, not a criminal trial. After all, relatively few lawyers try criminal cases. Thus, most lawyers confront the question of the perjurious client in a setting in which arguments based on constitutional concerns peculiar to criminal trials do not apply (the right to effective assistance of counsel, the defendant's privilege to refuse to testify and the corresponding right of a defendant to take the stand). Without the constitutional concerns attendant to criminal prosecutions or the drama of a client facing extended imprisonment or execution, the arguments in favor of lawyers assisting or passively acquiescing in client perjury lose much of their force.

Moreover, given how few civil cases ever get to trial, most lawyers confront the question of client perjury in the context of a civil deposition, not in the middle of a trial. In the deposition context it is unnecessary to worry about whether it is possible for a lawyer to correct perjurious testimony given on the stand without revealing to the fact-finder that the lawyer does not believe her own client on some matter. Any such revelation, according to some, might so unduly prejudice the finder of fact against the entirety of the client's case as to deprive the client of a fair trial. This concern evaporates once we imagine the false testimony is given outside the presence of the finder of fact, as is true in all depositions.

The second assumption common to discussions of client perjury, that the lawyer will generally be uncertain about whether what the client has said is a lie or not, may be true in many civil and criminal cases, but it is not always true. Sometimes, as in the next case, the lawyer knows, as surely as anyone can know anything, that what the client has said under oath is false. In that case, the lawyer knows because the client's testimony involves the lawyer's own conduct; in other cases the lawyer knows because the client has told her that the truth is otherwise[4] or because broad discovery has provided documents or other evidence that make it evident that the client's story is untrue. We begin then where many students will someday find themselves: representing a client whom they know to be lying in a civil deposition.

---

3. See, e.g., 18 U.S.C. § 1623 ("Whoever under oath in any proceeding before or *ancillary* to any court ... knowingly makes any false material declaration ...)(emphasis added); United States v. Moreno, 815 F.2d 725 (1st Cir.1987) (prosecution for false deposition testimony in a civil action).

4. See, e.g., In re Attorney Discipline Matter, 98 F.3d 1082 (8th Cir.1996) (court reporter inadvertently left her tape recording running during a break in the deposition documenting that the client told lawyer the truth and the lawyer told the client to "deny" it). See also In re Mack, 519 N.W.2d 900 (Minn.1994) .

Committee on Professional Ethics and Conduct of the Iowa State Bar Association v. William R. Crary

Supreme Court of Iowa, En Banc, 1976.
245 N.W.2d 298.

■ UHLENHOPP, JUSTICE.

This proceeding involves a determination of charges of unethical conduct on the part of an attorney, respondent William R. Crary. The record establishes the following by a convincing preponderance of the facts and circumstances in evidence . . . . .

Respondent [Crary] who was himself involved in litigation with his former wife over their children, became enamoured with Sue Evans Curtis, the wife of and mother of three children by Maury Wetzel Curtis. [Crary] . . . and Mrs. Curtis spent nights, weekends, and longer periods together, and engaged in sexual intercourse. . . . At the time, respondent and the Curtis family resided in Cedar Rapids, Iowa, about four blocks apart.

Unknown to respondent and Mrs. Curtis, Mr. Curtis employed private investigators to observe Mrs. Curtis.

About March 13, 1970, Mrs. Curtis told her husband she was going to Vail, Colorado, to stay at Tivoli Lodge. Instead, she went to respondent's home on that date and stayed with him until March 22.

On April 29, 1970, Mrs. Curtis commenced a suit against her husband, seeking a divorce, custody of their children, alimony, and child support. She alleged that she had conducted herself as a dutiful and loving wife. Her attorney was Mr. William O. Gray, assisted by respondent who was then Mr. Gray's associate. Mr. Gray was unaware at the time of the relationship between respondent and Mrs. Curtis.

. . .

On Wednesday, June 3, 1970, Mr. Justin W. Albright, attorney for Mr. Curtis in the divorce suit, commenced taking the discovery deposition of Mrs. Curtis at the office of Mr. Gray and respondent. In the course of this deposition in respondent's presence, Mrs. Curtis testified falsely regarding the period between March 13 and 22, 1970, when she was in respondent's home. Mrs. Curtis, respondent, and Mr. Albright knew the testimony was false, but Mrs. Curtis and respondent did not realize that Mr. Albright knew of the falsity. Mrs. Curtis did not assert the privilege against self-incrimination, but testified in part concerning the March 13 to 22 period:

Q. [by Mr. Albright] And as I understand it, you told Mr. Curtis that you were going to Vail, Colorado on this trip and that you were going to stay at the Tivoli Lodge, is that correct?

A. That's correct . . .

Q. Well, where did you go?

A. I went to Chicago. . . .

. . .

Q. And as I understand it then, you stayed all that period of time, from March 13th until March 22nd when you returned home, with Mrs. Richard Needham in Chicago, is that correct?

A. I did.

Q. Is that correct?

A. Yes.

. . .

Q. Who did you leave with . . . on the morning of Friday of March 13th [to get to the airport to go to Chicago?]

A. Mr. Crary. . . .

Q. And where did you go?

A. Downtown . . . [to the Roosevelt Hotel to get a cab.]

. . .

Q. And then he did not take you to the airport, is that correct?

A. Oh, no; heavens no.

. . .

At no time during this portion of the deposition did respondent request a recess or interrupt the perjury.

At 3:00 p.m. on June 3, 1970, the parties recessed the deposition until 1:00 p.m. on Friday, June 5, 1970. During that interim, respondent, knowing that Mrs. Curtis' Wednesday testimony was false, took no measure to correct it, to withdraw from the case as an attorney, to warn Mrs. Curtis she should lie no further, to inform Mr. Gray of the perjury, or to reveal the true situation to anyone.

The deposition resumed on June 5 with the same individuals present. At that time Mrs. Curtis testified falsely regarding the weekend of May 15 to 17, 1970, which she actually spent in Minneapolis with respondent. Again Mrs. Curtis, respondent, and Mr. Albright knew the testimony was false, but again Mrs. Curtis and respondent did not realize that Mr. Albright knew it was false—until later in the deposition. Mrs. Curtis testified in part:

Q. [by Mr. Albright] Well, did you go with anyone?

A. No.

Q. Well, just tell us where you went.

A. I went to Chicago to see Mrs. Needham . . .

Q. Well now, the second passenger who was right behind you was Mr. William R. Crary, was that correct, getting off this flight?

A. I have no idea who was getting off behind me. . . .

Q. Did you happen to see him on the plane on Ozark Flight No. 917?

A. Not that I recall. . . .

Q. And then at the bottom of the steps after you got off the plane, you were observed to meet with Mr. William R. Crary and walked together with him into the terminal, is that correct?

A. I don't remember....

. . .

Respondent did not seek to recess the deposition during this perjury or to hold Mrs. Curtis from falsely testifying.

As the deposition progressed, Mr. Albright's questions made evident that investigators had followed Mrs. Curtis and that Mr. Albright knew the truth. Respondent's testimony in later proceedings revealed what then happened at the Friday session of the deposition:

It became obvious, from the questions and the answers that I—or the questions that were being asked, that she had been followed by private detectives and that ... her husband at that time [Mr. Curtis] knew everything that she had done and where she had been and who she had seen.

Q. Was the deposition then adjourned?

A. Yes, it was. Actually what happened is that she became very shaken about the whole thing and asked to go to the ladies' room, and Bill Gray said, come on, let's go and find out about this. And he and I went into an office, and he said, is she lying about these things with you and with her? And I said, yeah, she is, and I was. And he said, we can't go on with this. She can't sit there and tell this story. And he said, what do you think we ought to do? And I said, I think we ought to recess the deposition, and we can't go on. I know we can't go on with it, no way. And so he went back into the office—or into the library, where we had been taking the deposition, and I gather adjourned it or recessed it or whatever.

Respondent later testified additionally:

Well, the deposition, as I said, terminated sometime in the middle or late Friday afternoon. Saturday morning I went back down, and, of course, our office was open Saturday morning, so everybody was there, and I discussed it with Bill Gray, ran through the thing with him, and he said, well, I think you better tell the other members of the firm what has happened. He said, obviously we have got a really sticky mess on our hands. And I said, obviously we do. And so I went around and told [the other members of the firm] ... what had occurred, that she had lied on her deposition and she had been seeing me and that I was sitting there in the deposition when she did it ...

Q. At that time had you formulated a plan as to what you should do, other than the fact that you were getting out of the case?

A. Well, what I should do with regard to her testimony?

Q. Right.

A. Well, the first thing that was necessary to do was to get her an attorney, because Bill said, I will not represent her any longer. I will have no part of it. You and I have to withdraw from the case, which we did.

Mrs. Curtis thereupon obtained other counsel, and in subsequent proceedings she testified that her testimony at the deposition was false.

. . .

... [T]he Committee on Professional Ethics and Conduct of The Iowa State Bar Association investigated the case and then filed a complaint against respondent before the Grievance Commission of this court. The Committee charged respondent with unethical conduct in connection with (1) the perjury incident, (2) the frustration of the custody decree [granted to Mrs. Curtis after her divorce], and (3) a combination of the first two. In the present proceeding we find no necessity to consider the third count.

The Third Division of the Commission heard the case and held regarding the perjury incident that respondent was relieved from reporting the perjury because of his privilege against self-incrimination and because the opposing party knew the testimony was false. The Commission held regarding the second count that respondent condoned Mrs. Curtis' acts in frustrating the decree. The Commission also held, "Respondent has committed certain acts of misconduct involving moral turpitude and placed himself where his silence or inaction could be misinterpreted as counseling violation of Court orders." The Commission reprimanded respondent.

The Commission accordingly made its report to this court and served the report on respondent, pursuant to our rules. Neither party took exceptions or an appeal.

Our preliminary examination of the report suggested possible disagreement with the Commission's decision. We therefore set the case for oral argument and invited briefs from the parties. We have now heard the parties orally and examined their briefs. The Committee argued before us that respondent should receive severer discipline, while respondent urged the contrary. We find that we cannot accept the Commission's findings, conclusions, and disposition.

. . .

II.   The Deposition Perjury.

. . .

What are the facts of the matter? Mr. and Mrs. Curtis were husband and wife, lived together, and had three children. Respondent began to see Mrs. Curtis and stayed with her at various places and slept with her—both before and after Mrs. Curtis commenced her divorce suit against Mr. Curtis.

After Mrs. Curtis commenced that suit, defense counsel in that case took her discovery deposition. Respondent, as associate of Mr. Gray, assisted with Mrs. Curtis' case. Respondent personally knew of Mrs. Curtis' misconduct, for he himself was her paramour. This was at a time when recrimination was a defense to divorce, and Mrs. Curtis' conduct would be in issue.... Moreover, the suit involved child custody, which in turn involved the spouses' conduct.... These are basic legal principles which a practicing attorney handling the divorce case would have in mind. But more than that, respondent had been personally involved in child custody litigation himself. He must have considered these legal principles; Mrs. Curtis faced a discovery deposition and respondent was himself sexually involved with her.

Yet in the present disciplinary proceeding, respondent testified:

Q. At the time of the deposition on June 3rd and 5th of 1970 and immediately prior to that, had you in any way discussed with Sue Crary what her testimony should be with reference to your association with her?

A. No. Didn't come up.

We do not believe this testimony that the matter did not come up.

Respondent also testified [that he just sat there when Mrs. Curtis was asked about the weekends that Crary knew she had spent with him. He testified that he had been surprised that she was asked about these weekends away from her husband:]

A. ... I had fully expected them to go into her background. She had been married for 17 years to Mr. Curtis, and obviously over 17 years many things happen, and I expected them to explore into their relationship and what was going on there. When they switched over into what she was doing two months after she filed for divorce and that sort of thing, it caught me by surprise, it caught her by surprise, I'm sure. At least she said it did afterwards. That seemed to be the tenor of the examination, as to what she was—done following the time she filed for divorce.

We do not believe this latter answer either.

Respondent contends, however, that the record contains no express testimony by him or Mrs. Curtis that he put her up to the false stories she related in the deposition. Yet those stories did not come out of thin air; they took some contriving. We doubt that Mrs. Curtis simply developed those stories about Mrs. Needham as the deposition progressed or that she developed them alone.

We think respondent was involved in the whole shameful episode, but we will accept arguendo his contention that he did not contrive the perjury with Mrs. Curtis. Then we have a situation in which respondent as an attorney at a deposition listened, his client started to lie under oath, he knew she was lying, and he just "sat there" and let her lie. More than that, the deposition recessed over Thursday, and respondent did nothing to stop Mrs. Curtis from lying some more. She resumed her lying on Friday and respondent still just sat there.

What is the law of this matter? We are not disposed to read §§ 610.14 (3) and 610.24(3)* of the Iowa Code in a narrow, technical, or legalistic manner. Assuming respondent did not know in advance that Mrs. Curtis was going to lie, his guilt was in failing to stop her or otherwise to call a halt when she started to lie.

Central to the administration of justice is the fact-finding process. Legislatures and courts can devise the finest rules of law, but if those rules are applied to false "facts," justice miscarries.

The attorney functions at the heart of the fact-finding process, both in trial and in pre-and post-trial proceedings. If he knowingly suffers a witness to lie, he undermines the integrity of the fact-finding system of which he himself is an integral part. Thus the fundamental rule is unquestioned that an attorney must not knowingly permit a witness to lie. In re Hardenbrook, 135 App. Div. 634, 121 N.Y.S. 250, affd. 199 N.Y. 539, 92 N.E. 1086, app. den. 144 A.D. 928, 129 N.Y.S. 1126 (disbarment where attorney learned after first day of trial that client lied, but nevertheless recalled client to testify on second day); In re Crary, 223 App. Div. 277, 228 N.Y.S. 340; In re Barach, 279 Pa. 89, 123 A. 727 (disbarment where attorney permitted witnesses to testify they were present at injury when he knew they were not present); 7 C.J.S. Attorney & Client § 23 at 753–754 ("There is no recognized rule of law or ethics which justifies the conduct of counsel in any case, civil or criminal, in endeavoring by dishonest means to mislead the court or jury, even if to do so might work to the advantage of his client, and such conduct will constitute a ground for suspension or disbarment.... An attorney may be suspended or disbarred for perverting, or attempting to pervert, a decision of a cause on the merits, by ... introducing evidence or allowing evidence to be given which he knows to be false or forged" ...).

But respondent contends he was not required to volunteer to opposing counsel or the court that Mrs. Curtis' testimony was false, since this could have provided evidence for building an adultery case against him. He cites authority that an attorney like others is privileged not to produce evidence which will incriminate him. Spevack v. Klein, 385 U.S. 511.

Respondent does not seem to grasp the point here. We do not place the decision on respondent's failure to inform opposing counsel or the court of the truth. In the present case no need really existed for this. Opposing counsel was not misled. His subsequent questions revealed he knew the facts; he made Mrs. Curtis' perjury patent. The vice of respondent's

---

* [Editors' Note:] Section 610.14 (3) of the Iowa Code stated:

It is the duty of an attorney and counselor: ... 3. To employ, for the purpose of maintaining the causes confided to him, such means only as are consistent with truth, and never to seek to mislead the judges by any artifice or false statement of fact or law.

Section 610.24 (3) provided:

The following are sufficient causes for revocation or suspension [of an attorney's license]: ... 3. A willful violation of any of the duties of an attorney or counselor as hereinbefore prescribed.

conduct was not in failing to reveal the truth but in participating in the corruption of the fact-finding system by knowingly permitting Mrs. Curtis to lie. Indeed if Mr. Curtis had not had private investigators, the falsity of this testimony might never have come to light; Mrs. Curtis' perjury, countenanced by respondent, might have subsequently carried the day in court. Contrast with respondent's conduct the acts of Mr. Gray. When that attorney suspected on Friday that Mrs. Curtis was lying he confronted respondent and upon learning the truth said, "She can't sit there and tell this story." He thereupon recessed the deposition.

Apart from self-incrimination, respondent contends that his duty to protect his client, Mrs. Curtis, conflicted with his duty to the justice system to divulge the falsity, and that he properly placed his duty to his client first. He bases this contention on the attorney-client privilege.

Respondent confuses the duty to divulge the truth after perjury is committed with the duty not to permit a witness to give false testimony in the first place. We will proceed on this contention, however, ... as though respondent's breach was in not divulging the truth to opposing counsel or the court after the false testimony was given. We address respondent's contention as he does under the attorney-client privilege and without reference to any other privilege.

The difficulty with respondent's contention is that it proceeds from a false premise. He cites the article entitled Perjury, The Lawyer's Trilemma, in Litigation (Winter 1975 Journ. of A.B.A. Litigation Section) [by Professor Monroe Freeman]. From this article, he concludes that a conflict between two duties exists: one to the client, the other to the justice system.

The flaw in respondent's reasoning is that no duty exists to the client when the client perjures himself to the knowledge of the attorney. Such conduct by the client falls outside the attorney-client relationship. When a prospective client approaches an attorney, he may expect that the attorney will assist him to the best of the attorney's ability. He may not expect, however, that the attorney will tolerate lying or any other species of fraud in the process. Prior to the present Code of Professional Responsibility, Canon 15 stated:

> Nothing operates more certainly to create or to foster popular prejudice against lawyers as a class and to deprive the profession of that full measure of public esteem and confidence which belongs to the proper discharge of its duties than does the false claim, often set up by the unscrupulous in defense of questionable transactions, that it is the duty of the lawyer to do whatever will enable him to succeed in winning a client's cause....

> The office of attorney does not permit, much less does it demand of him for any client, violation of law or any manner of fraud or chicane. He must obey his own conscience and not that of his client. Canons of Professional Ethics (A.B.A. 1957).

Correspondingly, the present rules state that "A lawyer shall not ... engage in conduct involving dishonesty, fraud, deceit, or misrepresentation," "engage in conduct that is prejudicial to the administration of justice," "participate in the creation or preservation of evidence when he knows or it is obvious that the evidence is false," or "counsel or assist his client in conduct that the lawyer knows to be illegal or fraudulent." Iowa Code of Professional Responsibility for Lawyers (1971) DR1–102 (A)(4) and (5), DR7–102(A)(6) and (7).

We hold that respondent acted unethically in knowingly permitting Mrs. Curtis to commit perjury on the first day of the deposition and to resume the perjury two days later, and that in so doing he violated §§ 610.14(3) and 610.24(3) of the Iowa Code.

. . .

[The court then discussed a lawyer's duty to observe a custody decree until it is set aside. Crary "acted unethically in proceeding in concert with Mrs. Curtis to nullify the custody decree" by luring the children away from Mr. Curtis' home and making them difficult to locate by taking them on trips out of state when they were supposed to return to Mr. Curtis' home.]

IV.   Discipline.

Reprimand is wholly inadequate discipline in this case. Respondent participated in the debasement of the fact-finding process and he took part in the overthrow of a decree of a court. His conduct was diametrically opposed to the fundamental duties of attorneys to bring truth rather than untruth to light and to uphold rather than bring down the judgments of courts.

The first requisite of an attorney is basic character. Uppermost in our minds is the question whether respondent possesses the character necessary to qualify him as an attorney.

We have placed in the balance all of the factors shown in evidence. After doing so, we conclude that respondent's license should be revoked, and we so order.

———

Ethics Rules on Presenting False Evidence

A lawyer who deliberately corrupts court process is subject to criminal prosecution and severe disciplinary sanctions. Unlike the ethics rules dealing with prevention or rectification of transactional fraud, the ethics rules concerning fraud on the court, particularly under the Model Rules, express a normative message similar to that expressed by the criminal and civil law.

Model Rule 3.3(a) specifies several situations in which the lawyer's duty of candor to the tribunal overrides the duty of confidentiality. The prohibition in M.R. 3.3(a)(1) against a lawyer making false statements to a court applies equally to oral and written statements[5] and the prohibition against submission of false evidence in M.R. 3.3(a)(4) applies equally to oral testimony and documentary evidence, as does the concomitant duty included in M.R.3.3(a)(4) for the lawyer to act upon discovery that evidence she thought was truthful when submitted is not. Notice that the duty to take "remedial" measures, when one discovers after the fact that false evidence has been offered, extends only to evidence that is "material." On the other hand, the duty to refrain from offering false evidence extends to all evidence, whether or not it is material.

Model Rule 3.3(b) makes explicit that the lawyer's duty of candor to the court, as detailed in M.R. 3.3(a), trumps the duty of confidentiality when the two conflict. The lawyer's duty to disclose that evidence she has offered is false is, however, limited to those instances in which the lawyer learns of the falsity "prior to the conclusion of the proceeding."[6] Should the duty extend further—until after the proceedings are over? Forever? How does Comment [13] justify the time limit? Is any statute of limitations justified?

Despite the time limit in M.R. 3.3(b), a lawyer has the discretion to disclose fraud she learns about after the proceedings are over, if disclosure is necessary to establish a defense against an accusation that the lawyer participated in the fraud, M.R. 1.6(b)(2). Comment [16] to M.R. 1.6 also provides that nothing in Rule 1.6 prevents a lawyer from withdrawing or disaffirming "any opinion, document, affirmation, or the like." Would this apply to a judgment or settlement procured by fraud?

M.R. 3.3(c) gives the lawyer discretion to refuse to offer evidence that the lawyer "reasonably believes is false." M.R. 3.3(d) requires the lawyer in an ex parte proceeding to inform the judge of "all material facts known to the lawyer" that, as Comment [15] explains, "the lawyer reasonably believes are necessary" for the judge to reach "an informed decision," "whether or not the facts are adverse."

In 1987, an ABA ethics opinion discussed the lawyer's duties under M.R. 3.3:

> If, prior to the conclusion of the proceedings, a lawyer learns that the client has given testimony the lawyer knows is false, and the lawyer cannot persuade the client to rectify the perjury, the lawyer must disclose the client's perjury to the tribunal, notwithstanding the fact that the information to be disclosed is information relating to the representation.

> If the lawyer learns that the client intends to testify falsely before a tribunal, the lawyer must advise the client against such course of action, informing the client of the consequences of giving false testimo-

---

5. People v. Bertagnolli, 861 P.2d 717 (Colo. 1993) (punishing lawyer for referring in closing argument to expert testimony that expert had asked lawyer to recant); Mississippi Bar v. Land, 653 So.2d 899 (Miss. 1994) (suspending lawyer for submitting false and deceptive answers to interrogatories).

6. See M.R. 3.3(b) and Comment [13] to 3.3.

ny including the lawyer's duty of disclosure to the tribunal. Ordinarily, the lawyer can reasonably believe that such advice will dissuade the client from giving false testimony and, therefore, may examine the client in the normal manner. However, if the lawyer knows, from the client's clearly stated intention, that the client will testify falsely, and the lawyer cannot effectively withdraw from the representation, the lawyer must either limit the examination of the client to subjects on which the lawyer believes the client will testify truthfully; or, if there are none, not permit the client to testify; or, if this is not feasible, disclose the client's intention to testify falsely to the tribunal.[7]

Why is the ABA's current position on fraud on a tribunal so different from that on fraud involving financial harm to third persons? Doesn't the absence in the transactional context of the safeguards of the adversary process—impartial judge, jury as fact finder and testing of evidence by the opposing party's lawyer—suggest that more protection rather than less should be accorded when these protections are not present?

Unlike the Model Rules, the Model Code treated fraud on third parties and fraud on the court as one problem, calling for one standard of conduct to be followed by the lawyer no matter whether the victim of the client's fraud was a court or a third party. Unfortunately, that is where the simplicity ends. In Chapter 4, we discussed how the 1974 amendment to DR 7–102(B)(1) tried to flip-flop the meaning of that rule as it applies to client fraud on third parties, see p. 284 supra; that discussion is equally applicable to DR 7–102(B)(1)'s treatment of client fraud on the court.

The ABA ethics opinions on fraud on the court, interpreting the Model Code provision, like the ethics opinions on fraud on third parties issued under the Code, conveyed mixed messages about the "right" approach to fraud on the court. Despite the language of DR 7–102(B)(1), i.e., "lawyer ... shall reveal ...", ABA ethics opinions took the position that when the lawyer learns of the client's false testimony after the fact, the lawyer may not disclose,[8] but has a duty to cease further representation of the client.[9] On the other hand, if the lawyer learned of the client's *intent* to commit perjury before the fact, the lawyer was required to advise the client that the lawyer would either withdraw prior to the submission of the false testimony, or report the client's intent to the tribunal, if the client made it plain her resolve to commit perjury was unshakeable.[10] See the note in Chapter 4 at p. 283.

The President's Lawyer's Disclosure to the Court

President Clinton's lawyer in the Paula Jones lawsuit, Robert Bennett, provided a very public example of a lawyer acting to notify a court that he had offered false evidence. During the President's deposition in that case,

---

7. ABA Comm. on Prof. Ethics Formal Op. 353 (1987).

8. See Informal Op. 1314 (1975) and Formal Op. 341 (1975).

9. See Formal Op. 287 (1953) (interpreting the Canons).

10. See ABA Informal Op. 1314 (1975).

Bennett had referred to an affidavit that Monica Lewinsky had submitted, which denied a sexual relationship with the President and falsely described the frequency and nature of her contacts with the President. In her later grand jury appearance, Lewinsky testified that the affidavit was false. On September 30, 1998, Bennett wrote the following letter to the federal judge presiding over the Jones lawsuit:

> Dear Judge Wright,
>
> As you are aware, Ms. Monica Lewinsky submitted an affidavit dated January 7, 1998 in the above-captioned case in support of her motion to quash the subpoena for her testimony. The affidavit was made part of the record of President Clinton's deposition on Jan. 17, 1998.
>
> It has recently been made public in the Starr Report that Ms. Lewinsky testified before a federal grand jury in August 1998 that portions of her affidavit were misleading and not true. Therefore, pursuant to our professional responsibility, we wanted to advise you that the court should not rely on Ms. Lewinsky's affidavit or remarks of counsel characterizing that affidavit.
>
> Very truly yours,
>
> Bob Bennett[11]

Throughout the impeachment proceedings one of President Clinton's defenses to charges that he committed perjury during the Jones deposition, suborned Lewinsky's perjury in the affidavit or obstructed justice by arranging for false testimony to be offered on his relationship with Lewinsky was that evidence on his relationship with Lewinsky was not material to the Jones lawsuit. As will be discussed later, this is a defense to a criminal charge of perjury, although it is not a defense to a criminal charge of obstruction of justice.[12] Does Bennett's letter undercut this claim by implicitly admitting that the affidavit is material? In following Rule 3.3(b), how should the lawyer assess what is material? One way to understand Bennett's letter is that he concluded that his duty to notify the court that evidence he offered was false extended to evidence a reasonable lawyer might view as material, not merely to evidence that the offering lawyer believed was material. Another possibility is that Bennett was not even conceding that a reasonable person could view the Lewinsky affidavit as material, but rather was disclosing the falsity of the affidavit to the court with his client's consent. Notice that his knowledge that the affidavit was false would be a confidence under Rule 1.6 whether or not that knowledge was communicated to him by his client or was known to half the civilized world, which is why we are assuming that he wrote the letter either under 3.3(b)'s exception to Rule 1.6 or pursuant to client consent.

---

11. New York Post, October 10, 1998 at 10.
12. See discussion infra at 353. Whether in an impeachment proceeding it should matter (and, if so, how much) that something is or is not recognized as a defense to a criminal charge is an open (and largely political) question, which is outside the scope of this book. We note it here merely for the sake of completeness.

Instead of disclosing too much information, did Bennett disclose too little? While the President claimed he had not committed perjury in the Jones deposition, White House Counsel Charles Ruff admitted before the House Judiciary Committee that reasonable people could conclude that the President had crossed the perjury line, although he maintained that the President had managed to tread on the edge of the line, while remaining in the lawful zone. Should Bennett's letter have disclosed to the court that some of the President's answers, such as his denial that he had been alone with Lewinsky, were not to be relied on by the court? What role, if any, should the fact that a prosecutor, Independent Counsel Kenneth Starr, was investigating Bennett's client, the President, for perjury and obstruction of justice have played in his decision to report to the Jones' court? Given that Bennett knew that the Independent Counsel was already investigating his client for perjury and obstruction of justice and that those allegations might lead to his client's impeachment and prosecution, is Bennett's letter a "reasonable remedial measure" for any false answers the President might have given as well as for having offered Lewinsky's affidavit? Reread Bennett's letter. Given what it communicates about the Lewinsky affidavit, is it not clear that it is putting the court on notice that some of the President's answers might very well be false too? Did Bennett manage to write the perfect letter, adequately notifying the court of the unreliability of certain evidence while doing as little damage to his client as possible?

Disciplining Lawyers Who Actively or Tacitly Participate in the Presentation of False Evidence

As the *Crary* case demonstrates, if it is discovered that a lawyer has sat silently by while her client or witness testified falsely, the discipline is likely to be severe. See also In re Mack[13] (indefinite suspension for lawyer who neither advised his client to correct false testimony, nor himself disclosed to the court or his adversary that the proffered testimony was untrue).

The court in *Crary* suspects, although it does not find, that the lawyer did more than sit passively by; it suspects that the lawyer helped create the false story told by the witness or at least encouraged her to offer the false testimony. In In re Attorney Discipline Matter, the court had conclusive proof that the lawyer encouraged the client to testify falsely.[14] In the middle of the trial of a divorce and custody case, a witness called by the husband's lawyer testified that the witness and the wife had had sex in front of the couple's young daughter. This testimony came as a complete surprise to the wife's lawyer who immediately requested a recess to confer with his client. The courtroom was cleared of all but the wife and her lawyer who proceeded to discuss the damaging testimony that had just been offered. However, unbeknownst to them or anyone else, the court reporter had inadvertently left the tape recorder running:

13. 519 N.W.2d 900 (Minn. 1994).   **14.** 98 F.3d 1082, 1084 (8th Cir. 1996).

Lawyer (L): ... What about this business about the [motel]? Did that happen?

Client (C): Yeah, it happened.

L: God-damn. What were you thinking about?

C: She was only three months—I mean 18 months. I couldn't leave him. I don't know. I don't know.

L: You better deny this. Eighteen months old, Jesus.

C: Well, she wasn't even 18 months in '86. She was a little bitty baby. She was still in diapers. ...In '85 she was about a year, but I wasn't seeing him in '86 because ... me and [my husband] still were talking, and I did see him then. [Non-sequitur in original.]

L: So that didn't happen in October of '86?

C: No, it wouldn't have been October.

L: You better deny this, buddy. You better deny it. ...

. . .

L: ... I think the thing that hurts you is taking the kid in the room and screwing with the kid in the room. ...You're going to have to do something with it.

C: What can I do with it that won't make it seem like I'm lying?

L: I don't know. That's up to you. It could be your word against his. It's up to you.

C: Are you saying if I deny it then—

L: If you said it didn't happen, it didn't happen.

. . .

L: Well, it's up to you. It's up to you. Well, you're telling the truth when you say it didn't happen in '86. Okay.

C: I don't remember it happening in '86, no.

The state of Illinois prosecuted this lawyer for suborning perjury, but he was acquitted—a matter we shall return to in a moment. Despite that acquittal, however, the Illinois Supreme Court suspended the lawyer from practice for two years; and the Missouri bar, to which the lawyer was also admitted, disbarred him. The United States District Court for the Eastern District of Missouri likewise disbarred the lawyer from practicing before it, and the Eighth Circuit affirmed that sanction as well as the sanction of the Missouri bar, which the lawyer had challenged on the ground that Missouri's disbarment order was somehow collaterally estopped by the lawyer's acquittal of criminal charges in Illinois.[15]

---

15. Under the Full Faith and Credit Clause, the Missouri court was required to give the Illinois acquittal only that effect that it would be given by an Illinois court. In Illinois, however, as everywhere else, "an acquittal in a criminal proceeding against an attorney will not act as a bar to subsequent disciplinary proceedings based upon

Because the attorney-client relationship is normally shielded from the observation of outsiders, transcripts of actual conversations between lawyers and clients are rare. There is, therefore, no reliable way to gauge whether the colloquy reprinted above is aberrational or representative of a common phenomenon. What is your guess?

While disciplinary sanctions against a lawyer who assists or passively acquiesces in a client's perjury are likely to be severe, demonstrating that the lawyer knew that the testimony proffered was false is often quite difficult, which makes the chance that discipline will be imposed relatively slim. Does the difficulty of "catching" lawyers in this misconduct argue for harsher discipline or more lenient treatment?

During his grand jury testimony, President Clinton was asked why he didn't correct his lawyer, Robert Bennett, when Bennett, presumably having been misled by his client into believing there was "no sex of any kind" between Lewinsky and the President, said as much to the judge. The President responded that clients were not normally responsible for monitoring what their lawyers said. Is that true? Later the President and his lawyers emphasized not his lack of responsibility for Bennett's innocent misrepresentations but the fact that, according to the President, he was not paying attention when Bennett made those representations. At the time of the deposition, President Clinton was a member of the Arkansas bar. If it is established through the videotape record and the testimony of those present at the deposition that the President was paying attention, what discipline, if any, should the Arkansas courts impose on him?[16]

Criminal Penalties for Presenting False Evidence[17]

Advising another to testify falsely is a crime.[18] The offense of subornation of perjury, see, e.g., 18 U.S.C. § 1621, requires that perjury actually have been committed, but a lawyer may be convicted of obstructing justice or conspiracy to obstruct justice for advising a client or witness to lie even if the perjurious testimony is never offered in court.[19] A lawyer may also be held criminally liable for submitting false documents on behalf of a client.[20]

---

substantially the same conduct." In re Attorney Discipline Matter, 98 F.3d at 1086 (citing, inter alia, In re Ettinger, 538 N.E.2d 1152, 1160 (Ill.1989)).

16. Cf. In Matter of Application of Charles M., 545 A.2d 7 (Md.1988) (denying bar admission to a person who as a layperson had lied in a deposition).

17. For a discussion of perjury, see Richard H. Underwood, False Witness: A Lawyer's History of the Law of Perjury, 10 Ariz. J. Int'l & Comp. L. 215 (1993); and Perjury! The Charges and the Defenses, 36 Duquesne L. Rev. 1 (1998).

18. See e.g., United States v. Vesich, 724 F.2d 451 (5th Cir.1984) (lawyer convicted of obstruction of justice, 18 U.S.C. § 1503, for advising a client to testify falsely before a grand jury).

19. See United States v. Silverman, 745 F.2d 1386 n. 7 at 1394 (11th Cir.1984) (citing cases).

20. For example, in United States v. Lopez, 728 F.2d 1359 (11th Cir.1984), a lawyer was convicted under 18 U.S.C. § 1001 for falsifying the dates on his client's application for permanent resident status. See also United States v. Vaughn, 797 F.2d 1485 (9th Cir.1986).

Any lie under oath may constitute perjury, as long as the lie was willful and about a matter material to the proceeding. Materiality is, however, viewed broadly and is assessed as of the time the statement was made. As to whether a particular statement was a lie and whether that lie was "willful," these elements generally are interpreted more stringently. The leading case under the federal perjury statute is Bronston v. United States.[21]

In *Bronston* the defendant's alleged perjury had occurred in a bankruptcy proceeding. When Bronston testified in the bankruptcy case, he was asked about Swiss bank accounts. At the time of his testimony, Bronston did not have a Swiss bank account, but he had once had one. He testified as follows:

Q. Do you have any bank accounts in Swiss banks, Mr. Bronston?

A. No, sir.

Q. Have you ever?

A. The company had an account there for about six months, in Zurich.

Q. Have you any nominees who have bank accounts in Swiss banks?

A. No, sir.

Q. Have you ever?

A. No, sir.

The Supreme Court reversed Bronston's conviction for perjury on the ground that his non-responsive answer to the second question was literally true, albeit misleading. The questioner should have listened more carefully and followed up. This result makes good sense when one considers that a nonresponsive answer is as likely to represent a witness's failure to understand the question (or appreciate precisely what is being asked) as it is to represent a willful intent to lie. Seen this way, the *Bronston* Court was merely stating that no reasonable jury could conclude beyond a reasonable doubt that a witness willfully intended to lie when the answer given was both nonresponsive and literally true. That is how the Sixth Circuit interpreted *Bronston* in United States v. DeZarn, a 1998 case upholding a perjury conviction based on materially misleading answers.[22]

Witness DeZarn had been interviewed under oath by federal investigators looking into allegations of political corruption. The investigation was focused on allegations that in 1990, a General Wellman had held a party at his home on the day the Preakness horse race was run. Allegedly, the main purpose of the party, according to the government, was to solicit campaign contributions from the guests who were later allegedly granted better treatment by army officials than the treatment afforded those who had not made contributions. The contributions were to support Lieutenant Governor Jones' run for the governorship; about 60 people attended the Preak-

21. 409 U.S. 352 (1973).   22. 157 F.3d 1042 (6th Cir.1998).

ness party, including the candidate Jones. All those contacted by the investigators were informed and apparently understood that the Preakness Party of 1990 was the subject of the inquiry. Moreover, the evidence showed that DeZarn helped planned the Preakness party as a fundraising event and accepted contributions for Jones from the guests.

During DeZarn's questioning, however, the interrogator messed up, referring to the Preakness party as if it had occurred in 1991 instead of 1990. In 1991, General Wellman had held a small dinner party at his home on the day the Belmont horse race was run. It had nothing to do with politics and candidate Jones was not present. DeZarn's perjury conviction was based on those facts and the following series of answers given by him under oath.

> Q: Okay, sir. My question is going to deal with General Wellman, though. Was it traditional for General Wellman to hold parties at his home and invite Guardsmen to attend?
>
> A: Well, I suppose you could say that for a number of years that going back to the late 50s he has done this on occasion.
>
> Q: Okay. In 1991, and I recognize this is in the period that you were retired, he held the Preakness Party at his home. Were you aware of that?
>
> A: Yes.
>
> Q: Did you attend?
>
> A: Yes.
>
>   . . .
>
> Q: Okay. Sir, was that a political fundraising activity?
>
> A: Absolutely not.
>
> Q: Okay. Did then Lieutenant Governor Jones, was he in attendance at the party?
>
> A: I knew he was invited. I don't remember if he made an appearance or not.
>
> Q: All right, sir. You said it was not a political fundraising activity. Were there any contributions to Governor Jones' campaign made at that activity?
>
> A: I don't know.
>
> Q: Okay. You did not see any, though?
>
> A: No.
>
> Q: And you were not aware of any?
>
> A: No.

The Sixth Circuit upheld DeZarn's conviction for perjury, stating that "a defendant may be found guilty of perjury if a jury could find beyond a reasonable doubt from the evidence presented that the defendant knew what the question meant and gave knowingly untruthful and materially misleading answers in response."[23]

The lawyer who was caught on tape advising his client to deny having committed adultery in front of her young child[24] (and who, as a consequence, lost his right to practice in Missouri's state and federal courts and was suspended from practice in Illinois) was prosecuted in Illinois for suborning perjury prior to being suspended and disbarred. After his "private" conversation with his client, the client took the stand. The lawyer began by asking her "Now, in 1986, what would possess him to tell that you went to a motel with him with your daughter?" The response: "I don't know." The testimony continued:

L: Do you ever—under oath now, do you ever remember going to a motel with your daughter with [the witness]?

C: No.

L: That's a lie, isn't it?

C: Yes.

L: What would possess him to tell that?

C: I don't know.

The lawyer was acquitted of the subornation charge. As to the October 1986 question and answer, the tape suggests that the answer might have been true. What about the subsequent testimony denying any memory of having gone to a motel with the daughter? Presumably the follow-up question and answer, about "that" being "a lie" were sufficiently ambiguous to justify acquitting the lawyer. The client might have been referring to her own previous answer and not the testimony of the male witness or the lawyer might have meant the question as a correction to the prior answer. Had the lawyer been convicted would the conviction have been upheld under *Dezarn*? Would you stake your freedom on that opinion?

False Evidence Offered by the Opposing Party

Under the Model Rules, the duty not to offer false evidence and the duty to remedy the introduction of false evidence by disclosure to the court is limited to the offering lawyer. Thus the Model Rules permit a lawyer to attack false testimony offered by the opposing lawyer through cross-examination, which preserves the strategic advantage that might otherwise be lost by advance disclosure to the tribunal.[25] However, once the proceedings lose their adversary character, as in a joint application to the court to

---

23. See also United States v. Robbins, 997 F.2d 390, 395 (8th Cir.), cert. denied, 510 U.S. 948 (1993) (upholding a perjury conviction, despite the fact the questioner had mangled the name of the company about which he was questioning the witness, making the witness's answers literally true as to the nonexistent company referred to by the questioner but nonetheless willful lies in that a jury could and did conclude beyond a reasonable doubt that the witness understood precisely to which company the questioner was referring).

24. See discussion infra at p. 350.

25. See e.g., Flynn v. Edmonds, 602 N.E.2d 880 (Ill.App.1992).

approve a settlement, both lawyers may have a duty to correct the false representations of the other party. That result makes sense whether one considers all evidence (and statements) made in a joint application as evidence that is *offered* by both lawyers or whether one analyzes the situation as an ex parte proceeding in which lawyers must disclose all material facts, even if adverse, to the court. See Model Rule 3.3(d).

In jurisdictions that maintain some version of the Model Code, the lawyer might be found to have a duty to inform the court that the opposing party has offered false evidence. DR 7–102(B)(2) requires lawyers to reveal "information clearly establishing" that one other than the client has perpetrated a fraud on the tribunal. Interpreting New York's version of that provision, the Second Circuit reversed the suspension of a lawyer who had failed to inform the trial court of his opponent's use of false evidence.[26] While the Second Circuit held that, at least in theory, a lawyer might be disciplined under DR 7–102 (B)(2) for such conduct, discipline could only be imposed when the lawyer had "actual knowledge" that the information was false—a mere belief or suspicion would not suffice. The opinion makes it clear that lawyers would rarely, if ever, be found to have "actual knowledge" of the falsity of their opponent's evidence. As the court put it: "The proper forum for resolving [whether an adverse witness lied] is not a collateral proceeding, but is the trial itself."[27] In other words, cross-examination is the way to approach this problem.

2.   PERJURY IN CRIMINAL CASES

Nix v. Whiteside

Supreme Court of the United States, 1986.
475 U.S. 157.

■ CHIEF JUSTICE BURGER delivered the opinion of the Court.

We granted certiorari to decide whether the Sixth Amendment right of a criminal defendant to assistance of counsel is violated when an attorney refuses to cooperate with the defendant in presenting perjured testimony at his trial.[1]

---

26. Doe v. Federal Grievance Committee, 847 F.2d 57 (2d Cir.1988).

27. Id. at 63.

1. Although courts universally condemn an attorney's assisting in presenting perjury, Courts of Appeals have taken varying approaches on how to deal with a client's insistence on presenting perjured testimony. The Seventh Circuit, for example, has held that an attorney's refusal to call the defendant as a witness did not render the conviction constitutionally infirm where the refusal to call the defendant was based on the attorney's belief that the defendant would commit perjury. United States v. Curtis, 742 F.2d 1070 (C.A.7 1984). The Third Circuit found a violation of the Sixth Amendment where the attorney could not state any basis for her belief that defendant's proposed alibi testimony was perjured. United States ex rel. Wilcox v. Johnson, 555 F.2d 115 (C.A.3 1977). See also Lowery v. Cardwell, 575 F.2d 727 (C.A.9 1978) (withdrawal request in the middle of a bench trial, immediately following defendant's testimony).

I

A

Whiteside was convicted of second degree murder by a jury verdict which was affirmed by the Iowa courts. The killing took place on February 8, 1977 in Cedar Rapids, Iowa. Whiteside and two others went to one Calvin Love's apartment late that night, seeking marihuana. Love was in bed when Whiteside and his companions arrived; an argument between Whiteside and Love over the marihuana ensued. At one point, Love directed his girlfriend to get his "piece," and at another point got up, then returned to his bed. According to Whiteside's testimony, Love then started to reach under his pillow and moved toward Whiteside. Whiteside stabbed Love in the chest, inflicting a fatal wound.

Whiteside was charged with murder, and when counsel was appointed he objected to the lawyer initially appointed, claiming that he felt uncomfortable with a lawyer who had formerly been a prosecutor. Gary L. Robinson was then appointed and immediately began investigation. Whiteside gave him a statement that he had stabbed Love as the latter "was pulling a pistol from underneath the pillow on the bed." Upon questioning by Robinson, however, Whiteside indicated that he had not actually seen a gun, but that he was convinced that Love had a gun. No pistol was found on the premises; shortly after the police search following the stabbing, which had revealed no weapon, the victim's family had removed all of the victim's possessions from the apartment. Robinson interviewed Whiteside's companions who were present during the stabbing and none had seen a gun during the incident. Robinson advised Whiteside that the existence of a gun was not necessary to establish the claim of self defense, and that only a reasonable belief that the victim had a gun nearby was necessary even though no gun was actually present.

Until shortly before trial, Whiteside consistently stated to Robinson that he had not actually seen a gun, but that he was convinced that Love had a gun in his hand. About a week before trial, during preparation for direct examination, Whiteside for the first time told Robinson and his associate Donna Paulsen that he had seen something "metallic" in Love's hand. When asked about this, Whiteside responded that

"in Howard Cook's case there was a gun. If I don't say I saw a gun I'm dead."

Robinson told Whiteside that such testimony would be perjury and repeated that it was not necessary to prove that a gun was available but only that Whiteside reasonably believed that he was in danger. On Whiteside's insisting that he would testify that he saw "something-metallic" Robinson told him, according to Robinson's testimony,

"we could not allow him to [testify falsely] because that would be perjury, and as officers of the court we would be suborning perjury if we allowed him to do it; ... I advised him that if he did do that it would be my duty to advise the Court of what he was doing and that I felt he was committing perjury; also, that I probably would be allowed to attempt to impeach that particular testimony."

Robinson also indicated he would seek to withdraw from the representation if Whiteside insisted on committing perjury.[2]

Whiteside testified in his own defense at trial and stated that he "knew" that Love had a gun and that he believed Love was reaching for a gun and he had acted swiftly in self defense. On cross examination, he admitted that he had not actually seen a gun in Love's hand. Robinson presented evidence that Love had been seen with a sawed-off shotgun on other occasions, that the police search of the apartment may have been careless, and that the victim's family had removed everything from the apartment shortly after the crime. Robinson presented this evidence to show a basis for Whiteside's asserted fear that Love had a gun.

The jury returned a verdict of second-degree murder and Whiteside moved for a new trial, claiming that he had been deprived of a fair trial by Robinson's admonitions not to state that he saw a gun or "something metallic." The trial court held a hearing, heard testimony by Whiteside and Robinson, and denied the motion. The trial court made specific findings that the facts were as related by Robinson.

The Supreme Court of Iowa affirmed respondent's conviction. State v. Whiteside, 272 N.W.2d 468 (1978). That court held that the right to have counsel present all appropriate defenses does not extend to using perjury, and that an attorney's duty to a client does not extend to assisting a client in committing perjury. Relying on DR 7–102(A)(4) of the Iowa Code of Professional Responsibility for Lawyers, which expressly prohibits an attorney from using perjured testimony, and Iowa Code § 721.2 (now Iowa Code § 720.3 (1985)), which criminalizes subornation of perjury, the Iowa court concluded that not only were Robinson's actions permissible, but were required. The court commended "both Mr. Robinson and Ms. Paulsen for the high ethical manner in which this matter was handled."

B

Whiteside then petitioned for a writ of habeas corpus in the United States District Court for the Southern District of Iowa. In that petition Whiteside alleged that he had been denied effective assistance of counsel and of his right to present a defense by Robinson's refusal to allow him to testify as he had proposed. The District Court denied the writ. Accepting the State trial court's factual finding that Whiteside's intended testimony would have been perjurious, it concluded that there could be no grounds for

---

2. Whiteside's version of the events at this pretrial meeting is considerably more cryptic:

"Q. And as you went over the questions, did the two of you come into conflict with regard to whether or not there was a weapon?

"A. I couldn't—I couldn't say a conflict. But I got the impression at one time that maybe if I didn't go along with—with what was happening, that it was no gun being involved, maybe that he will pull out of my trial."

habeas relief since there is no constitutional right to present a perjured defense.

The United States Court of Appeals for the Eighth Circuit reversed and directed that the writ of habeas corpus be granted. Whiteside v. Scurr, 744 F.2d 1323 (C.A.8 1984). The Court of Appeals accepted the findings of the trial judge, affirmed by the Iowa Supreme Court, that trial counsel believed with good cause that Whiteside would testify falsely and acknowledged that under Harris v. New York, 401 U.S. 222 (1971), a criminal defendant's privilege to testify in his own behalf does not include a right to commit perjury. Nevertheless, the court reasoned that an intent to commit perjury, communicated to counsel, does not alter a defendant's right to effective assistance of counsel and that Robinson's admonition to Whiteside that he would inform the court of Whiteside's perjury constituted a threat to violate the attorney's duty to preserve client confidences. According to the Court of Appeals, this threatened violation of client confidences breached the standards of effective representation set down in Strickland v. Washington, 466 U.S. 668 (1984). The court also concluded that *Strickland*'s prejudice requirement was satisfied by an implication of prejudice from the conflict between Robinson's duty of loyalty to his client and his ethical duties. A petition for rehearing en banc was denied. . . . We granted certiorari . . . and we reverse.

II

A

The right of an accused to testify in his defense is of relatively recent origin. Until the latter part of the preceding century, criminal defendants in this country, as at common law, were considered to be disqualified from giving sworn testimony at their own trial by reason of their interest as a party to the case. . . .

By the end of the nineteenth century, however, the disqualification was finally abolished by statute in most states and in the federal courts. . . . Although this Court has never explicitly held that a criminal defendant has a due process right to testify in his own behalf, cases in several Circuits have so held and the right has long been assumed. . . .

B

In *Strickland v. Washington*, we held that to obtain relief by way of federal habeas corpus on a claim of a deprivation of effective assistance of counsel under the Sixth Amendment, the movant must establish both serious attorney error and prejudice. . . .

In *Strickland*, we acknowledged that the Sixth Amendment does not require any particular response by counsel to a problem that may arise. Rather, the Sixth Amendment inquiry is into whether the attorney's conduct was "reasonably effective." A court reviewing a claim of ineffective assistance must "indulge a strong presumption that counsel's conduct falls within the wide range of reasonable professional assistance." In giving shape to the perimeters of this range of reasonable professional assistance, *Strickland* mandates that

> "Prevailing norms of practice as reflected in American Bar Association Standards and the like, ... are guides to determining what is reasonable, but they are only guides."

Under the *Strickland* standard, breach of an ethical standard does not necessarily make out a denial of the Sixth Amendment guarantee of assistance of counsel. When examining attorney conduct, a court must be careful not to narrow the wide range of conduct acceptable under the Sixth Amendment so restrictively as to constitutionalize particular standards of professional conduct and thereby intrude into the State's proper authority to define and apply the standards of professional conduct applicable to those it admits to practice in its courts. In some future case challenging attorney conduct in the course of a state court trial, we may need to define with greater precision the weight to be given to recognized canons of ethics, the standards established by the State in statutes or professional codes, and the Sixth Amendment, in defining the proper scope and limits on that conduct. Here we need not face that question, since virtually all of the sources speak with one voice.

C

We turn next to the question presented: the definition of the range of "reasonable professional" responses to a criminal defendant client who informs counsel that he will perjure himself on the stand. We must determine whether, in this setting, Robinson's conduct fell within the wide range of professional responses to threatened client perjury acceptable under the Sixth Amendment.

In *Strickland*, we recognized counsel's duty of loyalty and his "overarching duty to advocate the defendant's cause," Plainly, that duty is limited to legitimate, lawful conduct compatible with the very nature of a trial as a search for truth. Although counsel must take all reasonable lawful means to attain the objectives of the client, counsel is precluded from taking steps or in any way assisting the client in presenting false evidence or otherwise violating the law. This principle has consistently been recognized in most unequivocal terms by expositors of the norms of professional conduct since the first Canons of Professional Ethics were adopted by the American Bar Association in 1908. The 1908 Canon 32 provided that

> "No client, corporate or individual, however powerful, nor any cause, civil or political, however important, is entitled to receive nor should any lawyer render any service or advice involving disloyalty to the law whose ministers we are, or disrespect of the judicial office, which we are bound to uphold, or corruption of any person or persons exercising a public office or private trust, or deception or betrayal of the public.... He must ... observe and advise his client to observe the statute law...."

Of course, this Canon did no more than articulate centuries of accepted standards of conduct. Similarly, Canon 37, adopted in 1928, explicitly acknowledges as an exception to the attorney's duty of confidentiality a client's announced attention to commit a crime:

"The announced intention of a client to commit a crime is not included within the confidences which [the attorney] is bound to respect."

These principles have been carried through to contemporary codifications of an attorney's professional responsibility. Disciplinary Rule 7–102 of the Model Code of Professional Responsibility (1980), entitled "Representing a Client Within the Bounds of the Law," provides that

"(A) In his representation of a client, a lawyer shall not: . . .

"(4) Knowingly use perjured testimony or false evidence. . . .

"(7) Counsel or assist his client in conduct that the lawyer knows to be illegal or fraudulent."

This provision has been adopted by Iowa, and is binding on all lawyers who appear in its courts. See Iowa Code of Professional Responsibility for Lawyers (1985). The more recent Model Rules of Professional Conduct (1983) similarly admonish attorneys to obey all laws in the course of representing a client:

"*Rule 1.2* Scope of Representation

. . . "(d) A lawyer shall not counsel a client to engage, or assist a client, in conduct that the lawyer knows is criminal or fraudulent. . . ."

Both the Model Code . . . and the Model Rules . . . also adopt the specific exception from the attorney-client privilege for disclosure of perjury that his client intends to commit or has committed. DR 4–101(C)(3) (intention of client to commit a crime); Rule 3.3 (lawyer has duty to disclose falsity of evidence even if disclosure compromises client confidences). Indeed, both the Model Code and the Model Rules do not merely *authorize* disclosure by counsel of client perjury; they *require* such disclosure. See Rule 3.3(a)(4); DR 7–102(B)(1); Committee on Professional Ethics and Conduct of Iowa State Bar Association v. Crary, 245 N.W.2d 298 (Iowa 1976).

These standards confirm that the legal profession has accepted that an attorney's ethical duty to advance the interests of his client is limited by an equally solemn duty to comply with the law and standards of professional conduct; it specifically ensures that the client may not use false evidence. This special duty of an attorney to prevent and disclose frauds upon the court derives from the recognition that perjury is as much a crime as tampering with witnesses or jurors by way of promises and threats, and undermines the administration of justice.

The offense of perjury was a crime recognized at common law, and has been made a felony in most states by statute, including Iowa. An attorney who aids false testimony by questioning a witness when perjurious responses can be anticipated, risks prosecution for subornation of perjury under Iowa Code § 720.3 (1985).

It is universally agreed that at a minimum the attorney's first duty when confronted with a proposal for perjurious testimony is to attempt to dissuade the client from the unlawful course of conduct. Model Rules of Professional Conduct, Rule 3.3, Comment; Wolfram, Client Perjury, 50 S.Cal.L.Rev. 809, 846 (1977). A statement directly in point is found in the commentary to the Model Rules of Professional Conduct under the heading "False Evidence" [M.R. 3.3, Comment ¶ 5]:

> "When false evidence is offered by the client, however, a conflict may arise between the lawyer's duty to keep the client's revelations confidential and the duty of candor to the court. Upon ascertaining that material evidence is false, the lawyer *should seek to persuade the client that the evidence should not be offered* or, if it has been offered, that its false character should immediately be disclosed." (emphasis added).

The commentary thus also suggests that an attorney's revelation of his client's perjury to the court is a professionally responsible and acceptable response to the conduct of a client who has actually given perjured testimony. Similarly, the Model Rules and the commentary, as well as the Code of Professional Responsibility adopted in Iowa expressly permit withdrawal from representation as an appropriate response of an attorney when the client threatens to commit perjury. Model Rules of Professional Conduct, Rule 1.16(a)(1), Rule 1.6, Comment (1983); Code of Professional Responsibility, DR 2–110(B), (C) (1980). Withdrawal of counsel when this situation arises at trial gives rise to many difficult questions including possible mistrial and claims of double jeopardy.[6]

The essence of the brief *amicus* of the American Bar Association reviewing practices long accepted by ethical lawyers, is that under no circumstance may a lawyer either advocate or passively tolerate a client's

---

6. In the evolution of the contemporary standards promulgated by the American Bar Association, an early draft reflects a compromise suggesting that when the disclosure of intended perjury is made during the course of trial, when withdrawal of counsel would raise difficult questions of a mistrial holding, counsel had the option to let the defendant take the stand but decline to affirmatively assist the presentation of perjury by traditional direct examination. Instead, counsel would stand mute while the defendant undertook to present the false version in narrative form in his own words unaided by any direct examination. This conduct was thought to be a signal at least to the presiding judge that the attorney considered the testimony to be false and was seeking to disassociate himself from that course. Additionally, counsel would not be permitted to discuss the known false testimony in closing arguments. See ABA Standards for Criminal Justice, 4–7.7 (2d ed. 1980). Most courts treating the subject rejected this approach and insisted on a more rigorous standard, see, e.g., United States v. Curtis, 742 F.2d 1070 (C.A.7 1984); McKissick v. United States, 379 F.2d 754 (C.A.5 1967), aff'd after remand, 398 F.2d 342 (C.A.5 1968); Dodd v. Florida Bar, 118 So.2d 17, 19 (Fla. 1960). The Eighth Circuit in this case and the Ninth Circuit have expressed approval of the "free narrative" standards. Whiteside v. Scurr, 744 F.2d 1323, 1331 (C.A.8 1984); Lowery v. Cardwell, 575 F.2d 727 (C.A.9 1978).

The Rule finally promulgated in the current Model Rules of Professional Conduct rejects any participation or passive role whatever by counsel in allowing perjury to be presented without challenge.

giving false testimony. This, of course, is consistent with the governance of trial conduct in what we have long called "a search for truth." The suggestion sometimes made that "a lawyer must believe his client not judge him" in no sense means a lawyer can honorably be a party to or in any way give aid to presenting known perjury.

D

Considering Robinson's representation of respondent in light of these accepted norms of professional conduct, we discern no failure to adhere to reasonable professional standards that would in any sense make out a deprivation of the Sixth Amendment right to counsel. Whether Robinson's conduct is seen as a successful attempt to dissuade his client from committing the crime of perjury, or whether seen as a "threat" to withdraw from representation and disclose the illegal scheme, Robinson's representation of Whiteside falls well within accepted standards of professional conduct and the range of reasonable professional conduct acceptable under *Strickland*.

. . .

The Court of Appeals' holding that Robinson's "action deprived [Whiteside] of due process and effective assistance of counsel" is not supported by the record since Robinson's action, at most, deprived Whiteside of his contemplated perjury. Nothing counsel did in any way undermined Whiteside's claim that he believed the victim was reaching for a gun. Similarly, the record gives no support for holding that Robinson's action "also impermissibly compromised [Whiteside's] right to testify in his own defense by conditioning continued representation ... and confidentiality upon [Whiteside's] *restricted* testimony." The record in fact shows the contrary: (a) that Whiteside did testify, and (b) he was "restricted" or restrained only from testifying falsely and was aided by Robinson in developing the basis for the fear that Love was reaching for a gun. Robinson divulged no client communications until he was compelled to do so in response to Whiteside's post-trial challenge to the quality of his performance. We see this as a case in which the attorney successfully dissuaded the client from committing the crime of perjury.

Paradoxically, even while accepting the conclusion of the Iowa trial court that Whiteside's proposed testimony would have been a criminal act, the Court of Appeals held that Robinson's efforts to persuade Whiteside not to commit that crime were improper, *first*, as forcing an impermissible choice between the right to counsel and the right to testify; and *second*, as compromising client confidences because of Robinson's threat to disclose the contemplated perjury.

. . .

Whatever the scope of a constitutional right to testify, it is elementary that such a right does not extend to testifying *falsely*. In *Harris v. New York*, we assumed the right of an accused to testify "in his own defense, or to refuse to do so" and went on to hold that

"that privilege cannot be construed to include the right to commit perjury. See United States v. Knox, 396 U.S. 77 (1969); cf. Dennis v. United States, 384 U.S. 855 (1966). Having voluntarily taken the stand, petitioner was under an obligation to speak truthfully...." 401 U.S., at 225.

In *Harris* we held the defendant could be impeached by prior contrary statements which had been ruled inadmissible under Miranda v. Arizona, 384 U.S. 436 (1966). *Harris* and other cases make it crystal clear that there is no right whatever—constitutional or otherwise—for a defendant to use false evidence. See also United States v. Havens, 446 U.S. 620, 626–627 (1980).

The paucity of authority on the subject of any such "right" may be explained by the fact that such a notion has never been responsibly advanced; the right to counsel includes no right to have a lawyer who will cooperate with planned perjury. A lawyer who would so cooperate would be at risk of prosecution for suborning perjury, and disciplinary proceedings, including suspension or disbarment.

Robinson's admonitions to his client can in no sense be said to have forced respondent into an *impermissible* choice between his right to counsel and his right to testify as he proposed for there was no *permissible* choice to testify falsely. For defense counsel to take steps to persuade a criminal defendant to testify truthfully, or to withdraw, deprives the defendant of neither his right to counsel nor the right to testify truthfully....

On this record, the accused enjoyed continued representation within the bounds of reasonable professional conduct and did in fact exercise his right to testify; at most he was denied the right to have the assistance of counsel in the presentation of false testimony. Similarly, we can discern no breach of professional duty in Robinson's admonition to respondent that he would disclose respondent's perjury to the court. The crime of perjury in this setting is indistinguishable in substance from the crime of threatening or tampering with a witness or a juror. A defendant who informed his counsel that he was arranging to bribe or threaten witnesses or members of the jury would have no "right" to insist on counsel's assistance or silence. Counsel would not be limited to advising against that conduct. An attorney's duty of confidentiality, which totally covers the client's admission of guilt, does not extend to a client's announced plans to engage in future criminal conduct.... In short, the responsibility of an ethical lawyer, as an officer of the court and a key component of a system of justice, dedicated to a search for truth, is essentially the same whether the client announces an intention to bribe or threaten witnesses or jurors or to commit or procure perjury. No system of justice worthy of the name can tolerate a lesser standard.

The rule adopted by the Court of Appeals, which seemingly would require an attorney to remain silent while his client committed perjury, is wholly incompatible with the established standards of ethical conduct and the laws of Iowa and contrary to professional standards promulgated by that State. The position advocated by petitioner, on the contrary, is wholly consistent with the Iowa standards of professional conduct and law, with the overwhelming majority of courts,[8] and with codes of professional ethics. Since there has been no breach of any recognized professional duty, it follows that there can be no deprivation of the right to assistance of counsel under the *Strickland* standard.

E

We hold that, as a matter of law, counsel's conduct complained of here cannot establish the prejudice required for relief under the second strand of the *Strickland* inquiry. . . .

Whether he was persuaded or compelled to desist from perjury, Whiteside has no valid claim that confidence in the result of his trial has been diminished by his desisting from the contemplated perjury. Even if we were to assume that the jury might have believed his perjury, it does not follow that Whiteside was prejudiced.

In his attempt to evade the prejudice requirement of *Strickland*, Whiteside relies on cases involving conflicting loyalties of counsel. In Cuyler v. Sullivan, 446 U.S. 335 (1980), we held that a defendant could obtain relief without pointing to a specific prejudicial default on the part of his counsel, provided it is established that the attorney was "actively represent[ing] conflicting interests."

Here, there was indeed a "conflict," but of a quite different kind; it was one imposed on the attorney by the client's proposal to commit the crime of fabricating testimony without which, as he put it, "I'm dead." This is not remotely the kind of conflict of interests dealt with in *Cuyler v. Sullivan*. Even in that case we did not suggest that all multiple representations necessarily resulted in an active conflict rendering the representation constitutionally infirm. If a "conflict" between a client's proposal and counsel's ethical obligation gives rise to a presumption that counsel's assistance was prejudicially ineffective, every guilty criminal's conviction would be suspect if the defendant had sought to obtain an acquittal by illegal means. Can anyone doubt what practices and problems would be spawned by such a rule and what volumes of litigation it would generate?

Whiteside's attorney treated Whiteside's proposed perjury in accord with professional standards, and since Whiteside's truthful testimony could not have prejudiced the result of his trial, the Court of Appeals was in error to direct the issuance of a writ of habeas corpus and must be reversed.

■ JUSTICE BRENNAN, concurring in the judgment.

8. See United States v. Curtis, 742 F.2d 1070 (C.A.7 1984); Committee on Professional Ethics v. Crary, 245 N.W.2d 298 (Iowa 1976); State v. Robinson, 290 N.C. 56, 224 S.E.2d 174 (1976); Thornton v. United States, 357 A.2d 429 (D.C.1976); State v. Henderson, 205 Kan. 231, 468 P.2d 136 (1970); McKissick v. United States, 379 F.2d 754 (C.A.5 1967); In re King, 7 Utah 2d 258, 322 P.2d 1095 (1958); In re Carroll, 244 S.W.2d 474 (Ky.1951); Hinds v. State Bar, 19 Cal.2d 87, 119 P.2d 134 (1941). Contra, Whiteside v. Scurr, 744 F.2d 1323 (C.A.8 1984); Lowery v. Cardwell, 575 F.2d 727 (C.A.9 1978).

This Court has no constitutional authority to establish rules of ethical conduct for lawyers practicing in the state courts. Nor does the Court enjoy any statutory grant of jurisdiction over legal ethics.

Accordingly, it is not surprising that the Court emphasizes that it "must be careful not to narrow the wide range of professional conduct acceptable under the Sixth Amendment so restrictively as to constitutionalize particular standards of professional conduct and thereby intrude into the State's proper authority to define and apply the standards of professional conduct applicable to those it admits to practice in its courts." I read this as saying in another way that the Court *cannot* tell the states or the lawyers in the states how to behave in their courts, unless and until federal rights are violated.

Unfortunately, the Court seems unable to resist the temptation of sharing with the legal community its vision of ethical conduct. But let there be no mistake: the Court's essay regarding what constitutes the correct response to a criminal client's suggestion that he will perjure himself is pure discourse without force of law. As Justice Blackmun observes, *that* issue is a thorny one, but it is not an issue presented by this case. Lawyers, judges, bar associations, students and others should understand that the problem has not now been "decided."

I join Justice Blackmun's concurrence because I agree that respondent has failed to prove the kind of prejudice necessary to make out a claim under *Strickland*.

■ JUSTICE BLACKMUN, with whom JUSTICE BRENNAN, JUSTICE MARSHALL, and JUSTICE STEVENS join, concurring in the judgment.

How a defense attorney ought to act when faced with a client who intends to commit perjury at trial has long been a controversial issue.[1] But I do not believe that a federal habeas corpus case challenging a state criminal conviction is an appropriate vehicle for attempting to resolve this thorny problem. When a defendant argues that he was denied effective assistance of counsel because his lawyer dissuaded him from committing perjury, the only question properly presented to this Court is whether the lawyer's actions deprived the defendant of the fair trial which the Sixth Amendment is meant to guarantee. Since I believe that the respondent in this case suffered no injury justifying federal habeas relief, I concur in the Court's judgment.

·   ·   ·

1. See, e.g., Callan and David, Professional Responsibility and the Duty of Confidentiality: Disclosure of Client Misconduct in an Adversary System, 29 Rutgers L.Rev. 332 (1976); Rieger, Client Perjury: A Proposed Resolution of the Constitutional and Ethical Issues, 70 Minn.L.Rev. 121 (1985); compare, e.g., Freedman, Professional Responsibility of the Criminal Defense Lawyer: The Three Hardest Questions, 64 Mich.L.Rev. 1469 (1966), and ABA Standards for Criminal Justice, Proposed Standard 4–7.7 (2d ed. 1980) (approved by the Standing Committing on Association Standards for Criminal Justice, but not yet submitted to the House of Delegates), with Noonan, The Purposes of Advocacy and the Limits of Confidentiality, 64 Mich.L.Rev. 1485 (1966), and ABA Model Rules of Professional Conduct, Rule 3.3 and comment, at 66–67 (1983).

B

The Court approaches this case as if the performance and prejudice standard requires us in every case to determine "the perimeters of [the] range of reasonable professional assistance," but Strickland v. Washington explicitly contemplates [that "a court need not determine whether counsel's performance was deficient before examining the prejudice suffered by the defendant as a result of the alleged deficiencies...."]

... In this case, respondent has failed to show any legally cognizable prejudice. Nor, as is discussed below, is this a case in which prejudice should be presumed.

The touchstone of a claim of prejudice is an allegation that counsel's behavior did something "to deprive the defendant of a fair trial, a trial whose result is reliable." *Strickland....* The only effect Robinson's threat had on Whiteside's trial is that Whiteside did not testify, falsely, that he saw a gun in Love's hand.[4] Thus, this Court must ask whether its confidence in the outcome of Whiteside's trial is in any way undermined by the knowledge that he refrained from presenting false testimony.

... [T]he Court has viewed a defendant's use of [perjured] testimony as so antithetical to our system of justice that it has permitted the prosecution to introduce otherwise inadmissible evidence to combat it.... The proposition that presenting false evidence could contribute to (or that withholding such evidence could detract from) the reliability of a criminal trial is simply untenable.

... [T]he privilege every criminal defendant has to testify in his own defense "cannot be construed to include the right to commit perjury." Harris v. New York, 401 U.S., at 225. To the extent that Whiteside's claim rests on the assertion that he would have been acquitted had he been able to testify falsely, Whiteside claims a right the law simply does not recognize. "A defendant has no entitlement to the luck of a lawless decisionmaker, even if a lawless decision cannot be reviewed." *Strickland....* Since Whiteside was deprived of neither a fair trial nor any of the specific constitutional rights designed to guarantee a fair trial, he has suffered no prejudice.

The Court of Appeals erred in concluding that prejudice should have been presumed. Strickland v. Washington found such a presumption appropriate in a case where an attorney labored under " 'an actual conflict of interest [that] adversely affected his ... performance,' ".... In this case, however, no actual conflict existed. I have already discussed why Whiteside had no right to Robinson's help in presenting perjured testimony. Moreover, Whiteside has identified no right to insist that Robinson keep confidential a plan to commit perjury.... Here, Whiteside had no legitimate

---

4. This is not to say that a lawyer's threat to reveal his client's confidences may never have other effects on a defendant's trial. Cf. United States ex rel. Wilcox v. Johnson, 555 F.2d 115 (C.A.3 1977) (finding a violation of Sixth Amendment when an attorney's threat to reveal client's purported perjury caused defendant not to take the stand at all).

interest that conflicted with Robinson's obligations not to suborn perjury and to adhere to the Iowa Code of Professional Responsibility.

In addition, the lawyer's interest in not presenting perjured testimony was entirely consistent with Whiteside's best interest. If Whiteside had lied on the stand, he would have risked a future perjury prosecution. Moreover, his testimony would have been contradicted by the testimony of other eyewitnesses and by the fact that no gun was ever found. In light of that impeachment, the jury might have concluded that Whiteside lied as well about his lack of premeditation and thus might have convicted him of first-degree murder. And if the judge believed that Whiteside had lied, he could have taken Whiteside's perjury into account in setting the sentence. *United States v. Grayson,* 438 U.S. 41, 52–54 (1978). In the face of these dangers, an attorney could reasonably conclude that dissuading his client from committing perjury was in the client's best interest and comported with standards of professional responsibility.[7] In short, Whiteside failed to show the kind of conflict that poses a danger to the values of zealous and loyal representation embodied in the Sixth Amendment. A presumption of prejudice is therefore unwarranted.

C

In light of respondent's failure to show any cognizable prejudice, I see no need to "grade counsel's performance." *Strickland . . . .* The only federal issue in this case is whether Robinson's behavior deprived Whiteside of the effective assistance of counsel; it is not whether Robinson's behavior conformed to any particular code of legal ethics.

Whether an attorney's response to what he sees as a client's plan to commit perjury violates a defendant's Sixth Amendment rights may depend on many factors: how certain the attorney is that the proposed testimony is false, the stage of the proceedings at which the attorney discovers the plan, or the ways in which the attorney may be able to dissuade his client, to name just three. The complex interaction of factors, which is likely to vary from case to case, makes inappropriate a blanket rule that defense attorneys must reveal, or threaten to reveal, a client's anticipated perjury to the court. Except in the rarest of cases, attorneys who adopt "the role of the judge or jury to determine the facts," *United States ex rel. Wilcox v. Johnson,* 555 F.2d 115, 122 (C.A.3 1977), pose a danger of depriving their clients of the zealous and loyal advocacy required by the Sixth Amendment.[8]

---

7. This is not to say that an attorney's ethical obligations will never conflict with a defendant's right to effective assistance. For example, an attorney who has previously represented one of the State's witnesses has a continuing obligation to that former client not to reveal confidential information received during the course of the prior representation. That continuing duty could conflict with his obligation to his present client, the defendant, to cross-examine the State's witnesses zealously. See Lowenthal, Successive Representation by Criminal Lawyers, 93 Yale L.J. 1 (1983).

8. A comparison of this case with Wilcox is illustrative. Here, Robinson testified in detail to the factors that led him to conclude that respondent's assertion he had seen a gun was false. The Iowa Supreme Court

I therefore am troubled by the Court's implicit adoption of a set of standards of professional responsibility for attorneys in state criminal proceedings. The States, of course, do have a compelling interest in the integrity of their criminal trials that can justify regulating the length to which an attorney may go in seeking his client's acquittal. But the American Bar Association's implicit suggestion in its brief *amicus curiae* that the Court find that the Association's Model Rules of Professional Conduct should govern an attorney's responsibilities is addressed to the wrong audience. It is for the States to decide how attorneys should conduct themselves in state criminal proceedings, and this Court's responsibility extends only to ensuring that the restrictions a State enacts do not infringe a defendant's federal constitutional rights. Thus, I would follow the suggestion made in the joint brief *amici curiae* filed by 37 States at the certiorari stage that we allow the States to maintain their "differing approaches" to a complex ethical question. The signal merit of asking first whether a defendant has shown any adverse prejudicial effect before inquiring into his attorney's performance is that it avoids unnecessary federal interference in a State's regulation of its bar. Because I conclude that the respondent in this case failed to show such an effect, I join the Court's judgment that he is not entitled to federal habeas relief.

■ JUSTICE STEVENS, concurring in the judgment.

Justice Holmes taught us that a word is but the skin of a living thought. A "fact" may also have a life of its own. From the perspective of an appellate judge, after a case has been tried and the evidence has been sifted by another judge, a particular fact may be as clear and certain as a piece of crystal or a small diamond. A trial lawyer, however, must often deal with mixtures of sand and clay. Even a pebble that seems clear enough at first glance may take on a different hue in a handful of gravel.

As we view this case, it appears perfectly clear that respondent intended to commit perjury, that his lawyer knew it, and that the lawyer had a duty—both to the court and to his client, for perjured testimony can ruin an otherwise meritorious case—to take extreme measures to prevent the perjury from occurring. The lawyer was successful and, from our unanimous and remote perspective, it is now pellucidly clear that the client suffered no "legally cognizable prejudice."

Nevertheless, beneath the surface of this case there are areas of uncertainty that cannot be resolved today. A lawyer's certainty that a change in his client's recollection is a harbinger of intended perjury—as

found "good cause" and "strong support" for Robinson's conclusion. State v. Whiteside, 272 N.W.2d at 471. Moreover, Robinson gave credence to those parts of Whiteside's account which, although he found them implausible and unsubstantiated, were not clearly false. By contrast, in *Wilcox*, where defense counsel actually informed the judge that she believed her client intended to lie and where her threat to withdraw in the middle of the trial led the defendant not to take the stand at all, the Court of Appeals found "no evidence on the record of this case indicating that Mr. Wilcox intended to perjure himself," and characterized counsel's beliefs as "private conjectures about the guilt or innocence of [her] client." 522 F.2d at 122.

well as judicial review of such apparent certainty—should be tempered by the realization that, after reflection, the most honest witness may recall (or sincerely believe he recalls) details that he previously overlooked. Similarly, the post-trial review of a lawyer's pre-trial threat to expose perjury that had not yet been committed—and, indeed, may have been prevented by the threat—is by no means the same as review of the way in which such a threat may actually have been carried out. Thus, one can be convinced—as I am—that this lawyer's actions were a proper way to provide his client with effective representation without confronting the much more difficult questions of what a lawyer must, should, or may do after his client has given testimony that the lawyer does not believe. The answer to such questions may well be colored by the particular circumstances attending the actual event and its aftermath.

Because Justice Blackmun has preserved such questions for another day, and because I do not understand him to imply any adverse criticism of this lawyer's representation of his client, I join his opinion concurring in the judgment.

"Court Truth" and "Real Truth"

Did Whiteside see a metallic object in the victim's hand? How do we "know" what he did or didn't see? How did Robinson, Whiteside's lawyer, know that his client intended to perjure himself? How does the Court in *Whiteside* conclude that the testimony would have been perjurious? Justice Stevens' concurrence concentrates on the difficulty of being sure that a client intends to commit perjury. How can Justice Stevens be sure that Whiteside did not "after reflection ... sincerely believe" that he saw a metallic object?

What is the relationship between "court truth" and "real truth?" Although there were questions from the bench in *Whiteside* on how a lawyer is to "know" that the client intends to commit perjury, the opinions did not resolve the question of how certain a lawyer must be before acting on her judgment that the client will perjure herself.[1]

Model Rule 3.3(c) gives the lawyer discretion to refuse to offer evidence that she *reasonably believes* is false. In exercising this discretion, the lawyer is not permitted to reveal client confidences. Only when the lawyer "knows" that the evidence is false does the duty in 3.3(a)(4) override the obligations of confidentiality, see M.R. 3.3(b). The Terminology Section states that "Knowingly ... or Knows denotes actual knowledge," but adds that "a person's knowledge may be inferred from circumstances." ABA Formal Op. 353 (1987) emphasizes that M.R. 3.3's obligation to disclose

---

1. See Monroe H. Freedman, Client Confidences and Client Perjury: Some Unanswered Questions, 136 U.Pa.L.Rev. 1939 (1988); and Brent Appel, The Limited Impact of Nix v. Whiteside on Attorney–Client Relations, 136 U.Pa.L.Rev. 1913 (1988) (both describing the oral argument in *Whiteside*).

client perjury "is strictly limited" to situations when the lawyer "knows" the testimony offered was false. "[O]rdinarily [this knowledge will be] based on admissions the client has made to the lawyer. The lawyer's suspicions are not enough." Should the lawyer in a criminal case have to "know" with more certainty before acting to prevent or rectify client perjury than a lawyer in a civil case?

Judge Frankel has written that "[T]he sharp eye of the cynical lawyer becomes at strategic moments a demurely averted and filmy gaze," leaving him "unfettered by clear prohibitions that actual 'knowledge of the truth' might expose."[2] Does the "actual knowledge" standard include things the lawyer "should have known"? In *United States v. Benjamin*, printed in Chapter 2 at p. 62, the Second Circuit imposed criminal liability when a professional "deliberately closes his eyes to facts he has a duty to see." Can a lawyer avoid the responsibilities of M.R. 3.3 by deliberately closing her eyes?[3]

St. Thomas Aquinas said concerning a confession to a priest:

Whatever the priest knows through confession he, in a sense, does not know, because he possesses this knowledge not as man, but as the representative of God. He may, therefore, without qualms of conscience, swear to his ignorance in court, because the obligation of a witness extends only to his human knowledge.[4]

At trial a lawyer acts in the fact finder's presence, and is expected to act, as if she were incapable of knowing that her client is guilty. Should this expectation of willful blindness be extended to whether offered testimony is perjurious?

After being reversed in *Whiteside*, the Eighth Circuit decided United States v. Long.[5] In *Long*, the criminal defense lawyer told the trial judge, out of the presence of the jury, that his client wanted to testify but that the lawyer was "concerned about his testimony." In camera, the lawyer reiterated his concern "about the testimony that may come out." The judge informed the defendant that he had a right to testify but that his lawyer had an obligation not to offer evidence "which he believed to be untrue." Although the judge stated that the defendant could take the stand and offer a narrative statement without questioning from his lawyer, the defendant did not testify.

2. Marvin E. Frankel, The Search for Truth: An Umpireal View, 123 U.Pa.L.Rev. 1031, 1039 (1975).

3. Consider ABA Formal Op. 353 n. 9 (1988), which states:

The Committee notes that some trial lawyers report that they have avoided the ethical dilemma posed by Rule 3.3 because they follow a practice of not questioning the client about the facts in the case and, therefore, never "know" that a client has given false testimony.

Lawyers who engage in such practice may be violating their duties under Rule 3.3 and their obligation to provide competent representation under Rule 1.1. ABA Defense Function Standards 4–3.2(a) and (b) are also applicable.

4. Kurtscheid, A History of the Seal of Confession 194–95 (F.A. Marks, transl., 1927).

5. 857 F.2d 436 (8th Cir.1988), cert. denied, 502 U.S. 828 (1991).

The Eighth Circuit, reversing the conviction, distinguished *Long* from *Whiteside* in three respects, each of which required an evidentiary hearing. First, in this case, unlike *Whiteside,* the basis for the lawyer's belief that his client would perjure himself was unknown. Second, because the defendant did not testify, the court could not determine whether the lawyer's actions prevented his client from testifying *truthfully.* Third, in *Long* but not in *Whiteside* the lawyer "reveal[ed] his belief about his client's anticipated testimony to the trial court." The court stated that "a clear expression of intent to commit perjury is required before an attorney can reveal client confidences."[6]

The Eighth Circuit considered two procedural mechanisms that might be used in criminal cases to resolve whether a client's proposed testimony would be perjurious: (1) a hearing held by a judge other than the one presiding at trial, in which the defendant would get the benefit of the reasonable-doubt standard of proof;[7] and (2) establishment of a board of attorneys to decide the issue.[8] The Eighth Circuit implied, but did not hold, that some such safeguards might be constitutionally required.[9] Are there problems with implementing either of these solutions?

Government Use of Perjured Testimony to Obtain a Conviction

If the government knowingly uses perjured testimony to secure a conviction, the defendant is entitled to a new trial if "the false testimony could ... in any reasonable likelihood have affected the judgment of the jury...."[10] Even the government's *unwitting* use of perjured testimony violates due process if truthful testimony would "most likely change the outcome of the trial."[11]

What Should a Criminal Defense Lawyer Do?

What are the holdings in *Whiteside?* One holding, in which all nine justices concur, concerns the prejudice prong of the *Strickland* test; the other holding, in which five justices join, concerns the lawyer-performance aspect of that test. Is Justice Brennan correct in stating, in his concurrence, that "the Court's essay regarding what constitutes the correct response to a criminal client's suggestion that he will perjure himself is

---

6. 857 F.2d at 445 (quoting from the Eighth Circuit opinion in *Whiteside*).

7. See Carol T. Rieger, Client Perjury: A Proposed Resolution of the Constitutional and Ethical Issues, 70 Minn.L.Rev. 121, 153 (1985).

8. See William H. Erickson, The Perjurious Defendant: A Proposed Solution to Defense Lawyer's Conflicting Ethical Obligations to the Court and to His Client, 59 Den.L.J. 75, 88 (1981).

9. 857 F.2d at 446–47 and n. 10. But see Jackson v. United States, 928 F.2d 245 (8th Cir.1991) (unless lawyer had no basis for

believing client would commit perjury, informing the court of that belief to alert it to possible need of lawyer to withdraw did not violate criminal defendant's rights).

10. Giglio v. United States, 405 U.S. 150, 154 (1972) (quoting Napue v. Illinois, 360 U.S. 264, 271 (1959)). See also Avery v. Procunier, 750 F.2d 444 (5th Cir.1985); United States v. Jones, 730 F.2d 593 (10th Cir.1984).

11. Sanders v. Sullivan, 863 F.2d 218 (2d Cir.1988).

pure discourse without force of law?" Chief Justice Burger's statement that "both the Model Code and the Model Rules do not merely *authorize* disclosure by counsel of client perjury; they *require* such disclosure" has been severely criticized.[12] Who has the better of this debate, Burger or his critics?

Whiteside itself does not say what a criminal defense lawyer *must* do when faced with client perjury in a criminal case. It merely states what a lawyer *may* do, in conformity with the state's ethical standards, without unconstitutionally violating the defendant's rights.

When the client accedes to the lawyer's decision not to testify falsely, either before the trial as in *Whiteside* or during the trial, the courts have had little difficulty rejecting claims of interference with the right to counsel or to testify.[13] But what if the lawyer is initially unsuccessful in convincing the client not to testify falsely and some form of disclosure to the judge ensues? What is the judge supposed to do then?

In *Wilcox*,[14] decided before *Whiteside,* the lawyer believed that the defendant's proposed alibi testimony would be perjurious, and she informed the judge. The court ruled that, if the client insisted on testifying, it would permit counsel to withdraw and the defendant would have to proceed without counsel for the remainder of the trial. The defendant then agreed not to testify. The Third Circuit held that the trial judge's ruling, threatening a loss of counsel, violated the defendant's right to counsel and his right to testify.[15]

In Lowery v. Cardwell[16] the defense lawyer was surprised during his client's testimony in a bench trial by what he was convinced was perjury. The lawyer immediately requested permission to withdraw. The lawyer offered no reason for his request and the judge sought none, but refused the request. The Ninth Circuit held that the lawyer's motion to withdraw was tantamount to an announcement to the trier of fact that his client had lied and thereby deprived the client of a fair trial. The court suggested that

12. See Carl A. Auerbach, What Are Law Clerks For?: Comments on Nix v. Whiteside, 23 San Diego L.Rev. 979, 982–87 (1986) (arguing that the statement is inaccurate and rests on an "unsupported dictum in a civil, not a criminal case"—the Crary case discussed supra); and Monroe H. Freedman, The Aftermath of Nix v. Whiteside: Slamming the Lid on Pandora's Box, 23 Crim.L.Bull. 25, 26–27 (1987) (discussing the "manifest errors" in Chief Justice Burger's opinion).

13. For example, in United States v. Rantz, 862 F.2d 808 (10th Cir.1988), the court found that the lawyer's belief that the testimony would be false and ultimately detrimental to the defense was an adequate basis for the lawyer's refusal to call the defendant. The lawyer's belief was based on the overwhelming evidence offered by the prosecution, showing that the defendant was the initiator of the conspiracy.

14. United States ex rel. Wilcox v. Johnson, 555 F.2d 115 (3d Cir.1977).

15. The lawyer's behavior was criticized on two grounds. First, the lawyer requested to withdraw only if the defendant insisted on testifying. If there was an obligation to withdraw because of suspected future perjury, it applied whether or not the defendant continued to insist on testifying. Second, without a "firm factual basis" for her belief that the client intended to perjure himself, it was improper to disclose the intended perjury to the court.

16. 575 F.2d 727 (9th Cir.1978).

the lawyer could fulfill his obligation not to offer false evidence by letting the defendant testify in a narrative style without questioning from counsel.

> While a knowledgeable judge or juror, alert to the ethical problems faced by attorneys ... might infer perjury from [this procedure], counsel's belief [that the testimony was perjury] would not appear in the clear and unequivocal manner presented by the facts here.... The distinction we draw is between a passive refusal to lend aid to perjury and such direct action as we find here—the addressing of the court in pursuit of court order granting leave to withdraw.[17]

Is this a realistic distinction? *Whiteside* suggests that disclosure to the court in some circumstances is appropriate, but in *Whiteside* the court was not the fact-finder.[18]

Is a lawyer's request to withdraw essentially the same as informing the court of the lawyer's suspicions? May defense counsel in a criminal case seek to withdraw (or threaten to withdraw) only upon a "firm factual basis" for her belief that the client will commit perjury?[19]

The Narrative Approach

The narrative solution endorsed in *Lowery* was proposed by the ABA's Criminal Justice Section in its draft of the ABA Standards of Criminal Justice. Defense Function Standard 4–7.7 provided that if the lawyer could not dissuade the defendant from committing perjury, the lawyer should have the defendant tell her story in a narrative without further questioning by counsel. Before putting the client on the stand, the lawyer was supposed to make a private record of the fact that the defendant was taking the stand against the lawyer's advice. Under this Standard, the lawyer was prohibited from arguing the defendant's false version of the facts to the jury.

The ABA now firmly rejects the narrative approach.[20] ABA Formal Opinion 353 (1987), interpreting the Model Rules, states: "[T]he lawyer can no longer rely on the narrative approach to insulate the lawyer from a charge of assisting the client's perjury." The narrative approach, however, is embodied in the ethics rules in the District of Columbia[21] and is endorsed

---

17.   575 F.2d at 731.

18.   Compare Butler v. United States, 414 A.2d 844 (D.C.App.1980) (recusal of judge required where trial judge, sitting as trier of fact, learns from defense counsel that defendant plans to commit perjury). See also Garrett v. United States, 642 A.2d 1312 (D.C.App.1994) (lawyer's statement that "if ... [client] ... take[s] the stand, there would be problems with me continuing his representation," did not amount to an unequivocal declaration that client would commit perjury and thus judge did not have to recuse himself).

19.   See M.R. 1.16(a)(1) requiring withdrawal if a violation of the rules or other law will result; and M.R. 1.16(b)(1) permitting withdrawal if the lawyer reasonably believes the client's proposed course of action is criminal or fraudulent. See also M.R. 3.3(a)(4) and (c).

20.   Standard 4–7.7 was omitted from the second edition of the Standards in 1979 and the "narrative" solution was rejected by the Model Rules for reasons stated in Comments [8]-[10] to M.R. 3.3.

21.   The version of M.R. 3.3 adopted in the District of Columbia is similar to Standard 4–7.7. See D.C. Rule 3.3(b). Unlike M.R.

in some case law.[22] The narrative approach may have more acceptance in actual practice than in formal recognition.

After *Whiteside*, the Supreme Court recognized the constitutional right of a criminal defendant to testify, but repeated the *Whiteside* statement that this does not include the right to testify falsely.[23] Given the defendant's right to testify, what else can the trial court do, when informed by the defense counsel that she believes the defendant will lie, except let the defendant testify after proper warnings? The only question then would be whether the court should permit a narrative statement or order defense counsel to question the witness in the regular fashion.[24]

The Continuing Debate on Client Perjury in Criminal Trials

While commentators have argued extensively about whether a criminal defense lawyer who is convinced that her client intends to commit perjury, should act decisively in an effort to prevent that from happening,[25] the courts have been clear that the lawyer must do something. The cases are unanimous in requiring the lawyer at least to remonstrate with the client and to withdraw if the client insists on perjuring herself.[26] No court opinion

3.3, a D.C. lawyer may not disclose fraud on the tribunal if disclosure would reveal confidential client information protected by Rule 1.6.

22. See e.g., People v. Gadson, 24 Cal. Rptr.2d 219 (Cal.App.1993) (approving use of narrative testimony by defendant and two witnesses); Pennsylvania v. Jermyn, 652 A.2d 821 (Pa.1995) (defendant not denied effective assistance of counsel when lawyer had him testify by narrative without asking questions). People v. Guzman, 755 P.2d 917 (Cal.1988), held that the narrative approach was neither inconsistent with the defendant's rights nor apparently a violation of the lawyer's duty to refrain from offering false evidence. In *Guzman* defense counsel informed the court, outside the jury's presence, that the defendant would testify against his advice and would use the narrative approach. The court advised the defendant to follow the lawyer's advice and not testify, but, when the defendant insisted, permitted the defendant to testify in narrative format. Lead counsel made no mention of this testimony. The court found no violation of defendant's constitutional rights.

23. Rock v. Arkansas, 483 U.S. 44 (1987).

24. See United States v. Henkel, 799 F.2d 369 (7th Cir.1986) (lawyer moved to withdraw just before defendant's testimony; trial judge correctly understood this to

mean counsel believed the defendant would commit perjury; the court offered the defendant the chance to testify through a narrative statement without assistance of counsel, which the client declined; held: no violation of defendant's rights because no right to have counsel's assistance to testify falsely).

25. The following contributions to the debate are noteworthy: John T. Noonan, Jr., The Purpose of Advocacy and the Limits of Confidentiality, 64 Mich.L.Rev. 1485 (1966); Marvin E. Frankel, The Search for Truth: An Umpireal View, 123 U.Pa.L.Rev. 1031 (1975); Norman Lefstein, The Criminal Defendant Who Proposes Perjury: Rethinking the Defense Lawyer's Dilemma, 6 Hofstra L.Rev. 665 (1978); Wayne D. Brazil, Unanticipated Client Perjury and the Collision of Rules of Ethics, Evidence, and Constitutional Law, 44 Mo.L.Rev. 601 (1979); Charles W. Wolfram, Client Perjury, 50 S.Cal.L.Rev. 809 (1977); Monroe H. Freedman, Understanding Lawyers' Ethics (1990); Jay Sterling Silver, Truth, Justice and the American Way: The Case Against Client Perjury Rules, 47 Vand. L. Rev. 339 (1994); Marvin E. Frankel, Clients' Perjury and Lawyers' Options, 1 J. Inst. for Study Legal Ethics 25 (1996).

26. See, e.g., *Crary*, printed supra at p. 339, and *Long*, discussed supra at p. 371.

suggests that it is proper for a lawyer to act as if testimony that she knows to be false is true. While a few cases, and a number of commentators, suggest that remonstration and withdrawal are a lawyer's only duties,[27] the majority of courts state, as the majority of the Justices in *Whiteside* did, that at some point a lawyer has a duty to disclose client perjury so as to avoid assisting fraud on the tribunal.[28]

Nonetheless, a debate that was ignited over 30 years ago by Monroe Freedman rages on. In 1966, Freedman published an article entitled "Professional Responsibility of the Criminal Defense Lawyer: The Three Hardest Questions."[29] One of the three questions was whether it was right to suggest through questions posed on cross-examination that a witness the lawyer knew to be telling the truth was not. The two remaining "hardest" questions involved perjury: Is it proper for a criminal defense lawyer to put a witness on the stand who the lawyer knows will commit perjury? Is it proper to give the defendant legal advice that the lawyer believes will tempt the client to commit perjury? Freedman answered each of theses questions in the affirmative—a position he continues to advocate today[30] and one, we dare say, that is embraced by many trial lawyers. His initial assertion, however, caused a firestorm. Warren E. Burger, then a court of appeals judge, pushed for Freedman to be disciplined by the D.C. Bar for having advocated such views.

Monroe H. Freedman "Perjury: The Lawyer's Trilemma"

1 Litigation 26 (No. 1, Winter 1975).[31]

Is it ever proper for a lawyer to present perjured testimony?

One's instinctive response is in the negative. On analysis, however, it becomes apparent that the question is exceedingly perplexing. In at least

---

27. State v. Lee, 689 P.2d 153 (Ariz.1984) (en banc) (criminal case: defense lawyer should move to withdraw but should not inform the court of the specific basis for the request; lawyer should state only that an "irreconcilable conflict" makes continued representation extremely difficult); In re A., 554 P.2d 479, 486 (Or.1976) (civil case: lawyer should encourage the client to permit the lawyer to disclose the fraud on the court, inform the client that the lawyer will have to withdraw if there is no disclosure and then withdraw if the client refuses to disclose). Cf. Norman Lefstein, Reflections on the Client Perjury Dilemma and Nix v. Whiteside, Crim.Just., Summer 1986, at 27, 28 (accusing the majority opinion in *Whiteside* of "a shocking misstatement of the law pertaining to client perjury").

28. See, e.g., *Doe*, supra at p. 356, and *Crary*, supra p. 339.

29. 64 Mich. L. Rev. 1469 (1966).

30. See e.g., Monroe Freedman, Understanding Lawyers' Ethics 109–41 (1990).

31. Copyright © 1975 by the American Bar Association, Section of Litigation. Reprinted with permission. Professor Freedman has expanded his views and modified them somewhat in his book, Lawyers' Ethics in an Adversary System (1975), and a subsequent book, Understanding Lawyers' Ethics (1990). See also Freedman, Personal Responsibility in a Professional System, 27 Cath.U.L.Rev. 191 (1978); and Freedman, Legal Ethics and the Suffering Client, 36 Cath.U.L.Rev. 331 (1987).

one situation, that of the criminal defense lawyer, my own answer is in the affirmative.

    ... As an officer of the court, participating in a search for truth, what is the attorney obligated to do when faced with perjured testimony? That question cannot be answered properly without an appreciation of the fact that the attorney functions in an adversary system of justice which imposes three conflicting obligations upon the advocate. The difficulties presented by these obligations are particularly acute in the criminal defense area because of the presumption of innocence, the burden on the state to prove its case beyond a reasonable doubt, and the right to put the prosecution to its proof.

[The three conflicting obligations of the lawyer in the adversary system are: first, to learn everything the client knows about the case; second, to hold in strictest confidence what the client reveals; and third, to act with candor toward the tribunal.]

As soon as one begins to think about these responsibilities, it becomes apparent that the conscientious attorney is faced with what we may call a trilemma—that is, the lawyer is required to know everything, to keep it in confidence, and to reveal it to the court.

      .   .   .

If we recognize that professional responsibility requires that an advocate have full knowledge of every pertinent fact, then the lawyer must seek the truth from the client, not shun it. That means that the attorney will have to dig and pry and cajole, and, even then, the lawyer will not be successful without convincing the client that full disclosure to the lawyer will never result in prejudice to the client by any word or action of the attorney. That is particularly true in the case of the indigent criminal defendant, who meets the lawyer for the first time in the cell block or the rotunda of the jail....

However, the inclination to mislead one's lawyer is not restricted to the indigent or even to the criminal defendant. Randolph Paul has observed a similar phenomenon among a wealthier class in a far more congenial atmosphere. The tax adviser, notes Mr. Paul, will sometimes have to "dynamite the facts of his case out of the unwilling witnesses on his own side—witnesses who are nervous, witnesses who are confused about their own interest, witnesses who try to be too smart for their own good, and witnesses who subconsciously do not want to understand what has happened despite the fact that they must if they are to testify coherently." Mr. Paul goes on to explain that the truth can be obtained only by persuading the client that it would be a violation of a sacred obligation for the lawyer ever to reveal a client's confidence. Of course, once the lawyer has thus persuaded the client of the obligation of confidentiality, that obligation must be respected scrupulously.

      .   .   .

[A]nother way to resolve the difficulty . . . [is] by "selective ignorance." The attorney can make it clear to the client from the outset that the attorney does not want to hear an admission of guilt or incriminating evidence from the client. According to the [ABA Criminal Defense] Standards, that tactic is "most egregious" and constitutes "professional impropriety." On a practical level, it also puts an unreasonable burden on the unsophisticated client to select what to tell and what to hold back, and it can seriously impair the attorney's effectiveness in counseling the client and trying the case.

·   ·   ·

. . . [T]he ABA Standards have chosen to resolve the trilemma by maintaining the requirements of complete knowledge and of candor to the court, and sacrificing confidentiality. . . . [But] the Standards ignore the issue of whether the lawyer should [warn the client at the outset of the relationship that incriminating facts may have to be revealed to the tribunal]. The Canadian Bar Association, for example, takes an extremely hard line against the presentation of perjury by the client, but it also explicitly requires that the client be put on notice of that fact. Obviously, any other course would be a gross betrayal of the client's trust, since everything else said by the attorney in attempting to obtain complete information about the case would indicate to the client that no information thus obtained would be used to the client's disadvantage.

On the other hand, the inevitable result of the position taken by the Canadian Bar Association would be to caution the client not to be completely candid with the attorney. That, of course, returns us to resolving the trilemma by maintaining confidentiality and candor, but sacrificing complete knowledge. . . .

·   ·   ·

. . . I continue to stand with those lawyers who hold that the lawyer's obligation of confidentiality does not permit him to disclose the facts he has learned from his client which form the basis for his conclusion that the client intends to perjure himself. What that means—necessarily, it seems to me—is that, at least the criminal defense attorney, however unwillingly in terms of personal morality, has a professional responsibility as an advocate in an adversary system to examine the perjurious client in the ordinary way and to argue to the jury, as evidence in the case, the testimony presented by the defendant.

Freedman's Trilemma

Freedman's position has been adopted in the District of Columbia. Its version of M.R. 3.3 gives the lawyer discretion to reveal a client's intent to bribe or intimidate judges, witnesses or jurors, but prohibits disclosure of intended client perjury of a criminal defendant or past fraud on the court when disclosure would reveal client confidences.[32] Did D.C. get it right?

Freedman's argument is in part dependent on positing three duties—knowing all the facts, keeping confidences and candor to the court. What about the lawyer's responsibility under the criminal law and under the ethics rules to refrain from assisting criminal activity? To withdraw when continued representation will violate ethical rules or other law?

Freedman argues that "it is simply too much to expect of a human being ... facing loss of liberty and the horrors of imprisonment not to attempt to lie...." Do different considerations apply to lawyers in civil matters? If Freedman's central concern is the criminal defendant's right to tell her story, why is his argument not one for freeing the criminal defendant from the penalties of perjury or from the requirement of an oath? This is the path taken in Germany and other countries using nonadversarial procedural systems.[33]

At common law until the 19th century, a party, including a criminal accused, was disqualified from testifying on the ground that the temptation to falsify would put his soul in jeopardy. Today a criminal defendant has a due process right to testify in her own behalf.[34] If a state gives a defendant the option of testifying either on oath or unsworn, and the defendant elects an unsworn statement, should the jury be told by the judge or the prosecutor that this testimony is given without threat of penalty if found to be false?[35]

Freedman's argument implicitly rests on the proposition that perjury is unlike other crimes that corrupt court processes. In a subsequent article, Freedman returned to the question of how perjury can be distinguished from other crimes that corrupt court processes:

> [B]ribery is clandestine, usually not suspected when committed, and difficult to detect. Perjury, by contrast, takes place in the goldfish bowl of the courtroom, before a skeptical judge and jury, and is subject to immediate impeachment. Also, when perjury is detected by the court, the defendant faces the likelihood of an increased sentence.

---

32. See D.C. R.Prof.Conduct, specifically Rules 1.6(c)(2); 3.3(b); 3.3(d).

33. See, e.g., Mirjan R. Damaska, Presentation of Evidence and Fact Finding Precision, 123 U.Pa.L.Rev. 1083, 1088–90 (1975); and John H. Langbein, The German Advantage in Civil Procedure, 52 U.Chi.L.Rev. 823 (1985).

34. See Ferguson v. Georgia, 365 U.S. 570 (1961) (defendant may not be limited to giving unsworn testimony); and Whiteside, reprinted above, assuming that "a criminal defendant has a due process right to testify in his own behalf"). For a discussion of the historical transition from a rule of defendant's incompetency to testify to a rule of competency, see Ferguson, 365 U.S. at 573–582.

35. Several cases have agreed with Justice Frankfurter, concurring in Ferguson, 365 U.S. at 599–600, who stated that giving a defendant the option of testifying under oath or making an unsworn statement is not a violation of constitutional rights. See, e.g., Bontempo v. Fenton, 692 F.2d 954, 959–61 (3d Cir.1982); and United States v. Robinson, 783 F.2d 64, 66 (7th Cir.1986).

Further, as *Whiteside* illustrates, the lawyer ordinarily learns about the defendant's intended perjury as a result of a series of interviews with the client about the very offense that has been charged. That is, the lawyer's knowledge of the client's perjury is usually the direct outcome of lawyer-client communications about the crime that has been charged. Thus, knowledge of the "future crime" of perjury is inextricably interwoven with the crime that is the subject of the representation. A client's announcement of an intent to kill a witness, on the other hand, is a fact that stands separate and apart from communications about the crime that is the subject of the representation, such as what Whiteside did or did not see in the victim's hand just before he stabbed him.[36]

In *Whiteside* the Court rejected the distinction:

The crime of perjury in this setting is indistinguishable in substance from the crime of threatening or tampering with a witness or juror. A defendant who informed his counsel that he was arranging to bribe or threaten witnesses or members of the jury would have no "right" to insist on counsel's assistance or silence. Counsel would not be limited to advising against that conduct. An attorney's duty of confidentiality, which totally covers the client's admission of guilt, does not extend to a client's announced plans to engage in future criminal conduct.... [37]

Numerous commentators assert that perjury is pervasive and under-prosecuted.[38] Other evidence suggests that when the crime of perjury is prosecuted it is taken very seriously by the courts. Courts are more likely to imprison a convicted perjurer than a defendant convicted of other white collar crimes.[39] Judges often express the view that perjury is a most serious crime because it thwarts and potentially destroys the search for truth.[40]

The failure to devote prosecutorial resources to prosecutions for perjury may reflect, in part, that prosecutors share Freedman's expectation that people charged with crimes will lie and that prosecutors have doubts, like his, about punishing defendants for doing so. Perjury is a difficult crime to prove. Many courts require that corroborating evidence be nearly indisputable.[41] Also, alternatives to prosecutions for perjury are seen as viable. One is to increase the sentence of a defendant who has perjured herself during trial. In United States v. Grayson,[42] the Supreme Court held that a judge's

---

36. Monroe H. Freedman, Client Confidences and Client Perjury: Some Unanswered Questions, 136 U.Pa.L.Rev. 1939, 1951 (1988).

37. Nix v. Whiteside, 475 U.S. 157, 174 (1986).

38. See, e.g., Richard H. Underwood, Perjury! The Charges and the Defenses, 36 Duquesne L. Rev. 1–2 (1998) (citing other articles).

39. See Sourcebook of Criminal Justice Statistics (1982), Tables 5.18 and 5.19, at 461 and 466.

40. See, e.g., United States v. Otto, 54 F.2d 277, 279 (2d Cir.1931); Edwards v. State, 577 P.2d 1380 (Wyo.1978).

41. See, e.g., United States v. Neff, 212 F.2d 297 (3d Cir.1954); United States v. Thompson, 379 F.2d 625 (6th Cir.1967).

42. 438 U.S. 41 (1978). Sentence enhancement as a consequence of false testimony continues under the sentencing guidelines.

belief that the defendant had perjured herself is a valid sentencing consideration because it is seen as relevant to how likely the defendant is to be rehabilitated.[43]

If the lawyer is obligated not to present false testimony, is the defendant denied effective assistance of counsel when the lawyer presents a defense based on perjury?[44]

Freedman's "trilemma," posits a defendant falsely accused of robbery whose truthful testimony about his whereabouts (i.e., that he was near the scene at the time of the crime) might lead the jury to convict him. By positing this case, Freedman presents us with a scenario in which lying seems not only reasonable but, perhaps more important, not a clear moral wrong. How is it "known" in Freedman's case, except hypothetically, that the client has been *falsely* accused? Would it indeed be reasonable for a defendant in this situation to lie? What dangers are there for the innocent defendant who lies and is thought by the fact-finder to have lied?

Assuming there are some circumstances in which it is reasonable for an innocent defendant to lie, a number of questions remain. First, does the moral justification for the defendant's lying extend to the lawyer, giving lawyers who represent defendants in these circumstances a moral justification for assisting the lie? Second, if some defendants are morally justified in lying, must the lawyer assist all defendants to lie because any other stance would distinguish between clients according to whether the lawyer believed them to be truly innocent? Third, if the lawyer is morally justified in assisting at least some defendants to lie, does that mean that the ethics rules should leave it to the lawyer's discretion when to assist perjury and when not? Does it mean that the rules should *require* lawyers to assist perjury?

These questions are posed and insightfully discussed by Carl Selinger.[45] He concludes that an innocent defendant is morally justified in perjuring himself to avoid the greater wrong of unjustified imprisonment. Selinger argues, however, that a lawyer's oath to uphold the law places her under a

---

See United States v. Dunnigan, 507 U.S. 87 (1993).

43. See also David W. Eagle, Civil Remedies for Perjury: A Proposal for a Tort Action, 19 Ariz.L.Rev. 349, 369–72 (1977); and the note on perjury as a tort, below at p. 403.

44. See People v. Avery, 513 N.Y.S.2d 883, 887 (App.Div.1987) (defendant who "knowingly and willingly participated in an attempt to obstruct justice through perjured testimony ... is not in a position to ask this court to undo the consequences of [this wrongdoing]"); and North Dakota v. Skjonsby, 417 N.W.2d 818 (N.D.1987) (defendant, who had changed his story from time to time, claimed that he was denied effective assistance of counsel because his

trial lawyer failed to stop him from offering a perjurious defense; the court held that evidence available to the trial lawyer was not sufficient to find that he knew that the fabricated defense was a lie). But compare State v. Lee, 689 P.2d 153 (Ariz.1984) (calling of perjurious witnesses on the client's demand fell below the standard of minimally competent representation; witnesses testified by narrative statement and lawyer made no closing argument to jury).

45. Carl M. Selinger, The Perry Mason Perspective and Others: A Critique of Reductionist Thinking about the Ethics of Untruthful Practices by Lawyers for "Innocent" Defendants, 6 Hofstra L.Rev. 631 (1978).

special obligation not to break the rules for adjudicating disputes; and that by voluntarily participating in the criminal justice system the lawyer assumes two special obligations: (1) to conduct herself in accordance with the rules for finding the facts; and (2) to accept the judgments reached by the system when reached in accordance with the system's own rules. Selinger rejects a rule that would allow lawyers to assist "good" lying as opposed to "bad" lying because it would be difficult to administer such a rule in an evenhanded manner, and it would provide little guidance to lawyers trying to figure out what was prohibited.

B.   REMEDIES FOR ABUSIVE LITIGATION CONDUCT

INTRODUCTORY NOTE

When ordinary people are confronted with formal process, such as a summons in a legal proceeding, their emotions and anxieties are powerfully engaged. They are commanded in the esoteric language of formal law to respond within a stated period of time and are threatened with serious consequences if they do not do so or if the merits of the case go against them. To protect their interests, they must procure a lawyer in whom they have confidence—a difficult task for those whose contact with the legal system is limited or non-existent—and put their fate in the hands of this professional. The costs and anxieties that flow from being forced into the unwelcome role of a litigant are large, in psychic as well as economic terms. The loss of control over some aspects of one's future is itself a major problem; and if the litigation may result in serious losses, whether in money, reputation, marital status or personal freedom, the prospects are frightening. Lawyers often forget the truth stated by Judge Learned Hand:

> After now some dozen years of experience, I must say that as a litigant I should dread a lawsuit beyond almost anything else short of sickness and death.[1]

The American Rule on legal fees, discussed in Chapter 6 at p. 522 infra, requires each party to pay the costs incurred in pursuing or defend-

---

1. Learned Hand, The Deficiencies of Trials to Reach the Heart of the Matter (talk to ACBNY, Nov. 17, 1921), reprinted in 3 ACBNY Lectures on Legal Topics 1921–22 at 87, 105 (1926). This focus on defendants should not obscure the fact that potential plaintiffs also face difficult emotional and practical problems. For example, a woman who has been the victim of sexual harassment by her superior in an employment setting must make a series of difficult choices: Would she be better off ignoring the incident than pursuing the matter? Are informal remedies provided by the employer available or promising? How does one find a trustworthy lawyer who has the requisite skills and judgment? Will a lawyer think the case is worth her time? What happens to one's life while a lawsuit is making its way through cumbersome court procedures? Etc.

ing a legal proceeding.[2] The just claimant's recovery may be eroded or eliminated by the expense of vindicating the claim. The person forced to defend against an unfounded claim may be impoverished by a successful defense.

Given these realities, it is not surprising that criminal law, procedural law and ethics rules impose obligations on parties and their representatives not to abuse the judicial process. From the lawyer's point of view, the basic tension is between the lawyer's duties of loyalty to, and zeal for, a client and the battery of restraints that are imposed on a lawyer to protect the interests of the public, the courts and opposing parties. From the broader social point of view, the problem is one of devising social arrangements that permit the public expression of social norms while permitting accurate, efficient and fair resolution of disputes.[3]

1. FRIVOLITY, HARASSMENT AND DELAY: PROFESSIONAL RULES AND ATTITUDES

Professional rules, in dealing with frivolity, harassment and delay, impose limits on the "warm zeal" with which a lawyer is to urge a client's interests. The rule provisions must be considered in light of widely-shared professional attitudes, which strongly influence the behavior of lawyers and the actions of disciplinary bodies. Both ethics rules and professional attitudes are powerfully shaped by changes in procedural law.[4]

IN RE SOLERWITZ.[5] In 1982, shortly after 11,000 air traffic controllers were fired for participating in an illegal strike, Jack Solerwitz, a Long Island attorney, was retained by about 800 controllers to pursue reinstatement claims. When the Federal Merit System Protection Board rejected the claims, approximately 4600 petitions for review were filed in the United States Court of Appeals for the Federal Circuit. Because of the press of claims raising similar issues, the court designated twelve cases (including

---

2. The "court costs" often awarded to prevailing parties are typically small, fixed amounts that have no relationship to the real costs of litigating a matter. Attorneys' fees are the principal cost, but other litigation costs (investigations, expert witnesses, miscellaneous expenses) are often large and sometimes huge.

3. See Roger C. Cramton, A Comment on Trial–Type Hearings in Nuclear Power Plant Siting, 58 Va.L.Rev. 585 (1972) (discussing criteria for evaluating hearing processes); and Robert S. Summers, Evaluating and Improving Legal Processes—A Plea for Process Values, 60 Cornell L.Rev. 1 (1974).

4. An example is the change in procedural rules relating to use of general denials. Some years ago the law of pleading made it customary and acceptable for a plaintiff to make allegations in broad terms and for a defendant to respond with a general denial requiring plaintiff to prove all elements of the claim. Today procedural law generally requires the plaintiff to provide the defendant with better notice of the facts relied on and the defendant to respond in a particularized manner. A defendant who knows that some of the facts stated in the complaint are true may no longer make a general denial. M.R. 3.1 implicitly reflects this change by carving out an exception for the lawyer for the criminal defendant or a person subject to incarceration, who by a general plea (e.g., "not guilty") may require the state to prove every element of the case.

5. In re Solerwitz, 848 F.2d 1573 (Fed.Cir. 1988).

one of Solerwitz's) as "lead cases" that presented most of the common legal issues for review. These cases were given expedited hearing and review, and all others suspended. When the court decided the twelve lead cases (adversely to the controllers), it notified the petitioners and their lawyers in all of the other pending appeals, informed them that written notification was necessary to continue their appeals and warned them of the impropriety of maintaining frivolous appeals in cases that presented legal issues and fact patterns indistinguishable from those presented and decided in the lead cases.

Ignoring these warnings, Solerwitz filed or maintained appeals in 144 air traffic controller cases. The court directed Solerwitz to "show cause why he should not be suspended for two years from representing clients before this court." The show-cause order alleged that the briefs in Solerwitz's appeals (107 of which were virtually identical) were "devoid of any basis on which the precedents of this court could be distinguished in law or fact, and devoid of any effort to make such distinctions." At a hearing, there was evidence that Solerwitz pursued the appeals at the explicit request of his clients in the hope, which proved to be a vain one, that the Supreme Court would reverse the lead cases or that a political or legislative accommodation might come to the rescue of controllers whose cases were still pending.

According to the court's summary,

> Professor [Monroe] Freedman, [one of the ethics experts,] stated that "as long as counsel in good faith believes that his case is not frivolous, ... it is his duty to proceed with it notwithstanding any instructions to the contrary from the court" and that "the court is required to bend over backwards to defer to counsel's judgment with regard to what is filed and what is argued...." [The trial judge] found Professor Freedman "regards as frivolous only a paper that is fallacious on its face as distinguished from sham pleading in which the argument is plausible but the lawyer knows or should know that the underlying facts are not there to support it." ... Professor Hellerstein [a second ethics expert in the case, expressed the] opinion that "a lawyer has an obligation to persist in making and remaking the same argument to an intermediate court at least until the Supreme Court foreclosed that court on the merits." ... [He] testified that in his entire practice he never once turned down a client's request to bring an appeal because he believed it was frivolous, if [he] felt there was anything that could be argued....[6]

---

6. 848 F.2d at 1576–77. A more colorful summary of the positions of the ethics experts appears in a news report:

> Three ethics experts rose to [Solerwitz's] defense. A lawyer should argue that the earth is flat if a client so demands, said Monroe Freedman of Hofstra Law School. "What is today's joke is tomorrow's constitutional principle," said William Hellerstein of Brooklyn Law School, who, as chief of appeals for the Legal Aid Society of New York, once lost 54 cases in a row. Harvey Silverglate, a Boston lawyer who has taught ethics at Harvard Law School, described his own test for what is "frivolous": if nobody in the office giggles, it passes muster.

David Margolick, N.Y.Times, Jan. 20, 1989, at p. B4.

The court unanimously rejected these arguments: "Mr. Solerwitz's briefs ... did not attempt to convince the court that the lead cases, decided only a short time earlier, had been incorrectly decided and should be overruled. Instead, he merely repeated the same basic arguments that the court had rejected in the lead cases."[7] Solerwitz was suspended from practice before the Federal Circuit for a period of one year.

Screening Out Frivolous Claims

Model Rule 3.1 states that a lawyer (other than one for a criminal defendant or a person subject to incarceration) "shall not bring or defend a proceeding, or assert or controvert an issue therein, unless there is a basis for doing so that is not frivolous, which includes a good faith argument for an extension, modification or reversal of existing law."[8] M.R. 3.1 differs from its predecessor in the Model Code, DR 7–102(A)(1), in providing an objective rather than a largely subjective test for judging what is frivolous. The Model Code limited disciplinary sanctions to situations in which the lawyer *"knows or it is obvious* that such action would serve *merely* to harass or maliciously injure another." (Emphasis added.) Does the word "merely" make DR 7–102(A)(1) too lenient? Does the Model Code provision turn on whether a lawyer is clever enough to think up a plausible justification for the action that is non-harassing?

Comment [2] to M.R. 3.1 makes it clear that the Rule does not impose any duty on the lawyer to make a full inquiry about underlying facts before acting:

> The filing of an action or defense or similar action taken for a client is not frivolous merely because the facts have not first been fully substantiated or because the lawyer expects to develop vital evidence only by discovery. Such action is not frivolous even though the lawyer believes that the client's position ultimately will not prevail....

What about colorable claims brought "merely to harass ...'"? The Preamble to the Model Rules states that "A lawyer should use the law's procedures only for legitimate purposes and not to harass or intimidate others." In addition, M.R. 8.4(d) prohibits "conduct prejudicial to the administration of justice."[9] The most directly relevant provision, however, M.R. 4.4, states only that a lawyer "shall not use means that have *no substantial purpose* other than to embarrass, delay, or burden a third person...." (Emphasis added.) It is not surprising that these provisions lead to few disciplinary actions.

Lawyers may be expected to screen out frivolous claims and defenses when it is in their self-interest to do so. An unfounded claim or defense will result in legal fees that an unsuccessful client will be reluctant to pay and

7. 848 F.2d at 1579.

8. A separate rule, M.R. 3.4(d), provides that a lawyer should not make "frivolous" discovery requests or fail to make "reason-ably diligent" efforts to comply with proper discovery requests by another party.

9. See the discussion of this provision at p. 924 infra.

that may be unethical to exact.[10] Abuses are thus more likely when lawyers are tempted by self-interest to pursue frivolous matters or cheat their clients, and they are most likely when the abuse advances the interests of both client and lawyer. A lawyer, for example, may be tempted to file a damage action against a defendant solely to profit from a nuisance-value settlement entered into by a defendant to avoid the costs of a successful defense. Or she may assert a legally insupportable defense to earn fees while her client delays payment of a just claim or continues an illegal but profitable course of conduct.

What constitutes a "frivolous" claim or defense? Changes in the intellectual framework of American lawyers make this a more serious problem than it was in the past. Some streams of current legal theory, influenced by legal realism, critical legal studies and feminist and race theory, assert that law is culturally determined and highly contingent on existing social structures; that legal rules are themselves uncertain and legal outcomes indeterminate; and, consequently, that law is much more changeable than generally perceived.[11] To the extent that law is uncertain and constantly changing, general agreement on whether a lawyer's action is "frivolous" will frequently be lacking. In *Solerwitz* the "ethics experts" appear to have urged these post-modern views, but the court was confident that it could distinguish frivolous from non-frivolous actions.

Enforcement of the code provisions presents practical difficulties apart from getting agreement on the standard of judgment. If the professional rule requires a finding of subjective bad faith, as may be the case under DR 7–102(A)(1), an evidentiary hearing may be required to probe the attorney's motives. If the rule examines the objective merit of the pleading or motion, as does M.R. 3.1, either expert testimony is required or a court must resolve the issue as a question of law. Does the application of either standard turn on whether the lawyer is clever enough to think up a supporting argument that is not wholly implausible? Charles Wolfram concludes, not surprisingly, that "discipline is rarely imposed for violations of the antiharassment rules ... [which] can very likely do little to restrain advocates from taking steps that, based on other calculations, seem in the best interests of clients."[12]

---

10. Baranowski v. State Bar, 593 P.2d 613 (Cal.1979) (lawyer disciplined where, without making any independent legal or factual investigation of the client's claim, he had made an overzealous assessment of the legal worth of the claim and had received a large retainer from the client).

11. See Sanford Levinson, Frivolous Cases: Do Lawyers Really Know Anything at All?, 24 Osgoode Hall L.J. 353 (1986) (post-modern thought casts doubts on whether frivolousness can be determined with consistency and fairness).

12. Wolfram, Modern Legal Ethics § 11.2.2, at 595 (1986). See In re Bithoney, 486 F.2d 319 (1st Cir.1973) (suspension for repeated filing of bad faith appeals in immigration cases to delay deportation of clients); In re Jafree, 444 N.E.2d 143 (Ill.1982) (disbarment for filing over forty frivolous suits and appeals). In 1988 the West Virginia Supreme Court sent a strong message to the state's disciplinary committee that the filing of frivolous litigation should be taken more seriously. Committee on Legal Ethics of the West Virginia State Bar v. Douglas, 370 S.E.2d 325 (W.Va.1988).

Dilatory Tactics

Dilatory tactics are tempting to lawyers, especially when they serve interests of both the lawyer and the client. If the lawyer can earn additional fees while advancing the client's interest, delay becomes hard to resist. The legal profession has a schizophrenic attitude toward strategic use of delay, in part because its effective use involves professional skills that sometimes are admired. Bar leaders and professional codes speak out against the use of delay as a deliberate harassing tactic, but eminent lawyers often boast shamelessly at professional meetings of their skills in delaying cases. For example, Bruce Bromley of the Cravath firm, in a 1958 talk to an admiring audience of lawyers, said:

> Now I was born, I think, to be a protractor.... I quickly realized in my early days at the bar that I could take the simplest antitrust case that [the antitrust division] could think of and protract it for the defense almost to infinity.[13]

The point of Bromley's talk, aside from his amusing account of past exploits as a "protractor," was that procedural changes and more judicial control had made the life of the protractor much more difficult.

The Model Code's prohibition of lawyer delay, limited to delay that would "merely" serve to harass or maliciously injure another, implied that delay is permissible if it serves the client's interests. Model Rule 3.2, however, imposes on lawyers the affirmative obligation to "make reasonable efforts to expedite litigation consistent with the interests of the client." The test given in the comment to Rule 3.2 for resolving the tension between client interests and expeditious litigation is "whether a lawyer acting in good faith would regard the course of action as having some substantial purpose other than delay. Realizing financial or other benefit from otherwise improper delay in litigation is not a legitimate interest of the client." Would Bruce Bromley be subject to discipline under this standard?

2. TORT REMEDIES AGAINST LAWYERS FOR LITIGATION CONDUCT

Friedman v. Dozorc

Supreme Court of Michigan, 1981.
412 Mich. 1, 312 N.W.2d 585.

■ LEVIN, JUSTICE.

The plaintiff is a physician who, after successfully defending in a medical malpractice action, brought this action against the attorneys who had represented the plaintiffs in the former action. Dr. Friedman sought under a number of theories to recover damages for being compelled to defend against an allegedly groundless medical malpractice action. The trial

---

13. Bruce Bromley, Judicial Control of Anti-   trust Cases, 23 F.R.D. 417 (1959).

court granted the defendants' motions for summary and accelerated judgment.

The Court of Appeals affirmed in part and reversed in part. We granted leave to appeal to consider what remedies may be available to a physician who brings such a "countersuit".

We hold that: (1) The plaintiff has failed to state an actionable claim on a theory of negligence because an attorney owes no duty of care to an adverse party in litigation; (2) The plaintiff has failed to state an actionable claim on a theory of abuse of process because there is no allegation that defendants committed an irregular act in the use of the process issued in the prior case; (3) The plaintiff has failed to state an actionable claim on a theory of malicious prosecution because his complaint did not allege interference with his person or property sufficient to constitute special injury under Michigan law.

. . .

I

Leona Serafin entered Outer Drive Hospital in May, 1970, for treatment of gynecological problems. A dilation and curettage was performed by her physician, Dr. Harold Krevsky. While in the hospital, Mrs. Serafin was referred to the present plaintiff, Dr. Friedman, for urological consultation. Dr. Friedman recommended surgical removal of a kidney stone which was too large to pass, and the operation was performed on May 20, 1970. During the surgery, the patient began to ooze blood uncontrollably. Although other physicians were consulted, Mrs. Serafin's condition continued to worsen and she died five days after the surgery. An autopsy was performed the next day; the report identified the cause of death as thrombotic thrombocytopenic purpura, a rare and uniformly fatal blood disease, the cause and cure of which are unknown.

On January 11, 1972, attorneys Dozorc and Golden, the defendants in this action, filed a malpractice action on behalf of Anthony Serafin, Jr., for himself and as administrator of the estate of Leona Serafin, against Peoples Community Hospital Authority, Outer Drive Hospital, Dr. Krevsky and Dr. Friedman, as well as another physician who was dismissed as a defendant before trial. In December, 1974, the case went to trial in Wayne Circuit Court. No expert testimony tending to show that any of the defendants had breached accepted professional standards in making the decision to perform the elective surgery or in the manner of its performance was presented as part of the plaintiff's case. The judge entered a directed verdict of no cause of action in favor of Dr. Friedman and the other defendants at the close of the plaintiff's proofs. The judge subsequently denied a motion for costs brought by codefendant Peoples Community Hospital Authority, pursuant to GCR 1963, 111.6. The Court of Appeals affirmed and this Court denied leave to appeal.

Dr. Friedman commenced the present action on March 17, 1976 in Oakland Circuit Court. The following excerpt from his complaint summarizes his theories of recovery and the injuries he allegedly sustained as a result of the initiation and prosecution of the malpractice action:

> "13. That as a direct and proximate result of the negligence, malicious prosecution and abuse of process of these Defendants, the Plaintiff, Seymour Friedman, M.D., has endured grievous damages, including, but not limited to, the following: the cost of defending the aforesaid cause and the appeal, an increase in his annual malpractice insurance premiums for so long as he practices medicine, the loss of two young associates from his office who could no longer afford to pay the increased malpractice insurance premiums thereby requiring him to work excessive hours without relief, damages to his reputation as a physician and surgeon, embarrassment and continued mental anguish."

[The trial court granted the defendants' motion for summary judgment and Dr. Friedman appealed. The case was viewed by the parties, amici curiae, and the Michigan appellate courts as a test case involving the liability of a lawyer for filing and pursuing unfounded claims.]

. . .

II [Negligence]

Plaintiff and amici in support urge this Court to hold that an attorney owes a present or prospective adverse party a duty of care, breach of which will give rise to a cause of action for negligence. We agree with the circuit judge and the Court of Appeals that an attorney owes no actionable duty to an adverse party.

Plaintiff and amici argue that an attorney who initiates a civil action owes a duty to his client's adversary and all other foreseeable third parties who may be affected by such an action to conduct a reasonable investigation and re-examination of the facts and law so that the attorney will have an adequate basis for a good-faith belief that the client has a tenable claim. Plaintiff contends that this duty is created by the Code of Professional Responsibility and by the Michigan General Court Rules.[6]

Plaintiff further argues that an attorney's separate duty under the Code of Professional Responsibility to zealously represent a client is limited by the requirement that the attorney perform within the bounds of the law. [Here the court quoted DR 7–102(A)(1) and (A)(2); EC 7–4; and EC 7–10.] Acting within the bounds of the law is said to encompass refraining from asserting frivolous claims; this charge upon the profession imposes upon counsel a duty to the public, the courts and the adverse party to conduct a reasonable investigation. Plaintiff contends that since the duty to investigate already arises from the attorney-client relationship under the code and

---

6. Plaintiff's brief refers to Code of Professional Responsibility and Canons, Canon 1, DR 1–102(A), Canon 6, DR 6–101(A), Canon 7, DR 7–102(A), and various Ethical Considerations associated with Canon 7, especially EC 7–4 and EC 7–10, as well as to GCR 1963, 111.6 and 114.

court rules, recognition of a cause of action for negligence will impose no new obligation on the attorney.

. . .

In a negligence action the question whether the defendant owes an actionable legal duty to the plaintiff is one of law which the court decides after assessing the competing policy considerations for and against recognizing the asserted duty.

. . .

Assuming that an attorney has an obligation to his client to conduct a reasonable investigation prior to bringing an action, that obligation is not the functional equivalent of a duty of care owed to the client's adversary. We decline to so transform the attorney's obligation because we view such a duty as inconsistent with basic precepts of the adversary system.

The duties, professional and actionable, owed to the client by the attorney acting as advocate and adviser are broader than the obligation of reasonable investigation. . . . If an attorney were held to owe a duty of due care to both the client and the client's adversary, the obligation owing to the adversary would extend beyond undertaking an investigation and would permeate all facets of the litigation. The attorney's decision-making and future conduct on behalf of both parties would be shaped by the attorney's obligation to exercise due care as to both parties. Under such a rule an attorney is likely to be faced with a situation in which it would be in the client's best interest to proceed in one fashion and in the adversary's best interest to proceed contrariwise. However he chooses to proceed, the attorney could be accused of failing to exercise due care for the benefit of one of the parties.

. . .

In short, creation of a duty in favor of an adversary of the attorney's client would create an unacceptable conflict of interest which would seriously hamper an attorney's effectiveness as counsel for his client. Not only would the adversary's interests interfere with the client's interests, the attorney's justifiable concern with being sued for negligence would detrimentally interfere with the attorney-client relationship. . . .

. . .

. . . We reiterate what this Court said in State Bar Grievance Administrator v. Corace, 390 Mich. 419, 434–435, 213 N.W.2d 124 (1973):

> "[O]ur adversary system 'intends, and expects, lawyers to probe the outer limits of the bounds of the law, ever searching for a more efficacious remedy, or a more successful defense'."

We agree with those courts in other jurisdictions which have relied on the policy of encouraging free access to the courts as a reason for declining to recognize a negligence cause of action in physician countersuits.[12] No appellate court has yet approved such a cause of action.

. . .

III [Abuse of Process]

To recover upon a theory of abuse of process, a plaintiff must plead and prove (1) an ulterior purpose and (2) an act in the use of process which is improper in the regular prosecution of the proceeding. Spear v. Pendill, 164 Mich. 620, 623, 130 N.W. 343 (1911).[18]

Plaintiff contends he has pleaded that defendants' ulterior purpose in filing the former malpractice action was to coerce payments of large sums of money from plaintiff for defendants' financial gain by means of their contingent-fee arrangement with the former plaintiff. In addition, plaintiff alleges that irregular use of process was shown by defendants' filing of the complaint without adequate investigation.

. . .

We need not decide whether plaintiff's pleadings sufficiently allege that the defendants had an ulterior purpose in causing process to issue, since it is clear that the plaintiff has failed to allege that defendants committed some irregular act in the use of process. The only act in the use of process that plaintiff alleges is the issuance of a summons and complaint in the former malpractice action. However, a summons and complaint are properly employed when used to institute a civil action, and thus plaintiff has failed to satisfy the second element required in *Spear*, supra, 623, 130 N.W. 343, where the Court observed " '[t]his action for abuse of process lies for the improper use of process after it has been issued, not for maliciously causing it to issue.' "

. . .

IV [Malicious Prosecution]

Plaintiff relies upon the same allegations respecting defendants' conduct and their failure to meet professional standards which assertedly

---

12. Weaver v. Superior Court of Orange County, 95 Cal.App.3d 166, 156 Cal.Rptr. 745 (1979); Berlin v. Nathan, 64 Ill.App.3d 940, 21 Ill.Dec. 682, 381 N.E.2d 1367 (1978); Lyddon v. Shaw, 56 Ill.App.3d 815, 14 Ill.Dec. 489, 372 N.E.2d 685 (1978); Brody v. Ruby, 267 N.W.2d 902 (Iowa, 1978); Spencer v. Burglass, 337 So.2d 596 (La.App., 1976); Hill v. Willmott, 561 S.W.2d 331 (Ky.App., 1978).

18. The Restatement Torts, 2d, explains the tort of abuse of process as follows:

"The gravamen of the misconduct for which the liability stated in this section is imposed is not the wrongful procurement of legal process or the wrongful initiation of criminal or civil proceedings; it is the misuse of process, no matter how properly obtained, for any purpose other than that which it was designed to accomplish.... The subsequent misuse of the process, though properly obtained, constitutes the misconduct for which the liability is imposed under the rule stated in this section." 3 Restatement Torts, 2d, § 682, comment a, p. 474.

constitute negligence in contending that he has pled a cause of action for malicious prosecution. He argues that the question of probable cause in a malicious prosecution action against the attorney for an opposing party turns on whether the attorney fulfilled his duty to reasonably investigate the facts and law before initiating and continuing a lawsuit. If the attorney's investigation discloses that the claim is not tenable, then it is his obligation to discontinue the action.

Defendants respond that Michigan is among those jurisdictions that have not abandoned the special injury requirement in actions for the malicious prosecution of civil proceedings. . . .

[1.   Special Injury]

We agree with defendants that under Michigan law special injury remains an essential element of the tort cause of action for malicious prosecution of civil proceedings. . . .

. . .

A substantial number of American jurisdictions today follow some form of "English rule" to the effect that "in the absence of an arrest, seizure, or special damage, the successful civil defendant has no remedy, despite the fact that his antagonist proceeded against him maliciously and without probable cause." A larger number of jurisdictions, some say a majority, follow an "American rule" permitting actions for malicious prosecution of civil proceedings without requiring the plaintiff to show special injury.

The plaintiff's complaint does not allege special injury. We are satisfied that Michigan has not significantly departed from the English rule and we decline to do so today.

. . .

Most commentators appear to favor abrogation of the special injury requirement to make the action more available and less difficult to maintain.[34] Their counsel should, however, be evaluated skeptically. The lawyer's remedy for a grievance is a lawsuit, and a law student or tort professor may be particularly predisposed by experience and training to see the preferred remedy for a wrongful tort action as another tort action. In seeking a remedy for the excessive litigiousness of our society, we would do well to cast off the limitations of a perspective which ascribes curative power only to lawsuits.

[Eliminating the special injury requirement would make it much easier for plaintiffs to sue successfully for malicious prosecution. The court considered and rejected three arguments for making this cause of action easier to sustain. First, when a meritless lawsuit is brought, the defendant

---

34.   Prosser, supra, § 120, p. 851; Note, Promoting Recovery by Claimants in Iowa Malicious Prosecution Actions, 64 Iowa L.Rev. 408 (1979); Note, Malicious Prosecution: An Effective Attack on Spurious Medical Malpractice Claims?, 26 Case Western Reserve L.Rev. 653, 657–662 (1976); Birnbaum, Physicians Counterattack: Liability of Lawyers for Instituting Unjustified Medical Malpractice Actions, 45 Fordham L.Rev. 1003, 1090 (1977).

is entitled to reimbursement for costs, but "costs" as calculated in our system are trivial amounts and do not compensate the defendant for attorney's fees or other litigation expenses. That, however, "does not necessarily justify an award of compensation ... in a separate lawsuit." Second, vexatious suits known to be groundless are always against public policy. True, but other means of deterring groundless litigation "may be less intimidating to good-faith litigants." Third, the heavy burden of proof borne by a plaintiff in a malicious prosecution action will protect bona fide litigants from a second lawsuit. But that, according to the *Friedman* court, itself suggests that few plaintiffs will recover and, when they do not, the second action will be costly to the parties and to the court. Finally, the court noted, elimination of the special injury requirement would not be limited to medical malpractice cases, but would be available to any former defendant in any type of action.]

... In expanding the availability of such an action the Court would not merely provide a remedy for those required to defend groundless medical malpractice actions, but would arm all prevailing defendants with an instrument of retaliation, whether the prior action sounded in tort, contract or an altogether different area of law.

This is strong medicine—too strong for the affliction it is intended to cure. To be sure, successful defense of the former action is no assurance of recovery in a subsequent tort action, but the unrestricted availability of such an action introduces a new strategic weapon into the arsenal of defense litigators, particularly those whose clients can afford to devote extensive resources to prophylactic intimidation.

. . .

[2. Probable Cause]

Apart from special injury, elements of a tort action for malicious prosecution of civil proceedings are (1) prior proceedings terminated in favor of the present plaintiff, (2) absence of probable cause for those proceedings, and (3) "malice," more informatively described by the Restatement as "a purpose other than that of securing the proper adjudication of the claim in which the proceedings are based."[43]

. . .

The absence of probable cause in bringing a civil action may not be established merely by showing that the action was successfully defended.[44] To require an attorney to advance only those claims that will ultimately be successful would place an intolerable burden on the right of access to the courts.

---

43. See, generally, Prosser, supra, § 120, pp. 850–856, and 3 Restatement Torts, 2d, §§ 674–681B, pp. 452–473. Propriety of purpose is discussed in § 676.

44. See Prosser, supra, § 120. Cf. Drobczyk v. Great Lakes Steel Corp., 116 N.W.2d 736 (Mich.1962).

The Court of Appeals adopted, and plaintiff endorses, the standard for determining whether an attorney had probable cause to initiate and continue a lawsuit articulated in Tool Research & Engineering Corp. v. Henigson, 46 Cal.App.3d 675, 683–684, 120 Cal.Rptr. 291 (1975): . . .

> An attorney has probable cause to represent a client in litigation when, after a reasonable investigation and industrious search of legal authority, he has an honest belief that his client's claim is tenable in the forum in which it is to be tried.

In our view, this standard, while well-intentioned, is inconsistent with the role of the attorney in an adversary system.

Our legal system favors the representation of litigants by counsel. Yet the foregoing standard appears skewed in favor of non-representation; the lawyer risks being penalized for undertaking to present the client's claim to a court unless satisfied, after a potentially substantial investment in investigation and research, that the claim is tenable.

A lawyer may be confronted with the choice between allowing the statute of limitation to run upon a claim with which the client has only recently come forward, or promptly filing a lawsuit based on the information in hand. Such dilemmas are particularly likely to arise in connection with medical malpractice claims because a statute provides a six-month limitation period for bringing an action based on a belatedly discovered claim as an alternative to the normal two-year limitation period for malpractice actions. Time will not always permit "a reasonable investigation and industrious search of legal authority" before the lawyer must file a complaint to preserve the client's claim—and thus, perhaps, avoid an action by the client for legal malpractice.

In medical malpractice actions the facts relevant to an informed assessment of the defendant's liability may not emerge until well into the discovery process. Sometimes the relevant facts are not readily ascertainable. In the instant case, for example, defendants maintain that their efforts to acquire Mrs. Serafin's medical records were rebuffed until they commenced suit and thereupon became able to invoke established discovery procedures and the implicit power of the court to compel disclosure; it may be the practice of some doctors or hospitals to refuse to release medical records until a lawsuit has been commenced.

Moreover, the *Henigson* standard suggests rather ominously that every time a lawyer representing, say, a medical malpractice plaintiff encounters a fact adverse to the client's position or an expert opinion that there was no malpractice, he must immediately question whether to persevere in the action. An attorney's evaluation of the client's case should not be inhibited by the knowledge that perseverance may place the attorney personally at risk; the next fact or the next medical opinion may be the one that makes the case, and such developments may occur even on the eve of trial.

. . .

Indeed, whether an attorney acted without probable cause in initiating, defending or continuing proceedings on behalf of a client should not normally depend upon the extent of the investigation conducted. The Code of Professional Responsibility does not expressly impose any duty upon a lawyer to conduct an independent investigation of the merits of a client's claim. [Consider] DR 7–102(A), upon which plaintiffs in the instant action rely[.] [Text of rule omitted.]

DR 7–102(A) and the other professional standards to which plaintiff refers consistently incorporate a requirement of *scienter* as to groundlessness or vexatiousness, not a requirement that the lawyer take affirmative measures to verify the factual basis of his client's position. A lawyer is entitled to accept his client's version of the facts and to proceed on the assumption that they are true absent compelling evidence to the contrary.[53] The only general limitation on the lawyer's acceptance of employment is found in DR 2–109(A), the language of which parallels DR 7–102(A). And, although DR 6–101(A)(2) states that a lawyer shall not "[h]andle a legal matter without preparation adequate in the circumstances," that preparation need not entail verification of the facts related by the client.

Framed as it is in terms of "reasonableness", the *Henigson* standard is difficult to reconcile with the lawyer's obligation to represent his client's interests zealously. "Zealous representation" contemplates that the lawyer will go to the limits for his client, representing him loyally, tenaciously and single-mindedly. The question of whether a lawyer "abused that duty" is not a matter of what a hypothetical reasonable practitioner would have done in the same circumstances, but of whether the lawyer's conduct was beyond the limits of reason or the bounds of the law although another "reasonable" lawyer, or many such lawyers, might not have acted similarly.

The Restatement's definition of probable cause provides ample guidance whether damages are sought from a lawyer, his client or both:

> One who takes an active part in the initiation, continuation or procurement of civil proceedings against another has probable cause for doing so if he reasonably believes in the existence of the facts upon which the claim is based, and either (a) correctly or reasonably believes that under those facts the claim *may* be valid under the applicable law, or (b) believes to this effect in reliance upon the advice of counsel, sought in good faith and given after full disclosure of all relevant facts within his knowledge and information."[57] (Emphasis supplied.)

As applied to a plaintiff's lawyer, this standard would allow lack of probable cause to be found where the lawyer proceeded with knowledge that the claim had no factual or legal basis, but would impose no obligation

---

53. Cf. Murdock v. Gerth, 150 P.2d 489, 493 (Cal.App.1944): [lawyer "obligated to present" to a court any "fairly debateable" claim supported by "facts stated to him by his client" even though court subsequently determines that lawyer's "judgment was erroneous"].

57. 3 Restatement Torts, 2d, § 675, pp. 457–458.

to investigate if the lawyer could reasonably believe the facts to be as the client alleged.

[3. Malice]

This Court has said, in opinions addressed to the tort of malicious prosecution, that malice may be inferred from the facts that establish want of probable cause, although the jury is not required to draw that inference.[58] This rule, developed in cases where damages were sought from a lay person who initiated proceedings, fails to make sufficient allowance for the lawyer's role as advocate and should not be applied in determining whether a lawyer acted for an improper purpose.

A client's total lack of belief that the action he initiates or continues can succeed is persuasive evidence of intent to harass or injure the defendant by bringing the action. But a lawyer who is unaware of such a client's improper purpose may, despite a personal lack of belief in any possible success of the action, see the client and the claim through to an appropriate conclusion without risking liability. Restatement 2d, Torts, § 674, comment *d*, states:

> An attorney who initiates a civil proceeding on behalf of his client or one who takes any steps in the proceeding is not liable if he has probable cause for his action (see § 675); *and even if he has no probable cause and is convinced that his client's claim is unfounded, he is still not liable if he acts primarily for the purpose of aiding his client in obtaining a proper adjudication of his claim.* (See § 676). An attorney is not required or expected to prejudge his client's claim, and although he is fully aware that its chances of success are comparatively slight, it is his responsibility to present it to the court for adjudication if his client so insists after he has explained to the client the nature of the chances. (Emphasis supplied.)

While a client's decision to proceed with litigation although he knows that the facts are not as alleged, or that a proper application to the facts of existing law (or any modification thereof which can be advanced in good faith) will not support the claim, is indicative of the client's ulterior, malicious motive, that inference cannot so easily be drawn from conduct of a lawyer who owes his client a duty of representation and is unaware of the client's improper purpose. The lawyer who "acts primarily for the purpose of aiding his client in obtaining a proper adjudication of his claim," albeit with knowledge that the claim is not tenable, should not be subject to liability on the thesis that an inference of an improper purpose may be drawn from the lawyer's continuing to advance a claim which he knew to be untenable.[60]

---

58. Hamilton v. Smith, 39 Mich. 222 (1878); Drobczyk v. Great Lakes Steel Corp., supra; Renda v. International Union, UAW, 366 Mich. 58, 100–101, 114 N.W.2d 343 (1962).

60. In, most if not, all attorney-client relationships, decision-making authority ultimately rests with the client. A client may, in apparent good faith, insist upon pressing the claim although the attorney has explained that it has no chance of succeeding.

The Restatement defines the mental element of the tort of wrongful civil proceedings as "a purpose other than that of securing the proper adjudication of the claim in which the proceedings are based." A finding of an improper purpose on the part of the unsuccessful attorney must be supported by evidence independent of the evidence establishing that the action was brought without probable cause.[61]

We affirm that portion of the Court of Appeals decision which upheld summary judgment in favor of defendants on plaintiff's claims sounding in negligence and abuse of process. With respect to plaintiff's claim for malicious prosecution, we reverse the decision of the Court of Appeals and affirm the trial court's grant of summary judgment; we do so on the ground that an action for malicious prosecution of a civil action may not be brought absent special injury and the plaintiff failed to plead special injury.

■ Kavanagh, Williams and Ryan, JJ., concur.

■ Levin, Justice (concurring).

Much of the discussion of the problem of unjustified litigation suffers from an undue focus upon the need to compensate the injury suffered by the defendant subjected to a groundless and malicious action. Groundless civil litigation is, however, more than an affliction visited upon a few scattered individuals; it besets the judicial system as a whole. It is, therefore, appropriate to think of it as a systemic problem and to fashion a remedy which preserves and strengthens the integrity of the civil litigation system rather than randomly providing a fortuitous amount of compensation in a handful of isolated cases.

. . .

. . . [T]his Court can appropriately devise an approach to wrongful litigation which is capable of providing both an appropriate measure of deterrence and reasonable compensation for wronged litigants without imperiling the right of free access to the courts. The remedy, quite simply, is to recognize the inadequacy of existing provisions for the taxation of costs and to adopt a new and distinct court rule authorizing the judge to whom a civil action is assigned to order payment of the prevailing party's actual expenses, including reasonable attorneys' fees and limited consequential damages, where the action was wrongfully initiated, defended or continued.[5] Depending upon the circumstances, payment might be required of the attorney, the client or both. The factual questions implicit in such an

---

An attorney's ability to withdraw from representation is limited if the client objects.

61. A contingent fee arrangement or the expectation of the attorney that he will ultimately receive a fee for his services is not evidence of an improper purpose. In contrast, a purpose to secure an improper adjudication of the client's claim, as by coercing a settlement unrelated to the merits from an opponent who wishes to avoid the harassment, expense or delay of letting the lawsuit run its course, is an improper purpose. See 3 Restatement Torts, 2d, § 674, comment d, p. 453.

5. Adoption of such a rule appears to be an appropriate exercise of this Court's plenary power over practice and procedure in Michigan courts. See Perin v. Peuler (On Rehearing), 130 N.W.2d 4 (Mich.1964). . . .

evaluation of the losing side's conduct would be resolved by the judge after a prompt post-termination hearing at which the parties could call witnesses and they and their attorneys could testify.

The foundation for developing such a comprehensive structure for controlling vexatious litigation is already in place. GCR 1963, 111.6, [permits a court to impose sanctions on a party pleading facts unreasonably].

. . .

Having such a determination made by the judge to whom the original proceeding was assigned would have a number of advantages over assessment of these questions by judge and jury in a separate tort action:

First, a strategy for evaluating the propriety of litigation which is administered exclusively by judges is more susceptible of consistent application and careful supervision than a strategy which relies on a group of laymen chosen at random, often for one day and one trial. Confiding the question solely to the judge avoids the bifurcation of function associated with jury trial on the critical issue of probable cause in an action for malicious prosecution of civil proceedings. Limiting recovery to actual pecuniary loss, thereby eliminating recovery for emotional distress, and relying on a judge to assess damages, combined with the greater control that appellate courts exercise over a judge's findings as compared to a jury's verdict, should tend to avoid awards which might intimidate good-faith litigants.

Second, the judge would usually be familiar with the history of the case; the necessary evidence could be adduced and the relevant findings made in far more efficient fashion than if a new action and a separate trial before a different judge were required.

Third, parties who might be reluctant to initiate further litigation although they felt themselves wronged would be more likely to avail themselves of internal sanctions than of the opportunity to start a separate action which would take its place on the crowded docket and which the defendants would be likely to resist with all available means.

. . . By adopting a court rule this Court would address the problem directly and in a manner compatible with its responsibility to exercise close control and supervision.

. . .

The effectiveness of such a rule would depend upon the vigilance of the judges who would apply it. The opinion of the Court in the instant case describes certain instances in which sanctions should not be imposed against an attorney. Nothing in the opinion of the Court should, however, be understood as indicating that the Court is unwilling to commit itself to the imposition of sanctions against an attorney where it is appropriate.

[Chief Justice Coleman dissented from the portion of the majority opinion requiring an allegation of special injury to state a claim for malicious prosecution. He argued that the special-injury requirement was unrelated to whether the earlier suit was meritorious or frivolous; and that the court's concern for groundless malicious prosecution suits was "one-sided," demonstrating concern that such suits might cause legal malpractice insurance premiums to rise and ignoring the effect frivolous litigation has had on physicians' malpractice insurance premiums. Justice Moody's partial dissent also objected to the special-injury requirement as anachronistic. Formerly, most civil actions were accompanied either by civil arrest of the defendant or attachment or garnishment of the defendant's property. Thus the requirement of interference with the person or property of the defendant was routinely satisfied. Today these provisional and summary remedies are normally unavailable. The special injury requirement precludes most malicious suits and is unrelated to the actual damage caused by them.]

Civil Liability of a Lawyer for Pursuing a Frivolous Claim

Was the Claim Against Dr. Friedman Frivolous?

The *Friedman* case was litigated in the Michigan courts on the assumption that lawyer Dozorc brought an unfounded medical malpractice claim against Dr. Friedman. Presumably this is why medical associations and bar associations treated the litigation as a major case and filed amici briefs. Did Dozorc violate M.R. 3.1 or DR 7–102(A)(1)? See the discussion of the professional rules dealing with pursuing frivolous matters at p. 383 above. Do the limited facts suggest to the contrary that Dozorc was guilty of legal malpractice in failing to establish a prima facie case of medical malpractice against Dr. Friedman?

Negligence Claim

During the "medical malpractice crisis" of the 1970s, cases resembling *Friedman* were litigated in many states, with similar results.[14] The courts have uniformly rejected negligence claims brought against lawyers by people those lawyers had sued on behalf of a client.[15] The courts have likewise rejected the argument that the ethics rules, in particular the rules against maintaining frivolous suits, create a legal duty that extends to the opposing party.[16] Is there an inconsistency in relying on policies of "free access to the courts" to deny a civil recovery based on violations of M.R. 3.1 or DR 7–102(A)(1) when the purpose of those provisions is precisely to curtail frivolous filings?[17]

14. For discussion of Friedman v. Dozorc, see Gerald W. Boston, Liability of Attorneys to Nonclients in Michigan: A Re-examination of Friedman v. Dozorc and a Rule of Limited Liability, 68 U.Det.L.Rev. 307 (1991).

15. In addition to Friedman see: Morowitz v. Marvel, 423 A.2d 196 (D.C.App.1980);

Drago v. Buonagurio, 386 N.E.2d 821 (N.Y. 1978); Spencer v. Burglass, 337 So.2d 596, 600–601 (La.App.1976).

16. See Mozzochi v. Beck, 529 A.2d 171 (Conn.1987), discussed infra.

17. Charles Wolfram argues that standards of lawyer performance in ethics codes should be treated in much the same way

Do the reasons given in *Friedman* for rejecting the negligence claim apply with equal force to the type of claim allowed in *Greycas*, printed at p. 79 above? Why allow broader liability to third parties when the lawyer is acting as a facilitator of transactions than when the lawyer is acting as an advocate?

Abuse of Process

Why does the court in *Friedman* reject the abuse of process claim? The Restatement of Torts states that a party is liable for abuse of process when it uses legal process primarily to accomplish a purpose for which it is not designed.[18] A Comment explains that the word "primarily" was added to exclude liability "when the process is used for the purpose for which it was intended, but there is an incidental motive of spite or an ulterior purpose of benefit to the defendant."[19] As explained in *Friedman*, the tort has two elements: (1) an ulterior purpose; and (2) a willful act that is improper in the regular conduct of the proceeding.[20]

Mozzochi v. Beck[21] involved an abuse of process claim against lawyers. The plaintiff alleged that the lawyers had maintained suit despite learning that the allegations were untrue and that the suit therefore was wholly without merit. The court concluded:

> [A]lthough attorneys have a duty to their clients and to the judicial system not to pursue litigation that is utterly groundless, that duty does not give rise to a third party action for abuse of process unless the third party can point to specific misconduct intended to cause specific injury outside of the normal contemplation of private litigation. Any other rule would ineluctably interfere with the attorney's primary duty of robust representation of the interests of his or her client.[22]

Implicitly, *Mozzochi* states that factually baseless claims are within the "normal contemplation of private litigation." Given M.R. 3.1, Fed.R.Civ.P. 11 and state counterparts to these rules, how can maintaining a factually baseless claim be regarded as "normal"? Do M.R. 3.1 and Rule 11 "ineluctably" interfere with the attorney's primary duty of "robust" representation? Compare *Raine v. Drasin*,[23] upholding a jury verdict against a lawyer, including punitive damages, for filing a complaint against two doctors when

---

as criminal or regulatory standards are treated in tort litigation generally—as giving rise to a civil cause of action or as persuasive evidence of the standard of care. Because of the limited resources of disciplinary bodies, "judicial expansion of recoveries for professional civil liability may be necessary to achieve an acceptable level of attorney compliance with [professional codes]." Providing for civil liability for violation of professional rules prohibiting frivolous filings, Wolfram argues, would give bite to the professional rule. Charles W. Wolfram, The Code of Professional Re-

sponsibility as a Measure of Attorney Liability in Civil Litigation, 30 S.C.L.Rev. 281, 287–95, 310–314 (1979).

18. Restatement (Second) of Torts § 682.

19. Id., Comment b to § 682.

20. See W. Prosser and P. Keeton, Torts (5th ed.1984) § 121.

21. 529 A.2d 171 (Conn.1987).

22. 529 A.2d at 174.

23. 621 S.W.2d 895 (Ky.1981).

the lawyer had in his possession medical records showing the claim lacked substance.

Malicious Prosecution

The elements of a malicious prosecution cause of action are: (1) the defendant instituted a proceeding against the plaintiff; (2) the proceeding was terminated in favor of the plaintiff;[24] (3) the absence of probable cause for the proceeding; (4) the defendant acted out of malice or other improper purpose; and, in a minority of jurisdictions, (5) the plaintiff suffered damage of the type required for this cause of action.

(i) *Special injury requirement*. Isn't the special injury requirement an anachronism that should be eliminated from today's common law? When nearly all civil actions were initiated by arrest of the defendant or an attachment or garnishment of property, the requirement was easily met. Today, when those summary remedies may be employed constitutionally only in very special circumstances established after notice and hearing, the requirement has the effect of largely abolishing the malicious prosecution cause of action. Note that most American states have eliminated the special injury requirement.

(ii) *Absence of probable cause*. When, according to *Friedman*, does a lawyer's prior filing of a baseless suit satisfy the requirement that the suit was brought without probable cause? In *Friedman*, the court rejects the standard for judging probable cause articulated by the California court in *Henigson*. Why? One reason given is that "[t]ime will not always permit 'a reasonable investigation and industrious search of legal authority.' " If, as Justice Levin argues in his concurrence in *Friedman*, the answer to abusive litigation is sanctioning lawyers under a rule of court, why wouldn't the same concern about "time" argue against that solution?

The California Supreme Court has partially disapproved of the standard articulated in *Henigson*. *Henigson* said that probable cause had an objective component (reasonable investigation and industrious legal research) and a subjective component (honest belief). In *Sheldon Appel*[25] the court (1) rejected the subjective component, holding that it was irrelevant to the issue of probable cause whether the lawyer actually believed the suit was tenable; (2) held that probable cause was ordinarily for the court to decide as a matter of law and not for the jury; and (3) held that if there was such probable cause, it is immaterial that the attorney may not have made an adequate investigation.

How is a court to judge whether the prior action was instituted with probable cause? The standard, according to *Sheldon Appel*, is whether, on the facts as known to the lawyer at the time she instituted suit, the suit

---

24.   The requirement of termination means that a malicious prosecution claim cannot be asserted as a counterclaim. A favorable termination does not include a settlement, but only a successful adjudication.

25.   Sheldon Appel Co. v. Albert & Oliker, 765 P.2d 498 (Cal.1989).

was objectively tenable. Expert testimony on this question is not permitted.[26] How does the *Sheldon Appel* position on probable cause differ from that of the court in *Friedman?*

In Crowley v. Katleman,[27] the California Supreme Court held that a plaintiff may successfully maintain suit for malicious prosecution as long as one of the claims in the underlying case was filed without probable cause and with malice. In *Crowley,* there was probable cause for the defendants (a woman and her lawyer) to have alleged one of the six theories of liability that they had put forth in the underlying case. According to the California court, however, one valid claim does not immunize a lawsuit from being the basis of a later suit for malicious prosecution. Justice Arabian, dissenting, urged the virtues of rules that allowed judges to sanction lawyers for maintaining frivolous actions. Unlike the tort remedy, he argued, such rules promote judicial economy, infringe less on the principle of ready access to the courts and provide more appropriate penalties.

(iii) Malice. When does an attorney act with malice according to *Friedman?* In *Sheldon Appel,* the court held that once the judge finds that the prior action was *not* objectively tenable, then the fact that the lawyer never thought it tenable and the fact that she failed to do any research before filing become relevant to whether the suit was instituted with malice.

Note that when a *party* is sued for malicious prosecution, reliance on counsel's advice may serve to negate the element of malice.[28] However, reliance on counsel will not serve to negate malice when the client withholds facts from the lawyer.[29]

Other Tort Liability Issues

Immunity from Suit for Defamation

Lawyers and other participants in judicial proceedings are absolutely immune from suit for defamation based on statements made in the course of those proceedings or "reasonably related" thereto.[30] Some courts recognize only a qualified privilege for comments "preliminary to a proposed judicial proceeding."[31] Others recognize an absolute privilege for these comments.[32]

The broad reach of the privilege has been criticized:

26.   765 P.2d at 510.

27.   881 P.2d 1083 (Cal.1994).

28.   See, e.g., Noell v. Angle, 231 S.E.2d 330 (Va.1977).

29.   See, e.g., Derby v. Jenkins, 363 A.2d 967, 971 (Md.App.1976).

30.   See Restatement (Second) of Torts, § 586; W. Prosser and P. Keeton on Torts § 114 (5th Ed.1984).

31.   See, e.g., Pinkston v. Lovell, 759 S.W.2d 20 (Ark.1988) (comments by lawyer in conversation with clients on advisability of malpractice action are privileged if the initiation of proceedings in good faith is being seriously considered).

32.   See Arneja v. Gildar, 541 A.2d 621 (D.C.App.1988) (ethnic slurs).

In the hands of some courts, the privilege has been reshaped into something very much like a privilege for a lawyer to be bumptious and unrestrained in all matters vaguely related to litigation and regardless of whether the communication is calculated to advance or to retard justice or the proceeding.... Courts have employed the privilege beyond defamation and have held that suits are barred by the same immunity if they are based on negligent misrepresentation, invasion of privacy, or intentional infliction of emotional distress.[33]

Perjury as a Tort

The common law rule followed in most jurisdictions is that, in the absence of a statute, it is not a tort to commit perjury or suborn perjury.[34] A number of justifications are offered: The rule (1) protects society's interest in finality of judgments, (2) prevents multiplication of litigation, and (3) prevents the intimidation of witnesses and parties.[35] However, if the plaintiff otherwise states a cause of action, e.g., for malicious prosecution or conspiracy to defraud the plaintiff of property, proof of the use of perjury may establish other elements of the plaintiff's case.[36] In conspiracy cases, the courts usually require that the perjury be part of a larger scheme or plan to injure the plaintiff.[37]

Liability for perjury or suborning perjury may be predicated upon a statute. For example, N.Y. Jud. Law § 487 authorizes an injured person to recover treble damages in a civil action from an attorney "guilty of any deceit or collusion with intent to deceive the court or any party." This and similar statutes in other states, however, are interpreted narrowly and rarely invoked.

Tortious Spoliation of Evidence

A few states have imposed tort liability for the intentional or negligent destruction or loss of evidence. In cases involving the negligent destruction of evidence, the claim is usually that the defendant interfered with the plaintiff's efforts to sue some third party by negligently destroying or losing potential evidence. The plaintiff must show that the defendant had a special relationship to the plaintiff that entailed a duty to preserve the evidence, such as that of a health care provider to a patient.[38] The cases

---

33. Wolfram, Modern Legal Ethics 231 (1986).

34. See W. Prosser and P. Keeton, Torts (5th ed.1984) § 114; F. Harper, F. James and O. Gray, Torts § 5.22.

35. Shepherd v. Epps, 347 S.E.2d 289 (Ga. App.1986).

36. See, e.g., Snyder v. Faget, 326 So.2d 113 (Ala.1976) (perjury may be demonstrated to prove an overt act in furtherance of conspiracy to defraud).

37. See Stolte v. Blackstone, 328 N.W.2d 462 (Neb.1982) (collecting and discussing cases).

38. See, e.g., Bondu v. Gurvich, 473 So.2d 1307 (Fla.App.1984) (hospital failed to preserve certain medical records of the plaintiff; as a result plaintiff lost a medical malpractice lawsuit against doctors); Pirocchi v. Liberty Mutual Insurance Co., 365 F.Supp. 277 (E.D.Pa.1973) (action against claims adjuster for losing the chair that allegedly caused plaintiff's injuries, making it impossible for plaintiff to sue the chair's

generally involve parties that the plaintiff would have sued had the evidence not been destroyed.[39] Other jurisdictions reject this tort on the ground, among other things, that other remedies are available.[40]

Is Court Rule Better than Tort Rule?[41]

Courts have kept a tight rein on tort suits to redress frivolous litigation while enlarging the scope of court sanctions against lawyers who bring frivolous suits. Justice Levin, concurring in *Friedman*, argues for court rule instead of tort rule. Is a court rule preferable? Why?

After *Friedman* Michigan changed its rule on sanctions for frivolous litigation. M.C.R. 2.114 is substantially similar to Fed.R.Civ.P. 11 and is considerably more stringent than Michigan's old rule.[42]

3.   RULE 11 SANCTIONS

The Fight Over How Stringent Rule 11 Should Be

In 1983, Rule 11 of the Federal Rules of Civil Procedure was amended,[1] and litigation practice changed. The 1983 rule *required* judges to sanction lawyers whenever a paper filed in court by a lawyer was not well grounded in fact or not warranted by existing law or a good faith argument that existing law should be modified or reversed. The lawyer's belief in the facts alleged and the law argued was not enough to avoid the mandatory sanctions dictated by the amended rule; the test for avoiding sanctions was objective. The lawyer's belief in the facts had to be reasonable and the legal arguments had to be reasonable under existing law or reasonable arguments to extend or change the law. Moreover, the lawyer was required to

---

manufacturer). Compare, e.g., Parker v. Thyssen Min. Constr., Inc., 428 So.2d 615 (Ala.1983) (employer had no duty to preserve evidence for employee's potential civil action against third parties).

39. Hazen v. Municipality of Anchorage, 718 P.2d 456 (Alaska 1986) (claim that police intentionally altered a record of favorable evidence concerning person charged with crime stated a claim for relief).

40. For example, in Cedars–Sinai Medical Center v. Superior Court, 954 P.2d 511 (1998), the California court, emphasizing the value of finality in litigation and the availability of alternative remedies, such as instructing the jury on drawing negative inferences about lost evidence and awarding sanctions in the underlying case, overruled an earlier case, Smith v. Superior Court, 198 Cal.Rptr. 829 (1984), that had approved the tort of spoilation of evidence. See also LaRaia v. Superior Court, 722 P.2d 286 (Ariz.1986); and Miller v. Mont-

gomery County, 494 A.2d 761 (Md.App. 1985) (emphasizing that because destruction was by opposing party, plaintiff had other remedies available, i.e., negative inferences would be drawn about what the material would have shown).

41. For a discussion of tort liability and court sanctions, see John W. Wade, On Frivolous Litigation: A Study of Tort Liability and Procedural Sanctions, 14 Hofstra L.Rev. 433 (1986).

42. Another mechanism for reducing the number of frivolous medical malpractice cases is the use of medical malpractice screening panels in these cases. See, e.g., Howard Bedlin & Paul Nejelski, Unsettling Issues About Settling Civil Litigation, 68 Judicature 9, 11 (1984) (which also cites, at n. 5, state cases finding the panel system unconstitutional).

1. The full text of the amended rule is reproduced in the opening paragraphs of the Golden Eagle case, below at 407.

conduct a reasonable investigation into the facts and law before filing any papers in court, and sanctions for failing to conduct a reasonable investigation were mandatory too. Prior to 1983, sanctions were within the sound discretion of the trial court, and a lawyer's subjective belief in the soundness of the cause she was championing was enough to avoid them.

The stiffening of Rule 11 in 1983 resulted in a large increase in the frequency of sanctions and, not surprisingly, provoked a heated controversy.[2] Many judges and some lawyers lauded the constraints the rule placed on assertion of unmeritorious claims and defenses and other abusive litigation tactics. A few judges and many trial lawyers complained that the cure was worse than the disease, arguing the tactical use of the rule and the cost of collateral proceedings outweighed any benefits.[3] The plaintiffs' and civil rights' bar, as well as some legal scholars, also argued that Rule 11 limited the growth of new legal interpretations because it was sometimes used to penalize lawyers who challenged existing doctrine.[4]

At first the fight over Rule 11 as amended in 1983 was fought out in the courts. The *Golden Eagle* case, reprinted below, is an artifact of that fight. Many other judicial decisions, including nearly a half dozen by the Supreme Court, gradually narrowed the interpretive uncertainties. Attention then shifted to the rules committees of the Judicial Conference of the United States. These committees considered a large number of proposed amendments, some designed to broaden the rule and stiffen its requirements and others designed to narrow and moderate it. Finally the Judicial Conference sent a proposal to the Court. Over a vigorous dissent by Justice Scalia, the Court adopted a new version of Rule 11, which went into effect at the end of 1993.

The 1993 version of Rule 11 represented an elaborate compromise. On one hand, the lawyer's duty of candor was expanded somewhat. See the text of Rule 11(b) reprinted at p. 423 infra and the discussion that follows it. On the other, the rule no longer requires that sanctions be imposed for violations and a "safe harbor" provision has been added that immunizes violations as long as the violating lawyer withdraws or corrects the offending statements within 21 days of her opponent's calling them to her attention.[5]

---

2. Before the 1983 amendments Rule 11 motions had been filed in only nineteen reported cases; in the first four years after the rule was amended there were more than 600 reported Rule 11 cases. See William W. Schwarzer, Rule 11 Revisted, 101 Harv. L. Rev. 1013 (1988); Georgene M. Vairo, Rule 11: A Critical Analysis, 118 F.R.D. 189 (1988).

3. See, e.g., Judge Jack B.Weinstein "[Rule 11] has become another way of harassing the opponent and delaying the case. To date, the effects have been adverse." Tamar Lewin, A Legal Curb Raises Hackles,

N.Y. Times, Oct. 2, 1986, pp. D1, D8 (quoting Judge Weinstein).

4. See, e.g., Melissa L. Nelkin, Sanctions Under Amended Federal Rules 11: Some "Chilling" Problems in the Struggle Between Compensation and Punishment, 74 Geo. L. J. 1313, 1326 (1986). But see Jeffrey A. Parness, More Stringent Sanctions Under Federal Civil Rule 11: A Reply To Professor Nelkin, 75 Geo. L. J. 1937 (1987).

5. See 146 F.R.D. 577–92 (1993) for the full text of the 1993 version of the Rule and the accompanying Notes of the Advisory Committee on Civil Rules. For an in-depth anal-

Justice Scalia expressed strong objections to the changes in the sanctions provisions of the amended rule. Dissenting from the Court's adoption of the 1993 rule, he stated, "the proposed revision would render the rule toothless, by allowing judges to dispense with sanctions, by disfavoring the compensation for litigation expenses, and by providing a 21–day 'safe harbor' within which, if the party accused of the frivolous filings withdraws the filing, he is entitled to escape with no sanction at all."[6]

Scalia argued that empirical evidence showed that the 1983 rule was effective in deterring frivolous pleadings and motions, an important goal of the federal procedural system because it serves the fundamental purpose of the system—"just, speedy, and inexpensive determination of every action." Fed.R.Civ.P. 1. He cited data from a study by the Federal Judicial Center:

> Eighty percent of district judges believe [the 1983 version of] Rule 11 has had an overall positive effect and should be retained in its present form, 95 percent believed the Rule had not impeded development of the law, and about 75 percent said the benefits justify the expenditure of judicial time. . . . True, many lawyers do not like Rule 11. It may cause them financial liability, it may damage their professional reputation in front of important clients, and the cost-of-litigation savings it produces are savings not to lawyers but to litigants. But the overwhelming approval of the Rule by the federal district judges who daily grapple with the problem of litigation abuse is enough to persuade me that it should not be gutted as the proposed revisions suggests.[7]

In 1995 the Federal Judicial Center surveyed judges and lawyers on their experiences with and attitudes toward the 1993 version of the rule.[8] Most of the judges who were surveyed (68%), believed that the problem of frivolous litigation was much the same under the 1983 and 1993 versions of the rule, and most defense lawyers agreed (53%). Plaintiffs' lawyers (30%) were much more likely than judges (3%) or defense lawyers (5%) to deny that frivolous litigation was a problem.[9] The survey showed large support for the safe harbor provision added in 1993.[10] Only about one-fourth of each group of respondents supported the reintroduction of mandatory, as opposed to discretionary, sanctions. Significant percentages in all groups

ysis of the 1983 and 1993 amendments to Rule 11, see Carl Tobias, Common Sense and Other Legal Reforms, 48 Vand. L. Rev. 699 (1995).

6. See 146 F.R.D. at 507–08

7. 146 F.R.D. at 509–10.

8. Federal Judicial Center, Report of a Survey Concerning Rule 11, Federal Rules of Civil Procedure (1995).

9. Of the remaining 70% of plaintiffs' lawyers who thought frivolous litigation was or had been a problem, 44% reported that the problem had neither increased nor decreased after the 1993 amendments. Only 1% of plaintiffs' lawyers, 5% of "other lawyers" (lawyers who said they represented plaintiffs and defendants about equally), 9% of judges and 10% of defendants' lawyers thought the problem of frivolous litigation had gotten larger since the 1993 amendments to Rule 11 had been in force.

10. Eighty percent of the plaintiffs' lawyers, 70% of the judges, 67% of other lawyers and 61% of defense lawyers said they either strongly or moderately supported the safe harbor provision.

surveyed thought that the 1993 version of Rule 11 struck the right balance.[11]

In the years since 1993 various bills have been introduced in Congress that in effect would undo the 1993 changes and restore much or all of the 1983 regime. As of mid–1999, none of those bills had been enacted.

Does *Golden Eagle* suggest that the 1983 version was too strong? Too weak? Does it support a safe harbor provision?

Golden Eagle Distributing Corp. v. Burroughs Corp.

United States Court of Appeals, Ninth Circuit, 1986.
801 F.2d 1531.

■ BEFORE SCHROEDER, REINHARDT, AND BEEZER, CIRCUIT JUDGES.

■ SCHROEDER, CIRCUIT JUDGE.

I.   INTRODUCTION

This is an appeal from the imposition of sanctions under Rule 11 of the Federal Rules of Civil Procedure as amended in 1983. The appellant, a major national law firm, raises significant questions of first impression.

The relevant portions of the amended Rule provide:

> Every pleading, motion, and other paper of a party represented by an attorney shall be signed by at least one attorney of record in his individual name, whose address shall be stated. A party who is not represented by an attorney shall sign his pleading, motion, or other paper and state his address.... The signature of an attorney or party constitutes a certificate by him that he has read the pleading, motion, or other paper; that to the best of his knowledge, information, and belief formed after reasonable inquiry it is well grounded in fact and is warranted by existing law or a good faith argument for the extension, modification, or reversal of existing law, and that it is not interposed for any improper purpose, such as to harass or to cause unnecessary delay or needless increase in the cost of litigation. If a pleading, motion, or other paper is not signed, it shall be stricken unless it is signed promptly after the omission is called to the attention of the pleader or movant. If a pleading, motion, or other paper is signed in violation of this rule, the court, upon motion or upon its own initiative, shall impose upon the person who signed it, a represented party, or both, an appropriate sanction, which may include an order to pay to the other party or parties the amount of the reasonable expenses

---

11. General approval of the 1993 balance was given by 52% of judges, 41% of plaintiffs' lawyers, 40% of other lawyers, and 37% of defense lawyers. The same percentage of defense lawyers (37%) thought Rule 11 should be toughened to deter groundless filings, joined by 32% of judges, 24% of other lawyers and 11% of plaintiffs' lawyers. A question whether the 1993 version was too tough and thus deterred too many meritorious filings obtained agreement from 27% of plaintiffs' lawyers, 12% of defense lawyers, 16% of other lawyers, but only 7% of judges.

incurred because of the filing of the pleading, motion, or other paper, including a reasonable attorney's fee.

The appellant Kirkland & Ellis is the law firm that represented the defendant Burroughs in the underlying litigation. The sanctions which we review here stemmed from an unsuccessful motion for summary judgment filed by appellant on Burroughs' behalf....

. . .

The district court held that the positions taken by the appellant in its motions papers were supportable, both legally and factually. The district court concluded, however, ... that the appellant should have stated that a position it was taking was grounded in a "good faith argument for the extension, modification, or reversal of existing law" rather than implying that its position was "warranted by existing law." Second, the court held that the appellant's moving papers had failed to cite contrary authority in violation of the ABA's Model Rules of Professional Conduct, and that this breach constituted a violation of Rule 11.

. . .

II. PROCEDURAL BACKGROUND OF THIS DISPUTE

Golden Eagle Distributing Corporation filed the underlying action in Minnesota state court for fraud, negligence, and breach of contract against Burroughs, because of an allegedly defective computer system. Burroughs removed the action to the federal district court in Minnesota. Burroughs then moved pursuant to 28 U.S.C. § 1404(a) to transfer the action to the Northern District of California. The district court granted the motion, noting that all of the sources of proof, including the relevant documents and the computer system at issue, and almost all of the witnesses, were located in California.

Burroughs next filed the motion for summary judgment which gave rise to the sanctions at issue here. It argued that the California, rather than the Minnesota, statute of limitations applied....

. . .

A. The Statute of Limitations Argument

Kirkland & Ellis's opening memorandum argued that Golden Eagle's claims were barred by California's three-year statute of limitations. The question was whether the change of venue from Minnesota to California affected which law applied. Kirkland & Ellis essentially argued that under Van Dusen v. Barrack, 376 U.S. 612 (1964), California's law applied because a Minnesota court would have dismissed the action on forum non conveniens grounds....[12]

. . .

12. [Editors' note:] The Kirkland & Ellis memorandum in support of Burroughs' motion to dismiss stated:

In imposing sanctions, the district court held that Kirkland & Ellis's argument was "misleading" because it suggested that there already exists a forum non conveniens exception to the general rule that the transferor's law applies. *Golden Eagle*, 103 F.R.D. at 126–28. *Van Dusen* raised the issue but did not decide it. 376 U.S. at 640.[13]

Kirkland & Ellis's corollary argument, that a Minnesota court would have dismissed the case on forum non conveniens grounds, was found to be "misleading" because it failed to note that one prerequisite to such a dismissal is that an alternative forum be available. See Bongards' Creameries v. Alfa–Laval, Inc., 339 N.W.2d 561, 562 (Minn.1983). Burroughs had pointed out in its Rule 11 memorandum, however, that the meaning of the term "available forum" is not settled. Compare Wasche v. Wasche, 268 N.W.2d 721, 723 (Minn.1978) (statute of limitations bar may affect dismissal) with Hill v. Upper Mississippi Towing Corp., 252 Minn. 165, 89 N.W.2d 654 (1958) (suggesting available forum is where defendant is amenable to process).

. . .

B.   The Economic Damages Argument

Kirkland & Ellis also argued that Golden Eagle's claim for negligent manufacture lacked merit because Golden Eagle sought damages for economic loss, and such damages are not recoverable under California law. Kirkland & Ellis relied on Seely v. White Motor Co., 63 Cal.2d 9, 403 P.2d 145, 45 Cal.Rptr. 17 (1965). In *Seely*, the California Supreme Court limited recovery in negligence and strict liability tort actions to damages for personal injuries and harm to physical property.[14]

The district court sanctioned Kirkland & Ellis for not citing three cases whose holdings it concluded were adverse to *Seely*: the California Supreme Court's opinion in J'Aire Corp. v. Gregory, 24 Cal.3d 799, 598 P.2d 60, 157

The Minnesota courts have repeatedly applied the doctrine of forum non conveniens to dismiss claims of nonresident plaintiffs in circumstances strikingly similar to those in this case. ...[I]t would have been an abuse of discretion for a Minnesota trial court not to dismiss Golden Eagle's complaint.

103 F.R.D. 124, 126 (N.D.Cal.1984).

13. [Editors' note:] In *Van Dusen* the Supreme Court said: "In so ruling, however we do not and need not consider whether in all cases ... [the transferor's law should be applied].... We do not attempt to determine whether, for example, the same considerations would govern if a plaintiff ... contended that the transferor State would simply have dismissed the action on the ground of forum non conveniens." 376 U.S. at 639–40.

14. [Editors' note:] The Kirkland & Ellis memorandum in support of Burroughs' motion to dismiss used the following quote from *Seeley*: "[I]n actions for negligence, a manufacturer's liability is limited to damages for physical injuries and there is no recovery for economic losses alone." 103 F.R.D. at 128. The memo did not cite a more recent California Supreme Court case, *J'Aire*, which held that economic losses were recoverable in negligence actions, nor did it cite two California intermediate appellate cases applying *J'Aire* to allow economic damages. While *J'Aire* did not explicitly overrule *Seeley* and neglected to discuss or even cite it, at the time Kirkland & Ellis wrote its motion memo it was obvious that *J'Aire*, at a minimum, limited the language the law firm quoted from *Seeley*.

Cal.Rptr. 407 (1979), and two intermediate appellate court decisions interpreting *J'Aire's* effect on *Seely*, Pisano v. American Leasing, 146 Cal. App.3d 194, 194 Cal.Rptr. 77 (1983), and Huang v. Garner, 157 Cal.App.3d 404, 203 Cal.Rptr. 800 (1984).[1] The district court held that these omissions violated counsel's duty to disclose adverse authority, embodied in Model Rule 3.3, . . . which the court viewed as a "necessary corollary to Rule 11." *Golden Eagle*, 103 F.R.D. at 127.

Kirkland & Ellis continues to maintain vigorously that the cases are not directly adverse authority and that they are distinguishable. In this appeal we assume that they are directly contrary in order to reach the larger question of whether Kirkland & Ellis's failure to cite them was a violation of Rule 11.

III.   THE BACKGROUND OF THE 1983 AMENDMENTS TO RULE 11 AND THEIR INTERPRETATION IN THE COURTS

Under the 1983 amendments to Rule 11, an attorney signing any motion in federal court warrants that the motion is well-grounded in fact, that it is warranted by existing law or a good faith argument for an extension, modification or reversal of existing law, and that it is not filed for an improper purpose. . . .

The Advisory Committee Note to the amendments comments at length on their purpose. . . . All the comments make it clear that the amendments' major purposes were the deterrence of dilatory or abusive pretrial tactics and the streamlining of litigation. . . .

. . .

Th[e] expansion [of Rule 11] gave rise to concerns that the new Rule might have unfortunate results in at least two respects. The first was that the amended Rule might tend to chill creativity in advocacy and impede the traditional ability of the common law to adjust to changing situations. The Advisory Committee responded. . . .

> The rule is not intended to chill an attorney's enthusiasm or creativity in pursuing factual or legal theories. The court is expected to avoid using the wisdom of hindsight and should test the signer's conduct by inquiring what was reasonable to believe at the time the pleading, motion, or other paper was submitted.

Another major concern was that the broadened availability of sanctions might lead to protracted and expensive satellite litigation over the appropriateness of sanctions. . . .

. . . The leading decision in this circuit has identified the two major problems to which the amendments were directed as the problem of "frivolous filings" and the problem of "misusing judicial procedures as a weapon for personal or economic harassment." Zaldivar v. City of Los Angeles, 780 F.2d 823, 830 (9th Cir.1986). Along the same lines, the leading

---

1. Kirkland & Ellis did cite and discuss *J'Aire* in its reply brief after the case was called to its attention in plaintiff's response.

decision of the Second Circuit announced tests for the mandatory imposition of sanctions under both parts of the Rule. Sanctions should be imposed if (1) "after reasonable inquiry, a competent attorney could not form a reasonable belief that the pleading (or other paper) is well grounded in fact and is warranted by existing law or a good faith argument for the extension, modification or reversal of existing law" or if (2) "a pleading (or other paper) has been interposed for any improper purpose." Eastway [Construction Corp. v. City of New York] 762 F.2d [243] at 25 [(2d Cir.1985)]; . . . .

There is general agreement that whether the first of the two Rule 11 requirements has been satisfied is to be determined by use of an objective standard. . . .

As to the second, "not for improper purposes," part of Rule 11, we emphasized in *Zaldivar* the objective nature of the standard. We stated that a complaint which complies with the "well-grounded in fact and warranted by . . . law" clause cannot be sanctioned as harassment under Rule 11, regardless of the subjective intent of the attorney or litigant. *Zaldivar*, 780 F.2d at 832.

· · ·

IV. STANDARD OF REVIEW

[The court discussed Ninth Circuit decisions holding that the standard for appellate review in Rule 11 questions depended upon the issue involved and that de novo review was the appropriate standard when the issue, as in this case, involved "whether specific conduct violated the Rule." Subsequently, the Supreme Court in Cooter & Gell v. Hartmarx Corp., 496 U.S. 384 (1990), held that the standard of review for all issues arising under Rule 11 was whether the district court abused its discretion.]

V. THE APPLICATION OF RULE 11 IN THIS CASE

The district court's application of Rule 11 in this case strikes a chord not otherwise heard in discussion of this Rule. The district court did not focus on whether a sound basis in law and in fact existed for the defendant's motion for summary judgment. Indeed it indicated that the motion itself was nonfrivolous. 103 F.R.D. at 126. Rather, the district court looked to the manner in which the motion was presented. The district court in this case held that Rule 11 imposes upon counsel an ethical "duty of candor." *Golden Eagle*, 103 F.R.D. at 127. The court drew its principles from Rule 3.3 of the ABA's Model Rules and the accompanying comment. It said:

> The duty of candor is a necessary corollary of the certification required by Rule 11. A court has a right to expect that counsel will state the controlling law fairly and fully; indeed, unless that is done the court cannot perform its task properly. A lawyer must not misstate the law, fail to disclose adverse authority (not disclosed by his opponent), or omit facts critical to the application of the rule of law relied on.

Golden Eagle, 103 F.R.D. at 127.

. . .

We need not here definitively resolve the problems of the proper role of the courts in enforcing the ethical obligations of lawyers.[3] We must consider only whether Rule 11 requires the courts to enforce ethical standards of advocacy beyond the terms of the Rule itself.

The district court's invocation of Rule 11 has two aspects. The first, which we term "argument identification" is the holding that counsel should differentiate between an argument "warranted by existing law" and an argument for the "extension, modification, or reversal of existing law." The second is the conclusion that Rule 11 is violated when counsel fails to cite what the district court views to be directly contrary authority. We deal with each in turn, noting at the outset that many of our observations are applicable to both aspects of the court's interpretation of Rule 11.

A.   "Argument Identification"

. . .

The text of the Rule does not require that counsel differentiate between a position which is supported by existing law and one that would extend it. The Rule on its face requires that the motion be either one or the other. . . . It is not always easy to decide whether an argument is based on established law or is an argument for the extension of existing law. Whether the case being litigated is or is not materially the same as earlier precedent is frequently the very issue which prompted the litigation in the first place. Such questions can be close.

Sanctions under Rule 11 are mandatory. See, e.g., *Eastway*, 762 F.2d at 254 n. 7. In even a close case, we think it extremely unlikely that a judge, who has already decided that the law is not as a lawyer argued it, will also decide that the loser's position was warranted by existing law. Attorneys who adopt an aggressive posture risk more than the loss of the motion if the district court decides that their argument is for an extension of the law which it declines to make. What is at stake is often not merely the monetary sanction but the lawyer's reputation.

The "argument identification" requirement adopted by the district court therefore tends to create a conflict between the lawyer's duty zealously to represent his client, Model Code of Professional Responsibility Canon 7, and the lawyer's own interest in avoiding rebuke. The concern on the part of the bar that this type of requirement will chill advocacy is understandable.[4] . . .

---

3. Our judicial system reserves at least some role. See Roadway Express, Inc. v. Piper, 447 U.S. 752, 766–67 (1980); Eash v. Riggins Trucking Inc., 757 F.2d 557, 564–65 (3d Cir.1985) (en banc).

4. The ABA's litigation section has commented, for example, that the Golden Eagle decision "caused complete consternation in the practicing bar which sees vigorous advocacy, seemingly without regard to its possible misrepresentations to

Moreover, Rule 11 does not apply to the mere making of a frivolous argument. The Rule permits the imposition of sanctions only when the "pleading, motion, or other paper" itself is frivolous, not when one of the arguments in support of a pleading or motion is frivolous. Nothing in the language of the Rule or the Advisory Committee Notes supports the view that the Rule empowers the district court to impose sanctions on lawyers simply because a particular argument or ground for relief contained in a non-frivolous motion is found by the district court to be unjustified....

. . .

There is another risk when mandatory sanctions ride upon close judicial decisions. The danger of arbitrariness increases and the probability of uniform enforcement declines. The Federal Judicial Center recently studied the application of Rule 11 in fairly routine cases involving issues far less sophisticated than those involved in this case. The conclusion was as follows:

> Overall, we found that although the 1983 amendments appear to have increased judges' readiness to enforce the new certification requirements, their success thus far has been limited. Of specific concern are the findings that there is a good deal of interjudge disagreement over what actions constitute a violation of the rule, only partial compliance with the desired objective standard, inaccurate and systematically biased normative assumptions about other judges' reactions to frivolous actions, and a continued neglect of alternative, nonmonetary means of response.

. . .

B. The Failure to Cite Adverse Authority

. . .

Were the scope of the rule to be expanded as the district court suggests, mandatory sanctions would ride on close decisions concerning whether or not one case is or is not the same as another. We think Rule 11 should not impose the risk of sanctions in the event that the court later decides that the lawyer was wrong. The burdens of research and briefing by a diligent lawyer anxious to avoid any possible rebuke would be great. And the burdens would not be merely on the lawyer. If the mandatory provisions of the Rule are to be interpreted literally, the court would have a duty to research authority beyond that provided by the parties to make sure that they have not omitted something.

. . .

In rejecting the district court's broad interpretation of Rule 11, we do not suggest that the court is powerless to sanction lawyers who take positions which cannot be supported. A lawyer should not be able to

the court, as the hallmark of aggressive
and justified representation of the
client."

proceed with impunity in real or feigned ignorance of authorities which render his argument meritless. See, e.g., Rodgers v. Lincoln Towing Service, Inc., 771 F.2d 194, 205 (7th Cir.1985). In addition, Rule 11 is not the only tool available to judges in imposing sanctions on lawyers. However, neither Rule 11 nor any other rule imposes a requirement that the lawyer, in addition to advocating the cause of his client, step first into the shoes of opposing counsel to find all potentially contrary authority, and finally into the robes of the judge to decide whether the authority is indeed contrary or whether it is distinguishable. It is not in the nature of our adversary system to require lawyers to demonstrate to the court that they have exhausted every theory, both for and against their client. Nor does that requirement further the interests of the court. It blurs the role of judge and advocate. The role of judges is not merely to

> match the colors of the case at hand against the colors of many sample cases spread out upon their desk.... It is when the colors do not match, when the references in the index fail, when there is no decisive precedent, that the serious business of the judge begins.

B. Cardozo, The Nature of the Judicial Process 21 (1922). In conducting this "serious business," the judge relies on each party to present his side of the dispute as forcefully as possible. The lawyers cannot adequately perform their role if they are required to make predeterminations of the kind the district court's approach to Rule 11 would necessitate.

[The Ninth Circuit denied a sua sponte request for an en banc hearing in *Golden Eagle*. Judge Noonan's dissent from that denial, joined by four other judges, follows:]

Golden Eagle Distributing Corp. v. Burroughs Corp.

United States Court of Appeals, Ninth Circuit, 1987.
809 F.2d 584.

■ NOONAN, CIRCUIT JUDGE, with whom SNEED, ANDERSON, HALL, and KOZINSKI, CIRCUIT JUDGES, join dissenting from the denial of a sua sponte request for en banc hearing:

. . .

... The district judge had in front of him a brief which did three things. The brief flatly misrepresented Minnesota law as having definitively decided the issue of forum non conveniens in a way favorable to the defendant. The brief insinuated that federal law on the same issue was definitively established the way the defendant would have liked. The brief set out California law without qualification and without mention of later authority which for purposes of the present opinion is assumed to have been "directly contrary." The court sanctioned Kirkland, Ellis for these three statements of law, each of which was not "warranted." The truth or falsity of a statement is not merely a matter of "the manner" in which a position is presented. A false statement presented as a true statement is simply a misstatement. It is not warranted. It should be sanctionable.

. . . The opinion substitutes extreme hypotheticals for the case at hand. It imagines close cases where a judge might sanction a lawyer because the judge disagrees with his argument. But close cases exist that test the workability of any rule, civil or criminal. They are not a reason for repealing the rule. Here, on the opinion's own admission, the case was not close. Kirkland, Ellis failed to cite "directly contrary" authority.

. . .

How can a brief be warranted by existing law if its argument goes in the face of "directly contrary" authority from the highest court of the jurisdiction whose law is being argued? How can a brief be warranted to be "a good faith argument for the extension, modification, or reversal of existing law" when there is not the slightest indication that the brief is arguing for extension, modification or reversal?

. . .

The opinion puts the question as one of "argument identification," treating Kirkland, Ellis' failure as a failure to identify correctly its argument as one for extension of existing law. But Kirkland, Ellis' failure was far greater. Kirkland, Ellis made no argument at all for extending existing law. It simply misrepresented the law it cited.

. . .

. . . The Rule mandates sanctions for any legal papers filed in federal court with *any* improper purpose. The opinion reads "any" out of the Rule.

. . .

. . . The opinion says that the signatory attorney "warrants." "Warrants" is a verb meaning "to assure a person of the truth of what is said." Webster's, Meaning 2b.

How can a lawyer offer testimony to the truth of what he has filed, how can he assure a person of its truth, if it is a misrepresentation?

. . .

. . . The opinion goes on to cite with apparent approval the view of the American Bar Association's Litigation Section that "the practicing bar" sees vigorous advocacy "seemingly without regard to its possible misrepresentations to the court" as the mark of "justified representation of the client."

This vision of vigorous advocacy "seemingly" indifferent to misrepresentations is cited by the opinion as "understandable" concern by the bar that vigorous advocacy not be chilled. Identification of vigorous advocacy with indifference to misrepresentation reflects a one-sided view. It is a view that has been repudiated by modern legal ethics. There is no reason to revive the old, discredited view, much less to incorporate the old view into an interpretation of Rule 11. Vigorous advocacy is, necessarily, truthful advocacy.

A distinct shift from the old view was made in a report by the Joint Conference on Professional Responsibility established by the American Bar Association and the Association of American Law Schools. "Confronted by the layman's charge" that the lawyer is "nothing but a hired brain and voice," this committee undertook to set out the duties of lawyers in terms of social functions that made the lawyer's role understandable, acceptable, and even necessary. See Introductory Statement of Co-chairmen Lon L. Fuller and John D. Randall, "Professional Responsibility: Report of the Joint Conference," 44 ABA Journal 1159 (1958). The report, in large measure, reflected the jurisprudence, the insights, and the wisdom of Professor Fuller. The report stressed that "the integrity of the adjudicative process itself" depends upon the participation of the advocate in order to hold in suspense the mind of the judge, prevent premature closure of the judge's mind, and make a wise decision possible. The function of the advocate defined his responsibilities and the limits of advocacy. The report concluded that a lawyer whose "desire to win leads him to muddy the headwaters of decision" and who "distorts and obscures" the true nature of a case "trespasses against the obligations of professional responsibility." Id. at 1161.

Modern codes of ethics have followed this line of thought. The American Bar Association's Model Code of Professional Responsibility invoked the report of the Joint Conference in stating that a lawyer today "stands in special need of a clear understanding of his obligations and of the vital connection between these obligations and the role his profession plays in society." Preamble, fn. 3, ABA Model Code of Professional Responsibility (1974). The first disciplinary rule of the Code is that "a lawyer shall not ... engage in conduct involving dishonesty, fraud, deceit or misrepresentation." DR 1–102(A)(4). The Disciplinary Rule does not distinguish misrepresentation of fact and misrepresentation of law.

More specifically, under the general heading, "Representing a Client Zealously", the Model Code provides that a lawyer "shall not ... knowingly advance a claim or defense that is unwarranted under existing law, except that he may advance such claim or defense if it can be supported by good faith argument for an extension, modification, or reversal of existing law." DR 7–102(A)(2). Ethical Consideration 7–23 in the same Code declares, "Where a lawyer knows of legal authority in the controlling jurisdiction directly adverse to the position of his client, he should inform the tribunal of its existence unless his adversary has done so ..." EC 7–23.

The standards of the Model Code are substantially followed in the Model Rules of Professional Conduct of the American Bar Association. Rule 3.3 under the heading, "Candor Toward the Tribunal" makes it a black letter rule that a lawyer should not knowingly "fail to disclose to the tribunal legal authority in the controlling jurisdiction known to the lawyer to be directly diverse to the position of the client and not disclosed by opposing counsel." Model Rules 3.3(a)(3). The note on this Rule goes on to say, "Legal argument based on a knowingly false representation of law constitutes dishonesty toward the tribunal ... The underlying concept is that legal argument is a discussion seeking to determine the legal premises properly applicable to the case."

In black letters the Model Rules also provide, "A lawyer shall not bring or defend a proceeding, or assert or controvert an issue therein unless there is a basis for doing so that is not frivolous, which includes a good faith argument for an extension, modification, or reversal of existing law." Model Rule 3.1. Commentary on this Rule explicitly links it to DR 7–102(A)(2) of the Model Code.

Amazingly, the opinion of the court fails to acknowledge the source for the language of Rule 11 that a paper should be "warranted by existing law or a good faith argument for the extension, modification or reversal of existing law." Both the ABA's Model Rules, adopted on August 2, 1983, and Rule 11, which became effective August 1, 1983, are properly seen as based on DR 7–102(A)(2) of the Model Code in their treatment of what a lawyer should not do. If the objective standard of Rule 11 is higher than the subjective standard of Model Rule 3.3, that is no reason for the court to ignore the link between Rule 11 and the ethical standards of the bar.

It is equally surprising that the opinion of the court does not acknowledge that in the ABA's Model Rules, frivolousness is specifically defined by the absence of "a good faith argument for an extension, modification or reversal of existing law." Frivolousness does not only consist, as the court appears to assume, in making a baseless claim. Frivolousness also consists in making a legal argument without a good faith foundation.

. . . Not only does the opinion suggest a view of unrestrained advocacy repudiated by modern authorities, it favors a type of analysis sponsored by the Eighth Circuit and overruled by the Supreme Court [in *Nix v. White-side*, supra p. 356]. The opinion takes the position that a requirement of truthful argumentation "tends to create a conflict between the lawyer's duty zealously to represent his client" and "the lawyer's own interest in avoiding rebuke."

Precisely such an analysis was offered by the Eighth Circuit in relieving the lawyer of an obligation not to present perjury. That court found "a conflict of interest" between the lawyer's duty to represent his client zealously and the lawyer's ethical duty not to present perjury. Whiteside v. Scurr, 744 F.2d 1323 (8th Cir.1984); rehearing en banc denied, 750 F.2d 713 (8th Cir.1984). Reversing the Eighth Circuit, the Supreme Court noted that there was no conflict of duties when the lawyer was asked by his client to assist "in the presentation of false testimony." . . .

A client has as little right to the presentation of false arguments as he has to the presentation of false testimony. No conflict exists when a lawyer confines his advocacy by his duty to the court. The opinion is insensitive and unresponsive to the teaching of the Supreme Court that a restraint on the freedom of a lawyer to present falsity as truth does not create any true conflict. The lawyer has a duty to work within the boundaries of professional responsibility. He is not free to suborn testimony, to perjure himself, to offer perjured testimony, or to misrepresent facts or law. . . .

[A concluding section of Judge Noonan's dissent from the denial of en banc rehearing summarized "alternative avenues" for dealing with lawyer misconduct, including discipline for violating the ethics rules adopted by the federal district court and the inherent judicial authority to punish bad faith litigating conduct. A lawyer who misstates the law, Noonan concluded, may be sanctioned under these discretionary powers if Rule 11 is interpreted so as not to reach this behavior. He suggested it was not to late to reach the conduct in this case:]

Where a court has applied sanctions on a basis which is subsequently held to be mistaken, and the case is remanded, the court retains the power to award sanctions on a proper basis, such as the inherent power of the court to sanction the bad faith of counsel. Roadway Express, Inc. v. Piper, 447 U.S. at 767.[1]

Were Kirkland & Ellis's Legal Arguments Misleading?

Review the editors' notes 12–14 to the panel opinion. How would you characterize Kirkland & Ellis's arguments? Misleading? Creative Lawyering? Within the bounds of acceptable legal argument? Did any of the arguments in Kirkland & Ellis' memorandum in support of Burroughs' motion to dismiss violate M.R. 3.3? Did the firm's motion violate M.R. 3.1?

The earlier discussion of Spaulding v. Zimmerman, p. 5 supra, concluded that a lawyer has a professional duty not to volunteer information adverse to her client to the opposing party. The information may only be proffered if properly requested pursuant to procedural rules, such as those governing pretrial discovery. Model Rule 3.3(a)(3), on the other hand, imposes an affirmative duty "to disclose to the tribunal legal authority in the controlling jurisdiction known to the lawyer to be directly adverse to the position of the client and not disclosed by opposing counsel."[2] Why the different treatment of "law" as distinct from "fact"?[3] Did the Kirkland, Ellis brief in *Golden Eagle* violate M.R. 3.3(a)(3)? Does the professional rule in this instance require more or less candor than Rule 11?

Is the reference to the bar's view of "vigorous advocacy," see footnote 4 of the panel decision, cited with approval as Judge Noonan claims? How do the two opinions envision the role of the advocate?

1. [Editors' note:] Judge Schwarzer, the district judge, declined this invitation when the case was remanded. Subsequently, a jury trial resulted in a substantial verdict in favor of Golden Eagle against Burroughs.

2. DR 7–106(B)(1) of the Model Code is substantially identical.

3. The lawyer's obligation to disclose relevant authority that the opposing party has not cited is discussed in Geoffrey C. Hazard, Jr., Arguing the Law: The Advocate's Duty and Opportunity, 16 Ga.L.Rev. 821 (1982); Monroe H. Freedman, Arguing the Law in an Adversary System, 16 Ga.L.Rev. 833 (1982); and H. Richard Uviller, Zeal and Frivolity: The Ethical Duty of the Appellate Advocate to Tell the Truth about the Law, 6 Hofstra L.Rev. 729 (1977).

Some decisions of other circuits were directly in conflict with *Golden Eagle* on one or more of its three core propositions: (1) that Rule 11 sanctions applied only if the entire paper is frivolous;[4] (2) that the failure to cite controlling, adverse authority is not sanctionable;[5] and (3) that the failure to characterize a misleading statement of existing law as a request for a change of law is not sanctionable.[6] The 1993 amendments to Rule 11 reject, as did the bulk of the case law, the Ninth Circuit's position that individual allegations or contentions are not sanctionable if the paper as a whole is nonfrivolous. The amendments did not specifically address the "adverse authority" problem, but few courts before or after the 1993 amendments have emphasized the failure to cite adverse authority in sanctioning lawyers under Rule 11.[7] Finally, on the "argument identification" problem, the committee notes to the 1993 amendments had this to say:

> Arguments for extensions, modifications, or reversals of existing law or for creation of new law do not violate subdivision (b)(2) provided they are "nonfrivolous." This establishes an objective standard, intended to eliminate any "empty-head pure-heart" justification for patently frivolous arguments. However, the extent to which a litigant has researched the issues and found some support for its theories even in minority opinions, in law review articles, or through consultation with other attorneys should certainly be taken into account in determining whether paragraph (2) has been violated. Although arguments for a change of law are not required to be specifically so identified, a contention that is so identified should be viewed with greater tolerance under the rule.

How would *Golden Eagle* be decided under the 1993 version of Rule 11?

Rule 11: Experience, Problems and the 1993 "Solutions"

The tension between stability and change in the law is reflected in the arguments over Rule 11. One important question is whether courts can distinguish between creative lawyering that ensures that law can "adjust to changing situations," as the *Golden Eagle* court put it, and legal arguments

---

4. See e.g., Szabo Food Service Inc. v. Canteen Corp., 823 F.2d 1073, 1077 (7th Cir. 1987).

5. See e.g., Jorgenson v. County of Volusia, 846 F.2d 1350 (11th Cir.1988) (upholding the imposition of sanctions for failure to cite adverse, controlling precedent in support of a motion for a temporary restraining order and a preliminary injunction, although conduct might not have violated Model Rule 3.3 because opposing counsel later cited the case to the court). Cf. Thompson v. Duke, 940 F.2d 192 (7th Cir. 1991) (reversing sanctions for failure to cite adverse authority when counsel had "a principled basis for his argument" and opposing counsel brought the case to the court's attention).

6. See e.g., *Szabo*, 823 F.2d 1073; and De-Sisto College, Inc. v. Line, 888 F.2d 755 (11th Cir.1989).

7. Cf. Barth v. District of Columbia, 15 F.3d 1159 (D.C. Cir.1993 (unpublished opinion of divided panel reversing the imposition of sanctions for failure to cite adverse authority, where the cases were not dispositive of the action: "under no reasonable reading of Rule 11 are these cases within the range of citations whose omissions supports an award of sanctions"). On the use of Rule 11 to sanction lawyers for failing to cite controlling (or relevant) authority, see generally Daisy Hurst Floyd, Candor Versus Advocacy: Courts' Use of Sanctions to Enforce the Duty of Candor Toward the Tribunal, 29 Ga. L. Rev. 1035 (1995).

that are frivolous and thus appropriately sanctioned. The 1993 version of Rule 11 requires that legal arguments for the "extension, modification or reversal of existing law or [for] the establishment of new law"[8] be "nonfrivolous."[9] Does the passage quoted above on the meaning of nonfrivolous give enough guidance to courts on distinguishing legitimate creative lawyering from sanctionable argument?[10]

The 1993 amendments to Rule 11 were designed in part to respond to concerns that the 1983 version of the rule "chilled" legitimate advocacy.[11] A large body of information was collected about the use and effects of the 1983 version of the Rule, and this information played a large role in the debate that culminated in the 1993 amendments. A detailed study of motions made under the 1983 version of Rule 11 in the Third Circuit included the following findings and conclusions:[12]

First, application of Rule 11 was not uniform throughout the United States or within a judicial circuit. The variability was influenced not only by differing legal interpretations of the Rule, which might have diminished with time, but also by local legal culture and individual judicial attitudes towards sanctions as a case management device.

8. The "establishment of new law" phrase did not appear in the 1983 version of the rule.

9. The 1983 version of the Rule, instead of "nonfrivolous," had required that such arguments be "good faith" arguments. To avoid the subjective connotation of the words "good faith," the word "nonfrivolous" was substituted for it.

10. Ronald Gilson argues that "the fear that too rigorous a requirement of legal support will chill the development of the law ... results in an underinclusive definition" of strategic litigation, defined as "litigation moves that are designed not to vindicate a substantive legal right, but as a strategic device to secure a business advantage by imposing costs on the other party." Ronald J. Gilson, The Devolution of the Legal Profession: A Demand Side Perspective, 49 Md.L.Rev. 869, 875, 908 (1990). Because judges will lean over backwards in a desire not to discourage plausible claims, Rule 11 "remains a poor [gatekeeping] substitute [for advance screening by lawyers], albeit better than nothing." Id. at 909. The problem is that the more promising alternative—screening by lawyers—has been undercut by changes in the market for legal services:

> The traditional structure of professionalism, dominated by elite outside counsel and sheltered by information asymmetry, has been rent by changes in the market. ... [L]awyers functioning as private gatekeepers to enforce a Rawlsian agreement among clients—remains a desirable end which seemingly cannot be duplicated by public enforcement. ... [T]he segment of the profession most likely empowered to play this role is inside counsel, individuals hardly representative of the profession's traditional elite.

11. 146 F.R.D. at 402.

12. Third Circuit Task Force on Federal Rule of Civil Procedure 11, Rule 11 in Transition (Stephen B. Burbank, Reporter) Amer.Judicature Soc'y, 1989. See also Stephen B. Burbank, The Transformation of American Civil Procedure: The Example of Rule 11, 137 U.Pa.L.Rev. 1925 (1989). Major studies of Rule 11, apart from the Third Circuit study and the most recent study by the Federal Judicial Center, discussed in the following footnote, include: Lawrence C. Marshall et al., The Use and Impact of Rule 11, 86 Nw. U. L. Rev. 943 (1992); Melissa L. Nelkin, The Impact of Fed. Rule 11 on Lawyers & Judges in the Northern District of California, 74 Judicature 147 (1990); Georgene Vairo, Rule 11: A Critical Analysis, 118 F.R.D. 189 (1988); Saul M. Kassin, An Empirical Study of Rule 11 (Fed.Jud.Center 1985).

Second, counts of published decisions dealing with Rule 11 exaggerated the frequency of motions and sanctions. In the Third Circuit, Rule 11 sanctions were filed in less than 0.5% of all cases, and sanctions were imposed in 13.8% of cases in which motions were made.

Third, the perception that plaintiffs and their counsel suffered disproportionately under Rule 11 had some truth to it, but the statistics painted a picture less stark than some imagined. In the Third Circuit, plaintiffs or their counsel were the target of two-thirds of Rule 11 motions. Plaintiffs or their counsel were also sanctioned at a higher rate than their defense counterparts, but the two rates (15.9% and 9.1% respectively) were closer than many supposed.

Fourth, civil rights plaintiffs or their counsel were sanctioned at a rate (47.1% of motions) that was considerably higher than the rate (8.5%) for plaintiffs in non-civil rights cases. The report suggested that this difference was due in part to the inclusion in the civil rights category of some special types of cases (prisoner cases, pro se cases and cases involving duplicative litigation). Yet the Third Circuit report found the incidence of sanctions in § 1983 cases sufficiently troubling to recommend that judges should concentrate more on conduct (a lawyer acting with an improper purpose or failing to make a reasonable inquiry) and less on the legal merit of a filing.

Finally, the report concluded that the rule "has had widespread effects on conduct of the sort hoped for by the rulemakers," including encouraging greater care in making filings and an increase in case dismissal and settlement. The "directly associated costs (e.g., the costs of litigating Rule 11 issues to litigants and courts) do not appear to be clearly incommensurate with probable benefits;" "some other costs (e.g., chilling zealous but legitimate advocacy, poisoning attorney-client relations) are not presently a serious problem in the Third Circuit, but . . . some collateral consequences of Rule 11 (e.g., effect on insurance rates or availability) are imperfectly understood and may increase significantly in the future."[13]

---

13. The Federal Judicial Center's Study of Rule 11, 2 FJC Directions (Nov. 1991), reaches many of the same conclusions as the Third Circuit study. In an examination of Rule 11 in the district courts for Arizona, the District of Columbia, Northern Georgia, Eastern Michigan and Western Texas, the Center examined case files, reviewed published opinions and surveyed judges' attitudes towards the Rule. The Center's report confirmed that Rule 11 activity is modest and that plaintiffs are the most frequent target of sanctions. However, contrary to the criticism that Rule 11 has a disproportionate impact on represented plaintiffs and their attorneys in civil rights cases, the Center's study "found that the percentage of motions/orders . . . in civil rights cases was similar to . . . that in other types of cases with substantial Rule 11 activity. . . ." Id. at 22–23. The rate at which sanctions were imposed in civil rights cases was also "comparable to . . . that for all other types of litigants and cases." Id. at 23. The Center concludes that the five district courts have not sanctioned civil rights plaintiffs' attorneys where their arguments have been reasonable. The Center's study also generated interesting data regarding the sanctioning practices of individual judges. For example, in Arizona one judge had imposed no sanctions, while another judge in the same district had imposed sanctions in 57 percent of his Rule 11 rulings. The Center did not explore the reasons for the discrepancy, but it suggested some possible explanations: Some judges are more receptive to Rule 11

Unfortunately, there is no similarly detailed data available on the effects of the 1993 version of the Rule. One thing, however, is certain: the number of reported cases under Rule 11 has dropped dramatically since the 1993 amendments were adopted. A LEXIS search in the Newer File in the Genfed Library for the words "Rule 11 and sanctions" for the period between January 1, 1990 and January 1, 1992 yields 1684 cases; for the period January 1, 1997 to January 1, 1999 the same search yields only 924 cases, a 45 percent drop.

The "safe harbor provision" is the change most likely to have caused this decrease.[14] Under the 1993 amendments, a Rule 11 motion must be served separately from other motions and only after the targeted party has been given an opportunity to withdraw the challenged statement within 21 days of service of notice.[15] This means that "a party will not be subject to sanctions on the basis of another party's motion unless, after receiving the motion, it refuses to withdraw that position or to acknowledge candidly that it does not currently have evidence to support a specified allegation."[16] Does the safe harbor provision invite lawyers to try and get away with assertions that violate the rule? If so, is that a reason for concern?

Two other changes made in 1993 may also have contributed substantially to the drop in Rule 11 activity: First, under the 1983 rule, a motion for sanctions could be presented after final judgment, subject to the standards of local rules.[17] The 1993 amendments changed that.[18] While the text of the Rule does not explicitly state when a Rule 11 motion should be brought, the intent was to encourage prompt action on the part of the offended party:

> The revision leaves for resolution on a case-by-case basis, considering the particular circumstances involved, the question as to when a motion for violation of Rule 11 should be served and when, if filed, it should be decided. Ordinarily the motion should be served promptly after the inappropriate paper is filed, and, if delayed too long, may be viewed as untimely.[19]

Second, sanctions are discretionary and are to be imposed with the aim of deterring violations, not compensating the offended party.[20] Now that the

motions than others; when lawyers perceive a judge as being open to Rule 11 sanctions they file more motions in that judge's court; and some judges delegate Rule 11 activity to magistrates.

14. In the Federal Judicial Center's 1995 survey on Rule 11, 39% of the judges surveyed thought that the "safe harbor" provision had decreased Rule 11 activity in their courts; 37% thought Rule 11 activity remained the same; 23% could not tell; and only 2% of judges thought this provision had increased Rule 11 activity.

15. See Federal Judicial Center's Study of Rule 11, 2 FJC Directions 37 (Nov. 1991).

16. 146 F.R.D. at 591 (committee's notes explaining the amendment to Rule 11(c)).

17. See Cooter & Gell v. Hartmarx Corp., 496 U.S. 384, 397 (1990) (upholding sanctions awarded three and a half years after voluntary dismissal).

18. Ridder v. City of Springfield, 109 F.3d 288, 295 (6th Cir.1997).

19. Advisory Committee Notes to the 1993 Amendments.

20. See Advisory Committee Notes to the 1993 Amendments ("the purpose of Rule 11 sanctions is to deter rather than to compensate")

alleged violator must be given 21 days to fix the offending statement or paper before a motion for sanctions may be filed, should sanctions be mandatory? The Federal Judicial Center survey showed that only about one-quarter of each group questioned (judges, plaintiffs' lawyers, defense counsel and other lawyers) favored returning to a mandatory sanctions regime.[21] On the other hand, approximately two-thirds of all groups surveyed, other than plaintiffs' lawyers, supported making compensation, not just deterrence, a goal in determining an appropriate sanction.[22]

In an economic analysis of sanctioning frivolous suits, Mitchell Polinsky and Daniel Rubinfeld conclude that the proper level of deterrence often exceeds the cost of a sanctions hearing to the party forced to defend a frivolous action. If they are right, courts are not setting the level of sanctions at the appropriate level since most calculate the level of sanction based on the reasonable attorney's fees incurred by the offended party.[23] The authors also conclude that "the possibility of mistaken imposition of sanctions tends to discourage legitimate plaintiffs from suing." [24]

Interpretation and Application of Rule 11

Overview

The 1993 version of Rule 11(b) sets forth the following requirements for representations made to a court:

> *Representations to Court.* By presenting to the court (whether by signing, filing, submitting, or later advocating) a pleading, written motion, or other paper, an attorney or unrepresented party is certifying that to the best of the person's knowledge, information, and belief, formed after an inquiry reasonable under the circumstances,
>
> (1) it is not being presented for any improper purpose, such as to harass or to cause unnecessary delay or needless increase in the cost of litigation;
>
> (2) the claims, defenses, and other legal contentions therein are warranted by existing law or by a nonfrivolous argument for the extension, modification, or reversal of existing law or the establishment of new law;[25]

---

21. Federal Judicial Center, Report of a Survey Concerning Rule 11, Federal Rules of Civil Procedure (1995).

22. Id.

23. See Abner Realty, Inc. v. Administrator of GSA, 1998 WL 410958, *8 (S.D.N.Y. 1998) (reporting on the "typical sanction" imposed under the 1993 Rule and citing cases).

24. A. Mitchell Polinsky & Daniel L. Rubinfeld, Sanctioning Frivolous Suits: An Economic Analysis, 82 Geo.L.J. 397, 402 (1993). See also Lucian A. Bebchuk & How-

ard F. Chang, An Analysis of Fee Shifting Based on the Margin of Victory: On Frivolous Suits, Meritorious Suits, and the Role of Rule 11, 25 J. Legal Stud. 371, 376 (1996) (analyzing fee shifting as a way to deter frivolous plaintiffs who sue to exploit trial error). For a survey of the law and economics scholarship on frivolous suits, see Robert G. Bone, Modeling Frivolous Suits, 145 U.Pa.L.Rev. 519 (1997).

25. Note that a court may not fine a represented party under this section of the rule; it may only fine pro se parties and lawyers. Rule 11(c)(2)(A) (prohibiting monetary

(3) the allegations and other factual contentions have evidentiary support or, if specifically so identified, are likely to have evidentiary support after a reasonable opportunity for further investigation or discovery; and

(4) the denials of factual contentions are warranted on the evidence or, if specifically so identified, are reasonably based on a lack of information or belief.

The 1993 rule demands more of lawyers than the 1983 rule in one respect and less in another. The 1993 version is more demanding in that it makes plain that the rule extends to "later advocating" a paper filed with the court.[26] Prior to the 1993 amendments, case law was divided on this point. On the other hand, the rule allows lawyers to make certain factual assertions that might have been sanctioned under the 1983 rule as not well-grounded in fact. Specifically, the amended rule protects a plaintiffs' lawyer who, in making a factual allegation, notes that the allegation is "likely to have evidentiary support after a reasonable opportunity for further investigation." Similarly, a defense lawyer is protected when, in denying a factual contention, she notes that the denial is "reasonably based on a lack of information and belief." Both are protected, however, only to the extent it remains reasonable to have failed to discover the fact of the matter. The committee note states:

Sometimes a litigant may have good reason to believe that a fact is true or false but may need discovery, formal or informal, from opposing parties or third persons to gather and confirm the evidentiary basis for the allegation. Tolerance of factual contentions in initial pleadings ... does not relieve litigants from the obligation to conduct an appropriate investigation into the facts that is reasonable under the circumstances; it is not a license to join parties, make claims, or present defenses without any factual basis or justification.... [27]

The "reasonable ignorance" provisions are very popular with plaintiffs' lawyers.[28] According to the FJC study, judges and defense lawyers split almost evenly between support for the 1993 provisions and support for amending the rule to require that all factual contentions have evidentiary support when filed with a court.[29]

Rule 11 is not applicable to discovery motions or other papers filed in connection with discovery. Rule 11(d). Sanctions for discovery abuse must

sanctions against a represented party for violating (b)(2)).

26. The revised rule thus supposedly "emphasizes the duty of candor by subjecting litigants to potential sanctions for insisting upon a position after it is no longer tenable." 146 F.R.D. at 585.

27. 146 F.R.D. at 585.

28. According to the Federal Judicial Center's 1995 survey, 79% of plaintiffs' lawyers

and 68% of other lawyers supported these provisions.

29. Opposing and favoring the requirement of evidentiary support: 40% of judges against, 38% for; 45% of defense lawyers for, 40% against. Only 12% of plaintiffs' lawyers and 20% of other lawyers favored requiring evidentiary support.

be requested under Rules 26 and 37. See discussion infra p. 430 of discovery abuse.

Relying on the Client's Word

Under the 1983 version of the Rule: "Blind reliance on the client [would] . . . seldom [have constituted] a sufficient inquiry. . . ."[30] Interpreting the 1983 version of Rule 11, the Second Circuit concluded that a lawyer is entitled to rely on client statements that are "objectively reasonable," although relying on client statements without other pre-filing inquiry may be sanctionable conduct.[31] Elaborating on that last point, the court said: "In considering sanctions regarding a factual claim, the initial focus of the district court should be on whether an objectively reasonable evidentiary basis for the claim was demonstrated in pretrial proceedings or at trial. Where such a basis was shown, no inquiry into the adequacy of the attorney's pre-filing investigation is necessary."[32]

Under the Second Circuit's approach, a lawyer may "rely on the objectively reasonable representations of the client."[33] Pre–1993 decisions resting on the "reasonableness" of the lawyer's conduct continue to be relevant. The circumstances determine whether the lawyer's reliance on the client's words was reasonable.[34]

Papers Filed for an Improper Purpose

The "improper purpose" part of Rule 11 has been held to cover a variety of abusive litigation practices, including: filing repetitive papers;[35] pursuing harassing counterclaims;[36] and misstatements in papers as part of a persistent plan of discovery abuse.[37] Despite the word "purpose," courts

---

30. Southern Leasing Partners Ltd. v. McMullan, 801 F.2d 783, 788 (5th Cir. 1986); see Coburn Optical Industries v. Cilco, Inc., 610 F.Supp. 656, 659 (M.D.N.C. 1985) (lawyer sanctioned for not verifying his client's claim that it did not do business in the jurisdiction).

31. Calloway v. Marvel Entertainment Group, 854 F.2d 1452, 1470 (2d Cir.1988), rev'd on other grounds sub nom. Pavelic & LeFlore v. Marvel Entertainment Group, 493 U.S. 120 (1989).

32. Id. at 1470.

33. Hadges v. Yonkers Racing Corp., 48 F.3d 1320, 1329–30 (2d Cir.1995).

34. See, e.g., Gartenbaum v. Beth Israel Med. Ctr., 26 F.Supp.2d 645 (S.D.N.Y. 1998):

> Although an attorney may rely on "the objectively reasonable representations of the client . . . [he] cannot totally rely on the uncorroborated word of his client and hearsay witnesses for all of the key

contentions of the case." Forbes v. Merrill Lynch, Fenner & Smith, 179 F.R.D. 107, 109 (S.D.N.Y.1998). "When an attorney must rely on his client, he should question him thoroughly, not accepting his version on faith alone. . . . If all the attorney has is his client's assurance that facts exist or do not exist, when a reasonable inquiry would reveal otherwise, he has not satisfied his [Rule 11] obligation."

35. See, e.g., Deere & Co. v. Deutsche Lufthansa, 855 F.2d 385 (7th Cir.1988) (filing repetitive papers that refuse to accept judge's ruling on an issue and fail to address remaining issues in the litigation).

36. Hudson v. Moore Business Forms, Inc., 836 F.2d 1156 (9th Cir.1987) (counterclaim brought for purpose of harassing plaintiff into dropping the case and deterring others from bringing suit).

37. Perkinson v. Gilbert/Robinson Inc., 821 F.2d 686 (D.C.Cir.1987).

have held that this part of Rule 11, like the rest of the Rule, requires an objective determination of whether a reasonable lawyer acting as the lawyer did in this case would have been acting for improper purpose.

Who, If Anyone, Pays Sanctions?

The 1993 version of Rule 11 provides for penalties against the lawyer, the client or both except when the violation is of 11(b)(2) (unwarranted legal arguments) in which case monetary sanctions are not to be imposed on a represented party, but may be imposed against her lawyer or a pro se litigant. Rule 11(c)(2)(B). With the exception just noted, the rule allows but does not encourage monetary sanctions. "Since the purpose of Rule 11 sanctions is to deter rather than to compensate, the rule provides that, if a monetary sanction is imposed, it should ordinarily be paid into court as a penalty [as opposed to being paid to the moving party.]"[38] Only "if warranted for effective deterrence" does the rule allow the moving party to recover reasonable attorney's fees and expenses incurred as a result of the violation. Rule 11(c)(2)(B). This dramatically lessens the incentives of parties to seek sanctions, undercutting the deterrence goal of the rule.

Generally, courts seek to allocate sanctions between lawyer and client according to the relative responsibility of each for the Rule 11 violation. The 1993 amendments permit a sanction to be imposed upon a law firm whose partner or associate has violated the rule. Under the 1983 rule only the signing lawyer could be sanctioned.[39] Because Rule 11's central goal is to deter lawyer abuses, a federal court imposing a sanction on a lawyer may prohibit reimbursement from any source.[40]

Should Certain Types of Claims Be Judged More Leniently?

Dissenting in a case affirming sanctions against a civil rights plaintiff, Judge Cudahy of the Seventh Circuit suggested that courts should be more reluctant to sanction legal arguments in civil rights cases than in some other areas of law: "Due process ... is an area where creativity and frivolity sometimes threaten to merge; I would be more restrained than my brethren in handing out sanctions for civil rights claims."[41] Is there a principled justification for giving civil rights plaintiffs relatively lenient treatment under Rule 11?

38. 146 F.R.D. at 587–88.

39. See Pavelic & LeFlore v. Marvel Entertainment Group, 493 U.S. 120 (1989) (reading the 1983 version of the rule as allowing courts to sanction only the signing lawyer).

40. Derechin v. State University of New York, 963 F.2d 513 (2d Cir.1992) (lawyer for state agency must pay $250 sanction personally even though state statute permits reimbursement).

41. Szabo Food Service Inc. v. Canteen Corp., 823 F.2d 1073, 1086 (7th Cir.1987) (Cudahy, J., dissenting).Cf. Christiansburg Garment Co. v. EEOC, 434 U.S. 412, 422 (1978) (although fees are to be routinely awarded in favor of a prevailing plaintiff, attorney's fees may not be assessed against a plaintiff who fails to state a claim under 42 U.S.C. § 1988 or under Title VII of the Civil Rights Act of 1964 unless the complaint is frivolous).

Rule 11 does not apply to criminal proceedings. Should habeas corpus proceedings, which are civil, be subject to Rule 11 sanctions?[42] Repetitive pro se petitioners may be ordered not to file any more petitions without court approval. Read M.R. 3.1 and its comment. Should it have addressed the responsibilities of a lawyer representing a convicted person in a habeas proceeding? What should the standard be?

In Lopez v. Southeastern Tidewater Opportunity Project,[43] the court addressed the propriety of lawyers ghost-writing papers for litigants to file pro se, holding that the practice was "inconsistent with procedural, ethical and substantive rules of this Court."[44] While noting its belief that the lawyers involved should have known that the practice was improper, the court refused to sanction the lawyers, opting instead to make its view on the practice clear with the intent of sanctioning lawyers who engaged in the practice following the opinion in the instant case.[45]

Should lawyers employed by state or federal agencies be subject to Rule 11 sanctions? In Taylor v. Commonwealth of Pennsylvania,[46] the court imposed Rule 11 sanctions on government counsel for the state for having filed a frivolous motion to dismiss a habeas petition. A few cases hold that federal government lawyers may also be subject to Rule 11 sanctions.[47]

Harsher Treatment of Lawyers and Parties in Securities Cases

Under the Private Securities Litigation Reform Act of 1993, judges are required to make findings in all securities fraud cases on whether Rule 11 has been violated.[48] If the court finds a "substantial" failure to comply with any part of Rule 11(b), which details the requirements for statements presented to a court, the judge must impose a sanction which is presumed

---

42. Sanctions are rarely imposed in habeas proceedings absent special circumstances. See United States ex rel. Potts v. Chrans, 700 F.Supp. 1505, 1525 (N.D.Ill.1988) (spirit of habeas inconsistent with Rule 11 sanctions); United States v. Quin, 836 F.2d 654, 657 (1st Cir.1988) (sanctions appropriate when writ was used by retained counsel for "purely civil effect, the prevention of deportation"). But see Gelabert v. Lynaugh, 894 F.2d 746, 747 (5th Cir.1990) (per curiam) (sanctioning habeas corpus petitioner under Rule 11).

43. 968 F.Supp. 1075 (E.D.Va.1997), aff'd 172 F.3d 44 (4th Cir. 1999).

44. Id. at 1079–80.

45. Id. The few courts to have addressed this question agree that the practice is improper. See e.g., Ricotta v. State of California, 4 F.Supp. 2d 961 (S.D.Cal.1998) (holding the practice improper, but refusing to hold lawyer in contempt for reasons similar to those articulated in *Lopez*); Unit-

ed States v. Eleven Vehicles, 966 F.Supp. 361, 367 (E.D.Pa.1997) (condemning ghost-writing arrangement "wherein a party appears pro se while in reality the party is receiving legal assistance from a licensed attorney"); Ellis v. State of Maine, 448 F.2d 1325, 1328 (1st Cir.1971) ("[W]e cannot approve of such a practice. If a brief is prepared in any substantial part by a member of the bar, it must be signed by him.").

46. 686 F.Supp. 492 (M.D.Pa.1988).

47. See Adamson v. Bowen, 855 F.2d 668 (10th Cir.1988), holding that the Equal Access to Justice Act, 28 U.S.C. § 2412 (1981), waives the federal government's sovereign immunity as to Rule 11.

48. Section 101(b) of the Private Securities Litigation Reform Act (amending Section 27 of the Securities Act of 1933 and section 21D of the Exchange Act). See generally James D. Cox, Making Securities Fraud Class Actions Virtuous, 39 Ariz. L. Rev. 497 (1997).

to be "an award to the opposing party of the reasonable attorney fees and other expenses incurred in the action."[49] Thus, in all securities actions, including derivative suits,[50] Rule 11 sanctions are mandatory (at least upon a finding of substantial violation) and are not dependent on a motion from the opposing party. Moreover, the safe harbor provisions do not apply in securities cases.[51] Does it make sense to single out securities litigation for such treatment?

State Corollaries to Rule 11

State corollaries to Rule 11 run a wide gamut, although few, if any, make sanctions mandatory. Some states, following the lead set by the 1983 federal rule, have adopted an objective standard for assessing what representations to a court are subject to sanction. Those states include Illinois, North Carolina, Virginia and Wisconsin. Other states, including Florida and Pennsylvania, require courts to make a finding of subjective bad faith on the part of the lawyer or litigant before imposing sanctions (similar to the pre–1983 federal rule). Still other states, including New York, have no counterpart to Rule 11, leaving abusive conduct in litigation to vaguer and generally unenforced boundaries of the ethics rules. In general, lawyers run a greater risk of sanctions in federal court than in most states, even under the 1993 amendments.

4.   Other Procedural Sanctions

Unreasonably and Vexatiously Multiplying Proceedings

28 U.S.C. § 1927 provides:

> Any attorney or other person admitted to conduct cases in any court of the United States or any Territory thereof who so multiplies the proceedings in any case unreasonably and vexatiously may be required by the court to satisfy personally the excess costs, expenses, and attorneys' fees reasonably incurred because of such conduct.

The decisions are in conflict whether § 1927 requires subjective bad faith on the part of counsel.[52] Recklessness in pursuing a frivolous claim or defense, however, constitutes subjective bad faith. Bad faith is established when a lawyer " 'knowingly *or* recklessly raises a frivolous argument *or*

---

49.   Section 101(b) of the Private Securities Litigation Reform Act.

50.   See e.g., Simon DeBartolo Group, L.P. v. The Richard E. Jacobs Group, Inc., 985 F.Supp. 427, 430–31 (1997) (applying these provisions to a derivative action and joining other courts, which are cited, in holding that this provision is not limited to securities class actions but applies to all private securities litigation).

51.   See e.g., Smith v. Gerald Smith, Cytoferon Corp., 184 F.R.D. 420 (S.D.Fla.1998).

52.   Compare, e.g., Haynie v. Ross Gear Div. of TRW, Inc., 799 F.2d 237, 243 (6th Cir. 1986) (subjective bad faith not required), with e.g., Oliveri v. Thompson, 803 F.2d 1265, 1273 (2d Cir.1986) ("an award under § 1927 must be supported by a finding of bad faith ..."); and Barber v. Miller, 146 F.3d 707 (9th Cir.1998)(a finding of recklessness or bad faith is necessary; ignorance or negligence not enough).

argues a meritorious claim for the purpose of harassing an opponent' . . . [or undertakes t]actics . . . with the intent to increase expenses. . . . Even if an attorney's arguments are meritorious, his conduct may be sanctionable if in bad faith."[53]

Sanctions may be imposed under § 1927 even though the moving party failed to provide the offending lawyer with notice and 21 days to withdraw the representation as required by Rule 11's safe harbor provision.[54] In other words, Rule 11's safe harbor provision does not extend to sanctions under § 1927.

Inherent Judicial Authority to Sanction Bad Faith Conduct

Efforts to control unwanted litigation involve court decisions, procedural rules and statutes that empower courts to require a party or the party's lawyer to pay the legal fees of an adversary oppressed by bad-faith litigation. The inherent authority of a federal court to impose sanctions, including an award of attorney fees, was upheld in Roadway Express, Inc. v. Piper.[55] This "inherent power" permits a federal district court to assess attorney fees when "the losing party has acted in bad faith, vexatiously, wantonly, or for oppressive reasons." Since the power of a court over members of its bar is "at least as great as its authority over litigants," a federal court can tax counsel fees "against counsel who wilfully abused judicial processes."[56]

In Chambers v. NASCO, Inc.,[57] the Supreme Court upheld a sanction of $996,645 against a party who had attempted to deprive the district court of jurisdiction, filed false and frivolous pleadings and tried to wear down the opposing party through delay. The district court, concluding that the first and last of these grounds were not sanctionable under Rule 11 and that 28 U.S.C. § 1927 only applied to attorneys, relied on its inherent power to impose a monetary sanction equivalent to the total amount of the opposing party's litigation expenses, minus a contempt fee of $25,000 levied earlier.[58] The Supreme Court, in a 5–4 decision, upheld the sanction: A federal court may use its "inherent power to police itself, thus serving the dual purpose of 'vindicating judicial authority . . . and making the prevailing party whole for expenses caused by his opponent's obstinacy.' "[59]

Chambers' holding that federal courts have inherent power to sanction even when sanctions would be unavailable under either Rule 11 or § 1927

---

53. New Alaska Development Corp. v. Guetschow, 869 F.2d 1298, 1306 (9th Cir.1989).

54. See Ridder v. Springfield, 109 F.3d 288 (6th Cir.1997). See also Edwards v. General Motors, 153 F.3d 242 (5th Cir.1998) (sanctions under 1927 appropriate for failing to drop a lawsuit that lawyer does not intend to pursue, despite the fact that sanctions under Rule 11 not available because the filings were not frivolous as defined by that Rule).

55. 447 U.S. 752 (1980).

56. 447 U.S. at 766.

57. 501 U.S. 32 (1991)

58. The district court and the court of appeals also imposed sanctions on others connected to the case. In particular, one of Chamber's lawyers was disbarred, an issue the Supreme Court did not pass on.

59. 501 U.S. at 46.

allows judges to sanction lawyers, as well as nonlawyers, when the conduct that interferes with the administration of justice falls outside the four corners of other rules or statutes that authorize sanctions.[60]

Sanctions for Discovery Abuse

In 1976 the Court upheld a dismissal of an action under Fed.R.Civ.P. 37 upon a finding of failure in bad faith to comply with discovery.[61] This policy was reinforced by amendments to Rules 26 and 37 in 1980 and 1983. Rule 26(g) and Rule 37(b) provide that sanctions may include the award of attorneys fees. In addition, Rule 37(b) provides that negative inferences may be drawn from a party's refusal to comply with discovery, that the party may be prevented from contesting certain matters and that the court may dismiss the claim or enter a default judgment for noncompliance.[62]

Sanctions at the Appellate Level

Sanctions for frivolous legal arguments at the appellate level are most often levied under Fed.R.App.P. 38:

> If a court of appeals shall determine that an appeal is frivolous, it may award just damages and single or double costs.

Rule 38 does not make the imposition of sanctions mandatory upon a finding that the appeal is frivolous. Rule 38 sanctions require a determination that the appeal is frivolous and that sanctions are appropriate,[63] but a finding of subjective bad faith is not required.[64] An argument with merit enough to escape Rule 11 sanctions at the trial level may be sanctionable under Rule 38 if pressed on appeal.[65] On the other hand, appealing a Rule 11 sanction may result in additional sanctions under Rule 38.[66] Blatantly mischaracterizing a court opinion in an appellate brief may also lead to sanctions. "We can think of no better example of a pleading not well grounded in fact or law than a brief that falsely imputes a particular position to this court."[67] Courts have also imposed sanctions against

60. See e.g., Resolution Trust Corp. v. Dabney, 73 F.3d 262 (10th Cir.1995).

61. National Hockey League v. Metropolitan Hockey Club Inc., 427 U.S. 639 (1976).

62. See Apex Oil Co. v. Belcher Co., 855 F.2d 1009 (2d Cir.1988), discussing the relationship between Rule 11 and Rule 26(g), Rule 37(c) and § 1927. Also see Carlucci v. Piper Aircraft Corp., Inc., 775 F.2d 1440 (11th Cir.1985) (discussing statutes and rules authorizing sanctions for discovery abuse, including the court's inherent power).

63. Mays v. Chicago Sun–Times, 865 F.2d 134 (7th Cir.1989).

64. See, e.g., Sparks v. NLRB, 835 F.2d 705, 707 (7th Cir.1987) (subjective bad faith is not required).

65. See, e.g., Coghlan v. Starkey, 852 F.2d 806, 817 (5th Cir.1988) ("the unreasonableness of litigating [these] unsupported and meritless legal positions rose to a level appropriate for sanctions only after the opinion below elaborated why current law could not support the contention advanced").

66. See, e.g., Hale v. Harney, 786 F.2d 688, 692 (5th Cir.1986) (after Rule 11 sanctions were imposed counsel persisted by appealing a claim clearly barred by Supreme Court decisions).

67. See, e.g., *Mays*, supra at 140.

lawyers who file frivolous motions for Rule 38 sanctions.[68]

Rule 38 is not the only vehicle for sanctioning frivolous conduct on appeal. Although Rule 11 is not applicable on appeal unless incorporated into an appellate rule,[69] sanctions under 28 U.S.C. § 1927 and 42 U.S.C. § 1988 are available.[70] Sanctions on appeal may also be imposed under the court's inherent power.[71] See also 28 U.S.C. § 1912, which provides: "Where a judgment is affirmed by the Supreme Court or a court of appeals, the court in its discretion may adjudge to the prevailing party just damages for his delay, and single or double costs."[72]

The *Anders* Brief

Counsel should withdraw rather than pursue a frivolous appeal. But what about a court-appointed lawyer representing an indigent criminal defendant on appeal? In Anders v. California,[73] the Court held that counsel must accompany her request to withdraw with a brief setting forth "anything in the record that might arguably support the appeal." This brief is commonly referred to as an *Anders* brief. In the *McCoy* case, the Court upheld a Wisconsin Supreme Court rule that required that the *Anders* brief include "a discussion of why the issue lacks merit."[74] The defendant claimed that requiring his counsel to present the weaknesses in his cause deprived him of his Sixth Amendment right to effective assistance of counsel. The Court stated that the Wisconsin rule furthered the interest underlying *Anders*, i.e., protecting the defendant from counsel's mistaken conclusion that the appeal lacked merit, by assisting the court to make an independent determination. In dissent, Justice Brennan, joined by Justices Marshall and Blackmun, argued that the Wisconsin rule violated the lawyer's duty to advocate "the undivided interests of his client." The dissenters found this particularly troublesome because only indigent defendants would be affected by the rule.[75]

68. See, e.g., Meeks v. Jewel Cos., 845 F.2d 1421 (7th Cir.1988).

69. Braley v. Campbell, 832 F.2d 1504, 1510 n. 4 (10th Cir.1987) (en banc) (Rule 11 not applicable on appeal); but see In re Disciplinary Action Curl, 803 F.2d 1004 (9th Cir.1986) (Rule 11 applies on appeal through Rule 5 of the Ninth Circuit rules).

70. See, e.g., Limerick v. Greenwald, 749 F.2d 97 (1st Cir.1984).

71. NASCO, Inc. v. Calcasieu Tel. & Radio, Inc., 894 F.2d 696 (5th Cir.1990), aff'd Chambers v. NASCO, Inc., 501 U.S. 32 (1991); Trohimovich v. Commissioner, 776 F.2d 873, 876 (9th Cir.1985).

72. See Natasha, Inc. v. Evita Marine Charters, Inc., 763 F.2d 468, 472 (1st Cir.1985). 28 U.S.C. § 1912, however, is not interpreted to warrant fee shifting.

73. 386 U.S. 738, 744 (1967).

74. McCoy v. Court of Appeals of Wisconsin, 486 U.S. 429 (1988).

75. Apparently only one case has sanctioned a criminal defense lawyer for making frivolous arguments on appeal. See In re Becraft, 885 F.2d 547 (9th Cir.1989) (although sanctions are generally inappropriate in criminal appeals, defense counsel was sanctioned under Rule 38 for arguing in a petition for rehearing that the federal tax laws did not apply to resident U.S. citizens). The Supreme Court has, however, made it clear that lawyers who file frivolous petitions for certiorari are subject to sanctions under Supreme Court Rule 42.2. Austin v. United States, 513 U.S. 5 (1994) (per curiam) (advising courts of appeals who required counsel to file certiorari petitions when requested by an indigent

Given the *Anders* doctrine, lawyers taking an appeal on behalf of criminal defendants run little risk of Rule 38 sanctions.[76] Improper trial tactics by criminal defense lawyers are discussed later in this chapter.

5. HIGH STAKES LITIGATION AS A "PRISONERS' DILEMMA"

From an economic standpoint, the expenditure of resources on litigation is markedly different than such expenditures in the transactional context. Consensual transactions involve the creation of arrangements in which, at least in theory, everyone is better off:[77] Benefits are conferred on all of the participants and opportunities for the creation of new wealth or satisfaction enrich the rest of society. Litigation, on the other hand, marks the breakdown of social peace. In the jargon of game theorists, litigation is most often a zero-sum game in which there is a winner and a loser or, in many cases, because of the high costs of litigation, two losers. Consensual transactions have the capacity of making the social pie larger; litigation only divides a pie that itself is reduced by the high costs of litigation.[78]

An organization that expects to become involved in a certain number of disputes over a period of time will make arrangements, if it can, to control the expenditures involved in resolving those disputes. Thus in commercial settings, when manufacturers deal regularly with suppliers or buyers with the same sellers, contracts almost invariably provide for compulsory arbitration or another mode of dispute resolution that is less expensive than litigation. Each participant can expect a certain number of disputes to arise, e.g., whether particular goods conform to contract specifications, and each has an incentive to resolve such disputes accurately, expeditiously and cheaply. Winning one or losing another is less important than maintaining good long-term relationships with business partners and minimizing the transaction costs of disputes.[79] Dispute resolution costs in such settings are relatively low.

criminal defendant for whom counsel had been appointed to represent to change their rules to avoid subjecting lawyers to sanctions under Rule 42.2).

76. For more on the lawyer's responsibilities on appeal in a criminal case, see Jones v. Barnes, 463 U.S. 745 (1983), and the notes following it, infra at p. 480. Chapter 6 also addresses the allocation of authority between the defendant and the lawyer in the conduct of a criminal case.

77. Imperfect information and fraud sometimes leave those who trade worse off than they were before the bargain.

78. Again, however, one should keep in mind that arguments based on the economic paradigm, like most applications of Rawls' theory, tend to support the status

quo. Any argument that proceeds by comparing costs and benefits has a built-in bias for existing conditions. Put simply, rearranging existing institutions is almost always going to involve an initial cost that is higher than leaving them alone. Thus, unless we assume some kind of natural justice is reflected by existing societal arrangements, including existing distributions of wealth, a solution may be economically efficient without being just.

79. See, e.g., Stewart Macauley, Lawyers and Consumer Protection, 14 Law & Soc'y Rev. 115 (1979) (lawyers play a facilitating, mediating role in the consumer protection field, not the adversary role of the traditional professional model); Ian R. Macneil, The New Social Contract (1980).

When an organization's activities may result in litigation with an uncertain group of strangers, as in the product-liability context, and tort law prevents the organization from confining the claimant to a remedy provided in the contract, the organization is unable to control litigation expenditures. In a case involving a potential major liability, the organization has an incentive to spend additional amounts on legal services and other litigation costs as long as each expenditure marginally improves the overall outcome. Since it is known or suspected that the quality and extent of lawyering does affect the outcome of legal proceedings, the result is an escalation of expenditures on cases limited only by the magnitude of the stakes involved.[80]

The social problem is that each party has the same incentive to maximize its position by increasing litigation expenditures. The private problem is that, when both sides spend more on litigation, the benefits of those expenditures to each are reduced or eliminated. The situation is a classic "prisoners' dilemma" problem in which rational behavior by each participant (increasing expenditures in order to win a case) produces unfortunate results both for the litigants and for society.[81] The total expenditures on litigation sharply diminish the benefits of winning and multiply the burdens of losing. Because each party invests heavily in litigation expenses that counterbalance each other, outcomes are much the same as they would be if each spent less. As in the prisoners' dilemma, the litigants are worse off than if they had agreed in advance to cooperate with one another (i.e., to limit expenditures on litigation.) From the social standpoint the outcome is even more unfortunate: Resources that might be devoted to more productive uses are wasted on excessive litigation expenditures.[82]

The only group that benefits from this arrangement are lawyers engaged in high-stakes litigation—cases in which the amount at stake is large enough to justify large expenditures on legal services. The market for legal services of this type is a "winner-take-all" market in which slight differences in the perceived or actual ability of lawyers result in large variations in income.[83] Corporate managers, for example, faced with a $100 million damage suit or a hostile merger that will eliminate current manage-

80. In recent years defendants have devised another strategy: "settlement class actions." Settlement class actions are class actions that can be settled but not tried. These actions bring with them an increased risk of collusion between the defendant and class counsel. Once class counsel cannot threaten to go to trial and can only qualify for class counsel fees, the defendant in effect holds all the cards in the settlement "negotiation." Class counsel who balks at the defendant's idea of a fair settlement for the injured class can be passed over in favor of a more cooperative plaintiffs' lawyer willing to accept the settle-

ment in exchange for the chance to qualify for class counsel fees. Abuse in class actions is discussed infra at p. 815.

81. For a good introduction, see Robert D. Luce & Howard Raiffa, Games and Decisions 94–102 (1957), and Robert M. Axelrod, The Evolution of Cooperation (1983).

82. Orley Ashenfelter & David Bloom, Lawyers as Agents of the Devil in a Prisoner's Dilemma Game (mimeographed working paper, 1991).

83. Robert H. Frank & Philip J. Cook, Winner–Take–All–Society (1995).

ment, have little incentive to economize on legal services.[84] If lawyer X is perceived to have litigating abilities that are slightly better than Y or Z, thus increasing the probability of a successful outcome slightly, the managers will bid up X's services. This type of market produces an income distribution which resembles those observed in other "winner-take-all" markets, e.g., the disparity of earnings between Michael Jordan and other very good basketball players (e.g., the average NBA guard).[85]

Because the interests of the profession are not fully congruent with those of the general public, it is not surprising that legislators and judges generally are more supportive of measures designed to deter lawyers from pursuing or defending frivolous matters than are trial lawyers generally. Litigation is a vital aspect of the development of social norms and the struggle for a better social order. But litigation, like any other powerful medicine, is capable of abuse. Sanctions on lawyers who make unreasonable strategic use of litigation are therefore justified and necessary.

C.   HOW FAR FOR A CLIENT?

As to the "art" of the advocate, there is no inherent reason why it should be respectable at all. On the contrary, a cynic ... might define it as "Spokesmanship; or the art of misleading an audience without actually telling lies."

Cyril P. Harvey[1]

1.   WITNESS PREPARATION (COACHING)

There is very little law on the subject of witness preparation other than the criminal and ethical prohibitions on suborning perjury or using false evidence. Apparently the only ethics opinion is one responding to an

---

84. The corporation, as opposed to its managers, might be better off with a different strategy, which is only to say that agency problems may sometimes exacerbate the phenomenon described in the text.

85. The distribution of lawyer incomes has the characteristics of a "winner-take-all" market. The partners of major law firms that handle high-stakes litigation may average as much as $1 million per year while the median income of all lawyers is less than $70,000 per year. See John J. Wright and Edward J. Dwyer, The American Almanac of Jobs and Salaries 253 (1990) (median annual income of U.S. lawyers in 1987 was $68,922). Because this type of high-stakes litigation requires large staffs of

able younger lawyers who will work enormous hours under high pressure conditions to handle the voluminous documents and other complexities of such litigation, these firms bid up the beginning salaries of graduates of elite law schools to above the median salary for the profession as a whole. Similarly, on the plaintiffs' side, a relatively small number of plaintiffs' trial lawyers end up with most of the big-money cases and garner earnings that are the largest of any members of the legal profession.

1. Cyril P. Harvey, The Advocate's Devil 1–2 (1958) (Harvey was a prominent English barrister, 1923–1968).

inquiry concerning the proper level of lawyer involvement in preparing written testimony for regulatory proceedings. The committee, dealing more broadly with the subject, stated that "detailed, substantive consultations between lawyers and prospective witnesses are an expected part of trial preparation [and that] a lawyer's suggesting actual language to be used by a witness may be appropriate, as long as the ultimate testimony remains truthful and is not misleading."[2]

In *Anatomy of a Murder,*[3] a former prosecutor, Paul Biegler, defends a serviceman, Manion, accused of killing his wife's alleged rapist. At the initial interview with Manion, Biegler discovers that an hour elapsed between the time the serviceman learned of the assault on his wife and the time of the killing. The author of *Anatomy of a Murder,* then a justice of the Supreme Court of Michigan but writing under the pseudonym of Robert Traver, describes Biegler's thinking during the next meeting with his client:

> I paused and lit a cigar. I took my time. I had reached a point where a few wrong answers to a few right questions would leave me with a client—if I took his case—whose cause was legally defenseless. Either I stopped now and begged off ... or I asked him the few fatal questions and let him hang himself. Or else, like any smart lawyer, I went into the Lecture....

> And what is the Lecture?

> The Lecture is an ancient device that lawyers use to coach their clients so that the client won't know he has been coached and his lawyer can still preserve the face-saving illusion that he hasn't done any coaching. For coaching clients, like robbing them, is not only frowned upon, it is downright unethical.... Hence the Lecture, an artful device as old as the law itself, and one used constantly by some of the nicest and most ethical lawyers in the land. "Who, me? I didn't tell him what to say," the lawyer can later comfort himself. "I merely explained the law, see." It is a good practice to scowl and shrug here and add virtuously: "That's my duty, isn't it?"

In the famous lecture scene, Biegler explains that there are four ways to defend murder under Michigan law, and then suggests that the client's only hope is to have a legal excuse for the killing. The responsive client, led step by step by the lawyer's discussion of controlling legal principles, begins to understand that a form of insanity, temporary impaired mental capacity, may be the only defense under the facts. At the close of the interview, Biegler advises his client, "See if you can remember just how crazy you were."[4]

2. John S. Applegate, Witness Preparation, 68 Tex. L. Rev. 277, 279 (1989), discussing D.C. Legal Ethics Comm.Op. 79 (1979).

3. Robert Traver's Anatomy of a Murder (1958), a best-selling novel, was later made

into an award-winning movie by Otto Preminger.

4. Another movie, *The Verdict,* presents a different picture of witness preparation: a defendants' lawyer prepares the doctors he is defending in a medical malpractice case

Witness preparation does make a difference.[5] The most comprehensive recent discussion concludes:

> Witness preparation is not harmless. It provides opportunities for lawyers to encourage witnesses to adopt convenient, if not necessarily accurate, testimony. Even with the most honorable intentions, preparation may result in the distortion of witnesses' recollections. But witness preparation is integral to the lawyer's role in a judicial system that depends on partisan case development. Some preparatory activities are essential to a coherent and reasonably accurate factual presentation. More intensive preparation is required if the partisan advocate is to fulfill the ultimate responsibility to the client—presenting a persuasive case.... [6]

Given current practice in the United States, does a lawyer commit malpractice by failing to prepare witnesses? The purpose of witness preparation, according to one manual for trial lawyers, is that of "shaping the testimony, focusing on the significant, emphasizing helpful points, and structuring the presentation to minimize the damage caused by adverse information." The adversary system, the manual counsels, means that "It is not your job to bring all the facts to the attention of jury [but to] present the facts in the light most favorable to your side."[7]

Marvin Frankel, a distinguished lawyer, law teacher, and judge, comments critically on the American practice of witness preparation:

> [E]very lawyer knows that the "preparing" of witnesses may embrace a multitude of ... measures [other than the ordering and refreshing of recollection], including some ethical lapses believed to be more common than we would wish. The process is labeled archly in lawyer's slang as "horseshedding" the witness, a term that may be traced to utterly respectable origins in circuit-riding and otherwise horsy days but still rings a bit knowingly in today's ear. Whatever word is used to describe it, the process often extends beyond helping organize what the witness knows, and moves in the direction of helping the witness to

---

to testify in a vivid and direct manner that will be more effective with the jury. The movie, however, suggests that the hospital defendant may have been guilty of obstructing justice by encouraging a material witness to withhold testimony and that the defense lawyers may have known and acquiesced in this obstruction. The defense lawyers also obtained confidential information from the plaintiff's lawyer through seduction by a female agent.

5. Criminal trials in England, where the barristers who are examining witnesses have had no contact with them prior to the trial and have prepared solely on the basis of written statements supplied by a solicitor, are marked by witness testimony that has, to an American legal observer, a star-

tling spontaneity and tentativeness by contrast to that in American trials, which have a closer resemblance to staged dramatic presentations.

6. Applegate, supra, at 352. Applegate summarizes the large body of scientific studies to the effect that (1) witness preparation "intensifies the half-truth" problem by helping witnesses emphasize some facts and suppress others; and (2) distorts underlying memory both in terms of its content and the certainty with which the view is held. Applegate, supra, at 326–34.

7. Jeffrey L. Kestler, Questioning Techniques and Tactics § 9.14, at 332 (1988) (quoted in Applegate, supra, at 333).

know new things. At its starkest, the effort is called subornation of perjury, which is a crime, and which we are permitted to hope is rare. Somewhat less stark, short of criminality but still to be condemned, is the device of telling the client "the law" before eliciting the facts—i.e., telling the client what facts would constitute a successful claim or defense, and only then asking the client what the facts happen perchance to be. The most famous recent instance is fictional but apt: Anatomy of a Murder, a 1958 novel by Robert Traver.... It is not unduly cynical to suspect that this, if not in such egregious forms, happens with some frequency.

Moving away from palpably unsavory manifestations, we all know that the preparation of our witnesses is calculated, one way and another, to mock the solemn promise of the whole truth and nothing but. To be sure, reputable lawyers admonish their clients and witnesses to be truthful. At the same time, they often take infinite pains to prepare questions designed to make certain that the controlled flow of truth does not swell to an embarrassing flood. "Don't volunteer anything," the witnesses are cautioned. The concern is not that the volunteered contribution may be false. The concern is to avoid an excess of truth, where one spillover may prove hurtful to the case.... [8]

2. Fostering Falsity

A lawyer, faced with unfavorable evidence in a trial, may try to impeach the evidence or, alternatively or concurrently, she may draw on any ambiguities in the evidence in an effort to persuade the jury to draw a favorable inference. Impeachment seeks to persuade the jury that a witness is lying or mistaken; argument seeks to persuade the jury to draw favorable inferences. May she take either or both of these courses when she knows the witness is telling the truth and that the favorable inferences are in fact false?

Views of Commentators

Monroe Freedman discusses a hypothetical in which a lawyer's client is charged with a street robbery. Freedman assumes that the lawyer knows her client is innocent even though the client concedes he was one block away within five minutes of the crime, where he was seen by an elderly woman who is somewhat nervous and wears glasses. The woman testifies truthfully and accurately that she saw the client at this time and place.

What should the lawyer do? Freedman argues that the lawyer's duty in the adversary system is to make the truthful witness "appear to be mistaken or lying."[9] Preservation of the client's autonomy under our system of individual rights requires this conduct "unless tactics dictate otherwise."[10]

---

8. Marvin E. Frankel, Partisan Justice 15–16 (1980).

9. Monroe H. Freedman, Understanding Legal Ethics 167 (1990).

10. Id. at 168.

As soon as clients learned that confiding in their lawyers would result in less effective representation, such confidences [as the client's statement that he was near the scene of the crime] would rarely be given. The result would be selective ignorance, the practice in which the client is put on notice that he is not to tell his lawyer anything that might cause the lawyer to be less vigorous in her advocacy.[11]

But why do the interests of one human being justify a lawyer in inflicting harm on another, a well-meaning citizen who is cooperating in the pursuit of justice?[12] Why doesn't justice require that individuals bear the consequences of telling or not telling a lawyer truthful facts?

Harry Subin has envisioned a role for defense lawyers (a "monitoring" role, he calls it) that is sharply less adversarial than Freedman's conception.[13] In a criminal case, Subin would make it "improper for an attorney who knows beyond a reasonable doubt the truth of a fact established in the state's case to attempt to refute that fact through the introduction of evidence, impeachment of evidence, or argument." If the client nevertheless wants to go to trial, "the attorney would work to assure that all of the elements of the crime were proven beyond a reasonable doubt, on the basis of competent and admissible evidence." The attorney could also argue to the jury that the evidence does not "sustain the burden of proof."

John B. Mitchell, an experienced criminal defense lawyer, disagrees, arguing that the attempt to raise a reasonable doubt usually involves challenging the persuasiveness of certain inferences from the testimony of witnesses. Bringing out testimony, not itself false, to accredit a false theory, is not the same as arguing a false theory.[14]

Michigan Opinion CI–1164

A Michigan ethics opinion[15] provides a real-life situation to which these conflicting views may be applied:

11. Id. at 167.

12. A news story reports that elderly victims of crime are reluctant to become witnesses in New York City in part because they are aware that defense lawyers will engage them in grueling cross-examinations designed to "give the impression of faulty memory, obtuseness and senility." In one case discussed, a lawyer engaged in a rapid-fire, detailed and repetitive examination designed to confuse an 89 year-old witness, whose former lawyer was charged with stealing $129,000 from her. A mistrial resulted when the jury deadlocked 11–1 in favor of conviction. Although the victim died before the retrial, her testimony was provided by videotape. See In re Reisch, 474 N.Y.S.2d 741 (1st Dept.1984) (lawyer disbarred). E. R. Shipp, Fear and Confusion in Court Plague Elderly Crime Victims, N.Y. Times, Mar. 13, 1983, at p. A1.

13. Harry I. Subin, The Criminal Lawyer's "Different Mission": Reflections on the "Right" to Present a False Case, 1 Geo. J. Legal Ethics 125, 149–150 (1987).

14. John B. Mitchell, Reasonable Doubts Are Where You Find Them: A Response to Professor Subin's Position on the Criminal Lawyer's "Different Mission," 1 Geo.J.Legal Ethics 339, 343–46 (1987). See also Harry I. Subin, Is This Lie Necessary? Further Reflections on the Right to Present a False Defense, 1 Geo.J.Legal Ethics 689 (1988).

15. Michigan Ethics Op. CI–1164 (1987).

Client is charged with armed robbery. He proposes to call some friends as witnesses at trial, who will give truthful testimony that he was with them at the time of the crime. At the preliminary examination the victim had testified that the robbery occurred at the same hour and time to which the friends will testify. Client has confided to attorney that he robbed the victim; his theory on the time mix-up is that he stole the victim's watch and rendered him unconscious so that the victim's sense of time was incorrect when relating the circumstances of the robbery to the investigating detectives. Months later, at the preliminary examination, the victim relied on the detectives' notes to help him recall the time. Client and attorney have decided that client will not testify at trial. Would it be ethical for attorney to subpoena the friends to testify that client was with them at the alleged time of the crime?

The opinion concludes that the attorney may offer into evidence the testimony of the client's friends. The reasoning of the opinion runs as follows: The duty of zealous representation requires a criminal defense lawyer to use any truthful evidence that may help her client. If the friends' testimony is truthful and it will help the client, then the lawyer must use it. Defense counsel is not permitted to inform the prosecution that its evidence is inaccurate. Nor must defense counsel ignore truthful evidence simply because counsel knows the client is guilty—the lawyer is a partisan advocate, not an impartial fact-finder.

Although DR 7–102(4) [and M.R. 3.3(a)(4)] prohibits lawyers from introducing perjured testimony, in this fact situation the friends' testimony is truthful. A lawyer is not barred from using truthful testimony, even if that testimony will result in the acquittal of a defendant who has privately admitted his guilt to counsel. "One cannot suborn the truth." The burden is on the prosecution to prove the elements of the charge, and it must do so without the assistance of the defendant's lawyer.

Finally, the Opinion states that defense counsel should discuss with the client the decision of whether or not to use the testimony. Although the friends will testify truthfully, providing the defendant with an alibi, the prosecution may nonetheless have assembled overwhelming evidence against the defendant. If that is true, the testimony of the client's friends is unlikely to count for much with the jury. Under these circumstances, the defendant may be best advised to forego a trial and negotiate a plea bargain.

Is this reasoning sound? Is the conclusion just?

3.   DIRTY TRICKS IN COURT

Deliberate Injection of Impermissible Matter

The professional codes mandate that a "lawyer shall not ... allude to any matter that the lawyer does not reasonably believe is relevant or that will not be supported by substantial evidence ...".[16] In real life as well as in the courtroom scenes portrayed in movies and television, however, trial lawyers frequently make statements or ask questions that assume irrelevant or inadmissible facts. Robert Keeton (professor and then judge) states:

> Some lawyers frankly state, and still more endorse by practice, the ethically indefensible proposition that this kind of improper question should be asked unless it is of such prejudicial character that the refusal of the trial court to declare a mistrial would be reversible error. This practice is sometimes used for the very purpose of confronting adverse counsel with the difficult choice of waiving objection by failing to make it, or else make an objection that may lead the jury to conclude that he is attempting to withhold information from them.[17]

Keeton implies, without so stating, that the threat of professional discipline is not an adequate deterrent: "Protection against the deliberate use of clearly improper questions is inadequate under existing rules of law, unless the trial judge uses his discretionary powers to deal with the practice sternly." The primary constraint is a tactical one: If the jury perceives the tactic is unfair, its use may have a negative effect on lawyer and client.

Some matters are viewed as so prejudicial that their introduction will result in a mistrial or other sanctions. For example, severe sanctions may be imposed when a lawyer refers to the other's side's liability insurance or to concessions made in settlement discussions.[18] What should the lawyer do in more equivocal situations in which evidence is of doubtful admissibility but has large persuasive value? Keeton says:

> If you believe that the evidence of doubtful admissibility is likely to have a strong influence on the findings of the jury in the case, you may conclude that the chance of reversal is worth taking; the decision is based upon weighing the probable value of the evidence to you in its influence on the jury against the disadvantage of possible reversal of a favorable verdict and judgment.

Are you satisfied with this consequentialist approach?

A closely related issue involves the intentional use of leading questions to guide the witness.[19] The issue is complicated because under some circumstances leading questions may be employed. Leading questions, Keeton states, are "tempting" because their effect cannot be erased by

---

16. M.R. 3.4(e). DR 7–106(C)(1) is substantially identical. For a decision upholding contempt sanctions for repeated violation of forensic rules by a lawyer in a criminal trial, see Hawk v. Superior Court, 116 Cal. Rptr. 713 (Cal.App.1974).

17. Robert E. Keeton, Trial Tactics and Methods 59 (2d ed. 1973).

18. See, e.g., Fike v. Grant, 8 P.2d 242 (Ariz.1932) (liability insurance). See Richard H. Underwood & W. H. Fortune, Trial Ethics § 11.6 (1988).

19. Similar problems arise in connection with "speaking objections"—argumentative comments included in objections that are designed to put certain matter before the jury. Melvin Belli comments that a speaking objection "is not unethical if its purpose is further to emphasize, for example, the limited purpose of the introduction of certain testimony." Melvin M. Belli, Modern Trials 616 (Student ed. 1963).

objection or instruction. Even if the leading question is stricken, the witness has been tipped off about how to respond to a properly phrased question. After implying that general provisions of ethics codes are unlikely to deter lawyers from using leading questions, Keeton discusses "tactical" reasons why they should be avoided in some situations.[20]

Deliberate and flagrant appeals to bias and prejudice are likely to result in a mistrial. Skilled advocates, however, are frequently successful in introducing issues of socio-economic status, wealth, race, religion or ethnicity by one means or another. On some occasions the issues may be framed so as to permit introduction of evidence of a defendant's wealth or character.[21] Indirect allusions or the use of code phrases in questions or argument may pass without objection or judicial reprimand. If all else fails, use of a "dumb show" technique may get a point across to the jury.[22]

Asserting Personal Knowledge, Belief or Opinion

M.R. 3.4(e) prohibits a lawyer from "assert[ing] personal knowledge of facts in issue except when testifying as a witness, or stat[ing] a personal opinion as to the justness of a cause, the credibility of a witness, the culpability of a civil litigant or the guilt or innocence of an accused."[23]

Robert Keeton offers advice on this subject to law students contemplating a career in advocacy:

> Probably you will be at your best as an advocate when you cause the judge and jury to believe that the decision you are urging them to reach is a decision you would reach yourself. Yet the Code of Professional Responsibility, in one of its Disciplinary Rules, prohibits any direct statement of belief in your cause.... It seems more consistent

---

20. Id. at 48–52. M.R. 3.4(c), providing that a lawyer "shall not ... knowingly disobey an obligation under the rules of a tribunal," is violated by deliberate use of leading questions objectionable under a jurisdiction's evidence rules. DR 7–106(A) is substantially identical.

21. A punitive damage count may allow introduction of evidence of a defendant's wealth; character may become relevant if the subject is opened up by the adversary.

22. The most prevalent form of "dumb show" involves the dress and appearance of the client. The use of props, whether children or crutches, is frequent. Clarence Darrow, trying cases in a time when smoking was permitted in court, is reported to have distracted juries during the closing argument of his opponent by defying the law of gravity. A thin wire inserted in his cigar prevented the ash from falling.

Max Wildman, a well-known insurance defense lawyer in Chicago, used a creative strategy in a case in which his client, a widower, was suing Wildman's client for the wrongful death of his wife. Wildman employed a pretty young woman to sit immediately behind the plaintiff throughout the trial and to engage him in friendly conversation, in the presence of the jury, when the court was not in session. See Jeffrey O'Connell, The Lawsuit Lottery: Only the Lawyers Win c. 3 (1979) (discussing this and other "tricks of the trade" in tort cases).

23. For a discussion of the impropriety of prosecutors calling witnesses "liars," see Moore v. United States, 934 F.Supp. 724 (E.D.Va.1996) (distinguishing prosecutorial references to "lying" or "liars" that imply personal opinion or the possession by the government of extra-judicial evidence that supports the assertion of "lying," which are unethical, from assertions that the evidence or record support the conclusion that a witness has lied, which are proper).

with the apparent objectives of the rule, as well as the prevailing practice, to treat it as a regulation of the form and manner of your conduct ... rather than a regulation requiring that you not display, even indirectly, any appearance of commitment to your cause. Indeed, if interpreted as precluding even an indirect display of commitment to your cause, the rule could hardly be reconciled with your acknowledged duty as an advocate to bring "zeal" to your representation of your cause.[24]

Are you comfortable with this role of using non-verbal communication to portray your client as honest and her cause as just, without regard to your honest feelings and beliefs?

Intimidation and Harassment

Cross-examination of a witness that is harsh, unfair or oppressive carries its own deterrent effect. Even if the judge does not intervene, the jury may sympathize with the witness. For this reason, Keeton suggests that

> [I]t is better not to make [an objection to oppressive or misleading cross-examination] if the witness is able to take care of himself. . . . If the substantive content of your witness' testimony is not being weakened and your witness is not responding with angry or sarcastic answers, you may as well let your adversary have the freedom to err; you may finally object, but not until you are certain that your adversary has gone so far that the court will sustain the objection and thus convict your adversary in the presence of the jury of trying to take unfair advantage of the witness.[25]

Other versions of harassment, however, do not have this self-limiting quality. They are often referred to as "blaming the victim." Examples are legion. Consider the following:

Dalkon Shield Depositions

Women who used the intrauterine birth control device known as Dalkon Shield reported serious harms from pelvic infections allegedly caused by the device. Thousands of lawsuits were eventually filed against the manufacturer, A. H. Robins Company, which reportedly engaged in litigation tactics designed to encourage women to withdraw their claims and to discourage others from filing claims. The tactics ultimately proved to be unsuccessful. Persistent plaintiffs' lawyers proved that "Robins had marketed the Dalkon Shield without investigating its safety and that, after they had learned of the propensity of the device to cause life-threatening pelvic infections, company officials had withheld and even destroyed this information while the Dalkon Shield was still being sold and used."[26] The

24. Id. at 2–3.

25. Robert E. Keeton, Trial Tactics and Methods 175 (2d ed.1973).

26. Richard B. Sobol, Bending the Law: The Story of the Dalkon Shield Bankruptcy x (1991).

result was a succession of punitive damage awards that led to withdrawal of the product in 1980 and bankruptcy for Robins in 1985.

Morton Mintz's book on the Dalkon Shield controversy describes the deposition tactics of Robins and its lawyers:[27]

> No one disputes that certain sexual activities or unhygienic habits can enhance the environment for pelvic inflammatory disease [PID], even if they do not *cause* PID. This is why A. H. Robins had a right to make inquiries into highly private aspects of the lives of women who filed lawsuits blaming the Dalkon Shield for PID-related injuries. But it did not have a right to make *unreasonable and irrelevant* inquires.
>
> The record shows that Robins attorneys took depositions from Shield victims in which they asked not only intimate, but also demeaning and even intimidating questions. Although certain judges required defense-counsel to show a connection between the questions and women's injuries, others did not do so and allowed Robins to ask at public trials what plaintiffs' lawyers call "dirty questions."
>
> The following case is from the Shield suit of an Iowa mother of two children who had suffered PID and the consequent loss of her ovaries and womb. Robins's counsel took depositions from her and her husband, each in the presence of the other. To her, the company attorney put queries about her sexual relations before their marriage in 1963, *ten years before she was fitted with a Shield, and fifteen years before she was stricken with PID*. Her lawyer, Kenneth W. Green of Minneapolis, objected, calling such questions "disgusting as well as irrelevant."
>
> Robins then submitted written questions, to her and also to her husband. These, Green said in an affidavit, were "even worse," partly because they returned to the premarital period. Two written questions to the wife were: "Prior to your marriage in 1963", did you have sexual relations with anybody else other than [your husband]? and "Who were these sexual partners?"
>
> Green's own daughter had worn a Shield and suffered two episodes of PID, one of which almost killed her. But knowing of the invasions of privacy, he advised her not to sue Robins, and she didn't.
>
> Panty hose can't cause PID; not even defense experts suggested they could. But in a case involving another Shield litigant, a Robins attorney made pantyhose an issue. Among his questions was whether she wore them and what fabric was used in the crotch. To the latter query she replied, "I'll answer that, but this sounds more like an obscene phone call than anything else."
>
> During a deposition in Minnesota in May 1982, lawyers for a Boston woman directed her not to answer questions by Robins counsel about which way she wiped, and whether, and how often she engaged

27. Morton Mintz, At Any Cost: Corporate Greed, Women and the Dalkon Shield 194–   95 (1985).

in oral and anal intercourse and used so-called marital aids. Five months later, however, a judge compelled her to return to Twin Cities to answer the questions. As late as January 1984, a Midwestern woman was asked if before she was fitted with a Shield she had had any sexual partners in addition to her husband. By then the couple had adopted two children, her ability to bear a child of her own having been ruined by Shield-related PID.

Prego Cross–Examination

Dr. Veronica Prego brought suit against the public body operating a New York City hospital, claiming that she contracted AIDS by pricking a finger with a contaminated needle negligently left in a patient's bedding at defendant's hospital. Stanley Friedman, lawyer for the hospital authority, had the unenviable task of seeking to discredit Dr. Prego's testimony. He did so by challenging

> her sincerity, her stamina, her character, her veracity and her memory. He examined her love life and discussed her abortions. And as Dr. Prego, her mother and her sister sat nearby, he asked another witness to estimate her life expectancy.[28]

Columnists depicted Friedman as "an ogre, a sadist and a money-grubber," but he defended his cross-examination as only doing the job the adversary system required of him. Dr. Prego's pregnancies and love life were relevant because she might have contracted AIDs from transfusions or sexual contact; her life expectancy was relevant to damage issues. Lawyers for Dr. Prego predicted that Friedman's tactics would backfire. Perhaps they were right. Dr. Prego received a $1.35 million settlement award just before her case was to go to the jury.[29]

Countless other examples could be provided of tactics that some charge are improper: Tactics designed, it is said, to discourage or intimidate litigants or to prejudice the victim by blaming her for her harm.[30] Is a lawyer required to use tactics that are harsh or repugnant if the inquiry is legally relevant? Or do professional rules permit the lawyer's moral conscience to come into play? If the latter, should a lawyer inform a client in advance of representation that she will not use "repugnant" tactics?

Trickery

Perry Mason may get away with tricking an expert witness, for example, with a fingerprint that is not the one that has been introduced

28. David Margolick, Defense Tactics in the AIDS Doctor's Suit, N.Y.Times, Jan. 23, 1990, at p. B1.

29. Arnold H. Lubasch, Judge, in Shift, Discloses that Prego Will Get $1.35 Million, N.Y.Times, Mar. 10, 1990, at pp. B27–B28.

30. See Langlois v. Deja Vu, Inc., 1997 U.S. Dist. LEXIS 9327, *8–10 (W.D.Wash. 1997)

(describing questions by defense lawyers during a deposition, which were apparently designed to humiliate the plaintiff-witnesses, as "approach[ing] ... the outer-limits of the bounds of acceptable advocacy and warning all counsel "to tread well away from that line").

into evidence. But the use of trickery in a real trial is ill-advised because judges may view it as dishonesty toward the court. In United States v. Thoreen,[31] defense counsel in a criminal case, without the trial court's knowledge and permission, seated someone who looked like the defendant at the counsel table while the defendant sat immediately behind in the public section. Predictably, two government witnesses misidentified the defendant. The trial court allowed the government to reopen its case, the defendant was convicted and the lawyer was charged with and convicted of criminal contempt. On appeal, the court, conceding that the "line between vigorous advocacy and actual obstruction is close," upheld the contempt finding.[32]

4. Special Responsibilities of Prosecutors[33]

M.R. 3.8 outlines the special responsibilities of a prosecutor.[34] See also ABA Standards on the Administration of Criminal Justice (The Prosecution Function), particularly 3–3.9, Discretion in the Charging Decision.

In Brady v. Maryland,[35] the Supreme Court held that the prosecutor must reveal to the defense, upon request, exculpatory evidence "material either to guilt or to punishment." In United States v. Agurs,[36] the Court held that when the exculpatory evidence creates a reasonable doubt, the prosecution must disclose the evidence to the defense even if there is no request. However, the prosecution's failure to disclose evidence that could have effectively impeached government witnesses does not require automatic reversal; reversal is required only if there is "a reasonable probability that" had the defense known of the undisclosed evidence "the result of the proceeding would have been different."[37]

DR 7–103(B) requires the prosecutor to disclose to the defense, whether or not the defense makes a request, evidence "that tends to negate the guilt of the accused, mitigate the degree of the offense, or reduce the punishment." It does not tie this duty to "material" evidence, although one might read the "tends to" language as the substantial equivalent of a materiality requirement. See also M.R. 3.8(d), which adopts the same standard as DR 7–103(B), except that in connection with sentencing the

31. 653 F.2d 1332 (9th Cir.1981).

32. Id. at 1339.

33. The authors thank Kevin C. McMunigal of Case Western Reserve University School of Law for his helpful comments on this section of our book.

34. Criminal defense lawyers are subject to the general prohibitions against use of illegal means to gather evidence. For a revealing look at the ethics of white collar criminal defense lawyers, see Kenneth Mann, Defending White Collar Crime (1985). For reflections on the ethics of prosecutors, see

Fred C. Zacharias, Structuring the Ethics of Prosecutorial Trial Practice: Can Prosecutors Do Justice?, 44 Vand.L.Rev. 45 (1991); Stanley Z. Fisher, In Search of the Virtuous Prosecutor, 15 Am.J.Crim.Law 197 (1988).

35. 373 U.S. 83 (1963). See also Moore v. Illinois, 408 U.S. 786 (1972) (elaborating on the *Brady* rule).

36. 427 U.S. 97 (1976).

37. United States v. Bagley, 473 U.S. 667, 682, 685 (1985).

rule allows a prosecutor to withhold mitigating information that is privileged or is protected by order of a tribunal.

In People v. Jones,[38] the court held that the prosecutor did not violate the defendant's due process rights by failing to reveal during plea negotiations that the state's key witness had died. The court held that the prosecutor had neither a constitutional nor an ethical duty to reveal this information, as long as the prosecutor made no affirmative misrepresentation. The information was held to be outside the *Brady* rule because it was not exculpatory; the death of the witness merely made it difficult for the state to prove its case.

In Fambo v. Smith,[39] the court held that while the prosecutor did have a duty to disclose to the defendant that physical evidence critical to one of the counts of the indictment had been destroyed, the failure to do so did not affect the fairness of defendant's plea bargain. The Supreme Court has yet to abrogate a guilty plea based on the prosecution's failure to disclose *Brady* material and has never clearly articulated how, if at all, *Brady* applies to guilty pleas.[40]

Are these cases consistent with the *Brady* doctrine? With EC 7–13, which sets forth the justifications for the special responsibilities of a prosecutor? With ABA Standard 3–4.1, which says "[i]t is unprofessional conduct for a prosecutor knowingly to make false statements or representations in the course of plea discussion? . . ."[41]

The prosecution also has a duty to preserve evidence.[42] In the *Trombetta* case, the Court held that the loss or destruction of evidence does not violate the due process clause of the Constitution absent "official animus" or a "conscious effort to suppress exculpatory evidence."[43] In addition, the destroyed evidence must be "material" to the suspect's defense under a two-part test. First, the exculpatory value of the evidence has to have been apparent prior to the destruction of the evidence; and second, the evidence has to be such that the defendant would be unable to obtain comparable evidence by other reasonably available means.

5. USING IMPROPER MEANS IN GATHERING EVIDENCE

A lawyer may not use illegal means to gather evidence. The laws prohibiting fraud, burglary, theft, illegal use of the mail or wiretapping do not contain exceptions for lawyers. "It is unprofessional conduct for a

38.   375 N.E.2d 41 (N.Y.1978).

39.   433 F.Supp. 590 (W.D.N.Y.1977), aff'd, 565 F.2d 233 (2d Cir.1977).

40.   See, e.g., United States v. Matthews, 168 F.3d 1234, 1242 (11th Cir.1999) (refusing to decide whether, and, if so, to what extent *Brady* applies in cases when the defendant pleads guilty). See generally Kevin C. McMunigal, Disclosure and Accuracy in the Guilty Plea Process, 40 Hastings L. J. 958 (1989).

41.   ABA Standards on the Administration of Justice (Prosecution Function), Standard 3–4.1.

42.   California v. Trombetta, 467 U.S. 479 (1984).

43.   467 U.S. at 488.

lawyer knowingly to use illegal means to obtain evidence or information or to employ, instruct, or encourage others to do so.''[44]

In addition, the ethics rules prohibiting "dishonesty, fraud, deceit or misrepresentation" may place more stringent limits on the ways in which lawyers may gather evidence. For example, ethics opinions and some disciplinary cases state that a lawyer should not record conversations without the consent or prior knowledge of all the parties to the conversation.[45]

United States v. Ofshe,[46] involved charges that improper means had been used in gathering evidence by then Assistant United States Attorney Scott Turow (the author of *One L, Presumed Innocent* and other books). A lawyer, Glass, who was under investigation for racketeering in the Northern District of Illinois, approached Turow and offered to inform on suspected drug merchants. One of the individuals on whom Glass informed was Ofshe, for whom Glass was co-counsel in a pending federal cocaine charge in Florida. Turow warned Glass not to report or record any privileged communications or anything relating to Ofshe's pending case. A "body bug" produced information concerning ongoing money laundering and drug conspiracies. Turow also told Glass that Glass would have to withdraw from his representation of Ofshe after providing information, and, when Glass refused to withdraw, Turow told the district court, in camera, of Glass's conflict of interest.

On appeal from conviction of the original cocaine charges, Ofshe argued that the invasion of his attorney-client relationship with Glass required dismissal of the indictment. A panel of the Eleventh Circuit refused the defendant's motion to dismiss the indictment, stating that the appropriate remedy was suppression of the evidence thus garnered. Nevertheless, the court called Turow's conduct "reprehensible" and suggested referral to the state's disciplinary commission. When Turow defended his conduct, which had been reviewed and upheld by the Department of Justice, the court wrote a further opinion suggesting that he should be prosecuted for obstruction of justice.[47] Turow later wrote an article identifying his struggle with the Eleventh Circuit as the most bitter experience of his life as a prosecutor: "I believed—and continue to believe—that neither clients nor lawyers have the right to plan crimes secure from government law enforcement efforts.''[48]

44. ABA Standards Relating to the Administration of Criminal Justice: The Defense Function, Standard 4–4.2. See, e.g., Markham v. Markham, 272 So.2d 813 (Fla. 1973); Lucas v. Ludwig, 313 So.2d 12 (La. App.1975); and Tennessee Bar Association v. Freemon, 362 S.W.2d 828 (Tenn.App. 1961).

45. See, e.g., ABA Formal Op. 337 (1974) (lawyers should record conversations only with the consent or prior knowledge of all the parties to the conversation); ABA Informal Op. 1407 (1978) (in accord with

337). But see ABA Informal Op. 1357 (1975) (statements made at a public meeting may be recorded).

46. 817 F.2d 1508 (11th Cir.), cert. denied, 484 U.S. 963 (1987).

47. United States v. Ofshe, unpublished opinion, No. 86–5351 (11th Cir. Nov. 16, 1987).

48. Scott L. Turow, Law School vs. Reality, N.Y.Times Mag., Oct. 18, 1988, at p. 52. Richard Uviller agrees with Turow. Although Glass betrayed his client, he did so

On aiding and abetting the destruction or concealment of evidence see the *Stenhach* case in Chapter 1 and the notes following it.

———

under circumstances in which the client was seeking his assistance in on-going criminal conspiracies. In any event, Uviller argues, Glass's misconduct is not attributable to Turow either under ethics rules or as an accessory to crime. H. Richard Uviller, Presumed Guilty: The Court of Appeals vs. Scott Turow, 136 U.Pa.L.Rev. 1879 (1988).

CHAPTER 6

LAWYER–CLIENT RELATIONSHIP

INTRODUCTORY NOTE

The lawyer-client relationship is a complex one founded on contract and agency law but infused with professional ideals and governed in part by regulatory principles flowing from a lawyer's role as an officer of the court. Three simple models suggest facets of this complex relationship: (1) a fiduciary model, (2) a market model and (3) a regulatory or public utility model.[1] In the United States, the law and practice of the lawyer-client relationship have attributes of each model.

The fiduciary model draws on a legal and professional tradition that views a client as dependent upon her lawyer's skill and knowledge. According to that tradition, because a client cannot evaluate the quality of legal services, she must make a leap of faith and trust her lawyer to provide loyal, competent and diligent service at reasonable cost. Ideally, each lawyer's professional values prevent abuse of the client's trust. The lawyer becomes a fiduciary expected to put the client's interest ahead of other interests, especially the lawyer's self-interest.

The market model views the relationship between lawyer and client as a consensual exchange that benefits both lawyer and client: The client benefits from receiving services conforming to contract terms and market standards, and the lawyer benefits from receiving payment for services rendered. This approach presumes that a client can select an appropriate person to provide needed services, make satisfactory arrangements with that person and monitor the provision of service.[2]

The regulatory or public utility model views lawyers as quasi-public officials performing important public functions. This approach perceives dispute resolution and other legal tasks as so vital to the community that they must be closely regulated to serve public objectives of legitimacy, finality, fairness and efficiency. Under this model, more pervasive abroad

1. For useful discussion of various models of legal ethics, see John Leubsdorf, Three Models of Professional Reform, 67 Cornell L.Rev. 1021 (1982) (contrasting the approaches of market, public utility, and personal responsibility approaches to problems of professional reform); Anthony D'Amato & Edward J. Eberle, Three Models of Legal Ethics, 27 St. Louis U.L.Rev. 761 (1983) (applying autonomy, socialist and deontological models to the problem of confidentiality).

2. These assumptions are questioned by many people, including economists. See Kenneth Arrow, The Limits of Organization 61–79 (1974) (professional ethics are needed because patients lack information necessary to make the market model work in the health care field).

than in the United States, courts and legislatures provide detailed regulation of lawyers in the public interest.

What do ordinary Americans want from a lawyer? Empirical surveys performed by the American Bar Foundation indicate that the four principal qualities clients seek in their lawyers are commitment, integrity, competence and a fair and affordable fee.[3]

Who's in Charge?

Douglas E. Rosenthal, focusing on the dynamics of power, has contrasted a "traditional model" of the lawyer-client relationship with a "participatory model."[4] Considering a "professional" to be someone who does something that requires expert knowledge and skill, the traditional model stresses respect for professional knowledge, competence and autonomy. Because lay persons lack the knowledge to evaluate adequately the quality of what a professional does, they must trust that professional's judgment and responsibility. The traditional model thus expects clients to be cooperative, deferential and obedient.

The participatory model, on the other hand, posits a client of equal status who participates actively in the professional relationship, sharing control and decisional responsibility with the professional.[5] Rosenthal argues that the participatory model is preferable because it furthers client objectives and produces better results.[6] A lawyer, Rosenthal argues, "should be obligated to disclose to the client the relevant open choices involved in responding to his particular problem."[7] The lawyer should discuss with the client "the alternatives involved in identifying the problem, the alternatives for dealing with it, the professional's experience in employing these alternatives, and their anticipated difficulties and benefits."

---

3. See Barbara A. Curran, Surveying the Legal Needs of the Public: What the Public Wants and Expects in the Lawyer–Client Relationship, in Law in a Cynical Society: Opinion and Law in the 1980's 107–119 (Gibson & Baldwin eds. 1985).

4. Douglas E. Rosenthal, Lawyer and Client: Who's in Charge? 1–28 (1974).

5. Rosenthal argues that the two models take opposing positions on basic issues concerning the professional relationship and the provision of professional services. Id. The traditional model posits a passive, trusting and obedient client; assumes that ineffective professional service is rare; views professional problems as routine and technical, having a best solution inaccessible to lay understanding; assumes that professionals can and do make a client's interests their own and that professions and

courts set and maintain high professional standards; and posits that effective professional service is accessible to all paying clients. Rosenthal's participatory model provides opposing answers to these propositions.

6. The participatory model, Rosenthal found, produces larger awards in personal injury cases. In Rosenthal's study, a panel of experts evaluated the outcome of about 100 personal injury cases on the basis of a detailed workup of the facts, likely evidence, etc. The feature that most closely correlated with a good monetary outcome for a client was not the lawyer's education, experience, reputation, firm, professionalism or talent, but rather the aggressiveness of the client in monitoring the case.

7. Rosenthal, supra, at 155.

No action should be taken with respect to any of these choices until the client, aware of them, has given his consent."[8]

Paternalism and Manipulation

Lawyers, like physicians and other professionals, have passed through an arduous period of study and training. They view themselves, and others view them, as a relatively elite group. They typically earn more than those who work with their hands and enjoy greater prestige and social status. Their knowledge appears esoteric to ordinary people, in part because it employs a special language inaccessible to many clients. These features of the professional role, Richard Wasserstrom argues, "conspire to depersonalize the client in the eyes of the lawyer qua professional." As a result, lawyers tend to treat a "client as an object."[9]

> The lawyer qua professional is, of necessity, only centrally interested in that part of the client that lies within his or her special competency. And this leads any professional including the lawyer to respond to the client as an object—as a thing to be altered, corrected, or otherwise assisted by the professional rather than as a person. At best the client is viewed ... not as a whole person but as a segment or aspect of a person—an interesting kidney problem, a routine marijuana possession case, or another adolescent with an identity crisis.[10]

> Professional training, status and role, combined with the vulnerability and inexperience of many clients, also "operate to make the relationship a paternalistic one."[11] Because a lawyer knows some "things that the client doesn't know, it is extremely easy to believe that one knows generally what is best for the client."

> Invested with all of this power both by the individual and the society, the lawyer qua professional responds to the client as though the client were an individual who needed to be looked after and controlled, and to have decisions made for him or her by the lawyer, with as little interference from the client as possible.... [12]

8. Id.

9. Richard Wasserstrom, Lawyers as Professionals: Some Moral Issues, 5 Human Rights 1 (1975). Another portion of this essay was reprinted in Chapter 1 at p. 21.

10. Id. at 21.

11. A large philosophical and legal literature exists on paternalism. See Gerald Dworkin, Paternalism, in Morality and the Law 107 (Richard Wasserstrom, ed., 1971); Dennis F. Thompson, Paternalism in Medicine, Law, and Public Policy, in, Ethics Teaching in Higher Education 245 (Daniel Callahan and Sissela Bok, eds., 1980); David Luban, Paternalism and the Legal Profession, 1981 Wis.L.Rev. 454. See p. 487 infra.

12. Id. at 22. Wasserstrom's argument that professionals dominate their clients or patients relies upon an image of professional role that is somewhat more characteristic of medicine than of law: The client or patient as an inexperienced and sick or troubled lay individual who must rely on the physician's advice. Many lawyers, however, serve business clients, some of whom are experienced and knowledgeable in obtaining legal services. In addition, the medical profession encounters few analogs to in-house counsel, whose existence helps place many entity clients on a more even footing with their outside lawyers.

For discussion of the influence of images of professional role, see William F. May, The Physician's Covenant: Images of the Healer in Medical Ethics (1983). The medical pro-

Such paternalism may lead, even if inadvertently, to a lawyer's manipulating a client. Such manipulation can run the gamut from serving what a lawyer perceives as a client's best interest to furthering the lawyer's own interest. At either end of this spectrum some manipulation may be inevitable. For example, in translating unfamiliar legal reality for a client, a lawyer necessarily alters the client's expectations to conform to that reality. Similarly, lawyers often deploy their authority and articulateness to persuade clients to undertake an alternate course of conduct more consistent with legal and moral realities—a course of conduct that is either in the client's best interest or "the right thing to do": "If you persist in your plan to perjure yourself, I will be forced to withdraw from representing you in this case;" "The subpoena asks for all relevant documents. Although this memorandum is damaging, the consequences of divulging it now are far less serious than the later discovery, which I consider probable, that we have concealed it." This kind of counseling—attempting to guide a less-informed client along a morally and legally acceptable path—may demand of a lawyer extraordinary interpersonal skills, persuasiveness as an advocate and even courage.[13]

manipulation

A less justifiable form of paternalism involves more extreme control of information, slanted advice and occasionally deceit. Here, the lawyer does not convince or persuade a client to follow the lawyer's advice, but instead diverts the client from something she wants and intends to do. A lawyer deprives the client of effective choice by controlling the flow of information: "The settlement offer isn't perfect, but it's the best one you're going to get and better than a 50 percent chance of losing at trial; you should take it." "You can take the stand; but the jury won't believe you and the judge will hit you with a harder sentence." At the extreme, a lawyer may act without consulting the client, for example, rejecting a settlement offer or taking an important litigation step.

Another form of manipulation, clearly unjustifiable, involves situations in which a lawyer manipulates a client to serve the lawyer's self-interest. For example, a lawyer might pressure the client to accept a low settlement that provides the lawyer with a substantial fee on the basis of very little work.

Who Corrupts Whom?

Lawyer is the Bad Guy

Discussions of legal ethics are often predicated on opposing assumptions as to which side of the relationship poses danger to the other side or to the public interest. On the one hand, authors such as Rosenthal and Wasserstrom, focusing on the representation of injured or troubled individuals, view lawyers as dominant in the relationship and the locus of danger.

fession is discussed in Eliot Freidson, Profession of Medicine: A Study of the Sociology of Applied Knowledge (1970) and Paul Starr, The Social Transformation of American Medicine (1982).

13. This is particularly the case with a powerful client, such as a large corporation that generates and closely monitors a continuing volume of legal business, and is able to exercise control over the lawyer.

These authors assume that ethics rules should prevent lawyers from abusing or corrupting clients.[14]

Other authors, however, focusing generally on lawyers who serve corporate interests, view clients as the locus of danger—clients who exercise power over lawyers and bend those lawyers to the clients' will.[15] This view assumes implicitly that many clients are immoral, "bad" people who seek to use lawyers to further unjust causes by unjust means. Ethics rules thus should protect professional and public values, which are endangered when lawyers become merely "hired guns" or "mouthpieces" for clients.

Each of the competing stereotypes has some force in particular practice contexts, but both overlook the variety of law practice, individual variation and the powerful effects of the common culture shared by lawyers and clients. Assumptions that the morals of either lawyers or clients as a group are any worse (or any better) than the other are highly questionable. Both groups include a highly diverse segment of humanity, with a sampling of saints and scoundrels amid many ordinary, decent people who only occasionally succumb to temptation. A corruptive force—or a moral insight— may flow in either direction, although economic, legal and institutional incentives or controls may push behavior in one direction or another.

Clients also have strong temptations to manipulate their lawyers, for example, by presenting a favorable version of the facts.[16] In a deeper sense, it is impossible for the relationship to be wholly free of manipulation.[17] In any case, when the client has limited capacity, as in the case of a child, full participation of the client is impossible. See M.R. 1.14.

One Profession or Many?

Discussion of lawyers often proceeds on the assumption that the common characteristics of lawyers justify treating all lawyers the same—as

14. Stephen L. Pepper argues that three dichotomies influence how lawyers and legal scholars perceive lawyers' ethics: (1) whether legal ethics should be rule-based or virtue-based (general rule vs. discretion in application); (2) whether the goal is to serve individual autonomy or to advance community interests; and (3) whether the primary task of the ethical framework is to protect the client from the lawyer or to protect the lawyer from the client. An individual's position on these "fault lines" determines approaches to general issues and specific questions. Usually both sides of each dichotomy must be taken into account. The last factor, considered in the text at this point, generally turns on assumptions that are made about the lawyer-client relationship: are lawyers the pawns of informed, powerful clients or do they control and manipulate the client because

of their knowledge, control of information and monopoly over translation of general objectives into concrete legal steps. Pepper, Autonomy, Community, and Legal Ethics, 19 Capital Univ.L.Rev. 939 (1990).

15. Robert W. Gordon, David Luban and William H. Simon are examples of writers taking this position.

16. See Roy B. Fleming, Client Games: Defense Attorney Perspectives on Their Relations with Criminal Clients, 1986 Am.Bar Found.Res. J. 253.

17. See Stephen J. Ellmann, Lawyer and Client, 34 UCLA L.Rev. 717 (1987). Compare Marcy Strauss, Toward a Revised Model of Attorney–Client Relationship: The Argument for Autonomy, 65 N.C.L.Rev. 315 (1987).

members of a single profession governed by the same rules.[18] But is that the case?

The popular characterization of lawyers as "mouthpieces" for clients suggest a lawyer who is dependent upon or subservient to clients. Empirical studies of lawyer-client interaction conclude that large-firm corporate lawyers wield relatively little influence over their powerful and wealthy clients.[19] Lawyers in this sector of the profession tend to view themselves as technicians who do what their clients want. Corporate lawyers emphasize craft over counseling, allow their powerful business clients to set the agenda of corporate practice and "often seem to reject even the aspiration to serve as molders of corporate and public policy."[20]

On the other hand, studies of lawyers who deal with personal-plight practice (representation of individuals who face a legal problem and who have had little or no prior experience with lawyers or the legal system) emphasize the power and authority that lawyers exercise over clients.[21] One substantial study concluded that more participation by clients in this sector produces better results.[22]

Should legal ethics differentiate between sectors of practice?[23] David Wilkins argues that the institutions that regulate lawyers should differ

---

18. A major empirical study of the legal profession concludes that the profession is stratified, not by the type of services rendered, but by the socio-economic character of clients. The profession is divided into two hemispheres: those who serve corporate clients (and wealthy persons) and those who serve individuals. John P. Heinz & Edward O. Laumann, Chicago Lawyers: The Social Structure of the Bar (1983 and 2d ed.1998).

19. See, e.g., John P. Heinz, The Power of Lawyers, 17 Ga.L.Rev. 891, 904 (1983). Heinz writes:

> On the present state of our knowledge, ... I do not find much evidence that the lawyers who serve corporations enjoy a highly independent, autonomous role, a role that would permit the lawyers' own values (as distinct from those of their clients) to determine the positions taken, with the lawyers thus having important, independent effects on the allocation of scarce resources. In short, it appears to me that corporate lawyers usually do their clients' bidding, rather than the other way around.

See also Robert L. Nelson, Partners with Power: The Social Transformation of the Large Law Firm (1988) (reporting that corporate lawyers very rarely refuse a poten-

tial assignment because it was contrary to their personal values); and Robert A. Kagan & Robert E. Rosen, On the Social Significance of Large Firm Law Practice, 37 Stan.L.Rev. 399 (1985) (the predominant role performed by lawyers in corporate law firms is that of "nonjudgmental conduits").

20. Kagan & Rosen, supra, at 440.

21. See, e.g., William L.F. Felstiner & Austin Sarat, Divorce Lawyers and Their Clients (1995) (matrimonial lawyers); Hubert O'Gorman, Lawyers in Matrimonial Cases (1963) (same); Douglas E. Rosenthal, Lawyer and Client: Who's in Charge? (1974) (personal injury lawyers); Abraham S. Blumberg, The Practice of Law as a Confidence Game: Organizational Cooptation of a Profession, 1 L. & Soc'y Rev. 15 (1967) (criminal defense lawyers); Gary Neustader, When Lawyer and Client Meet, 35 Buffalo L.Rev. 177 (1986) (consumer bankruptcy lawyers).

22. See the discussion of Rosenthal's study supra at p. 450.

23. See, e.g., Ted Schneyer, Some Sympathy for the Hired Gun, 41 J. Legal Educ. 11, 22–27 (1991) (ethics rules should be more client protective in individual-client representation and more society-protective in corporate representation).

depending on the practice setting and the different dangers presented by those settings.[24] He suggests that courts and administrative agencies should exercise greater control over lawyers in corporate practice, to protect their professional independence and ensure compliance with legal norms, while professional discipline should play a stronger regulatory role in other settings, such as personal injury or criminal defense work.

Lawyer–Client Interaction

What actually occurs in the lawyer's office? Austin Sarat and William Felstiner observed, recorded and analyzed lawyer-client interaction in 40 divorce cases.[25] Among their findings were the following:

First, although the lawyers studied behaved adversarially in their negotiations with opposing parties, those same lawyers actively attempted to persuade their clients to reach negotiated settlements.

> [L]awyers work hard to sell settlement to their clients and to avoid contested hearings and trials. The negotiation between lawyer and client over how to understand the nature of the divorce dispute and the nature of the legal process is, in most cases, intertwined with the efforts of lawyers to sell settlement.[26]

Second, Sarat and Felstiner learned that "lawyer/client interaction in divorce occurs against a background of mutual suspicion, if not antagonism, between lawyers and clients."[27] Clients, frustrated by the slowness of the process and their lawyers' unresponsiveness to the moral or emotional aspects of their cases, "worry that their lawyers will be inattentive or disloyal." On the other hand, lawyers view their clients as emotional, demanding and having unreasonable expectations. "For divorce lawyers, the client is . . ., if not an enemy, an uncertain and unreliable partner and ally."[28]

Strains in the lawyer-client relationship in divorce cases, the study concluded, result from conflicting understandings about the nature of the dispute and the nature of the legal process. Clients view the underlying dispute from a retrospective and moral perspective. The failure of the marriage has left them feeling angry or hurt, victimized or guilty; and they attempt to enlist their lawyers in an effort to explain the marriage's failure and to assign blame. Their lawyers, viewing the question of who did what to whom and why as largely irrelevant in today's no-fault divorce regimes,

---

24. David B. Wilkins, Who Should Regulate Lawyers?, 105 Harv.L.Rev. 799 (1992).

25. See Austin Sarat & William L.F. Felstiner, Divorce Lawyers and Their Clients (1995). This important empirical study is discussed by David L. Chambers, 25 Divorce Attorneys and 40 Clients in Two Not So Big but Not So Small Cities in Massachusetts and California: An Appreciation, 22 Law & Soc. Inquiry 209 (1997). The

summary of their findings presented here is taken from Austin Sarat, Lawyers and Clients: Putting Professional Service on the Agenda of Legal Education, 41 J.Legal Educ. 43 (1991).

26. Sarat, supra, at 46.

27. Id. at 47.

28. Id.

tend to be emotionally unresponsive to their clients' concerns.[29] Yet the same lawyers engage in extensive counseling in efforts to fashion an appropriate "legal self" for the client. Divorce lawyers thus urge their clients not to trust their own feelings, not to be short-sighted and not to act on short-term emotions; the emphasis is on the financial, not emotional, aspects of the divorce.

> Thus, divorce lawyers can be seen as helping clients who will in the long run be more interested in the economics of settlement than in the vindication of immediate emotions.... [Lawyers] define their professional role so as to avoid assuming a sense of responsibility for the human consequences of being unresponsive to emotion. Clients, however, come to the divorce process expecting that their emotions will matter and that lawyers will care; they come away disappointed.[30]

Lawyers present law in action from the vantage point of legal realism, "trashing" the legal system and its actors and rules, while clients expect that the legal system will deal impartially with the facts, follow its own rules and arrive at fair and correct results. "[W]hat clients buy is knowledge of the ropes rather than knowledge of the rules; when they describe the legal system as idiosyncratic and personalistic, they endow themselves with the mystique of inside knowledge."[31]

Lawyer codes and discussions of "professionalism" tend to view the lawyer-client relationship in a romantic and idealized form: a relationship of trust and confidence between a responsible adult client and a competent lawyer who will vigorously and unselfishly advance the client's goals. Some empirical study and much anecdotal evidence, however, describe a reality pervaded instead by fear, suspicion and mistrust: a relationship characterized from time to time and in varying degrees by hostility, anger and suspicion as well as by respect, confidence and trust.[32] A more realistic view of the relationship, especially between unsophisticated individual clients and their lawyers, also suggests that lawyer understandings of what clients expect diverge from the expectations of the clients themselves. Lawyers think clients want a trickster; clients hope to have a helper. Because "lawyers misread clients as expecting bad behavior," they act out their own "cynical fallacy," serving their clients aggressively as Holmes's "bad man" would want to be served.[33]

---

29. "Client and lawyer are like performer and bored audience: although the lawyer will not interrupt the aria, she will not applaud too much either for fear of inviting an encore.... [W]hen lawyers refuse to engage with clients' efforts to give meaning to the past, clients often end up dissatisfied because they believe their lawyers do not understand or empathize with them." Id. at 48–49.

30. Id. at 50.

31. Id. at 52.

32. See Robert A. Burt, Conflict and Trust Between Attorney and Client, 69 Geo.L.J. 1015 (1981).

33. Marvin W. Mendes, Trickster, Hero, Helper, A.B.A. J. 14 (May–June 1983) (a summary of a larger empirical study, Marvin W. Mindes & Alan C. Acock, Trickster, Hero, Helper, Helper: A Report on the Lawyer Image, 1982 Am. B. Found. Res. J. 177).

A.   FORMING AND ENDING THE RELATIONSHIP

1.   FORMING THE RELATIONSHIP

Togstad v. Vesely, Otto, Miller & Keefe

Supreme Court of Minnesota, 1980.
291 N.W.2d 686.

■ PER CURIAM.

This is an appeal by the defendants from a judgment of the Hennepin County District Court involving an action for legal malpractice. The jury found that the defendant attorney Jerre Miller was negligent and that, as a direct result of such negligence, plaintiff John Togstad sustained damages in the amount of $610,500 and his wife, plaintiff Joan Togstad, in the amount of $39,000. Defendants (Miller and his law firm) appeal to this court.... We affirm.

In August 1971, John Togstad began to experience severe headaches and on August 16, 1971, was admitted to Methodist Hospital where tests disclosed that the headaches were caused by a large aneurism[1] on the left internal carotid artery.[2] The attending physician, Dr. Paul Blake, a neurological surgeon, treated the problem by applying a Selverstone clamp to the left common carotid artery. The clamp was surgically implanted on August 27, 1971, in Togstad's neck to allow the gradual closure of the artery over a period of days.

In the early morning hours of August 29, 1971, a nurse observed that Togstad was unable to speak or move. At the time, the clamp was one-half (50%) closed. Upon discovering Togstad's condition, the nurse called a resident physician, who did not adjust the clamp. Dr. Blake was also immediately informed of Togstad's condition and arrived about an hour later, at which time he opened the clamp. Togstad is now severely paralyzed in his right arm and leg, and is unable to speak.

Plaintiffs' expert, Dr. Ward Woods, testified that Togstad's paralysis and loss of speech was due to a lack of blood supply to his brain. Dr. Woods stated that the inadequate blood flow resulted from the clamp being 50% closed and that the negligence of Dr. Blake and the hospital precluded the clamp's being opened in time to avoid permanent brain damage....

About 14 months after her husband's hospitalization began, plaintiff Joan Togstad met with attorney Jerre Miller regarding her husband's condition. Neither she nor her husband was personally acquainted with

---

1. An aneurism is a weakness or softening in an artery wall which expands and bulges out over a period of years.

2. The left internal carotid artery is one of the major vessels which supplies blood to the brain.

Miller or his law firm prior to that time. John Togstad's former work supervisor, Ted Bucholz, made the appointment and accompanied Mrs. Togstad to Miller's office. Bucholz was present when Mrs. Togstad and Miller discussed the case.[3]

Mrs. Togstad had become suspicious of the circumstances surrounding her husband's tragic condition due to the conduct and statements of the hospital nurses shortly after the paralysis occurred. One nurse told Mrs. Togstad that she had checked Mr. Togstad at 2 a.m. and he was fine; that when she returned at 3 a.m., by mistake, to give him someone else's medication, he was unable to move or speak; and that if she hadn't accidentally entered the room no one would have discovered his condition until morning. Mrs. Togstad also noticed that the other nurses were upset and crying, and that Mr. Togstad's condition was a topic of conversation.

Mrs. Togstad testified that she told Miller "everything that happened at the hospital," including the nurses' statements and conduct which had raised a question in her mind. She stated that she "believed" she had told Miller "about the procedure and what was undertaken, what was done, and what happened." She brought no records with her. Miller took notes and asked questions during the meeting, which lasted 45 minutes to an hour. At its conclusion, according to Mrs. Togstad, Miller said that "he did not think we had a legal case, however, he was going to discuss this with his partner." She understood that if Miller changed his mind after talking to his partner, he would call her. Mrs. Togstad "gave it" a few days and, since she did not hear from Miller, decided "that they had come to the conclusion that there wasn't a case." No fee arrangements were discussed, no medical authorizations were requested, nor was Mrs. Togstad billed for the interview.

Mrs. Togstad denied that Miller had told her his firm did not have expertise in the medical malpractice field, urged her to see another attorney, or related to her that the statute of limitations for medical malpractice actions was two years. She did not consult another attorney until one year after she talked to Miller. Mrs. Togstad indicated that she did not confer with another attorney earlier because of her reliance on Miller's "legal advice" that they "did not have a case."

On cross-examination, Mrs. Togstad was asked whether she went to Miller's office "to see if he would take the case of [her] husband...." She replied, "Well, I guess it was to go for legal advice, what to do, where shall we go from here? That is what we went for." Again in response to defense counsel's questions, Mrs. Togstad testified as follows:

Q And it was clear to you, was it not, that what was taking place was a preliminary discussion between a prospective client and lawyer as to whether or not they wanted to enter into an attorney-client relationship?

---

3. Bucholz, who knew Miller through a local luncheon club, died prior to the trial of the instant action.

A I am not sure how to answer that. It was for legal advice as to what to do.

Q And Mr. Miller was discussing with you your problem and indicating whether he, as a lawyer, wished to take the case, isn't that true?

A Yes.

... Miller testified that "[t]he only thing I told her [Mrs. Togstad] after we had pretty much finished the conversation was that there was nothing related in her factual circumstances that told me that she had a case that our firm would be interested in undertaking."

Miller also claimed he related to Mrs. Togstad "that because of the grievous nature of the injuries sustained by her husband, that this was only my opinion and she was encouraged to ask another attorney if she wished for another opinion" and "she ought to do so promptly." He testified that he informed Mrs. Togstad that his firm "was not engaged as experts" in the area of medical malpractice, and that they associated with the Charles Hvass firm in cases of that nature. Miller stated that at the end of the conference he told Mrs. Togstad that he would consult with Charles Hvass and if Hvass's opinion differed from his, Miller would so inform her. Miller recollected that he called Hvass a "couple days" later and discussed the case with him. It was Miller's impression that Hvass thought there was no liability for malpractice in the case. Consequently, Miller did not communicate with Mrs. Togstad further.

. . .

Kenneth Green, a Minneapolis attorney, was called as an expert by plaintiffs. He stated that in rendering legal advice regarding a claim of medical malpractice, the "minimum" an attorney should do would be to request medical authorizations from the client, review the hospital records, and consult with an expert in the field. John McNulty, a Minneapolis attorney, and Charles Hvass testified as experts on behalf of the defendants. McNulty stated that when an attorney is consulted as to whether he will take a case, the lawyer's only responsibility in refusing it is to so inform the party. He testified, however, that when a lawyer is asked his legal opinion on the merits of a medical malpractice claim, community standards require that the attorney check hospital records and consult with an expert before rendering his opinion.

Hvass stated that he had no recollection of Miller's calling him in October 1972 relative to the Togstad matter. He testified that:

A ... when a person comes in to me about a medical malpractice action, based upon what the individual has told me, I have to make a decision as to whether or not there probably is or probably is not, based upon that information, medical malpractice. And if, in my judgment, based upon what the client has told me, there is not medical malpractice, I will so inform the client.

Hvass stated, however, that he would never render a "categorical" opinion. In addition, Hvass acknowledged that if he were consulted for a "legal opinion" regarding medical malpractice and 14 months had expired since the incident in question, "ordinary care and diligence" would require him to inform the party of the two-year statute of limitations applicable to that type of action.

This case was submitted to the jury by way of a special verdict form. The jury found that Dr. Blake and the hospital were negligent and that Dr. Blake's negligence (but not the hospital's) was a direct cause of the injuries sustained by John Togstad; that there was an attorney-client contractual relationship between Mrs. Togstad and Miller; that Miller was negligent in rendering advice regarding the possible claims of Mr. and Mrs. Togstad; that, but for Miller's negligence, plaintiffs would have been successful in the prosecution of a legal action against Dr. Blake; and that neither Mr. nor Mrs. Togstad was negligent in pursuing their claims against Dr. Blake. . . .

1. In a legal malpractice action of the type involved here, four elements must be shown: (1) that an attorney-client relationship existed; (2) that defendant acted negligently or in breach of contract; (3) that such acts were the proximate cause of the plaintiffs' damages; (4) that but for defendant's conduct the plaintiffs would have been successful in the prosecution of their medical malpractice claim. See, Christy v. Saliterman, 179 N.W.2d 288 (Minn.1970).

. . .

We believe it is unnecessary to decide whether a tort or contract theory is preferable for resolving the attorney-client relationship question raised by this appeal. The tort and contract analyses are very similar in a case such as the instant one,[4] and we conclude that under either theory the evidence shows that a lawyer-client relationship is present here. The thrust of Mrs. Togstad's testimony is that she went to Miller for legal advice, was told there wasn't a case, and relied upon this advice in failing to pursue the claim for medical malpractice. In addition, according to Mrs. Togstad, Miller did not qualify his legal opinion by urging her to seek advice from another attorney, nor did Miller inform her that he lacked expertise in the medical malpractice area. Assuming this testimony is true, as this court must do [in assessing whether the verdict is supported by the evidence], we

4. Under a negligence approach it must essentially be shown that defendant rendered legal advice (not necessarily at someone's request) under circumstances which made it reasonably foreseeable to the attorney that if such advice was rendered negligently, the individual receiving the advice might be injured thereby. See, e.g., Palsgraf v. Long Island R. Co., 162 N.E. 99 (N.Y.1928). Or, stated another way, under a tort theory, "[a]n attorney-client relationship is created whenever an individual seeks and receives legal advice from an attorney in circumstances in which a reasonable person would rely on such advice." 63 Minn.L.Rev. 751, 759 (1979). A contract analysis requires the rendering of legal advice pursuant to another's request and the reliance factor, in this case, where the advice was not paid for, need be shown in the form of promissory estoppel. See, 7 C.J.S., Attorney and Client, § 65; Restatement (Second) of Contracts, § 90.

believe a jury could properly find that Mrs. Togstad sought and received legal advice from Miller under circumstances which made it reasonably foreseeable to Miller that Mrs. Togstad would be injured if the advice were negligently given. Thus, under either a tort or contract analysis, there is sufficient evidence in the record to support the existence of an attorney-client relationship.

Defendants argue that even if an attorney-client relationship was established the evidence fails to show that Miller acted negligently in assessing the merits of the Togstads' case. They appear to contend that, at most, Miller was guilty of an error in judgment which does not give rise to legal malpractice. ...However, this case does not involve a mere error of judgment. The gist of plaintiffs' claim is that Miller failed to perform the minimal research that an ordinarily prudent attorney would do before rendering legal advice in a case of this nature. The record, through the testimony of Kenneth Green and John McNulty, contains sufficient evidence to support plaintiffs' position.

In a related contention, defendants assert that a new trial should be awarded on the ground that the trial court erred by refusing to instruct the jury that Miller's failure to inform Mrs. Togstad of the two-year statute of limitations for medical malpractice could not constitute negligence. The argument continues that since it is unclear from the record on what theory or theories of negligence the jury based its decision, a new trial must be granted. ...

The defect in defendants' reasoning is that there is adequate evidence supporting the claim that Miller was also negligent in failing to advise Mrs. Togstad of the two-year medical malpractice limitations period and thus the trial court acted properly in refusing to instruct the jury in the manner urged by defendants. One of defendants' expert witnesses, Charles Hvass, testified:

Q Now, Mr. Hvass, where you are consulted for a legal opinion and advice concerning malpractice and 14 months have elapsed [since the incident in question], wouldn't—and you hold yourself out as competent to give a legal opinion and advice to these people concerning their rights, wouldn't ordinary care and diligence require that you inform them that there is a two-year statute of limitations within which they have to act or lose their rights?

A Yes. I believe I would have advised someone of the two-year period of limitation, yes.

Consequently, based on the testimony of Mrs. Togstad, i.e., that she requested and received legal advice from Miller concerning the malpractice claim, and the above testimony of Hvass, we must reject the defendants' contention, as it was reasonable for a jury to determine that Miller acted negligently in failing to inform Mrs. Togstad of the applicable limitations period.

Obligations to a Prospective Client

Togstad demonstrates that a lawyer's interaction with a potential client may invoke some of the lawyer's duties to clients, such as confidentiality or due care, without becoming a full-fledged representation.[34]

What legal advice did lawyer Miller give the Togstads? How did that advice depart from the ordinary care standard? What should Miller have done instead? Should Miller have been disciplined professionally for his negligence?

A lawyer often works intermittently over a period of time on various matters for a client. Does such intermittent work establish a *continuing* attorney-client relationship? In North Carolina Bar v. Sheffield,[35] a lawyer who had worked intermittently for a person failed to file an answer to a complaint that that person left at his office. The court disciplined the lawyer for neglecting duties owed to a "client."

Limiting Liability by Limiting Scope of Employment

Model Rule 1.2(c) allows a lawyer to limit the objectives of representation with client consent. Comment [4] states: "The terms upon which the representation is undertaken may exclude specific objectives or means. Such limitations may exclude objectives or means that the lawyer regards as repugnant or improper." But Comment [5] continues, an agreement to limit the scope of employment

> must accord with the Rules of Professional Conduct and other law. Thus the client may not be asked to agree to representation so limited in scope as to violate Rule 1.1, requiring competent representation, or to surrender the right to terminate the lawyer's services or the right to settle litigation that the lawyer might wish to continue.

The Rule and Comment thus preclude an agreement limiting the scope of representation to a lawyer's off-the-cuff opinion based on no research or investigation, such as the advice provided by attorney Miller in *Togstad*. But could an agreement properly specify that a lawyer will provide only limited research in return for a reduced fee?[36] Would such an agreement comport with M.R. 1.1? May a lawyer require a client to sign a contract stating that in exchange for a free initial consultation the client waives the right to sue for any malpractice arising out of the initial interview?[37]

---

34. For further discussion of factors that trigger an obligation to people or entities with whom a lawyer has not established a full, formal client relationship, see Westinghouse Elec. Corp. v. Kerr–McGee Corp., 580 F.2d 1311 (7th Cir.1978), printed infra in Chapter 7 at p. 581.

35. North Carolina State Bar v. Sheffield, 326 S.E.2d 320 (N.C.Ct.App.1985). See also Jacobson v. Pitman–Moore, 624 F.Supp.

937 (D.Minn.1985), aff'd, 786 F.2d 1172 (8th Cir.1986) (mix-up in transfer of case from one firm to another).

36. See Wolfram, Modern Legal Ethics § 5.6.7 (arguing that such an agreement is proper under M.R. 1.2.)

37. See M.R. 1.8(h) and DR 6–102(A), and the note on limiting one's liability for malpractice in Chapter 3 supra at p. 172.

Choice of Client

Unlike the English barrister, the legal profession in the United States does not operate under the "taxicab rank" rule. A lawyer is not a public utility required to take on all comers. This principle is not spelled out directly in ethics codes, which approach the subject first by stating when a lawyer has an ethical obligation to undertake representation (i.e., when a tribunal appoints the lawyer to represent a person) and then by carving out exceptions to that obligation. See Model Rule 6.2. Comment [1] to Rule 6.2 provides that "A lawyer ordinarily is not obliged to accept a client whose character or cause the lawyer regards as repugnant" and goes on to state that "the lawyer's freedom to select clients is ... qualified," mentioning a moral responsibility to provide pro bono publico service and to represent unpopular clients and persons unable to afford legal services. Is a lawyer subject to justifiable moral criticism for the lawyer's choice of client?

2. TERMINATING THE RELATIONSHIP

Mandatory Withdrawal

Model Rule 1.16 deals with mandatory and permissive withdrawal.[38] Withdrawal is required when the client discharges the lawyer and when the lawyer is too ill to continue the representation.[39] Finally and perhaps most important, withdrawal is required when the continuing representation will result in a violation of ethics rules or other law.[40]

How sure must the lawyer be that the representation will result in a violation of other law or the rules before withdrawal is mandatory? Does M.R. 1.16(b)(2) help answer the question? The provisions on withdrawal are part of the package of ethical rules dealing with client crime or fraud. They should be read in conjunction with other provisions of the codes: (1) the prohibition against lawyer participation in criminal or fraudulent conduct;[41] (2) provisions requiring or permitting disclosure of client fraud;[42] and (3) provisions requiring disclosure of fraud on the court.[43]

38. DR 2–110 is the comparable Model Code provision. Read literally, DR 2–110(B) seems not to require withdrawal except in a case before a tribunal. The better and common reading is that withdrawal is required under the Code in any of the situations listed in DR 2–110(B) whether or not the lawyer is before a tribunal.

39. M.R. 1.16(a)(2) and DR 2–110(B)(3). See also M.R. 1.1 and 1.3 and DR 6–101(A)(3) (dealing with lawyer competence and diligence).

40. M.R. 1.16(a)(1) and DR 2–110(B)(2). Note that while DR 2–110(B)(2) does not mention "other law," it is a violation of the Code to violate other law in the course of the representation, DR 7–102(B)(7), and

thus withdrawal is required under DR 2–110(B)(2).

41. M.R. 1.2(d) and DR 7–102(A)(7); see the discussion of prohibited assistance at p. 62 supra.

42. See M.R. 1.6(b) and its Comments [15]–[17] on giving notice of withdrawal and requiring withdrawal if the client continues criminal or fraudulent conduct; see the discussion of client fraud at p. 282 supra. See also DR 4–101(C)(3); DR 7–102(B)(1);

43. M.R. 3.3 and DR 7–102(B)(1) (on disclosing fraud on the court); see the discussion of client perjury at p. 337 supra. See also M.R. 2.3 (evaluations conducted for third parties); and M.R. 4.1 (honesty in dealing with nonclients).

Model Rule 1.16 requires a lawyer to decline employment in all the situations that would require withdrawal. The Model Code deals with the decision to accept employment in a separate provision, DR 2–109.

Permissive Withdrawal

Model Rule 1.16(b) and DR 2–110(C) state the circumstances under which a lawyer *may* withdraw from representation, in effect, "fire" the client. Lawyers do not have the same freedom as clients to withdraw from the relationship. If the matter is before a tribunal, withdrawal must be with the court's permission. In Kriegsman v. Kriegsman,[44] for example, a law firm agreed to represent a client in a divorce action, eventually receiving $2,000 from her in fees. The lawyer's fee and expenses, however, had exceeded $7,500 because the opposing spouse refused to comply with some court orders. The client, who was on welfare and unable to pay more than $2,000, successfully opposed her lawyers' motions to withdraw. Accepting a retainer, the court said, constitutes a lawyer's implied agreement "to prosecute the matter to a conclusion" unless reasonable cause for withdrawal exists or the client consents. A lawyer's "obligations do not evaporate because the case becomes more complicated or the work more arduous or the retainer not as profitable as first contemplated or imagined."[45]

Under M.R. 1.16(b), a lawyer may withdraw (or decline to undertake representation) for any reason or no reason as long as withdrawal can be accomplished without "material adverse effect" on the client. A lawyer may withdraw even if there is harm to the client if the withdrawal is for any of the six reasons listed in 1.16(b). M.R. 1.16(b) is clearer than DR 2–110(C) in differentiating between withdrawal for cause and withdrawal without cause. DR 2–110(C), on permissive withdrawal before a tribunal, also list six reasons, but they differ from those in the Rules. Compare DR 2–110(C) and M.R. 1.16(b).

In some sense, all of the items in the Code's list address client misconduct. On the other hand, M.R. 1.16(b)(5) and (6) do not necessarily involve client conduct at all. Do they give the lawyer too much latitude to abandon a client? Is M.R. 1.16(b)(6) so broad that it swallows the rest of 1.16(b)? Or is it balanced by M.R. 1.16(c), which gives the trial judge broad discretion to order a lawyer to "continue . . . notwithstanding good cause for" withdrawal?

Restatement § 44 describes the grounds that justify withdrawal in broad terms, but qualifies these grounds with a proportionality rule.[46]

44. 375 A.2d 1253 (N.J.Super.Ct.App.Div. 1977).

45. 375 A.2d at 1255–56.

46. Restatement § 44(3), subsections f–i, permit withdrawal even though it has "a material adverse effect on the interests of the client" if "the client insists on taking action that the lawyer considers repugnant or imprudent;" the client, after being warned, "fails to fulfill a financial or other substantial obligation to the lawyer;" or "the representation has been rendered unreasonably difficult by the client or by the irreparable breakdown of the client-lawyer relationship." However, a lawyer may

Smith v. R. J. Reynolds Tobacco Co.[47] illustrates the proportionality idea. *Smith* involved two law firms that were financially and emotionally exhausted by years of pioneering but unprofitable contingent fee litigation on behalf of smoking victims. On appeal, the trial court's order granting the withdrawal motion was remanded for reconsideration. To succeed, the appellate court held, the firms must show "through expert proofs that, more probably than not, foreseeable damages discounted by the likelihood of recovering them will be substantially less than the value of the additional attorney time and expenses that will have to be devoted from the time of the withdrawal application through trial."[48] The trial court must consider the adverse effect on the clients as well as the financial burden faced by the firms.

In Picker Int'l v. Varian Associates,[49] the court held that a lawyer could not withdraw from representation, even if the client would not be harmed, if the purpose was to take on representation in a matter hostile to the client but not related to the prior matter. Does this rule—prohibiting a lawyer from "dropping a client like a hot potato"—extend the duty of loyalty or merely state a corollary? Compare M.R. 1.7 and 1.9. See Chapter 7 generally.

Protecting a Client Upon Withdrawal

Whether a lawyer is required or permitted to withdraw, it must be accomplished in accordance with Model Rule 1.16(d).[50] In addition to M.R. 1.16, other rules regulate a lawyer's actions after withdrawal. In situations involving a client fraud on a tribunal or third person, disclosure obligations may accompany or continue after withdrawal.[51] Rule 1.9 prohibits future representations that are materially adverse to a former client on a substantially related matter, unless the former client consents, and requires a lawyer to keep in confidence the former client's secrets.

Client Access to Lawyer's File

The law governing client access to a lawyer's file varies from jurisdiction to jurisdiction. The question arises primarily when a client, dissatisfied with a lawyer, is contemplating or pursuing a malpractice action against the lawyer; when a client switches lawyers; or when a firm lawyer moves to another firm and her clients ask that the files be transferred to the new firm. Model Rules 1.15(b), on safekeeping property, and 1.16(d), on declining or terminating representation, provide little guidance; they merely provide that the lawyer should give the client what the client is "entitled"

---

withdraw for these reasons only "when the lawyer reasonably believes that the effect on the lawyer of the ground for withdrawal is significantly greater than the reasonably unavoidable effect on the client that withdrawal would cause."

47. 630 A.2d 820 (N.J. Super.Ct.App.Div. 1993).

48. Id. at 831–32.

49. 869 F.2d 578 (Fed.Cir.1989).

50. M.R. 1.16(d) is substantially identical to DR 2–110(A)(2) and (3).

51. See M.R. 1.16(a)(1); M.R. 3.3(a)(4) and Comments [15]—[17] to M.R. 1.6, dealing with notice and disclosure.

to receive under other law. In the malpractice situation, the issue is normally resolved by discovery requests that result in the client obtaining information that may be relevant to the malpractice suit.

Clients who switch lawyers often encounter difficulties in obtaining relevant documents and work product from the discharged lawyer. Most jurisdictions give a lawyer a common law or statutory retaining lien in client property when the lawyer's claimed fee has not been paid. Yet client concern about the lawyer's fee may have led in whole or in part to the discharge. In some jurisdictions but not others, the ethics rules prohibit a lawyer from refusing to provide documents and work product to the former client when the client is unable to pay or would suffer harm in the pending matter if the file was not provided.[52]

In Sage Realty Corp. v. Proskauer, Rose, Goetz & Mendelson,[53] a real estate developer parted company with the Proskauer firm, which had represented it in a complex $175 million real estate restructuring transaction. When the firm asked Proskauer for its file, Proskauer said it would turn over formal legal opinions, court filings and closing documents, but not its internal work product—175,000 or so pages of legal memoranda, drafts of instruments, and notes and appraisals. The developer, which had paid over $2 million in fees, sued to obtain copies of the complete file. The New York Court of Appeals reversed lower court decisions holding that a client was entitled only to closing documents and the client's own papers. The court followed decisions in a number of states that give a client broad rights to the contents of a file when representation ceases on a matter still pending. The opposing position that the client is not entitled to work product it has paid for, the court said, places an unfair and unrealistic burden on the client to demonstrate a need for specific work product documents. Moreover, a lawyer's fiduciary relationship with a client continues after the representation has ended, entailing duties of openness and conscientious disclosure. The client, the court held, is presumptively entitled to the complete file, save for limited exceptions such as documents intended only for internal law firm use.[54]

---

52. District of Columbia Rule 1.8(i), after providing that "a lawyer may acquire and enforce a lien granted by law to secure the lawyer's fees or expenses," states that the lien applies only to "the lawyer's own work product, and then only to the extent that the work product has not been paid for." But "[t]his work product exception shall not apply when the client has become unable to pay, or when withholding the lawyer's work product would present a significant risk to the client of irreparable harm."

53. 689 N.E.2d 879 (N.Y.1997). See also Dean Starkman, Clients' Right to Lawyers' Files Is Disputed, Wall St. J., Feb. 17, 1998, at B18.

54. The *Sage Realty* case relied on Restatement § 58(2), which provides: "On request, a lawyer must allow a client or former client to inspect and copy any document possessed by the lawyer relating to the representation, unless substantial grounds exist to refuse." Comment *c* to Restatement § 58 spells out some of the "substantial grounds" of refusal: when the lawyer reasonably believes that the client would be harmed by disclosure (e.g., a psychiatric report concerning a mentally ill client) and when documents were intended only for internal law firm review (e.g., memoranda discussing staffing issues, possible conflicts of interest, or whether withdrawal was required because of the client's misconduct).

3. DISCHARGE AND ITS CONSEQUENCES

The starting point is the well-established rule that a client may discharge a lawyer at any time with or without good cause. However, approval of the tribunal is required if the matter is a litigated proceeding and approval is likely to be denied when a client attempts to change lawyers on the eve of or during trial.[55] Further, courts are reluctant to allow indigent defendants to switch appointed counsel because judges suspect that this is merely a tactic to delay the proceedings. When the request is made after the trial has begun, the defendant "must show good cause, such as an actual conflict of interest, a complete breakdown in communication or an irreconcilable conflict with his attorney."[56] In some other situations, such as when a public agency or subsidy provides counsel to a poor person, practical and institutional limitations narrow or extinguish the client's freedom of choice, since the only alternative may be pro se representation.

The client's ability to discharge a lawyer at will does not mean that discharge does not have legal and financial consequences. For example, while an in-house lawyer may be summarily removed from representing her employer on legal matters, the lawyer's employment contract may protect against discharge without cause and provide for termination payments or other protections. Moreover, if the discharge is precipitated by conduct protected by a whistle-blower statute or the jurisdiction recognizes the discharge as a retaliatory one against public policy, the employer may be liable for damages to the fired lawyer. This problem is considered further at p. 948 below (considering some special problems of in-house lawyers).

Vincent Johnson has summarized some of the current rules relating to client discharge of a lawyer and its legal consequences: (1) a client's contractual waiver of the right to discharge a lawyer is generally unenforceable as against public policy;[57] (2) a reasonable contractual provision addressing liability for fees of terminated counsel may be enforceable if the client is an experienced user of legal services and the liquidated damages provision is reasonable in amount; and (3) in most jurisdictions, a discharged lawyer may recover only the quantum meruit value of the services performed.[58] The latter situation, most often arising when a plaintiffs'

---

55. See M.R. 1.16(c). In Ogala Sioux Tribe v. United States, 862 F.2d 275 (Fed.Cir. 1988), the tribe sought to fire lawyers who had handled a complex case for thirty years. The court had awarded the tribe over $40 million dollars for land ceded under an 1868 treaty and the sole remaining issue was the amount of government offsets. The court upheld the trial court's refusal to terminate the authority of the lawyers to stipulate to this amount, emphasizing that the tribe had not found substitute counsel who could handle the case without significant delay.

56. Wilson v. Mintzes, 761 F.2d 275, 280 (6th Cir.1985).

57. See, e.g., Demov, Morris, Levin & Shein v. Glantz, 428 N.E.2d 387, 389 (N.Y.1981) (law firm could not enforce a client promise to employ it in a condemnation proceeding).

58. Vincent R. Johnson, Client Liability for Fees of Discharged Counsel, Trial (Apr. 1990), at 99–103 (also discussing some other issues).

lawyer retained on a contingent fee is discharged, has gone through great change in the last 30 years. The old rule, still adhered to in a few states, treated a client's decision to change counsel, if the lawyer's discharge was without cause, as a breach of the contingent fee contract; therefore, the discharged lawyer could recover the agreed upon fee if the client subsequently received an award. If the discharged lawyer had had a one-third contingent fee agreement and the client, represented by another lawyer, received an award of $300,000, the discharged lawyer would be entitled to $100,000. On the other hand, if the lawyer had been discharged for cause, the lawyer could recover nothing.[59]

The Modern Rule on Discharge of a Contingent Fee Lawyer

The modern rule seeks to balance the client's right to discharge counsel—clearly discouraged by the monetary consequences of the old rule—with the lawyer's right to receive fair compensation for work done. The quantum meruit approach is thought to achieve that result. In Fox & Associates Co. v. Purdon,[60] for example, an associate informed a firm client that he was leaving the firm; the client, preferring the associate's services, then discharged the firm. When the case was settled, the discharged firm brought suit against its former client to recover its one-third contingency fee. The court, overruling precedents that stretched back many years, held "that where an attorney is discharged by a client with or without just cause, and whether the contract between the attorney and client is express or implied, the attorney is entitled to recover the reasonable value of services rendered prior to the discharge on the basis of quantum meruit."

> The right to discharge one's attorney would be of little value if the client were liable for the full contract price. To force such an agreement into the conventional status of commercial contracts ignores the unique, fiduciary relationship created by an attorney's representation of a client. . . . Under the rule of quantum meruit, the client is protected since the discharge of an attorney is not always caused by a client's dissatisfaction with the quality of service rendered but, rather, may result from the client's lack of faith and trust or confidence in the attorney. . . .
>
> Neither does the quantum meruit rule create a threat that the discharged attorney will not be compensated for services rendered before discharge occurs. . . . An attorney who substantially performs under the contract may be entitled to the full price of the contract in the event of a discharge "on the courthouse steps," or just prior to settlement. Similarly, it would be inequitable to force a client who has received no service from the discharged attorney to pay the full price of the contract.[61]

---

59. See Teichner v. W & J Holsteins, Inc., 478 N.E.2d 177, 178 (N.Y.App.Div.1985) (lawyer not entitled to a quantum meruit fee recovery if discharged for cause).

60. 541 N.E.2d 448 (Ohio 1989).

61. 541 N.E.2d at 450.

Does the modern rule make it too easy for a client to change counsel without cause? What happens if the quantum meruit amount is more than the contract amount? What happens if the contingency never occurs because a trial on the merits results in a defendant's verdict or the plaintiff decides to abandon the claim?[62]

The modern rule is now the majority rule. All recent cases have agreed that recovery in quantum meruit should replace recovery on the contract.[63] When the lawyer has committed a clear and serious violation of a duty owed to the client, the lawyer forfeits any right to compensation whether discharged by the client or not.[64] For consideration of special retainer fees purporting to make a portion of the retainer "non-refundable," see p. 501 below.

B. Scope of Lawyer's Authority

INTRODUCTORY NOTE

Who decides what in the lawyer-client relationship? This inquiry has an empirical dimension (how do lawyers and clients actually behave in various sectors of practice?), a normative dimension (how should authority be allocated between lawyer and client?), and a legal dimension (how do controlling principles of agency law, contract law and legal ethics allocate responsibility?).

The issue of decision-making authority is related to two matters already considered: (1) the scope of representation, discussed above, and (2) the duty of communication, see M.R. 1.4. The base line on scope of representation is the contractual agreement between a lawyer and her client: What have client and lawyer agreed that the lawyer should do? The contracting parties, however, do not have total freedom to shape the relationship. The client, for example, may not agree to a quality of service below the minimum standard required by the lawyer's duty to "provide competent representation."[1] Some conflicts of interest are so extreme that they cannot be cured by client consent.[2] Nor is the client bound by a lawyer-client agreement that has the effect of "prospectively limiting the lawyer's liability to a client for malpractice." See M.R. 1.8(h). The lawyer

---

62. Two leading cases, Fracasse v. Brent, 494 P.2d 9 (Cal.1972), and Rosenberg v. Levin, 409 So.2d 1016 (Fla.1982), hold that a discharged contingency-fee lawyer recovers nothing until and unless the contingency happens. There is some authority to the contrary.

63. See, e.g., Fox & Associates Co. v. Purdon, 541 N.E.2d 448 (Ohio 1989) (adopting quantum meruit rule when client discharges lawyer retained on a contingent fee).

64. Restatement § 49.

1. See M.R. 1.1 and Comment [5] to M.R. 1.2.

2. Comment [3] to M.R. 1.7 states that "loyalty to a client prohibits undertaking representation directly adverse to that client without that client's consent" and that "a lawyer ordinarily may not act as advocate against a person the lawyer represents in some other matter, even if [the other matter] is wholly unrelated."

cannot provide, nor the client seek, legal assistance "that the lawyer knows is criminal or fraudulent."[3] Moreover, the law, by delegating certain authority to lawyer or client—the issue discussed in this section—provides a structure for the relationship that removes certain matters from lawyer-client negotiation. The client's right to discharge a retained lawyer and the lawyer's opportunity to withdraw, when available, provide practical constraints on lawyer-client negotiations. Within these and other limitations on contractual choice, however, "[a] lawyer may limit the objectives of the representation if the client consents after consultation." M.R. 1.2(c).

Decision-making within the lawyer-client relationship depends upon two-way communication. A lawyer has a duty to provide a client with "sufficient information to participate intelligently in decisions concerning the objectives of the representation and the means by which they are to be pursued."[4] The duty of communication may not extend as far as the "informed consent" notion that tort law imposes on physicians, but the duty is now embodied in a weaker form in the text of M.R. 1.4.[5]

Model Rule 1.2(a), addressing allocation of decision-making authority between lawyer and client, states:

> A lawyer shall abide by a client's decision concerning the objectives of representation, subject to paragraphs (c), (d) and (e), and shall consult with the client as to the means by which they are to be pursued. A lawyer shall abide by the client's decision whether to accept an offer of settlement of a matter. In a criminal case, the lawyer shall abide by the client's decision, after consultation with the lawyer, as to a plea to be entered, whether to waive jury trial and whether the client will testify.

The Model Code has no counterpart to M.R. 1.2.[6] The Comment to M.R. 1.2 should be read at this point.

1.   ALLOCATION OF DECISION–MAKING AUTHORITY IN CIVIL CASES

Decisions must be made at every point in the handling of a civil claim. Should a lawsuit be brought? What claims and legal theories should be asserted against whom? Should pretrial procedures be extensively used to gather information? Should settlement negotiations be undertaken and, if so, on what terms? What evidence should be presented at the trial and in

---

3. M.R. 1.2(d) prohibits the lawyer from counseling or otherwise assisting a client to commit a fraud or crime; M.R. 1.2(e) states that if a client expects assistance prohibited by the rules of professional conduct, the lawyer should explain the limits imposed by the rules.

4. Comment [1] to M.R. 1.4.

5. The only direct counterpart in the Model Code is EC 9–2, stating that "a lawyer should fully and promptly inform his client of material developments in the matters being handled for the client."

6. But see EC 7–7 (on the client's right to make decisions "affecting the merits of the cause or substantially prejudicing the rights of the client"); EC 7–8 (on the client's right to decide whether to forego legally available means or objectives because of nonlegal factors); and DR 7–101 (lawyer shall not fail to seek the lawful objectives of the client except that she may avoid offensive tactics without violating this rule).

what order and manner? Should the client testify? Should an opposing witness be cross-examined and, if so, with what purpose? What issues should be stressed in closing argument? The questions vary from small matters of technical detail (e.g., should an objection be made to a leading question by opposing counsel on a fairly insignificant matter?) to large issues of overall strategy (what remedies are sought on the basis of what legal theories and evidence?). Who is legally empowered to decide these and other questions?

One important variable is the context in which the issue arises. Suppose an advocate, without consulting her client, takes one of the actions mentioned above. By the time the client learns of it and objects, the tribunal and the opposing party may have reacted to the action. Clients in civil cases generally are bound by the mistakes of their lawyers as well as their intended acts.

In holding that clients are bound by their lawyers' actions in a civil proceeding, courts are giving priority to concerns of judicial administration and to the interests of opposing parties. A mythic unity of lawyer and client is presumed, with the lawyer as the alter ego of the client. As Justice Harlan put it, "each party is deemed bound by the acts of his lawyer-agent and is considered to have 'notice of all facts, notice of which can be charged upon the attorney.' "[7]The presumption that the lawyer has communicated relevant information concerning the representation to the client is almost irrebuttable.[8]

Is it essential that the lawyer have the right to decide which witnesses to call? What stipulations to enter into? What objections to make? Doctors know more than their patients, but we accept the principle that if there are alternate treatments available, the patient should decide after consultation (assuming the patient is conscious, sane and of legal age). Is a trial lawyer analogous to the surgeon in an operating room? Should it be assumed that the lawyer has not considered specific points of trial strategy until after the trial has actually begun? Is it possible to explain trial strategy choices to the client clearly enough so that she can make the decision?

Comment [1] to M.R. 1.2 states:

A clear distinction between objectives and means sometimes cannot be drawn, and in many cases the client-lawyer relationship partakes of a joint undertaking. In questions of means, the lawyer should assume responsibility for technical and legal tactical issues, but should defer to the client regarding such questions as the expense to be incurred and concern for third persons who might be adversely affected.

---

7. Link v. Wabash R.R. Co., 370 U.S. 626, 634 (1962) (upholding involuntary dismissal of an injured railroad worker's FELA claim for failure of his lawyer to attend a pretrial conference).

8. Courts use metaphors such as "in the course of a trial there [must] be one captain per ship." See Blanton v. Womancare, Inc., 696 P.2d 645, 650 (Cal.1985) (lawyer's authority to make tactical decisions in litigation is implied in law because essential to performance of role).

Is this helpful?[9]

If clients had the right to decide on tactics, would increased ethical violations by lawyers be the result? In medicine this does not seem to have happened. It is understood that a patient's right to decide on treatment is bounded by the law, e.g., a doctor cannot prescribe an illegal drug. Would a similar understanding work for lawyers and clients?

The analogy to medicine fails to capture that the lawyer, unlike the doctor, practices her craft through language and posture, i.e., means that appear intelligible to the client. The language of court (or of contract) resembles the language of the outside world. It is easy to imagine a client, armed with decision-making authority, who insists on speaking out for herself in court (or in negotiation). It is more difficult to imagine a patient wanting to perform surgery on herself. Is it possible to explain how court-talk is different and thus convince the client that she is better off not interfering? Must legal institutions—through case law, court procedures and ethics rules—reinforce the client's subordinate role for her own good?

Commentators have criticized the principle that lawyers should have broad authority, arguing that this gives the client too small a role in deciding her fate. If one purpose of trial is to affirm the individual's dignity and autonomy, that goal is ill-served by giving lawyers control over the process.[10] One major stream of academic commentary maintains that the lawyer's principal goal is to further the client's dignity and autonomy.[11] Another group of commentators, sometimes associated with critical legal studies, urges "moral activism" on the lawyer.[12]

9. On the attorney-client privilege, the general rule is that a lawyer may not waive the privilege without the client's consent, but consent may be express or implied. See Comment [7] to M.R. 1.6:

> A lawyer is impliedly authorized to make disclosures about a client when appropriate in carrying out the representation, except to the extent that the client's instructions or special circumstances limit that authority. In litigation, for example a lawyer may disclose information by admitting a fact that cannot properly be disputed, or in negotiation by making a disclosure that facilitates a satisfactory conclusion.

10. See, e.g., Susan R. Martyn, Informed Consent in the Practice of Law, 48 Geo. Wash.L.Rev. 307 (1980); Mark Spiegel, The New Model Rules of Professional Conduct: Lawyer–Client Decisionmaking and the Role of Rules in Structuring the Lawyer–Client Dialogue, 1980 Am.B.Found.Res.J. 1003.

11. See, e.g., Monroe H. Freedman, Understanding Legal Ethics 43–64 (1990) (assist-

ing a client to maximize her autonomy, once a lawyer has undertaken a representation, is required professionally and morally); Judith L. Maute, Allocation of Decisionmaking Authority Under the Model Rules of Professional Conduct, 17 U.C.Davis L.Rev. 1049, 1050 (1984); and Stephen L. Pepper, The Lawyer's Amoral Ethical Role: A Defense, A Problem, and Some Possibilities, 1986 Am.Bar Found. Research J. 613 (defending the traditional conception that a lawyer may do immoral, but lawful, acts in furtherance of a client's interests).

12. See, e.g., David Luban, Lawyers and Justice: An Ethical Study (1988) (arguing that the lawyer's traditional amoral role is only weakly justified and hence that lawyers should follow their own moral principles in assisting clients, even if this means disclosure of confidential information or betrayal of a client); Robert W. Gordon, Corporate Law Practice as a Public Calling, 49 Md.L.Rev. 255, 258 (1990): "lawyers [should] develop some vision of the common good or public interest, and try to

Both groups agree, however, that it is morally and legally important that the client fully participate in decisions involved in the representation. Nevertheless, an equal participatory model is difficult to reconcile with several considerations. First, the lawyer usually knows more about the legal aspects of the problem than the client, and more than the client practically can be told. Second, the lawyer typically is inured to the emotional distress of conflict and can therefore deal with it more steadily—this may be the other side of being "sensitive." Third, the decisions in carrying out a legal matter often require unabashed assertiveness: Should an impecunious widow take bankruptcy to avoid paying back rent to a landlord who may need the money almost as much as she does? Lawyers are used to taking such measures, while ordinary people are not. Also, some clients expect the lawyer to take responsibility for a difficult choice: "What should I do?" "What would you do if you were in my position?" These things said, lawyers often have strong inclinations and temptations to manipulate clients.

Authority To Settle Civil Matters

INTERNATIONAL TELEMETER CORP. v. TELEPROMPTER CORP.[13] This case arose out of a patent infringement suit that ITC had brought against Teleprompter. The question on appeal was whether there was sufficient evidence to support the trial court's conclusion that Kirsch, Teleprompter's lawyer, had either actual or apparent authority to bind Teleprompter to a settlement. Principals for the two companies had participated in extended negotiations and agreed on the basic terms of settlement: Teleprompter would pay ITC $245,000 and both companies would dismiss their claims against each other. The lawyers, Kirsch for Teleprompter and Amster for ITC, were then asked to draft documents and handle the legal details. Various drafts of a settlement agreement were exchanged, with Kirsch sending copies of all communications to ITC officials.

After being informed that Bresnan, Teleprompter's president, had signed the final documents, Kirsch notified ITC of that fact and arranged for Teleprompter's local counsel in the case to file a stipulation of dismissal. Then Teleprompter's management changed. The new management refused to deliver the settlement documents Bresnan had signed and disavowed the deal. Kirsch then telephoned Amster to tell him that he had been mistaken in his earlier statement that Teleprompter had agreed to the settlement. Kirch followed up the oral report with a "Dear Mort" letter to the same effect. He then withdrew from further representation of Teleprompter.

In ITC's action to enforce the settlement, the trial court held that the parties had agreed to be bound by the settlement as of the date of exchange of the settlement documents, which Bresnan subsequently signed, and

realize it in their practices, if necessary against the immediate wishes of their clients"); and William W. Simon, Ethical Discretion in Lawyering, 101 Harv.L.Rev. 1083, 1113–19 (1988) (lawyers should exer- cise ethical discretion in representing clients).

13. 592 F.2d 49 (2d Cir.1979).

ordered Teleprompter to pay ITC $245,000 plus interest and costs for its breach of the agreement. On Teleprompter's appeal, the Second Circuit affirmed. Judge Lumbard's opinion stated:

> Kirsch ... was acting within the ambit of his apparent authority and ITC was entitled to rely upon Kirsch's authority so long as there was no reason to believe that he was exceeding it. Teleprompter knew that ITC believed that Kirsch had the requisite authority and did nothing to correct this impression. In fact, ITC has no reason to think that Kirsch was exceeding his authority and Teleprompter had no reason to correct any misimpression because, as the district court found, Kirsch had full authority to negotiate and consummate a settlement. That a lawyer should have such authority is not rare. In this case, moreover, Kirsch kept Teleprompter apprised at all times of what he was doing. ... Teleprompter officials failed to disavow Kirsch's actions even when Kirsch sent them copies of his October 31 letter announcing that the settlement was executed.[14]

Judge Friendly concurred on "the understanding that our decision rests on the unique facts here presented and that we are not entering a brave new world where lawyers can commit their clients simply by communicating boldly with each other."[15] Friendly preferred to view the case as one in which the principals had orally contracted and the lawyers' later work in producing the documents was "a memorialization of an oral agreement previously reached." The reality of complex transactions, he pointed out, is one in which, after an agreement on basic terms have been reached by the principals, the lawyers exchange successive drafts of documents that are then signed at a formal closing or completed by simultaneous exchange and delivery of the closing documents. Ordinarily a contract is not formed until the final copies of the agreement are signed and delivered.

What is Judge Friendly's concern? Why did Kirsch resign after sending the "Dear Mort" letter? What could a lawyer do to ensure that the opposing party understood that there was no deal until a written settlement agreement was signed?

Actual and Apparent Authority

Did Kirsch have *actual authority* (express or implied) to settle the case for his client, Teleprompter? Or is Teleprompter bound by the settlement because Kirsch had *apparent authority?*

Actual authority of a lawyer may be either express or implied. Implied authority flows from legal rules delegating authority on some matter to the lawyer. Express authority exists when the principal (the client) through words or deeds causes *the agent* reasonably to believe that she has the authority to act.[16] Express authority to settle a dispute continues until and

---

14. 592 F.2d at 55–56.

15. 592 F.2d at 58 (Friendly, J., concurring).

16. See Restatement (Second) of Agency § 26.

unless the client revokes the authority.[17] A client's grant of a general power to settle without specific limits or instructions is enough to constitute express authority to settle.[18] Does M.R. 1.2 or 1.4 require the lawyer to check with the client before entering into a settlement or may the lawyer proceed on the basis of the client's general direction "to settle the case?"[19]

Implied authority to take a lawful measure reasonably calculated to advance a client's objectives permits a lawyer, for example, to reveal confidential information when doing so will further the client's objectives in a settlement negotiation. See M.R. 1.6(a), Comment [7]. Except in a few states, lawyers do not have implied authority to settle a client's disputed matter. A minority of jurisdictions, but not others, presume authority to settle from authority to negotiate.[20] This rebuttable presumption fosters the judicial policies of encouraging settlements and supporting their finality, but at the expense of client direction and autonomy.[21] The client's knowing failure to disapprove of the settlement within a reasonable time will be construed as a ratification.[22]

As the *International Telemeter* case suggests, many jurisdictions hold that a client will be bound when the attorney has *apparent authority* to enter a settlement, even if she lacks actual authority. Apparent authority exists when the *principal* (i.e., the client) through words or deeds causes *a third party* reasonably to believe that the agent has the principal's authority to act.[23] For apparent authority, courts generally require a showing of reliance and good faith on the part of the third party.[24] Apparent authority, the cases hold, is created only by the representations of the principal to the

---

17. Restatement § 33 provides that the settlement decision is for the client and may not be irrevocably delegated to the lawyer. Comment *c* states that a client may "confer settlement authority on a lawyer, provided that the authorization is revocable before a settlement is reached. A client authorization must be expressed by the client or fairly implied from the dealings of lawyer and client."

18. See Smedley v. Temple Drilling Co., 782 F.2d 1357, 1360 (5th Cir.1986) (general authorization sustained).

19. Close questions arise of what constitutes a settlement of a client's case. For example, is a lawyer's consent to the issuance of a preliminary injunction prohibiting any party from filing bankruptcy until a final judgment is issued a "compromise or settlement" of the client's case or a decision on tactics? See Hunt v. Bankers Trust Co., 799 F.2d 1060 (5th Cir.1986) (lawyer had implied authority).

20. See, e.g., St. Amand v. Marriott Hotel, Inc., 430 F.Supp. 488, 490 (E.D.La.1977), aff'd, 611 F.2d 881 (5th Cir.1980) (lawyer's authority to enter into a binding settlement is presumed from authority to negotiated and "will be set aside only upon affirmative proof of the party seeking to vacate the judgment that the attorney had no right to consent to its entry").

21. See Surety Insurance Co. of California v. Williams, 729 F.2d 581, 582–583 (8th Cir.1984) (strong presumption that the lawyer acted within the scope of authority). A lawyer's statement that she had authority is "highly probative" although not conclusive. An evidentiary hearing should be held. *Mid–South Towing*, supra, 733 F.2d at 391.

22. Cf. Capital Dredge and Dock Corp. v. Detroit, 800 F.2d 525 (6th Cir.1986) (no ratification when the client does not understand that the claim has been compromised).

23. See Restatement (Second) of Agency § 27.

24. See Terrain Enterprises, Inc. v. Western Casualty and Surety Co., 774 F.2d 1320 (5th Cir.1985) (applying Mississippi law).

third party and cannot be created by the agent's own actions or representations; authority to represent a client and appear at conferences does not create apparent authority to settle.[25] Judicial decisions dealing with the circumstances that manifest apparent authority are fact-intensive and sometimes inconsistent.[26]

Authority to Settle on Behalf of Government

Most of the cases addressing the settlement authority of government lawyers hold that those dealing with the government "must turn square corners." Morgan v. South Bend,[27] concluding that a governmental unit is not bound by a settlement entered into by its lawyer in the absence of express authority, is illustrative. In White v. United States Dept. of Interior,[28] the district court refused to enforce a $2 million settlement entered into by a United States attorney, holding that the lawyer had no apparent authority. "[P]arties who deal with a Government agent are charged with notice of the limits of the agent's authority. The government is not bound by agreements of agents beyond the scope of their authority in part because of this constructive knowledge."[29]

In one well-known case, Delaware Valley Citizens' Council v. Pennsylvania,[30] the State of Pennsylvania was held bound by a consent decree entered by the state's lawyer agreeing to establish a system for testing vehicle emissions. The Supreme Court of Pennsylvania upheld the legislature's refusal to set up the system, holding that the consent decree was a "nullity" because the lawyer had no authority to enter it.[31] The Third

---

25. See, e.g., Fennell v. TLB Kent Co., 865 F.2d 498 (2d Cir.1989). In *Fennell* the client knew that his lawyers were engaged in settlement discussions with the opposing party, did not ask his lawyers to stop these discussions, would have accepted a higher settlement figure, and did not tell the opposing party's counsel that his lawyers' authority was limited in any way. The Second Circuit held that these facts did not create apparent authority. See also Auvil v. Grafton Homes, Inc., 92 F.3d 226 (4th Cir. 1996) (client did not manifest to the opposing party that lawyer had authority to make a binding settlement by leaving the room in which his lawyer had told him that he should accept a settlement the lawyer had negotiated and by subsequently requesting that modifications be made in the settlement).

26. *Compare* Edwards v. Born, Inc., 792 F.2d 387, 390–92 (3d Cir.1986) (settlement authority implied from the "totality of the relationship where client repeatedly declined the lawyer's request to specify a settlement amount, saying that was the lawyer's job) *with* Morgan v. South Bend Community School Corp., 797 F.2d 471, 478 (7th Cir.1986) (criticizing cases departing from requirement that "compromise judgments depend on the actual authority of the person purporting to compromise the claim").

27. Id. at 477.

28. 639 F.Supp. 82, 90 (M.D.Pa.1986), aff'd, 815 F.2d 697 (3d Cir.1987).

29. Id. at 90. U.S. Department of Justice regulations provide that settlements over $2,000,000 can be entered only by the Deputy Attorney General on the Attorney General's behalf. The appropriate Assistant Attorney General generally is authorized to settle for amounts below this, and United States Attorneys are authorized to settle for $500,000 or less. See 28 C.F.R. §§ 0.160–0.168, Appendix to Subpart Y.

30. 755 F.2d 38 (3d Cir.1985), reaffirming 678 F.2d 470 (3d Cir.1982).

31. Scanlon v. Commonwealth, Department of Transportation, 467 A.2d 1108, 1115 (Pa.1983).

Circuit, however, stating that federal courts determine the authority of litigants and their agents in federal court litigation, determined that Pennsylvania was bound by its lawyer's action.[32] Is this case inconsistent with the general approach?

Settlement Practices and Adversary Premises

Studies of lawyer behavior suggest that the adversarial model may be more of a myth than a reality in many common settings. First, nearly all civil and criminal cases (90–95 percent) are settled rather than tried.[33] The settlements are heavily influenced by lawyers' predictions of expected outcomes if the cases were to be fully litigated ("bargaining in the shadow of the court").[34] But factors other than the expected litigation outcome also have heavy influence on settlements: the resources or staying power of the litigants and their lawyers; their relative aggressiveness and risk-averseness; the differential effect on parties and lawyers of delay and increased cost; systemic matters such as multi-year delays for a civil jury trial or a crushing case load in the prosecutor's office or the fact that prisons are full; and many similar factors. The frequency of settlement suggests that cooperative modes of behavior, rather than purely adversarial ones, are dominant in many litigation contexts some or all of the time.

Second, empirical studies suggest that the "conflict" ethic is not the norm in routine matters handled on a high-volume basis, whether the setting is traffic court, criminal court or divorce court. Lawyers who are too compliant with opposing lawyers or judges are departing from the professional model of zealous and loyal representation, but the pressures on them to do so, especially in matters involving relatively small stakes, are large. Jerome Skolnick's study comparing the performance of appointed counsel in criminal cases with that of privately retained counsel concludes that both "see greater advantage in cooperativeness than in conflict."[35] Defendants are pressured to accept guilty pleas because their lawyers predict that they will be found guilty and, if so, given a stiffer sentence. The fact that these expert predictions are frequently correct "leads to a system where the principal combatants are continually 'regressing' to a state of coopera-

---

32. See *Delaware Valley,* 755 F.2d at 41. The Seventh Circuit criticized *Delaware Valley* in the *Morgan* case, 797 F.2d at 477–78:

> *Delaware Valley* held that the entry of the consent decree was conclusive on the question of authority. We doubt that the Third Circuit meant to allow any employee of a state to bind the entire state just by signing his name to a consent decree, though this would be the logical consequence of the decision.

See also Derrickson v. Danville, 845 F.2d 715 (7th Cir.1988) (again criticizing *Delaware Valley*).

33. See H. Laurence Ross, Settled Out of Court: The Social Process of Insurance Claims Adjustment 136 (1970) (90–95 percent of all civil damage cases settled without trial); James E. Bond, Plea Bargaining and Guilty Pleas 13–15 (1975) (estimating that plea bargaining dispositions occur in as many as 95 percent of criminal cases).

34. See Robert H. Mnookin & Lewis A. Kornhauser, Bargaining in the Shadow of the Law: The Case of Divorce, 88 Yale L. J. 950 (1979).

35. Jerome H. Skolnick, Social Control in the Adversary System, 11 J. Conflict Resolution 52, 68 (1967).

tion."[36] These tendencies, at odds with the adversarial ethic, become destructive "where cooperation may shade off into collusion, thereby subverting the ethical basis of the system."[37]

Social science studies of lawyers who handle minor criminal cases, simple divorces, minor personal injuries and many common legal transactions frequently find that lawyers act as "double agents": In addition to representing a client, lawyers cooperate with opposing lawyers and institutional actors to a high degree. The studies report, for example, the following common practices: a personal-injury lawyer "cooling the client off" to accept a low-end settlement involving very little work on the lawyer's part;[38] a criminal defense lawyer performing a similar function in pushing the client to accept a plea bargain;[39] and divorce lawyers seeking to dispose of cases with as little work as possible.[40]

Are these findings consistent with claims that the dominant professional ideology is one of total commitment to client? Or merely a realistic recognition that in many situations clients cannot afford the degree of partisanship and process that wealthy parties are willing to expend when the stakes are high?[41]

2.   ALLOCATION OF DECISION–MAKING IN CRIMINAL CASES

Decisions a Client Has a Right to Make

The rule of thumb in criminal cases is similar to that in civil cases, i.e., questions on tactics and procedural matters are ones the lawyer may decide, questions on whether to compromise the client's cause are for the defendant. However, in criminal cases "procedural matters" are often matters of the defendant's fundamental rights, and it has long been recognized that at least four key matters should be decided by the defendant. "[T]he accused has the ultimate authority to make certain fundamental decisions regarding the case.... [They are] whether to plead guilty, waive a jury trial, testify in his or her own behalf, or take an appeal."[42]

---

36. Id. at 68.

37. Id. at 69.

38. Douglas E. Rosenthal, Lawyer and Client: Who's In Charge? (1974) (study of plaintiffs' personal injury lawyers). The Rosenthal study is discussed infra at p. 450.

39. Abraham S. Blumberg, The Practice of Law as Confidence Game: Organizational Cooptation of a Profession, 1 Law & Soc'y Rev. 15 (1967); Jerome H. Skolnick, Social Control in the Adversary System, 11 J. Conflict Resolution 52 (1967).

40. See Austin Sarat & William L. F. Felstiner, Divorce Lawyers and Their Clients (1995) (divorce lawyers portray themselves as insiders who can facilitate successful disposition, work hard to persuade their clients to settle, and disparage the fairness and legitimacy of legal processes and officials), discussed at p. 455 supra.

41. See David Luban, Partisanship, Betrayal and Autonomy in the Lawyer–Client Relation, 90 Colum.L.Rev. 1004, 1012 (1990). Lawyers in high-volume, low-fee practice "accept the principle of partisanship, but ... they understand that partisanship comes in degrees, and marginal units of zeal cost marginally more; and they substitute a 'satisficing' conception of zeal [a strategy that seeks what is good enough under the circumstances rather than what would be possible in an ideal world]."

42. Jones v. Barnes, 463 U.S. 745, 751 (1983), reproduced below. See M.R. 1.2(a); ABA Standards Relating to the Administra-

Some jurisdictions add to the list of decisions that the defendant has a right to make: e.g., waiver of the right to speedy trial;[43] entry of an insanity plea;[44] and presentation of a diminished capacity defense in a death penalty case.[45] Should the decision on whether to present a defense or take an appeal be one a criminal defendant always has a right to make? What if there is no credible evidence or the defense is legally frivolous? Who decides what is credible or frivolous?

If a lawyer, without the client's consent, makes any of the decisions that can be made only by a client, a new trial will be ordered. On the other hand, a defendant who makes the decision against counsel's advice is held to it. In People v. Robles,[46] for example, the defendant insisted on taking the stand over his lawyer's objection. On appeal, the defendant argued that the trial court had erred in allowing his testimony because the decision was tactical and within the province of the lawyer. The court upheld the conviction, stating that "where ... a defendant insists that he wants to testify, he cannot be deprived of that opportunity."[47]

Courts consider conduct by a lawyer that is the "practical equivalent" of entering a guilty plea over the client's objection as ground for reversal.[48] See generally the notes following *Nix v. Whiteside* in Chapter 5 above.

Decisions a Criminal Defense Lawyer May Make

Outside the areas entrusted by M.R. 1.2(a) or other law to the client's control, courts have upheld the lawyer's authority to decide "strategic" matters in a criminal case, notwithstanding that the client has objected, that fundamental rights were waived or that the lawyer had ample opportunity to consult with the client but did not.[49] How would courts monitor a

tion of Criminal Justice (Defense Function), Standards 4–5.2 and 4–8.2(a).

43. See Townsend v. Superior Court, 543 P.2d 619 (Cal.1975).

44. People v. Gauze, 542 P.2d 1365 (Cal. 1975).

45. People v. Frierson, 705 P.2d 396, 403 (Cal.1985) (reversing a death penalty because decision to withhold presentation of any defense in guilt phase of a capital case, when defendant desires that a defense be presented and when there is some credible evidence to support it, is not one a lawyer may properly make).

46. 466 P.2d 710 (Cal.1970).

47. Id. at 716.

48. See Brookhart v. Janis, 384 U.S. 1, 7 (1966) (lawyer agreeing, over client's objection, that the trial should be conducted as a "prima facie trial," in which the defense would neither present evidence nor cross-examine witnesses, was "the practical equivalent of a plea of guilty"). But see

People v. Ratliff, 715 P.2d 665 (Cal.1986) (conceding client's guilt to a lesser charge without client's consent is a trial tactic, not tantamount to pleading guilty, and decision is properly vested in the lawyer). Does *Ratliff* make sense?

49. The 1990 version of ABA Defense Function Standard 4–5.2(b) provided: "(b) The decisions on what witnesses to call, whether and how to conduct cross-examination, what jurors to accept or strike, what trial motions should be made, and all other strategic and tactical decisions are the *exclusive province* of the lawyer after consultation with the client." [Emphasis added.] As amended in 1992, Standard 4–5.2(b) reads: "Strategic and tactical decisions should be made by defense counsel after consultation with the client where feasible and appropriate. Such decisions include what witnesses to call, whether and how to conduct cross-examination, what jurors to accept or strike, what trial motions should be made, and what evidence should be introduced."

requirement that counsel obtain the client's consent prior to waiving any constitutional rights? Are the practical difficulties insurmountable? How do courts monitor whether a defendant has freely agreed to waive the right to trial by jury, to testify or to plead guilty?

Decisions the lawyer may make without client consent include: which witnesses to call;[50] whether to agree to a mistrial;[51] whether a defense is plausible;[52] the nature of opening or closing argument or their waiver;[53] whether to waive objection to the racial composition of the grand jury;[54] and whether to seek a change of venue after extensive pretrial publicity.[55]

Jones v. Barnes

Supreme Court of the United States, 1983.
463 U.S. 745.

■ CHIEF JUSTICE BURGER delivered the opinion of the Court.

We granted certiorari to consider whether defense counsel assigned to prosecute an appeal from a criminal conviction has a constitutional duty to raise every non-frivolous issue requested by the defendants.... [David Barnes, who had been convicted of robbery and assault in a New York state court, asked his assigned counsel, Melinger, to raise a number of issues on appeal from the conviction. Melinger, after communicating his plans to Barnes by letter and not receiving a reply, concentrated in his brief and oral argument on three of the issues, rejecting two others requested by Barnes because he, Melinger, believed they were not based on evidence in the record and would not aid Barnes in obtaining a new trial. Barnes' submitted his pro se brief presenting the other issues to the appellate court, which affirmed the conviction. When various post-conviction remedies proved unavailing, Barnes brought this federal habeas corpus action claiming that Melinger's failure to assert all the non-frivolous arguments Barnes had requested was a denial of his Sixth Amendment right to the effective assistance of counsel.]

This Court in holding that a State must provide counsel for an indigent appellant on his first appeal of right, recognized the superior ability of trained counsel in the "examination of the record, research of the law, and marshalling of arguments on [the appellant's] behalf," Douglas v. California [372 U.S. 353, 358 (1963)]. Yet by promulgating a per se rule that the client, not the professional advocate, must be allowed to decide what issues are to be pressed, the Court of Appeals [in this case] seriously undermines the ability of counsel to present the client's case in accord with counsel's professional evaluation.

50. See Connecticut v. Davis, 506 A.2d 86 (Conn.1986).

51. See People v. Ferguson, 494 N.E.2d 77 (N.Y.1986).

52. See Moreno v. Estelle, 717 F.2d 171 (5th Cir.1983).

53. See United States v. Mayo, 646 F.2d 369 (9th Cir.1981).

54. See Winters v. Cook, 489 F.2d 174 (5th Cir.1973).

55. See Curry v. Slansky, 637 F.Supp. 947 (D.Nev.1986).

Experienced advocates since time beyond memory have emphasized the importance of winnowing out weaker arguments on appeal and focusing on one central issue if possible, or at most on a few key issues....

. . .

An authoritative work on appellate practice observes:

> Most cases present only one, two, or three significant questions.... Usually ... if you cannot win on a few major points, the others are not likely to help, and to attempt to deal with a great many in the limited number of pages allowed for briefs will mean that none may receive adequate attention. The effect of adding weak arguments will be to dilute the force of the stronger ones. R. Stern, Appellate Practice in the United States, 266 (1981).

There can hardly be any question about the importance of having the appellate advocate examine the record with a view to selecting the most promising issues for review. This has assumed a greater importance in an era when oral argument is strictly limited in most courts—often to as little as 15 minutes—and when page limits on briefs are widely imposed.... Even in a court that imposes no time or page limits, however, the new per se rule laid down by the Court of Appeals is contrary to all experience and logic. A brief that raises every colorable issue runs the risk of burying good arguments—those that, in the words of the great advocate John W. Davis, "go for the jugular." Davis, The Argument of an Appeal, 26 A.B.A.J. 895, 897 (1940)—in a verbal mound made up of strong and weak contentions.... [6]

The Court's decision in Anders [v. California, 386 U.S. 738], far from giving support to the new per se rule announced by the Court of Appeals, is to the contrary. *Anders* recognized that the role of the advocate "requires that he support his client's appeal to the best of his ability." 386 U.S., at 744. Here the appointed counsel did that. For judges to second-guess reasonable professional judgments and impose on appointed counsel a duty to raise every "colorable" claim suggested by a client would disserve the very goal of vigorous and effective advocacy that underlies *Anders*. Nothing in the Constitution or our interpretation of that document requires such a standard....

■ JUSTICE BRENNAN with whom JUSTICE MARSHALL joins, dissenting.

The Sixth Amendment provides that "[i]n all criminal prosecutions, the accused shall enjoy the right ... to have the *Assistance of Counsel*"

---

6. ... Respondent points to the ABA Standards for Criminal Appeals, which appear to indicate that counsel should accede to a client's insistence on pressing a particular contention on appeal, see ABA Standards for Criminal Justice 2–3.2, at 2–4.2 (2d ed.1980). The ABA Defense Function Standards provide, however, that, [with certain exceptions,] strategic and tactical decisions are the exclusive province of the defense counsel, after consultation with the client. See ABA Standards for Criminal Justice 4–5.2 (2d ed. 1980).... In any event, the fact that the ABA may have chosen to recognize a given practice as desirable or appropriate does not mean that that practice is required by the Constitution.

(emphasis added). I find myself in fundamental disagreement with the Court over what a right to "the assistance of counsel" means. The import of words like "assistance" and "counsel" seem inconsistent with a regime under which counsel appointed by the State to represent a criminal defendant can refuse to raise issues with arguable merit on appeal when the client, after hearing his assessment of the case and his advice, has directed him to raise them ...

. . .

... [I]n Faretta v. California, 422 U.S. 806 (1975) [holding a criminal defendant has a constitutional right to proceed without counsel] ... we observed:

> ... To force a lawyer on a defendant can only lead him to believe that the law contrives against him.... The right to defend is personal. The defendant, and not his lawyer or the State, will bear the personal consequences of a conviction. It is the defendant, therefore, who must be free personally to decide whether in his particular case counsel is to his advantage. And although he may conduct his own defense ultimately to his own detriment his choice must be honored out of that respect for the individual which is the lifeblood of the law. *Illinois v. Allen* (Brennan, J., concurring).

[T]he Court argues that good appellate advocacy demands selectivity among arguments. That is certainly true—the Court's advice is good. It ought to be taken to heart by every lawyer called upon to argue an appeal ... and by his client. It should take little or no persuasion to get a wise client to understand that, if staying out of prison is what he values most, he should encourage his lawyer to raise only his two or three best arguments on appeal, and he should defer to his lawyer's advice as to which are the best arguments. The Constitution, however, does not require clients to be wise, and other policies should be weighed in the balance as well.

It is no secret that indigent clients often mistrust the lawyers appointed to represent them. There are many reasons for this, some perhaps unavoidable even under perfect conditions—differences in education, disposition, and socioeconomic class—and some that should (but may not always) be zealously avoided. A lawyer and his client do not always have the same interests. Even with paying clients, a lawyer may have a strong interest in having judges and prosecutors think well of him, and, if he is working for a flat fee—a common arrangement for criminal defense attorneys—or if his fees for court appointments are lower than he would receive for other work, he has an obvious financial incentive to conclude cases on his criminal docket swiftly. Good lawyers undoubtedly recognize these temptations and resist them, and they endeavor to convince their clients that they will. It would be naive, however, to suggest that they always succeed in either task. A constitutional rule that encourages lawyers to disregard their clients "wishes without compelling need can only exacerbate the clients" suspicions of their lawyers. ...

. . .

... In many ways, having a lawyer becomes one of the many indignities visited upon someone who has the ill fortune to run afoul of the criminal justice system.

I cannot accept the notion that lawyers are one of the punishments a person receives merely for being accused of a crime. Clients, if they wish, are capable of making informed judgments about which issues to appeal, and when they exercise that prerogative their choices should be respected unless they would require lawyers to violate their consciences, the law or their duties to the court.

Violation of Client Instructions as Ineffective Assistance

Was attorney Melinger's refusal to follow his client's instructions a violation of professional ethics? Justice Blackmun, concurring separately, stated that, as an ethical but not constitutional matter, a lawyer is bound to argue all nonfrivolous issues on which the appellant insists.[7] Does the majority opinion rest on this distinction between unconstitutional lawyer conduct and unethical conduct? Or does it adopt a lawyer-centered view of the lawyer-client relationship in a criminal trial and appeal?

The backdrop of *Barnes* is the systemic problem of providing an appeal at public expense to each convicted indigent defendant. An indigent defendant has little incentive not to take an appeal, even if the prospects of success are low.[8] The *Anders* case attempted to make the right of appeal meaningful by requiring appointed counsel to discuss "anything in the record that might arguably support the appeal."[9] This constitutional requirement modifies the general ethics requirement that prohibits lawyers from pressing frivolous matters and requires them to withdraw rather than do so. *Anders* and its progeny suggest that the lawyer's advocacy function in this situation is infused with public responsibilities of assisting the court system in ensuring that a defendant's rights are adequately protected.

The modification in counsel's role was itself modified in McCoy v. Wisconsin,[10] dealing with a Wisconsin rule requiring the lawyer to include an explanation of why the lawyer believes the appeal is frivolous in any brief filed pursuant to *Anders*. The Court held that the Wisconsin rule does not deprive the defendant of effective assistance of counsel.

7. *Barnes*, 463 U.S. at 754 (Blackmun, J., concurring).

8. See Thomas Y. Davies, A Hard Look at What We Know (and Still Need to Know) About the "Costs" of the Exclusionary Rule, 1983 Am.B. Found.Res. J. 611 (California's First District Court of Appeal, which includes San Francisco, reversed only 26 of 544 criminal appeals in a one-year period; the California Supreme Court accepted only four cases for review).

9. Anders v. California, 386 U.S. 738 (1967), discussed in Chapter 5 above at p. 431.

10. 486 U.S. 429 (1988).

Accepting or Rejecting a Plea Bargain Offer

A guilty plea will be set aside and a new trial ordered if entered without client consent.[11] The defendant is given what she has lost: her right to a fair trial and all the other protections afforded by that process. But what happens when the defendant's lawyer *rejects* a plea bargain without client consent and the defendant is convicted? Would reversing that conviction and ordering a new trial be a sensible remedy? As the Iowa court has said: "One more fair trial, or even a series of them, would not necessarily revive the lost chance [for a plea bargain]."[12] Is the answer to provide no remedy?

Courts have had difficulty with this dilemma. Johnson v. Duckworth[13] held that a lawyer who rejects a plea bargain without client consent ordinarily violates the defendant's Sixth Amendment right to effective counsel; the lawyer's action was reasonable in this case, however, because the defendant was 17, confused and the lawyer talked to the client's parents before deciding. The court also noted that the defendant had made no showing that he would have accepted the proffered plea, which would ordinarily be required before relief was granted.[14]

Other courts have ordered new trials, perhaps to put the defendant once again in the position where she can attempt to bargain with the prosecutor.[15] The prosecutor, however, may not choose to repeat the offer. This possibility was addressed in Iowa v. Kraus;[16] the Iowa court remanded the case, directing that the trial court allow the accused to enter a plea on the terms his lawyer had rejected (a plea to a lesser offense). "If a guilty plea is entered, judgment shall be pronounced accordingly and defendant's conviction of second-degree murder shall stand as reversed. If the defendant fails or refuses to enter such a plea his conviction ... shall stand affirmed."[17]

Albert Alschuler's discussion of the realities of the plea bargaining process concludes that the client's right to decide whether to plead guilty is realized only in a technical sense. Many defense lawyers believe their judgment on the plea should prevail; if the client resists, she should find a new lawyer.[18]

---

11. See Boykin v. Alabama, 395 U.S. 238 (1969).

12. Iowa v. Kraus, 397 N.W.2d 671 (Iowa 1986). Other courts have noted the difference between accepting a plea and rejecting one. See, e.g., Johnson v. Duckworth, 793 F.2d 898 (7th Cir.1986).

13. 793 F.2d 898 (7th Cir.1986).

14. See, e.g., Lloyd v. State, 373 S.E.2d 1 (Ga.1988) (failure to communicate plea unreasonable but no prejudice where no evidence that defendant would have accepted the offer).

15. See, e.g., State v. Simmons, 309 S.E.2d 493 (N.C.App.1983).

16. 397 N.W.2d 671 (Iowa 1986).

17. Id. at 676; see also Turner v. Tennessee, 858 F.2d 1201 (6th Cir.1988) (state may not withdraw plea offer unless it can show no vindictiveness in doing so). But see Commonwealth v. Copeland, 554 A.2d 54, 60 (Pa.Super.1988) (court may only order "imperfect relief" of new trial and cannot order the state to reinstate its plea offer).

18. Albert W. Alschuler, The Defense Attorney's Role in Plea Bargaining, 84 Yale L.J. 1179, 1306–7 (1975).

Autonomy to Opt for Death

Does the autonomy argument made by Justice Brennan in his dissent in *Barnes* justify allowing a client to decide to forego legal tactics that might save her from the death penalty? In Gilmore v. Utah,[19] the Supreme Court affirmed the right of a person to refuse to appeal a death sentence. The Court had previously granted the petition for a stay filed by Bessie Gilmore, the defendant's mother, which it now vacated, dismissing the action brought by his mother as "next friend" to stop the execution. In Lenhard v. Wolff,[20] the defendant's lawyers sought a writ of habeas corpus and a stay of their former client's execution, which the client refused to fight. They argued that in this case, unlike *Gilmore*, their client had never been shown to be competent to waive his rights. The Ninth Circuit refused to stay the execution because no evidence in the record raised a doubt about the client's competence.

PEOPLE v. DEERE. If the defendant has the right to insist that a defense of diminished capacity be presented, as California has held, does the defendant have the right to insist that that defense or others not be presented? People v. Deere[21] placed a public defender in this situation. The defender's client, Deere, had killed the husband of a former lover and two young children. After Deere was found competent to plead guilty and waive jury trial, he did so and the court found him guilty of the multiple murders. Deere then waived a jury on the penalty issue and offered no mitigating evidence. The defender failed in efforts to persuade Deere to offer mitigating evidence. "[Deere] made a brief statement voicing remorse for his crimes and saying he deserved to die." The sentence of death was reversed and remanded by the California Supreme Court for a retrial of the penalty phase. A majority held that defense counsel's failure to present any mitigating evidence in the penalty phase of a capital trial deprived Deere of effective assistance of counsel.

> Counsel first permitted his client to make a brief statement to the court ... "I know what I done was wrong" ... "I always believed [in] an eye for an eye. I feel I should die for the crimes I done."
>
> ... [T]he defense attorney's honest but mistaken belief that he had "no right whatsoever to infringe upon his [client's] decisions about his own life" operated to deny defendant his right to the effective assistance of counsel. While counsel should of course endeavor to comply with his client's wishes to the maximum extent consistent with his legal and ethical responsibilities, he is not—contrary to popular misconception—a mere "mouthpiece." As we recently found it necessary to reiterate, "Once an attorney is appointed to represent a client, he assumes the authority and duty to control the proceedings. The scope of this authority extends to matters such as deciding what witnesses to call, whether and how to conduct cross-examination, what

---

19. 429 U.S. 1012 (1976).   **21.** 710 P.2d 925 (Cal.1985) [*Deere I*].

20. 603 F.2d 91 (9th Cir.1979).

jurors to accept or reject, what motions to make, and most other strategic and tactical determinations."[22]

On remand the defendant was represented by the same public defender and Deere remained "adamant" against any presentation of mitigating evidence. As the public defender said, "[h]e does not want any evidence presented on his behalf because in his heart that is his private life and to bring that evidence into court would violate his relationships with everybody he holds dear and respects in this world. And to him, those relationships are more important than anything else, including his life." The defender, faced with a choice between "his duty to his client ... and his obligation to the law ... chose his client."

> "I feel under the unique circumstances of this case I must make this decision.... [Deere] has never once altered his position. ...[B]ased on his true and sincere and honest beliefs about what is right for him.... I stand with him 100 percent. ...[So I cannot] accede to the Court's order to either offer mitigating evidence or state for the record that there is none available.... [23]

The defense presented no mitigating evidence other than that in the first penalty trial. The trial court held the lawyer in contempt, but subsequently reversed the contempt, reopened the penalty phase, and appointed an independent attorney to investigate and present a case in mitigation. After successor counsel presented mitigating evidence at the reopened penalty hearing, the judge again sentenced Deere to death. The case again found its way to the California Supreme Court.

The opinion for the court praised the public defender for performing his duty to his client "courageously" and "at personal risk." It affirmed the death sentence on the ground that the required mitigation evidence had been presented in the reopened penalty trial; therefore Deere had not been denied effective assistance of counsel. The court heard six mitigation witnesses and successor counsel "also introduced into evidence an example of defendant's art work [obtained from the public defender by subpoena]." The new defense lawyer "stressed defendant's artistic talent and the work he could accomplish in prison if his life were spared." Justice Mosk, concurring, stated that the public defender, by declining to present available evidence in mitigation, "violated his obligation to the court and the adversarial process."[24]

Did the public defender do the right thing in standing by the client in the client's darkest hour even though he believed his client was making the wrong choice? Or does life have to be spoken for, as the Supreme Court of

---

22. 710 P.2d at 929, 931. The court stressed the state's interest in the reliable and fair administration of penalty decisions in capital cases, reasoning that a penalty trial at which available mitigating evidence is not presented is "no penalty trial at all." Id. at 934. But see In re Guzman, 755 P.2d 917 (Cal.1988) (defense counsel's acquiescence in client's desire not to present mitigating evidence is not ineffective assistance of counsel).

23. People v. Deere, 808 P.2d.1181, 1187 (Cal.1991) [*Deere II*], cert. denied, 502 U.S. 1065 (1992).

24. Id. at 1196 (Mosk, J., concurring).

California has decided, whether or not the client wants that done?[25] Would your decision be different if you had doubts about the client's mental competence?[26]

3. DISABLED CLIENTS

The normal adult client may be presumed capable of making or participating in decisions concerning the scope, objectives or means of representation. But many clients have impaired mental capacity, some are suffering from mental disease and some are juveniles. How do these conditions or impairments affect what the lawyer should do?[27]

Model Rule 1.14 provides:

(a) When the client's ability to make adequately considered decisions in connection with the representation is impaired, whether because of minority, mental disability or for some other reason, the lawyer shall, as far as possible, maintain a normal client-lawyer relationship with the client.

(b) A lawyer may seek the appointment of a guardian or take other protective action with respect to a client, only when the lawyer reasonably believes that the client cannot adequately act in the client's own interest.[28]

Paragraph (a) of M.R. 1.14 and Comments [1] and [2] remind the lawyer that a client under a disability may still be capable of participating in the representation, even if the client is unable to participate as fully as other clients. As Comment [1] states:

[A]n incapacitated person may have no power to make legally binding decisions. Nevertheless, a client lacking legal competence often has the

25. *Compare* Foster v. Strickland, 707 F.2d 1339 (11th Cir.1983) (defense attorney, obeying his client's instructions and contrary to the attorney's advice, failed to present an insanity defense; the court held that carrying out a competent client's instructions was ethical duty, not ineffective assistance of counsel), *with* State v. Holland, 876 P.2d 357 (Utah 1994) (when defense counsel, following his client's instructions, refused to offer mitigating facts and argument in a capital sentencing hearing because his client preferred death to life imprisonment, the Utah Supreme Court disqualified the lawyer and appointed a new lawyer to do so). Justice Durham's concurring opinion in *Holland* criticized the original defense lawyer's failure to fight the defense penalty: "rather than [be] a mere friend of the court, an attorney [should] represent[] the interests of a client with zeal and loyalty." 876 P.2d at 362. But who defines the interest of the client?

Doesn't Utah require defense counsel to be a "friend of the court," serving its institutional purposes, not an advocate who fights with zeal for the client's interests as the client conceives them?

26. On representing mentally impaired criminal defendants, see Rodney J. Uphoff, The Role of the Criminal Defense Lawyer in Representing The Mentally Impaired Defendant: Zealous Advocate or Officer of the Court?, 1988 Wis.L.Rev. 65.

27. The lawyer's responsibilities when representing amorphous clients, such as a class or a government, are considered in Chapter 8 infra.

28. The Model Code has no rule on representing a client under a disability, although EC 7–12 does deal with the issue in less detail than is found in the Comment to M.R. 1.14.

ability to understand, deliberate upon, and reach conclusions about matters affecting the client's own well-being. Furthermore, to an increasing extent the law recognizes intermediate degrees of competence.

Comment [2] adds that "[t]he fact that the client suffers a disability does not diminish the lawyer's obligation to treat the client with attention and respect."

A number of decisions, but not all, hold that the lawyer must ordinarily respect the client's decision to contest a civil commitment proceeding or to refrain from asserting an incompetency defense in a criminal case.[29]

When a legally incompetent client is adjudged unable to make a decision such as whether to dispose of property, the lawyer cannot act unless the lawyer has been legally appointed as guardian. If a guardian already exists, the lawyer "should ordinarily look to the representative for decisions on behalf of the client."[30] Why does Comment [3] qualify this statement with the word "ordinarily"?[31] The presence of a guardian does not relieve the lawyer of the obligation to treat the disabled client as a client to the extent possible, particularly in maintaining communication. See Comment [2] to M.R. 1.14.

When there is no guardian, M.R. 1.14(b) cautions that the lawyer should seek the appointment of a guardian "only when the lawyer reasonably believes that the client cannot adequately act in the client's own interests." But as Comment [5] suggests, even if the lawyer believes the standard of 1.14(b) has been met, seeking a guardian and thereby raising the question of incompetency may on balance do more harm to the client than good. The Comment says: "The lawyer's position in such cases is an unavoidably difficult one." It advises that the lawyer might seek guidance from a mental health professional.

When the lawyer decides that on balance a guardian should not be sought, the lawyer acts as de facto guardian, making certain decisions for the client and sometimes deciding to act against the client's express wishes. In State v. Aumann,[32] for example, the court held it proper, given the extent of the client's disability, for the lawyer to have decided against the client's wishes to take an appeal.

---

29. See, e.g., In re Link, 713 S.W.2d 487 (Mo.1986) (in civil incompetency proceedings, where lawyer concludes that the client is capable of understanding the matter, the lawyer must abide by the client's decisions on whether to waive or exercise a right). But see In re the Marriage of Beverly C. Rolfe, 699 P.2d 79 (Mont.1985) (although lawyer representing disabled client ordinarily should be guided by client, in custody proceedings lawyer should advocate a child's best interests even where they are at odds with child's expressed desires).

30. Comment [3] to M.R. 1.14. EC 7–12 is much to the same effect.

31. See Richard Neely, Handicapped Advocacy: Inherent Barriers and Partial Solutions in the Representation of Disabled Children, 33 Hastings L.J. 1359 (1982) (arguing that lawyers for a disabled client should not accept without critical examination decisions made by a guardian on behalf of the client).

32. 265 N.W.2d 316 (Iowa 1978).

Paul Tremblay identifies six options available to the lawyer and finds that each one entails its own ethical problems: (1) follow the client's expressed wishes whatever the consequences; (2) seek a guardian; (3) allow the family of the disabled client to make the decisions usually reserved for the client; (4) act as a de facto guardian; (5) try to persuade the client to accept the lawyer's judgment on the appropriate course to follow; and (6) withdraw. He concludes that lawyer supersession of the client's right to make decisions is only warranted in emergencies, that only in extreme cases should the lawyer seek a guardian, that relying in part on the family is justifiable and that non-coercive persuasion is the appropriate course in moderate cases of disability.[33]

C. FEES

INTRODUCTORY NOTE

Four types of fee arrangements are frequently encountered, separately or in combination: (1) a flat fee for a particular legal matter (e.g., $700 for a simple uncontested divorce or $150 for a simple will); (2) an hourly rate fee (e.g., $100 per hour for work on a particular matter); (3) a proportional fee (e.g., handling a real estate transaction for a percentage of the purchase price); and (4) a contingent fee (e.g., a fee of $10,000 to be paid if a particular result is obtained). Combinations of hourly rates with contingent features are common. The classic contingent fee in the personal injury field is both contingent and proportional (e.g., one-third of any award after deduction of expenses).

Systematic studies of legal fees and the basis of their calculation are rare. Contingent fees, discussed below, have received some attention. The hourly rate fee is said to have become much more common since 1950. The fee resulting from an hourly fee is the product of the hourly rate times the number of hours. Generally, the hourly rate is standard and calibrated to the lawyer's experience, while the number of hours is the product of the adversariness of the matter, the stakes, client goals and the relative complexity of the matter.[1] However, as economic analysis would suggest,

---

33. See Paul R. Tremblay, On Persuasion and Paternalism: Lawyer Decisionmaking and the Questionably Competent Client, 1987 Utah L.Rev. 515. See also Rodney J. Uphoff, The Role of the Criminal Defense Lawyer in Representing The Mentally Impaired Defendant: Zealous Advocate or Officer of the Court?, 1988 Wis.L.Rev. 65 (exploring alternatives to raising competency for the lawyer representing a mentally impaired criminal defendant).

1. See Herbert M. Kritzer et al., Understanding the Costs of Litigation: The Case

of the Hourly–Fee Lawyer, 1985 Am. B. Found. Res. J. 559. The authors, in assessing how reform proposals might affect the costs of civil litigation, conclude that delay has relatively little effect on processing costs (though very costly to plaintiffs in other respects); that "the level of involvement and control exercised by the client can significantly reduce the amount of time the lawyer spends on the case"; that "lawyers who take cases because of the professional visibility they will gain appear to spend significantly more time per case

both the standard hourly rate and the number of hours committed are informed and constrained by the charges made by other lawyers in the same market.

1. AMOUNT OF THE FEE

DR 2–106(A) prohibits a lawyer from contracting for, charging or collecting a "clearly excessive fee," but goes on to define a "clearly excessive fee" in terms of whether the fee is "reasonable." Model Rule 1.5(a) eliminates mention of "excessive" and simply states that "[a] lawyer's fee shall be reasonable." Both DR 2–106 and M.R. 1.5(a), employing substantially identical language, list eight factors relevant "in determining the reasonableness of a fee." For an even more extensive list of factors see Calif. R. Prof. Conduct 4–200(B). The smorgasbord of relevant factors point in different directions and require a balancing judgment based on the facts of each representation. Does this characteristic deprive lawyers of adequate advance guidance of whether a fee is "reasonable"? The confusion over the standard is repeated in the cases. In addition, courts sometimes use words such as "fair" and "inequitable" when judging a fee.[2] The reference to "communicate" in M.R. 1.5(b) is a reminder that the duty of communication of M.R. 1.4 applies to fee arrangements and alternatives. Some states require that the fee agreement be in writing.[3]

In the Matter of Fordham

Supreme Judicial Court of Massachusetts, 1996.
423 Mass. 481, 668 N.E.2d 816.

■ Before LIACOS, C.J., and O'CONNOR, GREANEY and FRIED, JJ.

■ O'CONNOR, JUSTICE.

[In March 1989, Timothy Clark, age 21, was arrested and charged with operating under the influence of alcohol (OUI) and operating a motor vehicle after suspension. A partially filled bottle of vodka was discovered in his unregistered vehicle. Timothy submitted to two breathalyzer tests which registered .10 and .12 respectively. Timothy's father (Clark) consulted three lawyers, who offered to represent Timothy for fees between $3,000 and $10,000. Shortly after the arrest, Clark went to the home of Laurence Fordham to service an alarm system which he had installed several years before. He spoke of his son's predicament to Fordham's wife, who told him that Fordham was an experienced and capable litigator. (A former senior litigator and partner at one of Boston's largest and most elite firms,

(which then gets billed to the client)"; and that "clients with a strong desire to keep costs low should avoid the federal courts if they have the option." Id. at 592–93.

2. See, e.g., Ackermann v. Levine, 788 F.2d 830 (2d Cir.1986).

3. See, e.g., Cal. Bus. & Prof. Code §§ 6147–6148 (contingency fee agreements and engagements where costs to a client exceed $1000 must be in writing) and D.C. Rules of Professional Conduct Rule 1.5(b) (when lawyer has not regularly represented the client, the fee must be communicated in writing).

Fordham was then practicing in his own boutique litigation firm with several associates.) Clark arranged a meeting with Fordham.]

[At this meeting, Timothy described the incident and the charges against him. Fordham told Timothy and Clark that he had never represented a client in a criminal matter, an OUI case, or a case in the Massachusetts district court. He explained that he was a knowledgeable and experienced litigator who was "efficient and economic in the use of [his] time" and that he worked on an hourly rate basis of $200 per hour. Clark hired Fordham to represent Timothy and agreed to pay the fees.]

[Fordham, who worked on the case during seven months in 1989, filed four pretrial motions, one a creative motion to suppress the breathalyzer results on the ground that, although the two tests were exactly .02 apart, they were not "within" .02 of one another as required by Massachusetts regulations. At the subsequent bench trial in October 1989, the court found Timothy not guilty of driving while under the influence.]

[Fordham, in accordance with the fee agreement, sent six monthly bills to Clark totaling $50,022.25, reflecting 227 hours of billed time, 173 by Fordham and 74 by his associates. Clark expressed his concern about the amount of the bills after receiving the first two, when he paid Fordham $10,000. Although Clark made no subsequent payments, in October, at Fordham's request, he signed a promissory note evidencing his debt to Fordham. Fordham's October bill added a charge of $5,000 as a "retroactive increase in fees."]

[In March 1992, bar counsel charged Fordham with charging a clearly excessive fee under DR 2–106. After a five-day hearing, the hearing committee recommended against discipline. The committee concluded that Fordham's fee was not substantially in excess of a reasonable fee. The board of overseers accepted this recommendation by a 6–5 vote. Bar counsel then appealed to the Supreme Judicial Court. In these proceedings bar counsel stipulated that all the work billed for was done and that Fordham acted conscientiously, diligently and in good faith in representing Timothy.]

[The court's opinion quoted the "clearly excessive" standard of DR 2–106(B) and the eight factors to be considered in ascertaining the reasonableness of a fee.]

In reviewing the hearing committee's and the board's analysis of the various factors ... which are to be considered [in deciding] whether a fee is clearly excessive, we are mindful that, although not binding on this court, the findings and recommendations of the board are entitled to great weight.... We are empowered, however, to review the board's findings and reach our own conclusion.... In the instant case we are persuaded that the hearing committee's and the board's determinations that a clearly excessive fee was not charged are not warranted.

The first factor listed in DR 2–106(B) requires examining "[t]he time and labor required, the novelty and difficulty of the questions involved, and the skill requisite to perform the legal service properly." Although the hearing committee determined that Fordham "spent a large number of hours on [the] matter, in essence learning from scratch what others ... already know," it "[did] not credit Bar Counsel's argument that Fordham violated DR 2–106 by spending too many hours." The hearing committee reasoned that even if the number of hours Fordham "spent [were] wholly out of proportion" to the number of hours that a lawyer with experience in the trying of OUI cases would require, the committee was not required to conclude that the fee based on time spent was "clearly excessive." It was enough, the hearing committee concluded, that Clark instructed Fordham to pursue the case to trial, Fordham did so zealously and, as stipulated, Fordham spent the hours he billed in good faith and diligence. We disagree.

Four witnesses testified before the hearing committee as experts on OUI cases. One of the experts, testifying on behalf of bar counsel, opined that "the amount of time spent in this case is clearly excessive." ...

A second expert, testifying on behalf of bar counsel, expressed his belief that the issues presented in this case were not particularly difficult, nor novel, and that "[t]he degree of skill required to defend a case such as this ... was not that high." He did recognize, however, that the theory that Fordham utilized to suppress the breathalyzer tests was impressive and one of which he had previously never heard. Nonetheless, the witness concluded that "clearly there is no way that [he] could justify these kind of hours to do this kind of work." ...

An expert called by Fordham testified that the facts of Timothy's case presented a challenge and that without the suppression of the breathalyzer test results it would have been "an almost impossible situation in terms of prevailing on the trier of fact." ...

The fourth expert witness, called by Fordham, testified that she believed the case was "extremely tough" and that the breathalyzer suppression theory was novel.... [The time and labor on the case was more than usual, but were not excessive] because the case was particularly difficult due to the "stakes [and] the evidence." ... [T]he theory on which Fordham [challenged the breathalyzer evidence] was novel. Finally, she stated that she thought she may have known of one person who might have spent close to one hundred hours on a difficult OUI case; she was not sure; but she had never heard of a fee in excess of $10,000 for a bench trial.

In considering whether a fee is "clearly excessive" within the meaning of ... DR 2–106(B), the first factor to be considered pursuant to that rule is "the novelty and difficulty of the questions involved, and the skill requisite to perform the legal service properly." DR 2–106(B)(1). That standard is similar to the familiar standard of reasonableness traditionally applied in civil fee disputes. ...See also Restatement (Third) of the Law Governing Lawyers § 46 comment f (Proposed Final Draft 1996) ("The standards that apply when fees are challenged as unreasonable in fee disputes are also relevant in the discipline of lawyers for charging unreasonably high fees"). Based on the testimony of the four experts, the number of hours devoted to Timothy's OUI case by Fordham and his associates was substantially in excess of the hours that a prudent experienced lawyer would have spent. According to the evidence, the number of hours spent was several times the amount of time any of the witnesses had ever spent on a similar case. We are not unmindful of the novel and successful motion to suppress the breathalyzer test results, but that effort cannot justify a $50,000 fee in a type of case in which the usual fee is less than one-third of that amount.

... Fordham's inexperience in criminal defense work and OUI cases in particular cannot justify the extraordinarily high fee. It cannot be that an inexperienced lawyer is entitled to charge three or four times as much as an experienced lawyer for the same service. A client "should not be expected to pay for the education of a lawyer when he spends excessive amounts of time on tasks which, with reasonable experience, become matters of routine." Matter of the Estate of Larson, 694 P.2d 1051 (Wash.1985). "[An inexperienced lawyer] may accept [novel] employment if in good faith he expects to become qualified through study and investigation, as long as such preparation would not result in unreasonable delay or expense to his client." Model Code of Professional Responsibility EC 6–3 (1982). ...

DR 2–106(B) provides that the third factor to be considered in ascertaining the reasonableness of a fee is its comparability to "[t]he fee customarily charged in the locality for similar legal services." The hearing committee made no finding as to the comparability of Fordham's fee with the fees customarily charged in the locality for similar services. [However, there was expert testimony on the subject. Of bar counsel's two experts: one said a customary flat fee in an OUI case, including trial, was between $1,000 and $7,500; the other said the customary charge was between $1,500 and $5,000. The highest fee one had ever heard of was $15,000, the other, $10,000. One of Fordham's experts said the customary fee for a bench trial of a first offense OUI was $2,000 "and sometimes less." She had never charged more than $3,500 for such a case, and she considered a fee of $40,000 to $50,000 "unusual and certainly higher by far than any I've ever seen before," although she had heard a rumor about a $10,000 fee. The other of Fordham's experts said he had heard of a $35,000 fee, but himself had never charged more than $12,000, which the court pointed out was less than twenty-five percent of Fordham's fee.]

.   .   .

The [hearing committee's] finding that Clark had entered into the fee agreement "with open eyes" was based on the finding that Clark hired Fordham after being fully apprised that he lacked any type of experience in defending an OUI charge and after interviewing other lawyers who were experts in defending OUI charges. Furthermore, the hearing committee and the board relied on testimony which revealed that the fee arrangement had been fully disclosed to Clark including the fact that Fordham "would have to become familiar with the law in that area." It is also significant, however, that the hearing committee found that "[d]espite Fordham's disclaimers concerning his experience, Clark did not appear to have understood in any real sense the implications of choosing Fordham to represent Timothy. Fordham did not give Clark any estimate of the total expected fee or the number of $200 hours that would be required." The express finding of the hearing committee that Clark "did not appear to have understood in any real sense the implications of choosing Fordham to represent Timothy" directly militates against the finding that Clark entered into the agreement "with open eyes."

That brings us to the hearing committee's finding that Fordham's fee fell within a "safe harbor." The hearing committee reasoned that as long as an agreement existed between a client and an attorney to bill a reasonable rate multiplied by the number of hours actually worked, the attorney's fee was within a "safe harbor" and thus protected from a challenge that the fee was clearly excessive. . . .

The "safe harbor" formula would not be an appropriate rationale in this case because the amount of time Fordham spent to educate himself and represent Timothy was clearly excessive despite his good faith and diligence. Disciplinary Rule 2–106(B)'s mandate [, by referring to "a lawyer of ordinary prudence,"] creates explicitly an objective standard by which attorneys' fees are to be judged. We are not persuaded by Fordham's argument that [discipline requires that "dishonesty, bad faith or over-reaching of the client" must be established.] . . .

Finally, bar counsel challenges the hearing committee's finding that "if Clark objected to the numbers of hours being spent by Fordham, he could have spoken up with some force when he began receiving bills." Bar counsel notes, and we agree, that "[t]he test as stated in the DR 2–106(A) is whether the fee 'charged' is clearly excessive, not whether the fee is accepted as valid or acquiesced in by the client." Therefore, we conclude that the hearing committee and the board erred in not concluding that Fordham's fee was clearly excessive.

Fordham argues that our imposition of discipline would offend his right to due process. A disciplinary sanction constitutes "a punishment or penalty" levied against the respondent, and therefore the respondent is entitled to procedural due process. In re Ruffalo, 390 U.S. 544, 550 (1968). Matter of Kenney, 504 N.E.2d 652 (Mass.1987) ("attorney has a substantial property right in his license to practice law"). Fordham contends that the bar and, therefore, he, have not been given fair notice through prior decisions of this court or the express language of DR 2–106 that discipline may be imposed for billing excessive hours that were nonetheless spent diligently and in good faith. . . . It is true, as Fordham asserts, that there is a dearth of case law in the Commonwealth meting out discipline for an attorney's billing of a clearly excessive fee. There is, however, as we have noted above, case law which specifically addresses what constitutes an unreasonable attorney's fee employing virtually the identical factors contained within DR 2–106. . . . More importantly, the general prohibition in DR 2–106(A) that "[a] lawyer shall not enter into an agreement for, charge, or collect an illegal or clearly excessive fee," is followed by eight specific, and clearly expressed, factors, to be evaluated by the standard of "a lawyer of ordinary prudence," in determining the propriety of the fee. . . . In addition, nothing contained within the disciplinary rule nor within any pertinent case law indicates in any manner that a clearly excessive fee does not warrant discipline whenever the time spent during the representation was spent in good faith. The fact that this court has not previously had occasion to discipline an attorney in the circumstances of this case does not suggest that the imposition of discipline in this case offends due process. . . .

In charging a clearly excessive fee, Fordham departed substantially from the obligation of professional responsibility that he owed to his client. The ABA Model Standards for Imposing Lawyer Sanctions § 7.3 (1992) endorses a public reprimand as the appropriate sanction for charging a clearly excessive fee. We deem such a sanction appropriate in this case. . . . [4]

———

BROBECK, PHLEGER & HARRISON v. TELEX CORP.[5] This fee dispute arose out of Telex's antitrust litigation with IBM. At trial Telex had won a $259.5 million judgment but lost on IBM's counterclaim. On appeal, the Ninth Circuit reversed Telex's judgment but upheld IBM's $18.5 million counterclaim judgment. Its solvency threatened, Telex began a search for the lawyer who had the best chance of getting the Supreme Court to hear and reverse the appellate court decision. Telex chose Moses Lasky of the Brobeck firm in San Francisco. Brobeck agreed to file a petition for certiorari with the Supreme Court, and, if granted, argue the merits. The elaborate contingency fee agreement, negotiated by Brobeck with the president and general counsel of Telex, provided for fees that varied depending upon what happened (e.g., a $25,000 minimum fee for filing the petition for certiorari ranging to a maximum fee of $5 million if Telex won a large judgment). Brobeck filed the certiorari petition, but a few days before the Court was to rule on it, Telex agreed with IBM on a "wash settlement" in which each party relinquished its claim against the other. Brobeck sent Telex a bill for $1 million and, when Telex refused to pay, brought suit to enforce the fee agreement. The Ninth Circuit affirmed a trial court decision holding that Brobeck's interpretation of the fee agreement was correct—the agreement called for a $1 million fee in the contingency that had in fact occurred. In response to Telex's claim that the fee

---

4. [Editors' note:] For a report of a similar case, see Tom Schoenberg, The $26,000 Simple Assault, Legal Times p. 1, Apr. 14, 1997. A Georgetown student, Petrillo, while working part time as a bouncer, punched a patron while breaking up a bar brawl and was subsequently charged with criminal assault. Petrillo's defense by lawyers in the D.C. office of L.A.'s Manatt firm resulted in a fee of $26,677.85 for 125 hours of work. According to Schoenberg, "[e]xperienced D.C. criminal lawyers say cases like this are a cakewalk. Spend maybe six hours on it; the defendant typi-cally gets sent to a pretrial diversion program, does some community service, and has his record expunged. Cost to the client: around $2,000, these lawyers say—or $7,500 tops in the unlikely event that the matter went to trial." Petrillo filed a fee dispute with the D.C. Bar's Attorney/Client Arbitration Board. While Petrillo could file a complaint with D.C. Bar Counsel, "that office," according to Schoenberg, "has not disciplined an attorney solely for excessive fees in over a decade."

5. 602 F.2d 866 (9th Cir.1979).

was "unconscionable" under applicable California law, the court responded:

> In these circumstances, the contract between Telex and Brobeck was not [unconscionable under California precedents]. This is not a case where one party took advantage of another's ignorance, exerted superior bargaining power, or disguised unfair terms in small print. Rather, Telex, a multi-million corporation, represented by able counsel, sought to secure the best attorney it could find.... Although the minimum fee was clearly high, Telex received substantial value from Brobeck's services. For, as Telex acknowledged, Brobeck's petition provided Telex with the leverage to secure a discharge of its counterclaim judgment, thereby saving it from possible bankruptcy in the event the Supreme Court denied its petition for certiorari....[6]

BUSHMAN v. STATE BAR OF CALIFORNIA.[7] Barbara Cox, aged 16, retained Bushman to represent her in a divorce and custody proceeding brought by her husband, Neal Cox. The fee arrangements included a $5,000 promissory note signed by Barbara and her parents and a retainer agreement providing for an hourly rate of $60. The court awarded custody to Barbara on the basis of a stipulation of the parties, and the court ordered that the husband pay Bushman a fee of $300 and $60 in costs. Bushman, who did not inform the court of the promissory note or of the sums paid by his clients, had billed his clients for $2,800 plus $60 in costs, collected $600 from them and claimed the full amount due under the promissory note. Bushman was suspended for one year. The Supreme Court accepted the State Bar's recommendation:

> [U]nder all the circumstances, the fee charged by Bushman was so exorbitant and wholly disproportionate to the services rendered to the defendants as to shock the conscience. An examination of the file in the Cox matter reveals that only a simple, almost routine series of documents was filed by Bushman on Barbara's behalf. Although he asserts that the case was "quite involved," he is unable to articulate any complex issues which required extensive research or specialized skills.... Aside from interviews with the defendants and a doctor, the only additional services performed by Bushman were two appearances in court for hearings on orders to show cause. He failed to substantiate his claim of 100 hours spent on the Cox case.... Cox's attorney spent slightly more than five hours on the case.

WHITE v. MCBRIDE.[8] White, the lawyer for the estate of a deceased former client, after being discharged by the probate court, sought to collect on a quantum meruit basis a contingency fee agreement he had negotiated with the client before he died. The fee agreement provided that the lawyer would receive a fee of one-third ($108,000) of the client's statutory share of his wife's estate. The probate court found that the lawyer had devoted about 114 hours to the matter and, using $150 as the maximum rate

6. 602 F.2d at 875.   **8.** 937 S.W.2d 796 (Tenn.1996).

7. 522 P.2d 312 (Cal.1974).

allowable for probate matters, set the fee at $12,500. When the lawyer appealed, seeking the full fee of $108,000, the court first held that a fee arrangement giving a lawyer a one-third interest in the probate of a substantial estate was an "excessive fee" under DR 2–106. Then, overruling prior Tennessee cases, the court held that an excessive fee could not be enforced—the lawyer had forfeited any right to a fee:

> [A]n attorney who enters into a fee contract, or attempts to collect a fee, that is clearly excessive [has committed] an ethical transgression of a most flagrant sort ... [and should not be permitted] to fall back on the theory of quantum meruit when he unsuccessfully fails to collect a clearly excessive fee.[9]

Excessive Fees

Did the court in *Fordham* correctly apply the factors that determine the reasonableness of a fee? The Restatement states that the eight listed factors "respond to three questions":[10]

> First, when the agreement was made, did the lawyer afford the client a free and informed choice [such as whether the lawyer explained the probable cost and other implications of the proposed fee agreement and whether the client understood the alternatives available from this lawyer and others]? ...

> Second, does the agreement provide for a fee within the range commonly charged by other lawyers in similar representations? ...

> Third, was there a subsequent change in circumstances that made the fee agreement unreasonable? Although reasonableness is usually assessed as of the time the agreement was entered into, [subsequent events are relevant when the agreement makes the fee turn on later events, the lawyer provided better or worse than normally expected service, or events not contemplated render the agreement unreasonably favorable to the lawyer].

Note that the third issue introduces the hindsight evaluation rejected by the *Brobeck* decision, but utilized in a number of other contract cases involving a fee dispute.[11] Should subsequent events be the basis for discipline?

The necessarily vague criteria in M.R. 1.5 and DR 2–206 raise questions about the fairness of disciplining lawyers for "unreasonable" fees. In Attorney Grievance Commission v. Wright,[12] for example, three lawyers

---

9. Id. at 803.

10. Restatement § 46, cmt. c.

11. See, e.g., McKenzie Construction, Inc. v. Maynard, 758 F.2d 97, 102 (3d Cir.1985) (lawyer employed on a one-third contingency fee basis obtained substantial settlement of client's claim after relatively little work; held, in suit by client to recover most of the fee, trial court erred in failing to consider circumstances arising after the agreement was entered into: "events may occur after the fee arrangement was made so that '[a] contingent fee arrangement [that] ... was in the first instance a fair contract becomes unfair in its enforcement.' ").

12. 507 A.2d 618 (Md.1986).

testified that the fee was reasonable and three that it was not. The court described all six as "lawyer[s] of ordinary prudence." The court held that the disciplinary agency had failed to meet its burden of showing the fee was "clearly excessive." Should the conflict of expert testimony in *Fordham* have led to the same result?

California lawyers were involved in both *Brobeck* and *Bushman*? Why is a $1 million fee agreement for a certiorari petition enforceable while a $5,000 fee for a divorce and custody proceeding results in discipline? Do market principles control some lawyers and fiduciary principles others? Does *Brobeck* mean that no fee is excessive if the client is a sophisticated commercial player.[13] Reflecting the holding in *Brobeck*, Calif. R. Prof. Conduct 4–200(B)(2) provides that the client's "sophistication" is a factor to be considered in judging whether the fee is unconscionable. Is "sophistication" the right term? Shouldn't the idea be expressed in terms of a client who is "experienced and knowledgeable in using the type of legal services that are involved"?

Should the standard applied in fee litigation between lawyer and client, as in *Brobeck*, be different from that in discipline cases such as *Fordham* and *Bushman*? In McKenzie Construction, Inc. v. Maynard,[14] the court stated that "[I]n a civil action, a fee may be found to be 'unreasonable' and therefore subject to appropriate reduction by a court without necessarily being so 'clearly excessive' as to justify a finding of breach of ethics [in a disciplinary proceeding]."[15] Is *McKenzie* correct in stating that fee arrangements that may not warrant professional discipline may be unenforceable as between lawyer and client? In a dispute between lawyer and client over the fee, the lawyer generally has the burden of justifying the fee; the client, even when he is suing to recover part of the fee charged, does not bear the burden of proving that the fee was too high. "This allocation of the burden of proof is premised on the relationship of trust owed by a lawyer to his client."[16]

Does the *Fordham* case go too far in substituting a court's judgment for a contract agreed to by the parties? Note that Clark, the parent who paid the fee in the *Fordham* case, was not an indigent but ran a small business and shopped around before he made the decision to hire Fordham to represent his son. Some critics have argued that the law of lawyering treats lawyers unfairly by applying standards to lawyer-client contracts that are much harsher on lawyers than those applied to members of other occupations:

13. See Ackermann v. Levine, 788 F.2d 830, 843 (2d Cir.1986) ("... the American client was a sophisticated business person with competent American international legal counsel"). Martin Lipton of Wachtell, Lipton, one of the best-known specialists in merger-and-acquisition law, is reported to have earned a $20 million fee for representing Kraft Inc. in the Philip Morris–Kraft takeover negotiations—a fee of more than $5,000 an hour. Stephen J. Adler & Laurie P. Cohen, Even Lawyers Gasp Over the Stiff Fees of Wachtell Lipton, Wall St. J., Nov. 2, 1988, at A1.

14. 758 F.2d 97, 100 (3d Cir.1985), summarized in note 9 supra.

15. 758 F.2d at 100.

16. Id.

One searches ... in vain to discover precisely why a lawyer, acting without deceit, without coercion, and without any other form of untoward conduct is not free to price legal services at what a client is willing to pay, reasonable or otherwise. Most other actors in the marketplace can do that—why not lawyers? When professional rhetoric is set aside all that is left is an extraordinary, socialist maxim that lawyers should be ashamed of making "too much" money. ....[17]

Judicial Control of Fees

Whether a lawyer's fee or fee claim is excessive may come before a court in many ways. The lawyer may sue the client to recover a fee, as in *Brobeck* and *White*, or the client may sue to recover fees already paid, as in *Jacobson*, infra. Fee questions may also be raised in disciplinary proceedings, as in *Fordham* and *Bushman*, although discipline that turns on a lawyer's excessive fee, as in those cases, is exceedingly rare.[18] In addition, a court must approve class action settlements and this supervision entails examination of the fee claim. Court determination or approval of fees is also required by court rule or statute when courts must supervise outcomes, approve fees, and other situations.[19]

Critics complain that judges or disciplinary authorities rarely exercise initiative or authority in approving or determining fees; the standard complaint in bankruptcy, probate, class action and other arenas is that judges routinely rubber stamp lawyers' fee requests and take little or no initiative.[20] In the rare situations in which there is an adversary presenta-

---

17. Roy Ryden Anderson & Walter W. Steele, Jr., Ethics and the Law of Contract Juxtaposed: A Jaundiced View of Professional Responsibility Considerations in the Attorney–Client Relationship, 4 Geo.J.Legal Ethics 791, 815 (1991)

18. The *Fordham* court stated that that decision was the first Massachusetts case disciplining a lawyer for an excessive fee; newspaper reports state that the District of Columbia has not disciplined a lawyer for an unreasonable fee in the last decade or more. Lester Brickman asserts that in the last half-century "there have been, at most, three cases in which lawyers have been disciplined for charging standard contingency fees in tort cases when ethically mandated commensurate risk was absent." Brickman, Contingency Fee Abuses, Ethical Mandates, and the Disciplinary System: Case-by-Case Enforcement of Contingency Fees, 53 Wash. & Lee L.Rev. 1339, 1357 n.68 (1996).

19. E.g., proceedings in which courts must supervise outcomes on behalf of minors, beneficiaries of fiduciary arrangements,

etc. or approve award of fees out of estates or trusts (probate and bankruptcy proceedings); when fee-shifting statutes entitle the prevailing plaintiff to an award of attorney's fees; and when the appropriate judicial sanction imposed on a party or lawyer by a court is payment of the opposing party's fees.

20. See, e.g., Claudia MacLachlan, Anger Rises Over Bankruptcy Fees, Nat'l L.J., Mar.9, 1992, at pp. A1, A33: "[l]awyers blame judges for arbitrary fee rulings; debtors feel fleeced but are reluctant to go after the very people they need to make deals with; and creditors, the intended watchdog ..., are frequently silent on fees" which, according to an ABA study, vary tremendously from district to district"; and Thomas Dougherty, Estate-Handling Fees Challenged by Some as 'Double–Dipping,' Ithaca J., Aug. 11, 1987, at p. 4A: the practice of 'double-dipping'—a lawyer serving as executor bills the estate for her duties and as lawyer for the estate bills it again for some of the same duties—"persists in New York state because dual fees generally aren't challenged

tion on the fee matter, however, a dramatic fee reduction often occurs. In a heart-valve class action, for example, class counsel's fees were cut to less than one-third of their original claim (and the proposed settlement enriched by $20 million as a consequence) after lawyers for Public Citizen intervened. The proposed settlement had called for $165 million for the class and one fifth of that amount ($33 million) to go to the plaintiffs' lawyers. Although the trial court agreed with the settling parties that the proposed settlement offered "substantial and valuable benefits to the class," he held that the lawyers' work was "not even remotely commensurate" with the amount claimed. The court reduced the fee to $10 million (about 5% of the total award).[21]

In all of the situations discussed above, a court's jurisdiction includes authority to review or determine the lawyer's fee. A more controversial question is whether trial and appellate courts have a roving commission to initiate or respond to concerns that a lawyer's fee in a pending court proceeding is reasonable. Many courts hold that upon a client's complaint or on its own initiative, a court may review a lawyer's fee in a summary proceeding "without nice regard to jurisdictional, case or controversy, pleading, or other procedural requirements that normally govern suits."[22] Some decisions, however, hold that absent statutory or rule authority a court may not review a fee agreement on its own motion in a civil or criminal proceeding.[23]

The authority to examine lawyers' fees with greater care than ordinary commercial contracts is based on the courts' inherent and statutory power to regulate the profession.[24] In practice, court intervention concerning

by either the judge overseeing the estate nor by the beneficiaries," who do not receive a full accounting of the two sets of fees).

21. Bowling v. Pfizer, Inc., 922 F.Supp. 1261 (S.D.Ohio 1996), aff'd, 132 F.3d 98 (6th Cir.1998). See Henry J. Reske, Two Wins for Class Action Objectors, ABA J., June 1996, at 36. In a class action involving consumer fraud claims against Bank-America, the intervention of another public interest group, Trial Lawyers for Public Justice, led to substantial improvement in the merits of the settlement from that originally proposed by the settling parties and a huge reduction of class counsel's fees. The original settlement would have provided the class with $2 million on individual application by consumers and class counsel with $5.4 million in fees. When the objectors appeared to fight the settlement, it was replaced by one that would automatically pay claimants $7.9 million and give class counsel less than $2 million in fees. Graham v. Security Pacific Housing Services, Inc. (D.Miss. May 27, 1997).

22. Wolfram, Modern Legal Ethics § 9.1 at 499 (1986). See, e.g., Coffelt v. Shell, 577 F.2d 30 (8th Cir.1978) (trial judge acted on his own motion to reduce lawyer's fee).

23. In United States v. Vague, 697 F.2d 805, 808 (7th Cir.1983), the court held that a trial court erred in reducing a criminal defense lawyer's fee after summary proceedings on the court's own motion. The Seventh Circuit, stating it was "a mistake to graft onto a lawsuit an issue that the judge is neither asked nor required to resolve," stated that the judge, should have referred the excessive fee question to the appropriate bar committee or instituted disciplinary proceedings pursuant to rules of court. See also Gagnon v. Shoblom, 565 N.E.2d 775 (Mass.1991) (holding that trial court lacked statutory or rule authority to determine reasonable of a contingent fee of a plaintiffs' personal injury lawyer when the client did not object to the fee).

24. See, e.g., Smitas v. Rickett, 477 N.Y.S.2d 752 (N.Y.App.Div.1984); Watson v. Cook, 427 So.2d 1312 (La.App.1983); In re LiVolsi, 428 A.2d 1268 (N.J.1981).

lawyers' fees is largely limited to situations where the court believes that the client is in need of special protection. Thus, courts are more likely to find fees excessive and reduce them in cases where the client is a minor[25] or poor.[26]

Non-Refundable Retainer Fees

Lawyers often use the term "retainer" to refer to a variety of fee arrangements. A "general retainer" or "engagement fee" normally refers to an advance payment by a client that ensures the lawyer's availability and requires the lawyer to avoid conflicting interests. The fee is earned when received whether or not the client subsequently calls on the lawyer to perform specific work. On the other hand, a "special retainer" is an advance payment for performance of specific work to be charged against it; the amount must be deposited in the lawyer's trust account and should be drawn on only as payment becomes due for work performed. If the representation ceases before the advance payment is exhausted, the lawyer must return the balance to the client.

Some courts have become concerned with fee agreements that provide for a large initial "non-refundable" fee, particularly when the client has had little experience with lawyers. If the lawyer completes the task with very little effort, the lawyer gets a windfall; if the client becomes dissatisfied and discharges the lawyer, the lawyer keeps the advance payment. In In re Cooperman,[27] the New York Court of Appeals affirmed a two-year suspension of a lawyer whose fee contracts in criminal and probate proceedings featured a "non-refundable minimum fee" of $5,000 to $15,000, no matter how much or how little work the lawyer did before the client discharged him. Non-refundable fees of the type involved in *Cooperman*, the court said, interfere with the client's right to "walk away" from the attorney-client relationship.[28] Subsequently, the New York Court of Appeals issued rules prohibiting matrimonial lawyers from using non-refundable minimum fees. The rules do not prohibit all non-refundable fees. A general retainer, in which the client is only paying for the lawyer's availability and avoidance of conflicts, remains permissible and becomes earned when received. But when the lawyer-client contract calls for specific

---

25. Hoffert v. General Motors Corp., 656 F.2d 161 (5th Cir.1981) (lawyer voluntarily reduced 40% contingency fee to 33%; court further reduced it to 20%).

26. United States v. Strawser, 800 F.2d 704 (7th Cir.1986) (criminal defense lawyer's fee so high that defendant rendered indigent and therefore unable to hire counsel to pursue appeal).

27. 633 N.E.2d 1069 (N.Y.1994).

28. The court made it clear that "[m]inimum fee arrangements and general retain-

ers that provide for fees, not laden with the non-refundability impediment irrespective of any services, will continue to be valid [and ethical]." 633 N.E.2d at 1074. Some courts have declined to follow *Cooperman*; see, e.g., Cohen v. Radio–Electronics Officers Union, 679 A.2d 1188 (N.J.1996). For criticism of "blanket proscription" of non-refundable retainers, see Steven Lubet, The Rush to Remedies: Some Conceptual Questions About Nonrefundable Retainers, 73 N.C. L.Rev. 271 (1994).

legal services, the agreement is a "special retainer" and, under New York law, it cannot be made totally non-refundable.[29]

When a fee agreement is ambiguous, it is to be construed against the lawyer who drafted it.[30] In Jacobson v. Sassower,[31] for example, the agreement between client and lawyer to handle a divorce provided for an hourly fee of $100 and "a non-refundable retainer of $2,500 (which is not to be affected by any possible reconciliation between myself and my wife). Said retainer is to be credited against your charges. . . ." After the lawyer had completed 10 hours of work on the matter, the client discharged her without cause. The client sued to recover the difference between the retainer of $2,500 and the hourly fee charge of $1,000. The court held for the client, stating:

> This retainer agreement was ambiguous because it did not state clearly that the "non-refundable retainer of $2,500" was intended to be a minimum fee and that the entire sum would be forfeited notwithstanding any event that terminated the attorney-client relationship prior to 25 hours of service. In the absence of such clear language, defendant was required to establish that plaintiff understood that those were the terms of the agreement and she failed to do so.[32]

Most courts assert that they have a special obligation to scrutinize contingent fee arrangements with unsophisticated clients.[33] "The requirement that the client be fully informed applies especially to a contingent-fee contract. . . . Contracts for contingent fees generally have a greater potential for overreaching of clients than fixed-fee contracts [and] are closely scrutinized by the courts where there is a question as to their reasonableness."[34]

Minimum Fees

In *Wealth of Nations* Adam Smith wrote that, because "[w]e trust our . . . fortune and sometimes our life and reputation" to lawyers, "their reward must be such . . . as may give them that rank in society which so important a trust requires. The long time and expense which must be laid out in their education, when combined with this circumstance, necessarily enhance still further the price of their labour."[35] English barristers and American lawyers, sharing Smith's sentiments, have done what they could to make Smith's promise a reality. This effort has involved attempts to control the supply of, and increase the demand for, legal services, topics

---

29. See Lester Brickman & Lawrence A. Cunningham, Nonrefundable Retainers Revisited, 72 N.C. L.Rev. 1 (1993).

30. But see *Brobeck* in which the court, undoubtedly influenced by the fact that the client's general counsel had negotiated the fee contract, seemed to ignore this rule in interpreting the complex fee contract.

31. 489 N.E.2d 1283 (N.Y.1985).

32. 489 N.E.2d at 1284.

33. See, e.g., In re Teichner, 470 N.E.2d 972 (Ill.1984).

34. Committee on Legal Ethics of West Virginia State Bar v. Tatterson, 352 S.E.2d 107, 113–114 (W.V.1986).

35. Quoted in Rhode & Luban, Legal Ethics 683 (2d ed.1995).

that are treated in chapter 10.[36] In addition, for many years professional etiquette led lawyers to decline to advertise their services or to "haggle" with their clients about fees. In the twentieth century local bars established minimum fees for common services (e.g., $150 for a simple will) and enforced the minimum fees by peer pressure and the threat of professional discipline.

The regime of minimum fees ended in 1975 when the Supreme Court, applying the antitrust laws to the "learned professions," struck down minimum fee schedules established by the Virginia state bar. After the *Goldfarb* case,[37] voluntary bar associations became subject to treble-damage liability to those harmed by minimum fee schedules. Faced with this threat, bar associations abandoned them.

2. ILLEGAL FEES

Illegal fees are prohibited explicitly by DR 2–106(A) and implicitly by Model Rules 1.5(a) and 8.4. Illegal fees include: fees collected by a public official when a statute prohibits the private practice of law while in office;[38] fees above those awarded by the court in cases where the court has exclusive power to decide fees;[39] fees collected for an illegal purpose;[40] and fees above the maximum amount allowed by a statute. Fees that the lawyer knows have been paid with the proceeds of criminal activity have also been considered illegal fees.[41] Whether a lawyer may be required to forfeit such funds under the federal forfeiture statutes is discussed Chapter 4 at p. 259.

Fraudulent Billing and Fee Padding

A growing body of empirical evidence now supports anecdotal accounts suggesting that deceptive billing practices by lawyers are a common occurrence. The practices encompass a wide range of conduct: outright fraud, such as charging for time that was not devoted to a client's matter;[42] "double-billing" for the same time (e.g., a lawyer on a coast-to-coast flight charging the travel hours to both the matter on which he worked and to the client who was paying for the trip); "churning" or overstaffing a matter by billing a client for duplicative, excessive or unnecessary work; and

---

36. For an extensive theoretical and empirical effort to demonstrate the existence and effects of this "professional project," see Richard L. Abel, American Lawyers *passim* (1989) (pp. 158–65 assess the success of the effort to increase lawyer incomes by controlling supply and increasing demand).

37. Goldfarb v. Virginia State Bar, 421 U.S. 773, 787 (1975) (a county bar association's minimum fee for title examinations was illegal price-fixing under Section 1 of the Sherman Act and the state bar's promulgation of minimum fee schedules was an unlawful restraint of trade).

38. See State v. Stakes, 608 P.2d 997 (Kan. 1980).

39. See In re Crane, 449 N.E.2d 94 (Ill. 1983).

40. In re Connaghan, 613 S.W.2d 626 (Mo. 1981) (en banc) (lawyer collected fees to bribe state legislator).

41. See In re Prescott, 271 N.W.2d 822 (Minn.1978).

42. According to Leona Helmsley, her former real estate lawyer billed her for a 43–hour day. Andrew Blum, The Empress Strikes Back, Nat'l L.J., July 11, 1994, at A6.

charging the client for firm overhead (e.g., duplicating costs, fax charges or secretarial support).[43]

Of the many stories of outright fraud that have rocked the legal profession, two are worth mentioning:[44]

- Little Rock lawyer Webster Hubbell resigned as U.S. associate attorney general in February 1994 under charges by his former partners that he had billed associates' work under his own name, paid personal expenses from a client account, and "billed taxpayers more that $20,000 for work on a savings and loan case in which he claimed to have averaged more than eight billable hours every day for three weeks, without resting even one weekend day."[45] The total of fraudulent billings was at least $394,000. Hubbell went to prison for his fraud.[46]

- The former managing partner of Chicago's Winston & Strawn, Gary Fairchild, was found to have cheated his firm about $784,000 by padding expense accounts; ironically, Fairchild's fraud was discovered when another Chicago firm, Chapman & Cutler, reported that its partner, Fairchild's wife Maureen, had overcharged Winston & Strawn some $275,000 on business that Fairchild had referred to her. It was later discovered that Maureen's false billings and expenses exceeded $1.3 million. Both Fairchilds resigned from their firms and from the bar and spent time in prison.[47]

Chapman & Cutler had the dubious distinction of making further headlines when leaked billing records from the firm revealed that partner James Spiotto had billed at or close to 6,000 hours four years in a row. He claimed he never took a vacation or a day off, worked 52 "all-nighters" in 1993, and billed an average of only 12.2 hours per day on the remaining "ordinary days."[48]

43. When the South Florida Water Management District asked Skadden Arps to justify its $6 million fee for representing it in Everglades pollution litigation, the District discovered thousands of items such as coffee and Danish for four delivered by the in-house cafeteria for $23.80, marked up to $33.60. This seems like small change, but after the fee was audited Skadden reduced its charges for travel, meals, staffing, copying, attorney time spent in preparing or processing bills, etc. by $1.1 million. Susan Beck & Michael Orey, Skaddenomics—The Ludicrous World of Law Firm Billing, Am. Lawyer, Sept.1991, at 3.

44. Lisa Lerman states that 37 cases of billing fraud have been publicly reported during the ten-year period 1989–1998 in which lawyers went to jail, were disbarred, or were under investigation. She lists 16 of them in Lisa G. Lerman, Regulation of

Unethical Bill Practices: Progress and Prospects, Professional Lawyer, 1998 Symposium Issue, at 89–98.

45. Darlene Ricker, Greed, Ignorance and Overbilling, A.B.A. J., Aug.1994, at 62.

46. See Dennis Cauchon, Ripples of Whitewater in ex-Clinton Aide's Guilty Plea, USA Today, Dec. 7, 1994, at 6A (Hubbell pleads guilty to mail fraud and tax evasion charges for overbilling clients at least $394,000).

47. Stephanie B. Goldberg, An Unexpected Ouster, ABA J., July 1994, at 28; Randall Samborn, Fairchild's Sudden Fall Ends With Drop of a Gavel, Nat'l L. J., Jan. 9, 1995, at A11.

48. See Amy Stevens, Top Chapman & Cutler Partner Chalked Up Astronomical Hours, Wall St. J., May 27, 1994, at B3; Karen Dillon, 6,022 Hours, Am. Law., July 1994, at 57.

On the empirical side, the continuing surveys of William Ross paint a dismal picture that is corroborated by other studies.[49] In Ross' 1994–95 survey of practicing lawyers, more than one-half of respondents stated that they believe that at least five percent of the time billed by lawyers is padded. This is consistent with the experience of legal audit firms, which report that five to ten percent of bills they examine are fraudulent. Billing for unnecessary work is also a big problem: "half of outside counsel and two-thirds of inside counsel estimated that at least ten percent of the work done by lawyers is motivated more by a desire to inflate hours than by a desire to service the real needs of the client."[50]

In addition to Rule 1.5, a number of ethics rules are relevant to fee padding: Rules 8.4(c) (prohibiting "fraud, deceit or misrepresentation"); Rule 7.1 ("false and misleading communications" about legal services); Rule 1.4(a) (communication); Rule 1.2 (scope of representation); and Rule 8.3 (duty to report).[51]

Statutory Fee Limits

Various federal and state statutes limit the fees a lawyer can charge in particular types of legal work.[52] These limits generally have been upheld by the courts against contentions that they unconstitutionally interfere with the right to counsel and violate separation of powers by infringing upon the court's power to regulate the profession.[53] Walters v. National Association of Radiation Survivors,[54] for example, upheld the longstanding $10 fee limit for representing a veteran seeking benefits from the Veterans Administration (VA). The Court rejected veterans' claims that the fee limit "denied them any realistic opportunity to obtain legal representation in presenting

49. See William G. Ross, The Honest Hour: The Ethics of Time–Based Billing by Attorneys (1997). For a summary, see Ross, The Ethics of Time Based Billing by Attorneys, Professional Lawyer, 1998 Symposium Issue, 81–88. See also Lisa G. Lerman, Lying to Clients, 138 U.Pa.L.Rev. 659 (1990).

50. Id. at 82.

51. See also Model Rules 5.1 and 5.2, dealing with the responsibility of supervisory and subordinate lawyers. Under these rules, when a partner orders an associate to make a fraudulent billing, both are subject to discipline. The ABA ethics committee addressed billing problems in a 1993 opinion. ABA Formal Op. 93–379 (1993). The opinion condemns double billing and billing for recycled work; disapproves of charges and mark-ups for normal expenses (e.g., photocopying) unless clients have agreed in advance to pay them; and urges lawyers to provide enough detail in bills so that clients can make an informed judgment about their reasonableness.

52. See, e.g., Federal Tort Claims Act, 28 U.S.C. § 2678 (as approved by court with a limit of 25 percent of most awards and 20 percent under § 2672); Social Security Act, 42 U.S.C. § 406 (as approved with a limit of 25 percent of retrospective benefits); and Veterans Benefit Act, 38 U.S.C. § 5904(d)(1) (20 percent of the total amount of past due benefits).

53. The Black Lung Benefits Act is another federal law restricting legal fees in administrative proceedings. See United States Dep't of Labor v. Triplett, 494 U.S. 715 (1990) (reversing a West Virginia decision holding the limit violated due process).

54. 473 U.S. 305 (1985). Justice Stevens, joined by Justices Brennan and Marshall, dissented, arguing that the "totalitarian" approach of the statute violated due process by denying claimants the "priceless" liberty of effective representation.

their claims to the VA and hence violated their rights under the Due Process Clause of the Fifth Amendment and under the First Amendment."[55] The Court stated that the limit furthered Congress' goal of fostering an informal, efficient and non-adversarial process that would allow veterans to get their benefits without lawyers.[56] Legislation in 1988 responded to the issue by substituting a restriction limiting fees to 20 percent of past due benefits awarded.

State statutes placing limits on attorneys fees are also common, for example, worker's compensation laws.[57] Lawyers may be disciplined for violating such limits.[58] Many states have general limits on the percentage lawyers may charge as contingency fees: some provisions set ceilings on the percentage charged in all personal injury cases; others apply only in medical malpractice cases. Exceeding those limits is charging an illegal fee.[59]

Contracting With a Client for Rights to Client's Story

Another prohibited fee arrangement is a contract that gives a lawyer the literary or movie rights to a client's story. See M.R. 1.8(d) and DR 5–104(B). The reason for prohibiting such arrangements is that what makes "good copy" does not necessarily make a good defense. The movie rights, for example, may be worth more if the client receives the death penalty than if sentenced to a twenty-year term. Another problem with such arrangements is the broad advance waiver of client confidences that they imply. See *von Bulow II*, discussed above in Chapter 4 at p. 265.

The reasons for prohibiting these contracts apply with equal force when the lawyer contracts with a third party to produce a book, movie or other portrayal based on information relating to the representation. M.R. 1.8(d) extends the prohibition to cover these third party contracts. Cases coming before the courts have involved defendants seeking to have their convictions overturned. The claim is that the contract created a conflict of interest for the lawyer that resulted in ineffective assistance of counsel.

---

55. 473 U.S. at 308.

56. See Paul C. Weiler et al., Reporters' Study, Enterprise Responsibility for Personal Injury, v. 1, c. 13 (American Law Institute, Apr. 15, 1991) (about 95 percent of social security funds are paid out in benefits; 70–80 percent of workers' compensation costs are actually received by injured workers; but the tort system delivers less than 50 percent of insurance fund dollars to injured plaintiffs). Alternative dispute resolution is a fashionable topic and is relevant here. See Jethro Lieberman & James Henry, Lessons from the Alternate Dispute Resolution Movement, 53 U.Chi.L.Rev. 424 (1986).

57. See Mack v. City of Minneapolis, 333 N.W.2d 744 (Minn.1983) (noting that almost all worker's compensation laws impose limits on attorney's fees).

58. See Louisiana State Bar Association v. Thalheim, 504 So.2d 822 (La.1987); Hudock v. Virginia State Bar, 355 S.E.2d 601 (Va.1987).

59. Settlements in mass tort class actions commonly set up dispute resolution systems to resolve claims due to individual class members. Invariably these settlements set a maximum fee that lawyers may charge for handling claims within the dispute system. For a critique of these provisions, see Susan P. Koniak & George M. Cohen, Under Cloak of Settlement, 82 Va. L.Rev. 1051, 1098–1100 (1996).

Courts usually respond by criticizing the contract but upholding the conviction.[60]

In Maxwell v. Superior Court of Los Angeles,[61] however, the California Supreme Court held that the defendant's constitutional right to counsel gave him the right to transfer the rights to his story to his lawyer in exchange for legal representation as long as he did so knowingly, voluntarily and after full disclosure by counsel of the risks and benefits involved in such a transaction. Many of the laws that limit the extent to which a criminal defendant may profit from the story of her crime were struck down as violative of the first amendment in the "Son of Sam" case.[62]

3. FEE DISPUTES

Fee Sharing (Referral Fees)

A lawyer may split a fee with a lawyer who refers the matter to her—a rule very different than that applied to physicians.[63] The practice is most common in personal injury matters undertaken on a contingent fee basis. A claimant with a complex high-damage case (e.g., a product liability claim involving large damages) may first consult and retain a local practitioner under a standard one-third contingent fee agreement. Because the case has high value and is likely to be contested, referral to a trial specialist frequently occurs. Under the revised retainer agreement, the referring lawyer is to receive one-third of the total fee one-third contingency fee. The

---

60. See, e.g., United States v. Marrera, 768 F.2d 201 (7th Cir.1985) (the contract alone is insufficient to show ineffective assistance of counsel); Dumond v. State, 743 S.W.2d 779 (Ark.1988). Cf. People v. Corona, 145 Cal.Rptr. 894 (Cal.Ct.App.1978) (conviction reversed because of counsel's gross neglect of basic duties and failure to develop key defenses; an alternate ground for reversal was that the literary contract between lawyer and client created an impermissible conflict of interest).

61. 639 P.2d 248 (Cal.1982) (considering and upholding the detailed fee agreement).

62. See Simon & Schuster, Inc. v. Members of New York State Crime Victims Bd., 502 U.S. 105 (1991).

63. See 42 U.S.C. §§ 1320a–7b (1995) (making it a crime for a doctor to solicit, pay or receive a kickback for referring a matter covered by Medicare or Medicaid to another doctor or service provided). Laws in some states go further banning all self-referrals and kickbacks, not just those connected to services reimbursed by government health-care programs. See Cal. Bus. & Prof. Code § 650.01 (West 1997); and

N.J. Stat. Ann. § 45:9–22:5 (West 1991). Under federal law, doctor kickbacks not associated with payments from government programs may be prosecuted as mail fraud, if not disclosed to the patient, under a theory of depriving the patient of honest services. See Gregory D. Jones, Primum Non Nocere: The Expanding "Honest Services 'Mail Fraud Statute and the Physician–Patient Fiduciary Relationship, 50 Vand. L. Rev. 1029 (1998). Lawyer codes prohibit a lawyer from making payments to nonlawyers who recommend their services (see M.R. 7.2(c)), but not as referral fees from another lawyer (see M.R. 1.5(e)); the existence of the arrangement, but not the terms of the division, must be disclosed. The federal mail fraud statute led to the conviction of a Boston investment banker who failed to tell his municipal bond clients about an arrangement with a brokerage firm which resulted in his receiving $2.5 million in referral fees. See ABA J., Apr. 1997, at 37. If it is mail fraud when physicians and investment bankers fail to disclose referral arrangements, then it is mail fraud and not just an ethics violation when lawyers fail to disclose.

specialist completes preparation of the case for trial and, if successful, obtains a substantial settlement or jury award. This scenario, replicated in thousands of instances in every jurisdiction, presents a number of legal and ethical issues. What must the forwarding lawyer tell the client in obtaining the lawyer's consent to the referral? Is the forwarding fee "excessive" for disciplinary purposes if the forwarding lawyer does little or no work on the matter? Enforceable in court if the trial specialist refuses to pay the forwarding lawyer the agreed upon share?

The Model Code permits fee sharing only if: (1) the client consents to employment of the other lawyer after a disclosure that the client's fee payment will be split; (2) the fee is divided "in proportion to the services performed and responsibilities assumed" by each lawyer; and (3) the total amount of the fee is not unreasonable for the total amount of legal services rendered. DR 2–107(A). What should a court do when a forwarding arrangement meets the first and third of these requirements, but not the third (i.e., the forwarding lawyer did very little of the total work)? Perhaps because referral arrangements of this type are extremely common, professional discipline for violation of the fee-sharing prohibition is rare and most courts enforce such agreements where the forwarding lawyer provided substantial services.[64] A few courts have refused to enforce the fee agreement when the forwarding lawyers has not performed substantial work.[65] Not surprisingly, plaintiffs' lawyers, asserting that the Code's restrictions are "flagrantly violated" by lawyers and "do[] little good," argue that fee splitting "work[s] in a client's best interest by giving lawyers the incentive to refer their contingent fee clients to the most competent attorneys."

Fee splitting was one of the most contentious issues in the drafting of the Model Rules and their subsequent consideration by state rule makers. Rule 1.5(e) relaxes the preconditions for fee splitting. First, the share of each lawyer need not reflect the respective amounts of services performed if "by written agreement with the client, each lawyer assumes joint responsibility for the representation." Second, the provision for client disclosure and consent is more perfunctory than under DR 2–107(A)(1). The client need be advised only of "the participation of all the lawyers involved" and "not object." M.R. 1.5(e) does not require that the client be informed of the fact of fee splitting or its size, nor, as in the Model Code, a disclosure of how work is to be shared.

M.R. 1.5(e) requires disclosure only of the participation of the new lawyer but not of the fact of division or its details. A small number of

---

64. See, e.g., Macurdy v. Sikov & Love, P.A., 894 F.2d 818 (6th Cir.1990) (agreement enforceable where "substantial division of services or responsibility is found"); McNeary v. American Cyanamid, 712 P.2d 845 (Wash.1986) (where both lawyers perform very substantial amounts of work the fee agreement is enforceable). Some jurisdictions take an even more lenient approach: see, e.g., Oberman v. Reilly, 411 N.Y.S.2d 23, 25 (1978) (agreement enforceable if "the attorney who seeks his share of the fee contributed some work, labor or service toward the earning of the fee"—a circumstance that almost invariably is present).

65. See, e.g., Belli v. Shaw, 657 P.2d 315 (Wash.1983) (agreement for forwarding fee not enforceable by lawyer who had little, if any, involvement in the trial).

states, including California and Illinois, require communication of the terms of the division. Some commentators favor the latter approach as furthering competition in lawyer fees; providing clients full information about who will handle their matters and how the fees will be divided, permits clients "to shop for a better division of fees and responsibilities among other lawyers."[66]

Fee Arbitration[67]

Comment [5] to Model Rule 1.5 provides: "If a procedure has been established for resolution of fee disputes, such as an arbitration or mediation procedure established by the bar, the lawyer should conscientiously consider submitting to it."

No state requires a client to arbitrate a fee dispute, presumably because such a rule would violate the client's constitutional right to a jury trial. But some require the lawyer to arbitrate if the client requests it. Anderson v. Elliott[68] upheld a Maine bar rule requiring lawyers to arbitrate fee claims at the client's request. The court rejected the claim that the rule violated the lawyer's right to a jury trial, stressing "the uniqueness of the attorney's relation to the court and to the client."[69]

Should the courts enforce a contract between lawyer and client that requires the client to submit to arbitration in the event of a fee dispute? Once a lawyer and client submit to arbitration should the result be binding? In California, neither party is bound if either appeals the decision, unless there is a prior agreement to be bound. In New Jersey, both parties are bound.

A Massachusetts decision considers a client's attack on a bar-sponsored arbitration procedure.[70] The client appeared without counsel before an arbitration board composed only of lawyers. In going without a lawyer, the client had relied on information provided by bar association staff and publications stating that "these proceedings are informal." The court reversed the board's award of the total fee claimed by the lawyer on two grounds: the information provided the client did not adequately inform her of her rights to appeal; and the arbitration proceedings were not adequately described to her. These problems, the court concluded, could be cured by fully informing the client in advance of the nature of the proceedings. What information should be provided? Does the client need to be told that

---

66. Wolfram, Modern Legal Ethics at 511. Restatement § 59 follows M.R. 1.5(e) but, in addition, requires that "the client is informed of and does not object to the fact of division and the participation of the lawyers involved."

67. See James R. Devine, Mandatory Arbitration of Attorney–Client Fee Dispute: A Concept Whose Time Has Come, 14 U.Toledo L.Rev. 1205 (1986) (summarizing the various state procedures and enforcement mechanisms).

68. 555 A.2d 1042 (Me.1989).

69. Id. at 1047. Also see In re LiVolsi, 428 A.2d 1268 (N.J.1981); and Kelley Drye & Warren v. Murray Indus., Inc., 623 F.Supp. 522 (D.N.J.1985) (both upholding New Jersey's client-initiated mandatory fee arbitration system).

70. Marino v. Tagaris, 480 N.E.2d 286 (Mass.1985).

bringing a lawyer would be helpful? Would non-lawyers on the panel, required in a number of states, cure the problem?

Client Confidentiality in Fee Disputes

A lawyer may reveal client confidences to collect a fee or establish a defense in a dispute with the client over the fee, but only to the extent necessary to support the lawyer's claim or defense. See Comment [19] to M.R. 1.6(b)(2); and the discussion of this issue in Chapter 4 supra. Should a lawyer advise a client that confidential information may be disclosed if the client proceeds to challenge the lawyer's fee?[71]

4.   CONTINGENT FEES

In a contingent fee arrangement, the lawyer is compensated only if a positive result is obtained for the client—the fee is contingent on the result. A contingent fee is usually calculated as a percentage of the client's recovery, but a contract calling for the lawyer to receive a fixed amount if the client prevails is also a contingent fee contract. In most personal injury cases, the plaintiff's lawyer's fee is contingent, but contingent fees are not limited to personal injury work.[1] Contingent fees are common in tax refund practice, condemnation proceedings, suits challenging wills, debt collection cases and class action suits for damages. Although contingent fee arrangements are common for a plaintiff, they are sometimes used in civil cases by a defendant. In *Brobeck*, supra, p. 495, for example, Telex was in the position of a defendant with respect to the counterclaims against it.[2]

Contingent fees in this country originally were considered illegal as a form of champerty.[3] Many other countries still prohibit contingent fee agreements, although Great Britain since 1991 has moved cautiously and slowly to allowance of some contingent fees in personal injury cases.[4] In the United States, contingent fees are now universally accepted; Maine, the last

---

71. See Lindenbaum v. State Bar, 160 P.2d 9 (Cal.1945) (improper to threaten client with disclosure).

1. See Boston & Maine Corp. v. Sheehan, Phinney, Bass & Green, 778 F.2d 890 (1st Cir.1985) (contingent fee in an eminent domain case).

2. See Brobeck, Phleger & Harrison v. Telex Corp., 602 F.2d 866 (9th Cir.1979); see also Dunham v. Bentley, 72 N.W. 437 (Iowa 1897) (upholding defendant's agreement to pay 30 percent of her interest in any estate property that the lawyer successfully protected from creditor's claims). But see Wunschel Law Firm P.C. v. Clabaugh, 291 N.W.2d 331 (Iowa 1980) (invalidating a lawyer's contingent fee contract with a defendant in a personal injury case that calculated the defense lawyer's fee as a per-

centage of the difference between the amount of the plaintiff's prayer for relief and the amount actually recovered by the plaintiff; because the prayer for relief is often exaggerated for strategic purposes, it is misleading to use it as a measure of the defense lawyer's skills).

3. See generally Symposium: Contingency Fee Financing of Litigation in America, 47 DePaul L.Rev. 227 (1998) (containing articles and commentary on the history, use and effects of contingent fees).

4. Legislation permitting a 10 percent "conditional fee" in personal injury cases became effective in October 1992. It was extended to other types of cases in 1995. See John C. Evans, England's New Conditional Fee Agreements, 63 Def.Couns.J. 376 (1996).

C. FEES **511**

state to accept contingent fees, lifted its prohibition in 1965. At first, acceptance was grudging—contingent fees were disreputable although not illegal.[5] The disrepute was based on two fears: that lawyers would be tempted to use illegal or unethical means to win judgments, for example, manufacturing evidence or bringing frivolous suits in the hopes of coercing a settlement; and that lawyers would put their own interests before those of the client, e.g., settling a case early, thereby guaranteeing the lawyer the greatest return for the smallest amount of work, when the client would be better served by pursuing the matter through trial. Underlying the disrepute was a social desire to minimize contentious litigation, an attitude that has dissipated in the twentieth century. Contingent fees, however, are still prohibited in some types of cases, notably divorce and criminal defense work. See the notes infra at p. 518.

Contingent fees are most often justified as a necessary means of broadening access to justice, allowing those otherwise unable to afford counsel to obtain representation in the courts. They are often referred to as "the poor man's key to the courthouse door."[6] In countries that prohibit contingent fees, lawyers are paid by public funds to represent indigent civil litigants. What is wrong with that solution?[7]

The courts generally will enforce a contingent-fee agreement in customary form between parties who bargained and contracted. However, courts scrutinize unusual agreements and do not enforce those thought to be unfair. Compare *Brobeck* with *McKenzie Construction,* discussed supra at p. 498. The courts give closer scrutiny to contingent fee arrangements when the client is unsophisticated, particularly if the contingent fee is substantial and the work legally elementary.[8] The court on its own motion may review a contingent fee arrangement, at least if the client is entitled to the court's special protection.[9]

Empirical studies have largely answered the fear that the contingent fee encourages frivolous or non-meritorious litigation by showing that contingency fee lawyers turn down as many cases as they accept, acting generally as gatekeepers in the civil justice system.[10] Some reservations

---

5. See, e.g., Rooney v. Second Avenue R.R., 18 N.Y. 368 (1858). See generally Frederick B. MacKinnon, Contingent Fees (1964).

6. See, e.g., Leonard C. Arnold, Ltd. v. Northern Trust Co., 506 N.E.2d 1279, 1281 (Ill.1987); Matter of Swartz, 686 P.2d 1236, 1242 (Ariz.1984).

7. *The Economist*, in a lengthy article and editorial, reviewed the state of civil justice in the United Kingdom and called for adoption of contingency fees and abolition of the "loser pays" rule. As compared with the U.S., the magazine stated, access to justice in the U.K. is poor: the government-subsidized legal aid system is costly and encourages frivolous suits; legal procedure is outmoded and costly; lawyers are not accountable for their negligence or misconduct; and judges provide lax control. The Economist, Jan. 14, 1995 (British ed.), at 29.

8. See, e.g., Randolph v. Schuyler, 201 S.E.2d 833 (N.C.1974).

9. See, e.g., Schlesinger v. Teitelbaum, 475 F.2d 137 (3d Cir.1973) (client was a seaman); Cappel v. Adams, 434 F.2d 1278 (5th Cir.1970) (clients were children); Dunn v. H.K. Porter Co., 602 F.2d 1105 (3d Cir. 1979) (class action suits).

10. See, e.g., Herbert M. Kritzer, Contingency Fee Lawyers as Gatekeepers in the

remain: many observers believe, for example, that the huge damages potentially available in some matters may force defendants to make "grey-mail" settlements that are substantial in amount even when the claims are of limited merit. Examples are a "bet-the-company" class action proceeding or when treble-damage or fee-shifting provisions provide an incentive for a plaintiff's attorney to bankroll cases that are marginal on the merits, but require substantial costs of defense and threaten a large recovery if successful.[11]

Professional Rules on Contingent Fees

Model Rule 1.5(c) specifically authorizes contingency fees where not prohibited by 1.5(d) or other law, but requires that all contingency fees be in writing.[12] Under M.R. 1.5(c), the writing must include:

> the method by which the fee is to be determined, including the percentage or percentages that shall accrue to the lawyer in the event of settlement, trial or appeal, litigation, and other expenses to be deducted from the recovery, and whether such expenses are to be deducted before or after the contingent fee is calculated.

M.R. 1.5(c) also requires the lawyer to provide the client with a written statement upon completion of the representation detailing the outcome, the client's share, the lawyer's share and how the lawyer calculated the division of proceeds.

Should the rules require that all fee contracts be in writing? That the lawyer relate the proposed fee to the factors specified in M.R. 1.5(a)? As proposed by the Kutak Commission and as adopted in some states, Rule 1.5(b) provides: "When the lawyer has not regularly represented the client, the basis or rate of the fee shall be communicated to the client in writing, before or within a reasonable time after commencing the representation." The ABA's version of M.R. 1.5(b) says such an agreement shall be "preferably in writing."

Contingent Fee Abuses

COMMITTEE ON LEGAL ETHICS OF WEST VIRGINIA STATE BAR v. GALLAHER.[13] Neva Dillon, age 64, a passenger in a car driven by her son, was seriously injured when the vehicle slid on icy roads and struck

---

Civil Justice System, Judicature 20–29 (July–Aug. 1997).

11. Matter of Rhone–Poulenc Rorer, Inc., 51 F.3d 1293 (7th Cir.1995) (Posner, J., arguing that mass tort class actions have an in terrorem effect that may necessitate a substantial settlement award when the action is not meritorious); see the discussion of class action lawyers in Chapter 8, infra.

12. Contingent fees are given little specific attention by the Model Code. DR 5–

103(A)(2) allows them as an exception to the general prohibition to acquiring a propriety interest in litigation; DR 2–106(B)(8) provides that whether a fee is contingent or fixed should be a factor in considering its reasonableness; and DR 2–106(C) prohibits them in criminal defense work. EC 2–20 states that contingent fees are "rarely justified" in domestic relations cases.

13. 376 S.E.2d 346 (W.Va.1988).

an approaching vehicle. There was no indication of negligent conduct on the part of the other driver. Mrs. Dillon, who "was not well educated, lacked prior experience with lawyers, and was unable to read and write," sought to recover her medical bills of $2,300 from her son's liability insurer. When the insurer rejected her claim, she retained Gallaher. Mrs. Dillon told Gallaher she did not want to sue her son but wanted to recoup her expenses from her son's insurer. Gallaher informed her that the possibility of recovery was rather slim but that he would pursue it. Fees were not discussed. Gallaher obtained copies of Mrs. Dillon's medical records and bills and forwarded them, with a demand for $8,500, to the insurer. Three weeks later Gallaher informed Mrs. Dillon that a $4,500 settlement offer was the best available. Mrs. Dillon agreed to the settlement and executed a release of claims. Gallaher told her at this time that his fee would be 50 percent of the settlement, or $2,250; no written fee agreement was ever executed. Mrs. Dillon and her son also understood him to say that the insurer would pay any future medical bills (which he later denied saying). When the insurer subsequently rejected a $569 medical bill, the Dillons returned to Gallaher and complained about the amount of his fee. He said the case was "closed" and that their only remedy was to sue him or report him to the state bar.

In the subsequent disciplinary proceeding, the court concluded that the 50 percent fee was excessive under DR 2–106. The opinion mentioned several circumstances in support of this conclusion: because of the family relationship, there was never any anticipation that a suit would be filed; the claimant was prepared to accept a modest settlement covering her medical bills, but because the lawyer's fee was so large, this limited objective was not achieved; the lawyer's investment of time and skill was de minimus (Gallaher claimed to have worked 16.6 hours on the case, seven of which followed the settlement); and even though risk was involved, the fee was grossly disproportionate to that risk. The court found a one-third fee of $1,500 reasonable, ordered the lawyer to refund the difference, and reprimanded the lawyer.

Virtues and Defects of Contingent Fees

The major virtues of the contingent fee are: *first*, from the client's perspective, this fee arrangement appears to align the lawyer's interest in earning a fee with the client's interest in gaining a larger recovery; *second*, the contingent fee shifts the risk of the lawyer being paid from the client to the lawyer; and *third*, the arrangement permits the client to borrow the amount of the lawyer's services and the expenses of the litigation from the lawyer. These psychological and economic effects provide the basis for the large degree of public acceptance of contingent fee arrangements. The bar's enthusiasm for the contingent fee may be influenced by the fact that current contingent fee arrangements may result in higher transaction costs in high-stakes cases and larger-than-average returns on lawyer time in smaller cases.[14]

---

14. Lester Brickman summarizes the available evidence as of 1989 in Brickman, Contingent Fees Without Contingencies: *Hamlet* Without the Prince of Denmark?, 37

The deficiencies and dangers of contingent fees emerge from study of (1) the incentives of lawyers under this fee arrangement, (2) the realities of lawyer-client communication in situations like that involved in the *Gallaher* case, and (3) the fact that in many cases the lawyer is bearing little risk of non-recovery. Studies of lawyer incentives agree that the popular view that lawyer-client objectives are aligned under the contingent fee ignores a substantial conflict of interest between lawyer and client built into the standard arrangement.[15] Because lawyers assess their rate of return on a per-hour basis, the interests of the client diverge sharply when the lawyer, by devoting 10 hours to preparing a case, can negotiate a settlement that is a substantial portion of the recovery that would be expected after much more extensive preparation and perhaps a full trial. For example, if the lawyer can settle a personal injury case against a liability insurer for $3,000 on the basis of ten hours' work (the equivalent of $300 per hour), but is likely to receive an award of $6,000 after 100 hours of work (the equivalent of $60 per hour), it is clearly in the lawyer's interest, but not the client's, for the lawyer to talk the client into accepting the $3,000 settlement offer. Doing so minimizes both time and risk for the lawyer: a certain recovery now as against the likelihood of a larger recovery after a much larger expenditure of lawyer time.[16]

The resulting conflict of interest becomes more serious because most individual clients lack awareness of it and the lawyer-client communica-

---

U.C.L.A. L.Rev. 29, 105–111 and 132–34 (1989); Herbert M. Kritzer concludes that "lawyers who take a case on a contingency fee basis can expect to do somewhat better than they do on their hourly fee cases. The occasional good case will yield some significant profits over and above the balancing out of the typical better than average cases and the worse than average cases. Under certain circumstances, lawyers can do much better from contingency fee work than most lawyers do from hourly fee work." Kritzer, The Wages of Risk: The Returns of Contingency Fee Legal Practice, 47 DePaul L.Rev. 267, 303 (1998) (empirical study of Wisconsin personal injury lawyers).

15. See Murray L. Schwartz & Daniel J. B. Mitchell, An Economic Analysis of the Contingent Fee in Personal Injury Litigation, 22 Stan.L.Rev. 1125 (1970); Kevin M. Clermont & John D. Currivan, Improving on the Contingent Fee, 63 Cornell L.Rev. 529 (1987); and Douglas E. Rosenthal: Lawyer and Client: Who's in Charge?, 96, 112 (1974) ("The widespread assumption that the contingent fee makes the lawyer 'a

partner' of the client in his claim with complete mutuality of interest in the ultimate case disposition is, in dollars and cents, simply not true.").

16. The pioneering article is Murray L. Schwartz & Daniel J. B. Mitchell, An Economic Analysis of the Contingent Fee in Personal Injury Litigation, supra. The analysis was refined by Kevin M. Clermont & John D. Currivan, Improving on the Contingent Fee, supra (proposing a fee agreement contingent on a positive recovery but including an hourly rate component as a way to align the economic interests of lawyer and client). An important variable is the risk averseness of both lawyer and client. The prevailing academic view is that contingent fee lawyers have inadequate incentives to prepare and pursue a claim thoroughly in cases with low or modest stakes. Conversely, "in high stakes cases, once lawyers have spent substantial time in preparation, they may be more inclined to gamble for a large recovery than clients with marginal resources and pressing needs." Rhode & Luban, Legal Ethics 699 (2d ed. 1996) (summarizing views of scholars).

tions which precede the execution of the fee agreement usually do not provide a candid discussion of the options available to the client and the divergence in lawyer incentives from those of the client. The informed consent idea has come late to the legal profession. Although professional rules now include a duty of communication on important decisions the client is entitled to make (see M.R. 1.4 and M.R. 1.2(a)), court decisions in fee and discipline cases have not generally enforced this duty in the context of initial fee arrangements. The common practice of most lawyers using contingent fees is to present a form agreement to an inexperienced client as the "standard arrangement" in the community or sector of practice. It is essentially an adhesion contract situation in which the client is not informed of other alternatives that may be in the client's interest. Nor are most individual clients in a position to shop around or make inquiries about alternative arrangements.[17]

The basic justification of the contingent fee is that it shifts the risks of the transaction to the party who is best able to bear them—the lawyer. Lawyers who specialize in a particular field of practice are in a much better position to assess the merit and expected value of a potential claim than lay people who have been injured in an accident. In performing this function, lawyers make prudent risk-management decisions: they decide to undertake cases that involve at least some minimum level of damages and have a reasonably good chance of success. Lawyers also reduce their risks by having a portfolio of such cases, relying on the fact that the vast majority will produce a reasonable award, a few will be big winners and another small percentage will be a partial or total loss.[18] The rationale of the contingent fee is that it rewards the lawyer for her willingness to undertake those cases that, although non-frivolous and plausible, turn out to be legal or economic losers (i.e., that result in a defendant's verdict or an award that fails to cover litigation expenses and the value of the lawyer's time).

Gallaher[19] is one of a small number of decisions that have upheld discipline of a lawyer for charging a contingency fee in a *tort* case not involving a substantial risk of recovery (but note that Gallaher's fee was 50 percent of the award rather than the customary one-third). A larger number of decisions have disciplined lawyers in *non-tort* situations when risk of non-recovery was absent. These are primarily cases in which the beneficiary of a life insurance policy, the beneficiary or creditor of an

---

17. See, e.g., Lisa G. Lerman, Clients Should Get the Benefit of Full Disclosure, ABA J., July 1995, at 45.

18. See Samuel D. Gross & Kent D. Syverud, Getting to No: A Study of Settlement Negotiations and the Selection of Cases for Trial, 90 Mich.L.Rev. 319, 337 (1992) (the success rate of personal injury claimants is one-third, about what one would expect if their lawyers were accepting the riskier cases that justify using the contingent fee).

19. Lester Brickman states that during the last half-century in which millions of contingency-fee tort cases have been handled by U.S. lawyers, only three cases have meted out discipline when no substantial risk was involved; 20 or so cases fall into the non-tort category. Brickman, Contingency Fee Abuses, Ethical Mandates, and the Disciplinary System: The Case Against Case-by-Case Enforcement, 53 Wash. & Lee L.Rev. 1339, 1357 n. 68 (1996).

estate, or the like, use a lawyer to gain a sum that is generally fixed in amount and certain of recovery.[20] Was the court correct in *Gallaher* in invalidating the fee agreement between the lawyer and client? In giving restitution to the client of the excessive amount of the fee?

In Gagnon v. Shoblom,[21] the plaintiff, Gagnon, observing a young woman with a disabled vehicle in the breakdown lane of a highway, pulled off the traffic lane to assist her. Moments later, while Gagnon was underneath the disabled vehicle in attempting a repair, it was hit by a loaded garbage truck driven by Shoblom. Gagnon, rendered a paraplegic by the accident, retained lawyer Goodman under Goodman's standard one-third contingency fee agreement. After extensive discovery and preparation, the lawsuit against Shoblom and his employer was settled for almost $3 million. Goodman's share was almost $1 million. The trial judge held a hearing on the reasonableness of the fee and determined that any fee compensation over $695,000 would be "unreasonable and excessive." Although Goodman had "handled the case expeditiously and well," this was a case in which the injuries were "catastrophic" and defendants' liability was apparent. The Massachusetts high court reversed, holding that the trial judge erred in disregarding the fee agreement. The client was not complaining and no statute or court rule permitted "a judge to substitute his evaluation of the legal services rendered pursuant to a contingent fee agreement."[22] But suppose the defendant employer had $10 million of liability coverage, Goodman had settled the case after only 20 hours of work and the client, objecting to the result and the fee, was supported by expert witnesses willing to testify that the expected award at trial would have been at least $5 million?[23] Is $50,000 per hour (a $1 million fee divided by 20 hours) a reasonable fee? Should a lawyer employ a contingent-fee agreement in a case involving little or no risk of non-recovery? Inform the client of other alternative fee arrangements? How can such rules be enforced?[24]

20. See, e.g., Committee on Legal Ethics of the W. Va. State Bar v. Tatterson, 352 S.E.2d 107, 112 (W.Va.1986) (35% contingent fee to recover life insurance payment was "clearly excessive" when there was "never any legitimate doubt about the receipt of the proceeds").

21. 565 N.E.2d 775 (Mass.1991).

22. Id. at 777. The *Gagnon* case is discussed in Lester Brickman, A Massachusetts Debacle: Gagnon v. Shoblom, 12 Cardozo L.Rev. 1417 (1991).

23. See Peter Passell, Contingency Fees in Injury Cases Under Attack by Legal Scholars, N.Y.Times, Feb. 11, 1994, at A1, B12, gives another example of a windfall fee: a Texas school bus case in which 21 children were killed in an accident, liability and damages were uncontested, and the claims were quickly settled. Under a standard one-third contingency fee agreement, lawyers for the plaintiffs received hourly returns estimated at between $12,500 and $25,000 per hour.

24. Ted Schneyer discusses the legal process aspects of regulating lawyer's fee arrangements. Some devices, such as after-the-fact case-by-case consideration of a fee's reasonableness, impose burdens that courts and disciplinary bodies are unwilling to undertake; and proposed substantive and procedural reforms, such as that of the Manhattan Institute, will change behavior but in uncertain ways and at unacceptable costs. "[T]he search for worthwhile fee control techniques ... [should] be guided by an appreciation of the institutional limits that constrain courts, legislatures, and the bar as designers and enforcers of fee regulations." Ted Schneyer, Regulating

Commentators differ concerning the extent to which the absence of a substantial risk of non-recovery should effect the validity of a "standard" contingent fee agreement. Partly at issue is the underlying question of whether market forces lead to a competitive equilibrium in setting the contingency percentage employed in particular tort fields. Charles Silver argues that competition for profitable cases among the large number of plaintiffs' lawyers results in market pricing; Lester Brickman argues that information asymmetry (the lawyer knowing the value and prospects of a case while the client is ignorant of both) combined with a professional tendency to stick with the traditional percentage make it a case of market failure, justifying regulation.[25] Empirical data, as mentioned earlier, is hard to come by and inconclusive.

Reforming the Contingency Fee: Manhattan Institute Proposal and ABA Response

In February 1994, two legal scholars, Jeffrey O'Connell and Lester Brickman, joined with Michael Horowitz of the Manhattan Institute to propose a legislative or judicial reform of the contingency fee.[26] The proposal, endorsed by a number of leading lawyers, is designed to lower transaction costs in cases, or portions of cases, where no real controversy exists between the parties, i.e., situations in which a substantial contingency fee is not justified by the risk because no real value-adding services are required of claimants' counsel.

The proposal would give the defendant in a personal injury case an opportunity to make an early settlement offer within 60 days of a plaintiff's demand for such an offer. If the defendant chose not to make an offer, the proposal would not apply and the plaintiff's lawyer would be free to negotiate a contingent fee, subject to current ethical restrictions. However, if an offer was made and accepted, the compensation to the plaintiffs' attorney would be limited to 10 percent of the first $100,000 and 5 percent of any greater amounts. If a settlement offer was made and refused, it would set a baseline for assessing the reasonableness of the contingency fee. Plaintiffs' demands and defendants' offers would need to be accompanied by information that is routinely discoverable to allow each side to assess the other's demand or offer.[27]

Contingent Fee Contracts, 47 DePaul L.Rev. 371, 412 (1998).

25. See Charles Silver, Control Fees? No, Let the Free Market Do Its Job, Nat'l L.J., Apr. 18, 1994, at A17; Lester Brickman, Contingent Fees Without Contingencies, supra, at 102–114.

26. Lester Brickman, Michael Horowitz & Jeffrey O'Connell, Rethinking Contingency Fees (Manhattan Institute Monography Series No. 1, 1994). The proposal is dis-

cussed in Peter Passell, Contingency Fees in Injury Cases Under Attack by Legal Scholars, N.Y.Times, Feb. 11, 1994, at A1, B12. One of the authors of this book was a member of the group supporting the proposal.

27. This summary is adapted from Michael Horowitz, Making Ethics Real, Making Ethics Work: A Proposal for Contingency Fee Reform, 44 Emory L.J. 173, 175–76 (1995).

The intent of the proposal is to link fees to the degree of risk actually borne by personal injury lawyers and their defense counterparts, and, by providing incentives for both sides to arrive at an early settlement, to reduce transaction costs dramatically. In theory, at least, the savings (estimated at $10 billion a year in lawyer fees) would be split between the plaintiff and the defendant. The losers would be lawyers—their fees would be reduced in all cases in which there were no factual disputes or legal uncertainties that would justify a substantial further commitment of value-adding lawyer services. Predictably, the proposal was opposed by *both* plaintiffs' lawyers and defense lawyers, who otherwise rarely agree on "tort reform" issues. Should state legislatures adopt the proposal?[28] What about the more modest proposal that lawyers should be required to disclose in writing to a contingency-fee client the actual services performed and the number of hours spent on the case?[29]

Some elements of the Manhattan Institute proposal were also put to the ABA ethics committee. The committee was asked to declare that a contingent fee of one-third to one-half of a settlement is a "reasonable" and therefore ethical fee only if early settlement offers by the defendant are conveyed to, and rejected by, the client. In Formal Opinion 94–389,[30] the committee refused to take sides in "the inflammatory and divisive policy issues" surrounding proposals to reform contingent fees, but then went on to provide a ringing endorsement of the status quo: a contingent fee is not unethical "when liability is clear and some recovery is anticipated" or when "a client can afford to compensate the lawyer on another basis." The opinion, however, does state that the client should be fully informed of alternative billing arrangements before a fee agreement is made.

Prohibitions on Use of Contingent Fees

Divorce Cases

The rationale for prohibiting contingent fees in divorce cases is that it contravenes the strong public interest in preserving marriages because

---

28. The proposal almost became law in California in the form of a voter initiative in 1998. When polls suggested that the initiative would be adopted, plaintiffs' lawyers launched a multi-million dollar ad campaign that resulted in a narrow defeat of the initiative.

29. This proposal was included in the Common Sense Legal Reform Act of 1995, H.R. Rep. No. 104–50 (1995), an outgrowth of Republican concern about high legal costs and frivolous litigation. Id.

30. ABA Committee on Legal Ethics and Professional Responsibility, Formal Op. 94–389 (Dec. 8, 1994). The opinion is criticized by Lester Brickman, ABA Regulation

of Contingency Fees: Money Talks, Ethics Walks, 65 Fordham L.Rev. 247 (1996) (the opinion, in "declaring the legitimacy of standard contingency fees in virtually all settings," "reflects the mutual financial interests of the trial and defense bars in protecting windfall fees as a way of promoting litigation"), and partially defended by Susan P. Koniak, Principled Opinions: Response to Brickman, 65 Fordham L.Rev. 337 (1996) (agreeing that the opinion is unprincipled in failing to give guidance to lawyers who routinely use a standard contingent fee in all situations, but correct on two other ethics propositions).

such a fee may interfere with reconciliation.[31] Divorce itself used to be regarded as against public policy except in very limited situations and in many states could be obtained only upon proof of criminal misconduct or adultery. A contingent fee was considered an unduly dangerous inducement to legal dissolution of marriage. The prohibition undoubtedly worked to the detriment of women, who in the typical marriage held little property or income-producing capacity and therefore lacked means to pay a fixed fee. In most marriages, this meant the male partner had greater freedom to dissolve the relationship and was at less financial risk in doing so than he would otherwise have been. On the other hand, a contingent fee deters the lawyer from facilitating reconciliation, for that would eliminate the division of property from which the fee could be paid. Moreover, in most jurisdictions the impecunious spouse, still usually the wife, can require the other party to pay attorneys' fees, including a part payment at the beginning of the litigation.[32]

The interest in encouraging reconciliation does not explain cases that disallow contingent fees in actions to modify or enforce divorce agreements.[33] If a lawyer takes a divorce case on a contingent basis, most states allow the lawyer to recover on the basis of quantum meruit. A number of commentators have criticized the prohibition of contingent fees in divorce cases.[34]

Criminal Defense Work

Contingent fees for defending criminal cases have traditionally been prohibited, although the reasons for doing so have been criticized.[35] Because a damage award is not created by a defense lawyer's efforts and winning a criminal case does not ordinarily increase the client's assets, a fee contingent on success would rarely be a necessary means to employ private counsel. Unless carefully drafted, a contingent-fee agreement for criminal representation might affect the client's choice in accepting a plea bargain or risking a trial. Defense lawyers, who generally prefer advance payment of a flat fee, have not pushed for permission to employ contingent fees. Finally, some fear persists that contingent fees would promote unscru-

---

31. See, e.g., Florida Bar v. Winn, 208 So.2d 809 (Fla.1968); In re Fisher, 153 N.E.2d 832 (Ill.1958); Baskerville v. Baskerville, 75 N.W.2d 762 (Minn.1956); McCarthy v. Santangelo, 78 A.2d 240 (Conn.1951).

32. See Wolfram, Modern Legal Ethics § 9.4.4 (1986). Compare Marriage of Gonzales, 124 Cal.Rptr. 278 (1975).

33. See, e.g., Licciardi v. Collins, 536 N.E.2d 840 (Ill.App.1989) (contingent fee unethical and therefore void in action to modify a divorce decree seven years after its entry).

34. For an argument that contingent fees should be allowed in divorce cases, see Comment, Professional Responsibility—Contingent Fees in Domestic Relations Actions: Equal Freedom to Contract for the Domestic Relations Bar, 62 N.C.L.Rev. 381 (1984).

35. See Restatement § 47 (although the black-letter rule continues the traditional ban on contingent fees in criminal cases, the reporter's note to comment c(i) states that "[t]he Reporters believe that the prohibition of criminal contingent fees should be relaxed, but no jurisdiction has done this").

pulous representation. Is overzealous misconduct more likely in criminal than in civil cases? More dangerous?

All states prohibit contingent fees for the defense of a criminal case. If a defense lawyer employs a contingent fee, the fee agreement is unenforceable, but the illegality of the fee arrangement is not enough to establish a claim for ineffective assistance of counsel in a postconviction proceeding for a new trial.[36] In Schoonover v. Kansas,[37] although the trial judge refused the defendant a new trial, he referred the lawyer to the state bar, which imposed discipline.[38]

Stronger arguments support a ban on financial arrangements that would make the compensation of prosecutors dependent upon success. A lawyer whose pay depends on securing a conviction will be tempted to prize convictions more than justice.[39]

Public Litigation

Should contingent fees be prohibited for lawyers retained by governmental bodies to enforce civil claims? Does this situation invoke the same policies that lead to prohibition of contingent fees in criminal cases? Government employment of lawyers on a contingent fee basis has generated few cases, probably because full-time government lawyers are compensated on a salary basis so the issue of contingent fees does not arise. But the practice of hiring private lawyers to prosecute governmental claims is growing rapidly. Federal agencies seeking to recover from those responsible for savings-and-loan failures have employed numerous private law firms, paying out million of dollars per year in fees. A contingent-fee arrangement with the Cravath, Swaine & Moore firm, calling for premium billing of up to $600 per hour in successful cases, led to congressional criticism.[40] Since then, many states have made controversial arrangements with plaintiffs' trial lawyers to pursue remedies against tobacco companies seeking recovery of health care expenditures allegedly caused by the promotion and sale of tobacco products.

36. See, e.g., People v. Winkler, 523 N.E.2d 485 (N.Y.1988); Downs v. Florida, 453 So.2d 1102 (Fla.1984); Schoonover v. Kansas, 543 P.2d 881 (Kan.1975). But see United States ex rel. Simon v. Murphy, 349 F.Supp. 818 (E.D.Pa.1972) (new trial granted where counsel represented defendant on contingent fee basis, which provided no fee if a guilty plea was entered, and counsel failed to communicate in a timely fashion to defendant the prosecutor's offer of a plea bargain to a lesser offense and persistently advised defendant not to plead guilty).

37. 543 P.2d 881 (Kan.1975).

38. In re Steere, 536 P.2d 54 (Kan.1975).

39. See Young v. United States ex rel. Vuitton et Fils S.A., 481 U.S. 787 (1987) (appointment of lawyers who represented plaintiffs in the private action from which this contempt prosecution emerged was improper because of their interest in the matter).

40. See Marianne Lavelle, Cravath S & L Fees Under Fire, Nat'l L.J., Apr. 20, 1992, at p. 3: "[Six Democratic senators calling for renegotiation of the fee arrangement] say that Cravath stands to earn more than $80 million under its current agreement with the Federal Deposit Insurance Corp., under which senior partners will earn bonus compensation amounting to $600 per hour."

The California Supreme Court held that a contingent fee is improper in any category of government civil cases "that demands the representative of the government be absolutely neutral."[41] The category includes eminent domain actions and actions to abate a public nuisance.[42] Is the same policy applicable to "private attorney general" actions brought under fee-shifting statutes, such as those applicable to civil rights, consumer and environmental claims?

Contingent Fee Schedules

A number of states have enacted so-called "tort reform legislation" as a means of curbing tort suits. These statutes typically prescribe maximum fee schedules for lawyers. In some states, for example New Jersey and New York, the maximum fee schedules apply to all personal injury cases handled on a contingent basis; in others, the fee schedules are limited to a particular type of suit, most commonly medical malpractice.

The fee schedules vary in detail but generally provide a descending sliding scale. For example, in California the plaintiff's lawyer in a medical malpractice case may charge no more than: 40 percent of the first $50,000 of client's recovery; 33 1/3 percent of the next $50,000; 25 percent of the next $500,000; and 15 percent of any amount exceeding $600,000.[43] Florida's limits on attorney's fees in medical malpractice actions permit a larger percentage in later stages of pursuing a claim (e.g., 40 percent after the jury is sworn), but restrict the contingency fee to 15 percent of any recovery in excess of $2 million.[44]

Some federal laws specify a single maximum percentage fee no matter how large the client's recovery. For example, the Federal Tort Claims Act allows fees no greater than 25 percent of any recovery once a case has been filed and 20 percent of any recovery prior to filing. The schedule encourages lawyers to file suit to gain a greater part of the recovery. What incentives do the California and Florida systems provide?

The courts generally have upheld these fee schedules whether they apply only to medical malpractice cases or more broadly.[45] But some decisions have struck down legislative fee arrangements applicable only to medical malpractice.[46]

41. People ex rel. Clancy v. Superior Court of Riverside County, 705 P.2d 347, 352 (Cal.1985).

42. See 705 P.2d 347, 352.

43. See California Medical Injury Compensation Reform Act of 1975 (MICRA), Calif.Bus. & Prof.Code § 6146.

44. Fla.Stat. § 766.109 (1988 Supp.).

45. See, e.g., Bernier v. Burris, 497 N.E.2d 763 (Ill.1986) (medical malpractice only); Roa v. Lodi Medical Group, Inc., 695 P.2d 164 (Cal.1985) (same); American Trial Lawyers v. New Jersey Supreme Court, 330 A.2d 350 (N.J.1974) (all personal injury cases).

46. See, e.g., Carson v. Maurer, 424 A.2d 825 (N.H.1980) (statute limiting plaintiffs' rights in medical malpractice cases and imposing a fee schedule for such actions held unconstitutional); Heller v. Frankston, 475 A.2d 1291 (Pa.1984) (statute requiring arbitration of medical malpractice claims and limiting attorney's fees in such cases unconstitutional).

In sustaining a maximum fee schedule, the Florida court in The Florida Bar,[47] also provided that a client may cancel any contingent contract within three days of its execution and required lawyers to provide clients with an elaborate statement of their rights. The lengthy statement of eleven paragraphs informs a client that she is entitled, among other things, "to bargain about the rate or percentage as in any other contract," inquire about the lawyer's education, training and experience in general and in handling similar cases, and "make the final decision regarding settlement." The lawyer, the statement provides, should inform the client whether the lawyer plans to handle the case alone or to refer it to another lawyer and under what terms; the possible adverse consequences of losing the case; and communicate any settlement offers immediately to the client.

Why is such a statement required only in contingent fee cases? Compare M.R. 1.5. Would the statement be more understandable if it covered fewer eventualities and were a lot shorter? Does a client need a lawyer to deal with her lawyer?

D. WHO SHOULD PAY FOR LITIGATION?

1. THE AMERICAN RULE AND ITS ALTERNATIVES[1]

The American rule is that each litigant must absorb her own litigation expenses, including attorney's fees. The "costs" typically awarded to prevailing parties do not begin to cover the actual costs of litigation, of which attorney's fees are the largest component. The origins of the American rule are obscure but apparently were a reaction by lawyers and judges to legislative fee limitations in the nineteenth century.[2]

Throughout most of the civilized world a prevailing litigant, whether plaintiff or defendant, recovers reasonable legal fees and other litigation expenses. This position on litigation expenses, referred to in the United States as "the English rule" or as "loser pays," has origins in Roman law. The English rule (two-way fee shifting in favor of the prevailing party) rests primarily on considerations of reparative justice: a successful party should be made whole by recovering the expenses necessarily entailed in vindicating a just claim or defense. This indemnity argument is supported in some instances by a punishment argument: a losing party who, by failing to settle a just claim or abandon a meritless one, has caused the winning party to spend money on legal fees should be punished by reimbursing the costs of the opposing party. Utilitarian arguments are also advanced on behalf of two-way fee shifting: frivolous or vexatious litigation should be

---

47. 494 So.2d 960, 964 (Fla.1986).

1. See Wolfram, Modern Legal Ethics § 16.6 (1986), for a good introduction to this topic.

2. See John Leubsdorf, Toward a History of the American Rule on Attorney Fee Recovery, 47 Law & Contemp.Probs. 9 (1984) (arguing that anti-lawyer sentiment expressed in limitations on awardable "costs" gave rise to the rule that parties were liable for their own attorney fees, thus separating fees from the award of costs).

discouraged (a deterrence argument) and dilatory tactics should be penalized.

The American rule, however, is deeply entrenched and efforts to dislodge it on either rightness or utilitarian grounds have failed repeatedly.[3] Arguments in favor of the American rule include the following:

- *Fairness.* The outcome of litigation is highly uncertain, especially in the United States, where law is more malleable and the application of law to fact more unpredictable than it is in England and many other countries. If a jury trial can be characterized as a "lottery," as some torts scholars argue,[4] it may be unfair to penalize the party who loses.

- *Reduced access to justice.* Saddling the loser with the winner's fees may discourage those with little means or large caution from using the judicial system. Risk-averse individuals generally will be more reluctant to bring lawsuits when there is some chance of losing.[5]

- *Administrative convenience.* Determining attorney's fees is difficult and tends to be hotly contested. A great deal of wasted effort— peripheral litigation not involving the merits—is involved in making an attorney fee award in every case unless, as in most foreign countries, relatively arbitrary amounts are awarded automatically.[6]

One-way fee shifting—the award of attorney fees to a prevailing plaintiff—is yet another alternative to the American rule, an alternative that has been embodied in more than 100 federal statutes and thousands of state laws.[7] The major federal enactment, on which others have been modeled, is the Civil Rights Attorney's Fees Act of 1976 (Fees Act), 42 U.S.C. § 1988, which provides:

> In any action or proceeding to enforce [certain listed civil rights statutes], the court, in its discretion, may allow the prevailing party,

3. The 1991 report of the Quayle Commission was one of the latest of these efforts. President's Council on Competitiveness, Agenda for Civil Justice Reform in America (1991) (favoring two-way fee shifting, as in the English rule).

4. See, e.g., Jeffrey O'Connell, The Lawsuit Lottery: Only the Lawyers Win (1979).

5. Aversion to the risks of being required to pay an opponent's litigation expenses varies with individuals and with types of litigants. In general, a one-time participant in litigation is likely to be more risk-averse than a "repeat player." See Marc Galanter, Why the "Haves" Come Out Ahead: Speculation on the Limits of Legal Change, 9 Law & Soc'y Rev. 95 (1974). An institutional litigant, such as a liability insurer, a large corporation or a government agency, is likely to be risk-neutral; it can predict the costs on the basis of past experience and can spread them over a portfolio of cases. See Charles W. Wolfram, The Second Set of Players: Lawyers, Fee Shifting, and the Limits of Professional Discipline, 47 Law & Contemp.Probs. 293 (1984).

6. See Werner Pfennigstorf, The European Experience with Fee Shifting, 47 Law & Contemp.Probs. 37 (1984) (reporting the fixed amounts of attorney's fees awarded, for example, in Germany).

7. In his dissent in Marek v. Chesny, 473 U.S. 1, 42–51 (1985), Justice Brennan listed more than 100 federal fee-shifting statutes. A survey of all fee-shifting legislation at the state level reported almost two thousand statutes; see Note, State Attorney Fee Shifting Statutes: Are We Quietly Repealing the American Rule?, 47 Law & Contemp.Probs. 321 (1984).

other than the United States, a reasonable attorney's fee as part of the costs.

On its face, this provision might be viewed as adopting the English rule ("loser pays" or two-way fee shifting). The legislative purpose, however, was to ensure that civil rights plaintiffs are provided with competent representation. The Supreme Court, relying heavily on the legislative history, interpreted the Fees Act as *requiring* a fee award for a prevailing plaintiff and as *permitting* one for a prevailing defendant only under very limited conditions.[8] Hence the Fees Act as construed is an example of one-way fee shifting to prevailing plaintiffs.

The economic effects of fee-shifting statutes have been studied extensively. Some things are clear, such as that a one-way fee shifting statute, providing a fee award to prevailing plaintiffs, stimulates the enforcement of the underlying right. The risk of having to pay the injured party's fees encourages the calculating actor to conform to the law rather than to risk liability.[9] Presumably legislators are acting on this insight in adopting discrete fee-shifting statutes in consumer, environmental, civil rights and other areas. One-way fee shifting provisions have other predictable effects.[10]

On other issues relevant to social policy, however, the effects of the various alternative fee provisions are less predictable. Simplistic assertions that adoption of the English rule would discourage litigation, increase the settlement rate, reduce total litigation expenditures and the like have been rejected by most scholars.[11] The subject is a very complex one, requiring consideration of a number of variables. The scholarly consensus, contrary to common understanding, is that the English rule, if transplanted to the United States, might result in more litigation and greater total legal

---

8. Newman v. Piggie Park Enterprises, 390 U.S. 400, 402 (1968), held that prevailing plaintiffs in civil rights actions are entitled to fee awards as a matter of course even though the losing defendant acted in good faith. Christiansburg Garment Co. v. Equal Employment Opportunity Comm'n, 434 U.S. 412 (1978), held that a prevailing defendant should not ordinarily be awarded fees unless the plaintiff's case was or became groundless or frivolous, or was pursued in bad faith.

9. See Richard Posner, Economic Analysis of Law § 21.9 (5th ed. 1998) (useful discussion of the effect of contingent fees, class actions, indemnity of legal fees, and Rule 11 on access to legal remedies and "legal error").

10. More claims will be asserted if a one-way fee shifting statute applies to a particular right. It is not clear, however, whether the rate of settlement will be affected. A great deal of party and judicial effort will go into the fee-setting process, discussed below. To the extent that governmental units bear the costs, they are shifted to taxpayers, and this may lead to downward pressure on fees that may make certain areas unattractive to many lawyers (e.g., low rates of compensation under the Criminal Justice Act of $30–$50 per hour). The frequency of situations in which a normal lawyer-client relation does not exist will multiply, e.g., when a public interest lawyer acts as "private attorney general" and defines the cause and the ways to further it.

11. The best source is the symposium on Attorney Fee Shifting, 47 Law & Contemp.Probs. 1 (1984), especially the article by Thomas D. Rowe, Jr., Predicting the Effects of Attorney Fee Shifting, id. at 39, which summarizes the economic findings in nontechnical language.

expenditures than the American rule. Given the difficulties of comparative analysis, in which so many other things affect results, uncertainty remains. Perhaps, given other societal and legal differences, the English rule is best for England and the American rule for the United States. Displacement of the American rule in discrete areas, resting upon the importance of vindicating certain legal rights or the desirability of deterring certain misconduct or both, has been the choice of American legislators.

2. COURT AWARDED ATTORNEY'S FEES

Common law exceptions to the American rule that parties bear their litigation expenses include: (1) situations in which the parties have provided for fee shifting by contract; (2) when the losing party has litigated in bad faith;[12] and (3) the common fund doctrine, applicable when a litigant expends attorney fees in creating a common fund from which others—such as a class of shareholders, trust beneficiaries or the like—may benefit.[13] The last doctrine has its source in federal equity jurisprudence but has been generalized in some states to a broader "doctrine that permits an award of fees to a party who has prevailed in an action in a way that benefits many other litigants."[14] One example is litigation establishing a scenic easement that significantly increases the value of neighboring properties.

Statutes Authorizing Award of Attorney's Fees

As previously indicated, many statutes now provide that a court will determine the attorney's fees to be awarded to a prevailing plaintiff by a defendant who settles or loses on the merits. Two-way fee shifting occasionally is provided, but usually the statutes, as in the Fees Act, prefer plaintiffs (one-way fee shifting to prevailing plaintiffs). Calculation of a "reasonable fee" under such statutes has consumed innumerable hours at the trial court level, generated a formidable number of appellate court decisions and occasioned much comment in legal journals.[15]

For some years a multi-factor approach stemming from the Fifth Circuit's *Johnson* case was followed by a number of federal courts.[16] A

---

12. See the discussion of Roadway Express, Inc. v. Piper, 447 U.S. 752 (1980) (inherent federal judicial authority to require a litigant, or a litigant's lawyer or both, who litigates in bad faith to pay the attorney fees of an opposing party) in Chapter 5 supra at p. 429.

13. See generally Wolfram, Modern Legal Ethics § 16.6.2 (1986).

14. Id. at 924.

15. See, e.g., Symposium on Fee Shifting, 71 Chicago–Kent L.Rev. 415 (1995) (articles on all phases); Dan B. Dobbs, Awarding Attorney Fees Against Adversaries: In-

troducing the Problem, 1986 Duke L.J. 435; Thomas D. Rowe, Jr., The Legal Theory of Attorney Fee Shifting: A Critical Overview, 1982 Duke L.J. 651; John Leubsdorf, The Contingency Factor in Attorney Fee Awards, 90 Yale L.J. 473 (1981).

16. Johnson v. Georgia Highway Express, Inc., 488 F.2d 714 (5th Cir.1974), listed twelve factors the trial court should consider in setting a fee, including all those listed in ethics rules (see M.R. 1.5(a); DR 2–106(B)). The Senate Report on the Civil Rights Attorney's Fees Awards Act of 1976 approved the *Johnson* formula. S.Rep. No. 94–1011, at 4. However, Supreme Court

second major method for setting attorney fees, commonly referred to as the "lodestar" method, was developed by the Third Circuit in *Lindy I* and clarified in *Lindy II*.[17] Under this approach a basic figure or lodestar was derived by multiplying the number of hours reasonably expended by a reasonable hourly rate for the attorney's services. The "lodestar" sum would then be adjusted upward or downward to reflect the contingent nature of the case or the unusual quality (good or bad) of the legal service in the particular case.

In Pennsylvania v. Delaware Valley Citizens' Council for Clean Air,[18] the Court noted the advantages of the *Lindy*-lodestar approach, stating that it "provided a more analytical framework ... than the unguided 'factors' [in] *Johnson*." Other Supreme Court cases have approved the lodestar approach[19] and City of Burlington v. Dague[20] appears to require it.

Problems in Implementing One–Way Fee Shifting

Problems in interpreting the Fees Act, 42 U.S.C. § 1988, and other one-way fee-shifting provisions have largely been resolved. Some of the major issues in application of federal fee-shifting statutes are:

When does a plaintiff "prevail"? For example, suppose a civil rights plaintiff wins on one of six claims against one of five defendants. Is a plaintiff entitled to a fee award under these circumstances? In general, the plaintiff receives an award of reasonable attorney's fees on any prevailing claim for which fee shifting is allowed if the claim meets a substantiality threshold.[21]

What is a "reasonable attorney's fee"? The lodestar method (hours reasonably expended multiplied by a reasonable hourly rate) has become "the guiding light" of the Court's fee-shifting jurisprudence.[22] The "reasonable hourly rate" turns out to be a community standard rather than an actual hourly rate in many cases. In Blum v. Stenson,[23] the Court held that the reasonable hourly rate for attorneys' fees is the prevailing rate in the

decisions appear to require lower courts to follow the lodestar method. See City of Burlington v. Dague, 505 U.S. 557 (1992) (stating that the lodestar fee is *"the* 'reasonable fee' "and rejecting one of the *Johnson* factors—the contingency of recovery); Pennsylvania v. Delaware Valley Citizens' Council for Clean Air, 478 U.S. 546, 563 (1986) (*Delaware Valley I*).

17. See, Lindy Bros. Builders v. American Radiator & Stan. San. Corp., 487 F.2d 161 (3d Cir.1973) (Lindy I), 540 F.2d 102 (3d Cir.1976) (Lindy II).

18. 478 U.S. 546, 563 (1986) (Delaware Valley I).

19. In Blum v. Stenson, 465 U.S. 886 (1984), Justice Powell, for a unanimous court, declared that the lodestar generally is "presumed to be a reasonable fee." The

Supreme Court also approved the lodestar approach in Hensley v. Eckerhart, 461 U.S. 424 (1983).

20. 505 U.S. 557 (1992).

21. See Smith v. Robinson, 468 U.S. 992, 1006 (1984) (plaintiff not entitled to attorney's fees under Fees Act for successful claim under another federal statute); Maher v. Gagne, 448 U.S. 122 (1980) (plaintiff is a "prevailing party" when rights are vindicated by consent judgment or settlement).

22. See City of Burlington v. Dague, 505 U.S. 557 (1992) (stating "a 'strong presumption' that the lodestar represents *the* 'reasonable' fee.") (emphasis added).

23. 465 U.S. 886 (1984).

community for the type of work performed, even where the attorneys are employed by a non-profit legal services organization.[24] A lawyer who customarily charges below the prevailing market rate in serving particular types of clients may nonetheless recover attorneys' fees based on the prevailing rate.[25]

May the lodestar fee be multiplied or enhanced when the plaintiff's lawyer has taken a case on a contingent-fee basis or when the case is novel or difficult? After wobbling on the issue for a number of years, the Court held that federal fee-shifting statutes do not permit contingency enhancement of a lodestar award.[26] The Court reasoned that one of the factors that might justify a fee enhancement—the relative difficulty of the case—was already included in the number of hours or the hourly rate that make up the lodestar fee or would come "at the social cost of indiscriminately encouraging nonmeritorious claims to be brought...."

May the "reasonable attorney's fee" greatly exceed the money damages awarded to a prevailing plaintiff? In City of Riverside v. Rivera,[27] the Court dealt somewhat inconclusively with the proportionality question. Police in Riverside, California, broke up a private party of Chicanos and arrested some of them in violation of state and federal law. A lengthy lawsuit resulted in a jury award of $33,350 followed by the trial court's award of almost $279,000 as a "reasonable attorney's fee." The Court upheld the fee award in a no-clear majority decision.

Four members of the Court in an opinion by Justice Brennan argued that the purposes of the Fees Act are served by including all hours reasonably expended. Measuring the award by the work actually done, Brennan said, serves the "private attorney general" policies underlying the Fees Act, which include provision of competent counsel in cases in which damages are relatively small. Four other justices, in an opinion by Justice Rehnquist, argued that a fee award 7.4 times as large as the award on the merits was unreasonable under the Fees Act. Justice Powell, who cast the controlling vote upholding the fee award, agreed with both sides. His opinion emphasized the discretion of the district court and the special findings in this case of the public aspects of the litigation.[28]

---

24. A prevailing plaintiff represented by a legal services organization is entitled to a fee award even though legal services lawyers work on a salary and are prohibited by law from charging a fee. See Evans v. Jeff D., 475 U.S. 717 (1986).

25. See Save Our Cumberland Mountains, Inc. v. Hodel, 857 F.2d 1516 (D.C.Cir.1988) (en banc).

26. See City of Burlington v. Dague, 505 U.S. 557, 563 (1992) (a "reasonable" attorney's fee can never include an enhancement for cases taken on contingency). In an earlier case, Pennsylvania v. Delaware Valley Citizens' Council for Clean Air, 483

U.S. 711 (1987), the Court divided 4–1–4 on the question. Justice O'Connor, who stated that sometimes an enhancement might be permissible, provided the decisive vote. *City of Burlington* rejects *Delaware Valley II* by a 6–3 vote.

27. 477 U.S. 561 (1986).

28. Id. at 584–85 (Powell, J., concurring). Given the subsequent changes in the personnel of the Court, the status of *Rivera* is unclear. See Quaratino v. Tiffany & Co., 166 F.3d 422 (2d Cir.1999) (en banc) (district court erred in reducing attorneys' fee to one-half of award but stating that court was taking no position on whether district

The *Rivera* concern about proportionality in fee awards discourages civil rights claims involving relatively small or uncertain claims and rewards defendants who fiercely resist meritorious claims. On the other hand, it protects defendants from facing a litigant who is not restrained by the practical consideration of keeping the costs of litigation in proportion to what is at stake, an asymmetry that may give plaintiffs' lawyers leverage to coerce unfair settlements.

Should statutory awards of attorneys' fees be limited to the amount provided in a plaintiff's contingent-fee arrangement with her lawyer? The Court has held that the lawyer's compensation is determined by the fee contract, which may provide either a higher or lower amount than the statutory fee awarded to the plaintiff.[29] For example, if a lawyer takes a civil rights damage action on a one-third contingent-fee basis and the award on the merits is $90,000, the lawyer receives the contract amount ($30,000) from the client whether the reasonable attorney's fee found by the court is $10,000 or $50,000. The statutory fee award is the plaintiff's, not the lawyer's.

Criticism of Lodestar Approach[30]

Scholars and judicial bodies have criticized prevailing fee-setting standards and methods in statutory fee-shifting cases.[31] The administrative costs of setting fees in each individual case are heavy, especially because both parties have an incentive to litigate the fee question extensively. Although the lodestar method has an appearance of objectivity, the resulting awards are highly variable and appear to reflect the attitudes of individual judges more than anything else.[32] Even more serious, the lodestar method "encourages lawyers to expend excessive hours, and, in the case of attorneys presenting fee petitions, engage in duplicative and unjustified work, inflate their 'normal' billing rate, and include fictitious hours or

court could reduce a lodestar figure if plaintiff wins a nominal victory).

29. Venegas v. Mitchell, 495 U.S. 82 (1990) (private fee arrangement can coexist with statutory fee award); Blanchard v. Bergeron, 489 U.S. 87 (1989) (attorney's fee under 42 U.S.C. § 1988 not limited to private fee arrangement).

30. For more on court awarded fees see the discussion of plaintiffs' class actions in Chapter 8 infra.

31. See, e.g., Symposium on Fee Shifting, 71 Chicago–Kent L.Rev. 415 (1995); and Report of the Third Circuit Task Force on Court Awarded Attorney Fees, 108 F.R.D. 237 (1985). The Third Circuit report, as well as some judicial decisions (e.g., Skelton v. General Motors Corp., 860 F.2d 250 (7th Cir.1988)), distinguishes sharply between "common fund" cases and statutory fee-shifting cases. In common fund cases, in which a lawyer's efforts produce a fund to be distributed to certain claimants or beneficiaries, the court should require the opposing parties to negotiate a percentage fee agreement, subject to the court's approval, at the outset of the case. Although risk enhancement in statutory fee cases penalizes the defendant with a strong case, this is not a problem in common fund cases, because the fee is charged against the plaintiff's recovery, not to the defendant.

32. The Third Circuit study states that the claim that judges "manipulate" the fee-setting process to achieve a pre-determined overall result "appears to be supported" by some empirical evidence. Id. at 247 and n. 32.

hours already billed on other matters, perhaps in the hope of offsetting any hours the court may disallow."[33] Judges are not in a position to police the hours expended as they occur and after-the-fact scrutiny is difficult and time-consuming. A further concern is that the lodestar method discourages early settlement of cases because lawyers on both sides have an incentive to keep the litigation alive to log more hours. Finally, the public interest bar charges that lodestar fees in securities and antitrust cases are set higher than those under the civil rights Fees Act, with discouraging effect on the willingness of lawyers to take those cases.

The Third Circuit report discusses these concerns at length and concludes with recommendations that a standardized table of hourly rates, applicable to all lawyers within a judicial district, be uniformly applied to all lawyers in all statutory fee cases. Judges should attempt to control hours by providing estimates of the maximum hours that will be compensated "so that the attorneys understand that excessive discovery or any other lawyer hyperactivity will not be tolerated or compensated."[34] These recommendations, especially standardized fees and recognition of a contingency element, are also intended to reduce the bias in fee setting against public interest lawyers.

3. SETTLEMENT CONDITIONED UPON FEE WAIVER

Evans v. Jeff D.

In Evans v. Jeff D.,[35] a class of mentally handicapped Idaho children sought injunctive relief against Idaho state officials, claiming that the inadequacy of educational and health care services provided to them violated their civil rights. The chief complaint was that the children were being kept in adult psychiatric facilities where they were abused by older patients. The class was represented by Johnson, a legal services lawyer, on a no-fee basis. Shortly before trial on the health care claims, the state made a generous settlement offer conditioned on waiver by the plaintiffs of any claim to attorney's fees or costs. Johnson, who was next friend of the class of minor children, accepted the offer in that capacity, but argued that the "coerced" waiver of attorney's fees was violative of the Fees Act of 1976, 42 U.S.C. § 1988. The district court rejected this contention and approved the settlement offer. The court of appeals reversed, approving the substantive portion of the offer but not its waiver of attorney's fees.

The Court, in an opinion by Justice Stevens, held (6–3) that the Fees Act does not prohibit all settlement offers conditioned upon a fee waiver and that the district court did not abuse its discretion in approving the fee waiver in this case. The majority opinion reasoned as follows:

The power of a district court under Rule 23 to approve settlements in class action cases does not permit the court to enforce some parts of a settlement offer while disapproving others; if the settlement offer is not

---

33. Id. at 247–48.
34. Id. at 263.

35. 475 U.S. 717 (1986).

approved in its entirety, the case must be tried on the merits. So the question was whether the Fees Act, properly interpreted, requires disapproval of a settlement offer that is conditioned upon a waiver of attorney's fees. The fee award entitlement belongs to the plaintiff class and not to the lawyer, who has an ethical duty to advance the client's interests rather than the lawyer's own interests (there is no conflict of ethical duties, but only a possible conflict with the underlying policies of the Fees Act).

The text of the Fees Act is silent on the issue of fee waivers, but the fee remedy is one of the "arsenal of remedies" that plaintiffs may use in enforcing their civil rights. The ability to give up one claim or remedy in order to advance another is an important aspect of civil rights enforcement. Marek v. Chesny,[36] upholding a lump-sum settlement offer that included damages on the merits as well as attorney's fees, stressed the importance of settlement in furthering the interests of civil rights plaintiffs. Settlements are discouraged unless defendants can determine the cost of the settlement package; if fees are left open, uncertainty about the amount of fees—which can be more substantial than the damages sought or the cost of injunctive relief—will discourage settlements. The flexibility in determining fees under the lodestar approach (determining the hourly rate, the number of hours that are reasonably expended on what claims, and the possibility of a "multiplier" or other adjustment) will stand in the way of settlements. Civil rights litigants, as well as the judicial system, will be disserved. Attempts to ban the simultaneous negotiation of fee awards and claims on the merits, the *Prandini* rule,[37] are impracticable and lead to circumvention.[38]

The district court, Justice Stevens concluded, did not abuse its discretion in accepting a settlement offer conditioned on a complete fee waiver. A state law or policy requiring a fee waiver in all cases would be violative of the Fees Act; and there may be other situations in which fee waiver is inappropriate. In this case, however, the extensive relief provided by the settlement was an adequate quid pro quo for the waiver of attorney's fees.

---

36. 473 U.S. 1 (1985).

37. Prandini v. National Tea Co., 557 F.2d 1015 (3d Cir. 1977) (holding that a ban on simultaneous negotiation of the merits and attorney's fees was required to prevent plaintiffs' lawyers from trading relief benefitting the class for a more generous fee for themselves).

38. In a footnote, Justice Stevens struck a cautionary note:

We are cognizant of the possibility that decisions by individual clients to bargain away fee awards may, in the aggregate and in the long run, diminish lawyer's expectations of statutory fees in civil rights cases. If this occurred, the pool of lawyers willing to represent plaintiffs in such cases might shrink, constricting the 'effective access to the judicial process' for persons with civil rights grievances which the Fees Act was intended to provide. H.R.Rep. No. 94–1558, p. 1 (1976). That the 'tyranny of small decisions' may operate in this fashion is not to say that there is any reason or documentation to support such a concern at the present time. Comment on this issue is therefore premature at this juncture. We believe, however, that as a practical matter the likelihood of this circumstance arising is remote. See Moore v. National Assn. of Securities Dealers, Inc., 762 F.2d, at 1112, n. 1 (Wald, J., concurring in judgment).

Id., at 743.

The ability to waive fees as part of a settlement offer is "a powerful weapon that improves [the ability of civil rights' victims] to employ counsel, to obtain access to the court, and thereafter to vindicate their rights by means of settlement or trial."

Justice Brennan, joined by Justices Marshall and Blackmun, dissented, arguing that the purpose of the Fees Act was undercut by fee waivers. The purpose of fee awards was to allow civil rights' victims to attract competent counsel. Allowing defendants to condition settlement of the merits on a waiver of fees will diminish the expectations of lawyers of receiving fees and decrease their willingness to accept civil rights cases. Once fee waivers are permitted, defendants will seek them as a matter of course. The Court's emphasis on encouraging settlements is a *judicial* policy and not a *legislative* one embodied in the Fees Act, which was concerned with victims getting competent lawyers. Moreover, the Court exaggerates the effect on settlements of leaving fees open, since the parties can exchange information on this subject in connection with negotiation of the merits.

Client Waiver of a Statutory Fee Award

What is a lawyer's proper course when offered a more-than-generous settlement for her client on the condition that she waive her attorney's fee? Was part of the problem in *Jeff D.* that the lawyer, not anticipating such an offer from the defendant, had not reached an understanding with the client as to what the response should be? Given the nature of the client in *Jeff D.*, with whom would such an understanding have been made?

Prior to *Jeff D.*, several bar associations had issued opinions holding it to be unethical for defendants to request fee waivers in exchange for relief on the merits. The majority emphasizes that these opinions were based on interpretations of the Fees Act and its purposes. In large measure that is true. Are these opinions vitiated by the decision in *Jeff D.*?[39]

The effects of *Jeff D.* depend largely on whether (1) the plaintiff's lawyer is a privately-retained one operating under a fee agreement or a non-profit legal services organization that depends on outside funding and is prohibited from undertaking representation on a contingent fee basis; and (2) the plaintiff's complaint seeks monetary relief or only injunctive relief. Lawyers handling cases seeking a monetary award can protect themselves by contract by obtaining a fee agreement providing that the fee will be paid out of the plaintiff's award. A non-profit legal services organization in a case seeking only injunctive relief, as in *Jeff D.*, is in a more difficult situation. There is no award from which a fee can be deducted; federally funded legal services grantees operate under regulations that restrict them from taking certain fee-generating cases; and the governing bodies and granting agencies that control and support public interest law

---

39. A law review note argues that *Jeff D.* should be taken as superseding state ethics decisions on this matter. See Comment, *Evans v. Jeff D.* and the Proper Scope of State Ethics Decisions, 73 Va.L.Rev. 783 (1987).

firms may prohibit or strongly protest the firm (or agency) bringing suit against the disadvantaged clients whom it is dedicated to serve.

Contracts Purporting to Restrict a Client's Right to Settle

Justice Brennan's dissent suggested that civil rights lawyers might find a way to live with *Jeff D.* by asking their clients to agree not to accept any settlement conditioned on a fee waiver or that would result in the lawyer's receiving less than a "reasonable fee," noting that it is a matter of local law whether such agreements would be allowed. What if "local law" consists of Model Rule 1.2? Comment [5] to Rule 1.2 states, "[T]he client may not be asked to agree ... to surrender ... the right to settle litigation that the lawyer might wish to continue."[40] What is wrong with agreements that limit the client's right to settle?[41]

Negotiating Attorney's Fees

In *Jeff D.* the Supreme Court rejected the ban on simultaneous negotiations articulated in Prandini v. National Tea Co.[42] The Court emphasized the need for the defendant to know what its ultimate liability would be before settling. Can this need be satisfied without permitting simultaneous negotiation of fees? The defendant's need for certainty on its maximum exposure might be satisfied by having the plaintiff's lawyer supply information on the firm's hourly charge and the number of hours worked, as the dissent in *Jeff D.* argued. This approach is more plausible now that the Court in *City of Burlington*, supra, apparently has rejected the possibility of the court awarding a multiplier to the basic "lodestar" calculation.

4.   LAWYER FINANCING OF CLASS ACTIONS

DR 5–103(B) of the Model Code provides that a lawyer may advance court costs and litigation expenses "provided the client remains ultimately liable for such expenses." Model Rule 1.8(e) removes the requirement that the client remain liable, allowing the lawyer to advance costs that can be recouped only if the client is successful on the merits. The major reason for this change was to permit "private attorney general" class actions, in which no single member of the class can fund the action but the lawyer would be willing to do so when there is a strong enough probability of success.[43]

---

40.   See Lewis v. S.S. Baune, 534 F.2d 1115, reh'g den., 545 F.2d 1299 (5th Cir.1977) (clauses in contract between lawyer and client prohibiting a settlement without lawyer's consent are void as against public policy). But see La.Rev.Stat.Ann. § 37–218 (Supp.1976) (permits a lawyer by contract to prohibit client from settling without lawyer's written consent).

41.   For a discussion of this question see Emily M. Calhoun, Attorney–Client Con-

flicts of Interest and the Concept of Non–Negotiable Fee Awards under 42 U.S.C. § 1988, 55 U.Colo.L.Rev. 341 (1984).

42.   557 F.2d 1015 (3d Cir.1977) (lawyers' fees may not be negotiated until the parties have reached settlement on the damage award of the underlying claim).

43.   See Mark Lynch, Ethical Rules in Flux: Advancing Costs of Litigation, 7 Litigation 19 (1981). For criticism of the change see

Some commentators approve of M.R. 1.8(e), arguing that it vindicates the enforcement of law and results in greater access to courts, and suggest that the rules should allow the lawyer to acquire property interests in class litigation.[44] Although In re "Agent Orange" Product Liability Litigation[45] suggests a much more restrictive approach to the financing of class action litigation, subsequent contractual arrangements by plaintiffs' class action lawyers in the mass tort field have been frequent and usually enforced.[46]

E.   LAWYER'S RELATIONSHIP WITH NON-CLIENTS

1.   COMMUNICATING WITH ANOTHER LAWYER'S CLIENT (ANTI-CONTACT RULE)

The law protects the lawyer-client relationship in a variety of ways. In addition to requirements designed to ensure commitment,[1] confidentiality[2] and loyalty,[3] the ethics rule prohibiting a lawyer from communicating on a matter with another lawyer's client provides further protection. The rule has assumed large importance in recent years because of controversies over application of the rule to contacts with employees of entity clients and to public and private investigatory activities that precede litigation. Violations of the rule may lead to professional discipline, disqualification, suppression of improperly obtained information and other remedies.[4]

Janet E. Findlater, The Proposed Revision of DR 5–103(B): Champerty and Class Actions, 36 Bus.Law 1667 (1981).

44. See the discussion of plaintiffs' class actions in Chapter 8 below at p. 812. On the funding of mass tort litigation, see Vincent R. Johnson, Ethical Limitations on Creative Financing of Mass Tort Class Actions, 54 Brook. L.Rev. 539 (1988).

45. 818 F.2d 216 (2d Cir.1987).

46. See Castano v. American Tobacco Co., 160 F.R.D. 544 (E.D.La.1995), rev'd, 84 F.3d 734 (5th Cir.1996). "[A]pproximately sixty of the nation's most powerful plaintiffs' law firms ... agreed to put up $100,-000 per year to cover litigation costs" to overcome the defendants' aggressive defense of claims. Richard L. Cupp, Jr., A Morality Play's Third Act: Revisiting Addiction, Fraud and Consumer Choice, 46 U.Kan.L.Rev. 465, 472 (1998).

1. See, e.g., Rule 1.3 (requiring "reasonable diligence and promptness in representing a client") and Canon 7 of the Model Code (stating that "a lawyer should represent a client zealously within the bounds of the law").

2. See the discussion of the attorney-client privilege, work-product doctrine and professional duty of confidentiality in Chapter 4.

3. The lawyer's duty to avoid conflicting interests that may impair the lawyer's representation of a client are discussed in the section that follows (conflicts with the lawyer's own interests) and in Chapters 7 and 8. Other rules prohibit certain kinds of outside interference with the relationship and seek to ensure that the lawyer's independent judgment is exercised on behalf of the client and not in the interest of third persons (see, e.g., Rules 1.8(f) and 5.4(c), prohibiting interference with a lawyer's independent professional judgment by third-party payors).

4. Disciplinary proceedings for violation of the anti-contact rule were relatively rare until recent controversies gave the rule more visibility. See Cleveland Bar Ass'n v. Rossi, 690 N.E.2d 501 (Ohio 1998) (public reprimand). Sanctions for violations of the rule occurring during a proceeding are much more frequent. See, e.g., Shoney's Inc. v. Lewis, 875 S.W.2d 514 (Ky.1994)

Model Rule 4.2 states that "[i]n representing a client, a lawyer shall not communicate about the subject of the representation with a person[5] the lawyer knows to be represented by another lawyer in the matter, unless the lawyer has the consent of the other lawyer or is authorized by law to do so."[6] This seemingly simple statement has given rise to wide-ranging and bitter controversy.

The "anti-contact rule" requires that lawyers communicate with other represented persons through those persons' lawyers and not by speaking to them directly. The rule allows direct communication where the other person's lawyer has consented or the law otherwise authorizes direct communication. An example of the latter situation is when the other party is the government; the First Amendment's right to petition for grievances allows some direct communication with the government itself.[7]

Neither client can consent to a prohibited contact without their lawyers' knowledge and acquiescence. The anti-contact rule, however, does not, and indeed could not, prevent one client from communicating with another. A lawyer cannot circumvent the rule by getting a non-lawyer to communicate with the party in the lawyer's stead.[8]

The anti-contact rule continues to apply even if a lawyer knows or believes that the other lawyer is violating a duty owed to her client or the client wants to waive the protection. In *The Verdict*, a movie based on an actual medical malpractice case, the plaintiff's lawyer, played by Paul Newman, receives a substantial settlement offer from the liability insurer for the hospital and doctors accused of malpractice. Newman allows the settlement offer to expire without informing his client's guardian, who is outraged when she hears what he has done. What steps may the defendants' lawyer take to bring a settlement offer to the attention of the

---

(disqualification); Faison v. Thornton, 863 F.Supp. 1204 (D.Nev.1993) (evidence excluded and lawyer disqualified and ordered to pay $46,000 in fees as sanction).

5. In August 1995 the ABA amended Rule 4.2, substituting "person" for "party" throughout the rule and amending the comments. As of mid–1999, ten states had adopted the amendment. The case law and most commentaries continue to employ the term "party." The significance of the change is unclear. Comment [3] to the original rule stated that '[t]his rule also covers any person, whether or not a party to a formal proceeding, who is represented by counsel concerning the matter in question." Most decisions accept this broad interpretation of "party," but some rest on a narrower view of party status in a proceeding or transaction. See, e.g., Matter of Simels, 48 F.3d 640, 649–50 (2d Cir.1995) (a represented person who was a possible wit-

ness against a lawyer's client and who might be charged with offenses arising out of the same events was not a "party" within the meaning of DR 7–104(A)(1)).

6. DR 7–104(A)(1) is substantially identical. Restatement § 158(1) states the anti-contact prohibition similarly, but spells out some issues not dealt with in M.R. 4.2: contact with public officers, response to an emergency and when the lawyer is a party and represents no one else in the matter.

7. Vega v. Bloomsburgh, 427 F.Supp. 593 (D.Mass.1977).

8. M.R. 8.4(a) (violating a professional rule through the acts of another); People v. Hobson, 348 N.E.2d 894 (N.Y.1976) (police officer obtained incriminating statements from criminal defendant in police custody without notice to or presence of defendant's lawyer). But compare ABA Formal Op. 92–362 (1992), discussed infra.

plaintiff?[9] Direct communication is prohibited by the anti-contact rule, even if it takes the relatively non-obtrusive form of a copy of a letter sent to the plaintiff's lawyer. But what if the plaintiff calls the defendants' lawyer and states: "My lawyer tells me nothing and does not return my phone calls. Have you made a settlement offer?" May the lawyer handle the problem by advising his client to talk directly with the opposing party? A 1992 ABA ethics opinion provides an affirmative response and the Restatement takes the same position.[10]

The purpose of the anti-contact rule is to protect the lawyer-client relationship from outside interference, prevent deception of a lay person, and protect confidential information.[11] The fear is that an inexperienced client, such as the personal injury claimant in *The Verdict*, may relinquish legal rights or lose confidence in her lawyer if a skilled professional representing an opposing interest is free to make direct contact. But should that desirable policy extend to situations in which the lawyer who is being bypassed is violating duties to her client and the client initiates the contact? Why are clients prevented from making an informed waiver of the protection?

John Leubsdorf argues that the anti-contact rule is given too broad an application.[12] He proposes that a lawyer be allowed to communicate with any person by letter with a simultaneous copy to the person's lawyer or directly as long as that person's lawyer is informed prior to the contact. The anti-contact rule gives a lawyer control of the flow of information to her client. Does it make inexperienced individual clients more dependent on their lawyers?

The anti-contact rule is easy to apply and relatively non-controversial when the matter is a transaction or litigation involving individual clients on both sides. The problems arise primarily in situations in which a private lawyer or government agency needs or wants to make a factual inquiry

---

9. The presumably permissible steps are that a lawyer may urge the other party's lawyer to have her client present at a settlement conference, seek the opposing lawyer's consent to make direct contact with her client, try to obtain the court's assistance in communicating with the opposing party, and report the lawyer's failure to communicate the settlement offer to the state disciplinary agency. How useful or effective are these steps likely to be?

10. ABA Formal Op. 92–362 (1992) (lawyer may advise her client to communicate directly with the opposing party; good representation involves advising a client about lawful alternatives that may be in the client's interest); but cf. In re Marietta, 569 P.2d 921 (Kan.1977) (discipline for having "caused" client-client contact). Restatement § 158(2) provides that the anti-contact rule "does not prohibit the lawyer from assisting the client in otherwise proper communication by the lawyer's client with a represented non-client, unless the lawyer thereby seeks to deceive or overreach the non-client."

11. Restatement § 158, cmt. *b*, states three reasons for the rule: to "protect against overreaching and deception of non-clients," protect "the relationship between the represented non-client and that person's lawyer," and assure "the confidentiality of the non-client's communications with the lawyer."

12. John Leubsdorf, Communicating with Another Lawyer's Client: The Lawyer's Veto and the Client's Interest, 127 U.Pa. L.Rev. 683 (1979). On the anti-contact rule generally, see Restatement §§ 158–62; Wolfram § 11.6.2.

before instituting formal proceedings. How can a lawyer, after hearing the story of a potential client or victim, decide whether formal legal action is required without gathering information from possible witnesses, including participants and observers of the events in question? The lawyer's dilemma is heightened when the potential defendant is an organization and the potential witnesses are its agents or employees. Difficult issues also arise when public prosecutors, seeking to enforce regulatory or criminal statutes, send out investigators to interview potential witnesses or targets. Some informed potential targets may already have retained lawyers and informed the prosecutor of this fact; others may be employees of the organization that is the investigatory target. Issues of the appropriate meaning and scope of the anti-contact rule then move beyond the important concerns of protecting the lawyer-client relationship and become broader issues of public and private enforcement of legal obligations.[13] Should the balance be struck by courts, heavily influenced in rule-making by the organized bar, or by legislatures or the executive branch?

Niesig v. Team I

Court of Appeals of New York, 1990.
76 N.Y.2d 363, 559 N.Y.S.2d 493, 558 N.E.2d 1030.

■ KAYE, JUDGE.

Plaintiff in this personal injury litigation, wishing to have his counsel privately interview a corporate defendant's employees who witnessed the accident, puts before us a question that has generated wide interest: are the employees of a corporate party also considered "parties" under Disciplinary Rule 7–104(A)(1) of the Code of Professional Responsibility, which prohibits a lawyer from communicating directly with a "party" known to have counsel in the matter?[1] The trial court and the Appellate Division both answered that an employee of a counseled corporate party in litigation is by definition also a "party" within the rule, and prohibited the interviews. For reasons of policy, we disagree.

As alleged in the complaint, plaintiff was injured when he fell from scaffolding at a building construction site. At the time of the accident he was employed by DeTrae Enterprises, Inc.; defendant J.M. Frederick was the general contractor, and defendant Team I the property owner. Plaintiff thereafter commenced a damages action against defendants, asserting two causes of action centering on Labor Law § 240, and defendants brought a third-party action against DeTrae.

---

13. See Ernest Lidge, Government Civil Investigations and the Ethical Ban on Communicating with Represented Parties, 67 Ind.L.J. 549 (1992).

1. . . . Employees individually named as parties in the litigation, and employees individually represented by counsel, are not within the ambit of the question presented by this appeal. Nor, obviously, are direct interviews on consent of counsel, or those authorized by law, or communications by the client himself (unless instigated by counsel).

Plaintiff moved for permission to have his counsel conduct ex parte interviews of all DeTrae employees who were on the site at the time of the accident, arguing that these witnesses to the event were neither managerial nor controlling employees and could not therefore be considered "personal synonyms for DeTrae." DeTrae opposed the application, asserting that the disciplinary rule barred unapproved contact by plaintiff's lawyer with any of its employees. Supreme Court denied plaintiff's request, and the Appellate Division modified by limiting the ban to DeTrae's current employees.

. . .

In the main we disagree with the Appellate Division's conclusions. However, because we agree with the holding that DR 7–104(A)(1) applies only to current employees, not to former employees, we modify rather than reverse its order, and grant plaintiff's motion to allow the interviews.

We begin our analysis by noting that what is at issue is a disciplinary rule, not a statute. In interpreting statutes, which are the enactments of a coequal branch of government and an expression of the public policy of this State, we are of course bound to implement the will of the Legislature; statutes are to be applied as they are written or interpreted to effectuate the legislative intention. The disciplinary rules have a different provenance and purpose. Approved by the New York State Bar Association and then enacted by the Appellate Divisions, the Code of Professional Responsibility is essentially the legal profession's document of self-governance, embodying principles of ethical conduct for attorneys as well as rules for professional discipline (see, Code of Professional Responsibility, Preliminary Statement, McKinney's Cons.Law of N.Y., Book 29, at 355). While unquestionably important, and respected by the courts, the code does not have the force of law (see, Matter of Weinstock, 40 N.Y.2d 1, 6, 351 N.E.2d 647).

That distinction is particularly significant when a disciplinary rule is invoked in litigation, which in addition to matters of professional conduct by attorneys, implicates the interests of nonlawyers. . . . In such instances, we are not constrained to read the rules literally or effectuate the intent of the drafters, but look to the rules as guidelines to be applied with due regard for the broad range of interests at stake. . . .

DR 7–104(A)(1), which can be traced to the American Bar Association Canons of 1908, fundamentally embodies principles of fairness. "The general thrust of the rule is to prevent situations in which a represented party may be taken advantage of by adverse counsel; the presence of the party's attorney theoretically neutralizes the contact." (Wright v. Group Health Hosp., 103 Wash.2d 192, 197, 691 P.2d 564, 567.) By preventing lawyers from deliberately dodging adversary counsel to reach—and exploit—the client alone, DR 7–104(A)(1) safeguards against clients making improvident settlements, ill-advised disclosures and unwarranted concessions (see, 1 Hazard & Hodes, Lawyering, at 434–435 [1989 Supp.]; Wolfram, Modern Legal Ethics § 11.6, at 613 [Practitioner's ed. 1986]; Leubsdorf, Communicating with Another Lawyer's Client: The Lawyer's Veto and the Client's Interests, 127 U.Pa.L.Rev. 683, 686 [1979]).

There is little problem applying DR 7–104(A)(1) to individuals in civil cases. In that context, [the] meaning of "party" is ordinarily plain enough: it refers to the individuals, not to their agents and employees.... The question, however, becomes more difficult when the parties are corporations—as evidenced by a wealth of commentary, and controversy, on the issue [citing numerous articles].

The difficulty is not in whether DR 7–104(A)(1) applies to corporations. It unquestionably covers corporate parties, who are as much served by the rule's fundamental principles of fairness as individual parties. But the rule does not define "party," and its reach in this context is unclear. In litigation only the entity, not its employee, is the actual named party; on the other hand, corporations act solely through natural persons, and unless some employees are also considered parties, corporations are effectively read out of the rule. The issue therefore distills to *which* corporate employees should be deemed parties for purposes of DR 7–104(A)(1), and that choice is one of policy. The broader the definition of "party" in the interests of fairness to the corporation, the greater the cost in terms of foreclosing vital informal access to facts.

The many courts, bar associations and commentators that have balanced the competing considerations have evolved various tests, each claiming some adherents, each with some imperfection (see generally, Annotation, Right of Attorney to Conduct Ex Parte Interviews with Corporate Party's Nonmanagement Employees, 50 ALR4th 652 [1986] [collecting cases]). At one extreme is the blanket rule adopted by the Appellate Division and urged by defendants, and at the other is the "control group" test—both of which we reject. The first is too broad and the second too narrow.

Defendants' principal argument for the blanket rule[3]—correlating the corporate "party" and all of its employees—rests on Upjohn v. United States (449 U.S. 383). As the Supreme Court recognized, a corporation's attorney-client privilege includes communications with low-and mid-level employees; defendants argue that the existence of an attorney-client *privilege* also signifies an attorney-client *relationship* for purposes of DR 7–104(A)(1).

Upjohn, however, addresses an entirely different subject with policy objectives that have little relation to the question whether a corporate employee should be considered a "party" for purposes of the disciplinary rule. First, the privilege applies only to *confidential communications* with counsel (see, CPLR 4503), it does not immunize the underlying factual information—which is in issue here—from disclosure to an adversary (see also, Upjohn v. United States, 449 U.S. at 395–396 supra). Second, the

---

3. This rule was adopted only in one formerly reported decision and three bar association ethics committee opinions [but two are from New York and other opinion and decision are from California where] a new disciplinary rule ... permits attorneys to initiate ex parte interviews with certain employees of a corporation (see, Cal. Rules Prof. Conduct, rule 2–100; Triple A Mach. Shop v. State of California, 261 Cal.Rptr. 493).

attorney-client privilege serves the societal objective of encouraging open communication between client and counsel (see, Rossi v. Blue Cross & Blue Shield, 73 N.Y.2d 588, 592, 540 N.E.2d 703), a benefit not present in denying informal access to factual information. Thus, a corporate employee who may be a "client" for purposes of the attorney-client privilege is not necessarily a "party" for purposes of DR 7–104(A)(1).

The single indisputable advantage of a blanket preclusion—as with every absolute rule—is that it is clear. No lawyer need ever risk disqualification or discipline because of uncertainty as to which employees are covered by the rule and which not. The problem, however, is that a ban of this nature exacts a high price in terms of other values, and is unnecessary to achieve the objectives of DR 7–104(A)(1).

Most significantly, the Appellate Division's blanket rule closes off avenues of informal discovery of information that may serve both the litigants and the entire justice system by uncovering relevant facts, thus promoting the expeditious resolution of disputes. Foreclosing all direct, informal interviews of employees of the corporate party unnecessarily sacrifices the long-recognized potential value of such sessions. "A lawyer talks to a witness to ascertain what, if any, information the witness may have relevant to his theory of the case, and to explore the witness' knowledge, memory and opinion—frequently in light of information counsel may have developed from other sources. This is part of an attorney's so-called work product." (International Business Machs. Corp. v. Edelstein, 526 F.2d 37, 41 [citing Hickman v. Taylor, 329 U.S. 495]. Costly formal depositions that may deter litigants with limited resources, or even somewhat less formal and costly interviews attended by adversary counsel, are no substitute for such off-the-record private efforts to learn and assemble, rather than perpetuate, information.

Nor, in our view, is it necessary to shield all employees from informal interviews in order to safeguard the corporation's interest. Informal encounters between a lawyer and an employee-witness are not—as a blanket ban assumes—invariably calculated to elicit unwitting admissions; they serve long-recognized values in the litigation process. Moreover, the corporate party has significant protection at hand. It has possession of its own information and unique access to its documents and employees; the corporation's lawyer thus has the earliest and best opportunity to gather the facts, to elicit information from employees, and to counsel and prepare them so that they will not make the feared improvident disclosures that engendered the rule.

We fully recognize that, as the Appellate Division observed, every rule short of the absolute poses practical difficulties as to where to draw the line, and leaves some uncertainty as to which employees fall on either side of it. Nonetheless, we conclude that the values served by permitting access to relevant information require that an effort be made to strike a balance, and that uncertainty can be minimized if not eliminated by a clear test that will become even clearer in practice.

We are not persuaded, however, that the "control group" test—defining "party" to include only the most senior management exercising substantial control over the corporation—achieves that goal. Unquestionably, that narrow (though still uncertain) definition of corporate "party" better serves the policy of promoting open access to relevant information. But that test gives insufficient regard to the principles motivating DR 7–104(A)(1), and wholly overlooks the fact that corporate employees other than senior management also can bind the corporation. The "control group" test all but "nullifies the benefits of the disciplinary rule to corporations." ... Given the practical and theoretical problems posed by the "control group" test, it is hardly surprising that few courts or bar associations have ever embraced it.[4]

By the same token, we find unsatisfactory several of the proposed intermediate tests, because they give too little guidance, or otherwise seem unworkable. In this category are the case-by-case balancing test (see, B.H. v. Johnson, 128 F.R.D. 659 [N.D.Ill.]; Morrison v. Brandeis Univ. [125 F.R.D. 312 [D. Mass]]), and a test that defines "party" to mean corporate employees only when they are interviewed about matters within the scope of their employment (Committee on Professional Ethics, Ass'n of Bar of City of N.Y., Opn. No. 80–46 [1980]; Committee on Professional Ethics, Massachusetts Bar Ass'n, Formal Opn. No. 82–7 [1982]). The latter approach is based on rule 801(d)(2)(D) of the Federal Rules of Evidence, a hearsay exception for statements concerning matters within the scope of employment, which is different from the New York State rule....

The test that best balances the competing interests, and incorporates the most desirable elements of the other approaches, is one that defines "party" to include corporate employees whose acts or omissions in the matter under inquiry are binding on the corporation (in effect, the corporation's "alter egos") or imputed to the corporation for purposes of its liability, or employees implementing the advice of counsel. All other employees may be interviewed informally.

Unlike a blanket ban or a "control group" test, this solution is specifically targeted at the problem addressed by DR 7–104(A)(1). The potential unfair advantage of extracting concessions and admissions from those who will bind the corporation is negated when employees with "speaking authority" for the corporation, and employees who are so closely identified with the interests of the corporate party as to be indistinguishable from it, are deemed "parties" for purposes of DR 7–104(A)(1). Concern for the protection of the attorney-client privilege prompts us also to include in the definition of "party" the corporate employees responsible for actually effectuating the advice of counsel in the matter (see, Polycast Technology

---

4. A "control group" test was adopted in Fair Automotive Repair v. Car–X Serv. Sys. (128 Ill.App.3d 763, 84 Ill.Dec. 25, 471 N.E.2d 554), Maxwell v. Southwestern Bell Tel. Co. (No. 80–4239 [D.Kan., Oct. 28, 1980]), and three bar association opinions (Los angeles County Bar Ass'n Opn. No. 369 [1977]; Arizona State Bar Ass'n Opn. No. 303 [1966]; Idaho State Bar Ass'n Opn. No. 21 [1960]).

Corp. v. Uniroyal, Inc., 129 F.R.D. 621, 625, 628, 629 [S.D.N.Y.]; 1 Hazard & Hodes, op. cit., at 436–437).

In practical application, the test we adopt thus would prohibit direct communication by adversary counsel "with those officials, but only those, who have the legal power to bind the corporation in the matter or who are responsible for implementing the advice of the corporation's lawyer, or any member of the organization whose own interests are directly at stake in a representation." (Wolfram, op. cit., § 11.6, at 613.) This test would permit direct access to all other employees, and specifically—as in the present case—it would clearly permit direct access to employees who were merely witnesses to an event for which the corporate employer is sued.

Apart from striking the correct balance, this test should also become relatively clear in application. It is rooted in developed concepts of the law of evidence and the law of agency, thereby minimizing the uncertainty facing lawyers about to embark on employee interviews. A similar test, moreover, is the one overwhelmingly adopted by courts and bar associations[5] throughout the country, whose long practical experience persuades us that—in day-to-day operation—it is workable.[6]

... Defendants' assertions that ex parte interviews should not be permitted because of the dangers of overreaching ... impel us to add the cautionary note that, while we have not been called upon to consider questions relating to the actual conduct of such interviews, it is of course assumed that attorneys would make their identity and interest known to interviewees and comport themselves ethically.

■ [JUDGE BELLACOSA, concurring in the result, argued that the "control group" test was preferable as a matter of policy and because it was more easily applied:]

[T]he "control group" definition better balances the respective interests by allowing the maximum number of informal interviews among persons with potentially relevant information, while safe-guarding the attorney protections afforded the men and women whose protection may well be of paramount concern—those at the corporate helm and the fictional entity itself, the corporation. Also, this approach is more consistent with the ordinary understanding and meaning of "party", and more reasonably fits the purpose for which the disciplinary rule exists; a profes-

---

5. See, e.g., Wright v. Group Health Hosp., 691 P.2d 564 (Wash.1984); Bey v. Village of Arlington Hgts., 50 Fair Empl.Prac.Cas. (BNA) 1375 (N.D.Ill.); Chancellor v. Boeing Co., 678 F.Supp. 250 [D.Kan.]; ... see also, ABA/BNA Lawyers' Manual on Professional Conduct, at 71:303–71:304 (1984)....

6. Given the nationwide experience with the test we now adopt, we find no basis for the assertion made in the concurrence that the test will unnecessarily curtail informal fact gathering or itself generate litigation....

[W]e are reversing the Appellate Division's [blanket] prohibition and permitting interviews of employee-witnesses to an accident, which would not be allowed under a blanket ban. In order to put to rest any possible confusion, we make clear that the definition of "party" we adopt for the purposes of DR 7–104(A)(1) is not derived from the Official Comment to ABA Model Rule 4.2....

sional responsibility purpose quite distinct from enactments in public law prescribing the rights and protections of parties to litigation.

———

Who Is a Represented Person or Party for Purposes of Anti-Contact Rule?

What difference does it make whether the plaintiff's lawyer may interview employees who were at the injury site? Why did unions, public interest groups and the New York attorney general file amicus briefs on the issue before the court? How will conversations with these possible witnesses interfere with the relationship between DeTrae and its lawyer?

The court in *Niesig* describes the various interpretations that might be given to the term "party" as used in M.R. 4.2[14] and DR 7–104(A)(1). These interpretations range from prohibiting ex parte contact with any agents of the opposing party to prohibiting contact only with the control group of the corporation. What reasons does the court give for defining "party" as it does? Why does the court reject the *Upjohn* analogy? *Upjohn,*, supra p. 209, personified an organizational "client" for the purpose of the attorney-client privilege as including communications on a legal matter from low-level company employees to a company lawyer.

Is the court's statement that *former employees* may be interviewed consistent with the employee categories enumerated as protected, e.g., when vicarious liability for the employer may flow from the statement of a former employee? Judicial decisions on whether former employees may be considered as still under the organizational umbrella are inconsistent, but most recent cases follow *Niesig* in permitting the contact unless there is a special confidentiality agreement with the particular former employee.[15]

Comment [4] of M.R. 4.2 states that the rule prohibits communications to any organizational representative "whose statement may constitute an admission on the part of the organization." Some cases and commentators have interpreted this comment as extending to any employee whose statement would be admissible against the corporation even though it would not be a binding admission under agency law.[16] *Niesig* explicitly rejects this view (see the last sentence of footnote 6). Whether to read the "admission"

---

14. As indicated earlier, the ABA amended Rule 4.2 in 1995, substituting "person" for "party" throughout the rule and its comments. However, few states have adopted the amendment as yet, and ethics rules and judicial decisions continue to talk of a represented "party."

15. See, e.g., H.B.A. Management, Inc. v. Schwartz, 693 So.2d 541, 542 (Fla.1997); Aiken v. Business & Industry Health Group, 885 F.Supp. 1474 (D.Kan.1995) (reviewing authorities). Rule 4.2 makes no mention of former agents or employees in either text or comment, but two ABA ethics opinions state that the rule does not prohibit generally prohibit informal contacts with former employees: ABA Formal Op. 91–359, reaff'd, ABA Formal Op. 95–396.

16. See Sherman L. Cohn, The Organizational Client: Attorney–Client Privilege and the No–Contact Rule, 10 Geo.J. Legal Eth. 739, 776–78 (1997).

language of the Comment as referring to evidence law (which would extend the reach of 4.2 to all employees of a corporation whether or not their conduct is in issue) or to agency law (which would circumscribe the reach of 4.2 to a much smaller group of agents) is an important question.[17] Under the federal evidence rule, followed in a number of states but not in New York, "any statement by a party's agent or servant concerning a matter within the scope of the agency or employment" is admissible against that party even though not binding it.[18]

If the purpose of the anti-contact rule as applied to entities is to protect the organization, why is it that when an employee is separately represented, a lawyer seeking an interview need only obtain the consent of the employee's lawyer and not also that of the organization's lawyer?[19]

May a lawyer apply the *Niesig* test with ease and confidence that an informal interview will not lead to charges of misconduct, a disqualification motion or possible exclusion of the resulting evidence? *Niesig* places the responsibility on each lawyer to apply the court's rule; some other decisions ask the lawyer to seek judicial approval on a case-to-case basis before talking with witnesses.[20] Consider the implications of this case-by-case balancing approach, requiring the judge to decide in every case who a lawyer may interview, on the cost of litigation and the possibility of making the pre-filing investigation of facts called for by Rule 11.

Does a broad view of the employees who are protected from contact stack the decks against a party seeking facts in connection with a claim against the organization? In Weider Sports Equip. Co., Ltd. v. Fitness First, Inc.,[21] the court rejected the broad interpretation offered by the organizational party, stating:

> ... Rule 4.2 as [the corporate defendant] would have the court apply it, is not a matter of ethics but becomes, in reality, a rule of political and economic power that shelters organizations, corporations and other business enterprises from the legitimate less costly inquiry and fact-gathering process necessary to make a legitimate assessment of whether a valid claim for relief exists.

---

17. Restatement § 159(2), following *Niesig*, prohibits communication with an organizational representative "whose statements, under applicable rules of evidence, would have the effect of binding the organization with respect to proof of the matter," but not with one who is merely an occurrence witness (i.e., whose conduct is not alleged to give rise to imputed liability on the part of the organization).

18. Fed.R.Evid. 801(d)(2).

19. See the last sentence of Comment [4] of Rule 4.2.

20. See Morrison v. Brandeis University, 125 F.R.D. 14, 18 n. 1 (D.Mass.1989) (case-by-case balancing approach adopted in instructor's action against university for denial of tenure; plaintiff's counsel allowed to contact professors who were part of "control group" because of plaintiff's need for the information and the unlikelihood that professors would speak freely in front of university counsel). Compare Chancellor v. Boeing Co., 678 F.Supp. 250 (D.Kan.1988) (citing *Upjohn*, the court denied plaintiff's counsel ex parte contact with employees involved in denying plaintiff's promotion).

21. 912 F.Supp. 502, 508–09 (D.Utah 1996).

When Opposing Party Is a Class

In Kleiner v. First National Bank,[22] the bank's counsel tried to get members of the opposing class to opt out of the suit. The bank claimed that the First Amendment protected these communications with the members of the class, citing Gulf Oil Corp. v. Bernard.[23] The court distinguished *Gulf* on the ground that the speech in that case, between class counsel and the class, was associational and thus entitled to more protection under the First Amendment than the speech in *Kleiner*, which was commercially-motivated and thus subject to greater regulation. Is this distinction persuasive?[24]

In Haffer v. Temple University,[25] a class of women students brought an action against Temple University alleging sex discrimination in the intercollegiate athletic program. Temple's counsel and an associate director in its athletic department distributed a memo to class members at Temple attempting to dissuade women athletes from taking part in the suit. The memo argued the importance of loyalty to the school. Temple's lawyer also telephoned two class members to dissuade them from meeting with class counsel. The court sanctioned Temple and its counsel for communicating with members of the class directly and for attempting to discourage them from cooperating with class counsel.[26]

When Represented Party Is a Government Agency

M.R. 4.2 and DR 7–104(A)(1), prohibiting communication with the opposing party unless that party's lawyer consents, both provide that such communication is permissible when "authorized by law". Comment [1] to M.R. 4.2 explains: "Communications authorized by law include, for example, the right of a party to a controversy with a government agency to speak with government officials about the matter." The First Amendment protects the right to petition the government for a redress of grievances. Some jurisdictions go further in permitting lawyers, in representing a client in a matter, to communicate directly with responsible government officials in an effort to resolve the matter.[27] An ABA ethics opinion draws a line between litigation matters (e.g., a tort claim against a government), in which the anti-contact rule applies fully, and broad policy matters (e.g.,

---

22.   751 F.2d 1193 (11th Cir.1985).

23.   452 U.S. 89 (1981).

24.   Contrast In re School Asbestos Litigation, 842 F.2d 671 (3d Cir.1988) (applying *Bernard* to hold that an order which restricted defendants' communications on school asbestos matters with any group reasonably believed to include a member of the plaintiff class was overbroad).

25.   115 F.R.D. 506 (E.D.Pa.1987).

26.   Also see Tedesco v. Mishkin, 629 F.Supp. 1474 (S.D.N.Y.1986) (sanctioning lawyer for communicating directly with opposing class members and for communicating in a misleading and coercive manner).

27.   See, e.g., Cal. R. Prof. Conduct, Rule 7–103 (anti-contact rule "shall not apply to communications with a public officer, board, committee or body"); and D.C. R. Prof. Conduct, Rule 4.2(d) (anti-contact rule applies with respect to contacts with government employees whose acts are alleged to have caused government liability, but not to "redress of grievances" contacts with officials who have decision-making responsibility on the matter).

whether broad new regulations should be adopted), in which a lawyer may communicate directly to agency officials who are responsible for the decisions involved.[28]

Does this mean that a government lawyer has no right to control access to her client's agents to prevent them from making adverse disclosures? See M.R. 3.4(f). Contacts with high policy-making officials are clearly protected by the right of petition, unless they are improper ex parte contacts in an adjudicatory matter. Contacts with government employees who have non-privileged information (e.g., occurrence witnesses) are also permissible because they are not the "client" of the government lawyer. But direct contacts with government agents who are within the managing/speaking category of agency law may be treated as if they were the government lawyer's client. In Frey v. Department of Health and Human Services,[29] for example, the court held that the opposing party must be allowed direct access to all government employees except those "who are the 'alter egos' of the entity, that is, those individuals who can bind it to a decision or settle controversies on its behalf."[30] The court observed that "while for most litigation purpose the law treats a government entity just like any other party, . . . unlike a corporate party, the government also has a duty to advance the public's interest in achieving justice, an ultimate obligation that outweighs its narrower interest in prevailing in a law suit."[31]

Application of Anti–Contact Rule to Prosecutors[32]

A heated controversy between bar groups, on the one hand, and federal and state prosecutors, on the other, concerns the application of the anti-contact rule to criminal investigations and prosecutions. It is generally agreed that the rule applies once a formal charge has been made against a represented defendant, but many other questions are disputed. Some involve large issues of law enforcement policy and federalism. Others involve the interpretation of the anti-contact rule: (1) Does the anti-contact rule apply to contacts at the investigatory, pre-indictment stage? (2) May a prosecutor communicate with a represented defendant at the latter's initia-

---

28. ABA Formal Op. 97–408 (Oct. 1, 1997). The opinion states, however, that a lawyer should only contact officials about policy decisions they can make and should notify the government lawyer of the planned conduct before it occurs.

29. 106 F.R.D. 32, 35 (E.D.N.Y.1985).

30. Id. at 35.

31. Id. at 36. See also Vega v. Bloomsburgh, 427 F.Supp. 593, 595 (D.Mass.1977) (state's attempt to bar its employees from communicating with opposing counsel impermissibly infringed on the state employee's First Amendment rights where there

was no showing that any of the employees' "interests are adverse to those of the plaintiffs, or for that matter consistent with those of the defendants"). Also see Fusco v. City of Albany, 134 Misc.2d 98, 509 N.Y.S.2d 763 (1986) (state freedom of information law authorized direct contact with government employees without prior consent of the government's lawyers).

32. See Roger C. Cramton & Lisa K. Udell, State Ethics Rules and Federal Prosecutors: The Controversies over the Anti–Contact and Subpoena Rules, 53 U.Pitt.L.Rev. 291 (1992).

tive and request? And (3) what remedies are appropriate for violation of the anti-contact rule?

These issues are complicated by the rule's interrelation with the large body of law dealing with the accused's Sixth Amendment right to counsel. After a formal charge has been made, law enforcement officers may not question a criminal defendant in the absence of counsel unless the accused knowingly and intelligently waives her right to have defense counsel present.[33] Nor is violation of the anti-contact rule itself a constitutional violation that leads to the exclusion of resulting evidence.[34] The questions, then, are whether questioning permissible under the Sixth Amendment violates the anti-contact rule and, if so, what is the appropriate remedy. Does the defendant's informed consent waive the anti-contact rule as well as the Sixth Amendment right to counsel? Does the body of federal law dealing with waiver by the accused bring the contact within the "authorized by law" exception of the anti-contact rule?

Pre-indictment contacts. Does the anti-contact rule apply at the investigatory stage? When Ivan Boesky and Dennis Levine agreed to cooperate with federal law enforcement officials engaged in a wide-ranging grand jury investigation of securities fraud, other potential targets such as Michael Millken quickly retained counsel, who in turn wrote federal prosecutors that their clients were represented and all communication should be through counsel. Are their clients now immune from routine inquiries by FBI agents? M.R. 4.2 prohibits communication "about the *subject matter of the representation* with a *person* (formerly *party*)" whom the lawyer making the contact knows is represented by another lawyer in the "*matter.*" When does a proceeding take on the concrete form suggested by the term "party" (in a jurisdiction that has not amended its rule) and "matter?"[35] Does the anti-contact rule apply to investigatory personnel such as the FBI, who may have legal training but are not acting as lawyers? Or is it sufficient that another lawyer, a federal prosecutor, is providing supervision and direction?[36] Most decisions hold that pre-indictment investigatory activities

---

33. Patterson v. Illinois, 487 U.S. 285 (1988).

34. The Court has declined to hold that violation of the anti-contact rule is a violation of an accused's Sixth Amendment right to counsel. Patterson v. Illinois, 487 U.S. 285 (1988), and Michigan v. Harvey, 494 U.S. 344 (1990). Justice Stevens, dissenting in both cases, argued that the constitutional standard should incorporate the fairness aspect of the ethics rule—the danger of overreaching when an accused, even with adequate consent, communicates with law enforcement officials in the absence of appointed counsel.

35. *Compare* United States v. Ryans, 903 F.2d 731 (10th Cir.1990) (because the anti-contact rule contemplates "an adversarial

relationship between litigants," it is inapplicable to investigative contacts occurring before the proceedings become accusatory), and United States v. Guerrerio, 675 F.Supp. 1430 (S.D.N.Y.1987) (evidence obtained at investigatory stage not subject to suppression because the subject of representation "is nebulous until the time of the formal initiation of the prosecution"), *with* United States v. Hammad, 858 F.2d 834 (2d Cir.1988) (the anti-contact rule applies at the investigatory stage, but ordinary investigative activity is generally within the rule's "authorized by law" exception).

36. *Compare* United States v. Thomas, 474 F.2d 110, 112 (10th Cir.1973) (enforcement officials are agents of the prosecuting party), and United States v. Jamil, 707 F.2d

are not subject to the anti-contact rule barring unusual circumstances, but United States v. Hammad[37] and a few other cases agitated law enforcement officials.

In *Hammad,* the prosecutor furnished an informant with a false subpoena and a hidden tape recorder whereby the informant recorded conversations with the defendant. The prosecutor knew the defendant was represented by counsel in the matter under investigation. The Sixth Amendment was not at issue because the incident took place as part of an investigation, not after criminal proceedings had been instituted. The court held that the anti-contact rule applies to prosecutors, but that the legitimate use of informants in an investigation was within the "authorized by law" exception to the rule. Here, however, the use of the informant was held not legitimate because the prosecutor engaged in "egregious misconduct" in using a "specious and contrived subpoena" and hence violated DR 7–104(A)(1).[38] The court further held that exclusion of the evidence would be an appropriate remedy.

The extension of the anti-contact rule to pre-indictment investigations supervised by a prosecutor, combined with the exclusion of evidence, alarmed the U.S. Department of Justice. One issue is the extent to which pre-indictment investigatory tactics should be governed by the anti-contact rule. The Department's position is that limitations imposed by the Constitution and by the Department's guidelines and internal review provide sufficient protection to those under investigation and that decisions such as *Hammad* cripple law enforcement by giving special treatment to those who have retained a lawyer prior to a civil or criminal investigation. That group of potential targets, according to the Department, consists largely of corporate defendants in civil matters and, in criminal matters, either professional criminals or those engaged in organized or white collar crime.

The Department's efforts to control the meaning of the "authorized by law" exception to the anti-contact rule in state ethics codes or, failing that, circumvent the rule by an assertion of federal authority, raised federalism and turf issues. Should a federal government lawyer be governed by a national standard applicable in all federal courts or by the standard in

---

638, 646 (2d Cir.1983) (no ethics violations where prosecutor was neither involved in nor aware of surreptitious contact with represented defendant), *with* United States v. Scarpelli, 713 F.Supp. 1144, 1159 n. 25 (N.D.Ill.1989) (rule does not apply to FBI agents).

37. 858 F.2d 834 (2d Cir.1988).

38. The quoted statements are from the third opinion in *Hammad.* When all U.S. attorneys in the Second Circuit applied for rehearing, Judge Kaufman denied that request but revised the initial opinion to remedy "some confusion as to the thrust of our opinion." 855 F.2d 36, revising 846

F.2d 854 (2d Cir.1988). During the pendency of the government's request for a rehearing en banc, the panel issued a third opinion that is unpublished and now unavailable. The fourth opinion, 858 F.2d 834 (2d Cir.1988), cert. denied, 498 U.S. 871 (1990), eliminated language criticizing the prosecutor's conduct, declined to rule on sham subpoenas, and limited its holding to the statement that use of the subpoena "under the circumstances of this case contributed to the informant's becoming the alter ego of the prosecutor," thereby violating the anti-contact rule.

effect in the state in which the federal court sits? Who should influence or control the standard's creation and interpretation: the chief federal law enforcement agency or the professional organizations in the states operating through the promulgation of ethics rules by their high courts? The Department's efforts were embodied first in the Thornburgh Memorandum,[39] an unnecessarily provocative document, and then the more reasonable promulgation by Attorney General Reno of a regulation purporting to provide federal prosecutors with a nationwide standard rather than the patchwork of state interpretations.[40] Both actions aroused the ire of influential groups of lawyers: the American Bar Association, the American Corporate Counsel Association, and the National Association of Defense Lawyers. The *Hammad* decision and two others, especially the *Lopez* case next discussed, provided the incentive for the Department's effort to interpret, circumvent and preempt state anti-contact provisions.[41]

Post-indictment contacts with defendant's consent. United States v. Lopez[42] involved contact between an indicted defendant represented by counsel and a federal prosecutor who, after obtaining approval of a magistrate, held several conversations with the defendant without the consent or presence of the defendant's lawyer. The defendant, stymied by his lawyer's refusal to assist him in plea bargaining, initiated the contacts and waived his lawyer's presence, stating that his lawyer was not acting in his best

39. In 1989 Attorney General Richard Thornburgh issued a memorandum arguing that Department of Justice enforcement practices that were constitutionally permitted fell within the "authorized by law" exception of the states' anti-contact rules, and, to the extent they did not, the state rules were inapplicable because of federal supremacy. The situation was complicated by the fact that many U.S. district courts had adopted as their own ethics rules those promulgated by the particular state. Thus a question of "separation of powers" within the federal government was also involved: could a federal court, interpreting a state ethics rule, override longstanding investigatory practices of federal prosecutors?

40. See Communications with Represented Persons, 28 C.F.R. § 77 (promulgated by Attorney General Reno in Aug. 1994). The rule was initially proposed during the Bush Administration and extensively reconsidered and revised during the Clinton Administration after extensive public notice and comment.

41. The third case is United States v. Ferrara, 847 F.Supp. 964 (D.D.C.1993), aff'd, 54 F.3d 825 (D.C.Cir.1995) (holding that a federal prosecutor cannot remove a state

disciplinary proceeding to a state court). The *Lopez* case was of special concern. For a review of the controversy, see Rory K. Little, Who Should Regulate the Ethics of Federal Prosecutors?, 66 Fordham L.Rev. 355 (1996).

42. 765 F.Supp. 1433 (N.D.Cal.1991), rev'd in part and aff'd in part, 989 F.2d 1032 (9th Cir.1993), modified, 4 F.3d 1455 (9th Cir.1993). The initial opinion of the Ninth Circuit panel reversed the district court's dismissal of Lopez's indictment but contained damaging and erroneous statements concerning the prosecutor's conduct. These statements had led to disciplinary charges against the prosecutor in Arizona. When the government filed a petition for rehearing en banc, the panel modified its decision, remanding the case for a hearing by Judge Patel concerning the prosecutor's conduct. When the government stated that it had affidavits from another district judge and the magistrate supporting the government's view that the prosecutor had not misled the magistrate, the district judge decided not to hold a hearing and scheduled the case for trial. Lopez was convicted and is now serving his sentence. The disciplinary charges against the prosecutor in Arizona were then dismissed.

interests. After the plea negotiations failed, the defendant's successor counsel moved to dismiss the indictment for violation of California's version of the anti-contact ethics rule (also adopted by local rule of the federal district court). The district court dismissed the indictment on the ground that the prosecutor's communications with the represented defendant violated the "widely accepted and time-honored" anti-contact rule. The Ninth Circuit upheld the application of the anti-contact rule, relying on facts (later proven to be erroneous) that the prosecutor had misled the magistrate by not informing her of facts that she failed to elicit from the defendant in an in camera hearing.[43]

Does the holding in *Lopez* deprive the defendant of her right to petition the government in a situation in which she may believe that her interests are not being served by her lawyer? Why doesn't judicial approval of the conversations bring the case within the "authorized by law" exception to the anti-contact rule? Clients can waive constitutional protections; why can't they waive the anti-contact rule?

Remedying violations. What remedies are appropriate if a prosecutor violates the anti-contact rule? Ethics rules provide standards for professional discipline, yet prosecutors are rarely disciplined for violations of the anti-contact rule.[44] Should evidence be excluded in civil or criminal proceedings because of violation of the rule?[45] *Lopez* held that dismissal of a criminal indictment was normally inappropriate as a remedy for violation of the anti-contact rule, but scattered decisions have excluded evidence obtained by contacts violating the rule.[46]

43. The anti-contact rule, the court held, bars direct prosecutorial communication with represented defendants after indictment and the general statutory authority of federal prosecutors does not override the rule. Although a magistrate's approval of contact would normally bring it within the "authorized by law" exception, the magistrate in this case was misled by the prosecutor. However, because the defendant was able to secure competent replacement counsel, the district court erred in dismissing the indictment.

44. Prosecutors who bypass defense counsel are rarely disciplined. See In re Conduct of Burrows, 629 P.2d 820 (Ore.1981). For imposition of discipline for direct communication in civil litigation, see, e.g., Toledo Bar Ass'n v. Westmeyer, 520 N.E.2d 223 (Ohio 1988); Florida Bar v. Shapiro, 413 So.2d 1184 (Fla.1982). See Fred C. Zacharias, Structuring the Ethics of Prosecutorial Trial Practice: Can Prosecutors Do Justice?, 44 Vand.L.Rev. 45 (1991).

45. In Mills Land & Water Co. v. Golden West Refining Co., 186 Cal.App.3d 116, 230 Cal.Rptr. 461 (1986), the court refused to suppress any information gained in the improper conversation that was otherwise discoverable, stating that the exclusionary rule was inappropriate in *civil* litigation. In criminal prosecutions evidence obtained through direct communication with the accused would not be discoverable. Should this make a difference in fashioning a remedy?

46. United States v. Hammad, 902 F.2d 1062 (2d Cir.1990) (prosecutor's use of a sham subpoena might in a future case justify informant's secret recording; earlier opinions had upheld the district court's exclusion of the evidence); United States v. Thomas, 474 F.2d 110 (10th Cir.1973) (violation of anti-contact rule may justify exclusion of resulting evidence). Contra: Gentry v. Texas, 770 S.W.2d 780, 791 (Tex. Crim.App.1988) (en banc) (disciplinary action against the prosecution, not exclusion of evidence, is the appropriate remedy); People v. Green, 274 N.W.2d 448, 454 (Mich.1979) (same).

Efforts to Resolve the Confusion Concerning the Scope of the Anti-Contact Rule

The Department of Justice rule governing ex parte contacts by Department lawyers with individuals and organizations known to be represented by counsel[47] provides, subject to a number of exceptions, that a government lawyer may contact a represented person or organization as part of government investigatory activity prior to an arrest or commencement of a civil or criminal proceeding. On the other hand, an ex parte contact with the "target" of enforcement activity is generally prohibited, with some exceptions. Finally, Department lawyers may not contact ex parte a represented "party," i.e., an individual or organization that has been named as a defendant, but again with some exceptions, including the situation involved in *Lopez*, in which the contact is requested by the defendant and approved by a judicial officer after inquiry. Although the Department still defends the rule, the Eighth Circuit has held it invalid and unauthorized.[48]

Other groups have responded to the argument, made by lawyers for private plaintiffs as well as by federal and state prosecutors, that some states have gone too far in interpreting the anti-contact rule to bar virtually all informal contacts with current or former employees of organizations and with individuals under criminal investigation. The ABA, while extremely hostile to the Justice Department's attempt to interpret and override state ethics rules, has responded with a detailed ethics opinion dealing with the contested issues.[49] The 1995 amendment to Rule 4.2, substituting "person" for "party" in the text of the rule, was accompanied by some clarifying amendments to the comments (the amendment added current paragraphs [2], [5] and [6]). The most important was the concession in amended Comment [2] that "constitutionally permissible investigative activities of lawyers representing government entities, directly or through investigative agencies, prior to the commencement of criminal or civil enforcement proceedings, when there is applicable judicial precedent that has found the activity permissible under this Rule or has found this Rule inapplicable" fall within the "authorized by law" exception.[50]

47. Communications with Represented Persons, 28 C.F.R. § 77.

48. O'Keefe v. McDonnell Douglas Corp., 132 F.3d 1252 (8th Cir.1998) (upholding a district court's protective order barring lawyers for Department of Justice from interviewing any current employees of a government contractor who were suspected of facilitating the contractor's alleged overbilling; the state's anti-contact rule, adopted by the district court, was not displaced by a Department regulation that was not authorized by law). See also Rory K. Little, Who Should Regulate the Ethics of Federal Prosecutors?, 65 Fordham L.Rev. 355 (1996) (historical and legal argument that the Attorney General has legal authority to promulgate such a rule, but concluding that doing so may be undesirable); Fred C. Zacharias, Who Can Best Regulate the Ethics of Federal Prosecutors ..., 65 Fordham L.Rev. 429 (1996) (expressing doubts on the validity of the rule).

49. ABA Formal Op. 95-396 (1995).

50. The Conference of Chief Justices, after issuing press releases attacking the desirability and legality of the Department's regulation, undertook negotiations with the Department and reached a tentative agreement, now apparently abandoned, on a revised Rule 4.2. Under the agreement, the chief justices would recommend the revised rule to their respective courts for adoption

As of July 1999 the controversy continues. In late 1998 Congress enacted the Citizens Protection Act, 28 U.S.C. § 530B, which overrides the Department of Justice regulation by requiring federal prosecutors to comply with state laws and rules that govern lawyer conduct as well as local federal court rules. This legislation went into effect in April 1999, although Sen. Orrin Hatch has held hearings on a bill that would explicitly authorize the Attorney General to promulgate regulations necessary for federal prosecutors to conduct their work, superseding inconsistent state law or federal court rules. At the same time, committees of the Judicial Conference of the United States are considering whether to propose rule amendments that would provide a limited set of ethics rules for application in federal courts, with the primary rule one of reference to the rules of the state in which the federal court sits. A tentative draft of proposed federal rules would provide a uniform federal anti-contact rule for application in federal court proceedings.[51] Simultaneously, two ABA groups, the Ethics 2000 Commission and the Committee on Ethics and Professional Responsibility, are considering amendments to Rule 4.2.

2.   FAIRNESS TO PERSONS NOT REPRESENTED BY COUNSEL

Model Rule 4.3 provides that when the other person is not represented, "the lawyer shall not state or imply that the lawyer is disinterested." Further, if the lawyer "knows or reasonably should know that the unrepresented person misunderstands the lawyer's role in the matter, the lawyer shall make reasonable efforts to correct the misunderstanding." DR 7–104(A)(2) provides that a lawyer shall not give advice to someone not represented by counsel "other than the advice to seek a lawyer," a mandate that is included in the Comment to Rule 4.3 but not in the text of the rule itself. M.R. 8.4(c) and DR 1–102(A)(4), both prohibiting "conduct involving dishonesty, fraud, deceit or misrepresentation," are also relevant.

Ethics opinions state that before interviewing a potential defendant, a lawyer must advise her that the lawyer is counsel for the plaintiff; also,[52] a lawyer who interviews an employee of an opposing party or a nonparty witness must disclose the lawyer-client relationship.[53]

In mass disaster situations, such as an air crash or a hotel fire, plaintiffs' lawyers who attempt to bring their services to the attention of potential claimants are criticized by bar groups and the public for improper solicitation.[54] What about the lawyer representatives of potential defendants or their liability insurers, who interview accident victims or their relatives to obtain information or to settle claims? Assuming that the lawyer is careful to identify her role, may a lawyer seek to get a release of

and, once adopted by a state, the Department would observe the rule. See 14 Law.Man.Prof.Conduct 264–68 (June 10, 1998), 459 (Sept. 30, 1998).

51. See 14 Law.Man.Prof.Conduct 78–79 and 82–86 (March 4, 1998) (discussion of proposal and text of draft rules).

52. ABA Informal Op. 908 (1966).

53. ABA Formal Op. 117 (1934).

54. Solicitation of accident victims is considered infra, p. 1030.

liability or ask the potential claimant to accept a settlement offer? What if the contact is carried on by a non-lawyer insurance adjuster carrying forms and instructions prepared by the insurer's legal counsel? Is any effort at persuasion appropriate, even truthful statements that "hiring a lawyer and bringing a court proceeding will take much longer, and you will have to pay an attorney fee"?

Another situation in which issues of candor and fairness to an unrepresented person frequently arise occurs when an organization's officers ask a lawyer to investigate allegations that some employees have violated duties to the organization (e.g., embezzling funds or getting kickbacks from suppliers) or engaged in illegal activities for which the organization may be held legally responsible (e.g., the internal investigation in the *Upjohn* case, supra p. 209, involving illegal payments to obtain foreign business). What should a lawyer conducting such an investigation tell an organizational employee who is about to be interviewed?

In W.T. Grant, Inc. v. Haines,[55] a lawyer for a retail chain was conducting an internal investigation of company employees who were suspected of taking kickbacks and bribes in making store leases. Haines, one of the employees, was called to New York for a meeting scheduled as a ruse to get him to New York, and was then interviewed for five and one-half hours by the company's lawyer, who, with Haines' consent, recorded the conversation and later obtained Haines' consent for a lie detector test. The lawyer told Haines that he had been retained by the employer to look into commercial dealings with shopping centers, but did not inform Haines that a fraud case naming Haines as a defendant had been filed that morning. In that proceeding, Haines later moved to disqualify the lawyer's law firm on ground that the lawyer gave legal advice to Haines, who was an unrepresented person. The court was troubled by this sequence of events but thought that DR 7–104(A)(2) was not violated by statements to Haines that "candid answers to the inquiry might clear his name 'if that [was] possible.'"[56] Asking Haines to sign authorizations consenting to access to his tax, credit cards and financial accounts, however, presented a "close question."[57] Didn't the lawyer give "legal advice" by urging that cooperation might help alleviate Haines' legal problems?[58]

Model Rule 3.8(c) prohibits a prosecutor from seeking "to obtain from an unrepresented accused a waiver of important pretrial rights, such as the right to a preliminary hearing." Should this rule be limited to prosecutors?

55. 531 F.2d 671 (2d Cir.1976).

56. Id. at 675.

57. See ABA Formal Op. 84–350 (1984) (withdrawing two previous ABA Informal opinions, Op. 1140 (1970) and Op. 1255 (1940), both of which prohibited lawyers from presenting documents to adverse parties who were not represented by counsel).

58. See 2 Hazard & Hodes, Law of Lawyering 752 (2d ed.1990) (arguing that the law-

yer's conduct violated both DR 7–104(A)(2) and M.R. 4.3). The court in *Haines* went on to hold that, even if the ethics rule was violated, disqualification was an inappropriate remedy where the violation did not "taint" the trial of the case and would deprive the other party of its counsel of choice. Professional discipline was the only appropriate remedy.

Model Rule 3.4(f) provides that a lawyer shall not request a person, other than the client, "to refrain from voluntarily giving relevant information to another party." However, the lawyer can so advise a person who is a relative, employee or agent of the client, *if* "the lawyer reasonably believes that the person's interests will not be adversely affected by refraining from giving such information." A lawyer may not advise another to refrain from cooperating if that advice is in furtherance of the client's illegal activity.[59]

F. LAWYER–CLIENT TRANSACTIONS

1. HANDLING PROPERTY OF CLIENTS AND OTHERS

Commingling Funds

David Hoffman, the father of American legal ethics, stated in 1836:

I will on no occasion blend with my own my client's money. If kept *distinctly as his*, it will be less liable to be considered *as my own*.[1]

Although this simple rule has been recognized as fundamental for long before lawyers had written ethics codes, it is still one of the most frequent bases of lawyer disbarment. In Matter of Warhaftig,[2] for example, a lawyer "borrowed" $11,125 from trust accounts containing advance fee payments not yet earned on various real estate transactions; caught by New Jersey's random audit of lawyer's client trust accounts, Warhaftig was disbarred even though he had an unblemished record and was a highly respected lawyer.

The fiduciary obligations concerning property that comes into a lawyer's possession are segregation, notification, record keeping, delivery and accounting. Restatement § 56(1) states them as obligations to: (1) take reasonable steps to safeguard the funds or property and segregate them from the property of the lawyer; and (2) notify the client or owner of the property upon receipt and promptly render a full accounting upon request.[3] With respect to the first requirement, Restatement § 56(1) provides: "In particular, the lawyer must hold such property separate from the lawyer's property, keep records of it, deposit funds in an account separate from the

---

59. See In re Blatt, 324 A.2d 15 (N.J.1974) (lawyer disbarred for urging witnesses not to cooperate with federal investigation); In re Russell, 282 A.2d 42 (N.J.1971) (lawyer disciplined for advising witnesses, who were represented by another lawyer, to plead the Fifth Amendment to help lawyer's client).

1. David Hoffman (1784–1854) wrote the first statement of professional ethics for American lawyers. His fifty "Resolutions in Regard to Professional Deportment" were first published in 1817 and in a revised form in 1836. See Thomas L. Shaffer,

American Legal Ethics 59 (1985); and Maxwell Bloomfield, David Hoffman and the Shaping of a Republican Legal Culture, 38 Md. L. Rev. 673 (1979).

2. 524 A.2d 398 (N.J.1987).

3. See generally Restatement § 56 (safeguarding and segregating property) and § 57 (surrendering possession of property); Note, Attorney Misappropriation of Clients' Funds: A Study in Professional Responsibility, 10 U.Mich.J.L.Ref. 415 (1977).

lawyer's own funds, identify tangible objects, and comply with related requirements imposed by regulatory authorities." Responsibilities concerning client property, which includes property in which a client claims an interest, flow from state lawyer codes; responsibilities concerning property of third persons, such as funds held in escrow for the seller of property being purchased by the client, are addressed by other law and by many lawyer codes. The detailed treatment of these matters varies in its details from jurisdiction to jurisdiction. M.R. 1.15, Safekeeping Property, is substantially similar to DR 9–102, but unlike its predecessor also applies to property of a third person that is in the lawyer's possession in connection with the representation.

As to funds partly or potentially belonging to the lawyer, the lawyer may withdraw funds from the trust account when payment from the client is due *unless* the client disputes the lawyer's claim, in which case the disputed portion "shall be kept separate by the lawyer until the dispute is resolved." M.R. 1.15(c); DR 9–102(A)(2) is substantially identical. Most jurisdictions read these provisions as requiring the lawyer to deposit money received as a general retainer in a trust account and allowing withdrawal only as the fee is earned.[4] A minority of jurisdictions permit the lawyer to deposit advance fee payments in the general office account.[5]

The prohibition against commingling is violated whether the lawyer deposits the client's money in the lawyer's account or the lawyer's money is deposited in the client's trust account. A violation occurs even if the lawyer was merely negligent. "[I]t is essentially a per se offense."[6] Courts treat violations of the ban against commingling of funds very seriously;[7] in some jurisdictions a violation results in automatic disbarment. In New Jersey, for example, the court will not consider a lawyer's inexperience, an otherwise outstanding career or the lawyer's restitution of the funds as mitigating factors in cases of intentional commingling:[8] "[The lawyer] knowingly used his client's money as if it were his own. We hold that disbarment is the only appropriate discipline [and] . . . use this occasion to state that generally all such cases shall result in disbarment." The willingness of clients "to entrust their funds to relative strangers simply because they are lawyers," the court said, is "built on centuries of honesty and faithfulness," sometimes "reinforced by personal knowledge of a particular lawyer's integrity

---

4. See, e.g., In re Aronson, 352 N.W.2d 17 (Minn.1984); and Miele v. Commissioner, 72 T.C. 284 (1979) (interpreting Pennsylvania code to require segregation of retainer fees). For a more complete list see Lester Brickman, The Advance Fee Payment Dilemma, 10 Cardozo L.Rev. 647, 656.

5. See, e.g., N.Y. State Bar Assn.Comm. Prof.Ethics, Op. 570 (1985); and D.C. Bar Op. 113 (1982).

6. In re Hessler, 549 A.2d 700 n. 3 (D.C.App.1988); Fitzsimmons v. State Bar, 667 P.2d 700, 702 (Cal.1983).

7. See, e.g., In re Pierson, 571 P.2d 907, 908–09 (Ore.1977) (a single conversion of client funds will result in disbarment); Akron Bar Ass'n v. Hughes, 348 N.E.2d 712, 715 (Ohio 1976) (penalty for commingling of funds is either indefinite suspension or disbarment).

8. In Matter of Wilson, 409 A.2d 1153 (N.J. 1979).

or a firm's reputation." "The underlying faith, however, is in the legal profession, the bar as an institution."[9]

Restitution was not an adequate remedy for this criminal breach of trust—"Banks do not rehire tellers who "borrow" depositors' funds. Our professional standards, if anything, should be higher."[10]

Record Keeping

The Model Rules and the Model Code require that the lawyer maintain complete records of all funds and property maintained by the lawyer for another. M.R. 1.15(a) specifies that the records be kept for five years following the termination of the representation. New Jersey, for example, has detailed requirements for law office bookkeeping, including provisions on recording the flow of all entrusted funds, billing the client, paying others on behalf of the client, and reconciling ledger and bank statements. The records must be kept "in accordance with generally accepted accounting practice" and retained for seven years, along with "copies of those portions of each client's case file reasonably necessary for a complete understanding of the financial transactions pertaining thereto."[11] Many other states have adopted requirements going beyond those in the lawyer codes.[12]

New Jersey and ten other jurisdictions subject a lawyer's financial accounts to random inspection by the bar regulatory agency. Should all states adopt random audit procedures?

Client Protection Funds

As of 1999, every U.S. jurisdiction has established a client protection fund to provide some reimbursement for clients whose assets have been lost as a result of dishonest conduct by a lawyer admitted to the jurisdiction's bar. The funds are maintained by mandatory contributions from lawyers in the state or by state bar dues money. They are woefully inadequate as a means of providing full restitution to the victims of lawyer dishonesty. The amount maintained in client protection funds is far below the amount lawyers actually misappropriate each year. To qualify for reimbursement, the client must show that all avenues of relief against the lawyer have been exhausted to no avail. Usually the client must make other demanding showings to obtain compensation. Assuming the client surmounts those hurdles, ceilings in the state plans generally restrict the amount a client may recover and the amount paid out per lawyer who violates the rule no matter how many clients are injured and the amount per transaction.[13]

9. 409 A.2d at 1154–55.

10. Id. at 1156.

11. N.J.Court Rules 1:21–6.

12. See, e.g., N.H. Rule 37 § 7 (specifying accounting system, including separate ledger pages for each client and an index to all trust accounts).

13. See Harriet L. Turney & John A. Holtaway, Client Protection Funds—Lawyers Put Their Money Where Their Mouths Are, The Prof'l Lawyer 18 (Feb. 1998): states reporting had funds nationwide totaling $43 million in reserves as of 1995; the average maximum allowable reimbursement per claimant was $43,533 and per lawyer, $132,292; only four states do not

As of 1999, 26 states require financial institutions to notify the state's lawyer disciplinary agency when an overdraft has occurred in a lawyer's trust or escrow account (a fairly effective early warning device); eleven states provide for random audit of lawyer trust accounts; and nine states require insurers to provide written notice to a claimant that a payment was delivered to the claimant's lawyer. In addition to these protections, why shouldn't lawyers be required to obtain a fidelity bond covering loss or embezzlement of client funds? No state requires complete protection of this kind, although Iowa requires this of lawyers acting as fiduciaries.[14]

Keeping Money of Multiple Clients in One Account

The rules allow a lawyer to use one trust account to deposit the funds of multiple clients. This is necessary because for many clients the lawyer may hold amounts too small or too briefly to justify the maintenance of separate trust accounts. If, on the other hand, the client's funds are great enough and the time the lawyer is to hold those funds is long enough, or the funds are held in a separate capacity, the lawyer should put the money in a separate interest bearing account.[15] Comment [1] to M.R. 1.15 states that "[s]eparate trust accounts may be warranted when administering estate monies or acting in similar fiduciary capacities." A state statute or case law may require the maintenance of a separate account in those and other situations.[16]

IOLTA Funds

IOLTA stands for Interest On Lawyers' Trust Accounts. Trust accounts containing the funds of multiple clients were traditionally non-interest bearing accounts because the lawyer has no right to the interest, and calculating and distributing the interest to each client was not administratively feasible. Today, almost all states have IOLTA plans. Under these plans the funds of multiple clients are kept in interest bearing "IOLTA accounts." The state either requires the lawyer to maintain the money of multiple clients in these accounts or allows the lawyer to do so. When an IOLTA account has been established, the bank pays the aggregate interest on the account to the state bar's IOLTA program. The money is used primarily to fund legal services for the poor, but other uses include funding of client security accounts or projects relating to the administration of justice.

Where lawyers are required to participate, the funds raised by IOLTA programs are substantial, but fluctuate with changes in interest rates. California's mandatory program raised $40 million in a five-year period.

have reimbursement limits. During 1993–95, a nationwide average of $36 million per year was paid out.

14. Information has been provided by John Holtaway, Client Protection Counsel, ABA (312–988–5298).

15. See, e.g., In re Petition of Minn. State Bar Ass'n, 332 N.W.2d 151, 157 (Minn. 1982).

16. See, e.g., Attorney Grievance Commission v. Boehm, 446 A.2d 52 (Md.1982) (separate account necessary when administering an estate).

Where the plans are voluntary, lawyer participation is generally low perhaps due to the fact that lawyers who keep client funds in non-interest bearing accounts are favored customers of banks. Is it ethical to accept benefits from a bank in exchange for keeping a non-interest bearing account?

After the cutbacks in federal funding for legal services programs for the poor in the early 1980s (see Chapter 11), IOLTA programs were expected to help make up the shortfall. Revenue has, however, been far below expectations where IOLTA programs are voluntary. In 1988, responding to the great difference in effectiveness between mandatory and voluntary programs, the ABA House of Delegates adopted a resolution urging states to make their voluntary IOLTA programs mandatory.

State IOLTA programs were put in jeopardy by the Supreme Court's holding in Phillips v. Washington Legal Foundation, Inc.[17] *Phillips* reviewed the Texas IOLTA rule which requires a lawyer who receives client funds that are "nominal in amount or are reasonably anticipated to be held for a short period of time" to place them in an interest-bearing account with interest payable to the Texas Equal Access to Justice Foundation. The Court held that both the funds held in these accounts and "the interest income generated [by it were the 'private property' of the client] for purposes of the Takings Clause of the Fifth Amendment." The case was remanded for consideration of whether the state by enforcing the IOLTA program has taken private property without just compensation. If the interest belongs to the client and the lawyer has a fiduciary duty to protect that client interest, the implication of the decision is that IOLTA contributions are consistent with legal ethics only if each client consents to this use of their property. If the interest due a client is a fairly trivial amount, client consent is likely to be forthcoming. Technological innovation is largely responsible for the current threat. Financial institutions now have software that makes it cost effective to keep track of the interest earned by relatively small amounts of money deposited within larger accounts. A few banks have already made these sub-accounting services available to lawyers. If the interest can be returned to the client, are IOLTA plans justified?

2. TRANSACTIONS WITH CLIENTS

Business Transactions

Lawyer-client business dealings are addressed by Model Rule 1.8(a) and DR 5–104(A) of the Model Code.[18]

---

17. 524 U.S. 156 (1998). See Ralph Gregory Elliot, *Phillips*, IOLTA, and the Lawyer's Duty to Communicate, The Prof'l Lawyer 1, 8 (Summer 1998) (if the interest payments are the client's property, lawyers have a duty to "consult meaningfully with their clients about how they want interest on their funds handled" and to seek out the best "investment means for earning net interest for their clients' benefit before turning to IOLTA").

18. See generally Restatement § 207. See also 1 Hazard & Hodes, Law of Lawyering 262–68 (2d ed. 1990); Wolfram, Modern Legal Ethics § 8.11 (1986).

Rule 1.8(a) provides that:

A lawyer shall not enter into a business transaction with a client ... unless:

(1) the transaction and terms ... are fair and reasonable to the client and are fully disclosed and transmitted in writing to the client ...;

(2) the client is given reasonable opportunity to seek the advice of independent counsel in the transaction; and

(3) the client consents in writing thereto.

Committee on Professional Ethics and Conduct of Iowa State Bar Association v. Mershon

Supreme Court of Iowa, 1982.
316 N.W.2d 895

■ McCORMICK, JUSTICE.

This case involves review of a Grievance Commission report recommending that respondent be reprimanded for alleged ethical violations arising from a business transaction with a client. Because we find respondent's conduct violated the principle in DR5–104(A), we adopt the recommendation.

From our de novo review of the record, we find the facts as follows. Respondent [Mershon] is a Cedar Falls attorney. He began to do tax and property work for Leonard O. Miller, a farmer, in 1951. Miller owned 100 acres of farmland adjacent to a country club near the city. In 1969, when he was 68, Miller became interested in developing the land for residential purposes. He employed a landscape architect and R. O. Schenk, of Schenk Engineering Company, to prepare a preliminary plat and market study.

When the preliminary work was completed, Miller brought Schenk to meet with respondent to discuss the project. Miller wished to proceed with the development but did not have sufficient funds to pay engineering costs. Schenk suggested that the three men form a corporation to which Miller would contribute the land, Schenk would contribute engineering services, and respondent would contribute legal services. They agreed the land was worth approximately $400 an acre. Schenk estimated engineering costs at $400 an acre, and he said legal costs were usually one half that amount.

After several conferences in early 1970, the three men formed a corporation, Union Township Development, Inc. Subsequently Miller conveyed the farmland to the corporation at a capitalized value of $12,500 and received 400 shares of stock. Schenk gave the corporation a $12,500 promissory note and also received 400 shares of stock. Respondent gave the corporation a $6,250 promissory note and received 200 shares of stock. The promissory notes were interest free and due at the discretion of the corporation. They were to represent the services to be rendered by Schenk and respondent.

Development plans were premised on the corporation's ability to obtain financing on the security of the farmland. As it turned out, the corporation was unable to borrow money unless the three individuals would guarantee the obligation personally. They refused to do so, and financing was never obtained.

The trio met at least annually to discuss the development, but when Miller died on December 31, 1978, at the age of 77, the project was still at a stalemate. Respondent believed the parties had an oral agreement that if development did not occur he and Schenk would relinquish their interests in the corporation to Miller. Three days after Miller's death, he transferred his stock to the corporation. He asked Schenk to do the same thing, but Schenk refused, denying any obligation to do so.

Respondent was nominated in Miller's will as executor of his estate. He served in that capacity until Miller's two daughters expressed dissatisfaction with his role in Miller's conveyance of the farmland to the corporation. He then resigned as executor. Consistent with his view, he showed Miller as owner of all corporate stock in the preliminary probate inventory. The farmland was appraised at $4,000 an acre.

Although respondent had expended $900 in out-of-pocket expenses for the corporation and performed legal services worth more than $6,000, he did not intend to seek payment. Schenk, however, maintained at the time of the grievance hearing that he still owned one half of the outstanding stock of the corporation.

The determinative question in our review is whether this evidence establishes a violation of the principle in DR5–104(A), which provides:

> A lawyer shall not enter into a business transaction with a client if they have differing interests therein and if the client expects the lawyer to exercise his professional judgment therein for the protection of the client, unless the client has consented after full disclosure.

. . .

This court has recognized and applied the principle expressed in DR5–104(A) for many years. In Healy v. Gray, 168 N.W. 222, 225 (Iowa 1918), the court quoted the general rule under which all business transactions between an attorney and client are regarded with suspicion and disfavor:

> Transactions between attorney and client, as in all other cases where fiduciary relations exist between parties, one of whom possesses superior knowledge and ability and the other is subject to his influence, are regarded with a scrutinizing and jealous eye by courts of equity, and will be set aside and the clients protected, whenever advantage has been taken of them through the influence or knowledge of the attorneys, possessed by reason of their peculiar relations.

Before making a contract with a client, an attorney must fully disclose every relevant fact and circumstance which the client should know to make an intelligent decision concerning the wisdom of entering the agreement. Ryan Bros. v. Ashton, 42 Iowa 365, 369 (1876). "To prevent abuse of such confidential relationship by removing temptation the law presumes such contracts to be fraudulent." Reeder v. Lund, 236 N.W. 40, 44 (Iowa 1931). "The burden is on the attorney to show that in any contract or settlement with his client or dealing with his client's property he has acted in fairness and good faith with a disclosure of all the facts." Donaldson v. Eaton & Estes, 114 N.W. 19, 21 (Iowa 1907).

. . .

In order to establish a violation of DR5–104(A) it is necessary to show that the lawyer and client had differing interests in the transaction, that the client expected the lawyer to exercise his professional judgment for the protection of the client, and that the client consented to the transaction without full disclosure.

. . .

Miller and Mershon plainly had differing interests in at least two aspects of the transaction. One was the issue of giving respondent a present interest in the corporation in anticipation of future legal services. The fee agreement was made during the existence of the attorney-client relationship and thus was subject to the general principles governing attorney-client transactions. ...Because respondent's fee was tied to the amount of his stock in the corporation, he and Miller had differing interests concerning the extent of respondent's stock ownership. Another differing interest involved making respondent a debtor of the corporation to assure that the services would be performed. Because Miller's interest was aligned wholly with the corporation, he and respondent had differing interests with respect to respondent's promissory note. ...

No dispute exists that Miller relied on respondent to exercise his professional judgment to protect him. One respect in which respondent did so was in preparing a written agreement to assure that Miller was reimbursed from the first profits of the corporation for the preincorporation expenses of preliminary studies. This, however, was the only agreement of the parties that was reduced to writing.

The fighting issue before the Commission was whether respondent made full disclosure to Miller within the meaning of [DR 5–104(A)] before Miller entered the transaction. If full disclosure means only that respondent made Miller fully aware of the nature and terms of the transaction, this requirement was satisfied. Nothing was hidden from Miller, and he was an active participant in the transaction. Full disclosure, however, means more than this.

Because of the fiduciary relationship which exists, the attorney has the burden of showing that the transaction

> was in all respects fairly and equitably conducted; that he fully and faithfully discharged all his duties to his client, not only by refraining from any misrepresentation or concealment of any material fact, but by

active diligence to see that his client was fully informed of the nature and effect of the transaction proposed and of his own rights and interests in the subject matter involved, and by seeing to it that his client either has independent advice in the matter or else receives from the attorney such advice as the latter would have been expected to give had the transaction been one between his client and a stranger.

Goldman v. Kane, 329 N.E.2d 770, 773 (Mass.1975). . . .

Respondent acknowledges he did not suggest to Miller that he obtain independent advice. The record does not show he otherwise gave Miller the kind of advice Miller should have had if the transaction were with a stranger. See Lawrence v. Tschirgi, 57 N.W.2d at 50 ("Plaintiff did not give his clients such advice regarding it as a disinterested attorney could be expected to give them or such advice as plaintiff should have given them if the proposed contract were between them and a strange attorney."). Respondent let Schenk estimate the value of his legal services and thus the extent of respondent's stock ownership without any investigation to determine whether the estimate was accurate. Nor did he suggest to Miller that he make such investigation. If Schenk's estimate was generous, the effect may have been to chill respondent's scrutiny of the benchmark for the valuation, which was Schenk's valuation of his own services. Furthermore there was no discussion or investigation concerning the reasonableness or wisdom of tying respondent's fee for future services to a present twenty percent interest in the corporation. . . .

Nothing was done to assure that Miller would get his farm back if either Schenk or respondent did not perform or if the development should not be undertaken. Nothing was done to protect Miller or his estate in the event of the death of any of the parties. The promissory notes could hardly have been on more favorable terms to the debtors. The record does not show whether Miller was informed of the difficulty the corporation might have in enforcing respondent's obligation. So far as the record shows, Miller was not told of any possible effect of respondent's differing interests on the exercise of his professional judgment.

The Commission found respondent is forthright and honest and gained no profit from the transaction. The record confirms this finding. As the Commission also found, however, a violation of DR5–104(A) was nevertheless established. Respondent had three alternatives when the Schenk proposal was first made. The safest and perhaps best course would have been to refuse to participate personally in the transaction. . . . Alternatively, he could have recommended that Miller obtain independent advice. Finally, if Miller refused to seek independent advice or respondent did not recommend he do so, he could have made the least desirable choice. He could have attempted to meet the high standard of disclosure outlined in this opinion.

Having chosen to enter the transaction without recommending that Miller obtain independent advice, respondent was obliged to make full disclosure. Because the record does not show full disclosure was made before Miller consented to the transaction, a violation of DR5–104(A) has been established. This is true even though respondent did not act dishonestly or make a profit on the transaction. See Committee on Professional Ethics and Conduct v. Baker, 269 N.W.2d 463, 465–66 (Iowa 1978).

In accordance with the Commission recommendation, we reprimand him for the violation.

————

Business Dealings with Clients

Mershon's client, farmer Miller, was elderly and apparently inexperienced in real estate development transactions. If Miller had been a major real estate developer with extensive business experience, including the formation of corporations and many prior dealings with lawyers, would the decision have been the same? Was Miller the "client" of Mershon with respect to the land transaction? Suppose Mershon had restricted the scope of engagement to legal work for the new corporation. Would the result be different?

In Matter of Neville,[19] the client was an experienced real estate trader who had been represented by the lawyer in various real estate deals over a period of ten years. Dispute arose concerning an exchange of properties with a third person accompanied by the lawyer's purchase of the acquired property. Although the lawyer did not represent the client in the transaction in question, the lawyer was disciplined for failing to "disclose every circumstance and fact 'which the client should know to make an intelligent decision concerning the wisdom of entering the agreement.' "[20] Clients, the court said, "depend upon the confidentiality and fairness arising from their relationships with their attorneys. They do not take a transactional approach, turning their confidence on and off at the end of each transaction."

Do *Mershon* and *Neville* cast doubt on arrangements in which lawyers for cash-short entrepreneurs accept shares of stock in new and risky ventures in return for legal services performed in getting the corporation started? The travails of Anthony Passante provide an object lesson.[21] Passante was corporate attorney and a director of the Upper Deck Company, a fledgling baseball card manufacturer with a better idea: the invention of a hologram that, when imprinted on the cards, protected them from counterfeiting. Although the company was growing rapidly, it lacked $100,-000 to secure a paper order that was essential to its survival. Passante, as the court put it, "stepped up to the plate and homered on the Upper Deck's behalf" by arranging for the necessary loan. The directors accepted the loan and, in gratitude, agreed among themselves that Passante should receive three percent of the company's stock. Some years later, after the company had become worth more than $100 million, Passante, who had never sought repayment of the $100,000, asked for his shares. When the

19. 708 P.2d 1297 (Ariz.1985).
20. Id. at 1304, citing the *Mershon* case.

21. Passante v. McWilliam, 62 Cal.Rptr.2d 298 (Cal.App.1997).

company refused, he brought suit on the oral contract. A jury verdict for $33 million was set aside by the trial judge and the dismissal upheld on appeal.

If the oral promise was bargained for (and therefore enforceable under contract law), the court said,

> it was obtained in violation of Passante's ethical obligations as an attorney. If, on the other hand, it was not bargained for ... it was gratuitous ... [and therefore] legally unenforceable, even though it might have moral force.

> . . .

> [I]f the stock promise was truly bargained for, then [Passante] had an obligation to the Upper Deck, as its counsel, to give the firm the opportunity to have separate counsel represent it in the course of that bargaining [citing Cal.R.Prof.Conduct 3–300, business transaction with a client].

> Here it is undisputed that Passante did not advise the Upper Deck of the need for independent counsel in connection with its promise, either in writing or even orally. Had he done so before the Upper Deck made its promise, the board of directors might or might not have been so enthusiastic about his finding the money as to give away three percent of the stock. In a business transaction with a client, notes our Supreme Court, a lawyer is obligated to give "his client 'all that reasonable advice against himself that he would have given him against a third person.'" ... Bargaining between the parties might have resulted in Passante settling for just a reasonable finder's fee. Independent counsel would likely have at least reminded the board members of the obvious—that a grant of stock to Passante might complicate future capital acquisition [as subsequent events suggest it might have done].

The courts in *Mershon* and *Passante* state what is sometimes referred to as the "stranger rule:" The lawyer who enters into a business transaction with a client must give the client the same legal advice and guidance as would be given by a lawyer who is a stranger to the transaction. What advice should Mershon have given that he did not give? Note that giving the appropriate advice would not by itself be enough. The other requirements of Rule 1.8(a) also must be met: The terms and circumstances of the transaction must be fair and reasonable to the client, the client must be adequately informed about the terms of the transaction and the risks presented by the lawyer's involvement in it, and the client must consent in writing to the lawyer's role after being encouraged, and given a reasonable opportunity, to seek independent legal advice concerning the transaction.[22]

---

22. This statement paraphrases Restatement § 207 (business transaction between lawyer and client). The requirement that a client be given a reasonable opportunity to seek the advice of independent counsel is taken seriously. The New Jersey court, interpreting Rule 1.8(a)(2), stated that a "passing suggestion" that a client consult a

The focus is whether an ordinary person in the circumstances would look to the lawyer as a protector rather than an adversary or a person dealing at arms length.[23] A violation may be established whether or not the client suffers economic loss.[24] Even where the terms of the transaction are reasonable, failure to make full disclosure of the potential conflict of interest is a violation.[25]

Would Mershon have been required to give the same advice to, and gain the same informed consent from, Schenck, the third entrepreneur? Was Schenck a co-client of the joint venture who was owed the same duties as were owed to Miller?

Under common law, a lawyer in a transaction with a client is treated as a fiduciary. As such the lawyer has the burden of proving that the transaction is "fair and equitable" to the client. In some jurisdictions this requirement is augmented by a "presumption" that such a transaction is tainted by fraud.[26] It is not always clear whether the presumption means more than imposing on the lawyer the burden of proof. Remedies include rescission of a transaction, civil liability, professional discipline and others.[27]

The reported cases often involve the following common situations: (1) lawyer buying estate property from estate beneficiaries; (2) lawyer investing client funds;[28] (3) loan transaction between lawyer and client,[29] and (4) lawyer "taking a piece of the action" in incorporating a new venture.[30] In

second attorney does not discharge the lawyer's duty to explain carefully to the client the need for independent legal advice in lawyer-client transactions. Matter of Smyzer, 527 A.2d 857, 862 (N.J.1987).

23. Sexton v. Arkansas Supreme Court Committee on Professional Conduct, 774 S.W.2d 114 (Ark.1989); Matter of Spear, 774 P.2d 1335 (Ariz.1989).

24. Committee on Professional Ethics and Conduct v. Baker, 269 N.W.2d 463, 466 (Iowa 1978).

25. See In re Appeal of Panel's Affirmance, 425 N.W.2d 824 (Minn.1988).

26. See, e.g., Avianca, Inc. v. Corriea, 705 F.Supp. 666, 679 (D.D.C.1989), aff'd, 70 F.3d 637 (D.C.Cir.1995) (affirming a $1.4 million judgment against a lawyer who, although he did not represent the client on the transaction in question, did the client's other legal work; a lawyer is presumptively liable, although presumption is rebuttable).

27. M.R. 1.8(a) is not listed in M.R. 1.10(a) as one of the conflicts of interest that itself is imputed to a lawyer in the same firm. However, if the adversity of interest between lawyer and client created by the transaction disqualifies the lawyer doing business with a client from representation,

other lawyers in the same firm are likely to be disqualified under the general rule stated in M.R. 1.7 (conflicts with the lawyer's own interest), a conflict imputed to other lawyers by M.R. 1.10(a).

28. See, e.g., Matter of Smyzer, 527 A.2d 857 (N.J.1987) (lawyer disciplined for convincing client to invest proceeds from the sale of her home in a holding company without disclosing his interest in the company); and Matter of Wolk, 413 A.2d 317 (N.J.1980) (lawyer advised a widow to invest $10,000 of her inheritance in a second mortgage on property worth one-half that amount which was owned by a company in which the lawyer owned a 25 percent interest, concealing from her the recent purchase price of the property, its real value and that the taxes on it were unpaid).

29. Sexton v. Arkansas Supreme Court Committee on Professional Conduct, 774 S.W.2d 114 (Ark.1989) (client loaned money to her lawyer on terms found to be usurious; the lawyer failed to disclose risks of nonpayment).

30. On the risks to a law firm of a firm lawyer becoming an active participant in a client's business, consider the huge settle-

some "easy" cases the client is an individual who is inexperienced in business transactions, the terms of the transaction are clearly unfair to the client, and disclosure was totally lacking. But in other cases, as in *Neville* and *Passante*, the client cannot be characterized as "unsophisticated" or the transaction clearly unfair.[31] Is the "hard law" involved in cases of this type unfair to lawyers?[32]

In light of this sad experience, it would be defensible to prohibit any business transaction with a client except transactions in the client's ordinary course of business, such as buying a car from a client in the automobile business. At one point California case law outlawed any business dealings between lawyer and client, but subsequent amendments to the court rules provided an approach similar to that under M.R. 1.8(a).[33] Some cases, such as *Neville*, come close to holding that any substantial transaction between lawyer and client runs a grave risk of being voidable at the client's option. Opinions from courts in Arizona,[34] Iowa[35] and other jurisdictions state that the only safe course is for a lawyer to avoid all business transactions with a client.

Acquiring an Interest in Litigation

Both the Model Rules and the Model Code prohibit the lawyer from acquiring a proprietary interest in litigation. M.R. 1.8(j) and DR 5–103(A). Important exceptions are the contingent fee, considered earlier in this chapter, and attorney's liens. A lawyer may acquire a lien against the client's property to secure the lawyer's fee or expenses when other law so

ments paid by two Philadelphia firms stemming from illegal acts of firm partners who had become active in a client's business: $50 million by Blank, Rome in connection with the failure of Sunrise Saving & Loan (see Nat'l L.J., April 25, 1988, p. 2); and $35 million by Morgan, Lewis & Bockius in connection with a partner's fraud on an insurance company which he both managed and represented (Wall St.J., Feb. 24, 1998, at B9).

31. See also Matter of Pascoe, 549 A.2d 1247, 1248 (N.J.1988) (holding that client's long experience in transactions of this type does not exonerate the lawyer who otherwise violates the rule). Cf. Alala v. Peachtree Plantations, Inc., 355 S.E.2d 286 (S.C.App.1987) (after carefully scrutinizing lawyer-client transaction court found that it was acceptable given that the clients were three experienced land developers and the terms of the contract were fair).

32. See Roy R. Anderson and Walter W. Steele, Jr., Ethics and the Law of Contract Juxtaposed: A Jaundiced View of Professional Responsibility Considerations in the Attorney–Client Relationship, 4 Geo.J.Legal Ethics 791 (1991) (arguing that "outmoded, unrealistic concepts" impose responsibilities on lawyers that are far more restrictive than those applied to other professions or fiduciaries).

33. See Ames v. State Bar, 506 P.2d 625 (Cal.1973) (interpreting court rule stating that a lawyer "shall not acquire an interest adverse to his client" as an absolute bar against acquisition of any such interest; subsequently replaced by Rule 3–300, California's version of M.R. 1.8(a)).

34. Matter of Spear, 774 P.2d 1335, 1344 (Ariz.1989): "The better rule may be to prohibit entirely lawyer-client business dealings.... As a general rule ... no lawyer should allow a client to invest or otherwise participate in the lawyer's business ventures unless the client obtains independent legal advice.

35. Committee on Professional Ethics v. Postma, 430 N.W.2d 387, 391–92 (Iowa 1988): "[W]e have done our best to discourage business ventures between attorneys and their clients...."

provides.[36] Further, a lawyer may advance litigation costs when and to the extent that professional rules allow. See M.R. 1.8(e) and DR 5–103(B).

An attorney's retaining lien allows a lawyer to keep possession of a client's property, but not to sell it, until the client pays what is owed to the lawyer.[37] The major issue here is the opportunity that a lawyer has to coerce a dissatisfied client into paying a fee the client does not believe the lawyer has earned by retaining client documents that are needed by successor counsel.[38] A charging lien attaches to the legal proceeding and allows the lawyer to recover expenses and fees incurred in that litigation from the proceeds. Lawyers may be disciplined for asserting charging liens that are the equivalent of illegal contingent fees.[39]

Advancing Funds to a Client

Lawyers subsidize litigation on an extensive basis. The contingent fee has the effect of loaning the value of the lawyer's services to the client, to be repaid only if and when the lawyer produces a substantial award from which the interest-free loan may be repaid. In addition, professional rules and longstanding practice permit the lawyer to advance litigation expenses (e.g., filing fees, investigation costs, fees for expert witnesses). DR 5–103(B) provides:

> While representing a client in connection with contemplated or pending litigation, a lawyer shall not advance or guarantee financial assistance to his client, except that a lawyer may advance or guarantee the expenses of litigation, including court costs, expenses of investigation, expenses of medical examination, and costs of obtaining and presenting evidence, provided that the client remains ultimately liable for such expenses.

Although the Model Code requires that "the client remains ultimately liable" for litigation expenses, lawyers are not required to press clients to recover these expenses. In most situations in which lawyers advance litigation expenses—usually where the retainer is on a contingent-fee basis for a person of moderate or limited means—the possibilities of recovery from the client if the case fails are remote and are rarely pursued.

---

36. On attorneys' liens generally, see Wolfram, Modern Legal Ethics § 9.6.3, pp. 558–562 (1986).

37. For guidelines on whether to invoke a retaining lien, see ABA Inf.Op. 1461 (1980). See also Rubel v. Brimacombe & Schlecte, P.C., 86 B.R. 81 (E.D.Mich.1988) (using the guidelines to decide whether to allow an attorney's charging lien).

38. See discussion of this issue at p. 465 supra. Restatement § 58(2) states that "a lawyer must allow a client or former client to inspect and copy any document pos-

sessed by the lawyer relating to the representation, unless substantial grounds exist to refuse." A number of states, however, give primacy to the lawyer's interest in compensation, by permitting a lawyer to retain documents when there is a dispute concerning outstanding fee charges.

39. See, e.g., State ex rel. Nebraska State Bar Ass'n v. Jensen, 105 N.W.2d 459 (Neb. 1960) (attorney's lien upon 15 percent of wife's alimony was in effect a contingent fee contract).

Model Rule 1.8(e) recognizes this reality by providing that the lawyer's investment in litigation expenses may also be contingent upon the result of the litigation. It provides:

A lawyer shall not provide financial assistance to a client in connection with pending or contemplated litigation, except that:

> (1) a lawyer may advance court costs and expenses of litigation, the repayment of which may be contingent on the outcome of the matter; and

> (2) a lawyer representing an indigent client may pay court costs and expenses of litigation on behalf of the client.

What purposes are served by these rules? Given that contingent fees are allowed in some cases, why not allow other means of acquiring an interest in litigation?

Both rules implicitly prohibit a lawyer from advancing money to a client for anything other than litigation expenses. The prohibition on advancing funds for living expenses or health care bills while litigation is pending raises a substantial issue of policy. An injured person, out of work and desperate for living and medical expenses, may be forced to settle a meritorious claim at a fraction of its real worth because the defendant, by claiming its right to jury trial and engaging in pretrial procedures, can postpone a recovery for a number of years. Under such circumstances, why shouldn't lawyers advance funds so that the plaintiff may obtain a more adequate award?

In Louisiana State Bar Ass'n v. Edwins,[40] the court held that a lawyer could provide financial assistance to a client under certain circumstances, provided that the advances were not used to solicit clients. A handful of other states, including California, take this approach.[41] The problems engendered by this approach are suggested in Sims v. Selvage,[42] In *Sims* the client discharged his lawyer, testifying that he did so because the lawyer refused to provide money to pay his medical fees. The court said of the *Edwins* rule:

> The obviously well intended interpretation of [DR] 5–103(B) in [*Edwins*] ..., to allow "a lawyer's guarantee of necessary medical treatment for his client, even for a non-litigation related illness ... if the lawyer for reasons of humanity can afford to do so", and to authorize as expenses of litigation, "the advance or guarantee by a lawyer to a client (who has already retained him) of minimal living expenses, of minor sums necessary to prevent foreclosures, or of necessary medical treatment" ... has created problems within the profession that override any benefit to the client. *Edwins*, in conjunction with [case law] allowing the client to withdraw from the contin-

---

40. 329 So.2d 437 (La.1976).

41. See, e.g., Cal.R.Prof.Conduct 4–210(A)(2) (lawyer may lend to client). The reporters for the Restatement urged this approach but were overruled by a narrow margin. See Restatement § 48(2).

42. 499 So.2d 325 (La.App.1986).

gency fee contract with relative impunity, pretty well guarantees that clients will not remain with the attorney who does not gear his practice to providing this type of service. No attorney solicitation is necessary. The reputation of providing these services is enough to draw the client.... The profession is demeaned [by this situation]. Surely, it is time to reconsider this whole area.[43]

Is the "problem" discussed in *Sims* one that should concern clients or only one of increased competition for lawyers? What is it that "demeans" the profession? Although the contingent fee in effect permits a lawyer to purchase a portion of a claim, ancient prohibitions of the assignment of tort claims continue to be enforced. Judge Posner argues that

> the existence of agency costs argues for ... allowing the outright sale of legal claims (contract claims already are assignable; tort claims, in general, are not).... [Assignment of claims would] make it easier for an illiquid or risk-averse person to bring a suit, yet it is not certain the result is more litigation. The likelier a suit is, the greater is the deterrent effect of whatever legal principle the suit would enforce, and hence the less likely are potential defendants to engage in the forbidden conduct that would create a right to sue.[44]

Why not permit a market in claims, so that able lawyers could buy up prospective claims and combine them for purposes of litigation?

Gifts From Clients

Courts have always looked at substantial gifts from clients, especially those solicited by the lawyer or conferred by means of an instrument drafted by the lawyer, with a highly skeptical eye and have invalidated them on a theory of presumptive fraud unless the lawyer has clearly demonstrated that the gift was not the result of undue influence or overreaching.[45]

The problem is one of distinguishing between a Christmas present of a bottle of expensive wine from a grateful client who has become the lawyer's friend and situations in which the lawyer has used her influence with the client to induce a substantial gift. The cases record the sad reality that temptation seduces intelligent and successful lawyers who clearly knew better.[46]

---

43. Id. at 329.

44. Richard A. Posner, The Economic Analysis of Law 625–26 (5th ed.1998). For other critical views of the prohibition against acquiring an interest in litigation, see the discussion, infra at p. 815, of proposals by Professors Macey, Miller and Coffee supporting the creation of a market in small claims that could be brought as class actions.

45. See, e.g., Matter of Putnam's Will, 177 N.E. 399 (N.Y.1931); McDonald v. Hewlett,

228 P.2d 83 (Cal.App.1951). See Gerald P. Johnston, An Ethical Analysis of Common Estate Planning Practices—Is Good Business Bad Ethics?, 45 Ohio State L.J. 57 (1984) (discussing legality and propriety of a lawyer drafting a will naming lawyer as a beneficiary, executor or as attorney for the estate).

46. See Committee on Professional Ethics v. Randall, 285 N.W.2d 161 (Iowa 1979) (former ABA president disbarred for drafting a client's will making him sole beneficiary); In re Cohn, 503 N.Y.S.2d 759 (1st Dept.

Although the Model Code lacks a disciplinary rule on the subject, the courts read the strictures of EC 5–5 into general disciplinary provisions to provide a basis for disciplinary sanctions.[47] The underlying transaction is voidable under decisional law that presumes overreaching and undue influence when a lawyer solicits a valuable gift or prepares an instrument effectuating it.[48]

Model Rule 1.8(c) states:

> A lawyer shall not prepare an instrument giving the lawyer or a person related to the lawyer as parent, child, sibling, or spouse any substantial gift from a client including a testamentary gift, except where the client is related to the donee.

This absolute prohibition goes beyond the pre–1983 case law, which permitted a lawyer to draft such an instrument, if the lawyer had urged the client to seek independent legal assistance, provided full disclosure and the client continued to insist that the lawyer do so.[49] M.R. 1.8(c), however, is narrower than the cases in that the rule only applies to substantial gifts transferred by instruments drafted by the lawyer-beneficiary. What about gifts transferred without papers?

Comment [2] to M.R. 1.8 assumes that any substantial gift will require the preparation of documents and thus will fall under 1.8(c). As for smaller gifts, the Comment states that these may be accepted as long as "the transaction meets general standards of fairness." When a lawyer is disqualified under M.R. 1.8(c), those in practice with the lawyer are likewise disqualified. See M.R. 1.10, discussed in Chapter 7 below.

Model Rule 1.8(c) provides an exception for instruments drafted by a lawyer for people to whom the lawyer is related. This exception, however, does not apply to friends of the lawyer. Lawyers must insist that friends who wish to make a gift to the lawyer retain other counsel to draft the documents of transfer. Even relatives of the lawyer (and the lawyer herself)

1986) (Roy Cohn disbarred for assisting an elderly, bedridden and probably incompetent client in signing his name to an instrument giving Cohn a substantial property interest).

47. Language in EC 5–5 was read into provisions of the Model Codes disciplinary rules. See, e.g., Matter of Rentiers, 374 S.E.2d 672 (S.C.1988) (public reprimand under DR 5–101(A) for drafting a will in which the lawyer/draftsman was named as executor, trustee of a testamentary trust and given an option to purchase real estate at below market value; lawyer failed to disclose that the will would be vulnerable to attack upon grounds of undue influence); Mahoning County Bar Association v. Theofilos, 521 N.E.2d 797 (Ohio 1988) (lawyer disciplined under DR 1–102(A)(6) for drafting a will that provided a $200,000

bequest for lawyer and his son and provided nothing for the client's relatives; lawyer failed to insist that independent counsel draft the will).

48. See, e.g., Radin v. Opperman, 64 A.D.2d 820, 407 N.Y.S.2d 303 (1978) (lawyer forced to give up Totten Trust accounts opened by client for lawyer's benefit, where no evidence of independent advice overcomes presumption of undue influence).

49. Restatement § 208(3) follows the case law rather than M.R. 1.8 in validating client gifts if the lawyer has not unduly influenced or overreached the client and has urged and given the client a reasonable opportunity to seek competent, independent advice, which need not be from another lawyer.

are well advised to have independent counsel draft any documents of transfer whenever possible, the exception in 1.8(c) notwithstanding. If the relative wishes to make a substantial gift to the lawyer or there is any chance that the gift will be challenged, independent counsel should be obtained.

Sexual Relationship With Client[50]

A growing body of case law deals with sexual relations between a lawyer and an individual client during the course of representation. In Drucker's Case[51] a lawyer was suspended for two years for sexual relations with a divorce client who suffered from an anxiety disorder; the court held that the lawyer's conduct violated M.R. 1.7(b) (conflict with the lawyer's own interests), M.R. 1.8(b) (use of client information to disadvantage the client), and M.R. 1.14(a) (failure to maintain a normal lawyer-client relationship with an impaired client). In People v. Gibbons[52] a criminal defense lawyer, who represented both a woman and her husband, initiated a sexual relationship with the female client; the lawyer, who had also engaged in other misconduct, was disbarred on conflict of interest grounds.

The number of reported discipline complaints involving sexual contact, formerly quite small,[53] has increased rapidly in recent years. Studies of psychotherapists' sexual involvement with patients reveal that 12 percent of psychotherapists nationwide report sexual contact with patients despite a flat professional prohibition.[54] Although Arnold Becker, the philandering divorce lawyer of *L.A. Law*, may not be typical, accumulating evidence suggests that sexual relationships between lawyers and divorce clients occur quite frequently. Manipulation and exploitation are especially probable when a client is vulnerable or in distress.

A 1992 ABA ethics opinion reviews the ethics rules that may be violated by a sexual relationship with an individual client during the course of representation.[55] First, the lawyer may breach fiduciary obligations to the client if the sexual relationship results from the client's dependence and vulnerability or the lawyer's manipulation of the client's trust.[56] Second, a lawyer's independent professional judgment may be lost due to sexual involvement with a client. M.R. 2.1. Third, a prohibited conflict with the lawyer's own interest results if that interest impairs or materially limits the representation. M.R. 1.7(b). Finally, client confidences are protected by the attorney-client privilege only when communications are made

50. See generally Abed Awad, Attorney Client Sexual Relations, 22 J. Legal Prof. 131 (1998) (surveying state ethics rules); and Note, Keeping Sex Out of the Attorney–Client Relationship: A Proposed Rule, 92 Colum.L.Rev. 887 (1992) (discussing and proposing a per se rule banning lawyer-client sexual relationships with limited exceptions).

51. 577 A.2d 1198 (N.H.1990).

52. 685 P.2d 168 (Colo.1984).

53. See Linda M. Jorgenson & Pamela K. Sutherland, Lawyer–Client Contact: State Bars Polled, Nat'l L. J., June 15, 1991, at p. 26 (only 90 complaints filed in 47 responding states, but low report is characteristic of sexual harassment).

54. Id. at 27.

55. ABA Standing Comm. on Ethics and Prof.Resp., Formal Op. 92–364 (July 6, 1992).

56. See M.R. 1.7(b), 1.8(a), (b), and 1.14(a).

for the purpose of receiving legal advice, imperiling statements made during a sexual relationship. The opinion advises lawyers to refrain from sexual relationships with clients. If such a relationship occurs and actually impairs the lawyer's representation, a disciplinary violation has occurred.

As of 1998, ten states had adopted express ethics rules on lawyer-client sexual relations. California was the first state to adopt a rule specifically addressing the problem, but its rule may add little to the existing prohibitions summarized in the 1992 ABA opinion.[57] A few states have followed the California example, emphasizing the exploitative character of sexual relations with a current client. At least six states have a per se ban on all sexual relations with current clients regardless of its exploitative character.[58]

Should a per se rule prohibit lawyer-client sex during the period of representation? Opponents of a per se rule argue that existing ethics provisions deal satisfactorily with the problem, privacy and autonomy interests of lawyers will be impaired, and sexual harassment charges and damage actions against lawyers will be encouraged.[59] Does the constitutional right of privacy stand in the way of regulation of lawyer-client sexual relationships?[60] Note that a professional rule would not restrict a lawyer's sexual relationships, but only require that she withdraw from representation before commencing a sexual relationship.

The Advocate–Witness Rule[61]

When, if ever, may the trial lawyer act as a witness in the case she is trying? Many firms offer wide-ranging services to their clients, e.g., negoti-

---

57. Rule 3–120(B) of the California Rules of Professional Conduct provides that members of the California bar shall not:

(1) Require or demand sexual relations with a client incident to or as a condition of any professional representation; or (2) Employ coercion, intimidation, or undue influence in entering into sexual relations with a client; or (3) Continue representation of a client with whom the member has sexual relations if such sexual relations cause the member to perform legal services incompetently in violation of rule 3–110.

58. See, e.g., Wisconsin Supreme Court Rule 20:1.8(k)(2): "A lawyer shall not have sexual relations with a current client unless a consensual sexual relationship existed between them when the lawyer-client relationship commenced." The rules generally provide exceptions for sexual relationships with spouses or that preexisted the representation. Some have limited or no application to sexual relationships with agents of a corporate or organizational client. The New York rule is limited to matrimonial representation.

59. See Note, Colum.L.Rev., supra (per se ban needed); Philip Corboy, No, It's Already Covered, A.B.A.J., Jan. 1992, at p. 35; William C. Barker & C. Harker Rhodes, Jr., Draconian Sex Rules Premature, Nat'l L.J., June 29, 1992, at p. 17.

60. See Carey v. Population Services International, 431 U.S. 678, 684 (1977) (one aspect of the "liberty" protected by the due process clause of the Fourteenth Amendment is the right to certain zones of privacy); but cf. Bowers v. Hardwick, 478 U.S. 186 (1986) (state may regulate sodomy).

61. Articles on the advocate-witness rule include: Barbara J. Moss, Ethical Prohibitions Against a Lawyer's Serving as Both Advocate and Witness, 23 Mem. St. U. L. Rev. 555 (1993); Jeffrey A. Stonerock, The Advocate–Witness Rule: Anachronism or Necessary Restraint?, 94 Dick. L. Rev. 821 (1990); Richard C. Wydick, Trial Counsel as Witness: The Code and the Model Rules, 15 U.C. Davis L. Rev. 651, 659 (1982); Arnold N. Enker, The Rationale of the Rule That Forbids a Lawyer to Be an Advocate and Witness in the Same Case, 1977 Am. B. Found. Res. J. 455.

ating contracts, establishing pension funds, handling tax matters and defending or prosecuting litigation. The lawyer who negotiated the contract or set up the tax plan may have relevant testimony to offer in later litigation on those matters. Should the lawyer be allowed to serve as trial counsel? In many firms, that lawyer would not handle litigation matters, although in some small shops one lawyer may do all these things. In firms with litigation departments, may the lawyers in the department continue as trial counsel when a lawyer in the same firm should be called as a witness on matters at issue in the litigation?

Model Rule 3.7(a) prohibits a lawyer from acting as trial counsel when she is "likely to be a necessary witness" in the case, although it lists some exceptions; a lawyer may continue as trial counsel when the testimony she may have to provide "relates to an uncontested matter," 3.7(a)(1), or "to the nature and value of legal services rendered in the case," 3.7(a)(2). A lawyer may also serve as trial counsel, despite the likelihood of being a necessary witness, when "disqualification ... would work substantial hardship on the client," 3.7(a)(3). These exceptions are virtually identical to those found in the Model Code. See DR 5–102(B).

There are, however, differences between the Model Rules' approach to the lawyer/witness scenario and that of the Model Code. First, the Model Code provision is triggered when it is "obvious" that the lawyer "ought to be called as a witness." Compare the "likely to be ..." standard used in the Model Rules.[62] Second, the Model Code prohibits a lawyer from accepting or continuing *representation* when she "ought to be called...." The Model Rules prohibits the lawyer, who is likely to be a witness, only from acting as trial counsel, not from other forms of representing the client. Thus, the lawyer may be able to perform case related pre-trial work under Model Rule 3.7, whereas the Code would prohibit that.[63] The most important difference between the Code and the Rules concerns the question of whether all lawyers in a law firm are disqualified from acting as trial counsel (or under the Code, from representing the client in any capacity) when any one lawyer in the firm is disqualified under the advocate-witness rule. The ethics rules, courts and lawyers refer to questions involving one lawyer's disqualification tainting other lawyers as "imputed disqualification" questions. In the next chapter, after considering what conflicts of interest suffice to get the first lawyer disqualified, we take up the subject of imputed disqualification.

Here, it is enough to note that, unlike the Model Code, Model Rule 3.7(b) does not automatically disqualify all lawyers in a firm from acting as trial counsel whenever one of them is "likely to be a necessary witness."

---

62. See Cannon Airways v. Franklin Holdings Corp., 669 F.Supp. 96,99 (D.Del.1987) (holding that the Model Rules standard covers fewer situations than the standard used in the Code).

63. See Culebras Enterprises v. Rivera–Rios, 846 F.2d 94., 98 (1st Cir.1988) (holding that under 3.7 a lawyer may do case-related pretrial work and noting that the result would be different under the Code).

Contrast DR 5–101 (accepting employment) and 5–102 (withdrawing from employment) both referring to a lawyer *or any member of the lawyer's firm.* On the other hand, Model Rule 3.7(b) does not allow other lawyers in the firm to proceed in every instance in which one of their colleagues is likely to be a witness. It provides that other conflicts rules may operate to disqualify the rest of the firm. When? You should be able to answer that question after studying the conflicts materials presented in the next chapter. As prologue to that material, think about the difference between a lawyer-witness whose testimony is completely favorable to the client and a lawyer-witness whose testimony will hurt the client's cause. In the second scenario, it would be the trial lawyer's job to examine or cross-examine the lawyer-witness in a manner designed to combat whatever damage that lawyer's testimony had done the client's cause. If the lawyer-witness and the trial lawyer were partners, isn't it reasonable to think the trial lawyer might not do as effective a job at impeaching the damaging testimony? If you were a client, how much would you trust the firm representing you to be "doing its best" for you, when one of its lawyers was likely to offer testimony damaging to your case?

CHAPTER 7

Conflicts of Interest

A. Introduction

An early statement by Justice Joseph Story (1779–1845) suggests the concerns underlying the law of conflicts of interest:

> An attorney is bound to disclose to his client every adverse retainer, and even every prior retainer, which may affect the discretion of the [client]. No [client] can be supposed to be indifferent to the knowledge of facts, which work directly on his interests, or bear on the freedom of his choice of counsel. When a client employs an attorney, he has a right to presume, if the latter be silent on the point, that he has no engagements, which interfere, in any degree, with his exclusive devotion to the cause confided to him; that he has no interest, which may betray his judgment, or endanger his fidelity.[1]

The rules on conflicts of interest do not aim at elimination of all possible conflicts; this is impossible. Even if we envisioned lawyers as ascetics, renouncing all self interest, devoted only to their calling—and we have no such vision—even if our notion of a lawyer was someone who served one client for the entirety of her career—and, of course, it is not—conflicting interests would be present: The client's interest would still sometimes conflict with the interests of third parties or with the law itself. Dealing with conflicting interests is inherent in a lawyer's life.

Conflicting interests are not unique to the lawyer-client relationship. The practice of law is a social relationship comparable to partnership, a joint venture or friendship. Any such relationship between two people carries the potential for a conflict of interest: Each party has her own interests, which may conflict with the interests of the other person.

Although everyone faces similar questions, the conflicts questions faced by lawyers are perhaps greater in number and intensity than those faced by most other people. Nor are the conflicts rules in non-lawyer relationships (e.g., a business partnership) a sure guide in analyzing lawyer conflicts of interest. The lawyer-client relationship is unique by definition, i.e., it is a relationship whose object is the rendering of legal advice and counsel. The most striking implication of this fact is that the rendering of illegal aid is, by definition, outside the bounds of the relationship. This is not true in the same sense for other relationships. In addition, a lawyer has a special legal duty of confidentiality to the client, recognized in importance by a corresponding attorney-client privilege protecting client confidences in court.

---

1. Williams v. Reed, 3 Mason 405, 418, Fed. Case No. 17,733 (C.C.Maine 1824).

All voluntary social relations are based on some measure of loyalty, commitment and trust. Loyalty stands in opposition to betrayal. The measure of loyalty required to sustain the relation depends on the purpose of the relation itself and the stakes. Less commitment is required to have a viable or satisfactory employment relationship than a satisfactory marriage. It is therefore necessary to speak of loyalty and trust specifically between lawyer and client. We are not here addressing the general question of whether clients ever "really" do or should trust their lawyers: about mistrust engendered by stereotypes (true or false) about the profession; about mistrust that might arise from difference between the lawyer's class, economic status or race and that of the client. These important issues are touched on elsewhere in this book. Here we are talking only about mistrust created when a lawyer acts as the client's agent in the face of serious conflicting interests. Ideal lawyer-client relationships in this respect may be impossible, but "reasonable loyalty" is not.

Questions of loyalty, commitment and trust speak both to the quality of the lawyer-client *relationship* and to the quality of the *representation*. If the client does not see the conflict as a betrayal, i.e., fails to appreciate the conflict or chooses to disregard it, the representation might nevertheless suffer. That is, there is a good chance that the lawyer with a serious conflict will shortchange her client, even if inadvertently. This aspect of conflict of interest rules reinforces competency in representation.

The Several Faces of Conflicts

Lawyers are exposed to two primary categories of conflicts: conflicts between clients and conflicts between lawyer and client. The latter category was considered in Chapter 6 above.

Conflicts between clients can be divided into two major subcategories: concurrent and successive representation. Conflict in concurrent representation involves conflict between two present or prospective clients or between one present and one prospective client. Conflict in successive representation involves conflict between a former client and a present or prospective client. Concurrent representation is taken up first, followed by successive representation. Some more complex situations are considered in Chapter 8.

Akin to conflicts in concurrent representation are conflicts between a client's interests and some third party who is not a client but to whom the lawyer owes some duty. For example, what should a lawyer for a corporation do when the interests of shareholders appear to conflict with the interests of management? What about a lawyer being paid by an insurance company to represent an insured who discovers that the insured's interests and the insurance company's interests are in conflict? What should a lawyer for a partnership do when one or more partners seem determined to oust another partner? Some of these problems are dealt with later in this chapter; others are introduced here and considered more fully in Chapter 8 below.

A further question is whether an entire firm is disqualified because one lawyer within the firm has a disqualifying conflict. This question involves the subject of imputed disqualification: some conflicts are imputed to other lawyers in the firm; others are not. In studying imputed disqualification one must also consider whether lawyers tainted by another's conflict remain disqualified when they sever their practice relationship with the disqualified lawyer. After studying the basic conflicts rules, we turn in this chapter to these imputed disqualification questions.

———

B.   CONCURRENT REPRESENTATION IN LITIGATION

INTRODUCTION: DIVERGING INTERESTS AND ANTAGONISM

The rules governing conflicts of interest in concurrent representation address two situations: when the interests of one client run (or have the potential to run) counter to those of another client and when the antagonism between two clients is great. As to the first problem, diverging interests, it is easiest to imagine the problem if you contemplate two clients who seek representation jointly on a matter of common purpose, for example, the city of New York and one of its police officers seeking a common defense against a civil rights suit caused by the officer's actions in causing a person's death. Some defenses available to the city involve implicating the officer. The interests of the two clients in the lawyer investigating the facts to develop those defenses or researching the law on those defenses diverge. It is in the city's interest, but not in the interest of the officer. Indeed, it is in the interest of the officer for the lawyer instead to be spending time developing theories that shift responsibility for the harm from the officer to superiors in the department, i.e., to the city. The more the interests of two clients diverge (or have the potential to diverge), the more the lawyer's representation of each client is restricted by her duty not to harm the other client. This is the problem of divergent interests.

As to the second problem, antagonism, it too is present in the example just given. Is it reasonable to expect the officer to trust her lawyer to be devoted to her cause if that lawyer is expending energy for another client on how to harm the officer? The more divergent the interests of two clients are (or are likely to become) the greater the potential for antagonism to interfere with the relationship between a lawyer and client. But the problem of antagonism may exist in situations that do not involve the lawyer in representing divergent interests, namely when a lawyer seeks to represent two clients in matters completely unrelated to one another.

Imagine a lawyer representing corporation X in a suit brought against it by its employees alleging sex discrimination. That lawyer is now approached by corporation Y which wants to sue corporations X and Z for conspiring to restrain trade. The interests of X in the first suit, which the lawyer is bound to protect, and the interests of Y in the second suit, which Y seeks to have the lawyer further, are not divergent. It is difficult to see how the decisions, advice, strategy or actions of the lawyer in defending X in the first suit would be affected by the fact that it was bound to protect Y's interest in the second suit, which distinguishes this situation from the city/officer situation described above. Given that the two matters (the sex discrimination case and the antitrust suit) are completely unrelated to one another, the problem of representing divergent interests does not arise. But were the lawyer to accept Y's invitation to sue its own client, X, the lawyer would be taking as antagonistic a stance against one of its own clients as it is possible to take. After being sued by its own lawyer, would it be reasonable for corporation X to trust that lawyer, even in unrelated litigation, to be dedicated to its cause? What client would believe it wise to confide freely in or take advice offered by a lawyer representing an opponent, even in an unrelated cause?

1.   PROFESSIONAL RULES ON CONCURRENT REPRESENTATION

The central provision in the Model Code on conflicts of interest, DR 5–105, and the Ethical Considerations that accompany it, are broadly written.[2] Case law on conflicts issues filled the gaps left by the Model Code. To a large extent, Model Rules 1.7 through 1.15, and 2.2 and 2.3 codify that case law. M.R. 1.16, Declining and Terminating the Representation, and M.R. 2.1, Advisor, are also relevant to conflicts problems. A conflict of interest is presented whenever a lawyer wants to withdraw and her client wants her to continue or would be harmed by her withdrawal. Similarly, M.R. 2.1 speaks of professional judgment that is unaffected by conflicting interests. Consideration of conflicts problems also raises issues of confidentiality under M.R. 1.6, such as when a lawyer wants to communicate a client's confidence to a prospective client to obtain consent to a concurrent or successive representation that would otherwise be prohibited, but the client does not agree.

Interests "Directly Adverse"

Model Rule 1.7(a) prohibits the representation of a client whose interests are directly adverse to another client's interests, unless:

> 1) the lawyer reasonably believes that the representation will not adversely affect the *relationship* with the other client; and

> 2) each client consents after consultation. (Emphasis added.)

When can a lawyer "reasonably believe" that the *relationship* will not be adversely affected? The use of the word "relationship" here instead of "representation" is significant. It is difficult to represent interests directly adverse to an individual client without the relationship with that client

---

2. DR 5–105 provides that a lawyer may not concurrently represent clients with "differing interests," unless (1) the lawyer ob-   tains consent after full disclosure and (2) it is "obvious" that the lawyer can "adequately represent" both clients.

being "adversely affected", even if the matters are wholly unrelated.[3] Consider the discussion of X and Y corporations discussed above. Is the client consent proviso empty?

As Comment [8] to M.R. 1.7 points out, client consent permits the adverse representation in some situations, particularly where the clients are organizations. For example, suppose a lawyer represents corporation X in all its securities matters; corporation Y, a bakery, is one of 30 subsidiaries of Corporation X; the lawyer is hired by corporation Z which wants to sue Y for breaching a delivery contract. The lawyer may reasonably believe that this suit will not have any adverse effect on the relationship with corporation X. The lawyer would then be able to proceed, if after explaining the potential problems (consultation), corporations X and Z gave their consent. That is, the lawyer would be able to proceed assuming that it is reasonable to believe that neither the relationship with X nor that with Z would be adversely affected and consent is obtained from *both* clients after consultation.

The paradigm of direct adversity is one client suing another: A lawyer may not, without consent, represent her client's opponent in any matter, no matter how unrelated to the client's suit.[4] Apart from litigation, it seems clear that when two clients are involved in a hostile negotiation their interests are also directly adverse. Further along the continuum situations

---

3. The Texas ethics rules permit a lawyer to engage in concurrent representation for and against a current client, without the consent of both clients, if the matters are not substantially related and the lawyer's responsibilities to one client do not "reasonably appear to be or become adversely limited by the lawyer's . . . responsibilities to another client." Tex.R.Prof.Conduct 1.06(b). When a district court, following the Texas rule, permitted a law firm to represent a class in an antitrust case against a company the firm was currently representing in other litigation, the Fifth Circuit granted mandamus and reversed. In re Dresser Industries, Inc., 972 F.2d 540 (5th Cir.1992). The applicable conflicts law governing disqualification in a federal court, the court said, is not the state ethics rule, whether or not it is adopted as a local rule by the district court, but the national law of professional responsibility interpreted and applied in Fifth Circuit decisions. Under that law "a law firm may [not] sue its own client, which it concurrently represents in other matters . . . and most certainly not here, where the motivation appears only to be the law firm's self-interest."

4. In Cinema 5, Ltd. v. Cinerama, Inc., 528 F.2d 1384, 1386–87 (2d Cir.1976), a leading case on concurrent representation, the firm argued that it should be allowed to proceed against a present client because the matter in which it represented the client bore no "substantial relationship" to that in which it was suing the client. The court said:

> Putting it as mildly as we can, we think it would be questionable conduct for an attorney to participate in any lawsuit against his own client without the knowledge and consent of all concerned. . . .
>
> Whether such adverse representation, without more, requires disqualification in every case, is a matter we need not now decide. We do hold, however, that the 'substantial relationship' test does not set a sufficiently high standard by which the necessity for disqualification should be determined. That test may properly be applied only where the representation of a former client has been terminated. . . . Where the relationship is a continuing one, adverse representation is prima facie improper . . . and the attorney must be prepared to show, at the very least, that there will be no actual or *apparent* conflict in loyalties or diminution in the vigor of his representation.

become more difficult to assess: How adverse are the interests of two
parties in friendly negotiations? The parties always have some divergent
aims, for example, one wants to buy for the least amount of money and the
other wants to sell for the greatest. The interests here do not seem directly
adverse, but are they nevertheless adverse enough to preclude one lawyer
representing both parties? Consider Model Rule 1.7(b).

Representation "Materially Limited"

M.R. 1.7(b) provides that a lawyer shall not represent a client if the
representation may be "materially limited" by the lawyer's responsibilities
to another client or to a third person, or by the lawyer's own interests. The
lawyer may, however, proceed in such situations if: (1) she reasonably
believes the *representation* will not be affected; and (2) the client consents
after consultation.

Under M.R. 1.7(b) the emphasis is on the quality of the representation
to be provided. The rule does not use the term "adverse" to describe the
other interests that might trigger the rule. This is because responsibilities
of a lawyer to another client might interfere with a concurrent representation even where the clients' interests are not so opposed as to be called
"adverse." Thus, the duty of loyalty might cause the lawyer to be less
committed to a client with a different interest in the matter; the duty of
confidentiality might result in hesitancy to discuss related issues with a
second client; and the duty of due diligence might cause the lawyer to
neglect one matter in favor of another that is more demanding of her time
or more lucrative.

The Restatement states the general rule on conflict of interests in
terms of the adverse affect on the representation. "A conflict of interest is
involved if there is a substantial risk that the lawyer's representation of the
client would be materially and adversely affected by the lawyer's own
interests or by the lawyer's duties to another current client, a former client
or a third person." Restatement § 201 (prohibiting a lawyer from proceeding in the face of a conflict of interest unless consent is obtained in
accordance with § 202 and the other requirements of 202 are met). In
other words, whether the representation is directly adverse or somewhat
less than directly adverse to an existing client is not the first question to be
asked under the Restatement's approach.[5] Under the Restatement once a
conflict, as defined in § 201 exists, whether the lawyer may proceed
depends on whether the criteria of § 202 can be met. Section 202 provides:

> (1) A lawyer may represent a client notwithstanding a conflict of
> interest prohibited by § 201 if each affected client or former client
> gives informed consent to the lawyer's representation. Informed con-

---

5.   Comment *e* to § 209 discusses suing a
client in an unrelated matter and seems to
take a more permissive approach than that
embodied in the comments to 1.7(a). Comment *e* emphasizes that confidential information is unlikely to be implicated when
suing a client in an unrelated matter, although the client might not believe that
the lawyer will prosecute (or defend) its
interests as fully in deference to the client
who is suing the first client.

sent requires that the client or former client have reasonably adequate information about the material risks of such representation to that client or former client.

(2) Notwithstanding the informed consent of each affected client or former client, a lawyer may not represent a client if:

(a) the representation is prohibited by law;

(b) one client will assert a claim against the other in the same litigation, . . .; or

(c) in the circumstances, it is not reasonably likely that the lawyer will be able to provide adequate representation to one or more of the clients.

How, if at all, does this formulation differ from that of Model Rule 1.7. Is it better? Contrast § 202(2) with M.R. 1.7(a). Do those two provisions cover the same range of conduct? Notice that § 202(2)(c) preserves the concept embedded in M.R. 1.7 that more than consent is necessary to cure conflicts that affect a current representation. On the other hand, the objective belief component of the Restatement's provision is not as prominently placed as it is in the Model Rules. Or, to put this point another way, the Restatement's structure suggests a more prominent role for consent than the structure of the Model Rules.[6]

The conflict provisions in the Model Rules and the Restatement share a similar structure: general rule (§§ 1.7 and M.R. 201–202) followed by more specific rules that represent application of the general rules in common situations. Thus, Model Rule 1.8 covers a series of situations involving conflicts between a lawyer's own interests and those of a client and details the conditions under which a lawyer may proceed, if at all, in each of those situations. See e.g., M.R. 1.8(a) concerning business transactions between lawyers and clients. Restatement § 207 parallels the subject matter of 1.8(a), and § 211 (multiple representation in non-litigated matters) covers substantially the same ground as Model Rule 2.2.

Model Rule 2.2 deals with the lawyer who acts as an intermediary between two clients. It may be considered a specific application of 1.7(b), giving the lawyer who contemplates acting as an intermediary between two clients more specific guidance than 1.7 alone.

Per Se Bans on Concurrent Representation

Although courts are quick to disapprove "unconsented" concurrent representation, they are reluctant to overrule client consent to the representation of conflicting interests. Respect for client consent recognizes the importance of a client's right to select counsel of her own choosing and, within limits, to select the kind of representation as between full-blown partisanship and intermediation.

6. See Fred C. Zacharias, Waiving Conflicts of Interest, 108 Yale L.J. 407 (1998) (contrasting various approaches to the role of consent in curing concurrent conflicts of interests).

The Supreme Court of New Jersey, for example, refused to approve a New Jersey ethics committee opinion that would have imposed an absolute ban on the joint representation of a government entity and individual government officials as defendants in § 1983 actions.[7] The ethics committee was concerned that a case-by-case approach was too uncertain. The court thought the absolute ban was overinclusive, i.e., that there are some situations where the dual representation does not present an actual conflict:

> Only in the most sensitive circumstances have we imposed a per se rule of disqualification. In the past we have by administrative directive prohibited the joint representation of driver and passenger in automobile negligence cases (other than those involving husband and wife or parent and child).

Why is the driver-passenger situation "sensitive" enough to adopt a per se rule and not the § 1983 situation?[8]

2. Concurrent Representation in Civil Litigation

Westinghouse Elec. Corp. v. Kerr–McGee Corp.

United States Court of Appeals, Seventh Circuit, 1978.
580 F.2d 1311.

■ Before Fairchild, Chief Judge, and Sprecher and Bauer, Circuit Judges.

■ Sprecher, Circuit Judge.

The novel issues on this appeal are (1) whether an attorney-client relationship arises only when both parties consent to its formation or can it also occur when the lay party submits confidential information to the law party with reasonable belief that the latter is acting as the former's attorney and (2) whether the size and geographical scope of a law firm exempt it from the ordinary ethical considerations applicable to lawyers generally.

The four separate appellants are some of the defendants in this antitrust case who were each denied their motions to disqualify the law firm of Kirkland and Ellis ("Kirkland") from further representing the plaintiff Westinghouse Electric Corporation ("Westinghouse"). Whether fortuitously or by design, on the same day, October 15, 1976, Kirkland, while representing the American Petroleum Institute ("API"), of which three of the appellants, Gulf Oil Corporation ("Gulf"), Kerr–McGee Corporation ("Kerr–McGee") and Getty Oil Company ("Getty"), were members, released a report which took an affirmative position on the subject of competition in the uranium industry, while simultaneously filing this

---

7. In the Matter of Opinion 552 of Advisory Committee on Professional Ethics, 507 A.2d 233, 239, n. 3 (1986).

8. See also Fleming v. State, 270 S.E.2d 185 (Ga.1980) (absolute ban on representing more than one defendant in death penalty cases).

lawsuit, representing Westinghouse, seeking to establish an illegal conspiracy in restraint of trade in the uranium industry.

The fourth appellant, Noranda Mines Limited ("Noranda"), asserts a different conflict of interest in Kirkland resulting from its prior representation of Noranda from 1965 to 1967 in several matters. . . . [This part of the opinion is omitted. The court held that Kirkland's earlier representation of Noranda did not warrant disqualification because it was not substantially related to the current litigation.]

I

On September 8, 1975, Westinghouse, a major manufacturer of nuclear reactors, notified utility companies that 17 of its long-term uranium supply contracts had become "commercially impracticable" under § 2–615 of the Uniform Commercial Code. In response, the affected utilities filed 13 federal actions, one state action, and three foreign actions against Westinghouse, alleging breach of contract and challenging Westinghouse's invocation of § 2–615. The federal actions were consolidated for trial in the Eastern District of Virginia at Richmond. . . .

As an outgrowth of its defense of these contract actions, Westinghouse on October 15, 1976, filed the present antitrust action against 12 foreign and 17 domestic corporations engaged in various aspects of the uranium industry.

Kirkland's representation of Westinghouse's uranium litigation has required the efforts of 8 to 14 of its attorneys and has generated some $2.5 million in legal fees.

Contemporaneously with its Westinghouse representation in the uranium cases Kirkland represented API, using six of its lawyers in that project.

In October, 1975, Congress was presented with legislative proposals to break up the oil companies, both vertically by separating their control over production, transportation, refining and marketing entities, and horizontally by prohibiting cross-ownership of alternative energy resources in addition to oil and gas. Since this proposed legislation threatened oil companies with a potential divestiture of millions of dollars of assets, in November, 1975, the API launched a Committee on Industrial Organization to lobby against the proposals. On December 10, 1975, API's president requested that each company designate one of its senior executives to facilitate coordination of the Committee's activities with the individual companies.

The Committee was organized into five task forces. The Legal Task Force was headed by L. Bates Lea, General Counsel of Standard Oil of Indiana, assisted by Stark Ritchie, API's General Counsel.

On February 25, 1976, Ritchie wrote to Frederick M. Rowe, a partner in Kirkland's Washington office, retaining the firm to review the divestiture hearings and "prepare arguments for use in opposition to this type of legislation." On May 4, 1976, Ritchie added that the Kirkland firm's work for API "should include the preparation of possible testimony, analyzing the probable legal consequences and antitrust considerations of the proposed legislation" and "you should make an objective survey and study of the probable effects of the pending legislation, specifically including probable effects on oil companies that would have to divest assets." Ritchie noted that "[a]s a part of this study, we will arrange for interviews by your firm with a cross-section of industry personnel." The May 4 letter to Rowe concluded with:

> Your firm will, of course, act as an independent expert counsel and hold any company information learned through these interviews in strict confidence, not to be disclosed to any other company, or even to API, except in aggregated or such other form as will preclude identifying the source company with its data.

On May 25, 1976, Ritchie sent to 59 API member companies a survey questionnaire seeking data to be used by Kirkland in connection with its engagement by API. In the introductory memorandum to the questionnaire, Ritchie advised the 59 companies that Kirkland had "ascertained that certain types of data pertinent to the pending anti-diversification legislation are not now publicly available" and the API "would appreciate your help in providing this information to Kirkland...." The memorandum included the following:

> Kirkland, Ellis & Rowe is acting as an independent special counsel for API, and will hold any company information in strict confidence, *not to be disclosed to any other company, or even to API*, except in aggregated or such other form as will preclude identifying the source company with its data. (Emphasis in original).

The data sought was to assist Kirkland "in preparing positions, arguments and testimony in opposition to this type of legislative [divestiture]" and was not to be sent to API but rather to Kirkland.

Pursuant to the provision in Ritchie's May 4, 1976 letter to Rowe that interviews would be arranged with a cross-section of industry personnel, Nolan Clark, a Kirkland partner, interviewed representatives of eight oil companies between April 29 and June 15, 1976.

After going through several drafts, the final Kirkland report to API was released on October 15, 1976. The final report contains 230 pages of text and 82 pages of exhibits. References to uranium appear throughout the report and uranium is the primary subject of about 25 pages of text and 11 pages of exhibits. The report marshalls a large number of facts and arguments to show that oil company diversification does not threaten overall energy competition. In particular the report asserts that the relatively high concentration ratios in the uranium industry can be expected to decline, that current increases in uranium prices are a result of increasing demand, that oil company entry into uranium production has stimulated competition and diminished concentration, that oil companies have no incentive to act in concert to restrict coal or uranium production and that the historical record refutes any charge that oil companies have restricted uranium output. The report concludes that "the energy industries, both individually and collectively, are competitive today and are likely to remain so." 448 F.Supp. at 1296.

As noted at the outset of this opinion, the API report was issued on the same day as the present antitrust suit was filed against several defendants, including Gulf, Kerr–McGee and Getty.

The district court concluded that "[a] comparison of the two documents reveals a rather basic conflict in their contentions and underlying theories." 448 F.Supp. at 1295. The court also observed that "[p]erhaps in recognition of the diametrically opposing theories of the API report and the Westinghouse complaint, Kirkland does not attempt to rebut the oil companies' charges that it has simultaneously taken inconsistent positions on competition in the uranium industry." 448 F.Supp. at 1296.

Gulf, Kerr–McGee and Getty are substantial dues-paying members of API. Kerr–McGee and Getty are also represented on API's board of directors.

At Ritchie's request, the cross-section interviews were mainly arranged by Gerald Thurmond, Washington Counsel of Gulf Oil Company and a member of API's Antitrust Strategy Group. On May 11, 1976, Thurmond advised Gulf officials that Nolan Clark of Kirkland planned to visit them. Attached to Thurmond's letter were the questions "which will be covered" in the meeting.[2]

The meeting was held on May 28, 1976 in Denver. Nolan Clark represented Kirkland. In attendance for Gulf were six vice presidents, a comptroller and a regional attorney. Also present was a Harvard professor who "also is working with API on the same subject." The meeting lasted more than two hours followed by lunch, during which discussions continued. After the meeting and in three letters from Gulf vice president Mingee to Clark dated August 10, 11 and 13, Gulf submitted specific information sought by Clark through the questionnaire and other written questions and in each letter Mingee stressed the confidential basis upon which the information was supplied.

Nolan Clark's interview with two Kerr–McGee vice presidents took place in Oklahoma City on June 9, 1976 and lasted about three hours. Clark was given considerable background information on Kerr–McGee's uranium industry, including mining locations, uranium conversion process, and pellet fabrication. On the subject of uranium marketing and pricing, one of the Kerr–McGee vice presidents described the escalating prices and tightening supplies in the current market, and the reasons behind the trends. Kerr–McGee sent its completed questionnaire to Clark on August 25, 1976.

---

2. [The questions, prepared by Nolan Clark as "the kinds of questions I might want to ask", are included in a lengthy footnote to the court's opinion. They sought detailed information about "alternative energy businesses" and a number of them referred specifically to uranium. E.g., "Do you expect the same rate of return for oil drilling, coal production, uranium exploration?" "Do you attempt to sell oil, natural gas, coal and uranium at BTU equivalent prices?"]

Kirkland did not interview any Getty personnel. However, Getty received the confidential API questionnaire which requested it to estimate the value of its assets subject to proposed divestiture and its research and development outlays in alternative energy fields. Getty completed the questionnaire and mailed its data sheets to Nolan Clark on June 4, 1976, with the understanding that the data would be held in confidence.

II

The crux of the district court's determination was based upon its view that an "attorney-client relationship is one of agency to which the general rules of agency apply" and "arises *only* when the parties have given their consent, either express or implied, to its formation." 448 F.Supp. at 1300 (emphasis supplied). Although some courts have stated that the attorney-client relation is one of agency and that the general rules of law applicable to agencies apply, in none of those cases was an agency principle applied to assist an attorney to avoid what would otherwise be an obligation to his client. . . .

. . .

The district court first determined that there existed no explicit or express attorney-client relationship in that no oil company representative requested Kirkland to act as its attorney orally or in writing and Kirkland did not accept such employment orally or in writing. The district court found that "Kirkland sent its legal bills to the API, and was compensated only by the API." 448 F.Supp. at 1301. A professional relationship is not dependent upon the payment of fees[6] nor, as we have noted, upon the execution of a formal contract.[7]

The court then purported to determine whether the professional relationship "may be implied from the conduct of the parties." First, it found no "indicia" such as "the preparation of a legally-binding document like a contract or a will, or the attorney's appearance in a judicial or quasi-judicial proceeding." 448 F.Supp. at 1301. Second, the court searched for evidence of three fundamental characteristics of an agency relationship; the power to affect the legal relations of the principal and others; a fiduciary who works on behalf of his principal and primarily for his benefit; and a principal who has the right to control the conduct of the agent. 448 F.Supp. at 1301–03.

[handwritten marginalia: Test to determine a professional relationship btw. lawyer & client]

6. Allman v. Winkelman, 106 F.2d 663, 665 (9th Cir.1939), cert. denied, 309 U.S. 668 (1940) ("lawyer's advice to his client establishes a professional relationship though it be gratis"); Fort Meyers Seafood Packers, Inc. v. Steptoe and Johnson, 381 F.2d 261, 262 (D.C.1967), cert. denied, 390 U.S. 946 (1968) (attorney's fees paid by third party "If appellant is not obligated to pay appellees for their services, it does not follow that there was no attorney-and-client relation"); Dresden v. Willock, 518 F.2d 281, 286 (3d Cir.1975) ("The fact that Dresden was to be paid by receiving stock in the enterprise did not change the nature of the [attorney-client] relationship"); E.F. Hutton & Co. v. Brown, 305 F.Supp. 371, 388 (S.D.Tex.1969) (Relation of attorney and client "is not dependent on the payment of a fee").

7. Udall v. Littell, 366 F.2d 668, 676 (D.C.Cir.1966), cert. denied, 385 U.S. 1007 (1967); E.F. Hutton & Co. v. Brown, supra note 6, at 388.

Using these tests, the court concluded that "[v]iewed in its totality, we believe that the evidence shows that no attorney-client relationship has existed between Kirkland and the oil companies." As we have indicated, to apply only the agency tests is too narrow an approach for determining whether a lawyer's fiduciary obligation has arisen.

The district court also erroneously permitted itself to be influenced by the size of the law firm involved. In addition to identifying Kirkland as one of the largest law firms in Chicago with a two-city operation including 130 lawyers in the Chicago office and 40 lawyers in the Washington, D.C. office, the court observed that "[w]ith the modern-day proliferation of large law firms representing multi-billion dollar corporations in all segments of the economy and the governmental process, it is becoming increasingly difficult to insist upon absolute fidelity to rules prohibiting attorneys from representing overlapping legal interests." 448 F.Supp. at 1287–88.

Although the court recognized that "where courts have found a disclosure of client information to one member of a law firm, such knowledge has traditionally been imputed to all members of his firm," it opted in this case to reject "this rigid approach, in recognition of the changing realities of modern legal practice." 448 F.Supp. at 1304.

The district court abused its discretion in applying a narrow, formal agency approach to determining the attorney-client relation and in applying a different imputation of knowledge principle in the case of a large law firm than that "traditionally" and recently applied by this circuit to sole practitioners and smaller firms. Schloetter v. Railoc of Indiana, Inc., 456 F.2d 706, 710 (7th Cir.1976).

III

. . .

Three district courts have held that each individual member of an *unincorporated* association is a client of the association's lawyer. In Halverson v. Convenient Food Mart, Inc., 458 F.2d 927, 930 (7th Cir.1972), we held that a lawyer who had represented an informal group of 75 franchisees "[b]ecause . . . [he] in effect had represented and benefitted every franchisee, . . . could reasonably believe that each one of them was his client."

Here we are faced with neither an ordinary commercial corporation nor with an informal or unincorporated association, but instead with a nation-wide trade association with 350 corporate and 7,500 individual members (448 F.Supp. at 1290) and doing business as a non-profit corporation.

We need not make any generalized pronouncements of whether an attorney for such an organization represents every member because this case can and should be decided on a much more narrow ground.

There are several fairly common situations where, although there is no express attorney-client relationship, there exists nevertheless a fiduciary obligation or an implied professional relation:

(1) The fiduciary relationship existing between lawyer and client extends to preliminary consultation by a prospective client with a view to retention of the lawyer, although actual employment does not result.[12]

Fiduciary Relationship

(2) When information is exchanged between co-defendants and their attorneys in a criminal case, an attorney who is the recipient of such information breaches his fiduciary duty if he later, in his representation of another client, is able to use this information to the detriment of one of the co-defendants, even though that co-defendant is not the one which he represented in the criminal case, Wilson P. Abraham Const. Corp. v. Armco Steel Corp., 559 F.2d 250 (5th Cir.1977) (disqualification case).

example

(3) When an insurer retains an attorney to investigate the circumstances of a claim and the insured, pursuant to a cooperation clause in the policy, cooperates with the attorney, the attorney may not thereafter represent a third party suing the insured nor indeed continue to represent the insurer once a conflict of interest surfaces.[13]

(4) In a recent case, where an auditor's regional counsel was instrumental in hiring a second law firm to represent some plaintiffs suing the auditor and where the second firm through such relationship was in a position to receive privileged information, the second law firm, although having no direct attorney-client relationship with the auditor, was disqualified from representing the plaintiffs. Fund of Funds, Ltd. v. Arthur Andersen & Co., 567 F.2d 225 (2d Cir.1977).

(5) In a recent case in this circuit, a law firm who represented for many years both the plaintiff in an action and also a corporation which owned 20% of the outstanding stock of the defendant corporation, was permitted to continue its representation of the plaintiff but was directed to disassociate itself from representing or advising the corporation owning 20% of defendant's stock. Whiting Corp. v. White Machinery Corp., 567 F.2d 713 (7th Cir.1977).

In none of the above categories or situations did the disqualified or disadvantaged lawyer or law firm actually represent the "client" in the sense of a formal or even express attorney-client relation. In each of those categories either an implied relation was found or at least the lawyer was found to owe a fiduciary obligation to the laymen.

---

12. ABA Code of Professional Responsibility, EC 4 1: "Both the fiduciary relationship existing between lawyer and client and the proper functioning of the legal system require the presentation by the lawyer of confidences and secrets of one who has employed or sought to employ him." Cf. McCormick on Evidence (2d ed.1972), § 88, p. 179: "Communications in the course of preliminary discussion with a view to employing the lawyer are privileged though the employment is in the upshot not accepted." See also, Taylor v. Sheldon, 172 Ohio St. 118, 173 N.E.2d 892, 895 (1961).

13. ABA, Opinions of the Committee on Professional Ethics (1967 ed.), Formal Op. 247 (1942). See also, State Farm Mutual Automobile Ins. Co. v. Walker, 382 F.2d 548 (7th Cir.1967), cert. denied, 389 U.S. 1045 (1968). For general discussion of conflicts inherent in insurance matters, see H. Drinker, Legal Ethics (1953) 114–18; L. Patterson and F. Cheatham, The Profession of the Law (1971) 237–40.

The professional relationship for purposes of the privilege for attorney-client communications "hinges upon the client's belief that he is consulting a lawyer in that capacity and his manifested intention to seek professional legal advice."[14] The affidavits before the district court established that: the Washington counsel for Gulf "was given to believe that the Kirkland firm was representing both API and Gulf;" Kerr–McGee's vice president understood a Kirkland partner to explain that Kirkland was working on behalf of API and also its members such as Kerr–McGee; and Getty's vice president stated that in submitting data to Kirkland he "acted upon the belief and expectation that such submission was made in order to enable [Kirkland] to render legal service to Getty in furtherance of Getty's interests."

A fiduciary relationship may result because of the nature of the work performed and the circumstances under which confidential information is divulged.[18] The Supreme Court approved and transmitted to Congress in 1972 the Federal Rules of Evidence,[19] which included among the lawyer-client privilege rules eventually eliminated by Congress, the following definition:[20]

> A "client" is a person, public officer, or corporation, association, or other organization or entity, either public or private, who is rendered professional legal services by a lawyer, or who consults a lawyer with a view to obtaining professional legal services from him.

. . .

Although Kirkland asserted, and the district court agreed, that it constructed a "Chinese wall" between the 8 to 14 Chicago-based attorneys working for Westinghouse and the 6 D.C.-based attorneys working for API, both conceded that William Jentes, one of Kirkland's lead attorneys working on the Westinghouse antitrust complaint, in August 1976 agreed with API task force head Lea, to prepare a legal memorandum analyzing arguments which had been advanced to broaden the scope of existing antitrust laws to outlaw interlocking directorates. Lea forwarded the Kirkland memorandum to the API, which mailed it to its member-company contact officers on September 23, 1976. Despite this breach of the "wall," we do not recognize the wall theory as modifying the presumption that actual knowledge of one or more lawyers in a firm is imputed to each member of that firm.[27] Here there exists a very reasonable possibility of

---

14. McCormick on Evidence (2d ed.1972), § 88, p. 179. See also R. Wise, Legal Ethics (1970) 284: "The deciding factor is what the prospective client thought when he made the disclosure, not what the lawyer thought."

18. Note Attorney's Conflict of Interests: Representation of Interest Adverse to That of Former Client, 55 Bost.U.L.Rev. 61, 66 (1975).

19. Supreme Court Order, November 20, 1972.

20. Rules of Evidence for the United States Courts and Magistrates as approved by Supreme Court (West Pub. Co. 1972). Rule 503(a)(1).

27. Schloetter v. Railoc of Indiana, Inc., 546 F.2d 706, 710 (7th Cir.1976). See also, Fund of Funds, Ltd. v. Arthur Andersen & Co., 435 F.Supp. 84, 96 (S.D.N.Y.), rev'd in part and aff'd in part, 567 F.2d 225, 229, n. 10 (2d Cir.1977).

improper professional conduct despite all efforts to segregate the two sizeable groups of lawyers.[28]

Kirkland has argued that the oil companies were aware that Kirkland was representing Westinghouse while it was also representing API, inasmuch as Kirkland sought discovery from Kerr–McGee, Getty and abortively from Gulf, relating to the Richmond litigation, in the way of voluntary interviews, depositions and the production of documents. The point, however, is not that the oil companies were aware that Kirkland represented Westinghouse but whether the oil companies were aware that such representation would lead to Kirkland representing Westinghouse in a lawsuit in which the oil companies would be defendants. As the district court noted, "none of the [Kirkland] Washington attorneys working on the API divestiture assignment knew of the separate Westinghouse antitrust complaint until it was filed in court on October 15 [1976], after the stock exchanges closed on that day." 448 F.Supp. at 1296. If some of Kirkland's own partners were not aware of the Westinghouse antitrust complaint until it was filed, the oil companies can scarcely be presumed to have greater knowledge that it was impending with themselves as some of the defendants. It was Kirkland's duty to keep the oil companies advised of actual or potential conflicts of interest, not the oil companies' burden to divine those conflicts.

Gulf, Kerr–McGee and Getty each entertained a reasonable belief that it was submitting confidential information regarding its involvement in the uranium industry to a law firm which had solicited the information upon a representation that the firm was acting in the undivided interest of each company. . . .

The fact that the two contrary undertakings by Kirkland occurred contemporaneously, with each involving substantial stakes and substantially related to the other, outbalances the client's interest in continuing with its chosen attorney. However, we believe that Westinghouse should have the option and choice of dismissing Gulf, Kerr–McGee and Getty from the antitrust case or discharging Kirkland as its attorney in the case. Substitute counsel has represented Westinghouse in the case since February 17, 1978, so that the impact of any change-over has been somewhat eased.

. . .

---

28. Judge Fairchild notes that he has a different view on this point. It is his understanding that on appeal, Kirkland does not rely on a Chinese wall theory. In his opinion, if it had been established that there was real insulation in all relevant particulars between the lawyers working in the Washington office on the API Report and those working in the Chicago office on the antitrust action, imputation of knowledge to all partners would be eliminated from consideration and a different result may have been appropriate.

Understanding *Westinghouse*

Westinghouse is a complicated case with rich facts. To make the most of it, start by imagining that the three oil companies (Getty, Gulf and Kerr–McGee) rather than API had retained Kirkland. Analyze that problem under the Model Rules. Would the outcome have been the same if the lobbying effort for the trade association had no relationship to the uranium antitrust litigation? For example, if Kirkland's Washington office had been engaged in opposing legislative changes in oil depreciation allowances, rather than legislation involving the energy activities of oil companies, including uranium.

Now put API back into the mix. Did the court hold that the three oil companies were clients along with API? What created Kirkland's duty to the oil companies? Was that duty the same as the duty that Kirkland would have owed the oil companies had they retained Kirkland directly? To answer that last question, consider whether Kirkland (retained by API) would have been barred from suing the oil companies for employment discrimination. If API had gathered data on uranium activities by interviewing the oil companies itself and passed that information to Kirkland only in aggregated form, would Kirkland have been disqualified from suing the oil companies on behalf of Westinghouse? Would it depend on what API had told the oil companies to get the information? Would it make sense to transfer API's duty to the oil companies to its lawyers?

Why was screening (creation of a wall of separation of the lawyers and files concerned with the two matters) insufficient to cure Kirkland's conflict? Would it be appropriate for Kirkland to have advised Westinghouse on the choice the court gives the company at the end of the case?[9]

Should a different standard be used in deciding whether to discipline a lawyer for a conflict, as distinct from the standard in disqualification cases? The law codified in M.R. 1.7 and M.R. 1.9 by and large developed not in disciplinary cases but in court cases on motions to disqualify. Is this portion of the Model Rules then uniquely applicable to conflicts questions arising outside the disciplinary process?

Positional Conflicts

Could Kirkland, on behalf of API, have lobbied Congress not to break up the oil companies, assuming it received no confidences from any of its member oil companies, and at the same time have alleged on Westinghouse's behalf that the oil companies were engaged in an illegal monopoly? When a lawyer argues for client A that a particular law is valid, and at the same time in another case for client B that that same law is invalid, the

---

9. James B. Stewart, The Partners: Inside America's Most Powerful Law Firms c. 4 (1983), includes a fascinating discussion of Kirkland's representation of Westinghouse. Stewart reports that Westinghouse retained the Wall Street firm of Donovan, Leisure to take over the uranium antitrust litigation. The antitrust case was later settled for about $100 million in cash plus various options to acquire uranium ore. Id. at 199. An internal investigation by Westinghouse resulted in a decision not to seek to recover approximately $3 million in fees from Kirkland. A shareholders' suit to force Westinghouse to pursue this claim was subsequently abandoned. Id.

conflict is referred to as a "positional conflict." The professional tradition flowing from English barristers to present-day lawyers accords a lawyer great freedom to assert whatever reasonable legal arguments will advance a client's clause, leaving it to the tribunal to reach an appropriate result. But many lawyers under today's condition are concerned about arguing inconsistent positions or even those that a major client may believe are opposed to its interests.[10]

Comment [9] to M.R. 1.7 states:

A lawyer may represent parties having antagonistic positions on a legal question that has arisen in different cases, unless representation of either client would be adversely affected. Thus, it is ordinarily not improper to assert such positions in cases pending in different trial courts, but it may be improper to do so in cases pending at the same time in an appellate court.

Does this help answer the question posed at the beginning of this note about lobbying for API while suing the oil companies? Does the Comment mean that you should not assert contrary legal positions in unrelated cases in the same trial court? The conflict cannot be cured by foregoing a particular argument on behalf of one client so to avoid asserting contrary positions before the same court. The decision to forego the argument is tainted because it is influenced by obligations to another client. See the *Fiandaca* case printed below at p. 595 which involves decisionmaking tainted by an alleged conflict.

Who Qualifies as a Client for Purposes of the Conflicts Rules?

In *IBM v. Levin*,[11] a law firm was disqualified from representing a computer leasing firm in an antitrust action against IBM because the firm had represented IBM on various labor matters over a number of years. The court held that IBM was a present client of the firm, despite the fact that the firm "had no specific assignment from IBM on hand on the day that [the firm filed suit against IBM] and even though [the firm] performed services for IBM on a fee for services basis rather than pursuant to a retainer agreement." The court found that "the pattern of repeated retainers, both before and after the filing of the complaint, supports the finding of a continuous relationship."[12]

Is initial contact with a person seeking representation enough to establish an attorney-client relationship for purposes of the conflicts rules?

---

10. See John Dzienkowski, Positional Conflicts of Interest, 71 Tex.L.Rev. 457 (1993).

11. 579 F.2d 271, 281 (3d Cir.1978).

12. Id. at 281. See also Fund of Funds Ltd. v. Arthur Andersen & Co., 435 F.Supp. 84, 95 (S.D.N.Y.), aff'd in part, rev'd in part on other grounds, 567 F.2d 225 (2d Cir.1977) (representation should be treated as concurrent even if the firm, in an effort to avoid the conflict, ceases representation of one of the clients before the motion to disqualify is filed).

Advance Waiver of Conflicts

To avoid disqualifications, firms increasingly employ provisions in retainer agreements whereby the client agrees to waive certain future conflicts should they arise. These provisions usually relate to successive conflicts, i.e., conflicts that might occur after the firm has concluded representing the client who signs the waiver. But the provisions sometimes apply to concurrent representation.

An early case dealing with such a provision, *In re Boone*,[13] refused to enforce a release permitting the lawyer subsequently to represent his client's opponent in the same matter. The court said,

> the client may waive a privilege which the relation of attorney and client confers upon him, but he cannot enter into an agreement whereby he consents that the attorney may be released from all the duties, burdens, obligations and privileges pertaining to the duty of attorney and client.... Courts owe a duty to themselves, to the public, and to the profession which the temerity or improvidence of clients cannot supersede.

In another aspect of the *Westinghouse* case,[14] Gulf sought to disqualify a law firm representing a co-defendant, which firm had formerly represented Gulf in a matter held to be substantially related. Gulf had agreed that the firm could continue to represent another client even if a conflict developed between the two clients' interests. The court, citing *In re Boone*, disqualified the firm despite the agreement, holding that the agreement could not give the firm permission to use the client's confidences against its own interests in favor of another client.[15] What if the consent agreement provided for screening within the firm?

ABA Formal Opinion 93–372 suggests a narrow role for advance waivers. For an advance waiver to be effective, it must describe the future conflict "with sufficient clarity so the client's consent can reasonably be viewed as having been fully informed when it was given." The Restatement reflects a similar view. Comment *d* to § 202 states that advance waivers are subject to "special scrutiny."

> A client's open-ended agreement to consent to all conflicts normally should be ineffective unless the client possesses sophistication in the matter in question and has had the opportunity to receive independent legal advice about the consent.... On the other hand, particularly in a continuing client-lawyer relationship in which the lawyer is expected to act on behalf of the client without a new engagement for each matter, the gains to both lawyer and client from ... advance [waiver of] defined conflicts might be substantial.

What might be the benefits to the client of such an agreement?

---

13. 83 Fed. 944, 957 (N.D.Cal.1897).

14. Westinghouse Elec. Corp. v. Gulf Oil Corp., 588 F.2d 221 (7th Cir.1978).

15. See also Kennecott Copper Corp. v. Curtiss–Wright Corp., 584 F.2d 1195 (2d Cir. 1978).

Procedures to Discover Conflicts

The court in Hughes v. Paine, Webber, Jackson and Curtis, Inc., discussed at p. 666 infra, criticized the law firm's procedures for discovering conflicts. The procedure involved a clerk's survey of the current matter file titles to determine clients and matters represented by the firm. The court said that "it should be noted that a files check may not reveal even the most obvious conflict, e.g., a new client seeks to sue a person who, it later turns out, is the chief executive officer of a corporate client."[16] The court recommended that in addition to a files check, a "new cases" memorandum be circulated within the firm "briefly describing the subject matter and the parties" before finally accepting any new case. Would this be adequate? What about affiliated corporations? Recall that Gulf Oil was not an immediate client of the firm in the *Westinghouse* case but was a member of the trade association, the American Petroleum Institute, which was the client. What about adverse parties in non-litigation matters, such as contentious negotiations? What about the addition of new parties in litigation? See Comment [1] to M.R. 1.7 (calling on lawyers to adopt "reasonable procedures, appropriate for the size and type of firm and practice" to discover conflicts).

Definition of "Firm"

The law generally has treated lawyers in the same firm as a single lawyer for purposes of conflict of interest. Is this fiction too far from the reality of contemporary law practice, frequently involving large firms with offices in a number of cities? How much information is really shared? Would an office in one city be any less vigorous in presenting a case against a client represented in an unrelated matter by a branch office in another city than against the client of a firm two floors above it in an office complex? Would client confidentiality be less respected?

Decisions such as *Westinghouse* effectively limit the size of firms. At some point, expansion does not pay if it excessively multiplies the number of cases in which the firm will be disqualified. Can firms avoid this problem by forming relationships with "corresponding firms" in different cities rather than opening branch offices?[17] How close a relationship between one firm and another would signify that they are de facto the same firm for purposes of the conflicts rules?

With respect to lawyers who share office space but not fees, Comment [1] to M.R. 1.10 says:

> ... Whether two or more lawyers constitute a firm [for purposes of the conflicts rules] can depend on the specific facts. For example, two practitioners who share office space and occasionally consult or assist each other ordinarily would not be regarded as constituting a firm. However, if they present themselves to the public in a way suggesting

---

16. 565 F.Supp. 663, 673 (N.D.Ill. 1983).

17. See ABA Formal Op. 84–351 (1984) ("affiliated" firms are treated as one firm for conflicts purposes).

that they are a firm or conduct themselves as a firm, they should be regarded as a firm for the purposes of the Rules. . . .

Much will depend on factual details, especially those concerning how the lawyers' relationship has been presented to potential clients.[18] An ABA ethics opinion states that lawyers who share office space may represent conflicting interests if they "exercise reasonable care" to protect their clients' confidences.[19] We take up imputed disqualification in more detail below at p. 670.

Lawyers Related to Other Lawyers

Model Rule 1.8(i) states:

> A lawyer related to another lawyer as parent, child, sibling or spouse shall not represent a client in a representation directly adverse to a person who the lawyer knows is represented by the other lawyer except upon consent by the client after consultation regarding the relationship.

A lawyer disqualified under M.R. 1.8(i) does not taint other lawyers in the firm.

M.R. 1.8(i) has no counterpart in the Model Code. DR 5–101(A) and DR 5–105(D), the general provisions on conflicts and imputed disqualification give no specific guidance in this situation and would seem to require the disqualification of the entire firm whenever a lawyer in it is disqualified because married or otherwise closely related to an opposing lawyer. This was not, however, the reading given by the ABA ethics committee. The committee's opinion rejected a per se rule of imputed disqualification, but emphasized the need for the related lawyers to take special precautions to preserve client confidences.[20]

The reported decisions deal primarily with lawyers who are married to each other.[21] The cases on spouses generally accord with the Model Rules approach of requiring disqualification when interests are directly adverse but not insisting on imputed disqualification.[22] In Jones v. Jones,[23] the court refused to find impropriety even though the married lawyers represented clients whose interests were directly adverse.

---

18. See Shelton v. Shelton, 542 N.Y.S.2d 719 (N.Y.App.Div.1989) (lawyer who sublet office space within a firm not member of the firm for purposes of conflicts rules). Cf. United States v. Cheshire, 707 F.Supp. 235 (M.D.La.1989) (lawyers who maintained separate practice but shared office space and letterhead, which described them as an "Association of Attorneys," treated as one firm under conflicts rules).

19. ABA Informal Op. 1486 (1982).

20. ABA Formal Op. 340 (1975).

21. For a case involving a father and son representing opposing interests, see Peek v. Harvey, 599 S.W.2d 674 (Tex.Civ.App. 1980) (disqualification would have been proper but reversal not required because no showing of harm).

22. See generally: John J. Cross, III, Ethical Issues Facing Lawyer–Spouses and Their Employers, 34 Vand.L.Rev. 1435 (1981); James C. Word, Risk and Knowledge in Interspousal Conflicts of Interest, 7 Whittier L.Rev. 943 (1985).

23. 369 S.E.2d 478 (Ga. 1988).

M.R. 1.8(i) does not apply by its terms to people who are dating on a regular basis, but M.R. 1.7(b) would apply and would yield the same result as M.R. 1.8(i). As for imputed disqualification of dating lawyers disqualified under 1.7(b), the more sensible reading of M.R. 1.10 would be to treat those lawyers in the same way that 1.8(i) treats related lawyers, i.e., not requiring that the whole firm be disqualified. In People v. Jackson,[24] the question was whether the defendant was denied effective assistance of counsel because his lawyer was involved in an ongoing romantic relationship with the prosecutor that she did not disclose to the defendant. The court reversed the conviction.[25]

Fiandaca v. Cunningham

United States Court of Appeals, First Circuit, 1987.
827 F.2d 825.

■ Before COFFIN, DAVIS and SELYA, CIRCUIT JUDGES.

■ COFFIN, CIRCUIT JUDGE.

This opinion discusses two consolidated appeals related to a class action brought by twenty-three female prison inmates sentenced to the custody of the warden of the New Hampshire State Prison. The suit challenges the state of New Hampshire's failure to establish a facility for the incarceration of female inmates with programs and services equivalent to those provided to male inmates at the state prison. After a bench trial on the merits, the district court held that the state had violated plaintiffs' right to equal protection of the laws and ordered the construction of a permanent in-state facility for plaintiffs no later than July 1, 1989. It also required the state to provide a temporary facility for plaintiffs on or before November 1, 1987, but prohibited the state from establishing this facility on the grounds of the Laconia State School and Training Center ("Laconia State School" or "LSS"), New Hampshire's lone institution for the care and treatment of mentally retarded citizens.

One set of appellants consists of Michael Cunningham, warden of the New Hampshire State Prison, and various executive branch officials responsible for the operation of the New Hampshire Department of Corrections ("state"). They challenge the district court's refusal to disqualify plaintiffs' class counsel, New Hampshire Legal Assistance ("NHLA"), due to an unresolvable conflict of interest. See N.H.Rules of Professional Conduct, Rule 1.7(b). They also seek to overturn that portion of the district court's decision barring the establishment of an interim facility for female inmates at LSS, arguing that this prohibition is unsupported either by relevant factual findings, see Fed.R.Civ.P. 52(a), or by evidence contained in the record.

24. 213 Cal.Rptr. 521 (App.1985).

25. See also Gregori v. Bank of America, 254 Cal.Rptr. 853 (App.1989) (disqualification of firm not warranted when lawyer in firm dated secretary in opponent's firm unless confidences were likely disclosed).

The other group of appellants is comprised of the plaintiffs in a separate class action challenging the conditions and practices at the Laconia State School, *Garrity v. Sununu*, No. 78–116–D (D.N.H. filed April 12, 1978), including the New Hampshire Association for Retarded Citizens ("NHARC") and the mentally retarded citizens who currently reside at LSS (the "*Garrity* class"). This group sought unsuccessfully to intervene in the relief phase of the instant litigation after the conclusion of the trial, but prior to the issuance of the court's final memorandum order. See Fed. R.Civ.P. 24. On appeal, these prospective intervenors argue that the district court abused its discretion in denying their motion.

We begin by presenting the relevant facts and then turn to our analysis of the legal issues raised by each of these appeals.

I.   Factual Setting.

This case began in June, 1983, when plaintiffs' appellate counsel, Bertram Astles, filed a complaint on behalf of several female inmates sentenced to the custody of the state prison warden and incarcerated at the Rockingham County House of Corrections. NHLA subsequently became co-counsel for plaintiffs and filed an amended complaint expanding the plaintiff class to include all female inmates who are or will be incarcerated in the custody of the warden. In the years that followed, NHLA assumed the role of lead counsel for the class, engaging in extensive discovery and performing all other legal tasks through the completion of the trial before the district court. Among other things, NHLA attorneys and their trial expert, Dr. Edyth Flynn, twice toured and examined potential facilities at which to house plaintiffs, including buildings at the Laconia State School, the New Hampshire Hospital in Concord, and the Youth Development Center in Manchester.

Pursuant to Fed.R.Civ.P. 68, the state offered to settle the litigation on August 1, 1986, in exchange for the establishment of a facility for female inmates at the current Hillsborough County House of Corrections in Goffstown. The state had already negotiated an agreement with Hillsborough County to lease this facility and expected to have it ready for use by the end of 1989. Plaintiffs rejected this offer, however, primarily because the relief would not be available for over three years and because the plan was contingent on Hillsborough County's ability to complete construction of a new facility for the relocation of its prisoners. Plaintiffs desired an in-state facility within six to nine months at the latest and apparently would not settle for less.

The state extended a second offer of judgment to plaintiffs on October 21, 1986. This offer proposed to establish an in-state facility for the incarceration of female inmates at an existing state building by June 1, 1987. Although the formal offer of judgment did not specify a particular location for this facility, the state informed NHLA that it planned to use the Speare Cottage at the Laconia State School. NHLA, which also represented the plaintiff class in the ongoing *Garrity* litigation, rejected the offer on November 10, stating in part that "plaintiffs do not want to agree to an offer which is against the stated interests of the plaintiffs in the *Garrity* class." The state countered by moving immediately for the disqualification of NHLA as class counsel in the case at bar due to the unresolvable conflict of interest inherent in NHLA's representation of two classes with directly adverse interests. The court, despite recognizing that a conflict of interest probably existed, denied the state's motion on November 20 because NHLA's disqualification would further delay the trial of an important matter that had been pending for over three years. It began to try the case four days later.

The *Garrity* class filed its motion to intervene on December 11, ten days after the conclusion of the trial on the merits. The group alleged that it had only recently learned of the state's proposal to develop a correctional facility for women at the Laconia State School. The members of the class were concerned that the establishment of this facility at the school's Speare Cottage, which they understood to be the primary building under consideration, would displace 28 residents of the school and violate the remedial orders issued by Chief Judge Devine in *Garrity*, 522 F.Supp. at 239–44, as well as N.H.Rev.Stat.Ann. ch. 171–A. The district court denied the motion to intervene on December 23, assuring the applicant-intervenors that it would "never approve a settlement which in any way disenfranchises patients of LSS or contravenes the letter or intent of [Chief Judge] Devine's order in *Garrity*."

Meanwhile, the court agreed to hold up its decision on the merits pending the conclusion of ongoing settlement negotiations, permitting the principal parties to spend the month of December, 1986, engaged in further efforts to settle the case. Within approximately one week after the conclusion of the trial, the parties reached an understanding with regard to a settlement agreement which called for the establishment of a "fully operational facility at the present site of the Laconia State School for the incarceration of female inmates by November 1, 1987." The agreement also provided that all affected residents of LSS would receive appropriate placements at least two months prior to the opening of the correctional facility. After negotiating this agreement, NHLA moved to withdraw as class co-counsel on December 11 and attorney Astles signed the settlement agreement on plaintiffs' behalf. The state, however, refused to sign the agreement.

This collapse of the post-trial settlement efforts prompted Judge Loughlin, the district judge in the instant case, and Chief Judge Devine, the *Garrity* trial judge, to convene a joint settlement conference on December 22, 1986. At this conference, plaintiffs formally withdrew their consent to the original settlement agreement in light of the state's refusal to abide by the agreement. Both parties agreed, nevertheless, to try once again to settle the matter in a manner acceptable to all concerned and to report to the en banc court by January 12, 1987. Judge Loughlin, apparently believing that NHLA's conflict of interest prevented its effective performance as plaintiffs' class counsel, granted NHLA's pending motion to withdraw the day after the joint settlement conference. NHLA, however, had reconsidered its

598 CHAPTER 7 CONFLICTS OF INTEREST

withdrawal from the case in light of the state's failure to sign the settlement agreement and it immediately petitioned the court to be reinstated as class counsel. The court denied the motion for reinstatement, reasoning that the "doctrine of necessity," its purported justification for denying the state's earlier disqualification motion in the face of NHLA's conflict of interest, no longer had force because the case had been tried to a conclusion.

The district court finally announced its decision on the merits on January 13, 1987. Finding that the conditions of confinement, programs, and services available to New Hampshire female prisoners are not on par with the conditions, programs, and services afforded male inmates at the New Hampshire State Prison, the court held that such gender-based, inferior treatment violates the Equal Protection clause of the Fourteenth Amendment. As a primary remedy, it ordered the state to establish "a permanent facility comparable to all of the facilities encompassed at the New Hampshire State Prison ... to be inhabited no later than July 1, 1989." In crafting a temporary remedy, it reiterated that "there shall not be a scintilla of infringement upon the rights and privileges of the *Garrity* class," and proceeded to rule that the state had to provide plaintiffs with "a building comparable to the Speare Building," but that such facility "shall not be located at the Laconia State School or its environs." This appeal resulted.

II. Appeal of State Department of Corrections....

A. Refusal to Disqualify for Conflict of Interest.

The state's first argument is that the district court erred in permitting NHLA to represent the plaintiff class at trial after its conflict of interest had become apparent. As we recognized in Kevlik v. Goldstein, 724 F.2d 844 (1st Cir.1984), a district court is vested with broad power and responsibility to supervise the professional conduct of the attorneys appearing before it. Id. at 847. It follows from this premise that "[w]e will not disturb the district court['s] finding unless there is no reasonable basis for the court's determination." Id. We must determine, therefore, whether the court's denial of the state's disqualification motion amounts to an abuse of discretion in this instance.

The state's theory is that NHLA faced an unresolvable conflict because the interests of two of its clients were directly adverse after the state extended its second offer of judgment on October 21, 1986. The relevant portion of New Hampshire's Rules of Professional Conduct states:

A lawyer shall not represent a client if the representation of that client may be materially limited by the lawyer's responsibilities to another client ... unless:

(1) the lawyer reasonably believes the representation will not be adversely affected; and

(2) the client consents after consultation and with knowledge of the consequences.

. . .

N.H.Rules of Professional Conduct, Rule 1.7(b). The comment to Rule 1.7 prepared by the ABA goes on to state:

> Loyalty to a client is also impaired when a lawyer cannot consider, recommend or carry out an appropriate course of action for the client because of the lawyer's other responsibilities or interests. The conflict in effect forecloses alternatives that would otherwise be available to the client.

N.H.Rules of Professional Conduct, Rule 1.7, comment. In this case, it is the state's contention that the court should have disqualified NHLA as class counsel pursuant to Rule 1.7 because, at least with respect to the state's second offer of judgment, NHLA's representation of the plaintiff class in this litigation was materially limited by its responsibilities to the *Garrity* class.

We find considerable merit in this argument. The state's offer to establish a facility for the incarceration of female inmates at the Laconia State School, and to use its "best efforts" to make such a facility available for occupancy by June 1, 1987, presented plaintiffs with a legitimate opportunity to settle a protracted legal dispute on highly favorable terms. As class counsel, NHLA owed plaintiffs a duty of undivided loyalty: it was obligated to present the offer to plaintiffs, to explain its costs and benefits, and to ensure that the offer received full and fair consideration by the members of the class. Beyond all else, NHLA had an ethical duty to prevent its loyalties to other clients from coloring its representation of the plaintiffs in this action and from infringing upon the exercise of its professional judgment and responsibilities.[4]

NHLA, however, also represents the residents of the Laconia State School who are members of the plaintiff class in *Garrity*. Quite understandably, this group vehemently opposes the idea of establishing a correctional facility for female inmates anywhere on the grounds of LSS. As counsel for the *Garrity* class, NHLA had an ethical duty to advance the interests of the class to the fullest possible extent and to oppose any settlement of the instant case that would compromise those interests. In short, the combination of clients and circumstances placed NHLA in the untenable position of being simultaneously obligated to represent vigorously the interests of two conflicting clients. It is inconceivable that NHLA, or any other counsel, could have properly performed the role of "advocate" for both plaintiffs

---

4. The fact that the conflict arose due to the nature of the state's settlement offer, rather than due to the subject matter of the litigation or the parties involved, does not render the ethical implications of NHLA's multiple representation any less troublesome. Among other things, courts have a duty to "ensur[e] that at all stages of litigation ... counsel are as a general rule available to advise each client as to the particular, individualized benefits or costs of a proposed settlement." Smith v. City of New York, 611 F.Supp. 1080, 1090 (S.D.N.Y. 1985).

and the *Garrity* class, regardless of its good faith or high intentions. Indeed, this is precisely the sort of situation that Rule 1.7 is designed to prevent.

Plaintiffs argue on appeal that there really was no conflict of interest for NHLA because the state's second offer of judgment was unlikely to lead to a completed settlement for reasons other than NHLA's loyalties to the *Garrity* class. We acknowledge that the record contains strong indications that settlement would not have occurred even if plaintiffs had been represented by another counsel. For instance, in ruling on the intervention motion, the district court stated that, pursuant to its duties under Fed. R.Civ.P. 23(e), it would not approve a settlement that infringed in any way on the rights of the LSS residents. Furthermore, as plaintiffs contend, the second offer of judgment was unattractive because it was phrased in "best efforts" language and did not set a firm date for establishment of the facility. The question, however, is not whether the state's second offer of judgment would have resulted in a settlement had plaintiffs' counsel not been encumbered by a conflict of interest. Rather, the inquiry we must make is whether plaintiffs' counsel was able to represent the plaintiff class unaffected by divided loyalties, or as stated in Rule 1.7(b), whether NHLA could have reasonably believed that its representation would not be adversely affected by the conflict. Our review of the record and the history of this litigation—especially NHLA's response to the state's second offer, in which it stated that "plaintiffs do not want to agree to an offer which is against the stated interests of plaintiffs in the *Garrity* case"—persuade us that NHLA's representation of plaintiffs could not escape the adverse effects of NHLA's loyalties to the *Garrity* class.

Both the district court and plaintiffs on appeal have also advanced the belief that "necessity" outweighed the adverse effects of NHLA's conflict of interest in this instance and justified the denial of the state's pre-trial disqualification motion. See United States v. Will, 449 U.S. 200, 213–17 (1980). . . .

While it is surely laudable that the court was anxious to resolve a lingering dispute concerning an unfortunate state of affairs, we fail to see how the doctrine of *necessity* is implicated in a case such as this. As plaintiffs' counsel admitted at oral argument, there was no particular emergency at the time of the court's decision to ignore the conflict of interest and proceed to trial. Plaintiffs simply continued to suffer the effects of the same inequitable treatment that had persisted for many years. While it would have been desirable to avoid delaying the trial for up to a year or more, it certainly was not "necessary" in the sense of limiting the court to but one potential course of action. We realize that other courts occasionally consider the possible effects of delay in ruling on disqualification motions, see, e.g., Laker Airways Ltd. v. Pan American World Airways, 103 F.R.D. 22, 27–28 (D.D.C.1984) ("Were the motion to disqualify to be granted, the resulting additional delay might well be crippling."), but in this circuit, arguments premised on delay have been less availing. As we held in *Kevlik*, 724 F.2d at 844, "we cannot, in the face of a breach of professional duty, ignore the wrong because appellees' counsel neglected to discern the conflict earlier, *or even opted to delay litigation by raising the motion . . . .*" Id. at 848 (emphasis supplied).

Absent some evidence of *true* necessity, we will not permit a meritorious disqualification motion to be denied in the interest of expediency unless it can be shown that the movant strategically sought disqualification in an effort to advance some improper purpose. Thus, the state's motivation in bringing the motion is not irrelevant; as we recognized in *Kevlik*, "disqualification motions can be tactical in nature, designed to harass opposing counsel." Id. However, the mere fact that the state moved for NHLA's disqualification just prior to the commencement of the trial is not, without more, cause for denying its motion. See id. There is simply no evidence to support plaintiffs' suggestion that the state "created" the conflict by intentionally offering plaintiffs a building at LSS in an effort "to dodge the bullet again" with regard to its "failure to provide instate housing for the plaintiff class." We do not believe, therefore, that the state's second offer of judgment and subsequent disqualification motion were intended to harass plaintiffs. Rather, our reading of the record indicates that a more benign scenario is more probable: the state made a good faith attempt to accommodate plaintiffs by offering to establish a correctional facility in an existing building at the Laconia State School and, once NHLA's conflict of interest with regard to this offer became apparent, the state moved for NHLA's disqualification to preserve this settlement option.

. . .

B. Proper Remedy.

In light of the district court's error in ignoring NHLA's conflict of interest, we believe it necessary to remand the case for further proceedings. We must consider a further question, however: must the district court now start from scratch in resolving this dispute? The state argues that the court's failure to disqualify NHLA is plain reversible error, and therefore requires the court to try the matter anew. We subscribe to the view, however, that merely "conducting [a] trial with counsel that should have been disqualified does not 'indelibl[y] stamp or taint' the proceedings." Warpar Manufacturing Corp. v. Ashland Oil, Inc., 606 F.Supp. 866, 867 (N.D.Ohio, E.D.1985) (quoting Firestone Tire & Rubber Co. v. Risjord, 449 U.S. 368, 376 (1981)). With this in mind, we look to the actual adverse effects caused by the court's error in refusing to disqualify NHLA as class counsel to determine the nature of the proceedings on remand. Cf. Board of Education of New York v. Nyquist, 590 F.2d 1241, 1246 (2d Cir.1979) (courts should be hesitant to disqualify an attorney unless trial will be tainted); Smith v. City of New York, 611 F.Supp. at 1091–92 (same); SMI Industries Canada Ltd. v. Caelter Industries, Inc., 586 F.Supp. 808, 814 (N.D.N.Y.1984) (same).

We do not doubt that NHLA's conflict of interest potentially influenced the course of the proceedings in at least one regard: NHLA could not fairly advocate the remedial option—namely, the alternative of settling for a site at the Laconia State School—offered by the state prior to trial. The conflict, therefore, had the potential to ensure that the case would go to trial, a route the state likely wished to avoid by achieving an acceptable settlement. Nevertheless, we do not see how a trial on the merits could have been avoided given the manner in which the case developed below. Judge Loughlin stated on the record that he would not approve a settlement infringing on the rights of LSS residents, and under Rule 23(e), any settlement of this class action required his approval to be effective. It seems to us, therefore, that even if some other counsel had advised plaintiffs to accept the state's offer for a building at LSS, a trial on the merits would have been inevitable.

With respect to the merits of the equal protection issue, the state has been unable to identify any way in which the court's error adversely affected its substantial rights at trial. The state admits that it had long recognized the need to establish an in-state facility for female inmates comparable to the state prison and that it had already taken steps in this direction by negotiating an agreement for the use of the present Hillsborough County House of Correction beginning in 1989. The evidence adduced at trial confirmed what both parties had known all along—that female state inmates do not enjoy services, programs, and conditions of confinement similar to those afforded the male inmates at the state prison—and this evidence led the court to conclude that the state had violated plaintiffs' right to equal protection of the laws.

The state has not directly challenged any of the district court's findings, which were based on the overwhelming evidence of inequitable treatment, and there has been no suggestion that the proceedings on the merits and the court's holding on the issue of liability were tarnished in any way by NHLA's participation. Indeed, as the state had to concede at oral argument, if the trial had been bifurcated into liability and remedy phases, NHLA's conflict of interest would have tainted its representation of plaintiffs—and required disqualification—only in the second, remedial phase of the trial. It seems plain to us, therefore, that at least with regard to the court's determination on the merits of the equal protection issue, the error in refusing to disqualify NHLA as class counsel is not inconsistent with substantial justice and should not require retrial of this issue. For these reasons, we hold that, with regard to the merits of the case, the district court's failure to disqualify NHLA constitutes harmless error at most, Fed.R.Civ.P. 61, and we affirm the district court's holding that the state violated plaintiffs' rights to equal protection of the laws.

The situation is different, however, with respect to the remedy designed by the district court. We believe that it would be inappropriate to permit the court's remedial order—which includes a specific prohibition on the use of LSS—to stand in light of the court's refusal to disqualify NHLA. The ban on the use of buildings located on the grounds of LSS is exactly the sort of remedy preferred by NHLA's *other* clients, the members of the *Garrity* class, and therefore has at least the appearance of having been tainted by NHLA's conflict of interest. Consequently, we hold that the district court's remedial order must be vacated and the case remanded for a new trial on the issue of the proper remedy for this constitutional deprivation. This determination leads us to the question of which parties should be permitted to participate in this new trial, an issue that forms the heart of the appeal brought by NHARC and the other members of the *Garrity* class as prospective intervenors. [The court allowed the intervention].

Conflict Caused by Opposing Party's Action

How did the interests of the two client classes conflict? Will consent of each client class solve the problem or does the court hold that the conflict is so severe that it is nonconsentable? How does a class of mentally retarded persons who are institutionalized consent to a conflict? Who acts on their behalf?[1] Does M.R. 1.14 help answer this question?

Should the court have paid more attention to the fact that a legal services organization represented both classes? To the reality that alternate counsel might not have been available to either class? Should this be a factor in judging "true necessity?" Does the court too lightly dismiss the harm to the female prisoners caused by delay?

What about the state's motives in proposing the Laconia site? Why would the state have persisted in offering the Laconia site given the judge's statement that he would not approve it? Why did the state refuse to sign the settlement agreement? What other evidence could plaintiffs have offered to show the state acted with improper motives?

What about the remedy? Is it too harsh or too lenient? How important should deterring lawyer misconduct be in fashioning a conflicts remedy? Discipline for violating the conflicts rules is rare unless there are other ethical violations, such as self-dealing or dishonesty.[2]

Should the court have held the state lacked standing to raise the conflict? Most courts do not require any special showing of standing before entertaining a motion to disqualify based on a conflict of interest.[3] Typically, a motion to disqualify is made by an opposing party or interest.

Judicial Impatience with Disqualification Motions: Estoppel and Appealability

Earlier decisions holding that "mere delay or laches" is not a defense to a motion to disqualify[4] have been rejected by most courts. As disqualifi-

---

1. For more on conflicts of interest in representing a class, see p. 813.

2. See, e.g., Lake County Bar Assn. v. Gargiuolo, 404 N.E.2d 1343 (Ohio 1980) (simultaneous conflict and self-dealing); Codiga v. State Bar, 575 P.2d 1186 (Cal. 1978) (lying to conceal conflict).

3. See, e.g., Kevlik v. Goldstein, 724 F.2d 844, 847–48 (1st Cir.1984) (standing to raise a disqualification motion based on ethical responsibility of all lawyers to bring to the court's attention possible ethical violations).

4. See, e.g., Emle Industries, Inc. v. Patentex, Inc., 478 F.2d 562, 573–74 (2d Cir. 1973) (three-year delay did not bar disqualification motion because it is in the public

cation motions became widely used, often for tactical purposes, judges increasingly applied delay and estoppel arguments in ruling on them.[5] In United Sewerage Authority v. Jelco, Inc.,[6] disqualification was denied on the basis of client consent, coupled with delay and the finding that it was "obvious" that the firm could adequately conduct the present representation despite the fact that the two disputes involved the same contract, since different contract provisions were in issue.

Impatient with the frequency of disqualification motions and their use as instruments of delay, the courts have made it well nigh impossible for lawyers to obtain review of a trial court's disposition of a disqualification motion. In 1981 the Supreme Court held that orders denying disqualification of lawyers in civil cases are not immediately appealable under 28 U.S.C. § 1291 prior to judgment on the merits.[7] Several years later the Court held that orders granting disqualification motions in civil cases were not final orders under § 1291.[8] A third case holds that in a criminal case the granting of a disqualification motion is not immediately appealable.[9] State courts have by and large followed this approach.[10]

Hence most of the law on this subject is now made by district courts, not the federal courts of appeals, because a ruling on disqualification is rarely grounds for reversing a subsequent judgment on the merits. Occasionally, a disqualification ruling may be certified for interlocutory appeal pursuant to 28 U.S.C. § 1292(b) or satisfy the demanding conditions for issuance of a writ of mandamus from the court of appeals.[11]

If a client appeals after final judgment, claiming that the grant or denial of a disqualification motion was reversible error, how could it show that it was prejudiced? For discussion of what a criminal defendant must

interest to enforce lawyers' ethical obligations).

5. See, e.g., Cox v. American Cast Iron Pipe Co., 847 F.2d 725, 729 (11th Cir.1988); Trust Corp. of Montana v. Piper Aircraft Corp., 701 F.2d 85, 87 (9th Cir.1983); MacArthur v. Bank of New York, 524 F.Supp. 1205, 1209 (S.D.N.Y.1981) ("the burden on the party seeking disqualification may be greater as a result of his undue delay").

6. 646 F.2d 1339 (9th Cir.1981).

7. Firestone Tire & Rubber Co. v. Risjord, 449 U.S. 368 (1981).

8. Richardson–Merrell Inc. v. Koller, 472 U.S. 424 (1985).

9. Flanagan v. United States, 465 U.S. 259 (1984).

10. The impatience evident in the Supreme Court decisions cited above may also be found in state court cases. "Court resources are sorely taxed by the increasing use of disqualification motions as harassment or dilatory tactics." Gorovitz v. Planning Board of Nantucket, 475 N.E.2d 377, 380 n. 7 (Mass. 1985).

11. Richardson–Merrell, 472 U.S. at 435, suggested that disqualified lawyers whose reputations are "egregiously injured" by the disqualification order, but whose clients are satisfied by substitute counsel, "might be able to obtain relief from the Circuit Judicial Council pursuant to 28 U.S.C. § 332(d)(1)." See also Firestone Tire & Rubber Co. v. Risjord, 449 U.S. 368, 373 n. 13 (1981) (order disqualifying a law firm cannot be reviewed by mandamus unless patently erroneous, requiring a showing of both irreparable harm and the existence of a demonstrable injustice). Cf. Grand Jury Subpoena of Rochon, 873 F.2d 170 (7th Cir.1989) (order disqualifying Attorney General of the United States from participating in a criminal investigation is immediately appealable).

show on appeal, see the notes following *Cuyler v. Sullivan*, printed below at p. 608.

Disciplinary action for filing or resisting disqualification motions for strategic purposes is extremely rare. Rule 11, sanctions, however, might be imposed against a lawyer who files a frivolous motion to disqualify or defends against a motion to disqualify when there is no legal or factual basis for doing so,[12] but under the 1994 version of Rule 11 the threat of sanctions for any baseless motion, including a frivolous motion to disqualify, have been substantially reduced. See the discussion of Rule 11 above at p. 404.

Curing a Simultaneous Conflict

EC 5–19 suggests that a lawyer who represents multiple clients with potentially differing interests may cure the problem by deferring to the judgment of the client who objects to the multiple representation and withdrawing from representing that client. While courts have recognized that the prospective prohibitions on conflicts should not always be imposed after the fact to disqualify,[13] the general approach is that a concurrent conflict cannot be converted into a successive conflict by firing an objecting or unwanted client. In Picker International Inc. v. Varian Associates, Inc.,[14] for example, a newly merged law firm found itself representing clients directly adverse in unrelated matters. The court held that the conflict could not be cured by dropping one client. Had the lawyers successfully withdrawn from the litigation prior to the merger, the case would be analyzed as one of successive representation: Because a lawyer may oppose *former* clients in matters *unrelated* to the previous representation, the newly merged firm would have been allowed to proceed.[15] On the question of a lawyer's continuing to represent one of two joint clients on the subject matter of the joint representation after a conflict develops among the two, see the *Brennan's* case printed below at p. 642 and the notes that follow it.

3. REMEDIES FOR CONFLICTS OF INTEREST

Conflict of interest violations may lead to a number of sanctions and remedies. Lawyers may be disciplined for violation of professional rules.[16] A

---

12. See, e.g., Optyl Eyeware Fashion Int'l Corp. v. Style Companies, Ltd., 760 F.2d 1045 (9th Cir.1985) (sanctions for filing frivolous motion to disqualify); Analytica v. NPD Research, Inc., 708 F.2d 1263 (7th Cir.1983) (sanctions for defending against a motion to disqualify). The court may also sanction a lawyer under 28 U.S.C. § 1927 for vexatiously multiplying the proceedings by bringing a groundless motion to disqualify.

13. See, e.g., Bodily v. Intermountain Health Care Corp., 649 F.Supp. 468 (D.Utah 1986); and Pennwalt Corp. v. Plough, Inc., 85 F.R.D. 264 (D.Del.1980) (both involving simultaneous representation in unrelated matters).

14. 869 F.2d 578 (Fed.Cir.1989).

15. See the discussion of successive conflicts below at p. 646. For another case involving conflicts created by law firm merger, see Harte Biltmore Ltd. v. First Pennsylvania Bank, N.A., 655 F.Supp. 419, 421 (S.D.Fla. 1987).

16. See, e.g., In re Banks, 584 P.2d 284 (Ore.1978) (lawyer reprimanded for representing a corporation and its president after their interests became conflicting). For

conflict of interest is a breach of duty that may provide the basis for a malpractice action.[17] Fee forfeiture is also an available remedy—a lawyer may not be entitled to fees for work performed after the conflict arose.[18] A conflict of interest may also be the basis for setting aside a contract or gift, especially one between a lawyer and client.[19] Federal and state statutes impose criminal penalties for conflict of interest violations on the part of government employees, former government employees and those dealing with the government.[20] In situations in which a lawyer seeks to use as evidence information obtained from a former client, the evidence may be excluded to protect that client's confidentiality interests. Other remedies may also be appropriate.[21]

The most common sanction for conflicts of interest in litigation is disqualification of the client's lawyer, as in *Westinghouse* and *Fiandaca*, considered above.[22] "The sanction assures both that the case is well presented in court, that confidential information of present or former clients is not misused, and, where appropriate, that a client's interest in a lawyer's loyalty is not violated."[23]

Use of a Disqualified Lawyer's Work[24]

Sometimes, as in *Westinghouse,* a lawyer or law firm is disqualified in the middle of a transaction or litigation. May successor counsel make use of the work of the disqualified lawyers? This was the issue before the court in First Wisconsin Mortgage Trust v. First Wisconsin Corp.,[25] an early and frequently cited case on this question. The court rejected an absolute rule

general discussion of conflicts remedies, see C. Wolfram, Modern Legal Ethics § 7.1.7 (1986).

17. See, e.g., Woodruff v. Tomlin, 616 F.2d 924 (6th Cir.1980) (lawyer held liable for malpractice for representing insurer, driver, owner and passenger in an accident case and not telling passenger that she might have a claim against the driver and owner on which insurer would be liable).

18. See, e.g., Financial General Bankshares, Inc. v. Metzger, 523 F.Supp. 744 (D.D.C. 1981) (corporate lawyer who also secretly advised dissident shareholder denied fees for the period in question), rev'd on other grounds, 680 F.2d 768 (D.C. Cir.1982).

19. See the discussion of this question at p. 564 supra.

20. These issues are discussed below at p. 684.

21. For general discussion of remedies for conflicts of interest, see Restatement § 201, Comment *e* and Reporter's Note. Other remedies include dismissal of an ac-

tion. See, e.g., Doe v. A Corp., 330 F.Supp. 1352 (S.D.N.Y.1971), aff'd sub nom. Hall v. A Corp., 453 F.2d 1375 (2d Cir.1972) (facts in shareholders' suit against corporation were derived entirely from information acquired by lawyer while employed by the corporation).

22. See generally James Lindgren, Toward a New Standard of Attorney Disqualification, 1982 Am.Bar Found. Research J. 419.

23. Restatement § 201, Comment *e*.

24. On access to a disqualified lawyer's work see also: Developments in the Law—Conflicts of Interests in the Legal Profession, 94 Harv.L.Rev. 1244, 1484–86 (1981); Comment, The Availability of the Work-Product of a Disqualified Attorney: What Standard?, 127 U.Pa.L.Rev. 1607 (1979); Comment, Access to Work Product of Disqualified Counsel, 46 U.Chi.L.Rev. 443 (1979).

25. 584 F.2d 201, 204–05 (7th Cir.1978) (en banc).

that would preclude access by successor counsel to any of the work product of a disqualified lawyer or firm, opting instead for a flexible approach.

> No doubt it will frequently be that the lawyer who is unfortunate enough to become involved in the Goodwin Sands of simultaneously representing clients whose interests either are or thereafter come into conflict, and who ceases representation of one of the clients, will find that the work performed during the period subject to disqualification will have aspects of confidentiality or other unfair detriment to the former client arising from the very fact of the knowledge and acquaintanceship acquired during the period of the prior representation. This does not mean, however, that this is always the situation, or even that it is frequently so.

The court held that only that work product which is " 'tainted by virtue of having been based upon confidential knowledge or other advantage gained during or from the dual representation'"[26] should be unavailable to successor counsel.

Does the functional or utilitarian approach of *First Wisconsin* place too great a burden on the client who succeeds in disqualifying a lawyer, often that client's former lawyer? The court in *First Wisconsin* did not come down firmly on the question of how much evidence the prevailing client must amass to demonstrate that the lawyer's work product was "tainted." The court did, however, state that it had "no particular quarrel with the test proposed by the dissent that the cases would 'turn upon whether there exists a reasonable possibility of confidential information being used in the formation of, or being passed to substitute counsel through, the work product in question.'" Should the court at least apply a rebuttable presumption that the work product is "tainted?" In *First Wisconsin* the contested work product was summaries of complicated loan transactions that any competent lawyer could prepare without access to any confidential information of the former client. If the conflict is severe and obvious, should a prophylactic rule be applied denying the use of the lawyer's work?

Contrast *First Wisconsin* with EZ Paintr Corp. v. Padco, Inc. [27]In the latter case, two lawyers of the law firm representing Padco had formerly been members of the firm representing EZ Paintr. The court disqualified Padco's firm and limited the turn-over of work product from the disqualified law firm to successor counsel to that prepared before the two tainted lawyers joined the firm.[28]

What about consultation between the disqualified firm and substitute counsel? The general rule is that a disqualified lawyer may consult with successor counsel concerning work that may be turned over but not as to other matters.[29]

---

26. 584 F.2d at 207.

27. 746 F.2d 1459 (Fed.Cir.1984).

28. See also Capital City Publishing Co. v. Trenton Times Corp., 1983 WL 1958 (D.C.N.J.1983).

29. IBM v. Levin, 579 F.2d 271, 281 (3d Cir.1978) (disqualified counsel permitted to

4. CONCURRENT REPRESENTATION IN CRIMINAL LITIGATION

Cuyler v. Sullivan

Supreme Court of the United States, 1980.
446 U.S. 335.

■ MR. JUSTICE POWELL delivered the opinion of the Court.

The question presented is whether a state prisoner may obtain a federal writ of habeas corpus by showing that his retained defense counsel represented potentially conflicting interests.

I

Respondent John Sullivan was indicted with Gregory Carchidi and Anthony DiPasquale for the first-degree murders of John Gorey and Rita Janda. The victims, a labor official and his companion, were shot to death in Gorey's second-story office at the Philadelphia headquarters of Teamsters' Local 107. Francis McGrath, a janitor, saw the three defendants in the building just before the shooting. They appeared to be awaiting someone, and they encouraged McGrath to do his work on another day. McGrath ignored their suggestions. Shortly afterward, Gorey arrived and went to his office. McGrath then heard what sounded like firecrackers exploding in rapid succession. Carchidi, who was in the room where McGrath was working, abruptly directed McGrath to leave the building and to say nothing. McGrath hastily complied. When he returned to the building about 15 minutes later, the defendants were gone. The victims' bodies were discovered the next morning.

Two privately retained lawyers, G. Fred DiBona and A. Charles Peruto, represented all three defendants throughout the state proceedings that followed the indictment. Sullivan had different counsel at the medical examiner's inquest, but he thereafter accepted representation from the two lawyers retained by his codefendants because he could not afford to pay his own lawyer.[1] At no time did Sullivan or his lawyers object to the multiple representation. Sullivan was the first defendant to come to trial. The evidence against him was entirely circumstantial, consisting primarily of McGrath's testimony. At the close of the Commonwealth's case, the defense rested without presenting any evidence. The jury found Sullivan guilty and fixed his penalty at life imprisonment. Sullivan's post-trial motions failed, and the Pennsylvania Supreme Court affirmed his conviction by an equally divided vote. Commonwealth v. Sullivan, 446 Pa. 419, 286 A.2d 898 (1971).

turn over work to and consult with new counsel concerning it); Williams v. TWA, 588 F.Supp. 1037, 1610 (W.D.Mo.1984) (portions of the disqualified firm's work made available to new counsel but consultation limited to that necessary to explain the work).

1. DiBona and Peruto were paid in part with funds raised by friends of the three defendants. The record does not disclose the source of the balance of their fee, but no part of the money came from either Sullivan or his family. See United States ex rel. Sullivan v. Cuyler, 593 F.2d 512, 518, and n. 7 (CA3 1979).

Sullivan's codefendants, Carchidi and DiPasquale, were acquitted at separate trials.

Sullivan then petitioned for collateral relief under the Pennsylvania Post Conviction Hearing Act. He alleged, among other claims, that he had been denied effective assistance of counsel because his defense lawyers represented conflicting interests. In five days of hearings, the Court of Common Pleas heard evidence from Sullivan, Carchidi, Sullivan's lawyers, and the judge who presided at Sullivan's trial.

DiBona and Peruto had different recollections of their roles at the trials of the three defendants. DiBona testified that he and Peruto had been "associate counsel" at each trial. Peruto recalled that he had been chief counsel for Carchidi and DePasquale, but that he merely had assisted DiBona in Sullivan's trial. DiBona and Peruto also gave conflicting accounts of the decision to rest Sullivan's defense. DiBona said he had encouraged Sullivan to testify even though the Commonwealth had presented a very weak case. Peruto remembered that he had not "want[ed] the defense to go on because I thought we would only be exposing the [defense] witnesses for the other two trials that were coming up." Sullivan testified that he had deferred to his lawyers' decision not to present evidence for the defense. But other testimony suggested that Sullivan preferred not to take the stand because cross-examination might have disclosed an extramarital affair. Finally, Carchidi claimed he would have appeared at Sullivan's trial to rebut McGrath's testimony about Carchidi's statement at the time of the murders.

. . .

The Pennsylvania Supreme Court affirmed both Sullivan's original conviction and the denial of collateral relief. Commonwealth v. Sullivan, 472 Pa. 129, 371 A.2d 468 (1977). The court saw no basis for Sullivan's claim that he had been denied effective assistance of counsel at trial. It found that Peruto merely assisted DiBona in the Sullivan trial and that DiBona merely assisted Peruto in the trials of the other two defendants. Thus, the court concluded, there was "no dual representation in the true sense of the term." Id., at 161, 371 A.2d, at 483. The court also found that resting the defense was a reasonable tactic which had not denied Sullivan the effective assistance of counsel. Id., at 162, 371 A.2d, at 483–484.

Having exhausted his state remedies, Sullivan sought habeas corpus relief in the United States District Court for the Eastern District of Pennsylvania. . . .

. . .

The Court of Appeals . . . held that the participation by DiBona and Peruto in the trials of Sullivan and his codefendants established, as a matter of law, that both lawyers had represented all three defendants. The court recognized that multiple representation " 'is not tantamount to the denial of effective assistance of counsel. . . .' " But it held that a criminal defendant is entitled to reversal of his conviction whenever he makes "'some showing of a possible conflict of interest or prejudice, however remote....'" ... The court acknowledged that resting at the close of the prosecutor's case "would have been a legitimate tactical decision if made by independent counsel." Nevertheless, the court thought that action alone raised a possibility of conflict sufficient to prove a violation of Sullivan's Sixth Amendment rights. The court found support for its conclusion in Peruto's admission that concern for Sullivan's codefendants had affected his judgment that Sullivan should not present a defense. To give weight to DiBona's contrary testimony, the court held, "would be to ... require a showing of actual prejudice." 593 F.2d at 522.

[The Court considered in part II the scope of federal judicial review of state findings of fact in a federal habeas proceeding; part III rejected the argument that ineffectiveness of counsel claims were inapplicable when a criminal defendant was represented by privately retained counsel rather than appointed counsel.]

IV

We come [now] to Sullivan's claim that he was denied the effective assistance of counsel guaranteed by the Sixth Amendment because his lawyers had a conflict of interest. The claim raises two issues expressly reserved in Holloway v. Arkansas, 435 U.S. [475] at 483–484 [(1978)]. The first is whether a state trial judge must inquire into the propriety of multiple representation even though no party lodges an objection. The second is whether the mere possibility of a conflict of interest warrants the conclusion that the defendant was deprived of his right to counsel.

A

In *Holloway*, a single public defender represented three defendants at the same trial. The trial court refused to consider the appointment of separate counsel despite the defense lawyer's timely and repeated assertions that the interests of his clients conflicted. This Court recognized that a lawyer forced to represent codefendants whose interests conflict cannot provide the adequate legal assistance required by the Sixth Amendment. Id., at 481–482. Given the trial court's failure to respond to timely objections, however, the Court did not consider whether the alleged conflict actually existed. It simply held that the trial court's error unconstitutionally endangered the right to counsel. Id., at 483–487.

Holloway requires state trial courts to investigate timely objections to multiple representation. But nothing in our precedents suggests that the Sixth Amendment requires state courts themselves to initiate inquiries into the propriety of multiple representation in every case.[10] Defense counsel

---

10. In certain cases, proposed Federal Rule of Criminal Procedure 44(c) provides that the federal district courts "shall promptly inquire with respect to ... joint representation and shall personally advise each defendant of his right to the effective as-sistance of counsel, including separate representation." See also ABA Project on Standards for Criminal Justice, Function of the Trial Judge § 3.4(b) (App.Draft 1972).

have an ethical obligation to avoid conflicting representations and to advise the court promptly when a conflict of interest arises during the course of trial.[11] Absent special circumstances, therefore, trial courts may assume either that multiple representation entails no conflict or that the lawyer and his clients knowingly accept such risk of conflict as may exist. Indeed, as the Court noted in *Holloway*, trial courts necessarily rely in large measure upon the good faith and good judgment of defense counsel. "An 'attorney representing two defendants in a criminal matter is in the best position professionally and ethically to determine when a conflict of interest exists or will probably develop in the course of a trial.'" 435 U.S., at 485, quoting State v. Davis, 110 Ariz. 29, 31, 514 P.2d 1025, 1027 (1973). Unless the trial court knows or reasonably should know that a particular conflict exists, the court need not initiate an inquiry.

Nothing in the circumstances of this case indicates that the trial court had a duty to inquire whether there was a conflict of interest. The provision of separate trials for Sullivan and his codefendants significantly reduced the potential for a divergence in their interests. No participant in Sullivan's trial ever objected to the multiple representation. DiBona's opening argument for Sullivan outlined a defense compatible with the view that none of the defendants was connected with the murders. The opening argument also suggested that counsel was not afraid to call witnesses whose testimony might be needed at the trials of Sullivan's codefendants. Finally, as the Court of Appeals noted, counsel's critical decision to rest Sullivan's defense was on its face a reasonable tactical response to the weakness of the circumstantial evidence presented by the prosecutor. On these facts, we conclude that the Sixth Amendment imposed upon the trial court no affirmative duty to inquire into the propriety of multiple representation.

B

Holloway reaffirmed that multiple representation does not violate the Sixth Amendment unless it gives rise to a conflict of interest. See 435 U.S., at 482. Since a possible conflict inheres in almost every instance of multiple representation, a defendant who objects to multiple representation must

Several Courts of Appeals already invoke their supervisory power to require similar inquiries.... As our promulgation of Rule 44(c) suggests, we view such an exercise of the supervisory power as a desirable practice. See generally Schwarzer, Dealing with Incompetent Counsel—The Trial Judge's Role, 93 Harv.L.Rev. 633, 653–654 (1980)....

11. ABA Code of Professional Responsibility, DR 5–105, EC 5–15 (1976); ABA Project on Standards for Criminal Justice, Defense Function § 3.5(b) (App.Draft 1971).

Seventy percent of the public defender offices responding to a recent survey reported a strong policy against undertaking multiple representation in criminal cases. Forty-nine percent of the offices responding never undertake such representation. Lowenthal, Joint Representation in Criminal Cases: A Critical Appraisal, 64 Va.L.Rev. 939, 950, and n. 40 (1978). The private bar may be less alert to the importance of avoiding multiple representation in criminal cases. See Geer, Representation of Multiple Criminal Defendants: Conflicts of Interest and the Professional Responsibilities of the Defense Attorney, 62 Minn.L.Rev. 119, 152–157 (1978); Lowenthal, supra, at 961–963.

have the opportunity to show that potential conflicts impermissibly imperil his right to a fair trial. But unless the trial court fails to afford such an opportunity, a reviewing court cannot presume that the possibility for conflict has resulted in ineffective assistance of counsel. Such a presumption would preclude multiple representation even in cases where " '[a] common defense . . . gives strength against a common attack.' " Id., at 482–483, quoting Glasser v. United States, 315 U.S. 60 (1942) (Frankfurter, J., dissenting).

In order to establish a violation of the Sixth Amendment, a defendant who raised no objection at trial must demonstrate that an actual conflict of interest adversely affected his lawyer's performance. In Glasser v. United States, for example, the record showed that defense counsel failed to cross-examine a prosecution witness whose testimony linked Glasser with the crime and failed to resist the presentation of arguably inadmissible evidence. Id., at 72–75. The Court found that both omissions resulted from counsel's desire to diminish the jury's perception of a codefendant's guilt. Indeed, the evidence of counsel's "struggle to serve two masters [could not] seriously be doubted." Id., at 75. Since this actual conflict of interest impaired Glasser's defense, the Court reversed his conviction.

Dukes v. Warden, 406 U.S. 250 (1972), presented a contrasting situation. Dukes pleaded guilty on the advice of two lawyers, one of whom also represented Dukes' codefendants on an unrelated charge. Dukes later learned that this lawyer had sought leniency for the codefendants by arguing that their cooperation with the police induced Dukes to plead guilty. Dukes argued in this Court that his lawyer's conflict of interest had infected his plea. We found " 'nothing in the record . . . which would indicate that the alleged conflict resulted in ineffective assistance of counsel and did in fact render the plea in question involuntary and unintelligent.' " Id., at 256, quoting Dukes v. Warden, 161 Conn. 337, 344, 288 A.2d 58, 62 (1971). Since Dukes did not identify an actual lapse in representation, we affirmed the denial of the habeas corpus relief.

Glasser established that unconstitutional multiple representation is never harmless error. Once the Court concluded that Glasser's lawyer had an actual conflict of interest, it refused "to indulge in nice calculations as to the amount of prejudice" attributable to the conflict. The conflict itself demonstrated a denial of the "right to have the effective assistance of counsel." 315 U.S., at 76. Thus, a defendant who shows that a conflict of interest actually affected the adequacy of his representation need not demonstrate prejudice in order to obtain relief. See *Holloway*, supra, 435 U.S., at 487–491. But until a defendant shows that his counsel actively represented conflicting interests, he has not established the constitutional predicate for his claim of ineffective assistance. See *Glasser*, supra, 315 U.S., at 72–75.[15]

---

15. See Comment, Conflict of Interests in Multiple Representation of Criminal Co- Defendants, 68 J.Crim.L. & C. 226, 231–232 (1977).

C

The Court of Appeals granted Sullivan relief because he had shown that the multiple representation in this case involved a possible conflict of interest. We hold that the possibility of conflict is insufficient to impugn a criminal conviction. In order to demonstrate a violation of his Sixth Amendment rights, a defendant must establish that an actual conflict of interest adversely affected his lawyer's performance. Sullivan believes he should prevail even under this standard. He emphasizes Peruto's admission that the decision to rest Sullivan's defense reflected a reluctance to expose witnesses who later might have testified for the other defendants. The petitioner, on the other hand, points to DiBona's contrary testimony and to evidence that Sullivan himself wished to avoid taking the stand. Since the Court of Appeals did not weigh these conflicting contentions under the proper legal standard, its judgment is vacated and the case is remanded for further proceedings consistent with this opinion.

[Justices Brennan and Marshall, in separate partial dissents, argued that the Sixth Amendment required a state court on its own initiative to inquire in every case of joint representation, to warn defendants of the possible risks and to ascertain that the representation is the result of the defendants' informed choice.]

The *Cuyler* Standard

Cuyler requires a defendant to show both that counsel actively represented conflicting interests, and that the conflict "adversely affected" counsel's performance. The defendant need not show "prejudice," i.e., that the result would have been different but for the conflict. Contrast this to the rule in *Strickland v. Washington* discussed at p. 177 supra. What is the difference between "adversely affected" and "prejudice"? The Third Circuit on remand in *Cuyler* held that the representation was adversely affected in that the lawyer did not call the codefendant to testify because doing so would have been against that defendant's interest.[1] Contrast *Cuyler* with the standard in civil cases. *Westinghouse*, for example, did not require proof of adverse effect from the conflict.

What does it take to show an "actual conflict" that "adversely affected" the defense lawyer's conduct? Should a showing that defense counsel simultaneously represents an important prosecution witness suffice? The cases turn on their facts, but many do not find an actual conflict resulting in an adverse effect when a prosecution witness is a former client of the defense counsel.[2]

---

1. Sullivan v. Cuyler, 723 F.2d 1077, 1084–89 (3d Cir.1983, reh. denied 1984) (divided court held that decision not to call defendant was an actual conflict of interest).
2. See, e.g., Castillo v. Estelle, 504 F.2d 1243 (5th Cir.1974) (conviction reversed).

But see Wycoff v. Nix, 869 F.2d 1111 (8th Cir.1989) (concurrent representation of defendant and potential prosecution witness

The *Cuyler* standard has been found satisfied where, at the trial, a prosecution witness represented by defense counsel accused defense counsel of involvement in the defendant's crime,[3] and where collusion between the defense attorney and the prosecutor has been found.[4] How much more protection is actually afforded the defendant under *Cuyler* than under *Strickland*?

Some courts do not require a showing of adverse effect, reasoning that such an effect is likely to consist of an omission by the lawyer—options passed by, strategies neglected, etc. Proving a negative is difficult and should be unnecessary if the defendant can show an actual conflict existed. On this basis the Massachusetts court, interpreting the state constitution's guarantee of effective assistance of counsel, held that adverse effect will be presumed even if the defendant knew of the potential conflict before the trial began.[5] The defendant's lawyer also represented one of the prosecution's witnesses in an unrelated civil case. The court held that the possibility that the lawyer might go easy when cross-examining this witness warranted reversal without a showing of actual adverse effect.[6]

Disfavoring Multiple Representation in Criminal Cases

Multiple representation in criminal cases is strongly discouraged by ethics rules and case law.[7] The cases hold that any doubts as to potential conflict should be resolved in favor of separate counsel.[8] A number of commentators urge a complete ban on dual representation in criminal cases.[9]

Why is the predisposition against dual representation so strong? First, of course, a conflict in a criminal case may result in a defendant being convicted who should be acquitted. A co-defendant with more money (e.g., a higher-up in a criminal ring) may pay the lawyer's fee and call the shots.

not an actual conflict because witness was not called and matters in representation were unrelated); and United States v. Gambino, 864 F.2d 1064 (3d Cir.1988) (no reversal under *Cuyler* despite fact that defense counsel, without defendant's knowledge, was representing a third party and failed to advance argument for defendant that third party and not defendant was source of heroin).

3. Mannhalt v. Reed, 847 F.2d 576 (9th Cir.1988).

4. United States ex rel. Duncan v. O'Leary, 806 F.2d 1307 (7th Cir.1986).

5. Commonwealth v. Hodge, 434 N.E.2d 1246 (Mass.1982).

6. Also see People v. Spreitzer, 525 N.E.2d 30, 34 (Ill.1988) (describing categories of cases in which Illinois courts will presume adverse effect).

7. See the Comment to M.R. 1.7; ABA Standards for Criminal Justice, The Defense Function 3.5(b); Fed.Rule Crim.Proc. 44(c).

8. See, e.g., Lollar v. United States, 376 F.2d 243 (D.C.Cir.1967); State v. Bush, 493 P.2d 1205 (Ariz.1972). Also see Fleming v. State, 270 S.E.2d 185 (Ga.1980) (imposing an absolute ban on a lawyer representing more than one defendant in death penalty cases).

9. John S. Geer, Representation of Multiple Criminal Defendants, 62 Minn.L.Rev. 119 (1978); Gary T. Lowenthal, Joint Representation in Criminal Cases, 64 Va.L.Rev. 939 (1978); Peter W. Tague, Multiple Representation and Conflicts of Interest in Criminal Cases, 67 Geo.L.J. 1075 (1979).

Whenever a third person pays the lawyer's fee there is a potential conflict between that person's interests and the client's.[10]

Second, the courts and commentators may be worried about the possibility of cooperative perjury. Should that be a factor in considering the legitimacy of joint representation?

Finally, the issue arises in the context of what game theory refers to as the "prisoner's dilemma." Assume two prisoners are co-defendants. Each can either inform on the other to the prosecutor or keep quiet. The prosecutor promises each that if either informs she will be sentenced to no more than one year, but if one informs and the other remains silent, the one who keeps quiet will receive between 5 and 10 years. The best choice for each individual, acting alone, is to inform on the other (providing the other does not also do so). An even better result, however, is imaginable. If they could cooperate with each other they might both go free for lack of evidence. But cooperation as a practical matter may be impossible.

Prosecutors use divide-and-conquer tactics in plea-bargaining. A common defense strategy by a single defense lawyer can counter this tactic. But co-defendants in the real world are never in equal positions; the degree of their culpability and the penalties each faces are different. A lawyer who tries to counsel co-defendants in the real world, given their unequal position, cannot counsel the same course for both. Yet the choices made by one—particularly, whether to accept the prosecutor's offer—are crucial to the fate of the other.[11]

Denial of Defense Counsel of Choice

When a criminal defendant is denied counsel of her choice, the defendant's Sixth Amendment right to counsel is implicated.[12] In a federal criminal trial, the defendant must await appeal upon final judgment to pursue the claim that she was denied counsel of her choice.[13] Must prejudice be shown when a defendant is wrongly denied counsel of her choice, i.e., when the trial judge's order of disqualification was erroneous? The emerging case law is that "A defendant who is arbitrarily deprived of the right to select his own counsel need not demonstrate prejudice."[14]

---

10. For rules on third parties paying for a lawyer's representation of a client, see Model Rules 1.7(b), 1.8(f) and 5.4(c); DR 5–107(A) and (B).

11. See, e.g., Thomas v. Foltz, 818 F.2d 476 (6th Cir. 1987) (one lawyer represented three co-defendants; the prosecutor offered to reduce the charges to second degree murder if all three would plead guilty; defendant Thomas was quite resistant but eventually decided to plead guilty; held: counsel was operating under an actual conflict of interest that adversely affected his representation of Thomas).

12. United States v. Curcio, 680 F.2d 881 (2d Cir. 1982) (government's interest in disqualifying defendant's counsel does not override defendant's choice of counsel where defendant's waiver of the right to separate representation was knowing and voluntary).

13. Flanagan v. United States, 465 U.S. 259 (1984), held that an order disqualifying defense counsel is not immediately appealable under 28 U.S.C. § 1291.

14. United States v. Rankin, 779 F.2d 956, 960 (3d Cir.1986) (convicted defendant, erroneously deprived of counsel of choice, need not show that substitute counsel's

This leaves the question of when it is wrong, because of a conflict, to disqualify counsel over defendant's protest. In Wheat v. United States,[15] the district court denied Wheat's request to be represented by the same lawyer who was representing two other people charged with involvement in the drug distribution conspiracy that formed the basis for the charges against Wheat. Wheat, who was to be tried separately from the other parties, expressed his willingness to waive the conflict, as the other defendants had done, and asserted that the Sixth Amendment gave him the right to counsel of his choice. Nevertheless, the district court, citing the likelihood that the co-defendants would be witnesses at one another's trials, held that counsel would be operating with an irreconcilable conflict and thus refused to allow counsel to represent Wheat. Wheat appealed from a subsequent conviction, claiming that the court's rejection of his counsel of choice violated his Sixth Amendment rights. The Court (5–4) upheld the conviction:

> Unfortunately for all concerned, a district court must pass on the issue of whether or not to allow a waiver of a conflict of interest by a criminal defendant not with the wisdom of hindsight after the trial has taken place, but in the murkier pre-trial context when relationships between parties are seen through a glass, darkly. The likelihood and dimensions of nascent conflicts of interest are notoriously hard to predict, even for those thoroughly familiar with criminal trials. It is a rare attorney who will be fortunate enough to learn the entire truth from his own client, much less be fully apprised before trial of what each of the Government's witnesses will say on the stand. A few bits of unforeseen testimony or a single previously unknown or unnoticed document may significantly shift the relationship between multiple defendants. These imponderables are difficult enough for a lawyer to assess, and even more difficult to convey by way of explanation to a criminal defendant untutored in the niceties of legal ethics. Nor is it amiss to observe that the willingness of an attorney to obtain such waivers from his clients may bear an inverse relation to the care with which he conveys all the necessary information to them.

> For these reasons we think the District Court must be allowed substantial latitude in refusing waivers of conflicts of interest not only in those rare cases where an actual conflict may be demonstrated before trial, but in the more common cases where a potential for conflict exists which may or may not burgeon into an actual conflict as the trial progresses.[16]

Compare the concern in *Wheat* for potential conflicts of interest with the showing the defendant has to make under *Cuyler*. Justice Marshall, dissenting in *Wheat*, criticized the majority for its unwarranted deference to the district court's decision, given the importance of the Sixth Amend-

---

performance harmed the defendant). In accord: Anaya v. Colorado, 764 P.2d 779 (Colo.1988).

15.   486 U.S. 153 (1988).

16.   486 U.S. at 162–63.

ment right involved. Justice Stevens' dissent emphasized the voluntary nature of defendant's waiver of the conflict.

Should the defendant be allowed to waive any conflict, no matter how serious? If she makes the waiver for strategic purposes?[17] Should voluntary waiver bar any future claim of ineffective counsel based on the conflict? How would courts determine whether a waiver is voluntary or informed?[18] The Court in *Wheat* stated: "Nor does a waiver by the defendant necessarily solve the problem, for we note, without passing judgment on, the apparent willingness of Courts of Appeals to entertain ineffective assistance claims from defendants who have specifically waived the right to conflict-free counsel."[19] This statement does not sound particularly approving of the practice described, does it? Is the Court suggesting that waiver should cure all conflicts for post-conviction purposes?

A California decision holds that under the state's constitution, trial courts do not have the same wide latitude to disqualify defendant's counsel of choice that the federal courts have under *Wheat*.[20] "A court abridges a defendant's right to counsel when it removes retained defense counsel in the face of a defendant's willingness to make an informed and intelligent waiver of his right to ... conflict-free counsel." The court rejected any other rule as "paternalistic", quoting from John Stuart Mill's *On Liberty* and writing itself that "[a] right that is imposed, as compared to a right that is chosen, is an impoverished right."[21] Is the line between what is "chosen" and what "imposed" easy to discern in this context?

Judicial Inquiry to Determine Whether a Conflict Exists

In federal cases when one lawyer proposes to represent multiple defendants, the judge must hold a hearing to advise each defendant of her right to separate counsel. Fed.R.Crim.P. 44(c). Rule 44(c) further states that "[u]nless there is good cause to believe no conflict of interest is likely to arise, the court shall take such measures as may be appropriate to protect each defendant's right to counsel." The presumption is clearly against joint representation.

How can a court adequately satisfy itself that a defendant's waiver is voluntary and appropriate without breaching client confidences?[22] When

17. See United States v. Bradshaw, 719 F.2d 907 (7th Cir.1983) (co-defendants had strategic purposes in presenting a common defense).

18. See Duncan v. Alabama, 881 F.2d 1013 (11th Cir.1989) (one of defendant's court-appointed lawyers had represented the murder victim in her efforts to stop the defendant from harassing her; defendant's other lawyer had represented the district attorney in a divorce action and could foresee continuing to represent him; the court held that defendant's waiver of these con-

flicts barred him from raising them after conviction).

19. 486 U.S. at 161–62.

20. Alcocer v. Superior Court, 254 Cal.Rptr. 72, 75 (1988).

21. Id. at 74.

22. See In re Paradyne Corp., 803 F.2d 604 (11th Cir.1986) (granting mandamus against a proposed in camera inquiry by the trial court). Also see United States v. Roth, 860 F.2d 1382 (7th Cir.1988) (trial court's failure to probe possible conflicts does not invalidate defendant's waiver).

one counsel represents multiple defendants, should a failure to conduct a Rule 44(c) inquiry constitute per se reversible error?[23]

State courts are not bound to follow the procedure specified in Rule 44(c). However, when a defendant objects to representation on the basis of a conflict, the court must inquire into it and appoint independent counsel if there is a potential conflict.

C. Concurrent Representation in Transactions

1. Representing Both Parties to a Transaction

State v. Callahan

Supreme Court of Kansas, 1982.
232 Kan. 136, 652 P.2d 708.

■ Per Curiam:

This is an original proceeding in discipline. The proceeding is the result of a complaint filed on behalf of Mrs. Ruth Fulton.

Ruth Fulton, an elderly lady, owned 320 acres of land in Butler County which she had inherited from her father. Although she was born in Kansas, she has been a resident of California for over 60 years, and the land had been leased to a neighboring landowner for a number of years.

In 1974, Mrs. Fulton decided to sell her land. She first offered it to her tenant who declined the offer. He advised, however, that a Lowell Lygrisse was in the market for such property and offered to contact him.

Subsequently, Lygrisse called Mrs. Fulton by phone and a tentative agreement was reached. During this conversation, Lygrisse suggested that the respondent, John Callahan, handle the transaction for both of them. Mrs. Fulton agreed, and later called respondent and retained his services.

The interpretation of the parties as to respondent's scope of employment differed. Mrs. Fulton stated that she believed respondent would act as a California escrow officer would and protect the interests of both parties. Respondent testified that he believed that he represented both parties as a scrivener to draw the papers and close the sale only after the terms of the purchase agreement had been negotiated between the parties.

Respondent prepared two contracts controlling the sale in accordance with the terms provided by Lygrisse and without consulting Mrs. Fulton. The first contract was entitled "Real Estate Purchase Contract." It provided for a sale price of $96,000.00, to be paid $24,000.00 at the time of closing

---

23. See United States v. Colonia, 870 F.2d 1319 (7th Cir.1989) (no reversal in absence of showing of actual conflict).

and the balance in three annual installments of $24,000.00 each. The first annual installment was to be secured by a certificate of deposit.

The contract was unusual, however, in that it provided that the seller would execute and deliver a deed to the buyer at closing, and that the land would be included with other land in a mortgage to the Federal Land Bank. Although Mrs. Fulton did not fully understand the transaction, she signed the contract on November 14, 1974, in reliance upon respondent.

On December 11, 1974, respondent wrote to Mrs. Fulton enclosing a deed for her to sign and informed her that he would hold the deed until the first $24,000.00 was paid. He also informed her that when Lygrisse secured his loan from the Federal Land Bank, respondent would purchase a certificate of deposit in the amount of $24,000.00 and pledge it as security for the second payment, and that he would then formalize the agreement on the balance owing. Mrs. Fulton signed the deed and returned it to respondent.

Thereafter, respondent filed and conducted the necessary legal action to quiet title to the land and obtained inheritance tax clearance. He also advised Mrs. Fulton as to certain tax consequences of the sale. He billed Mrs. Fulton on March 14, 1975, for his services in clearing the title and was paid.

The second contract was entitled "Pledge, Escrow and Agreement." It recited the schedule of payments on the unpaid balance and set up an escrow of the certificate of deposit securing the first annual payment due April 1, 1976.

It differed from the first contract of sale in that Paragraph 7 provided for acceleration of the unpaid balance upon default and provided:

> "In the event of default and nonpayment of any judgment therefore the Fulton's shall have a specific lien on the real estate covered hereby subject only to the Federal Land Bank first mortgage of record."

Mrs. Fulton signed the agreement on May 21, 1975, in reliance on respondent's request as her attorney, without independent legal advice, believing that the provisions of paragraph 7 would effectively place her in the position of a second mortgagee. She further assumed respondent would record anything necessary to perfect her "specific lien." No such other documents were prepared or recorded by respondent.

For several years before and after 1974, respondent was Lygrisse's personal attorney, and they were each owners of 50% of the common stock of L–C Farm Co., Inc., a corporation engaged in buying and selling farms and other real estate. Respondent was required to and did personally guarantee some or all of the debts of the corporation which at times exceeded $500,000.00. The Fulton farm was not purchased for the account of L–C Farms Co., Inc., however, and no claim is made that respondent personally acquired any interest therein. Respondent admits that he did not disclose to Mrs. Fulton his business relationship with Lygrisse.

No problems arose until Lygrisse defaulted on the final payment due April 1, 1978. Mrs. Fulton called respondent several times for advice. He told her that Lygrisse had suffered some business reversals but that he was sure Lygrisse would make the final payment. Sometime in late 1978, she contacted respondent again and asked how long she had to file for foreclosure. Respondent advised her that she had five years from the date of default, but suggested again that she didn't need to foreclose, that he was sure Lygrisse would pay.

In May of 1979, Mrs. Fulton and her husband traveled to Wichita and met with respondent for the first time in person. They asked respondent to file a foreclosure action on what they perceived to be their second mortgage. Respondent declined, citing as his reason a conflict of interest, but he agreed to refer them to another attorney. He did not advise them at that time that they did not have a secured interest in the real estate.

The Fultons then went to see Lygrisse who promised to pay them within a few weeks. When the payment was not forthcoming, Mrs. Fulton again phoned respondent who again assured them that he believed Lygrisse would pay and advised them not to foreclose.

Finally, on March 1, 1980, Mr. Fulton called respondent and again asked for the name of an attorney to file foreclosure proceedings. During this conversation, respondent for the first time advised the Fultons that they had no mortgage and that all they had was a promissory note.

The Fultons were subsequently referred to Jim Lawing of Wichita who prepared and filed a malpractice action against respondent. Shortly thereafter respondent filed a voluntary petition in bankruptcy and was ultimately discharged.

In the spring of 1980, the Federal Land Bank foreclosed its mortgage against the Fulton farm. Mrs. Fulton was not a party to the action and learned of the action through independent inquiry. Included in the action was a second mortgage given to an El Dorado bank by Lygrisse around the time the down payment to Mrs. Fulton was made. She has never received the final payment of $24,000.00.

Following a letter of complaint from Jim Lawing to the disciplinary administrator, a formal complaint with Lawing's letter attached was filed by the disciplinary administrator before the Board for Discipline of Attorneys. A hearing was held on November 18, 1981, and the hearing panel found that respondent had violated disciplinary rules DR 5–105(B), DR 6–101(A)(3), and DR 1–102(A)(4). It recommended indefinite suspension of respondent. Respondent has taken exception to the report.

The hearing panel found that respondent had violated DR 5–105(B) in that he represented both the sellers and the buyer when a conflict of interest existed by failing to warn the sellers that they did not have a perfected second mortgage or security interest.

[The court quoted DR 5–105(B) and (C).]

It is respondent's contention that the terms of the sale were agreed upon between the parties before he was employed and that he only represented the parties, insofar as the contract of sale was concerned, as a scrivener to write up the contract and close the sale in accordance with the prior agreement of the parties. He asserts further that he was under no duty to suggest "better terms" for the seller or to make and record a second mortgage not called for by the terms of the contract.

Under the circumstances here, however, we fail to see how respondent could have been unaware that he was not exercising his independent professional judgment in behalf of the Fultons in preparing the contract solely on the terms dictated by Lygrisse without consulting the Fultons, or at least advising them of the risk inherent in not taking a second mortgage to secure the balance of the purchase price.

Furthermore, respondent did not make a full disclosure to the Fultons of his close business and professional associations with the buyer.

This court, in State v. Hilton, 217 Kan. 694, 698, 538 P.2d 977 (1975), stated:

"The unmistakable intent of DR 5–105(C) is exemplified in 'Ethical Considerations' [EC] 5–15 (ABA Standards, Code of Professional Responsibility). It reads in pertinent part:

" 'If a lawyer is requested to undertake or to continue representation of multiple clients having potentially differing interests, he must weigh carefully the possibility that his judgment may be impaired or his loyalty divided if he accepts or continues the employment. He should resolve all doubts against the propriety of the representation. . . .' "

The panel also found respondent guilty of violating DR 1–102(A)(4) in that he misrepresented to the sellers that they had a specific lien on the property sold, subject only to a first mortgage to the Federal Land Bank, when in fact they had no such lien.

DR 1–102(A)(4) provides [that a lawyer shall not] "Engage in conduct involving dishonesty, fraud, deceit, or misrepresentation."

Respondent contends that nothing in the pledge agreement provides for a second mortgage. Paragraph 7, he argues, refers only to a lien given to a judgment under K.S.A. 60–2202 (Corrick), and when considered with other provisions of the contract amounts to no more than a warranty that Lygrisse would not allow a subsequent lien or mortgage to attach.

Again, under the circumstances here, we fail to see how the Fultons could reasonably have given such an interpretation to this provision. They believed that they had a "specific lien," and on several occasions when the Fultons inquired of respondent about foreclosure proceedings, he failed to disclose to them that there was no valid foreclosable interest and advised them not to foreclose. He finally offered to give them the name of another attorney to handle such an action. They were not advised that they had no security interest to foreclose until almost two years after the final payment was due.

The duty of good faith imposed upon an attorney does not always cease immediately upon termination of his employment. It continues as long as the influence created by the relationship continues. Alexander v. Russo, 1 Kan.App.2d 546, 571 P.2d 350, rev. denied 222 Kan. 749 (1977). The Fultons still looked to respondent for aid, and his conduct in failing to disclose to them that they had no lien on the property to secure the balance due them clearly rises to the level of deceit and dishonesty.

"Full Disclosure" as Predicate of Consent[1]

Lawyer Callahan helped a California woman sell her Kansas farm land to a Kansas dealer in such land. What did Callahan do that violated the disciplinary rules? What should he have done? Do your responses assume the answer to the question whether a lawyer may represent both the buyer and seller in a real estate transaction?

Suppose Callahan revealed his long-term connection with Lygrisse and fully disclosed that the transaction, as proposed by Lygrisse, constituted an unsecured, interest-free loan of part of the purchase price. Will Mrs. Fulton's consent be adequate or is this a nonconsentable conflict? Can Callahan make the full disclosure required by M.R. 1.7 and D.R. 5-105(C) without violating his duties to his other client, Lygrisse?

In Financial General Bankshares v. Metzger,[2] the court said full disclosure means "[an] affirmative revelation by the attorney of all the facts, legal implications, possible effects, and other circumstances relating to the proposed representation." The fact that the client knows the lawyer represents another client whose interests are adverse does not constitute full disclosure.

Providing full disclosure is not easy and sometimes is impossible. The reasons include:

- The rules on confidentiality: How is a lawyer to make full disclosure without breaching the other client's confidences? The lawyer must have each clients' permission to share confidential information with the other client.

- Uncertainty about the facts: The lawyer is supposed to detail the facts relating to the proposed representations. But facts are often uncertain or undiscovered, especially at early stages of a transaction.

---

1. See generally Wolfram, Modern Legal Ethics § 7.2 (1986); and Nancy J. Moore, Conflicts of Interest in the Simultaneous Representation of Multiple Clients, 61 Tex. L.Rev. 211 (1982).

2. 523 F.Supp. 744, 771 (D.D.C.1981), rev'd on other grounds, 680 F.2d 768 (D.C.Cir. 1982), see p. 732 infra.

What the lawyer has been retained to do on behalf of either client is also often uncertain.

- Change of facts: Facts change as transactions move forward. Consequently, disclosure must be an ongoing process. Cycles of continuing disclosure and renewed consent may be required.

Comment *c(i)* to § Restatement 202 provides a detailed discussion of informed consent. It provides in part:

> ... In a multiple-client situation, the information [provided by the lawyer] should address the interests of the lawyer and other client giving rise to the conflict; contingent, optional, and tactical considerations and alternative courses of action that would be foreclosed or made less readily available by the conflict; the effect of the representation or the process of obtaining other clients' informed consent upon confidential information of the client; any material reservations that a disinterested lawyer might reasonably harbor about the arrangement if such a lawyer were representing only the client being advised; and the consequences and effect of a future withdrawal of consent by any client, including, if relevant, the fact that the lawyer would withdraw from representing all clients. . . .

Must a client get another lawyer's advice before consenting to representation by a lawyer with a conflict? In Aetna Cas. & Sur. Co. v. United States,[3] the court held that consent given without the advice of independent counsel may still be informed consent. Several states require the *written* consent of the parties before a lawyer may proceed to represent conflicting interests. See California Rule 3–310. In California, the requirement is interpreted in practice not to require that the predicate disclosure also be in writing. Should a writing be required? Or are the problems of providing written expression to the effort to gain informed consent too great?

Confidentiality and Joint Clients

As noted in Chapter 4 at p. 208 supra, joint clients have no attorney-client privilege to assert against one another in any later litigation involving the subject matter of the prior joint representation. The question remains whether one of two or more joint clients may insist that the shared lawyer keep information in confidence, i.e., not tell the other joint client some piece of information relevant to the joint representation. Comment [6] to Model Rule 2.2 ducks this question, content to assert that the lawyer must both keep each client informed and maintain confidences. Comment [12c] to Massachusetts Rule 1.7 is significantly more helpful, providing:

> [W]hile each client [in a joint representation] may assert that the lawyer keep something in confidence . . ., each client should be advised at the outset of the joint representation that making such a request will, in all likelihood, make it impossible for the lawyer to continue the

---

3. 570 F.2d 1197 (4th Cir.1978), rev'g 438 F.Supp. 886 (W.D.N.C.1977).

joint representation.... Each client has a right to expect that the lawyer will tell the client anything bearing on the representation that might affect that client's interests.... [A]t the outset of the joint representation the lawyer should advise both (or all) clients that the joint representation will work only if they agree to deal openly and honestly with one another on all matters relating to the representation, and that the lawyer will have to withdraw, if one requests that some matter material to the representation be kept from the other.[4]

The Massachusetts Comment suggests that should one client in a joint representation insist that critical information be kept from the other, the lawyer would be bound to keep that confidence, albeit while resigning from the joint representation, which at least would put the other client on notice that something was amiss. Is this the right resolution or should the lawyer be allowed or even required to disclose the material confidence to the other client?

Remarkably, there is almost no case law on this question. A 1999 decision of the Supreme Court of New Jersey is the rare exception. In A v. B[5] the question was whether a law firm that jointly represented a husband and wife in drafting their wills may reveal to the wife that the husband had an illegitimate child, a fact the firm learned, not from the husband but from another source, after the wills were executed. Upon learning of the child's existence, the firm wrote to the husband stating that it believed it had an ethical obligation to inform the wife of the child's existence, although not its identity, and to advise her that under the couple's current wills a portion of her assets might ultimately devise to that child through her spouse. The letter to the husband suggested he tell his wife of the child, stating that if he did not, the firm would. The intermediate appellate court ordered the firm not to tell the wife.

The New Jersey Supreme Court reversed, holding that the firm had discretion to make the disclosure under New Jersey's version of Rule 1.6, which permits, but does not require, lawyers to reveal such information as the lawyer reasonably believes necessary "to rectify the consequences of a client's criminal, illegal or fraudulent act" in which the lawyer's services were used. The court, noting that it construed the term "fraudulent act" in Rule 1.6 broadly, held that the husband's deliberate failure to inform his

---

4. Comment 12[d] to Massachusetts Rule 1.7 provides:

In limited circumstances, it may be appropriate for a lawyer to ask both (or all) clients, if they want to agree that the lawyer will keep certain information confidential, i.e., from the other client. For example, an estate lawyer might want to ask joint clients if they each want to agree that in the eventuality that one becomes mentally disabled the lawyer be allowed to proceed with the joint representation, appropriately altering the estate plan, without the other's knowledge. Of course, should that eventu-

ality come to pass the lawyer should consult Rule 1.14 before proceeding. However, aside from such limited circumstances, the lawyer representing joint clients should emphasize that what the clients give up in terms of confidentiality is twofold: a later right to claim the attorney-client privilege in disputes between them; and the right during the representation to keep secrets from one another that bear on the representation.

5. 726 A.2d 924 (N.J.1999).

wife of the child's existence while jointly planning the disposition of their estates constituted a fraud upon the wife in which the law firm's services were used. Thus, the firm had discretion to reveal the information to the wife over the husband's objections. While not grounding its decision on this fact, the court mentioned that upon initiation of the joint representation both clients had signed documents entitled "Waiver of Conflict of Interest," which explained, among other things, that information provided by one spouse might become available to the other. While the court did not read these documents as explicitly authorizing the lawyers to reveal one spouse's confidences to the other, it said that their "spirit ... supports the firm's decision to disclose."

The New Jersey court said it could find no dispositive decision from any other court on the question before it. As to secondary authority, the Restatement § 112, Comment *l* provides that an explicit agreement reached by joint clients upon the initiation of the joint representation on whether they want the lawyer to reveal the confidences of each to the other is binding upon the lawyer. Where there is no prior explicit agreement, the Restatement's Comment leaves the decision on disclosure to the lawyer's discretion, providing, however, that upon resigning from a joint representation the lawyer may disclose that she has learned information that the other client will not permit the lawyer to disclose but which the lawyer believes should be disclosed. The professional ethics committees of New York and Florida have concluded, contrary to the Restatement's approach, that absent explicit prior authorization the lawyer may not disclose one client's confidence to her joint client.[6]

Representing Buyer and Seller

The *Callahan* case is premised on the implicit assumption that a lawyer may represent a buyer and seller in at least some situations. In most states a lawyer may represent a buyer and seller in a routine residential real estate transaction if certain conditions are met. For example, a Colorado ethics opinion[7] permits joint representation if the material terms of the agreement have been agreed upon by the parties (e.g., price, time and manner of payment, status of title upon transfer, inclusion of personal property, status of any present leases or tenancies, amount of earnest money deposit and the treatment of amounts so deposited upon the default of either party). The lawyer must disclose to the parties the risks of joint representation, including a warning that if litigation develops the lawyer cannot represent either party and that the attorney-client privilege may not apply to their communications to the lawyer. Both parties must consent and the lawyer must determine that she can provide adequate

---

6. New York State Bar Ass'n Comm. On Professional Ethics, Op. 555 (1984); and Florida State Bar Ass'n. Comm. on Prof. Ethics, Op. 95–4 (1997). Both opinions are discussed in A v. B, 726 A.2d at 930, and the hypotheticals considered in those opin-

ions distinguished from the facts before the New Jersey court.

7. Colo. Bar Ass'n Ethics Op. 68, Resolving Multiple Representation Conflicts (Apr. 20, 1985).

representation to each. If the lawyer has represented one party in the past, this must be revealed and its effect on the representation considered. The lawyer may not serve as a mere scrivener, but must fulfill the full obligations of the attorney-client relationship.

Even if it is permissible to undertake the representation, the Colorado opinion warns that difficulties may arise during its course: First, material issues may arise that the parties have not considered. The lawyer must inform the parties of the available alternatives and leave the decision to them. Second, if a title defect is discovered, the lawyer must raise the matter for the mutual consideration of the parties. In general, the parties should be advised of the advantages of obtaining separate representation.

The case law is to much the same effect. In re Kamp[8] holds that a lawyer seeking to represent both the seller and buyer in a real estate or similar transaction must disclose to each his relationship to the other, the pitfalls of dual representation which might make it desirable for each party to have separate counsel, and "[t]he full significance of the representation of conflicting interests." The difficulties of obtaining an informed consent after full disclosure are illustrated by a subsequent New Jersey case in which a lawyer, who jointly represented the buyer and seller in a real estate transaction, obtained the consent of the seller to an extension of the buyer's obligation to close the transaction without informing the seller that the buyer had sold his interest to a third person.[9] After the lawyer settled the seller's claim against him for breach of fiduciary duty, the court held that the innocent buyer was not vicariously liable for the lawyer's wrongdoing.

Although concurrent representation of buyers and sellers has been conventional in many localities, it is risky and should not be undertaken without carefully examining the circumstances surrounding the proposed representation, including the lawyer's past relationships with both clients and the attitude of both clients towards the proposed representation and each other. In In re Banta,[10] for example, a lawyer was reprimanded for having relayed to the buyer inaccurate facts given to the lawyer by the seller.

It is proper in some circumstances for a lawyer to bring two clients together to facilitate a deal between them.[11] But when the lawyer has a longstanding relationship with one party and a new relationship with the other, it may be unreasonable to believe that she can be impartial between them.[12]

8. 194 A.2d 236 (N.J.1963).

9. Baldasarre v. Butler, 625 A.2d 458 (N.J. 1993).

10. 412 N.E.2d 221 (Ind.1980).

11. See, e.g., Atlantic Richfield Co. v. Sybert,, 456 A.2d 20 (Md.1983).

12. See M.R. 2.2, Comments [3] (addressing joint representation in transactions) and [7] (discussing impartiality). See also Attorney Grievance Commission v. Collins, 457 A.2d 1134 (Md.1983); In re Lanza, 322 A.2d 445 (N.J.1974); In re Nelson, 332 N.W.2d 811 (Wis.1983).

Ethics Rules on Lawyer as Intermediary

Model Rule 2.2 has an elaborate set of provisions on the lawyer as intermediary.[13] Subparagraph (a)(1) specifies issues the lawyer should discuss with the clients before obtaining their consent. Subparagraphs (a)(2) and (a)(3) require that the lawyer reasonably believe the following: the matter can be resolved on terms compatible with the clients' best interests; each client will be able to make informed decisions; material prejudice to either client's interests should the contemplated resolution fail is unlikely; and the common representation can be undertaken impartially and without improper effect on the responsibilities the lawyer has to either client.

M.R. 2.2(b) prescribes how the lawyer should proceed while acting as an intermediary. M.R. 2.2(c) requires the lawyer to withdraw if either client requests or if the lawyer can no longer meet the requirements of paragraph (a). After withdrawing, the lawyer may not represent any of the clients in the matter that was the subject of the intermediation. The Restatement continues this approach, but makes explicit that co-clients may agree at the onset of the representation that in the event the joint representation collapses the lawyer may continue to represent one of the two of them. Comment *d* to § 201.

The puzzle concerning M.R. 2.2 is when and to what extent it displaces the general rule governing concurrent representation stated in M.R. 1.7. Some commentators view it as a more elaborate statement of the principles governing joint representation in transactions; others criticize it as a source of confusion. The ABA Ethics 2000 Commission decided in early 1999 to recommend its deletion from the Model Rules with its content being added to the Comments to M.R. 1.7.[14]

A lawyer who decides to act as an intermediary faces serious risks. In Klemm v. Superior Court,[15] the court identified some of these risks:

- If the lawyer fails fully to inform the clients of the facts, risks and potential disadvantages of the joint representation, the lawyer may be civilly liable to those clients for any loss suffered;

- The lawyer lays herself open to charges, whether well founded or not, of unethical and unprofessional conduct;

- The validity of any agreement negotiated without independent representation of each of the parties is vulnerable to easy attack as having been procured by misrepresentation, fraud and overreaching.

---

13. EC 5–20 of the Model Code states "[a] lawyer is often asked to serve as an impartial arbitrator or mediator in matters which involve present or former clients." Little guidance is given for performing such a role. EC 5–20 says only that the lawyer "may serve in either capacity if he first discloses such present or former relationships." A lawyer must look to DR 5–105, the Code's general rule on conflicts of interest.

14. See 15 Law.Man.Prof.Conduct 171 (Apr. 28, 1999) (proposal to eliminate M.R. 2.2). For discussion of M.R. 2.2, see John Dzienkowski, Lawyers as Intermediaries: The Representation of Multiple Clients in the Modern Legal Profession, 1992 U.Ill.L.Rev. 741 (discussing ethical problems of the intermediary rule).

15. 142 Cal.Rptr. 509, 514 (App.1977).

The court concluded that "[i]t thus behooves counsel to cogitate carefully and proceed cautiously before placing himself/herself in such a position."[16] Wouldn't a lawyer seeking to adjust a matter between clients be better off to call it "adjustment" and be governed by M.R. 1.7? Or do both rules require the same things?

2.   Lawyer's Role in Matrimonial Matters

Matrimonial Dissolution

When a lawyer represents both spouses in some stage of matrimonial dissolution, the context suggests difficulties not encountered in friendly negotiations of potential contracts or startup of business ventures. First, the existence of marital difficulties suggests some degree of antagonism between the spouses, even if they concur in a preference for an "amicable" and inexpensive parting. Second, if a contract negotiation fails the parties may walk away, but spouses are legally bound to each other in "holy deadlock." If agreement is not possible, they can either continue their marriage or resort to litigation to end it. Third, in many marital situations one spouse is a dominant figure who may have greater experience in dealing with property or contentiousness or both.

The latter factor, one spouse's undue influence over the other, is a serious impediment to representing both husband and wife in domestic relations cases. Matrimonial agreements can be challenged on the ground of overreaching. Representation of both spouses by one lawyer is an invitation to such a challenge. On the other hand, presuming an incapacity on the part of one spouse, usually the wife, to make an informed consent to a cheaper and possibly more amicable parting is itself demeaning and paternalistic.

State courts agree that a single lawyer cannot represent both spouses in the courtroom phase of divorce cases. But there is disagreement on whether a lawyer, with the informed consent of both spouses, may negotiate a separation arrangement and draft other papers dealing with property division or child custody for subsequent submission to the divorce court. In some states it is permissible for a lawyer, after negotiating an agreement on these matters, to represent the moving spouse in an uncontested court proceeding. In other states the parties must act pro se in the divorce court or obtain other representation.

In Levine v. Levine,[17] a former wife sought to rescind a separation agreement prepared by a lawyer who jointly represented both spouses. Despite the presence of factors suggesting overreaching—the lawyer was related to the husband by marriage and had previously represented the husband's business—the separation agreement was upheld on the basis of findings that the agreement was fair, the lawyer acted in a neutral capacity and the lawyer made full disclosure of relevant facts:

---

16. Id. at 514.   **17.**   436 N.E.2d 476 (N.Y.1982).

... While the potential conflict of interests inherent in such joint representation suggests that the husband and wife should retain separate counsel, the parties have an absolute right to be represented by the same attorney provided "there has been a full disclosure between the parties, not only of all relevant facts but also of their contextual significance, and there has been an absence of inequitable conduct or other infirmity which vitiate the execution of the agreement." ...

Contrary to the determination below, the fact that the same attorney represented both parties in the preparation of the separation agreement does not, without more, establish overreaching on the part of the husband.... [18]

Although the separation agreement was upheld, the lawyer's clients were put to considerable trouble and expense litigating its validity. Was the joint representation worth the risks entailed?

Some states prohibit a single lawyer from representing both spouses in matrimonial mediation, negotiation or litigation. These jurisdictions reason that divorce actions are inherently adversarial and involve great potential of opposing interests on such issues as support, child custody, visitation, ownership and division of property; consequently, one attorney should not represent both the husband and the wife at either the negotiation or litigation stage.[19] If one or both spouses cannot afford to retain a lawyer, and publicly-funded civil legal assistance is not available, as is likely to be the case, one or both must go unrepresented.

Divorce Mediation

Under M.R. 2.2, a lawyer is engaged in joint representation of two or more clients on a common matter; "mediation," on the other hand, usually involves a distinct role in which a lawyer does not have a lawyer-client relationship with either party. Clarity at the outset concerning whether a lawyer-client role is contemplated is vital.[20]

Ethics opinions in a number of states permit a lawyer to act as a

---

18. 436 N.E.2d at 479. Compare Klemm v. Superior Court, 142 Cal.Rptr. 509 (App. 1977). In *Klemm*, one factor that may have led the court to sustain the dual representation was that the challenge to the support agreement was brought not by either spouse but by the County of Fresno, which wanted the husband to pay child support to offset the AFDC payments being made to the mother. The wife asserted that she was content with the agreement for no support.

19. Blum v. Blum, 477 A.2d 289 (Md.App. 1984) (facts relating to separation agreement prepared by a lawyer representing both parties should be examined for possible duress; even where separating parties

appear in full accord, lawyer may not represent them both due to seriousness of potential conflict).

20. When a lawyer agrees to serve as an arbitrator, it is understood that an impartial decisional role is involved rather than a partisan one. "Intermediation" under M.R. 2.2 contemplates a commitment to the shared goals of two clients; "mediation" is often unclear—it may contemplate an independent advisory role more like arbitration (no lawyer-client relationship with the parties) or one in which a lawyer owes the full duties of the lawyer-client relationship to each party.

mediator in some marital situations.[21] An opinion of the Association of the Bar of the City of New York,[22] for example, considers a structured divorce mediation service in which a trained therapist consults with a separating couple to aid them in working out aspects of the separation or divorce (e.g., property division, child custody, visitation and support). The opinion gives somewhat grudging approval to participation of a lawyer as part of the mediating team to give impartial legal advice to the parties and to draft a divorce or separation agreement approved by them.

Mediation, the opinion states, has a range of meanings from relatively passive listening and questioning to active involvement in framing a comprehensive resolution. Dangers in performing the mediation function arise because of: the divergent interests of parties, doubt as to whether one or both of the parties understand the risks and give an informed consent, inequalities of bargaining power of the parties and the potential for misunderstandings and later recrimination against the lawyer. On the other hand, the adversary process has legal, emotional and economic costs that may outweigh its advantages in some situations. If the parties are antagonistic or troubled, or there is inequality of bargaining position, the lawyer cannot serve as a mediator. If there are complex and difficult legal questions (e.g., tax consequences), separate representation is required.

In appropriate situations, the opinion concludes, a lawyer may participate in the non-legal aspects of mediation, provide impartial legal advice and assist in reducing the parties' agreement to writing if: (1) the parties are fully advised of the risks (including the sharing of confidences); (2) the lawyer is satisfied the parties understand the risks; (3) legal advice is given only to both parties in each others' presence; (4) the parties are advised of the advantages of seeking independent legal counsel before executing any agreement; and (5) the lawyer does not represent either party in any subsequent legal proceedings relating to the divorce. The opinion also warns that the lawyer must take care not to assist non-lawyers on the mediation team in the unauthorized practice of law.

Joint Representation in Estate Planning

One of the most common forms of joint representation is that of a husband and wife who want to embody in will and trust instruments an estate plan that, while recognizing their individual desires to leave small separate bequests to individuals or organizations, furthers their common desire to leave their estates, after the death of both, to their descendants and relatives, while minimizing estate taxes. When unanimity and harmony

---

21. For a review of bar association opinions on use of mediation in matrimonial dissolution, see Note, Model Rule 2.2 and Divorce Mediation: Ethics Guideline or Ethics Gap?, 65 Wash.U.L.Q. 223 (1987). The opinions in a number of states reflect hostility to mediatory representation in divorce proceedings. Part of the problem is the lack of clarity concerning whether the particular mediation involves legal representation or, like arbitration, is a distinct function not involving a lawyer-client relationship with the parties.

22. Ass'n of Bar of City of New York, Comm. on Prof. Ethics No. 80–23 (1980).

prevail within the marriage, the lawyer may undertake such representation with assurance that the shared goals justify the joint representation. Even in this situation, the implications of joint representation should be discussed and consents put in writing—steps that informed observers say are commonly omitted. Most important, the lawyer should make it clear that all material communications from each spouse relating to the estate plan are not confidential as to the other spouse. Trouble often arises when this basic precaution is omitted.

Suppose a lawyer meets with a husband and wife for estate planning purposes. They each express a desire to give each other a survivorship interest in the bulk of their joint property, make some relatively small separate bequests to charities and leave the residue in equal shares to their two children. Drafts are prepared and discussed at a meeting with both clients. After this conference, however, the husband returns to the lawyer and asks her to change the provision for the children by omitting their names and substituting a general reference to "their issue in equal shares." He explains that, unknown to his wife, he has been supporting a child whom he has fathered out of wedlock and wants this child to have a share of the estate. He also does not want the lawyer to communicate this information to his wife. What should the lawyer do?

Situations of this kind place the tacit assumption of joint representation—that all material information relating to it must be communicated to each client—in conflict with the duty of confidentiality to a client. In A v. B,[23] discussed above, the court said the lawyer was permitted to disclose the information to the wife. The court relied on New Jersey's ethics rule permitting disclosure to rectify past or ongoing fraud when the lawyer's services had been used to effectuate the fraud. The decision left open the question whether the lawyer was required to inform the wife of the husband's fraud. Assume, as the court held, that the husband's conduct was a fraud on the wife, the lawyer did not disclose the fraud to the wife, and as a result the two marital children lost one-third of their inheritance. Under these circumstances, would the law firm be liable to them for the harm?[24]

Some estate planning lawyers have suggested that separate and simultaneous representation of a husband and wife is appropriate if advance consents are obtained. The separate representation on a matter of common interest would be predicated on a specific agreement between the clients and the lawyer involved that the lawyer would not be required to share confidential information among the clients. Can a husband and wife, undertaking a joint estate planning venture, waive the lawyer's fiduciary and ethical duty to communicate relevant information concerning the representation to them? Geoffrey Hazard has commented that the concept of separate co-representation is "a legal and ethical oxymoron."[25] Others

---

23. 726 A.2d 924 (N.J.1999).

24. See Teresa S. Collett, Disclosure, Discretion, or Deception: The Estate Planner's Ethical Dilemma, 28 Real Prop., Prob. & Trust J. 683 (Winter 1994).

25. Geoffrey C. Hazard, Jr., Conflict of Interest in Estate Planning for Husband and

have urged that representation of a married couple be considered a form of entity representation.[26] Hazard accepts the underlying moral premise that a lawyer in family settings should take into account the ties of affection and obligation between spouses and between parents and children in counseling clients and deciding whether to withdraw. Going beyond that, Hazard argues, departs from legal rules that place rights and duties in individuals; the "family," unlike a corporation, is not a legal entity that is governed by a large and established body of substantive law. Family law duties generally run from one spouse to another or from parents to children. Hazard concludes that "husband and wife ... are legally autonomous jural persons and must be treated as such in lawyer-client relationships."

3.   JOINT REPRESENTATION IN BUSINESS VENTURES

The most frequent form of joint representation in transactions involves the lawyer's role in creating, advising and sometimes terminating a business venture involving a small number of participants. Usually this activity involves the creation of a legal entity which then becomes the client. The special problems of organizational representation are considered in Chapter 8 at p. 708. Here we deal with situations in which joint representation of the individual participants is contemplated: the individuals are each paying a part of the lawyer's fee and establish a personal lawyer-client relationship on the common matter (i.e., they are co-clients).

Starting a new venture is the easiest case for joint representation, but even here there are actual or potential conflicts of interest that must be recognized and overcome by the informed consent of all co-clients. Suppose a lawyer is asked by Tom, Dick and Harriet, three acquaintances that she has never previously represented, to assist them in setting up a new business venture. Tom (age 30 and unmarried) has specialized expertise in the field; he will be the full-time manager providing much of the know-how. Dick (age 45 and married with two teenage children) will handle marketing and sales. Harriet (age 60, a retired businesswoman) will participate as the principal investor. Tom and Dick will work full-time for the new venture, Tom on a modest salary and Dick on salary plus commissions. Harriet will receive no salary but a share of the profits. The three clients ask the lawyer to set up a corporation, to help them work out the detailed terms of the venture (investment understandings, employment contracts, stock holdings, buy-out arrangements, etc.) and to prepare necessary documents. May the lawyer undertake the representation?

Wife, 20 Prob. Law. 1, 13 (1994), responding to, among others, Jeffrey Pennell, Professional Responsibility: Reforms Are Needed to Accommodate Estate Planning and Family Counseling, 1991 Miami Inst. Est.Plan. 18–3, 18–29 (spouses should be able to select separate simultaneous representation by same lawyer).

26.   Thomas L. Shaffer, The Legal Ethics of Radical Individualism, 65 Tex.L.Rev. 963 (1987); and Russell G. Pearce, Family Values and Legal Ethics: Competing Approaches to Conflicts in Representing Spouses, 62 Fordham L.Rev. 1253 (1994) (urging that husband-wife representation should be considered under M.R. 1.13, considering the family as an entity).

When this hypothetical was posed to two experienced business lawyers, they reached opposing conclusions.[27] Richard H. Levin approved the lawyer's undertaking the joint representation: She should help the parties work out a happy future together. Concededly, the undertaking is a difficult one because representation of the differing interests of each client requires a good deal of disclosure of the risks, care in dealing with the personalities and problems as they arise and a sensitive awareness to developing conflicts. Joint representation, however, has many advantages: It focuses everyone on the promise of the future and getting the job done; it downplays conflict and accentuates agreement and cooperation; and it is less expensive. In many situations, if one lawyer cannot serve, parties will get along with non-lawyers. Separate lawyers can create controversy and break deals. In negotiation, Levin says, "defining a problem tends to establish it and discussing it tends to arouse fears, belligerence, and obstinacy."[28]

> Most transactions should be viewed primarily as to their opportunities, and only secondarily as to their problems. The lawyer is most useful in affirmative planning, and adding cooks does not necessarily improve the broth.[29]

Another experienced lawyer, Meyer J. Myer, concluded that the present and potential differences are so large that separate representation is required. The clients have not resolved many critical issues. How can the lawyer resolve them? For example, the allocation of shares is a difficult problem when the participation of money and energy of each of the three is different; the facts suggest the desirability, in Harriet's interest, of providing a preferred debt interest for at least part of her investment but that may not be in the interest of the other two participants; given the different ages and family situations of the parties, working out buy-out arrangements and current income payments is problematic. Given these and other divergent interests, the lawyer cannot adequately represent each client:

> Experience has shown that when more than slight differences in interest, present or potential, exist, a full explanation by the lawyer of their implications, and a firm stand against the representation, will not only dissolve the criticism of unnecessary duplication of legal services but in the long run will enhance respect for the lawyer and the profession.[30]

Divergent interests, if not antagonism, pose even more difficult problems when the co-clients seek to terminate a joint venture. Suppose business associates come to have different views about the course the business should take or are unhappy with the contribution of a participant. They come to the lawyer and ask her to work out a fair dissolution. What are the risks to the lawyer? To the clients? Consider this situation in the

27. Stanley A. Kaplan (ed.), Legal Ethics Forum: Representation of Multiple Clients, 62 A.B.A.J. 648 (1976).

28. Id. at 650.

29. Id.

30. Id. at 652.

light of those discussed below in which Justice Brandeis, as a practicing lawyer, acted as "a lawyer for the situation."

May a lawyer represent both the buyer and seller of a business? The general rule is that the divergent interests of the parties are such that a lawyer cannot be on both sides of the termination of a business. These transactions are too complex and the parties will not have considered all of the complexities even if they come to the lawyer with what they think is a completed deal.

4.   "LAWYER FOR THE SITUATION"

Justice Louis D. Brandeis, one of the great American lawyers of the first half of the 20th century, provides an inspiring example of living a great life in the law. His piercing intellect, passionate social commitment and enormous accomplishments continue to inspire many American lawyers. The focus here is on a less well-known aspect of Brandeis' life: His conception of the appropriate role of a lawyer during his years as a practicing attorney in Boston. Because Brandeis often preferred to facilitate a comprehensive resolution to a dispute rather than represent a single party in adversarial negotiations, he described his role on occasion as "lawyer for the situation."[31] Acting in this role involves either joint representation or a mediatory role, both a departure from advocacy of a single client's interest—the role primarily envisioned by the lawyer codes.

Our knowledge of these matters comes primarily from the Senate confirmation hearings on President Wilson's nomination of Brandeis in 1916 as an associate justice of the U.S. Supreme Court.[32] At the hearing, prominent members of the bar charged Brandeis with unethical behavior in several instances where he acted as lawyer for the situation. The Warren case is illustrative.[33]

Brandeis had served as lawyer for the family of Samuel Warren, his law partner. Sam Warren's father had owned a substantial paper manufacturing company. When the father died, he left an estate of some $2 million to his wife and children. Brandeis sought to dispose of the estate appropriately and represented both members of the family and the estate. Sam Warren wished to keep the family business going but the other children did not desire an active role in the business. To satisfy all the children's wishes, Brandeis created a trust from which Sam could lease and continue operating the business. Brandeis transferred the mills to an inter vivos trust with Sam, his mother and a Mr. Mason (superintendent of the mills) as trustees. The trust then leased the property to Sam, his brother Fiske and Mr. Mason, who operated the business. As the mills prospered, the

31. See Clyde Spillenger, Reconsidering Brandeis as People's Lawyer, 105 Yale L.J. 1445 (1996).

32. See Alpheus T. Mason, Brandeis: A Free Man's Life 465–508 (1946) (discussing the confirmation fight).

33. The *Warren* case is discussed in John P. Frank, The Legal Ethics of Louis D. Brandeis, 17 Stan. L. Rev. 683, 694–98 (1965).

lessees were entitled to keep some of the profits as compensation for their services. Another portion of profits passed to the trustees and eventually to all the Warren children as beneficiaries.

This arrangement worked well for nineteen years until Ned Warren (one of the beneficiaries) became unhappy with Sam's management of the mills. In 1909, Ned brought an action to void the lease and to secure an accounting. He alleged fraud and collusion on the part of Sam Warren and Brandeis, arguing the arrangement with Sam as both lessee and trustee gave Sam an unjust financial gain at the expense of Ned and other family members. In the litigation, Brandeis represented the lessees. Before trial, Sam Warren died, Ned sold his interest in the trust to other family members and the litigation was abandoned.

The Warren case came back to haunt Brandeis at his confirmation hearings. Why did he represent both lessees and trustees at the drafting stage of the trust? Why did he represent only the lessees when Ned filed suit? Why did he continue to accept annual retainers from both trustees and lessees while the trust arrangement was working successfully?

Another representation explored in the confirmation hearings was Brandeis' handling of a debtor-creditor relationship.[34] Brandeis was approached by the owners of a tannery business which was in financial difficulties. The tanners thought Brandeis undertook to represent them but Brandeis eventually helped the creditors of the tannery, who drove the tannery into bankruptcy. When pressed to identify for whom he was actually working, Brandeis replied, "I should say that I was counsel for the situation." This misty response has caught the attention of legal commentators. What exactly are the characteristics of a lawyer for the situation? Is such behavior ethical?

After five months of investigation of this and other alleged improprieties in Brandeis' law practice, the Senate judiciary committee approved his nomination by a narrow 10 to 8 vote. He was confirmed by the Senate by a 47–22 vote.[35]

Geoffrey Hazard describes a lawyer for the situation as follows:

> [N]o other lawyer is involved. Hence, the lawyer is no one's partisan and, at least up to a point, everyone's confidant.... [H]e undertakes to discern the needs, fears, and expectations of each [client] and to discover the concordances among them.... He can contribute historical perspective, objectivity, and foresight into the parties' assessment of the situation [and] discourage escalation of conflict.... He can articulate general principles and common custom as standards by which the parties can examine their respective claims. He is advocate, mediator, entrepreneur, and judge, all in one. He could be said to be playing God.[36]

---

34. This matter, referred to as the *Lennox Case*, is discussed in Frank, supra, at 698–703.

35. Mason, supra, at 505.

36. Geoffrey C. Hazard, Jr., Ethics in the Practice of Law 64–65 (1978).

John P. Frank's analysis of Brandeis's ethics, published in 1965, offers a straight-forward rejection of lawyering for the situation. Frank's thesis is simple: "Lawyers are not retained by situations, and the adversary system assumes that they faithfully represent one interest at a time."[37] A "situation" is too vague for intelligible representation. Only specific clients, who can articulate particular interests in particular matters, are proper "units" of representation. Frank, after studying the Brandeis record, advises "never be 'counsel for a situation.'"[38]

Thomas L. Shaffer writes approvingly of Brandeis' "disagreement with the profession's elaborate concern for conflicts of interest."[39] He defends the concept and the practice of acting as lawyer for the situation:

> The lawyer-for-the situation claim involves ... saying that the situation has reality.... [Married couples and other family groups] have reality; they are *something*; and it is possible for a lawyer to recognize the reality of such situations (units) and then to accord professional representation and defense to such situations (units).... [T]o recognize the risks and to acknowledge that there are in such representation opportunities for self-deception is not to say that "situations" lack reality.... If human associations have reality, then it is not the case that the typical lawyer's client is always a (lonely) individual.[40]

In Shaffer's world view, the ancient bonds of family properly subordinate individual interests; professional responsibility rules are corrupting, he argues, if they do not temper zealous advocacy for the individual with a healthy measure of respect for organic communities of persons.

Hazard takes a cautious intermediate position between Frank's rejection of lawyering for the situation and Shaffer's acceptance of it.[41] Hazard sees lawyers for the situation as playing a constructive role in certain situations, but sounds loud warnings about the potential for abuse, alienation of clients and confused professional responsibilities. Hazard notes that professional codes recognize lawyering for the situation to some extent. See M.R.s 2.1, 2.2 and 2.3. The active and creative role of lawyer of the situation, Hazard writes, can be

> ... perhaps the best service a lawyer can render to anyone ... Approximat[ing] the ideal forms of intercession suggested by the models of wise parent or village elder.... It rests on implicit principles of decision that express commonly shared ideals in behavior rather than strict legal right. The basis of decision is mutual assent and not external compulsion. The orientation in time tends to be a hopeful view of the future rather than an angry view of the past.[42]

---

37. John P. Frank, The Legal Ethics of Louis D. Brandeis, 17 Stan. L. Rev. 683, 702 (1965).

38. Id. at 708.

39. Thomas L. Shaffer, American Legal Ethics 302 (1985).

40. Id. at 302–03. See also Thomas L. Shaffer, The Legal Ethics of Radical Individualism, 65 Tex.L.Rev. 963 (1987).

41. Geoffrey C. Hazard, Jr., Ethics in the Practice of Law 58–63 (1978).

42. Id. at 65.

But the role has many dangers. First, the lawyer for the situation undertakes an amorphous function: representing the best interests of all. Second, the degree to which the attorney is an active participant in a situation may become worrisome. Unlike representation of a single interest, a lawyer for the situation has no structure of goals and constraints imposed from the outside. Third, lawyering for the situation strains client trust: Clients must accept the lawyer's actions and judgments without being able to verify their soundness. Fourth, the lawyer for a situation faces much harder moral choices than an attorney in an adversarial system. Short of violating law, the traditional role permits a lawyer to leave hard choices to the client. Reliance on the premises of the profession allows the lawyer to occupy a simplified moral universe. A lawyer for the situation, on the other hand, has "choices to make that obviously can go against the interest of one client or another.... "[43] The existence of these hard choices may explain why many lawyers are reluctant to become lawyers for the situation and why professional rules give little recognition of the propriety of such practice: "in the event of miscarriage [the lawyer for the situation] will have no protection from the law."[44]

5. REPRESENTING AN INSURED PERSON UPON REQUEST OF AN INSURER[45]

For many years the ABA waffled on the lawyer's responsibility in representing an insured through retainer by an insurer. A 1942 ethics opinion declined to say whether information given by the insured to the lawyer is confidential as against the insurer.[46] The opinion stated that this "is a question of law and not of ethics," a question on which the courts were divided.[47]

In 1950, however, the ethics committee took the position that "[t]he essential point of ethics involved is that the lawyer so employed shall represent the insured as his client with undivided fidelity.... "[48] This is the generally accepted rule today.[49]

43. Ibid.

44. Ibid.

45. For general commentary see Nancy J. Moore, The Ethical Duties of Insurance Defense Lawyers: Are Special Solutions Required?, 4 Conn. Ins. L.J. 259 (1997); Charles Silver & Kent Syverud, The Professional Responsibilities of Insurance Defense Lawyers, 45 Duke L.J. 255, 314–315 (1995). *Compare* Robert E. O'Malley, Ethics Principles for the Insurer, the Insured, and Defense Counsel: The Eternal Triangle Reformed, 66 Tulane L.Rev. 511 (1991), and Stephen L. Pepper, Applying the Fundamentals of Lawyers' Ethics to Insurance Defense Practice, 4 Conn. Ins. L.J. 27 (1997) (both preferring the insured as the sole client view), *with* Charles Silver, Does Insurance Defense Counsel Represent the Company or the Insured?, 72 Tex.L.Rev. 1583 (1994) (arguing for the dual client position).

46. ABA Formal Opinion 247 (1942).

47. See Annot. 108 A.L.R. 505 for court decisions on this issue contemporaneous with Opinion 247.

48. ABA Formal Opinion 282 (1950).

49. See e.g., Parsons v. Continental National American Group, 550 P.2d 94 (Ariz. 1976).

Model Rule 1.8(f) provides that a lawyer shall not accept payment from another for legal services to a client unless: (1) the client consents after consultation; (2) there is no interference with the lawyer's independence or professional judgment or with the client-lawyer relationship; and (3) information relating to representation of the client is protected as required by M.R. 1.6 (the rule on confidentiality). In addition, M.R. 1.8(b) provides that "[a] lawyer shall not use information relating to representation of a client to the disadvantage of the client unless the client consents after consultation." Observe that "use" of information may be made without disclosure of such information.[50]

Coverage Questions

A liability insurer may assign a case to a defense lawyer believing that the event is within policy coverage. The defense attorney subsequently may discover facts indicating that the insured's liability falls outside the policy (e.g., the insured acted intentionally rather than negligently). May the defense attorney reveal that information to the insurance company? The cases hold that defense counsel's duty of loyalty to the insured bars her from taking any action that may be adverse to her clients' interests.[51] Thus, if an investigating defense lawyer discovers defendant's wrongful act was intentional, the lawyer may not reveal that information to the insurance company. Liability insurers often protect themselves against this possibility by undertaking the defense under a reservation of rights, leaving open the possibility of litigating coverage in a separate proceeding against the insured. The insurer's reservation of rights warns the insured that it may be in the latter's best interest to obtain separate representation.[52]

Settling an Insurance Claim

In Crisci v. Security Insurance Co.,[53] the court said: "When there is a great risk of a recovery beyond the policy limits so that the most reasonable manner of disposing of the claim is a settlement which can be made within those limits, a consideration in good faith of the insured's interest requires the insurer to settle the claim."[54] The duty-to-settle doctrine poses dangers for insurance defense counsel who reject offers of settlement within policy limits. In Lysick v. Walcom,[55] the insurer authorized counsel to settle for the policy limit, $10,000. Defense counsel offered plaintiff $9,500, which plaintiff refused. When defense counsel finally tendered the policy limit, plaintiff rejected the offer. At trial, the jury returned a plaintiff's verdict of

---

50. DR 5–107(B) provides that "A lawyer shall not permit a person who recommends, employs, or pays him to render legal services for another to direct or regulate his professional judgment in rendering such legal services."

51. See Parsons v. Continental American Group, 550 P.2d 94 (Ariz.1976).

52. See e.g., New York State Urban Dev. Corp. v. VSL Corp., 738 F.2d 61 (2d Cir.

1984) (insurer may participate in selecting independent counsel for insured); and Nandorf Inc. v. CNA Insurance Companies, 479 N.E.2d 988 (Ill. App.1985) (insurer obliged to pay for insured's independent counsel).

53. 426 P.2d 173 (Cal.1967).

54. Id. at 176.

55. 65 Cal.Rptr. 406 (App.1968).

$225,000. The insured settled its bad faith claim against the insurer for $89,000. The insurer, in turn, sued defense counsel for malpractice. The court found for the carrier, holding counsel liable for the excess.[56]

May the insurer settle without the insured's consent? This fact pattern commonly arises in the malpractice setting, when a professional is interested in protecting her reputation. Some states treat the insurance policy as a binding waiver by the insured of her right to control settlement.[57] With that view contrast Rogers v. Robson, Masters, Ryan, Brumund & Belom.[58] In that case, the court held that, even though the insurance policy authorized the insurer to settle without the insured physician's consent, the insured had a cause of action against the lawyer who settled against the physician's instructions and without fully disclosing to him the intent to settle. The lawyer's duty concerning settlement stemmed from the attorney-client relationship, not the policy.[59] Which is the better approach? If insureds can purchase policies at higher premiums that give them the right to control settlement, as they generally can, why should those who forego that option have the right to sue the lawyer for settling against the insured's wishes?

ABA Formal Opinion 96–403 (1996) addressed the ethical responsibility of a laywer hired by an insurer to represent an insured under a policy that gives the insurer exclusive control of the defense and settlement of the claim. The opinion concludes that the lawyer may "represent" the insured as long as the lawyer discloses and explains to the insured the limited nature of the representation and the insurer's right to call the shots. According to the committee, disclosure was required by Rule 1.2. Why not by any of the conflicts rules?

In American Insurance Assn. v. Kentucky State Bar,[60] the court affirmed an ethics committee advisory opinion prohibiting lawyers from contracting with an insurance company to represent insureds for a flat fee to be paid by the company. The court held that such an arrangement violates Rules 1.7(b) and 1.8(f)(2): Rule 1.7(b) by materially limiting the representation without the client's informed consent; and Rule 1.8(f)(2) by

56. If the insurance company was responsible for refusing the settlement offer, neither the insured nor the insurer can recover from the lawyer. See Purdy v. Pacific Automobile Ins. Co., 203 Cal.Rptr. 524 (App.1984) (lawyer's actions were not the proximate cause of the insured's loss when the insurer, not the lawyer, rejected the settlement offer).

57. See Mitchum v. Hudgens, 533 So.2d 194 (Ala.1988) (lawyer not liable to insured for malpractice for settling without insured's consent when policy gave insurer exclusive power to handle settlement matters); the court distinguished L & S Roofing, supra, by noting that here the insurer had not reserved rights against the insured, who

therefore had no financial stake in the settlement). Feliberty v. Damon, 527 N.E.2d 261 (N.Y.1988) (malpractice insurer not liable to doctor for settlement within policy limits despite adverse publicity).

58. 407 N.E.2d 47 (Ill.1980). The court absolved the insurer from liability on contract grounds even though it had instructed defense counsel to settle.

59. See M.R. 1.8(g), M.R. 1.2(a); DR 5–106. Accord: L & S Roofing Supply Co. v. St. Paul Fire & Marine Ins. Co., 521 So.2d 1298 (Ala.1987); Lieberman v. Employers Insurance of Wausau, 419 A.2d 417 (N.J. 1980).

60. 917 S.W.2d 568 (Ky. 1996)

allowing one paying for another's legal services to interfere with the lawyer's independent judgment. This opinion has been criticized by some commentators.[61] After all, what compensation scheme perfectly aligns lawyer and client interests? Is that critique persuasive? Should flat fee arrangements be prohibited?

A lawyer representing insurer and insured during settlement negotiations faces difficult choices; one court states that "the ethical dilemma ... would tax Socrates, and no decision or authority we have studied furnishes a completely satisfactory answer."[62] The ABA negotiated a detailed set of "guiding principles" with major casualty and liability insurance companies during the 1970s.[63] Although later rescinded, apparently to avoid antitrust concerns, the principles continue to provide informal guidance to lawyers and insurers in some situations. In some respects they are in conflict with more recent court decisions holding that the lawyer retained by the insurer to represent an insured must treat the insured as the client when a conflict arises.[64]

D. SUCCESSIVE REPRESENTATION

The substantial relationship test, important in concurrent representation cases, is central in successive representation cases. In successive representation, if the matters are not the "same or substantially related," the lawyer may proceed without even consulting the former client. If the matters are substantially related and the lawyer will be adverse to the former client, the former client's consent must be obtained before going forward.

Oddly enough, the Model Code has no provision specifying whether, and if so when, it is proper for a lawyer to oppose a former client on behalf of a present client. The courts filled the gap, relying on pre-Code common

---

61. See Charles Silver, Flat Fees and Staff Attorneys: Unnecessary Casualties in the Continuing Battle Over the Law Governing Insurance Defense Lawyers, 4 Conn. Ins. L.J. 205 (1997) (expressing strong disagreement with the Kentucky court's reasoning and holding); and Nancy J. Moore, the Ethical Duties of Insurance Defense Lawyers: Are Special Solutions Required?, 4 Conn. Ins. L.J.286–90 (criticizing the court's reasoning, while expressing sympathy for the holding albeit on somewhat different grounds than those articulated by the court).

62. Hartford Accident & Indemnity Co. v. Foster, 528 So.2d 255, 270–273 (Miss. 1988). See also Moritz v. The Medical Protective Co. of Fort Wayne, Indiana, 428

F.Supp. 865 (W.D.Wis.1977); Hamilton v. State Farm Insurance Co., 83 Wash.2d 787, 523 P.2d 193 (1974).

63. Guiding Principles, reprinted in 20 Fed. Ins.Couns.Q. 95. (1972).

64. For example, the principles provide that if the lawyer discovers a question of coverage he must notify both the company and the insured, and the insured should be invited to retain her own counsel at her own expense to represent her separate interest, Paragraph IV. But if the lawyer's information is a confidential communication from the insured, the lawyer should neither disclose the coverage question to the insurer or discuss the issue with the insured, Paragraph VI.

law principles. The case law on this subject has multiplied in recent decades, largely in connection with motions to disqualify.[1]

Lacking a specific Code provision on conflicts with former clients, courts relied on Canon 4 (preserving client confidences), Canon 5 (exercising independent judgment) and Canon 9 (avoiding the appearance of impropriety) in fashioning the law on this subject. The basic test, which antedated the Code, was first enunciated by Judge Weinfeld in T.C. Theatre Corp. v. Warner Brothers Pictures, Inc.:[2]

> [T]he former client need show no more than that matters embraced within the pending suit wherein his former attorney appears on behalf of his adversary are substantially related to the matters or cause of action wherein the attorney previously represented him, the former client. The court will assume that during the course of the former representation confidences were disclosed to the attorney bearing on the subject matter of the representation. It will not inquire into their nature and extent. Only in this manner can the lawyer's duty of absolute fidelity be enforced and the spirit of the rule relating to privileged communications be maintained.

The Model Rules, unlike the Model Code, specifically deal with the question of successive representation. M.R. 1.9(a) provides that a lawyer shall not: "represent another person in the same or a substantially related matter in which that person's interests are materially adverse to the interests of the former client unless the former client consents after consultation."

The rule, which applies only when the new client's interests are *materially adverse* to those of the former client, adopts the substantial relationship test. In requiring material adversity of interests, it is a rule against "switching sides." Finally, the former client's consent (after consultation) is enough to cure the conflict. M.R. 1.9 is not a "consent plus" rule like M.R. 1.7, which requires that the representation be objectively reasonable.

M.R. 1.9(c) (originally adopted by the ABA and adopted in many states as M.R. 1.9(b)) is a reminder that the lawyer also has a continuing duty of confidentiality to a former client. Even if the former client consents under M.R. 1.9(a) to the new representation, that consent does not obviate the lawyer's continuing duty of confidentiality. M.R. 1.9(b), as amended in 1989, is concerned with imputed disqualification and will be addressed later in this chapter.

M.R. 1.9 applies to all lawyers, including those whose former client was the government. Lawyers who formerly worked for the government, however, are bound by M.R. 1.11 *in addition* to M.R. 1.9. As we will see later in this chapter, M.R. 1.11 restricts a lawyer's representation of new clients in the same or substantially related matters, even when the new client's interests are in harmony with that of the former government client.

1. See the discussion above at p. 604 of the misuse of motions to disqualify counsel.

2. 113 F.Supp. 265, 268–269 (S.D.N.Y. 1953).

1.   SUCCESSIVE REPRESENTATION OF JOINT CLIENTS

Brennan's Inc. v. Brennan's Restaurants, Inc.

United States Court of Appeals, Fifth Circuit, 1979.
590 F.2d 168.

■ Before BROWN, CHIEF JUDGE, and GEWIN and TJOFLAT, CIRCUIT JUDGES.

■ TJOFLAT, CIRCUIT JUDGE:

This is an action for trademark infringement and unfair competition. This appeal, however, concerns the disqualification of attorneys. The district court barred the appellants' attorneys from further representing them on grounds of conflict of interest. The correctness of this order is the only issue before us.

I

The underlying dispute in this case arises out of the business affairs of the Brennan family of New Orleans, Louisiana, who have been in the restaurant business for many years. All of the corporate parties are owned and closely held by various members of the Brennan family. Appellee Brennan's, Inc., the plaintiff below, owns and operates Brennan's restaurant at 417 Royal Street in New Orleans. The corporate appellants own and operate other restaurants in Louisiana, Texas, and Georgia....

Prior to 1974, all the members of the Brennan family were stockholders and directors of plaintiff, and some of them were stockholders and directors of the corporate defendants. All the corporations were independent legal entities in the sense that none held any of the stock of another, but they were all owned by members of the Brennan family and had interlocking boards of directors. In 1971, Edward F. Wegmann became general counsel for the family businesses, and his retainer was paid pro rata by all the corporations. He continued this joint representation until November 1973.

As part of his services, Mr. Wegmann, in close cooperation with trademark counsel in Washington, D.C., prosecuted applications for the federal registration of three service marks: "Brennan's," "Breakfast at Brennan's," and a distinctive rooster design. A registration for the rooster design was issued in February 1972, but the applications for the other two marks were initially denied on the ground that they were primarily a surname. On the advice of Washington trademark counsel, Mr. Wegmann collected data supporting a demonstration that the marks had acquired a secondary meaning,[2] and the applications were amended to include this material. Registrations were subsequently issued in plaintiff's name in March 1973. These registered service marks are the subject of this lawsuit.

---

2. This supporting data included numerous local and national advertisements, articles from several publications and letters commending the quality of Brennan's, and statements of the dollar volume of sales and advertising.

Later in 1973 a dispute developed within the Brennan family over the operation and management of the family businesses. This dispute was resolved in November 1974 by dividing the corporations' stock between the two opposing family groups. Plaintiff became 100% owned by one group and the corporate defendants became 100% owned by the second group, composed of the individual defendants. Mr. Wegmann elected to continue to represent defendants and severed his connections with plaintiff and its shareholders.

At no time during the negotiations which culminated in the November 1974 settlement was there any discussion of who would have the right to use the registered service marks. Both sides claimed ownership of the marks and continued to use them after the settlement. Attempts to negotiate a license or concurrent registration were unsuccessful. Plaintiff filed this suit for trademark infringement and unfair competition on May 21, 1976. In their answer and counterclaim defendants alleged that the marks were registered in plaintiff's name for convenience only, and, "in truth and actuality, the applications were filed and the registrations issued for the benefit and ownership of all of the Brennan family restaurants, including the corporate defendants." Defendants also alleged that the marks and registrations are invalid.

Upon the filing of this suit, Mr. Wegmann, on behalf of the defendants, retained the services of Arnold Sprung, a New York patent and trademark attorney, to assist him in the defense of the case. On October 22, 1976, plaintiff moved for the disqualification of both attorneys: Mr. Wegmann on the ground that his present representation was at odds with the interests of plaintiff, his former client, and Mr. Sprung by imputation of Mr. Wegmann's conflict. After a hearing, the district court granted the motion. It found that the subject matter of the present suit is substantially related to matters in which Mr. Wegmann formerly represented plaintiff, and to allow him now to represent an interest adverse to his former client creates the appearance of impropriety. It also found that "the close working relationship which has been shown to exist between Mr. Wegmann and Mr. Sprung creates a significant likelihood that Mr. Sprung would have had access to or been informed of confidential disclosures made to Mr. Wegmann by his former client."

II

. . .

Defendants argue that the district court failed to consider that in his prior representation of plaintiff, Mr. Wegmann also represented defendants. This fact of joint representation is crucial, they assert, since no confidences can arise as between joint clients. Hence, the argument goes, Mr. Wegmann violates no ethical duty in his present representation.

We have not addressed this precise question before. In Wilson P. Abraham Construction Corp. v. Armco Steel Corp., [559 F.2d 250 (5th Cir.1977)] we reaffirmed the standard that "a former client seeking to disqualify an attorney who appears on behalf of his adversary, need only to show that the matters embraced within the pending suit are *substantially related* to the matters or cause of action wherein the attorney previously represented him," 559 F.2d at 252 (emphasis in original),[4] but we acknowledged that "[t]his rule rests upon the presumption that confidences potentially damaging to the client have been disclosed to the attorney during the former period of representation," id. Defendants contend that this presumption cannot apply in this case. This argument, in our view, interprets too narrowly an attorney's duty to "preserve the confidences and secrets of a client." ABA Code of Professional Responsibility, Canon 4 (1970).[5] The fundamental flaw in defendants' position is a confusion of the attorney-client evidentiary privilege with the ethical duty to preserve a client's confidences. Assuming the prior representation was joint, defendants are quite correct that neither of the parties to this suit can assert the attorney-client privilege against the other as to matters comprehended by that joint representation. Garner v. Wolfinbarger, 430 F.2d 1093, 1103 (5th Cir.1970). But the ethical duty is broader than the evidentiary privilege: "This ethical precept, unlike the evidentiary privilege, exists without regard to the nature or source of information or the fact that others share the knowledge." ABA Code of Professional Responsibility, EC 4–4 (1970). "A lawyer should not use information acquired in the course of the representation of a client to the disadvantage of the client...." Id. EC 4–5. The use of the word "information" in these Ethical Considerations as opposed to "confidence" or "secret" is particularly revealing of the drafters' intent to protect all knowledge acquired from a client, since the latter two are defined terms. See id., DR 4–101(A).[6] Information so acquired is sheltered from use by the attorney against his client by virtue of the existence of the attorney-client relationship. This is true without regard to whether someone else may be privy to it. NCK Organization v. Bregman, 542 F.2d 128, 133 (2d Cir.1976). The obligation of an attorney not to misuse information acquired in the course of representation serves to vindicate the trust and reliance that clients place in their attorneys. A client would feel wronged if an opponent prevailed against him with the aid of an attorney who formerly represented the client in the same matter. As the court recognized in E.F. Hutton & Co. v. Brown, 305 F.Supp. 371, 395 (S.D.Tex.1969), this

---

4. Accord, Celanese Corp. v. Leesona Corp. (In re Yarn Processing Patent Validity Litigation), 530 F.2d 83, 89 (5th Cir. 1976); American Can Co. v. Citrus Feed Co., 436 F.2d 1125, 1128 (5th Cir. 1971); T.C. Theater Corp. v. Warner Bros. Pictures, 113 F.Supp. 265, 268 (S.D.N.Y. 1953).

5. As the profession's own expression of its ethical standards, the Code of Professional Responsibility, Ethical Considerations, and Disciplinary Rules provide substantial guidance to federal courts in evaluating the conduct of attorneys appearing before them. See NCK Organization v. Bregman, 542 F.2d 128, 129 (2d Cir. 1976); Woods v. Covington County Bank, 537 F.2d 804, 810 (5th Cir. 1976).

6. *DR 4–101 Preservation of Confidences and Secrets of a Client.*

(A) "Confidence" refers to information protected by the attorney-client privilege underapplicable law, and "secret" refers to other information gained in the professional relationship that the client has requested be held inviolate or the disclosure of which would be embarrassing or would be likely to be detrimental to the client.

would undermine public confidence in the legal system as a means for adjudicating disputes. We recognize that this concern implicates the principle embodied in Canon 9 that attorneys "should avoid even the appearance of professional impropriety." ABA Code of Professional Responsibility, Canon 9 (1970). We have said that under this canon there must be a showing of a reasonable possibility that some specifically identifiable impropriety in fact occurred and that the likelihood of public suspicion must be weighed against the interest in retaining counsel of one's choice. Woods v. Covington County Bank, 537 F.2d 804, 812–13 (5th Cir.1976). The conflict of interest is readily apparent here, however, and we think that the balance weighs in favor of disqualification. See Zylstra v. Safeway Stores, Inc., 578 F.2d 102 (5th Cir.1978) (adopting per se rule of disqualification in class action cases for attorneys who are members of the class or partners or spouses of named plaintiffs). The need to safeguard the attorney-client relationship is not diminished by the fact that the prior representation was joint with the attorney's present client. Accordingly, we find the rule of Wilson P. Abraham Construction Corp. v. Armco Steel Corp. fully applicable to this case. Since the district court's findings of prior representation and substantial relationship are not disputed, we affirm the disqualification of Mr. Wegmann.

III

Whether Mr. Sprung should be disqualified presents a more difficult case. He has never had an attorney-client relationship with plaintiff; the district court disqualified him by imputation of Mr. Wegmann's conflict. Up to this point we have accepted, for the sake of argument, defendants' assertion that they were formerly joint clients with plaintiff of Mr. Wegmann. There is no dispute that plaintiff and defendants were previously represented by Mr. Wegmann simultaneously, but plaintiff maintains that, at least with respect to the registration of the service marks, Mr. Wegmann was representing plaintiff alone. The district court made no findings on the issue. Because we think that the disqualification of Mr. Sprung may turn on this fact and others not found by the court below, we vacate that part of the court's order relating to Mr. Sprung and remand the cause for further proceedings. For the guidance of the court on remand, we set forth our view of the applicable ethical standards.

If the court finds that Mr. Wegmann previously represented plaintiff and defendants jointly, we can see no reason why Mr. Sprung should be disqualified. As between joint clients there can be no "confidences" or "secrets" unless one client manifests a contrary intent. See Garner v. Wolfinbarger, 430 F.2d 1093, 1103 (5th Cir.1970); ABA Code of Professional Responsibility, DR 4–101 (1970). Thus, Mr. Sprung could not have learned anything from Mr. Wegmann that defendants did not already know or have a right to know. Plaintiff argues that this permits the defendants indirectly to gain the benefit of Mr. Wegmann's services when they could not do so directly. If the representation was joint, however, defendants possess no information as to which plaintiff could have had any expectation of privacy in relation to the defendants. The only remaining ground for disqualification then would be an appearance of impropriety. In Part II of this opinion, we decided there is such an appearance when an attorney represents an interest adverse to that of a former client in a matter substantially related to the subject of the prior representation. Mr. Sprung has never been plaintiff's counsel, however; he is only the co-counsel of one who was. We are enjoined not to give Canon 9 an overly broad application and to maintain "a reasonable balance between the need to ensure ethical conduct on the part of lawyers ... and other social interests, which include the litigant's right to freely chosen counsel." Woods v. Covington County Bank, 537 F.2d 804, 810 (5th Cir.1976). In the case of Mr. Sprung, we think the balance weighs against disqualification. . . .[7]

If the district court finds that Mr. Wegmann did not previously represent these parties jointly, it does not necessarily follow that Mr. Sprung should be disqualified. The courts have abjured a per se approach to the disqualification of co-counsel of disqualified counsel. Akerly v. Red Barn System, Inc., 551 F.2d 539 (3rd Cir.1977); American Can Co. v. Citrus Feed Co., 436 F.2d 1125 (5th Cir.1971). In the absence of an attorney-client relationship between Mr. Sprung and plaintiff, a presumption of disclosure of confidences is inappropriate. Wilson P. Abraham Construction Corp. v. Armco Steel Corp., 559 F.2d 250, 253 (5th Cir.1977). Mr. Sprung should not be disqualified unless he has learned from Mr. Wegmann information the plaintiff had intended not be disclosed to the defendants. See id.

Loyalty and Successive Representation

Identify the two matters in *Brennan's*. Look at the elements of a successive conflict codified in Model Rule 1.9. Were all those elements present in *Brennan's*? Did the defendant deny that any of these elements were present? What was the plaintiff's argument? Why did it fail? How would *Brennan's* be decided under Model Rule 1.9?

One can agree with the holding in *Brennan's* without agreeing with the court's articulation of reasons. Isn't the explanation in part II that the duty of confidentiality is broader than the attorney-client privilege inconsistent with the holding of part III that Sprung need not be disqualified if both parties were joint clients in the 1973 trademark registration matter? Can you find a better way of stating why it might make sense to disqualify Wegmann but not Sprung?

---

7. It is very likely that Mr. Wegmann will be a witness in this case. He handled the registrations for the service marks which are the subject of this suit. Moreover, he prepared and notarized two affidavits that were executed at the time the registrations were issued. Defendants rely on these affidavits in support of their claim of ownership of the marks. The circumstances of their execution and the facts to which these affidavits purport to attest will undoubtedly be a subject of dispute at trial and Mr. Wegmann's knowledge may be relevant. If he represented all the family corporations at the time, however, none of his knowledge is privileged and his testimony could freely be sought by either side.

Restatement § 213, dealing with former client conflicts, provides that a lawyer may not proceed adversely to a former client in the same or a substantially related matter if *either* the lawyer acquired confidential information (that is not now generally known) during the first representation that would be useful in the second representation *or* the second matter "involves work the lawyer performed for the former client." § 213 (1).[3] Does the Restatement capture what the real problem in *Brennan*'s was? If so, does that formulation of the problem help explain why Sprung was not disqualified along with Wegmann?

In the court's last footnote it discusses the likelihood that Wegmann is likely to be a witness in the underlying litigation. For a discussion of the ethics rules on lawyers serving as witnesses while acting as counsel in the case, see p. 571 above.

Primary and Secondary Clients?

A few cases recognize a distinction between primary and secondary clients, and hold that when a joint representation terminates, the lawyer may continue representing the primary client against the secondary one. The genesis of the "primary client" analysis is Allegaert v. Perot.[4] In *Allegaert*, the court said "before the substantial relationship test is even implicated, it must be shown that the attorney was in a position where he could have received information which his former client might reasonably have assumed the attorney would withhold from his present client."[5] The court held that because the moving party "necessarily knew that information given to [the law firm] would certainly be conveyed to [its] primary clients ... , the substantial relationship test is inapposite," and the law firm need not now be disqualified.[6]

While the language of *Allegaert* would seem to contradict *Brennan's*, its facts suggest an important distinction. In *Allegaert* the law firm representing Perot had represented him for some time. Perot and Walston entered into an agreement for joint operation of a business. The firm represented both Walston and Perot's interests in a substantially related matter affecting that business—a stockholder derivative action which involved challenges to the business. Thereafter, Walston went into bankruptcy and its trustee in bankruptcy asserted a claim against Perot. With the exception of the stockholder derivative suit, Walston was independently represented. The trustee in bankruptcy for Walston moved to disqualify the firm because of the firm's prior representation of Walston in the stockholder action.

In refusing to disqualify Perot's counsel, the *Allegaert* court said:

Integral to our conclusion that [Perot's lawyers] were not in a position to receive information intended to be withheld from [Perot] is the

---

3. Under § 213, consent from both the former and current client cures the successive conflict.

4. 565 F.2d 246 (2d Cir.1977).

5. Id. at 250.

6. Id.

[lawyers'] continuous and unbroken legal relationship with their primary client [Perot]. In contrast with our earlier cases, the attorneys sought to be disqualified here have not changed sides from a former client to a current, adverse client.[7]

Allegaert and *Brennan's* are similar in that the former representation was not one in which client communications were protected from disclosure to the other party. Joint clients were involved in *Brennan's* and cooperating litigants sharing pooled information in *Allegaert*. In neither case did the party moving to disqualify the common lawyer have a reasonable expectation that information provided by that party would be withheld from the other party. The two cases are different, however, with respect to the duty of loyalty. In *Brennan's* the lawyer had an intimate professional relationship with each branch of the family prior to their breakup. In *Allegaert*, however, Walston knew that counsel's primary loyalty was to Perot. Indeed, in defending the stockholder suit (the prior "matter") Walston was essentially a free rider on the Perot representation.[8] Cf. M.R. 2.2.

Conventional doctrine is that a lawyer owes "equal" loyalty to every client. Does the notion of a "primary client" contradict this proposition? Compare Comment [7] to M.R. 2.2 which says that "intermediation is improper when . . . impartiality cannot be maintained. For example, a lawyer who has represented one of the clients for a long period and in a variety of matters might have difficulty being impartial between that client and one to whom the lawyer has only recently been introduced."

Whatever the problems with the primary client theory, some courts rely on *Allegaert* for the proposition that there is no expectation of confidentiality between joint clients and hence no basis for subsequent disqualification of a lawyer representing one client against the other in a related transaction. For example, in American Special Risk Insurance Co. v. Delta America Insurance Co.,[9] the district court, citing *Allegaert*, said:

> This Circuit has held, however, that the substantial relationship test is inapplicable where a law firm's alleged disqualification arises out of simultaneous representation of two clients if each client was aware of the other's relationship to the firm and had no reason to believe that confidences of one party would be withheld from the other.[10]

---

7. Id. at 251.

8. See also C.A.M. v. E.B. Marks Music, Inc., 558 F.Supp. 57, 59 (S.D.N.Y.1983) (motion to disqualify denied where the prior representation had been joint and, as in *Allegaert*, "the attorneys . . . had a longstanding relationship with a primary client and briefly represented both parties when their interests apparently coincided. . . . [T]he later representation of the primary client against the interests of the former joint client could not cause the disclosure of any secrets—there was no expectation that information would be concealed from the primary client."). See also Anderson v. Pryor, 537 F.Supp. 890, 895 (W.D.Mo. 1982).

9. 634 F.Supp. 112, 121 (S.D.N.Y.1986).

10. Id. at 121. See also Christensen v. U.S. District Court, 844 F.2d 694, 698 (9th Cir. 1988) (collecting cases); Kempner v. Oppenheimer, 662 F.Supp. 1271, 1277 (S.D.N.Y.1987) (collecting cases). But see Anchor Packing v. Pro–Seal, 688 F.Supp. 1215, 1217 (E.D.Mich.1988) (disapproving of this line of cases and adopting *Brennan's* approach); and United States v. Moscony,

Another factor noted by the *Allegaert* court was the sophistication of the parties involved: "[T]he parties were not only aware of their mutual relationship, but also were as sophisticated, perhaps, as the American corporate community can be."[11] Should the former client's sophistication be considered? Would the *Brennan's* court have given weight to that factor?

Duty of Loyalty to a Former Client

Brennan's recognizes two underlying concerns of the substantial relationship test: the duty to preserve confidences and the duty of loyalty to a former client. Lawyer Sprung is treated differently from Lawyer Wegmann because he has no duty of loyalty to clients whom he never represented.

Nevertheless, some courts seem to reduce the substantial relationship test to one designed solely to protect the former client's confidences. The opinion in Analytica v. NPD Research,[12] for example, stated that two matters are considered to be substantially related "if the lawyer could have obtained confidential information in the first representation that would be relevant to the second." But other courts still recognize a duty of loyalty apart from the duty of confidentiality in two types of cases: when the lawyer switches sides (attacking the former client) or launches an attack on the lawyer's own prior work ("fouling one's nest").

The standard stated in *Analytica*, supra, would seem to apply whether or not the matters are substantially related and hence could be read as *broader* than the "substantial relationship" test. That is, if the question is as *Analytica* states it, namely whether the lawyer "*could* have" obtained confidential information relevant to the second matter, does not that possibility exist no matter what the first matter involved? At the same time, the *Analytica* standard seems to require greater risk that confidences will be disclosed to prove that they might be used against the client. The Seventh Circuit cases are notable for this inversion of the substantial relationship test.[13]

The underlying reason for reducing the successive conflict question to one of protecting confidences may be the courts' growing impatience with disqualification motions used for tactical purposes. This impatience also has led to more frequent use of sanctions for frivolous motions to disqualify.[14]

A still deeper problem is that the courts are not of one mind on whether to demand relatively strict loyalty to a former client, at the cost of requiring one or both parties to get new lawyers if they have a falling out,

697 F.Supp. 888, 891 (E.D.Pa.1988) (*Brennan's* approach is appropriate in criminal cases especially when parties are not sophisticated).

11. 565 F.2d at 251.

12. 708 F.2d 1263, 1266 (7th Cir.1983).

13. For another example, see Lasalle Nat'l Bank v. County of Lake, 703 F.2d 252 (7th Cir.1983).

14. See, for example, Optyl Eyewear Fashion Int'l Corp. v. Style Companies, Ltd., 760 F.2d 1045 (9th Cir.1985), where the court imposed sanctions against the lawyer after finding that the disqualification motion was brought in bad faith. In *Analytica* the Seventh Circuit imposed sanctions for frivolously resisting a motion to disqualify.

or to avoid that cost through a more relaxed standard of loyalty. M.R. 2.2 is clear that, if intermediation fails, "the lawyer shall not continue to represent any of the clients in the matter that was the subject of the intermediation." One of the risks of joint representation is inability to represent either joint client if there is a falling-out between them. But see Comment *d* to § 201 of the Restatement, which makes explicit that co-clients may agree at the onset of the representation that in the event the joint representation collapses the lawyer may continue to represent one of the two of them.

2.   THE SUBSTANTIAL RELATIONSHIP TEST

In Re: American Airlines, Inc.

United States Court of Appeals, Fifth Circuit, 1992.
972 F.2d 605.

■ HIGGINBOTHAM, Circuit Judge:

American Airlines, Inc. petitions for a writ of mandamus directing the district court to disqualify its former counsel Vinson & Elkins [VE] from representing plaintiff Northwest Airlines, Inc. We hold that the district court erred in denying American's motion and issue the requested writ.

I

Continental Airlines filed a complaint against American in the United States District Court for the Southern District of Texas on June 8, 1992, charging American with attempted monopolization by predatory pricing in violation of the Sherman Act. American filed a declaratory judgment action against Continental and Northwest in the United States District Court for the Northern District of Illinois the following day. Three days later, Northwest sued American in the Southern District of Texas. The Continental and Northwest suits have been consolidated by order of the district court.

On June 9, 1992, the day after Continental filed its complaint ... American's in-house counsel, asked Alison Smith, a VE partner, if VE would represent American in this case. Smith accepted the American representation on June 10, unaware that four days earlier Harry Reasoner, another VE partner, had promised ... Northwest's counsel, that VE would not consider representing another airline until ... [Northwest] and Reasoner ... [explored the possibility of VE accepting Northwest as a client.] When Smith informed Reasoner of her acceptance of the American representation, Reasoner directed her to inform ... [American] that "there might be a problem with Northwest" and that Reasoner would make the final decision the next day. On June 11 Reasoner accepted the Northwest representation.

American asserted that VE's prior representation of American and its agreement to do so in this case made its representation of Northwest improper. It requested that VE withdraw from the case in letters sent on June 12 and June 19. Northwest refused and on July 1 American moved to disqualify VE. The parties at this time became aware that Weil, Gotshal & Manges, American's lead counsel, had previously represented Northwest and Continental. An exchange of "conflicts" was briefly considered. When American indicated that it would not withdraw its motion to disqualify VE, Northwest moved to disqualify Weil, Gotshal on July 13.

American rests its motion to disqualify Vinson & Elkins on VE's representation of American in prior antitrust matters and its alleged agreement to represent it in this case. According to American, Vinson & Elkins has served as its "Houston antitrust counsel" since 1987. In this role VE defended American in suits by Continental and a Continental affiliate. VE also provided antitrust advice in connection with American's possible acquisition of Continental.

On July 24, after extensive briefing and the submission of numerous affidavits, the district court denied both motions to disqualify counsel. The court held that VE's initial acceptance of the American representation was a "mixup," that the past matters in which VE had represented American were only "tangentially related to this litigation," and that any confidential information possessed by VE was "not sufficient to cause any material prejudice to [American]." The court directed the parties to submit a plan for a Chinese Wall to safeguard against adverse use of confidential information in the case. American then filed the petition for writ of mandamus now before us.

[The court determined that it had jurisdiction to entertain the writ. Reaffirming prior decisions, it also stated that ethics rules adopted by the relevant state were not the "sole authority" for a federal court deciding a disqualification motion, stating that "[f]ederal courts may adopt state or ABA rules as their ethical standards, but whether and how those rules are to be applied are questions of federal law...."

[The court then discussed whether VE had "switched sides" by first agreeing to represent American (Alison Smith's June 10 conversation) and then withdrawing a day later when it accepted the Northwest representation. Northwest argued that the side-switching rule was not applicable because American had known prior to its conversation with Alison Smith that VE had a commitment to Northwest, had hired Baker & Botts to represent it before hearing VE's final decision and provided VE with a confidential memorandum primarily to prevent VE from representing Northwest. American disputed this account. "We need not remand for further fact finding because we hold that VE must be disqualified on other grounds."]

V

American's final two contentions rest on VE's prior representations of the airline in antitrust matters. American contends that VE must be disqualified because VE has represented American in matters substantially related to the present case and VE's representation of Northwest in this case will likely involve the use to American's disadvantage of confidential information obtained during these earlier representations. We will first discuss the applicable ethical standards. We will then apply these standards to the prior representations alleged by American to warrant VE's disqualification.

A.

... Our review in previous cases involving prior representations has been governed by the "substantial relationship" test:

> A party seeking to disqualify opposing counsel on the ground of a former representation must establish two elements: 1) an actual attorney-client relationship between the moving party and the attorney he seeks to disqualify and 2) a substantial relationship between the subject matter of the former and present representations.

Johnston v. Harris County Flood Control Dist., 869 F.2d 1565, 1569 (5th Cir. 1989); In Re Corrugated Container Antitrust Litigation, 659 F.2d 1341, 1345 (5th Cir. 1981); Duncan v. Merrill Lynch, Pierce, Fenner & Smith, 646 F.2d 1020, 1028 (5th Cir.), cert. denied, 454 U.S. 895 (1981). Because it is not disputed that VE represented American in the matters under consideration, the sole issue is whether these prior representations are substantially related to the present case. Our inquiry may be narrowed to this single question because the substantial relationship test is governed by an irrebuttable presumption. Once it is established that the prior matters are substantially related to the present case, "the court will irrebuttably presume that relevant confidential information was disclosed during the former period of representation." Duncan, 646 F.2d at 1028; Corrugated, 659 F.2d at 1347.[15]

The test is categorical in requiring disqualification upon the establishment of a substantial relationship between past and current representations. But we have never applied the test in a mechanical way that might "prevent[] an attorney from ever representing an interest adverse to that of a former client." Duncan, 646 F.2d at 1027–28. Rather, a substantial relationship may be found only after "the moving party delineates with specificity the subject matters, issues and causes of action" common to prior and current representations and the court engages in a " 'painstaking analysis of the facts and precise application of precedent.' " Duncan, 646 F.2d at 1029 (quoting Brennan's, Inc. v. Brennan's Restaurants, Inc., 590 F.2d 168, 174 (5th Cir. 1979)). Finally, the party seeking disqualification bears the burden of proving that the present and prior representations are substantially related. Duncan, 646 F.2d at 1028.

This circuit adopted the substantial relationship test before the promulgation of the Rules of Professional Conduct. We must decide the

---

15. A second irrebuttable presumption is that confidences obtained by an individual lawyer will be shared with the other members of his firm. See Corrugated, 659 F.2d at 1346. This presumption is not at issue in this case, for all of the VE lawyers involved have previously represented American.

application of the substantial relationship test under these new Rules. Texas Rule 1.09 provides in relevant part:

(a) Without prior consent, a lawyer who personally has formally represented a client in a matter shall not thereafter represent another person in a matter adverse to the former client: . . .

(2) if the representation in reasonable probability will involve a violation of Rule 1.05; or

(3) if it is the same or a substantially related matter.

Rule 1.09(a)(2) incorporates Rule 1.05, which prohibits a lawyer's use of confidential information obtained from a former client to that former client's disadvantage. Rule 1.09 thus on its face forbids a lawyer to appear against a former client if the current representation in reasonable probability will involve the use of confidential information or if the current matter is substantially related to the matters in which the lawyer has represented the former client.[16]

In providing two distinct grounds for disqualification, the Rules expand the protections for former clients beyond those afforded by the substantial relationship test. The Rules are not, however, broader than the protections provided by our precedents. While the focus of our cases has been on the substantial relationship test, we have indicated that a former client could also disqualify counsel by showing that his former attorney possessed relevant confidential information in the manner contemplated by Rule 1.09(a)(2). As Duncan, for example, stated: "[The moving party may disqualify counsel on the basis of prior representations] either by establishing that the present and previous representations are substantially related or by pointing to specific instances where it revealed relevant confidential information regarding its practices and procedures." Duncan, 646 F.2d at 1032. Thus, it does not appear that the Texas Rules make material addition to the basic approach we have used in the past.

But do the Rules take something away? That is, do the Rules offer less protection to former clients than our precedents? Northwest offers two related arguments on this score. First, Northwest contends that a substantial relationship between past and current matters exists only where the two cases are so closely related that the risk of adverse use of the former client's confidences threatens to "taint" the trial. Northwest also argues that a close relation between a past and current representation is irrelevant if the attorney relied on publicly available information in advising the former client. These two arguments are rooted in Northwest's larger assertion that the substantial relationship test is solely concerned with protecting a former client's confidences.

. . .

---

16. ABA Rule 1.9 is identical to Texas Rule 1.09 in all important respects: [quoting Rule 1.9(a) and (c)(1)].

We reject both of Northwest's arguments. A party seeking to disqualify counsel under the substantial relationship test need not prove that the past and present matters are so similar that a lawyer's continued involvement threatens to taint the trial. Rather, the former client must demonstrate that the two matters are substantially related. Second, we adhere to our precedents in refusing to reduce the concerns underlying the substantial relationship test to a client's interest in preserving his confidential information. The second fundamental concern protected by the test is not the public interest in lawyers avoiding "even the appearance of impropriety," but the client's interest in the loyalty of his attorney.

. . .

... Northwest ... asserts that ... [disqualification, as opposed to discipline for violating the ethics rule, is not warranted] unless the cases are so similar that there is a genuine threat ... [that the trial will be] taint[ed]. We reject this argument. The substantial relationship test, as applied in this circuit and elsewhere, does not have its source in disciplinary rules. To the contrary, the test was developed at common law. Our precedents did not rely on the Model Code or Model Rules in formulating the substantial relationship test, but on the landmark T.C. Theatre Corp v. Warner Bros. Pictures, Inc., 113 F. Supp. 265 (S.D.N.Y. 1953), which predated the Model Code and of course the Model Rules. See, e.g., Wilson P. Abraham Construction Corp. v. Armco Steel Corp., 559 F.2d 250, 252 (5th Cir. 1977); In Re Yarn Processing Patent Validity Litigation, 530 F.2d 83, 89 (5th Cir. 1976).

The actual development of Rule 1.09's substantial relationship provision is just the opposite of the version Northwest gives. The initial drafts of both the ABA and Texas Rules did not include a rule barring representation in substantially related matters. In both cases, the substantial relationship rule was added as a reflection of case law. See Robert P. Schuwerk & John F. Sutton, Jr., A Guide to the Texas Disciplinary Rules of Professional Conduct, 27A Hous. L. Rev. 1, 152 n.20, 153 n.34 (1990); Note, In Defense of the Double Standard in the Rules of Ethics: A Critical Reevaluation of the Chinese Wall and Vicarious Disqualification, 20 U. Mich. J.L. Ref. 245, 257 & n.66 (1986) (ABA Rules). Schuwerk & Sutton's account is instructive:

> The Texas committee originally avoided [the substantial related matter language] in proposed Texas Rule 1.09.... Subsequently, however, a difficulty emerged as a result of failure to employ the substantial relationship test in a disciplinary context. A lawyer might accept or continue employment in a matter against a former client believing (correctly) that no disciplinary violation was involved under the initially proposed version of Rule 1.09, only to be disqualified subsequently—perhaps at great cost and expenses to the client—by a court employing the traditional substantial relationship test.... The drafting committee, therefore, concluded that the danger of having its narrowly drawn Rule 1.09 turn into a trap for the unwary outweighed its objections to the substantial relationship test as a standard of discipline. It would be

in keeping with the committee's thinking, however, to construe "substantially related" narrowly for disciplinary purposes.

Schuwerk & Sutton, supra, at 153 n.34 (emphasis added); see also Rule 1.09 Comment 9.

As this account suggests, the difficulty posed by Rule 1.09 does not concern the "literal and mechanical" application of a disciplinary rule in disqualification cases. Rather, the concern is the transfer of the substantial relationship test developed by courts to the disciplinary context. See also Charles W. Wolfram, Modern Legal Ethics 366 (1986) (discussing ABA Rules' "adoption of the substantial relationship standard as a disciplinary rule"). Contrary to Northwest's contentions, the Rules did not supplant, but adopted, the common law substantial relationship test. The argument thus provides no basis for applying the substantial relationship test through the "taint" filter it proposes.

Northwest's argument concerning the Rules' deletion of Canon 9's appearance of impropriety standard has more purchase. Northwest argues that the Model Rules' omission of the "appearance of impropriety" standard contained in the Model Code indicates that the substantial relationship test should be solely concerned with ensuring "actual fairness" in the proceedings. But Northwest does not mention loyalty, itself a substantial addition under the Rules. As several commentators have noted, the Model Code provided no express protection to the former client's interest in loyalty. See, e.g., Geoffrey C. Hazard & W. William Hodes, The Law of Lawyering 292 (1991); Wolfram, supra, at 363 (1986). This interest is singled out only under the Rules. See Texas Rule 1.06 Comment 1 ("Loyalty is an essential element in the lawyer's relationship to a client"); ABA Rule 1.9 Comment ("The second aspect of loyalty to a client is the lawyer's obligation to decline subsequent representations involving positions adverse to a former client arising in substantially related matters")....

. . .

The link between loyalty and the appearance of impropriety is most evident in Brennan's Inc. v. Brennan's Restaurants, Inc., 590 F.2d 168 (5th Cir. 1979), where the court disqualified a former counsel even though there was no chance that confidential information might be used against the former client....

. . .

... If the sole focus of the substantial relationship test was the possible adverse use of confidences, prior representations in which the attorney advised the client but received no confidential information would not warrant disqualification. Even if the subject matter of case one and case two is identical, a former client's adversary is not inevitably advantaged by virtue of his attorney's prior representation of the client. And yet this court has held that the provision of legal advice on a substantially related matter by itself requires disqualification. See Corrugated, 659 F.2d at 1346–47; Brennan's, 590 F.2d at 171–72.

Disqualification rules not only preserve the purity of particular trials but also unavoidably affect relationships among attorneys and clients in general. . . . The trust a lawyer's duty of loyalty inspires in clients encourages them freely to confide in the lawyer and freely to rely on the advice provided by the lawyer. The substantial relationship test aims to protect the adversary process but also, or as part of this concern, seeks to provide conditions for the attorney-client relationship. What credence, for example, might American have attached to VE's December 1990 counsel that the airline's interests would be better served by postponing the acquisition of Continental for at least a year if it even suspected that VE itself might soon be representing one of its competitors in a suit against American, charging that it had abused its market power to the detriment of competition in the airline passenger service markets?

These considerations preclude us from accepting Northwest's final argument. Northwest claims that because VE relied primarily on public, not confidential, information in advising American, these prior matters cannot be considered substantially related to the present case. It contends that " 'facts that are community knowledge or that are not material to a determination of the issues litigated do not constitute "matters involved" within the meaning of the law' governing the substantial relationship test". The record sharply contradicts Northwest's claim that all of the material obtained by VE was publicly available. As we discuss below, VE was privy to many of American's secrets. But Northwest's argument would fail even if it could show that all of the information provided by American was public knowledge. Our precedents, the Texas Rules, and the ABA Rules all reject the position Northwest advances. This court has held that "information [provided by a client] is sheltered from use by the attorney against his client by virtue of the existence of the attorney-client relationship. . . .

The Texas and ABA Rules supply the same standard. The Rules do contain an exception for public information, but in each case this exception applies only to the provision prohibiting the use of confidential information, not the rule prohibiting successive representation in substantially related matters. Texas Rule 1.05 provides that "a lawyer shall not knowingly

> (3) *use* confidential information of a former client to the disadvantage of the former client after the representation is concluded unless the former client consents after consultation or the confidential information has become generally known."

Texas Rule 1.05 (b) (3) (emphasis added). This provision, however, is incorporated by Rule 1.09(a) (2), not the substantial relationship rule contained in Rule 1.09 (a) (3). The same distinction exists between Rules 1.9 (a) and 1.9(c) of the ABA Rules, as commentators have indicated. See, e.g., Charles W. Wolfram, Modern Legal Ethics 360, 365 (1986).

B.

VE represented American in several matters in recent years, earning fees in excess of $676,000. Our review will be limited to three of VE's prior representations. VE defended American in two suits brought by Continental in Texas. The focus of each case, as in the larger California litigation to which they were related, was SABRE, American's computerized reservation system [CRS]. The first case, System One Direct Access, Inc v. American Airlines Inc., was an antitrust suit brought by a Continental affiliate in Houston federal court. VE served as counsel from November 1987 until withdrawing in July 1988 when the case was transferred to Dallas.

VE also served as lead counsel in Continental Airlines, Inc. v. American Airlines, Inc., a Texas state court case [the *Fort Bend* case]. Continental alleged that American had breached contractual relationships and committed other acts of misconduct in operating its CRS. VE represented American from March 1989 until the case was settled as part of the global settlement between Continental and American in May 1990.

In late 1990, VE advised American concerning whether the Antitrust Division of the Department of Justice would approve "Project Armadillo," a proposed acquisition of Continental Airlines. The primary question was whether a merger of the two airlines would run afoul of the Department's merger guidelines. The representation ended in January 1991, when American apparently chose not to pursue the merger.

The two Texas cases were related and subsidiary to a larger suit by Continental and Northwest, among others, against American and United Airlines in California federal district court in 1985. Continental and Northwest charged American and United with monopolization of both computerized reservation systems and various air transportation markets. In particular, they charged predatory pricing of CRS systems and air transportation, closely related to the claim advanced by Northwest and Continental here.

American asserts, and Northwest appears to concede, that the California case is substantially related to the present case. However, Gibson, Dunn & Crutcher, not VE, represented American in California, so the similarities between the California case and the present one provide no basis for disqualification. American's argument that VE's prior representations are substantially related to this case rests largely upon its claim that the Texas cases are substantially related to the California case.

Northwest argues that the Texas cases are not substantially related to this case because the allegations in these cases, unlike in California, pertained only to CRS services, not air transportation services. We disagree. While the focus was certainly CRS systems, the plaintiffs also raised claims involving air transportation markets. Moreover, as we will explain, the Texas cases involved two particular matters at issue in the present case.

(1) Fort Bend

[The] *Fort Bend* [case] involved the state-law claims over which the California district court ... had declined to exercise pendent jurisdiction. Continental alleged breach of contract, duress, tortious interference, misrepresentation, and violation of the Texas Deceptive Trade Practices Act. As in California, Continental's petition focused on American's CRS operations. But also as in California, Continental asserted that American's power in the CRS market could not be considered apart from its position in the air transportation market. Continental claimed that "American and United, by leveraging their dominance as air carriers and the enormous secret profits they received from bias-diverted revenues, established themselves as the dominant CRS providers." Continental charged that American, having achieved dominance in the CRS market, in turn used SABRE to "exclude[] Continental in whole or in part from specific airline passenger markets."

. . . Continental claimed that American had breached its contract by "secretly accessing TXI's [a Continental affiliate] data base and using it to study passenger traffic flow through the Dallas/Fort Worth hub. Reports developed by American through the use of the TXI data contributed to American's successful exclusion of TXI from the Dallas/Fort Worth hub and elsewhere." In its tortious interference claim Continental alleged that American had "interfered with Continental's prospective contractual relations with its travel agents and air passengers," causing damages in the form of "lost airline bookings through bias diversions and total exclusion from certain air passenger markets." Finally, Continental noted that the California district court had cited American President Robert Crandall's alleged 1982 price-fixing solicitation of Braniff as "a textbook example of anticompetitive conduct" in ruling that "Continental could proceed to trial on its claim that American illegally attempted to monopolize the Dallas–Fort Worth airport."

Continental's allegations and its reference to Crandall's alleged price-fixing solicitation apparently supplied the basis for the belief among VE and Gibson, Dunn lawyers that American's alleged attempted monopolization of DFW would be at issue in the case and that Continental might seek to introduce the price-fixing incident as evidence on this score. As such, they believed that *Fort Bend* was intimately related to the California case. For example, a VE partner stated at the time that the California and Fort Bend suits "involve the same parties, the same alleged acts, and the same alleged damages." Another VE lawyer noted that the two suits could be seen as "largely identical": "[The *Fort Bend* petition] asserts that AA and UA used their purported CRS monopolies to obtain monopoly power in certain air transportation markets. This claim is intertwined with both the CRS monopolization and DFW attempted monopolization claims pending in California." The perceived similarities between *Fort Bend* and the California case led VE and Gibson, Dunn to spend considerable time exploring the possibility of an abatement of the Fort Bend case until the California proceedings had concluded.

VE argues that Crandall's alleged price-fixing solicitation and Continental's claim that American had used its CRS to exclude it from the DFW market were not at issue in *Fort Bend*. This contention is contradicted by the accounts of Gibson, Dunn lawyers and by notes taken by a VE lawyer during one meeting between VE and Gibson, Dunn. . . .

. . .

... VE suggested at oral argument that Crandall's alleged solicitation is not substantially related to the present case because this ten-year old incident would not be admitted as evidence. This is helpful but not dispositive. As the *Corrugated* court stated, the subject matter "does not need to be 'relevant' in the evidentiary sense to be 'substantially related.' It need only be akin to the present action in a way reasonable persons would understand as important to the issues involved." *Corrugated*, 659 F.2d at 1346.... [In its complaint in the instant case] Northwest included the incident under the heading "Conduct Giving Rise to Violations Alleged"....

We are persuaded that VE's representation of American in the *Fort Bend* case is substantially related to the present case.

(2) System One

In *System One*, Continental affiliate System One, a CRS vendor, charged that American had violated antitrust laws in its provision of CRS services. System One alleged that American had engaged in a variety of acts designed to exclude it from the CRS market. But as in Fort Bend, plaintiff presented the CRS and air transportation markets as inextricably linked. The *System One* complaint alleged that "AA has used its monopoly power in the provision of air carrier services in various geographic markets to obtain, retain, and enhance its power in the provision of CRS systems." Again, "AA has achieved its dominant position in the market for CRS services, and continues to enforce anticompetitive practices in an effort to maintain that position, not only to reap monopoly profits from the sale and use of CRS systems, but to enhance profits from the provision of air transportation services."

The record reflects extensive discovery regarding SABRE's effects on air transportation revenues. System One requested all documents relating to "incremental revenues," the general effect of "airline ownership of a CRS on the airline's sale of air transportation services," and "any actual or possible loss of revenue or other detriment to any commercial air carrier as a result of the operation or installation of SABRE." ...

In the absence of this prior litigation, there is little doubt that Northwest would seek to introduce evidence of the incremental revenues generated by SABRE in support of the predatory pricing claims it raises in this case. Northwest's General Counsel recently asserted in congressional testimony that American's ability

> to restructure and reduce its fares dramatically is directly related to American's long-term, advantageous use of its CRS.... DOT studies repeatedly have documented the flow of hundreds of millions of dollars of incremental revenue diverted from other carriers to American and United as a result of their CRS market power ... In a very real sense, American has launched its predatory attack on the industry using our own money.

... [C]hallenges by Northwest and Continental of American's CRS use have been earlier terminated in ways restricting their present assertion,

Continental by settlement and Northwest by a final judgment. Pointing to these outcomes, VE states that it will not, because it cannot, raise any issues relating to CRS in this case. Any attempts to redress perceived CRS abuses by American will be confined, as the congressional testimony suggests, to the legislature. Since American's CRS operation will not be at issue, VE contends that its representation of American on this matter cannot be substantially related to this case. Northwest in particular claims that the issues of incremental revenue and costs addressed in System One relate to CRS use and are quite different from the general airline revenue and cost issues at the center of this case.

We recognize that several possible claims relating to CRS might be barred by res judicata and we do not question Northwest's representations in this court and below that the present litigation will involve no attacks on American's CRS use. We are not persuaded, however, by Northwest's argument that a [court is precluded from finding that two matters are substantially related when a party represents that it] cannot, or will not . . . introduce[] in the present case [material related to the former case.] The exact scope of categories such as "CRS matters," especially at the early stage of the litigation when motions to disqualify are often considered, is unclear, and leaves much room for good faith dispute among the parties. The party who either lost in the previous case or represented to the court that certain matters will not be raised will attempt to define the sphere of these issues narrowly, while the party who prevailed in the earlier case or filed an unsuccessful disqualification motion will naturally attempt to define the precluded matters quite broadly. In the particular case of res judicata, it places the former counsel in the position of attempting to minimize the beneficial results of her prior representations by limiting their effect in the present case.

The facts of this case disclose how such a dispute might arise. Northwest claims that *System One* involved the particular matter of incremental revenues obtained by American through ownership of a CRS. Northwest states that the focus in this case will be on wholly different matters such as American's marketing strategy, ticket pricing, and general airline costs and revenues. The line between incremental revenues and general revenues, however, does not appear as distinct as VE suggests. Moreover, American hotly disputes VE's contention that discovery in *System One* was limited to the narrow issue of incremental revenues. To the contrary, American asserts that the VE lawyers reviewed and discussed documents relating to marketing strategy and general air transportation revenues and costs, the very matters Northwest identifies as the heart of the instant case.

There is another matter involved in *System One* that Northwest has indicated will be at issue in this case. Northwest must focus at trial upon barriers to entry into the relevant markets. In its complaint, Northwest lists among these barriers "the role of travel agents in the industry and incentive commissions paid by airlines to travel agents and other marketing programs and devices." Incentive or override commissions in particular were at the center of the System One case.

System One charged that American used override commissions as a means to exclude it from the CRS market: "AA conditioned the payment to travel agents of commissions on AA ticket sales on their agreement to use the SABRE system." . . . In connection with this claim, American agreed to produce and searched for "documents that describe or discuss American's policies and procedures regarding participation by travel agencies in any override, special incentive or 'soft dollar' commission program offered by American." . . . A VE lawyer and several VE paralegals spent more than ten weeks reviewing documents at American's offices. Gibson, Dunn lawyers who were involved claim that a VE lawyer personally reviewed documents relating to marketing strategy and air transportation issues. . . . VE's . . . response is limited to a statement by the lawyer that he has no specific recollection of documents reviewed and that he does not believe, "given the nature of the case," that he "reviewed any documents relating to American's pricing of airline transportation."

. . . Northwest argues that the two cases are not related because in System One the commissions were alleged to be a barrier to entry into the CRS market, while here they represent a barrier to entry into the air transportation market. Regardless of the direction of the block the trial must focus on the exclusionary force of CRS—its power to exclude competition in CRS is the handmaiden of its exclusionary force on airline passenger service.

. . . *Corrugated* and *Duncan* provide that two representations need only involve the same "subject matter" in order to be substantially related. As the summary of the document request quoted above discloses, VE lawyers reviewed documents relating to travel agency commissions in general, not simply those documents referring to the alleged practice of tying such commissions to CRS use. A substantial relationship exists when the prior representation concerns "the particular practices and procedures which are the subject matter of [Northwest's] suit. Duncan, 646 F.2d at 1032. Both *System One* and the present case involve American's travel agency commission "practices and procedures." Given that the two cases sharing this "subject matter" allege similar antitrust violations, we find VE's representation of American in *System One* substantially related to its present representation of Northwest.

(3) Project Armadillo

VE represented American most recently in "Project Armadillo," an American proposal to acquire Continental. VE provided American with antitrust analysis of the proposal, focusing on whether a merger of the two airlines could avoid challenge under the Department of Justice antitrust merger guidelines. VE's representation began in late November 1990 and concluded in early January 1991, when American chose not to pursue the acquisition.

As a memorandum prepared by American explained, the Department of Justice merger guidelines' main concern is "whether the merger will likely create, enhance or facilitate the exercise of market power—the ability to raise prices to supracompetitive levels—by the remaining participants in the relevant market." Market power is more easily inferred under narrowly defined markets, and it was therefore in American's interest to avoid "[a] market definition that is improperly narrow," for this would "result in such a high level of concentration that, inevitably, a court will conclude the merger poses an incipient threat to competition."

These same issues are at the heart of the present case. Northwest alleges that American has monopolized or attempted to monopolize the national air transportation market as well as four smaller geographic markets involving city pairs and regions. Because American enjoys a greater share of particular regional markets, Northwest will no doubt attempt to prove at trial that these smaller markets are relevant. To this end, Northwest cites four instances where American has allegedly indicated that O & D [origin and destination] and regional passenger markets are relevant markets.

VE asserts that its "narrow, limited, and brief" role in Project Armadillo cannot serve as the basis for disqualification in the present case. Northwest contends that some VE lawyers alleged by American to have worked on Project Armadillo were not in fact involved. A VE memorandum summarizing the initial meeting between American and VE lawyers, however, includes a notation directing that a copy of the memo be sent to these same lawyers whose involvement in the matter VE denies. Similarly, VE attempts to minimize the significance of the materials it received from American by suggesting that the materials were not even read by certain VE lawyers involved in the representation. The billing statements submitted by VE to American, however, disclose that each of the VE lawyers in question devoted time to "reviewing materials furnished by [the] client."

We have no reason to suggest that VE's misstatements are other than oversights, and, because they pertain only to the degree of its involvement in Project Armadillo, are secondary to the main question of the subject matter of VE's representation. Northwest contends that VE's representation of American does not warrant disqualification for two related reasons. Northwest asserts that VE was charged with a single "narrow, straightforward question" to which the answer was "obvious": Would the Justice Department oppose a complete merger of Continental and American on antitrust grounds? Northwest claims that the problem posed to VE required little detailed analysis and that all the information needed by VE to reach its conclusion "was and is publicly available." Because VE required no confidential information to determine that the merger would not be approved by the Justice Department, Northwest contends that VE's representation provides no basis for disqualification.

The record sharply contradicts Northwest's claim that all of the material supplied by American to VE was publicly available. But Northwest's argument would fail even if it could show that all of the information provided by American was public knowledge. As we explained above, the substantial relationship test, as set out in our precedents and the Rules, contains no exception for prior representations in which an attorney's advice was based on public information. Accordingly, the question is not whether VE's representation of American in Project Armadillo involved matters of public knowledge but whether the subject matter of the prior representation is substantially related to the present case.

American argues that the primary issue in Project Armadillo, as in this case, was market definition. Not only did VE represent American on this same issue, but VE was also in a position to obtain information regarding American's views on the proper measure of markets, views which Northwest's complaint suggests are relevant to the present case. Northwest recognizes that market definition will be crucial in this case, but argues that VE's treatment of this issue in Project Armadillo was superficial and limited. While conceding that "more difficult questions could have been raised had American been interested in a partial acquisition," Northwest contends that the "only issue with which American was concerned was whether it would be challenged if it attempted to acquire all of Continental's operations." According to Northwest, "the answer to American's question was obvious . . . Anyone familiar with American's hub operations in Dallas and Continental's Houston hub operations would realize that American and Continental are major competitors in this region and that their combination would be subject to challenge."

The record demonstrates, however, that the subject matter was far more complex, and VE's analysis far more extensive, than Northwest's account suggests. A VE partner's notes from the first meeting between VE and American indicate that American was interested in a partial acquisition from the very start: "AA would be interested in the entire company but there are certain operations that are particularly important . . . They would be willing to divest some operations." VE's investigation could not have "rested largely" on Continental's strong Houston presence, for when this question was brought up in the first meeting, VE noted that "AA could sell the Houston hub." Thus, sometime after the meeting a VE partner sent a memo to American explaining that he had "spoken at some length" with American's economist and asked that the market share data be rerun on the assumption that American would not acquire Continental's Houston hub. While Northwest now asserts that VE's advice was based largely on the Houston hub, a VE partner at the time stated in yet another memo that even when Houston is removed from consideration, "substantial problems are created by Continental's other hubs—particularly New York City, Chicago, Cleveland, and Denver," as well as by the "substantial overlaps between Continental and American on flights to Mexico." Northwest's contention that Project Armadillo involved the single question of a complete merger and required study of only a few markets is simply belied by the record.

· · ·

In addition, Northwest contends that the Department of Justice's merger guidelines made the answer obvious. This is not the position that VE took during the representation, however. Upon receiving a memo prepared by American setting out the difficulties to merger under the city-pair analysis, a VE partner responded that the memo was "only the beginning of the analysis in my view." The VE lawyer then went on to suggest that American might be able to acquire Continental even though the merger might "violate" the guidelines.

We are forced to the conclusion that the question of market definition in Project Armadillo was more complex than Northwest now asserts. VE's representation of American necessarily required a detailed evaluation of American's operations in the various markets that might be deemed relevant. The instant case will involve similar issues.

VE was also privy to American's views of the relevant air transportation markets, a related matter that will also be at issue in the present case. American provided VE with materials reflecting AA's position on antitrust issues in prior merger/acquisition cases. Included in these materials were confidential "white papers" filed by American with the Justice Department.

In support of its claim that markets other than the national market are relevant in the present case, Northwest's complaint asserts that American "has repeatedly urged that O & D markets and regional airline passenger markets are relevant economic markets." Three of the examples cited by Northwest in support of this allegation appear to be taken from public testimony. The fourth is different: "AA argued to the Department of Justice in 1989 that city pair markets to and from O'Hare Airport constitute relevant markets." Northwest does not deny that this statement is contained in the materials obtained by VE from American during Project Armadillo. Nor does Northwest claim that this statement is a matter of public knowledge. Rather, Northwest states that it simply copied Continental's complaint in drafting its own. Since Northwest's complaint did not involve any independent research by VE, the argument seems to run, the allegation cannot possibly be based on confidential information supplied by American. We would first point out that Northwest's explanation remains plausible only so long as the complaint remains the sole document involved in the case. Northwest will eventually have to address the issues, including American's alleged views on the relevant market, on its own. More importantly, the answer given by Northwest is precisely one the substantial relationship test forbids. Once a substantial relationship has been established, former counsel is precluded from attempting to prove that he did not receive confidences. See, e.g., Corrugated, 659 F.2d at 1347. Northwest's response here—that VE might have obtained the information, but did not use it—is plainly barred by our precedents.

We appreciate Northwest's concern that an overly broad reading of "subject matter" can leave antitrust counselors with one client per industry—a result with little redemptive value. The nexus here is far more than case one and case two both presenting claims of attempted monopolization. Northwest contends that cases like Laker Airways Ltd. v. Pan American World Airways, 103 F.R.D. 22 (D.D.C 1984), preclude us from disqualifying VE. But American's showing in this case goes far beyond the same field, same party "points of contact" found insufficient in that case. See id. at 40. Rather, American has succeeded in "delineating with specificity the subject matters, issues and causes of action" common to prior and present representations in the manner demanded by our precedents. Duncan, 646 F.2d at 1029.

VI.

We hold that VE's prior representations of American in substantially related matters require the disqualification of VE in this case. We therefore issue a writ of mandamus directing the district court to vacate its order denying American's motion and enter an order disqualifying VE from representing Northwest.

Are the Matters "Substantially Related"?

The courts have employed different formulas for "substantially related." In *American Airlines*, the Fifth Circuit, citing earlier decisions, stated that to be "substantially related" the prior representation "need only be akin to the present action in a way reasonable persons would understand as important to the issues involved."

Broad view

The Second Circuit's formulation seems narrower. In Government of India v. Cook Industries, Inc.,[1] the Second Circuit stated that to count as "substantially related" the relationship between the two matters must be "patently clear," the issues "identical" or "essentially the same".[2]

narrow view

Restatement § 213 states:

> ... The current matter is substantially related to the earlier matter if:
>
> (1) the current matter involves the work the lawyer performed for the former client; or
>
> (2) there is a substantial risk that representation of the present client will involve the use of information acquired in the course of representing the former client, unless that information has become generally known.

Restatement

Competition as an Adverse Interest

In *American Airlines* the court rejects Northwest's concern that its ruling will restrict antitrust lawyers to one client per industry. Did Northwest have a point?

Suppose a lawyer has worked in the past for a software manufacturer on intellectual property problems. She is now asked to perform similar work for another software manufacturer, an economic competitor. The

---

1. 569 F.2d 737, 739–740 (2d Cir.1978).
2. Also see Federal Deposit Insurance Corp. v. Amundson, 682 F.Supp. 981, 988 (D.Minn.1988). But see Anchor Packing v. Pro–Seal, 688 F.Supp. 1215, 1220 (E.D.Mich.1988) (Sixth Circuit rejects this narrow view, citing General Electric Co. v. Valeron, 608 F.2d 265, 267 (6th Cir.1979)).

former client is not a party to the second matter, but the representation involves the same skills, legal principles and industry know-how. Is the lawyer barred from undertaking the representation? M.R. 1.9 does not deal with the issue directly, but Comment [3] of M.R. 1.7, in discussing adversity of interest, states: "representation in unrelated matters of clients whose interests are only generally adverse, such as competing economic enterprises, does not require consent of the respective clients."

In *Maritrans GP Inc. v. Pepper, Hamilton & Scheetz,*[3] a law firm dropped one client, a large maritime operator, and undertook representation of a number of its major competitors. Although Maritrans had consented to joint representation of a few minor competitors, provided effective screening was put in place, it sought an injunction and damages against the firm when the firm discharged Maritrans and undertook a broader representation of its major competitors. The trial court found that the firm, in handling Maritrans' labor work, became "intimately familiar with Maritrans' operations" and "gained detailed financial information, including Maritrans' financial goals and projections, labor cost savings, crew costs, and operating costs." An injunction was granted and the case remanded for consideration of damages even though Pennsylvania's version of the Model Rules permits screening in this situation. A lawyer's duty under common-law fiduciary principles to protect client confidences, the court held, is not displaced by the ethics rule provision:

> [W]hether a law firm can later represent competitors of its former client is a matter that must be decided from case to case and depends on a number of factors. One factor is the extent to which the fiduciary was involved in its client's affairs.... We do *not* wish to establish a blanket rule that a law firm may not later represent the economic competitor of a former client in matters in which the former client is not also a party to a suit. But situations may well exist when the danger of revelation of the confidences of a former client is so great that injunctive relief is warranted.... There is a substantial relationship here between [the law firm's] former representation of Maritrans and their current representation of Maritrans' competitors such that the injunctive relief here was justified.[4]

The parties settled on remand; Pepper, Hamilton paid Maritrans $3 million, an amount slightly less than Maritrans had incurred in bringing its suit.

Taint Shopping

Why didn't the court hold that Vinson & Elkins was disqualified because one of its partners had agreed to represent American Airlines?

In *Hughes v. Paine, Webber, Jackson and Curtis, Inc.,*[5] one of the defendants met with a partner in the law firm that was representing the plaintiffs. The defendant talked with the lawyer about the possibility of the

---

3.   602 A.2d 1277 (Pa.1992).

4.   602 A.2d at 1286–87.

5.   565 F.Supp. 663 (N.D.Ill. 1983).

lawyer representing him in an SEC investigation arising out of the acts at the heart of the plaintiffs' case against the defendant. But the defendant did not then seek to hire the firm; instead, he sought other counsel. The court refused to disqualify the firm from continuing to represent the plaintiffs. At the time the defendant consulted the plaintiffs' law firm, he had every reason to know that the firm was handling the case against him, having received a letter about the case written on behalf of the plaintiffs by the law firm on its stationery.

The court, citing *Westinghouse*, found that there had been an attorney-client relationship between the lawyer consulted and the defendant and that consequently an irrebuttable presumption arose that confidential information had been passed to that lawyer. But the court also held, contrary to *Westinghouse*, that the defendant had never been a client of the "firm", only of the lawyer consulted. Since the client had never been a "firm" client, the court held that the presumption that the lawyer passed information on to his partners could be rebutted.

Is *Hughes* the best analysis of the "taint shopping" problem? The Scope section of the Model Rules states that the client-lawyer relationship does not exist until the client has asked the lawyer to render service and the lawyer has agreed, but that "some duties, such as the duty of confidentiality ... may attach when the lawyer agrees to consider whether a client-lawyer relationship shall be established." Does this help? In situations in which a corporation is shopping for a law firm to handle a major case, both sides must exercise care.[6] A lawyer must be careful not to receive confidential information relating to the merits, but inquire only as to matters concerning potential conflicts and suitability of the firm for the case. The potential client must also act with caution, lest a court come to the conclusion that it is engaged in an effort to disqualify law firms from representing the adversary.[7]

E. Imputed Conflicts

1. Rules and Problems

DR 5–105(D) of the Model Code provides that if any lawyer in a firm is disqualified from representing a client or being involved in a case, all the lawyers in the firm are disqualified. This rule proceeds on the legal fiction that those who practice together are "one lawyer." No matter how large the firm or how far away the offices, no matter how tangential the first

---

6. See ABA Formal Op. 90–358 (1990) (discussing the measures a lawyer should take in initial conversations with a would-be client in order to avoid conflicts of interest problems arising from the firm's representation of other clients).

7. See B.F. Goodrich v. Formosa Plastics Corp., 638 F.Supp. 1050, 1052–53 (S.D.Tex.

1986) (attorney-client relationship not established in preliminary interview when firm was but one of five interviewed, demonstrating interviewing company did not intend attorney-client relationship; firm would only be disqualified if confidences were actually communicated).

lawyer's involvement, DR 5–105 specifies that if one lawyer is out, the firm is out. See, for example, the *Westinghouse* case printed above at p. 581. The broad sweep of the Code's imputed disqualification rule led courts to create limited exceptions.

What is the rationale for the imputation rule? First, lawyers who practice together talk to one another about their cases, and in doing so share client confidences. This collegial interchange is one of the benefits and enjoyments of group practice. To protect confidences from being revealed or used in an improper manner, all lawyers who have had access to them are disqualified. The rule carries this possibility further, and presumes that confidences have been shared. Second, lawyers who practice together share professional and financial interests and are concerned with furthering each other's interest. Where a lawyer's interests suggest that her loyalty to a client will be impaired, her colleagues' loyalty can be similarly affected. Third, whether or not the first and second dangers are real in a particular case, their specter could cause clients and the public to lose confidence in the system of legal representation were the firm of a disqualified lawyer allowed to proceed.

The merit of the Code approach is that it is simple and easily applied. But its problems are apparent in a world in which lawyers move with increasing frequency from firm to firm. A strict operation of the rule in this world creates what more than one commentator has called legal "Typhoid Marys." Consider the following problems:

Mr. Gulliver is with First & First. Ms. First, a partner in the firm, represented Sewer Corp. in its suit against Bland Construction. Motor Corp. comes to the First firm wanting to sue Sewer in a substantially related matter. The firm must turn down the case: Ms. First is disqualified so everyone in the firm is disqualified, including Mr. Gulliver who never worked on the Sewer trial.

Now Gulliver leaves First. He joins Second & Second, but when Motor was turned down by First, it went to the Second firm which is now representing it against Sewer. Is the disqualification imputed to Gulliver when he was at First to be imputed to all the lawyers at Second? Must Second now drop the Motor case?

The first question to be answered in this problem is whether Gulliver remains disqualified after leaving First. The applicable rule is that a lawyer may not be involved in suing a former client in a substantially related matter. But is that rule engaged in this situation? Was Sewer Gulliver's client? The Model Code did not address this question.

The original conflicts provisions in the Model Rules and the provisions as amended in 1989 are somewhat ambiguous on whether and under what circumstances Gulliver would remain personally disqualified when he moved to the Second firm. Under M.R. 1.9(a), Gulliver would be disqualified from opposing Sewer in the same or a substantially related matter if Sewer can be considered Gulliver's former client. But is Sewer to be considered to have been Gulliver's client? At one extreme, M.R. 1.9(b), as amended, [M.R. 1.10(b) as originally adopted][1] makes it clear that Sewer would be considered Gulliver's former client if Gulliver had "acquired information material to the matter" when at First. In this situation neither Gulliver nor any other lawyer at Second could proceed against Sewer in this matter; Second would have to drop the Motor case. But what if Gulliver while at First had learned no material confidences about Sewer or for that matter no confidences at all?

One reading of the Model Rules is that Gulliver is not considered as having represented Sewer at all or in a substantially related matter if no material confidences were learned. Another reading, however, is suggested by the original Comment to M.R. 1.10, now included in the Comment to M.R. 1.9. The Comment discusses the lawyer's duty of loyalty to the client (her obligation to avoid adverse representation in a related matter) separately from the duty to preserve confidences. It explains that this loyalty interest, while not requiring the new firm's disqualification, may nonetheless require that the individual lawyer refrain from opposing a former client even in cases where 1.9(b) [1.10(b)] would allow the firm to proceed, i.e., in cases where the lawyer had not actually acquired material confidences. Does this mean Gulliver is disqualified no matter how insignificant his involvement with the Sewer matter was while at First? According to the Comment [8] to M.R. 1.9 [Comment to 1.10] the answer is no. Comment [8] specifically states that when the lawyer has acquired "no knowledge of information relating to a particular client of the firm" then that lawyer is not personally disqualified.

The best reading of these provisions, then, is that Gulliver may be disqualified in some instances when Second is not, i.e., when he has been involved enough in the case to have been considered Sewer's lawyer but not enough to have learned any material confidences that he could pass on to Second. On the other hand, Gulliver may have had no contact or such insignificant contact with the Sewer matter while at First that he may work on the very same matter on behalf of Motor. This resolution is consistent with the case law. For example, in Silver Chrysler Plymouth, Inc. v. Chrysler Motors Corp.,[2] the tainted lawyer had been an associate while at the first firm. The court, evaluating the level of work by the associate, concluded that there was little or no possibility that the associate would have been privy to client confidences.[3]

---

1. In 1989, the ABA House of Delegates amended the conflicts provisions of the Model Rules. In effect, the amendments moved old M.R. 1.10(b) to new M.R. 1.9(b); made old M.R. 1.9(b) into new M.R. 1.9(c); and made old M.R. 1.10(c) into new M.R. 1.10(b). Because many states based their rule sections on the original numbering, in this introduction we indicate the original Model Rule section in brackets after the Model Rule section number as amended. Thus, new M.R. 1.9(b), will be referred to as M.R. 1.9(b) [1.10(b)]. The corresponding sections are not identical, but they are close enough that the analysis presented here is the same under either version of the Model Rules. After the introduction, we revert to the Model Rule numbers as amended, eliminating the brackets.

2. 518 F.2d 751 (2d Cir.1975).

3. A similar holding is Gas–A–Tron of Arizona v. Union Oil Co. of California, 534 F.2d 1322 (9th Cir.1976). See also Freeman v. Chicago Musical Instrument, 689 F.2d

The Restatement codifies this case law. Section 204(2), Removing Imputation, provides that when one lawyer is disqualified because of a successive representation problem, other lawyers in the firm may proceed provided:

> (a) any confidential information communicated to the personally-prohibited lawyer is unlikely to be significant in the subsequent matter;

> (b) the personally-prohibited lawyer is subject to screening measures adequate to eliminate involvement by that lawyer in the representation; and

> (c) timely and adequate notice of the screening has been provided to all affected clients.

M.R. 1.10(b) [1.10(c)] is exemplified by the next problem. While Gulliver was at First, he defended Landlord in a suit brought by a tenant, charging that the building was unsafe. After Gulliver leaves First, the city housing department asks First to represent it in a suit against Landlord for violating the housing code, which provides for civil penalties. Can First take the suit now that Gulliver is gone?

While Gulliver was at First, the firm would have had to turn down the suit whether or not Gulliver had ever talked about the case to any of the lawyers at First, M.R. 1.10(a). However, after Gulliver has gone, whether First remains disqualified is decided under M.R. 1.10(b) [1.10(c)]. Under these provisions, First can take the case, even though it is substantially related to a case in which Gulliver represented the other side, if none of the lawyers still with the firm has acquired confidential information about Landlord from Gulliver.[4]

2.   IMPUTED DISQUALIFICATION AND MIGRATORY LAWYERS

Nemours Foundation v. Gilbane

United States District Court, District of Delaware, 1986.
632 F.Supp. 418.

■ FARNAN, DISTRICT JUDGE.

At this late juncture in a long and complicated proceeding the plaintiff, The Nemours Foundation ("Nemours"), has filed a motion to disqualify counsel for the defendant in this case, Pierce Associates, Inc. ("Pierce").... In Nemours' motion to disqualify, filed on October 4, 1985, Nemours requests the disqualification of the entire firm of Biggs & Battaglia ("Biggs"), Pierce's local Wilmington counsel, from further representation of their client. Nemours alleges that Biggs has a conflict of interest due

---

715, 722 (7th Cir.1982) (factors to be considered include the size of the firm, lawyer's area of specialization and the lawyer's position in the firm).

4.   See Novo Terapeutisk v. Baxter Travenol Laboratories, 607 F.2d 186 (7th Cir.1979).

to the former involvement of one of its present associates in this litigation
as a former associate of Howard M. Berg & Associates ("Berg"), counsel for
Furlow [a co-party of Nemours'] and co-counsel for Nemours at the time.
[The litigation concerned a dispute arising out of construction of an
addition to a hospital. Nemours commissioned the construction; Gilbane
was the general contractor; Pierce was a subcontractor of Gilbane; and
Furlow was the firm responsible for mechanical engineering. At this stage
of the litigation, Furlow and Nemours were aligned in interest in the
litigation against Pierce.]

BACKGROUND

Much of the factual background is not in dispute. Paul A. Bradley, the
attorney whose former representation of Furlow has raised the issue of
disqualification in this case, was admitted to the practice of law in February 1983 while he was employed at Berg. He began his employment there
on September 7, 1982. Bradley became involved in the litigation in April
1984, when he assisted Howard M. Berg, who "made all decisions regarding
the representation of Furlow." Bradley's responsibilities as a low-level
associate involved preparing for a "mini-trial" among the parties in efforts
to reach a settlement agreement. Bradley prepared the materials for a set
of books to be distributed to the party participants and the arbitrator. Most
of his consultation with experts concerned these materials. Bradley also
reviewed documents for Berg's client, Furlow, which included documents
produced by Nemours, the party moving for the disqualification of Biggs in
this case. Bradley further attested in his affidavit submitted to the Court
that, having reviewed thousands of documents, he presently (November 1,
1985) has no recollection of the content or existence of any documents that
potentially were covered either by the work product doctrine or attorney-
client privilege. To the best of his knowledge, Bradley's involvement in the
Furlow case terminated after the end of the mini-trial.[3]

Bradley subsequently did not follow the litigation, review any discovery
materials, or attend depositions concerning Furlow. He stated that he had
no way to determine if any conversation he had while representing Furlow
or any document involved in that case has been disclosed beyond the
purview of the attorney-client privilege or work product doctrine. When he
interviewed for a position with Biggs, he did not know of its involvement in
the present litigation and had no conversation with anyone concerning his
work for Furlow before being hired.[4]

---

3. Bradley stated that to the best of his
knowledge he did not meet with Nemours'
attorneys or their clients at any time after
the mini-trial. He did attend a brief meeting to discuss settlement, but no attorneys
from Nemours, Pierce, or other clients
were present. Finally, he did some research
on the proper form of Release and Stipulation of Dismissal to be filed with the Court.

4. Since then, Bradley's contacts with anyone involved in the litigation were limited
to the following. He became aware that
Biggs represented Pierce when he met Jack
Rephan, of Braude, Margulies, Sacks & Rephan, at Biggs' offices, probably in May
1985. He merely greeted him and helped
him carry several sealed boxes to an eleva-
tor; they did not discuss the litigation. On
the same day, Victor F. Battaglia and Rob-

It is apparent that Biggs was completely innocent of any knowledge of Bradley's involvement in the litigation, as was Bradley of Biggs' until Bradley met Jack Rephan, an attorney for Braude, Margulies, Sacks & Rephan ("Braude, Margulies"), Pierce's main counsel, when Rephan visited Biggs' offices approximately in May 1985. Bradley and his superiors at Biggs immediately decided that Bradley would have no contact with the Pierce litigation whatsoever and would not discuss it. Bradley himself resolved that he would not discuss the litigation or prior representation of Furlow "in any way with anyone" at Biggs. He further attested that he has never been asked by anyone at Biggs or Braude, Margulies concerning his Furlow representation. He does not [know] nor . . . has [he ever] known the location of the Pierce files at Biggs.

Victor Battaglia described his firm's procedure of "screening" Bradley from the litigation. All attorneys in the Pierce litigation must report to him. Biggs has a central file room, but since the actions of the litigation were consolidated, and long before Bradley was hired, all Pierce files have been kept directly adjacent to Robert Beste's offices. Furthermore, the only documents in the file are pleadings and other documents filed and of record with the Court, and previous drafts of filed documents.

ANALYSIS

On this motion for disqualification of Biggs, this Court is faced with two major issues. The first question is whether Bradley's previous involvement on behalf of Furlow in this litigation calls for his disqualification. Pierce argues that an attorney-client relationship never existed between Bradley and Nemours and contends therefore that there is no conflict of interest. The Court must address this issue first to determine the extent of Bradley's own involvement in the litigation, a necessary step in addressing the second issue. The essential discordance between Nemours' and Pierce's positions centers on whether this involvement of Bradley, now associated with Biggs, requires the disqualification of the entire firm of Biggs, as Nemours argues it should. Biggs contends that it has effectively "screened off" Bradley from any involvement or contacts with the Nemours litigation. This defense has been commonly termed the "Chinese Wall" defense. In ruling on this motion, the Court has coined the term "cone of silence" as a more accurate description of the ethical commands involved and the policies at stake.

. . .

A.   Disqualification of Bradley

Nemours alleges that the conflict of interest originates with Bradley, thus leading ultimately to the disqualification of Bradley and his firm.

ert Beste, attorneys at Biggs, also became aware of Bradley's prior involvement. They briefly discussed only the fact of his representation of Furlow. All agreed, and Bradley was so advised, that he should not discuss the litigation with anyone. Finally, he walked a Pierce employee to a federal grand jury hearing after gaining permission from Victor Battaglia. To the best of his knowledge, the hearing had nothing to do with the Nemours and Pierce litigation.

Bradley, as an associate at Berg, worked on the current litigation as counsel for Furlow. At that time, Furlow was a co-defendant of Nemours. As counsel for Furlow, Bradley was privy to confidences of both Furlow and Nemours as both planned "strategy sessions" in concert against Gilbane. This "commonality of interest" necessitated a sharing of work product, attorney-client privileges, and other confidential information.... After intense negotiations, Gilbane, Furlow, and Nemours entered a series of agreements to settle or to dismiss claims. During this entire period, according to Nemours, the interests of Pierce—whose counsel is Biggs, Bradley's new employer—were adverse to those of Furlow. Applying the Rules to this set of facts, specifically Rule 1.6 on confidentiality, Bradley is disqualified because the information he gained from Nemours was confidential information which must be protected, because Nemours must be considered a "client" of Bradley. Under Rule 1.9, Bradley cannot represent a client whose interests are "materially adverse" to the interest of the former client.

Pierce argues that Nemours cannot be considered a former client of Bradley for purposes of Rules 1.6 and 1.9. Nemours was merely a co-party of Furlow. The presumption that confidential information has passed to an attorney, which arises in the context of the attorney-client relationship, therefore does not apply. Nemours must prove that confidential information actually did pass from Nemours to Bradley, which it has been unable to do. (D.I. 730 at 15.)

Analysis must begin with the Rules. Rule 1.9, which deals with conflict of interest, reads as follows: [The court then quoted M.R. 1.9 as it was in 1986, which is substantially identical to present M.R. 1.9(a) and (c)(1).]

Several requirements arise from this provision. First, the lawyer must have had an attorney-client relationship with the former client. Second, the present client's matter must either be the same as the matter the lawyer worked on for the first client, or a "substantially related" matter. Third, the interests of the second client must be materially adverse to the interests of the former client. Fourth, the former client must not have consented to the representation after consultation. The second part of the provision lists the conditions on the use of the information relating to representation of the former client.

Rule 1.7, which Rule 1.9 references, provides guidance for determining when the interests of two clients are adverse: [The court quoted M.R. 1.7 at this point.]

This provision applies to both simultaneous representation of two clients, or successive representation, where the attorney-client relationship has been formally terminated, which characterizes the case at hand. The duty involved is one of loyalty to the client.

[The court then discussed Third Circuit and other decisions under the Canons and Model Code dealing with conflict of interest.]

Resolving the question of whether to disqualify counsel cannot be accomplished through mechanical means, but requires a careful balancing of the goals and objectives of professional conduct. "The chosen mode of analysis is to carefully sift 'all the facts and circumstances'." Pennwalt Corp. v. Plough, Inc., 85 F.R.D. 264, 269 (D.Del.1980); Akerly v. Red Barn System, Inc., 551 F.2d 539, 543 (3d Cir.1977). The Third Circuit has long refused to adopt a per se rule in questions of disqualification. Akerly, 551 F.2d at 543.

There is no doubt that Nemours must be considered a former "client" of Bradley for the purpose of determining whether a conflict of interest exists. Bradley himself stated that he reviewed confidential documents of Nemours when he represented Furlow in the litigation. Although there was no express attorney-client relationship, a fiduciary obligation, or "implied professional relation" existed nevertheless because Nemours disclosed information acting on the belief and expectation that such submission was made in order for Berg to render legal service to Nemours in furtherance of Nemours' interests. Westinghouse Elec. Corp. v. Kerr–McGee Corp., 580 F.2d 1311, 1319–20 (7th Cir.1978).[7]

Regarding the second requirement, under the old Code the Third Circuit adopted the "substantial relationship" test, now formally incorporated into the Rules, in determining when an attorney is prohibited from accepting a subsequent representation. Disqualification of counsel is required "where it appears that the subject matter of a pending suit in which the attorney represents an interest adverse to a prior employer is such that during the course of the former representation the attorney 'might have acquired substantially related material.' " . . .

There is no doubt that the Pierce litigation in which the Biggs' firm is involved is substantially related to the matter in which Bradley was involved when he was representing Furlow; indeed, the matter is one and the same.

The third requirement of Rule 1.9 is also met: Pierce's interests are adverse to Nemours'. Finally, Nemours, the "former client," now moving for disqualification of Biggs, certainly has not consented to the continued representation of Pierce. Bradley is thus clearly disqualified from representing Pierce in this litigation.

B. Disqualification of Biggs & Battaglia

The next issue is whether the entire law firm of Biggs must be disqualified, given the disqualification of one of its associates. Pierce argues that an effective screening mechanism is an acceptable alternative to disqualification of an entire law firm when one of its associates formerly

---

7. There is no doubt that as far as Bradley's formal client, Furlow, was concerned, the confidences relayed to him from Furlow's co-party, Nemours, were "confidential" within this primary attorney-client relationship.

. . . Rule 1.6 which deals with confidentiality . . . "applies not merely to matters communicated in confidence by the client but also to all information relating to the representation, whatever its source." Such a source would certainly include a co-party such as Nemours.

represented a client whose interests are "substantially related," and adverse, to those of a present client of the law firm.

An attorneys' disqualification is normally "imputed" to the other attorneys in his law firm. [The court quoted M.R. 1.10(a) and (b), which are substantially the same as current M.R. 1.10(a) and 1.9(b).]

There is now an explicit exception to imputed disqualification. The Rules, unlike the Code, sanction the use of a screening mechanism in appropriate circumstances, specifically referring to former government attorneys. Rule 1.11 states: "A firm with which that lawyer is associated may undertake or continue representation in the matter only if the disqualified lawyer is screened from any participation in the matter and is apportioned no part of the fee therefrom." Rule 1.11(b). The policy supporting this rule is to enable the government to attract qualified lawyers and to prevent the disqualification rule from imposing too severe a deterrent against entering public service. Comment to Rule 1.11.

The Comment to Rule 1.10 indicates the firm intention of its draftsmen that a pragmatic approach is necessary to the question of vicarious disqualification. The Comment also extends the analysis of Rule 1.10 to disqualified lawyers in law firms generally, not only former government attorneys. In the section "Lawyers Moving Between Firms," the authors of the Rules adopt a "functional analysis" in determining questions of vicarious disqualification. The rigid formalism underlying Canon 9's injunction against an "appearance of impropriety" is strongly rejected in favor of a new philosophy of pragmatism which balances the expectations of confidentiality of a former client against the importance of allowing a client the representation of his choice and promoting the mobility of attorneys, particularly associates, from one private law firm to another. The language of the Comment merits extensive quotation:

[The court then quoted the Comments [3]—[5] of M.R.1.9(b) (formerly 1.10(b)); you should read them at this time.]

· · ·

... In INA Underwriters Insurance Co. v. Rubin, 635 F.Supp. 1 (E.D.Pa.1983), the "Chinese Wall" defense was raised against a motion to disqualify a law firm. In that case, a client contacted a partner of the law firm Wolf, Block & Schorr ("Wolf, Block"). The client confided certain confidential information to the partner, but the partner subsequently refused to represent the client because he found that a conflict of interest existed. The court refused to apply an irrebuttable presumption that confidences were shared by the partners of Wolf, Block, and to impute the disqualification firm-wide. Id. at 3. There was no question that the partner who had met with the client was disqualified. The court approved of the screening of secret documents and firm members possessing knowledge of secrets and confidences in order to avoid disqualification of an entire firm. Id. at 4. The partner had never discussed the substantive content of his meeting with the client with any of the attorneys inside or outside the Wolf, Block firm. Id. at 5. A refusal to disqualify Wolf, Block in this case would not only maintain public confidence and integrity of the legal system, but also promote the policies of respecting a litigant's right to retain counsel of its choice and of enabling attorneys to practice without excessive restrictions. Id. at 5–6.

Before the adoption of the Rules, case law in other circuits[8] and scholarly commentary[9] had already adopted a liberalized approach based on a functional analysis. In the Second Circuit, where this approach has received its most extensive development, the test is whether the conduct of the disqualified attorney taints the underlying trial. Armstrong v. McAlpin, 625 F.2d 433, 444 (2d Cir.1980) (en banc), vacated on other grounds and remanded, 449 U.S. 1106 (1981). Disqualification if based solely on the appearance of impropriety cannot be justified as long as a firm's representation does not pose a threat to the integrity of the trial process. Id. As the court in *McAlpin* stated:

> We recognize that a rule that concentrates on the threat of taint fails to correct all possible ethical conflicts.... However, absent a threat of taint to the trial, we continue to believe that possible ethical conflicts surfacing during a litigation are generally better addressed by the "comprehensive disciplinary machinery" of the state and federal bar [citation omitted] or possibly by legislation.

Id. at 445–46; Board of Education of New York City v. Nyquist, 590 F.2d 1241, 1246 (2d Cir.1979). A court should only reluctantly order disqualification because of the immediate adverse effect on the client of separating him from counsel of his choice. *Nyquist*, 590 F.2d at 1246. Such motions for disqualification are often made for tactical reasons, and even when made in the best of faith, inevitably cause delay.

Several circuits have extended this functional analysis to create a rebuttable presumption of shared confidences among attorneys in a law firm in order to avoid vicarious disqualification....

The factual circumstances of Lemaire v. Texaco, Inc., 496 F.Supp. 1308 (E.D.Tex.1980), closely resemble those of the case at bar. In that case, an

---

8. See Fred Weber, Inc. v. Shell Oil Co., 566 F.2d 602, 609 (8th Cir. 1977) (holding that every representation against a former client's co-defendant in a related matter raises an appearance of impropriety would unnecessarily restrict choice of counsel available to litigants); Woods v. Covington County Bank, 537 F.2d 804, 813 n. 12 (5th Cir.1976) (test is whether likelihood of public suspicion or obloquy outweighs social interests served by lawyer's continued participation in a particular case); Silver Chrysler Plymouth, Inc. v. Chrysler Motors Corp., 518 F.2d 751, 757 (2d Cir.1975) (underscoring importance of public's right to counsel of its choice and economic mobility).

9. See Liebman, The Changing Law of Disqualification: The Role of Presumption and Policy, 73 Nw.U.L.Rev. 996 (1979); Lindgren, Toward a New Standard of Attorney Disqualification, 1982 A.B.A. Found.Research J. 419 (1982); Comment, The Ethics of Moving to Disqualify Opposing Counsel for Conflict of Interest, 1979 Duke L.J. 1310 (1979); Note, The Chinese Wall Defense to Law–Firm Disqualification, 128 U.Pa.L.Rev. 677 (1980); Note, A Dilemma in Professional Responsibility: The Subsequent Representation Problem, 50 UMKC L.Rev. 165 (1982).

attorney switched law firms after having represented one party in a lawsuit to the limited extent of filing initial pleadings. His new law firm represented the opposite side in the *same* litigation. The screening was established immediately, even before the attorney accepted the position with the new firm. The attorney went to great lengths to insure that he would have no connection with any facet of the lawsuit. He also made certain he would receive no part of any attorneys' fees collected in the case or share in its expenses.[10]

The lawsuit was complex and very expensive to prepare. There was no other law firm in the area qualified or willing to take on the litigation. Id. at 1309. The court found that any appearance of impropriety was greatly outweighed by the plaintiffs' right to have counsel of their choice. Id. at 1310.

There is no substantial reason against extending the exception to vicarious disqualification from the case of a former government attorney to private attorneys generally although the complex of policy factors differs somewhat in the two situations:

> Once it is admitted that a Chinese Wall can rebut the presumption of imputed knowledge in former government attorney cases, it becomes difficult to insist that the presumption is irrebuttable when the disqualified attorney's previous employment was private and not public. To hold fast to such a proposition would logically require a belief that privately employed attorneys are inherently incapable of being effectively screened, as though they were less trustworthy or more voluble than their ex-Government counterparts. If former government attorneys can be screened effectively, it follows that former private attorneys can be too.

INA Underwriters Insurance Co. v. Rubin, 635 F.Supp. at 5 (quoting Note, The Chinese Wall Defense To Law–Firm Disqualification, 128 U.Pa.L.Rev. 677, 701 (1980)).

The Court holds that an appropriate screening mechanism, in the proper circumstances, may rebut the presumption of shared confidences that arises under Rule 1.10 in cases where the disqualified attorney's conflict of interest originated in private practice. The Court prefers to refer to this screening procedure figuratively as a "cone of silence"[11] rather than a "Chinese Wall." The conical image, a metaphor adopted from popular television, more appropriately describes the responsibility of the *individual* attorney to guard the secrets of his former client. He is commanded by the ethical rules to seal, or encase, these particular confidences within his own conscience. The term "Chinese Wall" is suggestive of attempts in the context of a large law firm to physically cordon off attorneys possessing

---

10. See Rule 1.11(b).

11. As explained at greater length later in this opinion, in this case, Bradley determined on his own initiative not to speak to anyone concerning the Furlow–Nemours representation. This self-imposed silence began immediately upon his gaining knowledge of the adverse representation at Biggs.

information from the other members of the firm who represent clients whose interests are adverse to interests of these attorneys' former clients. See Analytica, Inc. v. NPD Research, Inc., 708 F.2d 1263, 1269 (7th Cir.1983). Such an approach tends to cast a shadow of disrepute on attorneys separated in this manner from their professional colleagues. The implicit assumption is that the wall, if high and thick enough, will resist an errant attorney's lack of discretion, and calm public mistrust through prophylaxis. A firm of more moderate size must therefore erect a wall of greater impenetrability. Instead, the Court believes that the more logically consistent, honest, and straightforward approach is to credit members of the legal profession with a certain level of integrity. This emphasis on the ethical rules themselves, rather than a presumption that they will be circumvented, should more effectively promote public respect for the bar. In effect, the Rules enjoin the attorney to guard his client's secrets in an affirmative and deliberate manner, through self-imposed silence. Canon 4 and Rule 1.6, which mandate maintenance of a client's confidences, have an independent significance. Baglini v. Pullman, 412 F.Supp. 1060, 1064 n. 11 (E.D.Pa.), aff'd, 547 F.2d 1158 (3d Cir.1976). Moreover, the trend among courts now to rule out an "appearance of impropriety" as the sole basis for disqualification strongly supports this increased emphasis on the ethical rule of confidentiality. McAlpin, 625 F.2d at 444; Silver Chrysler Plymouth, 518 F.2d at 757.

On the other hand, certain objective circumstances, including the timing and physical characteristics of the screening, will in many cases require disqualification of an entire firm. The evidence of faithfulness to Rule 1.6 is only one factor in a balancing of the policy factors identified above against the likelihood that confidences will be violated. The size of the firm remains an important consideration, as well as the nature of the prior involvement of the tainted attorney and the extensiveness of the screening. The test is one that integrates subjective reliance on the Rules manifested by the attorney's "cone of silence," with objective evidence that the Rules are being followed.

As in *Rubin* and *Lemaire*, Biggs' and Bradley's deliberateness and speed in establishing a "cone of silence" in the instant case similarly help support denial of the motion to disqualify. The circumstances of this case strongly support such a finding. Bradley himself is required by Rule 1.6 to maintain the confidences of his former client. The Court harbors no doubt based on the present affidavits that he thus far has not violated this ethical norm. If he should disclose any information, although he claims that he has no recollection of any substantive confidences, he can be subject to the disciplinary machinery of the state bar. McAlpin, 625 F.2d at 446. The Court's primary task at this juncture is to ensure a fair and just trial. Id. at 445–46; Nyquist, 590 F.2d at 1246. Following Rule 1.6, Bradley immediately sealed himself in a "cone of silence," resolving not to say anything concerning the substance of any communication, documents, or information to which he may have had access. In addition, Bradley's present lack of access to the information helps to reinforce his fidelity to Rule 1.6. When he changed firms, Bradley did not personally retain any notes or documents with which to refresh his recollection. (Id. at ¶ 6.) Furthermore, the information he reviewed when he was with the Berg firm was primarily non-confidential and his memory of this information is now fading. The importance of the ethical precept against disclosure of client confidences as a prophylactic safeguard in instances where violation of confidences is possible was recognized by the district court in *Baglini v. Pullman*, 412 F.Supp. at 1064 n. 11. See *Silver Chrysler Plymouth, Inc. Chrysler Motors Corp.*, 518 F.2d 751, 757 (2d Cir.1975) (Canon 9 should not override delicate balance created by Canon 4).

Supplementing Bradley's own self-imposed silence, Biggs has established an effective screening mechanism which has been in place ever since Bradley's former involvement was discovered. No information was disclosed to other Biggs attorneys up to that time or since then. Bradley does not know where the Pierce files are located at Biggs. These files are not contained in Biggs' central filing system but are segregated in separate file cabinets, all adjacent to one partner's office. Only pleadings and correspondence are located in Biggs' offices. Although Biggs would be considered a medium-size firm by Wilmington standards, the limited nature of Bradley's contact with his "former client" and knowledge of the litigation effectively counterbalance this factor.[12]

Another factor indicating that the confidences and secrets of Nemours will remain inviolate is the extent of Bradley's previous involvement in the litigation. Bradley was not the lead counsel in this litigation when he was at Berg. He had only recently joined Berg after becoming a member of the Delaware Bar,[13] and was assigned the duties which typically characterize the life of a young associate in his position. In addition, his involvement was brief, lasting only about four months, and ended approximately eight months before he changed firms. The attorney's degree of prior involvement, whether he controlled strategy, whether he was an associate or partner, and whether he shared legal fees from his firm's representation are all important factors in evaluating the effectiveness of a "cone."[14]

Furthermore, the policies identified in the Comment to Rule 1.10 would be promoted by a decision denying disqualification in this case. As of October 1985, in the entire State of Delaware there were currently 856 attorneys in private practice, 710 of whom practice in New Castle County. Of the 710 attorneys, over 280, or over forty percent, work for only ten Wilmington law firms. Eleven different law firms have been involved directly in this case and eight of these are in the "top ten." Attorney mobility, especially among young associates, would be severely restricted if a per se rule against a "cone of silence" were adopted. The small number of

---

12. As reported by the law firms themselves, as of March 1986, Biggs & Battaglia had 16 attorneys; Richards, Layton & Finger and Morris, Nichols, Arsht & Tunnell, two of Wilmington's largest law firms, had 52 and 43 attorneys, respectively, in Wilmington.

13. Bradley became a member of the Delaware Bar in 1983, having graduated from law school in 1981. 1 Martindale–Hubbell Law Directory 3408B (1985).

14. As an associate, Bradley would receive only his fixed, annual salary.

private firms in Wilmington of substantial size, combined with the facts and circumstances of this case, cry out for a flexible approach to vicarious disqualification.

In addition, Pierce would be considerably prejudiced by the disqualification of Biggs at this point in the litigation, shortly before trial is scheduled to begin on March 31, 1986. When Pierce attempted to obtain local counsel in Wilmington, all the major law firms in Wilmington either were already representing parties or believed that a conflict existed. Jack Rephan, attorney for Braude, Margulies, stated that he was not aware of any other office in Delaware of "sufficient abilities or facilities equipped to represent Pierce" in this litigation other than Biggs, after the other firms were found to have a conflict of interest. This large, complex litigation requires a large law office locally located with sufficient facilities and manpower to adequately represent Pierce's interests. The Court has scheduled three full months for the trial. Moreover, an "excellent working relationship" has developed between Pierce and its local counsel. An abrupt withdrawal by Biggs would substantially prejudice Pierce in this litigation.[19]

In contrast, Nemours fails to adduce any convincing evidence of prejudice to its interests resulting from Biggs' continued representation of Pierce. Nowhere in presenting its argument does Nemours allege the slightest disadvantage or harm. Certainly, the fact that Nemours was only a co-party of Bradley's primary client has some significance. Furthermore, this is not the case of a partner who, as a major strategist, must be quarantined from contact with other members of his firm who are involved in a case from which he is disqualified. This representation of Pierce by Biggs therefore has no tendency to "taint the underlying trial." McAlpin, 625 at 444; Nyquist, 590 at 1246. This fact, in combination with the harm that would accrue to Pierce should Biggs be required to withdraw, and the other powerful arguments of policy, all support denial of Nemours' motion to disqualify.

In addendum, the Court takes note of a factor weighing against Nemours' motion involving possible delay. Courts have been extremely reluctant to disqualify attorneys when there is a possibility that a motion was made primarily for strategic purposes in a litigation. Even when made in the best of faith, such motions inevitably cause delay. McAlpin at 444. It is possible—but by no means proven—that counsel for Nemours knew already in April 1985 that Bradley had joined Biggs.[20] Nemours raised this

---

19. Indeed, if Biggs & Battaglia were to be disqualified in the circumstances of this case, it is quite possible that in view of the realignment of the parties which resulted in the disqualification of Bradley, other firms should be disqualified, including counsel for the moving party on this motion.

Gilbane and Pierce were originally aligned together and shared confidential informa-tion. Through settlement, Gilbane is now aligned with Nemours. The technical disqualifications resulting from this realignment would rapidly cause this litigation to become unmanageable.

20. In April 1985, notices were sent to all members of the Delaware Bar that Bradley had joined the Biggs firm.

issue five months later, in September. Shortly before that, Nemours had lost a motion to compel. The total absence of any prejudice to Nemours of Bradley's association with Biggs ... tends to strengthen the appearance of mere delay and harassment as the overriding motive for the plaintiff's motion to disqualify. Nevertheless, the evidence is not sufficient to show that delay was an intentional element. The other factors standing alone are sufficient to withstand a motion to disqualify.

Notes on *Nemours*

Suppose Bradley had not worked on the *Nemours* matter while an associate with the Berg firm. After moving to the Biggs firm, would he be personally disqualified from participating in the case?

Why was Bradley personally disqualified in *Nemours*? Why wasn't the Biggs firm disqualified? Is the court's reading of the Model Rules justified? Bradley seems to have had access to Nemour's confidences. Shouldn't that be enough to disqualify Biggs? There is no claim that the confidences that Bradley had access to were insignificant. Indeed, he could have reviewed documents that contained important confidences. The claims instead are that he doesn't remember anything anymore and that he had no significant responsibility for the Nemours/Furlow side of the case because he was a lowly associate. Would those claims allow Biggs to continue under Restatement § 204(2), quoted above at p. 670?

Why was it necessary for Bradley to maintain a "cone of silence"? Why did the court substitute this metaphor for "Chinese Wall?"[1] Does the "cone" metaphor give insufficient emphasis to the responsibilities of other lawyers in the firm? See M.R. 5.1 and M.R. 5.2

In Atasi Corp. v. Seagate Technology,[2] the court held that neither, in its words, a "Chinese Wall" nor a "cone of silence" could allow the firm to proceed. In the process of so holding the court described the "cone of silence" as a screening method in which "the attorney switching firms, but not the other members of the [new] firm, agrees not to share confidences of prior clients with his new associates." Is this what the *Nemours* court had in mind? Screening is discussed further in subsequent notes.

To avoid the disclosure of confidences during the inquiry into whether the tainted lawyer has knowledge, courts look at such factors as: the firm's size, the lawyer's position in the firm (partners are judged more likely than associates to have actual confidences on the cases of others in the firm), the formal and informal patterns of communication among those who work at the firm, the procedures on access to client files, the number of the firm's

---

1. See Employers Insurance of Wausau v. Albert D. Seeno Construction Co., 692 F.Supp. 1150, 1165 (N.D.Cal.1988) (using "ethical wall," noting that some find "Chinese Wall" offensive and others confuse it with a flimsy paper structure instead of the Great Wall of China).

2. 847 F.2d 826, 831–832 (Fed.Cir. 1988) (interpreting the law in the Ninth Circuit).

lawyers involved in the original matter, and the testimony of lawyers, both the lawyers involved in the original case as to whether they discussed it with the tainted lawyer, and the testimony of the tainted lawyer as to whether she has any information about the original matter. Outcomes depend to an important extent on the judge's own prior experience in practice and her sensitivity to "purity" versus "mobility".

Screening

Formal screening, otherwise known as building an "insulation wall" or establishing a "cone of silence," refers to physical and procedural barriers established in a firm to prevent the tainted lawyer from transmitting or receiving information on a particular matter, which that lawyer is disqualified from handling.[3]

The messy reality of life is rarely as straightforward as our logical concepts. Screening was instituted by the Biggs firm in *Nemours* but not until some months after Bradley joined the firm. He also, the court says in note 4, "walked a Pierce employee to a federal grand jury hearing."

In Schiessle v. Stephens,[4] the Seventh Circuit stated that the question to be asked when a tainted lawyer moves to a new firm is: "[W]hether the knowledge of the 'confidences and secrets' of [the client of the first firm] which [the attorney] brought with him has been passed on to or is likely to be passed on to the members of the [second] firm."[5] How is this question different from the question to be asked under the Model Rules? Is the *Schiessle* formulation of the test better than that in the Model Rules?

In Panduit Corp. v. All States Plastic Mfg. Co., Inc.,[6] a patent lawyer who had handled Panduit's foreign patent work later joined a firm that represented a company that Panduit was suing for infringing a related patent. The tainted lawyer worked briefly on the case, observing one deposition, before screening was instituted. Following Seventh Circuit law, see *Schiessle,* supra, the court reversed a disqualification order. The standard is likelihood that confidences have passed, not certainty that this had occurred; and the presumption that confidences have been shared may be rebutted by the testimony of the lawyers involved.

If the Seventh Circuit is right that the question is whether information has been transferred, why not use screening to cure all conflicts within a firm? Isn't the logic of screening to prevent taint as expansive as imputation is to attribute taint? Does the Restatement's limited acceptance of screening for former client conflicts that arise in purely private practice settings, i.e., screening allowed with timely notice to all affected parties

---

3. For general discussion of screening in conflicts cases, see Wolfram, Modern Legal Ethics § 7.6.4 (1986); and Thomas D. Morgan, Screening the Disqualified Lawyer: The Wrong Solution to the Wrong Problem, 10 U. Ark. (Little Rock) L. J. 37 (1987).

4. 717 F.2d 417 (7th Cir.1983).

5. 717 F.2d at 421.

6. 744 F.2d 1564 (Fed. Cir.1984) (applying Seventh Circuit law).

when the confidential information acquired by the disqualified lawyer is not likely to be significant in the current representation, make sense?

The difficulties created by the imputation rule have led to much dissatisfaction with it, especially on the part of large law firms. These difficulties are especially significant for young lawyers, who are more likely to move than their older colleagues. A lawyer seeking to move from one firm to another will have to account for all her prior involvements in representation and have those checked against the prospective firm's list of pending clients and matters. This makes it important for young lawyers to keep an accurate record of the matters on which they have worked. It also suggests that young lawyers should keep their noses out of cases being handled by their firms in which they have no direct involvement.

Nemours and a number of other cases depart from the general rule of imputed disqualification. Where do the courts get authority to permit screening in situations in which the ethical rules do not permit it? Courts may more readily permit screening where the opposing party acquiesces or the conflict arose from an unusual or unforeseeable chain of events.[7] Most courts continue the rigorous stance against screening.[8]

A minority of jurisdictions have amended Rule 1.10 to permit screening in many conflict situations.[9] The District of Columbia ethics rules specifically address the problems of law students moving between firms. The rules provide that law students are bound to keep the former client's confidences,[10] but that the new firm is not disqualified.[11] The D.C. Rules do not explicitly require that the firm implement screening procedures in this situation, but it would seem the prudent course. Law clerks to judges also have confidentiality and conflict of interest obligations.[12]

The Model Rules do not depend on whether material confidences were actually passed from the tainted lawyer to others in the second firm. If the tainted lawyer has such confidences the firm cannot proceed. Screening might still be advisable and even necessary under the Model Rules, if the tainted lawyer—despite the fact that she has no material confidential information—is still disqualified under M.R. 1.9(a). See p. 668 above.

---

7. See, e.g., Manning v. Waring, Cox, James and Sklar, 849 F.2d 222 (6th Cir.1988); Cox v. American Cast Iron Pipe Co., 847 F.2d 725 (11th Cir.1988).

8. See, e.g., Atasi Corp. v. Seagate Technology, 847 F.2d 826, 831–832 (Fed.Cir.1988) (interpreting Ninth Circuit law).

9. See the table prepared by Attorneys Liability Assurance Society (ALAS) and reprinted in T. Morgan and R. Rotunda, 1999 Selected Standards on Professional Responsibility 143 ("the overwhelming majority of

jurisdictions (42 out of 51) *do not* recognize screening of a tainted lawyer as a cure for imputed disqualification"). Most of the minority permit screening only in the migratory lawyer situation; see, e.g., Pennsylvania's version of M.R. 1.10.

10. D.C. Rule 1.6(g).

11. D.C. Rule 1.10(b).

12. See Richard W. Painter, Open Chambers?, 97 Mich.L.Rev. 101, 124–42 (1999) (discussing ethical obligations of judicial law clerks).

Conflicts When Law Firms Merge

The conflicts problems arising when a lawyer moves from one firm to another are compounded when two firms merge. In a merger, all the current clients of each firm become the current clients of the surviving firm under M.R. 1.7, and the former clients of both firms come within the purview of M.R. 1.9. In dealing with law firm mergers, the courts have refused to allow a firm simply to dump one of the clients who will not consent to a conflict and indeed have said that notice to the affected clients should be given when the negotiations reach the stage that merger has "reasonable likelihood."[13]

Conflicts Created by Paralegals and Secretaries Moving Between Firms

In Kapco Mfg. Co. v. C & O Enterprises, Inc.,[14] a secretary from one law firm moved to the opponent's law firm. Kapco moved to disqualify C & O's lawyers based on this secretary's move. The court held that the same conflict rules and tests applied when the conflict was created by a non-lawyer changing firms as those that apply when lawyers move. Note that the litigation was ongoing in *Kapco*, so the tainted person would have been disqualified under M.R. 1.7, not 1.9. Little case law deals with the conflicts issues posed by secretaries or paralegals migrating from one law firm to another. According to the court in *Kapco*, "the courts in both [prior] cases took the disqualification motions seriously and applied analysis similar to those applied in attorney-transfer cases."[15]

F.   GOVERNMENT LAWYERS AND THE REVOLVING DOOR

INTRODUCTION

A large and complicated body of law deals with the ethics, including conflicts of interest, of government lawyers.[1] Criminal statutes at the federal and state level are supplemented by agency regulations that dupli-

---

13. See, e.g., In re Eastern Sugar Antitrust Litigation, 697 F.2d 524 (3d Cir.1982); Picker International v. Varian Associates, 869 F.2d 578 (Fed.Cir.1989). Also see the discussion of curing simultaneous conflicts in Chapter 7 above.

14. 637 F.Supp. 1231 (N.D.Ill.1985).

15. 637 F.Supp. at 1236. The two prior cases dealing with secretaries and paralegals who change law firms, both discussed in *Kapco,* are: Williams v. Trans World Airlines, Inc., 588 F.Supp. 1037 (W.D.Mo. 1984); and Swanson v. Wabash, Inc., 585 F.Supp. 1094 (N.D.Ill.1984).

1. Most of this law does not deal with lawyers as such but is applicable to govern-ment officers and employees, whether act-ing in a legal or some other capacity. The professional rules, of course, apply only to persons admitted to practice, but extend to activities of a lawyer acting in a non-legal capacity (e.g., as an elected official or a political appointee of the executive branch). Finally, the hierarchy of law is such that the ethics rules cannot decriminalize con-duct prohibited by general statutes. See the Koniak article reprinted in Chapter 2. For an example of a lawyer arguing the ethics rules trump the general law on conflicts and losing, see Midboe v. Commission on Ethics for Public Employees, 646 So. 2d. 351 (La. 1994).

cate some requirements and impose additional ones. Judicial decisions interpreting and applying these provisions are a third source of law. Finally, the lawyer codes include provisions that treat the lawyer moving in or out of government somewhat differently than other lawyers who change their employment.[2]

The traditional concerns that infuse the law of conflicts of interest applicable to lawyers in the private sector apply to a government lawyer, but with modifications that reflect the special role. First, confidentiality interests are at stake even though the special characteristics of government legal practice give these interests somewhat different contours. A government agency's confidential information, like that of a private client, must be kept in confidence by the agency's lawyer. Information concerning material prepared in anticipation of litigation (e.g., strategy in litigation, settlement objectives and other work product) is protected by the work product doctrine. Much information possessed by the government, however, is publicly available under laws dealing with public records, open meetings and freedom of information. Moreover, other categories of material possessed by the government are specially protected by law, such as information obtained from private persons by required submission or compulsory process. Thus the tax, health and social security records of individuals, along with grand jury minutes and transcripts, are given special protection by law: It is ordinarily a crime to divulge them unless there is statutory authorization for doing so.

Second, a government lawyer must be loyal to her client but loyalty has a somewhat different meaning in this setting. The role of a government lawyer is different from that of an advocate who seeks to win for a client: "[T]he duty of the public prosecutor [is] to seek justice, not merely to convict, and the duty of all government lawyers [is] to seek just results rather than the result desired by a client."[3] Nor does the normal lawyer-client relationship prevail: The "client" is often amorphous and hard to define, whether it be viewed as the employing agency or the executive branch or "we, the people."[4] A government lawyer may shape and define the interests of her amorphous client more than the typical lawyer in private practice. Nevertheless, a government agency is entitled to protection against side-switching because loyalty continues to be a concern and because side-switching may contribute to a public impression that government decision-making is neither fair nor impartial.

Some additional concerns are operative when dealing with governmental ethics. The metaphor of the "revolving door" conveys at least two special concerns. First, a government official may make decisions not in the public interest to advance the official's future career in private life. She

2. For general discussion of conflicts of former government lawyers, see Wolfram, Modern Legal Ethics § 8.10 (1986); Robert H. Mundheim, Conflict of Interest and the Former Government Employer: Rethinking the Revolving Door, 14 Creighton L. Rev. 707 (1981).

3. ABA Formal Op. 342, reprinted in 62 A.B.A.J. 517, 521 (1976), discussed below at p. 689.

4. See the discussion of "who is the government lawyer's client" in Chapter 8 at p. 785.

may, for example, shape her positions to favor potential private employers or use governmental power to obtain information helpful to future private clients. Some special constraints are appropriate in order to assure the public that government decision-makers exercise public authority for public and not private purposes.

Second, the image of the revolving door suggests undue influence, favoritism and possibly corruption. A lawyer spends a number of years in a government agency acquiring specialized knowledge, skills and experience. They become part of the human capital that makes that person's services more valuable in the private sector. So far, so good.[5] The lawyer also may have acquired inside information, not available to the public or even to other lawyers in the specialty, concerning internal policies and procedures of the agency or leanings on pending matters. She may have personal friendships with agency staff that lead to special treatment in the handling or timing of matters. At the extreme she may have "connections" or "influence" with agency staff who worked for her or with her that shade off into outright corruption. The public is properly concerned with combatting favoritism of this type, which affects the legitimacy of governmental action.

The dangers of the revolving door must be weighed against the advantages to government and to the public of able lawyers moving in and out of public service. A strong theme of American democracy involves citizen participation in and control of government. The American experience has been hostile to the notion of a permanent civil service that dominates the executive branch. The flux of democratic political change and electoral upheavals is thought best served by private citizens moving in and out of governmental service.

In addition, federal and state governments have become dependent upon recruiting young lawyers some of whom do not plan to make government service a lifetime career. The government benefits by hiring a cadre of able young lawyers who carry out a substantial proportion of the government's total legal work. Not all of them could be promoted to leadership roles within the government legal service. Policies that narrowed prospects of private employment would adversely affect the recruitment and quality of new government lawyers. Such policies would also affect the career mobility of lawyers and diminish the opportunity of clients to obtain counsel of choice, particularly in specialized areas of practice.

1.   SOURCES OF LAW ON GOVERNMENT LAWYER'S CONFLICTS

Statutes and Regulations

Federal statutes regulating conflicts of interest fall into two categories: (1) restrictions governing activities during federal employment; and (2)

---

5.   ABA Formal Op. 342, 62 A.B.A.J. at 519, n. 21, states: "Many a lawyer who has served with the government has an advantage when he enters private practice because he has acquired a working knowledge of the department in which he was employed, has learned the procedures, the governing substantive and statutory law and is to a greater or lesser degree an expert in the field in which he was engaged. Certainly this is perfectly proper and ethical...."

restrictions on post-government activities. Examples of the former include: A government employee may not, with limited exceptions, "participate personally or substantially" in any matter in which she or her immediate family or business associates has a financial interest; receive compensation outside of government salary; make or retain certain investments; and receive certain gifts and entertainment.[6] Extensive financial reporting requirements enforce these and other restrictions.

The federal conflict of interest statute, 18 U.S.C. § 207, deals with disqualification of former officers and employees. Penalties for violating that section are set out in 18 U.S.C. § 216. Conduct violating § 207 is punishable by imprisonment for one year or a fine. Those who willfully violate § 207 may be imprisoned for not more than five years or fined. In addition to that punishment, § 216(c) provides that the Attorney General may bring a civil suit against one violating various provisions of the conflicts statute. If she demonstrates by a preponderance of the evidence that the statute has been violated, the defendant may have to pay a civil fine of not more than $50,000 per violation or the amount of compensation received or offered for the prohibited conduct. Any effort to summarize the act's complex provisions is a hazardous undertaking, but three separate bases of disqualification "of a former officer or employee of the executive branch of the United States" are provided:

- A *permanent bar* of the former employee from representing any client before a federal agency or court in "a particular matter" in which "the United States ... is a party or has a direct and substantial interest" when the employee "participated personally and substantially" in the matter while with the government.

- A *two-year bar* of the former employee from representing another in connection with "a particular matter" in which "the United States ... is a party or has a direct and substantial interest" when the employee had "official responsibility" over the matter during the employee's final year with the government.

- A *one-year bar ("cooling-off period")* against any appearances before the same agency or department for any client if the employee was a high-level executive officer.[7]

Regulations promulgated by federal departments and agencies mirror the statutory provisions and frequently add further requirements. Anyone working for the federal government should familiarize herself not just with the conflicts statute but with the relevant agencies particular regulations.[8]

---

6. See also the conflicts rules in the Integrity in Procurement Act, 41 U.S.C. § 423.

7. An executive order of the Clinton Administration required presidential appointees to agree to longer periods of bar as a condition for accepting appointment.

8. The Lobbying Disclosure Act of 1995, 2 U.S.C. 261, regulates lobbyists, requiring, inter alia, that they make semi-annual reports to Congress.

The Office of Governmental Ethics (OGE) provides advice to federal government employees regarding conflict of interest rules, and compiles information on prosecutions under the conflicts statute. OGE materials are available on the Internet at <www.usoge.gov>.

Virtually every state has statutory provisions governing conflicts of interest on the part of state and municipal employees and those acting on behalf of government agencies.[9]

Conflicts of interest statutes raise many difficult interpretive questions. For example, in United States v. Nofziger,[10] a former top assistant to President Reagan challenged his conviction for violating the one-year bar applicable to high-level government executives. Nofziger, who had established a political consulting firm after leaving his White House post, lobbied White House officials on behalf of three clients within the one-year period. Nofziger claimed that, while he knowingly lobbied the White House, the government had not proved that he did so with the requisite intent— *knowledge* that the White House had a "direct and substantial interest" in the matters. The court reversed Nofziger's conviction, stating that the government's view that intent to influence the White House violated the statute "would impose strict liability on a lobbyist who is misinformed." Doesn't the court's interpretation put a premium on staying misinformed? Why would Nofziger be communicating with the White House with the intent to influence it if he did not think it had a "direct and substantial interest" in the matter?

In addition to statutes and regulations governing members of the executive branch, legislatures have rules that govern their members with restrictions that may implicate lawyer members or lawyers who have dealings with legislators.[11] Federal and state provisions governing legislators are generally more porous than those governing executive branch officials, but on some matters, for example, the receipt of outside income and gifts, they are apt to be detailed and specific.

Judicial Creation of a Special Ethics Rule

The profession's ethics rules apply on their face to all lawyers, including government lawyers. Their provisions become enforceable against gov-

---

9. See generally Rachel E. Boehm, Caught in the Revolving Door: A State Lawyer's Guide to Post–Employment Restrictions, 15 Rev. Litig. 525 (1996) (cataloguing state statutes). Two states with strict provisions are New York and Missouri. See N.Y. Pub. Off.Law § 73 (proscribing a two year bar on former employees' practicing before the state agencies for whom they worked); Mo. Ann. Stat. § 105,454 (prohibiting former state employees from all "attempts to influence a decision of any agency of the state" for one year after leaving government employment).

10. 878 F.2d 442 (D.C.Cir.), cert. denied, 110 S.Ct. 564 (1989).

11. The 1990–91 Senate inquiry into the conduct of the "Keating Five"—five Senators who simultaneously received major campaign contributions from the savings-and-loan mogul and intervened on his behalf with federal regulatory authorities—raised novel questions concerning senatorial ethics. See Richard L. Berke, Appearances Worry Congress as S. & L. Shadow Lengthens, N.Y. Times, July 29, 1990, at p. 1.

ernment lawyers when adopted by a state in which a government lawyer is admitted to or engaged in practice; when adopted by a federal court before which the lawyer makes an appearance; and when adopted by an agency by which the lawyer is employed. More specific requirements of state or federal law, however, may displace an ethics rule.

DR 9–101 of the Model Code provides that a lawyer shall not accept employment in a private matter upon which she acted as a judge or in which she had substantial responsibility while a public employee. This rule disqualifies a lawyer from subsequent representation of a private party in a matter in which the lawyer had substantial responsibility while with the government, *even if the private party is on the "same side" as the government*. The prohibition is broader than the general rule on subsequent representation of private clients developed in the case law and codified in M.R. 1.9(a), which applies only when the present client's interests are *adverse* to the interests of the former client, i.e., when the lawyer has "switched sides." Moreover, this broader disqualification rule is continued in Model Rule 1.11(a). Why the stricter rule for government lawyers?[12]

DR 5–105(D) provides that when one lawyer is disqualified the whole firm is disqualified. When read together with DR 9–101, this would require the disqualification of the entire firm in any case in which the former government lawyer had substantial responsibility. Moreover, neither provision provided for removal of the disqualification by waiver, i.e., consent of the appropriate government agency. However, the ABA, the courts and state ethics committees interpreted these rules to allow firms to proceed if the disqualified former government lawyer was screened from participation.

ABA Formal Opinion 342 led the way in rejecting the imputed disqualification of a firm employing a former government lawyer: The "weighty policy considerations" that support the allowance of screening of a former government lawyer to cure the conflict are:

> the ability of government to recruit young professionals and competent lawyers should not be interfered with by imposition of harsh restraints upon future practice nor should too great a sacrifice be demanded of the lawyers willing to enter government service; the rule serves no worthwhile public interest if it becomes a mere tool enabling a litigant to improve his prospects by depriving his opponent of competent counsel; and the rule should not be permitted to interfere needlessly with the right of litigants to obtain competent counsel of their own

---

12. ABA Formal Op. 342 (Nov. 24, 1975), reprinted in 62 A.B.A. J. 517, 518 (1976) summarized the policy considerations supporting a broader restriction not requiring material adversity:

the treachery of switching sides; the safeguarding of confidential governmental information from future use against the government; the need to discourage government lawyers from handling particular assignments in such a way as to encourage their own future employment in regard to those particular matters after leaving government service; and the professional benefit derived from avoiding the appearance of evil.

choosing, particularly in specialized areas requiring special technical training and experience.[13]

The opinion noted that a literal reading of DR 5–105(D) would disqualify a government agency from handling a matter in the reverse situation of a private lawyer joining the government. "Necessity dictates that government action not be hampered by such a construction of DR 5–105(D)." The opinion concluded, "whenever the government agency is satisfied that screening measures will effectively isolate the individual lawyer from participating in the particular matter and sharing in the fees attributable to it, and that there is no appearance of significant impropriety affecting the interests of the government, the government may waive the disqualification of the firm." Shortly thereafter, Kesselhaut v. United States[14] went further in holding that the government agency's consent was not required.

ARMSTRONG v. MCALPIN.[15] This is the leading decision on screening of the former government lawyer under the Model Code. In 1974 Altman, while at the SEC, had supervised an SEC investigation growing out of the collapse of the Capital Growth investment companies, in which McAlpin was a principal figure. When the bubble burst, McAlpin fled to Costa Rica. In 1975 Altman left the SEC and joined the Gordon firm in New York City. Armstrong, the receiver of the corporation victimized by the fraud, had originally retained his own law firm (Barrett) in an effort to track down assets and claims of the bankrupt company against McAlpin and others. The SEC turned over its investigatory files to the receiver. When a conflict of interest problem required withdrawal of the Barrett firm, the receiver then sought to employ the Gordon firm because some of its lawyers had the specialized competencies required. Because Altman was personally disqualified, his presence in the Gordon firm was a problem but Armstrong and the firm, with the approval of the district court and the consent of the SEC, went ahead after screening Altman from the case.

The majority of the en banc panel upheld the district court's refusal to disqualify the Gordon firm under these circumstances. Although "reasonable minds may and do differ on the ethical propriety of screening in this context," imputed disqualification is not required absent a threat of taint to the trial. Because disqualification motions affect a client's choice of counsel, are used for tactical purposes and result in delay in reaching the merits, disciplinary standards should not be applied inflexibly. Unfair use of privileged government information was not involved since the SEC had made its files available to the receiver. Concerns about the "appearance of impropriety" are "disserved by an order of disqualification in a case such

---

13. Id. at 518–19.

14. 555 F.2d 791 (Ct.Cl.1977) (rejecting an inflexible rule of imputed disqualification of the former government lawyer's new firm and also rejecting a requirement of government consent to the representation). See also Comm. on Prof. & Jud. Ethics of Ass'n of Bar of City of New York, Op. 889, 31 Record 552 (1976).

15. 625 F.2d 433 (en banc, 2d Cir.1980), vacated 449 U.S. 1106 (1981). *Armstrong* is frequently cited even though the decision was vacated on jurisdictional grounds on the basis of Firestone Tire & Rubber Co. v. Risjord, 449 U.S. 368 (1981), holding denial of disqualification motions nonappealable. See, e.g., Telectronics Proprietary Ltd. v. Medtronic, Inc., 836 F.2d 1332, 1335 (Fed. Cir.1988).

as this, where no threat of taint exists and where appellants' motion to disqualify opposing counsel has successfully crippled the efforts of a receiver, appointed at the request of a public agency, to obtain redress for alleged serious frauds on the investing public."[16]

Judge Newman, dissenting to the rejection of imputed disqualification, argued that "[t]he purposes of DR 9–101(B) cannot be fully achieved unless there is no possibility that the government attorney can be (or seem to be) influenced by the prospect of later private employment."[17] Disqualification of the former government lawyer's firm was required to prevent unfair use of information unavailable to the other side and because of public fears that screening would be ineffective. "[T]he public will not believe ... [that] Altman will not in fact disclose to his partners anything he learned while exercising substantial government responsibilities for related matters."[18]

Armstrong's approval of screening is much more tentative than that of ABA Opinion 342. First, the case does not involve side-switching—the private action is a follow-up of the SEC enforcement effort and consistent with it. Second, according to the majority, no confidential government information was involved. Third, the decision states that "reasonable minds can differ" on the question involved and emphasizes the special circumstances and facts of the particular case.

Model Rules of Professional Conduct

Under the Model Rules, lawyers who move between the government and private practice are bound by the conflicts rules applicable to all lawyers. Thus, M.R. 1.7 applies not only to private lawyers but to government and former government lawyers, as does M.R. 1.9, as originally adopted, and M.R. 1.9(a) and (c), as amended in 1989.[19] In addition, the special provisions in M.R. 1.11 apply to lawyers moving between private and government practice.

Model Rule 1.11(a) does two things: first, for an individual lawyer formerly with the government and now in private practice, the rule augments the prohibitions on subsequent representation found in M.R. 1.9; second, for a firm hiring a lawyer formerly with the government, it limits disqualification by imputation.

As to the individual lawyer now in private practice, who formerly worked for the government, M.R. 1.11(a) provides that where a lawyer participated in a matter *personally and substantially* while working for the government, the lawyer may not later represent a private client in connection with that matter unless the government agency consents or other law expressly permits the representation. Like its predecessor provision in the Code, M.R. 1.11(a) applies whether or not the present client's interests are adverse to the former client (the government).

16. 625 F.2d at 446.

17. 625 F.2d at 453.

18. Id.

19. See the Comments to these rules, which make it clear that while M.R. 1.11 only applies to former and present government lawyers, rules 1.6, 1.7 and 1.9 apply to all lawyers, government and former government lawyers included.

Even though the lawyer's present involvement may not be prohibited by M.R. 1.11(a), the former government lawyer must also make sure that M.R. 1.9(a) does not prohibit the representation. M.R. 1.9(a) does not require "personal and substantial" involvement in the former representation before it is triggered. Thus, when a present client's interests are adverse to those of the government, the former government lawyer's disqualification in a substantially related matter is broader than the limitation of M.R. 1.11(a) alone.

Consent from the appropriate government agency (the former client) allows the individual lawyer to proceed under M.R. 1.11(a). As with consent under M.R. 1.9(a), the government's consent under M.R. 1.11(a) does not waive the government's right to preservation of its confidences. The lawyer's duty to preserve the government's confidences under M.R. 1.9(c) and M.R. 1.6 remains in effect unless expressly waived.

M.R. 1.11(a) provides that when a lawyer is disqualified under this subsection (because she participated personally and substantially in the matter while with the government), the lawyer's entire firm is disqualified unless:

> (1) the disqualified lawyer is screened from any participation in the matter and is apportioned no part of the fee therefrom; and

> (2) written notice is promptly given to the appropriate government agency to enable it to ascertain compliance with the provisions of this rule.[20]

Notice to, not consent of, the government agency is required before the firm may proceed. The government's consent is necessary for the *individual lawyer* to participate (to avoid screening) but is unnecessary for representation by the *lawyer's firm* once the firm screens the lawyer. Why this distinction? Bear in mind that some governmental bodies may lack authority to waive a conflict of interest objection and others prefer a notification procedure that does not require formal agency action.

2. DISQUALIFICATION OF FORMER GOVERNMENT LAWYERS

Securities Investor Protection Corp. (SIPC) v. Vigman

United States District Court, Central District of California, 1984.
587 F.Supp. 1358.

■ TASHIMA, DISTRICT JUDGE.

This is an action brought by the Securities Investor Protection Corporation ("SIPC").... The complaint names seventy-five individual and

---

20. D.C. R.Prof.Conduct, Rule 1.11 (1990) imposes stiffer notice requirements: The personally disqualified lawyer is required to file with the government agency involved and serve on all other parties to the proceeding a signed document attesting that she will not participate in or discuss the matter with any other lawyer in the firm and will not share in any fees attributable to the matter. Another lawyer from the disqualified lawyer's firm must also file with the government and serve on all other parties a signed document attesting that all affiliated lawyers are aware that the disqualified lawyer must be screened and describing the screening procedures which the firm is implementing. Should these notice provisions have been included in the Model Rules' provision?

corporate defendants and alleges numerous violations of § 10(b) of the Securities Exchange Act of 1934 (the "Exchange Act"), 15 U.S.C. §§ 78a et seq., and Rule 10b–5 promulgated thereunder, the Racketeer Influenced and Corrupt Organizations Act, 18 U.S.C. §§ 1961 et seq. ("RICO"), fraud and breaches of fiduciary duty under California common law.... I address here, the motion of defendant Isadore Diamond, joined in by five other defendants, to disqualify SIPC's counsel.

BACKGROUND

Gerald E. Boltz and Charles R. Hartman are members of the law firm of Rogers & Wells and counsel of record for plaintiff SIPC in this action. Both attorneys formerly were employed by the Securities and Exchange Commission ("SEC" or the "Commission"). Boltz was employed as an attorney by the SEC for approximately 20 years, from 1959 until 1979. From 1972 until 1979, he was Regional Administrator of the SEC's Los Angeles Regional Office. Hartman was employed as an attorney by the SEC for approximately 11 years, from 1969 to 1980. From 1972 until 1980, he was assigned to the SEC's Los Angeles Regional Office, where he held the position of regional counsel from 1976 to 1980.

During the early 1970s, two related proceedings were instituted by the SEC against, among others, certain of the defendants named in this action. The first was a Commission administrative proceeding brought by the SEC's Washington Office in March, 1971.... The second was a civil injunctive action filed in this court by the SEC's Los Angeles Regional Office [in 1973].... The gravamen of the complaint in that action was the alleged fraudulent manipulation of the common stock of DCS Financial Corporation ("DCS"). Although the scope of the responsibilities and actions of Boltz and Hartman in those proceedings is in dispute, it is uncontested that Boltz signed the complaint and trial brief in the 1973 civil action and that Hartman appeared as trial counsel for the SEC in that action.

The complaint in the instant action, filed July 22, 1983, was signed by Boltz and lists Rogers & Wells and, among others, Hartman as attorneys, for plaintiff SIPC. Like the 1973 civil action and the 1971 administrative proceeding, plaintiff alleges the manipulation of a number of securities. The instant action, however, alleges an extremely elaborate scheme, encompassing the manipulation of seven securities on the over-the-counter market, including the securities of Bunnington Corp. ("Bunnington"), the company into which DCS had merged. As stated, the complaint charges numerous violations of the anti-manipulative provisions of the Exchange Act and RICO, as well as other violations of law. Certain of the claimed violations are based on asserted securities manipulations which occurred prior to the 1971 administrative proceeding and the 1973 civil action.

Defendants seek to disqualify Boltz, Hartman and Rogers & Wells from further representing SIPC in this action on the ground that continued representation by these former government attorneys in a matter connected to their government work contravenes the ethical standards of the legal profession.

I. THE APPLICABLE STANDARD OF PROFESSIONAL RESPONSIBILITY

Defendants contend that Boltz and Hartman's representation of SIPC in this action violates Rule 1.11(a) of the American Bar Association's ("ABA") recently adopted Model Rules of Professional Conduct (1983) ("Model Rules"). [The court quoted the text of Rule 1.11(a).][1]

Since SIPC does not contend that Boltz and Hartman have been screened from participation in this action, disqualification of either of these attorneys would require that Rogers & Wells also be disqualified. Model Rule 1.11(a)(1).

The district court has primary responsibility for controlling the conduct of attorneys practicing before it. Trone v. Smith, 621 F.2d 994, 999 (9th Cir.1980). Although the ABA does not establish rules of law that are binding on this Court, it is the Court's prerogative to disqualify counsel based on contravention of the ABA Model Rules.... This is true, despite the fact that neither this Court's Local Rules nor the Rules of Professional Conduct of the State Bar of California expressly refers to the ABA Model Rules. As the Ninth Circuit has recently stated:

> Despite the deletion in 1975 of a reference to the ABA Model Code in the Rules of Professional Conduct of the State Bar of California ... the California courts continue to rely on the Model Code in addressing issues not covered precisely by the Rules of Professional Conduct of the State Bar of California.

... But see People v. Ballard, 104 Cal.App.3d 757, 761, 164 Cal.Rptr. 81 (1980) (dictum) ("conduct of California attorneys is governed by California Rules of Professional Conduct" not ABA Model Code).

Because California courts have consistently looked to the Model Code, the predecessor of the Model Rules, as a source of ethical principles governing the conduct of California lawyers, I conclude that Rule 1.11(a) is an appropriate standard to apply in this case. See Local Rule 2.5.1 (requiring lawyers to comply with "decisions of any court applicable" to "standards of professional conduct required of members of the State Bar of California"). As noted, Rule 1.11(a) is substantially similar to former DR 9–101(B). Thus, California attorneys are, or should be, apprised of the standard of responsibility encompassed by the rule, from decisions of California and federal courts applying former DR 9–101(B).[2]

---

1. Except for the provision allowing representation when "the appropriate government agency consents after consultation," Rule 1.11(a) is similar to former Disciplinary Rule ("DR") 9–101(B), which provided that "[a] lawyer shall not accept private employment in a matter in which he had substantial responsibility while he was a public employee." Model Code of Professional Responsibility DR 9–101(B) (1979). See also footnote 9, ante.

2. Although the ABA Model Rules were not adopted until Aug. 2, 1983, 11 days after this action was commenced, they are the

SIPC contends that Rule 1.11(a) was meant to apply only to "switching sides" cases, that is, situations where a former government attorney seeks to represent a private litigant whose interests are adverse to the government. SIPC argues that such a limitation is supported by the rule's allowance of an otherwise prohibited representation when "the appropriate government agency consents after consultation." I disagree. Nowhere in the Model Rules, the Comments, or the ABA draft proposals is there support for limiting Rule 1.11(a) to switching sides cases....

Neither *Woods* [v. Covington County Bank, 537 F.2d 804 (5th Cir. 1976)] nor *General Motors* [v. City of New York, 501 F.2d 639 (2d Cir.1974)—two cases cited in notes to the 1981 draft of the Model Rules—] involved an attorney switching sides. In fact, the focus in both of these cases was not on whether or not an attorney had switched sides, but instead, was on avoiding the "appearance of impropriety." In *General Motors*, the City of New York brought an action against a bus manufacturer alleging an unlawful nationwide monopoly. One of the City's attorneys formerly had been employed by the Department of Justice and during that time had substantial responsibility in the investigatory and preparatory stages of a similar antitrust action against the same manufacturer. The court, in disqualifying the attorney from further representation of the City, noted that the purpose behind former Canon 9 and DR 9–101(B), as stated in ABA Formal Opinion No. 37 (1931), was to avoid:

> the manifest possibility ... [that a former government lawyer's] action as a public legal official might be influenced (or open to the charge that it had been influenced) by the hope of later being employed privately to *uphold* or *upset* what he had done.

501 F.2d at 649 (emphasis in the original). The court further recognized that its responsibility was:

> to preserve a balance, delicate though it may be, between an individual's right to his own freely chosen counsel ... and the need to maintain the highest ethical standards of professional responsibility. This balance is essential if the public's trust in the integrity of the Bar is to be preserved.

Id., quoting Emle Indus., Inc. v. Patentex, Inc., 478 F.2d 562, 564–65 (2d Cir.1973). The disqualification was not based on actual impropriety, but in order to avoid the appearance of impropriety and to safeguard the "public's trust." Id.

In *Woods*, the Fifth Circuit found no such danger of public mistrust. There, a former naval reserve attorney, during service, had investigated a securities fraud allegedly perpetrated on returning ex-prisoners of war ("POWs") on behalf of the POWs. He later represented the POWs in a private fraud action. The district court's disqualification order was reversed because, the court concluded, the attorney's conduct could not conceivably

appropriate standard against which to test the *continued* representation of SIPC. Moreover, as the ensuing discussion will indicate, the outcome of the analysis under former Canon 9 and DR 9–101(B) would not differ.

impugn the public's trust in the Navy or the legal profession. This was due, in large part, to the fact that

> as a legal assistance officer … [the attorney] did not possess any investigative authority beyond that available to a private lawyer.… Neither is there any allegation that [the attorney] ever held himself out to be an investigating officer acting on behalf of the United States Navy or as having any special governmental authority.

537 F.2d at 817.

… SIPC's contention that the "government consent" provision was meant to limit the application of Rule 1.11(a) to switching sides cases is contrary to the drafters' reliance on *Woods* and *General Motors* and, therefore, must be rejected. I now turn to an examination of the substantive aspects of the rule.[3]

II.   APPLICATION OF RULE 1.11(a)

A.   Agency Consent

As indicated, Rule 1.11(a) appears to allow an otherwise prohibited representation by a former government attorney when "the appropriate government agency consents after consultation." When, at the hearing on the motion, the Court confirmed that agency consent had not been sought, SIPC was directed to consult with the Commission to ascertain whether it would consent to the continued representation of SIPC by Boltz and Hartman. The SEC was then contacted by Rogers & Wells, as well as a number of other counsel in this action. The Commission has declined to give its consent, stating:

> [T]he Commission believes that as a general matter, a policy of waiving the personal disqualification of former Commission lawyers to permit them to participate in the matters which they handled while on the staff could undermine the public's confidence in the activities of the Commission's lawyers. After reviewing the factors relevant to this case, the Commission sees nothing unique in this situation which would warrant deviating from that general principle. Therefore, the Commission has determined that it would not waive any disqualification personal to Messrs. Boltz and Hartman, pursuant to Rule 1.11(a).[4]

The Commission's declination to waive personal disqualification in this case must be accepted as that agency's discretionary determination, as contemplated by the rule, that this is not a situation where waiver of disqualification would be in the public interest. However, it remains to be

---

3.   SIPC argues that this motion is governed by Model Rule 1.11(b), rather than Rule 1.11(a). [The court then quoted M.R. 1.11(b).] Possible disqualification under this rule is independent of and in addition to any basis for disqualification under Rule 1.11(a). Because I conclude that disqualification is required under Rule 1.11(a), I do not reach the question of whether Rule 1.11(b) also applies.

4.   The Commission's determination was communicated to counsel in a letter signed by its General Counsel. A copy of that letter, dated February 28, 1984, is appended hereto.

considered whether the predicate requirements for the application of Rule 1.11(a) are here present.[5]

B.   Same Matter

Although the ABA Model Rules do not define the term "matter" as used in Rule 1.11(a), it can be said that a matter includes a "discrete, identifiable transaction or conduct involving a particular situation and specific parties." See ABA Formal Opinion No. 342 (1975). Opinion No. 342 provides the following examples:

> The same lawsuit or litigation is the same matter. The same issue of fact involving the same parties and the same situation or conduct is the same matter.... [T]he same "matter" is not involved [when] ... there is lacking the discrete, identifiable transaction or conduct involving a particular situation and specific parties.

SIPC contends that, under this definition, the 1973 civil action is not the same matter as the instant action. However, examination of the instant complaint belies this contention. In paragraph 200 of the complaint, in support of the first claim for violation of RICO, plaintiffs allege:

> that at various times prior to November, 1967, *and thereafter, Vigman ... and Diamond* participated in a fraudulent scheme to manipulate the prices of various securities, including ... *DCS Corporation (a corporation subsequently merged with Bunnington)....* *Said conduct violated Section 10(b) of the Exchange Act and Rule 10b–5.*

(Emphasis added.) In paragraph 211 of the complaint, plaintiffs further allege:

> that between November, 1967 and January, 1971, in furtherance of the racketeering enterprise, Vigman, Diamond, and others engaged in a scheme to defraud the public in violation of the Securities Act, the Exchange Act and Rule 10b–5. This scheme involved the placement of unregistered securities into the marketplace and the subsequent manipulation of the price of those securities for the benefit of the RICO Defendants.

The complaint also alleges that defendant Vigman, despite being barred from the securities business on November 1, 1967, "continued to exercise control over Newport Securities Corp.", as well as a number of issuers, including Bunnington, and that the racketeering enterprise was carried out through, inter alia, Newport Securities.

It must be remembered that the subject of the 1973 civil action was the alleged manipulation of DCS stock by, among others, Vigman and Diamond (defendants here) in violation of, inter alia, § 10(b) of the Exchange Act and Rule 10b–5. Although the subject of the 1973 civil action largely was

---

5. As explained in the SEC's letter, the Commission has "made no determination" that this action and the 1973 civil action "are the same particular matter and that Messrs. Boltz and Hartman had personal and substantial responsibility for both matters."

alleged manipulations occurring in 1972, the complaint in the 1973 civil action also alleged fraudulent manipulation of securities "since about September 15, 1970."

It is evident that paragraphs 200, 208, 211 and 212 of the instant complaint refer to the same matter that was the subject of the 1973 civil action. Although this is not a situation where the subsequent complaint was "lifted ad haec verba" from the SEC complaint, *General Motors*, 501 F.2d at 650, I find that a discrete series of transactions involving a specific situation and specific parties in the 1973 civil action is part and parcel of a subsequent, broader allegation of widespread securities fraud and racketeering in the case at bench. The essence of the complaint here is that, since 1967, Vigman, Diamond and others have engaged in a sophisticated conspiracy to manipulate the price of securities. Thus, the complaint includes among its allegations, the alleged manipulation of the price of DCS stock by, among others, Diamond and Vigman, which allegation was the precise subject of the 1973 civil action. Therefore, I find that Boltz and Hartman are representing SIPC "in connection with a matter" which the SEC prosecuted in the 1973 civil action, within the meaning of Rule 1.11(a).[7]

C. Personal and Substantial Participation

SIPC argues that neither Boltz nor Hartman personally and substantially participated in the 1973 civil action. However, it is uncontroverted that Boltz signed both the complaint and the trial brief in that action. Although in his declaration Boltz states that his signatures "merely reflect a general SEC practice and policy that a Regional Administrator should personally sign the initial complaint in any action filed by that office," his argument ignores that plain requirement of F.R.Civ.P. 11. At the time Boltz signed the complaint and trial brief, Rule 11 provided that "[t]he signature of an attorney constitutes a certificate by him that he has read the pleading; that to the best of his knowledge, information, and belief there is good ground to support it." The Ninth Circuit has interpreted this language to require an attorney, before filing a civil action, "to make an investigation to ascertain that it has at least some merit, and further to ascertain that the damages sought appear to bear a reasonable relation to the injuries actually sustained." ... Therefore, when Boltz, as Regional Administrator, signed the complaint and trial brief, he assumed, as a matter of law, the personal and substantial responsibility of ensuring that there existed good ground to support the SEC's case and that it had, at least, some merit.[9] The assumption and proper discharge of that responsi-

---

7. Because of this finding, it is unnecessary to and I do not reach the question of whether this action also involves the same matter as the 1971 administrative proceeding.

9. One reason the Model Rule employs the term "participated personally and substantially" is because the term "substantial responsibility" used in former DR 9–101(B), "could disqualify the former head of a large governmental agency from private employment with respect to any matter arising during his tenure. See Cleveland v. Cleveland Elec. Illum. Co., 440 F.Supp.

bility required his personal and substantial participation in the action. That Boltz had such responsibility under law is further indicated by former Rule 11's provision that an attorney who violated the rule "may be subjected to appropriate disciplinary action." I, thus, find that Boltz had personal and substantial responsibility over and participation in the 1973 civil action within the meaning of Rule 1.11(a).[10] Cf. Telos, Inc. v. Hawaiian Tel. Co., 397 F.Supp. 1314, 1316 n. 11 (D.Haw.1975) ("Signing a complaint, is, ... by itself, except in rare circumstances, the exercise of substantial responsibility" under former DR 9–101(B).).

With respect to Hartman, it is not contested that he appeared at the trial as counsel of record on each day of the three-day trial in the 1973 civil action. However, Hartman contends that his role at the trial merely was to supervise an attorney-colleague at the SEC, who had no prior trial experience. Hartman further declares that all of the legal work in the 1973 civil action, "including both the actual preparation and the trial itself, was performed by" the other trial attorney.

Be that as it may, it is unlikely that an experienced attorney would or could effectively and properly supervise an inexperienced colleague without familiarizing himself with the facts of the case and the applicable law. To this end, Hartman no doubt had access to records, both public and confidential, relating to the case. It is difficult to conceive how an experienced attorney could carry out the type of supervisory role assigned to Hartman without becoming familiar with the evidence to be presented both by and against the SEC and conferring with and advising his less-experienced colleague during the course of the three-day trial. Therefore, I find that Hartman also had personal and substantial responsibility over and participation in the 1973 civil action within the meaning of Rule 1.11(a).

III.   CONCLUSION

Because courts have differed as to whether the somewhat subjective standard of the "appearance of impropriety" under former Canon 9 and DR 9–101 was an appropriate one to guide the conduct of lawyers, Model Rule 1.11(a) "sets forth more specifically the circumstances in which concern for public confidence in government necessitates disqualification of a government lawyer." 1981 Draft Notes at 304. The concerns addressed, however, remain the same. The specific circumstances requiring disqualification

---

193 (N.D.Ohio 1977); ABA Formal Opinion 342 (1975) [other citations omitted]." Boltz's disqualification here is not based on his "substantial responsibility" as Regional Administrator of the SEC's Los Angeles Regional Office, but on his personal substantial responsibility and participation in the 1973 civil action as an attorney who, by signing the complaint and trial brief and other actions personally participated substantially in the 1973 civil action. An attorney who personally signs the pleadings in an action is not immunized from Rule 11's imposition of personal responsibility because he also happens to be the head of a governmental office.

10. Further evidence of Boltz's personal participation in the 1973 civil action is found in the response of the SEC staff attorney who deposed defendant Diamond to Diamond's request for a copy of his deposition transcript: "Mr. Boltz has asked me to assure you on behalf of the [SEC] staff" that such a copy would be provided.

under Rule 1.11(a) have been met here. Because I find that Boltz and Hartman are representing a private client in connection with a matter in which both of them participated personally and substantially while employed by the SEC, and because the Commission has declined to consent to such representation, these attorneys and Rogers & Wells must be disqualified from further representation of SIPC in this action. Of course, this ruling is intended in no way to suggest any actual wrongdoing on the part of the attorneys involved or their law firm. Rather, this ruling is intended to effectuate the prophylactic purpose of Rule 1.11(a). See General Motors Corp., 501 F.2d at 649.

[The letter from the SEC, declining to consent to any personal disqualification of Boltz and Hartman, included the following footnote:

While Model Rule 1.11(a) permits a government agency to waive the personal disqualification of its former lawyers, 18 U.S.C. § 207, the federal post-employment statute would, if applicable, presumably eliminate any such discretionary action by a federal agency. While authoritative interpretations of Section 207 are the province of the Office of Government Ethics and the Department of Justice, it appears that Section 207 does not apply in this instance.]

————

SIPC and Model Rule 1.11

Boltz and Hartman are prohibited from representing SIPC under M.R. 1.11(a) if the representation involves the same "matter," they "participated personally and substantially" in the government's handling of it, and the government has not consented to the representation.[1] Consider each of these elements of Model Rule 1.11(a).

The court in *SIPC* says that the Model Rules do not define the word "matter" as used in M.R. 1.11(a). The court is in error in this respect. M.R. 1.11(d) defines "matter" "as used in this rule" as including:

    (1) any judicial or other proceeding, application, request for a ruling or other determination, contract, claim, controversy, investigation, charge, accusation, arrest or other particular matter involving a specific party or parties; and

    (2) any other matter covered by the conflict of interest rules of the appropriate government agency.

---

1. *ACC/Lincoln*, printed at p. 745 infra, provides another example of "revolving door" representation by a former government lawyer. Lawyer Schilling, who as a government bank regulator had expressed concerns about Lincoln's "serious regulatory violations," was engaged six months later in soliciting Lincoln's business on behalf of his new employer, Jones Day. Settlement of the government's claims against Jones Day and Schilling included provisions barring Schilling from representing thrifts or holding positions in the banking industry. See Wade Lambert, Jones Day Settles Claim at Lincoln Thrift, Wall St.J., Apr. 20, 1993, at p. B12.

ABA Formal Opinion 342, discussed above at p. 689, gave some examples of government lawyering that did not constitute the "same matter":

> [W]ork as a government employee in drafting, enforcing or interpreting government or agency procedures, regulations, or laws, or in briefing abstract principles of law, does not disqualify the lawyer under DR 9–101(B) from subsequent private employment involving the same regulations, procedures, or points of law; the same "matter" is not involved because there is lacking the discrete, identifiable transactions or conduct involving a particular situation and specific parties.[2]

Are these examples consistent with "matter" as defined in M.R. 1.11(d)? Under 1.11(d) should a former government prosecutor be precluded from later representing someone whom he had prosecuted for the government on a similar charge?[3] Should a criminal defendant's right to counsel affect how broadly the court's read 1.11(d) to disqualify former prosecutors?[4]

The Department of Justice, in its comments to the Kutak Commission's draft of the Model Rules, argued that the final version of the Model Rules should make clear that the definition of "matter" does not include "such prior government activities as drafting proposed legislation, participation in rulemaking, or reviewing government contracts [because an] overly broad categorization of disqualifying activity could impede government hiring significantly."[5] Are these activities included in the definition of "matter" in M.R. 1.11(d)?

Suppose the lawyers involved in *SIPC* had participated only in an effort by the SEC to issue guidelines for prohibited forms of stock manipulation? An effort to issue formal regulations on this subject?

Personal and Substantial Participation

ABA Opinion 342, interpreting the Model Code language, stressed the government lawyer's participation in "investigative or deliberative processes:"

> "[S]ubstantial responsibility" envisages a much closer and more direct relationship than that of mere perfunctory approval or disapproval of the matter in question. It contemplates a responsibility requiring the official to become personally involved to an important, material degree, in the investigative or deliberative processes regarding the transactions or facts in question. Thus, being the chief official in some vast office or organization does not *ipso facto* give that government official or em-

---

2. ABA Formal Opinion 342, 62 A.B.A.J. at 599.

3. Note that Rule 1.9 might present an alternative ground for disqualification in this situation. This matter is explored further in the text under Personal and Substantial Participation.

4. See U.S. v. Escobar–Orejuela, 910 F.Supp. 92 (E.D.N.Y. 1995) (reading the conflicts rules narrowly in this context due to the defendant's right to counsel of his choice).

5. Letter from Ass't Att'y Gen. Jonathan C. Rose to Robert J. Kutak, July 23, 1982, p. 2.

ployee the "substantial responsibility" contemplated by the rule in regard to all the minutiae of facts lodged within that office. Yet it is not necessary that the public employee or official shall have personally and in a substantial manner investigated or passed upon the particular matter, for it is sufficient that he had such a heavy responsibility for the matter in question that it is unlikely he did not become personally and substantially involved in the investigative or deliberative processes regarding that matter. . . .

The Model Rules' provision, unlike the Model Code, adds the adverb "personally" to describe the kind of involvement that will trigger the rule. What difference does this make?

Suppose Boltz had been a commissioner of the SEC at the time of the Commission's investigation of Vigman and others. He had been briefed about the matter at a Commission meeting, but no formal agency action was required. Suppose, alternatively, that he had been head of the SEC's enforcement division and had signed papers permitting the investigation and formal proceeding to go forward, but without acquiring detailed familiarity with the facts. Do these constitute the requisite degree of participation?

Note that when the lawyer did not personally and substantially participate in a matter but did work on the matter (or a substantially related matter) while with the government, the lawyer may be disqualified from acting adverse to the government in a subsequent case under Rule 1.9.[6]

Government Consent and Screening

M.R. 1.11(a) permits the government to waive the individual lawyer's disqualification. If consent is either not requested or not granted, the firm may still continue the representation provided the disqualified lawyer is isolated from all involvement in the case. Unlike Opinion 342, however, M.R. 1.11(a) does not require the government's consent to continued representation and screening. The firm's only obligation is promptly to notify the government agency involved so that it may monitor the firm's compliance with the rule's dictates on screening the lawyer. Is Opinion 342's requirement of consent to the screening a better rule?

If the lawyers for SIPC had formerly represented another private party against Vigman, they could represent SIPC now because M.R. 1.9 only applies when interests of the former and present clients are adverse. When consent was requested in *SIPC*, the SEC refused on the basis of its general policy. Is the SEC's general policy wise? What would be wrong with a policy to grant consent, absent special circumstances, whenever the lawyer was on the same side of the matter in the private case as she was when she worked for the government?

If the SEC had consented to participation by Boltz and Hartman in *SIPC*, the question whether they were barred by M.R. 1.11(b) would need

---

6. See, e.g., Violet v. Brown, 9 Vet. App. 530 (1996) (applying 1.9 to disqualify a lawyer that did not personally and substantially participate but who did switch sides).

to be faced. How should it be resolved? See the discussion of "confidential government information" below.

Was the *SIPC* court correct in stating that a "prophylactic" disqualification does not "suggest any actual wrongdoing on the part of the attorneys or their law firm"? Doesn't violation of a "prophylactic" ethics rule subject a lawyer to potential discipline? And what about the criminal law? Did Boltz and Hartman violate the criminal prohibitions of 18 U.S.C. § 207, discussed above at p. 687? Why does the SEC say in its letter that the statute "appears" to be inapplicable?

Confidential Government Information

As used in M.R. 1.11(b), the phrase "confidential government information" protects the confidences of persons about whom the government has acquired information.[7] The confidences of the government itself are protected by M.R. 1.6.

M.R. 1.11(b) provides that a lawyer who, by virtue of her former government employment, has "confidential government information about a person ... may not represent a private client whose interests are adverse to that person in a matter in which the information could be used to the material disadvantage of that person." The government has no power to waive this provision. The trigger for M.R. 1.11(b) is not whether the matters are the same, but whether the lawyer has "confidential government information" about a third party.

In light of M.R. 1.11(b), consider again the question of whether one level of government should be treated as a private client with respect to 1.11(a)'s prohibitions. Should one agency of government be considered a private client with respect to former employment by a different agency of the same government? Bear in mind that government agencies are not free to share information gathered about private parties with other agencies at their own discretion. Other law may restrict the transfer of information between government agencies. See, e.g., Fed.R.Crim.P. 6(e) (dealing with grand jury and other protected material).

Complicated ethical questions arise when the government changes its position in a lawsuit, moving from one side of the controversy to another— usually due to a change in administrations.[8] This question is considered in Chapter 8 below at p. 809.

Why Limit Screening to Former Government Lawyers?

In *Nemours*, above at p. 670, the court argued that migratory lawyer situations involving movement between private law firms should be treated

---

7. M.R. 1.11(e) defines "confidential government information" as "information which has been obtained under governmental authority and which, at the time this rule is applied, the government is prohibited by law from disclosing to the public or has a legal privilege not to disclose, and which is not otherwise available to the public."

8. See Note, Professional Ethics in Government Side–Switching, 96 Harv.L.Rev. 1914 (1983).

the same as movement from government to private employment. Private lawyers, the court said, are as trustworthy as government lawyers. Yet the Model Rules and most of the case law reject this view, permitting screening to remove the imputed disqualification in the case of former government lawyers but not in that of migratory private lawyers.[9]

Why allow screening in the case of the tainted former government lawyer but not in the case of the tainted private lawyer who moves from one firm to another? Consider the following arguments (and unstated counter-arguments): First, a government lawyer's obligation to seek just results departs somewhat from the traditional adversarial model. Second, the boundaries of many government matters, which often involve expansive issues of law, policy or formulation of general rules, are more difficult to determine than those involved in private representation. Practical problems of administration and, perhaps, a reduced level of loyalty are suggested when interests of government are diffuse and widely shared. The government, unlike private persons, deals with everyone. Third, confidentiality is less of a concern when the government is involved because so much government information is available to the public. The confidentiality concern involves litigation strategy on the part of the government and flow of information about private persons held by government, an issue dealt with separately by criminal statutes and in M.R. 1.11(b). Fourth, government lawyers work on a fixed salary; they do not have the same economic incentive to use confidential information to win cases. Finally, the consistent position of the federal government (and most state governments) has favored the use of screening, arguing that the public interest in able, mobile lawyers is more important than the danger that government information will be used against the government. In a sense, the government has consented in advance to screening procedures.

Can Government Be Disqualified by Imputation?

If one lawyer in a government agency is disqualified because of prior representation of a private client (or for any other reason), is the entire office disqualified? M.R. 1.11(c) is silent on the question. M.R. 1.10 is inapplicable to government law departments. See M.R. 1.10 and the definition of "firm" in Terminology. Hence, no rule prohibits a government law department (e.g., a prosecutor's office or a city counsel's office) from proceeding when one of its lawyers is disqualified. Nor does any rule prescribe the manner in which such an office could proceed in this situation, e.g., by screening. Would it nevertheless be prudent for a government law office to screen a lawyer who had formerly represented a private client against whom the office is now engaged?

The case law in this area arises primarily out of criminal trials. Typically, the defendant seeks to disqualify the state prosecutor's office (or the U.S. Attorney's office) on the ground that one of the lawyers in that

9. Most commentators support the distinction. See, e.g., Wolfram, Modern Legal Ethics § 7.6.4 at 403–04 (1986). Most of the cases also limit screening to cases involving former government lawyers.

office formerly represented the accused or a co-defendant or a witness in connection with the same case. Most state courts hold that the government should be allowed to proceed as long as the disqualified lawyer is not personally involved.[10] Where the state prosecutor has multiple offices, courts sometimes require that the case be handled by an office in a different location.

Some cases suggest that the entire government might be disqualified. In People v. Shinkle,[11] for example, the Chief Assistant District Attorney in Sullivan County, the prosecuting office, had formerly been with the Legal Aid Society, where he had been actively involved with the representation of the defendant in the same matter. In vacating the conviction, the New York Court of Appeals implied that a special prosecutor would have to be appointed to reprosecute.

The federal courts have refused to require that an entire United States Attorney's office be disqualified because of one disqualified lawyer.[12] If the disqualified prosecutor has not been properly screened, the whole office may be disqualified.[13] But disqualification of one unit of government will not extend to another.[14]

3.   OTHER ISSUES OF GOVERNMENT LAWYER CONFLICTS

When the Former Client Is Another Level of Government

An oft-cited case involving "same side" representation by a former government lawyer is General Motors Corp. v. City of New York.[15] In that case the lawyer while working for the federal government helped develop an antitrust case against General Motors involving alleged monopolization of bus manufacturing. Later, in private practice, he was retained on a contingent-fee basis by New York City to handle a private damage case against General Motors involving the same charges. The Justice Department consented to this representation. The court held that the lawyer was disqualified because his prior involvement in the matter was substantial and his arrangement with New York City was private employment. The

---

10. See, e.g., Florida v. Cote, 538 So.2d 1356 (Fla.App.1989); People v. Lopez, 202 Cal. Rptr. 333 (App.1984); State v. Laughlin, 652 P.2d 690 (Kan.1982); Pisa v. Commonwealth, 393 N.E.2d 386 (Mass.1979).

11. 415 N.E.2d 909 (N.Y.1980). See also Collier v. Legakes, 646 P.2d 1219 (Nev. 1982).

12. See, e.g., United States v. Caggiano, 660 F.2d 184 (6th Cir.1981); In re Grand Jury Proceedings, 700 F.Supp. 626 (D.P.R.1988); United States v. Newman, 534 F.Supp. 1113 (S.D.N.Y.1982).

13. For example, in Arkansas v. Dean Foods Prods. Inc., 605 F.2d 380 (8th Cir.1979), the state's entire antitrust division was

disqualified from prosecuting an individual who had been the client of the division's new chief when the chief was in private practice.

14. See United States v. Weiner, 578 F.2d 757 (9th Cir. 1978), where defendant moved to disqualify the U.S. Attorney's Office in a securities case because his former lawyer was now working for the SEC. The court denied the motion, finding that the size and complexity of the two government offices made any imputation of knowledge inappropriate.

15. 501 F.2d 639 (2d Cir.1974). The case is discussed in *SIPC* at p. 695.

fact that New York City was on the "same side" as the federal government was not enough to eliminate the "appearance of impropriety". "[T]here lurks great potential for lucrative returns in following into private practice the course already charted with the aid of government resources."[16]

ABA Opinion 342 states that the restrictions on former government lawyers should not apply if the new employer is another government agency.[17] Comment [4] to M.R. 1.11, however, rejects this view:

> When the client is an agency of one government, that agency should be treated as a private client for purposes of this Rule if the lawyer thereafter represents an agency of another government, as when a lawyer represents a city and subsequently is employed by a federal agency.

What about a lawyer who transfers from one agency of government to another agency of the same government? Should one agency of government be treated as the same client as another agency of government—thereby mooting conflict questions? Would your answer change if the first "agency" was the Congress and the second "agency" was the White House legal team?

Moving From Private Practice into Government Service

Model Rule 1.11(c)(1) governs situations where a lawyer moves from private practice into government service. It is a counterpart to M.R. 1.11(a) and like that provision applies even if the present client (the government) is on the "same side" as the former client. The exception in M.R. 1.11(c) allows the present government lawyer to proceed in the same matter if law expressly allows *or* if "no one is, or by lawful delegation may be, authorized to act in the lawyer's stead in the matter." This exception prevents the conflicts rules from paralyzing the government in those rare cases where the only person able to take the case for the government has a conflict.

M.R. 1.11(c)(1) has no consent provision. Whether the government lawyer can proceed on the *same side* of a matter in which she worked for a private client is not determined by whether the private client consents. Whether a government lawyer can proceed in a matter in which her former private client's interests are *adverse* to the government, is governed by M.R. 1.9(a). Moreover, whenever a government lawyer proceeds in a matter she handled while in private practice M.R. 1.9(c) and M.R. 1.6 protect the former private client's confidences.[18]

Other Conflicts Rules for Those in Public Service

---

16. 501 F.2d 650.

17. See ABA Formal Op. 342, n. 18., stating that this construction is consistent with *General Motors* because in that case the court found that the lawyer's employment by the city constituted private employment.

18. Generally see Ronald D. Rotunda, Ethical Problems in Federal Agency Hiring of Private Attorneys, 1 Geo.J.Legal Ethics 85 (1987).

Model Rule 1.11(c)(2) prohibits government lawyers from negotiating "with any person who is involved as a party or as attorney for a party in a matter in which the lawyer is participating personally and substantially." M.R. 1.12 governs the conflicts faced by former judges or arbitrators. Law clerks, of course, have substantial ethical responsibilities.[19]

19. On the ethical responsibilities of law clerks, see Richard W. Painter, Open Chambers?, 97 Mich.L.Rev. 101, 124–42 (1999); Note, The Law Clerk's Duty of Confidentiality, 129 U.Pa.L.Rev. 1230 (1981).

CHAPTER 8

Who Is the Client?

A. Individual or Enterprise

INTRODUCTORY NOTE

A lawyer is required to communicate and confer with a client, to keep the client's secrets and to abide by the client's decision on whether to accept a settlement offer.[1] When a lawyer represents an entity rather than an individual, to whom are these and other professional duties owed?

- When a lawyer represents a corporation, is communicating with the chief executive officer always sufficient? Should the lawyer ever insist on communicating with the board of directors? The shareholders?

- When the CEO communicates with the lawyer, is the attorney-client privilege personally held by the CEO or may the corporation waive it against the CEO's wishes? Who may waive the privilege on the corporation's behalf?

A lawyer for an organization constantly faces these and other delicate questions. Similar issues confront lawyers for partnerships, lawyers for trustees and other fiduciaries, and lawyers for a government agency. This chapter deals with those questions.

When organizational peace reigns and all the organization's agents lawfully fulfill their responsibilities to the entity, deciding who personifies the client is not difficult: The person designated by the organization's powers-that-be to deal with the lawyer personifies the client. This is so not because it is the right answer but because harmony prevails within the organization. When no one within the organization will contradict the designee, the lawyer may safely rely upon that person's instructions. But harmony in large or small organizations is a sometime thing that can be fractured by economic hard times, problems of succession, changes in ownership and such chancy events as deterioration in personal relationships. Problems arise when there is infighting over control of an entity and when the person designated to speak for the entity acts in a way that may harm it. Who personifies the client then? What duties does the lawyer for the organization owe to whom? Will conflict among constituents of the

---

1. M.R. 1.4 (duty of communication); M.R. 1.6 (duty of confidentiality); and M.R. 1.2(a) (client makes settlement decision).

organization inevitably result in termination of the lawyer's employment because of conflicts of interest?

1. RELATIONSHIP BETWEEN ORGANIZATION'S LAWYER AND ITS OFFICERS

Meehan v. Hopps

District Court of Appeal, First District, Division 1, California, 1956.
144 Cal.App.2d 284, 301 P.2d 10.

■ BRAY, JUSTICE.

This is an appeal from a certain order in an action brought by respondents as plaintiffs, against appellants as defendants, for an accounting and other relief on behalf of the policyholders, creditors and stockholders of the Rhode Island Insurance Company, in which it is charged that Stewart B. Hopps, former director, member of the executive committee and chairman of the board of the company, dominated and managed the company's affairs for his own personal gain in violation of his fiduciary duties. Defendants moved the trial court to restrain and enjoin the Providence, Rhode Island, law firm of Edwards & Angell, ... from further participation in the case and from disclosing information pertaining thereto. The motion was based upon the alleged dual relationship of Edwards & Angell towards Hopps and a claim that Hopps had turned over to that firm as his lawyers certain files, documents and other information which plaintiffs have used and have threatened to use against him in the present action. After a hearing the motion was denied. Defendants appeal.

With legislative authority the Board of Governors of the State Bar of California have formulated rules of professional conduct approved by the Supreme Court. These rules are binding upon all members of the State Bar. Bus. and Prof.Code § 6077.[2] Applicable here are Rule 5: "A member of the State Bar shall not accept employment adverse to a client or former client, without the consent of the client or former client, relating to a matter in reference to which he has obtained confidential information by reason of or in the course of his employment by such client or former client"; Rule 7: "A member of the State Bar shall not represent conflicting interests, except with the consent of all parties concerned." Section 6068, Business and Professions Code, provides: It is the duty of an attorney "(e) To maintain inviolate the confidence, and at every peril to himself to preserve the secrets, of his client."

As the law is clear, we deem it unnecessary to cite the many cases holding that an attorney who attempts to use against the interests of his

---

2. The firm of Edwards & Angell are the attorneys for the receiver, and the attorneys of that firm representing the receiver in the action were admitted by the trial court to the California State Bar for the purpose of participating in this case. None of them appear of record on this appeal.

former client information gained while the attorney-client relationship existed, may be enjoined from so doing.

The question first to be determined is:

1.   Had There Been an Attorney–Client Relationship Between Counsel and Hopps?

The determination of that question is one of law. De Long v. Miller, 133 Cal.App.2d 175, 178, 283 P.2d 762. However, where there is a conflict in the evidence the factual basis for the determination must first be determined, and it is for the trial court to evaluate the evidence. Id., 133 Cal.App.2d at page 179, 283 P.2d at page 764.

On the question of whether counsel ever represented Hopps as his attorney, the evidence is directly conflicting. Concededly the firm never charged nor received payment from Hopps for any services whatever. The services which Hopps claims were for him personally were paid for by Rhode Island. Soon after Hopps became connected with the company, counsel ceased to act as general counsel for it. Thereafter they were employed on special matters from time to time. At the time counsel first met Hopps they were working for Rhode Island on a merger of the Merchants Insurance Company into the former. Rhode Island's chairman asked counsel to draw a contract for the employment of Hopps, which was done. Hopps claims that the attorney drawing the contract advised him as well as the company. The attorney denied this and claimed that Hopps consulted his own lawyer, Farber, exclusively concerning the contract. Hopps testified that he confided in and was advised by counsel concerning his personal involvement in the affairs of Rhode Island; that he turned over to counsel his personal files; that Attorney Winsor of the firm was a friendly advisor and legal confidant and familiar with Hopps' personal affairs; that the firm undertook to represent Hopps' personal interest in the California controversy[3] and in a number of other matters. We deem it unnecessary to detail the evidence concerning the matters testified to by Hopps as showing a personal attorney and client relationship between him and counsel. Suffice it to say that evidence to the contrary on all matters was presented by Edwards & Angell. The question is primarily one of credibility. The trial court obviously disbelieved Hopps.

There are four matters in which appellants particularly claim that counsel acted personally for Hopps.

(1) The preparation of the employment contract between Rhode Island and Hopps. While Hopps does not claim that he employed counsel in this behalf but that Gilman, of counsel, advised him personally, Gilman denied this. Gilman had been handling for Rhode Island a proposed merger of Merchants Insurance Company with it. Watson, Rhode Island's chairman,

---

3.   This was a conflict between the Insurance Commissioner of California and Rhode Island, see Rhode Island Ins. Co. v. Downey, 95 Cal.App.2d 220, 212 P.2d 965, in which the actions of Hopps were looked upon with disfavor by the commissioner.

asked Gilman to draw the employment contract. Gilman conferred with both Hopps and Watson, sending copies of the contract when prepared to both. In the letter to Hopps accompanying the proposed contract Gilman stated that if it was not satisfactory to Hopps Gilman would take up with Watson any proposed changes. It frequently happens that one retained by a client to draft an agreement between him and another, will send such agreement to the other, asking for the latter's suggestions concerning it, which suggestions the drafter will take up with his client. This statement did not convert Gilman's relationship from attorney for Rhode Island to attorney for Hopps in any respect. The agreement was not to become effective unless the merger was made, and provided that Hopps was to have the right to be interested in the Merchants Insurance Company's dealing with Rhode Island and was only required to give part of his time to the latter. Winsor, of counsel, called on Hopps in New York in connection with the merger. None of these matters changed counsel's relationship as attorney for Rhode Island into attorney for Hopps as well. In his deposition Hopps stated that the work done by counsel on the employment contract was done for Rhode Island. At the trial he retracted that statement....

(2) Approximately nine years after the contract was drawn, counsel were employed by Rhode Island in connection with a controversy with Cuban interests. It involved nine companies and individuals including Hopps and Rhode Island on the American side, and seven on the Cuban side. It was actually a fight for control. Although the controversy had been going on for approximately seven years, counsel had nothing to do with it until approximately three months prior to its settlement. At Watson's request, counsel were employed to represent Rhode Island. At counsel's request Hopps prepared and gave them data concerning the background and history of the controversy and his interest in it. One of the most important problems was whether a proxy held by Hopps or those held by the Cuban interests should prevail. Hopps prepared memoranda concerning these, sending copies to Rhode Island's executive committee as well as to counsel. Counsel advised Rhode Island that only Hopps' proxy could be considered. The fact that counsel so advised, and the other matters they did in connection with the controversy, did not make them attorneys for Hopps.

(3) The Pioneer Equitable Settlement. This involved a dispute between Rhode Island on one side, the Pioneer Equitable and other companies and an individual on the other. Hopps had interests on both sides. There were a number of lawyers representing Rhode Island in this matter including counsel, who were employed by Rhode Island as special counsel in connection with a suit over custodian funds included in the controversy. Counsel denied Hopps' assertion that their special duty in the controversy involved any consideration by them of Hopps' personal interests nor any advice to him concerning them.

(4) The California controversy. [T]his was a controversy between Rhode Island and the Insurance Commissioner of California.... In addition to proceedings in the federal court, counsel endeavored to work out a

settlement of the controversy with the commissioner. Richards, of counsel, after consultation with Hopps and the obtaining of data from Hopps and other company officers, went to California for that purpose. Richards was told by the California authorities that the commissioner objected to Hopps' association with the company. Richards testified that he told them that he would not discuss personalities, but wanted to work out an arrangement by which the company could continue in business in California. During the negotiations in California, Hopps came out as well as other members of counsel, and together they prepared memoranda to be submitted to the commissioner's counsel. Here again there was nothing done by counsel or information received by them, which in any way made them attorneys for Hopps. While they refused to agree to Hopps' removal from a position of authority in the company, or even to discuss such a change, they were not representing Hopps in so doing, but as attorneys for the company were refusing to discuss the matter of the removal of its president.

Appellants point out that the "contemporaneous record" is replete with instances where Hopps presented memoranda and material to counsel and spent considerable time in conference with counsel, all to assist them in the preparation of the various proceedings in which they were engaged for the corporation. These are matters which Hopps' position as an officer of the corporation, and particularly one who dictated, or at least was instrumental in determining, the policy of the corporation in the particular matter, required him to give the corporation.

Disregarding the testimony of Hopps, as we are required to do on this appeal, we can find nothing in the record to show any relationship of attorney and client between Hopps and counsel, nor that he gave them any data, or disclosed to them any information which he as an officer of the company was not required by his position to do, nor which they as attorneys for the company in the matters entrusted to them, were not entitled to receive.

2.   Effect of Representation of the Company

Appellant has not cited, nor have we found, any case holding that an attorney for a corporation is disqualified from representing it in an action brought by it against one of its officers, nor that in such an action the attorney may not use information received from such officer in connection with company matters. The attorney for a corporation represents it, its stockholders and its officers in their representative capacity. He in nowise represents the officers personally. It would be a sorry state of affairs if when a controversy arises between an attorney's corporate client and one of its officers he could not use on behalf of his client information which that officer was required by reason of his position with the corporation to give to the attorney.

Kingman, of counsel, testified that on May 26, 1950, White, the then president of the company, came to counsel's office and informed him that the company would have to go into receivership and that Hopps stated that he was going to get counsel appointed as co-counsel for the receiver with another firm of attorneys. . . . The fact that counsel, as attorney for the receiver, requested and received Hopps' cooperation in certain receivership matters, that prior to their appointment as receiver, counsel on behalf of the company had prepared an answer in which it alleged that the officers, directors and agents of the company were not at fault, in nowise affected their right to represent the receiver, nor to participate in an action in which the receiver claims that Hopps, one of the officers, was at fault. If Hopps' action in arranging for the appointment did not constitute a consent to counsel being appointed attorneys for the receiver and acting in all respects as their duty as attorneys for the receiver required, such action indicates at least that Hopps originally did not consider that counsel had been his personal attorneys nor that he had disclosed to them any information over and above what his position with the company required him to disclose.

Cases cited by appellants where attorneys were enjoined from proceeding against former clients are easily distinguishable from our case. In all of them the relationship of attorney and client actually had existed between the attorney and the party against whom the attorney was now acting. . . . Consolidated Theatres v. Warner Bros., 2 Cir., 1954, 216 F.2d 920: An attorney who had been in the office of the law firm defending a motion picture producer in anti-trust litigation attempted to represent an exhibitor's anti-trust damage suit against the producer. United States v. Bishop, 6 Cir., 1937, 90 F.2d 65: An attorney represented the government on the first trial of an action by a veteran on a war risk policy. On the second trial of the same issue he attempted to represent the veteran. Watson v. Watson, 1939, 171 Misc. 175, 11 N.Y.S.2d 537: A wife sued to annul a marriage on the ground of the husband's previous conviction of a crime. The attorneys who had defended the husband in the criminal proceeding and who had obtained from him the history of his life attempted to represent the wife in the annulment action. The other cases cited by appellants relate to situations where the attorney either had represented the person whom he was now appearing against in the same matter or one connected with it or had advised other counsel representing the person he was now proceeding against. In none of the cases was there a situation where the attorney for a corporation was appearing for the corporation adversely to a former officer thereof.

Assuming that some of the information obtained from Hopps by counsel as representative of the corporation is that upon which the receiver's contention that Hopps dominated the corporation, its officers and companies, to its damage, is partially based, nevertheless such fact would not prevent counsel from representing either the corporation or the receiver in a controversy with Hopps nor from using that information against him. . . . If this were true, then the attorney representing a corporation in any given matter becomes the personal attorney of each stockholder because the attorney's actions benefiting the corporation likewise benefit the stockholder. Such relationship would disqualify the attorney from acting adversely to the stockholder concerning that particular matter in any controversy between the stockholder and a third party, but obviously would not prevent the attorney from representing the corporation in any controversy between it and the stockholder. As attorneys for the corporation, counsel's first duty is to it. Likewise, as an officer of the corporation, it was Hopps' duty to disclose to it all information necessary for its purposes. To hold that the giving of such information in that more or less intimate relationship which necessarily must exist between an officer of the corporation and its attorneys would prevent the corporation attorneys from thereafter using it in favor of the corporation in litigation against the officer, would be unfair to the corporation and its stockholders, and would violate the above mentioned very important precept, namely, that the attorney's first duty is to his client. . . .

Notes on *Meehan*

On what ground did Hopps seek to disqualify Edwards & Angell? The opinion seems to take for granted that, if Hopps had been represented individually by the Edwards firm, the firm could not represent the corporation in the accounting proceeding. Is this assumption right?

Is the court's holding that no lawyer-client relationship existed between the Edwards firm and Hopps consistent with cases like *Togstad* and *Westinghouse*[1] where a relationship giving rise to fiduciary duties was found between a lawyer and persons who reasonably believed that an attorney-client relationship had been established? Might Hopps, after dealing with the Edwards firm on a number of matters over a long period of time, have felt betrayed when the firm attacked him in the accounting proceeding? Why wasn't his belief that the Edwards firm were "his lawyers" a reasonable one?

When the Edwards firm negotiated the employment contract between Hopps and the corporation, was it acting as lawyer for both parties? What must an officer show to prove that an organization's lawyer also represented him as an individual?

The rule in *Meehan* that a lawyer for a corporation represents the corporation and not the individual officers, directors or shareholders is the general rule followed by American courts. See M.R. 1.13(a) and EC 5–18. As the court notes in *Meehan*, the working relationship between counsel and the managing officers of a company can easily blur the distinction (in the mind and actions of lawyer and corporate official alike) between representing the company and representing the individual. M.R. 1.13(d) requires that a lawyer for an organization provide corporate officers or other constituents something like a Miranda warning about who it is the lawyer represents whenever "it is apparent that the organization's interests are adverse to those of the constituents with whom the lawyer is dealing."

---

1. *Togstad* is printed in chapter 6 at p. 457 supra; *Westinghouse* is printed in chapter 7 at p. 581 supra.

Assuming M.R. 1.13(d) was in effect during the events described in the court's opinion, when, if at all, should Edwards & Angell have "reminded" Hopps that it did not represent him personally?

Representing Both an Organization and Its Officer

In E.F. Hutton & Co. v. Brown,[2] the court disqualified the firm representing Hutton on the ground that previously the firm had jointly represented Hutton's former officer, Brown, in a personal capacity while serving as corporate counsel. The firm claimed that it had represented only the company and that its dealings with Brown were in his official capacity as an officer of Hutton.

As vice-president of Hutton, Brown had authorized a loan to a third person to be secured by Westec common stock. Shortly after the loan was made the SEC suspended trading in Westec stock because of suspected trading illegalities. One issue in a subsequent SEC investigation was whether Brown knew that the loan would be used to purchase stock. Brown was twice called to testify about this matter in the SEC investigation. Hutton's lawyers discussed with him his forthcoming testimony and told him that they would accompany him to the hearings. At both hearings, Brown was asked if the lawyers with him were his lawyers, and he responded that they were. Thereafter, Hutton fired Brown and sued him for negligence in authorizing the loan. When Brown claimed that his communications with Hutton's lawyers were privileged, the lawyers argued that his testimony at the hearings surprised them because they had previously explained to Brown that they represented Hutton and not him individually. (Brown disputed this.) The lawyers had not corrected Brown's assertion at either hearing.

The court placed great emphasis on these facts, stating:

> An attorney's appearance in a judicial or semi-judicial proceeding creates a presumption that an attorney-client relationship exists between the attorney and the person with whom he appears. This presumption shifts to Hutton, the party denying the existence of the relationship, the burden of persuasion. When the relationship is also evidenced by the entry of a formal appearance by the attorney on behalf of the person with whom he appears, the presumption becomes almost irrebuttable....[3]

The fact that Brown had not paid the lawyers' fee and that he had never asked the firm to represent him were held not to overcome the relationship implied by the conduct of the lawyers at the hearings.

The court rejected arguments that the lawyers represented Brown only in his official capacity at a time when the interests of Hutton and Brown were perceived as identical. The SEC was investigating both Hutton and Brown, hence his interests as well as Hutton's were at stake. Brown's assertions that the lawyers represented him, therefore, meant Brown as an

---

2. 305 F.Supp. 371 (S.D.Tex.1969).   **3.** Id. at 387.

individual. Brown's belief that he was represented individually was reasonable, given the failure of counsel to correct the record and the fact that Hutton faced civil penalties, but Brown faced a potential prison term. Corporate counsel, the court observed, have "an obligation to ensure that there is no misunderstanding by the officer." Fears of adverse effects on corporate representation were unjustified: "Only those counsel who permit the officer to believe that they represent him individually will disable themselves from appearing in subsequent litigation against him."[4]

In *Hutton* the court said that a corporate lawyer who becomes aware that a corporate officer might misconstrue the lawyer's participation as individual representation has two options: (1) joint representation of the officer and the corporation after obtaining the informed consent of both clients; or (2) representing the corporation's separate interest after informing the officer that she did not represent him and that his interest would go unprotected unless he employed personal counsel.[5] If joint representation had been chosen in *Hutton*, would Hutton's lawyers have been disqualified from suing Brown?[6]

The underlying issue in cases like *Meehan* and *Hutton* is whether the putative client had a reasonable belief that a lawyer-client relationship existed. In United States v. Keplinger,[7] a corporate officer who had been convicted of mail and wire fraud claimed that evidence admitted against him should have been excluded under the attorney-client privilege. The corporation's lawyers had accompanied him to a meeting with the Food and Drug Administration (FDA), and FDA officials had referred to the lawyers as "your counsel." The court distinguished *Hutton* on the grounds that the lawyers had not entered a formal appearance as counsel and that the officer's subjective belief that counsel was representing him as an individual was not sufficient to demonstrate that an attorney-client relationship existed: "[N]o individual attorney-client relationship can be inferred without some finding that the potential client's subjective belief is minimally reasonable."[8]

Who Controls a Corporation's Attorney–Client Privilege?

Corporations like natural persons may claim an attorney-client privilege. See Upjohn Co. v. United States.[9] The privilege belongs to the corporation, not individual corporate officers.[10] But who speaks for the

4. Id. at 398.

5. See 305 F.Supp. at 396–97.

6. See M.R. 1.9 and *Brennan's* case, p. 642; see also Cooke v. Laidlaw, Adams & Peck, 510 N.Y.S.2d 597 (App.Div.1987) (firm that had jointly represented corporation and officer disqualified from representing corporation against the now-former officer involving matter substantially related to joint representation even if no confidences were in fact communicated to lawyer by officer).

7. 776 F.2d 678 (7th Cir.1985).

8. 776 F.2d at 701; see also Bernstein v. Crazy Eddie, Inc., 702 F.Supp. 962, 988 (E.D.N.Y.1988).

9. 449 U.S. 383 (1981), printed in Chapter 4 at p. 209 supra.

10. See Citibank, N.A. v. Andros, 666 F.2d 1192, 1195 (8th Cir.1981); In re Grand Jury Proceedings, 434 F.Supp. 648, 650 (E.D.Mich.1977), aff'd, 570 F.2d 562 (6th

corporation? Corporate law generally provides that the board of directors or a person authorized by the board to act may act for the corporation, if approval of shareholders on the particular matter is not required. In general, decisions concerning routine litigation are delegated to particular officers, but settlement of a major litigation that threatens the continuance or profitability of a corporation requires board action (e.g., a merger or an event that may result in insolvency).

In Commodity Futures Trading Commission v. Weintraub,[11] the issue was whether the trustee for a bankrupt corporation could waive the privilege on the corporation's behalf and against the wishes of the former directors of the debtor. Weintraub had been counsel to the now-bankrupt company. When called before the Commodity Commission to testify about the company's transactions, Weintraub refused, citing attorney-client privilege. The trustee in bankruptcy then waived the privilege on the corporation's behalf, but former officers intervened and attempted to assert it.

The Supreme Court held that the trustee, as the company's current management, controlled the privilege on the company's behalf. The former directors argued that vesting control of the privilege with the trustee would leave shareholders' interests unprotected or at least always subservient to the interests of creditors. The Court stated that the trustee had fiduciary duties that ran to both creditors and shareholders. Although the privilege could be used by trustees in favor of creditors at the expense of shareholders, this posture was "in keeping with the hierarchy of interests created by the bankruptcy laws."[12]

Weintraub involved communications made in the ordinary course of business prior to bankruptcy. What about communications between corporate management and bankruptcy counsel relating to the filing of bankruptcy? Can the bankruptcy trustee subsequently waive the privilege as to those communications?

A Privilege for Individual Corporate Officers?

Unlike the court in *Meehan*, the court in *Hutton* found an attorney-client relationship between the corporate officer and corporate counsel. Nevertheless, *Hutton* also held that the officer had no privilege to assert against the company:

> Brown gave information to counsel concerning the . . . loan transaction long before counsel appeared with him at the SEC and bankruptcy hearings. As a corporate officer, Brown's duty to his corporate employer required him to furnish this information to counsel at Hutton's request. In fact, because Brown obtained his knowledge within the scope of his position as an officer of Hutton, the information which he conveyed to counsel was, as a matter of law, already known to Hutton. The attorney-client privilege is therefore not available to Brown against Hutton, since all information he gave to counsel already was known to Hutton, and since Brown gave the information to counsel

Cir.1978); United States v. Piccini, 412   **11.** 471 U.S. 343 (1985).
F.2d 591, 593 (2d Cir.1969).   **12.** 471 U.S. at 344.

knowing that counsel, in turn, would convey it to Hutton's New York management.[13]

The grounds for denying Brown the privilege—the timing of communications, the status of information possessed by a corporate agent and his duty as an officer to communicate information relating to corporate business—suggest that a corporate officer, who has been represented as an individual and joint client with the corporation, may never be able to assert a privilege against the corporation itself. Several courts have so held.[14]

Other courts have stated that an officer sometimes may assert the privilege against the corporation, but only as to personal matters not related to the officer's duties or the corporation's business (e.g., drafting an officer's personal will). In In re Grand Jury,[15] the court held that a corporate officer who claims a personal privilege must show, in addition to all the usual elements of the attorney-client privilege, "that the substance of their conversation did not concern matters within the company or the general affairs of the company."[16] In Matter of Bevill, Bresler & Schulman Asset Management Corp.,[17] the court held that a personal attorney-client privilege could not be asserted against the corporation as to communications made by the officer about matters within the officer's "roles and functions" within the corporation. Corporate officers could have a personal attorney-client privilege only as to communications "not related to their role as officers of the corporation."[18] Is the *Bevill/Grand Jury* test consistent with the general rules on privilege between joint clients? Review the note on this subject in Chapter 4 above at p. 208.

Read Model Rule 1.13(e) and Comment [9] to the rule. What more, if anything, might you add to the rule or comment?

2. REPRESENTING AN ORGANIZATION AND ITS AGENTS IN DERIVATIVE ACTIONS

Yablonski v. United Mine Workers of America

United States Court of Appeals, District of Columbia Circuit, 1971.
448 F.2d 1175.

■ Before McGOWAN, ROBINSON and WILKEY, Circuit Judges.

■ PER CURIAM:

This is an action under § 501 of the Labor–Management Reporting and Disclosure Act[1] brought by the late Joseph A. Yablonski and 48 other

---

13. 305 F.Supp. at 400–01.

14. See, e.g., *Piccini,* supra, 412 F.2d at 593; Polycast Technology Corp. v. Uniroyal, Inc., 125 F.R.D. 47, 49 (S.D.N.Y.1989); In re O.P.M. Leasing Services, Inc., 13 B.R. 64, 67–68 & n. 11 (S.D.N.Y.1981), aff'd, 670 F.2d 383 (2d Cir.1982).

15. In re Grand Jury Investigation No. 83–30557, 575 F.Supp. 777 (N.D.Ga.1983).

16. 575 F.Supp. at 780.

17. 805 F.2d 120, 123 (3d Cir.1986) (relying on *In re Grand Jury*).

18. Id. at 125.

1. 29 U.S.C. § 501(b) (1964) provides [that a union member may bring an action in a

members of the United Mine Workers of America against the UMWA and three named officers—Boyle, President; Titler, Vice President; Owens, Secretary–Treasurer—asking for an accounting of UMWA funds disbursed by them and for restitution of funds allegedly misappropriated and misspent.

No trial on the merits has been had. The issue on this appeal is whether the law firm regularly representing the UMWA [Williams & Connolly of Washington, D.C.], who originally entered an appearance for the UMWA and the three individual officer-defendants, should be allowed to continue its representation of the UMWA after it withdrew as counsel for the individual defendants. The District Court found that the regular UMWA outside counsel was not disqualified from continuing its representation in this action, but for reasons enunciated infra we hold that in the particular circumstances of this case such representation should be discontinued.

After the action was filed in December 1969, appellant-plaintiffs filed in May 1970 a motion to disqualify counsel on the grounds (1) that the compensation of the regular UMWA counsel would continue to come from the UMWA treasury and (2) that there existed a conflict between the UMWA and the individual defendant officers. A month later the UMWA counsel withdrew as counsel for the individual defendants but remained as counsel for the UMWA, which the District Court sustained as proper.

At the outset of the lawsuit the then counsel for all defendants set about with commendable diligence to delineate the real issues of the lawsuit, filing in behalf of the UMWA and the three individual defendants answers setting forth all customary general defenses, and filing 34 pages of interrogatories to develop more fully the scope of the case.

The appellants argue that this period of six months' prior representation in this same suit disqualifies the regular union outside counsel to continue its representation of the UMWA, even after its withdrawal as counsel for the three individual officer-defendants. With this we do not agree. It has been inferentially held that one lawyer can properly represent all defendants if a suit appears groundless, and that separate counsel is required only in a situation where there is a potential conflict between the interests of the union and those of its officers. We regard the actions of the regular UMWA counsel during its six-month representation of both the union and its officers as an effort to ascertain the exact nature of the lawsuit and protect the interests of all defendants, and by our ruling herein do not imply any censure of counsel's action during this period of joint representation. But there does exist in our judgment a more serious barrier to the continued representation of the UMWA by its regular outside counsel in this particular lawsuit.

federal or state court against a union officer who has violated fiduciary duties owed to the union "to recover damages or secure an accounting or other appropriate relief for the benefit of the labor organization."]

I. Effect of Other Litigation in Which Regular UMWA Counsel Represent Defendant President Boyle

Of far more concern is the existence of other litigation in which the regular UMWA counsel is representing Boyle, sometimes in conjunction with representation of the union, at other times not.

(1) The "reinstatement" or "reprisal" case—one of four "election" cases brought by Joseph A. Yablonski against the UMWA and its officers, alleging that the reassignment or severance of plaintiff Yablonski from certain union duties was a reprisal for his running for president against the incumbent Boyle. After the death of Yablonski the trial court dismissed the case as moot, and this action is on appeal in this court. Appellants here claim that if this court should hold that the trial court was wrong in dismissing the reprisal case as moot, then appellee Boyle may subsequently be required to pay substantial punitive damages to the estate of Yablonski, and thus Boyle has a personal, as distinguished from a union, interest in that appeal. Although initially the union and its officers were represented by the union general counsel in the District Court, the regular UMWA outside counsel represented both the UMWA and Boyle personally on the motion to dismiss as moot, and continues such representation on appeal in this court.

(2) Denial of attorney's fees—as an outgrowth of the UMWA election cases, attorneys for "the Yablonski group" applied for attorney's fees to be paid by the union, which the District Court denied, finding that "no malfeasance on the part of the officers has yet been established." These four cases are now on appeal. The regular UMWA counsel represents both the union and the individual officer-defendants here and did so on the merits in two of the cases in the District Court (the *"Journal"*and "fair election" cases, paragraph 3 infra) and on the motions to dismiss in all four cases, where the issue originally was the compliance of the incumbent officers with the Labor–Management Reporting and Disclosure Act. This series of cases is alleged to be related to the case at bar, inasmuch as paragraph 13 of the complaint herein alleges that Boyle and the other individual officer-defendants employed counsel to defend them on charges of breach of trust and paid such counsel from UMWA funds, the regular outside UMWA counsel here involved being one of those whose representation and compensation is being challenged in this present suit.

(3) The *"Journal"*and "fair election" cases—during the UMWA election campaign candidate Yablonski claimed that the union newspaper was being used to promote the candidacy of incumbent President Boyle. On appeals in this court the regular UMWA counsel represented Boyle and the union, although in one aspect in the District Court which was severed and consolidated with the instant case, whether Boyle should be made to pay for some of the costs of printing of the *Journal*, the regular UMWA counsel does not represent Boyle.

(4) Blankenship v. Boyle—a group of retired miners sued the Trustees of the UMWA Welfare and Retirement Fund of 1950, one of the Three Trustees being Boyle, alleging that the Fund had been mismanaged by the Trustees. Boyle was charged with using his position as a Trustee to increase pension benefits to assist his re-election campaign. The District Court ordered his removal as Trustee and this court has recently refused to stay the effectiveness of that order, although not deciding the appeal on the merits. Regular UMWA counsel represents Boyle individually in all three of the capacities in which he is sued, as Trustee of the Fund, President of the UMWA, and Director of the National Bank of Washington, as well as representing the union.

We have listed and briefly described the above actions of record in which the regular UMWA counsel represents Boyle individually. Each of these has been minutely examined by appellees' counsel to demonstrate that in no instance is the representation of Boyle individually in conflict with the good faith representation of the UMWA in this case; in effect, that the interests of the UMWA and of Boyle individually are the same. We are assured that if any conflict should arise appellees' counsel would be prompt to withdraw as counsel to the UMWA in this case.

While the issues involved in each of the individual cases, and the past or present existence or nonexistence of any conflict, are relevant to the propriety of the regular UMWA counsel continuing its representation of the union in the case at bar, yet we do not think that this analysis is determinative of the real problem here. It is undeniable that the regular UMWA counsel have undertaken the representation of Boyle individually in many facets of his activities as a UMWA official, as a Trustee of the Fund, as a Director of the Bank owned 74% by the union. With strict fidelity to this client, such counsel could not undertake action on behalf of another client which would undermine his position personally. Yet, in this particular litigation, counsel for the UMWA should be diligent in analyzing objectively the true interests of the UMWA as an institution without being hindered by allegiance to any individual concerned.

We are not required to accept at this point the charge of the appellants that the "true interest" of the union is aligned with those of the individual appellants here; this may or may not turn out to be the fact. But in the exploration and the determination of the truth or falsity of the charges brought by these individual appellants against the incumbent officers of the union and the union itself as a defendant, the UMWA needs the most objective counsel obtainable. Even if we assume the accuracy of the appellee's position at the present time that there is no visible conflict of interest, yet we cannot be sure that such will not arise in the future.

Whether facts are discovered and legal positions taken which would create such a conflict of interest between the UMWA position and the position of the individual defendant Boyle may well be determined by the approach which counsel for the UMWA takes in this case. We think that the objectives of the Labor–Management Reporting and Disclosure Act[8] would be much better served by having an unquestionably independent new counsel in this particular case. The public interest requires that the validity of appellants' charges against the UMWA management of breach of its fiduciary responsibilities be determined in a context which is as free as possible from the appearance of any potential for conflict of interest in the representation of the union itself.

II.   Objective Determination of the UMWA's Institutional Interest

Counsel for the appellees here have stressed the "institutional interest" of the UMWA in all of the issues raised, and particularly the institutional interest of the union in "repose." Counsel's interpretation of the "institutional interest" of the union appears to have been broad enough to authorize UMWA counsel to undertake practically everything worthwhile in the defense of this lawsuit. After the withdrawal of the regular union counsel from representation of Boyle individually in this case, the individual practitioner selected to represent Boyle has apparently contributed little to the defense.

By far the strongest laboring oar has been stroked by the regular UMWA counsel on behalf of the union. On oral argument appellees' counsel stated that it had prepared 94 pages of answers to interrogatories, that the individual practitioner representing Boyle had agreed they should do this, as the UMWA had a definite interest that all questions as to the conduct of union affairs previously were accurately answered and that the accurate answers were to be found in the union records. We can see the UMWA interest in having such interrogatories answered accurately, but we would think that since it is the individual defendants who are charged with the

---

8. 29 U.S.C. § 401 (1964) sets forth the congressional declaration of findings, purposes and policy of the LMRDA, including *inter alia* the statement that "in order to accomplish the objective of a free flow of commerce it is essential that labor organizations, employers, and their officials adhere to the highest standards of responsibility and ethical conduct in administering the affairs of their organizations. . . ." The legislative history of the Act makes plain that a major congressional objective was to provide union members, as well as the Government in the public interest, with a variety of means to ensure that officials of labor organizations perform their duties in accordance with fiduciary standards. . . . The House Committee strongly expressed its concern that:

  Some trade unions have acquired bureaucratic tendencies and characteristics. The relationship of the leaders of such unions to their members has in some instances become impersonal and autocratic. In some cases men who have acquired positions of power and responsibility within unions have abused their power and forsaken their responsibilities to the membership and to the public. The power and control of the affairs of a trade union by leaders who abuse their power and forsake their responsibilities inevitably leads to the elimination of efficient, honest and democratic practices within such union, and often results in irresponsible actions which are detrimental to the public interest. (H.R. No. 741, 86th Cong., 1st Sess. 6 (1959).

Appellants' complaint in the instant case alleges a state of affairs existing within the leadership of the UMWA of the magnitude of that which the House Report condemned.

misconduct, their counsel would be the one to initiate and to carry the burden. . . .

In the crucial area of discovery matters, clearly representing the vast bulk of the effort expended by the parties defendant at this stage of the litigation, UMWA counsel have prepared 174 pages of answers to plaintiffs' initial interrogatories which were directed to all defendants, while counsel for the individual defendants, until 2 April 1971, some 7½ months after the interrogatories were originally served, had contented himself with filing 2 pages of answers for each individual defendant, a total of 6 pages. On 2 April 1971 counsel finally filed additional answers on behalf of defendant Boyle; however, as of the date of argument of this appeal, answers on behalf of the other individual defendants had not been filed.

. . .

. . . It appears that in 18 months of representation (6 months for both the UMWA and Boyle individually, and 12 months for the UMWA alone), the regular UMWA counsel has not brought forth a single issue on which the UMWA and the Boyle individual interest have diverged.

We think the analogy of the position of a corporation and its individual officers when confronted by a stockholder derivative suit is illuminating here.[10] We believe it is well established that when one group of stockholders brings a derivative suit, with the corporation as the nominal defendant and the individual officers accused of malfeasance of one sort or another, the role of both the corporate house counsel and the regular outside counsel for the corporation becomes usually a passive one. Certainly no corporate counsel purports to represent the individual officers involved, neither in the particular derivative suit nor in other litigation by virtue of which counsel necessarily must create ties of loyalty and confidentiality to the individual officers, which might preclude counsel from the most effective representation of the corporation itself. The corporation has certain definite institutional interests to be protected, and the counsel charged with this responsibility should have ties on a personal basis with neither the dissident stockholders nor the incumbent officeholders.

Purportedly a stockholder derivative suit is for the benefit of the corporation, even though the corporation is a nominal defendant, just as the appellants here assert (yet to be proved) that their action is for the benefit of the UMWA and that the individual incumbent officers are liable to the union itself for their alleged misdeeds. And, under established corporate law, if the individual officers are successful in the defense of a suit arising out of the performance of their duties as corporate officers, then they may justifiably seek reimbursement from the corporation for the costs of their successful defense.

---

10. See Phillips v. Osborne, 403 F.2d 826, 831 (9th Cir.1968); Int'l Brotherhood of Teamsters, etc. v. Hoffa, 242 F.Supp. 246, 251 (D.D.C.1965). Indeed, as appellees themselves noted in a motion filed in the court below "The action by Mr. Yablonski and others is a derivative action on behalf of the union. . . ."

In the ordinary case the action taken here by the regular UMWA counsel in the District Court might well have been the proper one, i.e., after establishing the nature of the lawsuit by interrogatories and filing answers on behalf of both the union and the individual officers in order fully to protect the position of all parties, then to step aside as counsel for the individual defendants and continue the representation of the union. But this particular case is a derivative action for the benefit of the union, and furthermore must be viewed in its relationship to this entire complex of numerous cases already pending or decided in this and the District Courts in which the regular UMWA counsel has already undertaken the representation of Boyle individually. Each and every one of these cases either directly arises out of or is directly connected with the struggle for power in the UMWA being waged by the Yablonski group on one side and the incumbent officers headed by President Boyle on the other. In this situation, the best interests of the UMWA and the purposes of the Labor–Management Reporting and Disclosure Act will be much better served by the disqualification of the regular union counsel in this particular suit and its continued representation of the individual Boyle in the other lawsuits.

We are cognizant that any counsel to represent the UMWA selected by President Boyle will be to some degree under his control. But such counsel will still only have one client—the UMWA—to represent in matters growing out of the union's affairs. Such counsel would never be professionally obligated to consider Boyle's personal interests, because they would not be representing him individually in related matters. And the extent of their labors would be gauged by the need to protect the UMWA position in this litigation. . . .

———

Notes on *Yablonski*

An action under the Labor–Management Reporting and Disclosure Act is analogous to a shareholder derivative suit: Union members are seeking, on behalf of the union, to enforce the fiduciary duties of union officers to the entity. The union is a nominal defendant in a suit brought on its behalf.

Suppose the Williams & Connolly firm had not been representing Boyle in other cases involving the same parties and many of the same issues, i.e., breach of fiduciary duties owed by union officers to union members. Would the firm have been disqualified from representing the union? On the actual facts of *Yablonski*, what conflict prevents continued representation of the union?

Following the decision printed above, the Williams & Connolly firm withdrew from representation of the union, and the union's in-house general counsel and his staff attorneys entered appearances on behalf of the union. The Yablonski group immediately moved to disqualify these lawyers, but the District Court denied the motion. The Court of Appeals in a sharply critical opinion overturned the ruling and disqualified counsel.[1] In this second opinion, the court said:

> The record now reveals a new arrangement for union counsel which in final analysis does not differ essentially from the older [one].... UMWA general counsel and three members of his staff are representing or have represented to some extent union officers who are accused of wrongdoing in this case. One staff member is the son of one of such officers, and another is the son of a nonparty officer whom the charges conceivably could implicate. Atop that, three of the five attorneys are themselves named in appellants' complaint as recipients of payments allegedly made by officers in breach of fiduciary duties.

> Considerably more is both charged and largely denied, but merely to recite only these several uncontested circumstances is to demonstrate satisfactorily that house counsel as a group do not fit the specifications we previously laid down for those who would undertake representation of UMWA in this cause. They simply are not "unquestionably independent new counsel" whose contemplated appearance would enable resolution of the issues "in a context which is as free as possible from the appearance of any potential for conflict of interests in the representation of the union itself." It follows that the license the District Court gave them to remain union counsel is a grave departure from the terms of our prior mandate....

> The district court's ruling [was apparently based on its] belief that "a passive role" was in store for UMWA in this case....

> ... [T]here is no predicate for a present assumption that UMWA must or will remain an inactive party. UMWA may, but is not inexorably bound to, take and maintain a detached position on the merits....

> Much of appellees' presentation is devoted to attempted justification of UMWA's representation by its house counsel on the ground that its institutional interests as a union coincide with the individual defensive interests of the officers who are sued. That approach puts the cart before the horse....

> ... [A] sine qua non of permissible union representation ... is the absence of any duty to another that might detract from a full measure of loyalty to the welfare of the union. House counsel no less than outside counsel must survive that test.... [2]

The fight for control of the United Mine Workers union began in the late 1960s when a group of dissidents led by Yablonski challenged the corrupt leadership of Boyle. The Boyle faction and the union itself were represented by Williams & Connolly; the Yablonski faction was represented by Joseph Rauh.[3] After the Williams & Connolly firm was disqualified from

---

1. See Yablonski v. United Mine Workers, 454 F.2d 1036 (D.C.Cir.1971).

2. Id. at 1040–42.

3. See Evan Thomas, The Man to See: Edward Bennett Williams 308–309 (1991).

representing the union in the *Yablonski* case, the firm continued to represent Boyle and the other officers in other matters.

In the case printed above, the court refers to the "late Joseph A. Yablonski." In December 1969, Yablonski and his wife and daughter were murdered by gunmen who broke into their home. Boyle and other union officials were eventually convicted of conspiring to murder Yablonski, after one of the three men they hired to do the deed confessed.[4] The gunmen were paid with union funds.[5] While lawyers played no role in that illegal use of union funds, lawyers at Williams & Connolly reportedly advised Boyle that paying the salaries of two union employees while they were in jail awaiting trial for the Yablonski murders was legal.[6] UMW's in-house counsel had previously told Boyle he could not legally do this, but in this instance, at least, Boyle's outside counsel proved more compliant.

Role of Corporate Counsel in Shareholder Derivative Suits

The relationship between a corporation's shareholders, directors and officers is usually orderly and harmonious. In *Yablonski* and in all situations resulting in a shareholder derivative suit, this harmony has broken down: Shareholders, or some of them, are suing members of the control group in the name of the corporation to enforce an obligation allegedly due the corporation.[7] Somewhere in the fray stands counsel to the corporation, either an outside law firm, "inside" lawyers employed by the corporation on a full-time basis or both. What is the position of the corporation's lawyer

4. See Bob Robertson, Legacy to the UMW, Pittsburgh Post–Gazette, Dec. 30, 1994, p.C1.

5. See Prater v. United States Parole Commission, 802 F.2d 948, 949 (7th Cir.1986). Prater, a union official, pled guilty to conspiracy to deprive a citizen of civil rights for his role in transferring union pension funds to those who killed Yablonski and his family.

6. See David Remnick, Edward Bennett Williams, At Home Amid the Sunlight and Shadows of the Past, Wash. Post, April 10, 1986, p. C1.

7. A derivative action brought by a shareholder to redress an injury to the corporation must be distinguished from a direct action by a shareholder to redress an injury sustained by, or a duty owed to, the shareholder. See ALI, Principles of Corporate Governance: Analysis and Recommendations § 7.01 and comments (1994) [hereinafter "Principles of Corporate Governance"]. For example, a claim that seeks to enforce a shareholder's right to vote is direct, not derivative, as is the claim of a shareholder who bought shares on the basis of misleading or false statements in a prospectus. On the other hand, if an officer or director injures the corporation by a violation of the duty of fair dealing, the action is derivative. Some situations are difficult to classify or may lead to an overlap of the two remedies.

What difference does it make whether the claim is direct or derivative? A direct action is exempt from special procedural requirements generally applicable to a derivative action: e.g., demand, security for expenses, verification of the complaint (discussed below). In addition, a direct action, unlike a derivative action, may not be terminated on the basis of a board recommendation or shareholder action. Unless a direct claim is subject to a statutory fee-shifting provision, the plaintiff's lawyer must be compensated out of the award either on a contingent-fee or common-fund basis. Corporate law provides for the payment by the corporation of litigation expenses of a successful derivative suit. The application of the *Garner* exception to the attorney-client privilege, see p. 768 infra, may also depend on

when a derivative suit is brought, and what difference does that position make?

In a derivative suit, shareholders formally place themselves in the shoes of the corporation to enforce a corporate right. As the court points out in *Yablonski*, the corporation is a defendant in name only;[8] the real defendants are the named persons, usually one or more of the corporation's officers, directors and majority shareholders, i.e., those with control of the corporation.

Corporate law, supplemented by the procedural law governing class actions, generally permits a derivative action only if the following conditions are satisfied:[9] (1) The shareholder was such both at the time of the wrong and at the time of suit. (2) If not excused as futile, a demand is made on the board of directors to pursue the action, and the board's response does not have the effect of terminating the action. The board may respond either by (a) taking over the suit, (b) permitting the derivative suit to proceed, or (c), more likely in today's world, filing a motion to dismiss or stay the action. The last response flows from a determination, made by vote of a disinterested board or a special litigation committee composed of disinterested directors, that prosecution of the derivative action is not in the best interests of the corporation.[10] (3) Security for the corporation's expenses in defending the action is provided, usually in the form of an indemnity bond.[11] And (4) the plaintiff shareholders are representative of the class and are adequately represented by counsel. A further degree of

whether the action is a direct or derivative one.

8. See Ross v. Bernhard, 396 U.S. 531 (1970).

9. See ALI, Principles of Corporate Governance: Analysis and Recommendations § 7.02 (1994) (standing to commence and maintain a derivative action only if the owner of an equity security has been a contemporaneous and continuing owner and is "able to represent fairly and adequately the interests of the shareholders"); id. at § 7.03 (intracorporate remedies must be exhausted by a demand requesting the board to prosecute the action or take suitable corrective measures); id. at § 7.04 (special pleading and procedural rules applicable to derivative actions including verification of facts pleaded in the complaint and, in a minority of states, provision of security-for-expense bond by the plaintiff shareholder).

10. See ALI, Principles of Corporate Governance § 7.05 (1994) (authorizing delegation of board authority to seek dismissal of a derivative action, approve a settlement, or seek a stay to a special litigating committee of disinterested directors even if a majority of the board is interested); id. at

§ 7.10 (providing for court dismissal of a derivative claim if the board has so recommended and the claim is subject to the business judgment rule, but subjecting the board's action to more scrutiny when the claim may involve a knowing and culpable violation of law or a violation of the duty of fair dealing).

11. An indemnity bond is required only in a minority of states. The cost of providing a bond that will reimburse the corporation or individual defendants for legal expenses incurred in defending an action determined to be lacking in merit is considerable: It may cost $30,000 to provide a bond of $100,000. ALI, Principles of Corporate Governance § 7.04, comment *h* (1994), opposes the "security-for-expenses" requirement because it chills meritorious actions and discriminates unfairly against small shareholders. The problem of irresponsible derivative actions, the ALI concludes, is dealt with more directly and effectively by other legal devices: (1) award of costs against a lawyer who brings a derivative action without legal cause, and (2) use of litigation committee reports to terminate suits.

judicial control is provided by the requirement that any settlement of a derivative suit must be approved by the court.

Yablonski states that corporate counsel's proper role in a derivative suit is to protect the corporation's interests, as distinct from the interests of either the director-defendants or the plaintiff-shareholders. Following this approach, corporate counsel should not jointly represent the corporation and either the director-defendants or the plaintiff-shareholders; the corporation is entitled to "independent counsel." Nevertheless, the court approves counsel's having jointly represented all defendants in the initial stages of the lawsuit. Why?

Some courts have allowed joint representation when the plaintiffs' suit appears to lack merit. This is seen as necessary to handle nuisance suits.[12] Representation during preliminary stages when the interests of the corporation and the officers either coincide or are being defined also may be proper.[13] Other courts, however, have questioned the "meritless" lawsuit standard.[14]

In Cannon v. United States Acoustics Corporation,[15] a leading case on the issue of joint representation, the court concluded that a lawyer should be disqualified from simultaneously representing the corporation and the individual officer defendants:

> [T]his is a derivative shareholder action against four officer-directors and two corporations. The complaint alleges that certain directors misappropriated monies of the corporation and violated federal and state securities laws. These are serious charges. If they are proved, the corporations stand to gain substantially. The [Code of Professional Responsibility] unquestionably prohibits one lawyer from representing multiple clients when their interests are in conflict. The Code goes so far as to say that if the clients' interests are potentially differing, the preferable course is for the lawyer to refuse the employment initially. . . .
>
> . . . Nevertheless, defendants' counsel argue there is no present conflict and should one arise they will withdraw their representation of the individual defendants and represent only the corporations. There are a number of problems with this solution. First, the complaint on its

---

12. See, e.g., Schwartz v. Guterman, 441 N.Y.S.2d 597, 598 (1981) ("In a meritless . . . suit [retaining] separate counsel for the corporation . . . may delay the matter and cause a needless expense, ultimately borne by the shareholders."); In re Conduct of Kinsey, 660 P.2d 660, 669 (Ore.1983) (counsel may represent all defendants if the suit is "patently sham or patently frivolous").

13. See Hausman v. Buckley, 299 F.2d 696, 699 (2d Cir.1962).

14. In Lewis v. Shaffer Stores Company, 218 F.Supp. 238, 240 (S.D.N.Y.1963), the court stated, "I have no doubt that . . . [the law firm for the defendants believes] in good faith that there is no merit to this action. Plaintiff, of course, vigorously contends to the contrary. The court cannot and should not attempt to pass upon the merits at this stage." The court held the corporation should retain independent counsel for the litigation.

15. 398 F.Supp. 209 (N.D.Ill.1975), aff'd in relevant part, 532 F.2d 1118 (7th Cir. 1976).

face establishes a conflict that cannot be ignored despite counsel's good faith representations. Second, counsel overlooks the hardship on the court and the parties if in the middle of this litigation new counsel must be obtained because a conflict arises. Lastly, although counsel offers to withdraw its representation of the individual defendants and remain counsel for the corporations if a conflict should arise, the appropriate course ... is for the corporation to retain independent counsel. Under this procedure, once counsel has examined the evidence, a decision can be made regarding the role the corporation will play in the litigation. This decision will be made without the possibility of any influence emanating from the representation of the individual defendants, and will also eliminate the potential problem of confidences and secrets reposed by the individual defendants being used adverse to their interests by former counsel should new counsel have had to have been selected under the approach suggested by defense counsel. This solution, concededly, is not without its disabilities. The corporations' rights to counsel of their choice are infringed and in a closely held corporation, as here, the financial burden is increased. Nevertheless, on balance, the corporations must obtain independent counsel....[16]

In contrast to *Cannon*, Comment [11] to M.R. 1.13 suggests that joint representation is presumptively valid:

The question can arise [in a shareholder derivative suit] whether counsel for the organization may defend such an action. The proposition that the organization is the lawyer's client does not alone resolve the issue. Most derivative actions are a normal incident of an organization's affairs, to be defended by the organization's lawyer like any other suit. However, if the claim involves serious charges of wrongdoing by those in control of the organization, a conflict may arise between the lawyer's duty to the organization and the lawyer's relationship with the board. In those circumstances, Rule 1.7 governs who should represent the directors and the organization.

Under corporate law, however, a derivative suit is predicated on failure of the board to take legal action appropriate to protect the corporation. Such inaction, if it occurred, necessarily involves at least serious neglect. Isn't that "wrongdoing?"

Comment [11] to M.R. 1.13 may reflect the more relaxed practice of lawyers representing small corporations, usually closely held, a setting in which joint representation and serving as "lawyer for the situation" have been common in the past. The older case law provides some support for the Comment's approach.[17] But almost all of the more recent cases find joint

16. 398 F.Supp. at 220; see also Messing v. FDI, Inc., 439 F.Supp. 776, 772 (D.N.J. 1977); Murphy v. Washington American League Base Ball Club, Inc., 324 F.2d 394 (D.C.Cir.1963); Harry G. Henn, Corporations § 370 (2d ed. 1970); Developments in the Law: Conflicts of Interest in the Legal Profession, 94 Harv.L.Rev. 1244, 1339–40 (1981).

17. See Selama–Dindings Plantations, Ltd. v. Durham, 216 F.Supp. 104 (S.D.Ohio 1963), aff'd, 337 F.2d 949 (6th Cir.1964);

representation improper, except in cases involving claims that clearly lack merit on their face.[18] Restatement § 212, comment *g*, reflects the modern view: in a derivative action the lawyer for the organization ordinarily should not also represent the individual defendants.[19]

Because of greater awareness of conflicts problems and concerns about malpractice, joint representation of both the corporation and officer defendants is rare today in situations involving large publicly held corporations. The corporation's regular counsel arranges for separate representation of any independent litigation committee. Officers and directors who are targeted by the action are usually represented independently. Corporate counsel remains involved on behalf of the corporate entity, but the representation is independent of that of the officer defendants. The view expressed in *Yablonski*, that the corporation has an "institutional interest" not voiced by a specific "constituent," either stockholder, officer or director, now largely prevails.

For a discussion of the attorney-client privilege in derivative suits, see p. 768 below.

Choosing Independent Counsel for a Corporation and Directing the Litigation

After the first *Yablonski* case, the president of the union, Boyle, selected new counsel for the union who were no more independent of his influence than the counsel they were replacing. Should the court have appointed successor counsel instead of leaving it to Boyle? Should the court have ordered the board of the corporate defendant (here, the union) to delegate to a group of independent directors, i.e., directors not implicated in the present action, the power to appoint and work with corporate counsel? Most courts agree with the court in *Yablonski* that court appointment interferes with corporate governance.[20] In Messing v. FDI,[21] after regular corporate counsel was disqualified, the court declined either to appoint counsel, as requested by the plaintiff shareholders, or approve a plan proposed by the board for selection of counsel. "It is for [the board], in the first instance, to devise a method to accommodate the need to continue the

---

Otis & Co. v. Pennsylvania R. Co., 57 F.Supp. 680 (E.D.Pa.1944), aff'd, 155 F.2d 522 (3d Cir.1946) (per curiam).

18. See, e.g., In re Conduct of Kinsey, 660 P.2d 660 (Ore.1983); cases cited in *Cannon*, 398 F.Supp. at 218–19.

19. Comment *g*, however, provides that "if the advice of the lawyer acting for the organization was an important factor in the action of the officers and directors that gave rise to the suit, it is appropriate for the lawyer to represent, if anyone, the officers and directors and for the organization to obtain new counsel." The comment goes on to point out that because representing

individual defendants in a derivative action would (under the rationale of derivative actions) be considered adverse to the corporation's interests, the consent of the corporation would be required even if the lawyer withdrew from representing the corporation before undertaking the defense of the individual officers. Would a per se rule advising the corporation's regular counsel to abstain from involvement in derivative actions make more sense?

20. See, e.g., *Cannon* supra; Lewis v. Shaffer Stores Company, 218 F.Supp. 238 (S.D.N.Y.1963).

21. 439 F.Supp. 776 (D.N.J.1977).

corporate enterprise while refraining from participating in any corporate decision in which they might have a personal interest. They act, or fail to act, at their peril.''[22]

Should a board, the majority of whose members are named as defendants in a derivative suit, be permitted to appoint a committee to direct the litigation for the corporation, usually referred to as a "special litigation committee"? Almost all courts have approved this solution because a contrary rule would permit one shareholder to incapacitate the entire board by leveling charges against a majority of its members.[23]

Court decisions differ on the deference to be given the judgments of special litigation committees. The leading Delaware case, Zapata Corp. v. Maldonado,[24] requires the corporation to demonstrate that the special litigation committee was independent, acted in good faith and had a reasonable basis for its decision. If the corporation meets that burden, the court may nonetheless exercise its own judgment to determine whether dismissing the shareholder's suit was in the best interests of the corporation. New York takes an approach of extreme judicial deference to the decisions of special litigation committees; the court's review is limited to whether the committee was independent, its decision disinterested and its procedures for decisionmaking appropriate.[25] Other jurisdictions have adopted their own approaches, generally somewhere between Delaware's more active judicial role and New York's extremely deferential approach.[26]

Mediating Among Competing Interests Within an Organization

Corporations and other organizations may become battlefields of conflicting interests. How much involvement by the lawyer is appropriate? For example, is it proper for corporation counsel to advise the president of the corporation on how to conduct an upcoming election of directors so as to

22. Id. at 783–84.

23. See, e.g., Hasan v. CleveTrust Realty Investors, 729 F.2d 372 (6th Cir.1984) (applying Massachusetts law); Joy v. North, 692 F.2d 880 (2d Cir.1982) (applying Connecticut law); Lewis v. Anderson, 615 F.2d 778 (9th Cir.1979) (applying California law); Abbey v. Control Data Corp., 603 F.2d 724 (8th Cir.1979) (applying Delaware law); Zapata Corp. v. Maldonado, 430 A.2d 779 (Del.1981); see also Principles of Corporate Governance § 7.10, comment f (1994).

24. 430 A.2d 779 (Del.1981).

25. See Auerbach v. Bennett, 393 N.E.2d 994 (N.Y.1979)

26. For a review of the various approaches adopted by state and federal courts on the degree of deference accorded a special litigation committee, see In re PSE & G Shareholder Litigation, 718 A.2d 254 (Super. Ct. N.J.1998) (also summarizing the views embodied in the ABA Model Business Corporation Act and ALI Principles of Corporate Governance). In PSE & G the New Jersey court endorsed the Massachusetts approach, see Houle v. Low, 556 N.E.2d 51 (Mass.1990). That approach requires that the corporation demonstrate that the special litigation committee was "at a minimum ... independent, unbiased and act[ing] in good faith" when it conducted a "thorough and careful analysis" of the shareholders' claims. In addition, the court must determine whether the committee reached "a reasonable and principled decision." The Massachusetts court listed factors, based on those identified in the Principles of Corporate Governance, that the court should consider in assessing the committee's decision.

frustrate a minority attempt to gain representation on the board? An ABA ethics opinion,[27] advising that such advice was appropriate, declared:

> In acting as counsel for a corporation a lawyer not only may but should give legal advice to its officers in all matters relating to the corporation as long as they are in office, except in situations where to his knowledge the interests of the officers are adverse to the interests of the corporation and the giving of the advice would be contrary to the interests of the corporation.

Would M.R. 1.13 or its Comment suggest a different conclusion? How is a lawyer to judge when the "giving of such advice would be contrary to the interests of the corporation?"

Questions such as those just discussed are infrequently presented to courts or disciplinary boards. Something has to go very wrong before a lawyer's decisions on such matters are reviewed in a formal setting. Even then, the lawyer's decisions are unlikely to be second-guessed except in egregious cases. Courts and disciplinary boards justifiably perceive that they cannot recreate the inner workings of organizations and their relationships with counsel. The reality that confronts corporate counsel is ordinarily too idiosyncratic, amorphous and dynamic to dissect in an adversary proceeding.[28]

This is not to suggest that courts should ignore gross misconduct. If the courts will not examine gross misconduct by lawyers, who will? In *Financial General Bankshares, Inc. v. Metzger*,[29] the district court found that attorney Metzger had breached his fiduciary and ethical duties to his corporate client by secretly engaging in attempts to seize or sell control of the company. The court held that Metzger's involvement with a group of minority shareholders who were plotting to take over the corporation with the aid of outside investors violated "the requirement that a corporate advisor remain neutral when confronted with an internecine conflict."[30] The court rejected Metzger's claim that his status as a shareholder gave him the right "to express his views on the management of the company." The court of appeals reversed, holding that the district court abused its discretion in exercising pendent jurisdiction over the local claim of lawyer misconduct after the federal securities law claims had been settled or dismissed.

---

27. ABA Informal Op. 1056 (1968).

28. On the inner workings of corporate bureaucracies, see Robert Jackall, Moral Mazes: The World of Corporate Managers (1988) (focusing on mid-level management); Geoffrey C. Hazard, Jr., Ethics and Politics in the Corporate World, 6 Yale J.Reg. 155 (1989) (reviewing Jackall's book).

29. 523 F.Supp. 744 (D.D.C.1981), rev'd for lack of jurisdiction, 680 F.2d 768 (D.C.Cir. 1982).

30. Id. at 765. The court cited Canon 5 of the Model Code; several ABA opinions, including Informal Op. 1056; and *Yablonski*, supra.

"Switching Sides" in a Derivative Suit: Representing Shareholders Against Management

Because shareholder derivative suits are brought on behalf of the corporation, it has been argued that a lawyer formerly engaged in representing the corporation would not be switching sides, i.e., opposing a former client, if she subsequently represented shareholders in a derivative suit. Most courts considering this argument have rejected it.[31] How would the Model Rules resolve this question? How would the corporate bar do so?

May an organization's lawyer, who also owns shares in the corporation, sue the corporation as a plaintiff-shareholder after terminating representation of the company? In Doe v. A. Corp.,[32] Doe had been an attorney with the law firm that represented the A. Corporation; he had worked on the corporation's business and had access to its confidential files. Two weeks before he left the firm, he bought one share of A. Corporation stock. He admitted that he bought this stock for the purpose of trying to oust current management by initiating a shareholder-derivative suit. He further conceded that "every fact alleged in the complaint" was acquired by him through his employment as A.'s lawyer. The court held: "[I]f an attorney believes that executives of a corporate client are engaging in wrongful conduct, he may disclose this to the corporation's board of directors; but he infringes [the professional duty of confidentiality] if he himself institutes suit."[33]

May an Organization's Lawyer Be a Plaintiff Against It?

In Hull v. Celanese Corp.,[34] Hull, an employee of Celanese, brought suit against the company alleging sex-based discrimination under Title VII of the Civil Rights Act of 1964. Delulio was a member of Celanese's in-house counsel staff, who had done some work on the Hull suit for Celanese. Delulio contacted Hull's lawyers and asked them to represent her in the lawsuit as another plaintiff. Celanese sought to disqualify the firm based on the risk that confidential information received by Delulio in her role as one of the corporation's lawyers would be used by the firm against Celanese. The firm argued that in its dealings with Delulio it had "cautioned [her] not to reveal any information received in confidence as an attorney for Celanese, but rather to confine her revelations ... to the facts of her own case."[35] The court, after commending the firm for the care it had taken, disqualified it from representing either plaintiff, and then added that its

31. See, e.g., Richardson v. Hamilton International Corporation, 469 F.2d 1382 (3d Cir.1972); Doe v. A. Corp., 330 F.Supp. 1352 (S.D.N.Y.1971), aff'd sub nom. Hall v. A. Corp., 453 F.2d 1375 (2d Cir.1972). But see Jacuzzi v. Jacuzzi Bros., Inc., 32 Cal. Rptr. 188, 191 (App.1963) (former attorney for the Jacuzzi company could represent shareholders in a derivative suit that sought to restore assets to the corporation; attorney acted "for the benefit of the cor-poration he previously represented" and, therefore, "is not representing an interest adverse to the corporation").

32. 330 F.Supp. 1352 (S.D.N.Y.1971), aff'd sub nom. Hall v. A. Corp., 453 F.2d 1375 (2d Cir.1972).

33. 330 F.Supp. at 1355, citing ABA Formal Op. 202 (1940).

34. 513 F.2d 568 (2d Cir.1975).

35. Id. at 571.

decision "should not be read to imply that either Hull or Delulio cannot pursue her claim of employment discrimination."[36]

How should Delulio's new lawyer proceed?

Protections for Corporate Officers and Agents[37]

Arrangements for protecting corporate directors and other top corporate officials from the legal risks of their decisions affect the decisions of lawyers engaged in suing and representing corporations. Corporate officials have two basic protections: First, the judicially developed "business judgment rule" shields directors from liability based on mere bad judgment.[38] Second, a complicated array of law and practice provides for indemnification from the corporation, for liability insurance or for both in many situations.

An officer or director who incurs expenses or liabilities while acting in good faith on the corporation's behalf has a strong claim to indemnification. On the other hand, the deterrent effect of legal sanctions is undercut and illegal conduct furthered if law permits officers and directors who have breached their fiduciary obligations to be indemnified at the expense of the corporation. State statutes govern a corporation's authority to make advance arrangements or after-the-fact decisions to indemnify officers and directors.[39]

The indemnification arrangements affect the incentives of parties and their lawyers in bringing and settling derivative suits. If the plaintiff's lawyer, who usually finances the litigation, loses on the merits, a fee-shifting provision may impose the defendants' costs on the plaintiff's lawyer. On the other hand, if the case is settled, the settlement may provide for an attorney's fee award. From the defendants' point of view, in a jurisdiction following the Delaware pattern, a settlement that includes no award on the merits but is limited to a fee award is also advantageous, because expenses may be indemnified or covered by insurance while a judgment on the merits cannot. Thus both sides have an incentive to agree on a settlement that limits relief to prospective procedural changes on the part of the corporation combined with a handsome fee award to the plaintiff's lawyer. Is this a form of collusion that violates professional ethics?[40] The lawyer for a corporation who agrees to a settlement that

36. Id. at 572.

37. For discussions of director and officer liability, see Reinier H. Kraakman, Corporate Liability Strategies and the Cost of Legal Controls, 93 Yale L.J. 857 (1984); John C. Coffee, Jr., Beyond the Shut–Eyed Sentry: Toward a Theoretical View of Corporate Misconduct and an Effective Response, 63 Va.L.Rev. 1099 (1977); Coffee, Corporate Governance and Directors' Liabilities: The Legal, Economic, and Sociological Analysis of Corporate Social Responsibility (K. Hopt & G. Teubner eds. 1984).

38. See generally ALI, Principles of Corporate Governance § 4.01 (1994).

39. See Dale A. Oesterle, Limits on a Corporation's Protection of Its Directors and Officers from Personal Liability, 1983 Wis. L.Rev. 513, 520–21 (with footnotes containing citations to statutory provisions).

40. Settlement patterns suggest the possibility of collusive settlements in which the plaintiff's lawyer recovers generous attorney's fees in return for a settlement that permits the defendants to be indemnified

relieves the directors of liability and transfers that liability to the corporation may later face a suit for malpractice, assuming, that is, that the corporation's management changes.[41]

Another protection available to corporate officers and agents is the "reliance on counsel" defense. Good faith reliance on advice of counsel allows corporate officers to escape liability for acts taken in their official capacity if such reliance negates relevant intent. On the other hand, permitting this defense puts a premium on an opinion that shields the officer and may encourage "opinion shopping."[42]

Lawyers Serving on Client's Board of Directors and Firms Investing in Client Stock

Comment [14] to Model Rule 1.7 reads in part:

A lawyer for a corporation or other organization who is a member of its board of directors should determine whether the responsibilities of the two roles may conflict. The lawyer may be called on to advise the corporation in matters involving actions of the directors. Consideration should be given to the frequency with which such situations may arise, the potential intensity of the conflict, the effect of the lawyer's resignation from the board and the possibility of the corporation's obtaining legal advice from another lawyer for such situations. If there is material risk that the dual role will compromise the lawyer's independence of professional judgment the lawyer should not serve as a director.

In an informal opinion in 1966,[43] the ABA stated that it was not an ethical violation for a lawyer for a bank also to serve on the bank's board of directors. The brief opinion stated that the dual role is a common practice "which to our knowledge has not been criticized" and that it did not involve the representation of conflicting interests. Since then, commentators have argued that the dual role is risky, unsound and should be prohibited by law.[44]

Lawyers who serve in dual roles as outside counsel and member of the client's board of directors may jeopardize the attorney-client privilege. The privilege is not available for information communicated to or learned by counsel through membership on the board.[45] The dual role may also create

by the corporation for their expenses. See Janet Cooper Alexander, Do the Merits Matter? A Study of Settlements in Securities Class Actions, 43 Stan.L.Rev. 497 (1991). ALI, 2 Principles of Corporate Governance 4–16 (1994), discusses policy arguments concerning the derivative action and summarizes available empirical studies.

41. See, e.g., Durkin v. Shea & Gould, 92 F.3d 1510 (9th Cir.1996), cert. denied 520 U.S. 1197 (1997).

42. See Douglas W. Hawes and Thomas J. Sherrard, Reliance on Advice of Counsel as a Defense in Corporate and Securities Cases, 62 Va.L.Rev. 1 (1976).

43. ABA Informal Op. 930 (1966).

44. See, e.g., Wolfram, Modern Legal Ethics 738–40 (1986); Simon Lorne, The Corporate and Securities Adviser, the Public Interest, and Professional Ethics, 76 Mich. L.Rev. 423, 490–95 (1978).

45. See, e.g., Securities and Exchange Commission v. Gulf & Western Industries, Inc., 518 F.Supp. 675 (D.D.C.1981).

conflict of interest and disqualification questions, risks whether the law firm's advice will be considered, for purposes of the business judgment rule, that of an "independent" director, and exposes the law firm to much greater risks of liability to the client and to third persons.[46] Some law firms prohibit their members from sitting on the boards of client corporations; others have lawyers on the boards of almost all clients. Malpractice insurers oppose the practice and sometimes decline to insure firms following the practice, arguing that it greatly increases a law firm's risk of civil liability.

What about having a client pay for legal services, at least in part, with its stock instead of cash? Some firms routinely offer this option to clients who seek legal assistance in connection with an initial public offering (IPO) of the clients' stock. Ostensibly this practice makes it easier for fledgling companies to afford high quality legal services. The practice, however, is fraught with danger. First, there is the danger of lawyer over-reaching, which is present in all lawyer-client business transactions. See Model Rule 1.8(a) and the discussion of business transactions with a client at p. 557 supra. In response to that danger, case law shifts the risk to the lawyer (or law firm) of any ambiguity in the lawyer-client contract or any misstep in the formation or execution of the transaction. Thus, the law firm may find itself deprived of the benefit of the bargain it makes with the client. Next, failure to disclose the details of the payment-in-stock arrangement may leave the firm and its client liable to investors for misrepresentation. Third, the law firm's stake in the client may give lawyers within the firm an incentive to blind themselves to client wrongdoing in a misguided attempt to protect the firm's investment. Recall how Singer, Hutner's dependence on its client OPM gave the firm an incentive to bend over backwards to keep the client afloat, i.e., to keep the fraud from being discovered, with the result that the firm's liability continued to grow. See p. 304 above. Fourth, the firm's stake in the client will constitute evidence from which a factfinder may legitimately infer the lawyer's intent to aid any subsequently-discovered client illegality resulting from the lawyer's (perhaps unknowing) assistance.

3.   DUTIES OF CORPORATION'S LAWYER FACED WITH CORPORATE WRONGDOING

A lawyer for a corporation learns that the corporation, under the direction of incumbent management, is planning or is engaged in serious wrongdoing. The officers in control refuse to recognize the problem or to do anything about it. What should the lawyer do? The alternatives include: remaining silent while continuing to represent the corporation, withdrawing from representation but remaining silent, seeking review within the corporate structure and, finally, making a "noisy withdrawal," one which discloses the problem to affected persons or the public.

---

46. For a summary of the risks, see Micalyn S. Harris and Karen L. Valihura, Is Dual Service Unethical?, Prof.Lawyer 2 (Fall 1998).

The Model Code's primary provision on the organizational client, EC 5–18, provides little guidance on these matters. The Model Rules contain a more elaborate provision.

Model Rule 1.13: Organization as Client

Model Rule 1.13(a) states that a lawyer for an organization represents the organization not its constituents.[1] M.R. 1.13(b) addresses what a lawyer should do when a constituent, e.g., an officer or employee, is acting in a way that may legally harm the organization:

> (b) If a lawyer for an organization knows that an officer, employee or other person associated with the organization is engaged in action, intends to act or refuses to act in a matter related to the organization that is a violation of a legal obligation to the organization, or a violation of law which reasonably might be imputed to the organization, the lawyer shall proceed as is reasonably necessary in the best interest of the organization. . . .

Note that only those acts harmful to the *organization* trigger the rule: An act must either be a violation of a legal obligation owed to the organization, such as a fiduciary duty or contractual obligation, or a violation of law that might reasonably be imputed to the organization.

Assuming the rule is triggered, M.R. 1.13(b) continues:

> In determining how to proceed, the lawyer shall give due consideration to the seriousness of the violation and its consequences, the scope and nature of the lawyer's representation, the responsibility in the organization and the apparent motivation of the person involved, the policies of the organization concerning such matters and any other relevant considerations. . . .

The rule further requires that "[a]ny measure taken shall be designed to minimize disruption of the organization and the risk of revealing information relating to the representation to persons outside the organization."

What may the lawyer do? The rule has a non-exhaustive list ("such measures may include among others"): (1) asking reconsideration of the matter; (2) advising that a separate legal opinion on the matter be sought for presentation to appropriate authority in the organization; and (3) referring the matter to higher authority in the organization, including, if warranted by the seriousness of the matter, referral to the highest authority that can act in behalf of the organization as determined by applicable law.

What should the lawyer do if the highest authority (which, in the case of a corporation, is usually the board of directors) refuses to act in the best

---

1. See George C. Harris, Taking the Entity Theory Seriously: Lawyer Liability for Failure to Prevent Harm to Organizational Clients Through Disclosure of Constituent Wrongdoing, 11 Geo.J. Legal Eth. 597 (1998); Stephen Gillers, Model Rule 1.13(c) Gives the Wrong Answer to the Question of Corporate Counsel Disclosure, 1 Geo.J.Legal Ethics 289 (1987).

interests of the corporation to prevent the harm? Should the lawyer inform the shareholders? A government agency? Rule 1.13, as proposed by the Kutak Commission[2] provided that the lawyer's options "may include revealing information, otherwise protected by Rule 1.6 *only if* the lawyer reasonably believes that:"

(1) the highest authority in the organization has acted to further the personal or financial interests of members of that authority which are in conflict with the interest of the organization; *and*

(2) revealing the information is necessary in the best interest of the organization.

The Kutak Commission proposal was rejected by the ABA House of Delegates, and M.R. 1.13(c) as adopted reads:

If, despite the lawyer's efforts in accordance with paragraph (b), the highest authority that can act on behalf of the organization insists upon action, or a refusal to act, that is clearly a violation of law, and is likely to result in substantial injury to the organization, the lawyer may resign in accordance with Rule 1.16.

Is M.R. 1.13 as adopted a "board as client" concept more than one of "organization as client"? Consider the approach suggested by the American Trial Lawyers Association (ATLA) in the American Lawyer's Code of Conduct (ALCC). ALCC Rule 2.5 provides that the board of directors of a corporation shall instruct the lawyer on how to resolve conflicts of interests that might arise among the interests of the board, officers and shareholders and that the lawyer shall follow those instructions whenever a conflict among the organization's constituents arises. The Comment to ALCC 2.5 explains that "one board might prefer to maximize candor between its officers and the lawyer" by instructing the lawyer to keep the officers secrets from the board. "Another board might prefer to know everything the lawyer knows." Are board members free under other law to prefer ignorance of an officer's secrets? Recall the reckless scienter standard discussed in Chapter 2.

Does M.R. 1.13 sufficiently protect the lawyer from liability under other law? Consider the standards in *Benjamin* and *Greycas*, Chapter 2 supra, and the *Klein* and *O.P.M.* cases in Chapter 4. Consider the adequacy of M.R. 1.13 in reading *ACC/Lincoln (Jones Day)*, the next principal case.

In the real world of corporate practice, lawyers often see the client as management (the real-life people who run the company), not some abstract entity. The "organization as client" approach embodied in Rule 1.13 is out-of-sync with that experience. However, the approach is grounded in both the law of corporations and the law of agency. The law of corporations recognizes the corporation as a "person" capable of holding privileges and entering into relationships;[3] the law of agency describes and delineates the

---

2. Revised Final Draft M.R. 1.13(c), June 30, 1982 (emphasis added).

3. See Dartmouth College v. Woodward, 17 U.S. (4 Wheat.) 518, 636 (1819); New Colo-

relationships among agents that serve a common principal (the lawyer, the CEO, the directors, etc. and the corporation).[4] This grounding in substantive law apart from the ethics rules provides a structure of legal relationships in which to locate the lawyer's role.[5]

Reality's intrusion on the idea of "organization as client" is perhaps most acute when one person dominates the organization. For example, in *Carter and Johnson,* discussed in the next note, the manager calling the shots, Hart, had a controlling stockholder interest and held the major offices in the company. Should this make a difference in the lawyer's analysis of who the client is? If not, what can the lawyer who is faced with such a dominant figure do to ensure some measure of independence?[6]

The Securities and Exchange Commission's View of the Corporate Lawyer's Duties

A number of years after taking on the organized bar by filing the complaint in *National Student Marketing,* reprinted in Chapter 2 at p. 104, the SEC opened up a second front. In *National Student Marketing* the SEC had charged the lawyers with substantive violations of the securities law (aiding and abetting securities fraud) and had sought injunctive relief to prevent future violations. In the next major action instituted against lawyers, the SEC employed a different tool, Rule 2(e), which has since become Rule 102(e).[7] This rule authorizes the SEC to discipline professionals in order to "protect the integrity of its own processes."[8]

IN RE CARTER AND JOHNSON.[9] Lawyers William R. Carter and Charles J. Johnson represented National Telephone Company, a telephone leasing company, from 1973 until the company stopped operations in 1975. There was no doubt who ran National: Sheldon L. Hart, who was a company founder, its controlling stockholder, CEO, chairman of the board of directors, president and treasurer all rolled into one. By 1974 National had big cash-flow problems, although it presented an outward picture of financial prosperity. To address its cash shortage, the company arranged for a $15 million loan from a consortium of banks in the spring of 1974. Before the loan could be finalized, however, National began taking short term advances on the loan and, by September 1974, had used up almost the entire line of credit. To placate the banks, National agreed that if the

---

nial Ice Co. v. Helvering, 292 U.S. 435, 442 (1933).

4. See Restatement (Second) of Agency generally and § 1, comment *e* (on the lawyer as agent) (1958); Floyd R. Mechem, Outlines of the Law on the Law of Agency, particularly § 12(a), 76 (4th ed.1952); see also William M. Fletcher, Cyclopedia of the Law of Private Corporations, §§ 275, 437, 466.3, 483 (rev.perm.ed.1982).

5. See the Koniak & Cohen excerpt reprinted at p. 848 infra.

6. The *O.P.M.* case, p. 304 supra, is another instance of dominant figures in an organization harming the entity.

7. See 17 C.F.R. 201.102(e) (1998). Amendment to Rule 102(e) of the Commission's Rules of Practice, Securities Act Release No. 33–7593, 63 Fed. Reg. 57164 (1998).

8. Touche Ross & Co. v. SEC, 609 F.2d 570, 581 (2d Cir. 1979).

9. Exchange Act Release No. 17,597 [1981 Transfer Binder] Fed. Sec. L. Rep. (CCH) ¶ 82,847 (Feb. 28, 1981).

company continued to experience cash shortages or tried to borrow more money, it would institute a "lease maintenance program" (LMP). Under the terms of the LMP, National would wind down its business by restricting sales and only maintaining leases which it had already sold.

During this period of financial crisis, National's president, Sheldon Hart, failed to disclose the financial problems that the company was facing and continued to issue optimistic reports to National's shareholders and the financial community. The lawyers, who were in "close and continuing contact with the company," clearly knew of its financial woes. In December of 1974, the lawyers helped Hart prepare a press release and a Form 8–K to be filed with the SEC. Neither of these documents disclosed the particulars of the loan agreement, the existence of the LMP or the potential consequences of both for National.

By March 1975, National's circumstances triggered its obligation to implement the LMP. Hart, without knowledge of counsel, falsely certified to the banks that the LMP had been initiated. Later in March and again in April, Carter and Johnson advised Hart that National should publicly disclose its obligation to implement the LMP. Hart, however, refused to follow that advice. In fact, the terms of the loan agreement, including National's obligation to implement the LMP were not disclosed until May 27, 1975, three days after Hart was forced to resign as National's president. A month later National declared bankruptcy.

The SEC staff charged that the attorneys had engaged in unethical and unprofessional conduct in their representation of National. After a hearing, the Administrative Law Judge (ALJ) found that the evidence supported the charges and suspended Carter from appearing before the Commission for one year and Johnson for nine months. The SEC reversed, holding that there was insufficient evidence of willfulness on the part of the lawyers to sustain the aiding and abetting charge.[10] As to the ethical violations, the Commission clearly considered the lawyers' conduct unacceptable, but reversed the ALJ nonetheless. The Commission explained that the ethical and professional responsibilities of securities lawyers had "not been so firmly and unambiguously established that ... all practicing lawyers ... [could] be held to an awareness of ... [the] norms."[11] Thus, it would not

10. Id. at ¶¶ 84,167–84,169. Dissenting, Commissioner Evans stated he would have found Carter had aided and abetted the primary violations of Hart and his company.

11. Recall the discussion of the state's weak commitment to enforcing its vision of the law of lawyering described in the Koniak excerpt at p. 133 supra. While arguing that the norms were too uncertain to justify holding Carter and Johnson to any particular standard, the Commission also stated that "while precise standards have not yet emerged, it is fair to say that there exists considerable acceptance of the proposition that a lawyer must, in order to discharge his professional responsibilities, make all efforts within reason to persuade his client to avoid or terminate proposed illegal action." Id. at 84,170. The statement that a proposition has garnered "considerable acceptance" does not state a particularly demanding or specific standard of conduct. More important, the Commission apparently did not believe it appropriate to punish Carter and Johnson for violating such a developing norm without having an-

hold Carter and Johnson responsible for any ethical lapses in their representation of National. Instead, the SEC used the case as a vehicle to announce standards to be applied in the future in Rule 2(e) proceedings against lawyers:

> When a lawyer with significant responsibilities in the effectuation of a company's compliance with the disclosure requirements of the federal securities laws becomes aware that his client is engaged in substantial and continuing failure to satisfy those disclosure requirements, his continued participation violates professional standards unless he takes prompt steps to end the client's noncompliance.[12]

According to the Commission, "counseling accurate disclosure" would suffice to keep a lawyer out of trouble even if the client did not follow; it would be enough, that is, as long as the client had not been engaged in a continuing pattern of nondisclosure. On the other hand, when the client engaged in a continuing pattern of nondisclosure sufficient to cause a reasonable lawyer to conclude that his advice was not going to be followed (or was not sought in good faith), the lawyer had to take "more affirmative steps ... to avoid the inference that he has been co-opted willingly or unwillingly into the scheme of non-disclosure."[13] At that juncture, the lawyer should consider a "direct approach" to members of the corporation's senior management or its board of directors. The lawyer should also consider resigning.

The Commission refused, however, to dictate any particular course of conduct to be followed, stating that the lawyer in the situation was best positioned to determine the precise steps to be taken. The SEC staff had hoped for a stronger ruling from the Commission, perhaps one imposing an affirmative duty of disclosure on lawyers faced with client intransigence.[74] The Commission had created a firestorm in *National Student Marketing* by allowing the staff to argue that sometimes lawyers were required to disclose fraud to the SEC.[75] In *Carter and Johnson,* a more cautious Commission did not mention disclosure as one of the possible actions a lawyer should consider when faced with a client engaged in a continuing pattern of securities fraud.

The SEC issued a request for comments on the rule laid down in *Carter and Johnson.*[76] In doing so, the SEC stated that the following rule taken from *Carter and Johnson* would apply to all conduct occurring after

---

nounced specifically that it would be holding lawyers to that norm.

12. Id. at ¶ 84,172.

13. Id.

74. SEC Commissioner A. A. Sommer startled the securities bar in 1973 by stating that "in securities matters (other than those where advocacy is clearly proper) the attorney will have to function in a manner more akin to that of the auditor than to that of the advocate." Sommer, Emerging Responsibilities of the Securities Lawyer, [1973–74 Transfer Binder] Fed.Sec.L.Rep. (CCH) ¶ 79,631 (Jan.1974). This and other statements suggested a duty of disclosure.

75. See the discussion of the bar's reaction to the complaint in *National Student Marketing* at p. 285, n. 9 supra.

76. Sec. Act Release No. 6344, Sec. Exchange Act Release No. 18106 (Sept. 21, 1981).

February 28, 1981 and would remain the rule unless modified by the SEC: "What is required, in short, is some prompt action that leads to the conclusion that the lawyer is engaged in efforts to correct the underlying problem, rather than having capitulated to the desires of a strong-willed, but misguided client."

The ABA responded by challenging the SEC's authority to discipline lawyers under Rule 2(e) and objecting to the *Carter and Johnson* rule, as it had been summarized by the SEC.[77] Commentators also criticized the SEC's use of 2(e) in cases like *Carter and Johnson*, arguing that lawyers would become over-cautious in order to protect themselves from liability, which would in turn result in clients keeping more and more information from their lawyers.[78] After the comment period, the SEC took no further official action on the *Carter and Johnson* rule release.

The SEC, however, continues to assert that it has the authority to issue and enforce what is now Rule 102(e), but it has brought very few cases against lawyers and has refrained from articulating general standards of conduct for securities lawyers.[79] In 1992, the SEC revisited the obligations of securities lawyers who have significant responsibilities for a client's compliance with the securities law:

IN RE GUTFREUND.[80] The case involved the failure of supervisors at Salomon Bros.—including Gutfreund, then Salomon's CEO—to respond adequately to the misconduct of a Salomon trader, which had come to their attention. The head of Salomon's government trading desk admitted to his supervisors that he had submitted false bids on Treasury securities. While the supervisors took almost no action and made inadequate disclosure of this wrong to federal authorities, the trader again made false bids. The SEC held that three Salomon officers had breached their duty to supervise

---

77. ABA Section of Corporation, Banking and Business Law, 37 Bus.Law. 915 (1982). So much for the "considerable acceptance" that the SEC had claimed existed for the norm it articulated.

78. See, e.g., Richard L. Miller, The Distortion and Misuse of Rule 2(e), 7 Sec.Reg.L.J. 54, 59 n. 13 (1979); Steven C. Krane, The Attorney Unshackled: SEC Rule 2(e) Violates Clients' Sixth Amendment Right to Counsel, 57 Notre Dame Lawyer 50 (1981); Note, SEC Disciplinary Proceedings Against Attorneys Under Rule 2(e), 79 Mich.L.Rev. 1270, 1275–77, 1285 (1981). SEC Commissioner Roberta Karmel, who had recused herself in *Carter and Johnson* because she formerly had been a partner with the law firm that had represented some of the directors of National Telephone, attacked the Commission's position in a series of dissenting opinions and articles. See, e.g., Joseph C. Daley & Roberta S. Karmel, Attorneys' Responsibilities: Adversaries at the Bar of the SEC, 24 Emory L.J. 747 (1975).

79. See Steve Nelson, Hushed SEC Voice Adds Little to Legal Ethics Debate, Legal Times, May 16, 1983, at p. 13. In 1991 the Commission ruled that it did not have authority to order a prominent New York City securities lawyer, George C. Kern, Jr., to comply with SEC rules requiring timely disclosure of developments that could affect the price of publicly traded securities. Kern, who served both as lawyer to and director of a company, failed promptly to disclose the company's talks with a third party during a takeover contest. See S.E.C. Drops Merger Case, N.Y.Times, June 22, 1991, at p. 45; Gregory A. Robb, S.E.C. Hears Arguments in Lawyer Case, N.Y.Times, June 9, 1989, at p. D1.

80. Exchange Act Release No. 31, 554, [1992 Transfer Binder] Fed. Sec. L. Rep. (CCH) ¶ 85,067 (Dec. 3, 1992).

under the Exchange Act.[81] Feuerstein, Salomon's chief legal officer, was not named in the *Gutfreund* complaint because he was not a direct supervisor of the trader whose conduct was in issue. But the SEC nonetheless addressed his role"to amplify [the SEC's] views on the supervisory responsibilities of legal and compliance officers in Feuerstein's position."[82] Despite the fact that he was not a direct supervisor of the trader, the SEC found that a lawyer in Feuerstein's position could be liable for a breach of the supervisory duty by virtue of having a position that invests the lawyer with substantial responsibility for compliance with the securities law.

The SEC emphasized that senior management had told the lawyer about the misconduct "to obtain his advice and guidance, and to involve him as part of management's collective response to the problem" and that the lawyer had recommended discipline and otherwise directed the company's response to misconduct in previous instances.[83] On these facts, the SEC concluded that the lawyer "shares the responsibility to take appropriate action to respond to the misconduct."[84] Once a lawyer with such general responsibility became involved in formulating the client's response to misconduct, he was "obligated to take affirmative steps to ensure" that the misconduct was adequately addressed. Moreover, if such a lawyer "takes appropriate steps but management fails to act and [the lawyer] . . . knows or has reason to know of that failure" she must consider what more can be done. According to the SEC, these additional steps might include "disclosure of the matter to the entity's board of directors, resignation from the . . . [representation], *or disclosure to regulatory authorities.*" Having raised the specter of disclosure to the government of client wrongdoing, the SEC added that applicable ethics rules "may bear upon what course of conduct the individual may properly pursue,"[85] an obvious reference to the differences among state versions of Rule 1.6.

The ABA and the securities bar often mischaracterize the SEC's position as one that converts a lawyer into a law enforcement officer bound to betray her client. Neither the *Carter and Johnson* standard nor the *Gutfreund* opinion, however, obligates a securities lawyer to blow the whistle on a client. Both require only that some action consistent with the law and ethics of lawyering be taken by the lawyer. Is that too much for the government to ask?

The Lincoln Savings and Loan Frauds

The real estate binge of the 1980s combined with partial deregulation of federally-insured savings and loan institutions, along with other factors, resulted in the failure of hundreds of thrifts. Meeting the national obli-

---

81. 15 U.S.C. § 78o(b)(4)(E) (1994). Under this section, the SEC may impose liability where a broker-dealer has "failed reasonably to supervise, with a view to preventing violations [of the federal securities laws], another person who commits such a violation, if such person is subject to his supervision."

82. In re Gutfreund at ¶ 83,608.

83. Id. at ¶¶ 83–608 to 83–609.

84. Id. at ¶ 83–609.

85. Id. at ¶ 83,609 n.26.

gation to stand behind deposits cost federal taxpayers hundreds of billions of dollars. Federal agencies brought civil and criminal proceedings against many managers of failed thrifts and their professional advisers, including the lawyers who represented the thrifts. Investors in and creditors of the thrifts also brought civil suits which presented many of the same issues. The next case involves one of the more notorious savings and loan institutions, Lincoln, and its equally notorious owner/operator Charles Keating.

Lincoln Savings and Loan was a wholly owned subsidiary of American Continental Corporation (ACC) and both companies were under the direct control of Charles Keating. The following is a rough sketch of the central wrongdoing conducted through Lincoln. First, there was the land/tax scheme.[86] Lincoln had bought cheap land. This land was a Lincoln asset but not a profit generating one. If the land could be sold (or appear to be sold) at a huge profit, the tax sharing plan Lincoln had with its parent ACC would require Lincoln to upstream a portion of the profit to ACC, ostensibly for ACC to pass on to federal and state taxing authorities. Cash, once diverted to ACC, could then be used for other purposes such as paying high salaries to ACC officials and funding other Keating projects. Bogus land transactions, combined with the tax sharing plan, would make the cash transfer possible.

The scheme worked this way: Lincoln would lend X, for example, $500,000. X would, usually on the same day, turn around and loan Y $400,000. Y would then purchase land from Lincoln for, say, $350,000, also on the same day or a day later. The land "purchased" would be land Lincoln had bought for perhaps $50,000. Lincoln would then book a profit of $300,000 on this transaction, allowing it to upstream a portion of that $300,000 to ACC under the tax sharing plan. ACC would spend that money, not save it to pass on to taxing authorities. Y would then, invariably, default on its loan to X, and X would take possession of the land "purchased" by Y from Lincoln, which was the security for the loan X had made to Y. X would then default on Lincoln's loan to it, and the land would be transferred from X to Lincoln in lieu of the cash (with interest) that was "due" Lincoln under its loan agreement with X.

Thus, at the end of this series of "linked" transactions, Lincoln would have: (1) the land it had started with; (2) a "bad" loan on its books that had been settled by seizing the land ("security" for the loan); (3) a profit on its books from the "sale" of land it had bought "low" and sold "high;" and (4) less cash in its coffers due to the upstreaming of a portion of the "profit" just mentioned. A series of such transactions, combined with other factors, led to Lincoln's insolvency, seizure by banking regulators and taxpayer-funded payments to Lincoln depositors.

To pull off the land/tax scheme Lincoln had to portray the loan to X as unconnected to Y's purchase of the land, and the price Y paid as fair (not

---

86. For a detailed description of this scheme and the defense of the accountants on whose watch this scheme was perpetrated, see Hearing of the House Committee on Banking, Finance and Urban Affairs, Nov. 14, 1989.

inflated). If the bank regulators noticed how little reason Lincoln had to believe that X would repay its loan, i.e., how bad a credit risk X was, then the connection between the land and loan would be more apparent. The fact that the underwriting for X's loan was non-existent or poorly documented would have been the first sign to bank regulators that something was amiss. Thus, "fixing" Lincoln's underwriting files was a key concern, as the case below demonstrates. Providing appraisals to Lincoln showing that Y paid a fair price for the land was also important to the scheme's success.

Another Lincoln scheme involved the sale of ACC debentures (bonds) in Lincoln's branch offices in California. The investors in those bonds later alleged that the manner of sale led them to believe that the ACC bond obligations were actually Lincoln obligations that were either federally insured or guaranteed. Finally, there were Lincoln's efforts to keep federal bank regulators at bay and to influence regulatory policy so that relatively high-risk investment strategies (with federally insured dollars) could be pursued by Lincoln. The lobbying campaign gave rise to what became known as the Keating Five scandal.[87] This scandal involved five Senators who received major campaign contributions from Keating and simultaneously intervened on his behalf with bank regulators, seeking to short-circuit or stall their investigation of Lincoln and get them to adopt regulatory policies or interpretations of existing policies that would make Keating's risky investments easier to pursue. One of Keating's particular goals was to change federal regulations to allow savings and loans to allocate more federally insured deposit money into direct investments instead of more traditional activity, i.e., making mortgage loans to local homeowners. The case below refers to this goal as Keating's efforts to "sunset" the Federal Home Loan Bank Board's (FHLBB's) "direct investment regulation."

In Re American Continental Corp./Lincoln Savings and Loan Securities Litigation (Jones Day)

United States District Court, District of Arizona, 1992.
794 F.Supp. 1424.

■ Before BILBY, D.J.:

This Opinion describes the basis of this court's rulings by order of February 14, 1992, on motions for summary judgment filed by parties to these consolidated actions.

I. PROCEDURAL HISTORY

Five separate actions are consolidated before this court [including a class action by purchasers of securities of American Continental Corp.

87. See Richard L. Berke, Appearances Worry Congress as S. & L. Shadow Length- ens, N.Y. Times, July 29, 1990, at p. 1.

("ACC") and an action by Resolution Trust Co., as receiver for Lincoln Savings & Loan Association ("Lincoln"). The actions charged professionals who provided services to ACC and/or Lincoln with civil liability for violations of federal securities laws, RICO and its Arizona counterpart and also sought damages under various state law claims of fraud, negligent misrepresentation and breach of fiduciary duty.]

These actions originate from the business dealings of Charles H. Keating, Jr. ("Keating"), former chairman of ACC. The claims at issue here were brought principally against professionals who provided services to ACC and/or Lincoln Savings. These include [a long list of accounting firms, law firms, consulting firms and others. Among the defendants are Jones, Day, Reavis & Pogue ("Jones Day"), a Cleveland-based law firm, and two of its individual partners.]

On February 14, 1992, following lengthy discovery, extensive briefing and oral argument, and after a review of voluminous pleadings, depositions, exhibits, and other papers, this court ruled on numerous motions for summary judgment. . . . At that time, the court stated that it would in due course issue this Memorandum Opinion, setting forth its analysis supporting the decision to grant or deny, in whole or in part, the various motions for summary judgment.

· · ·

II. LAW OF GENERAL APPLICATION

Section 10(b) of the [Securities and] Exchange Act

· · ·

... In Hollinger v. Titan Capital Corp., 914 F.2d 1564 (9th Cir.1990), the Ninth Circuit adopted a standard for the minimal culpable mindset, referred to hereinafter by this court as "reckless scienter." The Ninth Circuit held:

> Reckless conduct may be defined as the highly unreasonable omission, involving not merely simple, or even inexcusable negligence, but an extreme departure from the standards of ordinary care, which presents a danger of misleading buyers or sellers that is either known to the defendant or so obvious that the actor must have been aware of it.

Id. at 1569. The *Hollinger* court observed that "the danger of misleading buyers must be actually known or so obvious that any reasonable [person] would be legally bound as knowing, and the omission must derive from something more egregious than even 'white heart/empty head' good faith." Id. at 1569–70. Thus, the court concluded, "recklessness is a lesser form of intent rather than a greater degree of negligence."

· · ·

Aiding and abetting securities fraud—or secondary liability—requires proof of the following elements: (1) the existence of an independent primary wrong; (2) knowledge by the alleged aider and abetter of the wrong and of his or her role in furthering it; and (3) substantial assistance in the wrong. Levine [v. Diamanthuset, Inc.], 950 F.2d at 1483; Roberts v. Peat, Marwick, Mitchell & Co., 857 F.2d 646, 652 (9th Cir.1988). As with a primary violation, a defendant must know of the fraud, or recklessly disregard it. Levine, 950 F.2d at 1483.

Proof of substantial assistance requires a showing that the defendant's assistance was a substantial factor in causing the plaintiff's harm. Mendelsohn v. Capital Underwriters, Inc., 490 F.Supp. 1069, 1084 (N.D. Cal.1979). "Substantial assistance means more than a little aid." Barker v. Henderson, Franklin, Starnes & Holt, 797 F.2d 490, 496 (7th Cir.1986). Where substantial assistance is premised on actual misrepresentations, the *Hollinger* standard applies. Levine, 950 F.2d at 1484.

. . .

. . . If aiding and abetting liability is to be premised exclusively on silence or inaction, it may be necessary for the court to consider whether a defendant operates under a duty of disclosure. . . . "When it is impossible to find any duty of disclosure, an alleged aider-abettor should be found liable only if scienter of the high 'conscious intent' variety can be proved. Where some special duty of disclosure exists, then liability should be possible with a lesser degree of scienter."

. . .

Racketeering Influenced and Corrupt Organizations Act

. . .

To establish a RICO claim, plaintiffs must prove defendants intended to devise and did devise a scheme to defraud. United States v. Bohonus, 628 F.2d 1167 (9th Cir.1980). "The scheme must be reasonably calculated to deceive persons of ordinary prudence and comprehension." Id. at 1172. "Thus, the fraud must be active, not merely constructive." Id. Intent may be shown by examining the scheme itself. Id. "The fraudulent scheme need not be one which includes an affirmative misrepresentation of fact, since it is only necessary [to prove] that the scheme was calculated to deceive persons of ordinary prudence." Id. at 1172. "[D]eceitful concealment of material facts is not constructive fraud but actual fraud." Id. (citing Cacy v. United States, 298 F.2d 227, 229 (9th Cir.1961)).

The standard for aiding and abetting a RICO violation parallels that under Section 10(b). . . . A defendant must have knowledge or act with reckless scienter. See discussion of Section 10(b) standards, supra. This court has previously applied the reckless scienter standard to a RICO aiding and abetting action. In re ACC/Lincoln Savings Securities Litigation, MDL 834 (D.Ariz.Dec. 12, 1991). . . .

. . .

Common Law Fraud and Negligent Misrepresentation

Under California common law, an action for fraud and deceit requires proof of: (1) a false representation; (2) knowledge of the falsity; (3) an intent to induce reliance; (4) actual and reasonable reliance; and (5) resulting damage to the plaintiff. Secondary liability, or aiding and abetting, is defined in Restatement (Second) of Torts, 876b. It requires proof of knowledge of the primary violation, which may be inferred from the circumstances, and substantial assistance, which may be in the form of encouragement or advice. Pasadena Unified School Dist. v. Pasadena Federation of Teachers, 72 Cal.App.3d 100, 140 Cal.Rptr. 41 (1977). The aider and abetter's conduct must be a substantial factor in causing the plaintiff's harm. Rest.2d of Torts § 876 and comments.

A negligent misrepresentation claim involves the following elements: (1) a misrepresentation of past or existing material facts; (2) a lack of reasonable grounds for believing in the truth of the representation; (3) an intent to induce reliance; (4) actual and justifiable reliance; and (5) resulting damage.

[After discussing the standard for summary judgment under Fed.R.Civ. Pro. 56(c), the court granted defendants' motions for summary judgment on claims under § 18 of the Securities and Exchange Act, the California Corporation Code and for aiding and abetting ACC/Lincoln in negligently misrepresenting the financial condition of the two companies. The opinion then considers the remaining claims against each defendant. The portion of the opinion discussing the liability of Jones Day and two of its lawyers is reproduced here.]

V.   RULINGS PERTINENT TO INDIVIDUAL DEFENDANTS

. . .

D. Jones, Day, Reavis & Pogue

Jones Day, a defendant in [four of the actions] focuses its summary judgment motion on an individual opinion letter given in connection with a 1986 registration statement. Jones Day claims this opinion letter was neither false, nor was it written in an expert capacity. Jones Day generally claims that it has not engaged in conduct for which it could be held liable because lawyers are obligated to keep their clients' confidence and to act in ways that do not discourage their clients from undergoing regulatory compliance reviews.

1. The Record

The record reveals the following facts concerning Jones Day's involvement with ACC and Keating.

Prior to joining Jones Day, defendant William Schilling was director of the FHLBB Office of Examinations and Supervision. In that capacity, he was directly involved in the supervision of Lincoln Savings. During the summer of 1985, he wrote at least one memorandum and concurred in another, expressing serious regulatory concerns about numerous aspects of Lincoln's operations. For example, he wrote:

Under new management, Lincoln has engaged in several serious regulatory violations. Some of these violations, such as the overvaluation of real estate and failure to comply with Memorandum R–41(b), are the same type of violations that have lead to some of the worst failures in FSLIC's history.

Later in 1985, Schilling was hired by Jones Day to augment its expertise in thrift representation. On January 31, 1986, Schilling and Jones Day's Ron Kneipper flew to Phoenix to solicit ACC's business. ACC retained Jones Day to perform "a major internal audit of Lincoln's FHLBB compliance and a major project to help Lincoln deal with the FHLBB's direct investment regulations."

During the regulatory compliance audit, which Jones Day understood to be a pre-FHLBB examination compliance review, the law firm found multiple regulatory violations. There is evidence that Jones Day knew that Lincoln had backdated files, destroyed appraisals, removed appraisals from files, told appraisers not to issue written reports when their oral valuations were too low, and violated affiliated transaction regulations. Jones Day found that Lincoln did no loan underwriting and no post-closure loan followup to ensure that Lincoln's interests were being protected. Jones Day learned Lincoln had multiple "loans" which were, in fact, joint ventures which violated FHLBB regulations, made real estate loans in violation of regulations, and backdated corporate resolutions which were not signed by corporate officers and did not reflect actual meetings. There is evidence that Jones Day may have tacitly consented to removal of harmful documents from Lincoln files. For example, one handwritten notation on a memorandum memorializing Jones Day's advice not to remove documents from files reads, "If something *is* devastating, consider it individually." (Emphasis in original).

There is evidence that Jones Day instructed ACC in how to rectify deficiencies so that they would not be apparent to FHLBB examiners. Jones Day attorneys, including Schilling, testified that they told ACC/Lincoln personnel to provide the Jones Day-generated "to do" lists only to the attorneys responsible for rectifying the deficiencies, and to destroy the lists so that FHLB–SF would not find them in the files. For the same reason, Jones Day's regulatory compliance reports to ACC/Lincoln were oral. Jones Day paralegals testified that responsibilities for carrying out the "to do" lists were divided among Jones Day and ACC staff. Jones Day continued this work into the summer of 1986.

The evidence indicates that Jones Day may have been aware that ACC/Lincoln did not follow its compliance advice with respect to ongoing activities. There are material questions of fact concerning the procedures Jones Day used—if any—to ascertain whether their compliance advice was being heeded. The testimony suggests that Jones Day partners knew ACC/Lincoln personnel were preparing loan underwriting summaries contemporaneously with Jones Day's regulatory compliance review, even though the loan transactions had already been closed. Moreover, the evidence reveals that Jones Day attorneys participated in creating corporate resolutions to ratify forged and backdated corporate records.

On April 23, 1986, Jones Day partner Fohrman wrote:

> I received Neal Millard's memo on ACC. In looking at the long list of people involved, it occurred to me that there will be times when individuals may be called upon to render legal services that might require the issuance of opinion letters from Jones, Day. As we all know, we now possess information that could affect the way we write our opinion letters and our actual ability to give a particular opinion may be severely restricted. However, this large list of individuals may not be aware of knowledge that is held by Messrs. Fein and Schilling. I would suggest that a follow up memo be issued by Ron Fein indicating that any work involving ACC which requires the issuance of opinions, must be cleared by Ron. . . .

Also in April 1986, ACC's Jim Grogan wrote to Jones Day's Kneipper, soliciting a strategy to "sunset" the FHLBB direct investment regulation. Jones Day subsequently made multiple Freedom of Information Act requests to FHLBB in furtherance of a direct investment rule strategy, for which Lincoln was billed. In a September 12, 1986 telephone conversation, Grogan allegedly told Kneipper: "[C]omment letters were great success— FHLBB picked it up 'hook, line and sinker' Charlie wants to do again. . . ."

The record indicates that the concept of selling ACC debentures in Lincoln Savings branches may have originated at an April 9, 1986 real estate syndicate seminar given by Jones Day Defendant Ron Fein. There is evidence that Fein may have contributed to the detailed bond sales program outline, attending to details such as explaining how the sales would work, and insuring that the marketing table was far enough from the teller windows to distinguish between ACC and Lincoln Savings employees. The evidence indicates that Jones Day reviewed the debenture registration statement and prospectus, which is corroborated by Jones Day's billing records. As a result, in January 1987, ACC was able to assure the California Department of Savings Loan that:

> The process of structuring the bond sales program was reviewed by Kaye, Scholer and Jones Day to assure compliance not only with securities laws and regulations, but also with banking and FSLIC laws and regulations.

Moreover, there is evidence which suggests that political contributions were made on behalf of ACC, in exchange for ACC's consent that Jones Day could "bill liberally." On June 23, 1986, Kneipper memorialized a phone conversation:

> (1) 1:15 p.m. Ron Kessler—in past, firm has given $amt. to PAC, has premium billed, & PAC contri. to candidate; concern that we're an out of state law firm and that a $# in excess of $5,000.00 would look like an unusual move; Barnett and Kessler have done before; question re whether and how we can get some busi. from GOV. for this.

(2) 3:40 p.m. Jim Grogan Ten tickets at $1,000.00 equals $10,-000.00 Barr wants limits of $5,000.00/contribution

Agreed that we could bill liberally in future in recognition of this.

At deposition, Kneipper testified that his note—"agreed could bill liberally in recognition for this,"—"is what it appears to be." Jones Day set up an Arizona Political Action Committee ("PAC") specifically for the purpose of making a contribution to an Arizona gubernatorial candidate. The PAC was opened on September 4, 1986 and closed in December, 1986, after the contribution was made.

In June 1986, Jones Day solicited additional work from ACC. Jones Day attorney Caulkins wrote, in part:

Rick Kneipper reports that ACC is very explicit that it does not care how much its legal services cost, as long as it gets the best. He states that Keating gave him an unsolicited $250,000 retainer to start the thrift work, and sent another similar check also unsolicited in two weeks. On the down side, he reports that he has never encountered a more demanding and difficult client, . . .

It appears to Rick and to me that American Continental is made for us and we for them.

On October 28, 1986, Jones Day provided an opinion letter, required by Item 601(b) of SEC regulation S–K for inclusion in an ACC bond registration statement. Jones Day's opinion letter stated that the indenture was a valid and binding obligation under California law.

2. [Bond Holders' Actions for Securities and Common Law Fraud]

Jones Day seeks summary judgment on Plaintiffs' claims under Section 10(b), RICO and common law fraud.

Jones Day contends that it may not be held liable for counseling its client. The line between maintaining a client's confidence and violating the securities law is brighter than Jones Day suggests, however. Attorneys must inform a client in a clear and direct manner when its conduct violates the law. If the client continues the objectionable activity, the lawyer must withdraw "if the representation will result in violation of the rules of professional conduct or other law." Ethical Rule 1.16 ("ER"). Under such circumstances, an attorney's ethical responsibilities do not conflict with the securities laws. An attorney may not continue to provide services to corporate clients when the attorney knows the client is engaged in a course of conduct designed to deceive others, and where it is obvious that the attorney's compliant legal services may be a substantial factor in permitting the deceit to continue. See Rudolph v. Arthur Andersen, supra.

The record raises material questions about whether Jones Day knew of ACC/Lincoln's fraud, but nevertheless provided hands-on assistance in hiding loan file deficiencies from the regulators, offered detailed advice about setting up the bond sales program, carried out a lobbying strategy with respect to the direct investment rule, made political contributions on

ACC's behalf, reviewed SEC registration statements and prospectuses, and lent its name to a misleading legal opinion. This evidence raises material questions concerning section 10(b), RICO, AZRAC, common law fraud and deceit, and violations of Cal. Corp. Code §§ 25401 and 25504.1.

3. Section 11 Liability

Section 11 imposes liability for misleading statements made in connection with registration statements. Jones Day offers two arguments. [The court first rejected arguments that these claims were barred by statute of limitations.]

. . .

Jones Day further contends that it cannot be held liable under Section 11 because it did not issue an "expert" opinion. Section 11 applies to misleading statements made by one "whose profession gives authority to statements made by him." 13 U.S.C. § 771. Jones Day concedes that its October 28, 1986 opinion letter was required by SEC Regulation S–K, which provides in part:

> (5) Opinion Re Legality—(i) An opinion of counsel as to the legality of the securities being registered, indicating whether they will, when sold, be legally issued, fully paid and non-assessable, and, if debt securities, whether they will be binding obligations of the registrant.

SEC Regulation S–K, Item 601(5).

The court holds that an attorney who provides a legal opinion used in connection with an SEC registration statement is an expert within the meaning of Section ii. See Schneider v. Traweek, 1990 U.S. Dist. LEXIS 15,563 (C.D. Cal. Sept. 5, 1990).

4. [Action by Resolution Trust Co. (RTC) for Breach of Fiduciary Duty to Lincoln]

a.   Statute of Limitations

Jones Day contends that claims for breach of fiduciary duty, brought by the RTC, are time-barred. RTC contends that its claims were preserved until the conservatorship was imposed.

Under the theory of adverse domination, the limitations period on a corporation's cause of action is tolled while wrongdoers control the corporation. Bornstein v. Poulos, 793 F.2d 444 (1st Cir.1986) (doctrine extends to attorney with fiduciary duty to corporation); Fed. Sav. and Loan Ins. Corp. v. Williams, 599 F.Supp. 1184 (D. Md.1984) (limitations statute tolled while corporation is dominated by wrongdoers). In this instance, ACC/Lincoln management would not have brought claims on behalf of ACC/Lincoln, for it would have brought their own misconduct to light. Furthermore, the court finds material questions as to whether Jones Day knowingly assisted in ACC's alleged fraud. Accordingly, it is equitable to toll the statute of limitations on Lincoln's behalf.

b.   Validity of Claims

An attorney who represents a corporation has a duty to act in the corporation's best interest when confronted by adverse interests of directors, officers, or corporate affiliates. It is not a defense that corporate representation often involves the distinct interests of affiliated entities. Attorneys are bound to act when those interests conflict. There are genuine questions as to whether Jones Day should have sought independent representation for Lincoln.

Moreover, where a law firm believes the management of a corporate client is committing serious regulatory violations, the firm has an obligation to actively discuss the violative conduct, urge cessation of the activity, and withdraw from representation where the firm's legal services may contribute to the continuation of such conduct. Jones Day contends that it would have been futile to act on these fiduciary obligations because those controlling ACC/Lincoln would not have responded. Client wrongdoing, however, cannot negate an attorney's fiduciary duty. Moreover, the evidence reveals that attorney advice influenced ACC/Lincoln's conduct in a variety of ways. Accordingly, summary judgment as to this claim is denied.

5. Professional Negligence Claims

Jones Day issued an opinion letter that was included with ACC'S 1986 shelf registration statement. California authority provides that independent public accountants have a duty to those who are foreseeably injured from representations made in connection with publicly held corporations. While this duty does not extend to confidential advice which an attorney gives to its clients, it would apply where an attorney issues an SEC opinion letter to the public. Roberts v. Ball, Hunt., Hart, Brown & Baerwitz, 128 Cal.Rptr. 901 (1976); see also Int'l Mortgage Co. v. Butler Accountancy Corp., 223 Cal.Rptr. 218 (4th Dist.1986).

Accordingly, a question of fact remains as to whether the Yahr Plaintiffs, who purchased bonds issued pursuant to the November, 1986 shelf registration and amendments, were injured by the Jones Day opinion letter.

6. Section 12 Liability

Section 12 imposes liability only on those who offer and sell securities. 15 U.S.C. § 771. The court concludes that Jones Day's contributions to the bond sales program were those of an expert consultant rather than those of an offeror or seller. Accordingly, Jones Day's participation is insufficient to impose Section 12 liability within the meaning of the Securities Act.

. . .

Accordingly, this Memorandum Opinion affirms the court's Order of February 14, 1992 granting and denying summary judgment.[1]

---

1. [Editors' note:] In March 1992 Jones Day   settled the claims of ACC bondholders and

The *Central Bank* Decision

One claim against Jones Day—aiding and abetting the managers of Lincoln in violating Section 10(b) of the Securities and Exchange Act of 1934—was abrogated by a surprising decision of the Supreme Court in 1994, Central Bank of Denver v. First Interstate Bank of Denver.[2] Since then Congress has legislated twice on remedies for securities violations. See the discussion of these developments in Chapter 2 at p. 119. If the *Central Bank* rule had applied to *ACC/Lincoln*, the aiding and abetting claim under federal securities law would have been dismissed, but the other claims would have survived the motion for summary judgment. If Jones Day had not settled, it would have faced trial on the state tort and regulatory claims (and perhaps on amended claims charging it with liability as a principal under federal securities laws).

Notes on *Jones Day*[3]

Source of duty. What is the source of Jones Day's duties to either the bond purchasers or to the federal conservator? The Jones Day case involves two separate sets of claims against the law firm: first, claims by persons who purchased ACC bonds in 1986 and 1987 and lost their investment; and second, claims by the federal conservator, acting as Lincoln's successor in interest, that Jones Day failed to provide proper representation to its client, Lincoln. What is the source of Jones Day's duties to the bondholders? To the government? Does the decision rest upon a holding that federal banking law creates duties on the part of a legal adviser to a regulated thrift to exercise due diligence in assisting Lincoln's parent in selling bonds in its branches? Or to protect the interests of Lincoln's depositors, and the federal government's interest in the deposit insurance fund, as distinct from those of the thrift?

Why doesn't the opinion discuss the law of lawyering? Note that the lengthy opinion contains only one reference to a legal ethics code (the

stockholders for $24 million. See Wall St.J., Mar. 3, 1992, p. A2. The government claims against Jones Day went to trial in April 1993 before Judge Bilby. After opening arguments, Jones Day agreed to pay $51 million to the government in settlement of this and other cases against it. The settlement also obligated the firm to follow specified procedures in any future thrift regulation and prohibited William Schilling, who worked on the Lincoln matter after leaving the government, from holding any position in the banking industry or representing clients before the Office of Thrift Supervision, the agency that now regulates the savings and loan industry. See John H. Cushman, Jr., Law Firm Settles S. & L. Case, N.Y.Times, Apr. 20, 1993, p. D1. Press reports have stated that as much as $20 million of the settlement with the government was borne by partners in the firm, with the remainder paid by the firm's malpractice insurer.

2. 511 U.S. 164 (1994).

3. The factual statement in Judge Bilby's opinion supports his denial of Jones Day's motion for summary judgment. Accordingly, it states the facts developed in pretrial proceedings viewed most favorably to the parties against whom the motion was made (i.e., the bond purchasers and the federal conservator). Many of these facts, and the implications drawn from undisputed facts, were disputed by Jones Day. If the case had gone to trial, the jury would have heard another version of the facts.

Arizona version of M.R. 1.16). Yet the case involves lawyering that occurred primarily in California by lawyers of an Ohio-based law firm, some of whom were admitted in California.

Scope of the engagements. The Jones Day representation of ACC and Lincoln had three parts: First, the regulatory compliance audit for Lincoln that began in early February 1986 and was concluded less than five months later by Jones Day's resignation or firing. Second, a group of miscellaneous matters for ACC during the same period that involved regulatory and lobbying activities (e.g., efforts to terminate the FHLBB's direct investment regulation). And third, the engagement by ACC in October–November 1986 that resulted in the Jones Day legal opinion that was included in ACC's shelf registration with California authorities. Kaye Scholer was responsible for the securities work in connection with the sale of ACC bonds; Jones Day was retained merely to provide a very limited opinion concerning the corporate authority of ACC to issue the bonds.

Conflict of interest. Was there a conflict of interest between Jones Day's concurrent representation of a holding company (ACC) and its wholly-owned subsidiary (Lincoln)? Lincoln was a wholly-owned subsidiary of ACC, which was controlled by Keating. Generally no conflict of interest exists in joint representation of a parent company and its wholly-owned subsidiary, even in a transaction between them, because the alignment of ownership means that the interests of the two entities are not at odds with one another. However, if a regulated thrift, such as Lincoln, owed fiduciary duties under federal banking law to Lincoln's depositors and the federal insurance fund, Lincoln's duties and interests might be in direct conflict with those of Lincoln's owner, ACC. See Model Rule 1.7(a) (direct adversity of interests between jointly represented co-clients may result in an unconsentable conflict). A breach of the fiduciary duty to avoid conflicting interests also may give rise to civil liability of the lawyer to a person (or entity) to whom that duty is owed who has suffered resulting harm.

Issuance of a legal opinion. What is the significance of the Jones Day opinion stating that ACC's bond issue was valid and authorized? The crux of the bondholders' claims against Jones Day was that the firm aided and abetted ACC in defrauding the bondholders because its legal opinion, made at a time when the firm allegedly had knowledge that ACC was engaged in a fraudulent course of conduct, assisted ACC in selling the bonds. The Jones Day opinion contained no representations concerning ACC's financial soundness or solvency and dealt with a narrow legal issue. Did Jones Day's prior representation of Lincoln during the regulatory compliance audit give it knowledge that made the issuance of *any* legal opinion in connection with an ACC transaction extremely risky?

Remedies under M.R. 1.13. Was Jones Day, before withdrawing from its representation of ACC/Lincoln in 1986, required to go up the corporate chain of command or make a public disclosure to prevent or rectify client fraud? The government case against Jones Day, if it had been tried to completion, would have turned largely on this issue. Note that M.R. 1.13 was not in effect in either Arizona or California in 1986. If it had been, would Jones Day have been required to climb the corporate ladder to the Lincoln and ACC boards of directors? Are the alternative steps mentioned in M.R. 1.13(a) discretionary or are there situations in which some steps are required? Do those steps ever include going outside the client entities as lawyer Goldberg did in the *Meyerhofer* case, see Chapter 4 at p. 274. Is *ACC/Lincoln* consistent with the securities cases discussed in the preceding note?

Embarrassing incidents. What is the relevance, if any, of the factual assertions that Schilling may have violated conflict-of-interest rules applicable to former government lawyers and that Jones Day may have made illegal campaign contributions for a client? Would this evidence have been admissible at trial? On what theory? See the discussion of M.R. 1.11 and 18 U.S.C. § 207 in Chapter 7, pp. 687, 691 supra.

The *Kaye Scholer* Matter[4]

The duties of a lawyer during a bank examination was a principal issue in the charges against Kaye Scholer. Kaye Scholer served as an outside counsel for Lincoln, the thrift involved in *ACC/Lincoln*, supra, in various matters from 1984 until shortly before Lincoln was seized by the government in 1989. In June 1986 the firm was retained by Lincoln, replacing Jones Day, to assist Lincoln through what was expected to be a difficult, perhaps hostile, bank examination. Treating the bank examination as "litigation," Fishbein,[5] the partner in charge, instructed bank examiners to channel all inquiries through Kaye Scholer rather than dealing directly with Lincoln.

Kaye Scholer's aggressive representation of Lincoln during this bank examination led the Office of Thrift Supervision (OTS) in March 1992 to file administrative charges against the firm and three of its partners.[6] Six of the ten charges alleged that Kaye Scholer had knowledge of, but failed to disclose to the bank examiners, material facts, thereby making false and misleading other factual representations that were made to the bank board by the firm as Lincoln's agent. By making such representations, OTS alleged, Kaye Scholer violated regulations prohibiting false and misleading

---

4. The reader should know that Geoffrey C. Hazard, Jr., one of the co-authors of this book, provided legal advice and a favorable legal opinion to the Kaye, Scholer firm in connection with the charges made against it.

5. You may recall Fishbein as the lawyer who became OPM's counsel after Hutner and the Singer, Hutner firm withdrew. Supra at p. 307.

6. This Office of Thrift Supervision administrative proceeding is not reported. For discussion and citation of relevant materials, see ABA Working Group on Lawyers' Representation of Regulated Clients, "La-

borers in Different Vineyards?"—The Banking Regulators and the Legal Profession 24–30, 197–212 (Jan.1993). For thorough discussion of the OTS action against Kaye Scholer, see The Kaye Scholer Affair: The Lawyer's Duty of Candor and the Bar's Temptations of Evasion and Apology, 23 Law & Soc. Inquiry 243 (1998) (article by William H. Simon and commentaries by seven scholars); Symposium, 66 S.Cal. L.Rev. 977 (1993) (including articles by Susan P. Koniak, Ted Schneyer and David B. Wilkins); Susan Beck & Michael Orey, They Got What They Deserved, Amer.Lawyer 68 (May 1992).

statements and omissions of material facts that have the effect of making a factual representation misleading. OTS sought "restitution" of losses of at least $275 million (Kaye Scholer had been paid about $13 million in fees); the administrative proceeding was accompanied by an asset preservation ("freeze") order that sought to prevent the law firm's assets from being dissipated while permitting it to carry on its law practice. Kaye Scholer settled the matter for $41 million within a week without contesting the freeze order or admitting or denying the allegations.[7]

One feature of *Kaye Scholer* is unique and is unlikely to recur: OTS argued that the law firm, by interposing itself between Lincoln and the bank examiners, had become an alter ego of its client, Lincoln, and was not acting merely as a lawyer.

A second feature of *Kaye Scholer*, however, is of great continuing importance: the scope of a lawyer's duty to disclose facts adverse to the lawyer's client to a regulatory agency.[8] For example, did the firm violate its ethical duties by submitting a required statement to the banking agency to the effect that the resignation of ACC/Lincoln's accounting firm was not related to the thrift's financial condition, a statement that was alleged by the government to be knowingly false.

Model Rule 4.1 provides a duty to be truthful in dealing with third persons, but there is no affirmative duty to inform an opposing party of relevant facts. However, if a "tribunal" is involved, even one that is non-adjudicative in character, the lawyer has affirmative duties of candor. Rules 1.2(d), 3.3(a). Information must be disclosed either to avoid assisting the client in a fraud on the tribunal or to correct evidence that the lawyer has already offered but comes to know is false, even if the information would otherwise be protected by the lawyer's duty of confidentiality. If the tribunal is adjudicative in nature and the proceeding is *ex parte*, the lawyer must disclose material facts known to be adverse to the client's position, even if this is not necessary to prevent fraud. Rule 3.3(d). The lawyer in this last situation has a responsibility to see that the adjudicator's decision is an informed one.

Should OTS have argued that the banking agency was a "tribunal" to which the lawyer owed a duty of truthfulness not met by its filing stating that the accounting firm's resignation was unrelated to ACC's operation? The ABA Working Group, reporting on a lawyer's ethical responsibilities in

---

7. See Amy Stevens & Paulette Thomas, How a Big Firm Was Brought to Knees by Zealous Regulators: At Kaye Scholer, Survival Prevailed Over Principle as Partnership Panicked, Redefining a Lawyer's Duty, Wall St.J., Mar. 13, 1992, at A1, A5.

8. Why weren't the charges against Kaye Scholer limited to the more well-established theories involved in other S & L cases, such as *ACC/Lincoln*? The available facts, disputed by Kaye Scholer, were at least as strong as those in the case involv-

ing Jones Day, and would probably have established a prima facie case against Kaye Scholer of professional negligence, breach of fiduciary obligations to the entity client and aiding and abetting client illegalities. See Beck & Orey, supra, Ame. Law. 68 (May 1992) (summarizing the available evidence). Harris Weinstein, then general counsel for OTS, has emphasized the unusual action of Kaye Scholer in placing itself between the banking regulators and Lincoln.

the banking regulatory field, concluded that a bank examination is neither an adjudicative nor legislative proceeding subject to the provisions of Rule 3.9.[9] That does not, however, answer the question of whether a bank examination is an ex parte proceeding or the agency a tribunal within the meaning of Rule 3.3.

Kaye Scholer also provides a repeat of the disagreement between federal regulators and the organized bar concerning a lawyer's duty when she discovers that her corporate client is engaged in an illegal or fraudulent course of conduct. The courts in *National Student Marketing* and *ACC/Lincoln (Jones Day)* upheld the regulators arguments that a lawyer must take "some action" to prevent the continuing non-compliance with law. Must the lawyer climb the corporate ladder to the board of directors, or is that action permissive, as M.R. 1.13 would have it?[10]

Protecting a Client Corporation From Management Wrongdoing

What inquiry concerning underlying circumstances must be made by a law firm that handles a transaction for the thrift during a period in which its financial situation is deteriorating? In Federal Deposit Insurance Corp. v. O'Melveny & Meyers,[11] the receiver of a failed thrift was held to have stated a claim for relief against a law firm that had assisted the thrift in two real estate syndications offered to investors. When the private placements were made, the thrift was in unsound financial condition; its officers

---

9. ABA Working Group on Lawyers' Representation of Regulated Clients, "Laborers in Different Vineyards?"—The Banking Regulators and the Legal Profession 24–30, 197–212 (Jan.1993). *Kaye Scholer* also raises questions about the interpretation and validity of the Financial Institutions Reform, Recovery, and Enforcement Act of 1989 ("FIRREA"), Pub.L. No. 101–73, 103 Stat. 183, and other banking regulations. These issues are discussed in the ABA Report.

10. *Kaye Scholer* also raised important questions about the proper use of summary and extraordinary governmental authority. Unlike Jones Day in *ACC/Lincoln*, the charge against Kaye Scholer was not brought in a federal court where a defendant would have the right to a jury trial before an Article III judge. Kaye Scholer's fate was to be decided in an administrative proceeding before the agency that had brought the charges, with subsequent opportunity for limited judicial review of the administrative determination. The asset preservation order had the effect, along with the size and plausibility of the OTS damage claim, of depriving Kaye Scholer of

working capital and bringing it quickly to settlement. Law firms and the organized bar worry that the bar's independence may be threatened by governmental exercise of such extraordinary powers. Summary provisional remedies in other contexts are now generally held to be unconstitutional, see Connecticut v. Doehr, 501 U.S. 1 (1991) (invalidating a state law that permitted prejudgment attachment of a defendant's assets without a hearing to determine whether the plaintiff established "probable cause"). But see United States v. Monsanto, Inc., 924 F.2d 1186 (2d Cir.1991) (pretrial forfeiture of attorney's fees on government's ex parte application permissible if an opportunity for an adversary hearing is available prior to trial). A number of the recommendations of the ABA Report, supra, are concerned with constraining the use against lawyers of such broad regulatory authority.

11. 969 F.2d 744 (9th Cir.1992) (the case incorrectly refers to O'Melveny & Myers as "O'Melveny and Meyers"). *O'Melveny* is discussed in George C. Harris, Taking the Entity Theory Seriously . . . , 11 Geo.J. Legal Eth. 597, 623–32 (1998).

had fraudulently overvalued assets, embezzled funds and generally "cooked the books."[12] The complaint alleged that O'Melveny, knowing of the recent resignations of the thrift's prior auditors and outside law firm, did not question the auditors, the law firm, federal or state regulators or the thrift's chief financial officer about the thrift's financial status before giving legal opinions and doing other work that assisted the thrift in soliciting investors. After the thrift failed, the FDIC, acting as conservator, rescinded the investments and was assigned the investors' claims against O'Melveny. The receiver then brought suit against O'Melveny for professional negligence and negligent misrepresentation.

The Ninth Circuit held that, under these circumstances, allegations that the law firm "failed to make a reasonable, independent investigation" established a claim of professional negligence:

> Part and parcel of effectively protecting a client, and thus discharging the attorney's duty of care, is to protect the client from liability which may flow from promulgating a false or misleading offering to investors. An important duty of securities counsel is to make a "reasonable independent investigation to detect and correct false or misleading materials." ... This is what is meant by a due diligence investigation.... The Firm had a duty to guide the thrift as to its obligations and protect it against liability. In its high specialty field, O'Melveny owed a duty of care not only to the investors, but also to its client.... [13]

B.   ALMOST CLIENTS

1.   REPRESENTING A CLOSELY HELD CORPORATION OR PARTNERSHIP

Fassihi v. Sommers, Schwartz, Silver, Schwartz and Tyler, P.C.

Court of Appeals of Michigan, 1981.
107 Mich.App. 509, 309 N.W.2d 645.

■ PER CURIAM.

... In his complaint, plaintiff asserted that he was a 50% shareholder, officer, and director of Livonia Physicians X–Ray, P.C., a professional medical corporation. The various allegations included breach of the attorney-client relationship, breach of fiduciary, legal, and ethical duties, fraud,

---

12.   969 F.2d at 746.

13.   969 F.2d at 749. Quoting a commentator, the court stated: "[A]ttorneys, in rendering opinions relating to the securities laws, are not justified in assuming facts as represented to them by their clients [are correct]. Rather ... the attorney must make a reasonable effort to independently verify the facts on which the opinion is based."

and legal malpractice. Defendant [law firm] filed a motion for summary judgment on the basis that ... no attorney-client relationship existed with plaintiff. This motion was denied....

Following the trial court's order denying defendant's motion for summary judgment, plaintiff deposed attorney Donald Epstein. However, during the deposition Epstein repeatedly refused to answer questions, claiming an attorney-client privilege. Plaintiff moved for an order compelling discovery, but the trial court denied the motion.... This order also extended to both parties the opportunity to take an interlocutory appeal from the denial of their respective motion.

This Court granted leave to take the interlocutory appeals....

The following factual recitation comes from plaintiff's complaint and the statement of facts appearing in his brief.... [W]e are obligated to consider the facts in the light most favorable to the nonmoving party when passing on a motion for summary judgment....

In the summer of 1973, plaintiff, a radiologist practicing medicine in Ohio, was asked by Dr. Rudolfo Lopez to come to Michigan and join him in the practice of radiology at St. Mary's Hospital in Livonia. In August, 1973, the doctors formed a professional corporation known as Livonia Physicians X–Ray. Each doctor owned 50% of the stock, was an employee of the corporation, and received an identical salary. Plaintiff contends that the by-laws adopted by the two shareholders made each of them a member of the Board of Directors and that the two of them constituted the entirety of the board. Dr. Lopez was president of the corporation, and Dr. Fassihi was the secretary-treasurer.

Shortly after the corporation was organized, plaintiff sought and obtained medical staff privileges at St. Mary's [Hospital]. For a period of approximately 18 months, the doctors practiced together at the hospital in the radiology department.

Some time on or before June 4, 1975, Dr. Lopez decided that he no longer desired to be associated with plaintiff. Consequently, Lopez requested that the attorney for the professional corporation, the defendant, ascertain how plaintiff could be ousted from Livonia Physicians X–Ray.

On or about June 6, 1975, defendant's agent, Donald Epstein, Esquire, personally delivered to plaintiff a letter dated June 4, 1975, purporting to terminate his interest in the professional corporation. The letter stated that this termination followed a meeting of the board of directors.[2] Plaintiff

2. Whether or not the by-laws of the professional corporation made Drs. Fassihi and Lopez the sole directors of the organization, Donald Epstein in a deposition contended that a Joseph Carolan was a third director. Mr. Carolan was apparently the business manager of Livonia Physicians X–Ray. We assume that at least defendant considers him a proper director. Otherwise, it would have been impossible for Lopez to effect his scheme of terminating Fassihi's association with the professional corporation as Fassihi would have undoubtedly opposed the plan. In any case, a corporate arrangement whereby one 50% shareholder can oust the other 50% shareholder—whether individually or with the assistance of a third director—seems highly unusual

denies that any such meeting ever occurred. On June 9, 1975, plaintiff went to St. Mary's to perform his duties as a staff radiologist. At this time officials at the hospital told him that, due to his "termination" from the professional corporation, he was no longer eligible to practice at St. Mary's.

Dr. Lopez had an agreement with St. Mary's Hospital prior to plaintiff's association with Livonia Physicians X-Ray giving him personal and sole responsibility for staffing the radiology department. This agreement necessitated membership in Livonia Physicians X-Ray, P.C.

Defendant was responsible for drafting all the agreements pertaining to membership in the professional corporation. Defendant, and specifically Donald Epstein, had knowledge of the arrangements between Dr. Lopez and the hospital but never disclosed these facts to plaintiff. Plaintiff finally states that defendant has represented both Lopez individually and the professional corporation without disclosing to him this dual representation.

This case presents us with the difficult question of what duties, if any, an attorney representing a closely held corporation has to a 50% owner of the entity, individually.[3] This is a problem of first impression in Michigan.

We start our analysis by examining whether an attorney-client relationship exists between plaintiff and defendant. . . .

A corporation exists as an entity apart from its shareholders, even where the corporation has but one shareholder. . . . While no Michigan case has addressed whether a corporation's attorney has an attorney-client relationship with the entity's shareholders, the general proposition of corporate identity apart from its shareholders leads us to conclude, in accordance with decisions from other jurisdictions, that the attorney's client is the corporation and not the shareholders. . . .

Although we conclude that no attorney-client relationship exists between plaintiff and defendant, this does not necessarily mean that defendant had no fiduciary duty to plaintiff. The existence of an attorney-client relationship merely establishes a per se rule that the lawyer owes fiduciary duties to the client.

A fiduciary relationship arises when one reposes faith, confidence, and trust in another's judgment and advice. Where a confidence has been betrayed by the party in the position of influence, this betrayal is actionable, and the origin of the confidence is immaterial. . . . Furthermore, whether there exists a confidential relationship apart from a well defined fiduciary category is a question of fact. . . . Based upon the pleadings, we cannot say that plaintiff's claim is clearly unenforceable as a matter of law.

Plaintiff asserts that he reposed in defendant his trust and confidence and believed that, as a 50% shareholder in Livonia Physicians X-Ray, defendant would treat him with the same degree of loyalty and impartiality extended to the other shareholder, Dr. Lopez. In his complaint plaintiff

---

and comes to us on a stipulated hypothetical for purposes of this appeal.

3. See L. Greenhouse, In Corporate Law, Who's the Client? The New York Times, Sunday, February 15, 1981, p. 20 E.

states that he was betrayed in this respect. Specifically, plaintiff asserts that he was not advised of defendant's dual representation of the corporate entity and Dr. Lopez personally.[5] Plaintiff also alleges that he was never informed of the contract between Lopez and St. Mary's which gave Lopez sole responsibility in the staffing of the radiology department and, more importantly, that defendant actively participated with Lopez in terminating plaintiff's association with the corporation and using the Lopez–St. Mary's contract to his detriment.

In support of his position that he has an attorney-client relationship with defendant, plaintiff cites a number of cases standing for the proposition that the corporate veil will be pierced where the corporate identity is being used to further fraud or injustice.... These cases are not factually similar to the instant matter as they involve claims against a corporate principal attempting to protect himself from personal liability through the corporate entity. At the same time, these cases are instructive as they point out the difficulties in treating a closely held corporation with few shareholders as an entity distinct from the shareholders. Instances in which the corporation attorneys stand in a fiduciary relationship to individual shareholders are obviously more likely to arise where the number of shareholders is small. In such cases it is not really a matter of the courts piercing the corporate entity. Instead, the corporate attorneys, because of their close interaction with a shareholder or shareholders, simply stand in confidential relationships in respect to both the corporation and individual shareholders.[6]

In addition to the claim for breach of fiduciary duties, plaintiff contends that his complaint states a cause of action for fraud. The elements of fraud are: (1) a material representation which is false; (2) known by defendant to be false, or made recklessly without knowledge of its truth or falsity; (3) that defendant intended plaintiff to rely upon the representation; (4) that, in fact, plaintiff acted in reliance upon it; and (5) thereby suffered injury. Hyma v. Lee, 338 Mich. 31, 37, 60 N.W.2d 920 (1953); Cormack v. American Underwriters Corp., 94 Mich.App. 379, 385, 288 N.W.2d 634 (1979). The false material representation needed to establish fraud may be satisfied by the failure to divulge a fact or facts the defendant has a duty to disclose. An action based on the failure to disclose facts is one for fraudulent concealment....

Plaintiff's fraudulent concealment claim is premised on defendant's failure to divulge its dual representation of Livonia Physicians X–Ray and

---

5. The Code of Professional Responsibility and Canons DR 5–105 requires full disclosure of dual representation of parties to the clients involved and forbids dual representation in some circumstances.

6. Although factually different, Prescott v. Coppage, 266 Md. 562, 296 A.2d 150 (1972), is illuminating in its discussion of an attorney's obligations to third parties apart from a specific attorney-client rela-

tionship. In *Prescott*, the Maryland court found that the attorney owed a duty to a preferred creditor on a third-party beneficiary theory. The question in any given case is whether, irrespective of an actual attorney-client relationship, plaintiff has pled sufficient allegations tending to show some legal duty on the part of the attorney to him personally.

the failure of defendant to disclose the existence of the contract between Dr. Lopez and St. Mary's Hospital. We agree with plaintiff that, irrespective of any other duty, defendant would have an obligation to divulge its dual representation of the corporation and Dr. Lopez individually. The failure to divulge this fact might serve as the basis for a fraudulent concealment action. We cannot agree, however, that defendant had an obligation to divulge the existence or contents of the Lopez–St. Mary's Hospital contract to plaintiff. Defendant's knowledge of this contract arose out of a confidential attorney-client relationship between [it] and Dr. Lopez.[7] This attorney-client relationship prohibited defendant from divulging facts learned during the course of representation of Dr. Lopez unless Lopez waived his right to the attorney-client privilege. While defendant should have, and likely did, consider the effect that its relationship with Lopez might have on the representation of the corporation and incidentally plaintiff, as a 50% shareholder, officer, and director, it was not prohibited from representing both if its employees' independent professional judgment on behalf of either would not likely be adversely affected by representation of the other. Code of Professional Responsibility and Canons DR 5–105(C).

We now turn to the issue of whether defendant has a privilege to refuse to answer questions relative to communications concerning the ouster of plaintiff from the corporation. Defendant contends that these communications are privileged because they were made on behalf of the majority of the board of directors and the attorney-client privilege belongs to the control group.

We hold that under defendant's own argument, the attorney-client privilege may not be asserted against plaintiff. As a member of the board of directors, plaintiff was a member of the corporate control group. See Diversified Industries, Inc. v. Meredith, 572 F.2d 596 (CA 8, 1977). Thus, with respect to any communications defendant had with Dr. Lopez while representing the corporation, as opposed to Lopez personally, plaintiff, as a member of the control group, is equally entitled to this information.

Additionally, defendant acknowledges that the attorney-client privilege does not protect communications made for the purpose of perpetrating a fraud. See Garner v. Wolfinbarger, 430 F.2d 1093 (CA 5, 1970). Although plaintiff's complaint does not use the magic word "fraud", the gist of his complaint rests on a species of fraud. Plaintiff asserts that defendant, while under the guise of representing the corporation, conspired to withhold information from him which he had a right to have as a 50% shareholder and member of the board of directors and to wrongfully deprive him of the benefits of a business opportunity. These allegations were sufficient to defeat the invocation of the attorney-client relationship pursuant to the fraud exception. . . .

---

7. This is not to say that Dr. Lopez's personal failure to divulge the existence of his contract with St. Mary's Hospital could not serve as the basis for a fraudulent concealment claim. . . .

Duty Arising From "Confidential Relationship"

According to Dr. Fassihi, lawyer Epstein had a duty to Fassihi, which he breached. What were the alleged breaches of duty? The court noted that the allegations suggest a "confidential relationship" between Fassihi and Epstein, and that, if such a relationship existed, Epstein owed Fassihi a duty of care.[1] What facts does the court use to support its conclusion that a confidential relationship has been alleged by Fassihi? Why does the court hold that Epstein was obligated to disclose to Fassihi his prior representation of Lopez, but not the existence of the contract with the hospital? The facts are somewhat murky on whether the contract was between Lopez and the hospital or the professional corporation and the hospital. At the least, however, the corporation appears to have been the third party beneficiary of a contract between the hospital and Lopez. If that is so, would not Fassihi, as one of the two (or three) members of the board of directors have a right to know of the contract?

Compare *Fassihi* to *Meehan*. Would the *Fassihi* court have found on the facts in *Meehan* that the corporation's law firm in *Meehan* owed fiduciary duties to Hopps during Hopps' tenure as chairman of the board? After the bankruptcy? Does not the CEO of a large publicly-held corporation "repose faith, confidence, and trust in [corporate counsel's] judgment and advice" as Fassihi did? Is a fiduciary relationship thus created between corporate counsel and the CEO?

The questions just posed are designed to highlight an ambiguity in *Fassihi*'s reasoning. The court is not clear on how much weight to give each of the following factors in determining whether a confidential relationship exists: the particulars of the relationship between the lawyer and the relevant corporate constituent; the stake of the constituent's interest in the corporation; and the number of shareholders, i.e., how closely-held the corporation is. For example, would this court have found a confidential relationship between corporate counsel and a 5% shareholder of a three-shareholder corporation? Even if that shareholder had never met, talked to or corresponded with corporate counsel? What about a 5% shareholder of a 20 shareholder corporation, who had been in one shareholder meeting attended by counsel?

Skarbrevik: Counsel for a Close Corporation with No Fiduciary Duties to Shareholders?

In Skarbrevik v. Cohen, England & Whitfield,[2] a California intermediate appellate court held, citing *Meehan*, that a lawyer for a four-shareholder corporation owed no legal duty to one of the four shareholders and thus could not be sued by that person for negligence. Each of the four sharehold-

---

1. See also Adell v. Sommers, Schwartz, Silver and Schwartz, P.C., 428 N.W.2d 26, 29 (Mich.App.1988) (lawyers for partnership owe fiduciary duties to limited partners); Nancy J. Moore, Expanding Duties of Attorneys to "Non–Clients": Reconceptualiz-ing the Attorney–Client Relationship in Entity Representation and Other Inherently Ambiguous Situations, 45 So.Car.L.Rev. 659 (1994).

2. 282 Cal.Rptr.627 (1991).

ers in *Skarbrevik* owned 25% of the corporation's stock. Three of the shareholders, disappointed with Skarbrevik's performance, obtained his resignation as an officer by agreeing to buy his stock. The buyout never occurred because the three shareholders had to use their money to keep the corporation afloat. The three, assisted by corporate counsel, then came up with a plan to dilute the value of Skarbrevik's interest in the corporation. They would issue large numbers of shares of stock to themselves as payment for their efforts in saving the corporation. The problem was that the corporate articles required that before additional stock could be issued to the three of them, 25% had to be offered to Skarbrevik. The lawyer explained that the shareholders could amend the articles to delete this requirement, but that Skarbrevik had to have notice of the proposed amendment and of the meeting at which the amendment would be voted upon.

No meeting was ever held. Nonetheless, the lawyer participated in the creation of corporate records that purported to memorialize the meeting and the vote to delete the bothersome provision of the corporate articles. The lawyer also knew that Skarbrevik had not been given notice of a meeting or a proposal to amend the articles. The three shareholders issued shares to themselves, offering Skarbrevik none and thereby diluted his ownership interest from 25% to 4.7%. When Skarbrevik found out what the other shareholders had done, he sued them and corporate counsel for conspiracy to defraud him and counsel for negligence.

Throwing out the negligence claim on the ground that corporate counsel owed Skarbrevik no duty, the court emphasized that corporate counsel represents the corporation and not its constituents. The court rejected Skarbrevik's counsel's invitation to follow the Michigan court's decision in *Fassihi*:

> The distinction between the *Fassihi* case and the case before us is evident. Plaintiff in this case did not have close interaction, or any interaction at all, with . . . [corporate counsel] during the time period in which the legal services sued upon were rendered. . . . *Fassihi* is a pleadings case in which there were specific allegations of a relationship of trust and confidence between plaintiff and defendant attorneys. In our case, evidence at trial established no such relationship of trust and confidence . . . that would give rise to a fiduciary duty.[3]

The California court's narrow reading of *Fassihi* seems to demonstrate its fundamental discomfort with the Michigan court's approach. More to the California court's liking was a Massachusetts case, Felty v. Hartwig,[4] which found no "authority in which a 'corporate attorney, even when representing a closely-held corporation, has been held to . . . have an [implied] attorney-client relationship with the shareholders.'"[5]

---

3. Id. at 636.

4. 523 N.E.2d 555 (Mass.1988).

5. 282 Cal.Rptr. at 637 (quoting *Felty*). In contrast to *Skarbrevik* and *Felty* is Schaef-

fer v. Cohen, Rosenthal, Price, 541 N.E.2d 997, 1002 (Mass.1989):

> [T]here is logic in the proposition that, even though counsel for a closely held

The California court not only dismissed the negligence claim, it rejected the claim against corporate counsel for conspiring with the majority shareholders to defraud Skarbrevik, while acknowledging that the evidence established that the majority shareholders committed the tort of fraudulent concealment. They "deliberately embarked on a scheme to diminish plaintiff's interest in the corporation by diluting his stock in violation of their fiduciary duties,"[6] and they hid their scheme from him. Moreover, the court found that the jury could have reasonably inferred from the evidence that corporate counsel "knowingly participated in ... [their] fraud."[7] The plaintiff's theory of the case was that the conspiracy was for fraudulent concealment and constructive fraud based on breach of a fiduciary duty to disclose relevant matter. To make out a claim of fraud based on concealment, the plaintiff must show a duty to disclose. The court held that the shareholders' duty to disclose could not be imputed to corporate counsel and that corporate counsel had no other fiduciary duty to Skarbrevik. "There was no basis for plaintiff to place special trust or confidence in ... [corporate counsel], or for him to rely on [corporate counsel] to act in his best interest in relation to the corporation or the other shareholders. Nor was there any evidence that he did so."[8] The court noted that had the case been tried as one for actual, as opposed to constructive fraud (i.e., breach of fiduciary duty), the result might have been different.

Is *Skarbrevik* fundamentally inconsistent with Roberts v. Ball, Hunt, Hart, Brown & Baerwitz?[9] In *Roberts,* the California intermediate appellate court held that borrower's counsel could be sued by a lender for negligently writing an opinion letter, plausible on its face, stating that all borrower's partners were general partners, because the letter omitted to mention a material fact: that some partners of the borrower believed themselves to be limited partners, despite counsel's legal opinion to the contrary.

Co-Client Approach to Shareholders of Closely Held Corporations

Some courts have held that a lawyer representing a closely-held corporation also represents the individual shareholders as joint clients. In re Banks[10] involved a closely-held family corporation that had been dominated

---

corporation does not by virtue of that relationship alone have an attorney-client relationship with the individual shareholders, counsel nevertheless owes each shareholder a fiduciary duty. See *Fassihi,* ... for a well-reasoned opinion supporting that view. Just as an attorney for a partnership owes a fiduciary duty to each partner, it is fairly arguable that an attorney for a close corporation owes a fiduciary duty to the individual shareholders.

6.   282 Cal. Rptr. at 637.

7.   Id.

8.   Id. Contrast the California court's reasoning with that of the New York court in *Newburger, Loeb & Co.,* discussed at p. 93 supra. In *Newburger* the court imposed liability for fraud on a lawyer for a partnership who had helped general partners breach their fiduciary duties to limited partners, despite the fact that New York, unlike California, still requires privity before persons may sue lawyers for negligence.

9.   128 Cal.Rptr. 901 (App.1976), discussed at p. 87 supra.

10.   584 P.2d 284 (Ore.1978). See Lawrence E. Mitchell, Professional Responsibility and

by one family member during most of its history. Other family members subsequently wrested control of the corporation from that one family member, and the corporation's lawyers brought suit against him on their behalf. The court held that "in closely held ... corporations where the operator of the corporation either owns or controls the stock in such a manner that it is reasonable to assume that there is no real reason for him to differentiate in his mind between his own and corporate interests," the lawyer for the corporation owes that person the same duty not to represent conflicting interests that she would owe a client.[11] In a subsequent case[12] the Oregon court went one step further:

> Where a small, closely held corporation is involved, and in the absence of a clear understanding with the corporate owners that the attorney represents solely the corporation and not their individual interests, it is improper for the attorney thereafter to represent a third party whose interests are adverse to those of the stockholders and which arise out of a transaction which the attorney handled for the corporation. In actuality, the attorney in such a situation represents the corporate owners in their individual capacities as well as the corporation unless other arrangements are clearly made.[13]

Which alternative makes the most sense: the co-client approach, the no-duty approach of *Skarbrevik*, or the *Fassihi* approach, which allows a fiduciary duty to be implied depending on the facts?[14] What difference does it make? These questions are examined further in the notes following the next case and in the Hazard article on triangular relationships printed below at p. 775.

Partnerships

As *Fassihi* demonstrates, troublesome questions of loyalty and confidentiality arise in a partnership, joint venture or closely-held corporation when one of the entrepreneurs seeks to defraud or otherwise exploit

---

the Close Corporation, 74 Cornell L.Rev. 466 (1989) (ethics codes should be amended to provide that lawyer for close corporation also represents the individual shareholders); Note, An Expectations Approach to Client Identity, 106 Harv.L.Rev. 687 (1993) (urging reasonable expectations of a partner or constituent of a close corporation as the appropriate test).

11.   584 P.2d at 292.

12.   See In re Brownstein, 602 P.2d 655 (Ore.1979).

13.   602 P.2d at 657. In Rosman v. Shapiro, 653 F.Supp. 1441, 1445 (S.D.N.Y.1987), the court held that it is reasonable for a 50 percent shareholder in a closely-held corpo-

ration, where there is only one other shareholder, to believe that the lawyer for the corporation "is in effect his own individual attorney." See also Margulies v. Upchurch, 696 P.2d 1195 (Utah 1985) (lawyer for partnership may be found to have an attorney-client relationship with limited partners that would preclude him from suing them as individuals).

14.   Cf. Stainton v. Tarantino, 637 F.Supp. 1051, 1077 (E.D.Pa.1986) (in deciding whether attorney-client relationship exists with individual partners, jury should consider whether individual partners confided in, relied on and had partnership counsel perform legal services for them as individuals; if no attorney-client relationship existed, no fiduciary duty exists either).

another. An ABA ethics opinion[15] states that a lawyer representing a general or limited partnership normally represents the entity, not individual partners; that dual representation of the partnership and individual partners raises serious problems of conflict of interest and confidentiality; and that "information received by a lawyer in the course of representing the partnership ... normally may not be withheld from individual partners." A 1986 New York ethics opinion concluded that a lawyer representing a limited partnership, upon discovering that a general partner has committed acts adversely affecting the interests of limited partners, may disclose those facts to the limited partners "so that they will be able to take steps to protect their interests."[16] A subsequent opinion discussing the same situation goes further: the lawyer's duty to the partnership entity requires the lawyer to disclose the general partner's wrongdoing to the individual partners.[17] Although there is authority both ways, a number of cases hold that a limited partner may sue the partnership's lawyer for malpractice.[18] A failure to disclose may constitute fraud.[19]

Piercing the Privilege for Almost Clients: The *Garner* Doctrine

Consider the *Fassihi* court's treatment of the privilege question. The court gives two separate reasons why Epstein must answer deposition questions "relative to communications concerning the ouster of [Dr. Fassihi]" from the corporation: (1) as a corporate director, he is entitled to information concerning Epstein's representation of the corporation; and (2) the crime-fraud exception to the privilege. Is the court correct on the latter point? Are allegations in a plaintiff's complaint a sufficient basis for overriding the privilege?

While the *Fassihi* court says it is relying on the crime-fraud doctrine, it cites a case that stands for a different proposition: Garner v. Wolfinbarger.[20] In *Garner* the Fifth Circuit recognized an exception to the corporation's attorney-client privilege, holding that shareholder-plaintiffs in derivative suits may gain access to information protected by the corporation's attorney-client privilege if they can "show cause why [the privilege] should not be invoked in the particular instance."[21] To determine what counts as "good cause" for shareholder access to corporate information, *Garner* lists

---

15. ABA Formal Op. 91–361 (July 12, 1991).

16. Ass'n Bar City of New York Op. No. 1986–2.

17. See Ass'n Bar City of New York Op. No. 1994–10.

18. *Compare* Johnson v. Superior Court, 45 Cal.Rptr. 312 (App.1995) (lawyer for partnership has obligation of loyalty to all partners); Arpadi v. First MSP Corp., 628 N.E.2d 1335 (Ohio 1994) (partnership lawyer represents every limited partner); Adell v. Sommers, Schwartz, Silver & Schwartz, 428 N.W.2d 26 (Mich.App.1988) (same), *with* Hackett v. Village Court Associates,

602 F.Supp. 856 (E.D.Wis.1985) (insufficient relationship).

19. See Roberts v. Heim, 123 F.R.D. 614, 625 (N.D.Cal.1988) (limited partners are clients of partnership's lawyer (at least for attorney-client privilege purposes) because general partner and partnership lawyer have a fiduciary duty to make full disclosure of material facts to limited partners; withholding such information would constitute fraud).

20. 430 F.2d 1093 (5th Cir.1970), on remand, 56 F.R.D. 499 (S.D.Ala.1972).

21. 430 F.2d at 1103–04.

various factors.[22] Those factors reflect exceptions to the attorney-client privilege and whether the shareholder-plaintiffs have made a plausible showing that the derivative claim seeks to remedy a serious, possibly meritorious, breach of duty that defendant agents of the corporation owed to the corporation.

The *Garner* exception rests on common law precedent: If a plausible showing is made of serious breach of fiduciary duty, the privilege may not be claimed by the fiduciary against the beneficiary for whose benefit the legal relationship exists. The *Garner* court reasoned that where management is charged with a breach of fiduciary responsibility, accountability to shareholders justifies interference with confidentiality.[23] Note that *Garner* is inapplicable to communications with counsel about the derivative suit itself on the theory that the true interests of the corporation (and thus its shareholders) is not necessarily aligned with those prosecuting the derivative suit.[24]

Although widely recognized,[25] the *Garner* "good cause" standard has been criticized as vague and overbroad.[26] One commentator has urged that the *Garner* exception to the attorney-client privilege be abandoned entirely, with its office performed by the crime-fraud exception.[27] But the crime-fraud exception may be too narrow for the purposes envisioned by *Garner*, which seeks to ensure the attorney-client privilege is asserted in the best

22. The listed factors are: the number of shareholders bringing the claim against the corporation and the percentage of stock they represent; the bona fides of the shareholders; the nature of the shareholders' claim and whether it is obviously colorable; whether the information is vital to the shareholders and whether it is available from other sources; whether the shareholders' claim alleges that corporate officers acted criminally, or illegally but not criminally, or in a way that is of doubtful legality; whether the communication related to past or to future actions, i.e., whether the communications might have been part of an ongoing fraud; whether the communication concerns advice about the litigation itself; the extent to which the shareholders are fishing for information; and the risk of revelation of trade secrets or other information in whose confidentiality the corporation has an interest beyond the present litigation. 430 F.2d at 1104.

23. The court also drew an analogy between shareholders, as constituents of the corporation, and joint clients, noting that the privilege is unavailable among joint clients.

24. See In re LTV Securities Litigation, 89 F.R.D. 595 (N.D.Tex.1981) (*Garner* exception inapplicable to "after-the-fact" communications concerning offenses already completed); see also In re International Sys. & Controls Corp., 693 F.2d 1235 (5th Cir.1982) (refusing to apply *Garner* to the lawyer's work-product concerning the pending litigation).

25. See, e.g., Quintel Corp. v. Citibank, N.A., 567 F.Supp. 1357, 1363–64 (S.D.N.Y. 1983); Panter v. Marshall Field & Co., 80 F.R.D. 718, 722–23 (N.D.Ill.1978); Cohen v. Uniroyal, Inc., 80 F.R.D. 480, 482–85 (E.D.Pa.1978); In re Transocean Tender Offer Sec. Litig., 78 F.R.D. 692, 695–97 (N.D.Ill.1978); Valente v. Pepsico, 68 F.R.D. 361, 366–68 (D.Del.1975).

26. See Note, The Attorney–Client Privilege in Shareholder Litigation: The Need for a Predictable Standard, 9 Loy.U.Chi.L.J. 731 (1978) (arguing that the criteria in *Garner* for determining good cause are vague and overbroad).

27. See Developments in the Law—Privileged Communication: III. Attorney–Client Privilege, 98 Harv.L.Rev. 1501 (1985) (arguing that instead of using the *Garner* exception, courts should rely exclusively on the crime-fraud exception to get at those communications that corporate managers should not be allowed to shield from shareholders or others).

interests of the organization rather than for the benefit of management. *Garner* is concerned with bad faith in asserting the privilege, not bad faith in communicating with counsel for an illegal purpose. After the Supreme Court's decision in *Upjohn*, p. 209 supra, affirming the corporation's strong interest in frank and confidential communications with counsel, some commentators predicted the demise of *Garner*,[28] yet the *Garner* exception has survived and prospered.[29]

As noted earlier, *Garner* rests on precedent that allowed those to whom a fiduciary duty is owed to gain access to communications between the fiduciary and her counsel.[30] Restatement § 134A provides:

> In a proceeding in which a trustee of an express trust or similar fiduciary is charged with breach of fiduciary duties by a beneficiary, a [privileged] communication ... is nonetheless not privileged if the communication:
>
> (a) is relevant to the claimed breach; and
>
> (b) was between the trustee and a lawyer ... who was retained to advise the trustee concerning the administration of the trust.

Valente v. Pepsico, Inc.,[31] applied the *Garner* doctrine when minority shareholders charged that the majority shareholder had violated duties to them. The court, agreeing that a majority shareholder owes fiduciary responsibilities, just as a corporation does, to minority shareholders, held that the minority shareholders could gain access to communications between the majority shareholder and corporate counsel about the minority's interests: "A fiduciary owes the obligation to his beneficiaries to go about his duties without obscuring his reasons from the legitimate inquiries of the beneficiaries."[32] The court stated that the purpose of the privilege to encourage frank communication between lawyer and client was outweighed by the "more general and important right of those who look to fiduciaries to safeguard their interests to be able to determine the proper functioning of the fiduciary."[33]

---

28. See, e.g., Thomas Kirby, New Life for the Corporate Attorney–Client Privilege in Shareholder Litigation, 69 A.B.A.J. 174 (1983); John E. Sexton, A Post–Upjohn Consideration of Corporate Attorney–Client Privilege, 57 N.Y.U.L.Rev. 443 (1982).

29. See Ward v. Succession of Freeman, 854 F.2d 780, 785 (5th Cir.1988) ("*Upjohn* does not undermine ... *Garner*"); Donald B. Lewis, Garner is Alive and Well in Securities Litigation, 69 A.B.A.J. 903 (1983).

30. Should the *Garner* doctrine be applied to direct actions by shareholders? Some courts have so held. See, e.g., *Cohen*, supra (following *Garner* approach in federal secu-

rities lawsuit brought by individual plaintiff on his own behalf). But other decisions hold the policy rationale of *Garner* does not apply where the plaintiff seeks a damage recovery for an injury to her own interests rather than a recovery for the benefit of the corporation. See, e.g., Weil v. Investment/Indicators, Research & Management, Inc., 647 F.2d 18, 23 (9th Cir.1981) ("*Garner's* holding and policy rationale simply do not apply [when plaintiff is seeking damages for herself]").

31. 68 F.R.D. 361 (D.Del.1975).

32. Id. at 370.

33. Id. n. 16.

In Quintel Corp., N.V. v. Citibank, N.A.,[34] Gajria contracted with Citibank to be his agent in acquiring certain investment property. His suit alleged that Citibank breached its fiduciary duties to him in acquiring the property. The court, in applying *Garner* to allow Gajria access to communications between Citibank and its lawyers, stated:

> [T]he fiduciary's duty to exercise its authority without veiling its reasons from the grantor of that authority outweighs the fiduciary's interest in the confidentiality of its attorney's communications. The *Garner* rule stems not only from the general proposition that a beneficiary is entitled to know how the authority he has granted has been exercised but on the recognition that because of the mutuality of interest between the parties, the faithful fiduciary has nothing to hide from his beneficiary.[35]

What are the dangers of allowing beneficiaries access to their fiduciaries' conversations with counsel? If the faithful fiduciary has "nothing to hide" from his beneficiary, why must the beneficiary show good cause before gaining access to the confidential communications between lawyer and fiduciary?[36] Some courts have held that the fiduciary does not have a privilege to assert against the beneficiary, i.e., that the beneficiary is a joint client for purposes of the privilege.[37]

The privilege still protects communications between fiduciary and lawyer that do not relate to the fiduciary relationship or that occur after the fiduciary relationship has been terminated.[38] As to communications

---

34. 567 F.Supp. 1357 (S.D.N.Y.1983).

35. Id. at 1363; see also Aguinaga v. John Morrell & Co., 112 F.R.D. 671, 681 (D.Kan. 1986) (*Garner* applies to allow union members access to communications between union counsel and union leadership); Donovan v. Fitzsimmons, 90 F.R.D. 583 (N.D.Ill. 1981) (*Garner* rule allows the Secretary of Labor, suing a pension fund on behalf of the fund's beneficiaries, access to communications between the pension fund trustee and its lawyers). Compare In re Atlantic Financial Management Securities Litigation, 121 F.R.D. 141, 146 (D.Mass.1988) ("Without a showing of a fiduciary relationship, the *Garner* exception does not apply."); In re Colocotronis Tanker Securities Litigation, 449 F.Supp. 828 (S.D.N.Y. 1978) (*Garner* exception inapplicable between parties to an arm's-length contract).

36. In *Valente,* supra, the court shifted the burden to the fiduciary, requiring that it show why the privilege should not yield. Is this middle position between *Garner* and no privilege a better alternative?

37. See, e.g., Roberts v. Heim, 123 F.R.D. 614 (N.D.Cal.1988) (limited partners are

joint clients of lawyer for partnership for purposes of the privilege); United States v. Evans, 796 F.2d 264, 265–66 (9th Cir.1986) (pension trustee may not assert privilege against pension plan beneficiaries because "trustee is not the real client in the sense that he is personally being served"). In California the courts have held that they are precluded by statute from adopting *Garner*. See Dickerson v. Superior Court of Santa Clara County, 185 Cal.Rptr. 97 (1982); and Hoiles v. Superior Court of Orange County, 204 Cal.Rptr. 111, 114–15 (1984). Hence, in that state, beneficiaries are denied access to fiduciary-lawyer communications unless the court finds that beneficiaries are joint clients, whereupon the joint client exception to the privilege provides free access. See Roberts v. Heim, supra; *Hoiles*, 204 Cal.Rptr. at 115 n.4 (1984).

38. As to communications between the fiduciary and counsel about forming the fiduciary relationship,.compare *Quintel,* 567 F.Supp. at 1364 ("Prior to the investor's entry on the scene the important mutuality of interest is absent since Citibank's inter-

between the fiduciary and its lawyers about the extent of its obligations to the beneficiary, the court in *Quintel* said these are available under *Garner* as they were made "as part of and in furtherance of . . . fiduciary obligations."[39]

Should *Garner* allow those who allege that government officers have violated their trust to discover communications of government lawyers upon a showing of good cause? Should a similar rule permit members of a class to obtain communications between class representatives and the lawyer for the class?[40]

2.   REPRESENTING A FIDUCIARY

Fickett v. Superior Court of Pima County

Court of Appeals of Arizona, Division 2, 1976.
27 Ariz.App. 793, 558 P.2d 988.

■ HOWARD, CHIEF JUDGE.

Petitioners are defendants in a pending superior court action filed by the present conservator (formerly guardian) of an incompetent's estate against the former guardian and petitioners, attorneys for the former guardian. The gravamen of the complaint was that petitioner Fickett, as attorney for the former guardian, was negligent in failing to discover that the guardian had embarked upon a scheme to liquidate the guardianship estate by misappropriation and conversion of the funds to his own use and making improper investments for his personal benefit.[1]

[Herbert Schwager, the former guardian, was an investment adviser with a "well-known" brokerage house. He had befriended Mrs. Styer, who was old and had failing eyesight. Schwager was appointed guardian of Mrs. Styer's $1.3 million estate, consisting almost entirely of common stock. Within little more than a year, Schwager had sold most of the stock to build a two-unit business building. The two tenants were Schwager's wife, who ran a beauty salon, and another business in which Schwager had an interest. Both businesses became bankrupt. A separate corporation, wholly owned by Schwager, managed the building. It paid large salaries to Schwager and other family members for "management services." Schwager also

---

est is in putting together a proposal that it can sell to the investor, an interest not shared by the investor," therefore, the privilege holds); with *Roberts*, supra (limited partners may later gain free access to general partner's communications with lawyer for partnership).

39. *Quintel*, 567 F.Supp. at 1357. Accord, *Valente*, 68 F.R.D. 361 (D.Del.1975).

40. See Note, The Attorney–Client Privilege in Class Actions: Fashioning an Exception to Promote Adequacy of Representation, 94

Harv.L.Rev. 947 (1984) (arguing that a *Garner*-like exception be created for class members who seek access to communication between class representatives and counsel).

1. The facts of the guardian's misconduct can be found in the case of In Re Guardianship of Styer, 24 Ariz.App. 148, 536 P.2d 717 (1975). There we affirmed a judgment surcharging the guardian in the sum of $378,789.62.

extensively commingled funds in his personal account. Within three years most of Mrs. Styer's assets were gone and those that remained had large liens for loans or taxes. The plaintiff, a successor conservator, was able to recover little for the estate from Schwager or third parties. The conservator then brought this proceeding against the law firm which had represented Schwager as guardian.]

Petitioners filed a motion for summary judgment contending that, as a matter of law, since there was no fraud or collusion between the guardian and his attorney, the attorney was not liable for the guardian's misappropriation of the assets of the guardianship estate. In opposing the motion for summary judgment, the present conservator conceded that no fraud or collusion existed. His position, however, was that one could not say as a matter of law that the guardian's attorney owed no duty to the ward. The respondent court denied the motion for summary judgment and petitioners challenge this ruling by special action.

The general rule for many years has been that an attorney could not be liable to one other than his client in an action arising out of his professional duties, in the absence of fraud or collusion. 7 Am.Jur.2d, Attorneys at Law, § 167. In denying liability of the attorney to one not in privity of contract for the consequences of professional negligence, the courts have relied principally on two arguments: (1) That to allow such liability would deprive the parties to the contract of control of their own agreement; and (2) that a duty to the general public would impose a huge potential burden of liability on the contracting parties. An annotation of cases dealing with an attorney's liability to one other than his immediate client for the consequences of negligence in carrying out his professional duties may be found in Annot., 45 A.L.R.3d 1181 et seq.

We cannot agree with petitioners that they owed no duty to the ward and that her conservator could not maintain an action because of lack of privity of contract. We are of the opinion that the better view is that the determination of whether, in a specific case, the attorney will be held liable to a third person not in privity is a matter of policy and involves the balancing of various factors, among which are the extent to which the transaction was intended to affect the plaintiff, the foreseeability of harm to him, the degree of certainty that the plaintiff suffered injury, the closeness of the connection between the defendant's conduct and the injuries suffered, the moral blame attached to the defendant's conduct, and the policy of preventing future harm. Biakanja v. Irving, 49 Cal.2d 647, 320 P.2d 16 (1958); Lucas v. Hamm, 56 Cal.2d 583, 15 Cal.Rptr. 821, 364 P.2d 685 (1961). . . .

We believe that the public policy of this state permits the imposition of a duty under the circumstances presented here. In the case of In re Fraser, 83 Wash.2d 884, 523 P.2d 921 (1974), the Supreme Court of Washington in considering a complaint concerning an attorney's refusal to withdraw as attorney for a client-guardian, stated:

"The respondent maintains and we agree that under the circumstances he would not have been justified in withdrawing as counsel until such time as the guardian had secured the agreement of some other attorney to take over the handling of the guardianship. As the respondent suggests, *the attorney owes a duty to the ward, as well as to the guardian.* Since the guardian in this case manifested a greater interest in obtaining money for herself than in serving the interest of the ward, it would have been hazardous to the interest of the ward to turn the assets of her small estate over to the guardian.

In In re Michelson, 8 Wash.2d 327, 335, 111 P.2d 1011, 1015 (1941), we said:

'It must be borne in mind that the real object and purpose of a guardianship is to preserve and conserve the ward's property for his own use, as distinguished from the benefit of others.'

We think that under the circumstances of this case, the respondent cannot be faulted for refusing to abandon the ward at the guardian's request." 523 P.2d at 928. (Emphasis ours)

We are of the opinion that when an attorney undertakes to represent the guardian of an incompetent, he assumes a relationship not only with the guardian but also with the ward. If, as is contended here, petitioners knew or should have known that the guardian was acting adversely to his ward's interests, the possibility of frustrating the whole purpose of the guardianship became foreseeable as did the possibility of injury to the ward. In fact, we conceive that the ward's interests overshadow those of the guardian. We believe the following statement in *Heyer v. Flaig*, supra, as to an attorney's duty to an intended testamentary beneficiary is equally appropriate here:

"The duty thus recognized in *Lucas* stems from the attorney's undertaking to perform legal services for the client but reaches out to protect the intended beneficiary. We impose this duty because of the relationship between the attorney and the intended beneficiary; public policy requires that the attorney exercise his position of trust and superior knowledge responsibly so as not to affect adversely persons whose rights and interests are certain and foreseeable.

"Although the duty accrues directly in favor of the intended testamentary beneficiary, the scope of the duty is determined by reference to the attorney-client context. Out of the agreement to provide legal services to a client, the prospective testator, arises the duty to act with due care as to the interests of the intended beneficiary. We do not mean to say that the attorney-client contract for legal services serves as the fundamental touchstone to fix the scope of this direct tort duty to the third party. The actual circumstances under which the attorney undertakes to perform his legal services, however, will bear on a judicial assessment of the care with which he performs his services." 74 Cal.Rptr. at 229, 449 P.2d at 165.

We, therefore, uphold the respondent court's denial of petitioners' motion for summary judgment since they failed to establish the absence of a legal relationship and concomitant duty to the ward....

———

Duty of a Lawyer for a Fiduciary Toward a Beneficiary

Did lawyer Fickett have any contact or dealings with Mrs. Styer? A lawyer-client relationship? If not, why does Fickett owe her duties of care and loyalty akin to those owed to a client? Does the decision require a lawyer for a fiduciary to make a reasonable inquiry concerning the fiduciary's conduct or merely require some action to be taken if the lawyer knows or reasonably should know that a breach of fiduciary duty is occurring? Assume lawyer Fickett learned of Schwager's misconduct; what should he have done?[1]

Corporate directors and officers have fiduciary responsibilities to shareholders. May a lawyer for a corporation be sued by shareholders for failing to discover (and stop) corporate fraud? Review the note on FDIC v. O'Melveny & Myers, p. 758 above.

3. TRIANGULAR LAWYER RELATIONSHIPS

Geoffrey C. Hazard, Jr., "Triangular Lawyer Relationships: An Exploratory Analysis"

1 Georgetown Journal of Legal Ethics 15 (1987).[2]

I. Introduction

This article examines the nature of a lawyer's responsibilities where the lawyer's client has a special legal relationship with another party that modifies the lawyer's "normal" professional responsibilities. This legal relationship is termed "triangular," denoting the coexistence of a linkage of legal responsibility between the lawyer's client and a third person along with a linkage of professional responsibility between the lawyer and the client. The combination results in a special legal relationship between the lawyer and the third person.

. . .

This exploration focuses on two types of triangular relationships. The first involves a client in a fiduciary relationship to a third party. The classic example is that of a lawyer representing a guardian in matters relating to the guardian's responsibilities to a ward. In that relationship, the client-guardian has a set of strong and well defined legal obligations. Given these obligations, what are the legal obligations of the lawyer to the ward?

The lawyer-guardian-ward triangular relationship can be diagrammed:

1. See Jeffrey N. Pennell, Representations Involving Fiduciary Entities: Who Is the Client?, 62 Fordham L.Rev. 1319 (1994); and Joel C. Dobris, Ethical Problems for Lawyers Upon Trust Terminations: Conflicts of Interests, 38 U.Miami L.Rev. 1 (1983) (conflicts of interest of lawyer who represents a trustee).

2. Copyright © 1987 by the Georgetown Journal of Legal Ethics.

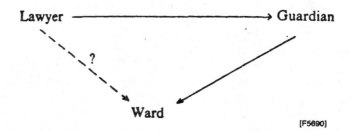

[F5690]

The second type of triangular relationship involves a third party who owes fiduciary duties to the lawyer's client, and the third party rather than the client is the one with whom the lawyer deals ordinarily. The classic situation is that of a lawyer who represents a corporation but who, in the ordinary course of professional service, deals with the corporation's officers, directors, and employees. To simplify terminology, we can treat the corporate officers, directors, and employees as a single category, even though important differences exist in their legal relationships to the corporation. Thus simplified, the corporate lawyer triangular relationship can be designated as lawyer-corporation-officer.

The lawyer-corporation-officer triangular relationship can be diagrammed:

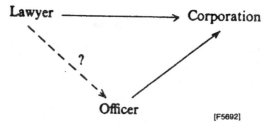

[F5692]

The difference in the vectors of obligation in these two triangular relationships is important. In the lawyer-guardian-ward triangular relationship, the ward is the dependent person and the obligee of the guardian, but the guardian is the dependent person and the primary obligee of the lawyer. In the lawyer-corporation-officer triangular relationship, the corporation is the dependent entity and the obligee of both the lawyer and the corporate officer. This structural difference in obligations can help identify and define the lawyer's role in the two triangular relationships....

Other triangular relationships can be classified into the two basic types:

I.	*II.*
Classic	*Classic*
Lawyer→Guardian→Ward	Lawyer→Corporation←Officer
Others	*Others*
Lawyer→General Partner→Partnership	Lawyer→Partnership←General Partner
Lawyer→Govt. Employee→Govt.	Lawyer→Govt.←Govt. Employee
Lawyer→Union Officer→Union	Lawyer→Union←Union Officer
Lawyer→Director→Corp.	Lawyer→Ward←Guardian

As the foregoing chart depicts, whether a triangular relationship falls into one or the other of the two basic categories depends on which party is the lawyer's client. If the lawyer represents the *guardian,* for example, the relationship is lawyer→guardian→ward and is of the first basic type. On the other hand, if the lawyer represents the *ward,* the relationship is lawyer→ward←guardian and is of the second basic type. Similarly, a lawyer retained to represent a corporate officer or director rather than the corporation falls under the first basic type, whereas the normal corporate lawyer relationship is lawyer→corporation←director and falls under the second basic type.

. . .

II. Traditional Concepts for Defining a Lawyer's Responsibilities

A. Three Possible Relationships

Part of the difficulty posed by triangular lawyer relationships lies in the traditional limitations in the definition of a lawyer's responsibilities. Generally, those responsibilities recognize only three relationships that a lawyer may have. One is with a client; the second is with the court; and the third is with a third party. In substance and orientation, these relationships differ from each other radically. In moral and existential quality, they are strangely alike in their radical simplicity. They characterize the lawyer's "relevant other" respectively as something like friend, father, and foe.

1. Clients

[Professor Hazard describes the lawyer's relationship with a client as legally both amorphous and secret. The lawyer's primary duty to the client is loyalty and the relationship may be analogized to that of limited-purpose "friendship."[3] Beyond the duty of loyalty, however, the lawyer-client relationship is largely unstructured, the only real limit being the "bounds of the law."]

2. Courts

[Starting with the basic proposition that "a lawyer is an officer of the court," Hazard suggests a lawyer owes the court only a minimal duty of diligence and candor. But while the lawyer's substantive responsibility to the court is minimal, the formal aspects of that relationship—the law of procedure and the rules of evidence—are highly detailed and exacting. Thus, where the lawyer's relationship with a client is legally unstructured and secret, the lawyer's relationship with the court is legally structured and visible.]

3. Third Party

The third kind of lawyer's relationship is that with a third party. In general, a third party is entitled to very little from the lawyer. If Broug-

---

3. Charles Fried, The Lawyer as Friend: The Moral Foundations of the Lawyer–   Client Relationship, 85 Yale L.J. 1060 (1976).

ham's dictum about the duty of the advocate is taken as the measure of the lawyer's legal duty to anyone but the client, a lawyer owes a third party nothing. The law concerning a lawyer's obligations to others is hard indeed, but not quite that hard. Against a lawyer, a third party is entitled to the protection of the criminal law and the law of fraud.... Rules against abusive litigation, such as rule 11 of the Federal Rules of Civil Procedure are essentially corollaries of the rule against fraud.

B.   Inadequacy of Conceptual Premises

The established conceptual system thus allows for only three parties with whom the lawyer may have a professional relationship: client, court, third party. As we shall see, the most difficult problems in triangular relationships are those in which the lawyer is performing a counseling function as distinct from the function of advocate. In counseling situations one thing is clear: none of the relevant others is a judge. Under the established scheme, that reduces the conceptual possibilities from three to two. The lawyer's relationship to the other person—the ward or the corporate office—must be characterized as either that between lawyer and client or that between lawyer and third party.

This is a stark choice. If the relationship is characterized as that with a client, then the duties of loyalty, zealous partisanship, and confidentiality are fully engaged. To say that when the lawyer represents a guardian he or she thereby also represents the ward, or that when a lawyer represents a corporation he or she also represents its corporate officers, is to implicate very serious practical and conceptual difficulties, indeed contradictions.

[Hazard describes three problems that would arise if we were to accept that guardian and ward were co-clients or that corporation and corporate officer were co-clients: (1) because potential conflict between the two clients (guardian and ward or corporation and corporate officer) is always present, concurrent representation of both would involve an impermissible conflict of interest; (2) similarly, the rules prohibiting representation adverse to a former client in the "same or a substantially related" matter would prevent a lawyer who was deemed to represent both from representing either the guardian or the ward if a subsequent dispute arose; and (3) confidential communications between the joint clients would not be protected either by professional rules or by the attorney-client privilege.]

. . .

The courts have rightly hesitated to embrace the foregoing implications. They have been confused, however, in knowing where to stop or even where to start. They evidently recognize that the lawyer in these triangular relationships has special protective responsibilities to the person who is not the client, but they do not wish to say that these responsibilities include the whole package owed to a client. Under the conventional conceptual system, the alternative is to say that the lawyer's relationship to the other person is that of lawyer and third party. In the guardian-ward situation, this would mean that the ward is merely a stranger. The same would be true of the corporate lawyer's responsibility to a corporate director, officer, or employee.

To treat the ward or the corporate officer as a mere stranger is unappealing and incoherent. It is unappealing because it affords the ward or the corporate employee, insofar as the lawyer is concerned, only the cold comfort provided by the laws of crime and fraud. It is incoherent in the guardianship situation because it calls for the lawyer as agent of the guardian to have an arm's length relationship with one to whom the guardian has an intimate and exacting fiduciary duty. That makes no sense under basic principles of the law of agency. Under the law of agency, the duty of an agent of the principal (i.e., the lawyer representing the guardian) to a third person (i.e., the ward) is a function of the duty of the principal (i.e., the guardian) to that person. To treat the ward as a stranger vis-á-vis the lawyer disregards that interconnection.

In the corporate situation an even more complicated set of difficulties is presented if the corporate officer is treated as a mere stranger. For one thing, the corporate officer is effectively the personification of the corporate client for most ordinary legal purposes. Corporate counsel and the corporate officer must maintain an intimacy that substantially replicates that between counsel and a flesh and blood client. It is simply impossible to hold that a person who is, in fact, a confidential intimate shall nevertheless be regarded in law as a total stranger. Moreover, under the law of agency, some kind of protective responsibility is owed by the principal to the agent in matters within the scope of the agency. A corporation owes a responsibility to its employees, sometimes something like that of guardian to ward. Thus, whatever the relationship between a corporation and its director, officer, or employee, it is not that of one stranger to another.

[Hazard argues that the unmodulated and polarized character of the alternative relationships (lawyer-client and lawyer-third party) are inappropriate when one of the two persons the lawyer is dealing with owes fiduciary duties to the other. The polar notions of friend or foe—the client as friend and the third party as foe) do not reflect the accommodation of competing values required by the situation. "The complex interdependencies in the[se] . . . situations do not lend themselves to analysis in terms of friend or foe."]

The inadequacy of these premises no doubt explains why the responses of courts and scholars to lawyer triangular relationships have been so baffled and baffling. Lacking an adequate conceptual system to address the problem, the courts have done what courts always do in such circumstances: They adhere to bad concepts and get poor results, or, as in the *Fickett* and *Yablonski* cases, they reach what may be good results but improvise on concepts. A variation of this technique is to marshal miscellaneous "factors," factors found in all the problematic situations, and then to maintain that the correct solution depends on "all the factors." . . . [See, e.g., the list of factors to be considered in deciding whether shareholders may gain access to the corporation's confidential communications with counsel. *Garner v. Wolfinbarger.*]

. . .

IV. Toward Better Conceptualizations

. . .

Neither the concept of "client" nor that of "third party" appropriately engages the complexities of triangular relationships, even a simple one such as that of guardian and ward involved in *Fickett v. Superior Court*. The client in such a triangular situation is not a person alone—the A of classical legal hypotheticals, where "*A*, the owner of Blackacre" does something to or is done something by *B*. One who has become another's guardian is no longer *A* but has become "*A* encumbered by duties to *B*." So long as the relationship between *A* and *B* exists, and for some purposes even after it ends, *A* is not a legal monad. Rather *A* is a member of an "institution," (as said in *Yablonski v. United Mine Workers*), that has a "whole purpose," (as said in *Fickett*). In legal terms, a guardian as such is an officeholder constituted by law, by court appointment as in the *Fickett* case or by private contractual designation. So also, and more obviously, the corporate director, officer, or employee is an officeholder constituted by legally sanctioned private ordering, and is a member of an "institution" that has a "whole purpose." As a matter of law, both guardian and corporate officer are not persons but personages, individuals who act in legal capacities.

. . .

The vocabulary and metaphorical geometry used in analyzing the "normal" lawyer-client relationship contemplate an intimate dyad of lawyer and client, facing outward toward an alien and presumptively hostile world of third parties. That vocabulary and geometry misdescribes relationships between a lawyer, a client who is a legal personage, and a third person whose very existence defines that personage. The problem is to develop concepts and vocabulary that intelligibly address relationships where the lawyer must care about two parties.

. . .

A. Client Openly Adverse to the "Other"

There are cases where a lawyer in a triangular situation has the same "arm's length" position vis-á-vis the "relevant other" as a lawyer "normally" should have on behalf of a client. The clearest is where the lawyer, not having been involved previously, is retained to represent a guardian or a corporate officer in litigation concerning that person's performance of duties [such as a proceeding initiated by the ward against the guardian to surcharge or remove the guardian].

There should be no equivocation or confusion about the nature of lawyer-client relationship and the lawyer's duties in this situation. An action for surcharge is a legal claim against the guardian in his or her individual capacity for alleged wrong committed in the course of an official capacity. The potential financial loss, moral obloquy, and civic disgrace faced by the guardian are real individual interests. Persons with that kind of exposure are entitled to legal representation, which means full service advocacy. The lawyer is obliged to make zealous efforts on the guardian's behalf; hold in confidence information garnered for the representation; and abstain from conflicting representation in the matter.

The same analysis applies where a lawyer, not previously involved, is retained to represent a corporate director, officer, or employee. Ordinarily, that kind of representation is arranged only when there is a significant possibility that the interests of the director, officer, or employee may diverge from the corporation's interests. When this possibility exists, there is also a risk that there will be legal or informal recrimination on behalf of the corporation. Persons with that kind of exposure are likewise entitled to full service advocacy.

The same analysis again applies where a lawyer, not previously involved, is retained to represent the corporation against a corporate director, officer, or employee to redress malfeasance in office. That was the situation in *Yablonski*, where the derivative suit sought to redress the officer's misspending of organization funds. The holding in *Yablonski* that the organization is entitled to the zeal of an uncompromised advocate is correct. . . .

[Other cases of "arm's length" relationships arise when a lawyer is retained to represent someone nominated as guardian or corporate officer in negotiating the terms of the office and when a lawyer with no prior involvement is brought into negotiations for termination or reformation of the special relationship. In both instances the lawyer is not involved in the conduct of the relationship, but only in negotiations concerning the creation, reformation, or termination of the relationship. In both cases the fiduciary is dealing at arm's length with a beneficiary, and the role of the lawyer becomes the typical one of negotiation or advocacy on behalf of the fiduciary-client.]

B.   Normal Protective Relationship

While the positions of the fiduciary and the "relevant other" are openly adverse in some situations, normally the fiduciary's protective responsibility is unambiguous. In the normal legal relationship between guardian and ward, or between corporation and corporate director, officer, or employee, the legal purpose of the relationship is being fulfilled and the fiduciary is conforming his or her conduct to legal requirements.

The lawyer's task in this normal situation is to assist the fiduciary in meeting his or her legal obligations, and to help minimize legal risks to the relationship from outside forces, such as persons with competing claims on the assets or the tax collector. Toward these ends the lawyer supplies advice and employs legally recognized techniques that further the undertaking. Thus, the lawyer provides the forms and procedures for board action in the corporation, for the proprieties where a director has a conflict of interest that disqualifies him or her from voting on a corporate matter, etc. In the guardianship, the lawyer similarly safeguards the proprieties. The lawyer represents the guardian *in taking care* of the ward—the "whole purpose of the relationship," to use the phrase from *Fickett*. In the corporate situation, the corporate counsel works with the corporate director, officer, or employee *in taking care* of the corporation's "institutional interests," to use the phrase from *Yablonski*. Neither a "guardianship" nor a "corporation" has material existence or autonomous identity. They are legal events, artifacts of the lawyer's endeavors in the representation. The relationship itself is an evolving legal event that the lawyer's services continuously create.

. . .

[T]he lawyer's responsibilities may well be analogized to multiple representation. The key rules are those of confidentiality and loyalty. In multiple representation, the rule of confidentiality includes all within the group and excludes all outside it. In the corporate situation, the rule of confidentiality applies to information the corporate lawyer obtains from corporate "constituents" in the course of the representation, as does the corresponding rule of attorney-client privilege.[51] The same principle would apply to information provided to a lawyer for a partnership and ought to apply to information received from a ward by a lawyer or a guardian.

Concerning the principle of loyalty, a lawyer may serve two or more clients in the same matter if they do not have adverse interests. In a triangular relationship in the normal state, the interests of the nonlawyer participants are not adverse; both, therefore, may be considered to be clients.

Conceptualizing both the "relevant others" as clients, and the lawyer as engaged in multiple representation, seems entirely natural when the triangular relationship is in its normal state. The question is whether there are reasons for refusing to conceptualize it in this way. Only one reason exists for such hesitancy: the implications that follow if the triangular relationship ceases to be normal and instead becomes antagonistic.

. . . Under standard doctrine, in multiple representation each client has the full rights of a client, including the power over confidentiality and the right to enforce the conflict of interest rules against the lawyer. Thus, if the corporate officer is treated in all respects as a client, then confidences he or she has imparted to the lawyer would not be usable against him or her *after* the normal triangular relationship has collapsed and the corporation and its officers become legal antagonists.[54] If the corporate officer is treated as a client in all respects, upon the collapse of his or her relationship with the

51. Upjohn Co. v. United States, 449 U.S. 383 (1981) (attorney-client privilege covers employee responses to questionnaires and interview notes of counsel).

54. The corporate officer does not have that right. E.g., Lane v. Chowning, 610 F.2d

1385 (8th Cir.1979) (defendant bank's attorney has no obligation to plaintiff-officer to refrain from using information acquired in representing bank).

corporation, the officer could then insist that the corporate lawyer not represent the corporation against him or her.[55] These are undesirable corollaries and their specter is a weighty objection.

This weighty objection indicates that the multiple representation concept should not operate fully once the triangular relationship has collapsed; indeed, that is the recognized rule. Ordinarily upon collapse of the relationship, the lawyer may continue to represent the person or entity that was his client in the full and formal sense, even though representation entails a position adverse to the other member of the triangle.[56] If both were treated as clients in the strict sense, that option would not be available.[57] The law should continue to recognize the lawyer's authority to continue representation of a guardian or a corporation after the relationship with the other party becomes antagonistic. On the other hand, the possibility that a triangular relationship might collapse into antagonism is an insufficient reason for rejecting the multiple representation analogy while the triangular relationship is still intact. It is also insufficient reason for denying the "relevant other" some of the rights of a full-fledged former client if the relationship does collapse, particularly where the lawyer had not made the ground rules clear earlier.[59]

C. Ambivalent and Unstable Situations

A triangular relationship may, then, be analyzed in two ways regarding the lawyer. One of the parties can be regarded as the client and the other as the third party, or both can be regarded as clients. Each interpretation fits traditional concepts and terminology, and each implies a firm set of legal consequences. While both interpretations are plausible, they result in radically different definitions of the lawyer's responsibilities. Under one

55. The corporate officer does not have that right either. E.g., Meehan v. Hopps, 144 Cal.App.2d 284, 301 P.2d 10 (1956) (attorney not precluded from representing client-corporation against officer where no prior attorney-client relationship existed between counsel and officer).

56. E.g., Commodity Futures Trading Comm'n v. Weintraub, 471 U.S. 343 (1985) (trustee of corporation in bankruptcy has power to waive corporation's attorney-client privilege with respect to communications that took place before filing petition in bankruptcy); Lane v. Chowning, 610 F.2d 1385 (8th Cir.1979); Meehan v. Hopps, 144 Cal.App.2d 284, 301 P.2d 10 (1956).

57. E.g., Opdyke v. Kent Liquor Market, Inc., 40 Del.Ch. 316, 181 A.2d 579 (1962) (attorney who organized and was retained by three man corporation owed fiduciary duty to stockholders, breached fiduciary duty to minority stockholder by buying ma-

jority stock to which minority shareholder had claim, and held stock as constructive trustee for minority stockholder).

59. Compare Model Rule 1.13 (Organization as Client), ... with E.F. Hutton & Co. v. Brown, 305 F.Supp. 371 (S.D.Tex.1969) (in-house counsel who had represented corporate officer in his individual capacity in prior separate litigation disqualified from representing corporation in negligence action against officer); see G. Hazard & W. Hodes, The Law of Lawyering 243–244, 262–264 (1985) (discussing fairness to non-clients within an organization and the *Miranda*-type warning required by rule 1.13(d)); but cf. W.T. Grant Co. v. Haines, 531 F.2d 671 (2d Cir.1976) (court has discretion to allow outside counsel to represent corporation in antitrust action against former employee even if counsel has had allegedly improper communication with employee unrepresented by counsel).

interpretation the "relevant other" is like a friend, under the second the "relevant other" is like a foe.

. . .

The difference between a "normal" triangular relationship and one contaminated by antagonism does not lie in the *structure* of the relationship. Until finally resolved or dissolved, the structure is ambiguously triangular, with the nonlawyer parties being fellow clients, or antipodal, with the nonlawyer parties being antagonists. The proper interpretation depends not on structure but on process—what has happened within the relationship. The relevant set of happenings include, above all, what the lawyer has done in the relationship.

In *Fickett,* the lawyer had done nothing when he should have been doing something. The "something" he should have been doing was neither mysterious nor extraordinary. If he had adhered to normal lawyer practice followed in a normal guardian representation, he would have satisfied himself that the guardian had at least some idea of the responsibilities concerning investments and of the requirements for periodic accounting, and would have activated the procedure for submitting such accounts. If the guardian had approached him to confide that some of the investments were irregular, normal lawyer practice would suggest that the lawyer should have said something like, "That could involve very serious difficulties." The lawyer would thereby not commit himself to representing the guardian versus the ward, or vice versa; the lawyer would only be suggesting the urgent need for redefinition of the relationship between the guardian and the ward. He or she should do nothing to further or conceal the guardian's misfeasance, because the law provides that doing so would constitute fraudulent conduct on the lawyer's part. If the guardian persisted in misconduct, under accepted standards of practice the lawyer could withdraw and advise the ward of the fact of withdrawal.

In *Yablonski,* the organization's lawyer did things when the situation was such that "the role of . . . counsel . . . becomes usually a passive one."[61] The lawyer should not have assisted the president in defending colorable claims of malfeasance toward the organization. If the lawyer had adhered to proper practice in this abnormal situation, he or she would have advised the president to get independent legal representation and perhaps have advised the board to get other independent representation for the organization. Indeed, as the law has now evolved, any other course by the lawyer could be regarded as furthering or concealing the president's malfeasance.

V.   Conclusion

The critical problem the lawyer faces in triangular relationships is that his or her professional responsibilities depend unavoidably on what the other two parties do for and to each other. The lawyer's duty cannot adequately be defined, as it normally is, by specifying *ex ante* the identity of "the client." Neither of the "relevant others" is a legally freestanding

---

61.   *Yablonski,* 448 F.2d at 1179.

person in the standard conceptual sense of "client." The guardian is not an individual alone but a person whose legal identity is expressed in terms of legal responsibilities ex officio. The corporation is not an individual at all, but exists only in law and through personification by others who act ex officio. If the other parties to the relationship conduct themselves as the law contemplates they should, then all the "relevant others" collectively can be considered "the client." That principle is already well established for corporations,[62] and there seems to be no reason not to think of guardianships and other triangular relationships in the same way. On the other hand, if the dominant party is guilty of misconduct toward the dependent one and if the lawyer behaves as though everything were still normal, the lawyer would then have at least an ethical problem and quite possibly legal liability.

. . .

The lawyer can see and act. Depending on what he or she sees and does, the dominant actor may have to be treated as something less than a client simpliciter and the lawyer himself or herself as something different from one who "knows no other duty." That definition of role entails being an active, visible participant in the transaction and exercising independent judgment. Such deportment does not fit the conventional mold.

C. LAWYERS FOR THE GOVERNMENT

INTRODUCTORY NOTE

Who is the client of the government lawyer? One way to begin the analysis is to ask who is the counterpart for the government lawyer of the constituents of organizational clients that make up a corporate lawyer's world. What government counterpart takes the place of the chief executive officer (CEO), the board of directors or the shareholders? For a lawyer in the United States Department of Justice is the Attorney General analogous to the CEO? Even when the lawyer is investigating illegal acts on the part of the Attorney General? Is the "public" comparable to shareholders? What duties, if any, does the lawyer owe to Congress?

As these questions demonstrate, the analogy to corporations is imperfect. Corporations are private organizations subject to public law and usually have a limited purpose (e.g., making money) and a limited ultimate constituency (e.g., the shareholders). Governments are themselves instruments of public law whose purpose cannot be expressed in a single formula. Further, the federal government, state governments and many local governments are organized on the basis of separation of powers, not integrated under one "board of directors." Finally, the public's interest is more amorphous than the shareholders' interest. While the law artificially re-

62. Upjohn Co. v. United States, 449 U.S.   383 (1981).

duces shareholders' interest to law-abiding profitability, reduction of the public's interest to a corruption-free, law-abiding government seems far too reductionist.

1. IDENTIFYING A GOVERNMENT LAWYER'S CLIENT[1]

The United States government employs more than 25,000 lawyers to handle its legal problems (two to three percent of all U.S. lawyers).[2] Most of these lawyers are employed full-time by one or another of the myriad departments or agencies of the executive branch. The variety of legal work performed by government lawyers is nearly as broad as the breadth of legal activity generally. Lawyers for the federal government are advisors, counselors and litigators; and they deal in virtually every legal specialty, although for obvious reasons administrative law and federal specialties have special prominence in their work.

The government lawyer functions within a complex federal system based on the principle of separation of powers.[3] It is an untidy structure of incredible complexity in which the President provides the principal focus of cohesion and unity while Congress, responding to interest groups, tends to further the centrifugal tendencies of a pluralistic society. The Constitution vests "executive power" in the President and legislative authority in the Congress, but in practice the functions are mixed, with independent agencies created by Congress having varying degrees of independence from presidential control and, conversely, the executive branch exercising delegated and inherent legislative authority in the form of executive orders, agency rules, and interpretive guidelines.... [A]lthough the President has broad power within the executive branch, there are independent agencies, officers with specific delegated functions and quasi-governmental corporations each operating within their own spheres of authority.

The Attorney General's control of litigation in which the United States is a party follows a similar pattern. Although the Attorney General has broad control over government litigation, Congress has passed more than one hundred statutes giving particular agencies separate litigating authority. The government lawyer in such a federal system must necessarily conform his conduct to statutes and regulations that do not apply to a lawyer in the private sector.[4]

1. Portions of this note are drawn, with permission from Roger C. Cramton, The Lawyer as Whistleblower: Confidentiality And The Government Lawyer, 5 Geo. J. Leg. Ethics 291, 292–306 (1991).

2. Federal Civilian Workforce Statistics, Occupations of Federal White–Collar and Blue–Collar Workers, tbl. W–A2 (reporting 25,385 "general attorneys" working for the federal government, Sept. 30, 1997).

3. See generally Geoffrey P. Miller, Government Lawyers' Ethics in a System of Checks and Balances, 54 U.Chi.L.Rev. 1293 (1987).

4. See, e.g., 18 U.S.C. § 205 (1982) (prohibiting government employees from representing parties in actions against the United States or the District of Columbia); 18 U.S.C. § 207 (1982) (placing restrictions on successive government and private employment); and 18 U.S.C. § 208 (financial conflict of interest statute).

In this unusual world, who is the government lawyer's client? The possibilities include: (1) the public, (2) the government as a whole, (3) the branch of government in which the lawyer is employed, (4) the particular agency or department in which the lawyer works and (5) the responsible officers who make decisions for the agency. The everyday answer for most government lawyers is (4) the particular agency or department in which the lawyer works. The special statutes and regulations that constitute the domain of that agency are the lawyer's daily concerns; the appointed officials and senior civil service officers who preside over its everyday work provide normally authoritative guidance. In special situations, however, when the policy views of the President come to bear on the agency or when trouble intervenes, such as an investigation of wrongdoing in the agency, the constitutional structure of the federal government suggests that the most appropriate answer is that a lawyer working for an agency within the executive branch represents the United States in the form of that branch.[5] An attitude of loyalty to the long term interests of the agency and the branch of which it is a part is appropriate for a government lawyer, but the amorphousness of "the public interest" cannot displace the concreteness of constitutional structure and agency law. At the other end of the spectrum, the agency lawyer, bound to serve the positions legitimately represented by officials within the executive branch, is responsive to but not the personal lawyer of agency heads. As is the case with a lawyer for a corporation, the government lawyer represents the institution not the personal interests of the politically appointed or elected official who temporarily is its chief officer.[6]

There is very little case law on the question of who the government lawyer represents.[7] Two recent cases arising out of the Whitewater Investigation, however, illuminate the subject.

---

5. See Michael S. Paulsen, Who "Owns" the Government's Attorney–Client Privilege?, 83 Minn.L.Rev.473 (1998).

6. Id. at 486–87 and n. 45.

7. For state cases see, e.g., Humphrey v. McLaren, 402 N.W.2d 535 (Minn.1987) (citing Minnesota's version of M.R. 1.13 and its Comment, and holding that the agency—and in some cases the entire government—is the client, not the individual head of an agency); and People ex rel. Deukmejian v. Brown, 624 P.2d 1206 (Cal.1981) (holding the state attorney general could not bring a case to enjoin the governor from implementing a statute, which the attorney general argued was unconstitutional). With *Deukmejian* contrast Feeney v. Commonwealth, 366 N.E.2d 1262 (Mass. 1977) (holding that the Massachusetts Attorney General could seek review against the objections of the head of the affected agency, the Governor, and the Massachusetts legislature—both houses of which passed resolutions asking that review not be sought—of a lower court decision holding that the state's civil service preference for veterans unconstitutionally discriminated against women.

For cases in accord with *Deukmejian*, see Manchin v. Browning, 296 S.E.2d 909 (W.Va.1982); and Arizona State Land Dept. v. McFate, 348 P.2d 912 (Ariz.1960). In accord with *Feeney* are State ex rel. Howard v. Oklahoma Corp. Commission, 614 P.2d 45 (Okl.1980); Connecticut Commission on Special Revenue v. Connecticut Freedom of Information Commission, 387 A.2d 533 (Conn.1978). Also see Ann B. Stevens, Can the State Attorney General Represent Two Agencies Opposed in Litigation? 2 Geo.J.Legal Ethics 757 (1989).

In re Lindsey

United States Court of Appeals, District of Columbia Circuit.
148 F.3d 1100 (1998).

■ Before: RANDOLPH, ROGERS and TATEL, CIRCUIT JUDGES.

■ PER CURIAM:

In these expedited appeals, the principal question is whether an attorney in the Office of the President, having been called before a federal grand jury, may refuse, on the basis of a government attorney-client privilege, to answer questions about possible criminal conduct by government officials and others. To state the question is to suggest the answer, for the Office of the President is a part of the federal government, consisting of government employees doing government business, and neither legal authority nor policy nor experience suggests that a federal government entity can maintain the ordinary common law attorney-client privilege to withhold information relating to a federal criminal offense. The Supreme Court and this court have held that even the constitutionally based executive privilege for presidential communications fundamental to the operation of the government can be overcome upon a proper showing of need for the evidence in criminal trials and in grand jury proceedings. See United States v. Nixon, 418 U.S. 683, 707–12 (1974); In re Sealed Case, 121 F.3d 729, 736–38 (D.C.Cir.1997). In the context of federal criminal investigations and trials, there is no basis for treating legal advice differently from any other advice the Office of the President receives in performing its constitutional functions. The public interest in honest government and in exposing wrongdoing by government officials, as well as the tradition and practice, acknowledged by the Office of the President and by former White House Counsel, of government lawyers reporting evidence of federal criminal offenses whenever such evidence comes to them, lead to the conclusion that a government attorney may not invoke the attorney-client privilege in response to grand jury questions seeking information relating to the possible commission of a federal crime. The extent to which the communications of White House Counsel are privileged against disclosure to a federal grand jury depends, therefore, on whether the communications contain information of possible criminal offenses. Additional protection may flow from executive privilege. . . . [Double brackets indicating deletion of material still under seal appear here and at numerous other places in the opinion. These marks, which appear to deal with material subject to a claim of executive privilege, are deleted in this reprinting.]

I.

On January 16, 1998, at the request of the Attorney General, the [special three-judge court] issued an order expanding the prosecutorial jurisdiction of Independent Counsel Kenneth W. Starr. Previously, the main focus of Independent Counsel Starr's inquiry had been on financial transactions involving President Clinton when he was Governor of Arkansas, known popularly as the Whitewater inquiry. The order now authorized Starr to investigate "whether Monica Lewinsky or others suborned perjury, obstructed justice, intimidated witnesses, or otherwise violated federal law" in connection with the civil lawsuit against the President of the United States filed by Paula Jones. . . .

On January 30, 1998, the grand jury issued a subpoena to Bruce R. Lindsey, an attorney admitted to practice in Arkansas. Lindsey currently holds two positions: Deputy White House Counsel and Assistant to the President. On February 18, February 19, and March 12, 1998, Lindsey appeared before the grand jury and declined to answer certain questions . . . [claiming government attorney-client privilege, executive privilege and work product protections related to the attorney-client privilege.]

On March 6, 1998, the Independent Counsel moved to compel Lindsey's testimony. The district court granted that motion on May 4, 1998. The court concluded that the President's executive privilege claim failed in light of the Independent Counsel's showing of need and unavailability. See In re Sealed Case, 121 F.3d at 754. It rejected Lindsey's government attorney-client privilege claim on similar grounds. . . .

The Office of the President appealed the [district court's opinion.] . . . The Independent Counsel then petitioned the Supreme Court to review the district court's decision . . . before judgment by this court. On June 4, 1998, the Supreme Court denied certiorari, while indicating its expectation that "the Court of Appeals will proceed expeditiously to decide this case." United States v. Clinton, 118 S.Ct. 2079 (1998). Following an expedited briefing schedule, on June 29, 1998, this court heard argument on the attorney-client issues. [No party appealed the district court's decision on executive privilege.] . . . In Part II we address the availability of the government attorney-client privilege. [Part III of the opinion is still under seal.]

II.

The attorney-client privilege protects confidential communications made between clients and their attorneys when the communications are for the purpose of securing legal advice or services. See In re Sealed Case, 737 F.2d 94, 98–99 (D.C.Cir.1984). It "is one of the oldest recognized privileges for confidential communications." Swidler & Berlin v. United States, 118 S.Ct. 2081, 2084–85 (1998).

The Office of the President contends that Lindsey's communications with the President and others in the White House should fall within this privilege both because the President, like any private person, needs to communicate fully and frankly with his legal advisors, and because the current grand jury investigation may lead to impeachment proceedings, which would require a defense of the President's official position as head of the executive branch of government, presumably with the assistance of White House Counsel. The Independent Counsel contends that an absolute government attorney-client privilege would be inconsistent with the proper role of the government lawyer and that the President should rely only on his private lawyers for fully confidential counsel.

Federal courts are given the authority to recognize privilege claims by Rule 501 of the Federal Rules of Evidence....

A.

Courts, commentators, and government lawyers have long recognized a government attorney-client privilege in several contexts. Much of the law on this subject has developed in litigation about exemption five of the Freedom of Information Act ("FOIA"). See 5 U.S.C. § 552(b)(5) (1994). Under that exemption, "intra-agency memorandums or letters which would not be available by law to a party other than an agency in litigation with the agency" are excused from mandatory disclosure to the public. ...We have recognized that "Exemption 5 protects, as a general rule, materials which would be protected under the attorney-client privilege." Coastal States Gas Corp. v. Department of Energy, 617 F.2d 854, 862 (D.C.Cir. 1980). "In the governmental context, the 'client' may be the agency and the attorney may be an agency lawyer." Tax Analysts v. IRS, 117 F.3d 607, 618 (D.C.Cir.1997); see also Brinton v. Department of State, 636 F.2d 600, 603–04 (D.C.Cir.1980). In Lindsey's case, his client—to the extent he provided legal services—would be the Office of the President.

Exemption five does not itself create a government attorney-client privilege. Rather, "Congress intended that agencies should not lose the protection traditionally afforded through the evidentiary privileges simply because of the passage of the FOIA." Coastal States, 617 F.2d at 862. ...Thus, when "the Government is dealing with its attorneys as would any private party seeking advice to protect personal interests, and needs the same assurance of confidentiality so it will not be deterred from full and frank communications with its counselors," exemption five applies. Coastal States, 617 F.2d at 863.

Furthermore, the proposed (but never enacted) Federal Rules of Evidence concerning privileges, to which courts have turned as evidence of common law practices, recognized a place for a government attorney-client privilege.... The Restatement also extends attorney-client privilege to government entities. See Restatement (Third) of the Law Governing Lawyers § 124 (Proposed Final Draft No. 1, 1996) [hereinafter Restatement].

The practice of attorneys in the executive branch reflects the common understanding that a government attorney-client privilege functions in at least some contexts. The Office of Legal Counsel in the Department of Justice concluded in 1982 that

> ... the privilege ... functions to protect communications between government attorneys and client agencies or departments, as evidenced by its inclusion in the FOIA, much as it operates to protect attorney-client communications in the private sector.

Theodore B. Olsen, Assistant Attorney General, Office of Legal Counsel, Confidentiality of the Attorney General's Communications in Counseling the President, 6 Op. Off. Legal Counsel 481, 495 (1982). The Office of Legal Counsel also concluded that when government attorneys stand in the shoes of private counsel, representing federal employees sued in their individual capacities, confidential communications between attorney and client are privileged. See Antonin Scalia, Assistant Attorney General, Office of Legal Counsel, Disclosure of Confidential Information Received by U.S. Attorney in the Course of Representing a Federal Employee (Nov. 30, 1976).

B.

Recognizing that a government attorney-client privilege exists is one thing. Finding that the Office of the President is entitled to assert it here is quite another.

It is settled law that the party claiming the privilege bears the burden of proving that the communications are protected. As oft-cited definitions of the privilege make clear, only communications that seek "legal advice" from "a professional legal adviser in his capacity as such" are protected. . . .

On the record before us, it seems likely that at least some of the conversations for which Lindsey asserted government attorney-client privilege did not come within the formulation just quoted. . . . [Some of the conversations occurred before the jurisdiction of the Independent Counsel was expanded to include the Monica Lewinsky matter; prior to that time advice concerning Jones v. Clinton, a lawsuit involving President Clinton in his personal capacity, "likely could not have been covered by government attorney-client privilege." Other conversations may have rested on executive privilege grounds, subsequently abandoned. And still others may have involved "political, strategic or policy advice" that is not protected by the attorney-client privilege. "With regard to most of the communications that were the subject of questions before the grand jury, it does not appear to us that" the proponent of the privilege made the required showing that particular questions sought "legal advice" from Lindsey "acting in his professional capacity as a lawyer" rather than in another capacity.] There is, however, no good reason for withholding decision on the issues now before us. We have little doubt that at least one of Lindsey's conversations subject to grand jury questioning "concerned the seeking of legal advice" and was between President Clinton and Lindsey or between others in the White House and Lindsey while Lindsey was "acting in his professional capacity" as an attorney.

The issue whether the government attorney-client privilege could be invoked in these circumstances is therefore ripe for decision.

. . . .

We therefore turn to the question whether an attorney-client privilege permits a government lawyer to withhold from a grand jury information relating to the commission of possible crimes by government officials and others. Although the cases decided under FOIA recognize a government attorney-client privilege that is rather absolute in civil litigation, those cases do not necessarily control the application of the privilege here. The grand jury, a constitutional body established in the Bill of Rights, "belongs to no branch of the institutional Government, serving as a kind of buffer or referee between the Government and the people," United States v. Williams, 504 U.S. 36, 47(1992), while the Independent Counsel is by statute an officer of the executive branch representing the United States. For matters within his jurisdiction, the Independent Counsel acts in the role of the Attorney General as the country's chief law enforcement officer. See 28 U.S.C. § 594(a) (1994). Thus, although the traditional privilege between attorneys and clients shields private relationships from inquiry in either civil litigation or criminal prosecution, competing values arise when the Office of the President resists demands for information from a federal grand jury and the nation's chief law enforcement officer. As the drafters of the Restatement recognized, "More particularized rules may be necessary where one agency of government claims the privilege in resisting a demand for information by another. Such rules should take account of the complex considerations of governmental structure, tradition, and regulation that are involved." Restatement § 124 cmt. b. For these reasons, others have agreed that such "considerations" counsel against "expansion of the privilege to all governmental entities" in all cases. 24 Charles Alan Wright & Kenneth W. Graham, Jr., Federal Practice and Procedure § 5475, at 125 (1986).

The question whether a government attorney-client privilege applies in the federal grand jury context is one of first impression in this circuit, and the parties dispute the import of the lack of binding authority. The Office of the President contends that, upon recognizing a government attorney-client privilege, the court should find an exception in the grand jury context only if practice and policy require. To the contrary, the Independent Counsel contends, in essence, that the justification for any extension of a government attorney-client privilege to this context needs to be clear. These differences in approach are not simply semantical: they represent different versions of what is the status quo. To argue about an "exception" presupposes that the privilege otherwise applies in the federal grand jury context; to argue about an "extension" presupposes the opposite. In Swidler & Berlin, the Supreme Court considered whether, as the Independent Counsel contended, it should create an exception to the personal attorney-client privilege allowing disclosure of confidences after the client's death. See Swidler & Berlin, 118 S.Ct. 2081, 2083–84 (1998). After finding that the Independent Counsel was asking the Court "not simply to 'construe' the privilege, but to narrow it, contrary to the weight of the existing body of caselaw," the Court concluded that the Independent Counsel had not made a sufficient showing to warrant the creation of such an exception to the settled rule. Id. at 2087–88.

In the instant case, by contrast, there is no such existing body of caselaw upon which to rely and no clear principle that the government attorney-client privilege has as broad a scope as its personal counterpart. Because the "attorney-client privilege must be 'strictly confined within the narrowest possible limits consistent with the logic of its principle,' " and because the government attorney-client privilege is not recognized in the same way as the personal attorney-client privilege addressed in Swidler & Berlin, we believe this case poses the question whether, in the first instance, the privilege extends as far as the Office of the President would like. In other words, pursuant to our authority and duty under Rule 501 of the Federal Rules of Evidence to interpret privileges "in light of reason and experience," Fed. R. Evid. 501, we view our exercise as one in defining the particular contours of the government attorney-client privilege.

When an executive branch attorney is called before a federal grand jury to give evidence about alleged crimes within the executive branch, reason and experience, duty, and tradition dictate that the attorney shall provide that evidence. With respect to investigations of federal criminal offenses, and especially offenses committed by those in government, government attorneys stand in a far different position from members of the private bar. Their duty is not to defend clients against criminal charges and it is not to protect wrongdoers from public exposure. The constitutional responsibility of the President, and all members of the Executive Branch, is to "take Care that the Laws be faithfully executed." U.S. Const. art. II, § 3. Investigation and prosecution of federal crimes is one of the most important and essential functions within that constitutional responsibility. Each of our Presidents has, in the words of the Constitution, sworn that he "will faithfully execute the Office of President of the United States, and will to the best of [his] Ability, preserve, protect and defend the Constitution of the United States." Id. art. II, § 1, cl. 8. And for more than two hundred years each officer of the Executive Branch has been bound by oath or affirmation to do the same. See id. art. VI, cl. 3; see also 28 U.S.C. § 544 (1994). This is a solemn undertaking, a binding of the person to the cause of constitutional government, an expression of the individual's allegiance to the principles embodied in that document. Unlike a private practitioner, the loyalties of a government lawyer therefore cannot and must not lie solely with his or her client agency.[8]

The oath's significance is underscored by other evocations of the ethical duties of government lawyers. The Professional Ethics Committee of the Federal Bar Association has described the public trust of the federally employed lawyer as follows:

> [T]he government, over-all and in each of its parts, is responsible to the people in our democracy with its representative form of government. Each part of the government has the obligation of carrying out, in the public interest, its assigned responsibility in a manner consistent with the Constitution, and the applicable laws and regulations. In contrast, the private practitioner represents the client's personal or private interest. . . . [W]e do not suggest, however, that the public is the client as the client concept is usually understood. It is to say that

---

8. We recognize, as our dissenting colleague emphasizes, that every lawyer must take an oath to enter the bar of any court. But even after entering the bar, a government attorney must take another oath to enter into government service; that in itself shows the separate meaning of the government attorney's oath. Moreover, the oath is significant to our analysis only to the extent that it underlies the fundamental differences in the roles of government and private attorneys—of particular note, the fact that private attorneys cannot take official actions.

the lawyer's employment requires him to observe in the performance of his professional responsibility the public interest sought to be served by the governmental organization of which he is a part.

Federal Bar Association Ethics Committee, The Government Client and Confidentiality: Opinion 73–1, 32 Fed. B.J. 71, 72 (1973). Indeed, before an attorney in the Justice Department can step into the shoes of private counsel to represent a federal employee sued in his or her individual capacity, the Attorney General must determine whether the representation would be in the interest of the United States. See 28 C.F.R. § 50.15(a). The obligation of a government lawyer to uphold the public trust reposed in him or her strongly militates against allowing the client agency to invoke a privilege to prevent the lawyer from providing evidence of the possible commission of criminal offenses within the government. As Judge Weinstein put it, "[i]f there is wrongdoing in government, it must be exposed.... [The government lawyer's] duty to the people, the law, and his own conscience requires disclosure...." Jack B. Weinstein, Some Ethical and Political Problems of a Government Attorney, 18 Maine L. Rev. 155, 160 (1966).

This view of the proper allegiance of the government lawyer is complemented by the public's interest in uncovering illegality among its elected and appointed officials. While the President's constitutionally established role as superintendent of law enforcement provides one protection against wrongdoing by federal government officials, another protection of the public interest is through having transparent and accountable government. As James Madison observed,

> [a] popular Government, without popular information, or the means of acquiring it, is but a Prologue to a Farce or a Tragedy; or, perhaps both. Knowledge will forever govern ignorance: And a people who mean to be their own Governors, must arm themselves with the power which knowledge gives.

Letter from James Madison to W.T. Barry (Aug. 4, 1822), in 9 the Writings of James Madison 103 (Gaillard Hunt ed., 1910). This court has accordingly recognized that "openness in government has always been thought crucial to ensuring that the people remain in control of their government." In re Sealed Case (Espy), 121 F.3d at 749. Privileges work against these interests because their recognition "creates the risk that a broad array of materials in many areas of the executive branch will become 'sequester[ed]' from public view." Id. (quoting Wolfe v. Department of Health & Human Servs., 815 F.2d 1527, 1533 (D.C.Cir.1987)). Furthermore, "to allow any part of the federal government to use its in-house attorneys as a shield against the production of information relevant to a federal criminal investigation would represent a gross misuse of public assets." In re Grand Jury Subpoena Duces Tecum, 112 F.3d 910, 921 (8th Cir.), cert. denied, 117 S.Ct. 2482 (1997).

Examination of the practice of government attorneys further supports the conclusion that a government attorney, even one holding the title Deputy White House Counsel, may not assert an attorney-client privilege before a federal grand jury if communications with the client contain information pertinent to possible criminal violations. The Office of the President has traditionally adhered to the precepts of 28 U.S.C. § 535(b), which provides that

> [a]ny information ... received in a department or agency of the executive branch of the Government relating to violations of title 18 involving Government officers and employees shall be expeditiously reported to the Attorney General.

28 U.S.C. § 535(b) (1994). We need not decide whether section 535(b) alone requires White House Counsel to testify before a grand jury.[6] The statute does not clearly apply to the Office of the President. The Office is neither a "department," as that term is defined by the statute, nor an "agency." However, at the very least "[section] 535(b) evinces a strong congressional policy that executive branch employees must report information" relating to violations of Title 18, the federal criminal code. As the House Committee Report accompanying section 535 explains, "[t]he purpose" of the provision is to "require the reporting by the departments and agencies of the executive branch to the Attorney General of information coming to their attention concerning any alleged irregularities on the part of officers and employees of the Government." Section 535(b) suggests that all government employees, including lawyers, are duty-bound not to withhold evidence of federal crimes.

Furthermore, government officials holding top legal positions have concluded, in light of section 535(b), that White House lawyers cannot keep evidence of crimes committed by government officials to themselves. In a speech delivered after the Kissinger FOIA case was handed down, Lloyd Cutler, who served as White House Counsel in the Carter and Clinton Administrations, discussed the "rule of making it your duty, if you're a Government official as we as lawyers are, a statutory duty to report to the Attorney General any evidence you run into of a possible violation of a criminal statute." Lloyd N. Cutler, The Role of the Counsel to the President of the United States, 35 Record of the Ass'n of the Bar of the City of New York No. 8, at 470, 472 (1980). Accordingly, "[w]hen you hear of a charge and you talk to someone in the White House ... about some allegation of misconduct, almost the first thing you have to say is, 'I really want to know about this, but anything you tell me I'll have to report to the Attorney General.'" Id. Similarly, during the Nixon administration, Solicitor General Robert H. Bork told an administration official who invited him to join the President's legal defense team: "A government attorney is sworn to uphold the Constitution. If I come across evidence that is bad for

---

6. 28 U.S.C. § 535(a) authorizes the Attorney General to "investigate any violation of title 18 [the federal criminal code] involving Government officers and employees." The Independent Counsel fills the shoes of the Attorney General in this regard because Congress has given the Independent Counsel "with respect to all matters in [his] prosecutorial jurisdiction ... full power and independent authority to exercise all investigative and prosecutorial functions and powers of ... the Attorney General." 28 U.S.C. § 594(a); see In re Sealed Case (Secret Service), 1998 WL 370584, at *7.

the President, I'll have to turn it over. I won't be able to sit on it like a private defense attorney." A Conversation with Robert Bork, D.C. Bar Rep., Dec. 1997–Jan.1998, at 9.

The Clinton Administration itself endorsed this view as recently as a year ago. In the proceedings leading to the Supreme Court's denial of certiorari with regard to the Eighth Circuit's decision in In re Grand Jury Subpoena Duces Tecum, the Office of the President assured the Supreme Court that it "embraces the principles embodied in Section 535(b)" and acknowledged that "the Office of the President has a duty, recognized in official policy and practice, to turn over evidence of the crime." Reply Brief for Office of the President at 7, Office of the President v. Office of Independent Counsel, 117 S.Ct. 2482 (1997) (No. 96–1783). The Office of the President further represented that "on various occasions" it had "referred information to the Attorney General reflecting the possible commission of a criminal offense—including information otherwise protected by attorney-client privilege." Id. At oral argument, counsel for the Office of the President reiterated this position. . . .

We are not aware of any previous deviation from this understanding of the role of government counsel. We know that Nixon White House Counsel Fred Buzhardt testified before the Watergate grand jury without invoking attorney-client privilege, although not much may be made of this.[7] On the other hand, the Office of the President points out that C. Boyden Gray, White House Counsel during the Bush Administration, and his deputy, John Schmitz, refused to be interviewed by the Independent Counsel investigating the Iran–Contra affair and only produced documents subject to an agreement that "any privilege against disclosure . . . including the attorney-client privilege" was not waived. However, the Independent Counsel in that investigation had not subpoenaed Gray or Schmitz to testify before a grand jury, and there is no indication that the information sought from them constituted evidence of any criminal offense. Independent Counsel Walsh apparently sought to question these individuals merely to complete his final report.

The Office of the President asserts two principal contributions to the public good that would come from a government attorney's withholding evidence from a grand jury on the basis of an attorney-client privilege. First, it maintains that the values of candor and frank communications that the privilege embodies in every context would apply to Lindsey's communications with the President and others in the White House. Government officials, the Office of the President claims, need accurate advice from government attorneys as much as private individuals do, but they will be inclined to discuss their legal problems honestly with their attorneys only if they know that their communications will be confidential.

7. President Nixon waived executive privilege and attorney-client privilege before the grand jury. See Special Prosecution Force, Watergate Report 88 (1975) [hereinafter Watergate Report].

We may assume that if the government attorney-client privilege does not apply in certain contexts this may chill some communications between government officials and government lawyers. Even so, government officials will still enjoy the benefit of fully confidential communications with their attorneys unless the communications reveal information relating to possible criminal wrongdoing. And although the privacy of these communications may not be absolute before the grand jury, the Supreme Court has not been troubled by the potential chill on executive communications due to the qualified nature of executive privilege. Compare Nixon, 418 U.S. at 712–13 (discounting the chilling effects of the qualification of the presidential communications privilege on the candor of conversations), with Swidler & Berlin, 118 S.Ct. 2081, 2086–87 (stating, in the personal attorney-client privilege context, that an uncertain privilege is often no better than no privilege at all). Because both the Deputy White House Counsel and the Independent Counsel occupy positions within the federal government, their situation is somewhat comparable to that of corporate officers who seek to keep their communications with company attorneys confidential from each other and from the shareholders. Under the widely followed doctrine announced in Garner v. Wolfinbarger, 430 F.2d 1093 (5th Cir.1970), corporate officers are not always entitled to assert such privileges against interests within the corporation, and accordingly must consult with company attorneys aware that their communications may not be kept confidential from shareholders in litigation. See id. at 1101. Any chill on candid communications with government counsel flowing from our decision not to extend an absolute attorney-client privilege to the grand jury context is both comparable and similarly acceptable.

Moreover, nothing prevents government officials who seek completely confidential communications with attorneys from consulting personal counsel. The President has retained several private lawyers, and he is entitled to engage in the completely confidential communications with those lawyers befitting an attorney and a client in a private relationship.

The Office of the President contends that White House Counsel's role in preparing for any future impeachment proceedings alters the policy analysis. The Ethics in Government Act requires the Independent Counsel to "advise the House of Representatives of any substantial and credible information ... that may constitute grounds for an impeachment." 28 U.S.C. § 595(c) (1994). In November 1997, a Congressman introduced a resolution in the House of Representatives calling for an inquiry into possible grounds for impeachment of the President. See H.R. Res. 304, 105th Cong. (1997). Thus, to the extent that impeachment proceedings may be on the horizon, the Office of the President contends that White House Counsel must be given maximum protection against grand jury inquiries regarding their efforts to protect the Office of the President, and the President in his personal capacity, against impeachment. Additionally, the Office of the President notes that the Independent Counsel serves as a conduit to Congress for information concerning grounds for impeachment obtained by the grand jury, and, consequently, an exception to the attorney-client privilege before the grand jury will effectively abrogate any absolute privilege those communications might otherwise enjoy in future congressional investigations and impeachment hearings.

Although the Independent Counsel and the Office of the President agree that White House Counsel can represent the President in the impeachment process, the precise contours of Counsel's role are far from settled.[10] In any event, no matter what the role should be, impeachment is fundamentally a political exercise. See the Federalist No. 65 (Alexander Hamilton); Joseph Story, Commentaries on the Constitution § 764, at 559 (5th ed.1905). Impeachment proceedings in the House of Representatives cannot be analogized to traditional legal processes and even the procedures used by the Senate in "trying" an impeachment may not be like those in a judicial trial. See (Walter) Nixon v. United States, 506 U.S. 224, 228–31 (1993); Story, Commentaries on the Constitution § 765, at 559–60. How the policy and practice supporting the common law attorney-client privilege would apply in such a political context thus is uncertain. In preparing for the eventuality of impeachment proceedings, a White House Counsel in effect serves the President as a political advisor, albeit one with legal expertise: to wit, Lindsey occupies a dual position as an Assistant to the President and a Deputy White House Counsel. Thus, information gathered in preparation for impeachment proceedings and conversations regarding strategy are presumably covered by executive, not attorney-client, privilege. While the need for secrecy might arguably be greater under these circumstances, the district court's ruling on executive privilege is not before us. In addition, in responding to the grand jury investigation and gathering information in preparation for future developments in accordance with his official duties, White House Counsel may need to interact with the President's private attorneys, and to that extent other privileges may be implicated.

Nor is our conclusion altered by the Office of the President's concern over the possibility that Independent Counsel will convey otherwise privileged grand jury testimony of White House Counsel to Congress.[11] Cf. Fed.

10. While a prior Comptroller General has thought that White House Counsel could properly be paid out of federal funds for representing the President in matters leading up to an impeachment, see Letter from Elmer B. Staats, U.S. Comptroller General, to Rep. John F. Seiberling 7 (Oct. 25, 1974), history yields little guidance on the role that White House Counsel would properly play in impeachment proceedings. The only President impeached by the House and tried by the Senate, Andrew Johnson, retained private counsel, and his Attorney General resigned from office in order to assist in his defense. See William H. Rehnquist, Grand Inquests 222 (1992). In contrast, after the House Judiciary Committee began an impeachment inquiry into the Watergate scandal, President Richard Nixon appointed James D. St. Clair as a special counsel to the President for Watergate-related matters. See Watergate Report 103. Although Nixon resigned before the House of Representatives voted on any articles of impeachment, St. Clair handled much of the President's defense until the President's resignation. See id. at 103–15. At the very least, nothing prevents a President faced with impeachment from retaining private counsel, and in turn this makes less clear what might be the division of labor between White House Counsel and private counsel.

11. Contrary to the Office of the President's suggestion, this is not a novel concern stemming from the Ethics in Government

R.Crim. P. 6(e). First, no one can say with certainty the extent to which a privilege would generally protect a White House Counsel from testifying at a congressional hearing. The issue is not presently before the court.[12] See Nixon, 418 U.S. at 712 n. 19. In re Sealed Case (Espy), 121 F.3d at 739 nn.9–10, 753. Second, the particular procedures and evidentiary rules to be employed by the House and Senate in any future impeachment proceedings remain entirely speculative. Finally, whether Congress can abrogate otherwise recognized privileges in the course of impeachment proceedings may well constitute a nonjusticiable political question. See (Walter) Nixon, 506 U.S. at 236.

The Supreme Court's recognition in United States v. Nixon of a qualified privilege for executive communications severely undercuts the argument of the Office of the President regarding the scope of the government attorney-client privilege. A President often has private conversations with his Vice President or his Cabinet Secretaries or other members of the Administration who are not lawyers or who are lawyers, but are not providing legal services. The advice these officials give the President is of vital importance to the security and prosperity of the nation, and to the President's discharge of his constitutional duties. Yet upon a proper showing, such conversations must be revealed in federal criminal proceedings. See Nixon, 418 U.S. at 713; In re Sealed Case (Espy), 121 F.3d at 745. Only a certain conceit among those admitted to the bar could explain why legal advice should be on a higher plane than advice about policy, or politics, or why a President's conversation with the most junior lawyer in the White House Counsel's Office is deserving of more protection from disclosure in a grand jury investigation than a President's discussions with his Vice President or a Cabinet Secretary. In short, we do not believe that lawyers are more important to the operations of government than all other officials, or that the advice lawyers render is more crucial to the functioning of the Presidency than the advice coming from all other quarters.

The district court held that a government attorney-client privilege existed and was applicable to grand jury proceedings, but could be overcome, as could an applicable executive privilege, upon a showing of need and unavailability elsewhere by the Independent Counsel. While we conclude that an attorney-client privilege may not be asserted by Lindsey to avoid responding to the grand jury if he possesses information relating to possible criminal violations, he continues to be covered by the executive privilege to the same extent as the President's other advisers. Our analysis,

---

Act. During initial discussions with the Watergate Special Prosecutor, "[James] St. Clair was primarily concerned that evidence produced for the grand jury not subsequently be provided by [the Special Prosecutor] to the House Judiciary Committee for use in its impeachment inquiry." Watergate Report 104–05. The Special Prosecutor eventually asked the grand jury to transmit an "evidentiary report" to the House Committee considering President Nixon's impeachment. Id. at 143.

12. The Office of the President cites no authority for the proposition that communications between White House Counsel and the President would be absolutely privileged in congressional proceedings, but rather merely suggests that they "should" be.

in addition to having the advantages mentioned above, avoids the application of balancing tests to the attorney-client privilege—a practice recently criticized by the Supreme Court. See Swidler & Berlin, 118 S.Ct. 2081, 2086–87.

In sum, it would be contrary to tradition, common understanding, and our governmental system for the attorney-client privilege to attach to White House Counsel in the same manner as private counsel. When government attorneys learn, through communications with their clients, of information related to criminal misconduct, they may not rely on the government attorney-client privilege to shield such information from disclosure to a grand jury.

. . .

■ TATEL, CIRCUIT JUDGE, dissenting from Part II and concurring in part and dissenting in part from Part III [a portion of the majority opinion still under seal].

The attorney-client privilege protects confidential communication between clients and their lawyers, whether those lawyers work for the private sector or for government. Although I have no doubt that government lawyers working in executive departments and agencies enjoy a reduced privilege in the face of grand jury subpoenas, I remain unconvinced that either "reason" or "experience" (the tools of Rule 501) justifies this court's abrogation of the attorney-client privilege for lawyers serving the Presidency. . . .

My colleagues and I have no disagreement concerning personal legal advice Lindsey may have given the President. We agree, and the White House concedes, that the official attorney-client privilege does not protect such communications, for as a White House employee Lindsey had no authority to provide such advice. Nor do we disagree about political advice given to the President by advisers who happen to be lawyers. Such advice is protected, if at all, by the executive privilege alone. Our disagreement centers solely on whether a grand jury can pierce the attorney-client privilege with respect to official legal advice that the Office of White House Counsel gives a sitting President. . . .

This court now holds that for all government attorneys, including those advising a President, the attorney-client privilege dissolves in the face of a grand jury subpoena. According to the court, its new rule "avoids the application of balancing tests to the attorney-client privilege—a practice recently criticized by the Supreme Court." But whether a court abrogates the privilege by applying the balancing test rejected in Swidler, or by the rule the court adopts today, the chilling effect is precisely the same. Clients, in this case Presidents of the United States, will avoid confiding in their lawyers because they can never know whether the information they share, no matter how innocent, might some day become "pertinent to possible criminal violations." Rarely will White House counsel possess cold, hard facts about presidential wrongdoing that would create a strong public interest in disclosure, yet the very possibility that the confidence will be breached will chill communications. As a result, Presidents may well shift their trust on all but the most routine legal matters from White House counsel, who undertake to serve the Presidency, to private counsel who represent its occupant.

Unlike Jaffee, 518 U.S. at 10–11 (recognizing a federal psychotherapy privilege), and In re Sealed Case, No. 98–3069, 1998 WL 370584, at *4 (D.C.Cir. July 7, 1998) (declining to recognize a protective function privilege for Secret Service agents), this case involves not the creation of a new privilege, but as in Swidler, the carving out of an exception to an already well-established privilege. See Swidler, 118 S.Ct. 2081, 2086–87. Denying that they are creating an exception, my colleagues say that they are "defining the particular contours of the government attorney-client privilege," but no court has suggested that the attorney-client privilege must be extended client by client to each new governmental entity, proceeding by proceeding. Rather, "[u]nless applicable law otherwise provides," Restatement § 124, the privilege applies to all attorneys and all clients, regardless of their identities or the nature of the proceeding, see Swidler, 118 S.Ct. 2081, 2086–87 (finding no case authority for civil-criminal distinction). The question before us, then, is whether either "reason" or "experience" (Fed. R. Evid. 501), calls for exempting the Presidency from the traditional attorney-client relationship that all clients enjoy with their lawyers.

As one of its reasons for abrogating the presidential attorney-client privilege, the court says that legal advice is no different from the advice a President receives from other advisers, advice protected only by executive privilege. I think the court seriously underestimates the independent role and value of the attorney-client privilege. Unlike the executive privilege—a broad, constitutionally derived privilege that protects frank debate between President and advisers,—the narrower attorney-client privilege flows not from the Constitution, but from the common law. The attorney-client privilege does not protect general policy or political advice—even when given by lawyers—but only communications with lawyers "for the purpose of obtaining legal assistance." Restatement § 122. Necessitated by the nature of the lawyer's function, the attorney-client privilege enables the lawyer as an officer of the court properly to advise the client, including facilitating compliance with the law. See Upjohn, 449 U.S. at 389. In other words, the unique protection the law affords a President's communications with White House counsel rests not, as my colleagues put it, on some "conceit" that "lawyers are more important to the operations of government than all other officials," but rather on the special nature of legal advice, and its special need for confidentiality, as recognized by centuries of common law. It therefore makes sense that the Presidency possesses both the attorney-client and executive privileges, and that courts treat them differently.

The court also cites 28 U.S.C. § 535(b). Although that statute generally supports qualifying—though not abrogating—the attorney-client privilege for government attorneys working in executive departments and agencies, the court acknowledges, as the Attorney General has told us in her amicus brief, that section 535(b) does not apply to the Office of the President. The court cites several statements, ... indicating that White House lawyers comply with the spirit of section 535(b). Nothing in those statements suggests, however, that their authors were referring to conversations between White House counsel and the President of the United States, i.e., that one presidential subordinate (White House counsel) would report a confidential conversation with a President to another presidential subordinate (the Attorney General). The court points to no other statutory basis for denying the President the benefit of the official privilege. Although the Independent Counsel statute ensures independent, aggressive prosecution of wrongdoing, nothing in that statute disables a President from defending himself or otherwise indicates that Congress intended to deprive the Presidency of its official privileges.

The court refers to actions of a few previous White House counsel.... In my view, these limited and contradictory examples reveal nothing about the standard we should apply where, as here, a President of the United States actually invokes the attorney-client privilege in the face of a grand jury subpoena.

Acknowledging the facial inapplicability of section 535(b) to the Office of the President, the court relies on the government lawyer's oath of office for the proposition that White House counsel cannot have a traditional attorney-client relationship with the President. But all lawyers, whether they work within the government or the private sector, take an oath to uphold the Constitution of the United States. ... No one would suggest that this oath abrogates a client's privilege in the face of a grand jury subpoena.

This court's opinion, moreover, nowhere accounts for the unique nature of the Presidency, its unique need for confidential legal advice, or the possible consequences of abrogating the attorney-client privilege for a President's ability to obtain such advice. Elected, head of the Executive Branch, Commander-in-Chief, head of State, and removable only by impeachment, the President is not just "a part of the federal government, consisting of government employees doing government business." As Justice Robert H. Jackson observed in the steel seizure case, the Presidency concentrates executive authority "in a single head in whose choice the whole Nation has a part, making him the focus of public hopes and expectations. In drama, magnitude and finality his decisions so far overshadow any others that almost alone he fills the public eye and ear." Youngstown Sheet & Tube Co. v. Sawyer, 343 U.S. 579, 653 (1952) (Jackson, J., concurring). ...

... By lumping the President together with tax collectors, passport application processors, and all other executive branch employees—even cabinet officers—the court bypasses the reasoned "case-by-case" analysis demanded by Rule 501.

A President's need for confidential legal advice may "know[ ] no parallel in government" for another reason. Because the Presidency is tied so tightly to the persona of its occupant, and because ... the Presidency's increased "vulnerability," stemming from "the visibility of [the] office and the effect of [the President's] actions on countless people," official matters—proper subjects for White House counsel consultation—often have personal implications for a President. Since for any President the line between official and personal can be both elusive and difficult to discern, I think Presidents need their official attorney-client privilege to permit frank discussion not only of innocuous, routine issues, but also sensitive, embarrassing, or even potentially criminal topics.

The need for the official presidential attorney-client privilege seems particularly strong after Watergate which, while ushering in a new era of accountability and openness in the highest echelons of government, also increased the Presidency's vulnerability. Aggressive press and congressional scrutiny, the personalization of politics, and the enactment of the Independent Counsel statute,—which triggers appointment of an Independent Counsel based on no more than the existence of "reasonable grounds to believe that further investigation is warranted," 28 U.S.C. § 592(c)(1)(A)—have combined to make the Supreme Court's fear that Presidents have become easy "target[s]," Fitzgerald, 457 U.S. at 753, truer than ever. No President can navigate the treacherous waters of post-Watergate government, make controversial official legal decisions, decide whether to invoke official privileges, or even know when he might need private counsel, without confidential legal advice. Because of the Presidency's enormous responsibilities, moreover, the nation has compelling reasons to ensure that Presidents are well defended against false or frivolous accusations that could interfere with their duties. The nation has equally compelling reasons for ensuring that Presidents are well advised on whether charges are serious enough to warrant private counsel. I doubt that White House counsel can perform any of these functions without the candor made possible by the attorney-client privilege. As I said at the outset, weakening the privilege may well cause Presidents to shift their trust from White House lawyers who have undertaken to serve the Presidency, to private lawyers who have not.

Preserving the official presidential attorney-client privilege would not place the President above the law, as the Independent Counsel implies. To begin with, by enabling clients—including Presidents—to be candid with their lawyers and lawyers to advise clients confidentially, the attorney-client privilege promotes compliance with the law. See Upjohn, 449 U.S. at 389, 101 S.Ct. 677. Independent Counsels, moreover, have powerful weapons to combat abuses of the attorney-client privilege. If evidence suggested that a President used White House counsel to further a crime, the crime-fraud exception would abrogate the privilege. See United States v. Zolin, 491 U.S. 554, 562–63 (1989). . . .

To be sure, a properly exercised attorney-client privilege may deny a grand jury access to information, see Swidler, 118 S.Ct. 2081, 2086–87 (justifying the burden placed on the truth-seeking function by the privilege), but Presidents remain accountable in other ways, see Fitzgerald, 457 U.S. at 757 (checks on Presidential action include impeachment, press scrutiny, congressional oversight, need to maintain prestige, and concern for historical stature). An Independent Counsel, moreover, can always report to Congress that a President has denied critical information to a grand jury. See 28 U.S.C. § 595(a)(2), (c). If the President continues to exercise his attorney-client privilege in the face of a congressional subpoena, and if Congress believes that the President has committed "high Crimes and Misdemeanors," U.S. Const. art. II, § 4, Congress can always consider impeachment. See H. Rep. No. 93–1305, at 4, 187–213 (1974) (recommending impeachment of President Nixon based on his refusal to turn over information in response to congressional subpoenas).

. . .

Accordingly, before abrogating the official attorney-client privilege for all future Presidents, this court should have remanded to the district court to allow the Independent Counsel to recall Lindsey to the grand jury to determine whether, with respect to each question that he declines to answer, he can demonstrate the elements of the attorney-client privilege, namely that each communication was made between privileged persons in confidence "for the purpose of obtaining or providing legal assistance for the client." If Lindsey failed to meet this burden, that would end the matter, leaving for another day the difficult question of presidential attorney-client privilege, with its consequences for the functioning of the Presidency, as well as its potential implications for possible impeachment proceedings (implications we have hardly begun to consider). On the other hand, if Lindsey demonstrated that his communications involved official legal advice, the district court could use the remand to enrich the record . . . [creating] an infinitely more useful record for us, or eventually the Supreme Court, to determine whether reason or experience justifies any change in the official presidential attorney-client privilege, and if so, whether the privilege can be modified without threatening a President's ability to "take Care that the Laws be faithfully executed." . . .

. . .

The Hillary Clinton Privilege Case

In In re Grand Jury Subpoena,[1] cited in the *Lindsey* case, the Eighth Circuit considered claims of attorney-client privilege by President Clinton and First Lady Hillary Rodham Clinton. A subpoena of the "Whitewater" grand jury required production of "[a]ll documents created during meetings attended by any attorney from the Office of Counsel to the President and Hillary Rodham Clinton (regardless whether any other person was present)" pertaining to several Whitewater-related subjects. The White House identified nine sets of notes responsive to the subpoena but refused to produce them, citing executive privilege, attorney-client privilege, and the attorney work product doctrine. Independent counsel Starr filed a motion to compel production of two of the nine sets of documents identified by the White House:

---

1. 112 F.3d 910 (8th Cir. 1997), cert. denied, Office of the President v. Office of   Independent Counsel, 117 S.Ct. 2482 (1997).

The first set of documents comprises notes taken by Associate Counsel to the President Miriam Nemetz on July 11, 1995, at a meeting attended by Mrs. Clinton, Special Counsel to the President Jane Sherburne, and Mrs. Clinton's personal attorney, David Kendall. The subject of this meeting was Mrs. Clinton's activities following the death of Deputy Counsel to the President Vincent W. Foster, Jr. The documents in the second collection are notes taken by Ms. Sherburne on January 26, 1996, during meetings attended by Mrs. Clinton, Mr. Kendall, Nicole Seligman (a partner of Mr. Kendall's), and, at times, John Quinn, Counsel to the President. These meetings, which took place during breaks in and immediately after Mrs. Clinton's testimony before a federal grand jury in Washington, D.C., concerned primarily the discovery of certain billing records from the Rose Law Firm in the residence area of the White House.[2]

The White House abandoned its claim of executive privilege before the district court, relying solely on the attorney-client privilege and the work product doctrine. Mrs. Clinton also entered a personal appearance through counsel and asserted her personal attorney-client privilege. The district court found it unnecessary to reach the broadest question presented by Starr's office, whether a federal governmental entity may assert the attorney-client privilege or the work product doctrine in response to a subpoena by a federal grand jury. Instead, the court concluded that because Mrs. Clinton and the White House had a "genuine and reasonable (whether or not mistaken)" belief that the conversations at issue were privileged, the attorney-client privilege applied. In addition, the court held that the work product doctrine prevented disclosure of the notes to the grand jury.

On expedited review, the Eighth Circuit considered and rejected three separate claims of privilege, with one judge dissenting. The majority rejected Mrs. Clinton's claim of personal attorney-client privilege: Mrs. Clinton and the White House did not share a common interest in the investigation sufficient to support a claim of a joint defense assertion of the privilege. Moreover, a mistake of law–such as a belief, however reasonable, that a conversation was privileged–did not make an unprivileged conversation a privileged one. The court also held that the White House could not protect the notes under the work-product doctrine because they were not prepared in "anticipation of litigation." The court reasoned that the special prosecutor was not investigating the White House and that anticipated congressional hearings did not rise to the level of adversarial proceedings.

More significant, the majority held that a governmental attorney-client privilege did not exist at all in the context of a criminal investigation. The court relied heavily on United States v. Nixon[3] to propound "the general principle that the government's need for confidentiality may be subordinated to the needs of the government's own criminal justice processes."[4] The court emphasized the public interest in government disclosure instead of

---

2.   112 F.3d, at 914.   **4.**   112 F.3d at 919.

3.   418 U.S. 683 (1974).

government concealment; the statutory duty of executive branch employees to report wrongdoing; the rarity of privileges in federal common law; and the inability of the actions of White House employees to expose the White House to criminal or civil liability as a result of the investigation. The court rejected arguments that an uncertain privilege was useless. It felt that any government official who feared that he had violated the criminal law should consult a private attorney, and that no harm would come to a government official from disclosures made of conversations with a lawyer in contemplation of future actions, assuming the lawyer gave accurate advice.

The Governmental Attorney–Client Privilege

All the judges in *Lindsey* and *Clinton* are in agreement that governments, like corporations, have an attorney-client privilege. Consider, for example, a routine case brought by an injured plaintiff against the "United States" under the Federal Tort Claims Act. Everyone agrees that communications between the government employee who is alleged to have caused the harm and the Justice Department lawyer who represents the United States in this action are protected by the governmental attorney-client privilege; any notes of that conversation would also be protected by the work product immunity. The two cases do not deal with the separate question whether the executive branch may exercise a valid privilege (executive privilege or attorney-client privilege) when congressional committees seek particular communications between the President and another government official. The inquiry in the two cases is confined to situations in which one part of the executive branch (the criminal law enforcement part) is seeking information through a federal grand jury of another part of the same branch.

Concentrating on the politically-charged scenario of an independent counsel investigating a President or First Lady may muddle one's thinking about government privilege. Consider then the more typical case, involving allegations that an agency official has abused authority by, for example, granting government contracts to a person from whom the officer received substantial gifts. If that officer comes to an agency lawyer and starts the conversation with "I think I'm in deep trouble and I want to talk to you in confidence," how should the government lawyer respond? If the lawyer receives information from the officer indicating that he has violated federal criminal law, what should the lawyer do with that information? Is the situation different if the information comes from the officer's secretary, who is not personally responsible for the allegedly wrongful action?

Who "Owns" the Government's Attorney–Client Privilege?

Who is right in *Lindsey*, the panel majority or the dissenter?[5] Is the notion that legal advice should be specially protected, as opposed to, say, a cabinet member's advice, a "conceit" of lawyers? Does the limited nature of

---

5. For an illuminating discussion of *Lindsey* and *In re Grand Jury Subpoena Duces Tecum*, see Michael Stokes Paulsen, Who "Owns" the Government's Attorney–Client Privilege, 83 Minn.L.Rev. 473 (1998).

executive privilege suggest a similarly limited understanding of the government attorney-client privilege? Does the dissent in *Lindsey* take adequate account of the statutory responsibilities of the Attorney General "as the country's chief law enforcement officer?" If the Independent Counsel Statute is constitutional, as the Supreme Court has held, doesn't that statute make the special prosecutor the chief law enforcement officer on the matters within her jurisdiction? In short, don't the *Nixon* case,[6] with its miserly interpretation of executive privilege, and the *Morrison* case,[7] with its endorsement of the statutory transfer to an independent counsel of the President's ultimate authority in the executive branch, support the results in *Lindsey* and *Clinton*?

Three separate questions should be distinguished: First, in the context of a federal criminal investigation of a federal officer believed to have violated federal law, may *the officer* invoke the attorney-client privilege *of the United States* against federal prosecutors acting within their authority? In the typical case involving an officer other than the Attorney General or the President, there is a powerful argument that the Attorney General should have the authority to waive or claim the government's privilege. Of course, the President, unless a valid statute provided otherwise, could always "persuade" the Attorney General not to exercise that authority or the reverse.[8]

Second, a 1954 statute, 28 U.S.C. § 535, requiring federal employees to inform the Attorney General of possible criminal law violations by federal officers, builds on a history in which a federal officer's claim that communications to a federal lawyer were personally privileged has never been upheld against a request from a federal grand jury investigating the officer's conduct. Communications with a private lawyer retained by the officer are privileged, but government lawyers are under the same duty to report law violations to the Attorney General as are non-lawyer federal employees. Does § 535(b) have the effect of abrogating the federal attorney-client privilege for all communications made by government employees to government lawyers concerning government business? Or does it merely provide an exception to the duty of confidentiality, leaving the attorney-client privilege unaffected? Is the government officer in the same position, vis-a-vis a government lawyer, as a corporation officer communicating with the corporation's lawyer?

---

6. United States v. Nixon, 418 U.S. 638, 694–95 (1974) (recognizing that a special prosecutor may contest the President's invocation of executive privilege). See William Van Alstyne, A Political and Constitutional Review of United States v. Nixon, 22 UCLA L.Rev. 116, 130–40 (1974) (the most important aspect of *Nixon* is its potential to "particle-ize" the executive power).

7. Morrison v. Olson, 487 U.S. 654 (1987) (upholding the Independent Counsel Act which vests any control the President might have over an independent counsel with the Attorney General).

8. Recall that President Nixon accomplished the firing of Archibald Cox, the special prosecutor he had earlier appointed, only after Attorney General Richardson and Deputy Attorney General Ruckelhaus had resigned rather than obey the President. At that point, the third in the line of succession, Solicitor General Bork, signed the order removing Cox.

Third, the Independent Counsel Statute transfers the Attorney General's statutory authority to speak for the United States in law enforcement to a properly appointed Independent Counsel acting within his jurisdiction. That transfer of authority to speak and act for the United States presumably includes the Attorney General's authority to claim or waive the government's attorney-client privilege. In the *Lindsey* case one part of the executive branch was seeking to assert the government's attorney-client privilege against the part of the executive branch—Independent Counsel Kenneth Starr—that by valid statute has been authorized in certain criminal investigations to represent "the United States."[9] Shouldn't the appeals court have made more of this?

The Independent Counsel Statute may well not survive the critical exposure it has received in recent years. If the statute is allowed to die, how will the principles stated in *Lindsey* and Clinton operate (assuming they are not overruled by the Supreme Court or by statute)?

Government Lawyer as Representing the "Public Interest"

In the introductory note to this section we provided an agency-centered answer to the question of who speaks for the government as client. Eric Schnapper takes an opposing view, arguing that a government lawyer may sometimes take a course of action or accept a settlement contrary to the wishes of agency heads:[29]

> The relationship of agency officials to government counsel is not that of client and attorney in any ordinary sense, for the identities and desires of those officials may vary with popular opinion, the vote of the electorate, or the whims of their superiors, while the law to which both officials and counsel owe their allegiance remains unaltered.[30]

Schnapper rejects the usual arguments in support of deferring to the legal and policy decisions of agency heads. Government officials, he argues, are entitled to the free representation of government lawyers only when "they are right." When the disputed conduct does not "in fact represent public policy," it is burdensome to opposing parties and the courts for government lawyers to advance positions that do not represent sound public policy.[31]

Does Schnapper assume that legal and policy questions faced by government agencies have a single, unambiguous answer? Are his views

9. See Douglas R. Cox, "Ken Starr, Not Hillary Clinton, Is the 'Client' Here," Wall. St.J., May 7, 1997, at A19.

29. Eric Schnapper, Legal Ethics and the Government Lawyer, 32 The Record 649 (1977). Other materials on the government lawyer's responsibilities include: Symposium: Government Lawyering, 61 L. & Contemp.Prob. (Winter & Spring 1998) (articles on government lawyers (1) shaping law and policy, (2) litigating on behalf of the United States, (3) congressional lawyers, and (4) executive branch lawyers); Geoffrey

P. Miller, Ethics in a System of Checks and Balances, 54 U.Chi.L.Rev. 1293 (1987); Jack B. Weinstein, Some Ethical and Political Problems of a Government Lawyer, 18 Me.L.Rev. 155 (1966); Luther A. Huston, Arthur S. Miller, Samuel Krislov & Robert G. Dixon, Jr., Roles of the Attorney General of the United States (1968); and Charles A. Horsky, The Washington Lawyer (1952).

30. Id. at 649.

31. Id. at 650–51.

applicable to the many situations in which law and policy are contested or uncertain? Why should a lawyer's view prevail over that of elected or appointed officials?

By statute, 28 U.S.C. § 518, the Solicitor General of the United States has authority to decide whether to petition the U.S. Supreme Court to review decisions in lower courts ruling against agencies and departments of the United States. A long tradition has vested substantial but not total discretion in the Solicitor General to control the government's decision to seek Supreme Court review and to determine the positions taken in cases before the Court.[32] Of course, the President may give directions to the Solicitor General or remove her from office.

When the Government Switches Sides in Litigation

The litigating position of "the United States" may change as a consequence of a presidential election. In 1979, for example, the Justice Department's Civil Rights Division intervened on behalf of the plaintiffs in an action against the Birmingham fire department to compel the city to implement an affirmative action hiring plan to correct past discrimination against blacks and hispanics. In 1981, after President Carter was defeated by President Reagan, while the suit was still in the discovery stage, the new head of the Civil Rights Division ordered a staff lawyer to seek court permission to withdraw the government's brief on behalf of the plaintiffs and to intervene instead on behalf of the fire department. What should such a lawyer do if she believes that "truth, justice, and the law" are with the plaintiffs?[33]

Does government side-switching raise conflict-of-interest or confidentiality concerns? In Washington v. Seattle School District No. 1,[34] the Supreme Court noted that the government had changed its position during the course of the litigation, but did not address the ethical or legal issues raised. The Department of Justice, on behalf of the United States, intervened on the side of the local school district in support of a voluntary school busing plan but, after a change in administrations, fought the plan. The school district argued that the Justice Department should be disqualified from further representation of the government because the government lawyers had access to the school district's confidences during the time

---

32. See United States v. Providence Journal Co., 485 U.S. 693 (1988) (attorney appointed by district court to prosecute criminal contempt charges cannot represent the United States before the Supreme Court without authorization from the Solicitor General, who declined to give such authorization). See generally Lincoln Caplan, The Tenth Justice: The Solicitor General and the Rule of Law (1987) (arguing the importance to the Supreme Court and "the rule of law" of the independent authority of the Solicitor General to define the interests of the United States in bringing and arguing cases in the Supreme Court). Cf. Ethics in Government Act, 28 U.S.C. § 594(a)(9) (authorizing independent counsel to appear before "any court of competent jurisdiction ... in the name of the United States").

33. See Stuart Taylor, Jr., Second–Class Citizens, American Lawyer, Sept. 1989, at p. 42, discussing the Birmingham fire department litigation.

34. 458 U.S. 457, 471 (1982).

of cooperation.[35] Should disqualification of individual government lawyers be limited to those cases in which the government has been aligned with another party that it now seeks to oppose?

Model Rules and Government Lawyers

The Scope section of the Model Rules states:

> Under various legal provisions, including constitutional, statutory and common law, the responsibilities of government lawyers may include authority concerning legal matters that ordinarily reposes in the client in private client-lawyer relationships. For example, a lawyer for a government agency may have authority on behalf of the government to decide upon settlement or whether to appeal from an adverse judgment. Such authority in various respects is generally vested in the attorney general and the state's attorney in state government, and their federal counterparts, and the same may be true of other government law officers. Also, lawyers under supervision of these officers may be authorized to represent several government agencies in intragovernmental legal controversies in circumstances where a private lawyer could not represent multiple private clients. They also may have authority to represent the "public interest" in circumstances where a private lawyer would not be authorized to do so. These Rules do not abrogate any such authority.

Comment [6] to Rule 1.13 states:

> The duty defined in this Rule applies to governmental organizations. However, when the client is a governmental organization, a different balance may be appropriate between maintaining confidentiality and assuring that the wrongful official act is prevented or rectified, for public business is involved.... Therefore, defining precisely the identity of the client and prescribing the resulting obligations of such lawyers may be more difficult in the government context. Although in some circumstances the client may be a specific agency, it is generally the government as a whole. For example, if the action or failure to act involves the head of a bureau, either the department of which the bureau is a part or the government as a whole may be the client for purpose of this Rule. Moreover, in a matter involving the conduct of government officials, a government lawyer may have authority to question such conduct more extensively than that of a lawyer for a private organization in similar circumstances. This Rule does not limit that authority.

2.   GOVERNMENT LAWYER AS WHISTLEBLOWER

"Whistleblower" is the modern term for an employee who makes public charges of wrongdoing against officials of that person's agency or

---

35. See Note, Professional Ethics in Government Side–Switching, 96 Harv.L.Rev. 1914 (1983), arguing that government lawyers should be disqualified when the government cooperates with one party and then switches sides to cooperate with that party's adversary. The Note urges use of presumptions to prevent misuse of confidential information shared with the government by a former ally.

organization. The dissent, accusation and disloyalty of whistleblowers often lead to job retaliation by those in control of the organization. Federal and state statutes seek to protect whistleblowers from such job retaliation, but moral issues remain:[36] What circumstances and what degree of certainty justify the breach of loyalty involved in "going public?" Should avenues of change within the organization be first exhausted? Must a whistleblower who is a lawyer also resign? How important is the whistleblower's intent in judging the propriety of her disclosure?

Many states have enacted laws protecting government-employee whistleblowers from retaliatory action.[37] Does a whistleblower statute supersede or nullify the ethical obligations otherwise governing a government lawyer?

At the federal level, the Civil Service Reform Act of 1978, as amended by the Whistleblower Protection Act of 1989,[38] prohibits a federal agency from taking an adverse personnel action against an employee's disclosure of information, not "specifically prohibited by law," that evidences: (1) a violation of law, rule or regulation, (2) gross mismanagement, (3) a gross waste of funds, (4) an abuse of authority, or (5) a specific and substantial danger to public health and safety. The disclosure, which may be made to anyone, including a journalist or a congressional staffer, is protected if the employee "reasonably believes" that the information "evidences" the specified wrongdoing. Government lawyers are covered by the Act, and the general prohibitions of disclosures of client information in ethics rules (e.g., M.R. 1.6) apparently do not fall within the Act's exception protecting information that Congress, by statute, has specifically protected, such as classified information. Does the Act have the effect, at least in some circumstances, of eliminating the government's right to discharge a lawyer for breach of confidentiality?[39]

In Taylor v. FDIC,[40] three government lawyers, who were working on cases seeking to hold the managers and advisers of failed thrifts liable for fiduciary wrongdoing, challenged a 1992 reorganization which moved them from one office to another. When the agency denied their objections, they "changed forum and theme," alleging before the Senate Banking Committee that the reorganization was intended to protect well-connected wrongdoers by hamstringing investigators. Later, in 1995, the lawyers resigned and brought suit under the Whistleblower Act for "constructive discharge." The court upheld dismissal of their action on the ground that the reorganization did not come within the statutory terms, as of 1992, limiting the

---

36. See Sissela Bok, Secrets 212–27 (1982) (discussing moral aspects of whistleblowing).

37. See, e.g., Cal.Gov.Code § 10543; Colo. Rev.Stat. 24–50.5–101; Me.Rev.Stat.Ann. tit. 26, § 831; N.Y. Labor Law § 740; Ohio Rev.Code Ann. § 4113.51; 43 Pa.Cons.Stat. § 1421.

38. See especially 5 U.S.C. § 3202(b).

39. Roger C. Cramton, The Lawyer as Whistleblower: Confidentiality and the

Government Lawyer, 5 Geo.J. Legal Ethics 291, 315 (1991), concludes: "Until and unless [federal government] lawyers avail themselves of the whistleblower provisions, forcing agency heads and the courts to wrestle with [the Act's uncertainties and] complexities, we will not have authoritative answers to these vexing questions."

40. 132 F.3d 753 (D.C.Cir.1998).

whistleblower protection to disclosures of "a possible violation of any law or regulation" (a 1993 amendment that stated broader grounds was inapplicable). Moreover, their disclosures to Congress, which may have involved violations of law, were not protected by the statute, which protects disclosures to agency superiors or the Attorney General but not to Congress.

In addition to whistleblower statutes, the First Amendment protects the speech of federal, state and local government employees. In Pickering v. Board of Education,[41] the Supreme Court held that an individual's exercise of his "right to speak on issues of public importance may not furnish the basis for his dismissal from public employment."[42] In Connick v. Myers,[43] the Court discussed the limits on this doctrine. Myers was a deputy district attorney who had circulated a questionnaire about internal office procedures regarding transfers and office morale; she was about to be transferred. The Court emphasized that the questionnaire focused not on "evaluat[ing] the performance of the office but rather [on] gather[ing] ammunition for another round of controversy with [Myers'] superiors."[44] Had the questionnaire involved the office's conduct of a particular case, could the prosecutor have been disciplined under M.R. 3.6? See the *Gentile* case, reprinted in Chapter 11 below.

3.   Government Lawyers Representing Individual Government Employees

In Dunton v. County of Suffolk,[45] the plaintiff sued the county and a county police officer to recover for the injuries received from a beating by the officer who had discovered the plaintiff with the officer's wife. At trial, the county attorney, who represented both the officer and the county, argued that the county was not liable because the officer was not acting within the scope of his employment but was an "irate husband." The verdict held the officer liable and the county not liable. On appeal, the Second Circuit remanded for a new trial based on an impermissible conflict of interest on the part of the county attorney. While the decision does not ban all joint representation in such situations, it emphasized that the "district court is under a duty to ensure that the [individual] client fully appreciates his situation."[46]

Under Monell v. New York City Department of Social Services,[47] liability may be imposed on a municipality under 42 U.S.C. § 1983 for a violation of civil rights resulting from the "execution of a government's policy or custom, whether made by its lawmakers or by those whose edicts

---

41. 391 U.S. 563, 574 (1968).

42. Also see Rankin v. McPherson, 483 U.S. 378, 383 (1987) (government employer may not discipline an "employee on a basis that infringes that employee's constitutionally protected interest in freedom of speech").

43. 461 U.S. 138 (1983).

44. Id. at 148.

45. 729 F.2d 903 (2d Cir.1984), modified, 748 F.2d 69 (1984).

46. Id. at 908. See also Clay v. Doherty, 608 F.Supp. 295, 305 (N.D.Ill.1985) ("[B]oth lawyer and judge must guard against any threatened interests ... in the *Dunton*-type cases.").

47. 436 U.S. 658 (1978).

or acts may fairly be said to represent official policy."[48] When municipal employees are sued as individuals along with the municipality, the latter can avoid liability by arguing that the employees' conduct was not official "policy or custom" but individual misconduct, and individual employees may avoid liability by arguing that their actions were taken pursuant to official policy, giving such employees qualified immunity.

Where employees may raise qualified immunity as a defense, courts generally have allowed joint representation only when the municipality embraces the employees' acts as municipal policy. Even in those situations, the court may require proof that the individual defendants have been adequately and fully informed of the potential conflict and its effect on the representation.[49] Within these contours, municipalities still rely on joint representation.[50]

None of these cases address whether the government, as opposed to the employee, could adequately consent to the joint representation; whether the decision to embrace the employee's acts, i.e., to waive a defense, was made free from conflict; or whether the government would be adequately defended. Who would have standing to challenge the government's consent to the joint representation? Do these concerns justify a per se rule?

D. Lawyers for a Class

"Experience teaches that it is counsel for the class representatives, and not the named parties, who direct and manage [class] actions. Every experienced federal judge knows that any statement to the contrary is sheer sophistry."[1]

Lawyer-client relationships with entities as clients can be arrayed according to how closely they resemble the paradigm of the individual client who defines the objectives of the representative: Lawyers for partnerships and small businesses are closest to the paradigm, then corporation lawyers, then government lawyers and finally lawyers for a class.[2]

---

48. Id. at 693.

49. See, e.g., Manganella v. Keyes, 613 F.Supp. 795 (D.C.Conn.1985).

50. Compare Shadid v. Jackson, 521 F.Supp. 87 (E.D.Tex.1981) (disqualifying government lawyer from representing individual defendants without inquiring whether defenses would be incompatible), with Coleman v. Smith, 814 F.2d 1142, 1147–48 (7th Cir.1987) (expressing reservations about the broad language condemning joint representation in *Dunton*). Also see Suffolk County Patrolmen's Benevolent Association, Inc. v. County of Suffolk, 751 F.2d 550 (2d Cir.1985) (upholding procedure creating panel of three independent lawyers from which police officers who were co-defendants with the county in civil rights actions had to choose counsel in order to get the county to reimburse their attorneys' fees).

1. Greenfield v. Villager Industries, Inc., 483 F.2d 824, 832 n. 9 (3d Cir.1973).

2. A different ordering would prevail if the client's ability to monitor the lawyer's performance were also considered. Experienced clients who regularly use the legal system ("repeat players") are now in the best position. Liability insurers and large corporations have the greatest ability to control their lawyers directly and indirectly through the funneling of repeat business.

As the Model Rules acknowledge, the lawyer for the government often acts as both client and lawyer at least in the office of state's attorney. However, the government lawyer is not free to make choices for the client because political constraints mean that public policies—the objectives of the representation—are never solely matters for the lawyer. Within accepted policy limits the government lawyer may have free rein, but at the limits the government lawyer still has a client.

Lawyers for a class, on the other hand, often construct the client by defining the objectives of the representation. A class often is defined in terms of a legal theory formulated by the lawyer. While the lawyer for a class appears in the mask of agent, the client may be solely the lawyer's creation and may exist only to serve the lawyer's ends.

When the lawyer is engaged in social advocacy or institutional reform, such as a lawyer for a public interest group or a legal services organization, the principal problem is that of paternalism—a lawyer shaping a dispute and making decisions on behalf of an otherwise unrepresented class of persons. Law reform litigation of this type is considered in Chapter 11 below at p. 1106.[3]

A second major type of class action lawyer is considered at this point: the entrepreneurial class lawyer. A lawyer who is engaged in enforcing the legal rights of a class but who is also strongly motivated by the hope of a substantial attorney's fee. Examples include a class derivative action brought by the shareholders of a company or a mass tort suit such as that by the victims of the chemical leak in Bhopal, India.[4]

Lawyers engaged in social advocacy and institutional reform (the lawyer as "social advocate") are both similar to and different from lawyers engaged in making a living from the attorney fees generated by successful class actions. Solicitation, financing of litigation and conflict of interest problems (conflicts within the represented class and conflicts between the interests of the lawyer and those of the class)[5] are problems shared by both types of lawyers. A valuable empirical study finds important differences, however, between the "social advocate" and the "entrepreneur."[6] They differ in terms of creativity in legal strategy (the entrepreneur prefers not to experiment), mobilization of the class (the entrepreneur prefers it to be

Individuals, especially those who face a personal plight requiring a lawyer, normally encounter more substantial "agency costs" in selecting, supervising and monitoring a lawyer.

3. For an insightful discussion of some ethical problems encountered in school desegregation cases, see Derrick A. Bell, Serving Two Masters: Integration Ideals and Client Interests in School Desegregation Litigation, 85 Yale L.J. 470 (1976).

4. See Deborah L. Rhode, Solicitation, 36 J.Legal Educ. 317, 319 (1986) (discussing the Bhopal incident and others).

5. For an early and often-cited discussion of conflicts of interest in class action practice, see Deborah L. Rhode, Class Conflicts in Class Actions, 34 Stan.L.Rev. 1183 (1982).

6. See Bryant Garth, Ilene H. Nagel & S. Jay Plager, The Institution of the Private Attorney General: Perspectives from an Empirical Study of Class Action Litigation, 61 S.Cal.L.Rev. 353 (1988).

inactive), and settlement approach (the entrepreneur covets the fee, the social advocate, the decree).

1.   OVERVIEW: THE PROBLEMS AND SOME PROPOSED SOLUTIONS

Jonathan R. Macey and Geoffrey P. Miller, "The Plaintiffs' Attorney's Role in Class Action and Derivative Litigation"
58 U. Chi. L. Rev. 1, 3–19, 116–118 (1991).[7]

[T]he single most salient characteristic of class and derivative litigation is the existence of "entrepreneurial" plaintiffs' attorneys. Because these attorneys are not subject to monitoring by their putative clients, they operate largely according to their own self-interest, subject only to whatever constraints might be imposed by bar discipline, judicial oversight, and their own sense of ethics and fiduciary responsibilities....

... In both the class action and the shareholder's derivative suit, the attorney's client is not actively involved in the conduct of the litigation on the plaintiff's side. But in other respects these devices are quite different in theory and rationale.

The class action is a tool for overcoming the free-rider and other collective action problems that impair any attempt to organize a large number of discrete individuals in any common project. These kinds of problems are prevalent ... when a large number of people have [each suffered some small injury.] In the absence of a class action device, such injuries would often go unremedied because most individual plaintiffs would not ... have a sufficient economic stake ... to incur the litigation costs....

The class action procedure partially overcomes these difficulties by providing an effective and inexpensive procedure for joining large numbers of individual plaintiffs. [Usually, but not always, this is done through a "(b)(3)" class action, which requires that "questions of law or fact common to the members of the class predominate over any questions affecting only individual members" and demands a showing that the class form "is superior to other available methods for the fair and efficient adjudication of the controversy."][8] ....

7. Copyright © 1991 The University of Chicago Law Review. Reprinted with permission.

8. [Editor's Note:] Since Macey and Miller wrote this article, class action practice has evolved to include not just the small claims class actions that the authors take as the paradigm, but also large-injury "mass tort" class actions in which the rationale for the class form is not the "collective action" problem discussed by the authors, but rather a supposed concern on the part of class members that the defendant's resources be fairly distributed among all those who are seriously injured and the justice system's concern for efficient resolution of mass tort cases. Moreover, more and more class actions are being brought not under Rule 23(b)(3), which the authors assume is the provision that governs, but under Rule 23(b)(1), a critical difference being that class members can opt out of

... Shareholder's derivative actions are not premised on collective action problems in the *litigation*. On the contrary, they presuppose the existence of a corporate form [capable of asserting it rights] that is already organized to overcome such ... problems.... The problem, rather, is with collective action *within* the corporate form itself.... [C]orporate managers typically have only a small ownership stake in the firms they manage. Thus, their interests deviate from those of shareholders: they may prefer to consume excessive perquisites or practice their golf whereas shareholders would want them to work diligently at maximizing profits.

The shareholder's derivative suit is one of many devices in corporate law for controlling these conflicts between managers and shareholders.... Unlike the class action, in which the relief is given to the plaintiff class members, any relief recovered in a derivative action (net of expenses including attorneys' fees) is returned to the corporation.

. . .

Both the class action and the shareholder's derivative lawsuit can thus be explained and rationalized in terms of modern economic theory.... The following discussion assumes that private enforcement of the applicable substantive laws represents sound social policy, or at least a policy preferred by those charged with making and enforcing the laws.

The role of the entrepreneurial attorney in class and derivative litigation can best be understood in terms of the economic theory of agency costs....

The attorney in litigation is, in theory and legal form, the agent of the client. As agent, the attorney is charged with the duty to advance the client's interests.... Yet attorneys do not always fulfill this responsibility, because their interests are rarely perfectly aligned with those of the client. The client pays the bill; the lawyer does the work. Many of the regulatory structures applicable to lawyers are designed to ensure that lawyers act as faithful agents of clients....

. . .

Plaintiffs' attorneys in class action and derivative suits occupy an uneasy place in the American legal system. The traditional image of the lawyer is ... [as] an agent of the client[,] ... subject to the client's control in ... important matters. [In contrast, p]laintiffs' class action and derivative attorneys ... are subject to only minimal monitoring by their ostensible "clients," who are either dispersed and disorganized (in the case of class action litigation) or under the control of hostile forces (in the case of derivative litigation). Accordingly, [these lawyers] ... function essentially as entrepreneurs who bear a substantial amount of the litigation risk and exercise nearly plenary control over all important decisions in the lawsuit.

the first kind of class action and are locked into any settlement or judgment in the second, (b)(1) class action. We return to these new developments later, see p. 826 infra.

The absence of client monitoring raises the specter that the entrepreneurial attorney will serve her own interest at the expense of the client. The existing regulatory system attempts to prevent such abuse—and to reduce what have been termed "agency costs"—in three principal ways. First, it allocates certain elements of litigating authority to persons other than the plaintiffs' attorney—absent class members, managers of corporations involved in derivative suits, representative plaintiffs, and the courts themselves. Second, it contains a number of special features ostensibly designed to weed out inappropriate representative plaintiffs. The representative plaintiff must assert claims that are typical of the claims being asserted, and must represent the class or corporation adequately. Third, plaintiffs' attorneys are subject to applicable rules of legal ethics that purport to constrain the attorneys' behavior in order to safeguard clients' interests.

We believe this regulatory structure is poorly designed ... , particularly when applied to "large-scale, small-claim" litigation in which the overall liability is large but the individual interests of the class members or corporate shareholders are small. The existing regulations are extraordinarily ineffective at aligning the interests of attorney and client ... Many regulatory shortfalls can be traced ultimately to a single fundamental error: the inappropriate attempt to treat entrepreneurial litigation as if it were essentially the same as standard litigation, in which the client exercises substantial influence. Even when the regulatory system acknowledges that entrepreneurial litigation poses special problems, it frequently attempts to resolve those problems by forcing class action and derivative litigation back into a standard model. The inevitable result is regulatory failure, simply because entrepreneurial litigation cannot be transformed into the traditional model even by brute regulatory force.

We propose revising the regulatory system ... with sensible rules that take into account the fact that the plaintiffs' attorney—not the client—controls the litigation. For example, the existing regulatory regime requires that all absent class members be given notice of a pending damages action and an opportunity to opt out of the suit—regardless of the size of the claim. The high cost of notifying absent class members when potential recovery is very small deters entrepreneurial attorneys from bringing meritorious suits. Thus, the rule harms, rather than protects, absent class members. We suggest that notice of class action in such cases should not be required for small claimants in advance of some authoritative disposition on the merits.

Another problem area is judicial review of settlements and fee requests, which is often haphazard, unreliable, and lacking in administrable standards. Although review of settlements is necessary so long as the entrepreneurial attorney's interests differ from those of the client, we suggest that review could be improved by the use of guardians ad litem to represent the interest of the class in large-scale, small-claim cases. As to fee requests, we join other recent commentators in finding that, despite serious drawbacks, a percentage-of-recovery method (in which the plaintiffs' attorneys are awarded some percentage of the class recovery as fees, either on a fixed percentage basis or according to some more complex sliding scale) is superior to the currently favored lodestar approach (which allows attorneys to recover according to the number of hours they spend on a case). The lodestar approach has three principal, related defects: it involves enormously burdensome calculation costs; it encourages attorneys to exaggerate their hours; and, because it guarantees that the attorneys will receive their fees if successful, it fails to give plaintiffs' attorneys the proper incentive to strike a settlement agreement that maximizes recovery for the plaintiff class.

We also criticize the current system for regulating the identity of the named plaintiff[: t]he existing requirements of typicality (under which the named plaintiff's claim must be similar to that of the other class members or shareholders) and adequacy (under which the named plaintiff must be capable of competently and adequately representing the absent class members or the corporation).... Given that the named plaintiff has little control over how the suit is conducted, the analysis should focus not on the appropriateness of the named plaintiff but rather on the reliability and competence of the plaintiffs' attorney.

Further, the regulatory system should acknowledge explicitly what is already the case, namely that ethics rules on solicitation, maintenance, fee-splitting and the acceptance of impropriety have virtually no current force or rationale in the large-scale, small-claim setting and are routinely circumvented with only the thinnest veneer of compliance. We recommend that these ethics rules be jettisoned in this group of cases. Instead of the current attempt to force the ethics analysis into standard, but inappropriate, doctrinal categories, the regulatory system should investigate whether the attorney's behavior poses real dangers to the interests of the class or corporation.

Underlying many of these observations is a more basic critique of the ... requirement that there be an actual identified individual plaintiff in large-scale, small-claim cases.... [T]he identified plaintiff operates almost always as a mere figurehead. The named plaintiff does little—indeed, usually does nothing—to monitor the attorney in order to ensure that representation is competent and zealous, or to align the interests of the attorney with those of the class or corporation. On the other hand, the requirement that there be an actual named plaintiff artificially limits the supply of attorneys able to bring large-scale, small-claim cases because in many cases "appropriate" representative plaintiffs are hard to find. The quality of representation is thereby diminished, and the private enforcement of law impaired. Further, attorneys ... routinely ... circumvent ethical restrictions on solicitation and maintenance ... to obtain named plaintiffs as their ticket into profitable litigation.... [T]he costs of requiring an actual named plaintiff greatly outweigh the benefits. Accordingly, we recommend that actual, identified named plaintiffs not be required in large-scale, small-claim litigation. Instead, a plaintiffs' attorney should be allowed to bring "Jane Doe" or "Richard Roe" complaint on behalf of a class or corporation.

Although we make several recommendations for ways in which the existing regulatory structure could be changed ... , we believe that a more fundamental change may be in order.... [T]he special problems of entrepreneurial litigation could be substantially overcome if the legal system were to allow some form of auction for plaintiffs' claims, under which attorneys (and others) could bid for the right to bring the litigation and gain the benefits, if any, that flow from success. A pure form of auction would simply sell the plaintiffs' claims outright to the winning bidder, with the proceeds to be distributed immediately to the class or corporation. Under such an approach, the winner of the auction would have litigation incentives ... very similar to those ... a claimholder would have in traditional ... litigation. There would be no need for any rules on typicality or adequacy of representation or for judicial scrutiny of settlements and fee awards. Class members would receive a certain and quick recovery rather than an uncertain and delayed one. The result would be more effective private enforcement of the law. Other possibilities we discuss involve partial bids or bids for lead counsel rights based on the percentage of the recovery that the attorney would be willing to take as a fee; these may be more feasible to implement, although they retain some of the problems of misalignment between the interests of the attorney and client.[3]

We do not advocate the auction approach as a panacea to the problem of attorney-client conflicts in class and derivative suits. There are a number of problems with an auction approach, including difficulties in defining the claim to be sold, the possibility that adequate financing will not be available to bidders, the problem of obtaining the cooperation of class members whose claims have been sold, and issues of consolidation of cases brought in different jurisdictions. Although we recognize these problems as serious, we believe there is considerable merit to the auction approach.

Market Approach to Class Action Claims

While the outright selling of class and derivative claims, advocated by Macey and Miller, has not yet been adopted anywhere, the more limited form of auction they discuss—auctioning the right to serve as class or derivative counsel—has been tried in a few cases.[9] Even with this limited

---

3. District Judge Vaughn Walker of the Northern District of California has recently conducted an auction of lead counsel rights based on fee percentages. See In re Oracle Securities Litigation, 131 F.R.D. 688 (N.D.Cal.1990) (setting up the bidding process); In re Oracle Securities Litigation, 132 F.R.D. 538 (N.D.Cal.1990) (awarding lead counsel rights to one of four bidders).

9. In addition to the *Oracle* case cited by Macey and Miller, see In re Wells Fargo Sec. Litig. 156 F.R.D. 223, 225 (N.D. Cal. 1994); and In re Amino Acid Lysine Antitrust Litig, 918 F.Supp. 1190 (N.D.Ill. 1996).

experience two problems have emerged: lawyers defeating the point of the auction by sharing bid information or agreeing to submit joint bids in lieu of competing;[10] and judges selecting counsel whose bid caps the maximum fee they can recover, eliminating counsel's incentive to seek any recovery greater than that necessary to justify the maximum fee.[11] The second problem could be remedied by judges refusing bids with caps. The first problem may prove more difficult to address.[12]

Susan Koniak and George Cohen have argued that the markets Macey, Miller and others seek to establish as a cure for some class action abuse will not work without a willingness to apply the antitrust laws to the practices of lawyers in class actions.[13] They argue that the fact that judges are acting for consumers (the class members) in purchasing lawyer services should not stop the application of the antitrust laws.[14]

While Macey and Miller argue that the existing regulatory structure fails in large part because it refuses to recognize the profound differences between the class/derivative lawyer and ordinary lawyers, in at least one sense class/derivative lawyers have until recently been treated quite differently by the regulatory structure: they have been virtually immune from malpractice suits.[15] Koniak and Cohen argue that this de facto immunity is,

---

10. See Susan P. Koniak & George M. Cohen, Under Cloak of Settlement, 82 Va. L.Rev. 1051, 1091–95 (1996) (describing the anti-competitive activities of the lawyers in the *Oracle* case).

11. In the *Amino Acid* case, supra, the judge appointed as class counsel a firm that had submitted the following bid: attorneys' fees of 20% of the first $5 million recovered; 15% of the next $10 million, and 10% of the next $10 million, and no additional fee for any recovery over $25 million. Thus, the fee was capped at $3.5 million and gave the lawyers no incentive to secure a recovery over $25 million. Moreover, given that bids are submitted pre-discovery, the lawyers would have had no reliable way of knowing that the claim was worth $25 million or less. The lawyers settled the case three months later and the headline in the Wall Street Journal read: "Bargain at the Bar: Archer–Daniels Cuts Surprisingly Good Deal in Price–Fixing Suit." The article was written by Laurie Cohen, Thomas M. Burton & Scott Kilman, Wall St. J., Apr. 12, 1996, at A1, A6.

12. Moreover, if the few instances of bidding are any guide to the future, anticompetitive activity by lawyers, if left unchecked, may be pervasive enough to undercut any benefits that these auctions might otherwise produce. In virtually every auction thus far held, the judge involved

has commented on the anticompetitive behavior of the lawyers supposedly competing to be class counsel. See Koniak & Cohen, supra, at 1094 nn. 353, 355 (citing and discussing the judges' comments).

13. Koniak and Cohen describe other anticompetitive aspects of class action practice, such as settlements negotiated by class counsel that guarantee class counsel's law firms unfair market advantage in the market for legal services created by the settlement—the market for clients to represent in the alternative dispute resolution process set up by the settlement. Id. at 1097–1102.

14. See id. at 1183–1269. Koniak and Cohen also argue that judicial approval of class settlements should not prevent subsequent application of antitrust laws to address anticompetitive activity countenanced by the settlement, such as caps on attorneys' fees and practices that tend to lock-in the market share of class counsel's firm. These practices tend to guarantee to counsel class a share of the after-settlement market for clients that is equal to or greater than class counsel's share of clients in the pre-settlement market of tort claimants. See id.

15. See Susan P. Koniak, Through the Looking Glass of Ethics and the Wrong with Rights We Find There, 9 Geo. J. Leg.

in large measure, the function of a widespread belief on the part of bench and bar that the requirement that a judge must find class counsel adequate to represent the class precludes subsequent litigation on all questions of lawyer incompetence, as well as constructive and actual fraud.[16] They argue that under generally accepted principles of preclusion law the class action judge's findings would not preclude later suits against class counsel for malpractice or fraud.[17] They point out that defense counsel could also be sued for fraud committed in negotiating a collusive settlement or for breach of fiduciary duty (or malpractice to the corporation), if the collusive settlement is in a derivative suit.[18] More generally, they argue that the threat of later liability for conduct in a class action might work much better than other proposed solutions to stem some of the abuses now present.[19]

Ethics 1 (1995) (analyzing how and why it has come to pass that the clients most vulnerable to lawyer misconduct, criminal defendants and class action plaintiffs, face legal obstacles to holding their lawyers accountable for malpractice not imposed on other clients). For a discussion of the obstacles confronting criminal defendants, see Chapter 3 supra at p. 201.

16. See Koniak & Cohen, supra, at 1140–41.

17. See id. at 1141–1180. For a thorough discussion of the preclusion issues involved, see Derrickson v. City of Danville, 845 F.2d 715 (7th Cir. 1988) (holding that court's prior approval of class action settlement did not preclude district attorney from indicting defendant's agents and its counsel for violating state ethics law by negotiating a settlement that inured to their personal benefit). The district attorney did indict and convict the defendant-city's agents and the conviction was sustained on appeal by the Illinois Supreme Court, which, like the federal appeals court, rejected the defense's preclusion arguments. See People v. Scharlau, 565 N.E.2d 1319, 1328–29 (Ill. 1990).

18. See Koniak & Cohen, supra, at 1150.

19. See id. at 1102–1140. In Kamilewicz v. Bank of Boston Corp., 1995 WL 758422 (N.D. Ill.1995), claims of fraud and negligence were brought against both class counsel and the defendant, a bank which had an independent fiduciary duty to safeguard the class members' bank accounts. See Koniak & Cohen at 1057–1068, 1270–1280. The allegations were that class counsel had secured defendant's assent to a class settlement that provided class counsel with attorneys' fees to be paid out of class members bank accounts by defendant deducting money from those accounts—the problem being, for some class members more money was deducted in attorneys' fees than was due them under the terms of the class settlement. In other words, many members of the class allegedly were charged more than 100% of their recovery in attorneys' fees. The case was dismissed by the federal district court on the ground that it could not hear an "appeal" from a state court's approval of a class settlement. The class appealed, arguing that claims like theirs, e.g., for malpractice in an earlier case, were not "appeals" of the first case. A panel of the Seventh Circuit affirmed the district court's dismissal unanimously, 92 F.3d 506 (7th Cir. 1996), and the class's request for rehearing en banc was denied. See 100 F.3d 1348 (1996), cert. denied 520 U.S. 1204 (1997). But Judge Easterbrook wrote a powerful dissent from that denial, which was joined by Chief Judge Posner and three other circuit judges. See 100 F.3d at 1349. The Vermont Attorney General, however, subsequently filed suit in a Vermont state court against the bank for participating in this alleged scam. The complaint alleged that many Vermont residents were defrauded by the settlement approved in this case by an Alabama state court (on behalf of a nationwide class). The trial court accepted the bank's argument that the Alabama court's approval of the fees precluded the suit. As of July 1999, the dismissal was pending on appeal before the Vermont Supreme Court, sub nom. State of Vermont v. Homeside Lending. Susan Koniak is providing pro bono assistance to the State of Vermont on this matter.

To date only a few such cases have been brought,[20] but each year seems to bring more than the previous year.

Macey and Miller suggest that appointing guardians for the class to help courts review class action settlements might help protect class members from collusive settlements, but they do not answer how and by whom these guardians will be compensated. Would they have sufficient funds to do a thorough and independent analysis of the settlement or would they end up relying on what class counsel and the defense counsel told them about the settlement? How and by whom would guardians be selected? No settling party and no judge interested in accepting a settlement and moving on to other matters would be likely to be interested in appointing those with a reputation for disapproving class settlements. Instead of a guardian, John Leubsdorf has proposed court appointment of a class advocate, whose job it would be to make all plausible arguments against a proposed settlement, which would introduce the benefits of adversarial process to the settlement approval stage when class counsel and the defendant's counsel are aligned in favor of the settlement.[21]

In theory, objectors to the settlement perform this function, but objectors who appear through counsel are rare. Moreover, when they appear they are not generally eligible for an award of attorneys' fees, particularly when their efforts have the effect of scuttling a settlement. From where would the money to pay such an award come? Thus, as things now stand objecting counsel (and their clients) have every incentive to accept a payment from class counsel and/or the defendant to go away.[22] Moreover, courts have little ability or incentive to monitor payoffs to objectors or their counsel.

Macey and Miller state that judicial oversight of class settlements and counsel's fees "is often haphazard, unreliable, and lacking in administrable standards." A 1996 study by the Federal Judicial Center, examining class action practice in four federal district courts, found that the average fairness hearing took up about 40 minutes of court time, putting aside two outlier class actions where objectors had vigorous and committed representation.[23] "Approximately 90% or more of the proposed settlements were

---

20. See. e.g., Durkin v. Shea & Gould, 92 F.3d 1510 (9th Cir.1996), cert. denied 520 U.S. 1197 (1997) (holding suit against defense counsel for malpractice against defendant corporation by agreeing to collusive settlement not precluded by court's approval of the settlement in the derivative action); Zimmer Paper Products Inc. v. Berger & Montague, P.C., 758 F.2d 86 (3d Cir.1985) (alleging negligence by class counsel in not providing timely notice to class member, a company with substantial stake in litigation, resulting in company's losing right to share in recovery; affirming grant of summary judgment for defendant, but acknowledging that a claim for mal-

practice might be made against class counsel despite class action court's approval of counsel's actions).

21. John Leubsdorf made this proposal in 1998 testimony to the Advisory Committee on the Federal Rules of Civil Procedure.

22. Of course, the lack of attorneys' fees for objecting counsel is in no small part responsible for their scarcity. For an analysis of the economic disincentives (and other obstacles) facing objecting counsel, see Koniak & Cohen, supra, at 1105–10.

23. The figures in the text are from E. Willging, Laural L. Hooper & Robert J. Niemic, Federal Judicial Center, Empirical

approved without any changes in each of the four districts."[24] With that high an approval rate, either the commentators, such as Macey and Miller above and Coffee below, drastically overestimate the problems that plague class action representation or the courts are poor monitors of the quality of representation and the settlements class counsel produce.[25]

As soon as a class action is filed, the lawyer for the class usually wishes to solicit potential class members to increase the likelihood of certification. Before and after certification, the lawyer has an interest in contacting class members to gather evidence and to discourage opting-out. Comment [4] to M.R. 7.2 on advertising states that "[n]either this Rule nor Rule 7.3 [on direct solicitation] prohibits communications authorized by law, such as notice to members of a class in class action litigation."

In Gulf Oil Co. v. Bernard,[26] Gulf petitioned the court for an order limiting the named plaintiffs and their lawyers from communicating with potential class members, alleging that counsel was telling potential class members that they could double their recovery by joining the suit and rejecting the back-pay offer. Without corroborating Gulf's allegations, the district court issued the order prohibiting such communication without prior court approval. The Supreme Court, while acknowledging the potential for abuse, held that the trial court had abused its discretion: "[A]n order limiting communications between parties and potential class members should be based on a clear record and specific findings that reflect a weighing of the need for a limitation and the potential interference with the rights of the parties."[27] The Court did not decide the case on First Amendment grounds, as the Court of Appeals had done,[28] but determined that any order limiting communications should be "carefully drawn ... to limit speech as little as possible. . . ."[29]

Study of Class Actions in Four Federal District Courts: Final Report to the Advisory Committee on Civil Rules (1996) at 57, 139 (Fig. 53) (hereinafter FJC Study). A preliminary version of the study's findings by the same authors is available in An Empirical Analysis of Rule 23 to Address the Rulemaking Challenges, 71 N.Y.U. L. Rev. 74 (1996). The FJC Study also showed that 42% to 64% of the fairness hearings in class actions in the four district courts were concluded without any presentation of objections. FJC Study at 57, 178 (Tbl. 38).

24. FJC Study at 58. Objections to attorneys' fees were made in 21 cases (18%), but in 19 of those cases the court nonetheless awarded the full fee requested by class counsel. See id. As to appeals, only 3 of the 90%-plus approved settlements,were ap-

pealed and in only one of those three cases was the approval of the settlement reversed. See id. at 191 (Tbl 51), 193 (Tbl. 53). There were 10 appeals of attorneys' fees awards with varied results. See id. at 77, 191–194 (Tbls. 51–54).

25. For a discussion of judicial incentives in class action suits, see Koniak & Cohen, supra, at 1122–30.

26. 452 U.S. 89 (1981).

27. 452 U.S. at 101.

28. 604 F.2d 449 (5th Cir.1979).

29. Id. at 102. See also Rossini v. Ogilvy & Mather, Inc., 798 F.2d 590 (2d Cir.1986) (upholding an order restricting communications between class counsel and the class against a challenge under Gulf Oil).

Collusion

While many commentators and the press describe the primary problem with class actions as too many frivolous suits,[30] John C. Coffee, Jr., an influential and prolific commentator on class and derivative suits,[31] identifies collusion as the greater threat. Coffee describes the plaintiffs' lawyer as an entrepreneur, performing the socially useful function of deterring undesirable conduct.

This arrangement encourages vindication of publicly-created rights that otherwise would not be enforced, but engenders two problems: (1) pursuit of some claims where the total social costs (public costs plus defendant costs) are greater than any social benefits (bad over-enforcement of law); and (2) collusive settlements that are in the interest of the plaintiffs' lawyer and the individual defendants but which sacrifice the interests of the plaintiff class (bad under-enforcement of law).

To make the case for collusion as the greater threat, Coffee starts with the observation that private and social incentives to litigate bear no necessary relationship to each other. Because the public bears a substantial portion of the costs of litigation, an excessive incentive to litigate may thus exist under some circumstances. He notes, however, that empirical evidence indicates that this is probably not the case in class and derivative actions. Although fee awards in these cases range between 20–30 percent of recoveries, they decrease in percentage as the recovery increases. Thus plaintiffs' lawyers have an incentive to settle more cheaply as the damages involved increase. Litigation stakes are asymmetric, with the defendant focusing on the total award and the plaintiff's attorney focusing on the fee, which is a declining percentage of the recovery.

Coffee emphasizes that by severing the fee award from the amount of the settlement or judgment, the lodestar method of determining the attorney's fee has unfortunate consequences. It provides incentive and opportunity for defendants and plaintiffs' attorneys to "arrange collusive settlements that exchange a low recovery for a high fee award."[32] He suggests that alternatives to the lodestar approach may be desirable: (1) allowing lawyers to buy claims and pursue them (lawyers would then have an incentive to expend effort up to the socially optimal position); (2) awarding damages that are a multiple of actual harm (dangers of over-deterrence are offset by the low risk of detection that accompanies many forms of illegal behavior); and (3) providing for an increasing percentage of fee as the recovery increases.

Plaintiffs' lawyers in derivative actions should be viewed as risk-preferring repeat players who hold a diversified portfolio of cases, whereas

30. A classic statement of this view can be found in Milton Handler, The Shift from Substantive to Procedural Innovations in Antitrust Suits—The Twenty–Third Annual Antitrust Review, 71 Colum.L.Rev. 1, 89 (1971).

31. See, e.g., John C. Coffee, Jr., Understanding the Plaintiff's Attorney: The Implications of Economic Theory for Private Enforcement of Law Through Class and Derivative Suits, 86 Colum.L.Rev. 669 (1986); John C. Coffee, Jr., The Regulation of Entrepreneurial Litigation: Balancing Fairness and Efficiency in the Large Class Action, 54 U.Chi.L.Rev. 877, 88389 (1987).

32. Id. at 691.

officers and directors are risk-averse one-time players. "The contrast is similar to that between a fully diversified investor and an investor who holds only a single speculative asset."[33] Coffee reasons that the best strategy for a plaintiff's lawyer in this field is to bring a substantial number of actions, but devote relatively little time to any of them. This behavior is "less an extortionate attempt to exploit the cost differential that favors plaintiffs' attorneys than a means of achieving the only form of risk spreading available to plaintiffs' attorneys in small firms."[34]

Coffee concludes that collusive settlements are the serious problem in the area, not extortion. One set of interests (that of plaintiff classes) is systematically sacrificed for the benefit of the other two (plaintiffs' lawyers and defendants). Courts are both unable and unwilling to prevent the "covert exchange of a cheap settlement for a high award of attorney's fees."[35] In shareholder derivative suits, for example, the fact that the officers and directors receive indemnification only if wrongdoing is not found provides a strong incentive for the control group to settle cases for a juicy fee award wholly apart from litigation merits. Officers and directors also have an incentive to pay an award on securities charges against the corporation in order to get off the hook on personal liability; and plaintiffs' attorneys have an incentive to go along with this strategy. "[S]ettlements that shift these costs from officers to their corporations both rob the law of its deterrent impact and, paradoxically, force shareholders, who are the intended beneficiaries of the substantive legal standard, to bear the costs of the actions."[36]

Two devices to deter nuisance actions (the bond requirement in derivative actions and the judicial reliance on the report of a special litigation committee) shift the odds against plaintiffs, but the latter has had the paradoxical effect of increasing the number of derivative suits. Because the special report procedure is extremely costly and time-consuming—often requiring two years and a cost of $1 million—its effect is to reduce the effort that a plaintiffs' lawyer devotes to cases while increasing their number. The cost of the process facilitates collusive settlements: The plaintiffs' lawyer can underbid the cost of the committee procedure.

Coffee argues that "good intentions"—the profession's and courts' desire to regulate the bounty hunter as a fiduciary—have had bad results. The lodestar fee encourages collusive settlements; other reforms (such as the litigation committee approach) may encourage the extortion of nuisance suits. Reforms that will be effective must operate on the incentives of the plaintiffs' attorney and be self-policing. To address these problems Coffee proposes that fee awards be stated in terms of percentage of recovery and provide either for multiple damages, prejudgment interest or a marginally increasing percentage.

---

33. Id. at 705.

34. Id. at 711–12.

35. Id. at 714.

36. Id. at 720.

As class action practice has evolved from the old small-claims class actions to new large-stakes, chiefly mass tort, class actions, new forms of collusion have arisen—forms that require new thinking about remedies. In the following excerpt, Coffee explains how the evolution of class actions has produced new forms of collusion and some variations on the old forms as well.

John C. Coffee, Jr., "Class Wars: The Dilemma of the Mass Tort Class Action"

95 Columbia Law Review 1343 (1995).[37]

. . .

... Throughout the 1980s, corporate defendants vigorously resisted the use of the mass tort class action, preferring even the alternative of a bankruptcy reorganization. But with the 1990s, their perception of the class action has changed dramatically. Defendants have not only adopted the class action as their preferred means of resolving their mass tort liabilities, but have also actually begun to solicit plaintiffs' attorneys to bring such class actions (as a condition of settling other pending litigation between them)....

... [T]his transformation is of historic significance: once a sword for plaintiffs, the modern class action is in some contexts increasingly becoming a shield for defendants. Rather than serving as a vehicle by which small claimants can aggregate their claims in order to make litigation economically feasible (and thereby also gain negotiating leverage vis-a-vis defendants), the mass tort class action now often provides a means by which unsuspecting future claimants suffer the extinction of their claims even before they learn of their injury.

Why is this happening? The one safe generalization about mass tort class actions is that the traditional safeguards used by courts to guard against collusive settlements have little value or relevance here. Three basic factors explain the unique vulnerability of the mass tort class action:

First, courts themselves are "conflicted" because of the threat of docket inundation from individual mass tort cases, and thus they may be more willing to countenance doubtful settlements that they probably would not otherwise accept....

Second, the court's primary tool for regulating plaintiffs' attorneys in class actions—judicial control over plaintiffs' attorneys' fees—is less effective in the mass tort context because defendants can (and do) offer inducements to settle that are largely beyond the court's control.

Third, even when individual class members hold legally meritorious claims for significant damages, client passivity may remain the norm because many (and sometimes virtually all) class members are "future claimants"—that is, persons who have not yet experienced any symptomat-

37. Copyright © Columbia Law Review. Reprinted with permission.

ic illness or disease, but rather share only a statistically enhanced risk of future illness or injury because of their exposure to a toxic product or process. To the extent that future claimants will remain rationally apathetic about a legal proceeding brought in their name (because they may have a low probability on an individual basis of experiencing actual, compensable injury), defendants have a strong interest in resolving such an action at an early stage well before any such class members experience injury and thus have an incentive to monitor their attorneys' conduct.

One other preliminary distinction needs to be understood about class actions. Although there are gray areas at the margin, class actions divide economically into "small claimant" classes and "large claimant" classes. In the former context, individual claimants lack legal claims that would be economically viable if asserted on an individual basis, while in the latter context most class members can attract competent counsel to represent them in individual actions on a contingency basis. Securities and antitrust class actions in particular tend to be thought of as "small claimant" classes, whose members cannot afford to opt out and pursue individual claims. Personal injury class actions, however, are populated by many class members with large individual claims. This distinction between "small claimant" and "large claimant" class actions helps to explain one other initially puzzling feature of class action practice and behavior: sometimes corporate defendants resist class certification vehemently, and sometimes they rush to embrace it (even soliciting the action). Under closer examination, defendants' behavior is consistent and rational. In "small claimant" class actions, defendants tend to resist class certification (because plaintiffs have no realistic alternative), whereas in "large claimant" classes, defendants increasingly prefer class certification for a variety of reasons, including both their desire to avoid repetitive awards of punitive damages and their hope to reach a "reasonable" global settlement with cooperative plaintiffs' attorneys.

. . .

C. The "Old" Collusion

Collusion within the class action context essentially requires an agreement—actual or implicit—by which the defendants receive a "cheaper" than arm's length settlement and the plaintiffs' attorneys receive in some form an above-market attorneys' fee. The mechanics of such an agreement varies with the litigation context. In the corporate and securities litigation settings, the standard means has been the nonpecuniary settlement: the plaintiff sues for money damages, but the final settlement awards only therapeutic relief—new bylaws, additional disclosure to shareholders, and other frequently cosmetic changes. In return for this bloodless settlement, defendants either pay the plaintiffs' attorneys' fees themselves or agree not to contest the plaintiffs' attorneys' application for court-awarded fees from the corporation. In the latter case, the plaintiff shareholder class suffers twice: first, by the abandonment of their claim for money damages, and second, by the payment of a fee by their corporation to a plaintiffs' attorney who has not performed any valuable service.

In the mass tort and antitrust contexts, a variation on the nonpecuniary settlement (known informally as a "scrip settlement") has become popular, involving discount coupons or certificates granting the injured class the right to buy the defendant's product at a discount. Often, the discount is no greater than what an individual plaintiff could receive for a volume purchase, or for a cash sale, or for using a particular credit card, and typically restrictions are placed on its transferability....

. . .

[M]ost of the cases in which dubious nonpecuniary consideration has been the primary basis for settlement have been "small claimant" class actions....

. . .

One "old" form of collusion is not limited to the "small claimant" class action. It involves what this Article will call a "reverse auction," namely a jurisdictional competition among different teams of plaintiffs' attorneys in different actions that involve the same underlying allegations. The first team to settle with the defendants in effect precludes [by granting a broad release in the settlement] the others(who may have originated the action and litigated it with sufficient skill and zeal that the defendants were eager to settle with someone else). A recent recurring scenario involves an inactively litigated action in state court being brought and settled so as to preclude a decision in a more aggressively litigated federal action....

The practical impact of this approach is that it allows the defendants to pick and choose the plaintiff team with which they will deal. Indeed, it signals to the unscrupulous plaintiffs' attorney that by filing a parallel, shadow action in state court, it can underbid the original plaintiffs' attorney team that researched, prepared and filed the action. The net result is that defendants can seek the lowest bidder from among these rival groups and negotiate with each simultaneously.... [38]

... No explicit agreement among the participants [in the reverse auction] is needed; all that is necessary is that each team of plaintiffs' attorneys sees that it can be divested of any participation in the action unless it reaches a settlement with the defendants first....

D. The "New" Collusion

1. Inventory Settlements. At least potentially, courts can respond to signs of collusion (or, more precisely, "non-adversarial" settlements) by reducing the plaintiffs' attorneys' fee award....

---

38. [Editor's Note:] A detailed example of this phenomenon can be found in Epstein v. MCA Inc., 126 F.3d 1235 (9th Cir.1997) (a collateral attack on a state settlement, holding absent class members are not bound to the sell-out state settlement because of class counsel's abysmal representation of their interests and are therefore free to pursue their federal claims in feder-al court). This rare (and we think correct) condemnation of class counsel's representation has, however, been withdrawn. The Ninth Circuit panel, with one changed judge, granted reargument and reversed the earlier decision, 2–1, but without a rationale that commanded a majority. 1999 WL 359511 (9th Cir. June 7, 1999).

... [But] the mass tort plaintiffs' attorney typically has an inventory of cases that the attorney represents on an individual basis. Often, the inventory may exceed several thousand cases. Thus, the plaintiffs' attorney's tactical goal is to expedite cases, pushing them through the pipeline to the eve of trial (and predictable settlement). Conversely, defendants in the mass tort setting are concerned less about existing cases than future claimants, who may dwarf the number of present claimants because of the long latency period associated with mass torts.

[Thus,] the possibilities for a deal ... [are present]: both sides have an incentive to trade a settlement of the plaintiffs' attorney's entire inventory (on terms favorable to the attorney) for a global settlement in a class action of all future claims (on terms favorable to the defendants). . . .

In return for the inventory settlement, the plaintiffs' attorney will be expected to serve as class counsel in a class action brought as a "settlement class" against the same defendants. By definition, a settlement class "action" cannot go to trial, and thus defendants need not fear litigation in the event that the two sides have a subsequent falling out. The critical step in this trade requires a special definition of the class: [all claimants who have not filed their claims by a certain date are members of the class]. This allows class counsel to exempt their inventory without looking too obvious and may forestall objectors because it allows the defendant to offer sweet inventory settlements to other plaintiffs lawyers in exchange for a tacit (or explicit) agreement not to object to the "future claimant" ("futures," for short) class action.]

To ensure that the plaintiffs' attorneys do not "welch" on their deal by settling their inventory cases and then refusing to file [or not object to the filing of] the "future claims" class action, the defendants may also require . . . plaintiffs' attorneys to sign an agreement that they will not in the future represent claimants against the defendants with regard to the same mass tort. . . .

. . .

2. Double–Dipping. . . . [T]he mass tort class action ... permits the attorney to receive two fees: one as class counsel and another as the legal representative of individuals filing claims under [the alternative claims resolution procedure established by the class settlement. Once the class settlement establishes a "claims resolution process," plaintiffs' lawyers, typically representing unsophisticated clients, can routinely charge a contingency fee of 25%, which is generally the cap on fees built into the class settlement] for doing almost no work and assuming no risk because recovery, albeit not too big a recovery, is virtually guaranteed by the alternate procedure and there is no chance of going to trial and losing. Moreover, class counsel has an advantage in recruiting clients to represent because after all that firm "negotiated" the very process the tort victims must now use.

. . .

3. Eligibility Restrictions and Illusory Benefits. Even if a self-interested plaintiffs' attorney is willing to enter into a "cheap" settlement, a problem remains: the court must approve the proposed settlement.... Few, if any, courts would approve a settlement that accorded desperately ill plaintiffs only nominal consideration.... Various tactics to [disguise how cheap the settlement is exist.] ... One is to impose rigorous eligibility criteria that would disqualify many or most within the plaintiff class—but in a manner that is not self-evident to the court or to other third parties.... In classes likely to be dominated by future claimants, another approach is to provide for a very low inflation factor.... Finally, the parties can simply underestimate the number and character of the claims likely to be filed against the settlement fund....

. . .

4. Settlement Classes. Nothing better facilitates collusion than the ability on the part of the defendants to choose the counsel who will represent the plaintiff class....

The new procedure involves negotiations between defendants and plaintiffs' attorneys prior to certification of the class action and, in some particularly dramatic cases, prior even to the filing of the class action. Obviously, this approach allows the defendants to test out settlement terms (potentially with several teams of plaintiffs' attorneys) before any action is filed. Then, when and if an agreement is reached, the action will be filed as a "settlement class." [A class that should the defendant object to certification would in all likelihood not be certified for trial. Sometimes a settlement class is either so big, so diverse or so filled with future claimants that it is a virtual certainty that no court would certify it for trial because it would not be "manageable," a requirement under Rule 23(b)(3).]

From the defendants' perspective, any attempt to reach an agreement by means of a settlement class is a "no lose" proposition: if defendants can obtain agreement from plaintiffs' attorneys and the court to a favorable settlement, the technique advances their interests; if they cannot, they are no worse off and can still object to any attempt by plaintiffs to obtain final class certification [and probably succeed.] More importantly, at least at the pre-filing stage, the plaintiffs' attorneys with whom the defendants are negotiating are always aware that if they do not reach agreement, the defense attorneys can move on and try their luck with a new team of plaintiffs' attorneys. Indeed, this is the critical difference between the evolving "settlement class action" procedure and negotiations between the parties in a conventional class action. In the latter context, if the defendants rebuff plaintiffs' counsel, the plaintiffs' team can litigate to a judgment. In the settlement class action, however, the plaintiffs' attorney has only a commission to settle and not to litigate. Such a plaintiffs' attorney has little more than a right of first refusal on the terms offered by the defendants. As this attorney must be painfully aware, a failure to exercise that option implies only that the option may pass to whomever is next in line.

5. *Restricting Opt Outs: Mandatory Classes and the Limited Fund Theory.* Probably the most aggressive tactic that has been attempted recently in connection with a "friendly" mass tort settlement is the certification of a "mandatory" class action from which class members may not opt out. Normally, a class action seeking money damages must be certified pursuant to Federal Rule of Civil Procedure 23(b)(3), and in such a case, class members have an express right to opt out.

Attempts to obtain certification of a mandatory class action under Rule 23(b)(1)(B) usually seek to rely on the justification that, absent pooling and proration among all claimants, the defendant's limited assets soon will be exhausted to the prejudice of future claimants, who will not receive compensation. There are at least two short answers to this justification: First, bankruptcy handles this pooling function much better, and with superior safeguards and procedures, than does the class action.[145] ... Second, the prediction that one's assets are insufficient to handle future claims is easily made, particularly by self-interested defendants. . . .

[To summarize, the recommendations for reform in this Article rest on] three fundamental principles. . . .

1. Settlement class actions must be monitored by the only participants with the appropriate incentives to monitor: namely, other plaintiffs' attorneys. Although the first step toward reform is the recognition of the same standards for class certification in the "settlement" class context as in "litigation" class actions, the more important and second step is to deny the defendant the ability to select the plaintiffs' counsel. The use of representative steering committees may be the simplest means by which to minimize the opportunistic discretion of the individual plaintiffs' attorney.

2. Future claimants are uniquely exposed in class actions. Time and time again, they have lost not only to defendants, but also to present claimants (and their attorneys). On balance, they appear to fare marginally better in bankruptcy proceedings, whereas the corporation's shareholders fare significantly better in mass tort class actions. Given the limited judicial ability to project either the number and character of future claimants in mass tort cases or the rate of inflation in the distant future, lump sum settlements should be accompanied by a safety valve: some right on the part of the individual litigant to opt out if actual economic benefits are less than projected. . . . [Earlier in the article Coffee raises other concerns about actions involving future claimants: whether they are justiciable controversies under Article III given that most class members have manifested no illness from their exposure to the allegedly toxic substance; and whether Rule 23, as it exists or as it might be amended, allows—or should allow— the certification of futures actions.]

3. The right to opt out needs to be modified and updated to the extent that "future claims" classes are permitted. A delayed right to opt out,

---

145. In particular, claimants in bankruptcy are protected by the "absolute priority" rule, which precludes the debtor's share- holders from participating in the reorga- nized company until all creditors have been paid in full.

triggered by the discovery of a previously latent mass tort injury or illness, would solve many of the problems of both future claimants and settlement classes.

. . .

_____

2.   CASE STUDY: GEORGINE V. AMCHEM PRODUCTS[1]

Georgine v. Amchem Products, Inc.

United States District Court, Eastern District of Pennsylvania.
157 F.R.D. 246 (1994).

■ Before REED, DISTRICT COURT JUDGE

. . .

INTRODUCTION

This is a class action claiming damages for asbestos-related personal injuries or wrongful death. Currently before the Court is the determination of whether the proposed settlement of the class action is fair to the class. . . .

. . .

History of this Litigation

[O]n January 15, 1993 . . . the complaint [in this case], an answer and [a proposed] settlement . . . [was filed with the court, instituting this action. The proposed settlement was between a class of persons exposed to the asbestos products of the] twenty defendant companies represented by the Center for Claims Resolution ("CCR" or the "CCR defendants"). Concurrent with the filing of the action, plaintiffs and defendants filed a joint motion for conditional class certification seeking temporary certification under Rule 23(b)(3) of an opt-out class only for the purposes of seeking approval of the proposed settlement. . . . [The class was composed of all persons (and those in their household) who had been exposed through their jobs to the asbestos products of the CCR defendants and who had not filed suit against those defendants before January 15, 1993. This class thus included some persons then ill from asbestos disease and many persons (the bulk of the class) who were not now ill from their exposure but who might

---

1. All the authors of this book were involved as paid experts on the ethics of class counsel in this case: Geoffrey Hazard, testifying on behalf of the proponents of the class settlement, the defendants and class counsel; Roger Cramton and Susan Koniak testifying on the other side, on behalf of the objectors to the settlement. Susan Koniak has written an extensive critique of the conduct of class counsel, the defendant and the district court in this case, see Susan P. Koniak, Feasting While the Widow Weeps: Georgine v. Amchem Products Inc., 80 Cornell L.Rev. 1045 (1995). Citations to the record are omitted from this reprinting of a portion of the district court's opinion.

become ill in the future. Some members of the proposed class objected to the certification of the class, claiming they were not adequately represented, and to the fairness of the settlement.]

. . .

Findings of Fact

I. THE CLASS AND THE CLASS REPRESENTATIVES

. . .

2. . . . Although the exact size of the class is unknown, it is undisputed that there are many tens of thousands of class members. Over the past fifteen years, the . . . defendant [corporations] have been named in over 180,000 asbestos personal injury claims.

. . .

II. BACKGROUND OF THIS CLASS ACTION

A. *History of the Asbestos Litigation*

13. The Court of Appeals for the Third Circuit has observed that asbestos litigation has been "an unparalleled situation in American tort law." In re School Asbestos Litig., 789 F.2d 996, 1000 (3d Cir.1986). The Judicial Panel for Multidistrict Litigation ("MDL Panel") has summarized what it terms the "most objectionable aspect of asbestos litigation":

> dockets in both federal and state courts continue to grow; long delays are routine; trials are too long; the same issues are litigated over and over; transaction costs exceed the victims' recovery by nearly two to one; exhaustion of assets threatens and distorts the process; and future claimants may lose altogether.

In re Asbestos Prods. Liab. Litig. (No. VI), 771 F. Supp. 415, 419 (J.P.M.L. 1991) (quoting Report of The Judicial Conference Ad Hoc Committee on Asbestos Litigation 1–3 (1991)).

14. The Court of Appeals adds the following, citing the observations of a Philadelphia Common Pleas Judge:

> Results of jury verdicts are capricious and uncertain. Sick people and people who died a terrible death from asbestos are being turned away from the courts, while people with minimal injuries who may never suffer severe asbestos disease are being awarded hundreds of thousands of dollars, and even in excess of a million dollars. The asbestos litigation often resembles the casinos 60 miles east of Philadelphia, more than a courtroom procedure.

In re School Asbestos Litig., 789 F.2d at 1001.

. . .

[By the mid–1980s asbestos litigation had grown into an industry. The plaintiffs asbestos bar was dominated by firms with large numbers of cases, called "inventories." Some cases went to trial, but most cases settled. CCR itself for the first years of existence made many "inventory settlements," block settlements of a plaintiff firm's entire inventory of asbestos cases. But as soon as an inventory settlement was reached, the plaintiffs' firm would start building a new inventory. So in 1991, CCR changed its strategy. It refused to settle any more cases without some guarantee about the future.

[Also in 1991 the Multi–District Litigation Panel, accepted the recommendation of eight judges with heavy asbestos dockets, and transferred all federal personal injury asbestos litigation to this district court for coordinated pretrial proceedings. The Panel voiced its hope that the MDL transfer might foster global settlements of the "asbestos mess," noting that transfer "offers a great opportunity to all participants who sincerely wish to resolve these asbestos matters fairly and with as little unnecessary expense as possible." The transfer made it easier for CCR to implement its no-settlement-of-inventories-without-some-guarantee-about-the-future strategy in that plaintiffs' leverage, the threat of going to trial, was minimized . . . because the MDL judge issued a stay of all trials and made it very difficult for any individual to secure a release from that stay. After the MDL transfer, plaintiffs' and defendants' steering committees were formed for the MDL litigation.

[CCR proposed the following plan: a class action to be filed against its member companies that would set up a framework for settling all future asbestos claims: which claims were worthy of payment, what range of money would be paid for each type of payment-worthy asbestos-caused illness, how many claims would be settled each year and the maximum amount of money that would be paid out each year. CCR proposed its idea to the MDL committee of asbestos plaintiffs' firms. The plaintiffs' committee rejected it, although two plaintiffs' firms seemed more receptive than the others. CCR then continued conversations with those two firms, who became class counsel in *Georgine*.

[CCR offered to settle all the cases in the inventories of the two firms, as soon as an agreement on the "futures" was reached. That "futures" agreement was the settlement proposed to the court in this case. CCR not only settled the inventory of cases in the two firms that became class counsel, it agreed to settle the inventories of any and all other asbestos lawyers who were willing to sign an agreement that purported to obligate those lawyers to advise all their future clients that the provisions included in the *Georgine* settlement were fair and should be accepted by those clients.

[Before the fairness hearing in this case, the court approved and oversaw an extensive campaign to give class members notice of the existence of the *Georgine* case and settlement and the terms of the settlement. Individual notice was sent to union members and some others who could be identified as having worked around the defendants' asbestos products. A considerable media notice campaign was also conducted. That campaign included ads that pointed out that anyone exposed to asbestos might be a member of the class, even if that person was now healthy. But the extent to which now healthy people paid attention is subject to serious question. Making the notice campaign even more problematic was the reality that some exposed to asbestos have no idea that they have been exposed until they contract an asbestos-connected illness.]

. . .

III.   FAIRNESS OF THE SETTLEMENT

A.   *Introduction*

37.   The Stipulation of Settlement in this proceeding is a 106–page document (with a 9–page amendment) which essentially sets up a schedule of benefits and an administrative procedure for compensating class members if and when they meet certain asbestos exposure and medical requirements.

B.   *The Negotiations Between CCR and Class Counsel*

40.   As is amply reflected by the complexity of the Stipulation, the testimony in the record and the parties' knowledge of this very mature litigation, the negotiations resulting in the Stipulation were difficult, lengthy, and time-consuming. Many discussions took place among parties of like interests to those here. Virtually no provision of the Stipulation was not the subject of significant negotiation.

[The Court then conducted an exhaustive review of the settlement terms, which ultimately the Court finds to be fair and reasonable to members of the class.]

. . .

IV.   ADEQUACY OF CLASS COUNSEL

177.   In considering whether it is appropriate to enter a final class certification order under Rule 23 and whether to approve the settlement negotiated on behalf of the class, this Court must evaluate the conduct and adequacy of Class Counsel. The following constitute the Court's findings of fact as to this issue.

A.   *Selection, Qualifications, and Conduct of Class Counsel*

178.   In or around November 1991, it became clear to the CCR defendants and Class Counsel that settlement negotiations in the MDL proceeding would not produce a global agreement among all plaintiffs and all asbestos defendants nationwide. Thus, CCR concluded that it wanted to pursue individual global settlement negotiations on its own behalf . . . [and] approached Mr. Motley and Mr. Locks[, now class counsel, to pursue this goal.] . . .

179.   . . . Mr. Motley and Mr. Locks had been appointed . . . [by the court] as the co-chairpersons of the Plaintiffs' Steering Committee. . . . And CCR was aware that the law firms of Ness, Motley and Greitzer and Locks had played prominent roles in representing thousands of asbestos victims in various national proceedings. . . .

[The court here recounted the impressive credentials of class counsel and their respective law firms, demonstrating their prominence among asbestos lawyers.]

184.   This Court finds that Messrs. Motley, Locks and Rice[, who is a partner of Mr. Motley's] are highly respected for their skills and experience in the asbestos litigation and had and have the knowledge and credibility necessary to negotiate on behalf of future asbestos victims in any global settlement effort. This Court also finds that CCR commenced negotiations with Class Counsel based on their reputation and experience in the asbestos litigation. There is no suggestion in the exhaustive discovery and litigated record that CCR executives or attorneys met and decided to "choose" plaintiffs' counsel with the largest inventory of unsettled claims in order to facilitate a global settlement by creating an atmosphere of collusion. That never happened.

· · ·

B.   *Conflict of Interest*

(1) Settlement of Present Cases and Future Claims

190.   ... CCR communicated to Mr. Motley, Mr. Rice, and Mr. Locks that once the CCR defendants "believed that there was some rational way of dealing with the futures [claims], that [they] were prepared to address the settlement of pending cases." ...

· · ·

197.   ... [T]his Court finds, that, in 1992, it was the CCR's policy not to settle pending cases without some protection for the future. With the negotiation of the settlement in this class action, CCR was exploring a different way to resolve the burgeoning number of asbestos claims, that is a different way of providing some protection for the future. The asbestos bar and the MDL Court were well aware of the CCR settlement policy. The evidence in the record also reflects, and this Court finds, that Class Counsel did not enter into the *Georgine* negotiations for the purpose of settling their pending cases.

198.   Moreover, the evidence reflects, and this Court finds, that the settlement of the inventory cases was not conditioned upon an agreement being finally reached in *Georgine*. It is clear on the face of the inventory settlement agreements, that if the Stipulation of Settlement had not been concluded after the negotiation of the inventory settlements, the inventory settlements nevertheless remained in full effect.

199.   This Court finds that in negotiating the inventory settlements for their present clients and the Georgine Stipulation for the futures class, Class Counsel and CCR bargained vigorously and at arms-length. The settlements reached for both groups of claimants were not negotiated against each other, and Class Counsel worked diligently to negotiate what they considered to be the best possible settlements achievable for each group of claimants. See ... Exhibit SP–300 ([providing critical terms of the

Settlement,] the fairness of the medical criteria and the compensation procedures is evidence of the adequacy of Class Counsel).

200. The Objectors argue that the simultaneous representation of present and future claimants by Class Counsel constituted an impermissible conflict of interest. They offered Professor Roger Cramton as an expert witness on this issue. . . .

201. Professor Cramton testified that, in his opinion, the concurrent representation of a very large number of present clients, whose asbestos cases Class Counsel wanted to settle, while negotiating on behalf of what became the Georgine class presented an impermissible conflict of interest under Model Rule 1.7(b) of the ABA Model Rules of Professional Responsibility. The Court rejects Professor Cramton's conclusion as to the existence of an impermissible conflict of interest because: (1) he lacks of experience in mass tort cases, class actions and asbestos litigation; and (2) because, as described below, the credible evidence in the record does not support his factual predicate.

202. Professor Cramton testified that, as he understood the facts, CCR demanded that "a large portion of the future claimants . . . get no or little monetary recovery" under the class action and that CCR wouldn't talk to Class Counsel "unless [they] agreed to that." [Referring to those with pleural plaque on their lungs but no other asbestos disease.] Professor Cramton's factual assumption that a large portion of future claimants who suffer from an asbestos-related disease will receive little or no monetary benefit under the Stipulation is contradicted by the evidence in the record. Rather, this Court has found that the eligibility criteria for cash compensation are fair and reasonable to the class as a whole and that, while non-impaired pleural claimants will not receive immediate cash compensation unless and until they meet certain medical criteria, these claimants receive a group of valuable benefits in lieu of immediate cash, including the right to claim future money benefits. . . . A significant percentage of these claimants will ultimately develop a compensable injury and receive compensation under the settlement. Further, this Court finds that Professor Cramton's conclusion was outweighed by the opinions of the experts offered by the Settling Parties.

203. The Settling Parties presented the expert testimony of Professor Geoffrey Hazard on this issue. . . .

204. Professor Hazard testified that, in his expert opinion, which this Court credits and accepts, Class Counsel did not have "a conflict of interest that impaired their ability or in any way disqualified them from performing the functions that they performed." The Court accepts Professor Hazard's conclusions: (1) that it was not a conflict for a lawyer to represent two groups of clients with similar claims against a common defendant, in this case, clients with pending claims and future claimants; (2) that this kind of concurrent representation was common practice and not a violation of Model Rule 1.7(b); and (3) that such representation "requires the lawyer to exercise proper judgment and fair mindedness in working out the negotia-

tions concerning allocation of any settlement, but that's part of the job. It doesn't mean you are out of the job.''

205.   This Court accepts Professor Hazard's testimony that in reaching his conclusion that there was no impermissible conflict of interest in this case, he took account of the settlement policy of the CCR defendants, which called for some assurances as to the resolution of future claims before the CCR defendants were willing to embark on a program to settle inventories of present cases. This Court finds persuasive Professor Hazard's explanation that CCR's interest in resolving the litigation, including both present and future claims, was not unlike a typical case where "defendants do not settle cases against the same lawyer involving similar or the same transactions unless they will settle them all, except under extraordinary circumstances.''

206.   Professor Hazard was aware that some of the inventory settlements included a few cases that were as yet unfiled, but were ready to be filed.[2] This Court accepts his opinion that this fact does not change the ultimate conclusion that Class Counsel did not have an impermissible conflict in settling their present cases at the same time that they negotiated the *Georgine* settlement.

207.   Professor Hazard also took into account the contention made by Objectors that since the terms of the proposed *Georgine* settlement were not identical to the settlement terms for the inventory claims, then Class Counsel had an impermissible conflict of interest in their concurrent representation of their present clients and the futures class.... This Court finds Professor Hazard's rejection of that contention persuasive when he explained that pending claimants are not identically situated to future claimants in that they have already incurred at least some of the transaction costs, delays and burdens of the tort system and that present claimants are in certain respects different than future clients. Based on this testimony, this Court finds that it was neither inappropriate nor evidence of a conflict to treat these two groups of claimants differently.

(2) Futures Provisions in the Inventory Settlement Agreements

213.   Objectors argued at the fairness hearing that the language of provisions in the inventory settlement agreements known as the "futures provisions" also created a conflict of interest for Class Counsel.

214.   Before entering into the inventory settlement agreements, Class Counsel had consulted with and had been advised by Professor John Freeman, an ethics expert, in connection with these futures provisions and the class action settlement generally. Professor Freeman advised Class Counsel that ethical propriety on the part of class counsel should be a keystone of any class action settlement. Specifically, as it relates to the issue of the futures provisions, Professor Freeman advised them that it was impermissible to enter into an agreement, known as a "lockout agree-

---

2. [Editor's note:] Review the class definition, which makes people with these claims technically members of the class.

ment," which would amount to an agreement to restrict their right to practice law in exchange for the settlement of pending cases in violation of Model Rule 5.6(b). Based upon Professor Freeman's testimony, this Court finds that before the original futures provisions in the inventory settlement agreements were drafted, it was the expressed intention of Class Counsel to act in accordance with the ethical rules governing the conduct of attorneys. Specifically, this Court finds that it was not the intention of Class Counsel to impermissibly restrict their right to practice law in exchange for the settlement of their pending cases.

[The "futures provisons" originally agreed to by class counsel were later modified. The first version signed by Ness, Motley said the "firm will not file any future asbestos personal injury claims ... against the CCR or any of its current members ... unless the medical evidence support one of the following asbestos-related diagnoses...."[3] The ABA then issued an ethics opinion, ABA Op. 93–371, which was requested by some of the counsel representing objectors in *Georgine,* to the effect that the "futures provisions" violated Model Rule 5.6(b). In light of this opinion, the futures provisions were redrafted.]

221. On June 11, 1993, the January 14, 1993 Ness, Motley inventory settlement agreement was revised and superseded. The amended agreement provided:

> Plaintiff Counsel believes that the criteria set forth in paragraph 5 [are] fair and reasonable criteria and acceptance of CCR's offer will be in the interest of its future clients who do not have a medical condition described in paragraph 5, in that it protects such clients from being forced prematurely to litigate, or settle and release their claims for asbestos injury. Plaintiff Counsel therefore agrees, unless in the exercise of its independent professional judgment, given some unforeseen circumstances, it determines otherwise, to recommend that its clients seriously consider, and accordingly will use its best efforts to encourage, each client to accept this alternative dispute resolution procedure. With respect to all clients who accept this alternative dispute resolution procedure, Plaintiff Counsel agrees to defer filing any asbestos-related personal injury claims against CCR or any of its current members until such time, if ever, as the claimant develops one of the asbestos-related diseases described in paragraph 5.

> · · ·

> ... [T]his agreement shall remain in full force and effect unless and until the Stipulation of Settlement in [*Georgine* ...] is finally approved by the Court, with all appeals, if any, exhausted. Upon final approval of the [*Georgine*] settlement, which includes medical criteria substantially comparable to the criteria of paragraph 5, this Agreement

---

3. [Editor's Note:] Here the futures provisions continued with a list of diseases that excluded pleural plaque claims, which were also excluded under the *Georgine* settlement. Pleural plaque claims were paid by CCR as part of the inventory settlements entered into by class counsel covering their present cases.

shall be superseded by [*Georgine*], except for those who have chosen to opt out in accordance with the orders of the Court.

. . .

223.   The Settling Parties presented the testimony of Professor Freeman, Professor Hazard, and Professor Sam Dash on the issue of the ethical propriety of the futures provisions. . . .

. . .

226.   Professor Hazard . . . testified [as had Professor Freeman] that these futures provisions did not violate Model Rule 5.6. The question, as analyzed by Professor Hazard, was whether it was inappropriate for lawyers who were handling a substantial number of asbestos cases, and who expect to handle a continuing flow of these cases, to state that in their professional judgment pleural cases should not be filed and agree to handle the pleural cases differently in the future. Professor Hazard concluded that the net effect of this statement is not a restriction; rather it is an affirmation about the standards that the lawyers will apply in screening the cases they handle in the future and an affirmation to the defendants that they should not be confronted with certain claims until the claimants are impaired.

227.   Professor Hazard further opined that, even if there were a violation of 5.6(b), it would be neither significant nor material, and that the futures provisions would not have undercut or impaired the loyalty with which Class Counsel acted on behalf of the class members. Rather, the futures provisions represent sober, sensible, humane professional judgment by the lawyers, reflecting experience in this kind of case, that will redound to the benefit of the lawyers' clients.

228.   . . . [T]he Court accepts Professor Dash's statement that the fact that the ABA Standing Committee issued Formal Opinion 93–371, which addressed a different but related futures agreement under Model Rule 5.6(b), indicates that the Standing Committee reached the conclusion that "the factual situation upon which they're opining is not clearly answered by the professional rule and it needs their guidance to lawyers on how to act in the future."

229.   In support of their contention that Class Counsel acted unethically when it entered into the inventory settlements agreements with the futures provisions, the Objectors presented the testimony of Professor Cramton and Professor Susan P. Koniak. . . .

230.   Professor Cramton testified that the [first] Ness, Motley agreement violated Model Rule 5.6 because "the document on its face is a restriction on future practice."[45]

---

45. Professor Cramton also opined that the futures provisions violate Model Rules 1.2(c) and 1.7(b). Having found that the futures provisions did not constitute binding obligations on Class Counsel, this Court finds that they could not have been a violation of Model Rules 1.2(c) and 1.7(b).

231. Professor Koniak testified that even the amended Ness, Motley inventory settlement agreement ... violates Model Rule 5.6 because Class Counsel are agreeing to restrict their advice to their future clients.

232. This Court rejects Professor Cramton's and Professor Koniak's conclusion as to the ethical propriety of the futures provisions because: (1) both lack experience in mass tort cases, class actions and asbestos litigation, such that neither understood how such a good faith commitment could reflect sensible professional judgment of lawyers with extensive experience in asbestos litigation; and (2) neither considered the intent of the lawyers and the parties when entering into the inventory settlement agreements.

233. This Court finds that the revised agreements more clearly reflect the parties' intent when entering into the original inventory settlement agreements, that is the parties originally intended that the futures provisions be a good faith commitment on the part of Class Counsel to recommend the Georgine medical criteria to their own clients. By "good faith commitment", the Court finds that the parties did not intend that the futures provisions create for Class Counsel a binding obligation not to represent clients who wished to sue CCR but who did not yet meet the Georgine medical criteria. [See also Dash Testimony] (intent is required to find a violation of Model Rule 5.6(b)). Indeed, the revised agreements made clear that Class Counsel had simply reached their own independent professional judgment that the terms of the agreement were in the best interest of their future clients.

. . .

C. Collusion

(1) Overview

247. The Objectors final argument as to adequacy of counsel is that the settlement in this class action was the product of collusion, i.e., that Class Counsel "sold out" the interests of the class members to benefit themselves and their present clients. This Court already found, without the benefit of the testimony presented at the fairness hearing, that the settlement appeared to be the product of non-collusive negotiations. Carlough v. Amchem Products, Inc., 834 F. Supp. at 1466. The following findings of fact are based on the evidence presented at the fairness hearing.

. . .

249. ... The Objectors ... argue, through the testimony of Professor John C. Coffee, Jr.,[46] that the inventory settlements are evidence that the settlement of this class action is collusive because they argue that: (1) Class Counsel were paid a premium for the settlement of their inventory cases in exchange for an agreement in this class action; (2) class members would

---

46. [Editors' note:] Professor Coffee provided expert testimony on a pro bono basis because he planned to write on settlement class actions and did not want the receipt of income to reflect on his objectivity. See Class Wars, supra.

have received more of a benefit in the tort system than they do under the Stipulation; and (3) claimants in the inventory settlements received more than they would have under the Stipulation.

. . .

252. This Court finds that when counsel represent a class they certainly can be in a position to sell out the class. For this and other reasons, courts are called upon to approve settlements of class actions to ensure that they are fair to the class. The opportunity to collude is not enough for a finding of collusion, however, especially given this Court's thorough analysis of the fairness of the terms of the class action settlement pursuant to Fed. R. Civ. P. 23. For this Court to find collusion in this case, the Court must find that there are some indications that Class Counsel did indeed negotiate the class action settlement for their own benefit. That is, this Court must find that Class Counsel would not have settled *Georgine* but for the opportunity to settle their inventory of unresolved cases for historical settlement values.

[After the *Georgine* complaint and settlement were filed, the court appointed Professor Stephen Burbank as Special Master to analyze the inventory agreements. Professor Burbank, as the court explained, "compared the value of the inventory settlements with the settlements reached historically between Class Counsel and CCR during the period 1988–92." He used confidential information supplied by the settling parties to make his analysis. He found that the inventory settlements were more or less the *same as, and in some cases lower than* the historical settlements he examined.

[Professor Coffee's objection to this analysis was that the MDL of 1991 had brought with it a stay of all asbestos cases and that stay constituted a significant intervening event, causing the value of asbestos claims to plummet, like a stock gone bad. The plaintiffs could not credibly threaten to go to trial: That was so because they could not secure the MDL judge's release from the stay order; he wanted global negotiations to proceed. Thus, according to Professor Coffee, the fact that the inventory settlements reflected pre-MDL value for cases stuck in the MDL demonstrated that class counsel had received a premium in the inventory settlements for their cooperation in bringing and settling a futures class action, *Georgine*, on terms acceptable to CCR. In addition, Professor Coffee noted that the inventory cases did not have trial dates, which should have reduced their value; that the inventory settlements included some cases that were unfiled, which should have reduced the overall value of the inventory; and that the CCR defendants received no "volume discount" in the inventory settlements, which in an arms-length transaction one might expect to see.]

. . .

266. [On Coffee's main claim, that the MDL changed the value of the inventories,] this Court finds that the CCR defendants never had a policy to seek a discount for the settlement of federal cases based upon the MDL

stay order, and never offered less than historical averages for the settlement of pending federal cases as a result of the MDL.

[The Court also noted that the majority of the inventory cases, between 70 and 90 percent, were state cases unaffected by the federal MDL stay. As to the unfiled cases, the Court emphasized that Coffee had no idea how many unfiled cases were in the inventories and that class counsel assured the Court that it was not a large number. Moreover, CCR had sometimes in the past settled unfiled claims. As to the last point on volume discounts, the Court found "no historical [sic] or otherwise compelling reason for expecting that Class Counsel would reduce their fee under the circumstances."]

. . .

272. In sum, . . . this Court finds that the settlement amounts in the inventory settlements were generally consistent with historical settlement averages for comparable settlements with CCR, were not inflated, did not include a premium paid to Class Counsel in exchange for the Georgine settlement, and were not the product of collusion.

278. Professor Coffee . . . [also based] his opinion on collusion . . . [on] a comparison of the value of the benefits to be received by the *Georgine* class members with the benefits received by similarly situated claimants in the inventory settlements. Professor Coffee argues that the claimants in the inventory settlements received more than they would have under the Stipulation. This valuation was based upon Exhibit O–170.[47]

. . .

281. This Court has . . . found that, during the course of the settlement negotiations in this class action, there were reasons for decreasing the values in the compensation schedules in the Stipulation from CCR's historical averages. These reasons included the fact that the Stipulation involves a waiver of defenses to qualifying claimants by the CCR defendants; that payments under the Stipulation should, in most cases, be made faster than under the tort system at considerably lower transaction costs, including attorneys' fees; and finally, that qualifying claimants with non-malignant conditions will be able to receive additional compensation if and when they contract cancer. Professor Coffee's inquiry . . . ignored these reasons, and thus the Court finds his opinion on this issue unpersuasive.

---

47. [Editors' Note:] Exhibit O, which Professor Coffee compiled, is a comparison of the total amount of money Class Counsel's inventory settlement clients would have received under *Georgine* had they each received the *high-end* of the negotiated average included in the settlement for each disease category. The exhibit is reproduced in full and analyzed in Koniak, supra, 70 Cornell L. Rev. at 1067. The chart shows that Ness, Motley's inventory clients did as a whole 54% better than the group would have done under *Georgine*; the inventory clients of Greitzer & Locks, the other class counsel firm, did 72% better than they would have under *Georgine*. See id. at 1067–68. *Georgine* and the inventory deals were negotiated simultaneously.

282.   In sum, the Court finds that an objective review of the record evidence does not persuade the Court that the Stipulation was the product of collusion. . . .

. . .

[The Court found the notice adequate and, as previously noted, the settlement fair and reasonable to all class members.]

Closing Discussion

No one disputes the notion that settlement is a preferred alternative to costly time-consuming litigation. This Court has been presented with an intricate comprehensive settlement plan on behalf of a nationwide opt-out class. . . .

Unlike the tort system, the settlement provides certain and prompt cash compensation to all class members who have suffered impairment or death as a result of their exposure to asbestos. The CCR defendants, in exchange, have waived all liability defenses except proof of exposure to one of their asbestos products. To all those class members who do not suffer an impairing asbestos-related disease, the settlement provides certain benefits, including the right to certain cash compensation if and when they become sick.

Also unlike the tort system, the claim procedures under the [settlement] are essentially non-adversarial; most qualifying claims of persons . . . will be settled for sums within a range of dollar values similar to the historical values paid by CCR over recent years. These settlements will include limitations on claimants' counsel fees and binding arbitration for most exceptional and extraordinary claims. A small number of unusually exceptional and difficult claims will be allowed to return to the tort system.

The CCR defendants have committed to the payment of a likely $1.289 billion (plus $317 million in costs) to settle anticipated claims under the Stipulation over the first ten years of its operation. And, because CCR was able to reach the settlement in this class action, it has further committed an additional $1.626 billion over the next four years to settle the inventory of cases presently pending in the tort system.

This case has received a great deal of attention from the press and from the asbestos bar and has been the subject of much debate. However, this Court has been determined to decide the fairness and jurisdictional issues assigned to it fairly and objectively and to stay removed from the fray. This Court has been constantly aware of whose interests are ultimately at stake in this lawsuit: the class members and the defendants. . . .

. . .

The inadequate tort system has demonstrated that the lawyers are well paid for their services but the victims are not receiving speedy and reasonably inexpensive resolution of their claims. Rather, the victims' recoveries are delayed, excessively reduced by transaction costs and relegated to the impersonal group trials and mass consolidations. The sickest of victims often go uncompensated for years while valuable funds go to others who remain unimpaired by their mild asbestos disease. Indeed, ... unimpaired victims have, in many states, been forced to assert their claims prematurely or risk giving up all rights to future compensation for any future lung cancer or mesothelioma. The plan which this Court approves today will correct that unfair result for the class members and the CCR defendants.

. . .

... This Court has determined that the terms of the settlement are fair and reasonable to the class and that the settlement itself is an innovative solution to a long-standing problem. The settlement calls for non-adversarial claims resolution procedures, sophisticated recognition of discreet asbestos-related diseases, and has been determined by some of the best medical experts in the field to cover almost all victims who are disabled or die as a result of their exposure to CCR asbestos products.

. . .

In sum, this settlement is a fair solution for these parties to a problem that left alone would cause unfair results for the asbestos victims and predictably unfortunate financial downfall for these defendants. Just as the CCR defendants have an interest in the fair compensation of all victims of asbestos disease as a result of exposure to their products, asbestos victims who are in this class have an interest in the continued financial viability of the defendant companies so that they will receive historically-based values for their claims. The settlement approved here resolves these concerns.

————

Supreme Court Rejection of *Georgine* in *Amchem Products*

The Third Circuit overturned the district court opinion in *Georgine*, holding that settlement classes had to meet all the requirements of ordinary class actions—actions that were filed to be litigated if no settlement were reached. The court of appeals held that, given the conflicts within the *Georgine* class and the circumstances that make the class unmanageable as a litigation class, the class could not be certified for purposes of settlement. The settlement proponents petitioned for certiorari, which was granted.

The Supreme Court also rejected the settlement class (and thus the settlement) in *Georgine*, although on somewhat narrower grounds. Under the rubric of Amchem Products, Inc. v. Windsor,[48] the Court held that settlement classes did not have to meet the "manageable for trial" requirement of Rule 23(b)(3), which ordinary classes have to meet, because settlement classes are not intended to be tried. On the other hand, settlement classes filed under Rule 23(b)(3) have to meet all other requirements of that section of the rule, just as ordinary classes do, as well as all

---

48. Amchem Products, Inc. v. Windsor, 521 U.S. 591 (1997).

the requirements of Rule 23(a), which opt-out and non-opt-out classes (those filed under Rule 23(b)(1) and 23(b)(2)) all have to meet. Rule 23(a) requires, among other things, that the class representatives be adequate, implementing the due process requirement that class members be adequately represented laid down in Hansberry v. Lee.[49] Longstanding judicial interpretation of the "adequacy" requirement insists that this means class counsel as well as the named class plaintiffs must be adequate.[50]

The Supreme Court said in part:

The safeguards provided by the Rule 23(a) and (b) class-qualifying criteria, we emphasize, are not impractical impediments—checks shorn of utility—in the settlement class context. First, the standards set for the protection of absent class members serve to inhibit appraisals of the chancellor's foot kind—class certifications dependent upon the court's gestalt judgment or overarching impression of the settlement's fairness.

Second, if a fairness inquiry under Rule 23(e) controlled certification, eclipsing Rule 23(a) and (b), and permitting class designation despite the impossibility of litigation, both class counsel and court would be disarmed. Class counsel confined to settlement negotiations could not use the threat of litigation to press for a better offer[51] . . .

. . .

. . . [T]he Third Circuit's appraisal is essentially correct[, a]lthough that court should have acknowledged that settlement is a factor in the calculus. . . . [W]ith or without a settlement on the table—the sprawling class the District Court certified does not satisfy Rule 23's requirements. . . .

The District Court concluded that predominance was satisfied based on two factors: class members' shared experience of asbestos exposure and their common "interest in receiving prompt and fair compensation for their claims, while minimizing the risks and transac-

---

49. 311 U.S. 32, 37 (1940).

50. See, e.g., Wagner v. Lehman Brothers Kuhn Loeb Inc., 646 F.Supp. 643 (N.D.Ill. 1986), counsel for the class engaged in unethical conduct by offering to pay a witness a percentage of any recovery in exchange for favorable testimony and interviewing the opposing party without informing that party's counsel. The court held that this unethical conduct barred the lawyer from representing the class: "An inquiry into the character of counsel for the class-representative is also necessary because he stands in a fiduciary relationship with the absent class." "Unethical and improper actions" by counsel for the plaintiff class,

Wagner holds, result in a determination that "he cannot adequately represent the putative class in accordance with his fiduciary duties." 646 F.Supp.at 661–62. See also, Greenfield v. Villager Industries, Inc., 483 F.2d 824, 832 (3d Cir.1973); Stavrides v. Mellon National Bank & Trust Co., 60 F.R.D. 634, 637 (W.D.Pa.1973).

51. [Editor's Note:] The Court cited Coffee's Class Wars article reprinted supra and quoted from Judge Easterbrook's dissent from the denial of rehearing en banc in Kamilewicz v. Bank of Boston Corp., 100 F.3d 1349 (7th Cir.1997): "[Parties] may even put one over on the court, in a staged performance."

tion costs ... in the tort system." 157 F.R.D. at 316. The settling parties also contend that the settlement's fairness is a common question, predominating over disparate legal issues that might be pivotal in litigation but become irrelevant under the settlement. The predominance requirement stated in Rule 23(b)(3), we hold, is not met by the[se] factors.... The benefits asbestos-exposed persons might gain from the establishment of a grand-scale compensation scheme is a matter fit for legislative consideration, but it is not pertinent to the predominance inquiry. That inquiry trains on the legal or factual questions that qualify each class member's case as a genuine controversy, questions that preexist any settlement.

[The court then went on to hold that the differences in this "sprawling class," including, different levels of exposure to asbestos, different illnesses (including no present illness), different medical histories, and different state laws applicable to the claims, made it apparent that common questions of law and fact did not predominate over differences.]

Nor can the class approved by the District Court satisfy Rule 23(a)(4)'s requirement that the named parties "will fairly and adequately protect the interests of the class." The adequacy inquiry under Rule 23(a)(4) serves to uncover conflicts of interest between named parties and the class they seek to represent....

As the Third Circuit pointed out, named parties with diverse medical conditions sought to act on behalf of a single giant class rather than on behalf of discrete subclasses. In significant respects, the interests of those within the single class are not aligned. Most saliently, for the currently injured, the critical goal is generous immediate payments. That goal tugs against the interest of exposure-only plaintiffs in ensuring an ample, inflation-protected fund for the future....

. . .

The settling parties, in sum, achieved a global compromise with no structural assurance of fair and adequate representation for the diverse groups and individuals affected....

Although the named parties alleged a range of complaints, each served generally as representative for the whole, not for a separate constituency.... "... [T]he adversity among subgroups requires that the members of each subgroup cannot be bound to a settlement except by consents given by those who understand that their role is to represent solely the members of their respective subgroups." In re Joint Eastern and Southern Dist. Asbestos Litigation, 982 F.2d 721, 742–743 (2nd Cir. 1992), modified on reh'g sub nom. In re Joint E. & S.Dist. Asbestos Litig., 993 F.2d 7 (2nd Cir.1993).

The Supreme Court did not rule on the alleged conflicts between the inventory clients and the class. However, its holding on the conflicts within the class and the need for subclasses means that class counsel cannot purport to represent at once presently-ill and the not-yet-ill because the interests of those two groups are seriously in conflict within the class. Does that imply that the same lawyer or set of lawyers are inadequate representatives of a class, if they simultaneously negotiate with the same defendant a class deal for the not-yet-ill (futures) and another deal for the presently-ill (their inventory clients)?

As the excerpt from the district court opinion makes plain, the authors of this book are not in agreement on the application of the conflict of interest rules to class actions. Hazard's position is heavily influenced by the practical need for sensible and efficient means of resolving the claims of those injured by "mass torts," and the lack of any legislative response to this need. Cramton and Koniak are respectively quite and mildly sympathetic to Hazard's concerns, but see the dangers of relieving class counsel from the conflicts rules as great enough to outweigh the benefits to be gained by using class actions to try and achieve a "more rational" system of handling mass torts. We leave further discussion and analysis to you.[52]

3. CLASS LAWYERS AND LAWYERS FOR OTHER ENTITY CLIENTS: COMMON PROBLEMS?

Susan P. Koniak and George M. Cohen, "In Hell There Will Be Lawyers Without Clients or Law," in Ethics in the Practice of Law (Deborah L. Rhode, ed.)

. . .

The less one's entity client resembles a large, publicly held corporation, the less sense the ethics rules [on representing entity-clients] make. The only rule specifically applicable to entity representation, Model Rule 1.13, addresses a particular crisis in the lawyer's relationship to an entity client: what a lawyer should do when she discovers that a constituent of the organization is violating duties to the organization or violating the law in a manner that might be imputed to the organization. In the representation of large, publicly held corporations this is *the* crisis, the crisis of the rogue manager or, worse yet, the rogue officers or directors. With its singular focus on this crisis, Rule 1.13 implies that in other situations, representing an entity is not much different from representing a person or at least so simple a matter that no particular guidance is required. When the client is a corporation, this position is at least tenable, because in the absence of lawless management, it is reasonable for a lawyer to defer to directions from management or the board just as the lawyer would defer to directions from an individual client. Such a stance is consistent with and, indeed

---

52. See also Ortiz v. Fibreboard. Inc., 119 S.Ct. 2295 (1999) (the Supreme Court's most recent pronouncement on class action practice, addressing, inter alia, class counsel's conflicts and the practice of locking victims of mass torts into non opt-out classes by asserting that the defendant's assets will be insufficient to pay all present and future claimants)

vindicates, the corporate form—a form that presumes that shareholders invest management and the board with the power to direct corporate activities, and insists that managers and directors act as faithful fiduciaries in exercising that power. The ethics rule on entity representation presupposes, and depends upon, the checks and balances that have evolved as a matter of corporate and agency law. To take an important example, corporate law is fuzziest when the corporation is on the verge of bankruptcy. With no clear answer in law on who speaks for the corporation in this situation, Rule 1.13 is of little use, as lawyers representing failing savings and loans discovered to their detriment. In general, however, the comprehensive legal backdrop makes it tenable to posit that only when management breaches its fiduciary duties must the lawyer cease to treat the decisions of managers as if they were comparable to the decisions of an individual client.

Not all entity-clients are corporations, however. They do not all share the same central crisis and, when an analogous crisis does present itself, lawyers for other entity clients may find that the remedial measures dictated by Rule 1.13 make little sense, despite the bold insistence of the rule's comment that the lawyer's duties "apply equally to unincorporated associations."

Let's start with partnerships. Two of the central crises in the representation of partnerships involve seemingly analogous situations to the crisis most likely to occur in corporate representation. When a majority of the general partners breach fiduciary duties owed the minority of general partners and when general partners breach fiduciary duties to limited partners, the lawyer for the partnership is in an analogous position to that of the corporate lawyer who discovers a manager engaged in illegal conduct. Rule 1.13, however, provides much more guidance to the corporate lawyer and is relatively unhelpful to her partnership-lawyer counterpart. The Rule presumes a formal hierarchy of control within the entity client, which the lawyer may use to help protect the entity from the lawlessness of its agents. In plain language, the Rule tells a lawyer to make her way up the entity's chain of command, bringing the misconduct to ever-higher levels of authority in an effort to bring the lawless agent into line. When general partners act in breach of fiduciary duties to limited partners or to a minority of their peers, to whom should the lawyer appeal? The partnership lawyer is likely to begin at the place Rule 1.13 marks as an end: advising the highest authority designated to act on behalf of the entity—typically all general partners—to abide by the law, and in all likelihood meeting resistance.

More troublesome, the crises central to the representation of other entity clients, like classes, are simply not analogous to those that plague corporations. In class actions, the big problem is not that those designated to represent the class as typical plaintiffs or defendants (the named representatives) are likely to act lawlessly and thereby harm the class; the problem is that class lawyers will subordinate the class's interest to their own. In fact, the class is entirely a creation of the lawyer: class counsel control its beginning, its end, its shape, its conduct. Rule 1.13 assumes that a well-defined entity exists with a hierarchical structure protected by legal checks and balances, and that an agent other than the lawyer is available to monitor the lawyer and direct the lawyer's effort. The Rule therefore simply does not speak to the problem of lawyer-domination of the entity client, which is at the core of all the difficult situations that confront class counsel.

Class actions are merely an extreme example of a more general point about the lawyer-entity relationship. That relationship depends on the law that structures or fails to structure the entity client. The more that internal and external rules structure an entity, for example, by designating the agents authorized to speak, listen and act on behalf of that entity, the easier it is for lawyers, authors of ethics rules, commentators and courts to conceptualize how lawyers should act in representing those entities, and to envision and address the crises likely to plague particular entities. On the other hand, the more formless the entity—the less defined it is by internal or external law—the more difficult it is to speak coherently about what lawyers should and should not do.

... [The] law [of class actions] condemns both collusion and inadequate representation, at least that's what the court opinions say.... [But we contend, along with Coffee, Macey, Miller and other commentators that both collusion and inadequate representation are rampant. How can that be?]

. . .

[A] court (or, for that matter any institution or individual) may say something is law and treat it as if it were not. To be law, as opposed to a string of words, ... two things must be true about them: they must divide actions that occur in the world into valid and void, lawful and unlawful; and they must entail real consequences. If any and all conduct meets a particular "standard," or if the violation of the standard never results in tangible consequences to the violator, we put it to you that the "standard" is no "standard" and certainly not a rule of law.

"Class counsel has adequately represented the class" is a mantra. Some form of that phrase can be found in virtually every class action settlement opinion, seemingly without regard to what class counsel has actually done. In most cases, the court does not even bother to construct a story describing class counsel's activities. Instead, courts content themselves by summarizing class counsel's resume in the most laudatory terms and by making conclusory statements about how well-respected, talented and above reproach class counsel is.[22] ... [E]ven in those cases [where the

---

22. See, e.g., ... South Carolina Nat'l Bank v. Stone, 139 F.R.D. 325, 331 (D.S.C.1991) ("Plaintiffs' counsel have now practiced before this court in a number of securities fraud class actions, and the court is aware from first-hand experience of their competency in this complex area of law. The Court is satisfied that the plaintiffs and their class counsel will fairly and adequately protect the interests of the class"); In re Washington Pub. Power Supply Sys. Secs. Litig., 720 F. Supp. 1379, 1392 (D.Ariz. 1989) ("Both Class Counsel and counsel for Chemical Bank deem the settlements to be

rare presence of objecting counsel forces a court to address the actions of class counsel,] the courts manage not to create any law of adequacy, leaping as they do from the actions of counsel to the conclusion that those actions are adequate without pausing to explain the content of the standard they purport to be applying.[23]

.   .   .

The extant "law" prohibiting collusion is as illusory as that guaranteeing adequacy. One must search high and low for a court decision rejecting a class settlement on the ground that it was collusive. Unlike adequacy, collusion is sometimes defined by the courts. Nevertheless, the definition sets such a high bar for "collusive" conduct, equating it with . . . criminal fraud, that the definition itself seems to guarantee the "no collusion" result. . . .

[The state of class action law is, of course, not lost on class counsel and other lawyers in the class action world. The dilemma for [these lawyers] is not that they are tempted to act immorally albeit, within the bounds of the law, which is the dilemma many legal ethics scholars insist is at the heart of the subject they teach and study. Nor is the dilemma simply that class action law is uncertain, and so lawyers are tempted to go beyond the bounds of the law. Rather, the ethical problem is that in a very real sense these lawyers are operating in a world without law. Their representation knows no bounds.]

The absence of law to control lawyer conduct in class action cases extends much further than we have thus far suggested. Class action "law" imposes little structure on the entity of the class, and to the extent it fails to do so, it leaves class counsel with what amounts in practice to virtually unlimited discretion to create, control, and manipulate her client: the class. A class is a unique entity in our legal system. Its true "owners," the class members, do not voluntarily form the entity. In fact, unlike any other legal entity, there is no law of class formation, save for the skimpy requirements of Rule 23. Nor, unlike any other legal entity, is there any law of "authority," that is decisionmaking power, within the class. Without this structural law as a foundation, ethics has nothing on which to build.

. . . While class action law demands that each class have named representatives, the law nowhere defines what the responsibilities of those representatives are either in relation to the rest of the class or in relation to class counsel. . . . In Amchem Products v. Windsor, the Supreme Court referred to the "representational responsibilities" of the named representatives and insisted that separate named representatives be appointed for

---

fair, reasonable, adequate and deserving of the Court's approval. Counsels' opinions warrant great weight both because of their considerable familiarity with this litigation and because of their extensive experience in similar actions").

23. See generally Susan P. Koniak, Feasting While the Widow Weeps: *Georgine v. Amchem Products, Inc.*, 80 Cornell L. Rev. 1045, 157, 1090–92 (1995).

subgroups within the class ... But the Supreme Court never said what those representational responsibilities were [nor did it speak of the responsibilities of counsel.] What point is there in insisting that separate named representatives be appointed for subgroups within a class, if class counsel need not follow the direction of the named representatives or even keep the named representatives informed of the case's progress [practices permitted under current law]? [Although the Supreme Court recently clarified that class counsel, not just the class representatives, must be free of serious conflicts of interests, it left quite vague the standards that lower courts should use in evaluating class counsel's adequacy; did nothing to clarify the appropriate relationship between counsel and the class representatives; and noticed but refrained from criticizing the practice of counsel negotiating a settlement before "appointing" class representatives to serve as named plaintiffs in the "settled" lawsuit counsel now intends to file.][24]

... [C]lass action law ... [also] says virtually nothing about the relation of objectors to the class or to class counsel.[53] Objectors are

24. [Editors' Note:] The Supreme Court in Ortiz v. Fibreboard Corp., 1999 WL 412604 (U.S., June 23, 1999), had an opportunity to address the conduct of class counsel, some of the same actors who had been counsel in Amchem Products. Ortiz like Georgine (Amchem) involved the settlement of inventory cases by class counsel while negotiating a "futures" class settlement. Geoffrey Hazard testified substantially as he had in Georgine (Amchem) that class counsel were adequate representatives of the class. John Leubsdorf testified on class counsel's conflicts on behalf of the objectors. Neither Koniak nor Cramton testified or otherwise worked for any party in Ortiz. The inventory settlements provided that the clients would be paid x dollars with one-half x due upon execution of the inventory settlement and the remaining one-half to be paid upon the occurrence of any one of three events. Two of the three events involved resolution of a case between Fibreboard and its insurers, matters that class counsel had no ability to control, and the third payout-triggering event was the negotiation of a class settlement for "futures" acceptable to Fibreboard. Class counsel negotiated such a settlement and the inventory clients benefitted. The Court rejected the Fibreboard class settlement on the ground that the class had been improperly certified as a non opt-out class under Rule 23(b)(1). The Court was urged by an amici brief filed on behalf of some law professors, including Cramton and Koniak, to address the responsibilities of class counsel, the conflict between inventory clients and the class and the conflicts of counsel in negotiating on behalf of a class as diverse as the class in Georgine (Amchem). The Court stated clearly that counsel, not just the class representatives, must be free of conflicts and that subgroups within the class in conflict with one another were entitled to independent counsel free of obligations to other subgroups within the class. The Court also mentioned with disapproval class counsel's competing obligations to clients outside the class, the inventory clients.

53. [Editors' Note:] In California Public Employees' Retirement System v. Felzen, 119 S.Ct. 720 (1999), the Court considered the long-neglected question whether objectors must intervene in the proceeding to have standing to appeal. The Seventh Circuit had held that objectors were required objectors to have intervened (or tried to do so) in the fairness hearing to have a right of appeal, Felzen v. Andreas, 134 F.3d 873 (7th Cir.1998). The Supreme Court affirmed by an equally divided court, with Justice O'Connor not participating. While it is true that class members can collaterally attack judgments and settlements in class actions on the ground that they were denied their due process rights to notice and adequate representation, see Hansberry v. Lee, 311 U.S. 32 (1940), prevailing in a collateral attack is no simple matter and many questions, notably the fairness of a

technically still members of the class, but the case law is silent on whether that means that objectors continue to be clients of class counsel ... [or whether or not clients, what counsel's duties to these people are].

The emptiness of the legal concepts of adequacy and collusion, together with the law's failure to define the rights and responsibilities of class counsel and the various constituent members of the class (named representatives, objectors, opt-outs and absent members) combine to create a free-zone of activity in which class lawyers can essentially do what they please. If one understands that in class action practice, defense counsel and plaintiffs' counsel have much to gain by cooperating to ensure that class counsel has wide discretion to dispose of the claims of the absent class, it is fairly easy to understand how this lawless state of affairs might result. Put simply, no subgroup within the bar has a strong interest in seeing any other subgroup involved in this area of practice constrained by the rule of law. With no subgroups within the bar to argue for or construct law constraining lawyer conduct in this field, we find no such law.

To decide what a class lawyer is supposed to do—what constitutes adequate representation—the relationship of the various components of a class to one another and then to the lawyer must be fleshed out. The more ephemeral the client, the more abstract and ultimately empty the lawyer's duty to that client will be. In short, class action abuse will thrive as long as the components of a class are as ill-defined as they are now. When one's client is unknowable or incoherent, one's duty will always be unclear. The law needs to make the class client coherent by explicating how its parts fit together and how they are designed to interact with the lawyer. With meaningless law and shapeless clients, the lawyer's self-interest is her only guide. The unchecked self-interest of lawyers drives class action practice today. That needs to change and asking the right questions is the first step.

In hell there will be lawyers without clients or law.[34] It is time legal ethics scholars talked about that.

---

settlement, are not properly the subject of collateral attack. Class members are presumptively bound by decisions in a class action, including approval of a class settlement; only certain issues may be raised on collateral attack; and, as a practical matter, class members have little access to the details of a settlement or the adequacy of counsel prior to the trial court issuing an opinion in the matter. Under these circumstances, the idea that class members are barred from appealing unless they first intervened, something not mentioned in any notice of a class action we have ever seen, borders on absurd. But cf. Marcel Kahan & Linda Silberman, The Inadequate Search for 'Adequacy' in Class Actions: A Critique of Epstein v. MCA, Inc., 73 N.Y.U. L. Rev. 765 (1998) (arguing against collateral attacks on the question of adequacy of counsel and for a requirement that all questions as to the representation be raised at the fairness hearing on the settlement or be deemed waived).

34. This warning (repeated in the title of this essay) is inspired by Grant Gilmore's famous closing to his book, The Ages of American Law: "In Heaven there will be no law, and the lion will lie down with the lamb.... In Hell there will be nothing but law, and due process will be meticulously observed." Grant Gilmore, The Ages of American Law 111 (1977).

CHAPTER 9

THE BAR AS A LEGAL AND SOCIAL INSTITUTION

A. INTRODUCTION

1. HISTORICAL SKETCH OF AMERICAN LEGAL PROFESSION

In their beginnings, the colonies had few trained lawyers, and their citizens dealt with legal formalities as best they could. In the absence of a regulatory system, anyone could be a lawyer who could use a set of legal forms and maintain a position in argument. Someone who did so more or less regularly for money could call himself a practicing lawyer. So much the better if one had, or pretended to have had, some kind of practice experience in the mother country, for example, serving as a justice of the peace.[1]

The practice of law, however, has been a regulated vocation almost from the time that an identifiable legal profession emerged in this country. As the political economy of the colonies expanded from 1620 to 1776, a legal profession evolved, concentrated in the wealthier and more populous colonies. The skills of practice were acquired primarily by the same means by which technical knowledge was usually transmitted in those days— apprenticeship with an established practitioner. Apprenticeship was essentially a contract whereby tutelage was provided by the master in return for scut work by the apprentice, such as scrivening documents and running errands. The apprenticeship system could accommodate only a limited number of new entrants, restraining competition within the profession. Quality of training necessarily varied widely. The system undoubtedly favored sons and relatives of existing practitioners. In time, weight was given to years of college education in place of apprenticeship years.

Concerning the colonial period, historian Michael Burrage says:

Seven colonies required periods of apprenticeship, ranging from three years in Delaware to seven in New York and New Jersey. New York and Massachusetts granted some exemption for college education and also set additional requirements for those wishing to practice as barristers in the higher courts. New Jersey, imitating the English bar,

---

1. For history of the beginnings of the English legal profession, see Symposium, 5 Law and History Rev. 1 (1987); Jonathan Rose, The Legal Profession in Medieval England: A History of Regulation, 48 Syr. L.Rev. 1 (1998). For a review of historical sources on the American legal profession, see Olavi Maru, Research on the Legal Profession c. 1 (2d ed. 1986).

had a third, higher coopted order of serjeants.[2] Virginia and South Carolina, with sizable number of lawyers, had no formal training requirements, probably because a large proportion of lawyers in both colonies qualified at the Inns of Court in London. Virginia seems to have expected those not trained in London, and certainly those who wished to appear in the higher courts, to serve a four-year apprenticeship. In sum, the principle of a specialist, trained, select bar seems to have been accepted in the majority of the colonies. However, it is not always clear whether the bar admission rules were imposed by the governor and the courts or by the practitioners themselves. Only in Massachusetts do we know for certain that the bar devised, administered, and enforced its own admission rules.[3]

Attempts to practice by those who lacked the requisite training, what is today called unauthorized practice of law, were little noticed or recorded. Although someone who represented himself as a lawyer, but who was not, would be subject to an action for deceit or perhaps malpractice,[4] such remedies were costly and worth pursuing only if damages could be both proved and collected. An alternative to a deceit action by the client might have been a suit by the bar to enjoin unauthorized practice by the unlicensed practitioner. As the law of unfair competition stood until the 20th century, however, members of the bar probably would have had no right of action against someone pretending to be qualified as a lawyer.[5]

Prior to enactment of statutes prohibiting the practice of law by unlicensed persons, the bar could do little to prevent untrained people from doing law office work, such as conveyancing and giving legal advice. The bar also could not prevent informal practice in the justice of the peace courts. However, those trained in law practice had two effective controls on law practice by those not admitted to the bar. One was ostracism. Thus, nonlawyers would be excluded from the formal and informal associations of practitioners, hence would be shut out from professional lore and professional gossip. Then as now this kind of access—being a member of "the club"—is important. Second, and relatedly, courts of general jurisdiction had control over the right to appear before them on behalf of others. Admission before the court in turn would be granted only to those recognized by their professional peers who had passed through the apprenticeship process. From an early date the key to entry into the profession was admission before the trial court of general jurisdiction under the auspices

---

2. [Editors' note:] "Serjeants" refers to serjeants at law, a small order of highest level barristers that originated in medieval times and became obsolescent in the 18th century.

3. Michael Burrage, Revolution and the Collective Action of the French, American, and English Legal Professions, 13 Law & Social Inquiry 225, 243 (1988) (containing an excellent summary of the history of the American legal profession).

4. See Wolfram, Modern Legal Ethics § 5.6.1 (1986).

5. See Milton Handler, False and Misleading Advertising, 39 Yale L.J. 22, 29 (1929). In the 20th century it was made a statutory offense for a person not a lawyer to engage in law practice. That prohibition is in turn a basis for injunctive proceedings by the bar to prevent such practice. See p. 992 infra.

of the apprenticeship system. This system apparently was fairly effective at the time the Constitution was adopted in 1787.

At the time of the Revolution, a hardy class of lawyers had established themselves in each of the original colonies. This generation of lawyers played an extraordinary role in creating the new republic (33 of the 55 participating members of the Constitutional Convention in 1787 were lawyers), molding the constitutional structure during the Federalist and Jeffersonian periods and expounding a vision of the "republican" lawyer-gentleman that two hundred years later remains at the heart of professional ideology.

Efforts to "do away with the lawyers" are often an aftermath of a successful revolution. Populist sentiment emanating from the American and French Revolutions culminated in the early 19th century in what was subsequently called the Jacksonian revolution.[6] Measures to abolish any special lawyer prerogatives arose in a few states and spread to others beginning as early as 1801.[7] Deregulation gained momentum over the next four decades: most states reduced or eliminated mandatory requirements for admission to the bar during the first half of the 19th century; professional associations largely disappeared; and opportunities arose in the profession for those of lower socioeconomic status.

> As a result, the American legal profession ... became a heterogeneous occupational category whose "members," if that is the right word, were stratified by their social and ethnic origins, law schools they attended, and places of work. Since they could no longer look to practitioners' organizations to confer distinctive professional honors or titles, they were obliged to earn their status like everyone else in American society by their educational qualifications, their incomes, and their lifestyles.[8]

Does the American legal profession continue to be a "heterogeneous occupational category" today?

Throughout most of the 19th century the practice of law, like the practice of medicine, was not an especially notable, highly rewarded or high-status endeavor.[9] There were no law schools similar to those of today; many lawyers did not have a college degree.[10] Some years later, during the

---

6. See Murray L. Schwartz, Lawyers and the Legal Profession 328–29 (2d ed.1985).

7. Georgia in 1801 required that admission to practice law be allowed simply on application to court; Ohio in 1802 abrogated all requirements for admission, Tennessee in 1809 and South Carolina in 1812. From 1851 to 1933, the Indiana Constitution provided that "Every person of good moral character, being a voter, shall be entitled to admission to practice law in all courts of justice."

8. Burrage, supra, 13 Law & Social Inquiry at 249, 252.

9. The classic discussion is J. Willard Hurst, The Growth of American Law: The Law Makers (1950). See also Maxwell Bloomfield, Lawyers and Public Criticism: Challenge and Response in Nineteenth–Century America, 15 Am. J. of Legal History 269 (1971); Bloomfield, The Texas Bar in the Nineteenth Century, 32 Vand. L. Rev. 261 (1979).

10. Terence C. Halliday & Mark W. Granfors, Class, Status, and Education in the

last decade of the 19th century, 88 percent of newly admitted Chicago lawyers had attended law school, and more than one-half of this group also had a college degree.[11] A major change in the "professionalism" of the bar had occurred gradually throughout the century, resulting in its last decades in changes that some scholars refer to as the "transformation" of the profession.[12]

> [T]he critical developments [in the evolution of the bar from a weak, corporate guild to a powerful, individualistic profession] came in the late nineteenth century as the forces of industrialization posed increasingly complex legal issues that only trained professionals could solve. Like the other [learned] professions, lawyers during these years fashioned a monopoly sanctioned by the state. This monopoly meant that lawyers set the standards for training and admission to the bar, the proper forms of practice, and code of conduct that practitioners were to follow.[13]

The three institutions central to the shaping of the professional ideology and practice environment of the modern legal profession were (1) the law school, (2) the large law firm and (3) the bar association. The American law school as we know it today dates from 1870 when Christopher Langdell became dean of the Harvard Law School. Entrance requirements were imposed (a college degree and competence in Latin); three years of instruction rather than two were required for graduation; and the case method of dialectical teaching replaced lectures and rote memorization of legal texts. This method encouraged the scientific study of law; systematization and rationalization provided an answer to the explosion of knowledge and waning cultural authority of traditional beliefs.

The graduates of the new law schools were largely responsible for another turn-of-the century innovation—the large law firm. The division of legal labor in a larger organization met the specialized needs of corporate clients. Counseling by senior lawyers assisted by the careful research of junior lawyers resulted in a new organizational form of practice, very different from the "oratory and showmanship" of the pre-Civil War generation.[14]

Bar associations as formal and powerful organizations flowed from the desire of relatively elite lawyers to respond to social change and to improve the profession and its standing. Local bar associations were first organized

Transition to Modern Professionalism, 1830–1900, Table 1.

11. Id.

12. See Gerard W. Gawalt (ed.), The New High Priests: Lawyers in Post Civil War America (1984); Wayne K. Hobson, The American Legal Profession and the Organizational Society, 1890–1930 (1986).

13. Kermit L. Hall (ed.), The Legal Profession: Major Historical Interpretations xi-xii (1987).

14. Hall, supra, at xiv. The structure of the large law firm owes much to Paul D. Cravath's organizing principles, which spread to other firms. See Robert T. Swaine, The Cravath Firm (3 vols., 1946–48). For contemporary discussion of the growth of large law firms, see Marc Galanter & Thomas Palay, Tournament of Lawyers (1991).

in the 1870s, beginning with the Association of the Bar of the City of New York in 1877. The number of local and state bar associations grew rapidly at the end of the century, but their activities were primarily social in character until the 1920s. Only 15 percent of all lawyers in 1915 belonged to state bars. The American Bar Association (ABA), formed in 1878, was a small and selective group of lawyers from across the country with a shared concern over preparation and admission to the bar. Its annual meetings at resort hotels in Saratoga, New York were pleasant social events attended by several hundred lawyers. Only after 1921 did the ABA, gradually growing in numbers and influence, begin to have a substantial effect on preparation for and admission to the bar.

Beginning in the 1920s the requirements for entry into the profession were increased.[15] Bar exams, which began in the late 19th century, were improved; requirements of prelegal college education were gradually put in place; and graduation from an ABA-approved law school became a prerequisite for bar admission. Alternatives, such as apprenticeship or study at unapproved schools, most of which were proprietary in character, were eliminated entirely in most states and drastically narrowed in the remainder. These developments were not completed until the 1950s.

2.   WHO REGULATES LAWYERS?

Occupational licensing is endemic in the United States, but the regulation of lawyers has distinct characteristics. First, it is generally created, revised and enforced by the highest court of a state. As the Florida Supreme Court said in Florida Bar v. Brumbaugh,[16] the court is not only an adjudicator but "acts in its administrative capacity as chief policy maker, regulating the administration of the court system and supervising all persons who are engaged in rendering legal advice to members of the general public." The regulatory regimes governing other occupations are created by statute and normally involve an administrative agency exercising delegated rulemaking and enforcement powers. Although "regulatory capture" of the responsible agency is a continuing problem with other licensed occupations, legislative oversight and public involvement may act as a check. In cases like *Brumbaugh,* on the other hand, the state supreme court combines the functions of legislator, enforcer and adjudicator.

Second, in most states the legislature is excluded from participation in the regulation of lawyers.[17] Early American courts, following English practice, assumed that determining the qualifications of those who appeared before them was part of inherent judicial authority. Decisions in many states draw negative implications from this doctrine of inherent authority:

---

15. See Richard L. Abel, American Lawyers 40–73 (1989) (discussing control of the production of lawyers); and Robert B. Stevens, Law School: Legal Education in America from the 1850s to the 1980s (1983).

16. 355 So.2d 1186, 1189 (Fla.1978).

17. For discussion of the inherent-powers doctrine, see Wolfram, Modern Legal Ethics 27–31 (1986); and Charles W. Wolfram, Lawyer Turf and Lawyer Regulation—The Role of the Inherent–Powers Doctrine, 12 U.Ark.Little Rock L.J. 1 (1989–90).

Because the regulation of lawyers is part of the "judicial power" vested in courts, any legislative act dealing with lawyers, unless it is fully consistent with the judicially imposed framework and policy, is said to violate the separation of powers provisions of state constitutions.[18] Why should the most broadly competent policy-making body be excluded from dealing with matters that have a large effect on the availability, cost and quality of legal services, such as group legal services, lawyer advertising and the like? Would the claim of exclusive authority make sense if confined to the lawyer's in-court representation of clients?

Third, bar associations retain a privileged and influential role in the formulation of professional standards. Standards and model codes promulgated by the ABA are studied by state bars, which issue reports that initiate rulemaking consideration by the high court of a given state. Because judges have heavy judicial caseloads, the rulemaking function may be treated in a perfunctory manner or delegated to the chief judge or a small group of judges. Although state supreme courts have exercised more independence in recent years, substantial deference typically is given to bar association views.[19]

Is self-regulation of the profession an essential element of "professionalism?" Or would it be desirable if public regulation of the practice of law were carried on by legislatively created bodies that included nonlawyers as well as lawyers?

Judicial Claim of Exclusive Authority

The highest courts of most states[20] view the grant of judicial power in state constitutions as giving the court the power to regulate lawyers.[21] In a sense, the high courts have inherited the traditional English and colonial practice of courts regulating lawyers through admission and disbarment. Declaration of standards for lawyer conduct in adjudicated cases is implemented by admission, disbarment and, in the twentieth century, the promulgation of ethics codes by the high courts.

In the late nineteenth century, fearing legislative intrusion on the "judicial" domain, many state courts went beyond a statement that they

---

18. See, e.g., Hustedt v. Workers' Compensation Appeals Bd., 636 P.2d 1139 (Cal. 1981) (invalidating a statute authorizing an administrative agency to discipline lawyers in agency proceedings).

19. Charles Wolfram states (too broadly?) that "lawyers, and *only* lawyers, now regulate the legal profession. Lawyers entirely control the process by which lawyer rules of conduct are written and adopted." Wolfram, Modern Legal Ethics 16 (1986).

20. The two largest states, California and New York, depart from the common pattern. In both states, legislative participation in regulation of the bar and the

practice of law has been more extensive than in most other states. In New York, in addition, the rulemaking authority concerning lawyers is divided between the highest court, the Court of Appeals, and the intermediate appellate courts.

21. See generally Charles W. Wolfram, Lawyer Turf and Lawyer Regulation: The Role of the Inherent–Powers Doctrine, 12 U.Ark. Little Rock L.Rev. 1 (1989–90) (viewing the judicial claim of exclusive authority to regulate the practice of law as a "shield behind which the legal profession has staked a claim to self regulation").

could regulate lawyers in the absence of legislation on the subject; the courts made claims of sweeping and exclusive judicial authority to regulate lawyers. Courts can and should protect judicial authority and independence by rejecting efforts of the executive and legislative branches to influence or control the judicial branch in the adjudication of disputes, but the claim of exclusive authority is extraordinary. In practice, the claim is an untenable one, since much general legislation can, does and should apply to lawyers. In many states a complex and inconsistent body of case law holds that in some instances judicial authority is exclusive (the court striking down legislation), in others the legislation is upheld under a comity principle (the court viewing the legislation as consistent with judicial policy), and yet a third category of cases enforce legislative regulation while ignoring the exclusive authority doctrine.

Consider the following illustrative cases:

IDAHO STATE BAR ASS'N v. IDAHO PUBLIC UTILITIES COMM'N.[22] After extensive notice and comment rulemaking proceedings, the state public utility commission adopted a rule concerning representation of parties in proceedings before the commission. The rule provided that a non-profit organization, motor carriers and utilities of small size could be represented by an officer, another representative or an attorney. All other parties could appear only by attorney or pro se. The Idaho State Bar challenged the rule as "in derogation of constitutionally granted Supreme Court control over legal practice in the state." The court held that "constitutionally granted judicial powers include supervision of the practice of law." Although the legislature may enact valid laws in aid of the courts' exclusive authority to regulate the practice of law, any legislation which attempts to alter "standards ... accepted or established by the courts ... is an invasion of the judicial power and violative of [separation of powers provisions in the state constitution]." Because of the quasi-judicial and administrative nature of the commission's proceedings, portions of the rule permitting an officer to represent a non-profit organization or a small utility were upheld (an application of the comity principle); but provisions permitting representation by a third person who was not a lawyer were set aside as infringing the judicial power.

In what way does non-lawyer representation of a party in an administrative proceeding (or a small claims court) involve or interfere with judicial powers?[23]

LLOYD & MICHEL v. FISHINGER.[24] Fishinger was seriously injured in a motorcycle accident. Two days after the accident, Lloyd, a Pennsylva-

---

22. 637 P.2d 1168 (Idaho 1981).

23. *Compare* Florida Bar v. Moses, 380 S.E.2d 412 (Fla.1980) (legislature may define unauthorized practice of law before administrative agencies), *with* Husfedt v. Workers' Compensation Appeals Board, 636 P.2d 1139 (Cal.1981) (legislature may not define who can practice before worker's compensation board).

24. 605 A.2d 1193 (Pa.1992), aff'g 552 A.2d 303 (Pa.Super.Ct.1989). For a discussion of the case and other Pennsylvania "inherent powers" decisions, see Recent Decisions:

nia lawyer, visited Fishinger in the hospital and offered to represent him. Fishinger signed a contingent fee agreement but more than a month later, when he was released from the hospital, Fishinger informed Lloyd orally and in writing that his services were no longer desired. Meanwhile, the liability insurer agreed to settle the claim for the policy limit of $100,000. Lloyd then brought suit against Fishinger claiming breach of the contingent fee agreement. Fishinger moved to dismiss; he relied on a Pennsylvania statute providing that "no attorney shall, during the first 15 days of the confinement of [an injured person in a hospital], enter ... into [a contingent fee agreement] with such patient in connection with his injuries." The equally divided court upheld an intermediate court's decision that the legislation invaded the judicial authority and was invalid under constitutional provisions authorizing the judiciary to regulate the legal profession. Recognizing that the lawyer's conduct violated the Code of Professional Responsibility, the court remanded the case for consideration of whether the lawyer's claim could be pursued consistent with that Code.

New York has never recognized the negative aspect of the inherent powers doctrine.[25] Other states hold that legislative regulation of law practice is unconstitutional only where it infringes directly and injuriously upon the core functions of the courts.[26] Federal legislative authority to regulate the practice of law in federal courts and agencies appears clear but is rarely exercised.[27] Although federal departments and agencies have dealt with representation and conduct issues in their own proceedings, Congress until recent years has left lawyer conduct almost entirely to the states. It remains uncertain whether the pressures flowing from today's world of highly competitive national and international practice will erode the legislative tradition of leaving lawyer regulation to the states. Some lawyer groups urge change, but the ABA and state bar groups strongly support state-based regulation of the profession by high court judges. Since bar groups have more influence with the state high courts than they do with state legislatures or the Congress, the dispute involves the continuing desirability of a substantial degree of "self-regulation" by the profession.

3. INSTITUTIONAL CONTROLS

Legal Structure of Law Practice

As Justice O'Connor suggests in her dissent in Shapero v. Kentucky State Bar, infra p. 1025, being a "lawyer" is a distinct social identity. A

Lloyd v. Fishinger, 66 Temple L.Rev. 499 (1993).

25. See Wolfram, Modern Legal Ethics § 2.2 (1986).

26. See, e.g., State ex rel. Robeson v. Oregon State Bar, 632 P.2d 1255 (Ore.1981) (statute requiring contributions to a professional liability fund and providing for suspension from practice for non-payment was constitutional).

27. See, e.g., Ex parte Garland, 71 U.S. (4 Wall.) 333, 379–80 (1866); Sperry v. Florida ex rel. Florida State Bar, 373 U.S. 379 (1963); see also Matter of Kerr, 424 A.2d 94 (D.C.App.1980) (legislative regulation of law practice flows from Constitutional grants to Congress of power to create the lower federal courts and to define their jurisdiction).

practitioner of law is someone who: (1) graduated from an accredited law school and thus underwent the socialization process of legal education; (2) successfully passed the bar admission requirements and has a certificate to prove it, thereby marking herself off from the large majority of the white collar workforce that does not have such a certificate; (3) primarily is engaged in work that is done exclusively or primarily by lawyers, including preparing and conducting various kinds of litigation and negotiating and documenting various kinds of transactions; (4) spends her day in lawyer work settings, particularly independent law firms and the law departments of government agencies and business corporations; and (5) talks and thinks "law" in shop talk, at professional meetings, in schmoozing with peers after work and in response to conversational gambits at cocktail parties.

Being a lawyer is sustained and influenced by complex institutional structures, far beyond admission requirements and the disciplinary system. Even in the absence of admission requirements and the disciplinary system, the practice of law would still be subject to general legal controls that operate on lawyers along with everyone else. These controls include criminal law, contract law and tort law, including the law of malpractice. Throughout this book we have seen these general legal controls applied to lawyers. Indeed, many of the central provisions in the Model Rules of Professional Conduct and the Model Code of Professional Responsibility reflect or correspond to general rules of common law, particularly the law of agency. These rules of law would continue to operate in the absence of specific regulation of the legal profession and would protect clients and third persons even if there were no restrictions on admission to practice law and no disciplinary machinery.

The common law position, however, is that trades and businesses generally are open to competition. Statutes prohibiting the unauthorized practice of law, i.e., doing what lawyers generally do without being admitted to the bar, have displaced this common law rule insofar as law practice is concerned. The regulation of competition in the delivery of legal services is considered in Chapter 10, but the topic is highly relevant to matters considered here.

Indirect Legal Controls on the Lawyer's Workplace

Law practice is also subject to indirect controls that have legal foundations. Particularly influential on the lawyer's environment are the atmosphere and routines in the law firm or law department in which the lawyer works day-to-day; in other law firms and law departments with which the lawyer interacts in her day-to-day work and by whom she might be employed if she changes jobs; in the courts and the government agencies with whom the lawyer interacts; and in the bar associations in which the lawyer participates. These institutions—the firms, the government agencies and the bar associations—all have political structures and agendas and are subject to economic incentives and constraints. They all have cultural characteristics. For example, some law firms are high pressure and earn high incomes; others are not. Some are very "pro bono" oriented; others are not. Some courts where lawyers appear are well-managed and on top of their calendars; others are bogged down and chaotic. Some government agencies with which lawyers deal have high technical competence and high esprit de corps; others are sluggish and incompetent. Together, these institutions are the matrix of life in which a lawyer tries to accomplish professional tasks, adjusts to the realities of practice and takes on her professional identity.

Systematic studies of careers in law are relatively few. One can imagine studies that take samples from cohorts of graduates from a cross-section of law schools ("elite," "national," state university, "local," etc.) at various years (1960, 1970, 1980, for example) and track their employment patterns over the years. Such studies would show what kinds of jobs graduates begin with (firms, prosecutor offices, sharing office space, etc.), when and where they shift jobs, and when they more or less settle into a permanent career. In 1985, seven law schools cooperated in such a study but only on the condition that the data not correlate the schools with their graduates.[28] Key findings were the following: 70 percent remain in the same metropolitan area in which they took their first law job; about 80 percent of law school graduates remain in law practice or a law-related vocation such as government; 40 percent work in a setting other than a private law firm; 75 percent of those who had been out 25 years had made at least one job change. Lawyers more than 15 years out of law school will have had on the average two or three different jobs. Those most likely to remain in the same work setting for long periods of time are large law firm lawyers and solo practitioners.

A study of Chicago lawyers by John Heinz and Edward Laumann provides the best conceptual formulation of lawyer employment in terms of the structure of contemporary law practice.[29] Heinz and Laumann conclude that the legal profession is highly stratified and has a relatively clear status hierarchy. Variation within the profession is best accounted for, not by the type of legal services rendered, but by the social and economic character of clients. The profession is organized in two hemispheres: lawyers who serve corporate clients and those who serve individuals. Corporate lawyers, who have fewer clients each year than those representing individuals, are often engaged in "symbol manipulation"; those who represent individuals are more often involved in "people persuasion."[30] Because lawyers respond to the interests and demands of their clients, "the nature of the clients served ... primarily determines the structure of social differentiation...."[31] Fields of practice that serve large corporate clients, such as securities, corporate tax, antitrust and banking, are at the top of the profession's

28. See Leona M. Vogt, From Law School to Career: Where Do Graduates Go and What Do They Do?, Harvard Law School Program on the Legal Profession (May 1986) ("Career Paths Study"). The schools were Boston College, Boston University, Columbia, University of Connecticut, Harvard, Northeastern and Suffolk.

29. John P. Heinz & Edward O. Laumann, Chicago Lawyers: The Social Structure of the Bar (1982) (reporting a study based on structured interviews of a random sample of 777 Chicago lawyers in 1975).

30. Id. at 61.

31. Id. at 83.

prestige structure while those serving individual clients in fields such as divorce, landlord and tenant, debt collection and criminal defense are at the bottom. Lawyers who serve the core economic values of American society are accorded more prestige than those who are people-oriented or cause-oriented.[32]

Although social science studies show that lawyers who practice in a particular context for particular clients tend to have many similarities, individual variation should not be overlooked. Consider, for example, the backgrounds of some Supreme Court Justices. For example, Chief Justice Earl Warren was a graduate of the law school of the University of California, Berkeley, and Justice William Brennan was a graduate of Harvard Law School, while Chief Justice Warren Burger was a graduate of William Mitchell Law School and Governors Cuomo of New York and Deukmejian of California went to St. Johns at the same time. This diversity indicates that a full account of the lawyer's vocational matrix would have to include a political, economic, sociological and historical analysis of American legal institutions.

The institutions constituting the lawyer's vocational matrix also have legal structures. Institutions such as law firms, courts and bar associations do not simply exist. They have been created by law or with the authority of law; they have legal powers that affect lawyers; and they are legally accountable in one way or another. See, e.g., Hishon v. King & Spalding (law firm), summarized infra; Shapero v. Kentucky State Bar (bar association), p. 1020. Model Rules 5.1 to 5.3, dealing with the roles and responsibilities of partners, subordinate lawyers and legal assistants, are considered at p. 944 infra.

The legal aspects of this institutional structure are as much a part of the system of professional regulation as are the rules governing admission to practice or those of professional discipline. For example, among the important institutional influences on law practice is the character of the courts in which a litigation lawyer practices and in which a transaction lawyer has to anticipate the transaction may ultimately be litigated. Contrast in this respect the Supreme Court of the United States, whose opinions make up a large part of today's law school curriculum, and the trial court in a state where judges are elected by popular vote.

Suppose, for example, a lawyer had a case involving the publishability of a literary work alleged to be pornographic. Would she handle the matter differently if she took it over after certiorari had been granted by the Supreme Court, as compared with the situation of a client who could not afford to litigate beyond a preliminary injunction in front of the local trial court? It would, of course, make all the difference in the world, or at least all the difference in the United States. Among the differences: The Supreme Court is the Supreme Court, not a one-person local trial judge; the Supreme Court is an instrument of the United States Government, and its judges have tenure effectively for life; the state trial judge faces an election

32. Id. at 127–34.

in the near future, and has to worry about the local news media and being able to raise campaign funding if necessary; the Supreme Court will have amicus briefs from all sectors of the national intelligentsia while the state trial judge may have nothing more than poorly drafted briefs by practitioners who have never before handled a First Amendment case. All these aspects of the case are "legal" in some sense—the rules governing tenure of the judges, the rules defining the participants in the litigation and the character of the forum that determines the kinds of argument that are submitted.

The institutions most directly influencing the lawyer are her situation of employment and her relationship to professional colleagues. Consider, first, the lawyer's employment situation: Although a lawyer's relationship with a client can be terminated by the client at any time and without reason, M.R. 1.16, it does not necessarily follow that the lawyer's employment relationship with a firm or law department similarly is merely "at will." See Hishon v. King & Spalding, summarized below, and the cases dealing with a fired lawyer's retaliatory discharge claim against her employer, p. 948 infra.

General Statutory Regulation of Lawyers' Work

HISHON v. KING & SPALDING[33] was a gender discrimination case brought by Elizabeth Hishon, a female associate at King & Spalding, an Atlanta law firm. The law firm, Hishon alleged, made representations to young associates that advancement to partnership was a "matter of course" for those "who received satisfactory evaluations." Further, the contract for employment provided that partnership decisions would be made on a "fair and equal basis." Of fifty partners at the firm, none were women, and no woman had ever been a partner at the firm. After she was twice rejected for admission to the partnership, the plaintiff filed suit. The question before the Court was whether Title VII applied to partner-selection decisions.[34]

The firm presented three arguments to the Court, all of which were rejected. First, the firm argued that advancement to partner can never be a "term, condition, or privilege of employment" under Title VII since elevation to partner necessarily involves a change in status from employee to employer. In a careful parsing of Title VII, the Court held that "[t]he benefit a plaintiff is denied need not *be* employment to fall within Title VII's protection; it need only be a term, condition, or privilege *of* employment" (emphasis in original). The Court summarily dismissed employer's second argument that Title VII exempted partnership decisions from scrutiny; "[w]hen Congress wanted to grant an employer complete immunity, it

---

33. 467 U.S. 69 (1984)

34. Title VII states in relevant part: "'"It shall be an unlawful employment practice for an employer—(1) to fail or refuse to hire or to discharge any individual, or otherwise to discriminate against any individ-ual with respect to his compensation, terms, conditions, or privileges of employment, because of such individual's race, color, religion, sex, or national origin." 42 U.S.C. § 2000e-2(a).

expressly did so." Employer's third argument that its partner-selection decisions were protected as constitutional rights of expression and association was equally unsuccessful: "[i]nvidious private discrimination ... has never been accorded affirmative constitutional protection.... There is no constitutional right, for example, to discriminate in the selection of who may attend a private school or join a labor union."

In setting out the elements of plaintiffs Title VII claim, the Court noted that a contractual relationship of employment is required to trigger the statute. As to what constitutes a term, condition, or privilege of employment under the statute, the Court stated: "A benefit that is part and parcel of the employment relationship may not be doled out in a discriminatory fashion...." The Court found that the benefit of partnership consideration was linked directly to the employment relationship at issue. Accordingly, the Court ruled that the plaintiff stated a claim under Title VII.

Justice Powell, concurring, relied on plaintiff's allegation that the law firm had obligated itself by contract to consider her for partnership on equal terms without regard to sex. The "enforcement of this obligation, voluntarily assumed, would impair no right of association." But, he cautioned:

> [T]he Court's opinion should not be read as extending Title VII to the management of a law firm by its partners. The ... opinion does not require that the relationship among partners be characterized as an "employment" relationship to which Title VII would apply. The relationship among law partners differs markedly from that between employer and employee—including that between the partnership and its associates. The judgmental and sensitive decisions that must be made among the partners embrace a wide range of subjects. The essence of the law partnership is the common conduct of a shared enterprise. The relationship among law partners contemplates that decisions important to the partnership normally will be made by common agreement ... or consent among the partners.

Why did a large Atlanta firm, King & Spalding, which boasted Jimmy Carter's attorney general as one of its partners, fight so hard to avoid the application of Title VII to partnership decisions? Is there anything to its free speech-free association argument? Is law firm autonomy related to the professional independence that is a celebrated ingredient of "professionalism?"

Gender Discrimination in Partnership Decisions

Ms. Hishon, who consulted nearly a dozen Atlanta lawyers before finding one who would take her case, settled her case against King & Spalding for a damage award. She subsequently practiced real estate law part-time in Atlanta.[31]

---

31. See Elizabeth A. Hishon: Unlikely Plaintiff, Nat'l L.J., Aug. 22, 1983, at p. 28; and Order Bares Partnership Process, Nat'l L.J., Dec. 10, 1990, at pp. 3, 15.

Three major questions were left unanswered by *Hishon* : (1) Does Title VII regulate the relationship among partners? (2) Who is a partner for Title VII purposes? (3) Will the courts grant specific performance in a Title VII partnership case?

As to the first question, Justice Powell's concurrence in *Hishon* states that the case does not speak to the relationship among partners. Powell's dictum is now supported by decisions of several courts of appeals holding that Title VII does not regulate the relationship among partners.[32] On the other hand, if the law firm is a corporation rather than a partnership, a discrimination claim may or may not be available, depending upon the circumstances, to a shareholder/professional who is discharged by the entity.[33]

Hishon did not seek an order directing the firm to make her a partner. Why? Price Waterhouse v. Hopkins,[34] discussed below, suggests that specific performance—an order requiring a firm to elect an employee to partnership—is an available remedy. A lower court decision subsequent to *Hishon* has held that the court has authority to award tenure to a college professor in an appropriate case.[35] But reported cases involving law firms have been limited to money damages;[36] none as yet has ordered specific relief in the form of partnership status.

Suppose a group of lawyers are considering the possibility of setting up a new firm; they want to restrict it on gender, ethnic or religious grounds (e.g., women who want to establish a "feminist" law firm or Mormons who want to practice with co-religionists). Is Title VII violated? What about state anti-discrimination statutes?[37]

---

32. See, e.g., Serapion v. Martinez, 119 F.3d 982 (1st Cir.1997) (discharged partner has no discrimination claim because partners are ""'employers"" and not ""'employees"" for Title VII purposes; citing and discussing cases).

33. *Compare* E.E.O.C. v. Dowd & Dowd, Ltd., 678 F.2d 1177 (7th Cir.1982) (partners of limited liability law partnership were not "employees" under Title VII) *with* Hyland v. New Haven Radiology Assocs., 794 F.2d 793 (2d Cir.1997) (radiologist/shareholder of professional corporation were employees of the corporation for purposes of Age Discrimination in Employment Act (ADEA)) and Wheeler v. Hurdman, 825 F.2d 257 (10th Cir.1987) (question of whether individual is a bona fide partner is decided on a case-by-case basis).

34. 490 U.S. 228 (1989).

35. Pyo v. Stockton State College, 603 F.Supp. 1278 (D.N.J.1985).

36. See, e.g., Ezold v. Wolf, Block, Schorr and Solis–Cohen, 983 F.2d 509 (3d Cir. 1992) (law firm, not the trial judge, determines weight to be given to particular performance criteria; trial court erred in awarding damages based on its own criteria when law firm regularly emphasized legal analytical ability in making partnership decisions), rev'g, 751 F.Supp. 1175 (E.D.Pa.1990).

37. A Massachusetts matrimonial lawyer who, desiring to represent only women had declined to represent a male, was fined $5,000 by the Massachusetts Commission Against Discrimination. Sropnicky v. Nathanson, Mass.Comm'n Against Discrimination, 91–BPA–0061 (Feb.25, 1997). See Judith Eilperin, Female Lawyer Fined for not Accepting Male Client, Nat'l L.J., May 12, 1997, at A7.

Causation and burden of proof in Title VII cases were considered in Price Waterhouse v. Hopkins.[38] Hopkins, described by partners at Price Waterhouse as "an outstanding professional ... with strong character, independence, and integrity," was denied partnership in the accounting firm. Virtually all of the criticism of Hopkins had to do with her "interpersonal skills." She was described as "sometimes overly aggressive" and "macho" and as someone who "overcompensated for being a women." One partner advised her to take a course in "charm school," and another objected to "a lady using foul language." The Court held that the evidence was sufficient to establish that sexual stereotyping played a part in evaluating Hopkins' candidacy for partnership. The plurality opinion held that once a plaintiff establishes that her gender played a part in the employment decision, the burden shifts to the employer to show by a preponderance of evidence that it would have made the same decision had it not taken gender into account. Justices O'Connor and White, who provided the concurring votes, stated that the plaintiff must demonstrate that gender was a substantial factor in the employment decision.

Gender Bias in the Courts

Reports of gender bias in the courts have led to studies and reports in a number of states. In California, for example, the state's judicial council adopted 67 recommendations in 1990 to redress gender discrimination in the operation of the courts and corrections facilities. They include a requirement that juries be instructed in gender-neutral language, a recruitment program to correct lopsided court appointments of lawyers and an ethics prohibition against judges belonging to discriminatory private clubs.[39] The allegations of sexual harassment in the work place by Anita Hill in the confirmation hearings of Clarence Thomas in 1991 focused professional and public attention on this issue.[40]

Other Applicable General Laws

Other federal statutes have been applied to the practice of law. In 1995, for example, the Supreme Court unanimously held that the plain language of the Fair Debt Collection Act's definition of debt collector includes "a lawyer who regularly tries to obtain payment of consumer debts through legal proceedings."[41] When applicable, federal law overrides any judicially-created state policies concerning the special regulation of the legal profession. But separation of powers issues are presented when general state legislation applies to lawyers. Consider a pair of cases decided in 1999 dealing with the question of whether state consumer fraud legislation

---

38. 490 U.S. 228 (1989).

39. See California Judiciary Acts in Effort To Redress Gender Bias in System, Wall St.J., Nov. 19, 1990, p. B8.

40. For discussion of the Thomas hearing, see David B. Wilkins, Presumed Crazy: The Structure of Argument in the Hill/Thomas Hearings, 65 So.Cal.L. Rev. 1517 (1992).

For general discussion of sexual harassment, see Marina Angel, Sexual Harassment by Judges, 45 U. Miami L.Rev. 817 (1991) (sexual harassment by judges is more widespread than most lawyers believe and little has been done to punish it).

41. Heintz v. Jenkins, 514 U.S. 291, 294 (1995).

applies to lawyers. The Texas Supreme Court allowed a claim against a lawyer by parents of twins who had died shortly after birth; the parents alleged that their lawyer had lied to them in saying that he had filed a medical malpractice complaint before the statute of limitations expired.[42] On the other hand, the Illinois Supreme Court rejected a daughter's claim that a lawyer had overcharged for moving two trust accounts of her incompetent mother from one bank to another.[43] Even though the commercial aspects of a service to consumers was involved, and the statute had been held to apply to accountants and physicians, the court stated that it alone regulated lawyer conduct, including billing, and the only remedy other than common law fraud and legal malpractice was professional discipline.

A number of state court decisions struggle with the question whether general statutes protecting consumers from abuses by service providers are consistent with those holding that the highest court of a state has exclusive authority to regulate the practice of law (see p. 839 supra). The Connecticut court, in upholding the application of the state's unfair trade practices act to lawyers, stated that the emphasis of disciplinary rules is ethical and regulatory, whereas that of general regulation is on the prevention of injury to consumers.[44] A number of states, including Massachusetts, have extended their sales taxes to legal services.[45]

B. ADMISSION TO PRACTICE

1. MODERN ADMISSION STANDARDS

Admission to the practice of law today takes the form of admission before the highest court of the state, except in New York, where it takes the form of admission to a lower court. Admission to the court carries with it the right of audience (i.e., to present matters on behalf of clients) in all courts of the jurisdiction, and to engage in law office practice.[1]

A parallel procedure governs admission to practice in federal courts. Admission to practice in a state does not of itself result in admission to practice in the federal courts in that state. Rather, a motion for admission to the federal court must be made. Separate admission is required to each

---

42. Latham v. Castillo, 972 S.W.2d 66 (Tex. 1999). See also Debakey v. Staggs, 605 S.W.2d 631 (Tex.Civ.App.1980), aff'd, 612 S.W.2d 924 (Tex.1981) (holding that treble-damage and fee-shifting provisions of the Texas Deceptive Trade Practices Act, which is intended to protect consumers by regulating ""'services'" as well as the sale of goods, applied when a lawyer acted unconscionably in botching a name change and refusing to return an advance fee payment).

43. Cripe v. Leiter, 703 N.E.2d 100 (Ill. 1998).

44. Heslin v. Connecticut Law Clinic of Trantolo, 461 A.2d 938 (Conn.1983).

45. See Massachusetts Imposes 5% Levy on Range of Services, Wall St. J., July 9, 1990, at p. A2.

1. On the problems created by state-by-state admission in a time of nationwide and international practice, see p. 1056 infra.

United States district court, to each United States court of appeals and to the Supreme Court of the United States. The basic requirement for admission to federal court is that the applicant have been admitted in a state. However, local federal court rules often require in addition a period of practice experience, participation in a number of trials, proof of familiarity with federal procedure or a combination of such requirements.[2]

Today, admission to practice in a state generally entails three requirements: (1) completion of the curriculum at a law school approved by the ABA; (2) passing a bar examination; and (3) meeting a requirement of "good character." Until invention of the bar exam in the latter half of the 19th century, admission required satisfying a judge that the applicant was conversant with the law, providing proof of good character and, in some states, fulfilling an apprenticeship requirement. As noted in the historical sketch, the apprenticeship system yielded uneven products under the best of circumstances. "Good character" was often interpreted to mean acceptability to the local establishment in the bench and bar. The requirement that the applicant demonstrate knowledge of the law could mean almost anything. One 19th century lawyer, who later was a member of the California Supreme Court, recalled that in 1836 the judge administered his rite of passage by "asking not a single legal question."[3] The modern admissions process may leave much to be desired, but it displaced a system that was uneven, frequently indifferent to any matters of qualification and often discriminatory against newcomers in society.

Accredited Law Schools[4]

Three national organizations participate in setting standards and procedures that govern law schools. The ABA, acting through its Section of Legal Education and Admissions to the Bar, has promulgated standards for "approved law schools" and applies these standards through extensive scrutiny of new schools and sabbatical inspections (once every seven years) of previously approved law schools. The ABA is recognized by the U.S. Department of Education as the only accreditation agency for degrees in law.

The Association of American Law Schools (AALS) has as its purpose "the improvement of the legal profession through legal education."[5] The AALS is an association of law schools; of the 183 ABA-approved J.D.-

2. See Wolfram, Modern Legal Ethics §§ 15.2 et seq. (1986).
3. Joseph G. Baldwin, The Flush Times of Alabama and Mississippi: A Series of Sketches (1858; 1957 ed.).
4. Comprehensive data on law schools, law school enrollments and bar admissions requirements are published annually by the ABA Section of Legal Education and Admissions to the Bar (entitled "A Review of Legal Education in the United States, Law Schools and Bar Admissions Requirements"). Bar admission requirements are compiled in an annual publication of the ABA section and the National Conference of Bar Examiners (NCBE) (entitled "Comprehensive Guide to Bar Admission Requirements").
5. See generally Robert B. Stevens, Law School: Legal Education in America from the 1850s to the 1980s (1983); AALS, Report of the AALS Long Range Planning Committee—May 1989.

granting law schools in 1999, 162 are AALS members. The AALS participates in ABA inspection of those law schools that are AALS members and applies membership standards through an accreditation committee. The AALS annual meeting in the first week of January features scholarly programs and other activities of interest to law teachers, librarians and administrators. The AALS also provides a faculty recruitment service, publishes the *Journal of Legal Education* and carries on many other activities.

The Law School Admission Council (LSAC) participates in selecting individuals for law practice through its administration of the Law School Admission Test (LSAT). An ABA standard provides that approved law schools require applicants to submit an LSAT score (with some limited exceptions).

Accreditation by the ABA requires maintenance of specified standards as to curriculum, law library, classroom facilities and faculty. Compliance is enforced by periodic inspections and by the sanction of withdrawal of accreditation. The standards permit a substantial range in faculty-student ratio (but no more than 30 students per full-time faculty member), pedagogical procedure (e.g., "lecture" versus "Socratic method"), clinical instruction, training in legal writing and research, subject matter of courses and relative balance between theory and "nuts and bolts."[6] The ABA Standards for the Approval of Law Schools require that a school "offer ... instruction" in certain areas: "subjects generally regarded as the core of the law school curriculum," "one rigorous writing experience," and "professional skills." However, students are not required to enroll in courses providing such instruction; the only instruction required of all J.D. graduates is "instruction in the duties and responsibilities of the legal profession."[7]

In 1995 the U.S. Department of Justice began an investigation of the ABA accreditation process, focusing on the setting of law faculty salaries. The Department, among other things, alleged that the exchange of data concerning faculty and professional salaries during the accreditation process was combined with ABA pressure on schools when their salaries fell below the median for schools in their region or type. In the law school world, as at Lake Woebegone, everyone must be above average. The investigation ended in June 1995 with the filing of an antitrust complaint along with an ABA consent decree settling the suit and requiring structural

6. ABA accreditation standards were extensively revised in 1996; the new standards are reprinted in ABA J., Aug. 1996, at 129. See generally, Symposium, The Regulation of Legal Education, 32 J. Legal Educ. 159–271 (1982); Barry B. Boyer & Roger C. Cramton, American Legal Education: An Agenda for Research and Reform, 59 Cornell L.Rev. 221 (1974); Note, ABA Approval of Law Schools, 72 Mich.L.Rev. 1134 (1974).

7. See Roger C. Cramton & Susan P. Koniak, Rule, Story, and Commitment in the Teaching of Legal Ethics, 38 Wm. & Mary L. Rev. 145, 146–63 (1996) (discussing the requirement, the failure of many law schools to take it seriously, and the ABA failure to provide meaningful enforcement).

and substantive changes in accreditation.[8] One consequence has been the removal of the ABA House of Delegates as the ultimate accreditation authority. Insofar as accreditation issues are concerned, the Council of the ABA Section on Legal Education and Admission to the Bar now acts as an autonomous body within the ABA .

According to the rules in every state, accreditation of a law school by the ABA constitutes accreditation for purposes of fulfilling that state's requirement of graduation from an approved law school. A few states, including California, separately accredit law schools, so that a law school may be accredited for purposes of admission in that state but not in other states. A handful of states still permit completion of study in a law office instead of completion of law school. This alternative, essentially an apprenticeship, was pursued by Justice Robert Jackson (Supreme Court of the United States, 1941 to 1954) and a good many others in his generation. Today the option is pursued by very few.

Bar Examination

With very limited exceptions, a second requirement for admission to practice is passing the bar exam. Several states recognize a "diploma privilege" under which graduation from a law school in the state fulfills the requirement of legal knowledge.

The legitimacy of the bar exam has often been disputed but remains generally accepted. It is acknowledged that the exam tests only part of the skills required to be a lawyer, and may test those skills imperfectly. However, the bar exam produces documentary evidence that can be reviewed without revealing the applicant's identity and compared with the performance of other applicants. The alternatives are: an interview system, in which personal identity would be important; an apprenticeship system, in which personal identity and family connections would heavily influence selection for the limited number of places; or no qualification test at all.

State bar exams have encountered two sometimes related legal challenges: the subjective grading of exams produces arbitrary results; and exam results are systematically adverse to African–Americans, Hispanics and other racial minorities.[9] The courts have uniformly rejected these challenges, once satisfied that grading was anonymous and conducted by a structured procedure. Charges of subjectivity in grading, even where grading is "blind," have been answered by adding or increasing the multiple-choice portion of the test and by giving an applicant who fails the right to

---

8. See Ken Myers, Settlement Will Mean Changes in ABA's Accreditation Process, Nat'l L.J., July 10, 1995, at A15; Henry J. Reske, One Antitrust Battle Over, ABA J., Aug. 1996, pp. 44–45.

9. Claims that the general "fail" rate on the bar exam had been raised in order to restrain competitive entry into the profession arose in the 1930s in many states, in Cali-

fornia in the 1950s and in Arizona in the 1970s. See Hoover v. Ronwin, 466 U.S. 558 (1984) (denied applicant alleged that Arizona's bar admissions committee had reduced the pass rate to restrain competition; complaint did not state a violation of federal antitrust law because of "state action" exemption).

repeat the exam. The theory is that any arbitrariness resulting from grader subjectivity is unlikely as a statistical matter to repeat itself against the same applicant.[10] Poats v. Givan[11] sustained an Indiana rule limiting an applicant to four attempts to pass the bar exam.

The problem of disparate impact of the bar exam on African–Americans and Hispanics has been raised in a number of states, including California, New York and Pennsylvania. The most systematic challenge appears to have been that litigated in Delgado v. McTighe,[12] involving the Pennsylvania bar exam. The Pennsylvania exam, like that in many other states, included one day of multiple-choice questions (the Multistate Bar Examination) and one day of essay questions formulated and graded by the state's bar examiners. The court found that the essay questions were graded "blind," that errors in grammar and spelling were not counted negatively and that the examiners had established adequate procedures for reviewing initial grades. The court placed heavy reliance on an outside study commissioned by the Pennsylvania Board of Bar Examiners, based on the 1972 exam. The study found that the lower pass rate for African–American candidates would have occurred at whatever combination of scores on the Multistate and essay portions were designated as a passing score.[13] The court in *Delgado* found that the disproportionate failure rate was not due to purposeful discrimination or to any invidious standards or grading procedures. *Delgado* appears to be the last court challenge to bar exams on the ground of discriminatory. The constitutional legitimacy of the current type of bar exam thus seems beyond successful legal challenge.

The court in *Delgado* noted: "The remedy for this situation is beyond the scope of the present inquiry. It seems clear, however, that further improvement in the Bar examination itself, through further increasing the reliability and the validity of the test, will not change the situation."[14] In an article surveying the case law and available data on disparate bar exam performance, Cecil J. Hunt, II, acknowledging that judicial challenges to the bar exam (at least in the near term) are not likely to succeed, argues that changes in legal education might make a significant difference.[15] Law school teaching methods, the heavy emphasis on first year grades and other

---

10. In Lucero v. Ogden, 718 F.2d 355, 358 (10th Cir.1983) for example, where an applicant challenged the Colorado bar exam, the court stated:

> Although the plaintiff asks for "an adversary hearing, an unbiased judge or hearing examiner, the opportunity to argue the facts and cross examine the other party, and the right to present evidence", ... there is nothing to indicate that any of these procedures would be any more effective in detecting grading errors than the absolute right to retake the exam.

11. 651 F.2d 495 (7th Cir.1981).

12. 522 F.Supp. 886 (E.D.Pa.1981).

13. "[A]s groups, the blacks and whites had different distribution of scores on both [portions of the examination]." Because the distribution of white scores was higher than that of blacks, "[n]o matter where the passing point is set, except at the very bottom, more blacks than whites will be failed." 522 F.Supp. at 893–94.

14. 522 F.Supp. at 893–894.

15. Cecil J. Hunt, II, Guests in Another's House: An Analysis of Racially Disparate Bar Performance, 23 Fla. St. U. L. Rev. 721 (1996).

factors, such as the impediments to learning of many students, take a particularly heavy toll on minority students. Hunt argues that the systematic demoralization that minority students are likely to experience in law school can and should be corrected and that doing so might have a significant effect on minority bar pass rates as well as other benefits.

2.   CHARACTER AND FITNESS

In addition to meeting educational requirements and passing a written bar exam, admission to the bar requires fulfillment of a "character and fitness" requirement.[16] Traditionally, proof was supplied through affidavits from people personally acquainted with the applicant, a mechanism still used. Although "character and fitness" are meaningful standards in extreme cases (e.g., prior convictions for embezzling money or mental incompetency), the terms are indeterminate and vague. It is unclear how someone, especially a young person, who has not yet undergone the strain of practice can show the capacity to handle such strain, but character committees in the past generally considered "good background" a propitious indicator. In the late 19th century, the requirement was sometimes employed to screen out applications by African–Americans and women; during the first decades of the 20th century, at least in some localities, the requirement effectively was employed to deter applications by Jews and those of immigrant origin.

Deborah Rhode's comprehensive empirical study documents and criticizes the character and fitness inquiry in operation.[17] The following matters are considered significant but not decisive and hence a basis for more intensive inquiry: criminal record, drug or alcohol abuse, repeated traffic offenses, dishonesty in business transactions, plagiarism and other cheating in school, unauthorized practice of law, psychiatric treatment and nondisclosure or false statements on the bar admission questionnaire. Do these comport with the "rational connection" standard discussed below? Rhode's findings suggest that the inquiry, although invoked fairly rarely, is explored with exasperating detail and troublesome policy implications in some cases. The elusiveness of "character" leads to arbitrary, unpredictable and intrusive results that maintain the profession's sense of shared values by excluding deviants. More troubling, today the inquiry into character for admission to practice is far more rigorous than the standards used for disciplining those already inside the bar.[18] Rhode urges that the inquiry

---

16. See generally Deborah L. Rhode, Moral Character as a Professional Credential, 94 Yale L.J. 491 (1985).

17. See Deborah L. Rhode, Moral Character as a Professional Credential, 94 Yale L.J. 491, 533–36 (1985).

18. Id. at 546. Bar application questions seem to have become increasingly intrusive; at least one state, Georgia, asks all applicants to waive all privacy rights to all medical records and any and all claims of physician-patient privilege, and a number of others ask all applicants to answer detailed questions about medical history. Can you imagine the bar's reaction to any state agency routinely asking a group of applicants for any government license or benefit to waive any and all claims of attorney-client privilege?

into character be entirely abandoned and that more attention be given to discipline of conduct that has harmed clients. Do you agree?

Consider the following cases:

- Prager was indicted in 1983 for organizing and leading a large-scale international marijuana smuggling operation for a number of years. After five years as a fugitive abroad, he returned to the United States, pled guilty and received a suspended sentence plus probation. After graduating from the University of Maine School of Law, he clerked for a justice of the Maine Supreme Court and then applied for admission in Massachusetts. The court denied his admission, but said that he could reapply in five years.[19]

- To finance his undergraduate and law school education, Gahan, an unmarried man without dependents, took out federally guaranteed student loans totaling about $14,000. After admission to practice in California in 1976, he worked for a law firm at an annual salary of $15,000 for six months. When his employer experienced financial trouble, Gahan was out of work for two months. During that period, he filed for bankruptcy. Because of other arrangements, "the only debts actually discharged in the bankruptcy proceedings were the Federally insured student loans." Gahan then applied and was denied admission to practice in Minnesota. The court, recognizing that there were "[n]o other grounds for showing lack of good moral character," held that "applicants who flagrantly disregard the rights of others and default on serious financial obligations, such as student loans, are lacking in good moral character if the default is neglectful, irresponsible, and cannot be excused by a compelling hardship that is reasonably beyond the control of the applicant." To avoid Supremacy Clause problems, the court said its decision was based "solely" on Gahan's failure to satisfy his financial obligations, not on his filing for bankruptcy.[20]

In Re Hale

Committee on Character and Fitness for the Third Appellate District of the Supreme Court of Illinois (1998).

■ JUDGE McCLINTOCK, CHAIRPERSON OF INQUIRY PANEL:

[Matthew F. Hale applied for admission to Illinois bar and passed the bar examination in 1998. His application was referred to the Committee on Character and Fitness of the Third District. A majority of the Inquiry Panel declined to certify Hale. Rule 4.1 of the applicable rules places the burden on the applicant to prove by clear and convincing evidence that he

19. 661 N.E.2d 84 (Mass.1996).
20. Application of Gahan, 279 N.W.2d 826 (Minn.1979). See also Matter of Anonymous, 549 N.E.2d 472 (N.Y.1989) (admission denied because of applicant's inability to handle personal finances, not because of bankruptcy); and Matter of C.R.W., 481 S.E.2d 511 (Ga.1997) (admission denied for failure to show satisfactory payment history on loans of over $35,000).

has the requisite character and fitness for admission to the practice of law. Because the reasons for denial "relate to the applicant's active advocacy of his core beliefs, "a heavy burden lies" upon the State to demonstrate that "a legitimate state interest" is sought to be protected. Baird v. Arizona, 401 U.S. 1, 6–7 (1971). Therefore the panel spelled out its reasons in some detail to guide the Hearing Panel which would now consider the matter.]

The Facts

Matthew F. Hale is 27 years old, attended undergraduate school in Bradley University in Peoria and received a J.D. degree in 1998 from Southern Illinois University School of Law at Carbondale. By his frank admission he is an avowed racist who, since his teenage days, has been actively involved in promoting white supremacy through organizations and by the distribution of literature. This literature portray blacks, Jews, and other minorities in an extreme negative light. . . .

Mr. Hale is currently the head of an organization called the World Church of the Creator which is claimed to be a religious organization. Hit title as head of this church is Pontifex Maximus (Supreme Leader). In the attached autobiography, Mr. Hale has stated that "he would dedicate his life to Creativity," referring to the World Church of the Creator. This religion, according to its founder, Ben Klassen, has as one of its major tenets the hatred of Jews, blacks and other colored people.

Mr. Hale's church admires Adolph Hitler and the National Socialism movement as practiced in Germany, except that it holds Hitler was mistaken in promoting only German nationalism. Instead, his church believes that Hitler's ideas relating to racial superiority should have been applied for the benefit of the entire "white race" as opposed to just Germans.

Mr. Hale and his church disavow violence and an intention to seek the forcible overthrow of the United States Government. However, Mr. Hale stated in his interview with us that if his organization would gain power by peaceable means it would call for the deportation of Jews, blacks and others whom his church refers to as "mud races." The United States would then become a country for members of the "white race" only.

The Inquiry Panel's interview with Mr. Hale occurred on November 25, 1998. At that time, Mr. Hale was extremely polite and answered all questions quite candidly. He is intelligent and articulate. He stated that after becoming a lawyer he would continue his activities as leader of his church, including his distribution of racist literature. He also plans to be active on the Internet to promote his church's racist views.

On the issue of moral character, he argued that his frank and open admission of the advocacy of racism shows greater moral character than do lawyers and others who are in fact racist but who utter such thoughts only in privacy.

Mr. Hale was asked whether or not he could take the oath to support the United States Constitution and the Constitution of the State of Illinois in good conscience. He unhesitatingly answered that he would have no difficulty even though, based on his beliefs, he obviously would be in substantial disagreement with current interpretations of the constitutions. He likened his situation to that of a judge or jury whose duty it is to follow the law even though they may disagree with it.

In connection with the oath, he was shown Article 1, § 20 of the Constitution of the State of Illinois which condemns "communications that portray criminality, depravity or lack of virtue in, or that incite violence, hatred, abuse or hostility toward, a person or group of persons by reason of or by reference to religious, racial, ethnic, national or regional affiliation." In response, Mr. Hale said that to the extent this Illinois constitutional provision limited "communications," it would run afoul of the First Amendment to the Constitution of the United States and therefore would not be binding on him.[1]

Additionally, Rule 8.4(a)(5) of the Rules of Professional Conduct for lawyers was brought to his attention. Mr. Hale was asked if he could abide by that rule if admitted to the Bar. The rule, in part, states that a lawyer shall not

> engage in conduct that is prejudicial to the administration of justice. In relation thereto, a lawyer shall not engage in adverse discriminatory treatment of litigants, jurors, witnesses, lawyers, and others, based on race, sex, religion, or national origin.

Again, Mr. Hale stated that he would have no problem with following this rule, reaffirming his statements that he would follow the law until such time as he could have it changed by peaceful means. He also said that in a recent employment in Champaign where he worked as a law clerk for a few months, he dealt with black clients and engaged in no acts of racism toward them. The accuracy of this statement was confirmed by independent inquiry.

Analysis of Moral Character

As noted, the applicant must establish his "good moral character and general fitness to practice law" "by clear and convincing evidence." (Supreme Court Rules 708(b), 709(b).... If these requisites may be established by simply showing an absence of criminal conduct in the past and having one or more persons vouch for one's character, Mr. Hale has established these requisites by clear and convincing evidence.[2]

On the other hand, if the lack of good moral character and general fitness to practice law may be judged on the basis of active advocacy that

---

1. This Illinois constitutional provision appears to be advisory only and not susceptible of being violated.

2. Mr. Hale was convicted of two city ordinance violations related to the advocacy of his beliefs. The Inquiry Panel attaches no significance to these convictions because countless individuals have been admitted to the Bar with more serious criminal violations. Additionally, the Inquiry Panel has doubts as to the legality or at least the appropriateness of these convictions because they related to the exercise of constitutionally protected activity and Mr. Hale may have been selectively prosecuted on account of his views.

attempts to incite hatred of members of various groups by vilifying and portraying them as inferior and robbing them of human dignity, Mr. Hale has not established good moral character or general fitness to practice law. As indicated, Mr. Hale's life mission is to bring about peaceable change in the United States in order to deny the equal protection of the laws to all Americans except perhaps those that his church determines to be of the "white race." Under any civilized standards of decency,[3] the incitement of racial hatred for the ultimate purpose of depriving selected groups of their legal rights shows a gross deficiency in moral character, particularly for lawyers who have a special responsibility to uphold the rule of law for all persons.[4]

However, even if the Illinois standards for considering moral character and general fitness to practice law allows the Committee to make a determination in this manner, the question remains as to whether or not denying certification for admission to the Bar is constitutional on that basis.

The Constitutional Analysis

At an earlier time the Committee on Character and Fitness might have desired to disqualify Mr. Hale on the ground that, despite his statements to the contrary, his views make it impossible for him to take the required oath "in good conscience." See, e.g., In re Anastaplo, 121 N.E.2d 826 (Ill.1954) and In Re Latimer, 143 N.E.2d 20 (Ill.1957). Also see In re Anastaplo, 163 N.E.2d 429 & 928 (Ill.1959), aff'd 366 U.S. 82 (1961).

Moreover, the Membership Manual for his church, which is on the Internet, describes 15 attributes of a church member under a heading entitled, "The Essence of a Creator." The number 1 essence listed is that "A CREATOR puts loyalty towards his own race above every other loyalty." (http://www.rahowa.com/manual.htm.) A reasonable question for the applicant is what happens when that loyalty conflicts with his oath to support the United States and Illinois Constitutions?

---

3. See references in the United Nations Charter and the UN's Universal Declaration of Human Rights at notes 8 & 9 infra.

4. In the recent case of In re A.L., No. 3–98–96 (3rd Dist. 11/13/98), the Appellate Court cited bigotry as evidence of depravity which has been defined as the opposite of good moral character. See In re Abdullah 423 N.E.2d 915, 917 (Ill.1991), which held that "depravity is 'an inherent deficiency of moral sense and rectitude.' "

Bigotry, as well as evil generally, is bottomed on irrationality. By contrast, our legal system is designed to produce rational results. Individual rights are at the cornerstone of law and justice. These rights are extolled in the Declaration of Independence, the Bill of Rights and other documents cited in this opinion. In our courts, facts matter so that each individual is entitled to be rationally judged on the particular circumstances of his or her case, with an impartial application of the law to the facts.

But the applicant regards these considerations as irrelevant. All that matters to him is whether someone is or is not a member of the "white race," as defined by his church. Such an irrational worship of race for the ultimate purpose of determining legal rights is not only depraved and immoral, but a rejection of all that law, lawyering and judging is meant to accomplish.

Additionally, even though Mr. Hale claimed to be able to abide by the Rules of Professional Conduct relating to non-discriminatory treatment, his activities in this regard arguably cast doubt on these representations. For example, in 1995, only a few weeks before he started law school, he wrote a letter to a woman who apparently had made comments in the Peoria Journal Star on racial issues that were contrary to his. In this letter he referred to "the nigger race" as "*inferior* in intellectual capacity" and condemned the "misbegotten equality myth" as "garbage" that was "destroying" "our whole country." (Emphasis in original.) He also suggested that this woman's rape or murder by a "nigger beast" might enlighten her.

With the applicant capable of such outrageous intemperate conduct, one might have concluded that he was insincere when he said he could comply with the Rules of Professional Conduct and conscientiously take the oath. However, later cases of the United States Supreme Court suggest that these very real questions about the applicant might be a frail reed upon which to deny certification. See, e.g., Bond v. Floyd, 385 U.S. 116, 132 (1966) and Law Students Research Counsel v. Wadmond, 401 U.S. 154, 163–164 (1971), which appear to hold that once an oath to support the Constitution is taken, others cannot urge that it was not taken sincerely.

Finally, an applicant cannot be denied admission to the Bar on a ground formerly announced by the Illinois Supreme Court—"that the practice of law is a privilege, not a right." In Re Anastaplo, 3 Ill.2d 471, 482 (1954). On the contrary, the United States Supreme Court later stated that "the practice of law is not a matter of grace, but of right for one who is qualified by his learning and his moral character." Baird v. Arizona, supra, 401 U.S. 1 at 8.

Absolute First Amendment Rights vs. A Balancing Test

The easiest resolution of Mr. Hale's application would be to certify him. This would be in accord with the view that the First Amendment is virtually absolute. . . .

Certainly statements found in some Supreme Court opinions, taken in isolation and without regard to the specific facts of the cases, might support this view. For example, in the bar admission case of Re Stolar, 401 U.S. 23, 28–29 (1971), it was stated that the State cannot "penalize petitioner solely because he personally . . . 'espouses illegal aims.'"

Nonetheless, on balance, a majority of the Inquiry Panel has concluded that the constitutional issues involving a case precisely like this one are open,[5] and that the Illinois requirement for moral character and general fitness to practice law precludes the applicant from being certified.

---

5. While First Amendment issues in this case are difficult and troublesome, we don't include "the free exercise" of "religion" among them. Our decision would be the same if Mr. Hale professed no religion, and his autobiography shows that his racist views evolved long before he discovered the World Church of the Creator. For an extensive discussion of the case law on the regulation of conduct stemming from religious beliefs, see Employment Division v. Smith, 494 U.S. 872 (1990). "*Smith* held that neu-

The latest United States Supreme Court decisions relating to bar admissions located by the Inquiry Panel are over 25 years old. In 1971, the year of its most recent cases on this subject, the Court characterized its earlier opinions as containing "confusing formulas, refined reasonings, and puzzling holdings." Baird v. Arizona, 401 U.S. 1, 4 (1971).

In that case, the Court, in a 5 to 4 split decision, held that "a State may not inquire about a man's views or associations solely for the purpose of withholding a right or benefit because of what he believes." 401 U.S. 1 at 7. The Court also said in that case:

> The First Amendment's protection of association prohibits a State from excluding a person from a profession or punishing him *solely* because he is a member of a particular political organization or because he holds certain beliefs. (Emphasis added.) 401 U.S. 1, at 6.

Neither [*Baird* or In Re Stolar, 401 U.S. 23, 31 (1971)] involved individuals who were actively involved in inciting racial hatred and who had dedicated their lives to destroying equal rights under law that all American currently enjoy. On the contrary, the applicants in those cases refused to reveal their views.

But in this case Matthew Hale has no interest in keeping his views a secret. In a 1997 interview that appears on the Internet, he said that "we have several websites going now. ...We are ... hoping to expand all these operations ... to give people full knowledge of Creativity...." (http://hate-watch.org/wcotc/haleinterview.html.) And his attached autobiography proclaims "that he looks forward to leading Creativity to worldwide White Victory!"

The case of Elrod v. Burns, 427 U.S. 347, 362 (1976), laid down the following formula for evaluating whether or not a public employee may have his First Amendment rights curtailed:

> It is firmly established that a significant impairment of First Amendment rights must survive exacting scrutiny.... The interest advanced must be paramount, one of vital importance, and the burden is on the government to show the existence of such an interest.

Assuming that the courts would apply the stringent *Elrod* formula for public employees to bar admission cases,[6] we believe that the impairment of First Amendment rights that the Panel's decision affects does survive exacting scrutiny and that the interest advanced with respect to the role of the legal profession, hereafter to be explained, is paramount. The Supreme Court has also utilized a balancing test in public employment cases.[7] In Pickering v. Board of Education, 391 U.S. 563 (1968), the Court said:

tral, generally applicable laws may be applied to religious practices even when not supported by a compelling governmental interest." City of Boerne v. Flores, 117 S.Ct. 2157, 2161 (1997). The latter case invalidated the Religious Freedom Restoration Act of 1993 (42 U.S.C. §§ 2000bb et seq.) which had been enacted for the purpose of overturning *Smith.*

6. This formula appears to be in accord with the Supreme Court's statement in the bar admission case of Baird v. Arizona ....

7. Public employment cases, unlike bar admission cases, usually arise where the par-

. . . it cannot be gainsaid that the State has interests as an employer in regulating the speech of its employees that differs significantly from those it possesses in connection with regulation of the speech of the citizenry in general. The problem in any case is to arrive at a *balance* between the interests of the teacher, as a citizen, in commenting upon matters of public concern and the interest of the State, as an employer, in promoting the efficiency of the public services it performs through its employees. (Emphasis added.)

The Commitment Of The Bar To Fundamental Truths

The balance that the majority chooses requires that a lawyer cannot, as his life's mission, do all in his power to incite racial and religious hatred among the populace so that it will peaceably abolish the rule of law for all persons save those of the "white race." Instead, and by rejecting Matthew Hale's application, let it be said that the Bar and our courts stand committed to these fundamental truths:

- All persons are possessed of individual dignity.[8]

- As a result, every person is to be judged on the basis of his or her own individuality and conduct, not by reference to skin color, race, ethnicity, religion or national origin.[9]

- The enforcement and application of these timeless values to specific cases have, by history and constitutional development, been entrusted to our courts and its officers—the lawyers—a trust that lies at the heart of our system of government.[10]

- Therefore, the guardians of that trust—the judges and lawyers, or one or more of them–cannot have as their mission in life the incitement of racial hatred in order to destroy those values.

Commencing with Jefferson's ringing declaration that all men are created equal, and continuing with the adoption of our Constitution, the Emancipation Proclamation and the Fourteenth Amendment, the moral, ethical and legal struggle for the precious values contained in those

ty seeking relief already holds a governmental position and is not applying for one. See, e.g., Perry v. Sindermann, 408 U.S. 593 (1972).

8. In condemning communications that incite racial hatred, the Illinois Constitution, Article I, § 20, commences with the phrase, "To promote individual dignity, ..." Similarly, the United Nation's Charter refers to "the dignity and worth of the human person" and the UN's Universal Declaration of Human Rights, which was 50 years old this month, recognizes "the inherent dignity . . . of all members of the human family."

9. The documents cited in the preceding footnote condemn discrimination in all

forms and in general echo our Declaration of Independence which holds that "all men" have "certain unalienable Rights," like "Life, Liberty and the pursuit of Happiness."

10. The Preamble to the Illinois Rules of Professional Conduct states that "The practice of law is a public trust." The Preamble later refers to lawyers "as officers of the court." Both of these concepts appear in Illinois Supreme Court cases throughout this century. See, e.g., People v. Payson, 74 N.E. 383 (Ill.1905) and In Re Both, 33 N.E.2d 213 (Ill.1941). Also see Justice Frankfurter's statement [infra].

writings has been costly, difficult and long. The Bar and our courts, charged with the duty of preserving those values, cannot allow Mr. Hale or any other applicant the use of a law license to attempt their destruction.

Finally, and this is the heart of our analysis, the majority's judgment is that to the extent its decision limits the First Amendment activities of lawyers, the fundamental truths identified above are so basic to the legal profession that, in the context of this case, they must be preferred over the values found in the First Amendment. The relationship of the profession to those truths was eloquently described in Schware v. Board of Bar Examiners, 353 U.S. 232, 246 (1957), by the late Justice Felix Frankfurter in a concurring opinion:

> . . . all the interests of man that are comprised under the constitutional guarantees given to "life, liberty and property" are in the professional keeping of lawyers.

The balance of values that we strike leaves Matthew Hale free, as the First Amendment allows, to incite as much racial hatred as he desires and to attempt to carry out his life's mission of depriving those he dislikes of their legal right.[11] But in our view he cannot do this as an officer of the court.

A preference for antidiscriminatory values over the First Amendment would not be new to Supreme Court decision making. Only five years ago the Court unanimously rejected First Amendment claims that "hate crimes" penalty enhancement statutes were invalid. . . . Wisconsin v. Mitchell, 508 U.S. 476.

. . . [T]he Supreme Court had no difficulty in finding the statute constitutional because "hate crimes" are "thought to inflict greater individual and societal harm." 508 U.S. 476 at 488. Arguably, the rationale in this case for preventing the applicant from becoming an officer of the Court is stronger than it was in the "hate crimes" case.

Conclusion

The late Supreme Court Justice Robert Jackson, America's chief war crimes prosecutor at Nuremberg, wrote during World War II in West Virginia Board of Education v. Barnette, 319 U.S. 624, 638 (1943):

> The very purpose of a Bill of Rights was to withdraw certain subjects from the vicissitudes of political controversy, to place them beyond the reach of majorities and officials and to establish them as legal principles to be applied by the courts. One's right to life, liberty and property, to free speech, a free press, freedom of worship and assembly, and other fundamental rights may not be submitted to vote; they depend on the outcome of no elections.

11. Under the First Amendment, a state may not criminalize Mr. Hale's actions in preaching racial hatred "except where such advocacy is directed to inciting or producing imminent lawless action and is likely to incite or produce such action." Brandenburg v. Ohio, 395 U.S. 444, 447 (1969).

Jackson's statement that the immutable principles of the Bill of Rights are to be "applied by the courts" has significance because "[t]here ... comes from the [legal] profession the judiciary." In re Anastaplo, 121 N.E.2d 826 (Ill.1954). Mr. Hale's life mission, the destruction of the Bill of Rights, is inherently incompatible with service as a lawyer or judge who is charged with safeguarding those rights.

The quotation from *Barnette* is important for another reason. Justice Jackson concluded that "fundamental rights may not be submitted to vote." But Mr. Hale wants to do exactly that, and it is a chilling thought indeed, considering that he and his church are admirers of Adolph Hitler, who acquired his absolute power peacefully, "quite legally" and "in a perfectly constitutional manner."[12]

If the civilized world had no experience with Hitler, Matthew Hale might be dismissed as a harmless "crackpot." However, history teaches a different lesson. In his defining study of Nazi German, William L. Shirer concluded his discussion of Hitler's death camps with the following passage:

> There were some ten million Jews living in 1939 in the territories occupied by Hitler's forces. By any estimate it is certain that nearly half of them were exterminated by the Germans. This was the final consequence and the shattering cost of the aberration which came over the Nazi dictator in his youthful gutter days in Vienna and which he imparted to—or shared with—so many of his German followers.[13]

While Matthew Hale has not yet threatened to exterminate anyone, history tells us that extermination is sometimes not far behind when governmental power is held by persons of his racial views. The Bar of Illinois cannot certify someone as having good moral character and general

---

12. The Rise and Fall of the Third Reich, A History of Nazi Germany, by William L. Shirer, Simon and Schuster, New York 1960, pp. 199 and 187. For purposes of our discussion, we find no meaningful difference between a destruction of the Bill of Rights that would accompany an election, as opposed to one that would follow a forcible overthrow of the government. As noted, Nazi Germany was created legally, but the Soviet Union arose out of revolution.

[M]erely holding private theoretical beliefs favoring either form of change is not a legal basis for disqualifying a bar applicant. Again, see Baird v. Arizona, supra, and Re Stolar, supra. Also see Keyishian v. Board of Regents of New York, 385 U.S. 589, 599–600 (1967). However, as Mr. Hale candidly admits, he has crossed a threshold from merely believing to actively inciting racial hatred for the avowed purpose of abolishing the Bill of Rights except for those of the "white race," and he plans to continue to do this as a lawyer.

Therefore, contrary to the dissent's statement, the majority decision does not require that future applications be scoured to determine each applicant's beliefs and opinions. Clearly, and as discussed, the foregoing Supreme Court cases preclude such an activity by a bar committee. Similarly, the majority concludes, contrary to the dissent, that there is a significant qualitative difference between a bar applicant who may disagree with some of our laws, like the Dram Shop Act for example, and one whose life mission is the incitement of racial hatred for the purpose of abolishing equal justice under law—the very principle that the Bar and our courts are charged with preserving.

13. Id., pp. 978–979.

fitness to practice law who has dedicated his life to inciting racial hatred for the purpose of implementing those views.

■ BAXTER, MEMBER OF INQUIRY PANEL, dissenting:

Matthew Hale, in his application and interview, plausibly asserts he can hold racist views and practice law in accordance with his oath as an attorney and there's no evidence of any conduct otherwise.

Until there is such conduct, the holding and even active advocacy of beliefs, no matter how repugnant to current law, cannot be the basis for denial of certification to an applicant who will subscribe to the oath. All lawyers disagree with some laws. Otherwise, character and fitness evaluations will have to review the beliefs and scrutinize the papers, speeches and opinions of every applicant to the bar. This type of scrutiny is not a requirement. It is replaced by the applicant's promise to subscribe to the oath and to comply with the Code of Professional Responsibility.

Time will tell if Matthew Hale can in fact practice law in accordance with his oath while holding extremist views. The Rules of the Attorney Registration and Disciplinary Commission of the Illinois Supreme Court are the profession's and the public's protection against any abuse. That such abuse may occur is only speculation at this time. Matthew Hale clearly understands the distinction.

Political Beliefs and Good Character

From 1947 to about 1970, Communist political beliefs were the concern of many character committee inquiries. Many serious people thought concern about Communist beliefs made some sense, on the ground that it would be difficult to be "an officer of the court" if one believed that law was inherently oppressive. Other serious people thought that there was no correlation between political radicalism, including membership in the Communist Party, and predisposition to violate standards of professional conduct. Moreover, some believed that excluding political radicals from law practice would change the pool of lawyers available to take various types of cases, particularly cases involving political radicals. That in turn would also change the kinds of causes and arguments that would be taken to the courts. The same arguments about the availability of lawyers and the variety of arguments brought to court could be made about lawyers with Hale's views.[1]

What tenets of Hale's beliefs made him unfit for admission according to the character committee? If Hale is unfit to be a lawyer for holding these

1. See Susan P. Koniak, When Law Risks Madness, 8 Cardozo L. & Lit. 65 (1996) (describing the radical constitutionalism of one branch of the militia movement and the troubling attempts by courts to stop the proliferation of this group's virulently racist and otherwise radical agenda, creating precedents that license broad injunctions against the dissemination of certain idea and extra punishment for violations of law that suggest disdain for the current constitutional regime).

beliefs, should the bar's disciplinary committee disbar those already admitted to the bar who hold similar beliefs? How would the committee find them? In any event, no one in Illinois or anywhere else has suggested such a project. Does that undermine the committee's position in *Hale*?

The battles over admitting Communists to the bar resulted in a series of decisions by a closely divided Supreme Court. Schware v. Board of Bar Examiners of New Mexico[2] involved an applicant who was denied admission because of prior membership in the Communist Party and related activities, including: participation in the 1930s in shipyard strikes that became embittered and violent; numerous arrests; use of aliases; and recruiting volunteers for the anti-Franco forces in the Spanish Civil War. Schware quit the Communist Party in 1940. After serving in the Army, he attended law school, graduating in 1953. His rabbi, his attorney, members of the law faculty, fellow students and law school staff testified to his current good character; no witnesses contradicted their testimony. The bar committee nevertheless denied him admission: "Taking into consideration the use of aliases by the applicant, his former connection with subversive organizations, and his record of arrests, he has failed to satisfy the Board as to the requisite moral character." The U.S. Supreme Court reversed the state court's denial of admission, saying:

> Any qualification must have a rational connection with the applicant's fitness or capacity to practice law.... There is nothing in the record which suggests that Schware has engaged in any conduct during the past 15 years which reflects adversely on his character.... During the period when Schware was a member, the Communist Party was a lawful political party.... Assuming that some members of the Communist Party during the period from 1932 to 1940 had illegal aims and engaged in illegal activities, it cannot automatically be inferred that all members shared their evil purposes or participated in their illegal conduct.... There is no evidence in the record which rationally justifies a finding that Schware was morally unfit to practice law.[3]

The "rational connection" rule remains the law. Is *Hale* consistent with *Schware*? Schware apparently had changed his political views by the time he sought admission. What if he had not?

In Konigsberg v. State Bar of California (*Konigsberg I*),[4] decided the same day as *Schware*, Konigsberg had relied on the First Amendment in refusing to answer whether he had been a member of the Communist Party. The Bar Examiners rejected his application, saying that he had failed to establish his good character, not that he had refused to answer questions about his party membership. The Supreme Court in a 5–4 decision reversed:

> Serious questions of elemental fairness would be raised if the Committee had excluded Konigsberg simply because he failed to an-

2. 353 U.S. 232 (1957).   **4.** 353 U.S. 252 (1957).
3. 353 U.S. at 239, 244, 246–47.

swer questions without first explicitly warning him that he could be barred for this reason alone....

If ... the Board had barred Konigsberg solely because of his refusal to respond to its inquiries into his political associations and his opinions about matters of public interest, then we would be compelled to decide far-reaching and complex questions relating to freedom of speech, press and assembly.[5]

On remand, the California bar examiners asked Konigsberg whether he was presently a member of the Communist Party, indicating clearly that refusal to answer would be regarded as obstruction of necessary inquiry into his fitness to practice law. Konigsberg refused to answer on the ground that the question was impermissible under the First Amendment. The Supreme Court by 5–4 vote affirmed the bar's denial of his admission (*Konigsberg II*).[6] In an opinion by Justice Harlan, the Court held that the question of Communist Party membership was legitimate even if its being asked might have some chilling effect on speech:

It would indeed be difficult to argue that a belief, firm enough to be carried over into advocacy, in the use of illegal means to change the form of the State or Federal Government is an unimportant consideration in determining the fitness of applicants for membership in a profession in whose hands so largely lies the safekeeping of this country's legal and political institutions.[7]

In re Anastaplo, decided the same day as *Konigsberg II* by the same 5–4 vote, raised essentially the same issue. Justice Harlan speaking for the Court said:

Where, as with membership in the bar, the State may withhold a privilege available only to those possessing the requisite qualifications, it is of no constitutional significance whether the State's interrogation of an applicant on matters relevant to these qualifications—in this case Communist Party membership—is prompted by information which it already has about him from other sources, or arises merely from a good faith belief in the need for exploratory or testing questioning of the applicant.[8]

Justice Black, joined by Chief Justice Warren and Justices Douglas and Brennan, bitterly dissented in both cases, arguing, among other things, that Anastaplo's principled refusal to answer questions that he believed to be invasive of individual liberty provided a record that demonstrated his fitness for practice. Denied admission to the Illinois bar, Anastaplo taught philosophy and later became a law teacher. In the 1980s, the Illinois Supreme Court, apparently bothered by its refusal to admit Anastaplo, invited him to reapply. He refused, replying in effect: "I applied before; if

---

5. 353 U.S. at 261.

6. Konigsberg v. State Bar of California, 366 U.S. 36 (1961).

7. 366 U.S. at 50–52.

8. 366 U.S. at 90.

you erred in denying me admission, you should reverse your prior decision."[9] The court took no further action.

The issue came up for reconsideration in a set of three cases in 1971: *Baird, Stolar,* and *Wadmond.*[10] All three cases were decided 5-4, with Justice Stewart being the decisive vote. In *Wadmond* the Court upheld a New York character and fitness inquiry into whether the applicant was a "knowing member" of an organization advocating violent overthrow of government. Stewart's opinion stated:

> It is ... well settled that Bar examiners may ask about Communist affiliations as a preliminary to further inquiry into the nature of the association and may exclude an applicant for refusal to answer.[11]

In *Stolar*, again without agreeing on an opinion, five members agreed that asking applicants to list all organizations to which they belong now or had belonged to since becoming a law student was unconstitutional. Should character committees be allowed to ask about, or attach significance to, membership in an anti-abortion organization that publicly professes "direct action" against abortion clinics? Should they be allowed to inquire into, and deny admission, based on membership in groups that espouse racist views? Based on dedication to such views, such as expressed by Hale?

No subsequent Supreme Court decisions have considered the "rational connection" standard in character and fitness determinations. State courts, however, have considered such questions as homosexuality[12] and psychological abnormalities.[13] Clearly proper subjects of inquiry include previous criminal convictions, financial dealings that have been legally questioned and involvement in litigation. Should any other inquiry be allowed?

Racist and Sexist Conduct

A number of states have adopted ethics rules, similar to that of Illinois discussed in *Hale*, which prohibit a lawyer from discriminatory conduct in the practice of law based on race, sex, religion, national original or other factors.[14] Efforts by groups within the ABA to amend the Model Rules to prohibit discriminatory conduct have thus far failed. The opposition has been based on free speech concerns,[15] supported by the view that existing rules (e.g., M.R. 4.3 (harassment) and M.R. 8.4(d) (conduct prejudicial to

9. In 1983 the Illinois State Bar Association petitioned the state Supreme Court to reconsider, on its own initiative, its prior decision to deny Anastaplo admission because he refused, as a matter of principle, to answer questions about whether he belonged to the Communist Party. David Rani, 30 Years have Passed . . ., Nat'l L. J., Aug. 22, 1983, at p. 8.

10. Baird v. State Bar of Arizona, 401 U.S. 1 (1971); In re Stolar, 401 U.S. 23 (1971); and Law Students Civil Rights Research Council, Inc. v. Wadmond, 401 U.S. 154 (1971).

11. 401 U.S. at 165-166.

12. Florida Board of Bar Examiners Re N.R.S., 403 So.2d 1315 (Fla.1981) (impermissible to inquire into sexual preference).

13. In re Florida Board of Bar Examiners, 443 So.2d 77 (Fla.1983) (inquiry proper).

14. Ill.R.Prof.Conduct 8.4(a)(5); see also Texas Rule 5.08, Washington Rule 8.4(g).

15. See Richard F. Duncan, A Speech Code for Lawyers, Wall St.J., Feb.3, 1994, at A14 (criticizing the proposed ABA rule on free speech grounds).

the administration of justice) cover most overt discriminatory conduct. In August 1998, however, Comment [2] was added to M.R. 8.4. The Comment makes it clear that a lawyer "who, in the course of representing a client, knowingly manifests by words or conduct, bias or prejudice based upon race, sex, religion, national origin, disability, age, sexual orientation or socioeconomic status" has committed conduct prejudicial to the administration of justice. The Comment exempts "[l]egitimate advocacy" and the discriminatory use of peremptory challenges. Is the latter exception warranted?

In United States v. Wunsch,[16] a criminal defense lawyer, unhappy when he was disqualified from a case on motion of a female assistant U.S. attorney, copied a heading from an issue of *California Lawyer* and sent it to the female prosecutor along with a letter stating that the disqualification was "neither just nor fair to the defendants." The photocopied legend read:

> MALE LAWYERS PLAY BY THE RULES, DISCOVER TRUTH AND RESTORE ORDER. FEMALE LAWYERS ARE OUTSIDE THE LAW, CLOUD TRUTH AND DESTROY ORDER.

At the request of the Department of Justice, the district judge ordered the lawyer to apologize and referred the matter to the court's disciplinary committee. The Ninth Circuit, on appeal, held that the lawyer's conduct did not impugn the integrity of the court in violation of local rules; was not conduct prejudicial to the administration of justice; and could not be punished under a California law prohibiting lawyers from engaging in "offensive personality" because the law was unconstitutionally vague.

Fitness of Applicants with Disabilities

The Americans with Disabilities Act (ADA)[17] provides that a person with a disability which substantially affects a major life activity, such as working, is entitled to a "reasonable accommodation." The ADA has created new problems and challenges for our state-based system of admission to the bar. Increasing the pool of paralyzed, blind, and hearing-impaired lawyers may bring with it many of the benefits that those advocating the admission of Communists envisioned: lawyers with more empathy for the problems of a particular subset of clients and the advocacy of positions that might otherwise go unheard or un-imagined. Law schools, bar examiners and law firms have made some progress, albeit in many cases reluctantly and slowly, in accommodating individuals with physical handicaps, including the deaf and the blind. On the other hand, there are serious questions about what should count as a "disability" that demands "accommodation" and what "accommodation" should be expected.

Application of Ronwin[18] illustrates the difficulties of evaluating whether an individual is so mentally ill that admission should be denied on

16.   84 F.3d 1110 (9th Cir.1996). See also Juliet Eilperin, Female Lawyer Fined for Not Accepting Male Client, Nat'l L.J., May 12, 1997, at A7 (reporting a decision of the Massachusetts Commission Against Discrimination fining a female lawyer, Judith Nathanson, because she limited her matrimonial practice to women).

17.   42 U.S.C. §§ 12101–12213 (ADA).

18.   Application of Ronwin, 555 P.2d 315, 317 (Ariz.1976), cert. denied, 430 U.S. 907 (1997).

fitness grounds. Ronwin, after graduating from Arizona State University College of Law, was denied the opportunity to retake the bar examination because the bar examiners were "unable to make the requisite finding that [he was] mentally and physically able to [practice law]." After a formal hearing on his fitness, the bar examiners found that "the applicant suffers from an established personality disorder ... which [c]auses him to be unreasonably suspicious [of the motives and intentions of others]; ... irresponsible and highly derogatory [in making] untrue public accusations and charges against persons in responsible positions; ... [and] to bring and pursue with great persistence groundless claims in court proceedings...." The Arizona Supreme Court rejected the examiners' reliance on Ronwin's "persistence," stating that "resorting [in good faith] to the legal system to express grievances" did not constitute unfitness. But the court held that Ronwin's personality disorder disqualified him for admission: "[Ronwin] has a 'paranoid personality' which is characterized by hypersensitivity, rigidity, unwarranted suspicion, excessive self-importance and a tendency to blame others and ascribe evil motives to them.... [O]n different occasions [in law school] he became enraged during discussions of academic matters and made serious threats of physical violence toward certain individuals and, in two cases, their wives...."

Claims of special treatment based on neurological and psychological disabilities (especially those related to learning, cognitive development and attention deficit disorder) pose difficult and unresolved problems.[19] Claimants who provide adequate documentation of such disabilities have received additional time on law school exams, but bar admission authorities have resisted departures from general rules for several reasons: concern about equity and fairness in testing; pressure from "a state judiciary that still sees itself as maintaining exclusive control over the admission process;" and lack of staff and funding to evaluate and administer the claims for special treatment.[20] The general language of the ADA does not resolve discrete issues such as when a disadvantage becomes a "disability; and what constitutes a "reasonable accommodation" for the particular disability. Courts have begun to address the interpretive and policy issues, but it will be some time before the law is settled on many of these important questions.[21]

---

19. The frequency of accommodation requests has increased rapidly. In New York, for example, 5 percent (402) of those taking the July 1998 bar exam requested accommodations; 4 percent (332) received them. See Tamar Lewin, U.S. Court Upholds Aid for the Disabled on State Bar Exams, N.Y. Times, Sept. 16, 1998, pp. A1, B12.

20. Erica Moeser, The Future of Bar Admissions and the State Judiciary, 72 Notre Dame L.Rev. 1169, 1171 (1997).

21. See Bartlett v. New York State Board of Law Examiners, 156 F.3d 321 (2d Cir.

1998), aff'g in part, vacating in part, 970 F.Supp. 1094 (S.D.N.Y.) (method by which bar examiners concluded that dyslexic applicant did not have a learning disability did not meet federal standards; applicant entitled to accommodations as a reading disabled person even though she had been able through "self-accommodation" to achieve average reading skills); cf. Florida Board of Bar Examiners re S.G., 707 S.E.2d 323 (Fla., Feb. 19, 1998) (bar applicant who requested and was allowed to take the two parts of the bar exam on separate occasions could not use score-av-

Admission of Foreign Lawyers

Efforts by U.S. lawyers to provide legal advice in foreign countries about United States law have led to proposals that U.S. jurisdictions permit lawyers admitted abroad to provide legal advice concerning that nation's law in the United States. A number of states have responded by allowing those admitted as "foreign legal consultants" to provide legal advice about the law of their home country in the state, but not advice concerning that state's law.[22] Foreign-trained lawyers are increasingly seeking full admission by motion or by passage of the bar exam and some states have responded with discretionary admissions or a general rule departing from the usual requirement of graduation from an ABA approved law school.[23] The economic forces of globalization, Erica Moeser warns, may make it easier for a German lawyer to be licensed in New York than it is for a New Jersey lawyer.[24] "If the gates of the profession," she warns, "are to be opened to persons other than those who have completed formal training at an institution meeting minimum educational standards, then the test or tests that are administered will need to provide more exhaustive coverage than they now do."[25]

3. WOMEN, AFRICAN–AMERICANS AND OTHER MINORITIES IN THE PROFESSION

Women

The history of women in the legal profession through the 19th century is essentially a story of frustration and exclusion.[26] The socio-legal attitude sustaining exclusion was stated in the high Victorian age by Justice Bradley, concurring in Bradwell v. State.[27] That decision affirmed denial of

eraging formula used for applicants who take both parts at the same time; doing so would constitute a preference that is not required by ADA).

22. Three states with a large component of international practice (California, Florida and New York) have led the way. The ABA adopted a model foreign legal consultant rule in 1993.

23. About one-half of U.S. jurisdictions permit a graduate of a foreign law school to take the jurisdiction's bar exam. Even in those jurisdictions, however, special restrictions apply. In New York, for example, if the foreign legal education is not in English in a common law jurisdiction, or not judged to be qualitatively as good as in ABA approved law schools, the applicant will be required to complete at least one year at an ABA approved law school (24 semester hours).

24. In 1999 a relatively small number of "foreign legal consultants" were registered in New York, but during 1994–98 alone 7,262 foreign lawyers took the New York bar exam and 2,757 passed (39%). Most were allowed to take the bar exam after one year of law school in the United States. In 1999 the ABA Section of Legal Education and Admission to the Bar urged state bar exam authorities not to admit foreign lawyers on the basis of a foreign law degree and one year of law school in the U.S.; the Section argues that at least two years of study in an ABA approved law school should be required for admission. Siobhan Roth, ABA Body Wants Tighter Rules . . ., Nat'l L.J., Apr.26, 1999, p. A12.

25. Moeser, supra, at 1175.

26. The story is recounted in Karen B. Morello, The Invisible Bar: The Woman Lawyer in America, 1638 to the Present (1986).

27. 83 U.S. (16 Wall.) 130 (1873).

admission to the Illinois bar of Myra Bradwell, who surely was better qualified than most of her contemporaries. Justice Bradley said:

> [T]he civil law, as well as nature herself, has always recognized a wide difference in the respective spheres and destinies of man and woman.... The natural and proper timidity and delicacy which belongs to the female sex evidently unfits it for many of the occupations of civil life. The constitution of the family organization, which is founded in the divine ordinance, as well as in the nature of things, indicates the domestic sphere as that which properly belongs to the domain and functions of womanhood.... So firmly fixed was this sentiment in the founders of the common law that it became a maxim of that system of jurisprudence that a woman had no legal existence separate from her husband, who was regarded as her head and representative in the social state; and, notwithstanding some recent modifications of this civil status, many of the special rules of law flowing from and dependent upon this cardinal principle still exist in full force in most States.... This very incapacity was one circumstance which the Supreme Court of Illinois deemed important in rendering a married woman incompetent fully to perform the duties and trusts that belong to the office of an attorney and counsellor.[28]

The available data indicate that the number of women lawyers rose from less than a dozen in 1870 to about 1,000 in 1910 but was still less than 10,000 by 1960, when women were about 3 percent of law students.[29] The increase in numbers whereby women have become a significant proportion of the profession has occurred since the 1960s. From 1973 to 1983, the size of the profession doubled; the number of women lawyers increased seven-fold.[30] As of 1991 about 22 percent of American lawyers were women;[31] and by 1998 the percentage had risen to about 27.[32]

A 1985 ABF study[33] showed that a higher fraction of women than of men had law jobs in government (other than the judiciary) and in legal

---

28. 83 U.S. (16 Wall.) at 141 (Bradley, J., concurring).

29. For an analysis of long-term demographic trends in the legal profession, giving special attention to gender, see Terence Halliday, Six Score Years and Ten: Demographic Transitions in the American Legal Profession, 1950–1980, 20 Law & Soc'y Review 53 (1986).

30. Donna Fossum, Women in the Law: A Reflection on Portia, 69 A.B.A.J. 1389 (1983).

31. ABA Section of Legal Education and Admissions to the Bar, Task Force Report on Law Schools and the Profession, Legal Education and Professional Development—An Educational Continuum 18–22 (1992). The proportion of women among the law school population rose from 3 percent in

1960 to 9 percent in 1970 to 34 percent in 1980 to 45 percent in 1998. As women have entered the profession in larger numbers, the proportion of women in the total lawyer population has grown from 2 percent in 1950 to 27 percent in 1998. Women lawyers, as a group, are substantially younger than men: In 1988 the median age for women lawyers was 34 and the median age for men lawyers 42. But the median age gap is gradually closing.

32. Elaine Friedman et al., Breaking Through, Nat'l. L. J., Mar. 30, 1998, p. C2.

33. Barbara A. Curran et al., Supplement to the Lawyer Statistical Report: The U.S. Legal Profession in 1985, Am.Bar Foundation (1986).

education and that the fraction in private law firms was lower for women than men.[34] As to wielding power in the institutions of which they are a part, the National Law Journal's 1998 list of the 50 most influential women in the profession includes very few women from large corporate law firms; one third of the list work in either academia or government. Six women on the list were practicing corporate/securities law within law firms, a traditionally male field. Women lawyers have attained more high status positions in corporations than they have in corporate law firms; almost 20 percent of the Journal's 50 most influential women were general counsels.[35]

The National Law Journal's 1991 survey of the 250 largest firms found that women made up 26.3 percent of all lawyers.[36] That percentage stayed about the same through most of the 1990s, but in 1997 an upward shift began and by 1998 the percentage of women in the 250 largest firms was 30.3. [37]The percentage of women partners in these large firms continues to climb, slowly but steadily, from 9 percent in 1989 to 16 percent in 1998. At firms with nonequity partnerships, in 1998 61 percent of women were equity partners, up dramatically from 54 percent in 1996. Of male partners, 75 percent had equity.

The earnings picture is not quite as cheerful. A 1998 report of the Massachusetts bar showed that women made up 34 percent of the lawyers in the state, but made on average only $40,000 a year compared to their male colleagues in the state who earned $72,000 on average.[38] Nationwide, women lawyers made 70 cents for every $1 a male lawyer made in 1998, according to the U.S. Bureau of Labor Statistics, and census figures support the AFL–CIO's finding that women lawyers make on average nearly $300 less per week than their male counterparts.[39]

Gender bias in the courtroom against women lawyers and women litigants has received attention by state court judges and state, local and women bar associations.[40] In 1984, New Jersey became the first state to

34. Judith S. Kaye, Women Lawyers in Big Firms: A Study in Progress Toward Gender Equality, 57 Fordham L.Rev. 111, 113 (1988).

35. Friedman et al., supra note 32.

36. See Progress Glacial for Women, Minorities, Nat'l L.J., Jan. 27, 1991, at p. 1.

37. The late 1990s data in this paragraph are from Michael D. Goldhaber, Woman's Numbers Rise at the Bigger Law Firms, Nat'l. L.J., Dec. 21, 1998, at A1.

38. Thomas Grillo, Rise in Women Lawyers Seen, Boston Globe, March 14, 1998, p. F2. The study also found that the average pay of all lawyers in the state dropped from $62,500 in 1990 to $62,000 in 1998. Earnings comparisons by gender, however, may be misleading unless they are corrected by gender for the relative frequency of part-

time work and the types of employment pursued. Many women work on a reduced schedule during child-bearing years; and women are more likely than men to choose jobs in sectors of the profession, such as government employment and solo practice, which are lower paid.

39. The Bureau of Labor numbers as well as the census and AFL–CIO findings are taken from: Becky Tiernan, Men vs. Women: Does 74 Cents Equal a Dollar, Tulsa World, May 9, 1999.

40. Generally see Note, Gender Bias in the Judicial System, 61 So.Calif.L.Rev. 2193 (1988). In 1980 the NOW Legal Defense Fund in cooperation with the National Association of Women Judges created the National Judicial Education Program to Promote Equality for Women and Men in the Courts.

issue a report on gender bias in the courts. Many other states have since undertaken studies of the problem. New York issued a report in 1986 which concluded that "gender bias," defined as "[d]ecisions made or actions taken because of weight given to preconceived notions of sexual roles rather than upon a fair and unswayed appraisal of merit as to each person or situation," is "pervasive." It operates against not only women lawyers but women litigants and court personnel. "[P]roblems are perpetuated by some attorneys' and judges' misinformed belief that complaints by women are contrivances of overwrought imaginations and hypersensitivities. More was found ... than bruised feelings resulting from rude and callous behavior. Real hardships are borne by women." Is suffering callous behavior not a real hardship? What audience is addressed by such terms as "bruised feelings?" Is this characterization itself a problem or merely a response to political realities?

As shown in the New York report, women litigants are accorded less credibility because of their gender and face a judiciary poorly informed and in many cases misinformed about matters integral to the welfare of women. As to women lawyers, the study found that they must brave a "verbal and psychological obstacle course" in the courtroom. Examples of overt sexism include: being ordered not to use Ms. and to use her husband's last name, not her own, under threat of "sleep[ing] in the county jail tonight;"[41] being told by a judge "I don't think ladies should be lawyers" and being asked what "her husband thought of her working here;"[42] and being referred to as "lawyerette" and "attorney generalette."[43] While it is difficult to measure whether gender bias has increased or decreased, the evidence is clear that bias persists in the late 1990s with little sign of easing in the near term.[44]

Deborah L. Rhode, "Perspectives on Professional Women"

40 Stan.L.Rev. 1163 (1988).[45]

In a variety of studies, female students have also expressed lower expectations for occupational success than males and have attached greater

---

41. See N.Y. Times, July 14, 1988, at p. A23 (comments made by United States District Court Judge Teitelbaum to attorney Barbara Wolvowitz who was trying a race discrimination case in federal court).

42. Nancy Blodgett, I Don't Think that Ladies Should be Lawyers, 72 A.B.A.J. 48 (1986) (reporting comments made by a Illinois state court judge to a woman lawyer from Mayer, Brown & Platt of Chicago in 1986).

43. Complaint Concerning the Honorable John J. Kirby, 354 N.W.2d 410 (Minn. 1984) (censuring state court judge for these remarks).

44. Jeannette F. Swent, Gender Bias at the Heart of Justice: An Empirical Study of State Task Forces, 6 S. Cal. Rev. L. & Women's Stud. 1 (1996) (at least thirty-five jurisdictions have reported finding significant gender bias). For a bibliography of reports on gender, ethnicity and race bias in the courts, see Judith Resnik, Asking About Gender in Courts, 21 Signs 952 (1996).

45. Copyright © 1988 by the Board of Trustees of the Leland Stanford Junior University. Reprinted with permission.

priority to relational aspects of employment such as opportunities for helping others than to opportunities for money, status and power. Family and peer pressure can also skew vocational choices and discourage career decisions that would compete with domestic responsibilities, require geographic mobility, or bring wives greater prestige and income than their husbands. Such pressures can be particularly intense within certain class, race, and ethnic groups.

Disparities between traits associated with femininity and traits associated with vocational achievement further reinforce these gender socialization processes. A wide array of experiential and clinical evidence indicates that profiles of successful professionals conflict with profiles of normal or ideal women. The aggressiveness, competitiveness, dedication, and emotional detachment traditionally presumed necessary for advancement in the most prestigious and well-paid occupations are incompatible with traits commonly viewed as attractive in women: cooperativeness, deference, sensitivity, and self-sacrifice. Despite substantial progress toward gender equality over the last several decades, these gender stereotypes remain remarkably resilient. Females aspiring to nontraditional or high-status positions remain subject to a familiar double bind. Those conforming to traditional characteristics of femininity are often thought lacking in the requisite assertiveness and initiative, yet those conforming to a masculine model of success may be ostracized in work settings as bitchy, aggressive, and uncooperative. As long as aspiring women are found wanting either as professionals or as women, they face substantial disincentives to aspire....

Of particular significance are the sexes' different priorities concerning family responsibilities. Although cultural commitments to equal opportunity in vocational spheres have steadily increased, these sentiments have not translated into equal obligations in domestic spheres. Most studies have indicated that women still perform about 70 percent of the family tasks in an average household. Employed wives spend about twice as much time on homemaking demands as employed husbands; men married to women with full-time jobs devote only 1.4 hours a week more to domestic duties than other husbands. When time spent in paid labor and domestic labor is combined, employed males average two hours less per day than employed females, and a disproportionate amount of male homemaking contributions involve relatively enjoyable activities such as playing with the children.... Women, particularly social and ethnic minorities, are also far more likely to become single parents, with all the associated demands. In the late 1980s, females headed 90 percent of the nation's single-parent households, and women of color were disproportionately likely to have such responsibilities....

Not only do women bear the vast majority of family obligations, they do so in occupational environments designed by and for men. As a result, career success has often meant compromise of caretaking values.

Female employees unwilling to make that sacrifice have paid a demanding professional price....

... [E]lite professionals also tend to impose longer and more unpredictable working hours, and are particularly resistant to extended leaves, part-time or flexible-time shifts, and home work. That resistance springs from a variety of sources. Many clients and colleagues object to the inconveniences and the apparent lack of commitment among employees working nonconventional hours....

Extended hours, unpredictable schedules, and frequent travel mesh poorly with childrearing responsibilities. Yet for women "on the road to success," no detours from standard workplace obligations are advisable....

The self, it appears, should conform to a male model with a vengeance....

Unconscious gender bias can operate on three levels: (1) prototypes, the images associated with members of a particular occupation; (2) schema, the personal characteristics and situational factors that are used to explain conduct; and (3) scripts, definitions of appropriate behavior in a given situation. Thus, when a female applicant for a given position (e.g., litigator) does not fit the evaluator's prototype (e.g., aggressive male), her credentials will be judged with greater skepticism. Many explanatory schema embody similar stereotypes: Men's success is more likely to be explained in terms of ability and their failure in terms of luck, while women's achievement is more often attributed to luck or effort and their failures ascribed to inability. Since evaluations of ability are most crucial in hiring and promotion decisions, these attribution biases entrench gender hierarchies. So too, the scripts defining appropriate social behavior often reflect patterns of gender dominance, deference, and accommodation. For example, in group conversation, male participants tend to speak and interrupt more often, and to hold the floor for longer periods than females. Women are expected not only to talk less but also to allow more interruptions, and those who deviate from their accustomed role provoke negative evaluations. Once again, these perceptual prejudices create a double bind: Women who conform to accepted stereotypes will appear to have less to contribute and less leadership potential than the male colleagues, while women who take a more assertive stance risk appearing arrogant, aggressive, and abrasive. How to seem "demure but tough" is particularly difficult when standards vary among those whose opinions are most critical. In male-dominated cultures, women are subject to criticism for being "too feminine" and not "feminine enough."

Unconscious gender prejudices affect not only the evaluation of individual performance, they also affect the performance itself. As both experimental and longitudinal studies have repeatedly demonstrated, low expectations of achievement frequently become self-fulfilling prophecies. Individuals often signal their assumptions in subtle or not so subtle ways. These forms of negative feedback, including lower salaries and less demanding assignments, can adversely affect self-confidence and job performance. Such consequences then reinforce the initial expectations, and a self-perpetuating cycle continues....

Women in Law Schools

The number of women on law school faculties in tenured or tenure-track position has increased substantially and regularly. In 1997–98, women were 51.1 percent of assistant professors, 44.2 percent of associate professors, and 19.7 percent of full professors at ABA approved law schools.[46] However, only about 8 percent of law deans are currently women, but they include some at high visibility schools (e.g., Cal–Berkeley, Georgetown and Stanford). In 1997–98, 28.3 percent of the associate deans with a professorial rank were women and 37.5 percent of assistant deans with that rank. Perspectives on the subject are often influenced by the history at a particular law school or the viewer's tendency to observe the glass as half full or half empty. But change has occurred, whether or not it counts as "progress" or is thought sufficient under the circumstances.[47]

On the tenure side of the tracks, some observers detect a troubling picture. A study of all tenure-track legal academics hired as entry-level candidates between the fall of 1986 and the spring of 1991, showed that during a time when law schools professed great commitment to affirmative action hiring, after controlling for credentials and other relevant characteristics, law schools: 1) hired men at significantly higher professorial ranks than women; 2) hired men to teach constitutional law at significantly greater rates than women with equivalent backgrounds; 3) hired women to teach courses such as trusts and estates and skills courses at a significantly higher rate than men with comparable credentials.[48] Anecdotal and avail-

46. AALS, Statistical Report on Law School Faculty and Candidates for Law Faculty Positions, tbl. 2A (<http://aals.org/statistics/t2a9798.htn>). Women were 37.6 percent of registrants in the 1997–98 AALS Faculty Appointments Register, tbl. 5A, but accounted for 47.0 percent of new assistant professor hires, tbl. 2A. Except for one of the last five years, women listed in the Register had a higher success rate than men; in two of the five years, the differences were statistically significant, tbl. 7A.

47. Richard H. Chused, The Hiring and Retention of Minorities and Women on American Law School Faculties, 137 U.Pa.L.Rev. 537, 548 (1988) (SALT study of faculty members at 149 schools in response to survey questionnaires). Chused's prediction in 1988 that legal writing was "on its way to becoming a 'woman's job'" has considerable support: eight years later 36 percent of

115 reporting law schools had 51 to 75 percent women staffing legal writing positions. See Maureen J. Arrigo, Hierarchy Maintained: Status and Gender Issues in Legal Writing Programs, 70 Temple L. Rev. 117, 120 (1997) (citing Jill J. Ramsfield & Bryan C. Walton, Survey of Legal Research and Writing Programs (unpublished survey) (1994)).

48. Deborah Jones Merritt & Barbara F. Reskin, Sex, Race and Credentials: The Truth About Affirmative Action in Law Faculty Hiring, 97 Colum. L.Rev. 199, 205 (1997) (study of tenure-track hires by accredited law schools for the five academic years from fall 1986–spring 1991 using AALS directory listings; dependent variables were the prestige ranking of law schools, initial rank conferred and relative status of courses taught; independent and control variables included gender and race;

able data indicates that women have experienced difficulties in receiving tenure.[49] Chused's study showed that although tenure and departure rates "were almost identical for men and women," women gain tenure more frequently in schools that already have a larger number of tenured women faculty members.

The presence of tenured women faculty member may result in "mentoring" relationships, provide a bloc of supporters or change the perceptions of male faculty members.[50] On the other hand, these mentoring responsibilities and greater committee work demands on women faculty members, resulting from the attempt to get a woman's presence on these bodies, adds up to greater burdens on women faculty members than their male counterparts and less time for scholarly pursuit.[51] The presence of senior women and the number of such women in firms and other practice settings may similarly affect the career progression of junior women and undoubtedly has an effect on how sensitive others in the workplace are to sexist attitudes and practices.[52] Like their counterparts in academia, however, women are also likely to be disproportionately burdened by mentoring and "representative" responsibilities.

Considerable attention has been focused on the experience of women students in law schools,[53] who now make up 43–45 percent of law students

control variables included measures of applicants' educational credentials, work experience and personal characteristics).

49. See, e.g., Marina Angel, Women in Legal Education: What It's Like to be Part of a Perpetual First Wave or the Case of the Disappearing Women, 61 Temp.L.Q. 799 (1988); Women Face Hurdles as Professors, Nat'l L.J., Oct. 24, 1988, at p. 1; and Richard H. Chused, Faculty Parenthood: Law School Treatment of Pregnancy and Child Care, 35 J.Legal Educ. 568, 584 (1985).

50. Chused Study at 550–52. See generally Lani Guinier, Michelle Fine & Jane Balin, Mentoring as a Way to End The Alienation of Women in Legal Academia: Becoming Gentlemen: Women, Law School And Institutional Change (1997).

51. American Bar Association Commission on Women in the Profession, Elusive Equality: The Experiences of Women in Legal Education 27 (1996) [hereinafter Elusive Equality]. The study found that these burdens were greatest on women of color, but were present for white women as well.

52. On women in legal academia, see Carrie J. Menkel–Meadow, Women as Law Teachers: Toward the Feminization of Legal Education, in Essays on the Application of a

Humanistic Perspective to Law Teaching (1981); Symposium on Women in Legal Education, 38 J. Legal Educ. 1–194 (1988).

53. Lani Guinier, Michelle Fine & Jane Balin, Becoming Gentlemen: Women's Experiences at One Ivy League Law School, 143 U.Pa.L.Rev. 1, 3, 32 (1994) (University of Pennsylvania study showing that women students are significantly underrepresented in the top echelons of their law school classes when ranked by grade point average, speak less often in class and are more alienated in law school than men); Catherine Weiss & Louise Melling, The Legal Education of Twenty Women, 40 Stan.L.Rev. 1299 (1988) (describing the alienation of women law students at Yale "from themselves, from the law school community, from the classroom, and from the content of legal education"); Linda F. Wightman, Women in Legal Education: A Comparison of the Law School Performance and Law School Experiences of Women and Men 11–12 (LSAC Research Report Series 1996) (stating that there was "no practical difference" in average performance of men and women during first year of law school, only some differences in certain grade ranges); Janet Ta-

nationwide.[54] Most studies show women participate less in law school and are more disaffected than men.[55] Some studies also show that when men and women enter law school with similar credentials, women end up performing less well in school, and that this disparity in performance increases as the years in law school go by.[56] More schools have now initiated gender bias studies, and "initial findings of some composite studies reveal that the existence and extent of gender disparities in academic performance vary widely among law schools."[57]

The problems encountered by women lawyers and the responses to these problems are mirrored in the experience of women in other fields, such as medicine and college teaching.[58] Women in the professions and women in academia have changed the focus in many substantive legal areas, in some areas have changed what is considered worthy of debate in law and have challenged the ground rules of traditional legal debate itself.[59] A large literature by and about women in the profession is now available, ranging from statistical demographics to narratives recounting personal experience.[60]

History of African–Americans in Law

The history of African–Americans in the law essentially parallels that of women, except that the pattern of events since the 1960s has been

ber et al., Gender, Legal Education, and the Legal Profession: An Empirical Study of Stanford Law Students and Graduates, 40 Stan.L.Rev. 1209, 1237–40 (1988) (finding few significant differences between male and female Stanford Law with the exception of class participation: men asked considerably more questions and volunteered more answers to professors' questions).

54. Elusive Equality, supra, at 1

55. In addition to the studies cited supra note 53, see ABA, Elusive Equality, supra note 51 (finding substantial alienation).

56. See, e.g., Guinier et al., Pennsylvania study supra; Legal Times, Apr. 1997, at 1 (reporting on potential gender disparity in grades at Georgetown).

57. Mary L. Clark, The Founding of the Washington College of Law: the First Law School established by Women for Women 47 Amer.U.L.Rev. 613, 675 (1998).

58. See Penina Glazer & Miriam Slater, Unequal Colleagues: The Entrance of Women into the Professions (1987).

59. See, e.g., Cynthia Grant Bowman & Elizabeth M. Schneider, Feminist Legal

Theory, Feminist Lawmaking, and the Legal Profession 67 Fordham L. Rev. 249 (1998) (describing the impact of feminist legal theory on legal practice and the legal profession); Rand Jack & Dana C. Jack, Moral Vision and Professional Decisions: The Changing Values of Women and Men Lawyers (1989); and Ann C. Scales, The Emergence of Feminist Jurisprudence: An Essay, 95 Yale L.J. 1373 (1986).

60. For bibliographies of this literature see Aviva Orenstein, Feminism and Evidence, in Feminist Jurisprudence, Women and the Law: Critical Essays, Research Agenda and Bibliography (Sharon Rush et al. eds., 1997); Paul M. George & Susan McGlamery, Women and Legal Scholarship: A Bibliography, 77 Iowa L.Rev. 87 (1991); Anthony P. Grech & Daniel J. Jacobs, Women and the Legal Profession: A Bibliography of Current Literature, 44 The Record 215 (March 1989) (covering the following subheadings: General, Bar Association Participation, Biographies, History, Networking, Part–Time Lawyering, Rise to Partnership, Studies and Reports, Surveys and Statistics, Women in the Study of Law, Women Judges).

morally more equivocal and far less encouraging to those who believe in "natural progress" toward human equality in opportunity and life realization.[61] The history of other minorities in the legal profession, particularly Hispanics and Asians, has not been as well-developed.[62]

Geraldine R. Segal, Blacks in the Law
Pp. 1–7, 16–19, 28–33, 76–77 (1985).[63]

Throughout the first half of the twentieth century, and even beyond, to become a black lawyer in America required an extraordinary measure of courage, determination, and vision. To most blacks it was a goal that seemed to defy social and economic realities. Indeed, at the turn of the century W.E.B. DuBois found that physicians and lawyers together comprised only 1.5 percent of the black population. According to the 1910 United States census, there were then only 798 black lawyers in the country, and by 1940 there were a mere 1,925—one black lawyer for every 13,000 blacks in America.

During those years blacks who did manage to become lawyers found themselves in a profession that was pervaded by racism and fundamentally segregated. Until 1937 there was no black federal judge in the nation, and even then it was a term appointment in the Virgin Islands; until 1949, none on a United States Circuit Court; until 1961, none on a United States District Court; and until 1967, none on the United States Supreme Court. Until 1936, blacks were not admitted to "white" law schools. Until 1943 color had to be stated on applications to the American Bar Association. Until 1946 there was no black teacher on the faculty of predominantly white law schools. . . .

Legal Education

Between 1877 and 1935 Howard [University Law School] was the only substantial source of legal education for blacks in the United States. During this period no black could obtain a legal education in an approved law school anywhere south of Washington, D.C.

During the next twelve years three other currently functioning accredited black law schools, all state institutions and all in the South, came into existence. The first of these was North Carolina Central University Law

61. J. Clay Smith Jr. has written a history of black lawyers through World War II, Emancipation: The Making of the Black Lawyer, 1844–1944 (1993); see also Smith, In Freedom's Birthplace: The Making of George Lewis Ruffin, The First Black Law Graduate of Harvard University, 39 Howard L.J. 201 (1995).

62. But see Leo M. Romero, Richard Delgado & Cruz Reynoso, The Legal Education of Chicano Students: A Study in Mutual Accommodation and Cultural Conflict, 5 New Mexico L.Rev. 177 (1975); Linda E.

Davila, "The Underrepresentation of Hispanic Attorneys in Corporate Law Firms," 39 Stanford L. Rev. 1403 (1987). Kiyoko Kamio Knapp, Disdain of Alien Lawyers: History of Exclusion, 7 Seton Hall Const. L.J. 103 (1996) (describing discrimination against and challenges faced by alien Asian lawyers in the United States).

63. Copyright © 1985 by Geraldine Segal. Published by the University of Pennsylvania Press. Reprinted with permission.

School in Durham, North Carolina, founded in 1939. The next two, both founded in 1947, were Texas Southern University Law School in Houston, Texas, and Southern University Law School in Baton Rouge, Louisiana. Howard and these three state black law schools have trained the majority of black lawyers in the nation.

Not content with the perpetuation of a situation that limited blacks to black law schools, skilled black advocates instituted suits beginning in the middle 1930s on the reasoning that blacks were entitled to a common education forum with whites if they were to practice the same law. Under the leadership of Charles H. Houston, and later Thurgood Marshall, and under the auspices of the NAACP Legal Defense and Educational Fund, a series of lawsuits were filed to obtain for blacks the right to attend predominantly white southern law schools. When Houston and Marshall took up the fight to enable Donald Murray, a 1934 black graduate of Amherst College, to enter the University of Maryland Law School, legal barriers restricting admission of blacks to white law schools began to fall, but only after persistent and effective advocacy produced court orders mandating this result. . . .

Undoubtedly, the decision of the United States Supreme Court in *Brown v. Board of Education,* handed down in 1954, had some significant impact on the thinking of white law schools. . . .

After this milestone was reached, changes came more rapidly. By the late 1960s most law schools, spurred on by the civil rights legislation and by the argument that minority leaders could benefit the country in numerous ways, had initiated minority recruitment and admissions programs. . . .

. . . .

In the mid–1960s a number of philanthropic organizations attempted to spur the interest of blacks in becoming lawyers by making grants to reduce the financial barriers to their entering law school. . . .

That the increased financial aid and remedial programs detailed above were successful to a significant degree is clear from the dramatic increases in black enrollment in law schools all over the country during the late 1960s and early 1970s. In 1965, Harvard Law School estimated that of the approximately 65,000 law students in accredited law schools in the nation, there were no more than 700 black students, or approximately 1 percent. By 1972 the 4,423 black students constituted 4.3 percent of all students attending accredited law schools in the country, and by the 1976–77 school year there were 5,503 black students, or about 4.7 percent of the total, in approved law schools.

In the succeeding three school years, however, black enrollment leveled off instead of continuing in its prior record of steady growth. . . .

Professional Associations

Although blacks have not yet achieved anything near proportional representation in the legal profession, the situation has improved markedly since Brown v. Board of Education (1954). Before that legal turning point, black attorneys were virtually isolated professionally. Opportunities to work with white colleagues or to represent white clients were almost nonexistent. Moreover, many blacks who needed legal representation feared that black lawyers would be unsuccessful against a white lawyer and before a white judge, regardless of the ability or the quality of the performance of the black lawyers. Those blacks who did retain black lawyers were usually too poor to furnish a lucrative practice. Black lawyers were largely confined to petty criminal cases and were rarely given the opportunity to prove their ability in other areas of the law.

In varying degrees this problem of professional segregation has beset black lawyers throughout the century. In 1912, racism within the legal community was so rampant that a storm arose over the "inadvertent" election of the first three black attorneys to the American Bar Association by its Executive Committee. When the Executive Committee discovered that it had unknowingly elected three members "of the colored race," the committee rescinded its prior action, stating that "the settled practice of the Association has been to elect only white men to membership." ...

In 1925, twelve black lawyers from around the nation (eleven men and one woman) met in Des Moines, Iowa, to organize and incorporate the National Bar Association (NBA). Although not restricting its membership to race, the NBA was designed to be, and became, the chief professional association of black lawyers....

In 1981, the NBA estimated that there were 12,000 black lawyers, of whom about 8,000 belonged to the NBA. From an American Bar Foundation estimate of a total of 535,000 lawyers in the United States in 1980, it appears that black lawyers comprise a little more than 2.2 percent of the American lawyer population....

[As Segal's study demonstrates, a "black lawyer," like all lawyers, lives and practices in a specific practice setting, in a specific community, during a specific historical period. Law practice tends to be highly localized, being bound up in an immediate socio-political context and tied to specific economic possibilities. Segal accordingly has subchapters on individual black lawyers and on several cities in which black lawyers have concentrated, including Atlanta, New York, Philadelphia and Washington, D.C.]

***

Lingering Racism

Despite the greater opportunity that blacks now have for entry into the legal profession, their life chances in the profession remain precarious.[64] In

64. For more general background, see also John Preston Davis, The American Negro Reference Book (1966); Marion S. Goldman, A Portrait of the Black Attorney in Chicago (1972); Richard Kluger, Simple Justice (1977). Also see Edward J. Littlejohn & Donald L. Hobson, Black Lawyers, Law Practice, and Bar Associations—1844 to 1970: A Michigan History, 33 Wayne L.Rev. 1625 (1987). On the special ethical

particular, the number of blacks making partner in predominantly white firms is small and increasing very slowly. In 1998 every firm on the National Law Journal's survey of the nation's 250 largest law firms had at least one minority lawyer (African–American, Asian or Hispanic), but 10 percent of those firms had precisely one.[65] As for associates, the top 250 law firms reported that 13 percent of associates were members of minority groups (6.1% Asian, 4% black and 2.8% Hispanic. In the two years between 1996 and 1998, the number of Asians in these law firms grew 72 percent. The number of Hispanic associates grew by 50 percent at a time when the number of associates overall grew by only 20 percent. African–American associates also did better than the general associate market, but not by much; they increased their ranks by 27.5 percent.

The number of African–Americans who were full-fledged equity partners in the largest 250 firms went from 236 the previous year to 247 in 1998, a gain of only 4.7 percent.[66] African–Americans made up only 1.2 percent of all equity partners at the 250 largest law firms; two years earlier the figure was 1.1 percent. In other words, the long-term picture for African–Americans in these firms is improving very slowly.

David B. Wilkins and G. Mitu Gulati, "Why Are There So Few Black Lawyers in Corporate Law Firms? An Institutional Analysis"[67]

84 California Law Review 493 (1996).

... Forty years after the Supreme Court's landmark decision in *Brown v. Board of Education*, society has made substantial progress toward eradicating the kind of overtly racist policies that excluded blacks from virtually every desirable sector of the economy. For many blacks, these changes have produced a dramatic growth in income and opportunity. In recent years, however, it has become painfully clear that simply dismantling America's version of apartheid has not produced economic parity between blacks and whites. Although poor blacks have benefitted the least from the civil rights revolution, "high level" jobs in business and the professions have also proved surprisingly resistant to change. The fact that blacks have made so little progress in breaking into the corporate law-firm elite—particularly at the partnership level—fits this larger pattern.

problems African–American lawyers may face, see David B Wilkins, Race, Ethics, and the First Amendment: Should a Black Lawyer Represent the Ku Klux Klan?, 63 Geo.Wash.L.Rev. 1030 (1995).

65. Michael D. Goldhaber, Minorities Surge at Big Law Firms, Nat'l. L, J., Dec. 14, 1998, p. A1. The remainder of numbers in this paragraph are from this source.

66. Blacks Underrepresented as Partners in Law Firms, Jet, Dec. 28, 1998, p.13 (reporting on the Nat'l. L. J. 1997 survey but providing data not included in Goldhaber's article). The numbers in this paragraph are all from this source.

67. Copyright 1995 © California Law Review. Reprinted with permission. Omitted paragraphs are not marked with ellipses.

Commentators generally offer one of two explanations for this "glass ceiling" effect. The first, generally proffered by firms, posits a shortage of black applicants with both the qualifications and the interest necessary to succeed in the demanding world of elite corporate practice. The second, most often articulated by blacks, blames the slow progress on continued racism both inside corporate firms and among the clients upon whom these entities depend for their livelihood.

As we argue below, both the "pool problem" and continuing racism against blacks play important roles in determining the employment opportunities available to African American lawyers. Standing alone, however, each explanation begs important questions. The "pool problem" explanation begs the question of whether the existing hiring and promotion criteria utilized by elite law firms to determine who is in the pool fairly and accurately predict future productivity. The racism story, on the other hand, fails to explain why firms that discriminate by refusing to hire or promote qualified black lawyers do not suffer a competitive disadvantage when those workers are employed by their competitors.

We present a stylized model of the contemporary elite corporate law firm, premised on two related features of professional work: the inherent subjectivity of quality assessments and the difficulty and expense of monitoring. In response to these realities, we posit that it is efficient for firms to adopt the following tripartite strategy: high wages to create a large pool of available workers and motivate those who are hired to work with relatively little supervision; a high associate-to-partner ratio, thus further encouraging associates to work hard in the hopes of becoming partners while at the same time allowing the firm to spread legal work among many lawyers with varying levels of knowledge and skill at the lowest possible cost; and a tracking system whereby the pool of associates is divided into those who will receive scarce training resources and those who will work on relatively undemanding assignments.

These features, we assert, disproportionately disadvantage black lawyers while also affecting whites. Two tendencies contribute to this result. First, because firms hire a large number of associates from a pool that has been artificially inflated by high salaries and ask many of them to do relatively undemanding work, these institutions have little incentive to invest in obtaining detailed information about the quality of potential employees. Hence, individuals within the firm can use race as a factor in their decision-making without hurting the firm's bottom line. The same goes for retention and promotion. Decisions to invest scarce training resources in average whites as opposed to average blacks will not hurt the firm's chances of producing the small number of high-quality partners that it needs to guarantee its productivity in future years. As a result, firms have little incentive to root out employment decisions that, either consciously or unconsciously, prejudice blacks or favor whites.

Second, because firms have no incentive to stop these practices, black lawyers in firms (as well as those contemplating joining firms) are more likely to choose human-capital strategies that, paradoxically, decrease their overall chances of success. Since blacks reasonably believe that they face an increased risk that their abilities will be unfairly devalued or overlooked, they have an incentive to overinvest either in avoiding visible negative signals or in obtaining easily observable positive signals that clearly identify them as superstars. Both of these strategies, however, are potentially counterproductive to the extent that they diminish a black lawyer's opportunity or incentive to obtain the skills upon which success at the corporate law firm ultimately depends.

MAPPING THE RACIAL LAW OF AVERAGES

We have supplemented the publicly available data with our own preliminary research on black Harvard Law School graduates in the classes of 1981, 1982, 1987, and 1988; a survey of 200 Harvard black alumni; a survey of 250 corporate law firms; and interviews. We divide our review of the data into two parts: recruiting and retention. Simply hiring more black lawyers is unlikely to change the racial composition of these institutions in light of the fact that virtually all of these new entrants leave before making partner. Retention, not recruitment, is therefore the key to increasing the number of black lawyers. Retention, however, is affected by the dynamics of the recruiting process. The fewer blacks a firm already has among its associates and partners, the more difficult it may be to recruit black students.

Firms now expend enormous resources on interviewing second-, third-, and even some first-year students for summer and full-time positions.... The on-campus interview consists of a brief twenty-minute discussion with a single lawyer, taken up almost entirely with the applicant's general interests, background, and experience and whatever questions the applicant has about the firm. Firms make call-back decisions based on the information that appears on an applicant's resume and transcript and this interview. Rather than ranking candidates by academic standing, firms tend to use loose grade cutoffs pegged to the academic standing of the applicant's school. More often than not, call-back interviews merely repeat this pattern. At some firms, this is a pro forma process in which most candidates receive summer offers; even firms that use call-back interviews as a screening device focus primarily on personality and fit. Although firms collect information about their summer associates, large firms in San Francisco, New York, and Chicago make permanent offers to more than 80 percent of summer associates. Many of the country's most prestigious firms extend offers to virtually all their summer associates.

... [T]o win the competition for [the coveted recruits with the best credentials], firms must both credibly signal their quality to these applicants and appear to treat applicants fairly. This helps to explain the division of the recruiting process into a "visible" stage, in which firms review a candidate's objective credentials, and an "invisible" stage dominated by subjective judgments about personality and fit. Because the call-back interview occurs out of sight, firms focus on assessing whether the applicant will fit its culture. The objective signals firms employ at the visible stage, although a highly imperfect measure of an applicant's potential, do a reasonably good job of reducing the pool and, more importantly, give clients, competitors, and law students an accessible and rankable method of rating firms.

The fact that firms rely on a few objective signals to identify qualified applicants at the visible stage and reserve the right to go behind these credentials to make judgments about personality and fit at the invisible stage doubly disadvantages black applicants. By relying on sorting devices such as law school status, grades, and law review membership, firms systematically exclude the majority of black applicants who do not have these standard signals. Thus, although blacks may be more likely to attend higher-status law schools than whites, the schools with the largest black populations are not ones from which large firms typically recruit. Even black students with superstar credentials from lower-status schools have little or no chance of being hired by a large firm. Those blacks who do attend elite schools face recognized barriers (e.g., poor primary and secondary school education, diminished expectations, hostile environments, and part-time work) to performing well in the classroom or in extracurricular activities such as law review. Given these added pressures, it is plausible that some black students who are currently admitted to schools would be more successful if they did not attend these academic institutions. However, given the nearly dispositive role that the status of an applicant's law school plays in the recruiting process, black students who want to have the option of working at an elite firm have little incentive to choose this option.

To the extent that firms make hiring decisions based on signals such as grade point averages, as opposed to the substantive content of the courses a student has taken, black applicants have an incentive to maximize the former at the expense of the latter. At the same time, the emphasis on personality and fit at the invisible stage (both on-campus and call-back interviews) can disadvantage black applicants with traditional signals. Although [overt racial] incidents . . . are undoubtedly rare, they underscore the fact that outright prejudice against blacks still exists at elite firms. A consistent line of empirical research demonstrates that when whites evaluate blacks, they frequently attribute negative acts "to personal disposition, while positive acts are discounted as the product of luck or special circumstances." Pervasive myths about black intellectual inferiority combined with lower than average levels of achievement in areas such as grades and test scores tend to make white interviewers question the credentials of blacks more than those of whites. In addition, interviewers generally expect to feel less comfortable when interviewing blacks. . . .

Since race is costless to observe, it provides a convenient mechanism, much like "personality" and "fit," for sorting applicants. Blacks, on average, have less access to influential contacts and other informal networks that allow some candidates to bypass the formal screening requirements. . . .

Ironically, these structural features of the recruiting process also lead us to predict that blacks who *are* hired will tend, on average, to be clustered in the superstar range. At the 73 elite firms who responded to our survey (29 percent response rate; 51 and 50 percent in New York and Washington, D.C., respectively) 5 percent more black than nonblack associates were graduates from elite schools. The black associates also tend to come from schools at the top of the elite range.... In New York firms, Harvard, Columbia, and NYU graduates were 51 percent of black associates; in the District of Columbia, Harvard, and Georgetown graduates were 52 percent.

When we look back to a period when there was less affirmative action, we find evidence that going to an elite law school was even more important for blacks. At five national law firms, 77 percent of black partners attended one of 13 elite law schools, compared with 70 percent of all white partners; the respective percentages who had attended Harvard or Yale were 47 and 33.

Because virtually all the blacks who start at a given elite law firm leave before becoming partner, we now examine how the institutional characteristics of those firms—high salaries, pyramiding, and tracking—affect a black associate's partnership prospects. Some associates report that they receive valuable training opportunities, while others do not. Once an associate acquires a reputation as being well trained, she will continue to receive training in the form of demanding work. An associate's perception about which track she is on will have a substantial impact on how long she decides to stay with the firm.

Black associates face three significant barriers to getting on the training track. First, an associate has to have mentors among the firm's partners or senior associates who can provide the royal jelly of good training. Less than 40 percent of our survey of black Harvard Law School graduates (only 24 percent of pre–1986 graduates) stated that a partner had taken interest in their work or career. Of those who did not find a mentor, 68 percent said this was a significant factor in deciding to leave the firm (79 percent of post–1986 graduates).... Chief among the factors that contribute to this problem is the bias that potential mentors have for proteges who resemble them. Because partners have little information about a new associate's actual skills, the decision about who is a superstar worthy of training will be made in the same way as it is done at the recruiting stage—based on a few easily observable signals. Blacks may also suffer from a general perception that they are "less interested" in corporate work than other lawyers. This sentiment may be reinforced by the fact that black associates appear to be more likely than their white peers to do more than the average amount of pro bono work, to hold skeptical views of the social utility of some of the goals of their corporate clients, and to leave corporate practice for jobs in the public sector. Finally, black associates will have difficulty getting onto the training track precisely because the generation of black associates before them did not.

Sociologists contend that when a group's representation in the workforce is small, individual members face increased pressures to perform and conform. Over 40 percent of our respondents reported that they were criticized more than white associates for making similar mistakes. If partners expect black associates to be average or unacceptable, then any mistake will be seen as confirming this initial assessment. Small numbers also increase the probability that group members will be tied together in the minds of members of the dominant group.

Lawyers wishing to move laterally face conflicting incentives: the longer they stay, the more they can claim to have accumulated valuable skills; but the closer they are to partnership, the greater the danger that potential employers may presume that they are leaving because they are not "good enough" to make partner. Only 15 percent of black Harvard respondents who had left their first elite firm went to another one; 33 percent went into government, 20 percent to corporate legal departments, and 17 percent to small nonelite firms. We hypothesize that the optimal time for black associates to leave firms is earlier than that for white associates.

Black associates therefore have strong incentives to choose career strategies that either minimize the danger of sending a negative signal or, conversely, maximize their opportunity for being regarded as superstars. The first requires the associate either to steer clear of demanding assignments or take fewer risks in completing the work. Only 32 percent of Harvard black alumni worked in corporate practice (24 percent of pre–1986 graduates). Only 14 percent of black partners work in general corporate practice, and less than 11 percent specialize in technical fields, such as banking (6 percent), bankruptcy (2 percent), and tax (1 percent). Anecdotal evidence also suggests that black associates may be overly cautious when performing their work. Those who study law firm interactions report that many black associates tend to speak less in meetings (particularly with clients), ask more clarifying questions when receiving work, are more likely to check assignments before handing them in, are more reluctant to disagree with partners or express criticism of their peers, and construe their assignments more narrowly. But successfully completing "difficult" work assignments is the best way for an associate to signal quality and thus worthiness for training.

At the opposite extreme, a black associate may seek out demanding assignments in order to overcome the presumption that she is "only" average—or worse. In response to our survey, 45 percent reported specializing in litigation (52 percent of pre–1986 graduates). These percentages are higher than those in all but the most litigation-oriented firms. This has been the most successful avenue to partnership: 56 percent of black partners at elite firms are litigators. Although many kinds of corporate work are handled exclusively by elite firms, litigators are needed in many different settings, including government, small firms solo practice, and in-house legal departments. The lower level of scrutiny in litigation, however, increases the risk that an associate will fall through the cracks. There also is a substantial amount of routine low-visibility work. These factors make litigation one of the least likely routes to partnership for associates as a whole.... Finally, litigation is generally less stable than corporate work, and dispute-specific factual knowledge is less transferrable to future cases.

In a study of successful minority managers in corporations, David Thomas concluded that even those who ultimately make it into the top ranks do not have the same smooth, linear progression as their white peers. This pattern of slow growth followed by relatively dramatic jumps in position is virtually impossible in a world in which both firms and associates make important career decisions within the first one or two years. There is, however, a way in which black lawyers have been able to replicate the success patterns Thomas outlines, although it involves leaving the firm. A substantial percentage of all black partners in our data set first worked in government (37 percent), in-house counsel's office (28 percent), and/or academia (II percent). Similarly in our survey, all four black Harvard graduates who had become partners in major firms first left their original firms and went into either government (three) or a small firm (one).

FINDING EFFICIENT RESPONSES TO EFFICIENT DISCRIMINATION

So long as firms continue to generate both a small number of high-quality partners and a steady supply of hardworking associates, they have little economic reason to alter the way they structure their business. Those who wish to break this cycle must therefore alter the incentives that firms presently face. Many commentators have documented the difficulty of applying Title VII and other similar anti-discrimination laws to high-level jobs in which quality judgments are inherently subjective. Nevertheless, the threat of liability undoubtedly encourages firms to pay more attention to their employment practices. Lawrence Mungin, a black Harvard Law School graduate, successfully sued the Washington, D.C., office of Katten, Muchin & Zavis for "constructively discharging" him on the basis of his race.* When Mungin, a senior associate, requested that he be evaluated along with the other associates in his class, he was working primarily on projects that would normally have been handled by second-and third-year associates. Not surprisingly, Katten's managing partner informed him that it would be impossible to make him a partner based on his current performance. Mungin's lawsuit revealed, however, that when Katten's Washington office lost most of its bankruptcy business (Mungin's area of specialization), he was told he would receive work from the Chicago main office, which never arrived. Nor was Mungin included in departmental meetings in Washington or Chicago or given a performance review during his first 18 months, even though Katten's policy was to review every associate twice a year. By shining light on the normally invisible world of law-firm staffing and work-assignment decisions, Mungin's case may encourage firms to pay more attention to whether black associates are getting access to challenging and productive work.

Formal training and mentoring programs might seem to be the ideal solution to the institutional dynamics we describe. But despite the fanfare with which firms announce their new training efforts, it is clear that those

---

* [Editors' Note:] But see Mungin v. Katten, Muchin & Zavis, 116 F.3d 1549 (D.C.Cir. 1997) (reversing the trial court).

wishing to succeed must still gain access to the traditional training track. These programs say nothing about who will actually get the type of work associates need to succeed. Formal assignment systems could break these patterns, but powerful partners routinely bypass them to grab superstar associates. Similarly, formal evaluation systems, while potentially providing valuable information and feedback, can also act as a diversion that allows partners to refrain from giving real feedback in the course of the working relationship.

. . . Anecdotal reports suggest that diversity consultants [hired by law firms] tend to concentrate on exposing how racist comments, unintended slights, and cliquish social patterns marginalize black lawyers. However, less than a third of the respondents to our survey mentioned explicit racist comments made in their presence, and less than 20 percent of those who did said the incident was a major reason for leaving the firm. Although a higher proportion (56 percent) did not feel welcome in the informal social networks within the firm, nearly half (46 percent) of these did not consider this a major factor in deciding whether to leave the firm. Moreover, there is a long history of firms and courts subtly transforming informal grievance procedures into mechanisms for suppressing conflict.

In 1988, the American Bar Association initiated the Minority Counsel Demonstration Project to encourage participating corporations to retain minority firms and to ensure that minority partners in majority firms do some of their legal work. In its first three years, 133 corporations, 39 major law firms, and 21 minority-owned firms participated, generating more than $100 million in billings for minority lawyers. Moreover, the number of minority associates at the 15 majority firms reporting increased by over 50 percent during the three years, and the number of minority partners by 57 percent. Nevertheless, there is reason to be skeptical. The claim that diversity is good for a corporation's bottom line has substantial force in sectors of the economy that sell consumer products, trade internationally, or do substantial business with the government. But when AT & T is considering a new joint-venture agreement, it wants lawyers who know how to operate in the complex world of strategic planning and corporate finance, a world that is still overwhelmingly white and male. It is not surprising, therefore, that most corporate participants in the ABA Program do little more than send the same letter every year "requesting information" and dole out a few small projects that are often below the pricing structure for most major firms. Yet anecdotal evidence suggests that black in-house lawyers are more likely to take an active interest in ensuring that work is fairly distributed to black lawyers inside firms, and black political clout has frequently been translated into opportunities for black lawyers.

At least since the 1970s, many elite firms have hired black lawyers whose rankable signals were lower than the average credentials of the firm's white associates. These affirmative action programs appear to have increased the presence of black lawyers in the elite firms. The most common objections raised to such programs—lowered standards, reduced worker effort, and stigmatized beneficiaries—do not provide persuasive grounds for abandoning them at elite firms. To the extent that goals and timetables or other affirmative recruiting measures give firms a reason to detect and prevent practices that favor whites over blacks with functionally *equal* qualifications, these measures will, in fact, serve rather than weaken the goal of "standards." Moreover, the standards critique ignores the tremendous growth in the size and quality of the law school applicant pool over the last few decades. Firms have an incentive to seek out superstars and to protect themselves against unacceptable workers. In the middle, however, they are (at least on efficiency grounds) indifferent since they know that differences among candidates in this range are not worth the trouble of investigating. Paradoxically, even in a world where some find the standards critique persuasive, the firm that hires the most black lawyers ought to be the one whose reputation among these skeptics suffers the least. Thus, firms such as San Francisco's Morrison & Foerster and New York's Cleary, Gottlieb, Steen & Hamilton can credibly claim that they are among the "best" firms for black lawyers. This, in turn, should signal to their clients, their competitors, and the general population of law students that the black lawyers they hire are likely to be the best in the available pool.

If affirmative action provides the average black associate, who today faces a low probability of success, with a somewhat greater probability, this can *only increase* her incentive to work. Associates are choosing some combination of signals and skills to help them both get a *ticket to the tournament* (where the price of the ticket is the level of signals the firm requires) and then have a chance of *winning the tournament* (where initial skills are necessary to help one be chosen by a partner for the training track). If as a result of affirmative action, blacks have to spend less of their scarce resources on purchasing the ticket, they can use those resources to acquire skills that will increase their chances of winning the tournament.

The logic of the stigma argument is straightforward and compelling. If it is widely known that at least some significant number of blacks have benefitted from affirmative action, employers will rationally discount any particular black candidate's credentials by the amount they think she has benefitted. The danger is that partners will choose to give routine projects to the black associates while assigning analytical-training-related ones to the white associates. The solution, however, is not to abandon voluntary affirmative action in hiring but to extend it to decisions regarding the choice of associates for projects and other internal firm decisions. Companies such as Procter and Gamble and AT & T rate their managers in terms of their success in promoting the firm's diversity goals and weigh these ratings in setting compensation and determining promotions. If elite firms were to institute policies of this kind, partners would have concrete incentives to insure that blacks make it onto the training track.

———————

African-Americans and Legal Education

The black experience in legal academia has been bleak. According to the Chused study, supra, "[in] 1986–87, a typical law school faculty had thirty-one members.... Of these ... thirty were white, one was black, Hispanic or other minority...."[68] In 1980, blacks constituted 2.8 percent of the faculty at other than the few traditionally black law schools. By 1986, the figure had risen only to 3.7 percent.[69] Compare the increase in the same period for women, discussed earlier; for Hispanics the percentage went from 0.5 to 0.7 percent; and for other minorities from 0.5 to 1.0 percent. "The data ... demonstrate that minority professors in general, and black professors in particular, tend to be tokens if they are present at all.... In sheer numbers, the increase has been very small ... only thirty-five more tenured black professors ... than there were in 1981."[70]

Of professors hired for tenure-track positions between 1986 and 1991, when law schools professed a high level of commitment to affirmative action hiring: about 17 percent were members of minority groups (9 percent male and 8 percent female).[71] Of those 17 percent, the best available data show that the majority were African–American (73.7%); Hispanic (16.7%); Asian (7.9%); and Native American (1.8%). About 30 percent of these hires were white women; and 53 percent were white men. White men were more likely to secure a job at an elite law school than any other group with women of color having the worst showing at elite schools.[72] From their exhaustive study of hiring between 1986 and 1991, Merritt and Reskin conclude that in those years white women and minority men enjoyed a small advantage in hiring over white men and minority women with comparable credentials.[73] On the other hand, preferences of schools for their own graduates swamped the effects of all other characteristics, including any advantage based on sex or race.[74]

---

68. Richard H. Chused, Hiring and Retention, supra, 137 U.Pa.L.Rev. at 538.

69. Id.

70. Id. at 539–40. On the experience of blacks in legal academia, see Andrew W. Haines, Minority Law Professors and the Myth of Sisyphus: Consciousness and Praxis Within the Special Teaching Challenge in American Law Schools, 10 Nat'l Black L.J. 247 (1988); Richard Delgado, Minority Law Professors' Lives: The Bell–Delgado Survey (Institute for Legal Studies Working Papers Series 39, Oct. 1988); Charles R. Lawrence, Minority Hiring in AALS Law Schools: The Need for Voluntary Quotas, 20 U.S.F.L.Rev. 429 (1986); Derrick A. Bell, Jr., Application of the "Tipping Point" Principle to Law Faculty Hiring Policies, 10 Nova L.J. 319 (1986); Derrick A. Bell, Jr., Strangers in Academic Paradise: Law Teachers of Color in Still White Law Schools, 20 U.S.F.L.Rev. 385 (1986).

71. Merritt & Reskin, supra, 97 Colum.L.Rev. at 229. All the figures in this paragraph are from this source.

72. Id. at 236. The top 16 law schools identified by Merritt & Reskin hired 11% of all professors in the time period of the study; 13.1% of white men won such an appointment; 10% of white women and minority men; and only 2% of minority women. As indicated earlier, AALS data for all ABA-approved law schools provides a somewhat different picture than this earlier snapshot of elite schools: In 1997–98, for example, 21.3% of new assistant professors were minorities, 13.3% of professors, and 10.3% of associate professors (tbl. 3A); minorities have the highest success rate in faculty hiring of all groups in the AALS Faculty Appointments Register. AALS Statistical Report, supra.

73. Id. at 282.

74. Id.

In 1996 California voters, by a 54 to 46 percent margin, approved Proposition 209, which declares that "the state shall not discriminate against, or grant preferential treatment to, any individual or group on the basis of race, sex, color, ethnicity, or national origin in the operation of public employment, public education, or public contracting;" That same year the Fifth Circuit in Hopwood v. Texas held that the University of Texas School of Law, and by extensions other institutions in its jurisdiction, could no longer use race as a decisive factor in the admission process.[75] These events obviously have implications far wider than our present focus, minorities and particularly African–Americans in the legal profession, but, if only because *Hopwood* involved a law school, the effect on the composition of the profession has been the subject of much heated debate. We have no intention of trying to resolve that debate here; indeed, among the three authors of this book, there is no consensus on the meaning of these events. But we do offer the following facts in the hope that they will help you consider the wisdom of the direction charted by the voters of California and the judges on the Fifth Circuit:[76]

- According to documents filed in *Hopwood*, out of the pool of resident applicants who scored between 189 and 192 inclusive on the law school's internal scoring system, which was based on grade point average and standardized law school admission tests, 100 percent of blacks and 90 percent of Mexican Americans, but only six percent of whites, were offered admission to the law school.

- The associate dean at Texas, in a draft letter prepared for the dean, described the results of the "radically different admission standards" applied to black applicants: "few of our Black students have been able to finish above the bottom quarter or third of the class in terms of law school grades." In addition, although about 90 percent of non-minority law graduates at Texas pass the bar on their first try, the figure for blacks was "consistently under 50 percent." "Even more seriously, half of our minority graduates who fail the exam fail again upon retaking."[77]

---

75. 78 F.3d 932 (5th Cir.), cert. denied, 116 S. Ct. 2581 (1996).

76. For a black law professor's views on affirmative action, see Stephen L. Carter, Reflections of an Affirmative Action Baby (1991). For a recent defense of affirmative action, see William G. Bowen and Derek Bok, The Shape of the River: Long–Term Consequences of Considering Race in College and University Admissions (1998) (drawing on student data from 28 elite colleges and concluding that preferentially admitted minority students have had successful subsequent careers). For a hopeful view of the substantial progress since 1930, combined with data that suggests doubts about preferential admissions in higher ed-

ucation, see Stephan and Abigail Thernstrom, America in Black and White: One Nation Indivisible (1997).

77. See Stephan Thernstrom, Diversity and Meritocracy in Legal Education: A Critical Evaluation of Linda F. Wightman's 'The Threat to Diversity in Legal Education,' 15 Const'l Comm. 11, 21, 24 (1998) (quoting from documents in the *Hopwood* record). The Wightman study of minority attrition put a favorable gloss on the subject, but the underlying data, analyzed by Thernstrom, indicated an attrition rate of 13 percent of white law students in the class of 1991 as against 43 percent of specially admitted black students. Id. at 40.

• Those in favor of Proposition 209 and *Hopwood,* argue that while minority enrollment has decreased at the most selective public universities in Texas and California, overall enrollment in universities (not law schools) of African–Americans and Hispanics has remained stable since 1996.[78]

• Those on the other side point out that in 1998, the first year in which Proposition 209 was effective, freshman minority enrollment in the nine-campus University of California system declined by 13 percent. However, that figure includes only blacks, Hispanics, and American Indians. Asian–American enrollment went up. Prior to Proposition 209, Asian–Americans had not been counted as "minorities" for purposes of affirmative action admission because of the high proportion of this group enrolled without any special consideration.[79]

• In an effort to correct the problem at the prestige universities, in 1998 the Texas state university system began admitting all Texas public high school students who graduated in the top tenth of their class into the state's flagship campuses, the University of Texas at Austin and Texas A & M. A somewhat similar plan is scheduled to go into effect in California in 2001.[80]

• Before *Hopwood* 40 to 60 Mexican–Americans enrolled in the University of Texas law school each year. The number of Mexican-Americans dropped to 26 the first year and 29 the second.

• Before *Hopwood* 20 to 40 African–Americans enrolled each year in the University of Texas law school; in 1997, there were four African–Americans; and in 1998, nine.[81] "Three years after [*Hopwood*] . . . there [were] a mere eight black students in a first-year class of 455 at the law school, a smaller percentage than in 1950."[82]

• In 1998 voters in Washington state passed a referendum similar to California's Proposition 209, banning racial preferences in college admissions.[83]

• "The conservative public law firm that brought [the *Hopwood* case and a similar suit pending against the University of Michigan has]

78. Affirmative Action: Living Without It, The Economist, March 13, 1999, p.34.

79. Siobhan Gorman, The 4 Percent Solution, Nat'l. L. J. March 20, 1999. This article also describes California's approach, scheduled to begin in 2001, of admitting the top 4 percent of high school graduates.

80. Yale Daily News, University Wire, March 23, 1999. See also Gorman, supra.

81. Lucy Hood, Bill to Dodge Hopwood Rule Filed in Austin, San Antonio Express-

News, Feb. 27, 1999, p.1B. This article also describes a bill introduced in the Texas legislature that makes findings on past discrimination in the Texas university system. The Fifth Circuit in *Hopwood* suggested that such legislature findings might be enough to justify an affirmative action program at the school.

82. The Economist, supra.

83. Gorman, The 4 Percent Solution, supra.

... sent out a handbook to students at elite universities, a step-by-step guide to suing colleges for 'illegal racial preferences.' "[84]

The issues suggested by this factual recital are among the most important facing American society. Catch phrases such as "affirmative action" or "preferential quotas" or "systemic racism" carry an emotional charge and may conceal discrete issues that would benefit from separate treatment. Underlying factual premises are disputed and normative positions debated. What vision of American life and of American law practice should be embodied in laws regulating these matters? Given that views are so fractured on these issues, what can law achieve?

Who counts as a minority? If we include people whose ancestry is Asian, Latin, African, Arabian, Native American ... , "people of color" constitute a majority of the people on earth and will, someday soon, constitute a majority of the American people. After Proposition 209, Asian enrollment at California's state universities increased, while African–American enrollment declined at the most selective public institutions. Similarly, the steady progress of "minorities" in law firms and legal academia looks a lot less steady and a lot less "progressive" when one focuses exclusively on the hiring and promotion of African–Americans. A powerful case can be made for the proposition that focusing on "minority" progress hides the magnitude of the problem confronting African–Americans in particular. No other "minority" in this nation's history has been subjected to so sustained an onslaught of private terror, public discrimination, educational deprivation and political exclusion as the African–American people.[85] Discrimination against other "minorities" has, in contrast, tended to be localized and relatively transitory. After the Civil War, African–Americans were understood for a brief moment in legal time to be the special concern of the Civil War Amendments to the Constitution and the federal legislation that accompanied those Amendments. But that moment was brief indeed. The entire project of affirmative action was built around the fungibility of minority groups. Was that a mistake?

Other Minorities

Discrimination on grounds of race, sex and ethnicity has affected many groups. Although discrimination against Jews has markedly eased in the last generation, it was a serious problem earlier. Jews in small number have been members of the American legal profession since the 19th century. Beginning with the large immigration from central and eastern Europe at the end of the 19th century, a substantial fraction of whom were Jews, the established legal profession became uneasy, widely hostile and discriminatory.[86] Similar attitudes were manifested toward Catholics on

---

84. The Economist, supra.

85. For a brilliant discussion and critique of the legal construct of "minority," in Supreme Court jurisprudence, see Robert M. Cover, The Origins of Judicial Activism in

the Protection of Minorities, 91 Yale L.J. 1287 (1982).

86. On Jewish lawyers, see Jerold S. Auerbach, Rabbis and Lawyers: The Journey from the Torah to the Constitution (1990);

religious grounds and toward Irish, Italians and Poles on ethnic grounds, but with less intensity. The same holds for all ethnic minorities in one degree or another.[87] At least since the mid–1970s, however, discrimination appears to have sharply declined in the legal profession, as much or more than in other vocational groups, as against people of European heritage.

Discrimination and differentials in opportunity evidently persist as against Hispanics, Asians and other ethnic minorities.[88] Lawyers who are physically disabled and gay and lesbian lawyers[89] also confront discrimination and barriers to entry into the "establishment" legal institutions in the United States. The high academic achievement of many Asians has improved their competitive position, but also engenders fear of competition. The moral challenge remains.

C. PROFESSIONAL DISCIPLINE

Introduction

Professional discipline is a substantial but controversial enterprise. A disciplinary complaint is filed each year against one out of ten of the nation's one million active lawyers. About one out of ten complaints lead to some form of discipline.[1] About 40 percent of disciplinary sanctions, however, are private censures or reprimands that remain invisible to clients, other lawyers and the general public. The available data indicates that about 5 percent of total complaints result in public or private sanctions; and that public and private reprimands are the only sanction in the

Comment, The Jewish Law Student and New York Jobs—Discriminatory Effects in Law Firm Hiring Practices, 73 Yale L.J. 625 (1964).

87. See generally Jerold S. Auerbach, Unequal Justice: Lawyers and Social Change in Modern America (1976).

88. See, e.g., Leo M. Romero, Richard Delgado & Cruz Reynoso, The Legal Education of Chicano Students: A Study in Mutual Accommodation and Cultural Conflict, 5 New Mex.L.Rev. 177 (1975); Linda E. Davila, The Underrepresentation of Hispanic Attorneys in Corporate Law Firms, 39 Stanford L.Rev. 1403 (1987). Kiyoko Kamio Knapp, Disdain of Alien Lawyers: History of Exclusion, 7 Seton Hall Const. L.J. 103 (1996) (describing discrimination against and challenges faced by alien Asian lawyers in the United States).

89. See, e.g., Symposium: Queer Studies I: An Examination of the First Eleven Stud-

ies of Sexual Orientation Bias by the Legal Profession, 8 UCLA Women's L.J. 343 (1998); The Los Angeles County Bar Association Report on Sexual Orientation Bias 4 S. Cal. Rev. L. & Women's Stud. 305 (1995); and Nancy D. Polikoff, Am I My Client?: The Role Confusion of a Lawyer Activist,31 Harv. C.R.-C.L. L. Rev. 443 (1996).

1. The information in this paragraph is drawn from conversations with Mary R. Devlin of the ABA Center for Professional Responsibility and the statistics on professional discipline published by the Center. See ABA Ctr.Prof.Resp., 1996 Survey on Lawyer Discipline Systems (1998) (compiling data from questionnaires sent to 56 U.S. disciplinary agencies; ten states did not respond and are not included). In the reporting jurisdictions, 6,486 sanctions were imposed in 1996, 3,852 of which were public sanctions and 2,634 private.

majority of investigated complaints. Less than one percent of investigated complaints result in disbarment.[2]

Disciplinary efforts vary enormously in staffing, resources and structure from state to state.[3] California, at one end of the spectrum, spent $372 per California lawyer in 1996[4] investigating 6,341 complaints and imposing public sanctions on 720 lawyers; the disciplinary body had a full-time staff of 289 lawyers, investigators and others. Missouri, on the other hand, which has about one-sixth the number of lawyers as California, spent $58 per lawyer investigating 1,679 complaints (a higher complaint rate than California) and imposed public sanctions on 37 lawyers with a full-time staff of ten (a much lower discipline rate). Missouri, along with a number of other states, relies heavily on the volunteer services of lawyers rather than a full-time professional staff.

How effective is professional discipline in protecting clients and deterring professional failure? This question should be borne in mind in considering this section. Some limitations on the effectiveness of professional discipline have been mentioned in prior chapters: (1) although clients are harmed by individual instances of a lawyer's departure from standards of due care, the nearly universal approach of disciplinary bodies is to investigate only instances of egregious and usually repeated instances of neglect and incompetence (Chapter 3); (2) similarly, one of the most common client complaints about lawyers concerns fee charges and demands, yet discipline for excessive fees is extremely rare (Chapter 6); (3) lawyers who are sanctioned by a court for misconduct in a proceeding are rarely disciplined for the same conduct (Chapter 5); and (4) lawyers who practice in large law firms are shielded from discipline by a culture that rarely reports violation of a firm lawyer and by difficulties in establishing the fault of an individual lawyer in situations of diffused responsibility. Thus professional discipline operates largely with respect to reckless or intentional wrongdoing on the part of individual lawyers, usually those who are solo practitioners or whose firm association is a small and loose affiliation of practitioners.

1.   THE DISCIPLINARY PROCESS

Evolution of Disciplinary Procedure

The old regime of disciplinary procedure was relatively informal.[5]

---

2. Id., charts I and II.

3. Id., charts I, II, VII and VIII.

4. California's expenditures on California State Bar activities led to a political crisis in 1997–1998. Governor Wilson attacked the State Bar for spending too much money on political and ideological activities; and a substantial proportion of the state's lawyers joined in one aspect of the criticism— bar dues were too high and too much was being spent on lawyer discipline. For part

of 1998 the State Bar was unfunded and activities largely ceased, but after the November 1998 elections the California Supreme Court ordered payment of sufficient dues to fund bar discipline. See Gail D. Cox, Latest in Calif. Bar Saga: a $396 Bar Bill, Nat'l L.J., Jan.18, 1999, p. A8.

5. Geoffrey C. Hazard, Jr. and Cameron Beard, A Lawyer's Privilege Against Self– Incrimination in Professional Disciplinary Proceedings, 96 Yale L.J. 1060, 1063–65 (1987).

Since the beginning of the nineteenth century, most American jurisdictions have required one who acts as a lawyer for others to be licensed. In the older parlance, and in the Hohfeldian sense, the practice of law is a "privilege," i.e., a capacity that is not an incident of citizenship but is conferred by law on a limited number of people who meet specified requirements. . . .

The term "privilege" has long been used as a predicate in analysis of the rules governing both admission to practice and lawyer discipline. The leading treatise on law practice of the early twentieth century . . . stated:

> The right to practice law is not a natural inherent right, but one which may be exercised only upon proof of fitness, through evidence of the possession of satisfactory legal attainments and fair character. The privilege of practicing law is not open to all, but is a special personal franchise limited to persons of good moral character, with special qualifications. . . . [Edward M. Thornton, A Treatise on Attorneys at Law 22–23 (1914)].

Under traditional legal doctrine, this characterization implied that constitutional law would require only a modicum of procedural formality for revocation of an attorney's license. . . .

According to Thornton, a petition for disbarment was to set forth verified allegations specifying with reasonable particularity the misconduct for which disbarment was sought. If the court found the allegations sufficient in law, it would ordinarily issue an order against the lawyer in question, directing him to show cause why he should not be disbarred. The burden of proof thus was on the attorney to prove his innocence. There was little or no pretrial discovery. Appellate review was nominally available, but the tenor of the decisions suggests that a lawyer found guilty of an offense warranting disbarment had little chance of obtaining reversal on either substantive or procedural grounds.[6]

The Supreme Court has considered remarkably few cases involving lawyer disciplinary proceedings, particularly compared with the number of bar admission cases it has considered. This suggests that the bar itself supports protective procedural standards in disciplinary matters, whatever its views might be on the rights of new applicants.

In re Ruffalo[7] involved charges that the respondent lawyer solicited personal injury claims to be brought under the Federal Employers Liability Act and hired a railroad employee to investigate claims against his employer railroad. The Court invalidated a disbarment based on a charge that was added only after the evidence had been received at the disciplinary hearing:

> [The lawyer] is entitled to procedural due process, which includes fair notice of the charge. . . . These are adversary proceedings of a quasi-criminal nature. . . . The charge must be known before the

---

6. Id. at 1063–65.   **7.** 390 U.S. 544 (1968).

proceedings commence. They become a trap when ... the charges are amended on the basis of testimony of the accused. He can then be given no opportunity to expunge the earlier statements and start afresh.[8]

Lawyer disciplinary procedure now adheres to a "due process" model. In most jurisdictions, the procedure is similar to a civil proceeding tried to a judge rather than a jury, with a preliminary prosecutorial review to determine probable cause:[9]

First, there is a required screening by the disciplinary agency to determine whether lodging a formal charge would be warranted. Functionally, this resembles the probable cause hearing in criminal procedure. It screens out those complaints for which the evidence is insufficient to get to a trier of fact, and synthesizes the evidence when it meets the sufficiency test, in the latter case laying the foundation for possible "plea bargaining." The second variation from the civil procedure model concerns discovery. In some jurisdictions, the accused lawyer has the same rights of discovery as are available in civil actions in the trial court of general jurisdiction, but the prevailing pattern gives the accused only informal access to the prosecution's dossier. Third, except in Texas and Georgia, there is no right to a jury trial.

The prevailing model thus may be described as a relatively formal version of administrative law procedure. Its elements include:

- The benefit of pre-charge screening by the disciplinary enforcement agency;

- The right to notice and a statement of the charge or grievance;

- The right to formal or informal discovery;

- The right to assistance of counsel;

- The rights to subpoena witnesses and evidence, to cross-examine adverse witnesses, and to exclude evidence inadmissible under the rules of evidence;

- The requirement of proof by a preponderance of the evidence or, in some jurisdictions, by clear and convincing evidence; and

- The right to judicial review.

The American Bar Association, after developing standards for lawyer discipline and rules for disciplinary enforcement, combined them in 1989 in the Model Rules for Lawyer Disciplinary Enforcement. The rules have influenced the development of disciplinary rules in many states.

Jurisdiction to Impose Discipline

Model Rule 8.5(a) provides:

---

8. 390 U.S. at 550–551.

9. Hazard and Beard, supra, 96 Yale L.J. at 1066–67.

A lawyer admitted to practice in this jurisdiction is subject to the disciplinary authority of this jurisdiction, regardless of where the lawyer's conducts occurs. A lawyer may be subject to the disciplinary authority of both this jurisdiction and another jurisdiction where the lawyer is admitted for the same conduct.

Rule 8.5(b), dealing with choice of law in the exercise of disciplinary authority, is considered infra p. 1062.

Discipline and the Fifth Amendment

Suppose a client charges that a lawyer converted funds the client had given the lawyer as a down payment on a transaction. At a subsequent disciplinary proceeding, the lawyer refuses to respond either to oral questions, relying on the Fifth Amendment, or to produce requested records concerning his client trust account. The lawyer's oral testimony cannot be compelled, but the trust account records are subject to compulsory process if specifically requested (the *Fisher* case, supra p. 227) or as "required records." Since the lawyer's failure to produce records does not rely on a valid privilege, the lawyer may now be charged additionally with refusal to cooperate with disciplinary authorities, providing proper notice and opportunity to defend are given as required by the *Ruffalo* case, supra. Professional discipline is infused with the idea that a lawyer, as an officer of the court, is obliged to cooperate with disciplinary authorities. But the duty to cooperate does not result in loss of the Fifth Amendment privilege or allow a state to discipline a lawyer for invoking the privilege.[10] The leading case is Spevack v. Klein.[11]

Spevack held that a lawyer could not be disbarred for refusing to produce records in a disciplinary proceeding concerning solicitation of personal injury cases. The decision rested on the ground that the Fifth Amendment's privilege against self-incrimination protected the lawyer against being compelled to give evidence in a disciplinary matter that could expose him to incrimination in a criminal prosecution. The premise was that the Fifth Amendment protects against being compelled to produce records because producing records is in effect being "compelled ... to be a witness against himself" within the meaning of the Amendment. That premise, however, has since been overruled by Fisher v. United States,[12] p. 227 supra. Two propositions stated in *Spevack* remain sound, however: (1) A lawyer cannot be disciplined for failure to respond in a disciplinary proceeding when the failure consists of invoking a constitutional privilege, and (2) the Fifth Amendment may be invoked in a disciplinary proceeding to avoid giving incriminating testimony.

---

10. May disciplinary authorities draw adverse inferences from a lawyer's invocation of the privilege? Several decisions answer in the affirmative. See, e.g., McInnis v. State, 618 S.W.2d 389, 392 (Tex.Civ.App. 1981), cert. denied, 456 U.S. 976), relying on Baxter v. Palmigiano, 425 U.S. 308 (1976) (prisoner's silence at prison disciplinary proceeding may be taken as adverse inference of guilt).

11. 385 U.S. 511 (1967).

12. 425 U.S. 391 (1976).

May a lawyer be punished for misconduct revealed in testimony the lawyer is required to give after being given immunity from criminal prosecution on the matters involved? In Anonymous Attorneys v. Bar Ass'n of Erie County,[13] several lawyers were called to testify before a Buffalo grand jury investigating the fixing of traffic tickets. They refused to testify on self-incrimination grounds. The grand jury granted the lawyers "immunity from any penalties or forfeitures arising out of the transactions" in question. The lawyers subsequently testified before the grand jury and at the criminal trials of certain officials. Their testimony indicated they participated in giving bribes. When disciplinary officials sought to initiate disciplinary proceedings against them for their involvement in ticket fixing, the lawyers claimed that the grant of immunity foreclosed any disciplinary proceedings involving the same matter.

The New York Court of Appeals rejected the lawyers' claim, holding (1) professional discipline is not a criminal "penalty or forfeiture" within the meaning of New York's use immunity statute, and (2) the Fifth Amendment and the grant of immunity apply only to "incrimination" in criminal proceedings and not to civil proceedings or sanctions such as professional discipline.

2.   GROUNDS FOR DISCIPLINE

In discussing "the uncertainty of the philosophy behind lawyer discipline," Charles Wolfram argues that two competing sets of standards create ambiguity:

> One set of standards attempts to predict the likelihood that a lawyer in the future will violate important norms. But another set of standards merely holds lawyers who have engaged in questioned conduct in the past to very high standards with little effort to assess the lawyer's ability to perform professional functions.[14]

The ABA Standards for Imposing Lawyer Sanctions summarize "the basic purpose of discipline:"

> [T]he primary purpose is to protect the public. Second, the . . . need to protect the integrity of the legal system. . . . Another purpose is to deter further unethical conduct and, where appropriate, to rehabilitate the lawyer. A final purpose . . . is to educate other lawyers and the public, thereby deterring unethical behavior among all members of the profession.[15]

Lawyer Crimes

Should a lawyer who has committed a crime be disciplined? Should the answer depend on the seriousness of the crime and whether or not it was related to the lawyer's representation of a client? Model Rule 8.4(b) limits

---

13. 363 N.E.2d 592 (1977).

14. Wolfram, Modern Legal Ethics § 3.3.1 (1986).

15. Commentary to ABA Standards for Imposing Sanctions § 1.1 (1986, amended in 1992).

discipline to those crimes "that reflect adversely on the lawyer's honesty, trustworthiness or fitness as a lawyer in other respects."[16] This fitness-to-practice standard suggests that felonies or other conduct involving dishonesty or breach of trust should result in discipline whether or not they occur in the practice of law. On the other hand, many misdemeanors, and perhaps even some felonies, may not reflect on a lawyer's fitness for practice.

The fitness-to-practice standard of M.R. 8.4(b) departs from the Model Code approach. DR 1–102(A)(4) states that a lawyer shall not "engage in illegal conduct involving moral turpitude." Crimes of violence involving premeditation and malicious intent clearly fall within the prohibited category as do those in which a lawyer deliberately violates a public or private trust. But what about a drunken bar room brawl, wilful tax evasion, or the growing of marijuana in one's back yard?[17] The vagueness of "moral turpitude" has led to inconsistency both in deciding that a disciplinary offense was committed and determining the appropriate sanction. Sanctions vary from a concealed slap on the wrist (private reprimand) to public censure, probation, suspension or disbarment.

The criminal conviction of a lawyer, especially for a felony, carries both procedural and substantive consequences. In all jurisdictions, a conviction (including a guilty plea) operates as proof of the facts on which the conviction was based. In many jurisdictions, including New York, a felony conviction results in automatic disbarment, and in the remainder it triggers a disciplinary inquiry. Discipline may be imposed for conduct that is also criminal even though the lawyer was acquitted in a criminal trial or the charges were dismissed or dropped.

Lawyers acting as public officials may be disciplined for official conduct that violates professional rules. During Senate confirmation hearings on his nomination as Attorney General, Acting Attorney General Richard Kleindienst was questioned about whether he had had conversations with anyone in the White House concerning a controversial antitrust case pending in the Supreme Court in which the government had sought a postponement.[18] Kleindienst responded negatively. Later, when the Nixon tapes became available, the Watergate Special Prosecutor discovered a tape-recorded telephone conversation in which President Nixon had ordered Kleindienst "don't file the brief," "drop the thing," etc. Kleindienst did not

---

16. Except for the "catch-all" provision of M.R. 8.4(d) (discipline for "conduct that is prejudicial to the administration of justice"), considered infra, the other provisions of M.R. 8.4 seem to imply the fitness-for-practice standard of M.R. 8.4(b) even though it is not specifically included. The conduct prohibited by M.R. 8.4(c) (dishonesty, fraud, deceit or misrepresentation) focuses on factors vital to lawyer integrity and client trust.

17. See Wolfram supra at 92–94, discussing the conflicting decisions on what constitutes "moral turpitude" and whether "illegal conduct" is limited to "criminal conduct."

18. The full story is reported in John T. Noonan, Jr. & Richard W. Painter, Professional and Personal Responsibilities of the Lawyer 179–212 (1997); see also Roger C. Cramton, On the Steadfastness and Courage of Government Lawyers, 23 John Marshall L.Rev. 165, 168–74 (1990).

obey the President's instructions (should he have done so?), but did not answer the Senate query truthfully.

Kleindienst pleaded guilty to a misdemeanor (making false statements) and received a suspended sentence. Disciplinary proceedings resulted in public censure in Arizona and a 30–day suspension in District of Columbia for violations of DR 1–102(A) which, like M.R. 8.4(c), prohibits "conduct involving dishonesty, fraud, deceit, or misrepresentation."[19] Should President Clinton, found to have lied in the Paula Jones case, be disciplined in Arkansas for his deposition testimony in the Paula Jones case and his subsequent federal grand jury testimony?[20] If disciplined, what sanction would be appropriate?

Deterring Lawyer Incompetence

The malpractice remedy is theoretically available to any client who is harmed by a lawyer's departure from standards of ordinary care. In practice, however, a plaintiff's lawyer will not undertake a legal malpractice case unless the client has suffered a large monetary harm and the chances of recovery are fairly good. Malpractice cases are generally hard fought and expensive; and a lawyer will not undertake one on a contingent fee basis, advancing expenses, unless the prospects of a substantial recovery are promising. These characteristics make the remedy unavailable when the client's harm is not large in amount and the client cannot advance expenses. Is professional discipline likely to give a client any solace? In general, as indicated in Chapter 3 supra, the current disciplinary system does not investigate and discipline individual instances of incompetence on the part of lawyers. Even when a disciplinary violation is found, restitutionary relief is generally unavailable or rarely given. Hence discipline is not an alternative to malpractice even when the latter remedy, as a practical matter, is unavailable.

A thoughtful study by Susan Martyn focuses on the problem of enforcing competence by punishing incompetence.[21] Martyn concludes that a disciplinary approach is unlikely to succeed in dealing with incompetence and hence that a malpractice remedy or more pervasive public regulation will be needed. The malpractice remedy, however, operates more or less

---

19. District of Columbia Bar v. Kleindienst, 345 A.2d 146 (D.C.Ct.App.1975) (recommended one-year suspension would be overly punitive considering Kleindienst's distinguished career and the stress created by a "highly charged political atmosphere"). The *Kleindienst* holding that a 30–day suspension was an appropriate disciplinary sanction for lying to an official body was overruled in In re Hutchinson, 534 A.2d 919 (D.C.Ct.App.1987) (one-year suspension for lawyer who lied to SEC about the source of insider trading information to shield himself and others from possible civil and criminal liability).

20. The federal district judge who was personally present when President Clinton was deposed found President Clinton guilty of civil contempt for "intentionally false" testimony about his relationship with Monica Lewinsky. She fined Clinton and reported his conduct to Arkansas disciplinary authorities. Jones v. Clinton, 36 F.Supp.2d 1118 (D.Ark.1999).

21. Susan R. Martyn, Lawyer Competence and Lawyer Discipline: Beyond the Bar?, 69 Geo.L.J. 705 (1981).

randomly, and more intensive public regulation seems an unlikely prospect. If the principal justification for licensure is protection against incompetence (as distinct from lawyer dishonesty, which is covered by criminal law in any event), and if effective policing against incompetency remains unattainable, what is the justification for licensure?[22]

A specific problem of great seriousness in the legal profession is incompetence and other misconduct resulting from substance abuse.[23] The impaired lawyer has given rise to peer review programs, rehabilitative arrangements and special disciplinary procedures and remedies.

Disciplinary Sanctions

As of 1989, disciplined lawyers in California had the following characteristics disproportionate to their representation in the bar as a whole: Disciplined lawyers are predominantly *solo practitioners* (50 percent of disciplined lawyers compared with 29 percent of the lawyer population); *male* (92 percent compared with 76 percent of lawyer population); *experienced* (82 percent in practice more than eleven years); had a *criminal record* (22 percent, presumably reflecting the fact that discipline usually flows from a lawyer's criminal conviction); and *substance abusers* (an estimated 20–40 percent of disciplined lawyers compared with an estimated 10 percent of all lawyers).[24].

The extent to which disbarment should be permanent is much debated. Contrary to popular understanding, only a small number of states make disbarment a permanent bar.[25] In the vast majority of states, disbarred lawyers are often readmitted on petition after a period of years. An extensive study by the National Law Journal found that, from 1991 to 1995, about one disbarred lawyer in the United States was readmitted for every 19 disbarred.[26] This rehabilitative approach has been strongly criti-

---

22. For a descriptive survey of studies of regulation of the legal profession, see Olavi Maru, Research on the Legal Profession: A Review of Work Done, c. 4 (2d ed. 1986). Also see Bryant G. Garth, Rethinking the Legal Profession's Approach to Collective Self–Improvement: Competence and the Consumer Perspective, 1983 Wis.L.Rev. 639.

23. For a review of the alcohol problem, see Michael A. Bloom and Carol L. Wallinger, Lawyers and Alcoholism: Is It Time for a New Approach?, 61 Temple L.Rev. 1409 (1988), which includes references to the related problem of drug abuse.

24. Deborah L. Rhode & David Luban, Legal Ethics 869 (2d ed.1995), summarizing James Evans, Lawyers at Risk, Cal.Law., Oct.1989, at 45–47; and Robert Fellmuth,

Fifth Progress Report of the State Bar Disciplinary Monitor (Sept. 1, 1989).

25. Ronald D. Rotunda & Mary M. Devlin, Permanent Disbarment: A Market Oriented Proposal, The Professional Lawyer, Nov. 1997, at 2, 12–16 (reporting that only eight states have permanent disbarment, including California, Illinois, New Jersey and Ohio).

26. Ann Davis' three-part series in Nat'l L.J., Aug. 5, 12, and 19, 1996. In a few states most disbarred lawyers are readmitted (e.g., Pennsylvania: 19 out of 22). Although the study does not look at the same lawyers over a period of time, it demonstrates that a substantial number of disbarred lawyers are readmitted and that some later cause substantial harm to their clients.

cized as offending the public understanding of values that are central to the justice system:

> [T]hieves, liars, perjurers, rapists and other serious criminal offenders [are] applying for, and sometimes securing, reinstatement to the practice of law. The specter of ever reinstating an attorney who has bribed a judge to fix a case, for example, or has committed other heinous crimes, is repulsive to most honest, ethical lawyers. To the public the prospect is inconceivable.[27]

Others stress the unevenness of the invocation and application of discipline and the disparity in sanctions applied to lawyers whose conduct was similar. This disagreement about the purposes of discipline and how to accomplish them, leads many to stress the importance of individualized decisions that center on rehabilitation: "giving the [disbarred] lawyer an incentive to mend his or her old ways."[28] The focus, in the view of proponents of readmission, should be on doing what is right for individuals, not a vain effort to improve the public image of the legal profession. Which approach do you favor and why? Ronald Rotunda and Mary Devlin support readmission that provides built-in protections for future clients: the disbarred lawyer should be required to retake and pass the state's bar examination and provide yearly proof for a number of years that the lawyer has adequate malpractice insurance and is bonded.[29]

Should disciplinary bodies have power to order a lawyer to pay restitution to a client who has been harmed? To fine a lawyer as a punitive sanction? Would these measures increase the deterrent effect of professional discipline? Another current issue, considered infra at p. 945, is whether law firms and other organizations of lawyers should be subject to discipline.

Conduct Prejudicial to the Administration of Justice

Model Rule 8.4(d) replicates the requirement of DR 1–102(A)(5) that a lawyer shall not "engage in conduct that is prejudicial to the administration of justice." What conduct is proscribed by this language?

IN RE MASTERS.[30] Masters, an experienced lawyer with extensive experience as a state prosecutor before entering private practice, was consulted by a construction company that was faced with an extortion demand made by Arambasich, a business agent for the Iron Workers' Union. Arambasich had visited the foreman at one of the client's construction jobs, placed a gun on the desk and told the foreman that "he was going to shut down the job" if he wasn't paid $1,000 every six months. Because of

---

27. David E. Johnson, Permanent Disbarment: The Case For ..., The Professional Lawyer, Feb.1994, at 22. Johnson emphasizes that lawyer violators are likely to be recidivists; his study of New Jersey lawyers who were disciplined but not disbarred for financial violations indicated that over one-fourth were subsequently found guilty of financial misconduct.

28. Ronald Rotunda, Permanent Disbarment: The Case Against ..., The Professional Lawyer, Feb.1994, at 22–24.

29. Ronald Rotunda & Mary M. Devlin, Permanent Disbarment: A Market Oriented Proposal, The Professional Lawyer, Nov. 1997, 2, 12–16.

30. 438 N.E.2d 187 (Ill.1982).

his service as a prosecutor, Masters had personal knowledge of Arambasich's reputation for violence; he feared for the safety of the foreman, himself, and his son, who had a summer job as an ironworker in the area. Masters advised the client to pay the extortion money; and he personally delivered a series of $1,000 payments to Arambasich over a five-year period. Masters then advised the client to end the payments and to report the extortion to law enforcement officials. A federal investigation resulted in indictment and conviction of Arambasich for extortion. Masters cooperated fully in the investigation and testified against Arambasich at the trial after receiving immunity from prosecution.

Masters was charged by the Illinois disciplinary body with violating the Illinois counterparts to DR 7–102(A)(7), counseling or assisting one's client in illegal activity; and DR 1–102(A)(5), engaging in conduct prejudicial to the administration of justice. The court agreed with Masters that he was not guilty of assisting a client's criminal conduct: the client in paying extortion money was a victim of crime, not a criminal. Yet the court rejected Masters' claim that good faith advice to cooperate with the extortion under the threat of serious injury should not be grounds for discipline under DR 1–103(A)(5):

> As an attorney [and as] former State's Attorney ... [Masters] was certainly aware of the fact that the proper course of conduct was to report the extortion demand to the appropriate authorities. For a lawyer of respondent's demonstrated ability and standing at the bar to serve as the conduit through which funds were passed from the alleged victim to the extortionist was unprofessional and unseemly and served to bring the legal profession into disrepute.[31]

Masters received a one-year suspension. A dissenting judge, argued that Masters had done "nothing illegal, immoral or unethical": "The record shows that Frank Masters did nothing worse than protect his client, an innocent victim of a criminal extortion, in the only way he believed was realistically available." The dissenting opinion argued that the rule prohibiting "conduct prejudicial to the administration of justice," which had previously been applied only to misconduct in a pending or contemplated legal proceeding, was unclear and that lawyers were given no guidance concerning its scope.

If Masters did not assist his client in the commission of a crime, why was he disciplined? Would the court have disciplined him if he had known his client was paying extortion to Arambasich but had not been personally involved in the payments? Does *Masters* obligate a lawyer to report a crime that the lawyer learns about because her client is its victim? One ABA ethics opinion implies that lawyers have a general duty to report crimes (even though lay people ordinarily do not), providing the lawyer's knowledge is based on unprivileged sources.[32]

---

31. 438 N.E.2d at 193.
32. See ABA Informal Op. 1210 (1972) (discussing the duty of lawyers to report crimes when knowledge is based on unprivileged sources).

What Conduct Prejudices the Administration of Justice?

The courts have generally invoked the prohibition on engaging in conduct prejudicial to the administration of justice in situations similar to those chargeable as obstruction to justice: advising clients to testify falsely,[33] paying a witness to be unavailable to testify,[34] threatening criminal prosecution and altering documents.[35] But the courts have also used the prohibition in other contexts, such as a lawyer's false statements about a judicial officer,[36] a lawyer's false statements to bar admissions authorities[37] and a lawyer's failure to appear at a contempt hearing for his failure to make child support payments.[38] Although some commentators have criticized the provision as overbroad and vague, the courts have nevertheless sustained applications of the prohibition.[39] Is it broader or vaguer than the federal obstruction of justice statute?

Another Illinois case, In re Corboy,[40] reflects much greater judicial tolerance of lawyer misconduct than was evidenced in *Masters* or *Himmel*, reproduced below. *Corboy* involved a substantial loan by several prominent Chicago lawyers to a Cook County circuit judge, ostensibly to pay a hospital bill of the judge's mother. In fact, unbeknownst to the lawyers providing the check, the judge used the money for other purposes. The Illinois ethics rule corresponding to DR 7–110(A) provided that a lawyer may not "give or lend anything of value" to a judge. The Illinois court held that the rule is a "per se" prohibition that does not require a corrupt purpose although, when read with Code of Judicial Conduct Rule 5(C)(4), the rule does not prohibit gifts implicit in "ordinary social hospitality." Even though the loan to the judge violated several ethics rules, including M.R. 8.4(d), the court imposed no sanction on the lawyers because they "acted without the guidance of precedent or settled opinion, and there was, apparently, considerable belief among members of the bar that they had acted properly."[41]

3. OBLIGATION TO REPORT PROFESSIONAL MISCONDUCT OF OTHER LAWYERS

One of the innovations of the Model Code was the inclusion in DR 1–103(A) of a broad mandatory obligation on the part of lawyers to report unprivileged knowledge of professional misconduct to disciplinary authori-

---

33. See, e.g., Florida Bar v. Simons, 391 So.2d 684 (Fla.1980).

34. People v. Kenelly, 648 P.2d 1065 (Colo. 1982).

35. In re Barrett, 443 A.2d 678 (N.J.1982).

36. State v. Nelson, 504 P.2d 211 (Kan. 1972).

37. In re Howe, 257 N.W.2d 420 (N.D. 1977).

38. People v. Kane, 638 P.2d 253 (Colo. 1981).

39. See, e.g., Donald T. Weckstein, Maintaining the Integrity and Competence of the Legal Profession, 48 Tex.L.Rev. 267, 275–76 (1970); Howell v. State Bar of Texas, 843 F.2d 205 (5th Cir.1988) (rule not vague); Office of Disciplinary Counsel v. Campbell, 345 A.2d 616, 621–22 (Pa.1975) (rule arguably vague but clear as applied to case at bar).

40. 528 N.E.2d 694 (Ill.1988).

41. 528 N.E.2d at 701.

ties.[42] The Model Rules narrow the scope of the obligation to report misconduct from that in the Code in two respects: (1) M.R. 8.3(a) requires a lawyer to report only those violations that raise "a substantial question as to the lawyer's honesty, trustworthiness or fitness as a lawyer in other respects"; and (2) the Rules do not require a lawyer to report if knowledge of the violation is based on information protected by the professional duty of confidentiality. See M.R. 8.3(c), referring to M.R. 1.6.[43] In contrast, the Code requires a lawyer to report all violations, with an exception only for information based on "privileged" communications. Use of the term "privileged" suggests the exception is limited to "confidences" protected by the attorney-client privilege and not, for example, information learned from a third party in the course of representing a client ("secrets").[44]

It is no secret that the duty to report professional misconduct is widely ignored. Although lawyers and judges are in the best position to learn of the wrongdoing of other lawyers, only a small proportion of disciplinary complaints are filed by them.[45] Prior to the *Himmel* case, reproduced below, lawyers had been disciplined for failure to report only in connection with other violations.[46] Should lawyers be disciplined for failing to report the misconduct of other lawyers?

In Re Himmel

Supreme Court of Illinois, 1988.
125 Ill.2d 531, 533 N.E.2d 790.

■ JUSTICE STAMOS delivered the opinion of the court:

This is a disciplinary proceeding against respondent, James H. Himmel. . . .

---

42.   The Canons of Professional Ethics contained much narrower reporting obligations: Canon 28 imposed a duty to report lawyers engaged in ambulance chasing, paying runners to drum up cases and related forms of stirring up litigation. Canon 29 imposed a duty but did not require lawyers to report perjury in litigation and "dishonest and corrupt conduct." General language admonished lawyers to "uphold the honor of the profession" by striving for its improvement by keeping out or removing "unfit persons."

43.   Rule 8.3(c) was amended in 1991 to protect information gained by a lawyer or judge "while serving as a member of an approved lawyer assistance program."

44.   ABA Formal Op. 341 (1975) interprets "privileged" as used in another provision of the Model Code, DR 7–102(B)(1), as including professional secrets as well as confidences protected by the attorney-client privilege, and its reasoning is also applicable to DR 1–103(A). Cf. the views of the Illinois court in the *Himmel* case, reprinted

below. See Chapter 4 below on the difference between confidential information and privileged communications. Formal Op. 341 is discussed at p. 284 supra.

45.   ABA Commission on Professionalism, In the Spirit of Public Service, A Blueprint for the Rekindling of Lawyer Professionalism 37 (1986): "reporting of serious misconduct of both lawyers and judges is essential [but] hardly any such reporting occurs." See generally F. Raymond Marks and Darlene Cathcart, Discipline Within the Legal Profession: Is It Self–Regulation?, 1974 Ill.L.Forum 193; Eric H. Steele and Raymond T. Nimmer, Lawyers, Clients, and Professional Regulation, 1976 Am.Bar Found. Research J. 917.

46.   See, e.g., Attorney Grievance Comm'n v. Kahn, 431 A.2d 1336 (Md.1981) (lawyer disbarred for aiding unethical conduct of his law firm and failing to report); Matter of Bonafield, 383 A.2d 1143 (N.J.1978) (lawyer disciplined for assisting another lawyer's misconduct and for failing to report).

We will briefly review the facts, which essentially involve three individuals: respondent, James H. Himmel, licensed to practice law in Illinois on November 6, 1975; his client, Tammy Forsberg ...; and her former attorney, John R. Casey.

[Forsberg retained Casey in 1980 to handle a personal injury claim arising out of a motorcycle accident. Casey settled the case for $35,000, but converted the portion of the settlement check ($23,233) belonging to Forsberg. Forsberg, after complaining about Casey's conduct to the Illinois disciplinary agency, retained Himmel in 1983 to collect her money and agreed to pay him one-third of any funds recovered above $23,233. Himmel then negotiated an agreement with Casey in which Casey agreed to pay Forsberg $75,000 in settlement of any claim she might have against Casey and Forsberg agreed not to initiate any criminal, civil or attorney discipline action against Casey. When Casey failed to pay the agreed amount, Himmel brought suit against him for breaching the agreement, resulting in a $100,000 judgment against Casey. Forsberg eventually received a total of $15,400 from Casey of which $10,400 was the result of Himmel's efforts. Himmel received no fee for his work.

[In 1985 Casey was disbarred by consent because of misconduct unrelated to Forsberg. In 1986 the Administrator of the Attorney Registration and Disciplinary Commission (the Commission) filed a disciplinary complaint against Himmel for failing to report Casey's misconduct in his representation of Forsberg. The Hearing Board determined that Himmel violated Rule 1–103(a) (the Illinois counterpart of DR 1–103(A)) and recommended a private reprimand. The Review Board recommended that the complaint be dismissed. The Administrator sought and obtained review in the Supreme Court.]

The Administrator now raises three issues for review: (1) whether the Review Board erred in concluding that respondent's client had informed the Commission of misconduct by her former attorney; (2) whether the Review Board erred in concluding that respondent had not violated Rule 1–103(a); and (3) whether the proven misconduct warrants at least a censure.

[The court first held that a client's complaint of attorney misconduct to the disciplinary commission is not a defense to an attorney's failure to report the same misconduct.]

... We have held that the canons of ethics in the Code constitute a safe guide for professional conduct, and attorneys may be disciplined for not observing them.... The question is, then, whether or not respondent violated the Code, not whether Forsberg informed the Commission of Casey's misconduct.

As to respondent's argument that he did not report Casey's misconduct because his client directed him not to do so, we again note respondent's failure to suggest any legal support for such a defense. A lawyer, as an officer of the court, is duty-bound to uphold the rules in the Code. The title of Canon 1 [of the Code] reflects this obligation: "A lawyer should assist in maintaining the integrity and competence of the legal profession." A lawyer may not choose to circumvent the rules by simply asserting that his client asked him to do so.

As to the second issue, the Administrator argues that the Review Board erred in concluding that respondent did not violate Rule 1–103(a)....

. . .

Our analysis of this issue begins with a reading of the applicable disciplinary rules. Rule 1–103(a) of the Code states: "(a) A lawyer possessing unprivileged knowledge of a violation of Rule 1–102(a)(3) or (4) shall report such knowledge to a tribunal or other authority empowered to investigate or act upon such violation."

Rule 1–102 of the Code states: "(a) A lawyer shall not (1) violate a disciplinary rule; (2) circumvent a disciplinary rule through actions of another; (3) engage in illegal conduct involving moral turpitude; (4) engage in conduct involving dishonesty, fraud, deceit, or misrepresentation; or (5) engage in conduct that is prejudicial to the administration of justice."

These rules essentially track the language of the American Bar Association Model Code of Professional Responsibility, upon which the Illinois Code was modeled.* Therefore, we find instructive the opinion of the American Bar Association's Committee on Ethics and Professional Responsibility that discusses the Model Code's Disciplinary Rule 1–103. Informal Opinion 1210 [1972] states that under DR 1–103(a) it is the duty of a lawyer to report to the proper tribunal or authority any unprivileged knowledge of a lawyer's perpetration of any misconduct listed in Disciplinary Rule 1–102. The opinion states that "the Code of Professional Responsibility through its Disciplinary Rules necessarily deals directly with reporting of lawyer misconduct or misconduct of others directly observed in the legal practice or the administration of justice."

This court has also emphasized the importance of a lawyer's duty to report misconduct. In the case In re Anglin (1988), 122 Ill.2d 531, 539, 524 N.E.2d 550, because of the petitioner's refusal to answer questions regarding his knowledge of other persons' misconduct, we denied a petition for reinstatement to the roll of attorneys licensed to practice in Illinois. We stated, "Under Disciplinary Rule 1–103 a lawyer has the duty to report the misconduct of other lawyers. Petitioner's belief in a code of silence indicates to us that he is not at present fully rehabilitated or fit to practice law." Thus, if the present respondent's conduct did violate the rule on reporting misconduct, imposition of discipline for such a breach of duty is mandated.

---

* [Editors' note:] The Illinois version of DR 1–103(A) narrows the duty to inform to "illegal conduct involving moral turpitude" and "conduct involving dishonesty, fraud, deceit, or misrepresentation." The Model Code requires that a lawyer to report *all* disciplinary violations of another lawyer.

The question whether the information that respondent possessed was protected by the attorney-client privilege, and thus exempt from the reporting rule, requires application of this court's definition of the privilege. [The court then quoted Wigmore's definition of the attorney-client privilege.] ... The record does not suggest that this information was communicated by Forsberg to the respondent in confidence. We have held that information voluntarily disclosed by a client to an attorney, in the presence of third parties who are not agents of the client or attorney, is not privileged information.... In this case, Forsberg discussed the matter with respondent at various times while her mother and her fiance were present. Consequently, unless the mother and fiance were agents of respondent's client, the information communicated was not privileged....

Though respondent repeatedly asserts that his failure to report was motivated not by financial gain but by the request of his client, we do not deem such an argument relevant in this case. This court has stated that discipline may be appropriate even if no dishonest motive for the misconduct exists.... In addition, we have held that client approval of an attorney's action does not immunize an attorney from disciplinary action.... We have already dealt with, and dismissed, respondent's assertion that his conduct is acceptable because he was acting pursuant to his client's directions.

Respondent does not argue that Casey's conversion of Forsberg's funds was not illegal conduct involving moral turpitude under Rule 1–102(a)(3) or conduct involving dishonesty, fraud, deceit, or misrepresentation under Rule 1–102(a)(4). It is clear that conversion of client funds is, indeed, conduct involving moral turpitude.... We conclude, then, that respondent possessed unprivileged knowledge of Casey's conversion of client funds, which is illegal conduct involving moral turpitude, and that respondent failed in his duty to report such misconduct to the Commission. Because no defense exists, we agree with the Hearing Board's finding that respondent has violated Rule 1–103(a) and must be disciplined.

The third issue concerns the appropriate quantum of discipline to be imposed in this case....

In evaluating the proper quantum of discipline to impose, we note that it is this court's responsibility to determine appropriate sanctions in attorney disciplinary cases.... We have stated that while recommendations of the Boards are to be considered, this court ultimately bears responsibility for deciding an appropriate sanction.... We reiterate our statement that "[w]hen determining the nature and extent of discipline to be imposed, the respondent's actions must be viewed in relationship 'to the underlying purposes of our disciplinary process, which purposes are to maintain the integrity of the legal profession, to protect the administration of justice from reproach, and to safeguard the public.' "

Bearing these principles in mind, we agree with the Administrator that public discipline is necessary in this case to carry out the purposes of attorney discipline.... [T]he evidence proved that respondent possessed unprivileged knowledge of Casey's conversion of client funds, yet respondent did not report Casey's misconduct.

This failure to report resulted in interference with the Commission's investigation of Casey, and thus with the administration of justice. Perhaps some members of the public would have been spared from Casey's misconduct had respondent reported the information as soon as he knew of Casey's conversions of client funds. We are particularly disturbed by the fact that respondent chose to draft a settlement agreement with Casey rather than report his misconduct. As the Administrator has stated, by this conduct, both respondent and his client ran afoul of the Criminal Code's prohibition against compounding a crime, which states in section 32–1: "(a) A person compounds a crime when he receives or offers to another any consideration for a promise not to prosecute or aid in the prosecution of an offender. (b) Sentence. Compounding a crime is a petty offense." (Ill.Rev. Stat.1987, ch. 38, par. 32–1.) Both respondent and his client stood to gain financially by agreeing not to prosecute or report Casey for conversion. According to the settlement agreement, respondent would have received $17,000 or more as his fee. If Casey had satisfied the judgment entered against him for failure to honor the settlement agreement, respondent would have collected approximately $25,588.

We have held that fairness dictates consideration of mitigating factors in disciplinary cases. . . . Therefore, we do consider the fact that Forsberg recovered $10,400 through respondent's services, that respondent has practiced law for 11 years with no record of complaints, and that he requested no fee for minimum collection of Forsberg's funds. However, these considerations do not outweigh the serious nature of respondent's failure to report Casey, the resulting interference with the Commission's investigation of Casey, and respondent's ill-advised choice to settle with Casey rather than report his misconduct.

Accordingly, it is ordered that respondent be suspended from the practice of law for one year.

————

Scope of Duty to Report

The *Himmel* case sent shock waves through the bar in Illinois and nationwide.[1] It was apparently the first case in which a lawyer had been disciplined *solely* for failing to report the misconduct of another lawyer. Bar associations and individual lawyers denounced the decision, arguing the following:[2] Himmel received confidential information from his client; he used that information to pursue the client's goal of monetary recompense

1. See Ronald D. Rotunda, The Lawyer's Duty to Report Another Lawyer's Unethical Violations in the Wake of *Himmel*, 1988 U.Ill.L.Rev. 977.

2. Three bar associations, including the Illinois Bar Association, unsuccessfully sought rehearing of the *Himmel* case. See Paul Marcotte, The Duty to Inform, ABA J., May 1989, pp. 17–18.

for Casey's wrongdoing; reporting a disciplinary violation or bringing criminal charges might have interfered with the client's objective of monetary recompense; therefore, Himmel had a duty to follow his client's instructions and not to report Casey's misconduct.[3] Does the *Himmel* opinion respond satisfactorily to this argument? Why does the duty to inform trump the explicit instructions of the client?

As indicated earlier, the term "privileged" has sometimes been interpreted to include both information protected by the attorney-client privilege and the larger category of information protected by the professional duty of confidentiality. Should the *Himmel* court have taken the broader view? Is *Himmel* also too restrictive in holding that Forsberg waived the attorney-client privilege because her mother and fiance accompanied her in meeting with Himmel? The *Himmel* case, if it arose in Illinois today, would apparently be decided the same way; the Illinois version of Rule 1.6 preserves the Model Code distinction between "confidences" protected by the attorney-client privilege and "secrets" learned during representation and its Rule 8.3 requires a lawyer to report information "not otherwise protected as a confidence by these Rules or other law."

Should the duty to report be limited to violations that raise a "substantial question" about another lawyer's "honesty, trustworthiness or fitness," as under M.R. 8.3, or apply to all ethical violations, as under the Model Code and the current Illinois version of M.R. 8.3?

Should the Duty Be Mandatory?

The broad question is whether lawyers should have a mandatory, rather than discretionary, duty to inform on other lawyers. The ABA's Commission on Professionalism, reporting in 1986, argued that increased reporting by lawyers and judges of professional misconduct was "essential" to protect the public from abuses that otherwise would not be detected or deterred. To put teeth into the report obligation, the Commission stated that "an improved attitude by lawyers with respect to reporting" would result if "proceedings [were] brought in appropriate cases against lawyers who fail to do so."[4] Perhaps the Illinois court heard this recommendation and took it seriously.[5] Or it may have been influenced by the outcry in

---

3. See Maryland State Bar Ass'n, Committee on Ethics, Op. 89–46 (1989) (lawyer suing client's former lawyer for breach of fiduciary duty is not required to report where client has asked lawyer not to file a complaint against the former lawyer).

4. Report of ABA Commission on Professionalism, supra, at 38.

5. The *Himmel* case did have the effect of stimulating the filing of disciplinary complaints by Illinois lawyers: the number of lawyer-initiated complaints skyrocketed to 922 (15.8 percent of all complaints) in 1989, immediately after *Himmel*, but has

since subsided to a steady flow of about 600 per year (8–9 percent of all complaints). It is thought that this figure is much higher than in many other states. According to disciplinary officials in the District of Columbia and New York, lawyers are responsible for about 30 reports per year (D.C) or "a handful" of complaints (New York); data concerning lawyer-initiated complaints is not available in many states. See Laura Gatland, The Himmel Effect, ABA J., Apr.1997, at 24–25; and Darryl van Duch, Best Snitches: Land of Lincoln Leads

Illinois flowing from Operation Greylord.[6]

Gerard Lynch is among those commentators who doubt the efficacy and desirability of a mandatory report obligation.[7] The pejorative aspect of words like "tattle," "snitch," "squeal" and "inform" reflects an inevitable and in part justifiable attitude arising from relational concerns:

> The impulse to protect one's friends and associates from harm, even from deserved punishment, is a moral and socially useful impulse precisely because it reaches beyond individual self-interest; it assimilates another's well-being to that of oneself.[8]

Lynch argues that relationships based on trust satisfy human needs of affiliation and identity; they also protect otherwise isolated individuals from the formal rigor of state power. A rigid legalism that requires a lawyer to report all professional misconduct of other lawyers, Lynch argues, is misconceived:

> Although it would sometimes be morally correct to report wrongdoing that comes to one's attention, such action would be morally incorrect in a great number of situations. The considerations relevant to sorting out these cases are highly complex. The preference for laws that are narrowly drawn and easy to apply would thus counsel that the law leave individuals free to follow their consciences in deciding whether or not to inform, except in a few carefully defined situations. Moreover, given the likelihood that people would disregard an unfocused and unpopular obligation to report the misconduct of others, little social benefit can be expected from a general rule even in those instances in which the moral obligation to inform is clearest.... [T]he law has generally declined—correctly I believe—to impose a duty to provide unsolicited information, except in situations in which the information is especially vital and a definable category of persons is particularly likely to obtain it. The possibility of harm is too great, and the rewards too slim, to justify a general duty to inform.... The ethical codes applicable to lawyers ought to reflect the same approach that has proved acceptable to society as a whole.[9]

Which approach is better, that of the ABA Commission on Professionalism or that of Lynch? Several jurisdictions do not have a report requirement, including California and Massachusetts.[10] And few state courts have followed Illinois in disciplining a lawyer solely for failure to report.[11]

the Nation ..., Nat'l L.J., Jan. 27, 1997, at A1, A25.

6. Martha Middleton, Chicago Courts Reel from Corruption Probe, Nat'l L.J., Mar. 2, 1987, p. 1, 39 (a federal investigation of widespread bribery and corruption in the Cook County Circuit Court resulted in at least 50 convictions, including those of seven judges and 25 lawyers).

7. Gerard E. Lynch, The Lawyer as Informer, 1986 Duke L.J. 491.

8. Id. at 531.

9. Id. at 535.

10. ABA/BNA Law.Man.Prof. Conduct 101:201 (1989).

11. An unpublished 1995 opinion of the Arizona Supreme Court is apparently the only other case disciplining a lawyer solely for failure to report (lawyer censured for failing to report that another lawyer had committed malpractice, embezzlement, and

Extortion as Prohibited Assistance

Although the disciplinary action in *Himmel* was grounded on the lawyer's failure to report, the Illinois court was troubled by another aspect of the case: Both Himmel and his client "ran afoul" of the criminal code's prohibition against compounding a crime, which prohibits receiving consideration in exchange for agreeing not to prosecute or report a crime, here the original theft of the client's money.

DR 7–105(A) of the Model Code provides that "A lawyer shall not present, participate in presenting, or threaten to present criminal charges solely to obtain an advantage in a civil matter."[12] The Model Rules do not contain a similar provision, presumably because it was thought unwise to go beyond the criminal prohibitions against threats constituting extortion, fraud or criminal abuse. These crimes usually would constitute "a criminal act that reflects adversely on the lawyer's honesty, trustworthiness or fitness as a lawyer in other respects" under M.R. 8.4(b).[13]

Does the criminal prohibition of extortion and the Model Code prohibition of threatening criminal charges prevent a lawyer from mentioning the possibility of criminal charges in civil negotiations? A 1992 ethics opinion and judicial holding give a negative response.[14] Extortion is further discussed in connection with the law governing negotiation, p. 1147 infra.

4. EFFECTIVENESS OF DISCIPLINARY ENFORCEMENT

The procedural protections afforded lawyers in disciplinary proceedings are substantial. The effectiveness of the enforcement process, however, has been repeatedly criticized. In 1970, the ABA sponsored a study of lawyer discipline by a special committee headed by former Supreme Court Justice Tom C. Clark. The Clark Report, as it is commonly called, found that the disciplinary machinery in most jurisdictions was in poor shape: inadequate staff, poor record keeping, feeble prosecution, erratically functioning grievance committees and other defects. It also found that sanctions were unequal and generally mild relative to the seriousness of offenses. The report called for comprehensive reform, including enlarged staff resources,

forgery). See Laura Gatland, The Himmel Effect, ABA J., April 1997, p. 25.

12. The California rule is even broader. It prohibits threats to present administrative and disciplinary charges as well as criminal charges. Calif.R.Prof.Conduct, Rule 5–100.

13. See 1 Hazard & Hodes, The Law of Lawyering § 4.4:103 (1990) (stating that the prohibition found in DR 7–105(A) was deliberately omitted from Model Rule 4.4 as redundant and also because its broad language appeared to prohibit "legitimate pressure tactics and negotiation strategies").

14. ABA Standing Comm. on Ethics and Prof. Responsibility, Formal Op. 92–363 (lawyer negotiating a civil claim is not barred from any mention of possible related criminal charges); Committee on Legal Ethics v. Printz, 416 S.E.2d 720, 727 n. 4 (W.Va.1992) (distinguishing between extortion and legitimate negotiations: "Receiving repayment of money taken from a victim is not extortion; however, asking a higher price (i.e., 'Give my money back and $20,000 or I'll call the cops!') in return for the victim's silence is extortion").

more hospitable concern for complainants, speedier preliminary investigations and trial and better calibrated sanctions.[15]

The course of events since the Clark Report has not been smooth. Most jurisdictions have introduced reforms along the lines recommended in the report. At the same time, the volume and backlog of disciplinary cases has rapidly increased in many jurisdictions, sometimes overwhelming the disciplinary system, as in California in the 1980s and New Jersey in the 1990s. The bar takes some satisfaction in its efforts to improve disciplinary enforcement, but many lawyers and much of the general public remain dissatisfied with many aspects of current disciplinary enforcement.

In 1992, the ABA adopted in watered-down form the recommendations of the Commission on Evaluation of Disciplinary Enforcement, which had spent three years studying the subject.[16] The Commission's study commended the changes that the Clark Report had stimulated and made recommendations on a number of recurring issues concerning professional discipline.

Who should control the disciplinary process? The ABA Commission accepted the view of consumer groups that control of the lawyer discipline system by state bar associations creates an appearance of conflict of interest and of impropriety. In many states, including Florida, New York and Texas, bar officials investigate, prosecute and adjudicate disciplinary cases, subject to judicial review. The Commission's recommendation that the state high court, and not some other governmental authority, should exclusively control the disciplinary process was adopted by the ABA House of Delegates in 1993 in a close vote.[17]

Should disciplinary proceedings be open to the public? The ABA Commission concluded that the effort to shield honest lawyers' reputations by holding disciplinary hearings behind closed doors contributed to public distrust of lawyer discipline. The Commission initially recommended that lawyer disciplinary records be open to the public from the time of the complainant's initial communication with the disciplinary agency (the procedure followed in Oregon). In the face of opposition, however, the Commission retreated to the position that records be kept confidential until a complaint has been dismissed or until a determination has been made that "probable cause" exists to believe that misconduct has occurred. The

15. See ABA, Special Committee on Evaluation of Disciplinary Enforcement, Problems and Recommendations in Disciplinary Enforcement (1970) (often referred to as the Clark Commission after its chairman).

16. ABA, Lawyer Regulation for a New Century: Report of the Commission on Evaluation of Disciplinary Enforcement (1992) (often referred to as the McKay Commission after its initial chairman).

17. The ABA rejected proposals that regulation of the legal profession should be turned over to state legislatures. The Com-

mission report, while urging that lawyers be regulated exclusively by state high courts, warned that "failure of the profession and the judiciary to act [to protect clients] imperils the inherent power of the court to regulate its officers [and] threatens the independence of counsel." Id. at xvi. For an argument that greater legislative participation in the regulation of lawyers would be desirable, see Deborah L. Rhode, The Rhetoric of Professional Reform, 45 Md.L.Rev. 274 (1986).

ABA House of Delegates rejected the view that dismissed complaints should be open to the public, resolving that a disciplinary matter should go public only upon a finding of probable cause. Should the disciplinary process be fully open to public view? At what stage?

What can be done to make professional discipline a more effective remedy for clients? Clients are largely unaware of the existence and details of disciplinary procedure.[18] Moreover, up to 90 percent of all complaints against lawyers are dismissed, and only a very small percentage of complaints result in significant sanctions.[19] Although a large number of complaints are properly dismissed as frivolous (e.g., client is unhappy with the outcome of litigation), a gap between client expectations and regulatory performance is responsible for a substantial portion of dismissals. The most common client grievances involve fee disputes, neglect and negligence. Clients expect that these matters will be taken seriously by disciplinary bodies, but disciplinary agencies view most such complaints as not within their jurisdiction[20] or lack resources to pursue them. The ABA endorses a system of expedited procedures for minor misconduct that is not subject to suspension or disbarment. It also has dealt with public concerns by recommending that states adopt a client protection fund, mandatory arbitration of fee disputes, voluntary arbitration of lawyer malpractice claims and random audits of lawyer trust accounts (the latter is in place in eleven states as of 1999).

Where will the needed resources come from? Everyone concedes that disciplinary agencies are understaffed and underfunded. Bar dues are now substantial in many states (e.g., $200–500 per year), and lawyers resist substantial further increases to finance disciplinary staff. Placing lawyer discipline under the court system rather than the legislature requires that government funding come through budgets for the judicial branch, many of which are experiencing serious funding problems.

The number of disciplinary complaints has risen markedly in recent years in virtually every jurisdiction. It is unclear what portion of the increase is due to increase in legal business (more lawyers serving more clients), an increased propensity of lawyers to violate professional rules, or a greater propensity of clients to file complaints; all three factors are probably involved. The increased disciplinary workload has overwhelmed the personnel and funds available to handle them. In New Jersey in 1994,

---

18. See Richard Abel, American Lawyers 144 (1989) (only 13 percent of clients found to be aware of disciplinary process); Eric H. Steel and Raymond T. Nimmer, Lawyers, Clients, and Professional Regulation, 1976 Am.Bar Found.Res.J. 917, 959–60 (individual clients aggrieved by lawyers do not know how to obtain redress; business clients pursue other options).

19. Lawyer Regulation for a New Century, supra, at xv: "Some jurisdictions dismiss up to ninety percent of all complaints."

20. Many fee disputes involves fees that are high but not so "unreasonable" or "clearly excessive" that they are disciplinary violations. Single instances of neglect and incompetence are generally viewed as not within the jurisdiction of the disciplinary system. See the discussion at p. 922 supra.

for example, it took four years to produce a suspension and five years to get a lawyer disbarred. New Jersey is one of the eleven states in which hearing boards are composed of bar volunteers; and was one of the 19 states that do not conduct hearings in public, waiting until final adjudication before a sanction is announced.[21] Yet recommendations to professionalize the volunteer lawyer staff, centralize intake of clients' complaints and completely eliminate the system's secrecy foundered after meeting with intense opposition from the organized bar. On the other hand, the New Jersey Supreme Court's 1994 action did streamline the process, eliminate private reprimands and open the process to public view once a grievance, after investigation, has become a formal complaint.[22]

As currently structured, the disciplinary process is largely invisible and reactive. Should it be made more visible and proactive? Should fee disputes, neglect and negligence be made disciplinary offenses? The disciplinary process would be more visible to clients if lawyers were required to include information concerning how to file a disciplinary complaint in fee retainer agreements. If adequately funded and authorized, disciplinary staff could initiate disciplinary proceedings on the basis of malpractice filings, judicial sanctions and random audits of trust accounts. Subjecting law firms to discipline might increase incentives of firms to maintain quality control of firm lawyers.[23]

The volume and vehemence of public criticism of lawyer ethics is hard to overestimate, as is the frustration and outrage of many clients at being unable to get recourse against misconduct and mistreatment by their lawyers, including overcharging, procrastination, refusal to respond, evasion and lying. Deborah Rhode, for example, argues that regulation of lawyers "rests on inconsistent premises:" Standards governing admission and provision of legal services "assume that a free market in legal services is inappropriate" because "clients are not in a position to make informed judgments about the quality and cost of services received." Yet professional discipline operates on the reality that client grievances will be the primary source of information about attorney misconduct. "In principle, the objective [of professional discipline] is protection of the public, not punishment of the lawyer. In practice, the system fails in both respects. Lawyers inevitably experience sanctions as punitive, and decision makers' reluctance to impose them prevents adequate protection. Less that 2% of complaints result in public sanctions, and they are rarely directed at practitioners from mainstream firms and organizations."[24]

21. See Rorie Sherman, Overhaul of Lawyer Discipline on Docket, Nat'l L.J., Mar.21, 1994, at pp. A5, A26; and Geoffrey C. Hazard, Discipline by Numbers, Nat'l L.J., Apr. 11, 1994, at A21, A22 (reviewing studies of the New Jersey recommendations).

22. See Kevin H. Michels, New Jersey Attorney Ethics 855 (1998).

23. See Ted Schneyer, Professional Discipline for Law Firms?, 71 Cornell L.Rev. 1 (1991) (professional discipline system should be extended to law firms).

24. Deborah L. Rhode, Institutionalizing Ethics, 44 Case West.Res.Rev. 665, 665–96 (1994).

D.   LAW FIRMS AND THE ORGANIZED BAR

1.   RESPONSIBILITIES OF JUNIOR AND SENIOR LAWYERS

Steven Brill, "When A Lawyer Lies"

Esquire 23–24 (Dec. 19, 1979).

Eighteen months ago, Joseph Fortenberry, Harvard College '66 and Yale Law '69, was on the perfect big-time lawyer's career path. At thirty-three, he had a federal court of appeals clerkship under his belt and was a senior associate at the New York law firm of Donovan Leisure Newton & Irvine working on the all-important antitrust case that Kodak was defending against Berkey Photo.

His prospects for being made a partner at the prestige firm the following year were excellent: He was regarded not only as brilliant but also as engaging and enjoyable to work with; Kodak was the firm's biggest case (occupying twenty lawyers full time, with gross billings of some $4 million a year); and he was working hand in hand with Mahlon Perkins Jr., one of the firm's most respected partners.

Then came April 20, 1977. That morning, in the middle of one of hundreds of depositions (on-the-record question-and-answer sessions with a witness prior to the trial) that he had sat through for months, Joe Fortenberry's career unraveled.

[Merton Peck, a well-known Yale economics professor, had been retained to offer an expert opinion that Kodak's dominance in the photography industry had resulted from its superior product innovations, not its acquisition of competitors or other monopolistic practices. Peck, in an early letter to Donovan Leisure, had stated that he was unable to explain how Kodak's early acquisitions could be irrelevant to its present market position. Berkey's lawyers had made numerous discovery requests for letters, reports and "interim reports" prepared by Peck.]

Alvin Stein, the lawyer for Berkey Photo, was questioning ... Peck, about files and other materials the professor had received from Kodak in order to prepare his testimony. In such suits, each side is allowed to obtain—or "discover"—almost any documents that the other side has used to prepare and bolster its case. Such materials can often be used to attack the credibility of witnesses.

Peck told Berkey lawyer Stein that he had shipped all the materials back to Perkins of Donovan Leisure earlier that year. What happened, then, to the documents, Stein asked Perkins. I threw them out as soon as I got them, the Donovan Leisure partner replied.

Perkins was lying. He'd saved all the documents in a suitcase, frequently taking them back and forth between his office at the firm and a special office he'd leased near the federal courthouse for the trial. And Joe Fortenberry, sitting at Perkins's side during this deposition, knew his boss was lying. He'd worked with the suitcase full of documents, and at least once he'd carried it between Perkins's two offices. Two weeks later, Perkins submitted a sworn statement to the court confirming he'd destroyed the documents. [The false affidavit was precipitated by a request to Perkins from lead lawyer John Doar to do something that would "satisfy" the court as to why the documents could not be produced; Doar failed to make specific inquiries about the documents.]

In January of 1978, [nine months later,] Perkins's perjury came to light when Stein, at the end of the Kodak–Berkey trial, asked Peck about any reports he had submitted prior to the trial to Kodak's lawyers. This led back to more probing questions about the materials Peck had used to prepare his testimony. Then—in what has since become a much-reported, pinstriped soap opera—on the Sunday night before the last week of the trial, a frightened Perkins broke down and confessed to Kodak lead lawyer John Doar that he'd never destroyed the documents but had actually hid them in a cupboard in his office. Perkins told the judge the next day, then resigned from the firm; Stein used Donovan Leisure's withholding of documents to help convince the jury of Kodak's bad faith and guilt; Kodak lost the case in a spectacular $113 million verdict (since reduced [by a settlement after Kodak, represented by new counsel, got a reversal on appeal]); Kodak dropped Donovan Leisure; and Perkins was convicted of contempt of court for his perjury and sentenced to a month in prison.

But what about Joe Fortenberry?

The rules by which the bar disciplines—the Code of Professional Responsibility—require that "a lawyer who receives information clearly establishing that ... a person other than his client has perpetrated a fraud upon a tribunal shall promptly reveal the fraud to the tribunal." [DR 7-102(B)(2); cf. MR 3.3(a)(4).] Moreover, the code requires that a lawyer who knows that another lawyer has engaged in dishonesty, deceit, or misrepresentation must report the offending lawyer to proper prosecutorial authorities. [DRs 8-102(A), 8-103; cf. MRs 8.3, 8.4(c).]

In short, Fortenberry was obligated to speak up when Perkins lied. Instead, he said nothing to anyone. To be sure, Perkins, perhaps thinking he was helping Fortenberry, told the federal prosecutors who later investigated the case that Fortenberry had whispered in his ear and reminded him of the existence of the documents when Perkins told Stein he'd destroyed them. Fortenberry denies this. What's undisputed, and more relevant, is that Fortenberry never said a word about Perkins's lie to the judge, as he was obligated to, or even to any other Donovan Leisure partner.

Throw the book at him, right? Wrong. Law firms teach young associates that they are apprentices to the partners, not whistle blowers. The partners, after all, are supposed to be the ones with the experience and standing to make decisions about right and wrong. Fortenberry had worked for Perkins for more than six months. In an environment like Donovan Leisure, this means that he respected the fifty-nine year-old "Perk," as his admiring partners called him, for the well-liked senior litigator that he was. It also means that he was intimidated by Perkins and, of course, that he knew Perkins was his ticket to a partnership when the firm partners would decide in the following year which of the associates at Fortenberry's level would be offered that golden prize. "What happened to Joe" says a close associate "was that he saw Perk lie and really couldn't believe it. And he just had no idea what to do. I mean, he knew Perkins was lying, but he kept thinking that there must be a reason. Besides, what do you do? The guy was his boss and a great guy!"

As stung as Donovan Leisure is by the Perkins affair, the firm's partners have treated Fortenberry with the compassion that suggests that they understand his dilemma. They've paid for him to retain his own lawyer for the investigation that resulted in Perkins's guilty plea and for possible bar association disciplinary action. (Federal prosecutors say there's no evidence of criminal misconduct on Fortenberry's part, but the Association of the Bar of the City of New York never comments on its own investigations regarding possible violations of the Lawyers Code of Professional Responsibility, even to the point of acknowledging whether there is one going on.) And they've kept him on at the firm and gone out of their way with signs ranging from work assignments to lunch invitations to show that they hold him blameless. In many ways, it hasn't helped. Friends say that Fortenberry—"a well-liked, personable genius," as one puts it—has been severely hurt emotionally by the Perkins episode. "He just looks and acts like a beaten man," as another associate explained.

There's one thing that Donovan Leisure could do to revive Fortenberry. They could make him a partner this June, when the decision on partners of his seniority is normally made. The odds are he'd have been made a partner had the Perkins affair never happened; so if, as Samuel Murphy of the firm's management committee told me recently, "in judging Joe for partnership, we're not going to hold the tragedy with Perk against him in any way," it stands to reason that he will get the offer. Then again, how does Donovan Leisure look, its reputation already hurt by the Perkins affair, offering a partnership to the man who apparently violated the Code of Professional Responsibility and kept quiet while Perkins perpetrated his fraud on the court?

With Donovan Leisure beginning to recover from the Perkins affair . . . the upcoming decision on what to do with Fortenberry may be the one last hurdle they have to pass. (A once-feared malpractice suit by Kodak is now unlikely, a source at the camera maker says.)

But there are larger questions, too, that Fortenberry's sad situation should raise. Donovan Leisure senior partner Murphy says that "the firm is trying to create an atmosphere in which associates in positions like Fortenberry's will feel free to take the story of one partner acting improperly to another partner." But Perkins's impropriety—a clear, deliberate lie—is an easy call. What about an associate who thinks his partner is filing a frivolous motion or is bilking a client? "You know, when you come to work at a big firm you do give up independence," Murphy concedes. "And a young lawyer's ideas about what is frivolous, for example, can't always be accepted, though we do encourage them to tell the partners they're working for what they think."

And what about firms other than Donovan Leisure that haven't been clubbed by a Perkins disaster into thinking about "open doors" and the like? I asked eight different associates, ages twenty-seven to thirty-two, at major firms around the country what they'd do in Fortenberry's situation. None said that they'd speak up to the judge in the case as their Code of Professional Responsibility requires; only four suggested that there was another partner at the firm they'd feel free to go to if their boss did something like that; and one told a story of watching a partner bill a client (a major utility) for three times the hours worked and, not knowing what to do, doing nothing.

Judge Marvin E. Frankel, the trial judge in the Kodak–Berkey case, was highly critical of Donovan Leisure's conduct during the trial and so outraged by Perkins's lie that he personally called it to the attention of the federal prosecutors. Frankel has since left the bench and become a partner at the midtown firm of Proskauer Rose Goetz & Mendelsohn. An associate there told me last week he'd "have no idea" what to do in a Perkins situation. "There isn't any way for an associate to handle that problem," Frankel concedes. Yet, unexplainably, the once-outraged judge shifts the direct responsibility from the individual law firms, where it belongs, to the organized bar generally: "All firms, including this one, should push the bar association to evolve procedures so that an associate doesn't have to be a hero to do what's ethical."

Every year more and more of the best brains in our society go from law school to firms like Donovan Leisure. And every year these firms get larger—and more competitive. Without some real effort from those at the top, this is an environment that is destined to make automatons out of those who get by and tragedies out of those, like Fortenberry, who have the bad luck to get tripped up.

––––––––

Aftermath of the *Berkey-Kodak* Incident

What should Fortenberry have done in April 1977 when Perkins, the partner in charge at Peck's deposition, lied to opposing counsel? Read Model Rules 5.1—5.3 and their Comments. Brill suggests that Fortenberry had a duty to report the falsity to the court. Might other actions, protecting both lawyers and client, have been taken before the false affidavit was filed with the court in May 1997?[1] What alternatives were available to Donovan

1. See James B. Stewart, Jr., The Partners 327–365 (1983) (suggesting that Perkins was moved to do very uncharacteristic things by a troubled relationship with the partner in charge of the Kodak–Berkey litigation, John Doar. Doar, who had a record

Leisure late in the trial when Judge Frankel pushed for an explanation of why documents returned by Peck had not been made available? The *Berkey-Kodak* incident had substantial consequences:

- The case was a major debacle for Donovan Leisure and the lawyers involved. The firm was fired by Kodak, one of its principal long-time clients, after the adverse jury verdict.[2]

- Mahlon Perkins pleaded guilty to a misdemeanor charge of contempt of court, spent 27 days in prison, but was never disbarred. Since then Perkins has devoted himself to volunteer service to educational, musical and legal organizations. In 1990 Perkins described his work as a volunteer at a public interest firm specializing in civil rights and criminal justice issues as the most satisfactory of his career. "Intellectually, the work here is every bit as satisfying as what I did before.... I'm helping in causes I believe in very deeply. This wasn't a good way to have gotten out, but at this point, I'm very happy not to be there, and very happy to be here."[3]

- Joseph Fortenberry was passed over for partner at Donovan Leisure (the firm states that the decision was made prior to the Kodak incident) and was not hired by any private law firm to which he applied for a job.[4] He died in his mid–40s after a number of years in the Antitrust Division of the Department of Justice.

MURPHY & DEMORY, LTD. v. MURPHY.[5] Admiral Daniel J. Murphy, U.S.N. (ret.), and Willard Demory were the two principals of Murphy & Demory, Ltd. (M&D), a consulting firm assisting government contractors in obtaining defense contracts. M&D brought this action against Admiral Murphy, alleging that he had breached his employment contract and his fiduciary duties by seeking to attract M&D employees and clients to a new organization, Murphy & Associates, in which he was the principal figure. The suit also named M&D's law firm, Pillsbury, Madison & Sutro (Pillsbury), and two lawyers in its Washington, D.C. office, Deanne Siemer and Keith Mendelson, as defendants, charging them with legal malpractice and breach of fiduciary duty. After a five-day non-jury trial, the presiding judge found that Murphy breached his employment contract with M&D and his fiduciary duties to it by attempting to induce employees and clients to leave

of distinguished government service, had never been in charge of a complex litigation and Donovan Leisure litigators found him "cold, distant, and morally arrogant"). See also Walter Kiechel III, The Strange Case of Kodak's Lawyers, Fortune 188 (May 8, 1978).

2. See Stephen Wermiel, Lawyers' Public Image Is Dreadful, Spurring Concern by Attorneys, Wall St. J, .Oct. 11, 1983, p. 1

(reporting that Donovan Leisure made a substantial payment to Kodak to fend off a malpractice action).

3. David Margolick, The Long Road Back for a Disgraced Patrician, N.Y.Times, Jan. 19, 1990, p. B6.

4. Stewart, supra at 24, 62.

5. Circuit Court, Fairfax County, Virginia, Chancery #128219 (June 6, 1994) (unreported decision).

M&D and join his new company, which offered consulting services in direct competition with M&D.

The court found that Pillsbury and its lawyers, Siemer and Mendelson, were guilty of legal malpractice for assisting Admiral Murphy in his efforts. They committed malpractice:

by accepting representation of Admiral Murphy in his efforts either to take control of M&D or to form, prior to his resignation from M&D, a new corporation to compete with M&D ...; by simultaneously representing Admiral Murphy in matters adverse to their client, M&D, without disclosing to the corporation or to Admiral Murphy the fact of the dual representation [and] obtaining the corporation's consent of such representation; [and] by filing on behalf of M&D a lawsuit seeking judicial dissolution of their by-then former client, M&D, based in part on the confidential information obtained from M&D employees during the course of their representation of M&D.

The Pillsbury Defendants ignored the warnings of junior associates at the law firm that the dual representation of Admiral Murphy was rife with conflicts of interest and the matters on which they were advising the Admiral entailed possible breaches of fiduciary duty and use of corporate opportunities. I was struck and disturbed by the fact that every inquiry by an associate into the propriety of the firm's actions was referred back to Ms. Siemer for resolution. Clearly, Pillsbury, Madison & Sutro's internal mechanisms for resolution of ethical issues are seriously deficient.

The partner in charge of the client relationship affected by the issue, who is least likely to be objective, is the ultimate arbiter of whether the firm has a conflict of interest. I found Ms. Siemer's testimony to lack credibility when she stated that she wrestled with the ethical issues posed by the joint representation of M&D and Admiral Murphy and concluded that there was no conflict because both clients had an identical interest in ensuring that Admiral Murphy had the best information possible as to what his options were, even if one option was to divert business from M&D and let the company wither.

... M&D had no interest in Admiral Murphy's knowledge of how to undermine the company.... Ms. Siemer willfully ignored the District of Columbia Rules of Professional Conduct with which she was well familiar, having written a treatise on legal ethics.... Pillsbury, Madison & Sutro is equally responsible for Ms. Siemer's lapses in this regard, particularly because in the face of warning bells from the associates, the firm allowed Ms. Siemer to be the final determiner of whether the firm had a conflict of interest.

Although I'm not unsympathetic to Mr. Mendelson's difficult position at the time of most of the activities complained of, I find that he too was equally responsible for the legal malpractice. Simply put, Mr. Mendelson was senior enough that he should have put a stop to the undisclosed dual representation of Admiral Murphy and M&D by disclosing the conflict to Admiral Murphy and M&D's board in obtaining their consent or, failing that, by withdrawing from the representation.

... I find that as a direct and proximate result of the Pillsbury Defendants' legal malpractice, M&D suffered compensatory damages in the amount of $500,000.[6]

Supervisory and Subordinate Lawyers

Lawyers acting under the direction of other lawyers are bound by lawyer codes, but a safe harbor is provided "if that lawyer acts in accordance with a supervisory lawyer's reasonable resolution of an arguable question of professional duty." M.R. 5.2. Was the conflict of interest question in M&D "an arguable question of professional duty?" Did Keith Mendelson, the associate, act in accordance with Deanne Siemer's "reasonable resolution" of that issue? Was his situation made more difficult because Ms. Siemer was a "rainmaker" and he was about to be considered for partnership? Do the professional rules governing conflicts of interest provide the standard for determining the standard of care for legal malpractice?

Law firms are required to establish reasonable procedures to identify conflicts and deal with other ethical issues. See M.R. 1.7, Comment [1]. The court in M&D criticized the Pillsbury procedures. Shortly after the case the Pillsbury firm issued a new directive governing "risk management and ethical concerns." Lawyers facing such a problem

should contact the Professional Responsibility Committee member resident in your office.... Additionally, if you feel it is necessary to discuss the matter with someone outside your office, you should contact the Chair of the Committee, or any other Committee member in the absence of the Chair. All conversations will be treated strictly on a confidential basis.

Many firms require an associate who has an ethical concern to raise it with the partner in charge and then, if the problem is not satisfactorily resolved, to take it to the firm's ethics committee.[7] Failure to take this step, some firms state, will jeopardize an associate's future in the firm. Suppose that you concluded, after working with a partner closely on a matter and reviewing the subsequent billings, that the partner had triple billed the client for attorney time, including your own. Would you feel comfortable raising this issue with the partner involved? Can it be raised without questioning the partner's integrity? How can confidentiality be maintained

---

6. Deanne Siemer left the Pillsbury firm shortly after the M&D case; Keith Mendelson was promoted to partnership. In 1994 Pillsbury totaled 593 lawyers firmwide, with 34 lawyers in the D.C. office.

7. Larry Smith, Firms Take Divergent Paths in Responding to Associates' Ethics Concerns, 13 Of Counsel 20–25 (August 15, 1994).

or the associate protected from retaliation from the partner when the partnership decision is being made?[8]

Firms can be badly hurt by incidents like that in *M&D*. Remaining silent prevents the firm from avoiding a problem while it was still possible to do so. The associate, however, is caught between the potential enmity of the supervising partner and censure by firm management. Perhaps there is truth in the old saying, "Being a lawyer is a tough way to make a living."

Discipline for Law Firms

Should professional discipline be extended to law firms? Professor Ted Schneyer argues that the steady growth of organizational law practice and changes in the regulatory process warrant imposing discipline on law firms.[9] At present, lawyers in firms of twenty lawyers or more are almost never subject to professional discipline. The nature of group practice militates against the application of the quasi-criminal process of professional discipline to individual firm lawyers:[10] First, even when a firm has clearly committed wrongdoing, the diffusion of responsibility in team practice makes it difficult to assign responsibility to individual lawyers. Second, disciplinary bodies are reluctant to single out one firm lawyer when others in the same firm may be equally responsible. And third, large law firms constitute an "ethical infrastructure" of attitudes, policies and operating procedures that either cause or can prevent ethical failures. For example, the absence of adequate conflicts-screening procedures and reviews in the *M&D* case was surely a factor in the failure of the Pillsbury firm to avoid a harmful conflict. Schneyer, relying on the analogy of corporate crime, concludes that disciplinary authority should be extended to law firms as a means of deterring law firm misconduct. Sanctions would generally be limited to public censure, probation periods and restitution for harms done.

One state, New York, has authorized law firm discipline but thus far used it very sparingly. As of mid–1999, the ABA was considering whether or not to adopt a rule permitting the discipline of law firms and other law practice organizations.

---

2. Declining Loyalty: Grabbing and Leaving

Increased competition for legal business and a "bottomline" mentality on profits has led to decreased loyalty: clients who parcel out work among

---

8. Smith, id., after interviewing prominent partners in a number of firms, reports: "No firm interviewed has concrete guarantees against recrimination. 'How can you guarantee something like that?' asks the chairman of an ethics committee at one 250–lawyer firm. Under the best of circumstances, he adds, associates only bring their questions to ethics committees 'with a dry mouth.' If the supervising partner is a rainmaker, the situation naturally gets worse; even the ethics partners or committee members might 'buckle' confronting big business getters."

9. Ted Schneyer, Professional Discipline for Law Firms?, 77 Cornell L.Rev. 1 (1991).

10. Id. at 8–11.

firms or combine it in a firm that is willing to provide a lower price; rainmakers who are lured from one firm to another; associates who jump ship and hope to take their clients with them. Legal ethics rules encourage some forms of opportunistic conduct, sometimes referred to as "grabbing and leaving:" (1) the right of a client to discharge one firm and hire another (M.R. 1.16, Comment [4]); (2) the right of a lawyer to solicit in person or in writing the legal business of "a prospective client with whom the lawyer has ... [a] prior professional relationship" (M.R. 7.3(a)); (3) the prohibition against covenants not to compete and related agreements that have the potential effect of discouraging clients from exercising freedom of choice (M.R. 5.6(a)); and (4) the ethics rules and law governing entitlement of a discharged firm's right to a quantum meruit fee for work done and the right of a successor lawyer to the agreed-upon fee. But other law is also very much in play: tort and agency rules governing fiduciary duties to clients and prohibiting tortious interference with existing contract relations; and partnership law that permits partners to make advance provision for some of these matters and provides default rules if the partnership agreement does not deal with the matter or does so in an invalid way.

Rosenfeld, Meyer & Susman v. Cohen,[11] illustrates both opportunistic conduct by departing lawyers and efforts to combat it. Rectifier Corp. hired the Rosenfeld firm on a one-third contingent fee basis to pursue an antitrust suit. Lawyers Cohen and Riorden spent five years working on the case; during this period they generated little in the way of fees but were paid a partnership share annually. As the antitrust case neared settlement, the two lawyers demanded a double share of the firm's profits. When the firm refused, they resigned from the firm and persuaded Rectifier to come with them, offering to reduce the company's fee to less than 10 percent of the award. The litigation settled for $33 million one year later. In the subsequent law suit, the Rosenfeld firm charged that the former partners had breached their fiduciary duty to the partnership. The appellate court agreed: the lawyers breached their duty not to "take any action with respect to unfinished business which leads to purely personal gain." The Rosenfeld–Rectifier fee agreement was "unfinished business" on the day the lawyers resigned; the right of the client to choose new lawyers did not eliminate the partners' duties to the partnership.

Robert Hillman, who has written extensively on the subject, states that "[g]rabbing and leaving is not in itself a fiduciary duty because no partner is permanently bound to a firm."[12] Rather, "[t]he manner in which partners plan for and implement withdrawal, ... is subject to the constraints imposed on them by virtue of their status as fiduciaries." A lawyer must provide reasonable notice of intent to withdraw from a firm, and may not solicit clients prior to making such a disclosure to the firm. Solicitation of clients prior to withdrawal breaches the loyalty obligations of the departing lawyer to the law firm. Following a lawyer's announcement regarding her

---

11. 194 Cal.Rptr. 180 (Cal.App.1994).

12. Robert Hillman, Loyalty in the Firm: A Statement of General Principles on the Duties of Partners Withdrawing from Law Firms, 55 Wash. & Lee L.Rev. 997, 999.

departure, the lawyer may solicit clients providing the following conditions are satisfied: "(a) Sufficient time has elapsed following the announcement to allow the firm an equal opportunity to compete for clients; (b) The solicitation is not done in secret; and (c) The client is advised or otherwise aware that it is free to choose the current firm or the partner's new firm (or any other lawyer or firm)."[13] A departing lawyer may also take client files that are reasonably related to the representation of a client and may recruit staff members. Following the partner's departure, the firm and former partner have a duty "to account to each other for income derived from cases pending at the time of withdrawal."

Forfeiture Provisions (Non–Compete Clauses)

Some law firms attempt to prevent losses caused by departing partners by including clauses in the partnership agreement that limit the share of firm capital the withdrawing partner can take or, more directly, prohibit the lawyer from competing for the same clients. These clauses may violate Model Rule 5.6(a), providing that a lawyer shall not be a party to or participate in a partnership or employment agreement that restricts the right of a lawyer to practice after the termination of the agreement. The rule seeks to protect the professional autonomy of lawyers and the right of clients to choose a lawyer. (M.R. 5.6, Comment [1].) In many states non-compete clauses are unenforceable. In Pettingell v. Morrison, Mahoney & Miller,[14] for example, the court found that a partnership provision that provided that departing partners would forfeit rights to the firm's cash profits and annual partnership interest credits should the partners compete with the firm was against public policy and unenforceable.

California, however, takes a different approach, permitting law firms to enter into agreements restricting competition by "attach[ing] economic consequence to a departing partner's unrestricted choice to pursue a particular kind of practice."[15] The court reasoned:

> Even the largest and most prestigious firms are fragile economic units, and there has been an increasing propensity of partners to leave, "grab clients," and set up a competing practice.... We are confident that our recognition of a new reality in the practice of law will have no deleterious effect on the current ability of clients to retain loyal, competent counsel.

The court added that "[a]n absolute ban on competition would be per se unreasonable."

---

13. Id. at 1013.

14. 687 N.E.2d 1237 (Mass.1997). See also Cohen v. Lord, Day & Lord, 550 N.E.2d 410 (N.Y.1989) (striking down a partnership provision that conditioned collection of partnership profits upon departing partner's promise not to compete in any state or jurisdiction where firm had an office; such agreements create a financial disincentive to leave the firm, thus "unfairly restricting [an attorney's] right to practice and the public's right to have access to any counsel").

15. Howard v. Babcock, 863 P.2d 150 (Cal. 1993) (upholding covenant forfeiting departure benefits of withdrawing partner who practices in same geographic area as law firm).

3.   WRONGFUL DISCHARGE OF IN-HOUSE COUNSEL

Balla v. Gambro, Inc.

Supreme Court of Illinois, 1991.
145 Ill.2d 492, 584 N.E.2d 104.

■ JUSTICE CLARK delivered the opinion of the court:

The issue in this case is whether in-house counsel should be allowed the remedy of an action for retaliatory discharge.

Appellee, Roger Balla, formerly in-house counsel for Gambro, Inc. (Gambro), filed a retaliatory discharge action against Gambro, its affiliate ... (Gambro Germany), [and] its parent company ... (Gambro Sweden) ... in the circuit court of Cook County (Gambro, Gambro Germany and Gambro Sweden [are] collectively referred to as appellants). Appellee alleged that he was fired in contravention of Illinois public policy and sought damages for the discharge. The trial court dismissed the action on appellants' motion for summary judgment. The appellate court reversed. (560 N.E.2d 1043.) We granted appellant's petition for leave to appeal and allowed amicus curiae briefs from the American Corporate Counsel Association and Illinois State Bar Association.

Gambro is a distributor of kidney dialysis equipment manufactured by Gambro Germany. Among the products distributed by Gambro are dialyzers which filter excess fluid and toxic substances from the blood of patients with no or impaired kidney function. The manufacture and sale of dialyzers is regulated by the United States Food and Drug Administration (FDA). . . .

Appellee, Roger J. Balla, is and was at all times throughout this controversy an attorney licensed to practice law in the State of Illinois. On March 17, 1980, appellee executed an employment agreement with Gambro which contained the terms of appellee's employment. . . . [Balla's duties as General Counsel and Manager of Regulatory Affairs included assuring "compliance with applicable laws and regulations."]

In July 1985 Gambro Germany informed Gambro in a letter that certain dialyzers it had manufactured, the clearances of which varied from the package insert, were about to be shipped to Gambro. Referring to these dialyzers, Gambro Germany advised Gambro:

> "For acute patients risk is that the acute uremic situation will not be improved in spite of the treatment, giving continuous high levels of potassium, phosphate and urea/creatine. The chronic patient may note the effect as a slow progression of the uremic situation and depending on the interval between medical check-ups the medical risk may be overlooked."

Appellee told the president of Gambro to reject the shipment because the dialyzers did not comply with FDA regulations. The president notified Gambro Germany of its decision to reject the shipment on July 12, 1985.

However, one week later the president informed Gambro Germany that Gambro would accept the dialyzers and "sell [them] to a unit that is not currently our customer but who buys only on price." Appellee contends that he was not informed by the president of the decision to accept the dialyzers but became aware of it through other Gambro employees. Appellee maintains that he spoke with the president in August regarding the company's decision to accept the dialyzers and told the president that he would do whatever was necessary to stop the sale of the dialyzers.

On September 4, 1985, appellee was discharged from Gambro's employment by its president. The following day, appellee reported the shipment of the dialyzers to the FDA. The FDA seized the shipment and determined the product to be "adulterated within the meaning of section 501(h) of the [Federal Act]."

On March 19, 1986, appellee filed a four-count complaint in tort for retaliatory discharge seeking $22 million in damages....

We agree with the trial court that appellee does not have a cause of action against Gambro for retaliatory discharge under the facts of the case at bar. Generally, this court adheres to the proposition that " 'an employer may discharge an employee-at-will for any reason or for no reason [at all].' " ... However, in Kelsay v. Motorola, Inc. (Ill.1978), 384 N.E.2d 353, this court first recognized the limited and narrow tort of retaliatory discharge. In *Kelsay*, an at-will employee was fired for filing a worker's compensation claim against her employer. After examining the history and purpose behind the Workers' Compensation Act to determine the public policy behind its enactment, this court held that the employee should have a cause of action for retaliatory discharge. This court stressed that if employers could fire employees for filing workers' compensation claims, the public policy behind the enactment of the Workers' Compensation Act would be frustrated.

Subsequently, in Palmateer v. International Harvester Co. (Ill.1981), 421 N.E.2d 876, this court again examined the tort of retaliatory discharge. In *Palmateer*, an employee was discharged for informing the police of suspected criminal activities of a co-employee, and because he agreed to provide assistance in any investigation and trial of the matter. Based on the public policy favoring the investigation and prosecution of crime, this court held that the employee had a cause of action for retaliatory discharge....

In this case it appears that Gambro discharged appellee, an employee of Gambro, in retaliation for his activities, and this discharge was in contravention of a clearly mandated public policy. Appellee allegedly told the president of Gambro that he would do whatever was necessary to stop the sale of the "misbranded and/or adulterated" dialyzers. In appellee's eyes, the use of these dialyzers could cause death or serious bodily harm to patients. As we have stated before, "[t]here is no public policy more important or more fundamental than the one favoring the effective protection of the lives and property of citizens." However, in this case, appellee was not just an employee of Gambro, but also general counsel for Gambro.

... [I]n Herbster v. North American Co. for Life & Health Insurance (Ill.App.1986), 501 N.E.2d 343, our appellate court held that the plaintiff, an employee and chief legal counsel for the defendant company, did not have a claim for retaliatory discharge against the company due to the presence of the attorney-client relationship. Under the facts of that case, the defendant company allegedly requested the plaintiff to destroy or remove discovery information which had been requested in lawsuits pending against the company. The plaintiff refused arguing that such conduct would constitute fraud and violate several provisions of the Illinois Code of Professional Responsibility. Subsequently, the defendant company discharged the plaintiff.

The appellate court refused to extend the tort of retaliatory discharge to the plaintiff in *Herbster* primarily because of the special relationship between an attorney and client. The court stated:

> The mutual trust, exchanges of confidence, reliance on judgment, and personal nature of the attorney-client relationship demonstrate the unique position attorneys occupy in our society.

The appellate court recited a list of factors which make the attorney-client relationship special such as: the attorney-client privilege regarding confidential communications, the fiduciary duty an attorney owes to a client, the right of the client to terminate the relationship with or without cause, and the fact that a client has exclusive control over the subject matter of the litigation and a client may dismiss or settle a cause of action regardless of the attorney's advice. Thus, in *Herbster*, since the plaintiff's duties pertained strictly to legal matters, the appellate court determined that the plaintiff did not have a claim for retaliatory discharge.

We agree with the conclusion reached in *Herbster* that, generally, in-house counsel do not have a claim under the tort of retaliatory discharge. However, we base our decision as much on the nature and purpose of the tort of retaliatory discharge, as on the effect on the attorney-client relationship that extending the tort would have. In addition, at this time, we caution that our holding is confined by the fact that appellee is and was at all times throughout this controversy an attorney licensed to practice law in the State of Illinois. Appellee is and was subject to the Illinois Code of Professional Responsibility (see the Rules of Professional Conduct which replaced the Code of Professional Responsibility, effective August 1, 1990), adopted by this court. The tort of retaliatory discharge is a limited and narrow exception to the general rule of at-will employment. ... The tort seeks to achieve " 'a proper balance ... among the employer's interest in operating a business efficiently and profitably, the employee's interest in earning a livelihood, and society's interest in seeing its public policies carried out.' "Further, as stated in *Palmateer*, *"[t]he foundation of the tort of retaliatory discharge lies in the protection of public policy...."* (Emphasis added.)

In this case, the public policy to be protected, that of protecting the lives and property of citizens, is adequately safeguarded without extending the tort of retaliatory discharge to in-house counsel. Appellee was required under the Rules of Professional Conduct to report Gambro's intention to sell the "misbranded and/or adulterated" dialyzers. Rule 1.6(b) of the Rules of Professional Conduct reads:

> A lawyer *shall* reveal information about a client to the extent it appears necessary to prevent the client from committing an act that would result in death or serious bodily injury. (Emphasis added.)

Appellee alleges, and the FDA's seizure of the dialyzers indicates, that the use of the dialyzers would cause death or serious bodily injury. Thus, under the above-cited rule, appellee was under the mandate of this court to report the sale of these dialyzers.

... [A]ppellee argues that not extending the tort of retaliatory discharge to in-house counsel would present attorneys with a "Hobson's choice." According to appellee, in-house counsel would face two alternatives: either comply with the client/employer's wishes and risk both the loss of a professional license and exposure to criminal sanctions, or decline to comply with client/employer's wishes and risk the loss of a full-time job and the attendant benefits. We disagree. Unlike the employees in *Kelsay* which this court recognized would be left with the difficult decision of choosing between whether to file a workers' compensation claim and risk being fired, or retaining their jobs and losing their right to a remedy, in-house counsel plainly are not confronted with such a dilemma. In-house counsel do not have a choice of whether to follow their ethical obligations as attorneys licensed to practice law, or follow the illegal and unethical demands of their clients. In-house counsel must abide by the Rules of Professional Conduct. Appellee had no choice but to report to the FDA Gambro's intention to sell or distribute these dialyzers, and consequently protect the aforementioned public policy.

In addition, we believe that extending the tort of retaliatory discharge to in-house counsel would have an undesirable effect on the attorney-client relationship that exists between these employers and their in-house counsel. Generally, a client may discharge his attorney at any time, with or without cause. . . . This rule applies equally to in-house counsel as it does to outside counsel. Further, this rule "recognizes that the relationship between an attorney and client is based on trust and that the client must have confidence in his attorney in order to ensure that the relationship will function properly." ... We believe that if in-house counsel are granted the right to sue their employers for retaliatory discharge, employers might be less willing to be forthright and candid with their in-house counsel. Employers might be hesitant to turn to their in-house counsel for advice regarding potentially questionable corporate conduct knowing that their in-house counsel could use this information in a retaliatory discharge suit.

We recognize that under the Illinois Rules of Professional Conduct [R. 1.6], attorneys shall reveal client confidences or secrets in certain situations, and thus one might expect employers/clients to be naturally hesitant to rely on in-house counsel for advice regarding this potentially questionable conduct. However, the danger exists that if in-house counsel are granted a right to sue their employers in tort for retaliatory discharge, employers might further limit their communication with their in-house counsel. As stated in Upjohn Co. v. United States (1981), 449 U.S. 383, 389, regarding the attorney-client privilege: " ... The privilege recognizes that sound legal advice or advocacy serves public ends and that *such advice or advocacy depends upon the lawyer being fully informed by the client.*" (Emphasis added.)

If extending the tort of retaliatory discharge might have a chilling effect on the communications between the employer/client and the in-house counsel, we believe that it is more wise to refrain from doing so.

Our decision not to extend the tort of retaliatory discharge to in-house counsel also is based on other ethical considerations. Under the Rules of Professional Conduct, appellee was required to withdraw from representing Gambro if continued representation would result in the violation of the Rules of Professional Conduct [1.16(a)] by which appellee was bound, or if Gambro discharged the appellee. In this case, Gambro did discharge appellee, and according to appellee's claims herein, his continued representation of Gambro would have resulted in a violation of the Rules of Professional Conduct. Appellee argues that such a choice of withdrawal is "simplistic and uncompassionate, and is completely at odds with contemporary realities facing in-house attorneys." These contemporary realities apparently are the economic ramifications of losing his position as in-house counsel. However difficult economically and perhaps emotionally it is for in-house counsel to discontinue representing an employer/client, we refuse to allow in-house counsel to sue their employer/client for damages because they obeyed their ethical obligations. In this case, appellee, in addition to being an employee at Gambro, is first and foremost an attorney bound by the Rules of Professional Conduct.... An attorney's obligation to follow these Rules of Professional Conduct should not be the foundation for a claim of retaliatory discharge.

We also believe that it would be inappropriate for the employer/client to bear the economic costs and burdens of their in-house counsel's adhering to their ethical obligations under the Rules of Professional Conduct. Presumably, in situations where an in-house counsel obeys his or her ethical obligations and reveals certain information regarding the employer/client, the attorney-client relationship will be irreversibly strained and the client will more than likely discharge its in-house counsel. In this scenario, if we were to grant the in-house counsel the right to sue the client for retaliatory discharge, we would be shifting the burden and costs of obeying the Rules of Professional Conduct from the attorney to the employer/client. The employer/client would be forced to pay damages to its former in-house counsel to essentially mitigate the financial harm the attorney suffered for having to abide by Rules of Professional Conduct. This, we believe, is impermissible for all attorneys know or should know that at certain times in their professional career, they will have to forgo economic gains in order to protect the integrity of the legal profession.

Our review of cases from other jurisdictions dealing with this issue does not persuade us to hold otherwise. [The court discussed Willy v.

Coastal Corp., 647 F.Supp. 116 (S.D.Tex.1986) (in-house counsel did not have a retaliatory discharge claim when he alleged he was fired because he required the defendant to comply with environmental laws); Nordling v. Northern States Power Co., 465 N.W.2d 81 (Minn.App.1991) (holding that plaintiff's status as in-house counsel precluded breach-of-contract and retaliatory discharge claims against his employer); Parker v. M & T Chemicals, Inc. 566 A.2d 215 (N.J.Super.1989) (New Jersey Whistleblowers Act provided a remedy to an employee who was discharged for urging compliance with state's health and safety laws); and Mourad v. Automobile Club Insurance Association, 465 N.W.2d 395 (Mich.App.1991) (upholding claim for breach of employment contract but not that for retaliatory demotion).]

For the foregoing reasons, the decision of the appellate court is reversed, and the decision of the trial court is affirmed.

■ JUSTICE FREEMAN, dissenting:

. . . [T]he majority first reasons that the public policy implicated in this case, i.e., protecting the lives and property of Illinois citizens, is adequately safeguarded by the lawyer's ethical obligation to reveal information about a client as necessary to prevent acts that would result in death or serious bodily harm [Ill.R. 1.6(b)]. I find this reasoning fatally flawed.

. . . [T]o say that the categorical nature of ethical obligations is sufficient to ensure that the ethical obligations will be satisfied simply ignores reality. Specifically, it ignores that, as unfortunate for society as it may be, attorneys are no less human than nonattorneys and, thus, no less given to the temptation to either ignore or rationalize away their ethical obligations when complying therewith may render them unable to feed and support their families.

I would like to believe, as my colleagues apparently conclude, that attorneys will always "do the right thing" because the law says that they must. However, my knowledge of human nature, which is not much greater than the average layman's, and, sadly, the recent scandals involving the bench and bar of Illinois are more than sufficient to dispel such a belief. Just as the ethical obligations of the lawyers and judges involved in those scandals were inadequate to ensure that they would not break the law, I am afraid that the lawyer's ethical obligation to "blow the whistle" is likewise an inadequate safeguard for the public policy of protecting lives and property of Illinois citizens.

. . . [T]his court must take whatever steps it can, within the bounds of the law, to give lawyers incentives to abide by their ethical obligations, beyond the satisfaction inherent in their doing so. We cannot continue to delude ourselves and the people of the State of Illinois that attorneys' ethical duties, alone, are always sufficient to guarantee that lawyers will "do the right thing." In the context of this case, where doing "the right thing" will often result in termination by an employer bent on doing the "wrong thing," I believe that the incentive needed is recognition of a cause of action for retaliatory discharge, in the appropriate case.

The majority also bases its holding upon the reasoning that allowing in-house counsel a cause of action for retaliatory discharge will have a chilling effect on the attorney-client relationship and the free flow of information necessary to that relationship. . . .

One of the basic purposes of the attorney-client relationship, especially in the corporate client-in-house counsel setting, is for the attorney to advise the client as to, exactly, what conduct the law requires so that the client can then comply with that advice. Given that purpose, allowing in-house counsel a cause of action for retaliatory discharge would chill the attorney-client relationship and discourage a corporate client from communicating freely with the attorney only where, as here, the employer decides to go forward with particular conduct, regardless of advice that it is contrary to law. I believe that, just as in-house counsel might reasonably so assume, this court is entitled to assume that corporate clients will rarely so decide. As such, to allow a corporate employer to discharge its in-house counsel under such circumstances, without fear of any sanction, is truly to give the assistance and protection of the courts to scoundrels. . . .

In holding as it does, the majority also reasons that an attorney's obligation to follow the Rules of Professional Conduct should not be the basis for a claim of retaliatory discharge. . . . It is incontrovertible that the law binds all men, kings and paupers alike. . . . An attorney should not be punished simply because he has ethical obligations imposed upon him over and above the general obligation to obey the law which all men have. Nor should a corporate employer be protected simply because the employee it has discharged for "blowing the whistle" happens to be an attorney.

. . . [T]he majority ignores the employer's decision to persist in the questionable conduct which its in-house counsel advised was illegal. It is that conduct, not the attorney's ethical obligations, which is the predicate of the retaliatory discharge claim. . . . [G]ranting the attorney a claim for retaliatory discharge simply allows recovery against the party bent on breaking the law, rather than rewarding an attorney for complying with his ethical obligations. . . .

[T]his case involves an attorney discharged from his employment, not one who has voluntarily resigned due to his ethical obligations. . . . [T]e majority overlooks the very real possibility that in-house counsel who is discharged, rather than allowed to resign in accordance with his ethical obligations once the employer's persistence in illegal conduct is evident to him, will be stigmatized within the legal profession. That stigma and its apparent consequences, economic and otherwise, in addition to the immediate economic consequences of a discharge, also militate strongly in favor of allowing the attorney a claim for retaliatory discharge.

———

Subsequent Cases

Two cases subsequent to *Balla* take a different position. *General Dynamics Corp. v. Superior Court*[16] attracted national attention as the first major decision recognizing the retaliatory discharge tort claim of a terminated in-house lawyer. The plaintiff, Andrew Rose, had worked as an attorney for General Dynamics for 14 years and alleged that he was fired in retaliation for his unwelcome legal advice on several sensitive matters, including drug use in the company and unlawful pay practices. The employer, relying on *Balla* and other cases, argued that an in-house lawyer, unlike other employees, was subject to discharge at any time for any reason. In its unanimous opinion, the California Supreme Court held that "there is no valid reason why an in-house attorney should not be permitted to pursue [a lack of "good cause"] contract claim in the same way as the nonattorney employee."[17] As to the tort cause of action, the court was more qualified. "[W]e conclude that there is no reason inherent in the nature of an attorney's role as house counsel to a corporation that in itself precludes the maintenance of a retaliatory discharge claim, provided it can be established without breaching the attorney-client privilege or unduly endangering the values lying at the heart of the professional relationship."[18]

A tort remedy for retaliatory discharge in violation of public policy was available, the court stated, in two situations: (1) when a lawyer was fired for refusing to violate a mandatory requirement of the profession's ethical rules; and (2) in other situations if two conditions were met: (a) the circumstances would support such a claim by a discharged non-lawyer employee; and (b) the claim could be established without violating the confidentiality obligations of lawyers. Although the court cited California's statutory duty of confidentiality in this connection (Business & Professions Code § 6068(e), containing no explicit exceptions to the duty of confidentiality), it dealt primarily with the attorney-client privilege, implying that any exception to the privilege was also an implied exception to the lawyer's duty of confidentiality.

Under what circumstances could a lawyer prove his claim without violating confidentiality or the attorney-client privilege? The court stated:

> ... Matters involving the commission of a crime or a fraud, or circumstances in which the attorney reasonably believes that disclosure is necessary to prevent the commission of a criminal act likely to result in death or substantial bodily harm, are statutory and well-recognized exceptions to the attorney-client privilege.... Although their revelation in the course of a retaliatory discharge suit may do lasting damage to the expectations of the corporate client (or, more likely, a corporate executive) that disclosures to counsel would remain inviolate, a concern for protecting the fiduciary aspects of the relationship in the case of a client who confides in counsel for the purpose of

16. 876 P.2d 487 (Cal.1994).   **18.** Id.

17. Id. at 490.

planning a crime or practicing a fraud is misplaced; such disclosures do not violate the privilege.[19]

In *GTE Products Corp. v. Stewart*,[20] the high court of Massachusetts followed the *General Dynamics* case. The court recognized a cause of action for retaliatory discharge brought by a former in-house lawyer, but upheld a summary judgment dismissing the claim because the lawyer failed to establish that his resignation was a constructive discharge. Stewart, who served as general counsel of GTE's lighting business, was well regarded by his supervisor, regularly promoted and given high annual performance ratings. In 1990–91 he addressed a series of communications to corporate officers concerning safety and liability issues related to three GTE lighting products (these attorney-client privileged documents were received by the trial court under a protective order of secrecy). In these communications Stewart urged "that the company take aggressive and (presumably) costly measures to protect consumer safety and guard against possible corporate liability."[21] He also advised GTE that the company's lighting maintenance service was required by federal hazardous waste regulations to treat fluorescent and incandescent light bulbs as hazardous waste for purposes of disposal. Stewart alleged that his advice was disregarded on some occasions and generally was not well received.

A few months before Stewart left the company, his immediate supervisor, Trevisan, GTE's general counsel, commended his performance, gave him a good rating, a raise and a bonus of over $30,000. Shortly thereafter, however, Trevisan lowered Stewart's performance rating drastically and told him that Lawson, the company's manager, was dissatisfied with Stewart's "confrontational" style, that Stewart's future with GTE was at risk unless he could get along with Lawson, and that Stewart should stop being the "social conscience" of the company. Stewart, believing that these actions were a precursor to discharge, resigned his employment. Trevisan tried unsuccessfully to persuade Stewart to return.

The Massachusetts court, rejecting the *Balla* case and following *General Dynamics,* concluded that the "public interest is better served if in-house counsel's resolve to comply with ethical and statutorily mandated duties is strengthened by providing judicial recourse when an employer's demands are in direct and unequivocal conflict with those duties." But a former in-house counsel's wrongful discharge claim "will be recognized only in narrow and carefully delineated circumstances." The in-house counsel must assert "that compliance with the demands of the employer would have required the attorney to violate duties imposed by a statute or the disciplinary rules governing the practice of law...." Moreover, the claim "depends on (1) explicit and unequivocal statutory or ethical norms (2) which embody policies of importance to the public at large in the circumstances of the particular case, and (3) the claim can be proved without any

---

19. Id. at 504.

20. 653 N.E.2d 161 (Mass.1995).

21. Id. at 164.

violation of the attorney's obligation to respect client confidences and secrets [under the Massachusetts version of DR 4–101(C)]."[22]

The court, however, after expressing doubt whether disagreements about the risks of a product or "advice relating to the avoidance of possible legal liability" could be the basis for a wrongful discharge claim, held that Stewart had not established the elements of "constructive discharge." The evidence that Stewart submitted in opposition to GTE's motion for summary judgment did not assert "that remaining in his position would have required him to violate his ethical obligations as an attorney ... [or] to further, commit, or conceal any illegal or fraudulent acts." The single unfavorable performance review was not sufficient to establish, as required by the law of constructive discharge, "that the new working conditions would have been so difficult or unpleasant that a reasonable person in the employee's shoes would have felt compelled to resign."[23]

Retaliatory Discharge Claims by Lawyers[24]

Why should a lawyer employed by an organization receive less protection against retaliatory discharge that violates a state's public policy than other employees of the organization? The *Balla* case links issues considered throughout this book: the lawyer's duties not to assist a client in violating the law (Chapter 2 on Conformity to Law), to maintain client confidentiality (Chapter 4 on Confidentiality), to withdraw if continued representation will violate law or a professional rule (Chapters 4 and 6, dealing with the obligation to withdraw) and the economic consequences of withdrawal for good cause (Chapter 6). Does the Illinois court correctly balance the competing interests involved? What might attorney Balla have done differently? See the discussion of Model Rule 1.13 in connection with the *ACC/Lincoln (Jones Day)* case, printed at p. 745 supra.

The Illinois version of the confidentiality rule, M.R. 1.6(b), unlike that adopted by the ABA, does not limit a lawyer's disclosure authority to situations in which the client's conduct is "criminal" and threatens "*imminent* death or substantial bodily harm." Further, Illinois imposes a mandatory duty of disclosure ("shall reveal") rather than a permission to disclose as in M.R. 1.6(b). If Illinois had adopted M.R. 1.6(b) as proposed by the ABA, would Balla have been under a professional duty to disclose? Suppose Gambro, Inc. had been engaged in an ongoing criminal fraud and the jurisdiction's professional rule *prohibits* disclosure (that is not the case in Illinois, which permits disclosure of "the intention of a client to commit a crime"). What result? Does the *Balla* court take the position that the ethics rule trumps other law?

Suppose lawyer Balla had been asked by his employer to forge a document or falsify a statement to a governmental body, both constituting

22. Id. at 167.

23. Id. at 169.

24. See Stephen Gillers, Protecting Lawyers Who Just Say No, 5 Georgia St.L.Rev. 1

(1988) (critique of the *Herbster* decision discussed in *Balla*). Also see Daniel S. Reynolds, Wrongful Discharge of Employed Counsel, 1 Geo.J.Legal Ethics 553 (1988).

criminal acts. Is a refusal to act in those situations more deserving of protection than the reporting issue in *Balla*, which involves a lawyer taking the initiative to "betray" a client's confidences? In a jurisdiction such as California or Massachusetts that recognizes an in-house lawyer's claim for retaliatory discharge, can the lawyer file a complaint revealing client confidences? Where do *General Dynamics* and *GTE Products* draw the line between permitted and prohibited disclosure of the corporation's confidential information?

To the extent that Balla's employment contract provides vested rights (e.g., employment for a term of years, pension rights), Gambro, Inc. cannot eliminate them by discharging him without cause. Claims with a statutory basis, such as a charge that the corporation's discharge involved age, sex or race discrimination, also are available.

Does an Outside Lawyer Have Any Protection Against Discharge Without Cause?

Suppose Balla had been an outside lawyer whose principal client was Gambro, Inc.? Does a discharged outside lawyer have any remedy against the former client? The retaliatory discharge tort is a common law development arising out of termination of employment. The agency relationship of a client with an independent contractor presumably is outside its purview. Because outside lawyers generally work for a number of clients, discharge by one client does not involve the same degree of economic dependency. May a law firm, having staffed up to handle a particular client's matters on a regular basis, protect itself by entering into a retainer agreement providing for liquidated damages reasonably related to those costs if suddenly discharged without cause? The economic consequences of discharge of lawyers who undertake a case on a contingent fee basis are discussed at p. 468 supra.

Do members of a law firm have a duty to report the violations of another lawyer in the firm? What steps should be followed before taking this step? In Wieder v. Skala,[25] an associate alleged in a breach of contract action against his former law firm that he was fired by the firm because he insisted that the firm report the professional misconduct of another lawyer in the firm.[26] The New York court relied on the disciplinary rule requiring a lawyer who knows about another lawyer's misconduct to report such conduct to the disciplinary authorities. Because of the disciplinary rule, the relationship between a lawyer and a legal employer is not merely that of employer and employee. Lawyers are also "independent officers of the court responsible in a broader public sense for their professional obligations." The disciplinary rules created an "implied understanding," on both sides, that neither will do anything to prevent the other from upholding the rule.

---

25. 609 N.E.2d 105 (N.Y.1992).

26. The court rejected the tort theory of retaliatory discharge, which has been construed in New York as limited to situations covered by a relatively narrow statute.

Firing a lawyer for acting ethically breaches this implied term of the law firm's employment contract with an associate.

4. BAR ASSOCIATIONS[27]

Charles W. Wolfram, Modern Legal Ethics

33–38 (1986).[28]

Bar Organizations as Bar Regulators

One whose reading about the legal profession was confined to appellate court reports might be led to believe that state supreme courts exercise both power and initiative in its regulation. In fact, courts serve as the largely passive sounding boards and official approvers or disapprovers of initiatives that are taken by lawyers operating through bar associations. Bar associations set and execute the agenda of business of the organized bar. Their power can be much the same regardless of the particular form or official status of the bar association. Formal and, to an extent, functional differences do exist between unofficial bar associations and those, called "integrated" or mandatory bars, that every lawyer must join as a condition of being eligible to practice law. At the end of the day, however, bar associations exercise pervasive influence over bar admission and discipline, whatever the form of their organization.

Bar Associations

Bar associations arose in the American colonies as eating clubs or similar social gatherings of lawyers.[91] Lawyer business was also their object, and early rules setting uniform fees and regulating the admission of lawyers to practice came from the bar associations. Bar associations fell into decline and ceased to exist during the early part of the nineteenth century. Little formal organization characterized the American bar until after the Civil War, although the groups of lawyers that accompanied judges on circuit undoubtedly had some cohesion and exercised some collective power.

The American Bar Association

Among the earliest groups of lawyers to band together in the orgy of occupational organization that swept the industrial world in the last third

---

27. For a description of studies of the organized bar, see Olivi Maru, Research on the Legal Profession c. 5 (2d ed. 1986). See also John A. Flood, The Legal Profession in the United States (3d ed., 1985, American Bar Foundation) (containing an annotated bibliography).

28. Copyright © 1986 West Publishing Co. Reprinted by permission.

91. Among histories of bar associations, see, e.g., R. Pound, The Lawyer from Antiquity to Modern Times (1953); C. Warren, A History of the American Bar (2d ed. 1966). Pound and, to an extent, Warren give laudatory, and largely uncritical, acceptance to the notion that the most highly organized and powerful forms of bar associations are the best.

of the nineteenth century was the American Bar Association.[92] The ABA was organized in the late summer of 1878 in Saratoga Springs, New York, a popular summering spot for the well-to-do.... The ABA started, and continues, as a private organization that controls its own membership and other affairs and is accountable to no public body for action it might take on organizational or policy matters.

The ABA can advance several reasons in support of a claim that it speaks for the entire legal profession. The ABA is the only national organization with significant lawyer membership from all areas of practice. It operates primarily through sections that are devoted to many fields of law or law practice.... Its membership in recent decades has averaged 45 to 55 percent of the nation's licensed lawyers. The ABA House of Delegates, its chief legislative arm, consists in large part of lawyers appointed from several sections or other parts of the ABA or elected from state and local bar associations that, in turn, exercise varying degrees of control over local lawyers. Historically, the leadership of the ABA and officials of both national and state governments have worked in harmony on a variety of projects, including many in the area of lawyer regulation.

. . .

Other Bar Associations

The ABA has several fellow and sister bar associations, but none compares in size or power. Most state and local bar associations are aligned with the ABA but some have no connections. Most other bar associations are devoted to the interests of lawyer specialists or to a particular issue, cause, or ethnic group. For example, the Federal Bar Association consists primarily of lawyers employed by the federal government. Lawyers are eligible for membership in the Association of Trial Lawyers of America (ATLA) only if they represent claimants in personal injury, products liability, or worker compensation claims. Lawyers who belong to the American College of Trial Lawyers, by contrast, predominantly defend large businesses and insurance companies. The National Bar Association is an organization of black lawyers. The National Lawyers Guild is primarily an organization of leftist lawyers interested in civil rights, civil liberties, and poverty issues.... Both in membership and in power, all other special-interest bar associations taken together cannot equal the power of the ABA.

State and local bar associations historically have operated much as the ABA—as autonomous, private organizations of largely like-minded lawyers within a state, county, city judicial district, or other geographical area.... Even as purely private organizations, state and local bar associations gained considerable power in the early decades of this century. With growing influence they began to lead more ambitious campaigns to influence the education and admission of lawyers, to restrict nonlawyer competi-

92. Accounts of the founding of the ABA are given in E. Sunderland, History of the American Bar Association and Its Work (1953); C. Goetsch, Essays on Simeon E. Baldwin (1981). See generally Brockman, The History of the American Bar Association: A Bibliographic Essay, 6 Am.J.Leg. Hist. 269 (1962).

tion through the creation of unauthorized-practice barriers, and to deal with disfavored practices such as solicitation and advertising by small-firm lawyers. Their power on those and other professional issues was exerted through public and private pressure on courts and legislatures to cede a wider regulatory role to bar associations.

The Operation of Bar Associations

While bar associations retained the formal status of private clubs, their legal powers widened increasingly as they came to gain political power over the profession. In recent decades, bar associations have turned to explicitly political activity such as legislative and administrative lobbying, public relations efforts, and the support of positions on issues. Some of those efforts relate to law reform, some relate to more controversial political issues, and much does not relate directly to the economic or professional status of bar members. Bar associations do not, however, overtly support candidates for political office, aside from the practice of some associations of expressing approval or regret concerning candidates for judicial offices.

As is true of other professional organizations, the majority of the members of bar associations are inactive on most organizational projects.... Most bar association business is conducted in private meetings of committees or boards. The general membership becomes simply the ratifier of predetermined menus of issues and proposals for their resolution. Of course, the general membership must remain content enough not to resign or to vote out a leadership that has struck off too far on its own. Such membership revolts are known among bar associations and serve to instill conservatism and timidity in bar leaders and executives.[5]

Mandatory Bars

The striving by local bars for more effective control of the legal profession resulted in an effort beginning in the early 1920s to "integrate"[7] the bars of the various states. The term does not refer to racial or gender diversity, which, at that time, was rejected by most bar associations and their members. Instead, integration referred to an organized bar effort to enact court rules or statutes to require every lawyer who actively practiced law to belong to the state bar association. Among other things, making bar membership mandatory would permit the bar association to exercise greater control over the admission and particularly the discipline of lawyers.

Typically the bar was made mandatory by an order issued by the state supreme court under its inherent power to regulate the practice of law,

---

5. The widely held lawyer belief is that bar associations tend to be conservative groups heavily dominated by large-firm lawyers unsympathetic to social change. A sociologist has argued, however, that the history of the positions taken by various bar groups on controversial social and political issues since the Second World War suggests that liberal as well as conservative causes are often espoused. Halliday, The Idiom of Legalism in Bar Politics: Lawyers, McCarthyism, and the Civil Rights Era, 1982 Am.B.Found.Research J. 913.

7. Mandatory bars were originally referred to as "integrated" bars and are now more commonly called "unified." The term "mandatory" is less euphemistic and more descriptive of their salient characteristic.

although several mandatory bars have been created by statute. Courts have uniformly upheld the power of the courts themselves or of bar associations to exact mandatory bar fees from lawyers and threaten suspension from practice as a penalty for a lawyer who, without excuse, does not pay.[10] In 1961 a divided Supreme Court in Lathrop v. Donohue[11] rejected federal constitutional attacks on mandatory lawyer membership in state bars. By the early 1980s thirty-three states and the District of Columbia had mandatory bars.

. . . . Because courts lack the time, staff, funds, or means of information gathering, they probably are not intimately aware of the actual operation of mandatory bars and supervise them only in a passive and reactive capacity by passing upon initiatives that are generated and shaped in detail elsewhere. . . .

Although mandatory bars have existed since 1921, they continue to generate controversy.[16] The concept of mandatory bar associations has been resisted for a number of reasons by many lawyers, primarily those in solo practice or small firms. Opponents have feared that annual dues would become too high and that funds taken from members' dues would be used to support projects opposed by a majority of members or to support political causes. . . .

———

Compulsory Membership in the Bar

The Wolfram excerpt discusses mandatory or unified bars and mentions the concern that "members' dues would be used to support . . . political causes."[1] That question came before the Supreme Court in the *Keller* case.

KELLER v. STATE BAR OF CALIFORNIA.[2] The State Bar, a state agency, imposed mandatory dues on members as a condition of practicing law in the state. Dues supported the agency's numerous activities, including setting standards for legal practice in the state, disciplining lawyer misconduct and examining applicants for admission to the bar. Additional-

---

10. Petition of Florida State Bar Ass'n, 40 So.2d 902 (Fla.1949); In re Unification of New Hampshire Bar, 109 N.H. 260, 248 A.2d 709 (1968); Petition of Rhode Island Bar Ass'n, 118 R.I. 489, 374 A.2d 802 (1977). . . .

11. 367 U.S. 820 (1961). . . .

16. See generally Schneyer, The Incoherence of the Unified Bar Concept: Generalizing from the Wisconsin Experience, 1983 Am.B.Found. Research J. 1. Professor Schneyer concludes that the contradictions inherent in the concept of a mandatory bar association should lead to their demise,

with their functions taken over by voluntary bar associations or, if necessary, by special-purpose agencies for bar discipline and the like that are financed by court assessment of dues on all lawyers.

1. Mandatory bars exist in 32 states and the District of Columbia; voluntary bars undertake the same functions in the other 18 states. In 19 of the 33 mandatory bar jurisdictions, the state bar is responsible for professional discipline.

2. 496 U.S. 1 (1990).

ly, the State Bar lobbied the legislature and filed amicus curiae briefs. These latter activities prompted a challenge by 21 members.

Plaintiffs argued that using mandatory membership dues to advance political and ideological causes to which they were opposed violated their First and Fourteenth Amendment freedoms of speech and association. The California Supreme Court rejected plaintiffs claim on the ground that the State Bar was exempt from scrutiny since it is a state agency. Overturning the state decision, the Supreme Court held that the State Bar was less like a state agency than a labor union for the purposes of the lawsuit. While state agencies may use unrestricted revenue ... for any purposes within its authority, the very specialized characteristics of the State Bar of California ... served to distinguish it from the role of the typical government official or agency.

The plan established by California for the regulation of the profession is for recommendations as to admission to practice, the disciplining of lawyers, codes of conduct, and the like to be made to the courts or the legislature by the organized bar. It is entirely appropriate that all of the lawyers who derive benefit from the unique status of being among those admitted to practice before the courts should be called upon to pay a fair share of the cost of the professional involvement in this effort.

But the very specialized characteristics of the State Bar of California discussed above served to distinguish it from the role of the typical government official or agency.... [I]t was created, not to participate in the general government of the State, but to provide specialized professional advice to those with the ultimate responsibility of governing the legal profession. Its members and officers are such not because they are citizens or voters, but because they are lawyers.... [Hence it is] subject to the same constitutional rule with respect to the use of compulsory dues as are labor unions representing public and private employees. ...

Petitioners assert that the State Bar has engaged in, inter alia, lobbying for or against state legislation (1) prohibiting state and local agency employers from requiring employees to take polygraph tests; (2) prohibiting possession of armor-piercing handgun ammunition; (3) creating an unlimited right of action to sue anybody causing air pollution; and (4) requesting Congress to refrain from enacting a guest worker program or from permitting the importation of workers from other countries. Petitioners' complaint also alleges that the conference of delegates funded and sponsored by the State Bar endorsed a gun control initiative, disapproved statements of a United States senatorial candidate regarding court review of a victim's bill of rights, endorsed a nuclear weapons freeze initiative, and opposed federal legislation limiting federal court jurisdiction over abortions, public school prayer, and busing.

Precisely where the line falls between those State Bar activities in which the officials and members of the Bar are acting essentially as professional advisors to those ultimately charged with the regulation of the legal profession, on the one hand, and those activities having political or ideological coloration which are not reasonably related to the advancement of such goals, on the other, will not always be easy to discern. But the extreme ends of the spectrum are clear: Compulsory dues may not be expended to endorse or advance a gun control or nuclear weapons freeze initiative; at the other end of the spectrum petitioners have no valid constitutional objection to their compulsory dues being spent for activities connected with disciplining members of the Bar or proposing ethical codes for the profession.

On remand in *Keller,* the California State Bar reexamined its expenditures and determined that only $3 of the typical 1991 dues of $478 were not germane to the bar's central purposes. Members who did not want to underwrite non-chargeable activities were permitted to take a $3 deduction. In Michigan, however, a similar evaluation resulted in an $18 rebate from total annual dues of $200.[3] Some mandatory bar jurisdictions, including the District of Columbia and North Carolina, deal with the *Keller* problem by spinning off lobbying and public interest advocacy to a voluntary state bar and limiting the mandatory bar to clearly permissible activities, such as bar admission, CLE and professional discipline.[4]

Which of the following activities are permissible under *Keller* : Resolutions or lobbying activities concerning the appointment rather than election of judges? Greater public funding of civil legal assistance for the poor? Longer periods of maternity leave for employees, including fathers? Extension of anti-discrimination laws to protect homosexuals against discrimination in housing, employment, education and public accommodations? Termination of China's "most favored nation" trade status because of that nation's human rights violations?"

Voluntary bar associations also face internal criticism and loss of membership if their political positions and legislative advocacy rile members. When the ABA came out in 1994 with a strong resolution supporting abortion on demand it added some younger lawyers and lost a substantial number of long-time members.[5] About 40 percent of U.S. lawyers belong to

---

3. Where Are the Big Savings?, A.B.A. J. 36–37 (March 1991).

4. See Kathleen O. Beatiks, Four Bifurcated Bars Say It Works, Calif.B.J., Apr. 1998, pp. 1, 12.

5. According to the Federalist Society, the ABA in 1998 opposed the following law reform issues: product liability and automobile insurance reform legislation, caps on punitive damages, safe harbor and other key aspects of securities litigation reform, mandatory Rule 11 sanctions, and regulation of contingent fee arrangements; in the same year the ABA supported the following law reform proposals: increased funding for the Legal Services Corp. and creation of mandatory mediation programs in federal courts. On social policy issues, the ABA opposed state or federal restrictions on abortion and endorsed public funding of abortions; endorsed adoption of needle exchange programs to reduce the spread of AIDs; urged governments at all levels to prohibit discrimination on the basis of sexual orientation in employment, housing and public accommodations; endorsed continued use of racial preferences in education and employment; called for a moratorium of the death penalty until additional habeas procedures are adopted; supported

the ABA; voluntary state bars vary from relatively low percentages of the state's bar (e.g., 30 percent) to relatively high (e.g., 70 percent). Voluntary state bars are facing stiff competition from specialized and local bar associations.[6]

5. "PROFESSIONALISM" AND CIVILITY

Roger C. Cramton, "On Giving Meaning to 'Professionalism' "[7]

Symposium on Teaching and Learning Professionalism (October 1996).

... Do we know what we are talking about when we talk about "lawyer professionalism?"[8] Our confusion about the meaning of professionalism leads us to portray the concept in terms that are both too abstract and too limited.

I. False Faces of Professionalism

Four false faces of professionalism masquerade as the real thing by treating a modest concern as the heart of the subject:

- "Professionalism" as "civility;"
- "Professionalism" as the absence of competition in legal services;
- "Professionalism" as limited to public or pro bono service; and
- "Professionalism" as a plea for self-regulatory authority of a kind that diminishes the accountability of lawyers to courts, lawmakers and the public.

A. *Professionalism as Civility*

Civility, of course, is a good thing: every lawyer should deal with other participants in the justice system with decency and courtesy, recognizing the dignity of each person. Civility reinforces the legitimacy and effectiveness of legal institutions by respecting the people and processes on which

enactment of federal and state gun control; supported adoption of universal health care; and called for rejection of a constitutional amendment prohibiting desecration of the American flag. Federalist Society, ABA Watch, Feb.1999.

6. See Darryl van Duch, Bar Associations Face Declining Member Rolls, Nat'l L.J., Jan.15, 1996, at A1.

7. Adapted with permission from a paper presented at the Symposium on Teaching and Learning Professionalism sponsored by the ABA Section of Legal Education and Admission to the Bar and the ABA Center

for Professional Responsibility, Oak Brook, Illinois, Oct. 2–4, 1996.

8. For book length treatments, see Mary Anne Glendon, A Nation Under Lawyers: How the Crisis in the Legal Profession is Transforming American Society (1994); Anthony T. Kronman, The Lost Lawyer: Failing Ideals of the Legal Profession (1993); and Sol Linowitz (with Mayer), The Betrayed Profession: Lawyering at the End of the Twentieth Century (1994). For citations to recent law review discussion of professionalism, see Rob Atkinson, A Dissenter's Commentary on the Professionalism Crusade, 74 Tex.L.Rev. 259 (1995).

our ordered liberty depends. Civility, however, is not the core of the enterprise. . . .

All too often, talk of civility displaces talk of fundamental issues and problems on which the legal profession cannot agree: Should the excessive zeal of current "hired gun" representation be tempered by recognition of limited duties to third persons? Should the absolutist notions of confidentiality found in many professional codes be modified to permit disclosure where other weighty interests are threatened? Should the unwillingness of professional discipline to deal with the two problems of most importance to clients—competent performance by lawyers and reasonable fees—lead to professional recognition of other mechanisms of making lawyers accountable to their clients?

The disarray and malfunctioning of the justice system need constructive criticism that is passionate, truthful, courageous and committed, which may sometimes require blunt or harsh language. Civility is a virtue, but courage, integrity and justice are more important virtues. When the profession talks as if civility is the heart of professionalism, it abandons a commitment to the real heart of professionalism: the difficult task of defining lawyer roles and attitudes that will result in a more just social order.

B.   Professionalism as the Absence of "Commercialism"

A second bastard form of modern professionalism is a version that restricts its content to complaints about "commercialism." Real-life stories of plaintiffs' lawyers rushing to accident scenes or touting their wares in tasteless advertisements become a metaphor for many lawyers' profound distaste for the commercial realities of the modern world. They become arguments for anti-competitive measures that are likely to harm consumers: attempts to exclude lawyers from outside the jurisdiction from competing for local business; restrictions on the flow of information about the availability and cost of legal services; and limitations on the provision of useful service by both lawyers and nonlawyers (the "ancillary business" controversy provides an example). Avoidance of "commercialism" becomes synonymous with "professionalism."

The rhetoric of commercialism assumes that those in business are morally inferior to lawyers and that their calling has no place for ethics or public responsibility. Simultaneously, it ignores the realities that lawyers earn their bread largely from the commercialism of their business clients and that the market for legal services today is fiercely competitive. A rhetoric of professional independence and autonomy from client has possibilities, but not a rhetoric built on disdain of profit-making activity in a competitive economy.

This image of professionalism assumes that the American virtues of risk-taking, private initiative and competitive markets are vices in the practice of law—a view that is inconsistent with both history and reality. The practice of law in this country has always been entrepreneurial in character. American lawyers have innovated novel structures and forms of legal practice; they have combined law practice with other endeavors; and they have been adaptive, expansionist and risk-taking in creating markets for legal services that are broader and deeper than elsewhere in the world. The corporate law firm, the contingent fee, the group services plan are illustrative of this energy and initiative.

The ideals of professionalism must accept the benefits—and the reality—of competition in legal services and provide practical solutions for situations in which competitive forces cannot provide adequate legal services.

C. Professionalism as Limited to Public Service

A third false face of professionalism presents it solely as public service. Public service and pro bono work are ways in which professional ideals can be put into practice, but they are not synonymous with a robust conception of professionalism. Most lawyers most of the time will be working for private clients, usually for the haves of this world, on business transactions or disputes involving money.[9] As the old saw puts it, "the practice of law deals mostly with the getting and keeping of money." Many will be doing so in law firms or organizations that are large and growing in size. While a pro bono commitment must be part of the message, meaning must be given to the everyday activities of private lawyers working for private clients.

Representation of private clients serves public goals when lawyer professionalism assists clients in pursuing lawful objectives, encourages lawyers to assist clients in refining their objectives in the light of moral concerns, and subordinates the interests of clients to the public interest in those less common situations in which a client's wrongful conduct threatens serious injury to third persons or to the integrity of judicial process.

The law office counseling and transaction work that constitutes most of what lawyers do often lacks the adversary structure, neutral umpire and represented parties that ensure the fairness of adversary proceedings. Even in contested proceedings, the claim that the invisible hand of the adversary system will maximize social good is undermined whenever the contest is an uneven one because one party is unrepresented or poorly represented. An adequate ethic of professionalism must reflect these realities. The good lawyer must be public-spirited and committed to access to justice. A pro bono contribution is an important component. But the representation of private clients must also be viewed as serving public purposes.

---

9. The work of most lawyers today lacks the elements of the narrative that has inspired American lawyers: "the fearless advocate who champions a client threatened with loss of life and liberty by government oppression." Today, the lawyer's partisan endeavors are usually applied in a quite different context: "The private client is more likely to be a business organization than a private individual; the transaction or proceeding is probably civil or regulatory rather than criminal; the outcome is more likely to be a matter of property or money than life of liberty; and the justice of the cause is probably indeterminate." Geoffrey C. Hazard, Jr., The Future of Legal Ethics, 100 Yale L.J. 1239, 1244–1245.

D. Professionalism as Self–Regulatory Freedom from Accountability

A fourth false face of professionalism is a preoccupation with "self-regulation" that has the effect of limiting the accountability of lawyers to clients and the public. Some versions of "professionalism" assume that only lawyers are in a position to assess the quality or cost of legal services and therefore only lawyers can make these judgments. Everyone recognizes that clients who regularly use particular kinds of legal services can and do evaluate the quality and cost of what they get. Professional discipline is in transition from a bar-controlled activity to a public process and the other forums that pass on a lawyer's conduct are public institutions: judges in applying sanctions in a proceeding; juries in malpractice or third-party liability cases; administrative agencies in enforcing agency rules of conduct.

Each lawyer should aspire to professional excellence, but aspiration alone is not enough. Regulatory structures must be adequate to enforce minimum standards of professional conduct.[10] The institution still most under the control of lawyers, professional discipline, depends on clients to report grievances, fails to deal with complaints of negligent performance or overcharging, and remains secretive and lawyer-protective in many jurisdictions. A professional recognition that accountability is a vital aspect of professionalism should lead to improvement of professional discipline and greater tolerance for other methods of controlling lawyer behavior: malpractice suits, judicial sanctions, and actions by administrative agencies.

The organized bar plays a vital role in defining standards of minimum conduct and in nurturing aspirational ideals of vocation, calling and service. But the bar cannot expect to have a monopoly of the prescription and enforcement of minimum standards of conduct. It can expect to influence its members by the inculcation of personal ideals of aspiration and excellence. If professionalism, under the rubric of self-regulation, is viewed as a ploy for opposing all forms of public accountability, it will be rejected by both lawyers and the public as mere special-interest pleading, undeserving of moral respect.

[The remainder of the article attempted an affirmative statement of the ideals of professionalism, concluding:] The central moral tradition of lawyering has been that a lawyer's primary obligation is to the procedures and institutions of the law. In recent decades, this earlier consensus has been largely, but not totally, replaced by ideology and behavior characterized by total commitment to client and a rejection of lawyers' public responsibilities. The need today is to regenerate the ideal of the law as a public profession with important public responsibilities and to give expression to those responsibilities through habitual behavior supported by principles and narratives that give meaning and life to them.

---

10. See Deborah L. Rhode, Institutionalizing Ethics, 44 Case Western Reserve L.Rev. 665 (1994).

Civility Codes

The legal profession has been transformed in recent decades. The factors of change in the conditions and structure of practice have included: growth in number of lawyers and size of law firms, intense competition for legal business, increased specialization and a perceived willingness of many lawyers to take the default position that anything that is not prohibited by ethics rules or other law is required by the lawyer's general obligation of zeal for client. The crisis of competitiveness and commercialism has generated seemingly endless discussion of "professionalism" and its companion, "civility." Many courts and bar associations have adopted civility creeds, codes or guidelines that exhort lawyers to behave with civility. They are intended to be enforced by individual conscience and peer criticism rather than by sanctions in proceedings. The student should examine one of the current creeds, such as the Guidelines for Litigation Conduct adopted by the ABA House of Delegates in August 1998.[11]

Monroe Freedman, a critic of this approach, attacks the underlying premise and worries that judges will use the codes to threaten or censure conduct that is permitted by ethics rules, but that some judges may consider to be "unprofessional."[12] The codes, Freedman fears, may disguise "subordination of zealous representation to vague and sometimes unethical notions of civility." Freedman worries that applications of the civility codes often prefer courtesy to fellow lawyers over loyalty to client. In effect, the codes ask a lawyer to voluntarily sacrifice client rights without the client's consent to avoid embarrassing an opposing lawyer who has made a mistake, such as failing to file a motion or brief within the required time period or returning a memorandum containing confidential information that was inadvertently sent by the opposing lawyer.[13] Freedman argues that civility creeds are not harmless when "given the force of law by judges who value courtesy to 'brother lawyers' above 'entire devotion to the interests of the client [and] warm zeal in the maintenance and defense of his rights.'"[14]

Future of Self-Regulation

When lawyers refer to "self-regulation," they usually have in mind the fact that, by and large, only lawyers regulate lawyers. Leaders of the bar

---

11. An early civility code has been influential in the drafting of others. See Standards for Professional Conduct Within the Seventh Federal Judicial Circuit (1992), reprinted in Morgan & Rotunda Standards Supplement along with several other codes.

12. Monroe H. Freedman, The Ethical Danger of 'Civility' and 'Professionalism,' 6 NYSBA Crim.Just.J. 17 (Spr.1998).

13. Freedman cites two examples: Dondi Properties v. Commerce Savings & Loan Ass'n, 121 F.R.D. 284 (N.D.Tex.1988) (in case in which defense lawyer was sanc-

tioned for using delaying tactics in violation of court rules, court also threatened to censure the incivility of plaintiff's lawyer who filed a motion to enforce the rule by striking the reply); and Sprung v. Negwer Materials, Inc., 727 S.W.2d 883 (Mo.1987), and 775 S.W.2d 97 (Mo.1989) (several opinions criticized plaintiff's lawyer by name for enforcing a default judgment against the client of a defense lawyer whose office had failed to file an answer, a default that a divided court enforced).

14. Id. at 18.

identify self-regulation as an essential component of "professionalism." The traditional view is that the responsible lawyer internalizes appropriate standards of conduct and supports institutional arrangements by which the profession implements and enforces these standards. The special expertise of the profession with respect to legal services, it is argued, permits it to perform this function better than an external regulatory body. Freedom of lawyers from oppressive state regulation permits the profession to maintain a degree of independence that supports challenges of official authority, a predicate of ordered liberty.[15]

Others challenge the profession's traditional view. The extreme claim is that professional rhetoric is a mask for self-interested activity that enhances lawyer status and earnings.[16] A more modest version of the same criticism notes the propensity of groups to view the world from a special perspective influenced by experience and sometimes by self-interest.[17] Developments since the 1960s, especially the rise of the consumer movement and the Watergate cover-up, have generated skepticism about authority, including that exercised by the organized bar. The response is a modern trend for greater openness, broadened participation and enlarged accountability. As applied to the legal profession, these developments involve a gradual shift from regulation by bar associations to judicial regulation, the use of notice-and-comment procedures in rulemaking, decreased secrecy in professional discipline and inclusion of nonlawyers on the official bodies responsible for admission and discipline. Yet the process remains a distinctive one in that legislative authority is either excluded entirely or rarely exercised, with the regulation of the profession largely committed to state high courts. Should state and federal legislatures play a larger role in regulation of the legal profession than they have in the past?

E. LEGAL EDUCATION

1. CRITICISM OF LEGAL EDUCATION

The legal profession in the United States is large, heterogeneous and fragmented. Law practice, which is increasingly specialized in character, is

15. See, e.g., the report of the ABA Commission on Professionalism, " ... In the Spirit of Public Service:" A Blueprint for the Rekindling of Lawyer Professionalism, 112 F.R.D. 243, 261–62 (1986), which includes in one of its definitions of "professionalism" the following: "That the occupation is self-regulating—that is, organized in such a way as to assure the public and the court that its members are competent, do not violate their client's trust, and transcend their own self-interest."

16. See, e.g., Richard Abel, American Lawyers 226–33 (1989), arguing that the evidence supports the "cynical view" that

lawyers have sought to control the supply and demand for legal services "in order to enhance both their earning power and their collective status." In Abel's view, the legal profession has "[sought] regulatory powers largely to immunize [itself] from external scrutiny." Id. at 232.

17. See, e.g., Thomas D. Morgan, The Evolving Concept of Professional Responsibility, 90 Harv. L. Rev. 702 (1977) (bar's ethical codes favor professional over public interests); and Deborah L. Rhode, Why the ABA Bothers: A Functional Perspective on Professional Codes, 59 Tex. L. Rev. 689 (1981) (same).

influenced by the nature of client needs and by the context of practice. Thus lawyers do very different things that require very different knowledge, skills and experience. Aside from the bar examination, the major shared experience of American lawyers is law school. To the extent that all lawyers, whatever work they do, share a common culture and ideology, legal education is a critical aspect of the common socialization of the bar.

Criticism of legal education has been constant and repetitious for many years.[18] The four principal categories of criticism, considered briefly below, are: (1) Law school does not adequately prepare its graduates for the practice of law; (2) the educational experience has a destructive effect upon the character or values of students; (3) law school fails to produce public-spirited and socially responsible lawyers; and (4) legal education is not accessible to all sectors of American society.

The lament that law school does not provide adequate preparation for the realities of practice is an old one that takes a number of forms. Critics charge that law school is too theoretical, too removed from the day-to-day context in which lawyers do their work. Academics respond that the distinction between theory and practice is meaningless (any good practice rests on a decent theory) and that learning how to learn throughout a long career is more important than memorizing information that will soon become outdated. Another form of the inadequate-preparation charge is that legal education concentrates too exclusively on cognitive analysis of appellate cases and manipulation of legal doctrine, providing insufficient exposure to other capacities required in lawyering, such as complex problem-solving skills (e.g., fact investigation, interviewing, negotiation, drafting, litigating).[19] Clinical legal education responds in part to this concern.[20] A related criticism is that law school omits development of the interpersonal skills that are so vital in lawyer-client relations, in working with other professionals and in persuading those with whom one is negotiating or dealing.[21]

A more fundamental version of the inadequate preparation criticism is that law teachers increasingly, especially at elite schools, have neither interest in nor capacity to prepare law students for practice. The result is a

---

18. Robert B. Stevens, Law School: Legal Education in America from the 1850s to the 1980s 278 (1983):

> Students will continue to reiterate the complaints about law schools that have been mouthed with remarkable regularity since ... the 1930s.... In practice, that remarkable and resilient vehicle, the case method, will continue to dominate legal education.

19. Two major studies have compared what practicing lawyers state are the skills needed in practice with those learned by these lawyers in law school. Leonard L. Baird, A Survey of the Relevance of Legal Training to Law School Graduates, 29 J.Legal Educ. 264 (1978); and Frances K. Zemans and Victor G. Rosenblum, The Making of a Public Profession, 55 et seq. (1981).

20. For discussion of the potential and problems of clinical legal education, see the articles in symposium, Clinical Legal Education, 33 J.Legal Educ. 604 et seq. (1983) (articles by Robert J. Condlin, Norman Redlich, Gary Bellow, Michael Meltsner and David Luban).

21. See, e.g., Thomas L. Shaffer and Robert S. Redmount, Lawyers, Law Students and People (1977).

growing dysjunction between legal education and the legal profession.[22] Scholarship is now "the name of the game" in the legal academy and especially scholarship in its most theoretical, abstract, creative and non-doctrinal aspects.[23] A decreasing proportion of law teachers have substantial experience in practice (the most common experience is a year or so as a law clerk to a judge). Much of the scholarship produced by today's scholars is not addressed to judges, lawyers or public officials but only to subsets of scholarly disciplines. An attitude of disinterest, even disdain, for doctrinal writing is evident; and many legal scholars not only know very little about law practice but have very little interest in it. They are not in a good position to serve as mentors to those entering the profession.[24]

The second charge, that law school has a destructive effect upon the character or values of students, also takes a variety of forms. One frequently expressed concern is that the teaching method—questions and answers based on appellate judicial decisions—is either too narrow, too stultifying or too humiliating.[25] Legal education reaches its height of interest and involvement in the first year, followed by a long downhill slide.[26] The decline of student interest, referred to by Professor Anthony Amsterdam as the MOPIE Syndrome (Maximum Obtainable Passivity in Education), means that the whole of the curriculum is less than the sum of its parts, many of which are excellent.[27] Students, Amsterdam argues, in coping with an instructor's surprise questions concerning judicial opinions, become solution-critics rather than problem-solvers. A variant of the same concern relies on humanistic, psychological or feminist arguments in concluding that law school narrows or warps law students.[28]

22. An article by Judge Harry Edwards criticizing "the growing disjunction between legal education and the legal profession" has led to an avalanche of commentary. See, e.g., Symposium, Legal Education, 91 Mich.L.Rev. 1921 (1993).

23. See Roger C. Cramton, Demystifying Legal Scholarship, 75 Geo.L.J. 1, 14 (1986) ("academic prestige seems to be the only game in town"); Kenneth Lasson, Scholarship Amok: Excesses in the Pursuit of Truth and Tenure, 103 Harv.L.Rev. 926 (1990); and David Bryden, Scholarship About Scholarship, 63 U.Colo.L.Rev. 641, 643 ("academic prestige derives almost entirely from one's reputation as a scholar").

24. See Patrick J. Schiltz, Legal Ethics in Decline: The Elite Law Firm, the Elite Law School, and the Moral Formation of the Novice Attorney, 82 Minn.L.Rev. 705 (1998) (mentoring disappears in both law firms and law schools as the former focus on money and the latter on prestige scholarship).

25. Critics charge that the controlled dialogue erodes students' self-respect, encourages cynicism and conveys an erroneous impression of the lawyer's role. See Paul N. Savoy, Toward a New Politics of Legal Education, 79 Yale L.J. 444 (1970).

26. In this respect it differs sharply from medical education, in which student interest and involvement increases as medical students become involved in patient care. See Roger C. Cramton, Professional Education in Medicine and Law: Structural Differences, Common Failings, Possible Opportunities, 34 Cleve.St.L.Rev. 349 (1985).

27. Anthony G. Amsterdam, Talk to SALT Annual Meeting (1989).

28. See Francis A. Allen, Law, Intellect, and Education (1979) (essays stressing the importance of a broad humanistic approach in legal education); Roger C. Cramton, The Ordinary Religion of the Law School Classroom, 29 J.Legal Educ. 247 (1978) (discussing the assumed value framework of contemporary legal education); J. B. Taylor, Law School Stress and the "Deformation Professionelle," 27 J.Legal Educ. 251

The effect of law school in shaping student values has been extensively studied, but the studies reach differing conclusions. Law students enter law school with strong commitments to social justice, it is said, but leave talking of jobs and choosing to serve as apologists of things as they are.[29] The bulk of the careful empirical studies, however, conclude that law school has only limited effect on student attitudes and values, but that market forces and contact with the practicing profession play a substantial role.[30]

Do law schools fail to produce public-spirited and responsible lawyers? This third deficiency is value-laden since it requires assumptions as to what constitutes a "good lawyer." Law graduates, if educated soundly and well, Richard Wasserstrom has said,

> would have and display a deep and abiding attachment to and concern for the moral worthiness and rightness of all that they do, of whatever they choose to do as lawyers, and a corresponding sense of responsibility for the justness and goodness of the legal system that their skills and training equip them to understand and to utilize.[31]

These graduates would care for their clients, treating them fairly and decently; they would also be concerned about persons affected by the client and with the justness and goodness of the actions and choices made on behalf of the client; and, finally, they would be interested and concerned for the justness and goodness of existing systems of law. Forming habits and

(1975) (psychological approach); Alan Stone, Legal Education on the Couch, 85 Harv.L.Rev. 392 (1971) (same); Andrew S. Watson, Some Psychological Aspects of Teaching Professional Responsibility, 16 J.Legal Educ. 1 (1963) (same); and Carrie Menkel–Meadow, Feminist Legal Theory, Critical Legal Studies, and Legal Education, or "The Fem–Crits Go to Law School," 38 J.Legal Educ. 61 (1988).

29. See Robert V. Stover, Making and Breaking It: The Fate of Public Interest Commitment During Law School (Howard S. Erlanger, ed., 1989) (law students' interest in public interest law declines significantly during law school; they become less interested in helping others and more interested in professional advancement); James C. Foster, The "Cooling Out" of Law Students, 3 Law & Policy Q. 243 (1981). But compare Murray L. Schwartz, The Reach and Limits of Legal Education, 32 J. Legal Educ. 543, 547 (1982), concluding on the basis of a number of studies that:

> Reasons for attending law school have not varied significantly over time. By far the most important are prestige, financial reward, and the achievement of a

stable, secure future—all indices of upward social mobility.... Legal education has little effect on personal attitudes of lawyers. Ethnic and religious backgrounds and type of practice far outweigh legal education in affecting their political and social values.

30. See E. Gordon Gee and Donald W. Jackson, Current Studies of Legal Education: Findings and Recommendations, 32 J.Legal Educ. 471, 494–501 (1982) (reviewing the studies and concluding: "law-school socialization operates within the constraints of the market for law graduates, where preferences meet hard realities"); Lawrence K. Hellman, The Effects of Law Office Work on the Formation of Law Students' Professional Values: Observation, Explanation, Optimization, 4 Geo.J.Legal Ethics 537 (1991) (law office intern experiences, which may involve contact with unprofessional conduct, have a powerful effect on students).

31. Richard Wasserstrom, Legal Education and the Good Lawyer, 34 J.Legal Educ. 155 (1984).

dispositions of this character would be a fundamental aim of legal education.

Do any American law schools fulfill a grand vision of this type? The excerpts from Duncan Kennedy and Stewart Macaulay that follow shed some light on this question and provide other perspectives on the goals and performance of law schools.

The fourth major criticism is that legal education is not accessible to all sectors of American society. Changes since 1960—growth in the demand for legal education, opening of opportunities for women and minorities and the increased cost of a legal education—have resulted in a major shift in the demographics of law students and lawyers. Paradoxically, these changes probably have reduced opportunities of non-minority individuals of lower socio-economic status to attend law school. As the number of applicants has grown, most law schools have become increasingly selective in admissions. Reliance on standard academic credentials, such as college grades, quality of college and LSAT score, favors applicants of higher socio-economic status because of the substantial correlation between those factors and socio-economic status. Similarly, the women who now take up 42 percent of the seats in American law schools generally are drawn from higher socio-economic backgrounds than the males they replaced. Given these constraints, the diversity of the law school population compares well with that of other fields of graduate and professional study. In few if any fields does the student population include 46 percent women, 7 percent blacks, and 20 percent total minorities, as was the case in law as of 1998.[32]

The cost of legal education, however, is a substantial barrier. Including the opportunity costs of foregoing employment during three academic years, the total cost ranges from $100,000 to $200,000 per student, depending on the school and other factors.[33] This is a major investment in human capital that graduates expect to recoup from earnings after law school. This fact, coupled with the need to borrow extensively to pay the costs, clearly has a powerful effect on choice of initial employment. Because these costs must be repaid from income generated in practice, lawyers become too expensive for some tasks and more expensive for all.[34]

32. ABA Section on Legal Education and Admissions to the Bar Fall 1998 Statistics. Women and majorities are a somewhat smaller percentage of J.D. graduates, indicating a slightly higher rate of attrition: Women (44.8%) and all Minorities (19.7%). African–Americans were 7.3% of all J.D. students in Fall 1998; Asian Americans 6.3%, Hispanics 5.6%, and Native Americans 0.8%. For current data see <www.abanet.org>.

33. For discussion of the costs of legal education, see John R. Kramer, Proceedings of the National Conference on Legal Education for a Changing Profession 93–114

(March 25–27, 1988) (law school tuition has increased much faster than the consumer price index; most of the increased revenues have gone to increased faculty salaries and expanded administrative staffs rather than to new faculty or the educational program).

34. Judge Richard A. Posner, in an excerpt that closes this section, argues that state requirements that require graduation from an ABA-approved law school as a prerequisite to admission to the bar provide law schools with a captive audience, insulating them from a true market test of the value of the services they provide. He urges de-

This array of criticisms suggests that legal education is in serious trouble. Yet the dominant fact is that legal education, despite the constant drumbeat of criticism, is somewhat of an American success story in terms of its growth, resources and prestige. It must be doing something reasonably well. For several generations law schools have prepared individuals who then exercised power and influence in American private and public life. The demand for legal education has grown steadily with the result that the number of college graduates who desire to attend law school has grown from about 12,000 per year in the 1950s to more than seven times that figure today. This number includes a major portion of college graduates who are the most highly qualified in academic credentials (academic achievement, test scores, membership in Phi Beta Kappa, Rhodes scholars and the like). Law schools have steadily garnered new resources and often occupy the newest or grandest physical facilities on university campuses. The law curriculum may be disorganized, the education inadequate in a number of ways, but somehow legal education has not only survived but prospered. Its characteristic structure, curriculum and teaching method have been highly resistant to change. For better or worse, it has muddled through.

Consider the excerpts that follow in light of the foregoing criticisms of legal education and your own experience.

2. PERSPECTIVES ON LEGAL EDUCATION

Duncan Kennedy, Legal Education and the Reproduction of Hierarchy

i, ii, 3, 5–7, 16–17, 20–22, 58, 65, 68, 70, 101–03 (1983).[35]

This is an essay about the role of legal education in American social life. It is a description of the ways in which legal education contributes to the reproduction of illegitimate hierarchy in the bar and in society. And it suggests ways in which left students and teachers who are determined not to let law school demobilize them can make the experience part of a left activist practice of social transformation.

The general thesis is that law schools are intensely *political* places, in spite of the fact that they seem intellectually unpretentious, barren of theoretical ambition or practical vision of what social life might be. The trade school mentality, the endless attention to trees at the expense of forests, the alternating grimness and chumminess of focus on the limited task at hand, all these are only a part of what is going on. The other part is ideological training for willing service in the hierarchies of the corporate welfare state.

regulation. If individuals could sit for the bar examination without law school training, law schools would have to convince them and their legal employers that the education was worth the time and money spent on it.

35. Copyright © Duncan Kennedy. Reprinted with permission.

To say that law school is ideological is to say that what teachers teach along with basic skills is wrong, is nonsense about what law is and how it works. It is to say that the message about the nature of legal competence, and its distribution among students, is wrong, is nonsense. It is to say that the ideas about the possibilities of life as a lawyer that students pick up from legal education are wrong, are nonsense. But all this is nonsense with a tilt, it is biased and motivated rather than random error. What it says is that it is natural, efficient and fair for law firms, the bar as a whole, and the society the bar services to be organized in their actual patterns of hierarchy and domination.

. . .

The First Year Experience

. . .

The initial classroom experience sustains rather than dissipates ambivalence. The teachers are overwhelmingly white, male, and deadeningly straight and middle class in manner. The classroom is hierarchical with a vengeance, the teacher receiving a degree of deference and arousing fears that remind one of high schools rather than college. The sense of autonomy one has in a lecture, with the rule that you must let teacher drone on without interruption balanced by the rule that teacher can't *do* anything to you, is gone. In its place is a demand for a pseudo-participation in which you struggle desperately, in front of a large audience, to read a mind determined to elude you.

. . .

The actual intellectual content of the law seems to consist of learning rules, what they are and why they have to be the way they are, while rooting for the occasional judge who seems willing to make them marginally more humane. The basic experience is of double surrender: to a passivizing classroom experience and to a passive attitude toward the content of the legal system.

The first step toward this sense of the irrelevance of liberal or left thinking is the opposition in the first year curriculum between the technical, boring, difficult, obscure legal case, and the occasional case with outrageous facts and a piggish judicial opinion endorsing or tolerating the outrage. The first kind of case—call it a cold case—is a challenge to interest, understanding, even to wakefulness. It can be on any subject, so long as it is of no political or moral or emotional significance. Just to understand what happened and what's being said about it, you have to learn a lot of new terms, a little potted legal history, and lots of rules, none of which is carefully explained by the casebook or the teacher. It is difficult to figure out why the case is there in the first place, difficult to figure out whether one has grasped it, and difficult to anticipate what the teacher will ask and what one should respond.

The other kind of case usually involves a sympathetic plaintiff, say an Appalachian farm family, and an unsympathetic defendant, say a coal company. On first reading, it appears that the coal company has screwed the farm family, say by renting their land for strip mining, with a promise to restore it to its original condition once the coal has been extracted, and then reneging on the promise. And the case . . . include[s] a judicial opinion that does something like awarding a meaningless couple of hundred dollars to the farm family, rather than making the coal company do the restoration work.

The point of the class discussion will be that your initial reaction of outrage is naive, non-legal, irrelevant to what you're supposed to be learning, and maybe substantively wrong into the bargain. There are good reasons for the awful result, when you take a legal and logical view, as opposed to a knee-jerk passionate view, and if you can't muster those reasons, maybe you aren't cut out to be a lawyer.

. . .

The Ideological Content of Legal Education

. . . Law schools teach . . . rather rudimentary, essentially instrumental skills in a way that almost completely mystifies them for almost all law students. The mystification has three parts. First, the schools teach skills through class discussions of cases in which it is asserted that law emerges from a rigorous analytical procedure called "legal reasoning," which is unintelligible to the layman, but somehow both explains and validates the great majority of the rules in force in our system. At the same time, the class context and the materials present every legal issue as distinct from every other, as a tub on its own bottom, so to speak, with no hope or even any reason to hope that from law study one might derive an integrating vision of what law is, how it works, or how it might be changed (other than in an incremental, case by case, reformist way).

Second, the teaching of skills in the mystified context of legal reasoning about utterly unconnected legal problems means that skills are taught badly, unself-consciously, to be absorbed by osmosis as one picks up the knack of "thinking like a lawyer." Bad or only randomly good teaching generates and then accentuates real differences and imagined differences in student capabilities. But it does so in such a way that students don't know when they are learning and when they aren't, and have no way of improving or even understanding their own learning processes. They experience skills training as the gradual emergence of differences among themselves, as a process of ranking that reflects something that is just "there" inside them.

Third, the schools teach skills in isolation from actual lawyering experience. "Legal reasoning" is sharply distinguished from law practice, and one learns nothing about practice. This procedure disables students from any future role but that of apprentice in a law firm organized in the same manner as a law school, with older lawyers controlling the content and pace of depoliticized craft training in a setting of intense competition and no feedback.

. . .

This whole body of implicit messages is nonsense. Legal reasoning is not distinct, *as a method for reaching correct results*, from ethical and political discourse in general (i.e., from policy analysis). It is true that there is a distinctive lawyers' body of knowledge of the rules in force. It is true that there are distinctive lawyers' argumentative techniques for spotting gaps, conflicts and ambiguities in the rules, for arguing broad and narrow holdings of cases, and for generating pro and con policy arguments. But these are *only* argumentative techniques. There is never a "correct legal solution" that is other than the correct ethical and political solution to that legal problem.

Put another way, everything taught, except the formal rules themselves and the argumentative techniques for manipulating them, is policy and nothing more. It follows that the classroom distinction between the unproblematic legal case and the policy oriented case is a mere artifact: each could as well be taught in the opposite way. And the curricular distinction between the "nature" of contract law as highly legal and technical by contrast, say, with environmental law, is equally a mystification.

These errors have a bias in favor of the center-liberal program of limited reform of the market economy and pro forma gestures toward racial and sexual equality. The bias arises because law school teaching makes the choice of hierarchy and domination, which is implicit in the adoption of the rules of property, contract and tort, look as though it flows from legal reasoning, rather than from politics and economics. The bias is reenforced when the center-liberal reformist program of regulation is presented as equally authoritative, but somehow more policy oriented, and therefore less fundamental.

The message is that the system is basically OK, since we have patched up the few areas open to abuse, and that it has a limited but important place for value-oriented debate about further change and improvement. If there is to be more fundamental questioning, it is relegated to the periphery of history or philosophy. The real world is kept at bay by treating clinical legal education, which might bring in a lot of information threatening to the cozy liberal consensus, as free legal drudge work for the local bar or as mere skills training.

. . .

The Modeling of Hierarchical Relationships

Yet another way in which legal education contributes causally to the hierarchies of the bar is through ... law teachers that model for students how they are supposed to think, feel and act in their future professional roles. Some of this is a matter of teaching by example, some of it a matter of more active learning from interactions that are a kind of clinical education for lawyer-like behavior.

. . .

Often, it boils down to law review. At first, everyone claims they aren't interested, wouldn't want to put in the time, don't work hard enough to make it, can't stand the elitism of the whole thing. But most students give about equal time to fantasies of flunking out and fantasies of grabbing the brass ring. And even though the class has been together for a semester or a year, everything is still different after the lightning of grades. An instant converts jerks into statesmen; honored spokespeople retire to the margins, shamed. Try proposing that law review should be open to anyone who will do the work. Within a week or two, the new members have a dozen arguments for competitive selection. Likewise at the hour of partnership.

. . .

The culmination of law school as training for professional hierarchy is the placement process, with the form of the culmination depending on where your school fits in the pecking order.

. . .

By dangling the bait, making clear the rules of the game, and then subjecting almost everyone to intense anxiety about their acceptability, firms structure entry into the profession so as to maximize acceptance of hierarchy. If you feel you've succeeded, you're forever grateful, and you have a vested interest. If you feel you've failed, you blame yourself, when you aren't busy feeling envy. When you get to be the hiring partner, you'll have a visceral understanding of what's at stake, but it will be hard even to imagine why someone might want to change it.

. . .

Strategy

In the absence of a mass movement of the left, the way to organize a left intelligentsia is in the workplace, around ideas and around the concrete issues that arise within the bourgeois corporate institutions where the potential members of such an intelligentsia live their lives.

. . .

... Organizing around ideas means developing a practice of left study, left literature and left debate about philosophy, social theory, and public policy that would give professional, technical and managerial workers the sense of participating in a left community.

Along with workplace organization around ideas there goes organization around the specific issues of hierarchy that are important in the experience of people in these institutions. This has to do with the authoritarian character of day-to-day work organization—with the use of supervisory power.... Selection, promotion and pay policies, along with a whole universe of smaller interventions, many of which are merely "social," maintain class/sex/race and also generational and meritocratic stratification within the cells of the hierarchy, while at the same time disciplining everyone to participate in the complex of hierarchical attitudes and behaviors.

. . .

What this means is that lawyers can have and should have workplace struggles, no matter where they are situated in the hierarchy of the bar, and whether or not they are actively engaged in political law practice. For law students, it means that it is important to have a law school struggle, even if they are spending most of their time on extra-curricular activities that support oppressed people.

Stewart Macaulay, "Law Schools and the World Outside Their Doors II:Some Notes on Two Recent Studies of the Chicago Bar"

32 Journal of Legal Education 506, 511–12, 521–25, 527 (1982).[36]

[The initial portion of Macaulay's article discusses two empirical studies of Chicago lawyers: (1) John P. Heinz and Edward O. Laumann, Chicago Lawyers: The Social Structure of the Bar (1982), discussed further at p. 922; and (2) Frances K. Zemans and Victor G. Rosenblum, The Making of a Public Profession (1981). Zemans and Rosenblum's book reports an appraisal of legal education by a sample drawn from the Chicago bar. Zemans and Rosenblum asked these lawyers to rank 21 skills and areas of knowledge related to the practice of law. They also asked where their respondents had gained these skills, what law schools tell their students about the importance of these skills and what they perceived as the goals of their law school. Zemans and Rosenblum found that lawyers see legal education as valuing and teaching "the ideal symbolic work of the legal profession." However, lawyers also thought that what was neglected in the law schools' self-defined mission were "the very competencies that practitioners find most important to the actual practice of law."]

. . . Those skills most closely identified with law school education [were considered surprisingly unimportant] when the responses of all of the lawyers are considered together. For example, "ability to understand and interpret opinions, regulations, and statutes" ranked fifth, trailing "fact gathering," "capacity to marshal facts and order them so that concepts can be applied," "instilling others' confidence in you," and "effective oral expression." 86.6 percent did rate such understanding and interpretive skill as important, but only 50 percent rated it extremely important. 77 percent said they learned this skill "essentially in law school." "Knowledge of theory underlying law" may seem critically important to law professors, but Zemans and Rosenblum's Chicago lawyers ranked it only thirteenth out of the twenty-one skills and areas of knowledge. 61.1 percent rated it as important but only 23 percent saw it as extremely important. 84 percent said they gained this knowledge in law school rather than in practice. 76.9

percent of the graduates of national law schools saw "providing the theoretical basis of law" as being a major goal of their school, while only 34.5 percent of the graduates of local law schools characterized such theoretical knowledge as a major goal of their education.

As might be expected, evaluations of skills and knowledge are not randomly distributed among lawyers. Zemans and Rosenblum conclude that the "lower prestige specialties seem to involve more interpersonal skills, while the higher prestige specialties are more likely to rate more purely 'analytic' skills as important to their practice." . . .

The lawyers acknowledged that many skills could not be taught easily in law school, but they criticized law schools for failing even to make their students aware of the importance of these parts of practice. . . .

[The concluding portion of Macaulay's article places empirical studies of legal education in the light of Duncan Kennedy's critique.]

What, then, are we to conclude? Few law professors, in all likelihood, would take their Duncan Kennedy neat; most would dilute his position greatly before they accepted it or, more likely, they would ignore it.[51] Most law professors probably would accept the picture painted by the two studies of the Chicago bar—perhaps quarreling about a detail here and there—and acknowledge that there is a gap between what lawyers do and what law

---

51. Those offended by Kennedy's position might consider Roger Cramton's The Ordinary Religion of the Law School Classroom, 29 J. Legal Educ. 247 (1978) which avoids Kennedy's "radical" or "left" vocabulary. Cramton finds the unarticulated fundamental assumptions of the American law school classroom to be: "a skeptical attitude toward generalizations; an instrumental approach to law and lawyering; a 'tough minded and analytical attitude toward legal tasks and professional roles; and a faith that man, by the application of his reason and the use of democratic processes, can make the world a better place." Id. at 248. He makes observations such as "The law teacher must stress cognitive rationality along with 'hard' facts and 'cold' logic and 'concrete' realities. Emotion, imagination, sentiments of affection and trust, a sense of wonder or awe at the inexplicable—these soft and mushy domains of the 'tender minded' are off limits for law students and lawyers." Id. at 250. "Instead of transforming society, the functional approach tends to become dominated by society, to become an apologist and technician for established institutions and things as they are, to view change as a form of tinkering rather than a reexamination of basic premises. Surface goals such as 'efficiency,' 'progress,' and

'the democratic way' are taken at face value and more ultimate questions of value submerged." Id. at 254. "Modern dogmas entangle education—amoral relativism tending toward nihilism, a pragmatism tending toward an amoral instrumentalism, a realism tending toward cynicism, an individualism tending toward atomism, and a faith in reason and democratic processes tending toward mere credulity and idolatry. We will neither understand nor transform these modern dogmas unless we abandon our unconcern for value premises. The beliefs and attitudes that anchor our lives must be examined and revealed." Id. at 262. Recognizing that Cramton and Kennedy are starting from such very different positions, I find the similarity in their views remarkable. But see William Stanmeyer, On Legal Education: The Selection of Faculty, 6 Law & Liberty—A Project on the Legal Framework of A Free Society 1–3 (Winter 1981) (describing legal education similarly but arguing students are indoctrinated against property and freedom). I think if one examined the "beliefs and attitudes that anchor our lives" as law teachers *in light of the two Chicago bar studies*, one would have to grant much of Kennedy's case. . . .

schools teach. Some, at least, would not be too troubled by this gap, seeing law school as properly specializing in teaching legal analysis. In essence, their reply to Zemans and Rosenblum would be that their lawyer respondents were wrong in rating the importance of analytical skill. These law teachers might see a division of labor, with law school teaching legal analysis while other skills are best learned elsewhere. Many law professors would be pleased by Francis Allen's view of legal education as one of the humanities, as a discipline concerned with the realization of the core values of the society through legal institutions.

My own view is what might be called a liberal straddle.... Duncan Kennedy's views must be faced. In many ways, legal education always risks being a kind of con game—an exercise in mystification, or a process of transforming idealistic students into hired guns. Allen's portrait flatters the subject greatly. His humanistic claim for legal education states an ideal while the reality—at least in others' classrooms—often is lip service to liberal values coupled with little concern for their realization in everyday affairs. Of course, all institutions have a kind of official picture of themselves, a version of their functions that gives them legitimacy. And given the nature of the world, there always is likely to be a gap between promise and performance. It also may be that legal education is trapped in a contradiction between the high ideals it sometimes considers and the inability of its subject matter—appellate cases—to tell us much about whether those ideals have any meaning within society. Whatever the source of the problem, we are unlikely to move much beyond empty symbolism if we are unwilling to reconsider many of our presuppositions and look beyond reported decisions.

Law school, for some students at least, does involve an important transformation of outlook. Some students still come into law school with "rhetorical visions, fantasy chains or organizational frames" concerning the profession they want to enter. They see lawyers as well paid in money and status. Moreover, their work is seen as involving defending core American values....

Most of these idealistic students are transformed into apprentice lawyers who will find it acceptable to represent those who are likely to be the best customers of their services.[54] Kennedy certainly is right that the first year of law school will be hard on students who question capitalism, liberal pluralism, or the existing distributions of wealth, privilege, and status in the society. The curriculum usually begins with a heavy dose of common law and ignores the many statutory rejections of its answers. The discussion in the classroom frequently celebrates individualism, efficiency, an incremental process, and protection of zones of freedom within which those with power can exercise it. A slightly idealistic first-year student often makes a statement in class which the professor can push into the form of "it is just to equalize wealth; X is the poorer of the parties and Y is

---

54. See James C. Foster, The "Cooling Out" of Law Students, 3 Law & Pol'y Q. 243 (1981). Some students, of course, do not get cooled out and are willing and able to find jobs involving idealistic elements.

a large corporation with a deep pocket; therefore X ought to win." When a master teacher is through, the student or one of his susceptible classmates will have asserted the virtues of rewards to the efficient who create wealth for all of us, the virtues of holding individuals responsible for their actions, and the evils of paternalism which robs the weaker of their choice and substitutes that of a purported expert. In a well-run class, all will see visions of grass growing in the streets if courts were to yield to softhearted sentiment. Other skilled teachers will drive home the message that the redistribution of wealth may be an appropriate function of legislatures in a pluralistic society but falls out of bounds for courts; however, they seldom examine seriously the likely consequences of this position. While such conclusions may flow from our political outlook, it would be hard to call them neutral or scientific with a straight face.

Even when the message of a first-year classroom is not so openly political, there is another message which is part of the process of transforming entering students into apprentice lawyers. A strong lesson is that there is always an argument the other way, and the Devil usually has a very good case. Heffernan has pointed out that law teaching tends to be Sophist rather than Socratic. Socrates asked questions in search of an understanding of justice. The Sophists, in contrast, played intellectual games and sought to make the weaker argument the stronger. Many law professors are famous for their skill in responding to whatever their students say by leaping to the other side. When a naive student thinks he can gain favor by joining the professor, the professor turns the argument on its head and leaps back to the original argument, perhaps stating it more persuasively. The successful student learns that there are no answers but just arguments. Of course, the really successful student learns that, as was true of Orwell's pigs, some arguments are more equal than others; indeed, the point may be that while there are few right arguments, there are many wrong ones. Nonetheless, the process is not a Socratic search for justice but a Sophist game. And if one is paid to play a game, it does not make much difference whether he plays for the Yankees, Brewers, Red Sox, or Orioles—or for IBM, General Motors, ITT, or the Department of Justice.

However, for many it would go too far to see lawyering as only a game. Part of the answer for them is supplied by comforting assumptions and ideas about the adversary system. Everyone involved in a controversy will have a lawyer pressing his case; the excesses of one will be canceled out by the zeal of another; thus, the unseen hand of competition in the marketplace of ideas will yield truth. If opposing lawyers play the intellectual game, nothing should be overlooked. A wise judge will be able to put aside bias and see all that is involved before making a decision. Thus, one who works for *any* client is serving an important social process, and, indeed, one has an obligation not to pull punches out of a misguided sense of social responsibility.

Kennedy certainly is right that law school tends to celebrate only part of the work and skills of attorneys and in this way reinforces the status hierarchies of the profession. However, when one looks at the two studies of the Chicago bar and other reports about the top end of the profession, one has to wonder if something else is not also involved. Law school does not track

perfectly with the needs of the largest law firms; it offers little training for much of their work.... General corporate practice also has high status, and occupies far more lawyers' time than corporate litigation. Nonetheless, law school tends to neglect training in planning transactions and drafting the needed legal documents to carry out the plan....

To a great extent, legal education has attempted to be all things to all people in order to claim status and rewards from both inside and outside the academy. However it is not easy to have it both ways....

Richard A. Posner, "Law School Should Be Two Years, Not Three"

Harvard Law Record, January 16, 1998.

In this article I will be discussing two dissatisfactions. The first is the dissatisfaction of many lawyers, particularly but not only recent law school graduates, with the conditions of the private practice of law, a dissatisfaction shared by a number of law professors. The second is the dissatisfaction of many lawyers and judges, and some law professors, with the changing character of legal scholarship and more broadly, with the growing estrangement between academia and law practice. This estrangement is nicely captured in the following statement by a professor at the Yale Law School. "Law professors are not paid to train lawyers, but to study the law and teach their students what they happen to discover."

These two phenomena have different causes and, I suspect, no cure. But both would be ameliorated by the deregulation of legal education and practice which I believe would lead to a two-year J.D. on the model of the two-year M.B.A. awarded by business schools, and would lead indirectly to a slight reduction in the pressure on young lawyers to recoup their investment in legal education by working ridiculously long hours. Although I favor complete deregulation of legal services, I shall for the sake of practicality confine my argument to the case for eliminating the requirement of a third year of legal education.

The deterioration in the working conditions of lawyers is a product in part of the increased competitiveness of the legal service industry. That increased competitiveness is part of a economy-wide movement toward greater competitiveness in service industries ranging from medical care to funerals, a movement that follows the movement in the 1980s to greater competitiveness in manufacturing. In the case of law, as earlier in the case of transportation, the trend to greater competitiveness has been helped along by a relaxation of regulatory controls, notably over the pricing and advertising of legal services and over the provision of substitute services by accountants, trust officers, paralegals and others. Since the tendency of competition is to transform producer surplus into consumer surplus, it is no surprise that one effect of the competitive revolution in legal services has been to make lawyers work harder.

Turning now to the changing character of legal scholarship, I think it is mainly though not entirely the product of causes internal to scholarly enterprise rather than having anything to do with the changes in the market for legal services, important and far-reaching as those changes have been. Beginning in the early 1960s, developments in economics, in political theory, in philosophy more generally, in history and even in literary criticism presented increasing opportunities to analyze law using the tools of other disciplines.

I had a conventional legal education and spent most of my time before I went into teaching of law in 1968 in fairly conventional law-type jobs. But when I became a law teacher I quickly became confirmed in the view that I had already formed that economic analysis of law was a lot more interesting than doctrinal analysis. Many others of my wave and subsequent waves of new law teachers had the same reaction, though the external discipline that fascinated them was not always economics. Eventually these people came to occupy positions of influence in academic law and began recasting legal scholarship in their image.

So, to summarize, law is becoming more like a business at the same time that law school is becoming less like a business school and more like a graduate department in the humanities and social science. The practice and the academy are indeed drifting apart. What if anything is to be done?

I want to consider what law schools can do about the drift, since there is very little law firms, subject as they are to intense competitive pressures, can do about it. I think that what law schools can do is to recognize that the public regulation of legal education, as a result of which lawyers cannot (with unimportant exceptions) be admitted to the bar without three years of residential study at a law school, is anachronistic, and to press for deregulation. The elite law schools at least can do this without grave jeopardy to their existence. They could attract more students to a shorter course of instruction, and many of their students would voluntarily elect a third year at such a school, though not perhaps until a later point in their career. And with the captive-audience character of the third year removed, those students who did stay (or come back) for a third year would be eager and attentive.

The main benefit of the abolition of a third-year requirement, however, would accrue to the students who decided not to stay for a third year. The shorter the course of instruction is, the lower the cost of law school to the students and hence less intense the pressure to work killing hours in order to pay off one's student loans. The student who obtained a J.D. (or call it an LL.B. and limit the J.D. to the three-year graduates, if you want) from an elite law school after completing the program that I have outlined would have saved himself as much as $100,000—$20,000 in tuition for the third year and $80,000 in foregone income in that year (less, of course, after taxes, but still considerable). In an age of specialization, is this so clearly an inferior alternative to the present system that it should be banned by the state?

I imagine that some will think me a Philistine and others will think that I have overlooked the humanizing or civilizing role of an extended legal education—the only hope, they argue, for restoring the fading ideal of the statesman lawyer. That would be a wistful hope, greatly exaggerating the moral effect of education, especially when the education is law school and the morals are those of lawyers. Law is fast becoming a business and the law schools cannot reverse the trend. As business ethics are not clearly inferior to legal ethics, I do not myself think that the trend should be regretted on moral grounds. [T]he law schools should adjust to it rather than fight it.

---

3.   Legal Profession's Messages About Legal Ethics

Professor Ronald Pipkin, on the basis of a substantial empirical study, argues that many law school courses in professional responsibility actually "desensitize students to legal ethics."[16] He begins by identifying the manifest and latent hierarchy of courses in law schools. The manifest hierarchy identifies important courses by such official indicators as the number of credits assigned to each course and whether a course is required or elective. The latent hierarchy is "less visible, less explicitly rationalized, and may either reinforce or work at cross-purposes to the official ... manifest structure. The latent hierarchies are communicated to students through the content of instruction, cues from the faculty, advice from practitioners and other students, feedback from the job market, bar exams and so forth."[17] Pipkin argues that the latent hierarchy works to undercut whatever importance the manifest hierarchy assigns to courses in professional responsibility.

Pipkin interviewed students at seven law schools in the academic year 1975–76. His data showed that students perceived courses in professional responsibility as requiring less time, as substantially easier, as less well-taught and as a less valuable use of class time. His data further suggested that courses in professional responsibility were held in low intellectual esteem in large measure because they were more likely to be taught by discussion method than by either lecture or the socratic method. Generally, courses taught by the Socratic method were considered by students to be the most intellectually demanding, with courses taught by lecture coming in second and courses taught by discussion coming in a poor third, no matter what the subject. Although students perceived professional responsibility as highly relevant to their later careers as practicing lawyers, a

---

16. Ronald Pipkin, Law School Instruction in Professional Responsibility: A Curricular Paradox, 1979 Amer.Bar Found.Research J. 247.

17. Id. at 252–53.

course's perceived relevance to life as a lawyer was irrelevant to how much time students expended on the course or whether or not they saw the course as intellectually challenging.

How does law school communicate messages about the importance of legal ethics? If professional responsibility issues have come up in other courses, how has the subject been treated by the professor? Is professional responsibility a theme that runs through your law school career? How do legal employers treat the subject? Fellow students? How have these messages affected your attitude toward legal ethics?

CHAPTER 10

REGULATION OF COMPETITION IN LEGAL SERVICES

INTRODUCTION: THE MARKET FOR LEGAL SERVICES

The legal profession is a service industry engaged in the production and distribution of legal services. An economic analysis of factors affecting the availability, cost and quality of legal services in the United States must consider both the demand for and the supply of legal services.

Demand for Legal Services

Major corporations encounter few problems in obtaining adequate legal services. They are experienced users of legal services and may choose who and how service is provided from a wide array of individual lawyers, outside law firms and inside staff counsel. Market forces operate fairly well in this sector of the legal services industry although corporations may complain about legal costs and others may complain that too many legal resources are devoted to corporations.

Ordinary Americans, however, face more difficulties. Recurrent studies report that low-and moderate-income Americans make little use of lawyers even though they report encounters with problems having legal aspects. Many have difficulty identifying a problem as one on which a lawyer might be useful; they also fear that the services will be more costly than they can afford; and they do not know how to find a competent, honest lawyer who handles the particular type of matter. For more detail, see p. 1122 below.

The social fairness of current patterns in the distribution of legal services has attracted much criticism and exhortation but little action. President Jimmy Carter, speaking to the Los Angeles County Bar Association in 1978, stated themes that have now become cliches from frequent repetition: the U.S. has more lawyers and more litigation than elsewhere in the world, but these resources are "wastefully [and] unfairly distributed.... Ninety percent of our lawyers serve 10 percent of our people. We are overlawyered and underrepresented." "Excessive litigation and legal featherbedding are encouraged [by an] organized bar [that] has fought innovations [that would make legal services more competitive and more widely available]." "Too often the amount of justice that a person gets depends on the amount of money that he or she can pay." "[B]y regarding the adversary system as an end in itself, we have made justice more cumbersome, more expensive, and less equal that it ought to be."[1]

Supply of Legal Services

Regulation of the supply of legal services takes a number of forms: (1) the prohibition on the practice of law by nonlawyers (unauthorized practice); (2) restraints on the flow of information about legal services (restrictions on lawyer advertising and solicitation of legal business); (3) restrictions on the form of delivery, such as limitations on group legal services, nonlawyer participation in or ownership of law firms and dual practice restrictions; and, finally, (4) the state admission and local counsel requirements that limit multistate practice. Direct regulation of access to the profession in the form of admission requirements, such as legal education, bar examination and character and fitness scrutiny was discussed in Chapter 9.

Market Imperfections in the Delivery of Legal Services

Is the professional monopoly in the best interests of society generally, or is it merely a tactic by which the legal profession seeks to protect its own turf? Both conservative economists and Marxist analysts view much of the profession's regulation of itself (through the instrumentality of the highest court of a state) as designed to enhance the incomes and status of lawyers. Milton Friedman, for example, argues that fears that consumers are incapable of making choices for themselves are paternalistic and wrong; registration or certification are adequate to overcome market imperfections such as inadequate information.[2] He "find[s] it difficult to see any case in which licensure [e.g., exclusion of competitors] rather than certification can be justified."[3] From Friedman's point of view, restraints on competition have adverse effects on the quality, variety and cost of services. Innovation is reduced, and the flow of information impeded. And it is almost inevitable that the producer group will dominate occupational licensing at the expense of the public.

The persistence of occupational licensing and the continuing public support for some types of regulation of legal and medical services have stimulated economic arguments in defense of at least some occupational regulation. Consider the following arguments:

Information imperfections in the legal services market may lead to consumer harm or a debasement of the quality of service.

- Some consumers of legal services need to be protected against their own ignorance. They may be harmed as a result of information deficiencies that are costly or impossible to correct. Individuals who have no experience with lawyers and are involved in a personal

---

1. Public Papers of the Presidents of the United States, Jimmy Carter, Book I, 834 (criticizing cost, delay, unfairness in distribution and lack of access). See also Derek C. Bok, A Flawed System of Law Practice and Training, 33 J.Legal Educ. 570 (1983).

2. Milton Friedman, Capitalism and Freedom 130–60 (1962).

3. Id. at 149.

plight, such as injury, divorce or a criminal charge, lack information necessary to choose or supervise a lawyer. The gap between the client's information and that of the lawyer requires the client to make a leap of faith, trusting that the lawyer is competent and honest. Professional regulation seeks to justify the client's trust by assuring a minimal level of integrity, competence and performance.

• If consumers cannot differentiate between high quality and low quality legal services, producers will not be compensated for the higher cost of high quality service. Information asymmetry may result in a "market for lemons," in the sense that producers are forced to make price and quality reductions that in turn lead to only cheap products being sold and the market shrinking.[4] The problem may be overcome by certification, advertising or other measures that remedy the typical consumer's information deficiencies. Alternatively, a regulatory regime may define performance standards and provide adequate incentives for lawyers to invest time, education and resources in providing quality services.[5]

Neighborhood effects (externalities) of sufficient size and frequency may justify governmental intervention. Even if it is paternalistic and undesirable to deny consumers the freedom to choose the type of service they want, costs to third persons or to the public generally may justify regulation. If an unlicensed and incompetent person builds a bridge or skyscraper that collapses, huge costs are imposed on others. After-the-fact remedies, such as negligence law, may not prevent a sufficient number of such incidents. In the context of legal services, externalities come into play most obviously when the issue is representation in litigation, which involves the interests of the court, opposing parties and the public in just and expeditious resolution of disputes. Regulation of advocates may serve those goals.

Finally, *free rider* problems may support some governmental intervention. Free riders are those who benefit from collective goods without contributing to their payment. In a sense, the public trust created by the profession's scheme of entry regulation and control of conduct is a collective good of the profession or the public. "[A]bsent effective regulatory structures, individual attorneys will have inadequate economic incentives to avoid cheating; they can benefit as free riders from the bar's general reputation without adhering to the standards that maintain it."[6]

How serious are these market imperfections? Are they applicable to all sectors of law practice or only a few? Would certification of lawyers be a

---

4. See George A. Akerlof, The Market for Lemons: Quality Uncertainty and the Market Mechanism, 84 Q. J. Econ. 488 (1970); Hayne E. Leland, Quacks, Lemons, and Licensing, 87 Pol.Econ. 1328 (1979); and Hayne E. Leland, Minimum Quality Standards and Licensing in Markets with Asymmetry of Information, in Simon Rottenberg (ed.), Occupational Licensure and Regulation 265 (1980).

5. See generally Robert Dingwall & Paul Fenn, 'A Respectable Profession'?, Sociological and Economic Perspectives on the Regulation of Professional Services, 7 Int'l Rev. Law & Econ. 51 (1987).

6. Deborah L. Rhode & David Luban, Legal Ethics 647 (1992).

satisfactory alternative to exclusive licensing? Would provision of public information about the practice and qualifications of lawyers solve the information problem?

A.   THE PROFESSIONAL MONOPOLY: UNAUTHORIZED PRACTICE OF LAW

1.   DEVELOPMENT OF THE UNAUTHORIZED PRACTICE RESTRICTION

In the United States many tasks of a more or less legal nature may be undertaken only by a lawyer. Statutes, court rules and judicial decisions restrict "the practice of law" to lawyers duly admitted in the jurisdiction. The only general exception to the professional monopoly of law practice is that persons who are directly affected may undertake to handle their own legal problems by arguing their own cases, writing their own wills or copying out their own deeds—a right of self-representation.[7] The law of unauthorized practice and its current status and justification are examined here.[8]

Until the 20th century, the doctrine of unauthorized practice of law meant only that a nonlawyer could not appear in court to represent another person. Courts enforced the doctrine mainly by regulating who could enter an appearance in litigation. Outside the courthouse, nonlawyers freely performed tasks that today would be called the unauthorized practice of law. Late in the 19th century, for example, title guaranty companies and debt collection agencies performed legal work as part of their services. Trust companies often drafted wills, and accountants gave tax advice. These and other activities on the part of nonlawyers encountered increasing resistance from the organized bar during the first half of the 20th century.

A vigorous and expansive doctrine of unauthorized practice did not appear on the American scene until sometime after the First World War. During the Depression of the 1930s, economic pressures on the bar and a political environment that was more hospitable to occupational licensing led to more vigorous enforcement of the expanded doctrine by bar unauthorized practice committees in virtually every state. During this period the present scope of unauthorized practice was embodied in judicial decisions, which state the modern rationale for, and breadth of, the doctrine.

7. See Faretta v. California, 422 U.S. 806 (1975) (criminal defendant who made a "knowing and intelligent" waiver of the constitutional right to the assistance of counsel had a constitutional right to self-representation).

8. The best general accounts of the bar's attempts to suppress unauthorized practice of law are Barlow F. Christensen, The Unauthorized Practice of Law: Do Good Fences Really Make Good Neighbors—Or Even Good Sense, 1980 Am.Bar Found.Research J. 159 (historical analysis); and Deborah L. Rhode, Policing the Professional Monopoly: A Constitutional and Empirical Analysis of Unauthorized Practice Prohibitions, 34 Stan.L.Rev. 1 (1981) (empirical study of bar association enforcement practice).

After judicial decisions had expanded the range of activities that constitute unauthorized practice, the organized bar, beginning in the 1930s, negotiated treaties with organized groups of competitors. The agreements divided the market for a broad range of services into two categories: services only lawyers could provide and services that accountant, architects, claims adjusters, collection agencies, liability insurance companies, lawbook publishers, professional engineers, realtors, title companies, trust companies and social workers were free to provide without being charged with the unauthorized practice of law. The growth of the consumer movement and the evolution of federal antitrust law brought an end to this market division strategy. The *Goldfarb* decision in 1975,[9] striking down the Virginia bar's suggested minimum fee schedules, made it clear that federal antitrust laws applied to anti-competitive activity by private bar associations. Subsequently, lower court decisions and the initiation of a federal challenge led to retrenchment and reorganization of unauthorized practice activity. The interprofessional treaties were abandoned because of fears of antitrust liability,[10] and a number of state bars disbanded their unauthorized practice committees. In other states, the state supreme court and mandatory state bars that had become state agencies took responsibility for regulatory activity.

Legal Remedies Against Unauthorized Law Practice

A nonlawyer who provides legal assistance to others may be subject to legal consequences. If the unlicensed person holds herself out as a lawyer, the law of fraud is violated.[11] Moreover, if sued for malpractice, an unlicensed person rendering legal services is held to the same standard of care and competence that a licensed lawyer must meet.[12] Another possible consequence is that fee contracts made by an unlicensed person may not be legally enforceable.[13] The unlicensed person could also be enjoined from continuing to provide legal services on the principle supporting injunction against a public nuisance.[14] Finally, practicing law without a license is defined as a crime in most states.[15] The quality of the services provided by

9. Goldfarb v. Virginia State Bar, 421 U.S. 773 (1975) (bar association's minimum fee schedules violate federal antitrust laws).

10. Committees of the ABA responsible for drafting such treaties gradually began to disband, although in 1999 (24 years after *Goldfarb*) some of these committees (composed of lawyers and representatives of some other profession's national group) were still in existence. Those committees no longer draft treaties, but the question is what, if anything, could they do without running afoul of the antitrust laws?

11. See, e.g., People v. Schreiber, 95 N.E. 189 (Ill.1911).

12. See Biakanja v. Irving, 320 P.2d 16 (Cal. 1958) (will drafting by notary public).

13. See, e.g., Ames v. Gilman, 51 Mass. (10 Metc.) 239 (1845); cf. Gesellschaft Fur Drahtlose Telegraphie M.B.H. v. Brown, 78 F.2d 410 (D.C.App.1935) (lawyer barred from recovering fees for services rendered in violation of ethical standards).

14. See, e.g., State v. Scopel, 316 S.W.2d 515 (Mo.1958) (injunction against unlicensed practice of medicine); W. Prosser & P. Keeton on Torts § 90 (5th ed. 1984).

15. See Deborah L. Rhode, Policing the Professional Monopoly, 34 Stan.L.Rev. 1, 11 n. 39 (1981) (collection of state statutes).

an unlicensed practitioner, an issue in malpractice cases, is not a defense to a criminal charge or the issuance or violation of an injunction.

2. What Constitutes "the Practice of Law"?

Unauthorized Practice of Law Committee v. Parsons Technology, Inc.

United States District Court, N.D. Texas, Dallas Division.
1999 WL 47235 (Jan. 22, 1999).

■ Sanders, Senior Judge.

· · ·

Having considered the motions, briefs, and arguments of both parties, and for the reasons set forth below, the Court concludes that there are no genuine issues of material fact and that Plaintiff Unauthorized Practice of Law Committee is entitled to judgment as a matter of law. Therefore, Plaintiff's Motion for Summary Judgment is granted and Defendant's Motion for Summary Judgment is denied.

I. BACKGROUND

The Plaintiff, the Unauthorized Practice of Law Committee ("the UPLC"), is comprised of six Texas lawyers and three lay citizens appointed by the Supreme Court of Texas. The UPLC is responsible for enforcing Texas' unauthorized practice of law statute, Tex. Gov't Code §§ 81.101–.106 (Vernon's 1998) ("the Statute").[1]

Parsons has published and offered for sale through retailers in Texas a computer software program entitled Quicken Family Lawyer, version 8.0, and its updated version Quicken Family Lawyer '99 ("QFL").

QFL is the product at the center of this controversy. In its most recent version, QFL offers over 100 different legal forms (such as employment agreements, real estate leases, premarital agreements, and seven different will forms) along with instructions on how to fill out these forms. QFL's packaging represents that the product is "valid in 49 states including the District of Columbia;" is "developed and reviewed by expert attorneys;" and is "updated to reflect recent legislative formats." The packaging also

---

1. Tex Gov't Code § 81.101 defines the practice of law, as follows:

(a) In this chapter the "practice of law" means the preparation of a pleading or other document incident to an action or special proceeding or the management of the action or proceeding on behalf of a client before a judge in court as well as a service rendered out of court, including the giving of advice or the rendering of any service requiring the use of legal skill or knowledge, such as preparing a will, contract, or other instrument, the legal effect of which under the facts and conclusions involved must be carefully determined.

(b) The definition in this section is not exclusive and does not deprive the judicial branch of the power and authority under both this chapter and the adjudicated cases to determine whether other services and acts not enumerated may constitute the practice of law.

indicates that QFL will have the user "answer a few questions to determine which estate planning and health care documents best meet [the user's] needs;" and that QFL will "interview you in a logical order, tailoring documents to your situation." Finally, the packaging reassures the user that "[h]andy hints and comprehensive legal help topics are always available."

The first time a user accesses QFL after installing it on her computer the following disclaimer appears as the initial screen:

> This program provides forms and information about the law. We cannot and do not provide specific information for your exact situation. For example, we can provide a form for a lease, along with information on state law and issues frequently addressed in leases. But we cannot decide that our program's lease is appropriate for you. Because we cannot decide which forms are best for your individual situation, you must use your own judgment and, to the extent you believe appropriate, the assistance of a lawyer.

This disclaimer does not appear anywhere on QFL's packaging. Additionally, it does not appear on subsequent uses of the program unless the user actively accesses the "Help" pull-down menu at the top of the screen and then selects "Disclaimer."

On the initial use of QFL, or anytime a new user name is created, QFL asks for the user's name and state of residence. It then inquires whether the user would like QFL to suggest documents to the user. If the user answers "Yes," QFL's "Document Advisor" asks the user a few short questions concerning the user's marital status, number of children, and familiarity with living trusts.[3] QFL then displays the entire list of available documents, but marks a few of them as especially appropriate for the user based on her responses.

When the user accesses a document, QFL asks a series of questions relevant to filling in the legal form. With certain questions, a separate text box explaining the relevant legal considerations the user may want to take into account in filling out the form also appears on the screen. As the user proceeds through the questions relevant to the specific form, QFL either fills in the appropriate blanks or adds or deletes entire clauses from the form. For example, in the "Real Estate Lease—Residential" form, depending on how the user answers the question regarding subleasing the apartment, a clause permitting subleasing with the consent of the landlord is either included or excluded from the form.

If a user selects a "health care document" (i.e., a living will, an advance health care directive, or a health care power of attorney) the following screen appears:

---

3. If the user answers "Yes" to the question concerning living trusts, she is asked one additional question concerning the amount of effort the user is willing to put into her estate plan.

Health Care laws vary from state to state. Your state may not offer every type of health care document. Family Lawyer assumes that you wish to have a health care document based on the laws of your state. When you select a living will, health care power of attorney, or advance health care directive, Family Lawyer will open the appropriate document based on your state.

When a Texas user selects a health care document a form entitled "Directive to Physicians and Durable Power of Attorney for Health Care" appears.

In addition to the separate text boxes providing question and form specific information, at any time throughout the program, the user may access various other help features which provide additional legal information. One such feature is "Ask Arthur Miller," where the user selects a general topic and then a specific question,[4] after which either a text-based answer is provided or, if the user's computer has a CD–ROM player, a sound card and a video card, a sound and video image of Arthur Miller answering the question appears.

The UPLC filed this action in state court alleging that the selling of QFL violates Texas' unauthorized practice of law statute, ... and seeking, among other things, to enjoin the sale of QFL in Texas. Parsons subsequently removed this case to this Court. Both parties now seek summary judgment. The UPLC argues that Parsons has violated the Statute as a matter of law. Parsons responds that the mere selling of books or software cannot violate the statute because some form of personal contact beyond publisher-consumer is required by a plain reading of the Statute. Alternatively, if the statute is not construed to require some form of personal relationship, Parsons argues that the application of the Statute to the mere sale and distribution of QFL would infringe upon Parsons' speech rights under the United States and Texas Constitutions. Parsons also argues that

---

4. The "Ask Arthur Miller" feature answers a number of predetermined frequently asked legal questions in the general topics of estate planning, family and personal, powers of attorney, health and medical, real estate, employment, financial, corporate, consumer and credit, and common questions. Some of the specific questions contained within these general topics are "What if I have a dispute, but don't want to go to the expense and delay of bringing a law suit?", "Why should I go to the trouble of writing a will?", "What is probate?", and "Doesn't a Premarital agreement take the romance out of marriage?". After the user clicks on the general question, a general response to the question appears. For instance, the response to the question, "Should a real estate lease be in writing?" is:

No matter how friendly the landlord-tenant relationship seems to be, it's usually best to have a written lease. In most states, an agreement to lease property must be in writing if the term of the lease is longer than one year. But even for shorter leases, a written lease can be very helpful in resolving issues that might arise later. Such issues might include the length of the lease, the amount of the rent, late charges, return of the security deposit, who pays for utilities and repairs, and whether pets are allowed. On the other hand, an oral lease may allow either party to terminate the lease upon much shorter notice.... Be sure you understand your state's landlord and tenant laws.

the Statute, if utilized to prevent the sale and distribution of QFL, should be void for vagueness. . . .

III. ANALYSIS

A. *Determination of This Suit on Summary Judgment.*

. . . Under Texas law, a court may determine whether the undisputed acts of a defendant fall within the statutory definition of the unauthorized practice of law. Unauthorized Practice of Law Committee v. Cortez, 692 S.W.2d 47, 51 (Tex.1985). While the right to trial by jury exists where the alleged acts purportedly constituting the unauthorized practice of law are disputed, the "courts ultimately decide whether certain undisputed activities constitute the unauthorized practice of law." Id. . . .

In this case, there are no genuine issues of material fact or disputed acts. Parsons' act of publishing QFL is undisputed. The contents of QFL are undisputed. All that remains to be determined is the legal consequences, if any, of these undisputed acts, and according to *Cortez*, the power to make this determination ultimately resides with the Court. Therefore, under both Texas law and the traditional federal summary judgment standards, this case is ripe for decision on summary judgment.

B. *The Violation of the Texas Unauthorized Practice of Law Statute.*

The UPLC moves for summary judgment because it claims, as a matter of law, the sale and distribution of QFL violates the Statute. The UPLC argues that QFL gives advice concerning legal documents and selects legal documents for users, both of which involve the use of legal skill and knowledge, and this constitutes the practice of law. Additionally, the UPLC argues that the Defendant's forms are misleading and incorrect. In sum, the UPLC alleges that QFL acts as a "high tech lawyer by interacting with its 'client' while preparing legal instruments, giving legal advice, and suggesting legal instruments that should be employed by the user." In other words, QFL is a "cyber-lawyer."

No one disputes that the practice of law encompasses more than the mere conduct of cases in the courts. See In re Duncan, 65 S.E. 210 (S.C.1909) (finding that the practice of law includes "the preparation of legal instruments of all kinds, and, in general, all advice to clients, and all action taken for them in matters connected with the law."). However, a comprehensive definition of just what qualifies as the practice of law is "impossible," and "each case must be decided upon its own particular facts." Palmer v. Unauthorized Practice of Law Committee, 438 S.W.2d 374, 376 (Tex.App.1969); see also State Bar of Michigan v. Cramer, 249 N.W.2d 1, 7 (Mich.1976) ("any attempt to formulate a lasting, all encompassing definition of 'practice of law' is doomed to failure.").

The UPLC, in arguing that the publication and sale of QFL constitutes the unauthorized practice of law, relies on two Texas Court of Appeals cases, Palmer v. Unauthorized Practice of Law Committee, 438 S.W.2d 374

(Tex.App.1969), and Fadia v. Unauthorized Practice of Law Committee, 830 S.W.2d 162 (Tex.App.1992).

Palmer held that the sale of will forms containing blanks to be filled in by the user, along with instructions, constituted the unauthorized practice of law. The *Palmer* court observed that the form sold by Mr. Palmer was "almost a will itself" and that the form purported to make specific testamentary bequests. The court feared that the unsuspecting layman "by reading defendants' advertisements, by reading the will form, and by reading the definitions that are attached, . . . [would be] led to believe that defendants' will 'form' is in fact only a form and that all testamentary dispositions may be thus standardized." Id. at 376. The *Palmer* court held that the preparation of legal instruments of all kinds involves the practice of law. The *Palmer* court further held that the exercise of judgment in the proper drafting of legal instruments, or even the selecting of the proper form of instrument, necessarily affects important legal rights, and thus, is the practice of law. In *Fadia*, the pro se defendant sold and distributed a manual entitled "You and Your Will: A Do–It–Yourself Manual." The defendant in *Fadia* attempted to get around *Palmer*'s conclusion that the selling of a will manual constitutes the unauthorized practice of law, by arguing that the court should reject *Palmer* in light of recent state court decisions requiring some form of personal contact or relationship between the alleged unauthorized lawyer and the putative client in order to violate the unauthorized practice of law statute. The court rejected the defendant's argument, stating that it would not overrule *Palmer* and if there were to be a pre-requisite of personal contact between the parties, such a change to the Statute would have to come from the legislature and not the courts. The *Fadia* court went on to hold that because a will secures legal rights and its drafting involves the giving of advice requiring the use of legal skill or knowledge, the preparation of a will involves the practice of law. Id. Since the selection of the proper legal form also affects important legal rights, the court reasoned that it too constituted the practice of law. Id. at 165. Therefore, since the will manual both purported to advise a layman on how to draft a will and selected a specific form for the layman to use, the court determined that the Defendant's selling of a will manual qualified as the unauthorized practice of law. Id.

. . . The Texas Supreme Court has since held that the mere advising of a person as to whether or not to file a form requires legal skill and knowledge, and therefore, would be the practice of law. Unauthorized Practice of Law Committee v. Cortez, 692 S.W.2d 47, 50 (Tex.1985).

Based on the interpretations of the Statute by the Texas courts, QFL falls within the range of conduct that Texas courts have determined to be the unauthorized practice of law. For instance, QFL purports to select the appropriate health care document for an individual based upon the state in which she lives. QFL customizes the documents, by adding or removing entire clauses, depending upon the particular responses given by the user to a set of questions posed by the program. The packaging of QFL represents that QFL will "interview you in a logical order, tailoring documents to your situation." Additionally, the packaging tells the user that the forms are valid in 49 states and that they have been updated by legal experts. This creates an air of reliability about the documents, which increases the likelihood that an individual user will be misled into relying on them. This false impression is not diminished by QFL's disclaimer. The disclaimer only actively appears the first-time the program is used after it is installed, and there is no guarantee that the person who initially uses the program is the same person who will later use and rely upon the program.

QFL goes beyond merely instructing someone how to fill in a blank form. While no single one of QFL's acts, in and of itself, may constitute the practice of law, taken as a whole Parsons, through QFL, has gone beyond publishing a sample form book with instructions, and has ventured into the unauthorized practice of law.

Parsons attempts to avoid the conclusion that it is guilty of the unauthorized practice of law by arguing that the Statute requires personal contact or a lawyer-client relationship. Parsons bases its argument first on the language of the Statute, which it contends requires that the prohibited services must be provided "on behalf of a client" in order to be the practice of law.

Even assuming that Parsons is correct that paragraph (a) of the Statute requires the prohibited services to be completed "on behalf of" a client, paragraph (a) of the Statute is not an exclusive definition of the unauthorized practice of law. Paragraph (b) of the Statute gives the Court the authority to determine that other acts constitute the unauthorized practice of law. Therefore, a judge could legitimately determine, under the authority granted in paragraph (b), that services provided to the public as a whole, as opposed to a singular client, qualify as the practice of law.

Next, Parsons argues that this Court should require a personal relationship between the party charged with the unauthorized practice of law and the party who benefits from the "advice" since this is the logic of almost every other court to consider the issue. (See ... also, e .g., New York County Lawyers' Association v. Dacey, 234 N.E.2d 459 (N.Y.1967)). However, as noted above, the pro se defendant in *Fadia* made this exact argument and the Texas Court of Appeals rejected it. Fadia, 830 S.W.2d at 164.

Nonetheless, Parsons contends that if the Texas Supreme Court were to consider the issue it would follow the lead of the other states. Although this Court is not *Erie* bound to follow the *Fadia* decision, it believes the Texas Supreme Court would find the *Fadia* decision a persuasive precedent. For this Court to be the first to impose a new interpretation of a state statute which has been on the books in its current form since 1987, and some form since 1939, would fly in the face of generally accepted notions of federal-state comity. If Parsons believes such a personal contact requirement should be included in the Statute, it should address these concerns to the Texas legislature. It is not appropriate for this Court to be the first to read such a requirement into the Statute.

Parsons' arguments to the contrary notwithstanding, QFL is far more than a static form with instructions on how to fill in the blanks. For instance, QFL adapts the content of the form to the responses given by the user. QFL purports to select the appropriate health care document for an individual based upon the state in which she lives. The packaging of QFL makes various representations as to the accuracy and specificity of the forms. In sum, Parsons has violated the unauthorized practice of law statute.

C. *Does the Statute Withstand Scrutiny Under the United States Constitution?*

Having determined that the publication of QFL violates the Texas unauthorized practice of law statute, the Court must now examine whether applying the Statute in such a manner infringes upon the rights guaranteed by the First Amendment of the United States Constitution. The First Amendment is plainly implicated by the UPLC's desire to halt the sale of QFL in the state of Texas. While there is no right of unlicensed laymen to represent another under the First Amendment's guarantees of freedom of association and freedom to petition one's government, Turner v. American Bar Ass'n, 407 F.Supp. 451, 478 (N.D.Tex.1975), Parsons' rights under the First Amendment's protections of a free press still apply.

1. Determining the Appropriate Level of Scrutiny: Content–Neutral v. Content–Based

The Court's initial First Amendment inquiry is to determine whether the Statute is a content-neutral or content-based restriction of speech.... If the Statute is determined to prevent speech based on its content, it is subject to strict scrutiny. If the Statute is merely a content-neutral restriction on speech, it is subject only to intermediate scrutiny.

The principal inquiry in determining content neutrality in speech cases is whether the government has adopted a regulation of speech because of disagreement with the message it conveys. Ward v. Rock Against Racism, 491 U.S. 781, 791 (1989). If the answer is "no," then the statute is content-neutral and subject only to intermediate scrutiny. The government's purpose is the controlling consideration in this inquiry. A regulation that serves purposes unrelated to the content of the expression is deemed neutral, even if it has an incidental effect on some speakers or messages but not others.

Parsons vehemently asserts that the Statute's prohibition is a content-based restriction on speech. It bases this assertion, not on the general purpose of the Statute, but on the deposition testimony of the UPLC's designated representative that the UPLC would not prosecute Parsons for the publication of its non-legal software titles. Thus, according to Parsons, since only its legal titles are subject to restriction, the Statute is based on the content of the software title, and therefore, the Statute is subject to strict scrutiny.

However, it is not what specific speech (or conduct) the Statute prohibits, but whether the government is evidencing a disagreement with the speaker's message, as well as the underlying purpose behind the statute, which determines content-neutrality. The mere fact that the Statute sanctions speech-based conduct does not make the Statute content-based. See Ohralik v. Ohio State Bar Ass'n, 436 U.S. 447, 456 (1978) ("it has never been deemed an abridgment of freedom of speech or press to make a course of conduct illegal merely because the conduct was in part initiated, evidenced, or carried out by means of language, either spoken, written, or printed.")

The Statute at issue is aimed at eradicating the unauthorized practice of law. The Statute's purpose has nothing to do with suppressing speech. The UPLC's decision to challenge some of Parsons' software titles but not others has less to do with their content than with the likelihood that the title has possibly violated the unauthorized practice of law statute. Of course, the UPLC would not subject Parson's non-legal titles to scrutiny under the Statute; it is unlikely that [its] Life Application Bible engages in the prohibited conduct of practicing law without a license. Such discrimination between products does not evidence a disagreement with the message of Parsons' software.

[T]he Court finds that the Statute is aimed at the noncommunicative impact of Parsons' speech, and therefore, is a content-neutral regulation which only incidentally affects speech and therefore is subject only to intermediate scrutiny.

2. Determining Whether a Content–Neutral Statute Overburdens Protected Speech Rights

Having determined that the Statute is content-neutral, the Court must still decide whether the Statute nonetheless overburdens protected speech. To make this determination, the Court subjects the Statute to intermediate scrutiny and the four part test of United States v. O'Brien, 391 U.S. 367 (1968). Under *O'Brien*, the UPLC must establish that: (1) the regulation is within the constitutional power of the state; (2) it furthers an important or substantial government interest; (3) the government interest is unrelated to the suppression of free expression; and (4) the incidental restriction of speech is no greater than is essential to the furtherance of that interest.

[The court held that the first three *O'Brien* factors were easily met: (1) Parsons conceded that Texas has the power to prohibit the unauthorized practice of law; (2) the court held that the state's interest in regulating the practice of law and protecting its citizens from being mislead was a substantial one; and (3) it held that the state interest is unrelated to the suppression of free expression. The case turned on (4) whether the incidental restriction of speech is no greater than is essential to the furtherance of the governmental interest.]

A regulation satisfies the final prong, often referred to as "the narrow tailoring requirement," "so long as the ... regulation promotes a substantial government interest that would be achieved less effectively absent the regulation." United States v. Albertini, 472 U.S. 675, 689 (1985). The regulation must also "not burden substantially more speech than is necessary to further the government's legitimate interest." Ward, 491 U.S. at 799.

The version of the narrow tailoring requirement for intermediate scrutiny does not require the government to chose the "least-restrictive alternative" in achieving its interests. Ward, 491 U.S. at 798. Furthermore, a court should not invalidate the government's preferred remedial scheme because some alternative solution is marginally less intrusive on a speaker's First Amendment interests. Turner Broadcasting System, Inc. v. F.C.C., 117 S.Ct. 1174, 1200 (1997) (*Turner II*). A statute should be struck down under intermediate scrutiny only when a "substantial portion of the burden on speech does not serve to advance [the State's content-neutral goals]." Simon & Schuster v. New York Crime Victims Bd., 502 U.S. at 122 n.* (quoting *Ward*, 491 U.S. at 799).

While the Court recognizes that the issue is close, it is of the opinion that the Statute does not "substantially burden" more speech than necessary, and that the government's interest would be achieved less effectively absent the regulation. Absent the regulation, as it is being applied in this case, the State's ability to combat the unauthorized practice of law in the computer age would be hindered. The State possesses an interest in protecting the uninformed and unwary from overly-simplistic legal advice. The UPLC does not seek to prevent the simple provision of information concerning legal rights; rather, it seeks to prevent the citizens of Texas from being lulled into a false sense of security that if they use QFL they will have a "legally valid" document that's "tailored to [their] situation" and "best meets their needs." If the UPLC is prevented from prosecuting Parsons, the State's interests in preventing those who are not authorized to practice law from giving legal advice would be less effectively achieved. Additionally, while the Statute burdens some speech, that burden does not rise to the level of a substantial burden. Moreover, the burden which the Statute does place on speech is necessary to serve the State's legitimate content-neutral interests. Thus, the Statute satisfies the fourth prong of *O'Brien*.

Since the Statute meets all four of *O'Brien'* s requirements, it survives review under intermediate scrutiny. The Statute does not violate the First Amendment to the United States Constitution.

Plaintiff's Motion for Summary Judgment is granted. Defendant's Motion for Summary Judgment is denied.

[After this decision, the Texas legislature amended § 81–101 to provide that the practice of law does not include "computer software or similar products ... [that] clearly and conspicuously state that ... [they] are not a substitute for the advice of an attorney." Based on that change, the Fifth Circuit vacated the injunction against Parsons' continued distribution of QFL and the judgment of the district court, remanding the case for "further proceedings, if any should be necessary." Unauthorized Practice of Law Committee v. Parsons Technology, Inc., 1999 WL 435871 (5th Cir., June 29, 1999).]

    PERKINS v. CTX MORTGAGE CO.[1] Ed and Jeanne Perkins, as representative plaintiffs, brought this class action on behalf of borrowers who, in connection with purchase of a home, had been charged a $250 document preparation fee by CTX, a large real estate financing company. The borrowers sought declaratory and monetary relief, asserting that CTX's fee constituted the unauthorized practice of law. The fee was charged to offset the overhead associated with the preparation of the extensive documentation necessary to process and complete loan transactions. CTX prepared 37 legal and nonlegal documents necessary to process and complete the Perkins' loan. In preparing these documents, CTX staff attorneys performed all tasks requiring the exercise of legal judgment. For example, CTX attorneys selected the loan products, created the documents necessary for each loan product, and supervised the programming of CTX's central computer, which then would generate form templates in the branch offices. At the branch offices, lay employees entered customer information such as Social Security numbers, employer information and bank account numbers in response to computer prompts depending on the type of loan the Perkinses had selected. Lay employees also entered the loan amount, interest rate, down payment and other factual data. Attorneys prepared the other documents requiring the exercise of legal judgment. For example, the Perkins' attorneys prepared the purchase and sale agreement, the earnest money agreement, the HUD–1, the excise tax affidavit, the warranty deed, and the escrow instructions.

    The court reviewed a line of Washington cases involving non-lawyer participation in residential real estate transactions. In Cultum v. Heritage House Realtors, Inc.,[2] one of the more recent cases, the court had held that a real estate broker could use a form contract that had been prepared by lawyers admitted to practice in Washington, but could not modify the form or insert a new provision into it. In the *Cultum* case, the lead opinion for a divided court had emphasized the consumer interest in convenient and low cost handling of residential real estate transactions by real estate professionals. Other cases had held that a finance or escrow company engaged in unauthorized practice when non-lawyer employees selected and modified the forms employed.[3] Drawing on these precedents, the *Perkins* court held that the selection and completion of legal documents, however the work was allocated between lawyers and non-lawyers employed by CTX, was the

1. 969 P.2d 93 (Wash.1999).

2. 694 P.2d 630 (Wash.1985) (real estate broker engaged in unauthorized practice when he inserted a structural contingency clause into a preprinted standard form real estate contract that Washington lawyers had drafted).

3. See, e.g., Hagan & Van Camp, P.S. v. Kassler Escrow, Inc. 635 P.2d 730 (Wash. 1981) (escrow company prepared earnest money agreements and other documents in real estate transaction).

"practice of law." However, it was "authorized" practice of law because only CTX lawyers exercised discretion. The court concluded:

> The resolution of this case, therefore, depends on balancing the competing public interests of (1) protecting the public from the harm of the lay exercise of legal discretion and (2) promoting convenience and low cost. Washington unauthorized practice of law cases are replete with instances of lay exercise of legal discretion causing public harm.[4] Yet, when the role of lay persons in selecting and completing form legal documents is reduced to entering objective data, the lay person's actions are unlikely to result in the uncertain legal rights with which this court has been concerned. Thus, the risk of public harm is low. Indeed, the Perkinses have never alleged that their loan documents were deficiently drafted or that their legal rights were prejudiced in the least.
>
> Moreover, permitting mortgage lenders to prepare loan documents in the way the CTX does relieves borrowers of the cost and inconvenience of having attorneys prepare their loan documents. Ironically, were the Perkinses to prevail, future borrowers would bear the additional cost of having attorneys prepare their loan documents, which would likely exceed that portion of the Perkinses' document preparation fee attributable to legal documents.
>
> Thus, we hold that, whether or not a fee is charged, lenders are authorized to prepare the types of legal documents that are ordinarily incident to their financing activities when lay employees participating in such document preparation do not exercise any legal discretion. Moreover, even though the Perkinses have not alleged any harm, in order to fully safeguard the public interest we further hold that lenders must comply with the standard of care of a practicing attorney when preparing such documents.[5]

Unauthorized Practice of Law in the Information Age

What does *Parsons Technology* permit a lay person to do by herself using books, software or other available information? What does *Perkins* permit a lay organization to do in connection with a real estate transaction? One proposition, not discussed in either case, is the constitutional right of any person to represent herself. The *Faretta* case[6] establishes that any person may engage in self-representation in any legal proceeding—even a

---

4. [Court's note:] See Cultum, 694 P.2d 630 (Wash.1985) (buyer's earnest money refund delayed because real estate agent prepared ambiguous contingency clause); Bowers v. Transamerica Title Ins. Co., 675 P.2d 193 (Wash.1983) (seller unable to execute against property upon buyer default because escrow agent prepared unsecured promissory note); Hogan v. Monroe, 684 P.2d 757 (Wash.App.1984) (lessors' repossession rights inadequately protected by lease-option agreement drafted by real estate agent); Hecomovich v. Nielsen, 518 P.2d 1081 (Wash.App.1974) (seller unable to recover personalty upon buyer default because real estate agent failed to provide for personalty in real estate sales contract).

5. 969 P.2d at 99–100.

6. Faretta v. California, 422 U.S. 806 (1975).

capital murder case.[7] The Comment to Model Rule 5.4 recognizes the right of self-representation by stating that "a lawyer may counsel nonlawyers who wish to proceed pro se." Does the pro se right apply to entities as well as individuals? Is the right of self-representation impaired by *Parsons?*

The unauthorized practice precedents of both Texas and Washington support a second proposition: any person may retain a lawyer to prepare legal forms and then publish and sell them to lay people. In Washington, but apparently not in Texas, a lay organization can go further: it can charge persons, for whom it is providing real estate financing, for the services of nonlawyer employees in filling out form documents which its staff lawyers have prepared. In both jurisdictions, a broker handling a real estate transaction cannot add or substitute different contract provisions for any of those in the real estate form contract which the broker uses as the basic framework for the deal.[8] Is *Perkins* a concession to the extraordinary growth of regulatory and bureaucratic complexity in handling ordinary residential real estate transactions?

A California organization, such as Nolo Press,[9] can use its in-house lawyers to create a book of forms (e.g., will forms) and can publish that book and sell it in California and most other states (what about Texas?). In most states, but not in Texas, the publisher can go further: it can add instructions on the use of the forms.[10] How useful are legal forms if the lay user is not given instructions on how to use them?

When a lay provider or an out-of-state lawyer wants to go even further, giving a lay person personalized advice concerning the selection and use of legal forms, many states treat the activity as unauthorized practice. In Florida Bar v. Brumbaugh,[11] for example, a former legal secretary used legal forms to assist couples who wanted a cheap and amicable no-fault divorce. In doing so, she obtained information from her clients (e.g., residency, name, address) and typed the information into the legal form; under the *Perkins* case that would be permissible since very little or no discretion was involved. But Brumbaugh also made choices among various forms and provisions depending upon the facts elicited from her clients. In doing so she encroached on legal turf or, as the bar would prefer to put it,

---

7. In early 1999 Dr. Jack Kevorkian represented himself (some pundits said incompetently) on charges that he had murdered a person who wanted to die; he was convicted of second-degree murder and given a lengthy prison sentence.

8. See Cultum v. Heritage House Realtors, Inc., 694 P.2d 630 (Wash.1985), discussed in *Perkins*.

9. Nolo Press of Berkeley, California is a leading publisher of legal information for the general public. It employs lawyers and others to prepare a wide range of books and computer programs to assist lay people in preparing legal documents, undertaking pro se litigation and the like. In mid–1999,

the Texas Unauthorized Practice of Law Committee was investigating Nolo Press. See Are Books Lawyers?, Nat'l L.J., April 4, 1998, at p. A4.

10. See State Bar of Michigan v. Cramer, 249 N.W.2d 1 (Mich.1976) (sale of form book with instructions was not unauthorized practice); New York County Lawyer's Ass'n v. Dacey, 234 N.E.2d 459 (N.Y.1967) (Connecticut lawyer who sold a book on how to avoid probate not engaged in unauthorized practice).

11. Florida Bar v. Brumbaugh, 355 So.2d 1186 (Fla.1978).

her incompetence threatened the interests of those using her services.[12] Although none of her hundreds of customers had complained and there was no evidence that her services were less competent than those of ordinary general practitioners, the court enjoined Ms. Brumbaugh from carrying on her trade in Florida.

The Florida court imprisoned another former legal secretary, Rosemary Furman, for contempt when she violated a court order enjoining her practice.[13] Furman's case led to national publicity and criticism of the Florida court, which then created a court-attached self-help advisory service for couples seeking simple no-fault divorces.[14] How much concern for those in need of legal services does the bar and court display when it takes steps to make services more available and simplifies procedures only after getting embarrassed by their joint (and extreme) efforts to stop nonlawyers from providing needed services at affordable rates?

Presumably it is permissible to do with computer software (an electronic medium) what one can do with a traditional book. However, this cannot be taken entirely for granted; a number of states impose much more restrictive requirements on radio and television advertising by lawyers than they do on advertising involving newspapers, flyers, billboards, etc., and the Supreme Court has dismissed appeals challenging the differential treatment on First Amendment and other constitutional grounds.[15] Suppose a lay person visits a public library to obtain help in drafting a simple will. The librarian directs the individual to the portion of the collection devoted to self-help books. Has the librarian engaged in unauthorized practice? What if the librarian goes further, attempting to explain the meaning of certain terms used in the book or, in answer to an inquiry, refers the user to another book in another section of the library dealing with probate procedures in the jurisdiction? Does regulation of this activity abridge the citizen's right to self-representation? Or the First Amendment rights of librarians or publishers?

12. *Brumbaugh* holds, in deference to First Amendment concerns, that a nonlawyer can disseminate written "how to" materials, including instructions on use, but may not give oral, personalized advice. In another context, lawyer solicitation of clients, the Supreme Court has drawn a line between sending out written materials to prospective clients, which the First Amendment usually protects, and personal contact with clients, which is not protected. See the *Shapero* case, p. 1020 infra.

13. Florida Bar v. Furman, 451 So.2d 808 (Fla.1984). The Supreme Court subsequently dismissed Furman's appeal for want of a substantial federal question, rejecting arguments that Florida's enforcement of its unauthorized practice statute violated her rights of self-representation, due process and free speech. Furman v. Florida, 444 U.S. 1061 (1980).

14. The Florida Supreme Court took two steps: a simplified dissolution procedure for couples who certify that they have no minor or dependent children and that they have made a satisfactory agreement regarding division of their property and payment of their debts; and a rule permitting non-lawyers to give advice regarding "routine administrative procedures" related to the completion of court-approved legal forms. Similar developments have occurred in other states. For example, as early as 1985, about one-half of divorces in Phoenix were accomplished without lawyers. See Self-Helpers on the Increase, ABA J., Mar. 1, 1988, at 40.

15. See p. 1034 infra.

Parsons Technology is different not only because an electronic medium is involved but because interactive software allows the user to search out possibilities and reach independent conclusions concerning what form is appropriate and what provisions should be included. (Cannot the same thing be done in a good public library by an intelligent user?) Moreover, Quicken Family Lawyer can be used for $29.95 to $59.95 rather than the general practitioner's fee of $500 or some such figure for many of the routine tasks that the software performs. Quicken Family Lawyer adds something else: cyber-lawyer Arthur Miller is there in video and voice to guide the user's choice of a form or a provision (or, more realistically, to pretend to do so). Is Miller engaged in assisting others in the unauthorized practice of law in all U.S. jurisdictions? In the unauthorized practice of law in all jurisdictions in which he is not a member of the bar? Notice that Professor Miller of the Harvard Law School has not been the target of any charges in connection with his involvement with Parsons.

Why not treat Quicken Family Lawyer, as Turbo–Tax and its competitors in the tax field are treated, as providing "legal information" rather than "legal advice," entitling it to constitutional protection under the First Amendment? Will many individuals harm themselves by attempting foolishly to do their own legal work? Of course they will. But others will be harmed by reading medical books and deciding to treat themselves. Isn't this inevitable in a society dedicated to preserving the right to speak and its counterparts, the right to hear and to know? Has the state bar shown that the frequency of mistakes and their seriousness are so great that state paternalism is justified?[16] Some lay people may be determined to write their own wills (perhaps they don't trust lawyers or cannot afford one). Deprived of the use of books and software, or of non-lawyers who could explain things to them, will these self-helpers choose to use lawyers or do it themselves with even worse results?

A lawyer not admitted in Texas engages in unauthorized practice when he gives a Texan advice by phone or e-mail concerning the selection of appropriate provisions for the Texan's will or other legal instrument. But what is the difference between getting the advice from questions posed to a robotic shrink-wrapped Arthur Miller rather than from the real-life Arthur Miller by telephone from his office in Cambridge, Massachusetts (other than the fact that the robotic Miller is available to all of the citizenry whereas the real-life one is available only to monied interests that are willing and able to pay pricey hourly fees)? Texas citizens and organizations who fall into the latter category can probably get personalized advice from

---

16. Deborah Rhode's comprehensive study of the enforcement of unauthorized practice regulation concludes that the burden of proof and persuasion rests on the legal profession to justify its monopoly rather than on actual or potential competitors: "Invoking standards that are conclusory, circular, or both, courts have typically inquired only whether challenged activity calls for 'legal' skills, not whether lay practitioners in fact possess them. At every level of enforcement, the consumer's need for protection has been proclaimed rather than proven." Deborah L. Rhode, Policing the Professional Monopoly: A Constitutional and Empirical Analysis of Unauthorized Practice Prohibitions, 34 Stan. L. Rev. 1, 99 (1981).

Miller (or some other fancy out-of-state legal consultant) by telephone. Is the Texas unauthorized practice committee dealing with that subvention of its unauthorized practice laws?

Another area in which enforcement of unauthorized practice restrictions is virtually non-existent is the advice given to poor people by social service agencies on complicated welfare and government benefits questions, where paralegals often do intake and handle routine filings, while supervisory personnel, usually nonlawyers, answer more complicated questions. Lawyers are generally not concerned with this area because (1) the clients cannot afford to pay and (2) even if an award can be obtained after a hearing, welfare statutes generally restrict the fees that lawyers can charge. See the discussion of statutory limits on fees in Chapter 6 at p. 505 above. For similar reasons, jailhouse lawyers are never the subject of unauthorized practice claims.

Imagine a bill proposed in your state's legislature and sponsored by the state medical society that would ban the "practice of medicine," broadly defined, by every organization other than those owned solely by licensed physicians.[17] All other health care providers, such as chiropractors, nurses, physical therapists, acupuncturists, sellers of herbal remedies would need to be employed and supervised by physicians. Would you oppose the legislation?

Defining the Professional Monopoly

Defining the activities that constitute the "practice of law" is no easy matter. The Model Rules and the Model Code prohibit a lawyer from assisting the unauthorized practice of law. See M.R. 5.5; DR 3–101(A). Although the Texas statute in *Parsons Technology* contains a bit more detail than many statutes or court rules that simply prohibit the "practice of law" by unlicensed persons, the standard Texas applies is the most common one: Is the activity one in which a lawyer's presumed special training and skills are relevant?[18] The test seems circular and thus not particularly helpful.[19]

17. Model Rule 5.4, discussed infra at p. 1041, provides that "a lawyer or law firm shall not share legal fees with a nonlawyer," "form a partnership with a non-lawyer" to practice law, and "practice law for a profit . . . if a nonlawyer owns any interest therein . . . ."

18. EC 3–5, after stating that "[i]t is neither necessary nor desirable to attempt the formulation of a single, specific definition of what constitutes the practice of law," provides a functional (but circular?) one: It is the practice of law when the "professional judgment of a lawyer" is involved in relating "the general body and philosophy of law to a specific legal problem of a client." The context suggests that this de-

termination is to be made in the light of public interest considerations, i.e., the sphere of exclusion is to be determined by the purposes to be served. Other common inquiries are: Whether a task is (1) difficult or complex, (2) involves legal skill and knowledge, or (3) something lawyers commonly do, or, on the other hand, is merely incidental or ancillary to what lay people or organizations commonly do.

19. D.C. Rule 49, adopted in 1997, is unusual it that it spells out a number of exceptions to the unauthorized practice prohibition. The exceptions apply to individuals practicing before federal and D.C. agencies and courts, to in-house counsel, to lawyers admitted elsewhere who are appearing pro

Case law has sometimes said that a matter having legal ramifications requires a lawyer's involvement only when it involves "difficult or doubtful legal questions."[20] Suppose a former legal secretary such as Brumbaugh, see discussion above, makes an arrangement with a lawyer under which any of her clients who has questions about filling out the forms could call the lawyer. Would the lawyer violate Model Rule 5.5 by participating in such an arrangement?

The boundaries of "practice of law" for purposes of enforcing the licensure requirement remain indistinct and vary from one state to another. The location of the boundaries is the product of political interaction between the organized bar and competing service providers, state law as formulated by state courts, constitutional law as formulated by the Supreme Court, inter-professional detente and market forces. In Colorado, Florida and Texas, for example, bar associations have been fairly aggressive, whereas in some other jurisdictions, such as California and Wisconsin, the bar has taken a much more "laissez-faire" approach.

The American law of unauthorized practice goes well beyond that of the remainder of the common law world in extending the prohibition to out-of-court legal services. Because law is such an omnipresent reality in today's world, it is impossible for individuals in myriad endeavors to carry on their work without dealing with "the law:" the police officer patrolling a neighborhood beat, the small business conforming to regulatory requirements, the contractor dealing with building codes and environmental requirements, the home owner who wants to build a fence or challenge his real estate assessment, the consumer dealing with an aggressive finance company or collection agency, or the spouse considering a no-fault divorce. Do these people need to be protected against their own inability to judge the quality of the services offered? If they are required to consult lawyers, is there any assurance that those lawyers will have the necessary competence, integrity and financial accountability?

Personalized Legal Assistance by Nonlawyers

Suppose an entrepreneurial lawyer builds a high-volume service to handle routine legal matters, calling it a "People's Law Center" or the like. At the Center, intake and basic work is done by paralegals specializing in various subject matter areas; a lawyer is consulted only when the paralegal considers such involvement necessary. Many law firms operate a high-volume practice in such matters as divorce, real estate closings, simple wills, probate of small estates, worker's compensation claims and personal bankruptcy.[21] In these firms, and in legal services organizations represent-

hac vice, and to lawyers moving to D.C. if they file an application and are supervised by a member of the D.C. bar.

20. Gardner v. Conway, 48 N.W.2d 788 (Minn.1951); Agran v. Shapiro, 273 P.2d 619 (Cal.Ct.App.1954).

21. See the detailed description of Raul Lovett's worker's compensation and personal

injury practice in Philip B. Heymann and Lance Liebman (eds.), The Social Responsibilities of Lawyers: Case Studies 258 (1988). A description of the high-volume practice of a legal clinic relying on exten-

ing the poor, intake and routine work is done almost entirely by paralegals. Unauthorized practice is not involved because the firm's lawyers prepared the standardized forms and are available to assist in their application to individual clients. Model Rule 5.4 prohibits an organization owned in part by nonlawyers from following the same practice. The rule, discussed further below, provides that "a lawyer or law firm shall not share legal fees with a nonlawyer," "form a partnership with a non-lawyer" to practice law, and "practice law for a profit ... if a nonlawyer owns any interest therein...." When nonlawyer organizations complain that law firm legal assistants exercise broad discretion and are given little supervision, the bar responds that professional codes require supervision and the supervising lawyer remains responsible for the work done. See M.R. 5.3 and EC 3–6.[22] Is this a satisfactory response?

The dramatic growth in the use of legal assistants and paralegals in recent decades has given rise to proposals that these individuals should be licensed by the state after demonstration of competence through education, examination or other entry requirements.[23] Is that a good idea? If licensing is required of legal paraprofessionals, should the legal profession control that process? Similar issues have arisen in the health care field, where nurse practitioner, nurses and other health care occupations have struggled to escape from the regulatory control of physicians.

The most controversial aspect of the 1986 report of the ABA Commission on Professionalism was language dealing with competition from paraprofessionals. Lawyers, the report stated, "should have to compete with properly licensed paraprofessionals" in "certain real estate closings, the drafting of simple wills, and selected tax services" if "clients of ordinary means are to be served at all." "[I]t can no longer be claimed that lawyers have the exclusive possession of the esoteric knowledge required and are therefore the only ones able to advise clients on any matter concerning the law.... Lawyer resistance to [inroads on lawyer exclusivity] for selfish reasons only brings discredit on the profession."[24] These sentences in the Commission's report, printed under the innocuous heading that lawyers

---

sive advertising is also included in the same volume. Id. at 49.

22. M.R. 5.3(b) governs the responsibilities of law firm partners and supervisory lawyers "regarding nonlawyer assistants" such as secretaries, investigators, law student interns and paraprofessionals. The basic responsibilities are reasonable efforts of training and supervision; under M.R. 5.3(c), a lawyer is responsible for an assistant's disciplinary violation if the lawyer ordered or ratified the conduct or is a partner who had direct supervisory authority over the employee "and knows of the conduct at a time when its consequences can be avoided or mitigated but fails to take reasonable remedial action.

23. Proposals to license paralegals have been considered but not yet adopted in California, where lay persons have been actively engaged in providing a variety of law-related services. For a review of the subject, see Carl M. Selinger, The Retention of Limitations on the Out-of-Court Practice of Law by Independent Paralegals, 9 Geo.J. Leg. Eth. 879 (1996).

24. ABA Commission on Professionalism, " ... In the Spirit of Public Service:" A Blueprint for the Rekindling of Lawyer Professionalism, 112 F.R.D. 243, 301 (1986).

should "encourage innovative methods which simplify and make less expensive the rendering of legal services," provoked a violent, critical reaction from lawyers and bar groups.

Nonlawyer Representation in Adjudicatory Proceedings

Representation of parties in proceedings in courts of general jurisdiction is the strongest case for the lawyer's professional monopoly. Here there is an unbroken tradition, flowing from the exclusive right of the English barrister to represent parties in high courts. Arguments of special skill and competence (the intricacies of court procedure and trial tactics), essential to protect clients from serious harm, are bolstered in this context by concerns about the efficient functioning of the legal system. The choice of one not trained to appear before a tribunal involves costs that must be borne by others—costs to the tribunal itself and to other litigants. The settlement and disposition of cases in an orderly and efficient manner is facilitated when a relatively small group of professional representatives deal with judges and each other on a regular basis.[25]

Even in the adjudicatory realm, however, statutes or custom carve out some exceptions for lower tribunals (e.g., justice of the peace courts, small claims courts) and some administrative tribunals. In most of these situations, the losing party is entitled to a de novo trial or further hearing before a constitutional court, in which nonlawyers will be forbidden from appearing on behalf of others.

Representation before tribunals has been an area of lively contest between lawyers and other interest groups. Courts have struck down state statutes or agency rules that have attempted to broaden the power of nonlawyers to represent others in agency proceedings.[26] Is the integrity of "judicial power" really threatened by legislative choices of this type?

Restrictions on Law Practice by Corporations

Most states prohibit the practice of law by corporations (other than "professional corporations" owned solely by lawyers). The prohibition prevents competition from banks, insurance companies, title insurance companies and others. It also forestalls attempts by national marketing chains to make law practice a true consumer product for the national market by installing law offices in retail stores.

The prohibition against law practice by corporations also prevents a corporation from appearing pro se in litigation; the corporation must always be represented by a lawyer who is properly admitted to practice. In

---

25. Thomas Ehrlich & Murray L. Schwartz, Reducing the Costs of Legal Service: Possible Approaches by the Federal Government, Subcomm. on Representation of Citizen Interests of the Comm. on the Judiciary, U.S. Senate, 93d Cong., 2d Sess. 3 (1974).

26. See, e.g., Idaho St. Bar Ass'n v. Idaho Pub. Utilities Comm'n, 637 P.2d 1168 (Idaho 1981) (agency rule authorizing representation in utility commission proceedings by nonlawyer representatives of consumer groups and trade associations held invalid).

Turkey Point Property Owners' Association, Inc. v. Anderson,[27] a neighborhood association of property owners filed a court challenge to a zoning variance given to a commercial developer. The association was represented by one of its officers (although a lawyer was in the room and "willing to assist"). Relying on the court rule requiring a corporation to be represented in court by a lawyer, the court dismissed the association's petition, denying it any review of the merits of the zoning variance. Do corporations, like individual consumers, need to be protected against their own ignorance? Or is the problem that, when non-lawyer agents represent a corporation, those agents may not provide a lawyer's independent judgment? Or is this feather-bedding for lawyers? Although corporations may be represented by lawyers in their employ (house counsel), the organized bar and some state courts take a dim view of efforts by liability insurers to handle the defense of insured tortfeasors through salaried lawyers.[28]

Turf Wars in Real Estate and Other Fields

All large accounting firms have large in-house legal staffs. These lawyers help in the services that accounting firms provide their clients. Similarly, all large banks have legal departments that help in the financial services that banks provide their customers. Further, all large corporations have legal departments that help in corporate operations. All these forms of legal service give legal shape to transactions involving the clients or customers of these organizations.

Are these business organizations involved in the "unauthorized practice of law"? The technical answer has been that the corporation is engaged in unauthorized practice if its lawyers provide legal assistance to *others,* such as the corporation's customers.[29] However, the corporation can provide legal assistance to *itself* without thereby engaging in practice of law. This conclusion has never been fully reconciled with the proposition that a corporation's law department lawyers are treated as full-fledged practitioners for purposes of the attorney-client privilege. That is, corporate law department attorneys are regarded as rendering legal advice to someone (the corporation) for purposes of the attorney-client privilege,[30] but are not regarded as providing legal services to that someone for purposes of the unauthorized practice of law prohibition.

---

27. 666 A.2d 904 (Md.App.1995).

28. See, e.g., American Ins. Ass'n v. Kentucky Bar Ass'n, 917 S.W.2d 568 (Ky.1996) (liability insurer's use of inside counsel to defend law suits brought against its insureds creates "impermissible conflicts of interest between the insurance defense attorney and the insured" and interferes with insured's right to an independent defense); Gardner v. North Carolina State Bar, 341 S.E.2d 517 (N.C.1986) (use of in-house claim litigation counsel constitutes unauthorized practice of law by insurer).

29. See, e.g., the case law discussed in *Perkins* supra; and In re Mid–American Living Trust Associates, Inc., 927 S.W.2d 855 (Mo. 1996) (corporation and its non-lawyer agents ordered to cease preparing or assisting in the preparation of estate planning instruments for Missouri residents without the direct supervision of a Missouri lawyer selected by and representing those individuals).

30. See Upjohn Co. v. United States, 449 U.S. 383 (1981), p. 209 supra.

Efforts by the bar to restrict the activities performed by staff lawyers of corporations engaged in other business have had mixed success. The ability of accounting firms to handle tax matters is rooted in federal law that displaces state unauthorized practice law. Statutes and regulations allow "tax practitioners" (a term that includes all certified public accountants) to give tax advice, prepare tax returns and, more recently, have an attorney-client privilege in most communications with clients. Financial institutions, however, have had only limited success in enlarging their business by offering estate planning services through staff lawyers that involve inter vivos or testamentary instruments. Competition between interests desiring to profit from the handling of residential real estate transactions has led to a variegated pattern reflecting local struggles and their judicial and political outcomes.

In 1962, for example, a much-publicized instance of conflict between realtors and lawyers arose in Arizona. The state bar succeeded in persuading the Arizona Supreme Court that the existing practice in which realtors, in conjunction with title insurance companies, prepared legal documents in real estate transactions, was unauthorized practice of law.[31] The realtors reacted with a petition campaign to reverse the court's decision by means of a constitutional amendment. The constitutional amendment was adopted by an overwhelming vote.

Three interest groups have fought to gain control of the market for residential real estate closings: lawyers, real estate brokers, and various business organizations (title companies, escrow agents and mortgage lenders). In the Northeast lawyers have generally reigned supreme. In California and other parts of the West, where brokers and escrow agents have been allowed to compete with lawyers, buyers and sellers have chosen escrow agents in preference to lawyers. In those states the only lawyer to review any portion of the transaction works not for the buyer or seller but for the escrow agent, the title company or the lender.[32]

In New Jersey a dual system evolved: in South Jersey brokers and title companies came to dominate all aspects of residential real estate closings; in North Jersey, lawyers remained in control of closings. The simmering turf war came to a boil in 1995, when the New Jersey State Bar Association renewed efforts to have the New Jersey Supreme Court determine that it was unauthorized practice for a lay person to represent others at a real estate closing.[33] The court upheld the South Jersey practice, while stating

---

31. State Bar of Arizona v. Arizona Land Title & Trust Co., 366 P.2d 1 (Ariz.1961), opinion on rehearing, 371 P.2d 1020 (Ariz. 1962). The controversy is described in Merton E. Marks, The Lawyers and the Realtors: Arizona's Experience, 49 A.B.A.J. 139 (1963).

32. Margaret A. Jacobs, More Home Buyers, Sellers Are Skipping the Lawyer, Wall St.J., Apr. 6, 1995, at B1 (estimating that fewer than 5% of buyers and sellers use a lawyer, preferring to pay the escrow agent a fee—usually 0.5% of the sale price).

33. In re Opinion No. 26 of the Committee on Unauthorized Practice of Law, 654 A.2d 1344 (N.J.1995) (asserting the court's "exclusive power of the practice of law" but deferring to the realities of consumer choice; a court-drafted standard form warning consumers of the risks was appended to the opinion).

its "strong" belief that "both parties should retain counsel for their own protection and that the savings in lawyers' fees are not worth the risks involved in proceeding without counsel." As a matter of public policy, the court concluded, home buyers and sellers should be free to choose brokers and title companies to assist them, providing they are adequately informed of the risks. The conflict of interest arising from the broker's interest in closing the transaction (no commission if no sale) could be handled by warning buyers of this risk as well as others. The decision was based on a factual record that showed that the use of standardized procedures by business organizations had not created significant problems and cost less than lawyers.[34]

Substantial conflict of interest problems arise when commercial entities such as insurers, trust companies or realtors perform legal services for their customers. The principal business of each is to sell something to the public, such as insurance in the case of insurance companies or trust services in the case of trust companies. If staff lawyers deal with customers in this setting, they may not provide the independent judgment expected of an outside lawyer. If competition is allowed, fiduciary and malpractice law, along with discipline of in-house lawyers, will have to be relied on to protect consumers against instances of impartial advice or impermissible conflict of interest.

An underlying issue, rarely discussed directly, is whether or not "professionalism," when properly understood, is inconsistent with, or threatened by, competition among lawyers and between lawyers and other service providers. This issue arises in connection with virtually every issue relating to regulation of what is offered to the public under the rubric of legal services: unauthorized practice, advertising and solicitation, group legal services, restrictions on form of practice, publicly subsidized legal services for the poor and other matters. What is the causal connection between the virtues of "professionalism," if they can be identified, and a competitive marketplace?[35]

B.   ADVERTISING AND SOLICITATION

1.   PROFESSIONAL TRADITIONS AND RULES

Traditional Ban on Lawyer Advertising[1]

The world has changed so much since 1976, when the Supreme Court first accorded free speech protection to "commercial speech,"[2] that today's

---

34. In South Jersey, where two-thirds of buyers and sellers relied on brokers exclusively, closing costs were $200–300, whereas lawyers charged $350–650 for the same services. Would the differential be larger if home buyers were required to use lawyers?

35. See the discussion of "professionalism" and civility at p. 965 supra.

1. For discussion of the history of lawyer advertising, see Lori B. Andrews, Birth of a Salesman: Lawyer Advertising and Solicitation (1980).

2. See Virginia State Bd. of Pharmacy v. Virginia Citizens Consumer Council, Inc.,

law students need to be reminded of the way things were when lawyer advertising was prohibited. In the 19th century lawyers sometimes advertised their services in newspapers or distributed business cards. But a professional tradition that it was unseemly for a lawyer to advertise, carried over from England, dominated the profession and was included in the ABA Canons of Professional Ethics in 1908.

Canon 27 stated in part (in its original form):

> The most worthy and effective advertisement possible, even for a young lawyer, is the establishment of a well-merited reputation for professional capacity and fidelity to trust. This cannot be forced, but must be the outcome of character and conduct.... [S]olicitation of business by circulars or advertisements, or by personal communications, or interviews not warranted by personal relations, is unprofessional.... Indirect advertisement for business by furnishing or inspiring newspaper comments concerning causes in which the lawyer has been or is engaged, ... the importance of the lawyer's positions, and all other like self-laudation, defy the traditions and lower the tone of our high calling, and are intolerable.

During the next six decades, ethics committees put substantial effort into defining the line between appropriate business-getting activities and impermissible ones. A lawyer could have a small, dignified sign ("shingle") to mark the office door, appear in a "reputable law list" (i.e., a directory, such as Martindale–Hubbell, primarily available to other lawyers), and make "customary use" of professional cards and business letterheads. But the sign could not be too large, any listings or advertisements in materials distributed to the public were prohibited and any identification of the lawyer's field of practice was improper (except for a traditional exception for three federal specialties—patent, trademark and admiralty lawyers). In an effort to deal with ingenious efforts at evasion, the professional rules became more and more elaborate. The longest and most detailed provisions of the 1969 Model Code dealt with advertising, solicitation and other efforts to provide information about legal services. See DRs 2–101 through 2–105 and ECs 2–6 through 2–15.

The reported decisions, which deal with such matters as whether distribution of a matchbook embossed with the lawyer's name is permissible,[3] often seem trivial. But the underlying issues were taken very seriously by leaders of the bar. They felt that a distinctive aspect of professionalism was a rejection of the commercial spirit, a posture that reinforced notions of the lawyer as serving larger interests than those of self. Moreover, they believed that advertising of legal services would inevitably be misleading to lay persons, resulting in deception, overreaching and incitement of litiga-

---

425 U.S. 748 (1976) (Virginia statute declaring it unprofessional conduct for licensed pharmacist to advertise prices of prescription drugs held invalid under First Amendment); Bates v. State Bar of Ari-

zona, 433 U.S. 350 (1977) (commercial speech protection extended to lawyer advertising of price of routine legal services).

3. See In re Maltby, 202 P.2d 902 (Ariz. 1949) (condemning matchbooks).

tion. "[P]ublic confidence in our legal system would be impaired by ... advertisements of legal services" because "it would inevitably produce unrealistic expectations in particular cases and bring about distrust of the law and lawyers." EC 2–9.

The scope of the ban on advertising and the profession's commitment to it are conveyed by the following cases:

• Berezniak distributed a calendar to "theatrical people" describing himself as specializing in "theatrical law" and containing testimonials praising his services (e.g., "Berezniak is one of the few lawyers who look for the interest of the client first and the money second"). In reprimanding Berezniak (and threatening disbarment if he persisted in such unprofessional conduct), the court said: "The advertisements of respondent are very obnoxious and disgusting, not only because they are gotten up after the manner of quack doctors and itinerant vendors of patent medicines ..., but because of the fact that they contain statements that cast reflections upon the common honesty, proficiency, and decency of the profession generally...."[4]

• Gray, a New York City lawyer, was censured for soliciting claims for collection and other legal business in letters addressed to businesses with which he had no professional relation (in one such letter he asked business firms to try his service by sending some of their "smaller business" to him). "Business men," who received such communications, the court said, "would be likely to [reach the repugnant conclusion] that the law was not, as consistently maintained, a learned *profession,* but had deteriorated into a mere *business,* where the most persistent and adroit self-advertiser would be the most successful."[5]

• Crocker published a classified advertisement in a daily newspaper offering to do "default divorces" for "$15 and costs." The Nebraska court suspended him for 30 days, saying that "[a]n advertisement in a newspaper by an attorney at law soliciting divorce cases is conduct requiring discipline."[6]

• In 1962 *LIFE* magazine published a feature article profiling the Olwine firm of New York City, describing the 25–lawyer firm in generally laudatory terms (e.g., a "blue chip" firm that enjoys "the cream of corporate business"). Four partners were censured for these self-promotion activities. The court said: "These actions tending prominently to publicize the names of these attorneys and their special qualifications, constitute indirect advertising[,] 'offend the traditions and lower the tone of our profession' ..., and require disciplinary action."[7]

4. People ex rel. Chicago Bar Ass'n v. Berezniak, 127 N.E. 36, 40 (Ill.1920).

5. In re Gray, 172 N.Y.S. 648, 652 (N.Y.App.Div.1918).

6. State ex rel. Hunter v. Crocker, 271 N.W. 444, 447 (Neb.1937).

7. Matter of Connelly, 240 N.Y.S.2d 126, 139 (N.Y.App.Div. 1963). As late as 1974, Marvin Belli, the self-styled "King of Torts," was suspended in California for 30 days for sending to *Time* and *Newsweek* a news release puffing the 20th anniversary of his annual seminar for trial lawyers and

Beginning in the 1960s forces within and without the profession began to challenge the total prohibition on advertising. The consumer movement, supported by the Department of Justice and the Federal Trade Commission, challenged paternalistic assumptions that consumers were incapable of intelligent use of the information provided by advertising.[8] The growth of the legal services movement, providing civil legal assistance to poor people, invoked concerns within and without the profession concerning the distribution of legal services. And some groups within a larger and more heterogeneous legal profession sought to develop new modes of delivery, such as legal clinics.[9]

Model Rules on Lawyer Advertising

Model Rules 7.1 and 7.2 make all advertising subject to requirements of truthfulness. The Rules also require that a lawyer maintain copies of all written solicitations for a specified period, such as two years, following their dissemination. This requirement allows enforcement authorities to verify the text of any such communications. Read the text of these rules and their comments at this time.

In 1983, when the American Bar Association adopted the Model Rules of Professional Conduct, the ABA rejected the Kutak Commission's recommendation that "targeted" letters be permitted along with newspaper advertisements, circulars distributed by a general mailing and other forms of written communication to the general public. Model Rule 7.3 allowed lawyers to send "non-targeted" letters but not "targeted" ones. This provision was attacked in the *Shapero* case, reprinted below, which quotes the 1983 rule. Following the *Shapero* case, M.R. 7.3 was amended. That rule and its Comment should be read at this time.

2.   FREE SPEECH AND LAWYER BUSINESS-GETTING ACTIVITIES

First Amendment Protection of Lawyer Advertising

Lawyer efforts to gain business by various forms of advertising and solicitation are now largely protected by authoritative interpretations of the First Amendment. The major current exception is in-person solicitation of legal business. Some state rules, however, impose special requirements on

---

for appearing in a *New York Times* advertisement endorsing Glenfiddich Scotch Whiskey. Belli v. State Bar, 519 P.2d 575 (Cal.1974).

8. See, for example, Justice Department testimony on the anticompetitive effect of the ban on advertising. See 60 A.B.A.J. 791, 792 (1974).

9. Critics argued that the premise that lawyers could build a practice by gradual growth of repute in the community was inappropriate in urban settings and was perpetuated by elite lawyers as a means of suppressing competition from new entrants. See Jerold S. Auerbach, Unequal Justice 43–44 (1976) ("The Canons especially impeded those lawyers who worked in a highly competitive urban market with a transient clientele ... [and reduced] the opportunity of an accident victim to recover damages"); Philip Shuchman, Ethics and Legal Ethics: The Propriety of the Canons as a Group Moral Code, 37 Geo. Wash.L.Rev. 244, 266–77 (1968) (attacking restrictions on advertising).

radio and television advertising and restrict written communication to accident victims or relatives within a stated period after an accident.

Even before the Supreme Court extended constitutional protection to commercial speech, two Arizona lawyers, Bates and O'Steen, who had opened a legal clinic in Phoenix "to provide legal services at modest fees to persons of moderate income who did not qualify for governmental legal aid," challenged Arizona's prohibition of all lawyer advertising on antitrust[10] and First Amendment grounds. Thus began the series of landmark cases putting First Amendment protection around lawyer advertising.

The current First Amendment standards for evaluating restrictions on commercial speech are set out in Central Hudson Gas & Electric Corp. v. Public Service Commission.[11] The *Central Hudson* test protects commercial speech (defined as "expression solely related to the economic interests of the speaker and its audience") that concerns lawful activity. Regulation is upheld only if: (1) the asserted government interest is "substantial," (2) the regulation "directly advances" that interest and (3) the regulation is no more extensive than necessary to serve that interest. Some of the leading cases are as follows:

- Bates v. State Bar of Arizona[12] involved newspaper advertising of a legal clinic that offered "legal services at very reasonable rates" and listed standard charges for certain matters (e.g., $175 plus $20 filing fee for an uncontested divorce). Such truthful advertising was held protected by the "commercial speech" component of the First Amendment.

- In re R.M.J.,[13] upholding First Amendment protection of truthful information in professional announcements circulated to potential clients, indicated that a state could require any such written communications to be labeled as an "advertisement."

- Zauderer v. Office of Disciplinary Counsel[14] held that lawyers could use "targeted" newspaper advertisements. The newspaper advertisement in that case invited Dalkon Shield claimants to contact the attorney concerning possible personal injury claims.

- Peel v. Attorney Registration and Disciplinary Commission[15] held that a truthful ad that identified a lawyer as certified by a particular

---

10. *Bates* rejected the antitrust challenge under the state action immunity, which permits an anticompetitive policy that is created and enforced by a state instrumentality, such as public utility regulation. Because Arizona's ban on lawyer advertising rested on a rule of its Supreme Court, it was within the state action immunity. *Compare* Hoover v. Ronwin, 466 U.S. 558 (1984) (a bar admission policy designed to limit the number of new entrants was a "clearly articulated state ... policy" "actively supervised" by a state agency and

therefore within the state action immunity), *with* Goldfarb v. Virginia State Bar, 421 U.S. 773 (1975) (minimum fee guidelines of state bar as a private association violate the antitrust laws).

11. 447 U.S. 557 (1980).

12. 433 U.S. 350 (1977).

13. 455 U.S. 191, 206, n. 20 (1982).

14. 471 U.S. 626 (1985).

15. 496 U.S. 91 (1990), a plurality decision in which Justice Marshall concurred on the

private lawyer association was not misleading. See M.R. 7.4 (communication of fields of practice) and discussion at p. 1034 infra.

In–Person Solicitation

The two leading cases on in-person solicitation were decided on the same day in 1978, one upholding discipline and the other striking it down.

OHRALIK v. OHIO STATE BAR ASSOCIATION.[16] Ohralik was indefinitely suspended for in-person solicitation of legal employment. Learning from a casual acquaintance that an 18–year old woman, Carol, had been injured in an auto accident, Ohralik contacted her parents, learned some details of the accident, and then visited the woman, who was hospitalized and in traction, and asked her to sign a contingent-fee agreement. Carol replied that she would have to speak to her parents first, but that he could "go ahead." A further visit to the parents led to an examination of the insurance policy and provided the name and address of Wanda, a passenger in the car driven by Carol. With a concealed tape recorder, Ohralik proceeded to Wanda's house and informed her that Carol's parents' insurance policy would provide her with a recovery of up to $12,500. Wanda agreed orally to representation. The following day Wanda's mother informed Ohralik that neither she nor Wanda wanted to sue nor did they wish him to represent them. Despite the discharge, Ohralik sued and obtained one-third of Wanda's insurance recovery, claiming that she had breached the oral fee agreement. A subsequent complaint to disciplinary authorities resulted in Ohralik's indefinite suspension for violating the solicitation rules.

On these facts the Court unanimously held that Ohio "has a legitimate and indeed 'compelling' interest in preventing those aspects of solicitation that involve fraud, undue influence, intimidation, overreaching, and other forms of 'vexatious conduct.' ... The facts in this case present a striking example of the potential for overreaching that is inherent in a lawyer's in-person solicitation of professional employment.[17] They also demonstrate the need for prophylactic regulation in furtherance of the State's interest in protecting the lay public."[18]

IN RE PRIMUS.[19] Edna Primus was employed as a legal consultant for a non-profit South Carolina organization and served as a cooperating lawyer with the American Civil Liberties Union (ACLU). In 1973, after reports that pregnant mothers in Aiken County, S.C., were being sterilized as a condition of receiving further benefits, an Aiken businessman asked the organization to send a representative to talk to the women who had

narrower ground that the state's total ban was too broad and also added that a state could require a disclaimer to accompany the certification by a private organization.

16.   436 U.S. 447 (1978).

17.   The opinion emphasized that Ohralik had approached the two young women when they were especially vulnerable; he urged his services upon them, describing his fee arrangement in a tantalizing way; he used a concealed tape recorder to preserve evidence of an oral fee agreement; and he refused to withdraw when asked to do so.

18.   Id. at 462, 468.

19.   436 U.S. 412 (1978).

been sterilized. Primus responded and later met with a number of women, including Mary Etta Williams. At the meeting, Primus advised the women of their legal rights and suggested the possibility of a lawsuit. Later, after being informed by the ACLU that it would provide representation for the sterilized mothers, Primus wrote Ms. Williams telling her that she would be coming back to Aiken in the near future, that the ACLU would support a lawsuit, and they could talk further at that time "[a]bout the lawsuit, if you are interested...." When Ms. Williams took a sick child to her physician, she was met with a lawyer who asked her to sign a release of liability in the physician's favor. Ms. Williams provided the lawyer with the letter from Primus and then called Primus to say that she did not want to sue. On the basis of the letter, the South Carolina Supreme Court upheld a public reprimand of Primus for improper solicitation of Ms. Williams.

Primus appealed, asserting that her activity was constitutionally protected expression and association. The Supreme Court agreed, noting that unlike *Ohralik*, Primus' activity "was not in-person solicitation for pecuniary gain," as "her actions were undertaken to express personal political beliefs and to advance the civil-liberties objectives of the ACLU, rather than to derive financial gain." The Court, quoting NAACP v. Button,[20] held that "[t]he First and Fourteenth Amendments require a measure of protection for 'advocating lawful means of vindicating legal rights,' ... including 'advising another that his legal rights have been infringed and referring him to a particular attorney or group of attorneys ... for assistance." Furthermore, although the state had an interest in regulating lawyer solicitation, its actions here were not narrowly tailored to further this interest: the application of the disciplinary rules had "a distinct potential for dampening the kind of 'cooperative activity that would make advocacy of litigation meaningful,' ... as well as for permitting discretionary enforcement against unpopular causes."[21]

Justice Rehnquist, dissenting in *Primus*, argued that a state should be free to prohibit in-person solicitation by lawyers whatever the motive of the lawyer; the *Button* case should be confined to solicitation for political purposes by lay members of organizations. The reliance on the assumed motives of lawyers, rather than on the nature of the conduct the state was regulating, was unprincipled and unsound. From Rehnquist's viewpoint, a personal injury lawyer, such as Ohralik, may act with lofty motives, and a public interest lawyer may be moved by considerations of power, status, or, when a fee-shifting statute is involved, money. Is Rehnquist right? Does *Primus* permit a lawyer to solicit the homeowners in a neighborhood to bring a toxic tort suit against a nearby industry? A damage action against the developer for failure to provide the common amenities promised in the sales contract? Does it depend upon whether monetary or injunctive relief

---

20. 371 U.S. 415 (1963) (collective activity undertaken to obtain meaningful access to courts is a fundamental right under the First Amendment).

21. 436 U.S. at 421–22, 437, 433.

is sought? Whether the lawyer employs a contingent fee retainer agreement or hopes for an attorneys' fee award from a class action?

The *Shapero* case, reprinted below, interprets *Ohralik* as supporting a categorical ban on all in-person solicitation for pecuniary gain. Thus a telephone call or home visit conveying the same information as a targeted letter would subject the lawyer to discipline. Yet those soliciting charitable contributions have a constitutionally protected right to do door-to-door solicitation.[22] So do accountants who seek to obtain new clients by direct, in-person and uninvited solicitation.[23] Are lawyers more dishonest than those who solicit for charities? Is abuse more likely with lawyers than accountants? Louise Hill argues that "the categorical proscriptions on in-person solicitation ... lack a firm historical basis and constitute a violation of the first amendment."[24]

Written Solicitation of Particular Matters

Shapero v. Kentucky Bar Association

Supreme Court of the United States, 1988.
486 U.S. 466, 108 S.Ct. 1916.

■ JUSTICE BRENNAN announced the judgment of the Court and delivered the opinion of the Court as to Parts I and II [considering the constitutionality of the Kentucky ethics rule] and an opinion as to Part III in which JUSTICE MARSHALL, JUSTICE BLACKMUN, and JUSTICE KENNEDY join [considering whether the particular advertisement was misleading].

This case presents the issue whether a State may, consistent with the First and Fourteenth Amendments, categorically prohibit lawyers from soliciting legal business for pecuniary gain by sending truthful and nondeceptive letters to potential clients known to face particular legal problems.

I

In 1985, petitioner, a member of Kentucky's integrated Bar Association, see Ky.Sup.Ct. Rule 3.030 (1988), applied to the Kentucky Attorneys Advertising Commission for approval of a letter that he proposed to send

---

22. Village of Schaumburg v. Citizens for a Better Environment, 444 U.S. 620 (1980) (ordinance prohibiting most door-to-door and on-the-street solicitation of charitable contributions invalid under First Amendment). The Court in *Schaumburg* distinguished *Ohralik,* stating, "charitable solicitation is not so inherently conducive to fraud and overreaching as to justify its prohibition." Id. at 637–38, note 11.

23. Edenfield v. Fane, 507 U.S. 761 (1993) (Florida's prohibition of in-person solicitation of clients violates the First Amend-

ment; lawyers, unlike accountants, are trained in the art of persuasion and an accountant's clients are not likely to be inexperienced, injured or distressed; privacy was not at issue because accountant Fane made his initial solicitation by mail). Does *Edenfield* mean that a lawyer's in-person solicitation of potential business clients cannot be prohibited?

24. See Louise L. Hill, Solicitation by Lawyers: Piercing the First Amendment Veil, 42 Maine L.Rev. 369, 369–70 (1990).

"to potential clients who have had a foreclosure suit filed against them." The proposed letter read as follows:

> "It has come to my attention that your home is being foreclosed on. If this is true, you may be about to lose your home. Federal law may allow you to keep your home by *ORDERING* your creditor [*sic*] to *STOP* and give you more time to pay them.

> "You may call my office anytime from 8:30 a.m. to 5:00 p.m. for *FREE* information on how you can keep your home.

> "Call *NOW*, don't wait. It may surprise you what I may be able to do for you. Just call and tell me that you got this letter. Remember it is *FREE*, there is *NO* charge for calling."

[The Commission declined to approve the proposal because the then-existing Kentucky Supreme Court Rule prohibited the mailing or delivery of written advertisements "precipitated by a specific event or occurrence involving or relating to the addressee or addressees as distinct from the general public." The Commission, believing that the rule's ban on targeted, direct-mail advertising was inconsistent with the *Zauderer* case, supra, recommended that the Kentucky Supreme Court amend its rules. On review, the Kentucky Supreme Court felt "compelled by the decision in *Zauderer* to order [its current rule] deleted," and replaced it with the ABA's 1983 version of Rule 7.3, which provided:

> A lawyer may not solicit professional employment from a prospective client with whom the lawyer has no family or prior professional relationship, by mail, in-person or otherwise, when a significant motive for the lawyer's doing so is the lawyer's pecuniary gain. The term 'solicit' includes contact in person, by telephone or telegraph, by letter or other writing, or by other communication directed to a specific recipient, but does not include letters addressed or advertising circulars distributed generally to persons not known to need legal services of the kind provided by the lawyer in a particular matter, but who are so situated that they might in general find such services useful.]

... We granted certiorari to resolve whether such a blanket prohibition is consistent with the First Amendment, made applicable to the States through the Fourteenth Amendment, and now reverse.

II

Lawyer advertising is in the category of constitutionally protected commercial speech. See Bates v. State Bar of Arizona, 433 U.S. 350 (1977). The First Amendment principles governing state regulation of lawyer solicitations for pecuniary gain are by now familiar: "Commercial speech that is not false or deceptive and does not concern unlawful activities ... may be restricted only in the service of a substantial governmental interest, and only through means that directly advance that interest." *Zauderer*, supra, 471 U.S., at 638 (citing Central Hudson Gas & Electric Corp. v. Public Service Comm'n of New York, 447 U.S. 557, 566 (1980)). Since state regulation of commercial speech "may extend only as far as the interest it serves," *Central Hudson,* supra, at 565, state rules that are designed to prevent the "potential for deception and confusion ... may be no broader than reasonably necessary to prevent the" perceived evil. In re R.M.J., 455 U.S. 191, 203 (1982).

In *Zauderer,* application of these principles required that we strike an Ohio rule that categorically prohibited solicitation of legal employment for pecuniary gain through advertisements containing information or advice, even if truthful and nondeceptive, regarding a specific legal problem. We distinguished written advertisements containing such information or advice from in-person solicitation by lawyers for profit, which we held in Ohralik v. Ohio State Bar Assn., 436 U.S. 447 (1978), a State may categorically ban. The "unique features of in-person solicitation by lawyers [that] justified a prophylactic rule prohibiting lawyers from engaging in such solicitation for pecuniary gain," we observed, are "not present" in the context of written advertisements. *Zauderer,* 471 U.S. at 641–642.

Our lawyer advertising cases have never distinguished among various modes of written advertising to the general public. See, e.g., *Bates,* supra (newspaper advertising); id., 433 U.S., at 372, n. 26 (equating advertising in telephone directory with newspaper advertising); *In re R.M.J.,* supra (mailed announcement cards treated same as newspaper and telephone directory advertisements). Thus, Ohio could no more prevent Zauderer from mass-mailing to a general population his offer to represent women injured by the Dalkon Shield than it could prohibit his publication of the advertisement in local newspapers. Similarly, if petitioner's letter is neither false nor deceptive, Kentucky could not constitutionally prohibit him from sending at large an identical letter opening with the query, "Is your home being foreclosed on?," rather than his observation to the targeted individuals that "It has come to my attention that your home is being foreclosed on." The drafters of Rule 7.3 apparently appreciated as much, for the Rule exempts from the ban "letters addressed or advertising circulars distributed generally to persons ... who are so situated that they might in general find such services useful."

The court below disapproved petitioner's proposed letter solely because it targeted only persons who were "known to need [the] legal services" offered in his letter, rather than the broader group of persons "so situated that they might in general find such services useful." Generally, unless the advertiser is inept, the latter group would include members of the former. The only reason to disseminate an advertisement of particular legal services among those persons who are "so situated that they might in general find such services useful" is to reach individuals who *actually* "need legal services of the kind provided [and advertised] by the lawyer." But the First Amendment does not permit a ban on certain speech merely because it is more efficient; the State may not constitutionally ban a particular letter on the theory that to mail it only to those whom it would most interest is somehow inherently objectionable.

The court below did not rely on any such theory.... Rather, it concluded that the State's blanket ban on all targeted, direct-mail solicitation was permissible because of the "serious potential for abuse inherent in direct solicitation by lawyers of potential clients known to need specific legal services." By analogy to *Ohralik*, the court observed:

> Such solicitation subjects the prospective client to pressure from a trained lawyer in a direct personal way. It is entirely possible that the potential client may feel overwhelmed by the basic situation which caused the need for the specific legal services and may have seriously impaired capacity for good judgment, sound reason and a natural protective self-interest. Such a condition is full of the possibility of undue influence, overreaching and intimidation.

Of course, a particular potential client will feel equally "overwhelmed" by his legal troubles and will have the same "impaired capacity for good judgment" regardless of whether a lawyer mails him an untargeted letter or exposes him to a newspaper advertisement—concededly constitutionally protected activities—or instead mails a targeted letter. The relevant inquiry is not whether there exist potential clients whose "condition" makes them susceptible to undue influence, but whether the mode of communication poses a serious danger that lawyers will exploit any such susceptibility. Cf. *Ohralik*, supra, 436 U.S., at 470 (Marshall, J., concurring in part and concurring in judgment) ("What is objectionable about Ohralik's behavior here is not so much that he solicited business for himself, but rather the circumstances in which he performed that solicitation and the means by which he accomplished it").

Thus, Respondent's facile suggestion that this case is merely "*Ohralik* in writing" misses the mark. In assessing the potential for overreaching and undue influence, the mode of communication makes all the difference. Our decision in *Ohralik* that a State could categorically ban all in-person solicitation turned on two factors. First was our characterization of face-to-face solicitation as "a practice rife with possibilities for overreaching, invasion of privacy, the exercise of undue influence, and outright fraud." *Zauderer*, supra, 471 U.S. at 641. See *Ohralik*, supra, 436 U.S., at 457–458, 464–465. Second, "unique ... difficulties," *Zauderer*, supra, 471 U.S. at 641, would frustrate any attempt at state regulation of in-person solicitation short of an absolute ban because such solicitation is "not visible or otherwise open to public scrutiny." *Ohralik*, 436 U.S. at 466. See also ibid. ("[I]n-person solicitation would be virtually immune to effective oversight and regulation by the State or by the legal profession"). Targeted, direct-mail solicitation is distinguishable from the in-person solicitation in each respect.

Like print advertising, petitioner's letter—and targeted, direct-mail solicitation generally—"poses much less risk of over-reaching or undue influence" than does in-person solicitation, *Zauderer*, 471 U.S. at 642. Neither mode of written communication involves "the coercive force of the personal presence of a trained advocate" or the "pressure on the potential client for an immediate yes-or-no answer to the offer of representation." Ibid. Unlike the potential client with a badgering advocate breathing down his neck, the recipient of a letter and the "reader of an advertisement ...

can 'effectively avoid further bombardment of [his] sensibilities simply by averting [his] eyes,' "*Ohralik,* supra, 436 U.S. at 465, n. 25 (quoting Cohen v. California, 403 U.S. 15, 21 (1971)). A letter, like a printed advertisement (but unlike a lawyer), can readily be put in a drawer to be considered later, ignored, or discarded. In short, both types of written solicitation "conve[y] information about legal services [by means] that [are] more conducive to reflection and the exercise of choice on the part of the consumer than is personal solicitation by an attorney." *Zauderer,* supra, 471 U.S. at 642. Nor does a targeted letter invade the recipient's privacy any more than does a substantively identical letter mailed at large. The invasion, if any, occurs when the lawyer discovers the recipient's legal affairs, not when he confronts the recipient with the discovery.

Admittedly, a letter that is personalized (not merely targeted) to the recipient presents an increased risk of deception, intentional or inadvertent. It could, in certain circumstances, lead the recipient to overestimate the lawyer's familiarity with the case or could implicitly suggest that the recipient's legal problem is more dire than it really is. Similarly, an inaccurately targeted letter could lead the recipient to believe she has a legal problem that she does not actually have or, worse yet, could offer erroneous legal advice. . . .

But merely because targeted, direct-mail solicitation presents lawyers with opportunities for isolated abuses or mistakes does not justify a total ban on that mode of protected commercial speech. See In re R.M.J., 455 U.S. at 203. The State can regulate such abuses and minimize mistakes through far less restrictive and more precise means, the most obvious of which is to require the lawyer to file any solicitation letter with a state agency, giving the State ample opportunity to supervise mailings and penalize actual abuses. The "regulatory difficulties" that are "unique" to in-person lawyer solicitation, *Zauderer,* supra, 471 U.S. at 641—solicitation that is "not visible or otherwise open to public scrutiny" and for which it is "difficult or impossible to obtain reliable proof of what actually took place," *Ohralik,* supra, 436 U.S. at 466—do not apply to written solicitations. The court below offered no basis for its "belie[f] [that] submission of a blank form letter to the Advertising Commission [does not] provid[e] a suitable protection to the public from overreaching, intimidation or misleading private targeted mail solicitation."

[The state concern that limited resources would prevent disciplinary bodies from scrutinizing a large volume of solicitation letters was not supported by evidence that scrutiny of such letters] will be appreciably more burdensome or less reliable than scrutiny of advertisements. . . . To be sure, a state agency or bar association that reviews solicitation letters might have more work than one that does not. But "[o]ur recent decisions involving commercial speech have been grounded in the faith that the free flow of commercial information is valuable enough to justify imposing on would-be regulators the costs of distinguishing the truthful from the false, the helpful from the misleading, and the harmless from the harmful." *Zauderer,* supra, 471 U.S. at 646.

III

The validity of Rule 7.3 does not turn on whether petitioner's letter itself exhibited any of the evils at which Rule 7.3 was directed. Since, however, the First Amendment overbreadth doctrine does not apply to professional advertising, see *Bates,* 433 U.S., at 379–381, we address respondent's contentions that petitioner's letter is particularly over-reaching, and therefore unworthy of First Amendment protection. In that regard, respondent identifies two features of the letter before us that, in its view, coalesce to convert the proposed letter into "high pressure solicitation, overbearing solicitation," which is not protected. First, respondent asserts that the letter's liberal use of underscored, uppercase letters (e.g., "Call *NOW,* don't wait"; "it is *FREE,* there is *NO* charge for calling") "fairly shouts at the recipient ... that he should employ Shapero." ... Second, respondent objects that the letter contains assertions (e.g., "It may surprise you what I may be able to do for you") that "stat[e] no affirmative or objective fact," but constitute "pure salesman puffery, enticement for the unsophisticated, which commits Shapero to nothing."

The pitch or style of a letter's type and its inclusion of subjective predictions of client satisfaction might catch the recipient's attention more than would a bland statement of purely objective facts in small type. But a truthful and nondeceptive letter, no matter how big its type and how much it speculates can never "shou[t] at the recipient" or "gras[p] him by the lapels," as can a lawyer engaging in face-to-face solicitation. The letter simply presents no comparable risk of over-reaching. . . .

To be sure, a letter may be misleading if it unduly emphasizes trivial or "relatively uninformative fact[s]," In re R.M.J., supra, at 205 (lawyer's statement, "in large capital letters, that he was a member of the Bar to the Supreme Court of the United States"), or offers overblown assurances of client satisfaction, cf. In re Von Wiegen, 470 N.E.2d 838, 847 (N.Y.1984) (solicitation letter to victims of massive disaster informs them that "it is [the lawyer's] opinion that the liability of the defendants is clear"); *Bates,* supra, 433 U.S. at 383–384 ("advertising claims as to the quality of legal services ... may be so likely to be misleading as to warrant restriction"). Respondent does not argue before us that petitioner's letter was misleading in those respects. Nor does respondent contend that the letter is false or misleading in any other respect. Of course, respondent is free to raise, and the Kentucky courts are free to consider, any such argument on remand.

The judgment of the Supreme Court of Kentucky is reversed and the case is remanded for further proceedings not inconsistent with this opinion. [Justices White and Stevens concurred in Parts I and II of the Court's opinion, but dissented from Part III, believing the question of whether the proposed letter was misleading "should be left to the state courts in the first instance."]

■ JUSTICE O'CONNOR, with whom CHIEF JUSTICE REHNQUIST and JUSTICE SCALIA join, dissenting.

Relying primarily on Zauderer v. Office of Disciplinary Counsel of Supreme Court of Ohio, 471 U.S. 626 (1985), the Court holds that States may not prohibit a form of attorney advertising that is potentially more pernicious than the advertising at issue in that case. I agree with the Court that the reasoning in *Zauderer* supports the conclusion reached today. That decision, however, was itself the culmination of a line of cases built on defective premises and flawed reasoning. As today's decision illustrates, the Court has been unable or unwilling to restrain the logic of the underlying analysis within reasonable bounds. The resulting interference with important and valid public policies is so destructive that I believe the analytical framework itself should now be reexamined.

I

Zauderer held that the First Amendment was violated by a state rule that forbade attorneys to solicit or accept employment through advertisements containing information or advice regarding a specific legal problem. I dissented from this holding because I believed that our precedents permitted, and good judgment required, that we give greater deference to the States' legitimate efforts to regulate advertising by their attorneys. Emphasizing the important differences between professional services and standardized consumer products, I concluded that unsolicited legal advice was not analogous to the free samples that are often used to promote sales in other contexts. First, the quality of legal services is typically more difficult for most laypersons to evaluate, and the consequences of a mistaken evaluation of the "free sample" may be much more serious. For that reason, the practice of offering unsolicited legal advice as a means of enticing potential clients into a professional relationship is much more likely to be misleading than superficially similar practices in the sale of ordinary consumer goods. Second, and more important, an attorney has an obligation to provide clients with complete and disinterested advice. The advice contained in unsolicited "free samples" is likely to be colored by the lawyer's own interest in drumming up business, a result that is sure to undermine the professional standards that States have a substantial interest in maintaining. . . .

II

[The dissent then discussed the *Central Hudson* test for commercial speech.] Applying that test to attorney advertising, it is clear to me that the States should have considerable latitude to ban advertising that is *"potentially* or demonstrably misleading,"* In re R.M.J., 455 U.S. 191, 202 (1982) (emphasis added), *as well as* truthful advertising that undermines the substantial governmental interest in promoting the high ethical standards that are necessary in the legal profession.

Some forms of advertising by lawyers might be protected under this test. Announcing the price of an initial consultation might qualify, for example, especially if appropriate disclaimers about the costs of other services were included. Even here, the inherent difficulties of policing such advertising suggest that we should hesitate to interfere with state rules designed to ensure that adequate disclaimers are included and that such advertisements are suitably restrained.

As soon as one steps into the realm of prices for "routine" legal services such as uncontested divorces and personal bankruptcies, however, it is quite clear to me that the States may ban such advertising completely. The contrary decision in *Bates* was in my view inconsistent with the standard test that is now applied in commercial speech cases. Until one becomes familiar with a client's particular problems, there is simply no way to know that one is dealing with a "routine" divorce or bankruptcy. Such an advertisement is therefore inherently misleading if it fails to inform potential clients that they are not necessarily qualified to decide whether their own apparently simple problems can be handled by "routine" legal services. Furthermore, such advertising practices will undermine professional standards if the attorney accepts the economic risks of offering fixed rates for solving apparently simple problems that will sometimes prove not to be so simple after all. For a lawyer to promise the world that such matters as uncontested divorces can be handled for a flat fee will inevitably create incentives to ignore (or avoid discovering) the complexities that would lead a conscientious attorney to treat some clients' cases as anything but routine. It may be possible to devise workable rules that would allow something more than the most minimal kinds of price advertising by attorneys. That task, however, is properly left to the States, and it is certainly not a fit subject for constitutional adjudication. Under the *Central Hudson* test, government has more than ample justification for banning or strictly regulating most forms of price advertising.

. . . Soliciting business from strangers who appear to need particular legal services, when a significant motive for the offer is the lawyer's pecuniary gain, always has a tendency to corrupt the solicitor's professional judgment. This is especially true when the solicitation includes the offer of a "free sample," as petitioner's proposed letter does. I therefore conclude that American Bar Association Model Rule of Professional Conduct 7.3 (1984) sweeps no more broadly than is necessary to advance a substantial governmental interest. . . .

III

The roots of the error in our attorney advertising cases are a defective analogy between professional services and standardized consumer products and a correspondingly inappropriate skepticism about the States' justifications for their regulations.

. . . The best arguments in favor of rules permitting attorneys to advertise are founded in elementary economic principles. See, e.g., Hazard, Pearce, & Stempel, Why Lawyers Should Be Allowed to Advertise: A Market Analysis of Legal Services, 58 N.Y.U.L.Rev. 1084 (1983). Restrictions on truthful advertising, which artificially interfere with the ability of suppliers to transmit price information to consumers, presumably reduce the efficiency of the mechanisms of supply and demand. Other factors being equal, this should cause or enable suppliers (in this case attorneys) to maintain a price/quality ratio in some of their services that is higher than would otherwise prevail. Although one could probably not test this hypothesis empirically, it is inherently plausible. Nor is it implausible to imagine that one effect of restrictions on lawyer advertising, and perhaps sometimes an intended effect, is to enable attorneys to charge their clients more for some services (of a given quality) than they would be able to charge absent the restrictions.

Assuming *arguendo* that the removal of advertising restrictions should lead in the short run to increased efficiency in the provision of legal services, I would not agree that we can safely assume the same effect in the long run. The economic argument against these restrictions ignores the delicate role they may play in preserving the norms of the legal profession. While it may be difficult to defend this role with precise economic logic, I believe there is a powerful argument in favor of restricting lawyer advertising and that this argument is at the very least not easily refuted by economic analysis.

One distinguishing feature of any profession, unlike other occupations that may be equally respectable, is that membership entails an ethical obligation to temper one's selfish pursuit of economic success by adhering to standards of conduct that could not be enforced either by legal fiat or through the discipline of the market. There are sound reasons to continue pursuing the goal that is implicit in the traditional view of professional life. Both the special privileges incident to membership in the profession and the advantages those privileges give in the necessary task of earning a living are means to a goal that transcends the accumulation of wealth. That goal is public service, which in the legal profession can take a variety of familiar forms. This view of the legal profession need not be rooted in romanticism or self-serving sanctimony, though of course it can be. Rather, special ethical standards for lawyers are properly understood as an appropriate means of restraining lawyers in the exercise of the unique power that they inevitably wield in a political system like ours. . . .

Imbuing the legal profession with the necessary ethical standards is a task that involves a constant struggle with the relentless natural force of economic self-interest. It cannot be accomplished directly by legal rules, and it certainly will not succeed if sermonizing is the strongest tool that may be employed. Tradition and experiment have suggested a number of formal and informal mechanisms, none of which is adequate by itself and many of which may serve to reduce competition (in the narrow economic sense) among members of the profession. A few examples include the great efforts made during this century to improve the quality and breadth of the legal education that is required for admission to the bar; the concomitant attempt to cultivate a sub-class of genuine scholars within the profession; the development of bar associations that aspire to be more than trade groups; strict disciplinary rules about conflicts of interest and client abandonment; and promotion of the expectation that an attorney's history of voluntary public service is a relevant factor in selecting judicial candidates.

Restrictions on advertising and solicitation by lawyers properly and significantly serve the same goal. Such restrictions act as a concrete, day-to-day reminder to the practicing attorney of why it is improper for any member of this profession to regard it as a trade or occupation like any other....

In my judgment, however, fairly severe constraints on attorney advertising can continue to play an important role in preserving the legal profession as a genuine profession. Whatever may be the exactly appropriate scope of these restrictions at a given time and place, this Court's recent decisions reflect a myopic belief that "consumers," and thus our Nation, will benefit from a constitutional theory that refuses to recognize either the essence of professionalism or its fragile and necessary foundations. Compare, e.g., *Bates,* 433 U.S., at 370–372, with id., at 400–401, and n. 11 (Powell, J., concurring in part and dissenting in part). In one way or another, time will uncover the folly of this approach. I can only hope that the Court will recognize the danger before it is too late to effect a worthwhile cure.

———

Targeted Mail After *Shapero*

How did lawyer Shapero plan to expand his law practice? What result if he had included the same information in a newspaper ad in a local newspaper? Are those who have a specific legal problem (e.g., someone facing a home foreclosure) more vulnerable to advertising than those among a newspaper's general readership who have the same problem? Is Justice Brennan correct in arguing that the state's interest in preventing deception or overreaching may be handled by requiring all letters to be deposited with the state disciplinary agency?

After the decision in *Shapero* invalidated M.R. 7.3 as promulgated in 1983, the ABA amended Model Rules 7.2 and 7.3. The revised rule, M.R. 7.3(c), adopts the suggestion in *In re R.M.J.* that the First Amendment does not preclude a requirement that advertising material be labeled as such. Also, M.R. 7.3(a) differentiates between in-person solicitation resulting in pecuniary gain and other solicitation. This attempts to track *Ohralik* and *Primus,* supra.

The Court's decision in *Shapero* suggested that, aside from possible issues concerning special rules for radio and TV advertising, the landscape of lawyer advertising had achieved stability. False and misleading ads were prohibited along with in-person solicitation for pecuniary gain; other forms of lawyer advertising were permissible. That assumption was challenged in 1995 by Florida Bar v. Went for It, Inc.

Targeted Mail to Accident Victims and Their Relatives

FLORIDA BAR v. WENT FOR IT, INC.[1] The Florida State Bar, concerned about the public image of the legal profession, conducted a two-year study that resulted in recommendations that Florida prohibit plaintiffs' lawyers from written solicitation of accident victims and their relatives. The Florida Supreme Court subsequently adopted two amendments to its Rules of Professional Conduct. The new provisions were intended to protect the privacy of victims and increase the public repute of the legal profession. One rule prohibited direct mail contact from a lawyer to a victim or the family of a victim within thirty days of an accident or disaster. The second rule prohibited a lawyer from accepting referrals from a service whose actions would violate the first rule if the lawyer had performed the activity.

A lawyer and his lawyer referral service (Went For It, Inc.) challenged the new rules on First Amendment grounds. After lower courts, relying on the *Shapero* case, had entered summary judgment for Went For It, Inc., the Supreme Court granted certiorari and reversed in a five-four decision. The two opinions, Justice O'Connor for the majority and Justice Kennedy for the dissent, disagreed on the application of the *Central Hudson* test to the commercial speech regulated by the Florida rules and the scope of the *Shapero* holding.

Justice O'Connor's majority opinion, applying the three-part test of *Central Hudson*, upheld Florida's restrictions on lawyer solicitation of accident victims and their families. The first prong, a substantial government interest in regulating commercial speech, was satisfied by Florida's interest in protecting potential clients' privacy and in "maintaining the professionalism of the members of the bar." The second prong, that the regulation must directly and materially advance the state's interest, was also satisfied. The Court relied on the Florida Bar's report of its two-year study of public attitudes toward the legal profession, which included survey and polling data, much anecdotal evidence, and many newspaper stories and clippings. The third prong, requiring that the regulation be narrowly tailored to fit the interest, was also met, primarily because the duration of the prohibition (thirty days) was short.

Although conceding that "some of *Shapero*'s language might be read to [control this case]," Justice O'Connor distinguished *Shapero* on three grounds:

> First and foremost, *Shapero*'s treatment of privacy was casual [because Kentucky in that case] did not seek to justify its regulation as a measure undertaken to prevent lawyers' invasion of privacy interests.... Second, in contrast to this case, *Shapero* dealt with a broad ban on all direct-mail solicitations, whatever the time frame and whoever the recipient. Finally, the State in *Shapero* assembled no

---

1. 515 U.S. 618 (1995). Both of the post-*Shapero* appointees who had not previously voted on a lawyer commercial speech case, Thomas and Breyer, joined the three dissenters in *Shapero* to create the majority.

For discussion of *Went for It*, see Ronald D. Rotunda, Professionalism, Legal Advertising, and Free Speech in the Wake of *Florida Bar v. Went for It, Inc.*, 49 Ark.L.Rev. 703 (1997).

evidence attempting to demonstrate any actual harm caused by target-ed direct mail.

In *Went for It*, Florida was protecting "the personal privacy and tranquility of [its] citizens from crass commercial intrusion by attorneys upon their personal grief in times of trauma." A letter confronting a victim or relative "while wounds are still open, in order to solicit their business," was very different from a written solicitation under other circumstances. The information gathered by the Florida Bar indicated both that direct solicitation within 30 days of an accident invaded privacy interests and, by impairing the public's view of lawyers, harmed the state's interest in the reputation of a state-regulated profession.[2]

Justice Kennedy's dissent, joined by three other justices, relied on the sweep of the Court's holding in the *Shapero* case, printed above. Written communications, the dissent stated, were not threatening speech, in part because, unlike an in-person solicitation, the letter could be "put in a drawer to be considered later, ignored, or discarded." Because of the nature of mail contact, the condition of the recipient is irrelevant and thus the state interest in protecting victims does not pass the first prong of *Central Hudson*. Restrictions on speech, Kennedy argued, are not justified merely because they offend the listener. This principle applied to commercial speech when the audience was not a captive one, but could deal with "objectionable mailings" by "taking the short journey from mail box to trash can."

The dissent also disagreed with the majority's reliance on the "un-scientific" surveys conducted by the Florida Bar, concluding that there was inadequate evidence that the regulation would materially advance any state interest, which could not include the improper interest of protecting the reputation of the bar. The "crass behavior of a few" lawyers could not be the basis for forbidding communications that "served vital purposes in the administration of justice," such as informing citizens of their rights and putting them in a position to vindicate those rights. Justice Kennedy also argued that the Florida rules were far too broad to be a reasonable fit with the state's asserted interest in the privacy of victims and their families. He emphasized the danger to accident victims if prompt investigations by counsel did not record and preserve relevant evidence.[3]

Went for It prohibits personal injury plaintiffs' lawyers (but not defense lawyers or liability insurers) from soliciting employment by sending target-

---

2. A subsequent Texas statute prohibiting any direct mail contact to accident victims and their families by attorneys, chiropractors, surgeons, physicians or private investigators until thirty days have elapsed from the time of the accident was upheld as to lawyers (other professionals were not considered) in *Moore v. Morales*, 63 F.3d 358 (5th Cir.1995). The court followed *Went For It*, but, in the absence of a bar study, relied on expert testimony of the potential detriment to victims and their families, a showing of a large number of complaints, and direct testimony of victims and relatives who received direct mail solicitations.

3. Cf. *Ficker v. Curran*, 119 F.3d 1150 (4th Cir.1997) (striking down a Maryland prohibition on lawyer solicitation of criminal and traffic defendants for 30 days after their arrest).

ed direct mail to accident victims and their relatives within 30 days of the accident. For the first time, the Court held that a state's interest in maintaining lawyer professionalism and the public perception of lawyers were substantial interests justifying a limitation on otherwise lawful commercial speech.[4]

In *Went for It* the Court said that a letter to an accident victim or relative soliciting legal employment shortly after the accident is "universally regarded as deplorable and beneath common decency." Is this the case without regard to the content of the letter? How about a letter that carefully and accurately summarizes legal rights, the importance of a prompt investigation that will discover evidence and witnesses before they disappear, alternative fee arrangements, the range of contingent fee percentages in the field and mentions the law firm only on the letterhead? Is it also "deplorable and beneath common decency" for a liability insurer to seek information concerning the accident through an investigator or send letters presenting a settlement offer? Can the insurance company's contacts be constitutionally prohibited?

Florida, following M.R. 7.3(c), requires solicitation letters to include the words "Advertising Material" on the outside envelope. If a recipient doesn't want to be bothered at the time, why isn't throwing the letter away unopened an adequate protection of privacy? Justice O'Connor's response was that the bar "is concerned not with citizens' 'offense' in the abstract," but is seeking "to forestall the outrage and irritation with the state-licensed legal profession that the practice of direct solicitation only days after accidents has engendered." Is that a "substantial" state interest?

In Ficker v. Curran,[5] a criminal defense lawyer, who customarily obtained clients by mailing letters to traffic defendants facing possible incarceration, challenged a Maryland criminal statute prohibiting such mail solicitation within thirty days of the criminal or traffic charge. A lawyer's direct-mail solicitation of a criminal defendant, the court held, is fundamentally different from that of a personal-injury plaintiff and is constitutionally protected speech. The court rejected arguments that privacy interests, the danger of overreaching, and protection of the repute of the profession were substantial enough interests in this context; the privacy interest of criminal defendants is minimal in light of the public nature of the charge, and criminal defendants, unlike potential tort claimants, must act promptly to preserve their rights. Don't potential tort claimants have to act promptly to discover and preserve evidence?

---

4. Cf. Zauderer v. Office of Disciplinary Counsel, 471 U.S. 626, 648 (1985): "[W]e are unsure that the State's desire that attorneys maintain their dignity in their communications with the public is an interest substantial enough to justify the abridgment of [lawyers'] First Amendment rights.... [T]he mere possibility that some members of the population might find advertising embarrassing or offensive cannot justify suppressing it. The same must be true for advertising that some members of the bar might find beneath their dignity."

5. 119 F.3d 1150 (4th Cir.1997).

Effect of Advertising on Public's Perception of Lawyers

Although it is widely assumed that lawyer advertising has contributed to the decline in repute of lawyers since 1976 (the year prior to *Bates*), careful examination of available studies suggests that there is no connection between advertising and public attitudes toward lawyer.[6] The decline since 1976 has been relatively small and most of it occurred in 1992–93, some fifteen years after lawyer advertising began.[7] The most elaborate study of the effects of various types of lawyer ads on public perceptions, research undertaken by the ABA Commission of Professionalism,[8] shows that the non-stylish "talking heads" ads, which are the only television ads some states allow, leave viewers believing that lawyers are less honest and knowledgeable. On the other hand, well-crafted television advertising by lawyers (the kinds of advertising that a number of states now prohibit) has a positive effect on public attitudes as to whether lawyers are honest, greedy, and caring. Surprisingly, viewers of a third type of ads—sensational or cartoonish commercials—increased viewers' perceptions of the professionalism, knowledge, helpfulness and effectiveness of lawyers.

Other Recent Developments

The *Went for It* decision reopened issues that many thought had been settled by *Shapero*. Given the deep feelings that many lawyers have about lawyer advertising, it was inevitable that some state bars would seek adoption of rules testing the limits on restricting solicitation. Most of the developments involve the same context as the *Went for It* case: written solicitation of an accident victim or relative shortly after the event.[9] But some promulgated rules have a broader sweep or a different context.

In 1996, a federal statute dealing with safety in air transportation also included a provision prohibiting unsolicited communications within thirty days of an air crash "concerning a potential action for personal injury or wrongful death ... made by an attorney or any potential party to the litigation to an individual injured in the accident, or to a relative of an individual involved in the accident...."[10] This prohibition, unlike that of

---

6. See William E. Hornsby, Jr. & Kurt Schimmel, Regulating Lawyer Advertising: Public Images and the Irresistible Aristotelian Impulse, 9 Geo.J.Leg.Eth. 325 (1996) (summarizing the research done by the ABA Commission on Advertising; reviewing and criticizing various state bar studies, including the Florida bar study relied on by the Court in *Went for It*); Rotunda, supra, Professionalism, Legal Advertising and Free Speech.

7. See Rotunda, Professionalism, Legal Advertising and Free Speech, supra at 729–32.

8. See Hornsby & Schimmel, supra; and ABA Commission on Advertising, Lawyer Advertising at the Crossroads: Professional

Policy Considerations (1995). Rotunda, supra at 731, notes that the only studies linking the public's negative attitudes toward lawyers with advertising or targeted mail have been carried out by state bar group and usually employing unscientific polling techniques; all objective studies, including that of the ABA, reach very different conclusions.

9. Nevada, Texas and other states have followed Florida in banning targeted mail to accident victims within a period after an accident or disaster; other states, including California, New York and Wisconsin, have decided not to act at this time.

10. Federal Aviation Reauthorization Act, 49 U.S.C. § 1136 (1996).

Florida in the *Went For It* case, applies to nonlawyer representatives of liability insurers or potential defendants, as well as to lawyers; its constitutionality has not been determined. Is it constitutional?

Texas has been active in addressing lawyer solicitation: First, a 1993 law made soliciting a potential client in person (or by telephone) by or on behalf of a lawyer a misdemeanor for a first offense but a felony for subsequent offenses. Second, the Texas lawyer disciplinary agency has experimented with "sting tactics" to enforce its prohibition of in-person solicitation of accident victims or their relatives. Third, discipline charges were brought against a prominent Texas plaintiffs' lawyer, John O'Quinn, for soliciting clients after the 1994 USAir crash in North Carolina; a jury subsequently acquitted him.[11]

Unresolved Questions

Some questions remain unresolved. The Court has upheld without argument or opinion the prohibition by some states of radio and television advertisements that are cast in symbolic, evocative and emotional terms or that employ dramatizations or celebrity endorsements.[12] Several states regulate lawyer advertising on the electronic media more stringently than print advertisement.[13] Should the Court, which has been careful to limit its general pronouncements to "written" ads, give states greater leeway in regulating lawyer advertising on radio and television?

Questions also remain concerning advertising containing qualitative claims not subject to verification. Ads that compare the quality of a lawyer's services to other lawyers (a matter not susceptible to objective determination) may be viewed as inherently misleading. Ads that recite past victories (e.g., "three million-dollar verdicts last year") may be deceptive because they give rise to unreasonable expectations.

Claims of special expertise may be regulated even though they cannot be entirely prohibited. In Peel v. Attorney Registration and Disciplinary

11. See Texas Makes Solicitation a Felony, ABA J., Sept. 1993, at 32; Lawyers Feel Bar's Sting, ABA J., Dec.1996, at 32; and Texas Lawyer Not Guilty of Solicitation, Nat'l L.J., Jan. 11, 1999, at A5. O'Quinn was also indicted for criminal solicitation in South Carolina and pled guilty to a misdemeanor.

12. A California lawyer was disciplined for a radio ad in which a former client described the lawyer's handling of a personal injury case and stated: "If I had any legal problem, car accident or anything, I would definitely go back...." Oring v. State Bar of California, 4 Law.Man.Prof.Conduct (ABA/BNA) 206 (July 6, 1988), appeal dismissed for want of a properly presented federal question, 488 U.S. 590 (1989). Subsequently, California changed its rule to permit

testimonials and endorsements if accompanied by a disclaimer that no "guarantee, warranty, or prediction" of outcome is involved.

13. See, e.g., Petition of Felmeister & Isaacs, 518 A.2d 188 (N.J.1986) (forbidding "drawings, animations, dramatizations, music or lyrics ... in connection with televised advertising"); Committee on Professional Ethics v. Humphrey, 377 N.W.2d 643 (Iowa 1985), appeal dism'd, 475 U.S. 1114 (1986) (prohibiting background sound, visual displays and more than one nondramatic voice in radio and television advertisements). Florida has special provisions dealing with ads on the electronic media. Rule 4–7.1(b).

Comm'n of Illinois,[14] the Court held that Illinois could not prohibit a lawyer's truthful statement that he had been "certified" as a "civil trial specialist" by the National Board of Trial Advocacy (NBTA). The NBTA is a private group that has "developed a set of standards and procedures for periodic certification of lawyers with experience and competence in trial work." The plurality opinion of Justice Stevens held that the letterhead was neither actually nor potentially misleading. Justice Marshall, however, who provided the fifth vote for reversal, indicated that a state could require disclaimers to protect against potentially misleading impressions that NBTA was a governmental body or that Peel's certification might "cause people to think that [Peel] is necessarily a better trial lawyer than attorneys without the certification."[15] Bar associations hostile to advertising may, however, require disclaimers in in an effort to destroy an ad's usefulness and thus stop lawyer advertising altogether.[16] Or they may use the lack of a disclaimer as a trap for the unwary. A Texas lawyer was disciplined because a newspaper ad offering to do uncontested divorces for $75–$175 did not include a disclaimer that he was "not certified [by the state] as a specialist in family law"—even though his ad did not claim that he was a specialist.[17]

Use of lay intermediaries to refer legal business may also be subject to state regulation. This is clearly the case when a lawyer pays someone, such as a paramedical, nurse or funeral home attendant, to inform potential clients of the lawyer's services. The prohibition of solicitation of professional employment by direct contact, stated in Model Rule 7.3, is extended to the use of agents by M.R. 8.4(a), which forbids a lawyer from violating a professional rule "through the acts of another."[18] But may a lawyer in person or in writing urge intermediaries to recommend her services? Discipline was upheld in Matter of Alessi,[19] involving a lawyer's letter to 1,000 realtors listing his fees for real estate closings and implicitly seeking referrals of those buying or selling homes. The court thought that conflict of interest considerations were brought in play when the broker acted as an intermediary.

14.   496 U.S. 91 (1990).

15.   496 U.S. at 114.

16.   *Compare* Tillman v. Miller, 133 F.3d 1402 (11th Cir.1998) (striking down a Georgia statutory provision requiring lawyers and others filing workers' compensation claims to put a large legend in their television ads saying that "willfully making a false ... representation to obtain ... benefits is a crime") *with* Office of Disciplinary Counsel v. Shane, 692 N.E.2d 571 (Ohio 1998) (lawyers publicly reprimanded for stating in TV ads that their contingent fee representation involves "no charge unless you win;" ads were misleading because

potential clients were not told that they were responsible for the costs of litigation).

17.   See Daves v. State Bar, 691 S.W.2d 784 (Tex.Ct.App. 1985), appeal dism'd, 474 U.S. 1043 (1986). See also Fight Over Bar Disclaimer Rule in Texas, Nat'l L.J., Feb. 2, 1997, at A6.

18.   See also DR 2–103(C), stating that a "lawyer shall not request a person or organization to recommend or promote the use of his services," with certain limited exceptions.

19.   457 N.E.2d 682 (N.Y.1983).

3.   IS "PROFESSIONALISM" CONSISTENT WITH COMPETITION IN LEGAL SERVICES?

Justice O'Connor's Critique

The *Went for It* case demonstrated that Justice O'Connor's critique of the Court's decisions on lawyer commercial speech (see her Shapero dissent above at p. 1025) may have more bite than appeared likely after the *Shapero* case. Justice O'Connor's views (and those of the Justices joining her in Shapero) reflect an understanding of lawyer "professionalism" that is quite different than that of the majority of Justices in *Shapero*, perhaps a minority today. Within the bar a similar disagreement exists. The differences involve such matters as whether solicitation of law suits vindicates legal rights (the view of Justices Brennan and Marshall) or stirs up costly and often frivolous litigation; and the question whether "commercialism" in law practice threatens the public service orientation of the profession (Justice O'Connor) or increased competition benefits consumers (Justice Blackmun in *Bates*).

The Report of the ABA Commission on Professionalism states that "professionalism" is an "elastic concept" that gets meaning from the historic traditions of the bar as a "learned profession." The Report quotes with approval Roscoe Pound's definition:

> The term refers to a group ... pursuing a learned art as a common calling in the spirit of public service—no less a public service because it may incidentally be a means of livelihood. Pursuit of the learned art in the spirit of a public service is the primary purpose.[20]

Justice O'Connor's dissent in *Shapero* states that professionalism "entails an ethical obligation to temper one's selfish pursuit of economic success" by giving primacy to interests of clients and the legal order. She argues that social arrangements dealing with the recruitment, preparation and conduct of lawyers need to reinforce this altruistic and public service orientation. Practices such as lawyer advertising will cause a diminution in the profession's public-service orientation: "[F]airly severe constraints on attorney advertising" will "act as a concrete, day-to-day reminder to the practicing attorney of why it is improper for any member of this profession to regard it as a trade or occupation like any other." O'Connor's opinion for the Court in *Went for It* also seems energized by a desire to improve the public's perception of the profession's special position.

Is Justice O'Connor correct in concluding that lawyer advertising gives rise to lawyer greed, which is antithetical to "professionalism?" Does her argument rest on the notion that something about the selection and socialization of lawyers makes them more altruistic than the population at large? Were lawyers less self-serving or more altruistic in the days prior to

---

20. ABA Commission on Professionalism, " ... In the Spirit of Public Service:" A Blueprint for the Rekindling of Lawyer Professionalism, 112 F.R.D. at 261.

lawyer advertising? How in concrete terms does lawyer advertising undermine professionalism?[21]

As Justice O'Connor's opinion indicates, the rule against advertising and solicitation helped sustain the special character of the practice of law. Another example of a rule having that effect is the custom in many other countries that an advocate, as well as a judge, must wear a black robe in court. Requiring certain attire in court may suppress one's freedom of expression; at the same time the rule may "say something" about the nature of the advocate's function. The third party effects of requiring certain attire are, however, quite different than those involved in restricting advertising or solicitation.

Other kinds of rules could more rigorously inhibit the "commercialization" of law practice. Lawyers could be prohibited from engaging in any other vocation or business as long as they are engaged in law practice.[22] Lawyers could be prohibited from holding public office or corporate directorships if they are also engaged in practice. They could be prohibited from forming law firms of "bureaucratic" size, for example larger than twenty members. (English barristers still are required to be solo practitioners; thirty years ago the largest firm in many states was no bigger than twenty lawyers.)

The present character of American law practice is significantly shaped by the *absence* of rules against the foregoing kinds of "commercialization" and "bureaucratization." Justice O'Connor does not mention any of these proposals (or the lack of any such rules) in her dissent in *Shapero*. Does allowing advertising "commercialize" the legal profession in different ways than allowing lawyers to sit on corporate boards? Are different socio-economic interests involved?

Use and Effects of Lawyer Advertising

According to a 1994 ABA poll: "Even as lawyers debate the propriety of advertising their services, the great majority [61 percent] is using some form of advertising and planning to do more of it."[23] The most common vehicles are brochures and Yellow Pages listings (used by the majority of lawyers); print ads and Yellow Pages display ads are used by more that one-fourth; and direct mail by 12 percent. Radio, television and billboards, primarily addressed to injury claimants and legal problems faced by large numbers of individual Americans, are employed by a much smaller percentage of the profession (radio, 5%; television, 2%; billboards, 1%), but receive

21. See Nancy J. Moore, Professionalism Reconsidered, 1987 Am.B.Found.Research J. 773, 788, criticizing the Report of the ABA Commission on Professionalism: lawyers "should immediately reject both the pious exhortation to renounce wealth as a primary goal of legal practice, as well as the more dangerous (if only implied) suggestion that any incursions on the tradition of self-regulation are inevitably inimical to

the public interest." See also Robert L. Nelson, David M. Trubek & Rayman L. Solomon (eds.), Lawyers' Ideals/Lawyers' Practices: Transformation in the American Legal Profession (1992).

22. See discussion of ancillary businesses and dual practice at p. 1042 infra.

23. Advertising Wars, ABA J., Feb.1994, at 72–73 (reporting results of Gallup Poll commissioned by ABA).

a larger share of total advertising expense. Lawyers, unlike consumers, say advertising has a negative effect on the image of the profession,[24] but younger lawyers are more likely to disagree.

Lawyers who provide individualized services to wealthy or corporate clients rarely use the forms of lawyer advertising that are criticized— billboards, newspaper ads, radio spots and television commercials. Lawyers in the corporate sector of practice, however, do use a variety of techniques to bring themselves to the attention of potential clients. Social connections through business and social clubs provide opportunities for informing clients of the experience and talents of firm lawyers. Newsletters that summarize current developments in fields in which a firm has expertise are distributed to potential clients. Many large law firms have engaged marketing and public relations consultants who seek to place stories or gain interviews in newspapers of general circulation or in the lawyer press.

Economic analysts generally conclude that advertising is an efficient means to market legal services that are capable of standardization but not those that require highly individualized treatment.[25] With respect to standardized services, advertising expands awareness of a legal need, provides information about which lawyers provide the service and communicates some information of possible cost. Even on the critical decision of choosing a particular lawyer, advertising adds to information coming from prior experience or word-of-mouth. "For the consumer of standardizable services, the probable result of permitting lawyers to advertise will be lower priced services of better quality."[26] Professor Macaulay agrees that "[l]awyer advertising may play some part in enlarging access to legal services," but warns against viewing it as either a devil or a panacea:

> Advertising alone is not likely to push the bar into crass commercialism or produce a nation of rational informed clients seeking to maximize utility. Recognizing this, we must be concerned that largely symbolic debates about lawyer advertising may divert us from concern with more pressing issues of access and equality.[27]

---

24. Paul Marcotte, Who Likes Lawyer Ads?, 74 A.B.A.J. 28 (Oct. 1, 1988).

25. See, e.g., Geoffrey C. Hazard, Jr., Russell G. Pearce & Jeffrey W. Stempel, Why Lawyers Should Be Allowed to Advertise: A Market Analysis of Legal Services, 58 N.Y.U.L.Rev. 1084 (1983); Timothy J. Muris & Fred S. McChesney, Advertising and the Price and Quality of Legal Services: The Case for Legal Clinics, 1979 Am.B.Found.Research J. 179 (comparing the price and quality of services offered by an advertising legal clinic and other law firms); Federal Trade Commission, Improving Consumer Access to Legal Services: The Case for Removing Restrictions

on Truthful Advertising (1984) (study concluding that state restrictions on price advertising of five routine legal services resulted in higher prices; "the dominant effect of advertising is to enhance price competition by lowering consumer search costs"). The empirical studies are reviewed in Stewart Macaulay, Lawyer Advertising: Yes But . . ., U. Wis. Inst. for Legal Studies: Working Paper 7–3 (1985).

26. Hazard, Pearce & Stempel, supra, at 1109.

27. Macaulay, supra, at 75.

C.   OWNERSHIP AND CONTROL OF LAW FIRMS

1.   GROUP LEGAL SERVICES

Consider the following departures from the traditional model of a lawyer or law firm providing fee-for-service legal assistance to private clients:

- A nonprofit advocacy group, e.g., NAACP, seeks to challenge racial discrimination in public education by seeking out blacks who would be willing to serve as plaintiffs in actions attacking racially segregated schools; the NAACP offers to provide legal services without cost to the plaintiffs.[1]

- A labor union, concerned about the quality and cost of legal services available to injured members of the union, advises its members not to settle worker's compensation or personal injury claims without consulting a lawyer and offers the services of designated attorneys who have agreed to handle claims on specified terms.[2] Alternatively, the union hires staff attorneys who are made available to handle the claims of members.[3]

- A nonprofit organization of motorists uses members' annual dues to hire a staff of lawyers and provide legal services, without charge, to members of the association in certain court proceedings arising out of the operation of members' automobiles.[4]

- A large retail chain, e.g., Sears or K–Mart, hires a staff of lawyers and opens law offices in many of its stores. The offices offer a limited menu of routine legal services (e.g., real estate closings, divorces, wills, individual bankruptcies) to customers at advertised rates.

1. See NAACP v. Button, 371 U.S. 415 (1963) (First Amendment protects NAACP's right to seek plaintiffs and provide them with counsel; state's interest in preventing barratry, maintenance and champerty are not a compelling state interest justifying limiting First Amendment freedoms).

2. See Brotherhood of Railroad Trainmen v. Virginia ex rel. Virginia State Bar, 377 U.S. 1, 8 (1964) ("[T]he First and Fourteenth Amendments protect the right of the members through their Brotherhood to maintain and carry out their plan for advising workers who are injured to obtain legal advice and for recommending specific lawyers.... And, of course, lawyers accepting employment under this constitutionally protected plan have a like protection which the State cannot abridge.")

3. See United Mine Workers of America, District 12 v. Illinois State Bar Assn., 389 U.S. 217 (1967) (reversing a lower court decision enjoining the union's program); United Transportation Union v. State Bar of Michigan, 401 U.S. 576 (1971) ("The common thread running through our decisions in NAACP v. Button, *Trainmen,* and *United Mine Workers* is that collective activity undertaken to obtain meaningful access to the courts is a fundamental right within the protection of the First Amendment.")

4. See People ex rel. Chicago Bar Assn. v. Motorists' Assn. of Illinois, 188 N.E. 827 (Ill.1933) (motorists' association enjoined from practicing law without a license).

- A large insurance company advertises "a prepaid legal services plan" under which, in return for an annual premium, the insured is entitled to receive a variety of legal services during the plan year, including telephone and office consultation with lawyers who have agreed with the insurance company to provide these services.

These arrangements for the provision of legal services to groups of people (hence the term "group legal services") differ in a number of important respects. The NAACP case involves the assertion of civil or political rights that are near the heart of freedom of expression; the union cases involve the assertion of employment-related rights; and the others involve the broad array of legal interests of ordinary Americans. Some of them (e.g., the NAACP case and the motorists' association) involve not-for-profit organizations, whereas the retail chain and the insurance company are engaged in profit-making activity. Should that make a difference? Some employ staff lawyers to deliver legal services, and others rely on members of the private bar who are affiliated with a particular plan. The insurance plan involves two distinctive features: prepayment and insurance.

Yet the common features of group legal services plans made them a center of controversy from the 1930s to the 1980s. In general, as with lawyer advertising, the ABA and state bar associations have attempted to prohibit or restrict arrangements for group legal services while the Supreme Court has forced the bar to accommodate them.[5] Yet the profession has not been monolithic in opposition: Important elements of ABA leadership have seen group legal services as a vital part of the long-term future of the legal profession because of their potential role in expanding the demand for legal services. Despite bar opposition, group and prepaid plans have grown rapidly, reaching millions of Americans by the mid–1980s. Much of the growth has been due to the recognition of lawyer advertising in 1977 and changes in federal law that made group and prepaid plans attractive as an employment-related fringe benefit.

Group legal services plans present a variety of standard professional responsibility problems. First, in most the lawyer is paid for and often selected by the organizers of the plan. Will the independent judgment of the lawyer in serving a client through the plan be distorted or controlled by the interests of the operator of the plan? The same possibilities are present whenever a third person selects and pays a client's lawyer (e.g., a liability insurer providing a defense to an insured) or an organization hires staff lawyers (e.g., corporate legal staff). Second, group legal services plans often rely on advertising, raising the same issues involved in other advertising of legal services. Should an insurance company be permitted to call or solicit

---

5. For discussion of the ABA's grudging response to the constitutional decisions requiring recognition of group legal services plans, see Wolfram, Modern Legal Ethics § 16.5.5 (1986). The 1969 Model Code limited lawyer participation in group legal service plans to those operated by a nonprofit organization that used "open panels" of lawyers (under an "open panel" a plan member is entitled to choose any lawyer from the private bar; under a "closed panel," a member is restricted to a staff lawyer or a group of lawyers selected by the plan).

members of the public to enroll in a prepaid legal services plan in the same manner in which those companies merchandise life and health insurance to the public? (See M.R. 7.3(d).) Third, many plans employ nonlawyers to administer plans and to perform paralegal functions. These staffing arrangements raise issues of unauthorized practice of law. Underlying all of these issues is one of competition with general practitioners in the provision of legal services to ordinary Americans.

Hostility to group legal services comes primarily from bar leaders who represent the interests of general practitioners who are threatened by competition from group legal services plans (e.g., the loss of work injury cases handled by a union plan). What similarities and differences are there between the group legal services problems and debate and the problems and debate concerning HMOs? What accounts for the differences?

2. FORM OF PRACTICE RESTRICTIONS OF MODEL RULE 5.4

The Kutak Commission's draft of what became Model Rule 5.4 eliminated the form of practice restrictions that restricted delivery of legal services to the public by groups and organizations primarily engaged in other activities or business. Under the proposal, a lawyer could be employed by any organization engaged in the delivery of legal services, such as an accounting firm or a financial institution, as long as the organization respected the lawyer's professional judgment, protected a client's confidential information, avoided impermissible advertising or solicitation and charged only reasonable fees. The Commission's proposal, however, was dropped from the Model Rules at the last minute by the ABA House of Delegates. Geoffrey Hazard, the reporter for the Kutak Commission, reports: "During the debate someone asked if [the Kutak] proposal would allow Sears, Roebuck to open a law office. When they found out it would, that was the end of the debate."[6]

Model Rule 5.4 forbids a lawyer to "form a partnership with a nonlawyer if any of the activities of the partnership consist of the practice of law," forbids a lawyer "to share legal fees with a nonlawyer," and says that a "lawyer shall not practice with or in the form of a professional corporation or association . . . if . . . a nonlawyer owns any interest therein . . .; a nonlawyer is a corporate director or officer thereof; or . . . a nonlawyer has the right to direct or control the professional judgment of a lawyer." The brief Comment states that these "[traditional] limitations are to protect the lawyer's professional independence of judgment." The restrictions are drawn from and substantially replicate DR 3–102(A), DR 3–103(A) and DR 5–107(C) of the Model Code and may be traced back to Canon 33 of the Canons of Professional Ethics.

Are the limitations of M.R. 5.4 justifiable? Why should nonlawyers be prohibited from investing in, managing and profiting from companies that provide legal services? Critics of form of practice restrictions argue that the legal services market would benefit from enlarged competition and in-

---

6. David Kaplan, Want to Invest in a Law Firm?, Nat'l L.J., Jan. 19, 1987, at p. 28.

creased investment.[7] Allowing banks, insurance companies or retailers to diversify into legal services would serve that purpose. On the other hand, especially when legal services are combined with another business activity, such as provision of banking or insurance services, legal advice may be distorted by the desire to sell the other services. Would malpractice liability provide a sufficient deterrent to such distortion?

M.R. 5.4 (and its Model Code antecedents) assumes that lay management of a legal services organization will be tempted, more than are lawyer managers, to interfere with the professional relationships of employed lawyers when it is profitable to do so and that the problem is so serious that a prophylactic rule prohibiting lay management is necessary. Are these assumptions correct? Why aren't after-the-fact remedies for violation of professional rules sufficient?

Do you think any of the problems associated with HMOs would be significantly reduced if only doctors were allowed to manage those organizations?

Dual Practice

Dual practice refers to two related problems: (1) a lawyer, who is also qualified in accounting, engineering or some other field, holds herself out as practicing in a dual capacity, and (2) a lawyer forms a partnership with a nonlawyer such as an accountant. DR 2–102(E) of the 1969 Model Code prohibited "a lawyer who is engaged both in the practice of law and another profession" from indicating the dual qualifications on a letterhead or sign. This prohibition was repealed in 1980, three years after the Supreme Court had held that the First Amendment protected truthful advertising. In Ibanez v. Florida Department of Business & Professional Regulation,[8] the Supreme Court held that a Florida lawyer who was also an accountant had a First Amendment right to list her status as a CPA and a certified financial planner in Yellow page ads and on business cards and stationery.

Dual practice in the form of a partnership of a lawyer and a nonlawyer presents additional problems: Is the lawyer aiding unauthorized practice by a nonlawyer (M.R. 5.5)? Is the lawyer sharing fees or management of a law firm with a nonlawyer (M.R. 5.4)? The combination of the two rules generally means that the nonlawyer must be supervised by the lawyer and may not act in a legal capacity, such as making a court appearance. Does this position that lawyers must be in charge reflect an assumption that lawyers are superior to other professionals?

---

7. For criticism of M.R. 5.4, see Stephen Gillers, What We Talked About When We Talked About Ethics: A Critical View of the Model Rules, 46 Ohio St.L.J. 243, 266–69 (1985). Gillers argues that M.R. 5.4 serves the interests of established firms, with accumulated capital and clientele, rather than the interests of lawyers generally, especially younger lawyers who would benefit from increased opportunities in salaried employment. Gillers also says that M.R. 5.4 harms consumers by suppressing competition in the supply of services.

8. 512 U.S. 136 (1994).

Ancillary Business Activities

During the 1990s the profession debated the desirability of a trend in major law firms to combine legal services with other types of consulting and business activities. A number of major firms created affiliated organizations to provide consulting and assistance in matters as varied as lobbying, employment practices, environmental planning, and many others. In general, professionals from other disciplines worked along with lawyers in teams designed to meet client needs. The restrictions of M.R. 5.4 were circumvented by separating the law firm's legal work from that of the affiliated organizations. Nonlawyers could be partners of the affiliated organization and share in its profits, but not those of the law firm. The controversy surrounding these activities, often referred to as "ancillary business activities," grew throughout the 1990s but as the century ended was largely displaced by the related issues concerning "multidisciplinary partnerships or practices" (MDPs), especially as conducted internationally by major accounting firms.[9]

Some segments of the bar, centered in the ABA Section of Litigation, charged that ancillary business activities presented serious professionalism concerns: compromising lawyers' independent judgment, endangering confidentiality and creating conflicting interests. Opponents of ancillary business activity feared that this "business" activity would impair lawyer professionalism by paving the way for nonlawyer ownership of or participation in law firms, distract lawyers from their professional responsibilities as lawyers and ultimately lead to a displacement of self-regulation. Lawrence Fox, a leading advocate of a professional rule prohibiting ancillary business activities, stated:

> [T]he ancillary business movement introduces non-lawyers into positions of influence and control of the profession. All the safeguards one can imagine do not overcome the reality that those who come to prominence and success in the operations of the ancillary business will end up with real power in the governance of the overall enterprise. Quite simply, money talks, and dependence on money changes perspectives in a way that people of the utmost good will cannot overcome....

> Also disquieting is the possibility that, if lawyers enter other fields of endeavor, non-lawyer enterprises such as Household Finance, Coldwell Banker, American Express and WalMart are likely to wish to add legal services to their array of consumer products. As lawyers cloak their drive for financial hegemony in arguments such as "it's a public service to offer the public one-stop shopping," it becomes a very small leap, if a leap at all, to argue that these other non-law-firm, non-

---

9. The ancillary business controversy is well described in Ted Schneyer, Policymaking and the Perils of Professionalism: The ABA's Ancillary Business Debate as a Case Study, 35 Ariz.L.Rev.363 (1963); the concerns about MDPs are considered at p. 1045 infra.

lawyer-controlled entities are entitled to an equal opportunity to provide this "public service".... [10]

Defenders of ancillary business operations countered that the activities are no different from others in which lawyers traditionally have been involved, that clients benefit from the broad array of services that are provided, that professional rules protecting confidentiality and prohibiting conflicting interests provide adequate protection against these very real dangers, and that efforts to define "the practice of law" for these purposes are unwise and counter-productive.

James Jones, the former managing partner of a firm that has offered non-law services in lobbying, public relations, real estate development and financial services, states that the future of the legal profession lies in these arrangements and that existing form-of-practice restrictions such as M.R. 5.4 should be revised to permit non-lawyers to become partners. Jones believes that the practice of law "has become far more complex and diverse" than could be imagined some years ago: the underlying economic and social activity is more complicated, requiring the tools and knowledge of other disciplines, and the law's effort to regulate under these circumstances is infinitely more complex and requires the skills of specialized lawyers "working in tandem" with professionals from other disciplines. This interdisciplinary collaboration, Jones argues, is best carried on in organizations that give equal status and rewards to nonlawyer participants. "[I]n all cases the motivation has been to improve the quality of service to clients by assuring that complex matters requiring interdisciplinary skills can be handled efficiently and economically." [11]

The ABA has reversed field on this issue several times. In August 1992 the House of Delegates rejected an amendment to the Model Rules that would have allowed ancillary services to be provided by law firm subsidiaries to nonclients, subject to a regulatory regime designed to ensure that lawyers' professional obligations toward clients were not impaired. The House, by a narrow margin, adopted a substitute prohibiting all ancillary services unless such services were provided by employees of the firms to clients of the firm in connection with the provision of legal services. M.R. 5.7 proved to be short-lived. General practitioners in smaller cities, who have always combined law practice with other activities, such as title search companies, service on corporate boards and real estate development, awoke to the fact that M.R. 5.7 might prohibit these long-standing activities. A renewed debate in August 1993 resulted in another narrowly divided vote, repealing M.R. 5.7. No state had adopted the 1992 version of M.R. 5.7 during its short life.

In 1994 the ABA adopted the current version of Rule 5.7. You should read this compromise position and its Comment at this time. A small number of states have adopted the rule. The District of Columbia deals

---

10. Lawrence Fox, Restraint Is Good in Trade, Nat'l L.J., Apr. 19, 1991, at p. 17.

11. James R. Jones, Law Firm Diversification, A.B.A.J. 52 (Sept. 1989).

with the issue differently: its version of M.R. 5.4 permits non-lawyers to become partners under certain circumstances.[12]

Why do powerful groups within the ABA seek to prohibit ancillary businesses when these groups do not oppose practices that involve an equal or greater interference with "independent professional judgment," such as lawyers serving on the board of directors of a corporation represented by the lawyer's firm or business transactions between lawyer and client?

"The MDPs Are Coming!"

In 1999 the American Bar Association created a special committee to make recommendations as to how the bar should respond to the "threat" posed by multidisciplinary practices.[13] "MDPs" are firms that provide various professional services under one organizational roof. Typically they originate as large accounting firms, expand to financial consultancy, and then to management consultancy, and include legal staffs to assist in serving client needs. Acting as accountants, MDPs are authorized to provide advice about tax matters and advocacy concerning tax matters before the Internal Review Service. By a 1998 federal statute they were given a limited evidentiary privilege in tax matters, similar to the attorney-client privilege under common law.[14]

In this country, the large accounting firms have long held the position that they and their lawyer-employees are not engaged in unauthorized practice of law but were providing tax advice, not legal advice, or were simply assisting their nonlawyer staff people with advice concerning the legal aspects of the accounting or management assistance being provided to the clients. The boundary is indistinct between (a) "tax" advice and (b) legal advice. "Tax" advice is not unauthorized practice of law but legal advice provided by an accounting firm to its clients is unauthorized practice of law and as such prohibited in all American jurisdictions. The boundary is also indistinct between (a) assisting an accountant with the legal aspects of the problems he is consulting about with the client and (b) providing legal advice to the client. Providing legal advice to a professional who is in turn providing other advice to a client is lawful, while providing legal advice directly to the client is improper if done by a lawyer who is employed in a firm that is not a law firm.

12. District of Columbia R.P.C. 5.4 provides that a lawyer "may practice law in a partnership or other form of organization in which a financial interest is held or managerial authority is exercised by an individual nonlawyer who performs professional services which assist the organization in providing legal services to clients" under several conditions, including that these persons "undertake to abide by these rules" and lawyer-partners or owners "undertake to be responsible for the nonlawyer participants to the same extent as if nonlawyer participants were lawyers under Rule 5.1." A number of law firms in the District of Columbia have named nonlawyer partners.

13. See 14 Law.Man.Prof. Conduct 390 (Aug. 19, 1998) (reporting creation of the ABA Commission on Multidisciplinary Practices headed by Sherwin P. Simmons).

14. This federal statute is discussed at p. 226 supra.

As a technical matter there is plausibility, within the foregoing framework, to the argument that the MDP staff lawyers are not engaged in unauthorized practice of law. As a political matter, the large accounting firms have signaled that they will fight efforts by the bar to restrict their activities. Furthermore, many accountants and lawyers in small towns, and in neighborhood practice in urban communities, closely cooperate in ways that amount to a mini-MDP. These firms report that they provide better services to their clients this way. Moreover, the lawyers in these arrangements note that they thereby get clients that they would not otherwise. The clients typically have more frequent contact with their accountants (at least once a year, for tax returns) and generally have a more positive attitude toward their accountants than they do toward lawyers. The foregoing situations, involving the big accounting firms and local joint practices, have been going on for years, notwithstanding sporadic protests by lawyers who consider them a threat to the independence of the legal profession.

The perceived threat of MDPs has become salient in the last few years because the accounting firms have become much more aggressive in recent years.[15] They have expanded the scope and size of their management consulting services and, in several countries elsewhere in the world where unauthorized practice of law is less an issue, have established various close relationships with law firms. These relationships range from outside absorption (for example in France and Spain) to contractual working relationships contemplating continuous cross-referral of clientele.[16] Possible responses by the bar are: (1) seek to terminate the MDP employment of lawyers in this country; (2) do nothing; and (3) amend the Model Rules to permit certain types of arrangements whereby lawyers can be employees of professional firms that are not law firms, i.e., an MDP, but will be governed by the rules of ethics in doing so.

The first alternative—seeking to terminate the MDP employment of lawyers—will be opposed both by the accounting firms and by many business clients. The second alternative will be resented by many lawyers and will leave lawyers employed by the MDPs outside the profession's ethical umbrella. The third alternative must focus on two key issues. The first is the restriction in Rule 5.4(a) against sharing fees with a nonlawyer and that in 5.4(b) against forming a partnership with a nonlawyer where the partnership provides services which include legal services. The second issue is the scope of imputation of conflicts of interest prescribed in Rule 1.10(a), which imputes a conflict of one lawyer to all other lawyers in a firm. The rule of imputation applicable to members of firms providing other services is much less exacting. For example, accounting firms general-

---

15. For discussion of the MDP threat, see 14 Law.Man.Prof. Conduct 269 (June 10, 1998).

16. See Charles W. Wolfram, Multidisciplinary Partnerships in the Law Practice of European and American Lawyers, in Lawyers' Practice and Ideals: A Comparative View (John J. Barcelo & Roger C. Cramton, eds.) (forthcoming 1999) (discussing the development of MDPs in Europe, the competitive pressures they place on American law firms competing for international business and the regulatory difficulties of accommodating them by the state-based regulation of lawyers in the U.S.).

ly take the position that "insulation walls" within the firm sufficiently protect the clients in matters of conflict of interest.[17]

Discussion of MDPs often proceeds on the premise that these organizations, if allowed to compete with law firms, will be preferred by clients. That premise has not become an established fact in the United States because competition has not yet given clients an unfettered choice. Enforcement of the ban on unauthorized practice of law seeks to deprive clients of that choice, an approach that may be implausible when the clients to be protected from their own incompetence are large multinational corporations who are advised by experienced in-house lawyers and other professionals. The form of practice restrictions also limit the ability of American law firms to attract the investment capital that may be necessary to compete on equal terms with the large accounting firms. In the individual-client sector of the market, the argument that clients lack competence to choose among professional service organizations has greater plausibility, but here also a relaxation or abandonment of the professional monopoly and the ownership restrictions would enhance the availability of services to moderate income people by organizations that are financially responsible and have an interest in developing a national reputation for quality. On the other hand, if the service organizations were outgrowths of corporations primarily engaged in another business (e.g., insurance or financial management), the alternatives they might provide to consumers might not provide an independent professional judgment (see p. 1013 above).

Regulatory change in this area is difficult in the United States because regulation is state-based and carried out largely through the high courts of the states. State-by-state action in 51 jurisdictions would be required. Federal legislation could accomplish the change on a national basis by a single piece of legislation. But the tradition of state control is hardy despite more frequent federal incursions in recent years. Change might also come about as part of a treaty in which the United States and the European Community dealt broadly with competition in the services field. As ever, the future remains uncertain.

D.   LOCAL CONTROL IN AN ERA OF MULTISTATE PRACTICE

Introduction

Admission to the bar and lawyer discipline are functions that from the earliest days have been carried on by state courts. Admission to the bar in a

---

17. Rule 102-2 of the Model Rules of Professional Conduct of the American Institute of Certified Public Accountants (AICPA) provides that a member may perform a professional service for a client when another member of the firm "has a relationship with another person, entity, product or service that could, in the member's professional judgment, be viewed by the client, employer or other appropriate parties as impairing the member's objectivity. If the member believes that the professional service can be performed with objectivity, and the relationship is disclosed to and consent obtained from such client . . ., the rule shall not operate to prohibit the performance of the professional service." It is unclear whether this language incorporates the "reasonable belief" standard stated in Model Rule 1.7(a)(1) and (b)(1) or turns solely on the subjective belief of the particular accountant. In any event, the conflict of one member of an accounting firm is not imputed to other members of the firm.

state carries authority to represent others in any state tribunal and in any transactions within the state coming within the state's definition of the "practice of law." Admission to the bar of a state is ordinarily a prerequisite to admission to the bar of a federal court within that state or which entertains appeals from that state. Admission in one state, however, does not authorize practice in another. Professional rules are violated when a lawyer "practice[s] law in a jurisdiction where doing so violates the regulation of the legal profession in that jurisdiction." M.R. 5.5(a); see also DR 3–101(B). For a New York lawyer to give advice on California law concerning a transaction with California contacts may be unauthorized practice.

Yet we are one nation with a national economy, bound together by a common language and a common legal culture. Federal law, increasingly important in everyday life and in law practice, is uniform throughout the nation. The legal systems of all states except Louisiana are based on the common law; uniform laws and the unifying effect of Restatements and legislative imitation provide sufficient commonality that legal education is relatively homogeneous everywhere. A substantial portion of the population moves each year, often across state lines, and business transactions involve people and events almost without regard to state lines. In this setting, clients want and expect their lawyers to handle all aspects of a transaction, even litigation, that crosses state lines.

In today's world the state-based control of admission and discipline is in tension with the reality of multistate legal problems and practice. This tension has produced fracture lines involving three questions: (1) When may a lawyer admitted to practice in one state be eligible for permanent admission in another (geographic restrictions based on local residence, a local office or association of local counsel)? (2) When may a lawyer admitted in one state be specially authorized to handle litigation in another state's courts (admission pro hac vice)? And (3) to what extent may an office lawyer provide advice to clients that crosses state lines (multistate practice)?

1.   EXCLUSION OF NONRESIDENTS

Supreme Court of New Hampshire v. Piper

Supreme Court of the United States, 1985.
470 U.S. 274.

■ JUSTICE POWELL delivered the opinion of the Court.

The Rules of the Supreme Court of New Hampshire limit bar admission to state residents. We here consider whether this restriction violates the Privileges and Immunities Clause of the United States Constitution, Art. IV, § 2.

I

Kathryn Piper lives in Lower Waterford, Vermont, about 400 yards from the New Hampshire border. In 1979, she applied to take the February 1980 New Hampshire bar examination. Piper submitted with her application a statement of intent to become a New Hampshire resident. Following an investigation, the Board of Bar Examiners found that Piper was of good moral character and met the other requirements for admission. She was allowed to take, and passed, the examination. Piper was informed by the Board that she would have to establish a home address in New Hampshire prior to being sworn in.

[Piper requested a dispensation from the residency requirement, due to inconvenience (she and her husband were new parents and had a favorable interest rate on their home mortgage), but the Clerk of the New Hampshire Supreme Court denied her request based on New Hampshire Supreme Court Rule 42, which excludes nonresidents from the bar. The state Supreme Court also denied her request. Piper then filed suit in the District of New Hampshire, alleging that Rule 42 violates the Privileges and Immunities Clause. The district court granted Piper's motion for summary judgment, reasoning that the opportunity to practice law is a fundamental right, and that Piper was denied this right with no substantial reason. The Court of Appeals affirmed, concluding that "there was no 'substantial reason' for the different treatment of nonresidents and that the challenged discrimination bore no 'substantial relationship' to the State's objectives."]

II

Article IV, § 2, of the Constitution provides that the "Citizens of each State shall be entitled to all Privileges and Immunities of Citizens in the several States."[6] This Clause was intended to "fuse into one Nation a collection of independent, sovereign States." Toomer v. Witsell, 334 U.S. 385, 395 (1948). Recognizing this purpose, we have held that it is "[o]nly with respect to those 'privileges' and 'immunities' bearing on the vitality of the Nation as a single entity" that a State must accord residents and nonresidents equal treatment. Baldwin v. Montana Fish & Game Comm'n, [436 U.S. 371, 383]. In *Baldwin*, for example, we concluded that a State may charge a nonresident more than it charges a resident for the same elk-hunting license. Because elk hunting is "recreation" rather than a "means of a livelihood," we found that the right to a hunting license was not "fundamental" to the promotion of interstate harmony.

Derived, like the Commerce Clause, from the fourth of the Articles of Confederation, the Privileges and Immunities Clause was intended to create a national economic union. It is therefore not surprising that this Court repeatedly has found that "one of the privileges which the Clause guarantees to citizens of State A is that of doing business in State B on

6. Under this Clause, the terms "citizen" and "resident" are used interchangeably. See Austin v. New Hampshire, 420 U.S. 656, 662, n. 8 (1975). Under the Four- teenth Amendment, of course, "[a]ll persons born or naturalized in the United States ... are citizens ... of the State wherein they reside."

terms of substantial equality with the citizens of that State." Toomer v. Witsell, supra, 334 U.S., at 396.... [I]n *Toomer* the Court held that nonresident fishermen could not be required to pay a license fee of $2,500 for each shrimp boat owned when residents were charged only $25 per boat. Finally, in Hicklin v. Orbeck, 437 U.S. 518 (1978), we found violative of the Privileges and Immunities Clause a statute containing a resident hiring preference for all employment related to the development of the State's oil and gas resources.

There is nothing in [these cases] suggesting that the practice of law should not be viewed as a "privilege" under Art. IV, § 2.[10] Like the occupations considered in our earlier cases, the practice of law is important to the national economy. As the Court noted in Goldfarb v. Virginia State Bar, 421 U.S. 773, 788, the "activities of lawyers play an important part in commercial intercourse."

The lawyer's role in the national economy is not the only reason that the opportunity to practice law should be considered a "fundamental right." We believe that the legal profession has a noncommercial role and duty that reinforce the view that the practice of law falls within the ambit of the Privileges and Immunities Clause. Out-of-state lawyers may—and often do—represent persons who raise unpopular federal claims. In some cases, representation by nonresident counsel may be the only means available for the vindication of federal rights. See Leis v. Flynt, 439 U.S., at 450 (Stevens, J., dissenting). The lawyer who champions unpopular causes surely is as important to the "maintenance or well-being of the Union," *Baldwin*, 436 U.S., at 388, as was the shrimp fisherman in *Toomer*, or the pipeline worker in *Hicklin*.

Appellant asserts that the Privileges and Immunities Clause should be held inapplicable to the practice of law because a lawyer's activities are "bound up with the exercise of judicial power and the administration of justice."[12] Its contention is based on the premise that the lawyer is an "officer of the court," who "exercises state power on a daily basis." Appellant concludes that if the State cannot exclude nonresidents from the bar, its ability to function as a sovereign political body will be threatened.

10. In Corfield v. Coryell, 6 F.Cas. 546 (No. 3,230) (CCED Pa.1825), Justice Bushrod Washington, sitting as Circuit Justice, stated that the "fundamental rights" protected by the Clause included ["professional pursuits" among other trades and occupations.] ... [W]e have noted that those privileges on Justice Washington's list would still be protected by the Clause. Baldwin v. Montana Fish & Game Comm'n, 436 U.S. 371, 387 (1978).

12. Justice Rehnquist ... asserts that lawyers, through their adversary representation of clients' interests, "play an important role in the formulation of state policy." He therefore concludes that the residency requirement is necessary to ensure that lawyers are "intimately conversant with the local concerns that should inform such policies." [This argument] is foreclosed by our reasoning in In re Griffiths, 413 U.S. 717, 729 (1973). There, we held that the status of being licensed to practice law does not place a person so close to the core of the political process as to make him a "formulator of government policy."

Lawyers do enjoy a "broad monopoly ... to do things other citizens may not lawfully do." In re Griffiths, 413 U.S. 717, 731 (1973). We do not believe, however, that the practice of law involves an "exercise of state power" justifying New Hampshire's residency requirement. In *In re Griffiths*, supra, we held that the State could not exclude an alien from the bar on the ground that a lawyer is an " 'officer of the Court who' ... is entrusted with the 'exercise of actual governmental power.' "We concluded that a lawyer is not an "officer" within the ordinary meaning of that word. 413 U.S., at 728. He " 'makes his own decisions, follows his own best judgment, collects his own fees and runs his own business.' "Moreover, we held that the state powers entrusted to lawyers do not "involve matters of state policy or acts of such unique responsibility as to entrust them only to citizens."

Because, under *Griffiths*, a lawyer is not an "officer" of the State in any political sense,[15] there is no reason for New Hampshire to exclude from its bar nonresidents. We therefore conclude that the right to practice law is protected by the Privileges and Immunities Clause.[16]

III

The conclusion that Rule 42 deprives nonresidents of a protected privilege does not end our inquiry. The Court has stated that "[l]ike many other constitutional provisions, the privileges and immunities clause is not an absolute." *Toomer v. Witsell*, 334 U.S., at 396.... The Clause does not preclude discrimination against nonresidents where (i) there is a substantial reason for the difference in treatment; and (ii) the discrimination practiced against nonresidents bears a substantial relationship to the State's objective. In deciding whether the discrimination bears a close or substantial relationship to the State's objective, the Court has considered the availability of less restrictive means.

[The Court rejected New Hampshire's justifications for its refusal to admit nonresidents: No evidence supported the assertion that nonresident lawyers would have less familiarity with local law or to behave unethically. The assertion that nonresidents would be unavailable for court proceedings called on short notice or participate in pro bono work had more merit, but would either not occur (nonresident members would live adjacent to the state and could be required to make pro bono contributions) or did not justify the exclusion of nonresidents.]

15. It is true that lawyers traditionally have been leaders in state and local affairs—political as well as cultural, religious, and civic. Their training qualifies them for this type of participation. Nevertheless, lawyers are not in any sense officials in the government simply by virtue of being lawyers.

16. Our conclusion that Rule 42 violates the Privileges and Immunities Clause is consis-

tent with Leis v. Flynt, 439 U.S. 438 (1979). In *Leis*, we held that a lawyer could be denied, without the benefit of a hearing, permission to appear pro hac vice. We concluded that the States should be left free to "prescribe the qualifications for admission to practice and the standards of professional conduct" for those lawyers who appear in its courts. Id., at 442....

[Justice White, concurring, thought the New Hampshire residency requirement was invalid as applied to Ms. Piper, given the facts of this case, but that it was unnecessary to reach the broader issue of the constitutionality of residency requirements generally.]

[Justice Rehnquist dissented, stating that "the practice of law should be treated differently [than other occupations because] law is one occupation that does not readily translate across state lines." A state's regulation of the practice of law, which is "distinctly and intentionally nonnational," is intended to further the distinctive law and social policy of the state. A state bar that resides locally, rather than commuting from Boston, only forty miles away from the New Hampshire's body, will have greater familiarity with state concerns, be available on short notice and otherwise serve the state's substantial interest in its own polity.]

Downfall of Exclusions Based on Citizenry and Residency

Until the 1970s, most states restricted eligibility to the bar to persons who were residents of the state or who affirmed an intention to become a resident upon admission or both. These restrictions were particularly rigorous in states adjacent to large metropolitan centers, e.g., New Jersey, and in "sunshine" states such as Florida. The former feared competition from nearby big city lawyers; the latter feared that senior lawyers from other states would come there to retire and engage in incidental practice. In the 1980s these restrictions were challenged on grounds of Equal Protection and the Privileges and Immunities Clause. The line of cases beginning with *Piper* has drastically curtailed these restrictions.[1]

Does Justice (now Chief Justice) Rehnquist advance a strong argument in his *Piper* dissent that substantial state interests support the residency requirement? How is a small state, nestled among large urban states, to preserve the special character of its law and bar unless it can impose a residency requirement?

Three other Supreme Court decisions have dealt with geographic restrictions and exclusions on bar admission. In Supreme Court of Virginia v. Friedman,[2] the Court struck down a Virginia provision permitting lawyers who were Virginia residents, but not those who maintained a nonresident status, to be admitted on motion without taking the bar examination. If Friedman, who lived in Maryland and worked on a corporation's legal staff, had moved to Virginia and affirmed an intention to practice full-time in Virginia, she could be admitted on motion, but not if she retained her Maryland residency. This differential treatment was held to violate the Privileges and Immunities Clause.

---

1. In re Griffiths, 413 U.S. 717 (1973), held citizenship requirements invalid; a state could not meet the heavy burden of sus-

taining the "suspect classification" of alienage under the strict scrutiny standard.

2. 487 U.S. 59 (1988).

In Barnard v. Thorstenn,[3] the Court invalidated on statutory grounds a rule of the Virgin Islands requiring for admission to the bar that an applicant reside for a year in the Islands and affirm an intention to reside there. A durational residency requirement of this type is virtually a ban on outsiders, who must spend a year in the Virgin Islands before becoming eligible for admission. The Court rejected as insubstantial five interests claimed to justify the residency requirement: the geographical isolation of the Virgin Islands, court delays flowing from any effort to accommodate the schedules of nonresident attorneys, difficulties of nonresidents in maintaining competence in local law given publication delays of Virgin Islands' legal materials, inadequacy of disciplinary resources to supervise nonresident lawyers, and difficulties in getting nonresidents to participate on a fair basis in assigned defense of indigent criminal defendants.[4]

In a third case, the Court invalidated a local rule of a United States district court that imposed a residency requirement for admission to that federal court.[5] The ground for the ruling was not the Privileges and Immunities Clause but the Court's inherent supervisory power over the lower federal courts.

Although the *Piper* line of cases eliminates residency requirements, other barriers still impede multistate practice. States need not permit nonresident lawyers to be admitted on motion, but may require all applicants to take the bar examination (about one-half of the states have reciprocity statutes that allow nonresidents to be admitted on motion if the applicant's state also does so). And a lawyer apparently can be required to maintain an office in a state as a condition of licensure.

New Jersey's Local Office Requirement

New Jersey rulemakers have attempted to avoid inundation by lawyers from Philadelphia and New York City by means of a local office requirement. New Jersey Court Rule 1:12–1(1) requires an attorney to maintain an office in New Jersey to practice in that state. A nonresident attorney may not satisfy the requirement merely by renting, but not actually using, office space in New Jersey. An attorney must have more than "occasional attendance" in the office and "more than an answering service unrelated to a place where business it conducted." The rule requires the presence of "a responsible person at the office to answer questions posed by courts, clients, or adversaries so that accurate information about the attorney's whereabouts and competent advice from the attorney can be obtained within a reasonable period of time."

The Third Circuit upheld the local office rule as "rationally related to the benefit [of assuring attorney competence, accountability, and accessibility] it is supposed to ensure." [6]Because in-state offices are required of nonresidents and residents alike, the rule does not favor resident attorneys.

3.   489 U.S. 546 (1989).

4.   489 U.S. at 553.

5.   Frazier v. Heebe, 482 U.S. 641 (1987).

6.   Tolchin v. Supreme Court of New Jersey, 111 F.3d 1099, 1109 (3d Cir.1997).

Can states reinvent the exclusion of nonresidents under the guise of the local office requirement?

2.   ADMISSION PRO HAC VICE

By long-established practice, a lawyer admitted in one jurisdiction may be permitted by a court of another jurisdiction to participate in a specific case. Normally, permission is sought through a motion by a lawyer already admitted to the court. This is called admission pro hac vice. A typical situation is bringing in a trial specialist from out of state to present a particularly difficult or important matter. Most courts have specific rules concerning such admissions, and the rules usually impose the requirement that a locally admitted lawyer also be associated in the case.[7]

In Leis v. Flynt,[8] an out-of-state lawyer claimed a right to appear on behalf of a criminal defendant (Larry Flynt of *Hustler* fame) without being admitted pro hac vice, on the ground that the right to practice constituted a constitutionally protected interest that other states had to recognize. This contention was rejected:

> We do not question that the practice of courts in most States is to allow an out-of-state lawyer the privilege of appearing upon motion, especially when he is associated with a member of the local bar. In view of the high mobility of the bar, and also the trend toward specialization, perhaps this is a practice to be encouraged. But it is not a right granted either by statute or the Constitution....
>
> A claim of entitlement under state law, to be enforceable, must be derived from statute or legal rule or through a mutually explicit understanding. The record here is devoid of any indication that an out-of-state lawyer may claim such an entitlement in Ohio, where the rules of the Ohio Supreme Court expressly consign the authority to approve a pro hac vice appearance to the discretion of the trial court....
>
> Nor is there a basis for the argument that the interest in appearing pro hac vice has its source in federal law. There is no right of federal origin that permits such lawyers to appear in state courts without meeting that State's bar admission requirements.... [9]

---

7. See generally Samuel J. Brakel & Wallace D. Loh, Regulating the Multistate Practice of Law, 50 Wash.L.Rev. 699 (1975).

8. 439 U.S. 438 (1979).

9. 439 U.S. at 441–43. The dissenting opinion of Justice Stevens, joined by Justices Brennan and Marshall, argues that a lawyer's right to "pursu[e] his calling is protected by the Due Process Clause ... when he crosses the border" of the State that licensed him. Justice Stevens identifies two "protected" interests that "reinforce" each other: the lawyer's interest in "discharging [his] responsibility for the fair administration of justice in our adversary system" and "the 'implicit promise' inhering in Ohio custom" of permitting out-of-state lawyers to handle particular cases. The dissent relies on the historic role of pro hac vice admissions in vindicating rights and in defending unpopular persons or causes.

Leis v. Flynt involved the lawyer's interest in pro hac vice admission. What about the client's right to be represented by counsel of choice?[10] In Ford v. Israel,[11] a Wisconsin criminal defendant was represented by a public defender because a Wisconsin rule required him to retain and pay local counsel if he was defended by the Chicago lawyer retained by his parents. He was unable to do so and, after being convicted, challenged the "local counsel" rule in a habeas proceeding. Judge Posner conceded that the rule "has about it the air of a guild restriction and may for all we know be motivated by a desire to increase the fees of Wisconsin lawyers."[12] But the attack on the conviction failed because the rule was not arbitrary, especially in a criminal case where a convicted defendant might well attack a conviction on ground that the out-of-state lawyer did not provide effective assistance. Thus the state had a legitimate reason to require local counsel.

The upshot is that pro hac vice admission is required for a lawyer to appear in a court to which she has not been regularly admitted. However, a court's refusal to admit pro hac vice a lawyer who meets the standard requirements, depriving the defendant of counsel of choice, may be reversible error under state law or ground for a collateral attack on the conviction.[13]

The absence of any constitutional protection for pro hac vice admission places a premium on the willingness of states to be receptive to out-of-state trial lawyers. Some states, such as New York, permit pro hac vice representation "in the discretion of the court" without requiring local counsel. Others, such as New Jersey, permit out-of-state lawyers to appear pro hac vice, but require that all papers filed in a court proceeding be signed by a lawyer authorized to practice in the state. Statutes and court decisions in a number of states set standards for pro hac vice admission and provide for hearings before denial.

In Hahn v. Boeing Co.,[14] two California lawyers brought suit in Washington on behalf of representatives of persons killed when a plane manufactured by Boeing crashed in Kenya. Boeing challenged the California lawyers' applications for pro hac vice admission on ground that they had solicited the plaintiffs in violation of Washington's professional rules. The trial court's order prohibiting the lawyers' pro hac vice admission until the court ruled on the solicitation charge was reversed on appeal. The appellate court stated that the required association of local counsel served

10. The abstention rule of Younger v. Harris, 401 U.S. 37 (1971), prevented defendant Flynt from seeking a federal court order enjoining Ohio's criminal prosecution of Flynt and *Hustler* magazine.

11. 701 F.2d 689 (7th Cir.1983).

12. 701 F.2d at 692.

13. See, e.g., Fuller v. Diesslin, 868 F.2d 604 (3d Cir.1989) (trial court's arbitrary denial of pro hac vice admission of two nonresident lawyers resulted in grant of habeas); Herrmann v. Summer Plaza Corp., 513 A.2d 1211, 1214 (Conn.1986) ("The right to have counsel of one's own choice, although not absolute, is important enough to require a legitimate state interest before a person can be deprived of that right.... In this period of greater mobility among members of the bar and the public, and the corresponding growth in interstate business, a court should reluctantly deny an application to appear pro hac vice").

14. 621 P.2d 1263 (Wn.1980).

one legitimate judicial interest: reasonable assurance that local rules of practice will be followed. The other interest—that "the attorney is competent and will conduct himself in an ethical and respectful manner in the trial of the case"—was met by the lawyers' out-of-state admission. Because Washington trial courts lack jurisdiction to try disciplinary matters and "[s]olicitation has no relevance per se to the conduct of the trial, nor is it prejudicial to the defendant," the trial court was required to grant pro hac vice admission unless it was shown that the out-of-state lawyer would not conduct a competent, ethical trial. This and other decisions support the view that pro hac vice admission may not be denied without substantial cause.[15]

Suppose a major state, such as California or Texas, enacted a statute or court rule providing that a lawyer may not be admitted pro hac vice in any state court proceeding unless the party makes a showing that competent legal service cannot be provided by a member of the state bar. Is the statute constitutional?

3.   MULTIJURISDICTIONAL PRACTICE

Denial of Fee to Out-of-State Lawyer

BIRBROWER, MONTALBANO, CONDON & FRANK, P.C. v. SUPE-RIOR COURT.[16] The Birbrower firm, a New York City firm, began representation of the Sandhu family in various business matters in 1986. Kamal Sandhu was the sole shareholder of ESQ Business Services Inc. (ESQ–NY), a New York corporation that produced business software. In 1990, the Birbrower firm worked on a software marketing agreement with Tandem Computers Inc. (Tandem) that granted Tandem worldwide distribution rights to ESQ–NY's computer software. The agreement provided that it would be governed by California law and that any dispute would be resolved under rules of the American Arbitration Association.

Thereafter, a second corporation with the same name was incorporated in California (ESQ–CAL), with Iqbal Sandhu, Kamal's brother, as a principal shareholder. In 1991 ESQ–CAL consulted Birbrower concerning Tandem's performance under the agreement. In 1992, ESQ–NY and ESQ–CAL jointly hired Birbrower to resolve the dispute with Tandem; the original fee agreement was executed in New York but was subsequently modified in California to a fixed fee agreement of $1 million.

The efforts of Birbrower lawyers to resolve the Tandem dispute included several brief trips to California in 1992–93. During these trips Birbrower consulted in California with officers of both ESQ–NY and ESQ–CAL concerning tactics and strategy, interviewed potential arbitrators, negotiat-

---

15. See Note, Due Process and Pro Hac Vice Appearances by Attorneys: Does Any Protection Remain?, 29 Buffalo L.Rev. 133 (1980) (suggested standards and procedures for handling pro hac vice applications); Comment, Leis v. Flynt: Retaining a Nonresident Attorney for Litigation, 79 Colum.L.Rev. 572 (1979).

16.   949 P.2d 1 (Cal.1998). The factual summary is largely drawn from the dissenting opinion of Justice Kennard.

ed with Tandem representatives, and in 1993 initiated an arbitration proceeding against Tandem on behalf of both companies with the American Arbitration Association office in San Francisco. Before an arbitration hearing was held, the dispute with Tandem was settled.

In 1994 ESQ–CAL and Iqbal Sandhu, its principal shareholder, sued Birbrower for malpractice. Birbrower cross-complained to recover its fee under the fee agreement. The plaintiffs' complaint was then amended to add ESQ–NY as a plaintiff. The plaintiffs' motion for summary judgment on the ground that the fee agreement was unenforceable because Birbrower had engaged in the unauthorized practice of law in California was sustained by the trial court and upheld by the intermediate court of appeals and the California Supreme Court.[17]

The high court's opinion held that California's unauthorized practice law, designed to ensure that legal services are competently performed, is not limited to preventing a nonlawyer (which includes a lawyer admitted in another state) from representing any one in a California court; it also prohibits anyone who is not a member of the California State Bar from giving legal advice and preparing contracts and other legal instruments in California. The court stated:

> In our view, the practice of law "in California" entails sufficient contact with the California client to render the nature of the legal service entails a clear legal representation. In addition to a quantitative analysis, we must consider the nature of the unlicensed lawyer's activities in the state. Mere fortuitous or attenuated contacts will not sustain a finding that the unlicensed lawyer practiced law "in California." The primary inquiry is whether the unlicensed lawyer engaged in sufficient activities in the state, or created a continuing relationship with the California client that included legal duties and obligations.[18]

Physical presence in California, the court said, is a relevant but not exclusive factor: an out-of-state lawyer would violate the statute by providing legal advice by telephone, fax or other means. Each case would be decided on its individual facts. In this case Birbrower engaged in "extensive practice" in California in advising ESQ–CAL on its dispute with Tandem, discussing strategy, negotiating with Tandem and initiating an arbitration proceeding. Under the statute, the court held, it is "irrelevant" whether an out-of-state lawyer "is, in fact, competent to practice in California." Any exception for out-of-state lawyers would have to be created by the California Legislature. Similarly, the law provided no exception for arbitration proceedings (other than a statutory one for international commercial disputes) and further legislation would be required to create one.

The court discussed the "limited exceptions" to California's unauthorized practice law. Statute or court rules permitted: (1) a trial judge to

---

17. The Supreme Court reversed one part of the lower court decision: the Birbrower firm was entitled to show that some of its services had been performed in New York and to recover for them on a quantum meruit basis, providing New York services could be severed from the fee agreement.

18. 949 P.2d at 5–6.

allow an out-of-state lawyer to make "a brief appearance" in a particular case; (2) a court to admit an out-of-state lawyer pro hac vice in a matter providing local counsel was attorney of record; (3) an out-of-state lawyer to practice before federal courts or certain federal agencies (but noting that each California district of the U.S. courts had a local rule limiting representation to members of the California bar); (4) a lawyer admitted in a foreign country might provide legal advice in California on the law of the that country, but not other legal advice, if admitted under a court rule dealing with "foreign legal consultants;" and (5) non-lawyers could participate in arbitration and conciliation of international commercial disputes under a California statute so providing. A footnote stated that "no statutory exception to [the unauthorized practice statute] allows out-of-state attorneys to practice law in California as long as they associated local counsel in good standing with the State Bar."[19]

RANTA v. MCCARNEY.[20] Ranta, a Minnesota lawyer, travelled to North Dakota to provide legal advice to McCarney. From time to time, Ranta billed McCarney the amount Ranta believed was fair and reasonable for the services rendered. McCarney paid Ranta regularly and referred him to "at least twenty clients" in Bismarck, where for a period Ranta opened what he called a "branch office." Ranta did not represent these clients in court proceedings but gave legal advice primarily on tax matters. In 1977 McCarney hired Ranta in connection with the sale of a Ford dealership. After the final documents were negotiated and signed in an all-day closing in Bismarck, Ranta billed McCarney for a balance due of $17,500. When Ranta brought suit to collect the unpaid fee, McCarney asserted that Ranta could not recover because he was not admitted to practice in North Dakota.

The trial court granted the motion to dismiss but stated that the equities favored Ranta since McCarney "received the total benefits of the contract and should not now be allowed to claim that Mr. Ranta is not entitled to his fee." On appeal, the court held that North Dakota's unauthorized practice statute, properly construed, barred recovery of compensation by an unlicensed attorney.

> The statute is intended to protect the public from unlicensed attorneys and is to be liberally construed "with a view to effecting its objects and to promoting justice." An out-of-State lawyer who is not authorized to practice law in this State (such as Ranta) sits in the same position as a suspended attorney previously admitted to practice law in this State . . .; such a person cannot lawfully practice law in this State, nor can that person charge a fee for such services.

The court stated that no exception for federal court or federal law practice was applicable because "Ranta's conduct did not involve an appearance in a federal court," and the court declined to recognize a "sister-state" exception. One dissenting justice stated that "[t]he only protection effected . . . in this case is the protection of the economic interests of the attorneys of this state and the estate of Mr. McCarney." A second dissenter

---

19. Id. at 4, n. 3.   **20.** 391 N.W.2d 161 (N.D. 1986).

argued that North Dakota should follow a New Jersey case[21] approving an award of fees to out-of-state counsel for a New Jersey estate for "federal tax matters, largely involving federal law and out-of-state activities." That case had said:

> Multistate relationships are a common part of today's society and are to be dealt with in common sense fashion. While the members of the general public are entitled to full protection against unlawful practitioners, their freedom of choice in the selection of their own counsel is to be highly regarded and not burdened by "technical restrictions which have no reasonable justification."

Local Control or National Bar?

Local control is enforced against trial lawyers by rules that limit court appearances to licensed local practitioners or those admitted pro hac vice for a specific litigation. The presence of an adversary in the courtroom setting provides an enforcement mechanism. A practical restraint on pro hac vice admission is also operative: In most states, the client must be willing to pay the additional cost of the associated local counsel.

Application and enforcement of local control is more difficult, however, with respect to counselors engaged in providing advice or facilitating transactions. Most of what they do occurs in the privacy of the law office. *Birbrower* and *Ranta* illustrate one enforcement device: denial of the opportunity to collect a fee for work performed. The out-of-state lawyer might also be disciplined by a jurisdiction in which she was practicing, the sanction being an order forbidding her from further practice in the state. Finally, it is possible, although highly unlikely, that the lawyer's conduct will be viewed as a disciplinary violation by her home state.

Lawyer Ranta attempted to justify his North Dakota practice on the ground that he was giving specialized advice on federal tax matters. Accounting firms can give tax advice nationwide, why can't lawyers? Ranta's problem was that his work for North Dakota clients involved all aspects of some business transactions, such as McCarney's sale of his Ford dealership. He had also established a branch office in North Dakota.[22] The *Ranta* decision made few waves partly because of these facts and also because North Dakota does not place high on the nation's legal services markets.

The law firm world was stunned, however, when the California Supreme Court held in *Birbrower* that a New York law firm could not collect a $1 million fee for work in connection with a California arbitration proceeding on behalf of a client, originally New York-based, that the firm had represented for a number of years. Business transactions in our national economy cross state lines without even noticing them and clients expect a

---

21. In Re Estate of Waring, 221 A.2d 193, 197 (N.J.1966).

22. Restatement § 3, cmt. e states that "a lawyer admitted in State A may not open an office in State B for the general practice of law there or otherwise engage in the continuous, regular, or repeated representation of clients within the other state."

law firm to deal with resulting legal issues wherever they may arise. *Birbrower* established that this common practice carries the risk that the law firm may be unable to collect the agreed-upon fee whenever the client is unwilling to pay and fee enforcement must be sought in the client's home state.

Are such restrictive rules justified by substantial local interests, or are they a form of economic protectionism for the local bar?[23] The interests generally relied on in defense of local control are those discussed throughout the domain of unauthorized practice: the harmful effects on local consumers of the provision of allegedly incompetent or unethical services by out-of-state practitioners; the relative ignorance of local substantive law and procedure on the part of out-of-state practitioners; and the difficulty of applying local disciplinary machinery to out-of-state lawyers. The restrictions pose the most difficulties for lawyers who move from one state to another for personal reasons, who are transferred by their corporate employers, who seek to develop a national practice in a specialty field and who are sought by unpopular clients who encounter difficulty in obtaining local representation.

In Fought & Co. v. Steel Engineering and Erection, Inc.,[24] an Oregon law firm acting as general counsel to an international client assisted local counsel in recovering damages for the client against the state of Hawaii arising out of construction of an airport on Maui. The Oregon firm sought and obtained a portion of the statutory attorney's fee for its work in preparing the litigation. The Hawaii Supreme Court distinguished *Birbrower* on the ground that local counsel had been retained and participated substantially. Hawaiian clients, the court also said, would have difficulty getting quality legal services at competitive fees if the unauthorized practice restriction made it impossible for mainland firms to collect fees.

Restatement § 3 (jurisdictional scope of practice by lawyer) provides that "a lawyer currently admitted in one jurisdiction may provide legal services to clients in a matter: ... (3) at a place within the jurisdiction in which the lawyer is not admitted to the extent the lawyer's activities in the matter arise out of or are otherwise reasonably related to the lawyer's practice [in the jurisdiction where admitted]." Comment *e* states that a lawyer may advise a home state client about the law of another state, conduct activities while physically present in another state for a client that has extensive contacts with the lawyer's home state, and do work ancillary to other representation of the client. Illustration 5 to Restatement § 3 indicates that an estate planning lawyer may draft a will and other documents for an out-of-state client, and may even travel to the client's state to have the documents executed, without engaging in the unautho-

---

23. See generally Charles W. Wolfram, Sneaking Around in the Legal Profession: Interjurisdictional Unauthorized Practice by Transactional Lawyers, 36 S.Tex.L.Rev. 665 (1995); Fred Zacharias, Federalizing Legal Ethics, 73 Tex.L.Rev. 335 (1994).

24. 951 P.2d 487 (Hawaii 1998).

rized practice of law. The reporter's note criticizes *Birbrower* and a New York case, Spivak v. Sacks,[25] as "unduly restrictive."

How could the Birbrower firm have protected itself from the risk that its clients would not pay? Consider the following: (1) associate a California lawyer as "local counsel;" (2) persuade the client to have the agreement with Tandem subject to New York law and arbitration in New York; (3) include a provision in the fee agreement that it was governed by New York law and that any fee dispute would be arbitrated in New York; and (4) ask the client to pay a substantial part of the fee in advance. Do any of these arrangements violate other ethics rules?

A National Solution?

The cases discussed above are inconsistent with the contemporary practice of law. Business lawyers give advice and handle transactions across state lines, bringing in lawyers from the jurisdiction only when a formal legal opinion is required. Even in litigation, national practice is carried on through liberal use of pro hac vice admission. If states fail to amend their unauthorized practice laws or state courts to interpret them more liberally, what can be done? Should the Commerce Clause or the Privileges and Immunities Clause be interpreted as protecting interstate law practice?[26]

May a lawyer who is handling a matter involving federal law engage in nationwide practice? In Spanos v. Skouras Theatres Corp.,[27] Judge Friendly encouraged an affirmative response by stating: "[U]nder the privileges and immunities clause of the Constitution, no state can prohibit a citizen with a federal claim or defense from engaging an out-of-state lawyer to collaborate with an in-state lawyer and give legal advice concerning it within the state."[28] Spanos, a California lawyer, assisted a theater chain in planning a

---

25. 211 N.E.2d 329 (N.Y.1965) (although "incidental and innocuous" practice by out-of-state lawyer is permissible, California divorce lawyer, called there by New York acquaintance to come to New York to assist her in developing strategy to resist husband's attempts to gain custody in Connecticut proceeding, could not recover fee for 14 days of work advising client and her local counsel in New York). See also El Gemayel v. Seaman, 533 N.E.2d 245 (N.Y. 1988) (Lebanese lawyer, residing in Washington, D.C., made phone calls to New York client and one trip to New York, in assisting her in regaining custody of child taken to Lebanon by father in violation of Massachusetts custody decree; fee recovered because New York contacts, unlike *Spivak*, were "incidental and innocuous").

26. Under the Treaty of Rome governing the European Community, an attorney licensed in one country may provide legal services in another on the basis of "home

title" or additional qualifications. Home title (the license in the other country) permits provision of advice on the local law of any nation of the community, except for activities specifically reserved to members of the local bar. In the United Kingdom, for example, activities specifically reserved include representation in court without assistance or undertaking probate and conveyancing work. See John Toulmin, Legal Practice in Europe, 8 Int'l Fin.L.Rev. 19 (1989). A 1997 law of the European Parliament entitles a lawyer qualified in one member country to become fully admitted in another if the lawyer has practiced the law of host country and EU law for more than three years. See EU Practice Rules Are Near Approval, Nat'l L.J., Dec. 15, 1997, p. A3.

27. 364 F.2d 161 (2d Cir.1966) (en banc).

28. 364 F.2d at 170. The per curiam opinion in *Leis v. Flynt*, discussed above at p. 1055, pointedly stated that this portion of the

major antitrust action in New York. Spanos did not seek admission pro hac vice but performed extensive work over several years, mostly in New York. After the case was settled, the client refused to pay. The court, in addition to its broad statement of constitutional principle, quoted above, held that the failure of the client's New York lawyer to move for Spanos' pro hac admission, which would have been granted as a matter of course by the federal court under its rules, could not be used to defeat the out-of-state lawyer from collecting his fee.

Commentators have proposed the legislative creation of a national bar examination qualifying those who pass for practice in any state. A less dramatic proposal would be a separate national admissions process for practice involving federal courts and federal law. Another possibility is to separate trial court representation from other aspects of the practice of law, with state admission (either permanent or pro hac vice) required for in-court representation, but legal advice and other practice of law opened to nationwide competition by judicial decision or federal legislation. Would one of these proposals be desirable? How likely is it that a change of this type will come about? Is this a fit subject for federal legislation?

What State's Law Governs a Lawyer's Conduct?

Multijurisdictional practice is an everyday activity of many litigators, business lawyers and in-house lawyers. Most of this practice is totally consistent with state prohibitions of unauthorized practice. Many lawyers are admitted in more than one state; firms that represent clients doing business across state lines often have branch offices in states where plants are located (with locally admitted attorneys in that office who participate in the representation); and out-of-state litigators are normally admitted pro hac vice to handle a particular matter. These and other circumstances give rise to a choice-of-law problem: which state's law of lawyering should govern the lawyer in a transaction or litigation?

Despite the growth and prevalence of multijurisdictional practice, there are astonishingly few judicial decisions and ethics opinions addressing choice of law. As some of the cases reprinted in this book indicate, the problem is often ignored by the parties and the court. In In re ACC/Lincoln Savings & Loan, for example, supra p. 745, the court cited only one ethics rule (Model Rule 1.13, adopted by Arizona, but not in effect in California or Ohio) in considering claims brought in an Arizona federal court that an Ohio-based law firm assisted the fraud of an Arizona mogul in its representation in California of a California savings and loan. The general tendency of lawyers and judges to ignore choice-of-law issues in legal ethics cases, often by assuming that the law of the forum applies, was understandable prior to 1983 because the ethics codes were largely uniform across the country. That is no longer the case. The state variations in adopting the

---

Spanos decision "must be considered to have been limited, if not rejected entirely, by [subsequent Supreme Court decisions]." 439 U.S. at 438, 442 n. 4. But *Leis* itself is impaired as a precedent by language of the Court in *Piper*, reprinted above at p. 1048. So the current status of Judge Friendly's view is in doubt.

Model Rules have created situations in which, for example, disclosure of client fraud is required in New Jersey and prohibited in nearby Delaware; and where screening to cure an imputed conflict of interest is recognized in Pennsylvania but not across the state line in New Jersey.

A small number of cases, usually involving malpractice or fee litigation between a lawyer and a former client, explicitly address the issue. In Bernick v. Frost,[29] for example, New Jersey's statutory limits on contingency fees were held to apply to a contingent fee contract executed in New Jersey between a New Jersey lawyer and a New Jersey client concerning litigation conducted in New York. The court held that the dominance of the New Jersey contacts "points unequivocally to the application of New Jersey law."

The problem also arises in the context of professional discipline. Model Rule 8.5(a)—the entirety of the rule that was promulgated in 1983 and adopted in most Model Rule jurisdictions—restates a traditional principle that a state may discipline a lawyer regardless of where the lawyer's misconduct occurs. Concern over the growing "balkanization" of the law of lawyering led to the addition of a disciplinary choice of law rule in 1993. The amended rule provides greater clarity and predictability to lawyers who practice across state lines, creates some new problems and fails to deal with others.[30]

M.R. 8.5(b) clarifies which jurisdiction's disciplinary rules applies to lawyers who are admitted and practice in more than one jurisdiction. M.R. 8.5(b)(1) provides that in litigation, a lawyer, including one admitted pro hac vice to handle a particular case, is subject to the professional rules of the forum state. In all other situations, dealt with in M.R. 8.5(b)(2), lawyers are subject to the rules of the jurisdiction in which they "principally" practice, with one exception—where the particular conduct in question "clearly has its predominant effect" in another jurisdiction. For example, Comment [4] states that a lawyer, principally practicing in State A but also admitted in State B, who handles an acquisition for a company whose headquarters and operations are in State B, would be subject to the professional rules of State B.

---

29. 510 A.2d 56, 59–60 (N.J.Super.Ct.App.Div.1986).

30. See Symposium, Ethics and the Multijurisdictional Practice of Law, 36 S.Tex. L.Rev. 657 (1995), especially articles by Jeffrey L. Rensberger (arguing that focus should be on who should be protected when lawyers fail to do what they should rather than what lawyers do); Mary C. Daly (arguing that contractual agreement on the law governing the relation should be permitted, providing the jurisdiction selected has a substantial relationship to the representation); Arvid Roach (analyzing and defending the choice-of-law rule of M.R. 8.5(b); and commentary of Mark H. Aultman, Kathleen Clark and David Luban on the same subject.

CHAPTER 11

LAW, LAWYERS AND JUSTICE

INTRODUCTORY NOTE

One tradition in Judaism explains the Jews' place as the chosen people with the following story. God's presence in the world, the Shekinah, was once whole in the form of a giant crystal globe. This globe was shattered into millions of tiny pieces of glass. The Jews were chosen as the people whose responsibility it is to collect the pieces of glass to try and restore God's presence in the world. In Hebrew this responsibility is captured by the words *"tikkun olum,"* which means to repair the world. The story explains that the Jews were given the Torah, the law, at Mount Sinai as the means to fulfill their responsibility. The moral of the tale is that by living a life dedicated to studying and living the law one helps to repair the world.

We begin our examination of law, lawyers and justice with this story because most law students and many lawyers believe that law is an important and necessary means of repairing the world and at its best a life in the law is devoted to this task of repair, to bringing justice into the world. In this chapter we investigate the connection between law and justice, between being a lawyer and repairing the world. We begin with the grand gesture, repairing the world, if you will, by shaking it. We move next to lawyers for the poor and public interest lawyers, repairing the world by trying to even out the odds. We conclude with the day-to-day work of ordinary lawyers—lawyers who draft contracts, litigate tort suits, negotiate messy divorces, advise corporations and the like. Are these lawyers, one of whom you will most likely be, helping to repair the world? Is the disappointment that many lawyers feel a function of the contradiction between their ideal of practice, that lawyers should help repair the world, and the reality of practice as they experience it? Do we need to abandon the ideal of repairing the world because the ideal does not correspond to reality or can we reformulate what it means to repair the world? Does picking up one tiny piece of glass at a time count?[1]

---

1. A Christian story provides an affirmative answer: Jesus is describing God inviting the righteous at the last judgment to "inherit the kingdom prepared for you," and saying to them: " 'for I was hungry and you gave me food, I was thirsty and you gave me something to drink, ... I was naked and you gave me clothing, I was sick and you took care of me, I was in prison and you visited me.' Then the righteous will answer him, 'Lord, when was it that [we did these things]?' And the Lord will answer them, 'Truly, I tell you, just as you did it to one of the least of us, you did it to me.' " Matt. 25: 31–40.

In Gideon v. Wainwright,[2] the Warren Court held that due process "cannot be realized if the poor man charged with a crime has to face his accusers without a lawyer to assist him."[3] In *Gideon*, the Court offered two explanations for the essential connection between lawyers and justice. First, quoting "the moving words of Justice Sutherland in Powell v. Alabama," the Court explained:

> The right to be heard would be, in many cases, of little avail if it did not comprehend the right to be heard by counsel. Even the intelligent and educated layman has small and sometimes no skill in the science of law. If charged with crime, he is incapable, generally, of determining for himself whether the indictment is good or bad. He is unfamiliar with the rules of evidence. Left without the aid of counsel he may be put on trial without a proper charge, and convicted upon incompetent evidence, or evidence irrelevant to the issue or otherwise inadmissible. He lacks both the skill and knowledge adequately to prepare his defense, even though he have a perfect one. He requires the guiding hand of counsel at every step in the proceedings against him. Without it, though he be not guilty, he faces the danger of conviction because he does not know how to establish his innocence.[4]

Justice Sutherland's explanation of the connection between lawyers and justice emphasizes commutative justice—justice envisioned as fairness through neutrality in adjudicating guilt and innocence, rights and duties. Lawyers, here, are part of justice itself. Adjudication that is fair and just normally requires the participation of a lawyer to be realized.[5] Is this less true in civil proceedings than in criminal proceedings?

A second quotation, from the *Gideon* case, emphasizes a different aspect of justice and thus a different connection between lawyers and justice.

> Governments, both state and federal, quite properly spend vast sums of money to establish machinery to try defendants accused of crime. Lawyers to prosecute are everywhere deemed essential to protect the public's interest in an orderly society. Similarly, there are few defendants charged with crime, few indeed, who fail to hire the best lawyers they can get to prepare and present their defenses. That government hires lawyers to prosecute and defendants who have the money hire lawyers to defend are the strongest indications of the widespread belief that lawyers in criminal courts are necessities, not luxuries.[6]

Justice here is distributive—justice as providing for the poor and unfortunate in society. Justice here is giving the poor what those with means have and consider essential, lawyers. Why those with means consider lawyers essential is explained by the connection between lawyers and commutative justice.

---

2. 372 U.S. 335 (1963).

3. 372 U.S. at 344 (1963). The evolution of an indigent criminal defendant's right to counsel at state expense is discussed in Chapter 3 at p. 176 supra.

4. 372 U.S. at 344–45, quoting Powell v. Alabama, 287 U.S. 45, 68–69 (1932) (in-volving the Scottsboro Boys), discussed at p. 176 supra.

5. But cf. Faretta v. California, 422 U.S. 806 (1975) (establishing the right to proceed without counsel).

6. 372 U.S. at 344.

Few, if any, well-to-do civil litigants would proceed to trial without a lawyer, and governments use lawyers in civil proceedings with the same regularity as in criminal proceedings. Thus the same widespread belief—that lawyers are necessities not luxuries in contested proceedings involving substantial stakes—extends to civil as well as criminal cases. Should a poor person have a right to a lawyer in a civil proceeding? This issue is discussed at p. 1091 infra.

Both aspects of justice, commutative and distributive, are included in the American concept of justice, meaning that the ideal of justice is that society will be even-handed in dealing with all litigants and decently open-handed in dealing with the poor. But there is yet a third aspect of the ideal of justice as it is conceived in this country that is important to this discussion and which complicates the picture drawn thus far. Substantively the ideal of justice in America affirms individual equality, notwithstanding that in practice a denial of equality to women, blacks and other minorities was and is an acknowledged fact. On the positive side, justice as the political equality of individuals signifies that everyone has an equal right to participate in various political and legal processes. On the negative side, however, the principle of individual political equality signifies that no class or group has a recognized and accepted special responsibility to carry the burden of social justice. It follows that no chosen people have a special duty to repair the world through pursuit of justice.

Fulfilling either the commutative or distributive aspects of justice entails great intellectual and practical difficulties. Enhancing these difficulties, however, is the very real tension between the special responsibility for justice that both the commutative and distributive aspects of justice assign to lawyers and the American ideal that rejects assigning such special responsibility to one group. Moreover, it is not just nonlawyers who have serious doubts about the justice of assigning lawyers a special responsibility for justice, lawyers too have such doubts. Who appointed *us* as the special guardians of justice? This question resurfaces in different forms in the materials discussed below: Why should lawyers have to volunteer to represent the poor without adequate compensation? Who anointed us to represent the public interest? What gives a lawyer the right to try to stop an individual client from doing something because the lawyer thinks it is of questionable legality or unjust or unwise? We return to these questions at the end of this chapter, but we raise them now so that you may consider them in thinking about the issues raised in the materials that follow.

A. SHAKING THE WORLD: LAWYERS FOR AND AS REVOLUTIONARIES

1. POLITICS AND THE COURTROOM

Professor Cover penetrates to the heart of the use of force that lies behind legal authority:[7]

---

7. Robert M. Cover, Violence and the Word, 95 Yale L.J. 1601, 1608–09 (1986).

The act of sentencing a convicted defendant is among [the] most routine of acts performed by judges. Yet it is immensely revealing of the way in which [legal] interpretation is shaped by violence. First, examine the event from the perspective of the defendant. The defendant's world is threatened. But he sits, usually quietly, as if engaged in a civil discourse. If convicted, the defendant customarily walks— escorted—to prolonged confinement, usually without significant disturbance to the civil appearance of the event. It is, of course, grotesque to assume that the civil facade is "voluntary" except in the sense that it represents the defendant's autonomous recognition of the overwhelming array of violence ranged against him, and of the hopelessness of resistance or outcry....[17]

There are societies in which contrition or shame control defendants' behavior to a greater extent than does violence.... But I think it is unquestionably the case in the United States that most prisoners walk into prison because they know they will be dragged or beaten into prison if they do not walk. They do not organize force against being dragged because they know that if they wage this kind of battle they will lose—very possibly their lives.

If I have exhibited some sense of sympathy for the victims of this violence it is misleading. Very often the balance of terror in this regard is just as I would want it. But I do not wish us to pretend that we talk our prisoners into jail. The "interpretations" or "conversations" that are the preconditions for violent incarceration are themselves implements of violence.

What then is the criminal defense lawyer's role—or for that matter, the role of a lawyer in a civil proceeding that threatens to divest a client of her child, her property or something else held dear—when the client decides to respond by breaking the rules of the proceeding as a protest, as a challenge, as a statement that what is going on will not be calmly accepted?

Norman Dorsen and Leon Friedman, Disorder in the Court

Pp. 56–64, 272, 276–277 (1973).[8]

The Chicago Conspiracy Trial

The most notorious disorderly trial in recent years was the Chicago conspiracy trial of 1969–70. In that case, eight leading members of the

---

17. ... Bobby Seale taught those of us who lived through the 1960's that the court's physical control over the defendant's body lies at the heart of the criminal process. The defendant's "civil conduct," therefore can never signify a shared understanding of the event; it may signify his fear that any public display of his interpretation of the event as "bullshit" will end in violence perpetrated against him, pain inflicted

upon him. Our constitutional law, quite naturally enough, provides for the calibrated use of ascending degrees of overt violence to maintain the "order" of the criminal trial. See, e.g., Illinois v. Allen, 397 U.S. 337 (1970)....

8. Copyright © 1973 by the Association of the Bar of the City of New York. Reprinted with permission.

Vietnam antiwar movement were indicted under the federal anti-riot statute of 1968 for conspiring, organizing, and inciting riots during the 1968 Democratic National Convention in Chicago. It appears from the evidence introduced at the trial that seven of the eight defendants—David Dellinger, Abbie Hoffman, Jerry Rubin, Rennie Davis, Tom Hayden, Lee Weiner, and John Froines—had planned to hold massive demonstrations in the streets and parks of Chicago at the time of the 1968 convention to protest the continuation of the Vietnam war. After extensive negotiations with city officials, permits for large-scale demonstrations were refused. Nevertheless, rallies were held, which led to violent confrontations between the demonstrators and the Chicago police.

Subsequent investigations by a special committee of the National Violence Commission concluded that the disturbances that ensued were the result of a "police riot"....

The trial drew considerable public notice because of the notoriety of the defendants and because this was the first use of a statute which was of doubtful constitutionality. From its inception numerous incidents occurred which attracted even more attention. In the week before the trial began, four of the attorneys who had appeared earlier in the case for specific pretrial motions telegrammed that they were withdrawing from further participation. On the motion of the United States attorney, Judge Julius Hoffman took the unusual step of issuing bench warrants to have all four arrested and brought before him. Five days later, after a storm of protest from lawyers and law professors, he vacated the order.

Additional contention arose because of the judge's refusal to postpone the trial until Charles Garry of California, who was engaged to act as Bobby Seale's lawyer, had recovered from a gall bladder operation. Seale insisted from the first days of the trial that he was unrepresented until Garry appeared. On September 26, he said to the court:

> If I am consistently denied this right of legal defense counsel of my choice who is effective by the judge of this Court, then I can only see the judge as a blatant racist of the United States Court.

On the same day the court reprimanded Tom Hayden for giving a clenched fist salute to the jury and Abbie Hoffman for blowing them kisses. On September 30, the court discharged one juror after reading to her the contents of a threatening letter signed "The Black Panther," which had been sent to her home. On October 15, the defendants asked to celebrate Vietnam Moratorium Day and tried to drape the counsel table with American and N.L.F. flags. On October 22 the defendants tried to bring a birthday cake into the courtroom for Bobby Seale....

Gagging and Binding of Bobby Seale

The most serious disorders occurred over the problem of representation for Bobby Seale. After Charles Garry became unavailable, William Kunstler filed an appearance for Seale ostensibly in order to see him at the county jail. On the first day of the trial, he also filed a general appearance for four of the defendants, including Seale. On September 26 Seale rejected Kunstler as his lawyer and thereafter insisted on his right to defend himself. The court and Seale argued about this issue at almost every opportunity. On October 14, [Seale engaged in an extended colloquy with Judge Hoffman, objecting to Kunstler's representation of him and insisting that if Garry could not represent him, he would represent himself. He continued talking after being directed to be silent.]

On October 20 Bobby Seale made a motion to act as his own lawyer. The U.S. attorney opposed the motion and Judge Hoffman ruled that Seale was represented by Kunstler and could not discharge him. The court of appeals later ruled that Judge Hoffman acted improperly in not inquiring whether Seale wanted Kunstler to represent him.

The conflict escalated on October 28, when Seale again insisted on his right to represent himself.

Mr. Seale:	. . . You are in contempt of people's constitutional rights. You are in contempt of the constitutional rights of the mass of the people of the United States. You are the one in contempt of people's constitutional rights. I am not in contempt of nothing. You are the one who is in contempt. The people of America need to admonish you and the whole Nixon administration.
Mr. Hayden:	Let the record show the judge was laughing.
Mr. Seale:	Yes, he is laughing.
The Court:	Who made that remark?
Mr. Foran [prosecutor]:	The defendant Hayden, your Honor, made the remark. . . .
The Court:	You are not doing very well for yourself.
Mr. Seale:	Yes, that's because you violated my constitutional rights, Judge Hoffman. That's because you violated them overtly, deliberately, in a very racist manner. Somebody ought to point out the law to you. . . .

On the next day, October 29, Seale addressed a group of his followers in the courtroom before the judge appeared. As soon as the court was called into session, Richard Schultz, the assistant United States attorney, spoke:

Mr. Schultz:	If the Court please, before you came into this courtroom, if the Court please, Bobby Seale stood up and addressed this group.

Mr. Seale: That's right, brother. I spoke on behalf of my constitutional rights. I have a right to speak on behalf of my constitutional rights. That's right.

Mr. Schultz: And he told those—people in the audience, if the Court please—and I want this—on the record. It happened this morning—that if he's attacked, they know what to do. He was talking to these people about an attack by them.

Mr. Seale: You're lying. Dirty liar. I told them to defend themselves. You are a rotten racist pig, fascist liar, that's what you are. You're a rotten liar. You are a fascist pig liar.

                              I said they had a right to defend themselves if they are attacked, and I hope that the record carries that, and I hope the record shows that tricky Dick Schultz, working for Richard Nixon and [his] administration all understand that tricky Dick Schultz is a liar, and we have a right to defend ourselves, and if you attack me I will defend myself.

Seale was forcibly put into his chair by the marshals. After he again insisted on his right to represent himself, the court took a brief recess. Seale was then taken out of the courtroom by the marshals and returned bound and gagged in his chair. The gag was not secure, and he could still speak through it. Kunstler described the scene for the record:

Mr. Kunstler: I wanted to say the record should indicate that Mr. Seale is seated on a metal chair, each hand handcuffed to the leg of the chair on both the right and left sides so he cannot raise his hands, and a gag is tightly pressed into his mouth and tied at the rear, and that when he attempts to speak, a muffled sound comes out.

Mr. Seale (gagged):   You don't represent me. Sit down, Kunstler.

The Court: Mr. Marshal, I don't think you have accomplished your purpose by that kind of a contrivance. We will have to take another recess.

On the next day, October 30, 1969, Seale was again bound and gagged.

Mr. Weinglass: If your Honor please, the buckles on the leather strap holding Mr. Seale's hand is digging into his hand and he appears to be trying to free his hand from that pressure. Could he be assisted?

The Court: If the marshal has concluded that he needs assistance, of course.

Mr. Kunstler:	Your Honor, are we going to stop this medieval torture that is going on in this courtroom? I think this is a disgrace.
Mr. Rubin:	This guy is putting his elbow in Bobby's mouth and it wasn't necessary at all.
Mr. Kunstler:	This is no longer a court of order, your Honor; this is a medieval torture chamber. It is a disgrace. They are assaulting the other defendants also.

The three days from October 28 through October 30 produced the most serious crisis in the trial. Of the 137 citations for contempt against the defendants, 47 occurred then. Seale was cited six times for his actions and the remaining defendants for their support of Seale and their protest against what was happening to him. One week later, on November 5, 1969, Seale was held in contempt by Judge Hoffman and severed—from the trial. He was sentenced to forty-eight months in jail—three months for each of sixteen acts of misconduct. The court of appeals later held that four of the sixteen specifications dealing with Seale's attempt to defend himself were insufficient to justify contempt charges. After the case was reversed and sent back by the court of appeals for retrial before a different judge, the government decided not to reprosecute the contempt charges because it did not wish to disclose information concerning wiretaps of Seale.

Ralph Abernathy Incident

Two other triggering events that led to numerous contempt citations were the refusal to allow Reverend Ralph Abernathy to testify and the revocation of the bail of David Dellinger. On Friday, January 31, the defense indicated it was prepared to rest its case on Monday, February 2, after submitting some television film. Over the weekend, another witness, Ralph Abernathy, became available. On Monday morning, Kunstler asked to reopen the case to allow Abernathy to testify. Judge Hoffman refused the request.

The Court:	There have been several witnesses called here during this trial . . . whose testimony the Court ruled could not even be presented to the jury— singers, performers, and former office holders. I think in the light of the representations made by you unequivocally, sir, with no reference to Dr. Abernathy, I will deny your motion that we hold—
Mr. Kunstler:	. . . Your Honor. . . . I think what you have just said is about the most outrageous statement I have ever heard from a bench, and I am going to say my piece right now, and you can hold me in contempt right now if you wish to. You have

violated every principle of fair play when you excluded Ramsey Clark from that witness stand. The New York Times, among others, has called it the ultimate outrage in American justice.

Voices:

Right on.

Mr. Kunstler:

I am outraged to be in this court before you. Now because I made a statement on Friday that I had only a cameraman, and I discovered on Saturday that Ralph Abernathy, who is the chairman of the Mobilization, is in town, and he can be here.... I am trembling because I am so outraged, I haven't been able to get this out before, and I am saying it now, and then I want you to put me in jail if you want to. You can do anything you want with me ... because I feel disgraced to be here.

Kunstler was then ordered to make no reference to Abernathy before the jury.

Mr. Schultz:

Your Honor, may the defendants and their counsel then not make any reference in front of this jury that they wanted Dr. Abernathy to testify?

Mr. Kunstler:

No, no.

The Court:

I order you not to make such a statement.

Mr. Kunstler:

We are not going to abide by any such comment as that. Dr. Ralph Abernathy is going to come into this courtroom, and I am going to repeat my motion before that jury.

The Court:

I order you not to.

Mr. Kunstler:

Then you will have to send me to jail, I am sorry. We have a right to state our objection to resting before the jury.

The Court:

Don't do it.

After the jury was brought into the court, Abernathy arrived and Kunstler immediately asked that he be allowed to testify. The request was refused....

Lawyer Contempts

The contempt citations against the two lawyers in the case did not involve abusive language or obscene remarks. The government said in its appellate brief, "The attorneys present a far different case; they did not heap vituperation upon the judge as did their clients, but rather repeatedly contested rulings by the judge to the point of obstructing the trial." Thus

Weinglass was cited for refusing to sit down immediately after being ordered to do so, for asking questions on cross-examination beyond the scope of the direct examination, for repeating citations of legal authorities, for continuing an argument after the judge had ruled on it, and for making disrespectful remarks about the prosecution. He also was cited for making "invidious comparisons" between the court's treatment of the government's case and of the defense's.

Kunstler was cited for similar transgressions, such as refusing to sit down or continuing to argue. The court also cited him for going into the substance of a document not introduced in evidence and for arguing about the time of recess. In addition he defied specific orders of the court not to mention before the jury certain matters which the court had ruled on. Kunstler was given the maximum sentence of six months for these transgressions and an additional six months for his intemperate remarks on the morning of the Abernathy affair. He also received four months for telling the court, "You brought this on [referring to fistfights between the marshals and spectators.] This is your fault," and four months for accusing the government of using violence in the courtroom and of liking to strike women. He was also cited for referring to the gagging of Bobby Seale as "medieval torture" and for expressing his approval of disapproving groans from the spectators.

Total Contempt Citations

Aside from the cluster of disruptions described above, the trial proceeded without significant interruption for four and a half months. There were individual incidents from time to time, produced in part by the unconventional life style and political activism of the defendants: Rubin was cited twice for wearing judicial robes in court; Hoffman, for blowing kisses to the jury and asking the court, "How is your war stock doing"; Dellinger, for requesting a moment of silence on Moratorium Day; and all of the defendants were cited for interrupting the court or making comments on political subjects or the proceedings. At the very end of the trial, immediately after the jury was charged, Judge Hoffman handed down a total of 159 citations for contempt, 121 against the defendants other than Seale and 38 against the two lawyers. The largest single category (36 citations) consisted of defendants refusing to rise at the beginning or close of a court session. In 27 cases they called the judge a name or accused him of prejudice or injustice or made sarcastic comments to him, mostly arising from the incidents described above. In 10 cases they interrupted or insulted the prosecution, and in 11 cases they applauded or laughed in the courtroom.

On May 11, 1972, all the contempt convictions of the defendants and the lawyers were reversed by the Seventh Circuit Court of Appeals.[9] The appellate court held that the judge cannot wait until the end of the trial to punish the defendants and the lawyers.

---

9. [Editors' note:] In Re Dellinger, 461 F.2d
389 (7th Cir.1972).

... the trial judge must disqualify himself if he waits to act until the conclusion of the trial. When the trial proceedings have terminated, the need for proceeding summarily is not present.

The court also determined that Bobby Seale could not be punished summarily by the judge.

The court of appeals sent the case back to the district court level for retrial of the contempt before a judge other than Judge Hoffman.... [Judge Gignoux of the District of Maine was designated to try the remanded contempt case. At the close of the government's case, two defendants and a number of contempt specifications were dismissed. The remaining defendants then testified. Weinglass, Davis and Hayden were acquitted; Dellinger, Hoffman, Rubin and Kunstler were found guilty of various contempts but no fines or sentences were imposed. In re Dellinger, 270 F.Supp. 1304 (N.D.Ill.1973). On appeal, the Seventh Circuit affirmed. The two contempt counts against lawyer Kunstler involved (1) a lengthy personal attack on the trial judge and (2) his statement before the jury objecting to the judge's decision not to permit Abernathy to testify).]

The Contempt Power

Federal and state courts possess authority to hold trial participants in contempt for conduct relating to the proceeding. Civil contempt, often employed for conduct occurring in the presence of the judge, is remedial in character—an effort to coerce a person to do something that person has refused to do. Criminal contempt, on the other hand, punishes the offending individual in an effort to vindicate the authority of the court.[10] A criminal sanction must be determinate, whereas a civil sanction must be remedial or coercive, and must be lifted immediately upon compliance.

In the Whitewater Investigation, for example, Susan McDougall was first committed to prison for up to 18 months for civil contempt. She had refused to testify about certain matters before the grand jury after having been given immunity from prosecution; if she had agreed to testify, she would have been immediately released. Instead, after the civil contempt effort to remedy her refusal had failed, she was charged with obstruction of justice and criminal contempt. The jury acquitted her on the obstruction of justice charge but deadlocked on the criminal contempt charges.[11] President Clinton was held in civil contempt for lying in his deposition in the lawsuit brought against him by Paula Jones.[12] The judge ordered that the President pay the costs to the court of the judge's having attended that deposition in D.C. and reasonable attorneys' fees of Jones' lawyers incurred

10. See, e.g., Gompers v. Buck's Stove & Range Co., 221 U.S. 418, 422 (1911).

11. Neil A. Lewis, Federal Jury Acquits McDougal on One Charge and Is Split on 2, N.Y.Times, Apr.13, 1999, p. A1.

12. See Jones v. Clinton, 36 F.Supp.2d 1118 (D.Ark.1999).

as a result of the President's false testimony. The theory was that these payments were remedial in nature and not punitive and thus could be imposed via the civil contempt process.

A civil contemnor is entitled to only minimal due process: notice and the opportunity to be heard. Neither proof beyond a reasonable doubt nor a jury trial is required. Those faced with criminal contempt, on the other hand, are entitled to most of the rights of criminal defendants generally:

> [T]he right to be advised of the charges; the right to the assistance of counsel; a right to a jury trial if the sentence imposed will exceed six months confinement or constitute a "nonpetty" fine; the presumption of innocence; the requirement that guilt be proved beyond a reasonable doubt; the right to be tried by an unbiased judge in a public trial in those cases deserving a trial; the opportunity to present a defense and call witnesses (except when the contempt is committed in open court and no serious sanction is imposed); the protection against double jeopardy; and the availability of a presidential pardon.[13]

Securing Courtroom Decorum[14]

The intertwined problems of judicial intemperance and lawyer misconduct are difficult to solve simply because the possible remedies and sanctions by which to control them are so limited as compared to those which may be invoked against a litigant or spectator. A disruptive spectator may simply be excluded from the trial. Members of the news media can be excluded if their presence intrudes on calm and orderly procedure. As to litigants, Illinois v. Allen[15] establishes that a defendant's presence at trial is a right that can be denied if he refuses to conform to elemental requirements of courtroom decorum. Accordingly, where a litigant's disturbances obstruct fulfillment of his opportunity to participate, he may be excluded and his trial conducted in absentia. But while in special circumstances bystanders and even litigants can be dispensed with and a trial still be held, the same is not true of the judge nor, in an adversary system, of counsel.

Should the trial judge preside over the criminal contempt hearing? The central question at the stage of adjudicating a criminal contempt is who shall preside. The traditional rule that the trial judge may ordinarily hear the contempt either immediately or after the conclusion of the proceeding has been eroded by decisions establishing that, if the defendant's conduct "includes a personal attack on the trial judge carrying such potential for bias that he is not 'likely to maintain that calm detachment necessary for fair adjudication,' the trial judge must disqualify himself if he waits to act until the conclusion of the trial."[16] As applied to misconduct by lawyers,

13. Joel M. Androphy & Keith A. Byers, Federal Contempt of Court, 61 Tex.B.J. 16, 26 (1998).

14. This note is adapted, with permission, from Geoffrey C. Hazard, Jr., Securing Courtroom Decorum, 80 Yale L.J. 433 (1970).

15. 397 U.S. 337 (1970).

16. In re Dellinger, 461 F.2d 389, 395 (7th Cir.1972), quoting Mayberry v. Pennsylvania, 400 U.S. 455, 465 (1971) (reversing contempt of pro se defendant and stating: "[w]here ... [a judge] does not act the instant the contempt is committed, but

this exception nearly swallows the rule. Where a lawyer's trial conduct has been grossly disruptive, the judge's efforts to control the trial may have been ineffectual, which is itself an involvement of a very disturbing kind; if the efforts were provocative, personal involvement becomes clear. Except in the most clear-cut instances, a criminal contempt trial should be held before another judge.

Lawyer's responsibility for courtroom decorum. What is a lawyer supposed to do if her client persistently misbehaves despite her advice to the contrary? It is no real answer to say the lawyer should resign from the case, for what will her successor do? The lawyer should tell the client to behave himself, and do so with sincerity or at least its reasonable imitation. It is sometimes argued that the client's courtroom conduct is none of the lawyer's business: the lawyer is but an agent to serve the principal's desires, and hence the agent's responsibility ends with giving the principal advice.[17] The client does have certain procedural initiatives which the advocate can neither waive nor exercise on the client's behalf: the right to speak before pronouncement of sentence, the right to advice on consequences before tendering a guilty plea, the right to be present and to confront witnesses, and the right to testify against his counsel's advice. Furthermore, the hippy or yippy defendant has a right to insist that the impartiality by which he is judged not depend on changing his life-style pending trial, just as the poor man should not have to change his clothes nor the black man his skin. It is also no doubt true that judges and prosecutors often confuse *dishabille* with disorder and perceive loud mannerisms as literally making noise.

Nevertheless, there are some trials in which the defendants have talked when they should have been silent, moved about when they should have been seated, gesticulated when they should have been in repose. The lawyer's duty to admonish her clients against such misbehavior is a component of the lawyer's own role as advocate. The role of advocate is that of speaking to questions of law and fact in a particular kind of forum in accordance with specified opportunities and sequences. It would be quite clear that the lawyer could not play her role if whenever she tried to speak she was ignored, or interrupted or drowned out by a bullhorn. The lawyer's part, however, is not soliloquy but a series of ordered exchanges with the judge and opposing counsel. If the judge and opposing counsel cannot speak without disruption or hindrance, then the lawyer's appearances and cues

waits until the end of the trial, on balance, it is generally wise where the marks of the unseemly conduct have left personal stings to ask a fellow judge to take his place;" and "a defendant in criminal contempt proceedings should be given [on due process grounds] a public trial before a judge other than the one reviled by the contemnor").

17. In his autobiography, William Kunstler, in a detailed discussion of his participation in the Chicago Eight trial, states: "We put the system on trial by mocking it at every turn." Kunstler, My Life as a Radical Lawyer (1995). In an interview he stated: "in a political trial, where the intent is to punish a defendant for his thoughts, my conception of a lawyer's obligation is that he must join with his client in presenting a political defense; that he should, in effect, be the political agent of his client in the courtroom." Playboy Magazine, Oct. 1970, at p. 76.

are lost or disordered and at some point her role and reason for being there simply collapse. If the advocate does not contribute to sustaining these forensic requirements, she has to that extent abdicated her role and literally has no place in the performance. And if she does not believe in her role and cannot live it, she should seek another calling, just as an atheist should leave the priesthood.

The same, of course, goes for the judge and the prosecutor. To some who observed the "Chicago Eight" trial, one of the appalling things was the noisome patter of witticism and jokes by Judge Hoffman. It is conceivable that if he had consistently avoided playing it like a minstrel show, the defendants might not have played it like a circus.[18]

"Political" trials. A political trial—one in which the defendants are tried for conduct that is interpreted by them and by the community at large as a challenge to the legitimacy of the political order—poses special problems. The challenge constitutes an appeal for some form of public support. From the viewpoint of the challenged authority, the issues in a political trial are defined by positive law: whether the challenge enjoys the immunity afforded to free speech; whether all defendants were accomplices to the illegal elements of the enterprise; and similar issues. From the viewpoint of the defendants, however, these are only some of the issues; they have "counterclaims" that may include a maddening combination of transcendental political or ethical issues and procedural technicality. One counterclaim is that the regime is illegitimate according to some theory of political justice so that the actions of its officials are not clothed with legal authority and therefore amount to naked coercion. A subsidiary count is that the court trying the case is part of the illegal system and that its proceeding is a juridical pretension and a farce, as indeed it is if the premise is accepted.

The second counterclaim is that the court will not try the case with proper observance of its own legal procedure. This claim depends on technical and sometimes hypertechnical interpretation of procedural law ·and may involve tactics which seek to make it a self-fulfilling prophecy. Like the first counterclaim, it asserts that the court is not really a court. But the second counterclaim is supported by an argument which is diametrically opposite to that supporting the first counterclaim. The argument is that according to the tribunal's own law, the tribunal is not functioning as one.

A political trial thus involves two and perhaps three concurrent proceedings. In the "straight" one, the prosecutor is the accuser, the defendants are the accused and the judge and jury are arbiters. In the trial of defendants' first counterclaim, the defendants are the accusers, the prosecutor and the judge (and sometimes the jury) are the accused, and the arbiter is indefinitely the jury (hence the struggles at voir dire), the defendants' circle of sympathizers, the world at large, or history. The alignment of the parties is the same in the defendants' second counterclaim except that the arbiter is the appellate courts.

---

18. An excellent docu-drama recreating the Chicago Eight trial is available in video form: Jeremy Kagan, Inter Planetary Productions, Conspiracy: The Trial of the Chicago Eight (1987).

The confusion over the participants' position is confounded by evidentiary problems. The evidence for the government in a political trial consists largely of the defendants' utterances—writings, speeches, discussions. These are what actuated the prosecution in the first place and what constitute the legal basis for regarding the defendants' conduct as peculiarly wrongful. Hence, in putting on its case the prosecution inevitably rebroadcasts the defendants' challenge of the regime and thus introduces evidence which defendants regard as relevant to their first counterclaim, that the tribunal is illegitimate. Defining the proper scope of these proofs involves continual rulings that are subject to the claim of prejudicial error. Sometimes the defendants seek to introduce even fuller accounts of their utterances. If this effort is successful, it buttresses their first counterclaim; if it is unsuccessful, it buttresses the contention that the court is not trying the case fairly.

The proceeding as a whole is thus suffused with ambiguity: proofs consisting of speeches, which bear simultaneously on issues that have been pleaded and others that have not been, which are punctuated by evidentiary and procedural issues laden with double or triple meaning, which are advanced by participants who are intermittently forgetful that the conflict encompasses the agenda and their respective roles. Rules that clarify the official roles and responsibilities in the hearing of such a case can help define the issues in the underlying struggle over whether the official version of the proceedings shall prevail. Reaffirmation of the contempt power confirms the consequences if the established order does prevail. The established order, however, by its own terms cannot win the struggle by the threatening mechanisms of legal prescription and penal sanction. It can win only through steadfast and unpretentious fulfillment of official roles, especially that of the judge.

Representing unpopular defendants. On the obligation to provide representation to "unpopular" clients, see Model Rule 1.2(b) and Comment [3]; see also EC 7–9 and EC 7–17.[11]

Lawyer as Revolutionary

During the 1960s Professor Richard Wasserstrom addressed the relationship of the lawyer to radical or revolutionary programs.[12]

> [L]awyers and revolution don't mix especially well.... [T]he legal system—any legal system—is an essentially conservative institution [in a fundamental sense].... First, the law is conservative in the same way in which language is conservative. It seeks to assimilate everything that happens to that which has happened.... Thus the lawyer's

---

11. See also Mark Green, The Other Government 270–88 (1975); Abe Krash, Professional Responsibility to Clients and the Public Interest: Is There a Conflict?, 55 Chicago Bar Record 31 (1974); Andrew L. Kaufman, Introduction: A Professional Agenda, 6 Hofstra L.Rev. 619 (1978) (describing how the ethics rules embody and have always embodied a tension between the obligation owed one's client and the obligation owed to the public at large).

12. Richard Wasserstrom, Lawyers and Revolution, 30 U.Pitt.L.Rev. 125 (1968).

virtually instinctive intellectual response when he is confronted with a situation is to look for the respects in which that situation is like something that is familiar and that has a place within the realm of understood legal doctrine.... [P]ersons who are genuinely concerned with far-reaching and radical ... solutions to social ills ought to be on guard against and ought to mistrust this powerful tendency on the part of the lawyer to transmogrify what is new into what has gone before or to reject as unworkable or unintelligible what cannot be so modified.

The second way in which the law is conservative comes about through the very basic character of the lawyer qua lawyer.... First, there is the obvious, but important, fact that when an individual is a lawyer he is playing an institutional role. As such, there are all sorts of explicit and implicit constraints upon his thought and action. As a *lawyer*, there are some things he simply cannot do—without ceasing to play the role of a lawyer.... Second, the lawyer qua advocate plays an essentially non-critical role. The very essence of the lawyer's institutional role is to submerge himself in his clients' position and to represent that interest in the legal arena as forcefully as possible.... [B]eing an advocate in our legal system—where one does not or need not choose one's causes—encourages a non-critical, non-evaluative, uncommitted state of mind....

... The attorney's role is intimately connected with securing for his client the greatest possible advantage that can be wrung for him from the institutional system. Paradoxically enough, this leads not to the single-mindedness of purpose that so typically characterizes the revolutionary and the radical, but leads rather to a penchant for compromise, accord and accommodation. The attorney is in many respects the system's broker.... [T]he processes of litigation and adjudication derive from and are infected by the model of the market place in which a good bargain consists in each of the parties making concessions and compromises.

[The lawyer's cast of mind] is at best neutral and more typically uncongenial to that of the revolutionary's.... The revolutionary may, for instance, simply not be interested in winning in any conventional sense. Or, he may be interested in winning if and only if certain very special conditions obtain. In either case, the tension that is latent in the lawyer's whole approach to problems becomes manifest and intense.

... [T]he lawyer's ambitions to try to get the best he can for client *within the legal order* can be not so much inconsistent with his client's interest as genuinely corruptive of them. For there are innumerable situations in which the lawyer's inclination to take what he can get leads to the compromise of interests and rights about which no accommodation ought ever be tolerated.

· · ·

[T]he third major issue that falls within the heading of the lawyer and revolution ... [is] whether we ought to be radical in respect to the law, and if so, of what such radicalism would consist.... [I]t is not very easy or very sensible to be radical in respect to the *idea* of a legal system.... The trouble begins when we move beyond ... [ameliorative] proposals to genuinely radical suggestions for social innovation and change.... [We can't get along without law or lawyers and intermediate steps, such as getting rid of the adversary system, are] an extraordinarily difficult undertaking, particularly for lawyers.[13]

In 1981 Professor Duncan Kennedy urged Harvard law students to subvert the "demonic" and "antisocial" practice of corporate law from within.[14] A leftist student might take actions within the corporate law firm, such as refusing to work on cases that are offensive to one's beliefs.

> ... I'm not advocating self-immolation—more like sly, collective tactics within the institution where you work, to confront, outflank, sabotage or manipulate the bad guys and build the possibility of something better.

> ... What I am suggesting is the politicization of corporate law practice, which means doing things and not doing things in order to serve left purposes, not because they fit or don't fit the Canons. The point is to turn down clients because they want you ... to delay implementation of environmental controls, even though it's all totally within the law. But the point also is to reconceive the internal issues of firm hierarchy as an important part of one's political life, fighting the oligarchy of senior partners, opposing the oppression of secretaries by arrogant young men who turn around and grovel before their mentors....

> ... If you fight now, if you come to stand for something now, you'll be able to make things different when you own the place.

> ... If you think before you act, if you are subtle, collusive, skillful and tricky, if you use confrontation when confrontation will work, you should able to do left office politics without being fired, and make partner.[15]

Among the many responses provoked by Kennedy's article was one from a Harvard colleague, Detlev Vagts:[16]

> ... In brief, the radical lawyer of 1982 has three choices: to go to a corporate law firm and resist through "sly" tactics, to go there and resist openly or to go somewhere else. I take Professor Kennedy to advise the first, though the layers of irony are so thick as to obscure the message. I would disagree. The disadvantages of the "sly" alternative start with the short-range problem that it is unlikely to work, given the perceptiveness of the opposition. It certainly won't work a second time. Meanwhile, the practice of using subtle and tricky messages corrupts one's ability to communicate with anybody....

---

13. Id. at 128–33.

14. Duncan Kennedy, Rebels from Principle: Changing the Corporate Law Firm from Within, Harvard L.S.Bull. 36 (Fall 1981).

15. Id. at 36, 37, 39.

16. Harv.L.S.Bull. (Winter 1991).

One can combine mild reformism with work in a high pressure law practice but one simply cannot survive in it if one is involved in a constant series of battles of conscience over what one is asked to do.

... One is left, then, with going elsewhere and taking up the very difficult task of building or creating a left organization.... [T]here are organizations—law firms, law communes, some government offices, some parts of law school faculties—that offer beginnings.... [T]his is where the talented young radical lawyer belongs. To hold out the alternative that one can keep one's leftist conscience and "still make partner" is to disguise an inescapable dilemma. Those who think that they can have both through a few sly schemes are likely to end up as weary court jesters in motley shaking their bells at the passing parade.[17]

2. FREE SPEECH RIGHTS OF LAWYERS

The degree of protection accorded to lawyer speech depends upon the context in which the speech occurs. Statements made by a lawyer in the course of representation of a client are protected by common law privilege. An absolute privilege protects statements made in or reasonably related to a judicial proceeding.[18] A qualified privilege protects statements in the course of representation outside of judicial proceedings.[19] See the discussion of these privileges in Chapter 5 above at p. 402.

In other contexts, however, lawyers are accorded less protection for their speech than nonlawyers. Lawyers' free speech issues arise in several recurring contexts. Disruptive and improper speech in the courtroom itself, discussed in the materials above, may be punished by civil or criminal contempt or by professional discipline. The materials below deal with, first, public comment about pending cases; second, extrajudicial comments of lawyers about judges generally or the administration of justice; and third, public criticism of particular judges.

Public Comment About Pending Cases

Gentile v. State Bar of Nevada

Supreme Court of the United States, 1991.
501 U.S.1030.

■ CHIEF JUSTICE REHNQUIST delivered the opinion of the court with respect to parts I and II, and delivered a dissenting opinion with respect to part III in which Justice White, Justice Scalia, and Justice Souter have joined.

---

17. Id. at 30.

18. See Restatement (Second) of Torts § 586; W. Prosser and P. Keeton on Torts § 114 (5th ed. 1984); e.g., DeVivo v. Ascher, 228 N.J.Super. 453, 550 A.2d 163 (1988) ("We ... favor a broad interpretation of the phrase 'in the course of a judicial proceeding.' ").

19. See Restatement (Second) of Torts § 595, Comment d; W. Prosser and P. Keeton, supra, § 115.

Petitioner was disciplined for making statements to the press about a pending case in which he represented a criminal defendant. The State Bar, and the Supreme Court of Nevada on review, found that petitioner knew or should have known that there was a substantial likelihood that his statements would materially prejudice the trial of his client. Nonetheless, petitioner contends that the First Amendment to the United States Constitution requires a stricter standard to be met before such speech by an attorney may be disciplined: there must be a finding of "actual prejudice or a substantial and imminent threat to fair trial." ... We conclude that the "substantial likelihood of material prejudice" standard applied by Nevada and most other states satisfies the First Amendment.

I

Petitioner's client was the subject of a highly publicized case, and in response to adverse publicity about his client, Gentile held a press conference on the day after Sanders was indicted. At the press conference, petitioner made, among others, the following statements:

"When this case goes to trial, and as it develops, you're going to see that the evidence will prove not only that Grady Sanders is an innocent person and had nothing to do with any of the charges that are being leveled against him, but that the person that was in the most direct position to have stolen the drugs and the money, the American Express Travelers' checks, is Detective Steve Scholl.

"There is far more evidence that will establish that Detective Scholl took these drugs and took these American Express Travelers' checks than any other living human being."

[Petitioner also stated at the press conference that a number of the witnesses against his client were "known drug dealers and convicted money launderers;" that his client was "an innocent man;" and he implied that Detective Scholl was a drug user.]

Articles appeared in the local newspapers describing the press conference and petitioner's statements. The trial took place approximately six months later, and although the trial court succeeded in empaneling a jury that had not been affected by the media coverage and Sanders was acquitted on all charges, the state bar disciplined petitioner for his statements.

The Southern Nevada Disciplinary Board found that petitioner knew the detective he accused of perpetrating the crime and abusing drugs would be a witness for the prosecution. It also found that petitioner believed others whom he characterized as money launderers and drug dealers would be called as prosecution witnesses. Petitioner's admitted purpose for calling the press conference was to counter public opinion which he perceived as adverse to his client, to fight back against the perceived efforts of the prosecution to poison the prospective juror pool, and to publicly present his client's side of the case. The Board found that in light of the statements, their timing, and petitioner's purpose, petitioner knew or should have known that there was a substantial likelihood that the statements would materially prejudice the Sanders trial.

The Nevada Supreme Court affirmed the Board's decision, finding by clear and convincing evidence that petitioner "knew or reasonably should have known that his comments had a substantial likelihood of materially prejudicing the adjudication of his client's case." Gentile v. State Bar of Nevada, 787 P.2d 386, 387 (Nev.1990). The court noted that the case was "highly publicized"; that the press conference, held the day after the indictment and the same day as the arraignment, was "timed to have maximum impact"; and that petitioner's comments "related to the character, credibility, reputation or criminal record of the police detective and other potential witnesses." The court concluded that the "absence of actual prejudice does not establish that there was no substantial likelihood of material prejudice."

II

[The Court first summarized the history of the efforts of bar and public groups to balance fair trial concerns against free speech interests.]

When the Model Rules of Professional Conduct were drafted in the early 1980's, the drafters ... adopted the "substantial likelihood of material prejudice" test. Currently, 31 States in addition to Nevada have adopted—either verbatim or with insignificant variations—Rule 3.6 of the ABA's Model Rules. Eleven States have adopted Disciplinary Rule 7–107 of the ABA's Code of Professional Responsibility, which is less protective of lawyer speech than Model Rule 3.6, in that it applies a "reasonable likelihood of prejudice" standard. Only one State, Virginia has explicitly adopted a clear and present danger standard, while four States and the District of Columbia have adopted standards that arguably approximate "clear and present danger."

Petitioner maintains, however, that the First Amendment to the United States Constitution requires a State, such as Nevada in this case, to demonstrate a "clear and present danger" of "actual prejudice or an imminent threat" before any discipline may be imposed on a lawyer who initiates a press conference such as occurred here.[4] He relies on decisions such as Nebraska Press Assn. v. Stuart, 427 U.S. 539 (1976), Bridges v. California, 314 U.S. 252 (1941), Pennekamp v. Florida, 323 U.S. 331 (1946), and Craig v. Harney, 331 U.S. 367 (1947), to support his position. In those cases we held that trial courts might not constitutionally punish, through use of the contempt power, newspapers and others for publishing editorials, cartoons, and other items critical of judges in particular cases. We held that such punishments could be imposed only if there were a clear and present danger of "some serious substantive evil which they are designed to avert." Bridges v. California, supra, 314 U.S., at 270. Petitioner also relies on Wood

---

4. ... Petitioner challenged Rule 177 as being unconstitutional on its face in addition to as applied.... The validity of the rules in the many states applying the "sub- stantial likelihood of material prejudice" test has, therefore, been called into question in this case.

v. Georgia, 370 U.S. 375 (1962), which held that a court might not punish a sheriff for publicly criticizing a judge's charges to a grand jury.

. . . [N]one of these cases involved lawyers who represented parties to a pending proceeding in court. . . .

. . . [T]he theory upon which our criminal justice system is founded [is that] the outcome of a criminal trial is to be decided by impartial jurors, who know as little as possible of the case, based on material admitted into evidence before them in a court proceeding. Extrajudicial comments on, or discussion of, evidence which might never be admitted at trial and *ex parte* statements by counsel giving their version of the facts obviously threaten to undermine this basic tenet.

At the same time, however, the criminal justice system exists in a larger context of a government ultimately of the people, who wish to be informed about happenings in the criminal justice system, and, if sufficiently informed about those happenings might wish to make changes in the system. The way most of them acquire information is from the media. The First Amendment protections of speech and press have been held, in the cases cited above, to require a showing of "clear and present danger" that a malfunction in the criminal justice system will be caused before a State may prohibit media speech or publication about a particular pending trial. The question we must answer in this case is whether a lawyer who represents a defendant involved with the criminal justice system may insist on the same standard before he is disciplined for public pronouncements about the case, or whether the State instead may penalize that sort of speech upon a lesser showing.

It is unquestionable that in the courtroom itself, during a judicial proceeding, whatever right to "free speech" an attorney has is extremely circumscribed. An attorney may not, by speech or other conduct, resist a ruling of the trial court beyond the point necessary to preserve a claim for appeal. Sacher v. United States, 343 U.S. 1, 8 (1952) (criminal trial); Fisher v. Pace, 336 U.S. 155 (1949) (civil trial). Even outside the courtroom, a majority of the Court in two separate opinions in the case of In re Sawyer, 360 U.S. 622 (1959), observed that lawyers in pending cases were subject to ethical restrictions on speech to which an ordinary citizen would not be. . . .

Likewise, in Sheppard v. Maxwell, [384 U.S. 333 (1966)] where the defendant's conviction was overturned because extensive prejudicial pretrial publicity had denied the defendant a fair trial, we held that a new trial was a remedy for such publicity, but

> "we must remember that reversals are but palliatives; the cure lies in those remedial measures that will prevent the prejudice at its inception. The courts must take such steps by rule and regulation that will protect their processes from prejudicial outside interferences. Neither prosecutors, counsel for defense, the accused, witnesses, court staff nor enforcement officers coming under the jurisdiction of the court should be permitted to frustrate its function. *Collaboration between counsel*

and the press as to information affecting the fairness of a criminal trial is not only subject to regulation, but is highly censurable and worthy of disciplinary measures." 384 U.S., at 363 (emphasis added).

We expressly contemplated that the speech of *those participating before the courts* could be limited. This distinction between participants in the litigation and strangers to it is brought into sharp relief by our holding in Seattle Times Co. v. Rhinehart, 467 U.S. 20 (1984). There, we unanimously held that a newspaper, which was itself a defendant in a libel action, could be restrained from publishing material about the plaintiffs and their supporters to which it had gained access through court-ordered discovery. In that case we said that "[a]lthough litigants do not 'surrender their First Amendment rights at the courthouse door,' those rights may be subordinated to other interests that arise in this setting," id., at 32–33, n. 18, (citation omitted), and noted that "on several occasions [we have] approved restriction on the communications of trial participants where necessary to ensure a fair trial for a criminal defendant." Ibid.

. . .

We think that the quoted statements from our opinions in In re Sawyer, 360 U.S. 622 (1959), and Sheppard v. Maxwell, supra, rather plainly indicate that the speech of lawyers representing clients in pending cases may be regulated under a less demanding standard than that established for regulation of the press in Nebraska Press Assn. v. Stuart, 427 U.S. 539 (1976), and the cases which preceded it. Lawyers representing clients in pending cases are key participants in the criminal justice system, and the State may demand some adherence to the precepts of that system in regulating their speech as well as their conduct. As noted by Justice Brennan in his concurring opinion in *Nebraska Press*, which was joined by Justices Stewart and Marshall, "[a]s officers of the court, court personnel and attorneys have a fiduciary responsibility not to engage in public debate that will redound to the detriment of the accused or that will obstruct the fair administration of justice." 427 U.S., at 601, n. 27. Because lawyers have special access to information through discovery and client communications, their extrajudicial statements pose a threat to the fairness of appending proceeding since lawyers' statements are likely to be received as especially authoritative. See, e.g., In re Hinds, 449 A.2d 483, 496 (N.J.1982) (statements by attorneys of record relating to the case "are likely to be considered knowledgeable, reliable and true" because of attorneys' unique access to information); In re Rachmiel, 449 A.2d 505, 511 (N.J.1982) (attorneys' role as advocates gives them "extraordinary power to undermine or destroy the efficacy of the criminal justice system"). We agree with the majority of the States that the "substantial likelihood of material prejudice" standard constitutes a constitutionally permissible balance between the First Amendment rights of attorneys in pending cases and the state's interest in fair trials.

When a state regulation implicates First Amendment rights, the Court must balance those interests against the State's legitimate interest in regulating the activity in question. See, *e.g., Seattle Times,* supra, 467 U.S.

at 32. The "substantial likelihood" test embodied in Rule 177 is constitutional under this analysis, for it is designed to protect the integrity and fairness of a state's judicial system, and it imposes only narrow and necessary limitations on lawyers' speech. The limitations are aimed at two principal evils: (1) comments that are likely to influence the actual outcome of the trial, and (2) comments that are likely to prejudice the jury venire, even if an untainted panel can ultimately be found. Few, if any, interests under the Constitution are more fundamental than the right to a fair trial by "impartial" jurors, and an outcome affected by extrajudicial statements would violate that fundamental right. See, e.g., *Sheppard*, 384 U.S., at 350–351; Turner v. Louisiana, 379 U.S. 466, 473 (1965) (evidence in criminal trial must come solely from witness stand in public courtroom with full evidentiary protections). Even if a fair trial can ultimately be ensured through voir dire, change of venue, or some other device, these measures entail serious costs to the system. Extensive voir dire may not be able to filter out all of the effects of pretrial publicity, and with increasingly widespread media coverage of criminal trials, a change of venue may not suffice to undo the effects of statements such as those made by petitioner. The State has a substantial interest in preventing officers of the court, such as lawyers, from imposing such costs on the judicial system and on the litigants.

The restraint on speech is narrowly tailored to achieve those objectives. The regulation of attorneys' speech is limited—it applies only to speech that is substantially likely to have a materially prejudicial effect; it is neutral as to points of view, applying equally to all attorneys participating in a pending case; and it merely postpones the attorney's comments until after the trial. While supported by the substantial state interest in preventing prejudice to an adjudicative proceeding by those who have a duty to protect its integrity, the rule is limited on its face to preventing only speech having a substantial likelihood of materially prejudicing that proceeding.

[Part III of Chief Justice Rehnquist's opinion, which was joined by three other justices, argued that Model Rule 3.6 was not overbroad or void for vagueness. "The Rule provides sufficient notice of the nature of the prohibited conduct." M.R. 3.6(c), allowing an attorney to state "the general nature of the claim or defense," uses terms of degree ("general" and "elaboration"), but "convey[s] the very definite proposition that the authorized statements must not contain the sort of detailed allegations that petitioner made at his press conference" (referring to the specific charges against Detective Scholl and the other witnesses).]

■ JUSTICE KENNEDY announced the judgment of the Court and delivered the opinion of the court with respect to Parts III and VI, and an opinion with respect to Parts I, II, IV, and V in which JUSTICE MARSHALL, JUSTICE BLACKMUN and JUSTICE STEVENS join.

[In Parts I and II of his opinion, joined by three other justices, Justice Kennedy argued that the standard stated in M.R. 3.6 might be interpreted to be consistent with the "clear and present danger" test, but Nevada's interpretation and application of it violated the First Amendment. Petitioner's actions were preceded by pre-indictment publicity by law enforcement officials that were damaging to his client; in holding the press conference, petitioner acted deliberately and after investigating the ethics rule; at the conference he refused to elaborate on his description of his client's defense; most of the information in his "abbreviated, general comments six months before trial" had been published in one form or another. "There is no support for the conclusion that petitioner's statement created a likelihood of material prejudice, or indeed of any harm of sufficient magnitude or imminence to support a punishment of speech."]

III

As interpreted by the Nevada Supreme Court, the Rule is void for vagueness, in any event, for its safe harbor provision, Rule 177(3), misled petitioner into thinking that he could give his press conference without fear of discipline. Rule 177(3)(a) provides that a lawyer "may state without elaboration . . . the general nature of the . . . defense." Statements under this provision are protected "[n]otwithstanding subsection 1 and 2(a-f)." By necessary operation of the word "notwithstanding," the Rule contemplates that a lawyer describing the "general nature of the . . . defense" "without elaboration" need fear no discipline, even if he comments on "[t]he character, credibility, reputation or criminal record of a . . . witness," and even if he "knows or reasonably should know that [the statement] will have a substantial likelihood of materially prejudicing an adjudicative proceeding."

Given this grammatical structure, and absent any clarifying interpretation by the state court, the Rule fails to provide " 'fair notice to those to whom [it] is directed.' "Grayned v. City of Rockford, 408 U.S. 104, 112 (1972). A lawyer seeking to avail himself of Rule 177(3)'s protection must guess at its contours. The right to explain the "general" nature of the defense without "elaboration" provides insufficient guidance because "general" and "elaboration" are both classic terms of degree. In the context before us, these terms have no settled usage or tradition of interpretation in law. The lawyer has no principle for determining when his remarks pass from the safe harbor of the general to the forbidden sea of the elaborated.

· · ·

. . . The fact Gentile was found in violation of the Rules after studying them and making a conscious effort at compliance demonstrates that Rule 177 creates a trap for the wary as well as the unwary.

The prohibition against vague regulations of speech is based in part on the need to eliminate the impermissible risk of discriminatory enforcement, Kolender v. Lawson, 461 U.S. 352, 357–358, 361 (1983); Smith v. Goguen, 415 U.S. 566, 572–573 (1974), for history shows that speech is suppressed when either the speaker or the message is critical of those who enforce the law. The question is not whether discriminatory enforcement occurred here, and we assume it did not, but whether the Rule is so imprecise that discriminatory enforcement is a real possibility. The inquiry is of particular relevance when one of the classes most affected by the regulation is the criminal defense bar, which has the professional mission to challenge actions of the State. Petitioner, for instance, succeeded in preventing the conviction of his client, and the speech in issue involved criticism of the government. . . .

Gentile and Trial Publicity

Was there a "substantial likelihood" that lawyer Gentile's televised charges would "materially prejudice" the jury voir dire in the impending trial? Note that Gentile charged that a police detective was responsible for the crime with which his client had been indicted and that specific prosecution witnesses were "money launderers and drug dealers." Should a "clear and present danger" test be applied rather than the looser test of "substantial likelihood of material prejudice" to an adjudication? Are the "safe-harbor" provisions of Model Rule 3.6(c) unconstitutionally vague, as Justice Kennedy and four of his colleagues held?

Justice Kennedy stated that "an attorney may take reasonable steps to defend a client's reputation and reduce the adverse consequence of indictment . . . including an attempt to demonstrate in the court of public opinion that the client does not deserve to be tried." Does this permission (duty?), if taken seriously, undermine any effort to restrict pretrial publicity?[1]

In August 1994, partly because of the *Gentile* case, the ABA significantly amended Model Rule 3.6. At the same time, the ABA added M.R. 3.8(g), applicable to prosecutors. Read these rules at this time. The 1994 amendment to M.R. 3.6: (1) restates in paragraph (b) the types of information that a lawyer may disclose outside of court despite the general ban in paragraph (a) of extrajudicial statements likely to prejudice a court proceeding; (2) authorizes a lawyer to protect a client by responding to recent publicity initiated by others (paragraph (c)); and (3) makes clear that all lawyers in a firm or government agency are governed by the rule (paragraph (d)). The 1994 amendments also substantially rewrote the Comment and Code Comparison to reflect changes in the text of the rule. California, moved by criticism of the use of the press by both sides in the O. J. Simpson case, promulgated a trial publicity rule for the first time; California R. Prof. Conduct 5–120 is modeled on the 1994 revision of M.R. 3.6.

Extrajudicial Criticism of Administration of Justice

Legal systems invariably require or expect lawyers to treat judges with courtesy and respect. Deference to judges is part of the ritual aspect of public judicial proceedings and contributes to their public acceptance and

---

1. See Kevin Cole & Fred Zacharias, The Agony of Victory and the Ethics of Lawyer Speech, 69 S.Cal.L.Rev. 1627 (1996) (analyzing *Gentile* in the light of the publicity blitz in the O.J. Simpson case).

legitimacy. Lawyers who participate in these public ceremonies conform themselves to the tribunal's customs of dress, demeanor and deference either out of conviction or self-interest or both. For similar reasons, lawyers are hesitant to make public criticisms of judges. The judicial tradition of not being drawn into public controversies leaves judges unable to defend themselves against groundless public charges. Yet the official conduct of an occasional judge is subject to just censure of a kind that a lawyer may be in the best position to make. The lawyer codes express a special obligation of lawyers not to criticize judges through false accusations,[2] as well as the hope that lawyers might come to the defense of judges unfairly accused.[3]

The permissible limits on extrajudicial criticism of judges by lawyers have expanded in recent decades. Formerly, a number of decisions took the position that vigorous public criticism of judges was sanctionable, regardless of the truth or falsity of the criticism, because it created public disrespect for the law or the judiciary. In those cases it was the tone of criticism rather than its factual content that was considered objectionable. For example, in In re Snyder,[4] a lawyer was suspended from practice in all federal courts in the circuit for six months for a private letter sent to a district judge's secretary criticizing the court's system of compensating court-appointed lawyers. The lawyer's letter referred to the "extreme gymnastics" required to receive "puny amounts" and expressed "extreme disgust" at his treatment by the court of appeals, which twice rejected his undocumented requests for additional compensation. Without reaching First Amendment issues, the Supreme Court reversed.[5] Speaking for a unanimous court, Chief Justice Burger stated:

> We do not consider a lawyer's criticism of the administration of the [Criminal Justice] Act or criticism of inequities in assignments under the Act as cause for discipline or suspension. . . . Officers of the court may appropriately express criticism on such matters.

> The record indicates the Court of Appeals was concerned about the tone of the letter; petitioner concedes that the tone of his letter was "harsh," and, indeed it can be read as ill-mannered. All persons involved in the judicial process—judges, litigants, witnesses, and court officers—owe a duty of courtesy to all other participants. The necessity for civility in the inherently contentious setting of the adversary process suggests that members of the bar cast criticisms of the system in a professional and civil tone. However, even assuming that the letter exhibited unlawyer-like rudeness, a single incident of rudeness or lack of professional courtesy—in this context—does not support a finding of contemptuous or contumacious conduct, or a finding that a lawyer is "not presently fit to practice law in the federal courts." Nor does it rise to the level of "conduct unbecoming a member of the bar" warranting suspension from practice.[6]

---

2. M.R. 8.2(a); DR 8–102(B).
3. M.R. 8.2 comment [3]; EC 8–6.
4. 734 F.2d 334 (8th Cir.1984).
5. In re Snyder, 472 U.S. 634 (1985).

6. 472 U.S. at 646–47. See also Justices of Appellate Division, First Dep't v. Erdmann, 333 N.Y.S.3d 863 (1972), rev'd, 301 N.E.2d

Criticism of Particular Judges

Although general criticism of the judiciary or of the administration of justice will receive a great deal of constitutional protection, lawyers who make false charges against a particular judge are subject to professional discipline.[7] Model Rule 8.2(a) prohibits a lawyer from making a statement "that the lawyer knows to be false or with reckless disregard as to its truth or falsity concerning the qualifications or integrity of [judicial officers and candidates for such office]." The special requirements applicable when public figures sue speakers for defamation—proof of both falsity and "actual malice"—[8] have not been applied to a lawyer's accusations against a judge that turn out to be false.

Elizabeth Holtzman, a prominent political figure in New York, was reprimanded for a press release made while she was serving as a prosecutor.[9] Holtzman charged a named judge with judicial misconduct by staging a replay of a pending sexual assault incident. The judge, she stated,

> asked the victim to get down on the floor and show the position she was in when she was being sexually assaulted.... The victim reluctantly got down on her hands and knees as everyone stood and watched. In making the victim assume the position she was forced to take when she was sexually assaulted, Judge Levine profoundly degraded, humiliated and demeaned her.[10]

Holtzman had relied on the memorandum of a trial assistant reporting the incident, but she did not obtain the minutes of the criminal trial, discuss the incident with the trial assistant or speak with persons present during the alleged misconduct. Members of her staff counseled her to delay publication until the trial minutes were received. The court accepted the lower court's finding that the accusation was false.

> Petitioner's act was not generalized criticism but rather release to the media of a false allegation of specific wrongdoing, made without any support other than the interoffice memoranda of a newly admitted trial assistant, aimed at a named judge who had presided over a number of cases prosecuted by her office. Petitioner knew or should have known that such attacks were unwarranted and unprofessional,

426 (N.Y.1973) (reversing censure of a lawyer whose critical quotes about New York trial and appellate judges—the latter as "the whores who became madams"—were published in a magazine article; the court held that "isolated instances of disrespect for ... Judges and courts expressed by vulgar and insulting words ... uttered ... outside the precincts of the court are not subject to professional discipline").

7. See, e.g., Ramirez v. State Bar, 619 P.2d 399 (Cal.1980) (accusations against state court of appeals judges in federal court pleadings); In re Crumpacker, 383 N.E.2d 36 (Ind.1978) (disbarment for intemperate and unfounded attacks upon character and integrity of judge who had ruled against lawyer in emotion-laden litigation).

8. Harte–Hanks Communications, Inc. v. Connaughton, 491 U.S. 657 (1989) (actual malice defined as knowledge of a statement's falsity or reckless (i.e., conscious) disregard for its truth); New York Times v. Sullivan, 376 U.S. 254 (1964).

9. Matter of Holtzman, 577 N.E.2d 30 (N.Y. 1991).

10. Id. at 31.

serve to bring the bench and bar into disrepute, and tend to undermine public confidence in the judicial system.

Therefore, petitioner's conduct was properly the subject of disciplinary action under DR 1–102(A)(6) [prohibiting "conduct that adversely reflects on his fitness to practice law"]. . . .

Petitioner contends that her conduct would not be actionable under the "constitutional malice" standard enunciated by the Supreme Court in New York Times v. Sullivan (376 U.S. 254). Neither this Court nor the Supreme Court has ever extended the *Sullivan* standard to lawyer discipline and we decline to do so here.

Accepting petitioner's argument would immunize all accusations, however reckless or irresponsible, from censure as long as the attorney uttering them did not actually entertain serious doubts as to their truth. . . .

. . .

In order to adequately protect the public interest and maintain the integrity of the judicial system, there must be an objective standard, of what a reasonable attorney would do in similar circumstances. It is the reasonableness of the belief, not the state of mind of the attorney, that is determinative.[11]

B. LAWYERS SERVING POOR PEOPLE AND "THE PUBLIC INTEREST"

1. A CONSTITUTIONAL RIGHT TO CIVIL LEGAL ASSISTANCE?

After Gideon v. Wainwright,[1] it seemed possible that a similar right to counsel might be recognized for civil matters. The high water mark of this development was Boddie v. Connecticut,[2] in which the Court on due process grounds struck down a state statute requiring prepayment of a $45 filing fee by divorce plaintiffs. *Boddie* was subsequently narrowed to situations where judicial process provided the only means for vindicating a fundamental interest[3] and was then displaced by a balancing-of-factors approach in

---

11. 577 N.E.2d at 33–34. For another case involving reprimand of a prosecutor for public criticism of a particular judge, see Matter of Westfall, 808 S.W.2d 829 (Mo. 1991) (lawyer stated that a judge's opinion was "somewhat illogical" and "a little bit less than honest," the judge "distorted the statute," and represented a conclusion the judge had reached before he wrote the decision). The Supreme Court denied review in both the *Holtzman* and *Westfall* cases.

1. 372 U.S. 335 (1976) (Fourteenth Amendment due process requires states to provide counsel to indigent defendants in criminal trials threatening imprisonment).

2. 401 U.S. 371 (1971).

3. United States v. Kras, 409 U.S. 434 (1973) (bankruptcy not a fundamental interest); Ortwein v. Schwab, 410 U.S. 656 (1973) (upholding a $25 filing fee to obtain

Lassiter v. Department of Social Services.[4]

In *Lassiter* the Court held that a state's failure to appoint counsel for an indigent, imprisoned mother, before terminating her parental rights to custody of her minor child as an unfit parent, did not violate due process. The Court's three-part balancing process, carried over from other due process cases, considers (1) the private interests at stake, (2) the government's interests and (3) the extent of the risk that the claimed procedural right, here the absence of publicly provided counsel, will lead to erroneous results in the litigation. In *Lassiter*, however, the Court added something to the balancing process. The Court identified a presumption that there is a right to appointed counsel only when the indigent person faces a loss of personal liberty in the form of confinement by the state. After balancing the three elements identified above, the Court "set[s] their net weight in the scales against the presumption"[5] that there is a right to appointed counsel only when confinement is a possibility. This thumb-on-the-scales form of balancing sounded the death knell for a right to counsel in most civil cases.

Four dissenting justices asserted that termination of parental rights involves a more important interest than is involved in many misdemeanor cases. They also argued that appointment of counsel is particularly important for a fair adjudication of cases of this type, which involve the application of an imprecise standard in formal adversarial proceedings in which the opposing party, the state, is represented. As the dissenters predicted, few situations under *Lassiter's* balancing-of-interests approach turn out to require the appointment of counsel in civil cases.[6] States are free to provide counsel to indigents in civil cases either generally or in specific categories of cases, but with limited exceptions have not done so.[7]

David Luban argues that the premises of the American political system require the provision of counsel to indigents in important civil matters, and especially in civil enforcement proceedings against a poor person.[8] Equality before the law is a fundamental principle embodied in constitutional text. Its effective implementation requires access to the legal system, which in turn is dependent upon the assistance of lawyers. In Luban's view, the failure to provide counsel impairs the legitimacy of government.

state court appellate review of a state agency's reduction of welfare benefits).

4.   452 U.S. 18 (1981).

5.   Id. at 27.

6.   See, e.g., United States v. Bobart Travel Agency, 699 F.2d 618 (2d Cir.1983) (civil contempt charges that may lead to imprisonment require the appointment of counsel).

7.   In Payne v. Superior Court, 553 P.2d 565 (Cal.1976), a prisoner seeking to defend a civil action was held entitled to appointed counsel. *Payne* was reaffirmed in Yarbrough v. Superior Court, 702 P.2d 583 (Cal.1985) (expressing a hope that the legislature would provide funding for representation that otherwise depended on appointed counsel serving without compensation).

8.   David Luban, Lawyers and Justice: An Ethical Study c. 11 (1988) (equality-of-rights-not-fortunes is a basic legitimation right of society; its denial undermines the legitimacy of the system and may generate a right of resistance).

Geoffrey Hazard states some of the reasons why "[t]he notion that due process meant lawyer-assisted process never took hold in civil matters:"[9]

> For one thing, there was a long tradition, exemplified in worker's compensation proceedings, juvenile court, and small claims, that legal dispute resolution could be more just, more expeditious and less expensive if lawyers were kept out. For another thing, in civil cases there was no apparatus of legal assistance provided by the state to assist one side, as was provided for the prosecution in criminal cases.

> There was a more fundamental difficulty in fixing the provision of civil legal aid. The measure of necessary legal aid in criminal cases was the quantum provided the prosecution. There was no similar measure for civil legal aid. To provide a lawyer to an indigent civil grievant was in effect to confer a subsidy in the amount of nuisance settlement value to beneficiaries arbitrarily selected in terms of income or wealth and self-selecting in terms of disposition to litigate. Implicitly recognizing this, the courts were willing to say that due process required legal aid only in narrowly limited civil categories.

Are Hazard's arguments persuasive? While the "measure of necessary legal aid in criminal cases" may be "the quantum provided to the prosecution," is that what the Constitution guarantees? Review the notes at p. 191 that follow *Strickland* in Chapter 3.

In the absence of any constitutional entitlement, provision of counsel to indigents in civil matters depends upon the volunteered services of lawyers, judicial actions appointing lawyers for indigents and legislative provision of subsidized legal services.

Steven Brill, "The Stench of Room 202"

The American Lawyer, Pp. 1, 15–18, 20 (April 1987).[10]

Tracy Miller, NYU Law class of '85, Order of the Coif and Root–Tilden scholar, steps through the cigarette butts and heads up the dark, graffiti-lined stairway. At the top of the landing, she pushes open the door just lightly enough not to hit any of the several dozen blacks and Puerto Ricans lingering in the corridor, then whirls around through another door.

This room, with the paint peeling, with the fluorescent lights half out, with the yellow newspapers stacked in the soot against the window sill under the "In God We Trust" sign, with the white people with briefcases in front of the bench and the nonwhites, clutching pieces of official-looking paper, milling around in the back, is the seat of justice every day for hundreds of Americans: Brooklyn housing court, room 202.

It is also a place, as I'll explain below, that I would like the American Bar Association's president . . . to think about every day he is in office.

9. Geoffrey C. Hazard, Jr., After Professional Virtue, 1989 Sup.Ct.Rev. 213, 219–20.

10. Copyright © 1993 The American Lawyer.

As Miller waits for her case to be called, a short, wiry white man in a dark, double knit suit, his tie already loosened at 9:30 in the morning, stands in front of the bench calling out names. The first ten bring no answer. The eleventh yields an eager black man with a mock-fur hat. He rushes up to the white man and identifies himself.

"Yes, that's me, sir," he whispers.

There is some discussion, apparently about money, which I cannot hear completely, then: "Sign this stip, and you can go," the white man explains, not looking at him.

The black man signs quickly, says, "Thank you, Your Honor," and rushes out.

His Honor is not a judge. He is Kenneth Mintz, counsel to the landlord in this case. Mintz has just gotten his tenant-opponent to sign some sort of stipulation in an eviction proceeding that the tenant had—by virtue of his having shown up in this courtroom—been fighting.

Mintz's firm, Gutman & Mintz of Queens, counts among its clients J. Leonard Spodek, known in New York as the "Dracula Landlord" for the way he has rendered heatless, threatened with goon squads, and otherwise abused tenants so brazenly that he has been jailed twice recently.

Mintz later said that the stipulation involved a client other than Spodek and was "probably just an adjournment." The man who signed it could not be found by the time I realized what had happened and went looking for him in the corridor.

(Asked why he had allowed the man to think he was the judge, Mintz said, "I always introduce myself. . . . You must not have . . . heard me. It's impossible that he thought I was the judge. . . . Sometimes people in court call lawyers 'Your Honor,' "Mintz added.)

"It could have been an adjournment, or a stip waiving all defenses and promising to be out," Tracy Miller explains, "or it could be a stip saying he'll pay on time from now on. . . ." It could also, Miller notes, have been a stipulation saying that although the rent was withheld because the landlord didn't make repairs, those repairs have now been made and the rent will be paid.

"It could have been anything," Miller concludes.

But, adds Miller, because this particular courtroom is, in part, for tenants who have gotten notices of dispossession and have then filed papers asserting some kind of defense, it's likely the stipulation was a substantive waiver of something.

Mintz, now joined by a red-nailed, white-bloused associate who hands him file after file, calls out a half dozen more case names, then lets another member of the landlords bar have his turn.

"The only lawyers other than us," says Miller, are landlord lawyers. "Except for us, it's a landlords bar versus pro se tenants."

Miller is a staff attorney with Brooklyn Legal Services Corporation B. She is one of ten attorneys in the housing unit. (Brooklyn Legal Services Corporation A, the citywide Legal Aid Society, and other legal services organizations together have about two dozen more lawyers working on housing cases in Brooklyn, which has a larger population than Houston.)

Last year there were 111,000 cases in Brooklyn housing court, making estimates by Miller and her colleagues that 95 percent of all tenants in housing court go without lawyers seem conservative. As a result, Legal Services lawyers are reduced to providing what they call "triage service"— taking only one in ten housing cases that come through the door, and trying to make sure those cases have unusually strong fact situations, such as a landlord harassing a tenant in a gentrifying neighborhood in order to get him to move out so that the building can be turned into a co-op or a luxury rental.

At about 10 a.m. civil court judge Richard Goldberg and a clerk enter the room. Goldberg, a small white-haired man who seems almost frightened by the proceedings, sits quietly while the clerk, Norman Botwin, takes over. Botwin orders everyone to "listen carefully, because if you miss your name when it is called you will be in default," and then calls out a series of 30 case names. In only one instance does he get an answer from both parties, whereupon Judge Goldberg sends them up to a sixth-floor courtroom.

"This [courtroom] is just so the judge can assign motions to the other judges," explains Miller, who apparently has been doing this work long enough—15 months—for that explanation to make sense.

In the 29 cases where one or both parties don't answer, the clerk dismisses the tenants' motions if they don't answer but holds over the motions if the landlords don't answer.

"He figures the landlord's lawyer is somewhere in the building," says Miller, who like her colleagues I will meet later, seems so coolly professional about how unhallowed these hallowed halls of justice are that you suspect she's been emotionally numbed by it all. "I know, it's not fair," she adds matter-of-factly, "but it's the way it works."

After Miller's case has been sent up to the sixth floor, she hurries down to a first-floor auditorium-like courtroom where tenants first come when they've received eviction notices.

Miller says that she's "trying to round up" the landlord's lawyer who has the case with her on the sixth floor so that she can get out before lunch. "These guys are handling maybe a hundred cases at a time, and the judge will never dismiss if they don't show. He'll just hold it over," she explains.

I count 121 blacks and Hispanics, mostly women, among the 124 people sitting on bridge chairs. (Brooklyn is about 50 percent black and Hispanic.) All but one of the lawyers—including Mintz, who has found his way to the bench here, too—are white.

It is almost impossible to hear the names called above the wailing of two infants, one bundled on a bridge chair, another sleeping fitfully on the linoleum floor under his mother's feet.

Down a hallway outside this first-floor "courtroom" is the waiting area where tenants will be sent if they are lucky enough to hear their names in the auditorium and answer correctly "tenant by the court" (which means the tenant is here and wants the case adjudicated by the court rather than by arbitration) and to have the landlord's lawyer answer as well.

Here, these people who believed enough in our system to show up when sent that piece of paper saying, in the name of our justice system, that they were about to become homeless will wait for their cases to be assigned to another judge, after which time they will wait, again, for one of the landlord's lawyers to decide to show up.

The room's light bulbs are all out except one. The place looks like the arcade of an abandoned subway station. It is dark. Filthy. Virtually chairless. An affront to justice.

It is not simply a matter of people holding out on rent that they owe. New York, especially many areas of Brooklyn, is in the midst of a real estate upheaval that has seen values skyrocket in many neighborhoods where the renters are the working poor or lower middle class. So many landlords are doing anything they can—claiming rent hasn't been paid, raising rents illegally, claiming leases don't exist, and not offering to renew leases when they are obligated to—in order to bring dispossession actions.

Other tenants face dispossession even though they are only withholding rent because repairs to which they are entitled have not been made. Still others may, indeed, be far behind on their rents for no reason other than inability or unwillingness to pay. But even they could—if they had lawyers—raise defenses ranging from the landlord's not having kept up his end of the bargain because of some significant fault in the building (such as no heat or no locks on the doors), to invalid or just plain nonexistent service by the process server. A lease, after all, is supposed to be a contract, and due process is supposed to be due process.

Russell Engler, who works with Miller at the Brooklyn Legal Services housing unit, may be exaggerating when he says, "We could successfully fight ninety percent of all evictions if we could take the cases." But he may not be far off.

But because Miller, Engler, and their cohorts can't take all the cases, they pick their fights carefully. Engler—who graduated from Harvard Law School in 1983 and clerked for Fourth Circuit Court of Appeals Judge Francis Murnaghan, Jr., before coming to Brooklyn in 1984—splits his time between individual cases having what he says are particularly compelling facts and what he calls "impact litigation," which are suits designed to improve things generally for his clients.

Thus, last December Engler began attacking the kangaroo-court aspects of Brooklyn housing court by suing the chief judge of civil court, as well as the administrator of the overall state court system, among others, for not acting on complaints he had made that one judge—Ferdinand Pellegrino—was particularly biased.

Engler charged that Pellegrino, who declined comment on the case, "enters orders granting judgments of possession to landlords against unrepresented tenants without conducting a trial or making a record of the proceeding; approves stipulations prepared by landlords' attorneys without reading the stipulations ... to unrepresented tenants; ... [and] rules against tenants after having heard an ex parte communication from the landlord's attorney...."

This kind of impact litigation can yield broad results, and its logic as a client service is compelling. (For example, in 1985 Engler's colleagues won a suit requiring the city's Housing Authority to overhaul its procedures for accepting and acting upon applications for its scarce apartments.) It's also exactly the kind of litigation that the Reagan administration has attacked when brought by Legal Services lawyers, claiming it represents political activism rather than the lawyering that a taxpayer-paid program is meant to support.

Miller and another lawyer, Sheryl Karp, also do work that is strategically well-targeted, but controversial: "They're a two-lawyer illegal eviction unit established with a grant from the city last year to help tenants who are threatened with illegal evictions or who have already been evicted illegally." Thus, the two young women often end up representing and even helping to organize tenants' associations that are fighting landlord harassment.

As Miller and I leave a courtroom up on the fourth floor, we run into Karp. They stop and talk just long enough in the crowded hall under the "Pay All Fees To Court Cashiers Only" signs to attract two women who need help. Legal Services lawyers are not supposed to pick up cases in the courthouse. But Miller takes ten minutes to advise the first woman informally; and Karp, realizing that the second woman's case may fall within the scope of their special unit's work—the woman claims she is being harassed in a building where Karp knows the landlord is trying to force everyone out—darts into a courtroom to tell a judge that she's just taken the case and needs a postponement.

"Wall Street lawyers work nights, and I work nights," says Karp as we walk back to her office two blocks from the courthouse. "Only we work different places. I'm usually at a tenants' association meeting or in a client's apartment."

. . .

"I figure we're saving the city money by keeping people from becoming homeless," explains Miller, having come back from court and settled into her small office. "It costs the city thousands to take care of people who become homeless. But, of course, what we do is much more important than the money it saves."

Does she ever feel so frustrated or worn down that she'd like to move on, say, to a more conventional Wall Street job? "No, I love what I do," Miller answers quickly. "I can see the law I practice have an effect on people. I can work in a subject area that I love"—Miller got a master's in urban planning at Columbia before going to law school and wrote her thesis on rent control—"and I get more freedom and responsibility than just about any lawyer I know from my law school days."

"I know that what I'm doing is what I want to do for the rest of my life," says Karp, who is 31 and came to Brooklyn Legal Services in 1986. "And I have to tell you that I used to be embarrassed to admit that, because I don't know too many people my age who feel that way."

"This is the only type of legal work I think I could ever enjoy," echoes Engler, who spent part of the summer between his second and third years at Harvard at San Francisco's McCutchen, Doyle, Brown & Enerson. "I would guess that fifty percent of the people we represent would become the homeless people everyone's reading about if we didn't represent them," he adds. "Or they'd be one more stop—maybe a relative's home or one more rental—away from being homeless. I spend my time preserving what is probably a man's most basic property right, his home." . . .

One could argue that a rough measure of our commitment to justice is the difference between what we, in the way we organize our legal and economic systems, pay Engler or Miller and what we pay a starting associate on Wall Street. In 1971, a few years before the Legal Services Corporation started, the going rate on Wall Street was roughly $16,000. That year, staff lawyers at Brooklyn Legal Services were paid $12,000. That's about 4:3; starting salaries on Wall Street [in 1987] are about $75,000 including bonuses, or about three times what Engler and Miller make. And on Wall Street Miller and Engler, it should be remembered, would be getting second-and fourth-year salaries, not starting salaries.

[Brill then argues that the American Bar Association should propose "practical, relatively radical measures" to achieve equal justice: First, encourage law graduates to work for the non-rich by requiring ABA-approved law schools to provide full student loans to any student who wants one combined with a substantial loan forgiveness program for graduates who work for "a nonprofit organization providing legal services to the poor." The program would be paid for out of tuition charges, thus shifting the cost to students who take higher paying jobs after graduation. Second, a "justice tax" of 0.5–1.0 percent of law firms' gross revenues be imposed to finance legal services for the poor. Third, companies that make money by selling things to lawyers, such as *The American Lawyer* (Brill's publication) and LEXIS, should be asked to contribute the same percentage.]

No one is ever going to even things up so that the mirror in Tracy Miller's tiny office can become a window with a harbor view, her linoleum a carpet, her subway token a Dialcab voucher. She doesn't expect that.

But she and every other lawyer and every other American has a right to expect that the rest of her profession will do more. That her profession won't allow Americans to go homeless because they didn't have a lawyer to nag a judge into doing his job. That her colleagues at the bar will remember that more people see room 202 in a week than see a deposition room in a month, and that for these people the "litigation crisis" isn't about docket delay, interrogatories, and hourly rates but about simple justice.

Miller and every other lawyer and every American have a right to expect that places like room 202—scenes that seem taken from Soviet propaganda texts—won't continue to be the true images of justice in our country.

And we all have a right to expect that the justice profession in the country that is supposed to stand for equal justice will push itself, reexamine itself, even tax itself, to produce more [lawyers] like Miller and Engler.

---

2.   PROFESSIONAL OBLIGATION TO REPRESENT POOR PEOPLE

The legal profession in the United States has regarded itself, uniquely among legal professions in the world, as charged with a responsibility to provide legal assistance to the poor. Various rationales are offered. One is that a lawyer, as an officer of the court, has a concern that justice be done, and that representing an indigent person who requires legal assistance is an obvious way to act upon this concern. Another rationale is that the bar has a monopoly of law practice, and as a monopolist it should reallocate its monopoly profits to a manifest public need that is related to the monopoly. A third rationale is that representation of the poor is a special kind of continuing legal education that exposes the lawyer to the realities of justice as administered to the poor.[11]

The bar's commitment to representing the poor has always been and remains more rhetorical than actual. The scope and depth of the legal needs of the poor began to be taken more seriously by the public and the bar after the upheavals of the 1960s and the development of the federal legal services program. Even before that, however, "legal aid" organizations in many communities provided poor people with some free legal help. This aid was provided by private lawyers who would volunteer their time and effort. Although lawyers in other countries recognized some similar obligation, the obligation was not treated as seriously, in legal or moral terms, as in this country. Is this different response rooted in an aspect of the American concept of justice?

11. For discussions of the "pro bono" obligation see Barlow F. Christensen, The Lawyer's Pro Bono Public Responsibility, 1981 Am.Bar Found.Research J. 1; Geoffrey C. Hazard, Jr., The Lawyer's Pro Bono Obligation, in ABA Proceedings of the Second National Conference on Legal Services and the Public (1981); David L. Shapiro, The Enigma of the Lawyer's Duty to Serve, 55 N.Y.U.L.Rev. 735 (1980).

Mandatory Pro Bono

Volunteered services may have worked reasonably well in small-town America at an earlier time. Lawyers were general practitioners who had contacts with a wide range of people in their communities. A poor person who came to a lawyer's office with a substantial and meritorious legal problem may have had a decent chance of getting necessary help. A competent general practitioner could tell a meritorious case when he saw it, especially if he was free to decline it. Toward the end of the 19th century, the face-to-face character of American society gave way in urban centers. During the 20th century legal practice increasingly became specialized in character. Absent institutional arrangements channeling willing lawyers to needy clients, volunteered efforts proved ineffective.

Lawyers have embodied their aspirations concerning access to justice in their codes of professional ethics, but have not stated them in mandatory terms.[12] The wording of Model Rule 6.1, as adopted in 1983, reflects an explicit rejection of earlier drafts which mandated 40 hours per year of pro bono service from each lawyer. A 1993 amendment to M.R. 6.1 edges back toward the original Kutak Commission proposal: "A lawyer *should aspire* to render at least [50] hours of pro bono publico legal services per year [primarily to persons of limited means or organizations that address the needs of such persons]." Read Rule 6.1 and its comment at this time. Note that M.R. 6.1 departs from the general pattern of the Model Rules in stating an aspirational rather than a disciplinary standard.

Mandatory pro bono proposals have arisen in states and localities with increasing frequency since the 1980s, partly stimulated by cutbacks in federal funding of the Legal Services Corporation. Thus far state-wide proposals have been defeated or tabled after extensive discussion.[13] Florida, however, went part way in 1993 by imposing a report requirement on all lawyers.[14]

A New York proposal provides a specific focus for discussion. In 1990 a committee appointed by the chief judge of the New York Court of Appeals proposed that the courts adopt rules compelling New York lawyers to donate 40 hours every two years to advance the legal needs of the poor.[15]

12. See Model Rule 6.1 and its comment; and Model Code ECs 2–25, 8–3 and 8–9.

13. For discussion of mandatory pro bono proposals, see Symposium, 19 Hofstra L. Rev. 739 et seq. (1991); David Luban, Lawyers and Justice: An Ethical Study 240–89 (1988); Steven B. Rosenfeld, Mandatory Pro Bono: Historical and Constitutional Perspectives, 2 Cardozo L. Rev. 255 (1981); Michael A. Millemann, Mandatory Pro Bono in Civil Cases: A Partial Answer to the Right Question, 49 Md.L.Rev. 18 (1990).

14. Fla.R.Prof.Conduct 4–6.1 states that every lawyer has a professional obligation to "render pro bono legal services to the poor or ... participate ... in other pro bono service activities that directly relate to the legal needs of the poor;" although the duty is "aspirational rather than mandatory," it is stated as a minimum 20 hours annually or a contribution of $350 to a legal aid organization, and an annual report concerning its fulfillment must be made on a form attached to the annual dues statement. See 630 So.2d 501 (Fla.1993).

15. Committee To Improve the Availability of Legal Services, Final Report to the Chief Judge of the State of New York (April 1990), reprinted in 19 Hofstra L. Rev. 755

The mandatory pro bono proposal contained the following details: Law firms could credit the excess hours of some firm lawyers to meet the obligations of others. Lawyers in small firms of less than ten lawyers could satisfy their obligation by paying $1,000 each, in lieu of time, to support legal services for the poor. A third alternative permits law firms or unaffiliated lawyers to hire an attorney to discharge their collective obligation to devote time. Is this proposal desirable and fair?

The proposal, like mandatory pro bono plans elsewhere, divided the New York bar. Most bar associations opposed it, but individual lawyers and a few bar associations supported it. The Association of the Bar of the City of New York, which is representative of New York City's largest firms, " 'reluctantly' but forcefully endorsed the proposal as essential to meet a 'desperate' need." In light of this mixed reaction, Chief Judge Wachtler postponed action on the report for a period of time in the hope that the stimulus it provided to voluntary pro bono would suffice to meet the problem.

No one knows the proportion of the legal needs of the poor that are now going unmet, an issue discussed further below. In the modern administrative/welfare state, however, corporations and poor people may be two groups in society most in need of competent legal assistance. The corporate need is obvious to most law students, undoubtedly because law school courses that explicate the corporation's legal and regulatory problems abound. On the other hand, few law students take courses that study the complex law and practice of Aid for Dependent Children, Social Security disability, federal and state housing laws or any of the multitude of other legal areas that directly impinge on the lives of poor people. Corporations, however, able to pay for needed legal services, receive the legal assistance they want.

The federally-funded national legal services program meets a portion of the legal needs of the poor, although funding cuts since 1981 have seriously reduced the number of lawyers and and the quantity of service that the program provides.[16] Efforts to encourage and support private bar involvement in local legal services programs have met with some success. Various studies show that most lawyers do participate in some pro bono work, as long as one takes a broad definition of activity that qualifies. In other words, much of the time lawyers spend on "pro bono" work is directed toward activities that build relations with other lawyers, such as bar association work, or work that is designed to attract clients, such as free or reduced-fee work for local charities.[17]

(1991) (generally referred to as the Marrero Report after its chairman).

16. See discussion infra at p. 1106

17. Although most lawyers donate some free services, little of it involves the representation of indigents. Miskiewicz, Mandatory Pro Bono Won't Disappear, Nat'l L.J. 1 (Mar. 23, 1987). Some reports indicate that as many as 16 percent of lawyers participate in pro bono services for the poor, but other studies report that only about 6 percent of lawyer time is pro bono, much of it devoted to charities rather than poor people. See the materials cited in Roger C. Cramton, Mandatory Pro Bono, 19 Hofstra L.Rev. 1113, 1121, 1124 (1991).

The argument for mandatory pro bono usually proceeds along the following lines: (1) Many individuals, and especially the poor, have an unmet need for vital legal services. (2) A lawyer is necessary for meaningful access to the justice system. (3) The American ideal of equal justice under law is undermined by lack of access to justice. (4) Although voluntary pro bono is commendable, it has proven insufficient even when supplemented by modest public funds in the form of the national legal services program. Therefore (5) lawyers must satisfy the unmet need with mandated services at least until other alternatives, such as adequate provision of publicly-funded services, are put in place.[18]

Even if one accepts the premises of this argument, serious legal, moral and practical questions are raised when a general moral obligation of lawyers to represent the poor is converted into a detailed legal requirement. The legal objections rest on various constitutional provisions, including freedom of speech and association, the takings clause, equal protection and involuntary servitude. The legal arguments have generally been rejected in the context in which they have the greatest force: court-appointment programs which require an appointed lawyer to devote a substantial amount of time to handling a particular matter.[19] Such appointments commit a lawyer to a specific client and cause, bear heavily on trial lawyers and may require a large amount of uncompensated time. On the other hand, the imposition of a modest annual pro bono obligation on lawyers who are extensively regulated and have an exclusive license to practice is hard to perceive as involuntary servitude.[20] If the lawyer is given a great deal of choice concerning how the required service is performed, as is the case in most mandatory proposals, a claim that free speech and associational rights are impaired is also difficult to maintain. Whether mandatory pro bono is wise or desirable is perhaps a more important inquiry than whether it would pass constitutional muster.

18. For a more extended argument, see David Luban, Lawyers and Justice 267–89 (1988).

19. See, e.g., Unites States v. Shackney, 333 F.2d 475, 485–87 (2d Cir.1964) (only physical restraint or legal confinement constitutes involuntary servitude); United States v. Dillon, 346 F.2d 633 (9th Cir.1965) (compulsory appointment of a lawyer not a taking); Family Div. Trial Lawyers v. Moultrie, 725 F.2d 695 (D.C.Cir.1984) (compulsory appointment of lawyers for uncompensated representation of parents in child neglect and parental termination cases was not a taking; but case remanded for a further hearing on an equal protection claim arising out of limitation of that obligation to juvenile defenders). But see State ex rel. Scott v. Roper, 688 S.W.2d 757 (Mo.1985) (suggesting that uncompensated service presents a constitutional question); and DeLisio v. Alaska Superior Court, 740 P.2d 437 (Alaska 1987) (court appointment was a temporary taking requiring just compensation). See David L. Shapiro, The Enigma of the Lawyer's Duty to Serve, 55 N.Y.U.L.Rev. 735, 765 (1980) (arguing that compelling a lawyer to represent a particular client or to assert certain positions is "more troublesome than a tax in dollars"). See Note, Court Appointment of Uncompensated Legal Assistance in Civil Cases, 81 Colum.L.Rev. 366 (1981).

20. Although the practice of law is a property interest protected by the takings clause of the Fourteenth Amendment, Konigsberg v. State Bar, 353 U.S. 252 (1957), a requirement that a relatively small number of hours be devoted to public service each year is supported by the bar's historic tradition of response to court appointment and falls short of a "taking."

The moral objections to mandatory pro bono are that mandated service intrudes on personal autonomy; that it converts a gift of volunteered services into the duty of a compelled exaction, thus depriving the actor of the moral significance of the gift of service;[21] and that in application it tends to be regressive and inequitable, falling with a heavier hand on less affluent and less successful lawyers.[22] Consider these arguments in the context of the New York mandatory pro bono proposal summarized above.

The legal and moral objections to mandatory pro bono reflect an underlying theme discussed earlier: the emphasis on the political equality of individuals in the American concept of equality, which entails a rejection of elitism and of assigning of special responsibilities for justice to one group.[23]

The principal practical objections to mandatory pro bono rest on concerns about the quality and efficiency of mandated services, the burdensome problems of administration and enforcement, the discouragement of charitable and bar association work if these activities are excluded from the required pro bono category, as in the New York proposal, and, finally, a concern that, if adopted in only one jurisdiction, lawyers in that state will be adversely affected vis-a-vis their competitors in other states. A pro bono obligation imposed on New York lawyers will operate essentially as a tax on legal services, putting New York lawyers in a less favorable position with respect to clients who can go elsewhere for legal services.

21. The idea that activity performed out of obligation deprives the activity of moral significance is not universal. In Jewish Law "obligation" holds the cherished place of "right" in Western law. Those in the community with the most obligation are considered the most privileged, just as in Western law those with the most rights are the most privileged. So in Jewish law men have more obligations than women, the rich more than the poor, and professionals such as teachers more than nonprofessionals. Recall the "chosen people" story told on the first page of this Chapter. Being specially "obligated" to do justice and repair the world is precisely what gives the Jews their claim to being "chosen." Being especially blessed, "chosen," means to have more obligations than others, not fewer. For a discussion of how legal ethics in this country has been distorted by the privileged notion of "right" and the disparaged place of "obligation" in Western law, see Susan P. Koniak, Through the Looking Glass of Ethics and the Wrong with Rights We Find There, 9 Geo. J. Legal Ethics 1 (1995) (arguing the absurdity of giving two groups of clients a "right" to adequate representation, while simultaneously di-minishing the "obligation" of their lawyers to provide adequate representation, i.e., simultaneously limiting the ability of those clients to sue their lawyers for malpractice).

22. Moral philosophers and economists have debated whether the provision of blood for transfusions may best be met exclusively by voluntary donation (as in the United Kingdom) or by purchase as well as gift. Richard Titmuss's comparative study concludes that the British approach, forbidding the development of a market for blood, fosters "the gift relationship" and is more effective in providing blood, while the more commercial approach in the United States results in chronic shortages. See Richard Titmuss, The Gift Relationship: From Human Blood to Social Policy (1971); Kenneth Arrow, Gifts and Exchanges, 1 Phil. & Pub. Affairs 343 (1972); and Peter Singer, Altruism and Commerce: A Defense of Titmuss Against Arrow, 2 Phil. & Pub. Affairs 312 (1973). The altruistic impulse was the target of President Bush's frequent references to "a thousand points of light."

23. See discussion above at p. 1066.

Doubts about the quality and efficiency of mandatory services rest on the specialized character of the legal needs of poor people. Is an office lawyer engaged in bond debenture work likely to be an effective advocate for poor people?[24] The most common legal problems faced by poor people involve highly technical subjects with which most lawyers are unfamiliar. Law schools generally do not teach these subjects, at least in any depth.[25] Representation of indigent criminal defendants requires familiarity with criminal law and its local practice. Representation of poor people in disputes with a welfare department requires familiarity with a complicated body of federal and state law and with local administrative practice in administering that law. The law of landlord and tenant, which affects many poor people, is similarly complicated. From a political-economic viewpoint, most poor people exist in a semi-socialist regime in which their lives are continuously dependent on government regulation and discretion. Hence, in most localities, certainly in all major cities, a very sophisticated system would be required to provide a lawyer to every poor person facing a legal problem.

A related problem is equalizing the burden of service on all members of the bar. Although the bar as a whole may have a monopoly of law practice, no single lawyer or law firm does. If the burden of discharging the collective responsibility were not equitably apportioned, widely disparate burdens would be involved. Lawyers who had undertaken to learn a specialty in the "law of the poor" would be particularly vulnerable, and that would create perverse incentives to remain unskilled in poverty law.[26] The difficulties could be ameliorated if lawyers were exposed in law school or through continuing legal education and practice to some field of "poverty law." But the acceptance of such a duty would require the bar to take seriously its rhetorical claim that it has a special responsibility for justice in this country, a notion that many lawyers and much of the public resist.

Should law students be required during law school to assist in providing legal assistance to the poor?[27] A substantial and growing number of law schools now impose a public service requirement. In addition to law

24. Some believe that the costs of arranging and supervising pro bono opportunities (training, administering referrals and monitoring performance) exceed the benefits. Esther Lardent, Pro Bono in the 1990s, in American Bar Association, Civil Justice: An Agenda for the 1990s (1990) (mandatory pro bono programs will make a "very small dent in a very large problem").

25. Presumably, however, law schools could and would teach these subjects, if lawyers were obligated to practice this law some number of hours each year to keep their licenses and that obligation was enforced.

26. See, e.g., Family Division Trial Lawyers v. Moultrie, 725 F.2d 695 (D.C.Cir.1984), in which lawyers who had signed up to re-

ceive compensated court assignments as juvenile defenders were required, as a condition of receiving compensated assignments, to accept court appointments for uncompensated representation of indigent parents in child neglect and parental termination proceedings.

27. See John R. Kramer, Law Schools and the Delivery of Legal Services—First, Do No Harm, in American Bar Association, Civil Justice: An Agenda for the 1990s (1991) ("the best way to alter attorneys' attitudes is from the ground up by instilling in law students a sense of the responsibilities they must shoulder when they become members of the bar").

students, should all law professors have to engage in pro bono activity? Some schools with public service requirements for students also impose requirements on professors, but it is our understanding that more schools have student-only requirements. Would a professor-only requirement make more sense?

The *Mallard* Case[28]

John Mallard, an Iowa lawyer with a securities and bankruptcy practice, was appointed by a federal magistrate in Iowa to represent inmates of a state prison in their civil suit against prison officials seeking redress for brutalities and other wrongs. The appointment was pursuant to a program, begun as a voluntary pro bono effort by the Iowa bar and the state legal services organization, subjecting every lawyer who had been admitted to the federal district court's bar to compulsory appointment, which worked out to one appointment about every three years. Mallard refused the appointment, stating that "he had no familiarity with the legal issues presented in the case, that he lacked experience in deposing and cross-examining witnesses, and that he would be willing to volunteer his services in an area in which he possessed some expertise, such as bankruptcy and securities law."[29] After being ordered by the magistrate, the district judge and the court of appeals to provide service, Mallard sought certiorari from the Supreme Court, which heard the case and reversed.

In *Mallard* the Court held, 5–4, that the federal statute empowering a federal judge to "request" an attorney to represent an indigent in a civil case[30] did not create a legally binding obligation on the part of the attorney. Justice Brennan's opinion for the majority relied on the fact that other provisions of the same statute imposed mandatory duties; the opinion did not reach the question whether a district court had inherent authority apart from the statute to require a lawyer to serve. Justice Brennan acknowledged the tradition that members of the bar have an obligation to represent indigents,[31] but interpreted the history as establishing an ethical rather than legal obligation: " 'To justify coerced, uncompensated legal services on the basis of a firm tradition in England and the United States is to read into that tradition a story that is not there.' "[32]

Justice Stevens' dissenting opinion argued that the statute was using polite language to describe an order an attorney was legally obliged to accept. Citing the history of court appointments in England and the United

---

28. Mallard v. United States District Court for the Southern District of Iowa, 490 U.S. 296 (1989). The case is discussed in Geoffrey C. Hazard, Jr., After Professional Virtue, 1989 Sup.Ct.Rev. 213.

29. 490 U.S. at 299.

30. 28 U.S.C. § 1915(d), which provides: "The court may request an attorney [to represent the indigent in certain proceedings]."

31. "In a time when the need for legal services among the poor is growing and public funding for such services has not kept pace, lawyers' ethical obligation to volunteer their time *pro bono publico* is manifest." 490 U.S. at 310.

32. 490 U.S. at 304 (quoting from David L. Shapiro, The Enigma of the Lawyer's Duty to Serve, 55 N.Y.U.L.Rev. 735, 753 (1980)).

States, as well as that of the statute, Stevens quoted Justice Field's statement in 1860: "Counsel are not considered at liberty to reject ... the cause of the defenseless, because no provision for their compensation is made by law."[33] Brennan's opinion reflects the American ideal of individual political equality, whereas Stevens' opinion reflects an acceptance of the bar's special obligation to see justice done.

3.   PUBLICLY FINANCED CIVIL LEGAL ASSISTANCE

Background[34]

Legal aid in various forms began around 1900, sometimes as self-help associations of worker and immigrant groups, sometimes as charities. Through the 1950s legal aid programs were funded almost entirely by charity and subscription of members of the bar. The programs usually had a small staff, often one person, assisted by volunteers and law students. The agencies were few in number, located almost exclusively in major cities, thinly funded and relatively passive, concentrating on individual cases and having the aura of a charity. In the 1960s the Ford Foundation made legal aid a major undertaking and infused it with new money, new stature and new assertiveness. In 1964, the Office of Economic Opportunity (OEO) of President Lyndon Johnson's "war on poverty" program provided funding for a quantum leap in civil legal assistance. The federal legal services program, discussed more fully below, originated in the OEO initiative.

Public defender programs originated in the western states, notably California, in the early part of the 20th century. They are publicly funded law offices providing representation to indigent criminal accused and to juveniles.[35]

Development of Federal Legal Services Program

The visionaries and activists who started the legal services movement in the turbulent 1960s had three missions in mind: (1) the individual client-service mission of traditional legal aid, (2) law reform and institutional change and (3) empowering poor people by creating organized groups that

---

33. 490 U.S. at 313–14, quoting from Rowe v. Yuba County, 17 Cal. 61, 63 (1860).

34. For general and historical background, see Earl Johnson, Jr., Justice and Reform: The Formative Years of the OEO Legal Services Program (1974); Reginald Heber Smith, Justice and the Poor (1919); Emery A. Brownell, Legal Aid in the United States (1951); Elliot Cheatham, A Lawyer When Needed (1963); Jerome E. Carlin, Jan Howard & Sheldon L. Messinger, Civil Justice and the Poor (1966); Barlow F. Christensen, Lawyers for People of Moderate Means (1970).

35. For discussion of public defenders, see Lisa J. McIntyre, The Public Defender: The Practice of Law in the Shadows of Repute (1987) (empirical study of Cook County, Illinois, public defender office); Michael McConville and Chester L. Mirsky, Criminal Defense of the Poor in New York City, 15 N.Y.U.Rev. of Law & Soc. Change 581–964 (1986–87); and Lee Silverstein, Defense of the Poor in Criminal Cases in American State Courts (1965).

might engage in direct action such as boycotts, demonstrations and political activity. The activists in the legal services movement ridiculed individual-client assistance as "band-aid" work that failed to get at fundamental problems.[36] They sought to direct the program's resources into social advocacy and organizational activity. The provision of lawyers for otherwise represented persons in dealing with public or private institutions resulted in numerous decisions requiring fuller procedure or establishing new substantive law. The ultimate objective—a substantial redistribution of societal wealth and power—proved to be too large and too politically controversial to be accomplished by lawyers through the mechanism of the courts.

The social reform potential visualized in the 1960s for the federal legal assistance program excited hopes of reformers and fears of conservatives, both greatly exaggerated. The result was a political struggle for control of the program, involving the organized bar at various levels, political action groups, factions in Congress and a variety of governmental agencies. Broadly speaking, the reformers sought to make legal aid programs a vehicle for structural legal reform, through test cases, class actions and legislative activity, in such areas as housing, civil rights, education, welfare benefits and employment. The conservatives sought to maintain legal aid as a service program for needy individuals in such traditional matters as child support and custody, landlord-tenant disputes, debtor-creditor disputes and securing governmental benefits.[37]

In 1974, a detente of sorts was reached. The federal legal services program was established on a permanent basis through the Legal Services Corporation Act.[38] The statutory objectives are stated in politically neutral terms of "equal access to justice" and "high-quality legal assistance" for the poor. Political and organizational activities on the part of legal services lawyers are largely excluded by specific restrictions: a ban on political activity by lawyers in the field, a prohibition on participation in organizational activity (as distinct from legal advice concerning it) and procedural constraints on the use of class actions. These restrictions suggest that individual-client service and test-case litigation arising out of it constitute the central statutory mission.

---

36. See Stephen Wexler, Practicing Law for Poor People, 79 Yale L. J. 1049, 1053 (1970) ("If all the lawyers in the country worked full time, they could not deal with even the articulated problems of the poor.... In this setting, the object of practicing poverty law must be to organize poor people, rather than to solve their legal problems.").

37. For one view at the time, see Carlin, Howard & Messinger, supra; for another, see Geoffrey C. Hazard, Jr., Social Justice Through Civil Justice, 36 U.Chi.L.Rev. 242 (1970); Hazard, Law Reforming in the Anti–Poverty Effort, 37 U.Chi.L.Rev. 242 (1970).

38. Pub.L. 93–355, 88 Stat. 378, codified as 42 U.S.C. § 2996 et seq. Roger Cramton, one of the authors of this book, served as the initial chairman of the board of directors of the Legal Services Corporation, July 1975–July 1998, as an appointee of President Ford, and as a member of the Board until May 1979. Thomas Ehrlich, then dean of the Stanford Law School, was selected to head the full-time staff of the Corporation.

The structure of the national program involves the Legal Services Corporation (LSC) as a funding agency for local non-profit organizations that actually represent clients and deliver legal services. LSC is forbidden to provide legal services to poor people directly, but it has an uncertain extent of regulatory authority over the operation of local programs. Restrictions on the matters that could be undertaken by local programs were included in the original Act (e.g., abortion and school desegregation cases). These restrictions have since been modified, elaborated and fought over, each time in highly political battles. Parallel struggles over the level of funding regular recur.[39]

President Reagan was strongly against any reformist tendency in legal aid and favored abolishing the Legal Services Corporation. Major bar associations, led by the American Bar Association, in company with various civil rights and other activist groups, held out for continuing the program. Since the 1980s, the program has survived but with funding diminished by budget cuts and inflation and more restrictions on the services the program's lawyers may provide. The federal legal services program has achieved permanence with modest funding, a distinctive structure, significant restrictions on practice and a legacy of bitter political controversy.

Funding and Caseloads[40]

Annual funding of the Legal Services Corporation rose to $321 million in the Carter Administration, struggled for survival at annual funding of about three-fourths of that amount during the Reagan years, then climbed to $400 million in 1995 under President Clinton before being cut again to $278 million in 1996. The funding for fiscal year 1999 is $300 million. These figures do not reflect the ravages of inflation, especially heavy in the 1980s, on the value of the dollar.[41]

One development since the Reagan years has been the increased funding of local programs from non-LSC sources. In 1997, for example, 269 LSC grantees received $275 million from LSC (55%) and $228 million (45%) from other sources (e.g., state IOLTA programs, local funding, foundations, charitable gifts). This development has led to legislative restrictions and LSC regulations subjecting most of the legal representation under non-LSC funds to the same restrictions applicable to LSC funds (see below).

---

39. See generally Roger C. Cramton, Crisis in Legal Services for the Poor, 26 Vill. L.Rev. 521 (1981); Carrie Menkel–Meadow, Legal Aid in the United States: The Professionalization and Politicization of Legal Services in the 1980s, 22 Osgoode Hall L. J. 28 (1984).

40. Data in this paragraph is from Legal Services Corporation, 1997 Annual Report; and Alan D. Houseman, The Future of Legal Services: Legal and Ethical Implictions of the LSC Restrictions, 25 Fordham Urban L.J. 286 (1998). Alan Houseman

estimates that the national resources for civil legal assistance totaled about $711 million in 1999: ($289 million from LSC; $115 million from state IOLTA plans; and $317 million from other sources).

41. Phillips v. Washington Legal Foundation, Inc., 524 U.S. 156 (1998), discussed supra at p. 557, threatens to further decrease the funding of legal services by reducing the contribution from state IOLTA plans.

Local legal service programs closed about 1.5 million cases in 1997. The 269 local programs had over 8,000 full-time employees. The majority of cases closed in 1997 were related to family law and housing issues. Other significant areas of representation included consumer fraud and income maintenance (e.g., welfare benefits). Over two-thirds of clients are women.

A major revision of the underlying legislation in 1996 added further restrictions on cases that could be handled or methods of representation. The 1996 legislation also ended funding for the state and national centers that supported local programs by providing specialized information, training programs and assistance in handling major cases (these so-called "backup centers" are struggling along on funding from other sources).

Legislative and Regulatory Restrictions[42]

Some restrictions on legal services programs and lawyers have been in effect since the program began in 1974 while others have been added subsequently, most notably in 1996.

Legislative advocacy (lobbying). The 1974 Act prohibited use of LSC funds to "directly or indirectly" influence the passage or defeat of federal, state or local legislation or regulation except where "necessary to the provision of legal advice and representation with respect to such clients' legal rights and responsibilities" or where a government agency or legislative body or committee or member thereof requested assistance.[43] A recipient legal aid agency was also prohibited from using private funds for lobbying. The 1996 revision prohibits all legislative advocacy, even in agency rule-making, although non-LSC funds may be used by a recipient to participate in a public rule-making proceeding or to respond to requests for information from government agencies, legislative bodies and elected officials.

Organizing. The LSC Act forbids use of LSC funds "to organize, assist to organize or encourage to organize or to plan for the creation or formation of, or the structuring of, any organization, association, coalition, alliance, federation, confederation or any similar entity."[44] Changes in 1977 made it clear that local programs may give legal advice to those seeking to organize a group of poor people or to such an organization once it is formed. But legal services lawyers may not themselves organize the group.

Restrictions on cases. Since the 1980s LSC recipients have been prohibited from representing clients in matters involving non-therapeutic abortions, aliens in deportation and other immigration matters, voter redistricting cases and other matters. The 1996 legislation added further restrictions: challenges to welfare reform laws or regulations, and civil litigation on behalf of prisoners. A new provision also requires programs to identify potential clients by name to the defendant if the program is going

42. See Houseman, supra and Alan D. Houseman, Legal Representation and Advocacy Under the Personal Responsibility and Work Opportunity Reconciliation Act of 1996, 30 Clearinghouse Rev. 932 (1997).

43. Public Law 93–335, § 1007(a)(5).

44. Pub.L. 93–355, § 1007(b)(6).

to file litigation or engage in pre-complaint settlement negotiations where litigation is anticipated.

Restrictions on advocacy. Prior to 1996 class actions were permitted subject to procedural requirements; under the 1996 legislation, LSC recipients are barred from filing Rule 23–type class actions in a federal or state court. In addition, recipients cannot claim, collect or retain statutory attorney's fees in cases initiated after April 25, 1996. Another 1996 prohibition prevents LSC recipients from legally challenging a new statutory law or regulation amending state or federal welfare laws; on the other hand, a recipient that represents an individual welfare client who is seeking relief from a welfare agency because of a threatened adverse action (e.g., terminating benefits) may challenge agency policies and practices as violative of law or Constitution. See the *Velasquez* case, summarized below.

Monitoring provisions. The 1996 legislation also gives LSC monitors and auditors access to financial records, time records, retainer agreements, eligibility records and client names if they appear in those records, unless the information in those records is protected by the attorney-client privilege. Efforts are being made by local legal services programs to design their financial records so that neither client names nor confidential information are included in them.

Restrictions on use of non-LSC funds by recipients. Most of the above restrictions are applicable to the use of non-LSC funds by an LSC recipient. In other words, a local program that takes federal money must comply with the same restrictions in the use of money that it obtains from other sources. One result of this is the development of a dual delivery system in ten states, creating two sets of legal service providers in the same city or state, one operating on federal money and the other operating on money from other sources. LSC regulations permit a recipient to set up an affiliated legal services program, with the same or an overlapping board of directors, and carry out restricted activities through that affiliate from non-LSC funds providing: (1) the affiliate is a separate legal entity; (2) no LSC funds are involved; and (3) the affiliate is physically and financial separate.[45]

In Velazquez v. Legal Services Corporation,[46] the Second Circuit considered a facial challenge to the LSC regulations implementing the 1996 legislation and the constitutionality of the legislative restrictions on lawyer advocacy. The challenged regulations permitted LSC recipients to fund affiliates that engaged in restricted activities with non-LSC funds and restricted the scope of legal services that legal services lawyers could provide to their clients both by case subject matter and by method of advocacy. The court, following the Ninth Circuit in an earlier case,[47] upheld

---

45. See 45 C.F.R. § 1610 (implementing statutory restrictions on the use of non-LSC funds by LSC recipients).

46. 164 F.3d 757 (2d Cir.1999).

47. Legal Aid Society of Hawaii v. Legal Services Corp., 145 F.3d 1017 (9th Cir. 1998).

nearly all of the statutory and administrative restrictions against First Amendment challenge.

The court relied on Rust v. Sullivan,[48] in which a facial challenge to restrictions on federal family planning services was upheld by the Supreme Court. "Just as Congress is entitled to provide a limited range of medical services under Title X, it is free to offer a limited menu of legal services." The program integrity rules, limiting the use of non-LSC funds, did not impose an unconstitutional condition on the receipt of LSC funds: "in appropriate circumstances, Congress may burden the First Amendment rights of recipients of government benefits if the recipients are left with adequate alternative channels for protected expression." The court noted that the program integrity rules allow some LSC grantees with substantial non-federal funding to "provide the full range of restricted activity through separately incorporated affiliates without serious difficulty." The court, relying on the *Rosenberger* case,[49] held that the restrictions on lobbying and welfare reform activity did not discriminate on the basis of viewpoint in violation of the First Amendment.

One provision of the welfare reform restrictions, however, was struck down as "inescapably viewpoint-based." The suit-for-benefits exception allowed LSC-funded lawyers to represent an individual seeking welfare benefits, provided that the relief sought "does not involve an effort to amend or otherwise challenge existing law in effect on the date of the initiation of the representation." This provision, by discouraging challenges to the status quo, "discriminates on the basis of viewpoint." Forbidding a lawyer from arguing the unconstitutionality or illegality of a welfare law in court "effectively drives the idea from the marketplace where it can most effectively be offered," and thus is an impermissible governmental restriction on speech.[50]

Aside from constitutionality and policy, do these legislative restrictions on the legal techniques that may be employed on behalf of poor clients lead to representation by legal services lawyers that violates professional rules? Do they require incompetent representation (M.R. 1.1) or constitute an interference by a third party payor with the lawyer's independent professional judgment (M.R.s 1.8(f) and 5.4(c))? Or are these potential problems cured by viewing the restrictions as a reasonable limitation on the scope of representation permitted by M.R. 1.2(c), providing the client is informed of the restrictions and consents to them?[51]

---

48. 500 U.S. 173 (1991).

49. Rosenberger v. Rector and Visitors of the Univ. of Virginia, 515 U.S. 819 (1995).

50. The court noted that the Ninth Circuit had come to a contrary conclusion on the basis of a dictum in the *Rust* case. The Second Circuit panel, however, with one judge dissenting on this point, relied instead on National Endowment for the Arts v. Finley, 118 S.Ct. 2168 (1998). A petition for rehearing en banc is pending (May 1999).

51. These issues are discussed by Stephen Ellmann and Stephen Gillers in Ethical Issues Panel, 25 Fordham Urban L.J. 357–92 (1998). Similar issues arise in insurance defense representation and advocacy by lawyers for public interest organizations. See Restatement § 215(2), permitting with a client's consent "direction [by someone other than the client when] reasonable in

Stephen Wexler, "Practicing Law for Poor People"

79 Yale Law Journal 1049, 1049–1059 (1970).[52]

Poor people are not just like rich people without money. Poor people do not have legal problems like those of the private plaintiffs and defendants in law school casebooks. People who are not poor are like casebook people. In so far as the law is concerned, they lead harmonious and settled private lives; except for their business involvements, their lives usually do not demand the skills of a lawyer. Occasionally, one of them gets hit by a car, or decides to buy a house, or lets his dog bite someone. The settled and harmonious pattern of life is then either broken or there is a threat that without care it may be broken. This is the law school model of a personal legal problem; law schools train lawyers to take care of such problems and to understand the role of a lawyer in those terms.

Poor people get hit by cars too; they get evicted; they have their furniture repossessed; they can't pay their utility bills. But they do not have personal legal problems in the law school way. Nothing that happens to them breaks up or threatens to break up a settled and harmonious life. Poor people do not lead settled lives into which the law seldom intrudes; they are constantly involved with the law in its most intrusive forms. For instance, poor people must go to government officials for many of the things which not-poor people get privately. Life would be very difficult for the not-poor person if he had to fill out an income tax return once or twice a week. Poverty creates an abrasive interface with society; poor people are always bumping into sharp legal things. The law school model of personal legal problems, of solving them and returning the client to the smooth and orderly world in television advertisements, doesn't apply to poor people.

. . .

Poverty will not be stopped by people who are not poor. If poverty is stopped, it will be stopped by poor people. And poor people can stop poverty only if they work at it together. The lawyer who wants to serve poor people must put his skills to the task of helping poor people organize themselves. This is not the traditional use of a lawyer's skills; in many ways it violates some of the basic tenets of the profession. Nevertheless, a realistic analysis of the structure of poverty, and a fair assessment of the legal needs of the poor and the legal talent available to meet them, lead a lawyer to this role.

If all the lawyers in the country worked full time, they could not deal with even the articulated legal problems of the poor. And even if somehow lawyers could deal with those articulated problems, they would not change very much the tangle of unarticulated legal troubles in which poor people live. In fact, only a very few lawyers will concern themselves with poor people, and those who do so will probably be at it for only a while. In this setting the object of practicing poverty law must be to organize poor people,

scope and character, such as by reflecting obligations borne by the person directing the lawyer...."

rather than to solve their legal problems. The proper job for a poor people's lawyer is helping poor people to organize themselves to change things so that either no one is poor or (less radically) so that poverty does not entail misery.

Two major touchstones of traditional legal practice—the solving of legal problems and the one-to-one relationship between attorney and client—are either not relevant to poor people or harmful to them. Traditional practice hurts poor people by isolating them from each other, and fails to meet their need for a lawyer by completely misunderstanding that need. Poor people have few individual legal problems in the traditional sense; their problems are the product of poverty, and are common to all poor people. The lawyer for poor individuals is likely, whether he wins cases or not, to leave his clients precisely where he found them, except that they will have developed a dependency on his skills to smooth out the roughest spots in their lives.

The lawyer will eventually go or be taken away; he does not have to stay, and the government which gave him can take him back just as it does welfare. He can be another hook on which poor people depend, or he can help the poor build something which rests upon themselves—something which cannot be taken away and which will not leave until all of them can leave. Specifically, the lawyer must seek to strengthen existing organizations of poor people, and to help poor people start organizations where none exist. There are several techniques for doing this, but all of them run counter to very deeply rooted notions in law school training, professionalism and middle-class humanism. I shall say something about the techniques which have already been used by lawyers to help organize poor people; but the techniques are not nearly so important as the mentality of the lawyer who uses them. The techniques will prove unsuccessful if applied by a lawyer who misunderstands his role; and the lawyer who knows what he is about will find the techniques to do his job.

The starkest picture of the "proper" mentality for a poor people's lawyer is painted in a story told by a very successful welfare rights organizer:

> I once found a recipient who worked hard at organizing, and was particularly good in the initial stages of getting to talk to new people. I picked her up at her apartment one morning to go out knocking on doors. While I was there, I saw her child, and I noticed that he seemed to be retarded. Because the boy was too young for school and the family never saw a doctor, the mother had never found out that something was seriously wrong with her son. I didn't tell her. If I had, she would have stopped working at welfare organizing to rush around looking for help for her son. I had some personal problems about doing that, but I'm an organizer, not a social worker.

I have heard this story related several times; each time, the people who have not heard it before gasp, fidget in their seats, and shrink away from the organizer. It is natural for them to be repelled, for this story embodies the very hardest line about organizing. Not everyone can handle the "personal problems" which arise from a primary commitment to organizing. The very things which make a lawyer want to work for poor people make it difficult to help them in the most effective way. Few can accept the organizer's model fully; but the more one is able to accept it, the more he can give poor people the wherewithal to change a world that hurts them.

If organizing is the object of a poverty practice, what are the methods for achieving that object? One method by which an existing organization can be strengthened is for a lawyer to refuse to handle matters for individuals not in the organization. A lawyer is a valuable piece of property in a poor community; an organization that can command his skills for its members, and deny them to non-members, has a powerful means of building its membership.

Turning people away is difficult: The values which made a lawyer want to help poor people will make it hard to turn away a person with a problem; the professional ethic is full of talk about representing all who need representation; moreover, the government, which often pays the lawyer, has guidelines designed to ensure that all who come get served. The latter points are weakened when one realizes that there are too many poor people seeking or in need of aid to help them all. A seemingly neutral policy of "first-come, first-served" cuts against the least informed, the least mobile, and the most oppressed. Some sieve is inevitably applied to the work a poverty lawyer does; that sieve can be one he chooses consciously in order to serve a particular end, or it can be one he chooses without thinking, and with no aim at all....

Selection of clients is only the first step; the cornerstone of a practice is the kind of service a lawyer provides for his clients. The hallmark of an effective poor people's practice is that the lawyer does not do anything for his clients that they can do or be taught to do for themselves. The standards of success for a poor people's lawyer are how well he can recognize all the things his clients can do with a little of his help, and how well he can teach them to do more.

There are several reasons for building a practice with these goals. First, there aren't enough lawyers to serve poor people, so poor people must be helped and taught to serve themselves. Second, it is better for poor people to acquire new skills than new dependencies. Third, poor people can often do what lawyers cannot or will not do. Finally, the law ought to be demystified for all laymen, but especially for the poor. More important than the specific techniques is the lawyer's belief that his clients are able to do a great many "legal" things for themselves. Most people who are not poor believe that poor people are unable to take care of themselves, let alone do work traditionally reserved for professionals. In addition to this general belief in the incompetence of poor people, lawyers are taught to believe, and have a three-year investment in believing, that what they have learned in law school was hard to learn, and that they are somehow special for having learned it. It is difficult for a lawyer to commit himself to believing that poor people can learn the law and be effective advocates; but until he believes that, a lawyer will create dependency instead of strength for his clients, and add to rather than reduce their plight.

Four ways in which a lawyer can help his clients use his knowledge are (1) informing individuals and groups of their rights, (2) writing manuals and other materials, (3) training lay advocates, and (4) educating groups for confrontation. None is particularly glamorous, but all are extremely important.

These techniques are some of the possible ways in which a lawyer can help poor people to use his knowledge and skills. While these techniques are important, the most important thing for a poor people's lawyer is to avoid playing the "lawyer's game." From all that one hears in law school, one comes to believe that a lawyer is doing his job and being a good person if he is honest and works as hard as he can for the interests of his client. This technical "morality" is a fraud; it is a way to avoid, rather than to address, the real moral questions which a lawyer ought to face. It is morality within a game.

The chief theoretical justification for the game is the adversary notion of law: each side has an advocate, each advocate is competent and fully devoted to the interests of his client, and from this structure justice will emerge. Among the not-poor, the adversary system might lead to justice; the most usual criticism of lawyers from not-poor people concerns their dishonesty and failure to be fully committed and fully competent advocates. But if justice can be obtained for the not-poor through an adversary system of law, it is because they are involved with the law on a case-by-case basis. But a case-by-case injustice is not what poor people face; they confront a host of unjust institutions, acting for and within an unjust society. The whole notion of an adversary proceeding is unsuited to dealing with social problems.

---

4. RECURRING POLICY ISSUES

Staff–Attorney System or Judicare System?

The United States is distinctive in that civil legal assistance to the poor is provided primarily by organizations that employ "poverty lawyers"— lawyers who are employed full time by local non-profit organizations engaged in delivering legal services to eligible poor persons (generally defined as persons whose household incomes are below 125 percent of the federal "poverty line"). In other countries eligible poor persons are referred to members of the private bar, who are then paid by the state at rates fixed by statute or regulation. The latter system, by analogy to Medicare, is referred to as "judicare" in the United States.

The staff-attorney system, which is favored by virtually all participants in the U.S. legal services movement, provides a cadre of lawyers who are intellectually and personally committed to serving the poor; the delivery of service may be organized so that clients are served by experienced specialists in various areas of poverty law, such as welfare, housing or education; and it permits more aggressive pursuit of institutional reform that benefits groups of poor people rather than merely an individual client.

Proponents of judicare as a replacement of or alternative to the staff-attorney system argue that use of private lawyers permits a more normal lawyer-client relationship (the client chooses the lawyer and controls the objectives of the representation) and leads to greater client satisfaction.[53] Some proponents favor judicare for precisely the reasons that those enamored of law reform litigation prefer the staff-attorney system: Judicare is more likely to stick to individual-client service. Studies performed by the Legal Service Corporation indicate that both systems are feasible, the existence of some staff component is essential in controlling costs and the staff system offers a potential of having a larger impact on the legal rights and living conditions of eligible clients.[54]

Who Should Be Served?

The demand for free goods, even if their use involves time and inconvenience, is likely to exceed the available supply. The result is an inevitable rationing problem. Because lawyers cannot and will not be provided to all poor people who feel aggrieved and who lack the resources or capacity to seek relief on their own, someone must decide who will be served. Local legal services programs are required to establish priorities after consultation with representatives of client groups, but it is recognized that staff lawyers play a large role in shaping and then administering priorities. The establishment of a priority in one area, such as public housing issues, may lead to refusing service in categories of other cases. A number of legal services programs, for example, refuse to accept matrimonial cases. Critics of the current program advocate adoption of more neutral principles, such as queuing or some effort to replicate the private market, as with a voucher system or client copayments.[55]

Current arrangements rely on utilitarian arguments of *triage* : Because funding is so limited, scarce resources must be devoted to handling the

53. Samuel J. Brakel, Judicare: Public Funds, Private Lawyers, and Poor People (1974); Brakel, Styles of Delivery of Legal Services to the Poor, 1977 Amer.Bar Found. Research J. 219. For an empirical study of the relationship of legal services lawyer to their clients, see Ann Southworth, Lawyer–Client Decisionmaking in Civil Rights and Poverty Practice: An Empirical Study of Lawyers' Norms, 9 Geo.J.Legal Eth. 1101, 1105 (1996) (legal services lawyers "played significant roles in decisions affecting their clients and sometimes chose strategies without consulting clients").

54. Legal Services Corporation, The Delivery Systems Study: A Policy Report to the Congress and President of the United States (1980).

55. See Douglas J. Besharov, Legal Services for the Poor: Time for Reform xiv, xvi (1990) (staff lawyers, who dominate priority setting, devote little effort to the problems associated with family breakdown, which are the most critical problem of poor people today; client copayments would force clients to choose among their needs); and Marshall J. Breger, Legal Aid for the Poor: A Conceptual Analysis, 60 No.Car. L.Rev. 282 (1982) (utilitarian justifications of a lawyer-centered rationing of service should be replaced by an individual-rights approach).

most serious problems that will do the most good for poor people as a whole. This argument places group interests above the right of individuals to obtain access to justice to defend or enforce their legal rights.[56] Inevitably, it places authority in staff lawyers who decide what cases to take and, in doing so and in handling the subsequent representation, to make decisions as to what is in the best interests of poor people.[57] Finally, critics argue, it departs from the traditional lawyer-client relationship by putting lawyers too much in control. A poor client, unlike a rich one, is unable to choose her lawyer, define the objectives of representation and the resources devoted to it and to select a new lawyer if the initial one is unsatisfactory.

What Should Be the Standard of Service?

Ordinary people who desire a lawyer to prepare a will, get a divorce or facilitate a transaction must pay the customary charge of lawyers for that service. Numerous studies indicate that many of them forego the use of legal services because of cost, inconvenience or fear of becoming involved in the legal machinery. Those with little choice, who are cast as defendants in a proceeding brought by someone else, reluctantly hire lawyers, but generally push them to handle the matter as cheaply as possible. The result is a world in which most people "lump it" on many legal matters and get low-cost or minimal representation on many others. That is the reality of the legal market place in which most private persons make their decisions.

The most ambitious vision of legal services for the poor, however, looks to the representation provided to wealthy individuals and large corporations in high-stakes matters as the appropriate analogy. Earl Johnson, who headed the OEO legal program in the 1960s, states that he learned what full-servicing lawyering for a client really meant from a partner at Covington & Burling who represented American Airlines in major controversies. Poor people, Johnson concluded, are entitled to the same quality and extent of legal service that is provided to a wealthy client in a high-stakes matter: aggressive advocacy at every stage, including appeals; representation in administrative and legislative matters, including lobbying; and use of representative or class actions when in the interest of clients as a group. The implication is that eligible clients of publicly-funded legal services offices are entitled to what only a few wealthy persons and large corporations actually receive and then only in high-stakes matters: unrestricted

---

56. Breger, supra, argues that the claims of poor people of access to justice are best protected through allocation and litigation procedures that give equal weight to each person's complaint, not by procedures that turn on the group impact of a given poor person's case. Marie A. Failinger & Larry May, Litigating Against Poverty: Legal Services and Group Representation, 45 Ohio State L. J. 1 (1984), responding to Breger's argument, dispute his claim that access rights are more important than welfare rights.

57. See Paul R. Tremblay, Toward a Community–Based Ethic for Legal Services Practice, 37 U.C.L.A. L.Rev. 1103, 1111 (1990) (legal services lawyers face the dilemma of choosing between "allegiance to the individual client" and making choices that serve interests of groups of poor people.

full-service lawyering that leaves no stone unturned and is largely unre-strained by considerations of cost.

The stakes involved in some test cases or class actions clearly justify full-service lawyering. The aggregation of small, related claims may collec-tively constitute a major claim that justifies a substantial commitment of legal resources whether the case is pursued by a legal services lawyer, without fee, or a class action lawyer who anticipates a fee award from a successful action. See the discussion of class action lawyers in Chapter 8 above at p. 813.

Other matters, however, present issues of proportionality and fairness. A private litigant ordinarily will not pursue a $1,000 matter by expending more than some fraction of that amount on legal services. But a publicly-funded lawyer is not similarly constrained in litigation on behalf of a poor client. As Gary Bellow and others have recognized, this fact confers enormous leverage on legal services lawyers in dealing with private persons and some leverage in dealing with government agencies. Because the costs of litigation from the point of view of a private person may be larger than the amount at stake, the possibility of extortionate settlements exist. The constraints on this behavior on the part of legal services lawyers are the practical ones of heavy caseloads and limited staffs, constraints that advo-cates of full-service lawyering on behalf of the poor vigorously lament and want removed.

Social Advocacy v. Individual Client Service[58]

The activist vision is one in which lawyers improve the lives of poor people by redistributing power to them to influence decisions that will affect them. Gary Bellow, for example, criticized the tendency of most legal service organizations to devote most of their effort to individual client service.[59] Poorly trained and inexperienced lawyers were thrown into frustrating and tension-laden situations that resulted in minimal service and did little to ease the larger problems of the poor. The legal services program's potential for social change, he argued, could not be achieved unless its priorities were reversed, so that political organization of the poor would come first, followed by aggressive pursuit of strategic priorities in a way that would apply maximum pressure in favor of institutional and legal changes that affect large numbers of poor people.

A massive expansion of minimal, routinized legal assistance throughout the low-income areas of the country, mediated by selective efforts at "law reform", is potentially a powerful system of social

---

58. The best single discussion of the current legal services program is Alan W. House-man, Political Lessons: Legal Services for the Poor—A Commentary, 83 Geo.L.J. 1669 (1995); see also Marshall J. Breger, Legal Aid for the Poor: A Conceptual Anal-ysis, 60 No.Car. L. Rev. 282 (1982); Failing-er and May, supra.

59. Gary Bellow, Turning Solutions Into Problems: The Legal Aid Experience, 34 N.L.A.D.A. Briefcase 106, 122 (1977). See also Gary Bellow, Legal Aid in the United States, 14 Clearinghouse Rev. 337 (1980).

control, capable of defining and legitimating particular grievances and resolutions and ignoring others. Legal aid lawyers, unwilling or unable to respond to client concerns in ways which link them to a larger vision of social justice, can readily become purveyors of acquiescence and resignation among the people that they are seeking to help. Clients can be literally "taught" that their situations are natural, inevitable, or their own fault, and that dependence on professional advice and guidance is their only appropriate course of action; that is, legal assistance for the poor can become a bulwark of existing social arrangements. To echo a now familiar phrase, a profession that is not part of the solution can soon become part of the problem. The legal aid experience may soon be a troubling illustration of the modern homily.[60]

One of the ironies of modern political debate is that some members of the political right, such as Jack Kemp, HHS Secretary under President Bush, have appropriated the term "empowerment" to describe their approach to the problems of the poor. They view the liberal programs of the 1960s, including the legal services movement, as disempowering the poor and empowering instead liberal do-good program employees, such as legal services lawyers. This critique reflects the American suspicion of groups who see themselves as having a special obligation to serve social justice. This suspicion is grounded in the belief that members of such groups are really serving their individual needs and not the needs of others. The irony is that this same charge can be and is leveled against the "new right" advocates of empowerment.

David Luban provides an elaborate philosophical defense of a vision of politicized legal services.[61] As a foundation for doing so, he constructs a worst-case scenario of public housing representation in order to then argue that, even in the occasional instances of worst-case social activism, the activity is needed and desirable. In considering the issues raised here, the student should recall two cases previously considered that involved social advocacy by legal services lawyers: *Fiandaca,* printed in Chapter 7 at p. 595 supra, and *Jeff D.,* summarized in Chapter 6 at p. 529 supra.

Luban's scenario involves a legal services program (the Center) in a metropolitan area that decides to focus its attention on reforming the city's public housing program. The agency responsible for public housing has allowed the housing to deteriorate, has not maintained basic services and has violated state and federal law in perpetuating racial patterns. The staff attorneys in the program decide to mount an attack against the agency's

---

60. Bellow, Turning Solutions Into Problems, at 122. See also Jack Katz, Poor People's Lawyers in Transition (1982). Katz's study of the legal services program in Chicago finds that during the 1970s "law reform" activities replaced an earlier emphasis on organizing and community education. The result was what Katz calls the "legalization of poverty." Legal services lawyers helped create government pro-

grams for the poor that were professionally administered, confined by formal procedures and limited by rules and standards. Poverty lawyers became poverty managers and "helped rationalize the state's organization of the poor as a homogeneous segregated social class."

61. See David Luban, Lawyers and Justice (1990).

tenant-selection practices, its failure to correct project conditions and its construction policies for new units. The Center cuts back on provision of other legal aid to handle the tenants who are well-situated to raise these issues. To build the morale and loyalty of housing clients who agree to accept representation on the Center's terms, a broad range of legal services other than housing is provided to them. A series of lawsuits over a period of years results in a federal judge appointing a receiver to administer the housing agency, ousting the elected officials who have been unresponsive to prior court orders. The existing units are fully integrated and new construction is targeted for transitional areas mixed in racial composition. The Center's activities produce a great deal of hostility in the city, including some from poor groups who are declined service or who disagree with the Center's housing location policies.

Luban's example graphically raises all the important objections to politicized public interest law practice:

> The Center's lawyers manipulated clients, took sides in a dispute within the client community (over whether the development should be built in an integrated neighborhood), spent public money to take a partisan stand on several divisive and politically controversial issues, switched from a general legal services practice to a politicized legal campaign, and used the courts to take control of a political institution. All of these are highly debatable tactics. . . . [62]

Luban's conclusion, however, is that, choice of tactics aside,

> There is absolutely nothing illegitimate about impact work being done by legal services lawyers, even highly politicized legal services lawyers. On the contrary, law reform of this sort is at once an admirable attempt to further social justice and a professional responsibility to help more clients rather than fewer. It is precisely what lawyers ought to be doing.[63]

Luban argues that successful law reform solves the problems of many poor people at once and is therefore the most efficient use of scarce legal resources. Although Luban concedes that client control and manipulation are sometimes involved, "one cannot succeed in political action without dirtying one's hands."[64] Moreover, the people and groups served by the lawyer's political use of the legal machinery are aware of what is going on. Their free and mutual commitment to the lawyer's cause justifies the unusual degree of lawyer control. Winning the battle in the courts rather than in the legislatures does not violate democratic principles because the courts are intervening on behalf of groups that are under-represented in the legislatures. Luban concludes that public interest lawyers, by helping "fragmented constituencies to organize themselves, . . . serve the highest

---

62. Id. at 297–98. The authors do not believe that Luban's scenario reflects the attitudes and conduct of the legal services lawyers in the one housing receivership case of which they are aware.

63. Id. at 302.

64. Id. at xiv.

goal of democracy: to engage citizens in responsible deliberation about the ends of action."[65]

Is the lawyering described by Luban consistent with the role of the lawyer envisioned by professional ideology and ethics rules? With the role for which legal education prepares law students? Do public interest lawyers work to correct democratic failures?[66] Public interest lawyers might be seen instead in republican versus democratic terms: an elite group working toward some vision of the public good. Is this description more accurate, if less appealing? If it is less appealing, how so?

Compare Brill's description of the work of legal services' lawyers in his article on Room 202, p. 1093, Wexler's description of what the ideal poor person's lawyer would do, p. 1112, and Luban's description of the tactics necessary in the name of social justice. Would Wexler approve of the lawyers Brill praises or those Luban critiques and defends? Would Luban approve of Brill's lawyers? What responsibility do you think the bar has to stop the Stench of Room 202? To remedy conditions in public housing projects? To organize the poor so that they get a bigger piece of the American promise?

Or are housing conditions in a city such as New York the result of political, legal and financial structures that are unlikely to be amenable to lawyering activity (e.g., unrealistic and unenforced building codes, inequities and shortages resulting from a rent-controlled housing market and absence of social provision for homeless people)? William Simon, in addressing the role of legal services lawyers in public housing matters, argues that the reliance on procedural formalities by legal services lawyers is a two-edged sword: legal formalism benefits the poor when lawyers are available to exploit procedural options and landlords carry the burden of proof in eviction proceedings.[67] The same procedural restraints, however, interfere with enforcement of housing codes when the burden of proof falls on tenants. Similarly, elaborate procedures hobble tenant groups when they seek to improve their living conditions by evicting tenants who are selling drugs. In some situations, the legal services program has been politically hurt when local programs opposed the efforts of tenant groups to use more expeditious procedures to evict those believed to be responsible for crime-ridden conditions.[68]

65. Id. at xv.

66. In Democracy in America, Alexis deTocqueville made a quite different claim: democratic institutions, he said, could not survive unless the powerful "influence" of lawyers protected democratic institutions "against the excesses of democracy."

67. William Simon, Legal Informality and Redistributionist Politics, 19 Clearinghouse Rev. 384, 385 (1985).

68. See Dennis J. Saffron, Comments, 25 Fordham Urban L. J. 308–14 (1998) (describing the opposition of legal services programs in New York City to the attempt of elected public housing tenant officials and the Dinkins Administration to modify a 25–year-old consent decree to make it easier for tenants to evict drug dealers from public housing); see also Escalera v. New York Housing Authority, 924 F.Supp. 1323 (S.D.N.Y.1996).

C.   Justice and Ordinary Lawyering

1.   Access to Justice for the Non–Poor

Is there too much or too little access to justice in the United States? Are lawyers the problem of or the solution to the contemporary problems of access and litigiousness? In 1983 Derek Bok, former dean of the Harvard Law School and then president of Harvard University, expressed widely-held views in a broad critique of the American legal system, the legal profession and legal education.[1] "The legal system," Bok said, is "grossly inequitable and inefficient; . . . there is far too much law for those who can afford it and far too little for those who cannot."[2] Legal rules and procedures, he argued, are unclear and unnecessarily complex; lawyers are too numerous and too litigious;[3] legal uncertainty and conflict, combined with overelaborate procedures, fuel more (and more complex) regulation and litigation, resulting in social expenditures on legal services that have grown to over $100 billion annually.[4] The excessive cost and delay have harmful effects on everyone; they tax the well-to-do and deprive the poor and the middle class of effective access to justice. Bok urged a combined program of simplification of law (delegalization) and enlarged access, cautioning that either by itself will only make things worse. Society, he asserted, needs simpler procedures and fewer rules which are "more fundamental, better understood, and more widely enforced throughout society."[5] Simultaneously, new forms of delivery of legal services could provide access to justice to the poor and the middle class at reasonable cost and quality.

The underlying issues are important, complex and highly controverted.[6] The argument that American society is excessively litigious and over-lawyered is attacked by leaders of the bar and by a substantial group of legal scholars. Marc Galanter's studies of available historical and comparative data on the volume and frequency of litigation demonstrate that patterns of litigation vary over time and place, but that current figures in the United States are not markedly different from those of the American

---

1. Derek C. Bok, A Flawed System of Practice and Training, 33 J.Legal Educ. 570 (1983), reprinted from Harvard Magazine 38–45, 70–71 (May–June 1983).

2. Id. at 571.

3. Bok lamented that the wastefulness of our legal system "attracts an unusually large proportion of the exceptionally gifted" college graduates, resulting in "a massive diversion of exceptional talent into pursuits that often add little to the growth of the economy, the pursuit of culture, or the enhancement of the human spirit. . . ." Id. at 573–74.

4. In 1982, when Bok wrote, annual expenditures on legal services in the United States were estimated at $30–40 billion; seventeen years later they are probably closer to $120 billion. In 1996 legal services contributed $100 billion to the gross domestic product. Statistical Abstract of the United States 452 (1998).

5. Id. at 580.

6. For a good survey of this subject, see Thomas D. Rowe, Study on Paths to a "Better Way": Litigation, Alternatives, and Accommodation, 1989 Duke L. J. 824.

past or of other countries with a similar legal system.[7] Recent decades have shown, however, an increase in the volume, complexity, length and cost of high-stakes litigation, especially in the federal courts.

Do the benefits of litigation outweigh its costs? Americans resort to court because other mechanisms of social control—the family, the church, the neighborhood—have lost some of their effectiveness. Some matters that other countries handle without adjudication, such as compensation for accidental injuries, are left to the courts in the United States. The unwillingness or inability of other branches of government to deal decisively with social problems—witness abortion, deficit spending, or conditions in schools or prisons—relegates problems to the courts or encourages efforts to do so. The diffusion of authority among federal, state and local governments adds complexity, uncertainty and opportunities for manipulation.

But are these aspects of American society vices or virtues? An alternative vision converts what critics view as vices into virtues.[8] Governmental authority is diffused in order that liberty may flourish. The complex blend of reliance on private economic activity and public regulation is designed to provide opportunity and material well-being. The quest for equality in a society characterized by racial, ethnic and religious pluralism centers on the pursuit of individual legal rights. The quest for accountability presses for fairer procedures and better outcomes in private and public institutions. From this point of view, justice through law is a distinctive American virtue rather than a vice. Those who share this vision point to problems of access and conclude that America is underlawyered rather than overlawyered, or at least that the distribution of legal services is badly skewed. In any event, the intangible and immeasurable benefits of litigation should also be considered: expanded opportunities for women and minorities, expansion of civil liberties, fair procedures within institutions, limits on government. "Who would deny that these are significant gains? Whether they are worth the cost is a question that models and equations cannot answer."[9]

---

7. See Marc Galanter, Reading the Landscape of Disputes: What We Know and Don't Know (and Think We Know) About Our Allegedly Contentious and Litigious Society, 31 U.C.L.A. L. Rev. 4 (1983); Marc Galanter, The Day After the Litigation Explosion, 46 Md. L. Rev. 3 (1986) ("civil court filings are [not] dramatically higher than in the recent past" and are comparable to those of countries with similar legal systems; settlement rates remain high; and the greatest single sources of increased filings are divorce cases in state courts and social security cases in federal courts, which are not brought because people are "enamored of litigation or beguiled by lawyers").

8. For example, determining whether a particular claim is frivolous may turn on normative judgments that are warped in time.

In 1976 a prominent legal educator and public official cited sex discrimination suits against Little Leagues as an example of "legal pollution" that endangered the legal system. Thomas Ehrlich, Legal Pollution, New York Times 17 (Feb. 8, 1976). Today, gender stereotyping in the provision of athletic opportunities is viewed as raising important social and legal issues. See Deborah L. Rhode, Justice and Gender 299–301 (1989).

9. Lawrence Friedman, Litigation in Society, 15 Am.Rev.Sociol. 17, 27 (1989). Marc Galanter states that the "consternation about litigation" is partly due to the heightened sense on the part of corporate managers and public officials of increased accountability to public standards that is fostered by litigation. Galanter, supra, 46 Md. L. Rev. at 38.

The purpose here is not to resolve the unanswerable questions posed by differing attitudes concerning the American reliance on law, lawyers and litigation, but to put more specific and perhaps answerable questions against the backdrop of the larger normative controversy. Who uses the services of lawyers? Are some important "legal needs" left unserved by current patterns of availability and distribution? How, why and at what cost can these needs be met?[10]

Use of Legal Services by Low-and Moderate Income Americans

A 1974 study, updated in 1989, reports that about 70 percent of the adult population consult a lawyer at least once in a lifetime.[11] For most Americans the exposure to lawyers is very infrequent: one-quarter have never consulted a lawyer; only about 40 percent have consulted a lawyer within the past three years. The type of legal problem that is taken to lawyers varies depending upon the age and income level of the individual; and frequency of use increases with income.[12]

A 1994 ABA study of the legal needs of low-and moderate-income Americans explores and confirms the prevailing conception that there a vast, untapped demand for legal services that is not being handled for one reason or another.[13] "Legal need" refers to specific situations confronted by members of households that raised legal issues, whether or not they were recognized as "legal" or taken to some part of the civil justice system. About one-half of all households surveyed faced some situation that raised a legal issue. The most frequent categories of need were problems characterized as financial-consumer, housing-property, community-regional, family-domestic, personal or economic injury, estates-wills, health related, or public benefits (this overall order of frequency varied by income level).

Four of ten households deal with legal need by handling it on their own. Moderate-income households turned to some aspect of the civil justice system (usually consulting a lawyer) as a second response, but not low-income households, who took no action at all. The least likely course of action was turning to a non-legal third party (e.g., a service providing agency or community organization). Nearly three-fourths of the legal needs

10. For an excellent collection of materials on topics treated more summarily here, see Deborah L. Rhode and David Luban, Legal Ethics 784–894 (1992).

11. Barbara A. Curran & Francis O. Spaulding, The Legal Needs of the Public 79–81 (1974) and ABA Consortium on Legal Services, Two Nationwide Surveys 3–4, 57–60 (1989).

12. Frequency of use of lawyers for home buying and wills increases with age and income; consumer and government benefits problems often affect younger persons with lower incomes. Gender and race differences

include: incidence of torts is greater for men, but women are somewhat more likely to consult a lawyer; minorities are more likely to consult lawyers for tort problems but in general use lawyers less than whites.

13. American Bar Association Consortium on Legal Services and the Public's Legal; Needs: Comprehensive legal Needs Study (1994). Low-income households were defined as the bottom one-fifth in household income; moderate-income households as the middle three-fifths in household income.

of low-income households and two-thirds of those of moderate-income households were not taken to the civil justice system.

The predominant reasons of low-income households for not seeking legal assistance were that it would not help and that it would cost too much. For moderate-income households, the dominant reasons included that they could handle the situation on their own and that a lawyer's involvement would not help. Buried in the volunteered "other reasons" is the comment that the respondents did not know how to find a lawyer.

Those who sought the help of the legal system were more satisfied with the outcome than those who did not. About three-fourths of legal needs brought to the justice system involved a lawyer in one way or another. Those who used lawyers reported fairly high rates of satisfaction (60–70% on most items) with their lawyer's honesty, attention, concern, etc. Other efforts to measure the public's legal needs show that many people think they have been legally wronged by another;[14] and that some grievances (e.g., a tort matter) are much more likely to be pursued than others (e.g., a discrimination claim).[15]

The time and energy of lawyers is primarily devoted to relatively well-to-do individuals, small businesses and large organizations. Lawyers in private practice spend only a small portion of their time in the representation of low income clients.[16] Only about 4,000 lawyers work for the legal services organizations that provide free civil legal assistance to eligible poor people. The Council for Public Interest Law reported in 1989 that about 1,000 lawyers employed by some 200 tax-exempt non-profit groups were working on public interest concerns.[17] Thus less than 1 percent of U.S. lawyers are engaged full time in representing poor people or otherwise unrepresented interests in civil matters. Social advocacy litigation—efforts to vindicate the collective interests of groups such as prisoners, welfare recipients and victims of institutional discrimination—is largely dependent on the efforts of this small band of public interest lawyers.

Alternative Prescriptions

How important are the unserved needs described above in social and individual terms? Poor people have many needs and the pursuit of legal

14. Richard E. Miller and Austin Sarat, Grievances, Claims, and Disputes: Assessing the Adversary Culture, 15 Law & Soc'y Rev. 525 (1980–81) (reporting that 40 percent of randomly selected households experienced a grievance involving $1,000 or more during a three-year period; 79 percent of those experiencing a grievance made a claim and 68 percent obtained some recovery, but only 11 percent filed a lawsuit).

15. William Felstiner, Richard Abel, and Austin Sarat, The Emergence and Transformation of Disputes: Naming, Claiming, and Blaming, 15 Law & Soc'y Rev. 631 (1980).

16. See Joel Handler, Ellen Hollingsworth, and Howard Erlanger, Lawyers and the Pursuit of Legal Rights (1978) (estimating that only about 10 percent of the effort of those lawyers who represent individual clients is devoted to those with incomes in the bottom one-third of the population).

17. Nan Aron, Liberty and Justice for All: Public Interest Law in the 1980's and Beyond 55–56 (1989).

claims with the help of lawyers may be much less important than other needs, such as housing, education and employment. Social resources are finite and other programs and benefits for poor people compete with the provision of lawyers. Moreover, legal services are different from other professional services in two respects: First, because equality in their provision is important (the adversary system operates best when both parties have advocates of equal skill and resources), it is argued that poor or limited services carry some negatives and limited benefits.[18] Second, the availability to one party of subsidized legal services imposes costs on other persons, who are forced to hire lawyers to defend their interests, and on the public.

If all needs cannot be met because of cost or normative objections, who should decide what needs will be met? In Europe, where a right to civil legal assistance is generally recognized, its actual provision is restricted by screening mechanisms and by severe restrictions on the fees lawyers earn in handling matters that survive the screening process.[19]

If some specific needs should be met, perhaps because they enable poor people to take control over their own lives, does it follow that law, lawyers and litigation are the best or most desirable approach? Alternatives include the simplification or modification of legal rules or processes so that individuals could handle their own problems. This approach, often referred to as "delegalization," is favored by Bok and other commentators because it reduces the need for legal intervention by substituting an alternative regime. Drastic simplification of transactions or events that now require the use of lawyers, such as probate of wills, sale of houses and divorces, might reduce the need for lawyers for millions of routine matters. Simpler statutes and regulations written in "plain English" might be followed without resort to professional advice. Changes in substantive law would also eliminate the need for lawyers and lawsuits, for example, the substitution of national health care for most personal injury and accident losses. All of these proposals are highly controversial. In each case the legal profession tends to resist substantive or procedural change, whether out of concern for the substantive or procedural rights that would be sacrificed or out of economic self-interest. In each area lawyers opposing change (e.g., probate lawyers opposing simplified probate or personal injury lawyers opposing compensation plans) are joined by powerful economic and social interests (e.g., insurance companies and health care providers who oppose compensation and health care proposals that would affect their interests).

A second set of reform proposals seeks to reduce the cost of legal services and court proceedings by handing them more efficiently. Alternative dispute resolution (ADR) is a favorite proposal. Frank Sander, for

18.   Richard L. Abel, Legal Services (1981), reprinted in G. Hazard and D. Rhode, The Legal Profession: Responsibility and Regulation 417 (2d ed. 1988) (unlike health care and other services, "the services of a lawyer are valuable only if they are roughly equal, in quality and quantity, to the services possessed by adversaries").

19.   See Earl Johnson, Jr., The Right to Counsel in Civil Cases, 19 Loy.-L.A. L.Rev. 341 (1985) (comparative study).

example, proposes extensive use of ADR techniques in a multi-door courtroom, with some official deciding which technique, or series of techniques, are appropriate for a particular dispute.[20] Repetitive and routinized adjudicatory functions would be handled by procedures less cumbersome than normal adjudication. Most cases, even the complex ones, would be disposed of in arbitration or mediation stages that would precede the trial stage. Skeptics respond that the efficiency gains will occur only if the parties waive constitutional rights or the procedures deal effectively with intractable procedural dilemmas. Others attack the fundamental premises of ADR. Owen Fiss, for example, argues that social values inherent in judicial declaration of public norms are sacrificed by substitution of more informal processes of private settlement.[21] Richard Abel and others worry that compulsory ADR will be confined in practice primarily to poor people, resulting in second-class justice for those who are already deprived.[22]

Another way to reduce the cost of legal services, favored by a number of commentators, involves deregulation of the practice of law. Increased competition within the legal profession and with nonlawyer service providers, it is argued, would lower the cost of routine legal services and make them more available to the public at acceptable levels of quality. This approach would eliminate the professional monopoly and the remaining restrictions on form of practice. Nonlawyers would be able to compete with lawyers in the provision of legal services by delivering services directly to clients (with a possible exception for representation of criminal defendants) or by employing various combinations of lawyers and paralegals to perform legal tasks on a high-volume, low-cost basis.

2. JUSTICE IN THE LAW OFFICE: DRAFTING CONTRACTS

Do private lawyers have an obligation to see that justice is done? It is fairly well accepted that trial lawyers may and should leave justice to the judge and jury. In the stylized world of a trial, lawyers are expected to play the role of partisan advocate; judges and juries are to worry about just results. Because partisanship must be kept "within the bounds of law," law constrains the trial lawyer's partisanship. For example, the law on suborning perjury, Rule 11 on honesty in papers filed in civil proceedings, the prosecutor's obligations to provide the defense with exculpatory information and not to seek the conviction of the innocent, all set limits on the partisanship of trial lawyers.

Nonetheless, the theory of adversary proceedings is that each side's lawyers will be partisan—through adversary representation under the supervision of an impartial referee (the judge), the fact finder, be it judge or jury, will arrive at a just result. The advocate should not supplant the fact

---

20. See Frank Sander, Varieties of Dispute Processing, 70 F.R.D. 111 (1976); Stephen Goldberg, Eric D. Green and Frank Sander, Dispute Resolution (1985).

21. Owen Fiss, Against Settlement, 93 Yale L.J. 1073 (1984).

22. Richard Abel, Delegalization, reprinted in G. Hazard and D. Rhode, The Legal Profession: Responsibility and Regulation 388 (2d ed. 1988). See also Jerold Auerbach, Justice Without Law? Resolving Disputes Without Lawyers 115–37 (1983).

finder's role in the name of justice. Justice in American society is in large part defined by the assumption that lawyers will play the role of partisan at trial, and citizens in the form of a jury, not professionals, will decide the litigants' fate.

Most lawyering, however, is other than trial lawyering. The vast majority of lawyering occurs in the offices of lawyers and consists of lawyers helping clients arrange their affairs or transact business with other people. No referee charged with keeping partisanship within the limits of the law is present in the lawyer's office; no entity charged with determining facts or applying law to concrete situations passes on assertions. Those present are limited to the lawyer, her client, sometimes the opposite party and sometimes a lawyer for that party. Whose job is it in this situation to see that justice is done? That the law is followed? That the parties operate in good faith? Should it be anyone's job?

Lawyer's Role in Drafting Contracts

The American concept of justice, emphasizing as it does individualism and autonomy, reserves much room for the private ordering of relations among citizens, including citizens acting through business organizations. This private law is created for the most part by lawyers acting for individual fee-paying clients. Are these lawyers, who create law for the parties, responsible for the justice and injustice of the law they create? When both parties to a contract are represented by competent counsel, lawyers may relinquish some responsibility for the justice of what they create by relying on the adversary excuse: "It's my job to further my client's interest and it's the other side's job to further her client's interest." Of course, the private contracting model lacks some features of an adversary proceeding that are important to the excuse, such as an effective referee and discovery procedures to ensure the availability of material information. The adversary excuse is thus only partially available in reciprocally lawyered contract formation. It fails completely, however, when only one party to a contract is represented by a lawyer.

Standard form contracts are particularly troublesome because they threaten the premise that contracting parties have engaged in meaningful bargaining and given mutual assent to the terms. Although the consumer assents to some aspects of the transaction—procuring particular goods or services for a specified price—assent to the standardized terms is questionable. Even if the terms are available in advance, they are often numerous, buried in fine print and difficult to understand and evaluate (they often deal with factual and legal contingencies outside the experience of the typical consumer). The matters at stake, from the consumer's vantage point, are not worth the time and trouble of evaluating them. As Arthur Leff said, the standard form contract, which "is designed *not* to be read or pondered" leads to "aggrandizement by form."[23]

23. Arthur A. Leff, Unconscionability and the Code—the Emperor's New Clause, 115 Pa.L.Rev. 485, 504 (1967).

Everyone concedes that standard form contracts have many advantages. Negotiating individual contracts is a costly and time consuming process. Form provisions are efficient and afford businesses with certainty and predictability about potential legal hazards. They allow market forces to concentrate on the central aspects of the particular transaction, such as the price and quality of the good or service involved. The dangers of standard form contracts, however, lead to legislative, regulatory and judicial attempts to eliminate overreaching.

In most other Western democracies the terms of contracts, particularly adhesion (take-it-or-leave-it) contracts, are closely regulated and often specified in detail by legal codes. In this country, government specification of contract terms is exceptional, although it occurs in insurance regulation and some other areas. As a result, the fairness and justice of the private law created by contracts are far more dependent on the lawyers who draft such agreements.

A few studies and some knowledgeable observers conclude that business lawyers draft contracts to favor their clients and, in doing so, take a partisan and one-sided view as to what the law will allow. Karl Llewellyn, discussing the routine practice of lawyers in drafting form contracts, said: "Any engineer makes his construction within a margin of safety, and a wide margin of safety ... [but] [b]usiness lawyers tend to draft to the edge of the possible."[24] Commentators argue that efforts at legislative, administrative and judicial control of the imbalances of the form contract system "have been imperfect, costly, and slow."[25] Should lawyers be enlisted in the effort to prevent the use of unreasonable, unconscionable and illegal provisions in form contracts?

Form Leases in Landlord–Tenant Situation[26]

In 1973, the Massachusetts Supreme Judicial Court held in litigation between a landlord and tenants that an implied warranty that the premises are fit for human occupation was part of all rental agreements for dwellings and that this implied warranty of habitability could not be waived by any contract provision.[27] Landlords eager to escape the implications of this

---

24. As quoted in William T. Vukowich, Lawyers and the Standard Form Contract System: A Model Rule That Should Have Been, 6 Geo.J.Legal Ethics 799, 813 n. 72 (1993) (Llewellyn's testimony before the New York Law Revision Commission in 1954). See also Todd D. Rakoff, Contracts of Adhesion: An Essay in Reconstruction, 96 Harv.L.Rev. 1173, 1244 (1984): "The lawyer drafts to protect the client from every imaginable contingency. The real needs of the business are left behind; the standard is the latitude permitted by the law." See also Curtis J. Berger, Hard Leases Make Bad Law, 74 Colum.L.Rev. 791 (1974) (standard form residential leases

contain only tenant duties and landlord remedies and immunities; tenant rights and landlord duties are absent).

25. See Vukowich, supra, 181–24 (discussing social control of standard form contracts and citing the views of others).

26. See Daniel E. Wenner, Note, Renting in Collegetown, 84 Cornell L.Rev. 543 (1999) (use of unconscionable and illegal lease provisions in form leases provided to student tenants in a college town).

27. Boston Hous. Auth. v. Hemingway, 293 N.E.2d 831, 843 (Mass.1973). Similar rules are in effect in many other jurisdictions.

ruling set their lawyers to work. One landlord included in his lease the following provision, presumably drafted by his lawyers:

> There is no implied warranty the premises are fit for human occupation [are habitable] *except so far as governmental regulation, legislation or judicial enactment otherwise requires.* (Emphasis in original).[28]

The landlord's lawyer argued that this provision was not deceptive because it included "in small print, [the words] 'except so far as governmental regulation, legislation or judicial enactment otherwise requires.' "Was it unethical for the lawyers to have included this provision? In thinking about this question, consider the following proposed Model Rule, which was rejected by the ABA House of Delegates when adopting the Model Rules:

> Proposed Rule 4.3: Illegal, Fraudulent, or Unconscionable Transactions
>
> A lawyer shall not conclude an agreement, or assist a client in concluding an agreement, that the lawyer knows or reasonably should know is illegal, contains legally prohibited terms, would work a fraud, or would be held to be unconscionable as a matter of law.[29]

Presumably one of the reasons the ABA rejected Proposed Rule 4.3 was the uncertainty about which terms "would be held to be unconscionable as a matter of law."[30] Prior to a court ruling on a specific term, how is a lawyer to assess which terms would be held unconscionable? Should a lawyer assess contract terms favorable to her client as if the lawyer were a judge called upon to rule on the conscionability of the term in question? Does it matter whether the other side is represented? Is represented competently?

What of the justification for the habitability clause offered by the lawyers for the Massachusetts landlord? In *Leardi* the Massachusetts court held that the habitability clause quoted above violated the state's consumer protection law.[31] The Massachusetts consumer protection law expressly incorporates judicial interpretations of the Federal Trade Commission Act.[32] Under the federal statute (and many state consumer laws like the one in Massachusetts), a practice is deceptive if it possesses "a tendency to deceive."[33] Moreover, in judging whether an act is deceptive "regard must

---

28. Leardi v. Brown, 474 N.E.2d 1094, 1099 (Mass.1985).

29. The comments to the proposed rule stated that "[a]lthough a lawyer is generally not responsible for the substantive fairness of the result of a negotiation, the lawyer has a duty to see that the product is not offensive to the law.... As an officer of the legal system, a lawyer is required to observe [legal requirements prohibiting certain contract provisions].... A lawyer is not absolved of responsibility for a legally offensive transaction simply because the client takes the final step in carrying it out...."

30. See Geoffrey C. Hazard, Jr., The Obligation to Be Trustworthy, 33 S.Car.L.Rev. 181 (1981) (discussing the rejection of the Kutak proposal); Gary T. Lowenthal, The Bar's Failure to Require Truthful Bargaining by Lawyers, 2 Geo.J.Legal Ethics 411 (1988).

31. Mass. General Laws c. 93A.

32. 15 U.S.C. § 45 (1982).

33. Trans World Accounts, Inc. v. FTC, 594 F.2d 212, 214 (9th Cir.1979).

be had, *not to fine spun distinctions and arguments that may be made in excuse,* but to the effect which it might reasonably be expected to have upon the general public."[34] The Massachusetts Supreme Judicial Court thus held the clause deceptive, rejecting the fine spun distinctions offered by the landlord's lawyers. The court said that the clause suggested that the implied warranty of habitability was

> "the exception and not the rule, if it exists at all." Indeed, the average tenant, presumably not well acquainted with [the court's precedent on the implied warranty] is likely to interpret the provision as an absolute disclaimer of the implied warranty of habitability.[35]

If it is unlawful for landlords to include such provisions in leases, may lawyers include them in rental agreements drafted for landlords? DR 7–102(A)(7) of the Model Code prohibits assistance "that the lawyer knows to be illegal or fraudulent." Model Rule 1.2(d) narrows the prohibition to "conduct that the lawyer knows is criminal or fraudulent." Inclusion of an unlawful and deceptive contract provision may be unfair and unconscionable, but is it "criminal," "fraudulent" or "illegal?" Even if it is, how does a lawyer "know," before a court rules, that a particular clause is unconscionable?[36]

On the other hand, if landlords and other providers of consumer goods can be fined for violating consumer protection laws by including provisions that are later declared unconscionable, then surely it is not unfair to expect lawyers to exercise reasonable foresight in deciding which clauses are likely to be ruled unconscionable. Of course, the exercise of such foresight assumes that a lawyer is able to exercise nonpartisan judgment. An ingenious advocate can articulate "fine spun distinctions" in defense of virtually any provision. But it is another matter for an office counselor to write such clauses into contracts. Was the ABA thus unwise to reject Rule 4.3?

––––––––

Carnival Cruise Lines v. Shute

Supreme Court of the United States, 1991.
499 U.S. 585.

■ JUSTICE BLACKMUN delivered the opinion of the Court.

In this admiralty case we primarily consider whether the United States Court of Appeals for the Ninth Circuit correctly refused to enforce a forum-

---

34. P. Lorillard Co. v. FTC, 186 F.2d 52, 58 (4th Cir.1950) (emphasis added).

35. *Leardi,* 474 N.E.2d at 1099 (quoting the trial judge in the case).

36. In addition to the rules prohibiting a lawyer from assisting crime or fraud and requiring withdrawal in such situations, other ethics provisions confer discretion on the lawyer. See M.R. 1.2(c) (agreed-upon limits on the objectives of the representation); M.R. 1.16(b)(3) (withdrawal when client insists on repugnant or imprudent objectives); M.R. 2.1 (lawyer may advise on moral, economic, social and political factors); and M.R. 4.3 (dealing with unrepresented party).

selection clause contained in tickets issued by petitioner Carnival Cruise Lines, Inc., to respondents Eulala and Russel Shute.

I

The Shutes, through an Arlington, Wash., travel agent, purchased passage for a 7–day cruise on petitioner's ship, the *Tropicale*. Respondents paid the fare to the agent who forwarded the payment to petitioner's headquarters in Miami, Fla. Petitioner then prepared the tickets and sent them to respondents in the State of Washington. The face of each ticket, at its left-hand lower corner, contained this admonition:

"Subject to Conditions of Contract on Last Pages Important!

PLEASE READ CONTRACT—ON LAST PAGES 1, 2, 3"

The following appeared on "contract page 1" of each ticket:

Terms and Conditions of Passage Contract Ticket

. . .

3. (a) The acceptance of this ticket by the person or persons named hereon as passengers shall be deemed to be an acceptance and agreement by each of them of all of the terms and conditions of this Passage Contract Ticket.

. . .

8. It is agreed by and between the passenger and the Carrier that all disputes and matters whatsoever arising under, in connection with or incident to this Contract shall be litigated, if at all, in and before a Court located in the State of Florida, U.S.A., to the exclusion of the Courts of any other state or country."

The last quoted paragraph is the forum-selection clause at issue.

II

Respondents boarded the *Tropicale* in Los Angeles, Cal. The ship sailed to Puerto Vallarta, Mexico, and then returned to Los Angeles. While the ship was in international waters off the Mexican coast, respondent Eulala Shute was injured when she slipped on a deck mat during a guided tour of the ship's galley. Respondents filed suit against petitioner in the United States District Court for the Western District of Washington, claiming that Mrs. Shute's injuries had been caused by the negligence of Carnival Cruise Lines and its employees.

[The court of appeals reversed the district court's grant of defendant's motion for summary judgment. It held that defendant's contacts with Washington were sufficient for personal jurisdiction and that the forum-selection clause was unenforceable because it "was not freely bargained for." 897 F.2d 377 (9th Cir.1990).]

III

We begin by noting the boundaries of our inquiry. First, this is a case in admiralty, and federal law governs the enforceability of the forum-selection clause we scrutinize.... Second, we do not address the question whether respondents had sufficient notice of the forum clause before entering the contract for passage. Respondents essentially have conceded that they had notice of the forum-selection provision....

Within this context, respondents urge that the forum clause should not be enforced because, contrary to this Court's teachings in The Bremen [v. Zapata Off–Shore Co., 407 U.S. 1 (1972)], the clause was not the product of negotiation, and enforcement effectively would deprive respondents of their day in court. Additionally, respondents contend that the clause violates the Limitation of Vessel Owner's Liability Act, 46 U.S.C.App. § 183c. We consider these arguments in turn.

IV–A

. . .

In *The Bremen*, this Court addressed the enforceability of a forum-selection clause in a contract between two business corporations. An American corporation, Zapata, made a contract with Unterweser, a German corporation, for the towage of Zapata's ocean-going drilling rig from Louisiana to a point in the Adriatic Sea off the coast of Italy. The agreement provided that any dispute arising under the contract was to be resolved in the London Court of Justice. After a storm in the Gulf of Mexico seriously damaged the rig, Zapata ordered Unterweser's ship to tow the rig to Tampa, Fla., the nearest point of refuge. Thereafter, Zapata sued Unterweser in admiralty in federal court at Tampa. Citing the forum clause, Unterweser moved to dismiss. The District Court denied Unterweser's motion, and the Court of Appeals for the Fifth Circuit, sitting en banc on rehearing, and by a sharply divided vote, affirmed. 446 F.2d 907 (1971).

This Court vacated and remanded, stating that, in general, "a freely negotiated private international agreement, unaffected by fraud, undue influence, or overweening bargaining power, such as that involved here, should be given full effect." 407 U.S., at 12–13. The Court further generalized that "in the light of present-day commercial realities and expanding international trade we conclude that the forum clause should control absent a strong showing that it should be set aside." Id., at 15. The Court did not define precisely the circumstances that would make it unreasonable for a court to enforce a forum clause. Instead, the Court discussed a number of factors that made it reasonable to enforce the clause at issue in *The Bremen* and that, presumably, would be pertinent in any determination whether to enforce a similar clause.

In this respect, the Court noted that there was "strong evidence that the forum clause was a vital part of the agreement, and [that] it would be unrealistic to think that the parties did not conduct their negotiations, including fixing the monetary terms, with the consequences of the forum clause figuring prominently in their calculations." Id., at 14 (footnote omitted). Further, the Court observed that it was not "dealing with an agreement between two Americans to resolve their essentially local disputes in a remote alien forum," and that in such a case, "the serious inconvenience of the contractual forum to one or both of the parties might carry greater weight in determining the reasonableness of the forum clause." Id., at 17. The Court stated that even where the forum clause establishes a remote forum for resolution of conflicts, "the party claiming [unfairness] should bear a heavy burden of proof." Ibid.

In applying *The Bremen*, the Court of Appeals in the present litigation took note of the foregoing "reasonableness" factors and rather automatically decided that the forum-selection clause was unenforceable because, unlike the parties in *The Bremen*, respondents are not business persons and did not negotiate the terms of the clause with petitioner. Alternatively, the Court of Appeals ruled that the clause should not be enforced because enforcement effectively would deprive respondents of an opportunity to litigate their claim against petitioner.

. . .

In evaluating the reasonableness of the forum clause at issue in this case, we must refine the analysis of *The Bremen* to account for the realities of form passage contracts. As an initial matter, we do not adopt the Court of Appeals' determination that a nonnegotiated forum-selection clause in a form ticket contract is never enforceable simply because it is not the subject of bargaining. Including a reasonable forum clause in a form contract of this kind well may be permissible for several reasons: First, a cruise line has a special interest in limiting the fora in which it potentially could be subject to suit. Because a cruise ship typically carries passengers from many locales, it is not unlikely that a mishap on a cruise could subject the cruise line to litigation in several different fora. See *The Bremen*, 407 U.S., at 13 and n. 15; *Hodes*, 858 F.2d, at 913. Additionally, a clause establishing ex ante the forum for dispute resolution has the salutary effect of dispelling any confusion about where suits arising from the contract must be brought and defended, sparing litigants the time and expense of pretrial motions to determine the correct forum, and conserving judicial resources that otherwise would be devoted to deciding those motions. See *Stewart Organization*, 487 U.S., at 33 (concurring opinion). Finally, it stands to reason that passengers who purchase tickets containing a forum clause like that at issue in this case benefit in the form of reduced fares reflecting the savings that the cruise line enjoys by limiting the fora in which it may be sued. Cf. Northwestern Nat. Ins. Co. v. Donovan, 916 F.2d 372, 378 (CA7 1990).

We also do not accept the Court of Appeals' "independent justification" for its conclusion that *The Bremen* dictates that the clause should not be enforced because "[t]here is evidence in the record to indicate that the Shutes are physically and financially incapable of pursuing this litigation in Florida." 897 F.2d, at 389. We do not defer to the Court of Appeals' findings of fact. In dismissing the case for lack of personal jurisdiction over petitioner, the District Court made no finding regarding the physical and financial impediments to the Shutes' pursuing their case in Florida.... Furthermore, the Court of Appeals did not place in proper context this Court's statement in *The Bremen* that "the serious inconvenience of the contractual forum to one or both of the parties might carry greater weight in determining the reasonableness of the forum clause." 407 U.S., at 17. The Court made this statement in evaluating a hypothetical "agreement between two Americans to resolve their essentially local disputes in a remote alien forum." Ibid. In the present case, Florida is not a "remote alien forum," nor—given the fact that Mrs. Shute's accident occurred off the coast of Mexico—is this dispute an essentially local one inherently more suited to resolution in the State of Washington than in Florida. In light of these distinctions, and because respondents do not claim lack of notice of the forum clause, we conclude that they have not satisfied the "heavy burden of proof," ibid., required to set aside the clause on grounds of inconvenience.

It bears emphasis that forum-selection clauses contained in form passage contracts are subject to judicial scrutiny for fundamental fairness. In this case, there is no indication that petitioner set Florida as the forum in which disputes were to be resolved as a means of discouraging cruise passengers from pursuing legitimate claims. Any suggestion of such a bad-faith motive is belied by two facts: petitioner has its principal place of business in Florida, and many of its cruises depart from and return to Florida ports. Similarly, there is no evidence that petitioner obtained respondents' accession to the forum clause by fraud or overreaching. Finally, respondents have conceded that they were given notice of the forum provision and, therefore, presumably retained the option of rejecting the contract with impunity. In the case before us, therefore, we conclude that the Court of Appeals erred in refusing to enforce the forum-selection clause.

IV–B

Respondents also contend that the forum-selection clause at issue violates 46 U.S.C.App. § 183c, [which makes unlawful any contract provision for maritime passenger transportation "purporting ... to lessen, weaken, or avoid the right of any claimant to a trial by court of competent jurisdiction on the question of liability for [personal] injury, or the measure of damages therefor."]

By its plain language, the forum-selection clause before us does not take away respondents' right to "a trial by [a] court of competent jurisdiction" and thereby contravene the explicit proscription of § 183c. Instead, the clause states specifically that actions arising out of the passage contract shall be brought "if at all," in a court "located in the State of Florida," which, plainly, is a "court of competent jurisdiction" within the meaning of the statute.

... [R]espondents cite no authority for their contention that Congress' intent in enacting § 183c was to avoid having a plaintiff travel to a distant forum in order to litigate. The legislative history of § 183c suggests instead that this provision was enacted in response to passenger-ticket conditions purporting to limit the shipowner's liability for negligence or to remove the issue of liability from the scrutiny of any court by means of a clause providing that "the question of liability and the measure of damages shall be determined by arbitration." [Citing legislative history.] Because the clause before us allows for judicial resolution of claims against petitioner and does not purport to limit petitioner's liability for negligence, it does not violate § 183c.

The judgment of the Court of Appeals is reversed....

■ JUSTICE STEVENS, with whom JUSTICE MARSHALL joins, dissenting.

The Court ... implies that a purchaser of a Carnival Cruise Lines passenger ticket is fully and fairly notified about the existence of the choice of forum clause in the fine print on the back of the ticket.... I begin my dissent by noting that only the most meticulous passenger is likely to become aware of the forum selection provision. I have therefore appended to this opinion a facsimile of the relevant text, using the type size that actually appears in the ticket itself. A careful reader will find the forum-selection clause in the eighth of the twenty-five numbered paragraphs.

Of course, many passengers, like the respondents in this case, will not have an opportunity to read paragraph 8 until they have actually purchased their tickets. By this point, the passengers will already have accepted the condition set forth in paragraph 16(a), which provides that "[t]he Carrier shall not be liable to make any refund to passengers in respect of ... tickets wholly or partly not used by a passenger." Not knowing whether or not that provision is legally enforceable, I assume that the average passenger would accept the risk of having to file suit in Florida in the event of an injury, rather than canceling—without a refund—a planned vacation at the last minute. The fact that the cruise line can reduce its litigation costs, and therefore its liability insurance premiums, by forcing this choice on its passengers does not, in my opinion, suffice to render the provision reasonable....

Even if passengers received prominent notice of the forum-selection clause before they committed the cost of the cruise, I would remain persuaded that the clause was unenforceable under traditional principles of federal admiralty law and is "null and void" under the terms of Limited Liability Act, 49 Stat. 1480, as amended, 46 U.S.C.App. § 183c, which was enacted in 1936 to invalidate expressly stipulations limiting shipowners' liability for negligence.

Exculpatory clauses in passenger tickets have been around for a long time. These clauses are typically the product of disparate bargaining power between the carrier and the passenger, and they undermine the strong public interest in deterring negligent conduct. For these reasons, courts long before the turn of the century consistently held such clauses unenforceable under federal admiralty law....

Clauses limiting a carrier's liability or weakening the passenger's right to recover for the negligence of the carrier's employees come in a variety of forms. Complete exemptions from liability for negligence or limitations on the amount of the potential damage recovery, requirements that notice of claims be filed within an unreasonably short period of time, provisions mandating a choice of law that is favorable to the defendant in negligence cases, and forum-selection clauses[4] are all similarly designed to put a thumb on the carrier's side of the scale of justice.

Forum selection clauses in passenger tickets involve the intersection of two strands of traditional contract law that qualify the general rule that courts will enforce the terms of a contract as written. Pursuant to the first strand, courts traditionally have reviewed with heightened scrutiny the terms of contracts of adhesion, form contracts offered on a take-or-leave basis by a party with stronger bargaining power to a party with weaker power. Some commentators have questioned whether contracts of adhesion can justifiably be enforced at all under traditional contract theory because the adhering party generally enters into them without manifesting knowing and voluntary consent to all their terms. See, e.g., Rakoff, Contracts of Adhesion: An Essay in Reconstruction, 96 Harv.L.Rev. 1173, 1179–1180 (1983); Slawson, Mass Contracts: Lawful Fraud in California, 48 S.Cal. L.Rev. 1, 12–13 (1974); K. Llewellyn, The Common Law Tradition 370–371 (1960).

The common law, recognizing that standardized form contracts account for a significant portion of all commercial agreements, has taken a less extreme position and instead subjects terms in contracts of adhesion to scrutiny for reasonableness. Judge J. Skelly Wright set out the state of the law succinctly in Williams v. Walker–Thomas Furniture Co., 350 F.2d 445, 449–450 (D.C.Cir.1965):

> Ordinarily, one who signs an agreement without full knowledge of its terms might be held to assume the risk that he has entered a one-sided bargain. But when a party of little bargaining power, and hence little real choice, signs a commercially unreasonable contract with little or no knowledge of its terms, it is hardly likely that his consent, or even an objective manifestation of his consent, was ever given to all of the terms. In such a case the usual rule that the terms of the agreement are not to be questioned should be abandoned and the court should consider whether the terms of the contract are so unfair that enforcement should be withheld.

See also ... Henningsen v. Bloomfield Motors, Inc., 32 N.J. 358, 161 A.2d 69 (1960).

---

4. All these clauses will provide passengers who purchase tickets containing them with a "benefit in the form of reduced fares reflecting the savings that the cruise line enjoys by limiting [its exposure to liabili-ty]." See ante, at 8. Under the Court's reasoning, all these clauses, including a complete waiver of liability, would be enforceable, a result at odds with longstanding jurisprudence.

The second doctrinal principle implicated by forum-selection clauses is the traditional rule that "contractual provisions, which seek to limit the place or court in which an action may ... be brought, are invalid as contrary to public policy." See Dougherty, Validity of Contractual Provision Limiting Place or Court in Which Action May Be Brought, 31 A.L.R.4th 404, 409, § 3 (1984). See also Home Insurance Co. v. Morse, 20 Wall. 445, 451 (1874). Although adherence to this general rule has declined in recent years, particularly following our decision in The Bremen v. Zapata Off–Shore Co., 407 U.S. 1, the prevailing rule is still that forum-selection clauses are not enforceable if they were not freely bargained for, create additional expense for one party, or deny one party a remedy. See 31 A.L.R.4th, at 409–438 (citing cases). A forum-selection clause in a standardized passenger ticket would clearly have been unenforceable under the common law before our decision in *The Bremen*, see 407 U.S., at 9, and n. 10, and, in my opinion, remains unenforceable under the prevailing rule today.

The Bremen, which the Court effectively treats as controlling this case, had nothing to say about stipulations printed on the back of passenger tickets. That case involved the enforceability of a forum-selection clause in a freely negotiated international agreement between two large corporations providing for the towage of a vessel from the Gulf of Mexico to the Adriatic Sea. The Court recognized that such towage agreements had generally been held unenforceable in American courts, but held that the doctrine of those cases did not extend to commercial arrangements between parties with equal bargaining power.

The federal statute that should control the disposition of the case before us today was enacted in 1936 when the general rule denying enforcement of forum-selection clauses was indisputably widely accepted. The principal subject of the statute concerned the limitation of shipowner liability, but as the following excerpt from the House Report explains, the section that is relevant to this case was added as a direct response to shipowners' ticketing practices. "During the course of the hearings on the bill (H.R. 9969) there was also brought to the attention of the committee a practice of providing on the reverse side of steamship tickets that in the event of damage or injury caused by the negligence or fault of the owner or his servants, the liability of the owner shall be limited to a stipulated amount, in some cases $5,000, and in others substantially lower amounts, or that in such event the question of liability and the measure of damages shall be determined by arbitration. The amendment ... is intended to, and in the opinion of the committee will, put a stop to all such practices and practices of a like character." H.R.Rep. No. 2517, 74th Cong., 2d Sess., 6–7 (1936); see also S.Rep. No. 2061, 74th Cong., 2d Sess., 6–7 (1936).

. . .

The stipulation in the ticket that Carnival Cruise sold to respondents certainly lessens or weakens their ability to recover for the slip and fall incident that occurred off the west coast of Mexico during the cruise that originated and terminated in Los Angeles, California. It is safe to assume that the witnesses—whether other passengers or members of the crew—can be assembled with less expense and inconvenience at a west coast forum than in a Florida court several thousand miles from the scene of the accident.

. . . The forum-selection clause here does not mandate suit in a foreign jurisdiction, and therefore arguably might have less of an impact on a plaintiff's ability to recover. See Fireman's Fund American Ins. Cos. v. Puerto Rican Forwarding Co., 492 F.2d 1294 (CA1 1974). However, the plaintiffs in this case are not large corporations but individuals, and the added burden on them of conducting a trial at the opposite end of the country is likely proportional to the additional cost to a large corporation of conducting a trial overseas.[6]

Under these circumstances, the general prohibition against stipulations purporting "to lessen, weaken, or avoid" the passenger's right to a trial certainly should be construed to apply to the manifestly unreasonable stipulation in these passengers' tickets. Even without the benefit of the statute, I would continue to apply the general rule that prevailed prior to our decision in *The Bremen* to forum-selection clauses in passenger tickets.

I respectfully dissent.

Unconscionability

Congress briefly outlawed forum-selection clauses in passenger tickets, effectively overruling *Carnival Cruise*. This change was accomplished in late 1992 by a "technical clarification" of 46 App. U.S.C. § 183c "buried in a 68-page act which was passed under a motion to suspend the normal rules."[1] The swift congressional reversal of *Carnival* might be viewed as poetic justice (the fine print of a rider on a legislative enactment displacing the fine print of an adhesion contract), but the overruling was itself overruled the following year by another "technical clarification" returning to the statutory language involved in *Carnival*.[2]

6. The Court does not make clear whether the result in this case would also apply if the clause required Carnival passengers to sue in Panama, the country in which Carnival is incorporated.

1. Michael F. Sturley, Forum Selection Clauses in Cruise Line Tickets: An Update on Congressional Action "Overruling" the Supreme Court, 24 J. Maritime L. & Commerce 399, n. 5 (1993). The amendment invalidated any provision in a passenger contract that purports "to lessen, weaken, or avoid the right of any claimant to a trial by *any* court of competent jurisdiction."

(Emphasis added.) A year later the word "any" returned to the original "a."

2. See Smith v. Doe, 991 F.Supp. 781 (E.D.La.1998) (holding that the forum selection provision in the passenger's ticket, because of the second legislative change, was governed by *Carnival Cruise* and enforceable); see also Kurt A. Franklin & David A. Weldy, Dark of the Night Legislation Takes Aim at Forum Selection Clauses: Statutory Revisions in Relation to Carnival Cruise Lines, Inc. v. Shute, 6 U.S.F. Mar.L.J. 259 (1994).

On what grounds did the Court find the forum-selection clause "fundamentally fair?"[3] Contracts of pre-specified form, whose terms are not actually negotiated, are not in and of themselves unconscionable. Generally, courts will invalidate a contract on the ground that it is an adhesion contract only if unfairness is found both in the procedure by which the contract was formed and in the contract terms being challenged.[4] Should the Court in *Carnival* have paid more attention to the fairness of the contract process? Recall that before the Shutes ever saw the ticket, they were bound because the money they paid for the ticket was unrefundable. Under these circumstances, was the Shutes' lawyer negligent to have "conceded" notice?

Courts rarely, if ever, will find a contract void as an adhesion contract when both parties are business entities. When two business entities have entered into a contract, the first requirement, procedural unfairness, is rarely found. Notice that *The Bremen* case, on which *Carnival* is based, involved two business entities (sophisticated contractors, presumably, each represented by counsel). Business entities whose counsel fail to read and alert their clients to harsh provisions in "fine print" may sue their lawyers for malpractice if those provisions later come back and bite them.

Consider Justice Stevens' description of the ticket. Assuming the Shutes' money was refundable or that they had seen the ticket before purchasing it, should a lay person be expected to read, understand and comprehend the implications of the ticket terms? Do you read the fine-print contract terms on your airline tickets? The ticket you get when you park your car in a commercial lot?

Do you agree with the majority that no evidence of fraud or overreaching by Carnival was presented? Judge Posner, no big fan of unconscionability doctrine, had this to say about the Ninth Circuit's decision in this case, while the case was pending review before the Supreme Court:

The [Ninth Circuit's] opinion bristles with hostility to nonnegotiated form contracts, but the facts were special. A passenger was injured on a cruise ship and brought suit. The cruise line sought to dismiss the suit on the basis of a forum selection clause printed on the passenger's ticket. The ticket had not even been mailed to the passenger until after she bought the ticket and as a result she had had no knowledge of the clause until the transaction was complete. If ever there was a case for stretching the concept of fraud in the name of unconscionability, it was [*Carnival*]; and perhaps no stretch was necessary.... If a clause really is buried in illegible "fine print"—or if as in [*Carnival*] it plainly is

3. See Effron v. Sun Line Cruises, 158 F.R.D. 39 (S.D.N.Y.1994) (refusing to apply *Carnival Cruise* to a forum selection clause in fine print that required a U.S. passenger who purchased a ticket in the U.S. to bring suit in a foreign country unconnected with either the cruise or the place of injury).

4. See, e.g., Williams v. Walker–Thomas Furniture Co., 350 F.2d 445, 449 (D.C.Cir. 1965) (setting forth the standard of unconscionability as "includ[ing] an absence of meaningful choice on the part of one of the parties together with contract terms which are unreasonably favorable to the other party").

neither intended nor likely to be read by the other party—this circumstance may support an inference of fraud, and fraud is a defense to a contract.[5]

Carnival's Lawyers

Assuming that Carnival's lawyers wrote the forum-selection clause relying on *The Bremen*, was it reasonable at that time to believe that *The Bremen* justified the inclusion of such a clause in a consumer contract? If the law on what is conscionable is unclear, may the lawyer simply include the term and hope for the best, i.e., a decision like *Carnival* approving the clause after the fact? Is that "the best?" Or is "the best" outcome one that results in waiving the clause for those parties who threaten to challenge its enforceability and assuming that most people will adhere to the term on the (perhaps mistaken) belief that it is enforceable? Is the later strategy ethical?

A form contract prepared by lawyers has an air of legality about it. Why shouldn't unrepresented parties who sign such a document be entitled to believe—what most ordinary people do believe—that the terms included are lawful? Doesn't a lawyer who drafts a form contract implicitly represent as much, knowing that unrepresented persons will rely on that representation? Recall that in many jurisdictions, third parties who reasonably rely on a lawyer's negligent misrepresentations can now sue the lawyer.[6] Moreover, those who are intentionally deceived by someone else's lawyer have always been allowed to maintain an action for fraud against that lawyer.[7] Do these tort principles suggest that it is unlawful or unethical for a lawyer to intentionally or negligently include unconscionable terms in a form contract? Should lawyers who draft form contracts be expected to flag provisions of doubtful enforceability for consumers?

Consider now the lawyers' responsibility for the procedure employed by Carnival to sell its tickets. Assuming Carnival's lawyers believed the forum-selection clause was valid under *The Bremen* as long as ticket buyers had notice of the clause, should the lawyers have refused to include the clause so long as Carnival sold its tickets on a sight-unseen nonrefundable basis? Should the lawyers have insisted that some other notice of the provision be given, perhaps in the Carnival brochure?

What changes, if any, should Carnival's lawyers have recommended to their client after the Court's decision? Consider that in a later class action brought against Carnival by passengers injured on a cruise, a California intermediate appellate court held that the forum-selection clause was not enforceable against any plaintiff who did not have sufficient notice.[8] Of

5. Northwestern Nat'l Ins. Co. v. Donovan, 916 F.2d 372, 376, 377 (7th Cir.1990) (enforcing a forum selection clause in fidelity insurance contract between Wisconsin insurer and promoters of Texas tax-shelter investment transactions).

6. See, e.g., Greycas v. Proud, p. 79.

7. See the discussion of a lawyer's liability for intentional fraud at p. 92 supra.

8. Carnival Cruise Lines v. Superior Court of Los Angeles County, 286 Cal.Rptr. 323 (Cal.App.1991).

course, Carnival might not want to draw attention to such clauses because notice might frighten passengers or passengers might not agree to such terms for other reasons. On the other hand, if that is Carnival's reason for selling tickets without notice or hiding the clause, doesn't that suggest "overreaching or fraud?" Should a lawyer be a party to that?

Rescission and Mistake

Murray Schwartz argues that lawyers in nonadversarial settings should refrain from the use of "unconscionable" means and from assisting clients toward "unconscionable" ends:

> [T]he client has no "legal right" to a noncriminal or nonfraudulent result which would nonetheless be unenforceable or which could be avoided were a court to review the transaction, and ..., therefore, the client has no right to receive professional assistance for this purpose. A lawyer has a professional responsibility to decline to accomplish on behalf of a client that which the formal processes of the law themselves would not tolerate.[9]

Schwartz relies on an ethics opinion stating that it is unethical for a landlord's lawyer to insert in a lease a provision previously held void as against public policy.[10] Schwartz also relies on cases and ethics opinions involving inadvertent mistakes by one party's lawyer that are known to the other's party's lawyer. In Stare v. Tate,[11] for example, the spouses agreed on the principles that should govern the property settlement in their divorce proceeding. The wife's lawyer, however, made an arithmetic error of about $50,000 in a settlement offer incorporating these principles. The husband's lawyer, recognizing the error, prepared a counteroffer that was prepared in a way designed to minimize the possibility that the wife or her lawyer would discover the mistake. When the parties met, the counteroffer was accepted after some minor give and take. The upshot was that the wife received about $50,000 less than she would have received absent the arithmetical error.

Immediately after the divorce became final, the brash former husband mailed his former spouse a copy of the offer containing the erroneous computations, with an exultant note pointing out the "$100,000 mistake in your figures...." She brought an action to reform the property settlement agreement to reflect the parties' acceptance of her valuation of the disputed property. Established law, the court said, vitiated an agreement based on fraud, mutual mistake of the parties or a mistake of one party, which the other party knew of when the agreement was made. Since the husband's lawyer was aware of the mistake, the settlement agreement was set aside. The court stated:

---

9. Murray L. Schwartz, The Professionalism and Accountability of Lawyers, 66 Calif.L.Rev. 669, 687 (1978).

10. Comm. on Prof. Ethics, Ass'n of Bar of City of New York, Op. 722 (1948) (including unlawful provision purporting to waive

tenant's right to a sixty-day period in which to cancel an agreed-upon rent increase is unethical conduct).

11. 98 Cal.Rptr. 264 (App.1971).

... [It does not matter] what Joan would have done had Tim been more frank. By permitting her to enter into the contract in the belief that he had accepted her $550,000 value, he simply took the risk that if she discovered the mistake and sought judicial redress, the contract would be enforced on the terms which she mistakenly thought she had already received.

If substantive law will invalidate an agreement reached under circumstances of mistake or fraud, what implications does this have for lawyer behavior in negotiating the agreement?[12]

D.   THE LAW AND ETHICS OF NEGOTIATION[1]

1.   THE LAWYER AS NEGOTIATOR

Lawyers frequently justify partisan behavior in litigation on the ground that the adversary system requires such behavior in order to operate effectively. But most of what lawyers do takes place in the law office and not in court. Consider the differences between the two settings. In litigation settings, the partisan behavior of the lawyer on behalf of a client is countered by the similar behavior of the opposing lawyer; the proceeding is being conducted in accordance with elaborate procedural rules established in advance; an experienced and impartial judge is available to apply existing law, enforce limits and rule on alleged abuses; and an impartial trier of fact decides contested issues. None of these safeguards are available when a lawyer is counseling a client in the law office and the proposed estate plan, business transaction, or other legal arrangement will affect the interests of third persons, who often are not present and may also be unrepresented. In addition to deficiencies in participation and adverse representation, there is no neutral arbiter.

Do the norms of partisanship applicable in litigation settings extend to practice contexts lacking neutral arbiters and procedural safeguards? Can any single set of ethical standards deal with the diverse circumstances in which legal advice is given to clients? Should there be multiple rules of professional conduct, each designed for specific practice contexts and situations, rather than one overarching code?

These fundamental questions are raised by considering lawyers as negotiators. Negotiation, along with interviewing, fact investigation, counseling, and drafting, is one of the most pervasive of all lawyer activities. The fact that 90–95 percent of all civil and criminal cases are settled is one indicator of the importance of negotiation even to litigators. For office

---

12. See also Comm. on Prof. Ethics, Ass'n of Bar of City of New York, Op. No. 477 (1939) (when a lawyer negotiating a settlement makes an arithmetical error that hurts her client, the opposing lawyer, recognizing the inadvertent error, should urge her client to reveal the mistake and, if the client refuses, do so herself).

1. This textual material is designed to be considered in connection with a simulated negotiation. Material for the simulation will be distributed prior to the negotiation.

lawyers, the negotiation involved in structuring transactions is an everyday activity.

Negotiation takes place in an extraordinary variety of contexts. Consider, for example, the crucial significance of the variables suggested by the following circumstances:

Continuing relationships or one-shot encounters. In one negotiation a manufacturer may be seeking to work out a problem with a long-term major supplier. Each party has a strong incentive to reach an agreement that will not adversely affect future business relations. In another negotiation two strangers, who hope never to see each other again, are negotiating the aftermath of an automobile accident which unfortunately brought them into momentary contact with one another; their interest in cooperation is slight. Academics who study negotiation state that different styles of negotiation are encountered in these different settings:[2] When parties have a continuing relationship and strong ties, cooperative or consensus-oriented negotiation is more likely. When the parties are strangers and a one-shot negotiation is involved, competitive or concession-oriented negotiating techniques are more frequently employed. In a competitive negotiation, the parties and their lawyers seek to maximize their own interests.

Professional relationships. In either of the examples just given, the parties may be represented, on the one hand, by lawyers who are close professional friends with a great deal of mutual trust and respect; or, on the other hand, the parties may be represented by lawyers who have not encountered each other before, do not expect to again, and come from professional backgrounds that differ in legal culture and negotiating style.

Legal and social context of negotiation. Some negotiated settlements must be approved by judges (e.g., a property settlement in a divorce proceeding or a settlement of a minor's personal injury claim); others are examples of private ordering between competent adults that are subject to judicial scrutiny only if one participant provides evidence of fraud, illegality, or mutual mistake. The negotiations take place in radically different institutional and substantive contexts. Consider the implications for process and behavior of the following contexts: the plea bargaining process in the criminal justice field; labor negotiations in the union-management field; commercial negotiation in a particular industry or trade; negotiation of disputed matters in matrimonial and family controversies; and negotiation of personal injury claims between representatives of liability insurers and

---

2. For discussion of negotiation styles and strategies, see Donald G. Gifford, A Context–Based Theory of Strategy Selection in Legal Negotiations, 46 Ohio St. L. J. 41 (1984) (reviewing and comparing competitive and cooperative strategies); Carrie Menkel–Meadow, Toward Another View of Negotiation: The Structure of Legal Problem Solving, 31 UCLA L.Rev. 754 (1984) (arguing for a cooperative strategy); Roger Fisher & William Ury, Getting to Yes (1981) (arguing that a cooperative approach is more effective as well as better on ethical grounds); Robert J. Condlin, Bargaining in the Dark: The Normative Incoherence of Lawyer Dispute Bargaining Role, 51 Md.L.Rev. 1 , 12 (1992) ("[I]n any single negotiation, where there is no prospect of future dealing, it is usually irrational for individual bargainers to act cooperatively, and that is the bargainer's dilemma").

plaintiffs' lawyers. Apart from the reality that each context provides a substantive and procedural framework, the lawyers engaged in these separate fields have been socialized in very special ways. In a sense, each field is a distinct legal culture. Commentators state that the expectations and behavior of lawyers who represent clients in these distinct milieus are shaped more by these subcultures than they are by general professional codes.

Conduct of parties. "All's fair in love and war" is the popular saying. Is there truth in it? Informed observers argue that what adversaries do in negotiation is heavily influenced by their beliefs concerning the actual or potential conduct of their opponents. If they expect fair dealing from opponents, they will act accordingly. On the other hand, if they view the opposing party as advancing an unjust claim or of acting in bad faith, they may feel justified in retaliating in kind. Game theorists refer to this common strategy as "tit for tat." Should one's views of the merits or of the opposing party's tactics influence how a negotiator behaves?

Relative bargaining strength of the parties and their lawyers. External circumstances having nothing to do with the merits of a claim have dramatic effects on negotiating outcomes. A small business threatened by insolvency may not be in a position to hold out for trial; an impoverished accident victim with large and increasing obligations may feel compelled to take what an insurance company offers; an inexperienced lawyer lacking trial experience who is facing an experienced and stubborn litigator may settle a claim for less than its full worth. Many other circumstances place pressures of time, money, or emotion on one of the parties or lawyers. Moreover, events having nothing to do with the merits of a claim, such as the unrelated death of a principal witness, may dramatically effect the litigation value of a claim. Is there anything wrong with lawyers taking these facts of life into account in conducting negotiations? How could parties and courts, imagining themselves in an ideal world, attempt to determine the "true" value of a claim or defense apart from a shift in its "litigation" value as a result of the death of an important witness?

Use of deception by negotiators. Game theorists view bargaining as kindred to a child's game of chicken in which each side, concealing its bottom line, seeks to bluff the other into a favorable settlement. For each side, "[t]here is some range of alternative outcomes in which any point is better for both sides than no agreement at all. . . . Yet if both parties are aware of the limits to this range, *any* outcome is a point from which at least one party would have been willing to retreat and the other knows it. . . ."[3] If game theorists are correct, negotiating parties will have difficulty reaching an agreement if their bottom lines are not hidden from each other. It is for this reason that some negotiators, otherwise truthful in negotiation, view questions about "negotiating authority" and "resistance points" as so improper that lying is appropriate if evasion or a refusal to answer may communicate some information.

---

3. Thomas Schelling, The Strategy of Conflict 21–22 (rev. ed. 1980).

2.   TRUTHFULNESS IN BARGAINING[4]

How Truthful Are Lawyers in Negotiations?

Negotiating conduct is veiled by law office secrecy and protected by the attorney-client privilege. Our knowledge concerning day-by-day behavior is very limited. One of the only empirical studies of lawyer behavior in negotiations, a report by Steven D. Pepe, then a law professor, now a federal judge, presents a bleak view of the moral climate among one group of civil litigators.[5] Pepe asked two substantial samples of litigators (a group of Michigan lawyers and a national sample) and another group of judges (state and federal court judges) how they would handle a hypothetical negotiation problem. Under the scenario, a lawyer, shortly before entering settlement negotiations with the opposing lawyer, discovers that his client has given knowingly false evidence on a material issue during a deposition hearing. Nearly 60 percent of the total group of litigators responded that this information need not be disclosed to the other side if the client refused to authorize the disclosure. Judicial attitudes were somewhat different: 60 percent of federal judges thought the lawyer should disclose. Fifty percent of the Michigan lawyers thought it was proper to enter into a settlement without disclosing the false deposition testimony; and 38 percent thought it was permissible for the lawyer to refer to the false deposition testimony in negotiations. Less than one-half of the lawyers responded that they would be fully candid and truthful if they were asked a question about the false portion of the deposition. But this is one study of lawyer attitudes in a hypothetical situation. Actual lawyer behavior in negotiations may be better or worse.

Relevant Ethics Rules

There are very few cases discussing the circumstances under which a lawyer may have a duty or permission to disclose adverse information to an opposing lawyer or party in a bargaining situation. One fundamental principle is that the lawyer, as a representative of a client's interest, is obligated to advance the client's interest. Duties of competence, diligence, confidentiality, and loyalty (including both commitment to the client and avoidance of conflicting interests) all require a lawyer not to volunteer any information that the lawyer has learned in the course of representing a client, unless the disclosure is expressly authorized by the client or impliedly authorized because it serves the task the client has asked the lawyer to perform. See Model Rules 1.1, 1.3, 1.4, 1.6, and 1.7–1.9. In civil proceedings, opposing parties can discover relevant information through pre-trial discovery procedures. See Fed.R.Civ.Pro. 26; and M.R. 3.4(d) (prohibiting a

---

4.   Truthfulness in bargaining is the subject of a large literature. For a philosophic treatment, see Sissela Bok, Lying: Moral Choice in Public and Private Life (1978). In addition to the articles excerpted and summarized below, lying by lawyer negotiators is discussed by Gerald B. Wetlaufer, The Ethics of Lying in Negotiations, 75 Iowa L.Rev. 1219 (1990).

5.   Stephen D. Pepe, Standards of Legal Negotiations: Interim Report for ABA Commission on Evaluation of Professional Standards (1983).

lawyer from "fail[ing] to make reasonably diligent effort to comply with a legally proper discovery request by an opposing party)."

On the other hand, legal and ethical limitations on what a lawyer may do for a client may sometimes require disclosure even when doing so is harmful to the client. See M.R. 1.2(d) (lawyer prohibited from knowingly counseling or assisting a client in criminal or fraudulent conduct); M.R. 8.4(c) (prohibiting conduct involving dishonesty, fraud, deceit or misrepresentation); and M.R. 4.1 (lawyer prohibited from knowingly making a false statement of material fact to a third person or, in some circumstances, failing to disclose when doing so would assist client crime or fraud). Note that the application of the latter provision is affected by the breadth of the exceptions to confidentiality specified in the state' version of Rule 1.6(b), i.e., the disclosure of material facts required by Rule 4.1(b) to prevent misrepresentation is cancelled if the confidentiality rule prohibits the disclosure. On the other hand, if a state's ethics rules permit disclosure, M.R. 4.1(b) makes the disclosure mandatory because "disclosure is [not] prohibited by rule 1.6."

Conduct Assisting or Involving Illegal Conduct

Ethics rules are buttressed by laws imposing criminal and civil liability on lawyers who engage in criminal conduct, harm others by intentionally tortious conduct such as fraud, or, in many jurisdictions, negligently misrepresent material facts. Moreover, contracts negotiated under duress or coercion are unenforceable;[6] and rescission or reformation is an appropriate remedy in cases of mutual mistake or fraud.[7] Unconscionable terms in consumer contracts will not be enforced.[8] These general requirements of substantive law must be borne in mind in considering lawyer participation in the bargaining process.

The use of threats in negotiation may also involve the felony of extortion (blackmail is the colloquial term). The Model Penal Code provides that "A person is guilty of theft if he purposely obtains property of another by threatening to . . . cause an official to take or withhold action."[9] Section 223.4 adds that "It is an affirmative defense . . . that the property obtained by threat of . . . invocation of official action was honestly claimed as restitution or indemnification for harm done to which such . . . official action relates, or as compensation for property or lawful services." The official comments explain that this affirmative defense "firmly establishes the intention not to intrude into what many regard as legitimate negotiating tactics."[10]

DR 7–105(A) of the Model Code of Professional Responsibility dealt explicitly with a lawyer's use of unlawful threats: "A lawyer shall not

---

6. Restatement (Second) of Contracts §§ 174, 175 (1979).

7. Id., § 155 (mutual mistake), § 166 (fraud).

8. Id. § 208, Comment (e).

9. 2 Model Penal Code and Commentaries (Official Draft and Revised Comments) § 223.4 (Theft by Extortion) (1980).

10. Id. at 213.

present, participate in presenting, or threaten to present criminal charges solely to obtain an advantage in a civil matter." The Model Rules do not contain a similar provision for two reasons. First, the criminal prohibitions against threats constituting extortion or criminal abuse are included under M.R. 8.4(b), making it a professional violation to "commit a criminal act that reflects adversely on the lawyer's honesty, trustworthiness or fitness as a lawyer in other respects." Second, the drafters of the Model Rules, aware that the crime of extortion has a varying content from state to state, left the subject to be handled by Rule 8.4's general referral to state criminal law. In Committee on Legal Ethics v. Printz,[11] the court distinguished between extortion and legitimate negotiations: "Receiving repayment of money taken from a victim is not extortion; however, asking a higher price (i.e., 'Give my money back and $20,000 or I'll call the cops!') in return for the victim's silence is extortion."[12]

Restatement (Second) of Contracts § 161 provides that non-disclosure of a fact sometimes will be treated as an assertion that the fact does not exist. Disclosure is required when it is necessary to correct a previous assertion that is erroneous, or when the fact in question concerns a basic assumption of the negotiation and failure to disclose would violate "good faith and . . . reasonable standards of fair dealing." "Reasonable standards of fair dealing," according to Comment d, refers to prevailing business practices.[13] Compare a litigant's obligation under procedural rules to correct information supplied in response to discovery requests (see p. 11 supra).

Comment [2] to M.R. 4.1 implies that some factual statements made in negotiation (e.g., "puffery") do not constitute misrepresentations:

> Under generally accepted conventions in negotiation, certain types of statements ordinarily are not taken as statements of material fact. Estimates of price or value placed on the subject of a transaction and a party's intentions as to an acceptable settlement of a claim are in the category, and so is the existence of an undisclosed principal except where nondisclosure of the principal would constitute fraud.

Some commentators have argued that the law of misrepresentation and fraud is inconsistent with the above Comment.[14] First, a statement is fraudulent under the Restatement, even though ambiguous, if it is made "without any belief or expectation as to how it will be understood" or

---

11.   416 S.E.2d 720, 727 n.4 (W.Va.1992).

12.   See also State v. Harrington, 260 A.2d 692 (Vt.1969), in which a lawyer represented a woman in a bitter matrimonial dispute with her husband. The court held that the lawyer committed criminal extortion by sending the husband a letter which threatened to disclose unrelated illegal conduct of the husband to government agencies unless the husband consented to a no-fault divorce in another state and paid $175,000.

13.   See Rhode & Luban, Legal Ethics 429–30 (2d ed. 1995), relying on tort law as summarized in Restatement (Second) of Torts §§ 527, 529 and 551(1965).

14.   Id. Other commentators would argue that the Restatement of Contracts and Torts require too much candor. E.g., James J. White states that it may be "better to have no rule than to have one so widely violated as to be a continuing hypocrisy." Is hypocrisy a worse sin than deceit?

"with reckless indifference" as to its interpretation by the hearer.[15] Partially true statements that materially mislead because of the maker's failure to state qualifying information are also fraudulent.[16] Concerning intentions, the Restatement provides: "A representation of the maker's own intention to do or not to do a particular thing is fraudulent if he does not have that intention."[17] Concerning puffery, the Restatement provides that one party to a business transaction is under a duty to disclose to the other before the transaction is consummated "the falsity of a representation not made with the expectation that it would be acted upon, if [the maker] subsequently learns that the other is about to act in reliance upon it in [the] transaction...."[18] A party must also disclose "matters known to him that he knows to be necessary to prevent his partial or ambiguous statement of the facts from being misleading." Liability for nondisclosure exists in all these situations.

An early version of Model Rule 4.1 attempted to restate the tort and contract law summarized above as a professional duty of "candor toward other parties." The proposed rule stated: "In conducting negotiations a lawyer shall be candid in all representations to opposing parties." This affirmative duty was coupled with negative prohibitions which went well beyond the prohibitions on lying embodied in current M.R. 4.1. The proposed rule would have prohibited a lawyer from failing to disclose a fact known to the lawyer when "disclosure ... is necessary to correct a misapprehension resulting from a previous representation made by the lawyer or known by the lawyer to have been made by the client; or [when] manifestly necessary to prevent the resolution of the matter from being voidable on the ground of fraud or mistake."[19]

Note that the rule actually adopted, M.R. 4.1(b), if read literally, prevents a lawyer from disclosing any information relating to the representation, even if "disclosure is necessary to avoid assisting a criminal or fraudulent act by a client," *unless disclosure is permitted by the exceptions to confidentiality of M.R. 1.6(b)*." And the latter provision, as promulgated by the ABA, does not allow disclosure to prevent an ongoing or future client crime or fraud not involving a threat of imminent death or injury. In most states, however, disclosure to prevent financial injury from prospective or ongoing client fraud is permitted.

Judicial Decisions

In Spaulding v. Zimmerman,[20] defense lawyers entered into a settlement with the injured plaintiff without revealing that, unknown to the

15. Restatement (Second) of Torts § 527(b) and (c) (1965).

16. Id., § 529.

17. Id., § 530(a).

18. Id., § 551(2)(d).

19. This provision codified agency law, which imposes liability on a lawyer who fails to correct a misapprehension on the part of the opposing party that is based on earlier statements or misleading omissions of the lawyer as negotiator for a client. See Restatement (Second) of Agency § 348, comment c (1957).

20. 116 N.W.2d 704 (Minn.1962), reprinted at p. 5 supra.

plaintiff or his lawyer, the plaintiff had an additional injury caused by the accident: a life-threatening aortic aneurysm. Because the plaintiff was a minor and the court had been provided with incorrect information concerning the extent of the minor's injuries, the settlement was set aside. But the court made it clear that if the plaintiff had been an adult at the time of settlement (a settlement not requiring court approval), the plaintiff's only remedy would be a malpractice remedy against his lawyer or doctor. No fraudulent misrepresentation concerning the plaintiff's injuries were made at the settlement conference. Given the adversary relationship in the settlement negotiation, "no rule or duty rested upon defendants or their representatives to disclose this knowledge [or the life-threatening injury to the adverse party]." Thus the result in *Spaulding* turns on the special responsibilities of a court toward a minor and of lawyers to the court.[21]

Another relevant line of cases involves representations made by a lawyer that are either "reckless" (e.g., repeating to the opposing party easily verifiable material facts obtained from the client that turn out to be false) or "misleading." Some cases have held a lawyer civilly liable for negligent misrepresentation under these circumstances. A leading example is Roberts v. Ball, Hunt, Hart, Brown & Baerwitz,[22] holding that a negligent misrepresentation claim was stated when a lender, before making a large loan to a partnership, had received a legal opinion from the partnership's lawyer stating that all fourteen partners were general partners whose personal assets would be available to the lender. The lender's misrepresentation claim was based on the failure of the lawyer to reveal its knowledge that thirteen of the fourteen partners claimed they were limited partners and were prepared to litigate the issue.

3.   NEGOTIATING STRATEGIES AND THE TEMPTATION TO DECEIVE

Alvin B. Rubin, "A Causerie on Lawyers' Ethics in Negotiation"

35 Louisiana Law Review, 577–78, 580–86, 588–89, 591 (1975).

Litigation spawns compromise, and courtroom lawyers engage almost continually in settlement discussions in civil cases and plea bargains in criminal cases. We do not know what proportion of civil claims is settled by negotiation before the filing of suit, but it must be vastly greater than the number of cases actually filed [although settlement rates are extremely high].

Although less than one fourth of the lawyers in practice today devote a majority of their time to litigation, and most spend none at all in the

---

21.   Cf. Virzi v. Grand Trunk Warehouse & Cold Storage Co., 571 F.Supp. 507 (E.D.Mich.1983) (stating in dictum that lawyer has duty to reveal the death of his client before settling the deceased client's claim for personal injuries), discussed at p. 10 supra.

22.   128 Cal.Rptr. 901 (App.1976), discussed at p. 87 supra.

traditional courtroom, there are few lawyers who do not negotiate regularly, indeed daily, in their practice. . . .

There are a few rules [in the 1969 Code of Professional Responsibility] designed to apply to other relationships that touch peripherally the area we are discussing. A lawyer shall not:

- knowingly make a false statement of law or fact [DR 7–102(A)(5)].

- participate in the creation or preservation of evidence when he knows or it is obvious that the evidence is false [DR 7–102(A)(6)].

- counsel or assist his client in conduct that the lawyer knows to be illegal or fraudulent [DR 7–102(A)(7)],

- knowingly engage in other illegal conduct or conduct contrary to a Disciplinary Rule [DR 7–102(A)(8)], or

- conceal or knowingly fail to disclose that which he is required by law to reveal [DR 7–102(A)(3)].

In addition, he "should be temperate and dignified and . . . refrain from all illegal and morally reprehensible conduct [EC 1–5]." The lawyer is admonished "to treat with consideration all persons involved in the legal process and to avoid the infliction of needless harm" [EC 7–10].

Taken together, these rules . . . imply that a lawyer shall not himself engage in illegal conduct, since the meaning of assisting a client in fraudulent conduct is later indicated by the proscription of *other* illegal conduct. . . . [T]he lawyer is forbidden to make a false statement of law or fact *knowingly*. But nowhere is it ordained that the lawyer owes any general duty of candor or fairness to members of the bar or to laymen with whom he may deal as a negotiator, or of honesty or of good faith insofar as that term denotes generally scrupulous activity.

Is the lawyer-negotiator entitled . . . to depend on "cunning, precise calculation, and a willingness to employ whatever means justify the end of policy?" Few are so bold as to say so. Yet some whose personal integrity and reputation are scrupulous have instructed [law] students in negotiating tactics that appear tacitly to countenance that kind of conduct. In fairness it must be added that they say they do not "endorse the *propriety*" of this kind of conduct and indeed even indicate "grave reservations" about such behavior; however, this sort of generalized disclaimer of sponsorship hardly appears forceful enough when the tactics suggested include:

- Use two negotiators who play different roles. (Illustrated by the "Mutt and Jeff" police technique; "Two lawyers for the same side feign an internal dispute . . .").

- Appear irrational when it seems helpful.

- Raise some of your demands as the negotiations progress.

- Claim that you do not have authority to compromise. (Emphasis supplied.)

- After agreement has been reached, have your client reject it and raise his demands.

Another text used in training young lawyers commendably counsels sincerity, capability, preparation, courage and flexibility. But it also suggests "a sound set of tools or tactics and the know-how to use (or not to use) them." One such tactic is, "Make false demands, bluffs, threats; even use irrationality."

. . .

Let us consider the proper role for a lawyer engaged in negotiations when he knows that the opposing side, whether as a result of poor legal representation or otherwise, is assuming a state of affairs that is incorrect.... [Suppose] L, the lawyer is representing C, a client, in a suit for personal injuries. There have been active settlement negotiations with LD, the defendant's lawyer. The physician who has been treating C rendered a written report, containing a prognosis stating that it is unlikely that C can return to work at his former occupation. This has been furnished to LD. L learns from C that he has consulted another doctor, who has given him a new medication. C states that he is now feeling fine and thinks he can return to work, but he is reluctant to do so until the case is settled or tried. The next day L and LD again discuss settlement. Does L have a duty either to guard his client's secret or to make a full disclosure? Does he satisfy or violate either duty if, instead of mentioning C's revelation he suggests that D require a new medical examination?

Some lawyers avoid this problem by saying that it is inconceivable that a competent LD would not ask again about C's health. But if the question as to whether L should be frank is persistently presented, few lawyers can assure that they would disclose the true facts....

Interesting answers are obtained if lawyers are asked whether it is proper to make false statements that concern negotiating strategy rather than the facts in litigation. Counsel for a plaintiff appears quite comfortable in stating, when representing a plaintiff, "My client won't take a penny less than $25,000," when in fact he knows that the client will happily settle for less; counsel for the defendant appears to have no qualms in representing that he has no authority to settle, or that a given figure exceeds his authority, when these are untrue statements. Many say that, as a matter of strategy, when they attend a pre-trial conference with a judge known to press settlements, they disclaim any settlement authority both to the judge and adversary although in fact they do have settlement instructions; estimable members of the bar support the thesis that a lawyer may not misrepresent a fact in controversy but may misrepresent matters that pertain to his authority or negotiating strategy because this is expected by the adversary.

To most practitioners it appears that anything sanctioned by the rules of the game is appropriate. From this point of view, negotiations are merely, as the social scientists have viewed it, a form of game; observance of the expected rules, not professional ethics, is the guiding precept. But gamesmanship is not ethics....

The monopoly on the practice of law does not arise from the presumed advantages of an attorney's education or social status: it stems from the concept that, as professionals, lawyers serve society's interests by participating in the process of achieving the just termination of disputes. That an adversary system is the basic means to this end does not crown it with supreme value. It is means, not end.

If he is a professional and not merely a hired, albeit skilled hand, the lawyer is not free to do anything his client might do in the same circumstances. The corollary of that proposition does set a minimum standard: *the lawyer must be at least as candid and honest as his client would be required to be.* [Emphasis added.] The agent of the client, that is, his attorney-at-law, must not perpetrate the kind of fraud or deception that would vitiate a bargain if practiced by his principal. Beyond that, the profession should embrace an affirmative ethical standard for attorneys' professional relationships with courts, other lawyers and the public: The lawyer must act honestly and in good faith. Another lawyer, or a layman, who deals with a lawyer should not need to exercise the same degree of caution that he would if trading for reputedly antique copper jugs in an oriental bazaar. It is inherent in the concept of an ethic, as a principle of good conduct, that it is morally binding on the conscience of the professional, and not merely a rule of the game adopted because other players observe (or fail to adopt) the same rule. . . .

While it might strain present concepts of the role of the lawyer in an adversary system, surely the professional standards must ultimately impose upon him a duty not to accept an unconscionable deal. While some difficulty in line-drawing is inevitable when such a distinction is sought to be made, there must be a point at which the lawyer cannot ethically accept an arrangement that is completely unfair to the other side, be that opponent a patsy or a tax collector. So I posit a [third] precept: The lawyer may not accept a result that is unconscionably unfair to the other party.

A settlement that is unconscionable may result from a variety of circumstances. There may be a vast difference in the bargaining power of the principals so that, regardless of the adequacy of representation by counsel, one party may simply not be able to withstand the expense and bear the delay and uncertainty inherent in a protracted suit. There may be a vast difference in the bargaining skill of counsel so that one is able to manipulate the other virtually at will despite the fact that their framed certificates of admission to the bar contain the same words.

The unconscionable result in these circumstances is in part created by the relative power, knowledge and skill of the principals and their negotiators. While it is the unconscionable result that is to be avoided, the question of whether the result is indeed intolerable depends in part on examination of the relative status of the parties. The imposition of a duty to tell the truth and to bargain in good faith would reduce their relative inequality, and tend to produce negotiation results that are within relatively tolerable bounds. . . .

... It is inherent in the concept of professionalism that the profession will regulate itself, adhering to an ethos that imposes standards higher than mere law observance. Client avarice and hostility neither control the lawyer's conscience nor measure his ethics. Surely if its practitioners are principled, a profession that dominates the legal process in our law-oriented society would not expect too much if it required its members to adhere to two simple principles when they negotiate as professionals: Negotiate honestly and in good faith and do not take unfair advantage of another—regardless of his relative expertise or sophistication....

The ABA Rejects Judge Rubin's Proposal

The Kutak Commission, which drafted the Model Rules, proposed several versions of a rule that embodied Judge Rubin's proposal that the lawyer-negotiator "may not accept a result that is unconscionably unfair to the other party." The Discussion Draft of January 30, 1980, included the following formulation:[23]

[Proposed Rule] 4.2 Fairness to Other Participants

(a) In conducting negotiations a lawyer shall be fair in dealing with other participants.

(b) A lawyer shall not make a knowing misrepresentation of fact or law, or fail to disclose a material fact known to the lawyer, even if adverse, when disclosure is:

(1) required by law or the Rules of Professional Conduct; or

(2) necessary to correct a manifest misapprehension of fact or law resulting from a previous representation made by the lawyer or known by the lawyer to have been made by the client....

Proposed paragraph (a), by requiring that lawyers be "fair," went well beyond current law. However, the honesty and candor required by paragraph (b) were expressions of prior law: DR 7–102(A)(5) of the Model Code prohibited a "knowingly false statement of law or fact;" and Restatement (Second) of Agency § 348 imposes civil liability, under some circumstances, when a lawyer does not correct a manifest misapprehension on the part of the opposing party. Thus paragraph (b)(1) largely restated existing law. Moreover, such deliberately tortious conduct may constitute prohibited assistance, and aiding a client in fraudulent conduct was also prohibited by current law.

"The idea underlying the Kutak Commission's original proposal," according to Geoffrey Hazard, its drafter, "was not very complicated: the lawyer, as the instrument of a transaction, should be the guardian of its integrity. The proposal did not purport to hold lawyers strictly liable for the integrity of transactions or even burden them with a duty of reasonable care. Their only duty was to disclose facts of which an opposing party was

23. See Geoffrey C. Hazard, Jr., The Lawyers' Obligation to Be Trustworthy When Dealing with Opposing Parties, 33 So.Car. L.Rev. 181, 191–96 (1981), discussing the Kutak Commission proposals and the organized bar's response to them.

obviously ignorant and which might affect the integrity of the transaction."[24]

Nevertheless, bar groups responded to the proposed rule with extraordinary vehemence as involving a broad expansion of lawyer duties that were unduly vague and unenforceable, yet would expose lawyers to new civil liability. Faced with overwhelming opposition, efforts to regulate negotiating conduct were dropped except for the rule prohibitions against false statements and assisting fraud.

Can Lawyers' Negotiating Tactics Be Regulated?

If ethical behavior is costly, especially if the costs are large ones, many lawyers will succumb to the temptation to use deceptive tactics.[25] As baseball manager Leo Durocher put it, "Nice guys finish last."[26] Even if the lawyer avoids flat-out lies, she may mislead opponents into believing that material facts are otherwise than the lawyer knows them to be—an absence of candor that sometimes constitutes misrepresentation or fraud. Such conduct, experts acknowledge, often reaps rewards.

In part, the temptations are large because negotiation, as James J. White emphasizes, is nonpublic behavior.[27] There is no trial, no public testimony by conflicting witnesses, and, therefore, no opportunity to examine the truthfulness of assertions made during the negotiation: "If one negotiator lies to another, only by happenstance will the other discover the lie."[28] The temptation to deceive is fostered because of the low probability of punishment. If an increasing number of lawyers use deception, it becomes even more difficult for the honest lawyer to hold to a moral high ground.

Another challenge to truthfulness, White notes, arises out of the paradoxical nature of the negotiator's responsibilities. On the one hand the negotiator must be fair and truthful, and yet, on the other hand, she must mislead the opponent. "Like the poker player, a negotiator hopes that his opponent will overestimate the value of his hand. Like the poker player, in a variety of ways he must facilitate his opponent's inaccurate assessment. The critical difference between those who are successful negotiators and those who are not lies in this capacity both to mislead and not be misled."[29]

White suggests that rulemakers, in refusing to make lack of candor and misstatements of one's intentions actionable, are recognizing the bounds of law's control over human behavior. Geoffrey Hazard, discouraged by the profession's opposition to a rule attempting to restate the tort and contract

---

24. Id. at 192.

25. See Ronald J. Gilson & Robert H. Mnookin, Cooperation and Conflict between Litigators, 10 CDR Alternatives 1 (1994), a condensation of an article under the same title, 94 Colum.L.Rev. 509 (1994).

26. Leo Durocher, Nice Guys Finish Last 5 (1975).

27. James J. White, Machiavelli and the Bar: Ethical Limitations on Lying in Negotiation, 1980 ABF Research J. 926.

28. Id. at 926.

29. Id. at 927.

law of misrepresentation, now concurs with White. He concludes that the legal regulation of truthfulness cannot go much beyond the proscription of fraud. Hazard notes that while this fact is disquieting, it is "not necessarily occasion for despair."[30] Rather, it is indicative of the "limitations on improving the bar by legal regulations."[31]

Why is law so powerless to define and punish "unfairness" or "absence of candor" in negotiation? In part the answer is found in the enormous differences in negotiating context and the wide range of resulting customary behavior. For example, negotiating with armed terrorists who are holding hostages operates under different rules and customs than employer-union collective bargaining. And so on throughout an extraordinary variety of separate negotiating environments and cultures. A second underlying reality, mentioned above, is that negotiation is a process in which a negotiator seeks to lead the opposing party to overvalue the strength of the negotiator's position, or as White puts it, to mislead the opponent without actually lying. Faced with these realities, it is difficult or impossible to formulate and apply a single "truthfulness" standard to govern lawyer participation in negotiations. Consequently, it is argued, regulators must fall back on minimum prohibitions of dishonesty and the law of misrepresentation and fraud.

The Case for Cooperative Negotiating Strategies

Many of the ethical problems arising in negotiation result from the view that zealous hard bargaining requires an adversarial stance toward other parties. A prominent leader of the bar, Whitney North Seymour, stated that a professional ideology encouraging excessive advocacy mistakenly results in wasteful conflict that enriches lawyers but rarely advantages their clients.[32] Seymour and other experts claim that a more cooperative approach to bargaining is not only more attractive on ethical grounds but also a more effective tool for successful negotiations.

A form of cooperative negotiation referred to as "integrative bargaining" has received widespread attention as the result of the publication of Fisher and Ury's popular text, Getting to Yes.[33] The authors call for "principled negotiation" and identify four basic elements of this approach: people, interests, options and criteria. The successful principled negotiator will separate the people from the problem. She will focus on the interests that support each party's claims, not the position they take within the dispute. By focusing on options, the principled negotiator will generate a variety of possible solutions before committing herself to a single solution.

---

30. Hazard, op. cit. at 196.

31. Id.

32. Quoted in Gilson & Mnookin, op. cit., at 1.

33. Roger Fisher & William Ury, Getting to Yes: Negotiating Agreement Without Giving In (1981). For discussion of the negotiating approach of Fisher and Ury, see Donald Gifford, A Context–Based Theory of Strategy Selection in Legal Negotiations, 46 Ohio St.L.J. 41 (1985).

Finally, the criteria for the settlement will be based on objective rather than subjective standards.

Integrative bargaining strategy does not have universal applicability. It functions best, and is most used, when parties share an identifiable mutual gain or multiple issues can be traded off against one another. When the bargaining parties share a long-term interest in good relations and benefit from each other's well-being, integrative bargaining is at its best. It is less useful when the parties disagree only on a single issue and their interests are inherently opposed. In these "zero-sum" negotiations, competitive bargaining is common.

Proponents of cooperative negotiation, like Alvin Rubin, reject the use of threats, feigned or real anger, and the appearance of irrationality. Instead, cooperative negotiators look to the underlying needs and interests that led the parties to assert their positions in the first place. Settlements are then the result of an appeal to objective criteria rather than an exercise in offer/counteroffer and a test of will and bargaining power. By focusing on the client's real needs, not the money and goods that legal disputes usually emphasize, the competition of the moment is minimized and negotiators can achieve their client's ends without being trapped into senseless and futile game playing.

If cooperative negotiation is as effective a negotiating tool as its proponents claim, then why is it the exception rather than the norm? Robert Axelrod suggests a partial explanation can be found in the "prisoners' dilemma."[34] The prisoners' dilemma is a paradigm for situations in which no one cooperates, although all would be better off if everyone did, because unless *everyone* cooperates the cooperator(s) lose and the cut-throats win. Commentators argue that many situations in negotiation and litigation have similar qualities: cooperative behavior saves transaction costs and produces fair and reasonable results, but short-term advantages can be gained from competitive or aggressive behavior providing the other side is cooperative. If both sides are competitive, however, transaction costs are higher and the gains of aggression may be reduced or become negatives.

Axelrod explored solutions to the prisoner's dilemma through the use of a computer strategy tournament. The simplest and most effective strategy was "tit for tat." The user of this strategy cooperated so long as the other player cooperated. If the other player defected, the strategist defected; if the other player began to cooperate again, the strategist resumed cooperation. This strategy (and others like it) fared best in the tournament, although the premise of the tournament and a necessary condition for this strategy to succeed is that the two players are bound to play a series of games. Successful players combine four tactics: (1) They never initiated the use of "dirty tricks." (2) They did not let the other side use dirty tricks without retaliation. (3) After retaliating, they did not hold grudges—they

34. Robert M. Axelrod, The Evolution of Cooperation (1984). Axelrod's discussion of the "prisoner's dilemma" is summarized by Leo Herzel & Leo Katz, The Prisoner's Dilemma, 31 U.Chi.Law School Record 8 (1985).

returned to a "no-first-use" policy on dirty tricks. (4) They made it clear to the other side that their strategy followed the first three rules. More briefly, successful strategists are nice, retaliatory once provoked, forgiving, and transparent.

A bargainer who follows these rules may sometimes be exploited by a non-cooperative adversary's dirty tricks, and is particularly vulnerable in one-shot transactions. However, experiments have shown if negotiators encounter each other in repeat transactions, non-cooperative negotiators will generally be "punished" in future encounters for excessively competitive past behavior and cooperative negotiators usually fare better in the long run. Gilson and Mnookin argue that this process encourages cooperative negotiation. A trusting relationship between opposing lawyers in repeated contact with one another may develop. This relationship of trust permits lawyers to rely confidently on each other's representation and substantially improves the efficiency of the dispute resolution process. When opposing lawyers value their reputations with each other for trustworthiness and cooperation, they can create an environment for collaborative problem solving even in circumstances where their clients cannot.[35]

Robert Condlin, reviewing the literature about negotiation strategy, argues that strategy and competition are part of the very nature of the process.[36] It is, therefore, a mistake to hope that the strategic and competitive side of negotiation can be eliminated. Condlin points out that the long term effectiveness of cooperative bargaining stands in sharp contrast to the short-term, one-time advantage that successful competitive bargaining can sometimes confer. He argues that the duty of zealous advocacy for a current client requires lawyers to seek the one-time advantage. Otherwise they are trading off the client's interests for their own long-term bargaining effectiveness, which benefits only themselves, their future clients, and the present client's adversary. Condlin concludes: "[T]he bargainer's dilemma ... [i]n any single negotiation, where there is no prospect of future dealing, [is that] it is usually irrational for individual bargainers to act cooperatively...."[37]

Gerald Wetlaufer agrees with Condlin that it is self-deceiving to think that ethical conduct in negotiation can always be viewed as enlightened self-interest. Lies that are unlikely to be revealed may be highly effective and the world in which we live "honors instrumental effectiveness above all else."[38] However, Wetlaufer similarly notes that our common excuses for lying are equally self deceiving. Excuses such as "everyone does it" or "the other side is doing it" presupposes an impoverished view of morality, a

35. Gilson & Mnookin, supra at 527 (penalties imposed on non-cooperative lawyers) and 564 (cooperative strategies "damp conflict, reduce transaction costs and facilitate dispute resolution").

36. Robert F. Condlin, Bargaining in the Dark: The Normative Incoherence of Law-

yer Dispute Bargaining Role, 51 Md.L.Rev. 1 (1992).

37. Id. at 12.

38. Gerald Wetlaufer, The Ethics of Lying in Negotiations, 75 Iowa L.Rev. 1219, 1223–26, 1272–73 (1990).

view likely to be rejected in other contexts.[39] Moral theorists and negotiation experts have long pointed out that deceptive practices weaken fundamental values of trust and integrity. The social dilemma is that unrestrained selfishness destroys the social fabric.

Moral Restraint as Everyone's Task

Reed Elizabeth Loder argues that every lawyer has a role in transforming the ethical quality of negotiation practice.[40] She notes that excuses can never justify uncritical conformity to unethical prevailing practice. According to Loder, every practitioner bears some share of responsibility for perpetuating such practice over time. It is incumbent on each lawyer to seize opportunities to defy unethical customs when those chances realistically arise. Thus, every lawyer has a role in transforming questionable practices. If enough lawyers act honestly and fairly, questionable practices will be transformed over time.

Loder also emphasizes that informal sanctions already govern negotiation.[41] Professional reputations develop surprisingly easily and tend to stick like glue. A mistreated lawyer will not forget a humiliation and may warn others of danger. Furthermore, a large number of reported cases demonstrate that deceptions sometimes are exposed and that the consequences for the deceiving lawyer are grave. Even if a lawyer escapes detection in one case, repeated deceptions increase the overall risks to that lawyer. The risks are multiplied because a lawyer who successfully deceives once may be more inclined to take greater risks the next time. Such a lawyer may face direct sanctions, in the form of civil liability or other consequences, but may also faces business damage. A deceitful reputation may reduce her effectiveness and eventually result in other loss of reputation and business. In short, deception may lead to external sanctions as well as moral disquiet.

E.   DO LAWYERS HAVE A SPECIAL RESPONSIBILITY FOR JUSTICE?

INTRODUCTORY NOTE

American society has always been radically heterogeneous in terms of ethnic and religious identity. Locally, ethnic and religious groups provided social leadership in defining and working toward the public good and aiding the poor well until the 19th century. These groups still had considerable strength until World War II, when the accumulating effects of urbanization, the automobile and mobility through education broke down this pattern. While these groups were strong sources for justice on a local basis

---

39. Id. at 1248–51.

40. Reed Elizabeth Roder, Moral Truthseeking and the Virtuous Negotiator, 8 Geo.J. Leg.Ethics 45 (1994).

41. Id. at 90.

in the past and still retain some force today, they were not generally active agents at the state level, let alone the national level.

Instead, at various times and in various places in the United States there was a more or less recognized political aristocracy that professed responsibility for social justice at the state and national level—notably the New England church oligarchy in the late 18th and early to mid–19th centuries, and the planter aristocracy in the pre-Civil War South. deTocqueville saw lawyers as such an aristocracy[1] and to some extent the bar still sees itself that way.

Louis D. Brandeis, "The Opportunity in the Law" (1905)

In Brandeis, Business—A Profession (1914).

... Standing not far from the threshold of active life, feeling the generous impulse for service which the University fosters, you wish to know whether the legal profession would afford you special opportunities for usefulness to your fellow-men, and, if so, what the obligations and limitations are which it imposes....

For centuries before the American Revolution the lawyer had played an important part in England. His importance in the State became much greater in America. One reason for this, as deTocqueville indicated, was the fact that we possessed no class like the nobles, which took part in government through privilege. A more potent reason was that with the introduction of a written constitution the law became with us a far more important factor in the ordinary conduct of political life than it did in England. Legal questions were constantly arising and the lawyer was necessary to settle them. But I take it the paramount reason why the lawyer has played so large a part in our political life is that his training fits him especially to grapple with the questions which are presented in a democracy.

The whole training of the lawyer leads to the development of judgment. His early training—his work with books in the study of legal rules—teaches him patient research and develops both the memory and the reasoning faculties. He becomes practiced in logic; and yet the use of the reasoning faculties in the study of law is very different from their use, say, in metaphysics. The lawyer's processes of reasoning, his logical conclusions, are being constantly tested by experience. He is running up against facts at every point. Indeed it is a maxim of the law: Out of the facts grows the law; that is, propositions are not considered abstractly, but always with reference to facts....

If the lawyer's practice is a general one, his field of observation extends, in course of time, into almost every sphere of business and of life. The facts so gathered ripen his judgment. His memory is trained to retentiveness. His mind becomes practiced in discrimination as well as in

---

1. See the quote from deTocqueville at p. 1164 infra.

generalization. He is an observer of men even more than of things. He not only sees men of all kinds, but knows their deepest secrets; sees them in situations which "try men's souls." He is apt to become a good judge of men....

His experience teaches him that nearly every question has two sides; and very often he finds—after decision of judge or jury—that both he and his opponent were in the wrong. The practice of law creates thus a habit of mind, and leads to attainments which are distinctly different from those developed in most professions or outside of the professions. These are the reasons why the lawyer has acquired a position materially different from that of other men. It is the position of the adviser....

[B]y far the greater part of the work done by lawyers is done not in court, but in advising men on important matters, and mainly in business affairs. In guiding these affairs industrial and financial, lawyers are needed, not only because of the legal questions involved, but because the particular mental attributes and attainments which the legal profession develops are demanded in the proper handling of these large financial or industrial affairs. The magnitude and scope of these operations remove them almost wholly from the realm of "petty trafficking" which people formerly used to associate with trade. The questions which arise are more nearly questions of statesmanship. The relations created call in many instances for the exercise of the highest diplomacy. The magnitude, difficulty and importance of the problems involved are often as great as in the matters of state with which lawyers were formerly frequently associated. The questions appear in a different guise; but they are similar. The relations between rival railroad systems are like the relations between neighboring kingdoms. The relations of the great trusts to the consumers or to their employees is like that of feudal lords to commoners or dependents....

It is true that at the present time the lawyer does not hold as high a position with the people as he held seventy-five or indeed fifty years ago; but the reason is not lack of opportunity. It is this: Instead of holding a position of independence, between the wealthy and the people, prepared to curb the excesses of either, able lawyers have, to a large extent, allowed themselves to become adjuncts of great corporations and have neglected the obligation to use their powers for the protection of the people. We hear much of the "corporation lawyer," and far too little of the "people's lawyer." The great opportunity of the American Bar is and will be to stand again as it did in the past, ready to protect also the interests of the people....

For nearly a generation the leaders of the Bar have, with few exceptions, not only failed to take part in constructive legislation designed to solve in the public interest our great social, economic and industrial problems; but they have failed likewise to oppose legislation prompted by selfish interests. They have gone further in disregard of common weal. They have often advocated, as lawyers, legislative measures which as citizens they could not approve, and have endeavored to justify themselves by a false analogy. They have erroneously assumed that the role of ethics to be applied to a lawyer's advocacy is the same where he acts for private interests against the public, as it is in litigation between private individuals.

The ethical question which laymen most frequently ask about the legal profession is this: How can a lawyer take a case which he does not believe in? The profession is regarded as necessarily somewhat immoral, because its members are supposed to be habitually taking cases of that character. As a practical matter, the lawyer is not often harassed by this problem; partly because he is apt to believe, at the time, in most of the cases that he actually tries; and partly because he either abandons or settles a large number of those he does not believe in. But the lawyer recognizes that in trying a case his prime duty is to present his side to the tribunal fairly and as well as he can, relying upon his adversary to present the other side fairly and as well as he can. Since the lawyers on the two sides are usually reasonably well matched, the judge or jury may ordinarily be trusted to make a decision as justice demands.

But when lawyers act upon the same principle in supporting the attempts of their private clients to secure or to oppose legislation, a very different condition is presented. . . .

Here, consequently, is the great opportunity in the law. The next generation must witness a continuing and ever-increasing contest between those who have and those who have not. The industrial world is in a state of ferment ... The labor movement must necessarily progress. The people's thought will take shape in action; and it lies with us, with you to whom in part the future belongs, to say on what lines the action is to be expressed; whether it is to be expressed wisely and temperately, or wildly and intemperately; whether it is to be expressed on lines of evolution or on lines of revolution. Nothing can better fit you for taking part in the solution of these problems, than the study and preeminently the practice of law. Those of you who feel drawn to that profession may rest assured that you will find in it an opportunity for usefulness which is probably unequalled. There is a call upon the legal profession to do a great work for this country.

———

Is Brandeis' justification for the special responsibility of lawyers for justice persuasive? Has law school trained you as Brandeis suggests?

Robert W. Gordon, "The Ideal and the Actual in the Law"

In Gerald W. Gawalt, Ed., The New High Priests: Lawyers in Post–Civil War America (1984).[2]

[We can think of lawyers] as having "ideal interests" as well as material ones, and as struggling to work out a relationship between their

---

2.   Copyright © 1984 by Gerald W. Gawalt.

beliefs and their practices—between the ideal and the actual—with which they could live in comfort. Lawyers are perhaps ... double agents. They have obligations to a universal scheme of order, "the law," understood as some fairly coherent system of rules and procedures that are supposed to regulate social life in accordance with prevailing political conceptions of the good.

The law, to put this another way, is an artificial utopia of social harmony, a kind of collectively maintained fantasy of what society would look like if everyone played by the rules. But lawyers are also supposed to be loyal toward and advance the interests of clients pursuing particular ends. The lawyer's job, thus, is to mediate between the universal vision of legal order and the concrete desires of his clients, to show how what the client wants can be accommodated to the utopian scheme. The lawyer, thus, has to find ways of squeezing the client's plan of action into the legally recognized categories of approved conduct. Of course, the law's view of the client's reality is often a highly distorted one, since its categorizing forms are administratively manageable only if they drastically abstract and simplify from that reality, and legitimate only if they seem to be part of the system of universal normative order. Even so, the lawyer's job is selling legitimacy: reassurance to the client and its potential regulators, investors, or business partners that what it wants to do is basically all right; and the lawyer cannot deliver unless she can make plausible arguments rationalizing her client's conduct within the prevailing terms of legal discourse. She must, in short, be able to understand the day-to-day world of the client's transactions and deals as somehow approximating, in however decayed or imperfect a form, the ideal or fantasy world of legal order.

Reform-minded lawyers of 1870 had no trouble perceiving that their world was, from this point of view, in lots of trouble. The articulate ones are most easily described as modified or pragmatic classical liberals, that is, their ideal society was one in which (adult male) individuals were left free to pursue self-interest within a framework of property rights, exchange rules, and public order guaranteed by law—rules of general application, treating individuals as formally equal, and impartially and predictably applied.... Within their ideal scheme of order, all participants had definitely bounded rights and powers—the individual vis-á-vis other individuals and the state, the states vis-á-vis one another and the federal government, the separate branches of government vis-á-vis one another—which it was the role of the judiciary, the natural arbiter of the system as well as a player in it, to enforce.

Yet this scheme had for some years—since the '50s or '60s, depending on whether one blamed the railroads or Reconstruction—been in a process of total breakdown. Liberal lawyers analyzed the breakdown much as other reformers did, except that they were more prone to see it as the result of *legal* failure that was remediable by legal reform. The present evils could be summed up as lack of generality in framing laws, and lack of predictability and impartiality in applying them. Southern black codes, debtor's stay laws, legislation relieving municipalities from contracted bond obligations, handouts of subsidies, exemptions, and privileges to railroad corporations—all had in common the vice of *particularly* favoring or disfavoring special classes of citizens. Impartiality of application had been subverted by patronage appointments or machine-controlled election of corrupt judges or officials. Predictability was undermined by the same factors, as well as by sloppiness in statutory draftsmanship, judicial decision making, and administration of procedural rules, and by the wild variety of law-making jurisdictions.

The lawyers proposed to restore all this unruly mess to the dominion of the rule of law....

[H]igh-minded lawyers were embarked on a practical program of reform. As leaders of the bar, they belonged to a tradition, communicated through endless reiteration in formal speeches, of patrician Whig aspirations to play a distinctive role in American society as a Third Force in politics (in fact the role of "the few" in classical republican theory), mediating between capital and labor, between private acquisitiveness and democratic redistributive follies; thus, they kept looking for social stages on which to enact the role of Tocqueville's lawyer-aristocrats....

———

Lawyers as Aristocracy

Gordon suggests that the leaders of the New York bar of the 1870s faced a conflict between their idealized conception of the law and their role in its administration, on the one hand, and the seamy actuality they confronted in everyday life on the other hand. It seems clear that the same contradictions are confronted by all lawyers, not just those in New York City or a century ago.

Gordon refers to the underlying wish to "enact the role of deTocqueville's lawyer-aristocrats." In this he is referring to deTocqueville's famous observation:

> Men who have made a special study of the laws and have derived therefrom habits of order, something of a taste for formalities, and an instinctive love for a regular concatenation of ideas are naturally strongly opposed to the revolutionary spirit and to the ill-considered passions of democracy.

> Study and specialized knowledge of the law give a man a rank apart in society and makes of lawyers a somewhat privileged intellectual class. The exercise of their profession daily reminds them of this superiority; they are the masters of a necessary and not widely understood science; they serve as arbiters between the citizens.... Add that they naturally form *a body*....

> So, hidden at the bottom of a lawyer's soul one finds the tastes and habits of an aristocracy.[3]

3. Alexis deTocqueville, Democracy in America, P. 11, Ch. 8.

The problem with viewing lawyers or the ideal of the legal profession as aristocratic is that the concept of an especially responsible republican class implies a legitimate social inequality. But social inequality is presumed unjust in America, particularly since such cases as Brown v. Board of Education[4] and Baker v. Carr[5] elevated the concepts of social and political equality to positions of primacy in our constitutional order as that order exists in ideal form.

But the elevation of social and political equality to positions of constitutional primacy delegitimates claims of other groups to special positions of social and moral leadership and the First Amendment renders religious claims to social leadership suspect at the very time it protects the existence of religious groups. By default then, the norms that constitute our common reference points in the debate on social justice are norms supplied by positive law not the ethic of elite groups. The American judiciary's special role in the political order, expressed by the judiciary's expansive power to invalidate legislation as unconstitutional, enhances the role of positive law in the debate on social justice. And our federalist system, which celebrates diversity and decentralized power at the same time that it subordinates local decisions to federal ones within the federal government's legitimate sphere, also acts to transform questions of social justice and legitimate social action into complicated questions of law.

In this diffuse, complex and pluralistic system, lawyers are the caretakers of the law. Although the notion of a group charged with special responsibilities to see justice done inherently contradicts other premises of American society, the very structure of American justice elevates the bar to such a position. The question is whether we are worthy of the task given us and what happens to justice if we are not.

4. 347 U.S. 483 (1954).   5.   369 U.S. 186 (1962).

CHAPTER 12

BECOMING AND BEING A LAWYER

On the one hand ...

But the lawyer is always in a hurry.... The consequence has been, that he has become keen and shrewd; he has learned how to flatter his master in word and indulge him in deed; but his soul is small and unrighteous.... [F]rom the first he has practiced deception and retaliation, and has become stunted and warped [although he thinks of himself as] a master of wisdom.

—*Plato,* Theatetus

There was a society of men among us, bred up from their youth in the art of proving by words multiplied for the purpose, that white is black and black is white, according as they are paid.

—*Jonathan Swift,* Gulliver's Travels

On the other hand ...

When I think then of the law, I see a princess mightier than she who once wrought at Bayeux, eternally weaving into her web dim figures of the ever-lengthening past—figures too dim to be noticed by the idle, too symbolic to be interpreted except by her pupils, but to the discerning eye disclosing every painful step and every world-shaking contest by which mankind has worked and fought its way from savage isolation to organic social life.

—*Oliver Wendell Holmes, Jr.* (in steel letters on marble at the University of California School of Law, Berkeley)

[O]ur profession in its highest walks afforded the best employment in which any man could engage.... To be a priest, and possibly a high priest in the Temple of Justice; to serve at her alter and aid in her administration; to maintain and defend the inalienable rights of life, liberty and property upon which the safety of society depends; to succor the oppressed and defend the innocent; to maintain constitutional rights against all violations, whether executive, by the legislature, by the restless power of the press, or worst of all by the ruthless rapacity of an unbridled majority; to rescue the scapegoat and restore him to his proper place in the world— all this seemed to me to furnish a field worthy of any man's ambition.

—*Joseph H. Choate,* in an address delivered to the Bench and Bar of England, 1905

I have a high opinion of lawyers. With all their faults, they stack up well against those in every other occupation or profession. They are better to work with or play with or fight with or drink with, than most other varieties of mankind.

> —*Harrison Tweed,* accepting the Presidency of the Association of the Bar of the City of New York, 1945

INTRODUCTORY NOTE

This coursebook is about the law and morals of a profession, the practice of law. The law consists of the regulations and common law directly addressing the lawyer's conduct, and the substantive and procedural law that is the material with which the lawyer works and in which her practice is embedded. The moral issues are the questions of right and wrong that are unresolved by the law or which arise because the law, as written or as administered, does not correspond to a sense of justice.

In the course of addressing these problems, the materials herein convey a great deal of information about the practice of law. It is not a systematic presentation, for this is not a coursebook in the demographics, sociology or economics of the legal profession. Nevertheless, the cases report real-life vignettes in the practice of law and yield a composite picture that is fairly accurate. There are cameos of big firm practitioners, small firm and sole practitioners, corporate law department lawyers, lawyers in government practice and prosecutors and defenders. There are men and women, and individuals of various ethnic, religious and geographical backgrounds. Along with the other sources of information that a law student has, informal as well as formal, the whole is a reasonable description of the profession at work.

In very general terms, the professional activity of lawyers is directed primarily at protecting property and claims to property and wielding or seeking to deflect the coercive power of government. That is, law practice is concerned with the use of money and power. Yet the lawyer's relationship to money and power is secondary and mediatory. A lawyer is not an investment banker or a business entrepreneur, although many people trained as lawyers migrate into those lines of work. Nor is a lawyer a public official even though a lawyer is appropriately called, as in the Preamble to the Model Rules of Professional Conduct, "an officer of the legal system." A lawyer provides assistance to those who directly own or manage property and who directly exercise or are subject to political authority. In doing so, a lawyer acts with loyalty to the client, but a loyalty qualified by responsibilities to the legal system.

As Canon 7 of the Code of Professional Responsibility states, "A lawyer should represent a client zealously within the bounds of the law." This seemingly simple axiom reveals the conflicting commitments involved in the practice of law. The practice of law is a continual encounter with such personal conflict.

What are the rewards of practice? Why go through the labor, and bear the opportunity costs, of preparing to practice law? Why pursue it afterwards? There are some obvious answers. Entry into the practice of law is fairly open to people of a wide range of backgrounds and talents, so long as they have relatively high levels of verbal facility, stamina and diligence. Becoming a lawyer does not require a political constituency or extensive capital (other than the willingness to borrow against future earnings). The legal profession can be entered even without social or political connections, although those certainly can help. Work in law practice generally has considerable variety and novelty, and often involves an inside view of fascinating and sometimes bizarre human affairs. It usually requires active use of a person's intelligence. Most kinds of practice involve a relatively high degree of autonomy—freedom from bureaucratic or direct regulatory control—although employment in large organizations is becoming more common. Most practitioners make a decent living, certainly compared to the general population, and many achieve substantial influence in the councils of business, government or politics. Most find repeated satisfactions in using their abilities to help people plan their affairs or extricate themselves from messy situations.

So what are the discontentments in the practice of law, and how do they arise? The following materials seek to frame that problem and to suggest responses.

A. MORALITY OF RHETORIC

The first excerpt, from Gorgias, provides Socrates' moral critique of the lawyers of his day—rhetoricians—and more particularly, his moral challenge to those who practice or teach law. Gorgias was the most famous rhetorician of his age; he practiced and taught. The word "gorgeous" is derived from his name, bearing witness to the beauty and power of his speech.

Plato's Gorgias

Reprinted From the Dialogues of Plato, Translated Into English by B. Jowett.
(D. Appleton and Co.: New York 1898).

Gorgias: Rhetoric, Socrates, is my art.

Socrates: Then I am to call you a rhetorician?

Gor. Yes, Socrates, and a good one too, if you would call me that which, in Homeric language, "I boast to be."

Soc. I should wish to do that.

Gor. Then pray do.

Soc. And are we to say that you make other men rhetoricians?

Gor. Yes, that is exactly what I profess to make them, not only at Athens, but in all places.

Soc. And will you continue to ask and answer questions, Gorgias, as we are at present doing, and reserve for another occasion the longer mode of speech which Polus was attempting? and will you keep your promise, and answer shortly the questions which are asked of you?

Gor. Some answers, Socrates, are of necessity longer; but I will do my best to make them as short as I can; for a part of my profession is that I can be as short as any one.

Soc. That is what is wanted, Gorgias; exhibit the shorter method now, and the longer one at some other time.

Gor. Well, I will; and I am sure that you will commend my brevity of speech as unrivaled.

Soc. Well, then, as you say that you are a rhetorician, and a maker of rhetoricians, what is the business of rhetoric in the sense in which I might say that the business of weaving is making garments—might I not?

Gor. Yes.

Soc. Might I not say, again, that the business of music is the composition of melodies?

Gor. Yes.

Soc. By [the god] Here, Gorgias, I admire the surpassing brevity of your answers.

Gor. Yes, Socrates, and I do think that I am good at that.

Soc. I am glad to hear it; answer me in like manner about rhetoric: what is the business of rhetoric?

Gor. Discourse.

Soc. What sort of discourse, Gorgias?—such discourse as would teach the sick under what treatment they might get well?

Gor. No.

Soc. Then rhetoric does not treat of all kinds of discourse?

Gor. Certainly not.

Soc. And yet rhetoric makes men able to speak?

Gor. Yes.

Soc. And to understand that of which they speak?

Gor. To be sure.

Soc. But does not the art of medicine, which we were just now mentioning, also make men able to understand and speak about the sick?

Gor. Certainly.

Soc. Then medicine also treats of discourse?

Gor. Yes.

Soc. Of discourse concerning diseases?

Gor. Certainly.

Soc. And does not gymnastic also treat of discourse concerning the good or evil condition of the body?

Gor. Very true.

Soc. And the same, Gorgias, is true of the other arts: all of them treat of discourse concerning the subject of which they are the arts.

Gor. That is evident.

Soc. Then why, if you call rhetoric the art which treats of discourse, and all the other arts treat of discourse, do you not call them arts of rhetoric?

Gor. Because, Socrates, the knowledge of the other arts has only to do with some sort of external action, as of the hand; but there is no such action of the hand in rhetoric which operates and in which the effect is produced through the medium of discourse. And therefore I am justified, as I maintain, in saying that rhetoric treats of discourse.

Soc. I do not know whether I perfectly understand you, but I dare say that I shall find out: please to answer me a question; you would allow that there are arts?

Gor. Yes.

Soc. And in some of the arts a great deal is done and nothing or very little said; in painting, or statuary, or many other arts, the work may proceed in silence; and these are the arts with which, as I suppose you would say, rhetoric has no concern?

Gor. You perfectly conceive my meaning, Socrates.

Soc. And there are other arts which work wholly by words, and require either no action or very little, as, for example, the arts of arithmetic, of calculation, of geometry, and of playing draughts; in some of which words are nearly coextensive with things: and in most of them predominate over things, and their whole efficacy and power is given by words: and I take your meaning to be that rhetoric is one of this sort?

Gor. Exactly.

Soc. And yet I do not believe that you really mean to call any of these arts rhetoric; although the precise expression which you used was, that rhetoric is an art of which the effect is produced through the medium of discourse; and an adversary who wished to be captious might take a fancy to say, "And so, Gorgias, you call arithmetic rhetoric." But I do not think that you would call arithmetic rhetoric, any more than you would call geometry rhetoric.

Gor. You are quite right, Socrates, in your apprehension of my meaning.

Soc. Well, then, let me have now the rest of my answer: seeing that rhetoric is one of those arts which works mainly by the use of words, and there are other arts which also use words, tell me what is that quality of words by which the effect of rhetoric is given: I will suppose some one to ask me about any of the arts which I was mentioning just now; he might say, "Socrates, what is arithmetic?" and I should reply to him as you replied to me just now, that arithmetic is one of those arts in which the effect is produced by words. And then he would proceed: "Words about what?" and I should say, Words about odd and even numbers, and how many there are of each.... And suppose, again, I were to say that astronomy works altogether by words—he would ask, "Words about what, Socrates?" and I should answer, that the words of astronomy are about the motions of the stars and sun and moon, and their relative swiftness.

Gor. Very true, Socrates; I admit that.

Soc. And now let us have from you, Gorgias, the truth about rhetoric: which you would admit (would you not?) to be one of those arts which operate and produce all their effects through the medium of words?

Gor. True.

Soc. Tell me, I say, what are the words about? To what class of things do the words which rhetoric uses relate?

Gor. To the greatest, Socrates, and the best of human things.

Soc. That again, Gorgias, is ambiguous; I am still in the dark: for which are the greatest and best of human things? ...

Gor. That, Socrates, which is truly the greatest good, being that which gives men freedom in their own persons, and to rulers the power of ruling over others in their several States.

Soc. And what would you consider this to be?

Gor. I should say the word which persuades the judges in the courts, or the senators in the council, or the citizens in the assembly, or at any other public meeting: if you have the power of uttering this word, you will have the physician your slave, and the trainer your slave, and the money-maker of whom you talk will be found to gather treasures, not for himself, but for you who are able to speak and persuade the multitude.

Soc. Now I think, Gorgias, that you have very accurately explained what you conceive to be the art of rhetoric; and you mean to say, if I am not mistaken, that rhetoric is the artificer of persuasion, having this and no other business, and that this is her crown and end. Do you know any other effect of rhetoric over and above that of producing persuasion?

Gor. No; the definition seems to me very fair, Socrates; for persuasion is the crown of rhetoric.

Soc. Then hear me, Gorgias, for I am quite sure that if there ever was a man who entered on the discussion of a matter from a pure love of knowing the truth, I am one, and I believe that you are another.

Gor. What is coming, Socrates?

Soc. I will tell you: I am very well aware that I do not know what, according to you, is the exact nature, or what are the topics of that persuasion of which you speak, and which is given by rhetoric; although I have a suspicion both about the one and about the other. And I am going to ask—what is this power of persuasion which is given by rhetoric, and about what? But why, if I have a suspicion, do I ask instead of telling you? Not for your sake, but in order that the argument may proceed in such a manner as is most likely to elicit the truth. And I would have you observe, that I am right in asking this further question. If I asked, "What sort of a painter is Zeuxis?" and you said, "the painter of figures," should I not be right in asking, "What sort of figures, and where do you find them?"

Gor. Certainly.

Soc. And the reason for asking this second question would be, that there are other painters as well, who paint many other figures?

Gor. True.

Soc. But if there had been no one but Zeuxis who painted them, then you would have answered very well?

Gor. Certainly.

Soc. Now I want to know about rhetoric in the same way;—is rhetoric the only art which brings persuasion, or do other arts have the same effect? I mean to say this—Does he who teaches anything persuade of what he teaches or not?

Gor. He persuades, Socrates,—there can be no mistake about that.

Soc. Again if we take the arts of which we were just now speaking,—do not arithmetic and the arithmetician teach us the properties of number?

Gor. Certainly.

Soc. And therefore persuade us of them?

Gor. Yes.

Soc. Then arithmetic as well as rhetoric is an artificer of persuasion?

Gor. That is evident.

Soc. And if any one asks us what sort of persuasion, and about what,— we shall answer, of that which teaches the quantity of odd and even; and we shall be in a position to show that all the other arts of which we were just now speaking are artificers of persuasion, and of what kind of persuasion, and about what.

Gor. Very true.

Soc. Then rhetoric is not the only artificer of persuasion?

Gor. True.

Soc. Seeing, then, that not only rhetoric works by persuasion, but that other arts do the same, as in the case of the painter, a question has arisen which is a very fair one: Of what persuasion is rhetoric the artificer, and about what? is not that a fair way of putting the question?

Gor. I think that is.

Soc. Then, if you approve the question, Gorgias, what is the answer?

Gor. I answer, Socrates, that rhetoric is the art of persuasion in the courts and other assemblies, as I was just now saying, and about the just and unjust.

Soc. And that, Gorgias, was what I was suspecting to be your notion; yet I would not have you wonder if by and by I am found repeating a seemingly plain question; for as I was saying, I ask not for your sake, but in order that the argument may proceed consecutively, and that we may not get the habit of anticipating and suspecting the meaning of one another's words, and that you may proceed in your own way.

Gor. I think that you are quite right, Socrates.

Soc. Then let me raise this question; you would say that there is such a thing as "having learned"?

Gor. Yes.

Soc. And there is also "having believed"?

Gor. Yes.

Soc. And are the "having learned" and the "having believed," and are learning and belief the same things?

Gor. In my judgment, Socrates, they are not the same.

Soc. And your judgment is right, as you may ascertain in this way: If a person were to say to you, "Is there, Gorgias, a false belief as well as a true?" you would reply, if I am not mistaken, that there is.

Gor. Yes.

Soc. Well, but is there a false knowledge as well as a true?

Gor. No.

Soc. No, indeed; and this again proves that knowledge and belief differ.

Gor. That is true.

Soc. And yet those who have learned as well as those who have believed are persuaded?

Gor. That is as you say.

Soc. Shall we then assume two sorts of persuasion,—one which is the source of belief without knowledge, as the other is of knowledge?

Gor. By all means.

Soc. And which sort of persuasion does rhetoric create in courts of law and other assemblies about the just and unjust, the sort of persuasion which gives belief without knowledge, or that which gives knowledge?

Gor. Clearly, Socrates, that which only gives belief.

Soc. Then rhetoric, as would appear, is the artificer of a persuasion which creates belief about the just and unjust, but gives no instruction about them?

Gor. True.

Soc. And the rhetorician does not instruct the courts of law or other assemblies about just and unjust, but he only creates belief about them; for no one can be supposed to instruct such a vast multitude about such high matters in a short time?

Gor. Certainly not.

Soc. Come, then, and let us see what we really mean about rhetoric; for I do not know what my own meaning is as yet. When the assembly meets to elect a physician or a shipwright or any other craftsman, will the rhetorician be taken into counsel? Surely not. For at every election he ought to be chosen who has the greatest skill; and, again, when walls have to be built or harbors or docks to be constructed, not the rhetorician but the master workman will advise; or when generals have to be chosen and an order of battle arranged, or a position taken, then the military will advise and not the rhetoricians: would you admit that, Gorgias? As you profess to be a rhetorician and a maker of rhetoricians, I shall do well to learn the nature of your art from you. And here let me assure you that I have your interest in view as well as my own. For I dare say that some one or other of the young men present might like to become your pupil, and in fact I see some, and a good many too, who have this wish, but they would be too modest to question you. And therefore when you are interrogated by me, I would have you imagine that you are interrogated by them. "What is the use of coming to you, Gorgias?" they will say; "about what will you teach us to advise the State? about the just and unjust only, or about those other things also which Socrates has just mentioned?" How will you answer them?

Gor. I like your way of leading us on, Socrates, and I will endeavor to reveal to you the whole nature of rhetoric. You must have heard, I think, that the docks and the walls of the Athenians and the plan of the harbor were devised in accordance with the counsels, partly of Themistocles, and partly of Pericles, and not at the suggestion of the builders.

Soc. Certainly, Gorgias, that is what is told of Themistocles, and I myself heard the speech of Pericles when he advised us about the middle wall.

Gor. And you will observe, Socrates, that when a decision has to be given in such matters the rhetoricians are the advisers; they are the men who win their point.

Soc. I had that in my admiring mind, Gorgias, when I asked what is the nature of rhetoric, which always appears to me, when I look at the matter in this way, to be a marvel of greatness.

Gor. A marvel indeed, Socrates, if you only knew how rhetoric comprehends and holds under her sway all the inferior arts. And I will give you a striking example of this. On several occasions I have been with my brother Herodicus or some other physician to see one of his patients, who would not allow the physician to give him medicine, or apply the knife or hot iron to him; and I have persuaded him to do for me what he would not do for the physician just by the use of rhetoric. And I say that if a rhetorician and a physician were to go to any city, and there had to argue in the Ecclesia or any other assembly as to which should be elected, the physician would have no chance; but he who could speak would be chosen if he wished, and in a contest with a man of any other profession the rhetorician more than any one would have the power of getting himself chosen, for he can speak more persuasively to the multitude than any of them, and on any subject. Such is the power and quality of rhetoric, Socrates. And yet rhetoric ought to be used like any other competitive art, not against everybody,—the rhetorician ought not to abuse his strength any more than a pugilist or pancratiast or other master of fence; because he has powers which are more than a match either for enemy or friend, he ought not therefore to strike, stab, or slay his friends. And suppose a man who has been the pupil of a palestra and is a skillful boxer, and in the fulness of his strength he goes and strikes his father or mother or one of his familiars or friends, that is no reason why the trainer or master of fence should be held in detestation or banished,— surely not. For they taught this art for a good purpose, as an art to be used against enemies and evil-doers, in self-defense, not in aggression, and others have perverted their instructions, making a bad use of their strength and their skill. But not on this account are the teachers bad, neither is the art in fault or bad in itself; I should rather say that those who make a bad use of the art are to blame. And the same holds good of rhetoric; for the rhetorician can speak against all men and on any subject, and in general he can persuade the multitude of anything better than any other man, but he ought not on that account to defraud the physician or any other artist of his reputation merely because he has the power; he ought to use rhetoric fairly, as he would also use his combative powers. And if after having become a rhetorician he makes a bad use of his strength and skill, his instructor surely ought not on that account to be held in detestation or banished. For he was intended by his teacher to make a good use of his instructions, and he abuses them. And therefore he is the person who ought to be held in detestation, banished, and put to death, and not his instructor.

Soc. You, Gorgias, like myself, have had great experience of arguments, and you must have observed, I think, that they do not always terminate to the satisfaction or mutual improvement of the disputants; but disagreements are apt to arise, and one party will often deny that the other has spoken truly or clearly; and then they leave off arguing and begin to quarrel, both parties fancying that their opponents are only speaking from personal feeling. And sometimes they will go on abusing one another until the company at last are quite annoyed at their own condescension in listening to such fellows. Why do I say this? Why, because I cannot help feeling that you are now saying what is not quite consistent or accordant with what you were saying at first about rhetoric. And I am afraid to point this out to you, lest you should think that I have some animosity against you, and that I speak, not for the sake of discovering the truth, but from personal feeling. Now if you are one of my sort, I should like to cross-examine you, but if not I will let you alone. And what is my sort? you will ask. I am one of those who are very willing to be refuted if I say anything which is not true, and very willing to refute any one else who says what is not true, and just as ready to be refuted as to refute; for I hold that this is the greater gain of the two, just as the gain is greater of being cured of a very great evil than of curing the evil in another. For I imagine that there is no evil which a man can endure so great as an erroneous opinion about the matters of which we are speaking; and if you claim to be one of my sort, let us have the discussion out, but if you would rather have done, no matter; let us make an end.

Gor. I should say, Socrates, that I am quite the man whom you indicate; but, perhaps, we ought to consider the audience, for, before you came, I had already given a long exhibition, and if we proceed the argument may run on to a great length. And therefore I think that we should consider whether we may not be detaining some part of the company when they are wanting to do something else.

Chaerephon: You hear the audience cheering, Gorgias and Socrates, which shows their desire to listen to you, and for myself, Heaven forbid that I should have any business which would take me away from so important and interesting a discussion.

Soc. I may truly say ... that I am willing, if Gorgias is.

Gor. After this, Socrates, I should be disgraced if I refused, especially as I have professed to answer all comers; in accordance with the wishes of the company, then, do you begin, and ask of me any question which you like.

Soc. Let me tell you then, Gorgias, what makes me wonder at your words; though I dare say that you may be right, and I may have mistaken your meaning. You say that you can make any man, who will learn of you, a rhetorician?

Gor. Yes.

Soc. Do you mean that you will teach him to gain the ears of the multitude on any subject, and this not by instruction but by persuasion?

Gor. Certainly.

Soc. You were saying, in fact, that the rhetorician will have greater powers of persuasion than the physician, even in a matter of health?

Gor. Yes, with the multitude,—that is.

Soc. That is to say, greater with the ignorant; for with those who know, he cannot be supposed to have greater powers of persuasion than the physician has.

Gor. Very true.

Soc. And if he is to have more power of persuasion than the physician, he will have greater power than he who knows?

Gor. Certainly.

Soc. Though he is not a physician,—is he?

Gor. No.

Soc. And he who is not a physician is obviously ignorant of what the physician knows?

Gor. That is evident.

Soc. Then, when the rhetorician is more persuasive than the physician, the ignorant is more persuasive with the ignorant than he who has knowledge? is not that the inference?

Gor. In the case which is supposed, yes.

Soc. And the same holds of the relation of rhetoric to all the other arts; the rhetorician need not know the whole truth about them; he has only to discover some way of persuading the ignorant that he has more knowledge than those who know?

Gor. Yes, Socrates, and is not this a great blessing?—not to have learned the other arts, but the art of rhetoric only, and yet to be in no way inferior to the professors of them?

Soc. Whether the rhetorician is or is not inferior on this account is a question which we will hereafter examine if the inquiry is likely to be of any service to us; but I would rather begin by asking, whether he is as ignorant of the just and unjust, base and honorable, good and evil, as he is of medicine and the other arts; I mean to say, does he know anything actually of what is good and evil, base or honorable, just or unjust in them; or has he only a way with the ignorant of persuading them that he not knowing is to be esteemed to know more than another who knows? Or must the pupil know and come to you knowing these things before he can acquire the art of rhetoric? And if he is ignorant, you who are the teacher of rhetoric will not teach him, for that is not your business, but you will make him seem to know them to the multitude, when he does not know them; and seem to be a good man, when he is not. Or will you be wholly unable to teach him rhetoric unless he knows the truth of these things first? What is to be said, Gorgias, about all this? I swear that I wish you would, as you were saying, reveal to me the power of rhetoric.

Gor. Well, Socrates, I suppose that if the pupil does chance not to know them, he will have to learn of me these things as well.

Soc. Say no more, for there you are right; and so he whom you make a rhetorician must know the nature of the just and unjust, either of his own previous knowledge, or he must be taught by you.

Gor. Certainly.

Soc. Well, and is not he who has learned carpentering a carpenter?

Gor. Yes.

Soc. And he who has learned music a musician?

Gor. Yes.

Soc. And he who has learned medicine is a physician, in like manner. He who has learned anything whatever is that which his knowledge makes him.

Gor. Certainly.

Soc. And in the same way, he who has learned what is just is just?

Gor. To be sure.

Soc. And he who is just may be supposed to do what is just?

Gor. Yes.

Soc. And must not the rhetorician be just, and is not the just man desirous to do what is just?

Gor. That is clearly the inference.

Soc. Then the just man will surely never be willing to do injustice?

Gor. That is certain.

Soc. And according to the argument the rhetorician ought to be a just man?

Gor. Yes.

Soc. And will therefore never be willing to do injustice?

Gor. Clearly not.

Soc. But do you remember saying just now that the trainer is not to be accused or banished if the pugilist makes a wrong use of his pugilistic art; and in like manner, if the rhetorician makes a bad and unjust use of his rhetoric, that is not to be laid to the charge of his instructor, neither is he to be banished, but the wrong-doer himself who made a bad use of his rhetoric is to be banished—was not that said?

Gor. Yes, that was said.

Soc. And now it turns out that this same rhetorician can never have done any injustice.

Gor. True.

Soc. And at the very outset, Gorgias, there was an assertion made, that rhetoric treated of discourse, not about odd and even, but about just and unjust. Is not that true?

Gor. Yes.

Soc. And I thought at the time, when I heard you saying this, that rhetoric, which is always discoursing about justice, could not possibly be an unjust thing. But when you said, shortly afterwards, that the rhetorician might make a bad use of rhetoric, I noted with surprise the inconsistency into which you had fallen; and I said, that if you thought, as I did, that there was a gain in being refuted, there would be an advantage in discussing the question, but if not, I would leave off. And in the course of our examination, as you will see yourself, the rhetorician has been acknowledged to be incapable of making an unjust use of rhetoric, or of unwillingness to do injustice. By the dog, Gorgias, there will be a great deal of discussion, before we get at the truth of all this.

Polus : And do you, Socrates, seriously incline to believe what you are now saying about rhetoric? What! because Gorgias was ashamed to deny that the rhetorician knew the just and the honorable and the good, and that he could teach them to any one who came to him ignorant of them, and then out of the admission there may have arisen a contradiction; you, as you always do, having recourse to your favorite mode of interrogation. For do you suppose that any one will ever say that he does not know, or cannot teach, the nature of justice? The truth is, that there is great want of manners in bringing the argument to such a pass.

Soc. Illustrious Polus, the great reason why we provide ourselves with friends and children is that when we get old and stumble a younger generation may be at hand, and set us on our legs again in our words and in our actions; and now, if I and Gorgias are stumbling, there are you a present help to us, as you ought to be; and I for my part engage to retract any error into which you may think that I have fallen—upon one condition.

Pol. What is that?

Soc. That you contract, Polus, the prolixity of speech in which you indulged at first.

Pol. What! Do you mean that I am not to use as many words as I please?

Soc. Only to think, my friend, that having come on a visit to Athens, which is the most free-spoken State in Hellas, you of all men should be deprived of the power of speech—that is hard indeed. But then look at my case: should not I be very hardly used if, when you are making a long oration and refusing to answer what you are asked, I may not go away, but am compelled to stay and listen to you? I say rather, that if you have a real interest in the argument, or, to repeat my former expression, have any desire to set me on my legs, take back again anything which you please; and in your turn ask and answer, like myself and Gorgias—refute and be refuted: for I suppose that you would claim to know what Gorgias knows?

Pol. Yes.

Soc. And you, like him, invite any one to ask you about anything which he likes, and you will know how to answer him?

Pol. To be sure.

Soc. And now, which will you do, ask or answer?

Pol. I will ask; and do you answer me, Socrates, the same question which Gorgias, as you suppose, is unable to answer: What is rhetoric?

Soc. Do you mean what sort of an art?

Pol. Yes.

Soc. Not an art at all, in my opinion, if I am to tell you the truth, Polus.

Pol. Then what, in your opinion, is rhetoric?

. . .

Soc. I should say a sort of routine or experience.

Pol. Then does rhetoric seem to you to be a sort of experience?

Soc. That is my view, if that is yours.

Pol. An experience of what?

Soc. An experience of making a sort of delight and gratification.

Pol. And if able to gratify others, must not rhetoric be a fine thing?

Soc. What are you saying, Polus? Why do you ask me whether rhetoric is a fine thing or not, when I have not as yet told you what rhetoric is?

Pol. Why, did you not tell me that rhetoric was a sort of experience?

Soc. As you are so fond of gratifying others, will you gratify me in a small particular?

Pol. I will.

Soc. Will you ask me what sort of an art is cookery?

Pol. What sort of an art is cookery?

Soc. Not an art at all, Polus.

Pol. What then?

Soc. I should say a sort of experience.

Pol. Of what? I wish that you would tell me.

Soc. An experience of making a sort of delight and gratification, Polus.

Pol. Then are cookery and rhetoric the same?

Soc. No, they are only different parts of the same profession.

Pol. And what is that?

Soc. I am afraid that the truth may seem discourteous; I should not like Gorgias to imagine that I am ridiculing his profession, and therefore I hesitate to answer. For whether or no this is that art of rhetoric which Gorgias practises I really do not know: from what he was just now saying, nothing appeared of what he thought of his art, but the rhetoric which I mean is a part of a not very creditable whole.

Gor. A part of what, Socrates? Say what you mean, and never mind me.

Soc. To me then, Gorgias, the whole of which rhetoric is a part appears to be a process, not of art, but the habit of a bold and ready wit, which knows how to behave to the world: this I sum up under the word "flattery"; and this habit or process appears to me to have many other parts, one of which is cookery, which may seem to be an art, and, as I maintain, is not an art, but only experience and routine: another part is rhetoric, ... And Polus may ask, if he likes, for he has not as yet been informed, what part of flattery is rhetoric: he did not see that I had not yet answered him when he proceeded to ask a further question,—Whether I do not think rhetoric a fine thing? But I shall not tell him whether rhetoric is a fine thing or not, until I have first answered, "What is rhetoric?" For that would not be right, Polus; but I shall be happy to answer, if you will ask me, What part of flattery is rhetoric?

Pol. I will ask, and do you answer: What part of flattery is rhetoric?

Soc. Will you understand my answer? Rhetoric, according to my view, is the shadow of a part of politics.

Pol. And noble or ignoble?

Soc. Ignoble, as I should say, if I am compelled to answer, for I call what is bad ignoble,—though I doubt whether you understand what I was saying before.

Gor. Indeed, Socrates, I cannot say that I understand myself.

Soc. I do not wonder at that; for I have not as yet explained myself, and our friend Polus, like a young colt as he is, is apt to run away.

Gor. Never mind him, but explain to me what you mean by saying that rhetoric is the shadow of a part of politics.

Soc. I will try, then, to explain my notion of rhetoric, and if I am mistaken, my friend Polus shall refute me. Are there not bodies and souls?

Gor. There are.

Soc. And you would further admit that there is a good condition of either of them?

Gor. Yes.

Soc. Which condition may not be really good, but good only in appearance? I mean to say, that there are many persons who appear to be in good health, and whom only a physician or trainer will discern at first sight not to be in good health.

Gor. True.

Soc. And this applies not only to the body, but also to the soul: in either there may be that which gives the appearance of health and not the reality?

Gor. Yes, certainly.

Soc. And now I will endeavor to explain to you more clearly what I mean: the soul and body being two, have two arts corresponding to them: there is the art of politics attending on the soul; and another art attending on the body, of which I know no specific name, but which may be described as having two divisions, one of which is gymnastic, and the other medicine. And in politics there is a legislative part, which answers to gymnastic, as justice does to medicine; and they run into one another, justice having to do with the same subject as legislation, and medicine with the same subject as gymnastic, yet there is a difference between them. Now, seeing that there are these four arts which are ever ministering to the body and the soul for their highest good, flattery, knowing or rather guessing their natures, has distributed herself into four shams or simulations of them; she puts on the likeness of one or other of them, and pretends to be that which she simulates, and has no regard for men's highest interests, but is ever making pleasure the bait of the unwary, and deceiving them into the belief that she is of the highest value to them. Cookery simulates the disguise of medicine, and pretends to know what food is the best for the body; and if the physician and the cook had to enter into a competition in which children were the judges, or men who had no more sense than children, as to which of them best understands the goodness or badness of food, the physician would be starved to death. A flattery I deem this and an ignoble sort of thing, Polus, for to you I am now addressing myself, because it aims at pleasure instead of good. And I do not call this an art at all, but only an experience or routine, because it is unable to explain or to give a reason of the nature of its own applications. And I do not call any irrational thing an art; if you dispute my words, I am prepared to argue in defense of them.

Cookery, then, as I maintain, is the flattery which takes the form of medicine, and the art of tiring [cosmetics], in like manner, takes the form of gymnastic, and is a knavish, false, ignoble, and illiberal art, working deceitfully by the help of lines, and colors, and enamels, and garments, and making men affect a spurious beauty to the neglect of the true beauty which is given by gymnastic.

I would rather not be tedious, and therefore I will only say, after the manner of the geometricians (for I think that by this time you will be able to follow),

As the art of tiring : gymnastic :: cookery : medicine; or rather—

As tiring : gymnastic :: sophistry : legislation; and—

As cookery : medicine :: rhetoric : justice.

And this, I say, is the natural difference between them, but by reason of their near connection, the sphere and subject of the rhetorician is apt to be confounded with that of the sophist; neither do they know what to make of themselves, nor do other men know what to make of them. For if the body presided over itself, and were not under the guidance of the soul, and the soul did not discern and discriminate between cookery and medicine, but the body was made the judge of them and the rule of judgment was the bodily delight which was given by them, then the word of Anaxagoras, that word with which you, friend Polus, are so well acquainted, would come true: chaos would return, and cookery, health, and medicine would mingle in an indiscernible mass. And now I have told you my notion of rhetoric, which is in relation to the soul what cookery is to the body. I may have been inconsistent in making a long speech, when I would not allow you to discourse at length. But I think that I may be excused, as you did not understand me, and could make no use of my shorter answer, and I had to enter into an explanation. And if I show an equal inability to make use of yours, I hope that you will speak at equal length; but if I am able to understand you, let me have the benefit of your brevity, for this is only fair; and now this answer of mine is much at your service.

Pol. What do you mean? Do you think that rhetoric is flattery?

Soc. Nay, I said a part of flattery; if at your age, Polus, you cannot remember, what will you do by and by, when you get older?

Pol. And are the good rhetoricians meanly regarded in States, under the idea that they are flatterers?

Soc. Is that a question or the beginning of a speech?

Pol. I am asking a question.

Soc. Then my answer is, that they are not regarded at all.

Pol. How not regarded? Have they not very great power in States?

Soc. Not if you mean to say that power is a good to the possessor.

Pol. And I do mean to say that.

Soc. Then, in that case, I think that they have the least power of all the citizens . . . .

. . .

Soc. Well then, I say to you that here are two questions in one, and I will answer both of them. And I tell you, Polus, that rhetoricians and tyrants have the least possible power in States, as I was just now saying; for they do nothing, as I may say, of what they will, but only what they think best.

Pol. And is not that a great power?

Soc. Polus has already denied that.

Pol. Denied? Nay, that is what I affirm.

Soc. By the—what do you call him?—not you, for you say that great power is a good to him who has the power.

Pol. I do.

Soc. And would you maintain that if a fool does what appears best to him he does what is good, and would you call this great power.

Pol. I do not say that.

Soc. Then you must prove that the rhetorician is not a fool, and that rhetoric is an art and not a flattery,—that is the way to refute me; but if you leave me unrefuted, then the rhetoricians who do what they think best in States, and the tyrants, will be deprived of this power: for you assume that power is a good thing, and yet admit that the power which is exercised without understanding is an evil.

———

QUESTIONS

How do the tone and "rules" of the dialogue as conducted by Socrates differ from the "Socratic method" used in law school? What values are implicit in Socrates' style? In the "Socratic method"?

Gorgias concedes that if a student does not know the right and wrong of those things upon which he will argue, it is the law professor's responsibility to teach the student this. Do you agree?[1]

Is the practice of law a "routine" or "experience" as Socrates called "rhetoric"? Does Socrates' critique apply only to lawyers acting as advocates and not to counseling or other lawyer roles?

What arguments in defense of a lawyer's role would a modern lawyer make that Gorgias did not? James Boyd White has attempted to answer this question. White's dialogue features two American lawyers, Euerges and Euphemes, "successful attorneys in a firm with a diverse general practice," who seek to defend their lives and endeavors in a conversation with Socrates.[2]

White's Euerges argues that the lawyer's function is to advise people about their legal rights and duties, and to represent clients' interests or desires, by increasing their power, range of choices, liberty and wealth. A course of action is chosen only after a detailed consultation with clients, viewed as responsible and intelligent actors, concerning their needs and wants. In response to the charges equating lawyers with prostitutes, Euerges claims that a lawyer's work is part of an overarching system whose overall aim is justice. A lawyer serves justice by playing his part in such a system which, despite its imperfections, experience has shown to be the best. This is shown by the progress that our law has made over time, and by the ethical constraints and circumscribing rules of law that have evolved to control attorneys' misrepresentations. In appealing to a judge, the lawyer may use only the techniques of persuasion permitted by the system. This excludes, for example, appeals to bigotry. Finally, traditional legal procedures originate in a democratic form of government, founded with the people's consent, and thus are the most just. In sum, White's Euerges justifies the lawyer's role and function in a manner similar to that of the organized profession.[3]

White's Euphemes, on the other hand, justifies the modern lawyer's activity on a different basis. Euphemes, after rejecting the "idealistic" justifications of Euerges, claims instead that the practice of law specifically and uniquely enables one to attain the difficult-to-reach goal of becoming "trustworthy".[4] The most important factor in attaining such a character is

1. For contemporary discussion of the propriety or obligation of a law teacher addressing issues of "right and wrong," see Symposium, Beyond the Ordinary Religion, 37 J.Legal Educ. 509 (1987) (articles by Roger C. Cramton, Katherine T. Bartlett, James R. Elkins, Peter M. Shane and James Boyd White).

2. James Boyd White, The Ethics of Argument: Plato's *Gorgias* and the Modern Lawyer, in White, Heracles' Bow, c. 10 (1985), reprinting in modified form the ar-

ticle of the same title in 50 U.Chi.L.Rev. 849 (1983).

3. See the discussion of the views of Charles Fried, David Luban and Richard Wasserstrom on role morality and the "adversary system excuse" in Chapter 2.

4. Brandeis in his essay, The Opportunity in the Law, excerpted in Chapter 11 at p. 1160, also argues that everyday law practice cultivates judgment and virtue. For another contemporary argument to this ef-

the "ethical community that one establishes both with one's clients and with other lawyers and judges."[5] The function of lawyers in the community is to preserve and improve a language of description, value and reason—a culture of argument—without which it would be impossible even to ask the important questions, such as those about the nature of justice.[6]

In its practical application, a concept like that of justice is not ideal or universal, but rather culturally conditioned. Concepts concerning justice are the tools or materials lawyers use to "maintain the materials essential to these cultural activities and the conventions and understandings that make them possible." Cultural continuity requires a stable language, procedures to regulate it and a vocabulary of shared cultural norms, values and expectations. New facts and circumstances constantly test and reshape this language. Lawyers are essential participants in the cultural discourse and framework by which law is made and remade. Lawyers preserve and refurbish the law itself as "a way in which the community defines itself, not once and for all, but over and over, and in the process educates itself about its own character and the nature of the world."[7]

Euphemes then discusses the ethical dimensions of this approach to lawyering. The alleged "insincerity" of an advocate's assertions in the dynamic process described above is irrelevant because it is transparent; it deceives no one. It is but a small, recognized aspect of a formalized procedure that plays only a part in reaching the overall goal—well-known to the decision-maker—of achieving a lawful result. A given attorney's "best" argument does not reflect justice in the abstract, but rather the means that the culture allows one to use in attempting to reach a just result. In so doing, the lawyers also instruct the judge concerning the nature of the case and the scope of disagreement. The "trustworthy" lawyer is one who does this honestly and intelligently, and whose standards of argument are heightened by being addressed to an "ideal" judge. Such an approach justifies the activity of being a lawyer in any community, just or unjust, since it entails making the best case the materials of the culture will allow. Of course, no one can know whether the lawyer's arguments or her conception of the "ideal" judge are "best", but the important thing is to know how to approach these questions, and how to strive for the best possible use of cultural materials.

If, however, a culture appears so repugnant as to warrant its destruction, one must first evaluate "the materials for argument that the culture makes available."[8] Would it be possible to appeal to its "better" side? Is any improvement possible? Here Euphemes affirms the role of ideals, the values of equality and reason that make up the rule of law. How should one evaluate ideals? Certain basic standards exist, but in the case of more complicated issues the question is rather how best to engage in dialogue on such unresolved questions. To preserve this dialogue's useful character for

---

fect, see Anthony T. Kronman, Living in the Law, 54 U.Chi.L.Rev. 835 (1987).

5. Id. at 232.

6. Id. at 223.

7. Id. at 235.

8. Id. at 232.

others, one must encourage an interplay between a realistic and an idealistic language: the latter alone may be impractical and useless, whereas the former alone may devolve into a cynical instrumentalism.

Thus, one of the lawyer's functions is to preserve the tension between the two poles of realism and idealism. The language of the law must reflect both "factual congruence with reality" and the "element of aspiration"; and the lawyer must use these tools to "convert and translate" the facts of human experience into arguments about justice. A lawyer always remains an advocate during this process, but the "trustworthy" lawyer spells out to his client, implicitly or explicitly, the limits of his advocacy. The lawyer's credibility, and thus his effectiveness before the judge, actually depends upon such self-restraint. In sum, her duty is to present, and thus become, a "trustworthy" character, the very opposite of Socrates' amoral rhetorician. The uniquely equivocal situations that an attorney encounters offer her a unique opportunity to develop her character; such a career then becomes "not a life 'worthy of no one,' but a life worthy of anyone."[9]

Are White's arguments more persuasive to the modern lawyer than those offered in Plato's dialogue?

B.   FORMATIVE INFLUENCE OF LEGAL INSTITUTIONS

Erving Goffman's project in Asylums was the examination of "total institutions," e.g., prisons, monasteries and mental hospitals. The institutions in which lawyers train and work are not "total." Law schools, which come closest to his model, allow "inmates" to interact more or less freely with the outside world. Law firms, corporations and government bureaucracies are all further along the spectrum, controlling the lives of "inmates" and "staff" by less obvious, although not necessarily less effective, means. Finally, the court system is obviously not a "total" institution. Although some of its participants, judges and court personnel, are more or less "fixed" participants, parties and jurors are transitory actors; many lawyers and some parties are repeat players. There are, however, two factors that make the connection between courts and total institutions closer than it might appear at first. One, the power of courts, in civil and criminal matters, is dependent on their ability to transform people into inmates of total institutions. The power of law in the end *is* the power of total institutions. The court system may therefore be seen as the portal to society's involuntary total institutions. Second, courts, while ostensibly "open" to the public, are not open in the sense that Grand Central Station is open. The court wields enormous power on all within its domain: lawyers, litigants, jurors and even spectators to a lesser degree are expected to play by special rules and act in accordance with roles not appropriate in other settings.[10]

9. Id. at 237.

10. See the materials in Chapter 11 discussing the contempt charges against lawyers

Despite the sometimes striking parallels between legal institutions and total institutions, it is important to remember two important distinctions. First, "inmates" in legal institutions retain active membership in other "institutions" or communities—families, ethnic and religious groups, community-organizations, political parties and the like—which serve as continuing sources of traditions, norms and commitments that provide grounds by which the individual may critique, resist and revise the institutions of law. Second, an "inmate" in a law school or law firm, unlike one in a prison or asylum, can always choose to leave.

Erving Goffman, Asylums

Pp. 3–18, 44–45, 60–65, 99 (1961).[11]

INTRODUCTION

I

Social establishments—institutions in the everyday sense of that term—are places such as rooms, suites of rooms, buildings, or plants in which activity of a particular kind regularly goes on. In sociology we do not have a very apt way of classifying them. Some establishments, like Grand Central Station, are open to anyone who is decently behaved; others, like the Union League Club of New York or the laboratories at Los Alamos, are felt to be somewhat snippy about who is let in. Some, like shops and post offices, have a few fixed members who provide a service and a continuous flow of members who receive it. Others, like homes and factories, involve a less changing set of participants.... In this book another category of institutions is singled out and claimed as a natural and fruitful one because its members appear to have so much in common—so much, in fact, that to learn about one of these institutions we would be well advised to look at the others.

II

Every institution captures something of the time and interest of its members and provides something of a world for them; in brief, every institution has encompassing tendencies. When we review the different institutions in our Western society, we find some that are encompassing to a degree discontinuously greater than the ones next in line. Their encompassing or total character is symbolized by the barrier to social intercourse with the outside and to departure that is often built right into the physical plant, such as locked doors, high walls, barbed wire, cliffs, water, forests, or moors. These establishments I am calling *total institutions,* and it is their general characteristics I want to explore.

The total institutions of our society can be listed in five rough groupings. First, there are institutions established to care for persons felt to be

and defendants in the Chicago conspiracy trial and the note on courtroom decorum, pp. 1067, 1075 supra.

11. Copyright © 1961 by Erving Goffman.

both incapable and harmless; these are the homes for the blind, the aged, the orphaned, and the indigent. Second, there are places established to care for persons felt to be both incapable of looking after themselves and a threat to the community, albeit an unintended one: TB sanitaria, mental hospitals, and leprosaria. A third type of total institution is organized to protect the community against what are felt to be intentional dangers to it, with the welfare of the persons thus sequestered not the immediate issue: jails, penitentiaries, P.O.W. camps, and concentration camps. Fourth, there are institutions purportedly established the better to pursue some work-like task and justifying themselves only on these instrumental grounds: army barracks, ships, boarding schools, work camps, colonial compounds, and large mansions from the point of view of those who live in the servants' quarters. Finally, there are those establishments designed as retreats from the world even while often serving also as training stations for the religious; examples are abbeys, monasteries, convents, and other cloisters. . . .

Before I attempt to extract a general profile from this list of establishments, I would like to mention one conceptual problem: none of the elements I will describe seems peculiar to total institutions, and none seems to be shared by every one of them; what is distinctive about total institutions is that each exhibits to an intense degree many items in this family of attributes. In speaking of "common characteristics," I will be using this phrase in a way that is restricted but I think logically defensible. At the same time this permits using the method of ideal types, establishing common features with the hope of highlighting significant differences later.

III

A basic social arrangement in modern society is that the individual tends to sleep, play, and work in different places, with different co-participants, under different authorities, and without an over-all rational plan. The central feature of total institutions can be described as a breakdown of the barriers ordinarily separating these three spheres of life. First, all aspects of life are conducted in the same place and under the same single authority. Second, each phase of the member's daily activity is carried on in the immediate company of a large batch of others, all of whom are treated alike and required to do the same thing together. Third, all phases of the day's activities are tightly scheduled, with one activity leading at a prearranged time into the next, the whole sequence of activities being imposed from above by a system of explicit formal rulings and a body of officials. Finally, the various enforced activities are brought together into a single rational plan purportedly designed to fulfill the official aims of the institution.

Individually, these features are found in places other than total institutions. For example, our large commercial, industrial, and educational establishments are increasingly providing cafeterias and free-time recreation for their members; use of these extended facilities remains voluntary in many particulars, however, and special care is taken to see that the ordinary line of authority does not extend to them. Similarly, housewives or farm families may have all their major spheres of life within the same fenced-in area, but these persons are not collectively regimented and do not march through the day's activities in the immediate company of a batch of similar others.

The handling of many human needs by the bureaucratic organization of whole blocks of people—whether or not this is a necessary or effective means of social organization in the circumstances—is the key fact of total institutions. From this follow certain important implications.

When persons are moved in blocks, they can be supervised by personnel whose chief activity is not guidance or periodic inspection (as in many employer-employee relations) but rather surveillance—a seeing to it that everyone does what he has been clearly told is required of him, under conditions where one person's infraction is likely to stand out in relief against the visible, constantly examined compliance of the others. Which comes first, the large blocks of managed people, or the small supervisory staff, is not here at issue; the point is that each is made for the other.

In total institutions there is a basic split between a large managed group, conveniently called inmates, and a small supervisory staff. Inmates typically live in the institution and have restricted contact with the world outside the walls; staff often operate on an eight-hour day and are socially integrated into the outside world. Each grouping tends to conceive of the other in terms of narrow hostile stereotypes, staff often seeing inmates as bitter, secretive, and untrustworthy, while inmates often see staff as condescending, highhanded, and mean. Staff tends to feel superior and righteous; inmates tend, in some ways at least, to feel inferior, weak, blameworthy, and guilty.

Social mobility between the two strata is grossly restricted; social distance is typically great and often formally prescribed. Even talk across the boundaries may be conducted in a special tone of voice ... Although some communication between inmates and the staff guarding them is necessary, one of the guard's functions is the control of communication from inmates to higher staff levels ... Just as talk across the boundary is restricted, so, too, is the passage of information, especially information about the staff's plans for inmates. Characteristically, the inmate is excluded from knowledge of the decisions taken regarding his fate. Whether the official grounds are military, as in concealing travel destination from enlisted men, or medical, as in concealing diagnosis, plan of treatment, and approximate length of stay from tuberculosis patients, such exclusion gives staff a special basis of distance from and control over inmates.

All these restrictions of contact presumably help to maintain the antagonistic stereotypes. Two different social and cultural worlds develop, jogging alongside each other with points of official contact but little mutual penetration. Significantly, the institutional plant and name come to be identified by both staff and inmates as somehow belonging to staff, so that when either grouping refers to the views or interests of "the institution," by implication they are referring (as I shall also) to the views and concerns of the staff.

The staff-inmate split is one major implication of the bureaucratic management of large blocks of persons; a second pertains to work.

In the ordinary arrangements of living in our society, the authority of the work place stops with the worker's receipt of a money payment; the spending of this in a domestic and recreational setting is the worker's private affair and constitutes a mechanism through which the authority of the work place is kept within strict bounds. But to say that inmates of total institutions have their full day scheduled for them is to say that all their essential needs will have to be planned for. Whatever the incentive given for work, then, this incentive will not have the structural significance it has on the outside. There will have to be different motives for work and different attitudes toward it. This is a basic adjustment required of the inmates and of those who must induce them to work.

· · ·

There is an incompatibility, then, between total institutions and the basic work-payment structure of our society. Total institutions are also incompatible with another crucial element of our society, the family. Family life is sometimes contrasted with solitary living, but in fact the more pertinent contrast is with batch living, for those who eat and sleep at work, with a group of fellow workers, can hardly sustain a meaningful domestic existence. Conversely, maintaining families off the grounds often permits staff members to remain integrated with the outside community and to escape the encompassing tendency of the total institution.

· · ·

THE INMATE WORLD

I

It is characteristic of inmates that they come to the institution with a "presenting culture" (to modify a psychiatric phrase) derived from a "home world"—a way of life and a round of activities taken for granted until the point of admission to the institution.... Whatever the stability of the recruit's personal organization, it was part of a wider framework lodged in his civil environment—a round of experience that confirmed a tolerable conception of self and allowed for a set of defensive maneuvers, exercised at his own discretion, for coping with conflicts, discreditings, and failures.

The full meaning for the inmate of being "in" or "on the inside" does not exist apart from the special meaning to him of "getting out" or "getting on the outside." In this sense, total institutions do not really look for cultural victory. They create and sustain a particular kind of tension between the home world and the institutional world and use this persistent tension as strategic leverage in the management of men.

II

The recruit comes into the establishment with a conception of himself made possible by certain stable social arrangements in his home world. Upon entrance, he is immediately stripped of the support provided by these arrangements. In the accurate language of some of our oldest total institutions, he begins a series of abasements, degradations, humiliations, and profanations of self. His self is systematically, if often unintentionally, mortified. He begins some radical shifts in his *moral career,* a career composed of the progressive changes that occur in the beliefs that he has concerning himself and significant others.

The processes by which a person's self is mortified are fairly standard in total institutions; analysis of these processes can help us to see the arrangements that ordinary establishments must guarantee if members are to preserve their civilian selves.

The barrier that total institutions place between the inmate and the wider world marks the first curtailment of self. In civil life, the sequential scheduling of the individual's roles, both in the life cycle and in the repeated daily round, ensures that no one role he plays will block his performance and ties in another. In total institutions, in contrast, membership automatically disrupts role scheduling, since the inmate's separation from the wider world lasts around the clock and may continue for years. Role dispossession therefore occurs. In many total institutions the privilege of having visitors or of visiting away from the establishment is completely withheld at first, ensuring a deep initial break with past roles and an appreciation of role dispossession. . . . I might add that when entrance is voluntary, the recruit has already partially withdrawn from his home world; what is cleanly severed by the institution is something that had already started to decay.

Although some roles can be re-established by the inmate if and when he returns to the world, it is plain that other losses are irrevocable and may be painfully experienced as such. It may not be possible to make up, at a later phase of the life cycle, the time not now spent in educational or job advancement, in courting, or in rearing one's children. A legal aspect of this permanent dispossession is found in the concept of "civil death": prison inmates may face not only a temporary loss of the rights to will money and write checks, to contest divorce or adoption proceedings, and to vote but may have some of these rights permanently abrogated.

The inmate, then, finds certain roles are lost to him by virtue of the barrier that separates him from the outside world. The process of entrance typically brings other kinds of loss and mortification as well. We very generally find staff employing what are called admission procedures, such as taking a life history, photographing, weighing, fingerprinting, assigning numbers, searching, listing personal possessions for storage, undressing, bathing, disinfecting, haircutting, issuing institutional clothing, instructing as to rules, and assigning to quarters. Admission procedures might better be called "trimming" or "programming" because in thus being squared away the new arrival allows himself to be shaped and coded into an object that can be fed into the administrative machinery of the establishment, to be worked on smoothly by routine operations. . . .

Because a total institution deals with so many aspects of its inmates' lives, with the consequent complex squaring away at admission, there is a special need to obtain initial co-operativeness from the recruit. Staff often feel that a recruit's readiness to be appropriately deferential in his initial face-to-face encounters with them is a sign that he will take the role of the routinely pliant inmate. The occasion on which staff members first tell the inmate of his deference obligations may be structured to challenge the inmate to balk or to hold his peace forever. Thus these initial moments of socialization may involve an "obedience test" and even a will-breaking contest; an inmate who shows defiance receives immediate visible punishment, which increases until he openly "cries uncle" and humbles himself.

An engaging illustration is provided by Brendan Behan in reviewing his contest with two warders upon his admission to Walton prison:

> "And 'old up your 'ead, when I speak to you."
>
> " 'Old up your 'ead, when Mr. Whitbread speaks to you," said Mr. Holmes.
>
> I looked round at Charlie. His eyes met mine and he quickly lowered them to the ground.
>
> "What are you looking round at, Behan? Look at me."
>
> I looked at Mr. Whitbread. "I am looking at you," I said.
>
> "You are looking at Mr. Whitbread—what?" said Mr. Holmes.
>
> "I am looking at Mr. Whitbread."
>
> Mr. Holmes looked gravely at Mr. Whitbread, drew back his open hand, and struck me on the face, held me with his other hand and struck me again.
>
> My head spun and burned and pained and I wondered would it happen again. I forgot and felt another smack, and forgot, and another, and moved, and was held by a steadying, almost kindly hand, and another, and my sight was a vision of red and white and pity-coloured flashes.
>
> "You are looking at Mr. Whitbread—what, Behan?"
>
> I gulped and got together my voice and tried again till I got it out. "I, sir, please, sir, I am looking at you, I mean, I am looking at Mr. Whitbread, sir."

Admission procedures and obedience tests may be elaborated into a form of initiation that has been called "the welcome," where staff or inmates, or both, go out of their way to give the recruit a clear notion of his plight. As part of this rite of passage he may be called by a term such as "fish" or "swab," which tells him that he is merely an inmate, and, what is more, that he has a special low status even in this low group.

The admission procedure can be characterized as a leaving off and a taking on, with the midpoint marked by physical nakedness. Leaving off of course entails a dispossession of property, important because persons invest self feelings in their possessions. Perhaps the most significant of these possessions is not physical at all, one's full name; whatever one is thereafter called, loss of one's name can be a great curtailment of the self.

Another clear-cut expression of personal inefficacy in total institutions is found in inmates' use of speech. One implication of using words to convey decisions about action is that the recipient of an order is seen as capable of receiving a message and acting under his own power to complete the suggestion or command. Executing the act himself, he can sustain some vestige of the notion that he is self-determining. Responding to the question in his own words, he can sustain the notion that he is somebody to be considered, however slightly. And since it is only words that pass between himself and the others, he succeeds in retaining at least physical distance from them, however unpalatable the command or statement.

The inmate in a total institution can find himself denied even this kind of protective distance and self-action. Especially in mental hospitals and political training prisons, the statements he makes may be discounted as mere symptoms, with staff giving attention to non-verbal aspects of his reply. Often he is considered to be of insufficient ritual status to be given even minor greetings, let alone listened to. Or the inmate may find that a kind of rhetorical use of language occurs: questions such as, "Have you washed yet?" or, "Have you got both socks on?" may be accompanied by simultaneous searching by the staff which physically discloses the facts, making these verbal questions superfluous. And instead of being told to move in a particular direction at a particular rate, he may find himself pushed along by the guard, or pulled (in the case of . . . mental patients), or frog-marched. . . .

. . .

VI

Although there are solidarizing tendencies such as fraternalization and clique formation, they are limited. Constraints which place inmates in a position to sympathize and communicate with each other do not necessarily lead to high group morale and solidarity. In some concentration camps and prisoner-of-war installations the inmate cannot rely on his fellows, who may steal from him, assault him, and squeal on him, leading to what some students have referred to as anomie. In mental hospitals, dyads and triads may keep secrets from the authorities, but anything known to a whole ward of patients is likely to get to the ear of the attendant. (In prisons, of course, inmate organization has sometimes been strong enough to run strikes and short-lived insurrections; in prisoner-of-war camps, it has sometimes been possible to organize sections of the prisoners to operate escape channels; in concentration camps there have been periods of thoroughgoing underground organization; and on ships there have been mutinies; but these concerted actions seem to be the exception, not the rule.)

But though there is usually little group loyalty in total institutions, the expectation that group loyalty should prevail forms part of the inmate culture and underlies the hostility accorded those who break inmate solidarity.... The same inmate will employ different personal lines of adaptation at different phases in his moral career and may even alternate among different tacks at the same time.

First, there is the tack of "situational withdrawal." The inmate withdraws apparent attention from everything except events immediately around his body and sees these in a perspective not employed by others present. This drastic curtailment of involvement in interactional events is best known, of course, in mental hospitals, under the title of "regression."
. . .

Secondly, there is the "intransigent line": the inmate intentionally challenges the institution by flagrantly refusing to co-operate with staff. The result is a constantly communicated intransigency and sometimes high individual morale. Many large mental hospitals, for example, have wards where this spirit prevails. Sustained rejection of a total institution often requires sustained orientation to its formal organization, and hence, paradoxically, a deep kind of involvement in the establishment. Similarly, when staff take the line that the intransigent inmate must be broken (as they sometimes do in the case of hospital psychiatrists prescribing electroshock or military tribunals prescribing the stockade), then the institution shows as much special devotion to the rebel as he has shown to it. Finally, although some prisoners of war have been known to take a staunchly intransigent stance throughout their incarceration, intransigence is typically a temporary and initial phase of reaction, with the inmate shifting to situational withdrawal or some other line of adaptation.

A third standard alignment in the institutional world is "colonization": the sampling of the outside world provided by the establishment is taken by the inmate as the whole, and a stable, relatively contented existence is built up out of the maximum satisfactions procurable within the institution. Experience of the outside world is used as a point of reference to demonstrate the desirability of life on the inside, and the usual tension between the two worlds is markedly reduced, thwarting the motivational scheme based upon this felt discrepancy which I described as peculiar to total institutions. Characteristically, the individual who too obviously takes this line may be accused by his fellow inmates of "having found a home" or of "never having had it so good." The staff itself may become vaguely embarrassed by this use that is being made of the institution, sensing that the benign possibilities in the situation are somehow being misused. Colonizers may feel obliged to deny their satisfaction with the institution, if only to sustain the counter-mores supporting inmate solidarity. They may find it necessary to mess up just prior to their slated discharge to provide themselves with an apparently involuntary basis for continued incarceration. Significantly, the staff who try to make life in total institutions more bearable must face the possibility that doing so may increase the attractiveness and likelihood of colonization.

A fourth mode of adaptation to the setting of a total institution is that of "conversion": the inmate appears to take over the official or staff view of himself and tries to act out the role of the perfect inmate. While the colonized inmate builds as much of a free community for himself as possible by using the limited facilities available, the convert takes a more disciplined, moralistic, monochromatic line, presenting himself as someone whose institutional enthusiasm is always at the disposal of the staff. In Chinese P.O.W. camps, we find Americans who became "Pros" and fully espoused the Communist view of the world. In army barracks there are enlisted men who give the impression that they are always "sucking around" and always "bucking for promotion." In prisons there are "square johns." In German concentration camps, a long-time prisoner sometimes came to adapt the vocabulary, recreation, posture, expressions of aggression, and clothing style of the Gestapo, executing the role of straw boss with military strictness....

The alignments that have been mentioned represent coherent courses to pursue, but few inmates seem to pursue any one of them very far. In most total institutions, most inmates take the tack of what some of them call "playing it cool." This involves a somewhat opportunistic combination of secondary adjustments, conversion, colonization, and loyalty to the inmate group, so that the inmate will have a maximum chance, in the particular circumstances, of eventually getting out physically and psychologically undamaged. Typically, the inmate when with fellow inmates will support the counter-mores and conceal from them how tractably he acts when alone with the staff.[124] Inmates who play it cool subordinate contacts with their fellows to the higher claim of "keeping out of trouble"; they tend to volunteer for nothing; and they may learn to cut their ties to the outside world just enough to give cultural reality to the world inside but not enough to lead to colonization.

· · ·

An interesting institutional ceremony, often connected with the annual party and the Christmas celebration, is the institutional theatrical. Typically the players are inmates and the directors of the production are staff, but sometimes "mixed" casts are found. The writers are usually members of the institution, whether staff or inmate, and hence the production can be full of local references, imparting through the private use of this public form a special sense of the reality of events internal to the institution. Very frequently the offering will consist of satirical skits that lampoon well-

---

124. This two-facedness·is very commonly found in total institutions. In the state mental hospital studied by the writer, even the few elite patients selected for individual psychotherapy, and hence in the best position to espouse the psychiatric approach to self, tended to present their favorable view of psychotherapy only to the members of their intimate cliques. For a report on the way in which army prisoners concealed from fellow offenders their interest in "restoration" to the Army, see the comments by Richard Cloward in Session Four of New Perspectives for Research on Juvenile Delinquency, eds. Helen L. Witmer and Ruth Kotinsky, U.S. Dept. of Health, Education, and Welfare, Children's Bureau Publication No. 356 (1956), especially p. 90.

known members of the institution, especially high-placed staff members. If, as is frequent, the inmate community is one-sexed, then some of the players are likely to perform in the costume and burlesqued role of members of the other sex. Limits of license are often tested, the humor being a little more broad than some members of the staff would like to see tolerated. . . .

————

QUESTIONS

How do law schools use admission procedures and obedience tests to initiate recruits? Why are these techniques necessary? What lines of adaptation have you used in your career as a law student? Why? Have you perceived among your fellow students variations on the lines of adaptation described by Goffman? What values does the structure of law school inculcate? Are these necessary for "good" lawyering? What changes in law school would you suggest?

What are the admission procedures and obedience tests used by law firms and other institutions in which lawyers work? Are there similar lines of adaptation present? In what ways are clients like inmates in the lawyer's office? Since neither the model of inmate or staff works well to describe the client in a law firm, how would you go about describing the client's relationship to the institution?

How are lawyers like inmates in the courts? How are they like staff? What role do the litigants play in the court system? The jurors?

C. SATISFACTIONS AND DISSATISFACTIONS OF PRACTICE

Patrick J. Schiltz, "On Being a Happy, Healthy, and Ethical Member of an Unhappy, Unhealthy, and Unethical Profession"

52 Vanderbilt Law Review 871 (1999).[1]

Dear Law Student:

I have good news and bad news. The bad news is that the profession that you are about to enter is one of the most unhappy and unhealthy on the face of the earth—and, in the view of many, one of the most unethical.

1. Copyright 1999 © Vanderbilt Law Review. Reprinted by permission. This adaptation of a lengthy article reduces part of the text to summary, deletes other portions, eliminates most of the footnotes and renumbers the retained footnotes. Law students and young lawyers are encouraged to read the original version of the article, which appears in the Vanderbilt Law Review with commentaries on it by a number of academic and practicing lawyers. Readers desiring supporting information should consult the extensive documentation in the article.

The good news is that you can join this profession and still be happy, healthy, and ethical. I am writing to tell you how. But first the bad news:

1. Lawyers are more unhealthy than most other occupational groups

The importance of the role lawyers play in our society suggests that many would be concerned about the mental and physical health of lawyers. That is not the case. One needs to look hard at medical and psychological studies to discover that lawyers are in remarkably poor health.

Depression. Lawyers are among the most depressed people in America. In 1990, researchers studied the prevalence of major depressive disorder ("MDD") across 104 occupations.[2] When the results were adjusted for age, gender, education, and race/ethnic background to determine to what extent those in each occupation were more depressed than others who shared their most important socio-demographic traits, only three occupations were discovered to have statistically significant elevations of MDD: lawyers, pre-kindergarten and special education teachers, and secretaries. Lawyers topped the list, suffering from MDD at a rate 3.6 times higher than non-lawyers who shared their key socio-demographic traits. The researchers did not know whether lawyers were depressed because "persons at high risk for major depressive disorder" are attracted to the legal profession or because practicing law "causes or precipitates depression." They just knew that, whatever the reason, lawyers were depressed.

Other studies have produced similar results. A study of Washington lawyers found that, "[c]ompared with the 3 to 9 percent of individuals in Western industrialized countries who suffer from depression, 19 percent of . . . Washington lawyers suffered from statistically significant elevated levels of depression."[3] Another study—this one of law students and practicing lawyers in Arizona—discovered that when students enter law school, they suffer from depression at pretty much the same rate as the general population. However, by the spring of the first year of law school, thirty-two percent of law students suffer from depression, and by the spring of the third year of law school, the figure escalates to an astonishing forty percent. Two years after graduation, the rate of depression falls, but only to seventeen percent, roughly double the level of the general population.[4] And finally, a study of North Carolina lawyers found that twenty-four percent reported suffering symptoms of depression—such as appetite loss, insomnia, suicidal ideation, and extreme lethargy—at least three times per month during the previous year.[5]

---

2. William W. Eaton et al., Occupations and the Prevalence of Major Depressive Disorder, 32 J. Occupational Med. 1079 (1990).

3. G. Andrew H. Benjamin et al., The Prevalence of Depression, Alcohol Abuse, and Cocaine Abuse Among United States Lawyers, 13 Int'l J.L. & Psychiatry 233, 240 (1990) [hereinafter Benjamin et al.].

4. Id. at 234 (citing G. Andrew H. Benjamin et al., The Role of Legal Education in Pro-

ducing Psychological Distress Among Law Students and Lawyers, 1986 Am. B. Found. Res. J. 225).

5. North Carolina Bar Ass'n, Report of the Quality of Life Task Force and Recommendations 4 (1991) [hereinafter North Carolina Bar Report].

Anxiety and other mental illness. Depression is not the only emotional impairment that seems to be more prevalent among lawyers than among the general population. The Arizona study found elevated rates of anxiety, hostility, and paranoia.[6] Over twenty-five percent of North Carolina lawyers reported that they had experienced physical symptoms of extreme anxiety—including trembling hands, racing hearts, clammy hands, and faintness—at least three times per month during the past year.[7] And the Washington study found indicia of anxiety, social alienation, obsessive-compulsiveness, paranoid ideation, interpersonal sensitivity, phobic anxiety, and hostility in "alarming" rates among lawyers—rates many times the national norms. Needless to say, these studies "give[] substantial indication of a profession operating at extremely high levels of psychological distress."[8]

Alcoholism. Lawyers, more than the population generally, are prodigious drinkers. The North Carolina study reported that almost seventeen percent of lawyers admitted to drinking three to five alcoholic beverages every day. One researcher conservatively estimated that fifteen percent of lawyers are alcoholics.[9] The study of Washington lawyers found that eighteen percent were "problem drinkers," a percentage "almost twice the approximately 10 percent alcohol abuse and/or dependency prevalence rates estimated for adults in the United States."

Drug abuse. Very little is known about the frequency with which lawyers use illegal drugs, but the little that is known is not encouraging. The Washington study found that *one third* of lawyers in Washington suffer from depression, problem drinking, or cocaine abuse.[10] Thus, when you show up for your first day of work in a year or two, and you're taken around the office to meet your new colleagues, one out of every three of the hands you will shake may belong to a lawyer who is depressed or who abuses alcohol or cocaine.[11]

Divorce. Marriage is good for you. "The married live longer and have a lower risk of a variety of physical and psychological illnesses than the unmarried."[12] Also, those who are married report higher levels of career satisfaction than those who are single.[13] The North Carolina study con-

6. Amiram Elwork, Stress Management for Lawyers 14–15 (2d ed.1997) [hereinafter Elwork].

7. North Carolina Bar Report, supra at 4.

8. Connie J.A. Beck et al., Lawyer Distress: Alcohol–Related Problems and Other Psychological Concerns Among a Sample of Practicing Lawyers, 10 J. L. & Health 1, 23, 49 (1995–96) [hereinafter Beck et al.].

9. *See* Eric Drogin, Alcoholism in the Legal Profession: Psychological and Legal Perspectives and Interventions, 15 Law & Psychol. Rev. 117, 127 (1991).

10. Id. at 242.

11. See Elwork, supra, at 15–16; Benjamin Sells, The Soul of the Law 99 (1994) [hereinafter Sells]; Deborah L. Rhode, The Professionalism Problem, 39 Wm. & Mary L. Rev. 283, 297 (1998).

12. David B. Larson et al., The Costly Consequences of Divorce: Assessing the Clinical, Economic, and Public Health Impact of Marital Disruption in the United States 1 (1995) [hereinafter Larson et al.].

13. David L. Chambers, Accommodation and Satisfaction: Women and Men Lawyers and the Balance of Work and Family, 14 J.L. & Soc. Inquiry 251, 255, 274 (1989).

firmed that what is true for people generally is also true for lawyers specifically: Among lawyers, "changing from single to married status directly increases happiness and satisfaction with life. Marriage also leads to greater job and career satisfaction . . . and improves health."[14] The North Carolina study identified unmarried lawyers as one of three categories of lawyers least satisfied with their lives.

Likewise, divorce is bad for you physically and psychologically (and, if you are a woman, economically).[15] Those who divorce die younger than either those who never marry or those who stay married; indeed, the effect of getting divorced on life expectancy is "only slightly less harmful . . . than smoking a pack or more of cigarettes per day."[16] Divorced people suffer from severe diseases more frequently than do single, married, or widowed people. Divorced people are far more likely to abuse alcohol than those who have never been divorced. Psychologically, divorce is devastating: The separated and divorced suffer from psychiatric illness (such as depression and schizophrenia) far more than do the single, married, and widowed. For example, men who are divorced or separated are admitted to hospitals for treatment of psychiatric disorders twenty-one times more frequently than married men. And, not surprisingly, the suicide rate of those who are divorced is almost triple the rate of those who are married, and significantly higher than the rates of those who have never married or been widowed.

Although empirical data comparing the divorce rates of lawyers to those of either the general population or other professionals is limited, there is evidence that the divorce rate among lawyers is higher than among other professionals. A study by Felicia Baker LeClere found that the percentage of lawyers who are divorced is indeed higher than the percentage of doctors who are divorced and that the difference is particularly pronounced among women. For example, 16.2% of female attorneys between the ages of thirty-five and forty-nine are divorced, as compared to 11.0% of female doctors in the same age range. Similarly, among ages fifty to sixty-four, 24.3% of female lawyers are divorced, as compared to 15.3% of female doctors.

LeClere's findings are consistent with an earlier study of divorce rates among women attorneys. That study found that women who have completed six or more years of post-secondary education, a category that obviously includes lawyers, have a substantially higher divorce rate than women generally.[17] Among well educated women, the divorce rate for women lawyers was twice that for women doctors and about one-third higher than

---

14. North Carolina Bar Report, supra, at 7.

15. See generally Larson et al., supra, at 41–88; Judith S. Wallerstein & Sandra Blakeslee, Second Chances: Men, Women, and Children a Decade After Divorce (1989); Judith S. Wallerstein & Joan Berlin Kelly, Surviving the Breakup: How Children and Parents Cope With Divorce (1980).

16. Id. at 1.

17. Teresa M. Cooney & Peter Uhlenberg, Family–Building Patterns of Professional Women: A Comparison of Lawyers, Physicians, and Postsecondary Teachers, 51 J. Marriage & Fam. 749, 751 (1989).

the divorce rate for women professors. After their first marriages end, women attorneys are significantly less likely to remarry than women physicians and professors.

Suicide. Lawyers reportedly think about committing suicide and commit suicide far more often than do non-lawyers.[18] A review of the death certificates of over 26,000 white male suicide victims by the National Institute for Occupational Safety and Health suggested that the suicide rate for white male lawyers may be over twice that of other white males.[19] The Washington and North Carolina studies report a greater risk of suicide among lawyers.

Physical health. The extremely limited information that is available indicates that the physical health of lawyers may not be much better than their emotional health. Lawyers do not exercise much[20] and suffer from ulcers, coronary artery disease, and hypertension in substantial numbers.[21] One troubling study of women attorneys who had graduated from the University of California at Davis School of Law between 1969 and 1985 found that those who worked more than forty-five hours per week while pregnant suffered three times more miscarriages than those who worked less than thirty-five hours per week.[22] Yet working forty-five hour weeks is not only common in the legal profession, but in some sectors, particularly big firms, that work week is almost considered part-time.

In sum, attorneys seem to be an unhealthy lot. Researchers do not know whether lawyers are unhealthy because unhealthy people are attracted to the legal profession or because something about the practice of law turns healthy people into unhealthy people. But the few researchers who have studied the legal profession are unanimous that lawyers are, as a group, in remarkably poor health.

2. People who are this unhealthy are likely to be unhappy

People who are this unhealthy—people who suffer from depression, anxiety, alcoholism, drug abuse, divorce, and suicide to this extent—are almost by definition unhappy. It should not be surprising, then, that lawyers are indeed unhappy, nor should it be surprising that the source of their unhappiness seems to be the one thing that they have in common: their work as lawyers. "Work satisfaction affects life satisfaction."[23] Almost a century ago, Russian playwright Maxim Gorky wrote: "When work is a

18. *See* Deborah K. Holmes, Learning from Corporate America: Addressing Dysfunction in the Large Law Firm, 31 Gonz. L. Rev. 373, 377 (1995–1996).

19. Carol A. Burnett et al., Suicide and Occupation: Is There a Relationship?, Paper Presented at the American Psychological Association—National Institute for Occupational Safety and Health Conference on Workplace Stress in the 90's, at 2 (Nov. 19–22, 1992) (on file with author).

20. Half of lawyers do not exercise regularly. *See* North Carolina Bar Report, supra,

at 4; Young Lawyers Div., American Bar Ass'n, The State of the Legal Profession 1990, at 51 (1991) [hereinafter State of the Legal Profession].

21. North Carolina Bar Report, supra, at 4.

22. Marc B. Schenker et al., Self–Reported Stress and Reproductive Health of Female Lawyers, 39 J. Occupational & Envtl. Med. 556 (1997).

23. Myers & Diener, supra, at 15.

pleasure, life is a joy! When work is a duty, life is slavery."[24] If Gorky was right, then life for many lawyers is "slavery," as job dissatisfaction among lawyers is frequent, intense and increasing.

A Rand study of California lawyers found that "only half say if they had to do it over, they would become lawyers."[25] On the whole, California lawyers were reported to be " 'profoundly pessimistic' about the state of the legal profession and its future."[26] A survey of the North Carolina bar produced similar results. Almost a quarter of North Carolina lawyers said that, if given the choice, they would not become attorneys again; almost half said that they hope to leave the practice of law before the end of their careers; and over forty percent said that they would not encourage their children or other qualified persons to enter the legal profession.[27] Along the same lines, a nationwide poll of attorneys conducted by the *National Law Journal* found that less than a third of those surveyed were "very satisfied" with their careers.[28] Surveys of University of Michigan Law School graduates five years after graduation report the "gloomy" picture that the proportion of those graduates working in large law firms who were "quite satisfied" with their careers after five years declined from a high of 54% for the classes of 1978–79 to 30% for those of 1990–91.[29]

The most comprehensive data on career satisfaction of lawyers were produced by three ABA national surveys. The first survey, conducted in 1984, asked 3000 lawyers of all ages—some of whom were ABA members and some of whom were not—about job satisfaction and many other matters.[30] The second survey, conducted in 1990, resurveyed those who had responded to the 1984 survey, and also questioned just over 1000 lawyers who had been admitted to the bar after the 1984 survey had been concluded.[31] The third survey, conducted in 1995, was more limited: Only "young lawyers" who belonged to the ABA were questioned—"young lawyers" being defined as those who were under the age of thirty-six or who had been admitted to practice for less than three years.[32]

24. Maxim Gorky, The Lower Depths act I, in Four Modern Plays 289 (Henry Popkin ed., Alexander Bakshy trans., Holt, Rinehart & Winston, 1961).

25. Nancy McCarthy, Pessimism for the Future: Given a Second Chance, Half of the State's Attorneys Would Not Become Lawyers, Cal. B.J., Nov. 1994, at 1, 1.

26. Id. See also "It's Become a Miserable Profession", Cal. Law., Mar. 1992, at 96. Almost three-quarters of the California lawyers responding to the survey agreed that they "enjoy practicing law less now than [they] did when [they] first began," and a similar percentage said that they would not advise their children to become attorneys. Id.

27. North Carolina Bar Report, supra, at 4.

28. Margaret Cronin Fisk, Lawyers Give Thumbs Up, Nat'l L.J., May 28, 1990, at S2.

29. The University of Michigan Law School: A Report on the Class of 1991 Five Years After Graduation 1 (unpublished report, on file with author) [hereinafter Michigan Law School Survey].

30. State of the Legal Profession, supra, at 1.

31. Id. at 2–3.

32. Young Lawyers Div., American Bar Ass'n, Career Satisfaction 1995, at 1 & n.1 (1995) [hereinafter Career Satisfaction].

Taken together, the surveys show a steady decline in the job satisfaction of attorneys. The 1990 study reported that "the extent of lawyer dissatisfaction has increased throughout the profession [and] is now reported in significant numbers by lawyers in all positions—partners as well as junior associates."[33]

The decrease in job satisfaction was even more dramatic among those lawyers who were surveyed in both 1984 and 1990. Forty percent of them had been "very satisfied" and three percent "very dissatisfied" in 1984; just six years later, only twenty-nine percent of these same lawyers (that is, the lawyers who were questioned in *both* 1984 and 1990) were "very satisfied," and the number who were "very dissatisfied" had risen to eight percent.[34] The 1995 survey of new lawyers found that over twenty-seven percent were already "somewhat" or "very" dissatisfied with the practice of law; only about one in five was "very" satisfied.[35]

3.   Lawyers are unhappy primarily because they work too much

Why are lawyers so unhealthy and unhappy? Lawyers give many reasons why their work is less satisfying: the increased pressure to attract and retain clients in a ferociously competitive marketplace; working in an adversarial environment in which aggression, selfishness, hostility, suspiciousness and cynicism are widespread; the lack of control over their lives; the demands of unreasonable clients; lack of civility among lawyers; decline of collegiality and loyalty among their partners; and lawyers' poor public image. Mostly, though, lawyers complain about the hours. Everyone who writes or talks about life as a practicing lawyer reports that lawyers complain mostly about the long hours they have to work.

A *National Law Journal* survey reported that "most attorneys in the survey believed their careers were putting too much of a burden on their personal lives. When asked what they especially disliked about practicing law, more than half (54 percent) mentioned too many hours/not enough time for a personal life."[36] The 1990 ABA study, after describing increasing job dissatisfaction among attorneys, said that "[t]his increased dissatisfaction is directly caused by a deterioration of the lawyer workplace.... In particular, the amount of time lawyers have for themselves and their families has become an issue of major concern for many lawyers."[37] The North Carolina study identified as "a major factor" in attorney dissatisfaction "[l]ack of enough time to balance work with time for self, family, the

---

33. Id. at 81.

34. Id. at 53 tbl.68.

35. A recent study of Chicago lawyers by John Heinz, Kathleen Hull, and Ava Harter, however, reported levels of job satisfaction that were similar to those reported by Americans in other lines of work. John P. Heinz et al., Lawyers and Their Discontents: Findings from a Survey of the Chicago Bar, 74 Ind.L.J. 735 (1999). The study, which utilized extensive interviews of individual lawyers and inquired into numerous subjects, was not focused on job satisfaction but asked a small number of questions concerning it. Large numbers of lawyers could be relatively dissatisfied with their work, even if most were satisfied.

36. Margaret Cronin Fisk, Lawyers Give Thumbs Up, Nat'l L.J., May 28, 1990, at S12 [hereafter Fisk].

37. State of the Legal Profession, supra, at 81.

community, *pro bono*, etc."[38] Respondents to the Michigan Law School survey reported themselves far less satisfied with "[t]he balance of their family and professional lives" than with "[t]heir career as a whole" or any of four other measures of "[l]ife [s]atisfaction."[39] And an ABA report singled out as a "significant" cause of the decline in lawyer's quality of life the fact that lawyers "do not have enough time for themselves and their families—what many have come to call 'the time famine.'"[40]

When it comes to their brutal work schedules, lawyers have reason to believe that their workload has increased. "Conventional wisdom just a few decades ago was that lawyers could not reasonably expect to charge for more than 1200 to 1500 hours per year."[41] Thirty years ago, most partners billed between 1200 and 1400 hours per year and most associates between 1400 and 1600 hours.[42] As late as the mid–1980s, even associates in large New York firms were often not expected to bill more than 1800 hours annually.[43] Today, many firms would consider these ranges acceptable only for partners or associates who had died midway through the year.

A 1991 study by William Ross discovered that fifty-one percent of associates and twenty-three percent of partners billed at least 2000 hours in 1993.[44] Seventy percent of those responding to the Michigan Law School survey worked an average of fifty or more hours per week; over a quarter of the respondents worked more than sixty hours per week.[45] The ABA's 1990 study found that forty-five percent of attorneys in private practice billed at least 1920 hours per year, and sixteen percent billed 2400 or more hours.[46] The same study also found that, although seventy percent of attorneys are *permitted* to take more than two weeks of vacation every year, only forty-eight percent actually do so.[47]

Workloads, like the job dissatisfaction to which they so closely relate, are not distributed equally throughout the profession. Generally speaking, lawyers in private practice work longer hours than those who work for corporations or for the government.[48] In the 1990 ABA survey, for example, only fifty-six percent of those in private practice agreed that they had

---

38. North Carolina Bar Report, supra, at 11.

39. Michigan Law School, supra, at 3 tbl.1.

40. At the Breaking Point, supra, at 3.

41. Deborah L. Rhode, Institutionalizing Ethics, 44 Case W. Res. L. Rev. 665, 711 (1994).

42. See William G. Ross, The Honest Hour: The Ethics of Time–Based Billing by Attorneys 2–3 (1996); see also Walt Bachman, Law v. Life: What Lawyers Are Afraid to Say About the Legal Profession 103 (1995) ("Twenty years ago ... [l]awyers with average billings of 1,500 hours per year often became partners[.]"); Carl T.Bogus, The Death of an Honorable Profession, 71 Ind.

L.J. 911, 924 ("[I]n the 1960's the median number of billable hours was about 1500 per year for partners and associates alike.").

43. Ross, supra, at 20.

44. Id.

45. Michigan Law School Survey, supra, at 3 tbl.1.

46. State of the Legal Profession, supra, at 22 tbl.19.

47. Id. at 23 tbl.21. The North Carolina study found that 17.3% of lawyers did not take more than *one* week of vacation in 1989. North Carolina Bar Report, supra, at 4.

48. *See* Elwork, supra, at 30.

enough time to spend with their families, compared to seventy-four percent of corporate lawyers and seventy-nine percent of government lawyers. "Time for family and self is a real problem for lawyers in private practice. Far fewer lawyers in corporate counsel and government settings have insufficient time."[49]

Within private practice, the general rule of thumb is the bigger the firm, the longer the hours.[50] For example, a recent study found that 41.3% of associates in firms of under 101 lawyers billed fewer than 1800 hours, as compared to 16.3% of associates in firms of over 250 lawyers.[51] At the biggest firms in the biggest cities, associates commonly bill 2000 to 2500 hours per year. Big firm partners don't have it much better. Junior partners at the nation's 125 largest law firms average 1955.5 billable hours per year, almost 300 hours per year more than partners in small firms. At some big firms, the average number of hours billed by partners and associates alike is 2000.

The long hours that big firm lawyers must work is a particular source of dissatisfaction for them. While roughly half of all attorneys in private practice complain about not having enough time for themselves and their families,[52] in big firms the proportion of similarly disaffected lawyers is about three quarters.[53]

At first blush, these billable hour requirements may not seem particularly daunting. You may think, "To bill 2000 hours, I need to bill only forty hours per week for fifty weeks. If I take an hour for lunch, that's 8:00 a.m. to 5:00 p.m., five days per week. No sweat." However, there is a big difference—a painfully big difference—between the hours that you will *bill* and the hours that you will spend at *work*. If you're honest, you will be able to bill only the time that you spend working directly on matters for clients. Obviously, you will not be able to bill the time that you spend on vacation, or in bed with the flu, or at home waiting for the plumber. But you will also not be able to bill for much of what you will do at the office or during the workday—going to lunch, chatting with your co-workers about the latest office romance, visiting your favorite websites, going down the hall to get a cup of coffee, reading your mail, going to the bathroom, attending the weekly meeting of your practice group, filling out your time sheet, talking with your spouse on the phone, sending e-mail to friends, preparing a "pitch" for a prospective client, getting your hair cut, attending a funeral,

49. State of the Legal Profession, supra, at 17.

50. See Altman Weil Pensa, Inc., The 1996 Survey of Law Firm Economics, at III–2, III–6 [hereafter Altman Weil Pensa]; Task Force on Professional Fulfilment, Boston Bar Ass'n, Expectations, Reality and Recommendations for Change 9 (1997) [hereinafter Boston Bar Study]; David B. Wilkins & G. Mitu Gulati, Reconceiving the Tournament of Lawyers: Tracking, Seeding, and Information Control in the Inter-

nal Labor Markets of Elite Law Firms, 84 Va. L. Rev. 1581 (1999).

51. National Ass'n for Law Placement, Employing Associates in 1997: Patterns & Practices 11, 15 (1997).

52. See North Carolina Bar Ass'n, supra, at 4; State of the Legal Profession, supra, at 17.

53. See Fisk, supra, at S12; Chris Klein, Big–Firm Partners: Profession Sinking, Nat'l L.J., May 26, 1997,at A24.

photocopying your tax returns, interviewing a recruit, playing Solitaire on your computer, doing pro bono work, reading advance sheets, taking a summer associate to a baseball game, attending CLE seminars, writing a letter about a mistake in your credit card bill, going to the dentist, dropping off your dry cleaning, daydreaming, and so on.

Because none of this is billable—and because the average lawyer does a lot of this every day—you will end up billing only about two hours for every three hours that you spend at "work."[54] To bill 2000 hours per year, you will have to spend about sixty hours per week at the office, and take no more than two weeks of vacation/sick time/personal leave. If it takes you, say, forty-five minutes to get to work, and another forty-five minutes to get home, billing 2000 hours per year will mean leaving home at 7:45 a.m., working at the office from 8:30 a.m. until 6:30 p.m., and then arriving home at 7:15 p.m.—and doing this *six days per week*, every week. That makes for long days and for long weeks. And you will have to work these hours not just for a month or two, but year after year after year.

What makes people happy is the *nature* of the work they do and the quantity and quality of their lives outside of work. Long hours at the office have no relationship to the former and take away from the latter. Every hour that lawyers spend at their desks is an hour that they do not spend doing many of the things that give their lives joy and meaning: being with their spouses, playing with their children, relaxing with their friends, visiting their parents, going to movies, reading books, volunteering at the homeless shelter, playing softball, collecting stamps, traveling the world, getting involved in a political campaign, going to church, working out at a health club. There's no mystery about why lawyers are so unhappy: They work too much.

4. Lawyers work too much because they get caught in a rat race that makes money and status the only shared goals

Why do lawyers work too much? No one knows for certain why so many lawyers work so hard, although many people have opinions. My answer to the question of why so many lawyers work so much, based on eight years in a big firm as both an associate and as a partner, is simple: It's the money, stupid. The explanation begins with law students, who, like most Americans, seem to be more materialistic than they were twenty-five or thirty years ago. In 1970, thirty-nine percent of students entering college said that " 'being very well off financially' " was either an " 'essential' " or a " 'very important' " life goal; in 1993, the figure had almost doubled to seventy-five percent.[55] Of nineteen possible life goals suggested to incoming college students, getting rich was selected most often—even more often than " 'raising a family.' " Not surprisingly, then, "the most coveted jobs amongst [law students] are high-paying large law firm jobs."[56] The vast

54. *See* Bachman, supra, at 108; Elwork, supra, at 19; Sol M. Linowitz, The Betrayed Profession 107 (1994).

55. David G. Myers & Ed Diener, Who Is Happy?, 6 Psychol.Sci. 10, 12 (1995).

56. Roger E. Schechter, Changing Law Schools to Make Less Nasty Lawyers, 10 Geo. J. Legal Ethics 367, 386 (1996).

majority of law students—at least the vast majority of those attending the
more prestigious schools (or getting good grades at the less prestigious
schools)—want to work in big firms. And the reason they want to work in
big firms is that big firms pay the most.

Of course, students deny this—they don't like to admit that they've
"sold out," so they come up with "rationalizations, justifications, accounts,
and disclaimers" for seeking big firm jobs.[57] They insist that the *real*
reason they want to go to a big firm is the training, or the interesting and
challenging work, or the chance to work with exceptionally talented colleagues, or the desire to "keep my doors open." They imply that the huge
salaries are just an afterthought—mere icing on the cake. Or they reluctantly admit that, yes, they really are after the money, but they have no
choice: Because of student loan debt, they *must* take a job that pays
$80,000 per year. $60,000 per year just won't cut it.

Most of this is hogwash for two reasons: almost all of the purported
non-monetary advantages of big firms either do not exist or are vastly
overstated and, more fundamentally, there are few lawyers who could not
live comfortably on what most corporations or government agencies pay,
whatever their student loan debt.[58] Students are after the money, pure and
simple. The hiring partner of any major firm will tell you that if his firm
offers first year associates a salary of $69,000, and a competitor down the
street offers them $72,000, those who have the choice will flock to the
competitor, even if the competitor will require them to bill 200 hours more
each year.[59]

If this were *not* true, would big firms get into bidding wars for the
services of the best law school graduates? But big firms do get into bidding
wars—all the time—and, as a result, the salaries of first year associates get
pushed to extraordinary levels.[60] In 1997, the median starting salary for
first year associates in firms of over 250 lawyers was $71,502. First year
associates in some California firms now earn $95,000 per year. And in 1997
some New York firms broke the magic $100,000 barrier and began paying
six figure salaries to first year associates. As the salaries of first year
associates go up, the salaries of senior associates must rise to keep pace; no
sixth year associate wants to be paid less than a first year associate. And as

57. Robert Granfield, Making Elite Lawyers: Visions of Law at Harvard and Beyond 149 (1992).

58. If a law student has children, an unem-
ployed spouse and $60,000 or more in
debts, the student may need a big firm
income. But economic circumstances do not
restrict the choices of most law students.
First, one-third of law students graduate
with no student loan debt. Second, an unmarried student with $50,000 in loan debt
(the average debt load is $40,000) can meet
the required loan payments of $487 per
month ($5,480 annually) from the many
thousands of entry-level jobs that pay $40,-

000–60,000 per year: take-home pay on a
$50,000 job would be about $36,000 or
$3,000 per month; after making a loan
payment of $487, the young lawyer would
be left with $2,500 per month to live on. A
lawyer who is spending more money than
most Americans are earning will not be
living in poverty!

59. See Bachman, supra, at 106.

60. See Marc Galanter & Thomas Palay,
Tournament of Lawyers: The Transformation of the Big Firm 56–57 (1991) (describing bidding wars among New York firms).

the salaries of senior associates go up, the salaries of junior and senior partners must also rise.

Firms pay for this ever-spiraling increase in salaries by billing more hours. Instead of demanding 2000 billable hours per year from first year associates, they can demand 2100, and instead of demanding 1900 billable hours per year from junior partners, they can demand 1950. Because the market for lawyers' services has become intensely competitive, raising billing rates to pay for spiraling salaries is simply not an option for most firms. As a result, firms get the extra money to pay for the spiraling salaries in the only way they can: They bill more hours. Everyone has to work harder to pay for the higher salaries. And when salaries go up again, everyone has to work still harder. Associate compensation has increased 1000% in the past thirty years, while billing rates have increased only 400%.[61] Obviously, "law firms have paid for the higher salaries by increasing billable hours rather than charging higher rates."[62]

The economics of law firm "leverage" maintains the pace of increased income for senior partners. Big firms "buy associates' time 'wholesale and sell it retail.'"[63] As a new associate in a large firm, you will be paid about one third of what you bring into the firm.[64] About a third of the amount generated by your billable hours will be paid to you. Another third will go toward paying the expenses of the firm. And the final third will go into the pockets of the firm's partners. Firms make money off associates. That is why it's in the interests of big firms to hire lots of associates and to make very few of them partners. The more associates there are, the more profits for the partners to split, and the fewer partners there are, the bigger each partner's share.

It should not surprise you that, generally speaking, the bigger the firm, the more the leverage. As a result of the disparity in leverage between big and small firms, partners in big firms make dramatically more money than partners in small firms. In 1995, the median income of partners in firms of seventy-five or more attorneys was $190,408—almost forty-two percent higher than the median income of partners in firms of eight or fewer lawyers.[65] (By contrast, the median income of *associates* in firms of seventy-five or more attorneys was $76,263, just twelve percent higher than the median income of associates in firms of eight or fewer lawyers.[66]) The stark relationship between firm size and partnership compensation cannot be explained by differences in hourly rates, hours billed, or quality of legal services.[67] Rather, it results from the skim.

61. See William G. Ross, The Honest Hour: The Ethics of Time–Based Billing by Attorneys 2 (1996).

62. Id.; see also North Carolina Bar Report, supra, at 12.

63. Robert L. Nelson, Partners with Power: The Social Transformation of the Large Law Firm 77 (1988).

64. See Richard L. Abel, American Lawyers 192 (1989) [hereafter Abel].

65. Id. at IV–6.

66. Id.

67. Id. at 193–94.

This, then, is life in the big firm: It is in the interests of clients that senior partners work inhuman hours, year after year, and constantly be anxious about retaining their business. And it is in the interests of senior partners that junior partners work inhuman hours, year after year, and constantly be anxious about retaining old clients and attracting new clients. And it is in the interests of junior partners that senior associates work inhuman hours, year after year, and constantly be anxious about retaining old clients and attracting new clients and making partner. And most of all, it is in everyone's interests that the newest members of the profession, the junior associates, be willing to work inhuman hours, year after year, and constantly be anxious about *everything*—about retaining old clients and attracting new clients and making partner and keeping up their billable hours.[68] The result? Long hours, large salaries, and one of the unhealthiest and unhappiest professions on earth.

The profession that you are about to enter is absolutely obsessed with money. "[M]oney is not just incidental to the practice, but at its core."[69] Money is at the root of virtually everything that lawyers don't like about their profession: the long hours, the commercialization, the tremendous pressure to attract and retain clients, the fiercely competitive marketplace, the lack of collegiality and loyalty among partners, the poor public image of the profession, and even the lack of civility. Almost every one of these problems would be eliminated or at least substantially reduced if lawyers were simply willing to make less money. The North Carolina Bar Association had it exactly right: "[T]he misguided view of money as the sole goal of practice, sole measure of success and sole measure of self-worth is directly and indirectly responsible for many of the problems in practice today."[70]

The notion that lawyers could get by with less money is not exactly absurd. In 1994, the median income for American men employed full-time during the entire year was $31,612; for women, the comparable figure was $23,265.[71] In the largest firms (those of seventy-five or more lawyers), partners' median income in 1995 was $190,408, and a quarter of big firm partners made over $261,425.[72] These 1995 figures do not reflect the dramatic increases in law firm compensation since then. For example, at those firms qualifying for the "Am Law 100,"[73] the average profits per partner rose to $587,000 in 1997.[74] It's not as if lawyers are just scraping by.

68. See Douglas N. Frenkel et al., Introduction: Bringing Realism to the Study of Ethics and Professionalism, 67 Fordham L.Rev. 697, 704 (1998) (describing how, in large firms facing increasingly competitive markets, "[f]irm-wide insecurity trickles down") [hereafter ABA Litigation Study Report].

69. American Bar Ass'n, The Report of At the Breaking Point: A National Conference ... 12 (1991) [hereafter At the Breaking Point].

70. North Carolina Bar Report, supra, at 9.

71. Bureau of the Census, U.S. Dep't of Commerce, Statistical Abstract of the United States 1996, at 469 tbl.725 (116th ed. 1996).

72. Altman, Weil Pensa, supra, at IV–6.

73. Every year, in its July/August issue, the *American Lawyer* provides highly detailed financial information on the 100 largest American law firms—the "Am Law 100."

74. John E. Morris, Too Good to Be True?, Am.Law., July/Aug.1998, at 5.

At the same time that lawyers are enjoying these fantastic incomes, many are dissatisfied with their professional lives, and their single biggest complaint is the long hours they have to work. Lawyers could enjoy a lot more life outside of work if they were willing to accept relatively modest reductions in their incomes. Take, for example, a partner who is billing 2000 hours and being paid $200,000. If we assume that a twenty percent reduction in billable hours will translate into a twenty percent reduction in pay, this lawyer could trade $40,000 in income for 600 more hours of life outside work. Our hypothetical partner has a choice, then: He can make $200,000 per year and work many nights and most weekends—routinely getting up early, before his children are awake, driving to the office, eating lunch at his desk, leaving the office late, picking up dinner at the Taco Bell drive-through window, and then arriving home to kiss the cheeks of his sleeping children. Or he can make $160,000 per year and work few nights and weekends. He can spend time with his spouse, be a parent to his children, enjoy the company of his friends, pursue a hobby, do volunteer work, exercise regularly, and generally lead a well balanced life—*while still making $160,000 per year*. If those lawyers asked themselves, "What will make me a happier and healthier person: another $40,000 in income (which, after taxes, will mean another $25,000 or so in the bank) or 600 hours to do whatever I enjoy most?," it's hard to believe that many of them would take the money.

But many of them *do* take the money, including nearly all who remain in big firm practice. Thousands of lawyers choose to give up a healthy, happy, well-balanced life for a less healthy, less happy life dominated by work. And they do so merely to be able to make seven or eight times the national median income instead of five or six times the national median income. Why? Are lawyers just greedy?

Well, some are, but it's more complicated than that. For one thing, lawyers don't think in these terms. They don't see their lives as crazy. Very few lawyers are working extraordinarily long hours because they need the money. They're doing it for a different reason.

Big firm lawyers are, on the whole, a remarkably insecure and competitive group of people. Many of them have spent almost their entire lives competing to win games that other people have set up for them. First they competed to get into a prestigious college. Then they competed for college grades. Then they competed for LSAT scores. Then they competed to get into a prestigious law school. Then they competed for law school grades. Then they competed to make the law review. Then they competed for clerkships. Then they competed to get hired by a big law firm.

Now that they're in a big law firm, what's going to happen? Are they going to stop competing? Are they going to stop comparing themselves to others? Of course not. They're going to keep competing—competing to bill more hours, to attract more clients, to win more cases, to do more deals. They're playing a game. And *money* is how the score is kept in that game.

Why do you suppose sixty year old lawyers with millions of dollars in the bank still bill 2200 hours per year? Why do you suppose lawyers whose children have everything money can buy but who need the time and attention of their parents continue to spend most nights and weekends at the office—while continuing to write out checks to the best child psychologists in town? Why do you suppose one big firm partner I know flew into a rage after learning that his year-end bonus would be only—*only*—$400,000, while the bonus of one of his rivals in the firm would be $425,000?

It's not because these lawyers *need the money*. Any of these lawyers could lose every penny of his savings and see his annual income reduced by two-thirds and still live much more comfortably than the vast majority of Americans. What's driving these lawyers is the desire to *win the game*. These lawyers have spent their entire lives competing and measuring their worth by how well they do in the endless competitions. And now that they're working in a law firm, money is the way they keep score. Money is what tells them if they're more successful than the lawyer in the next office, or in the next office building, or in the next town. If a lawyer's life is dominated by the game—and if his success in the game is measured by money—then his *life* is dominated by money.[75] For many, many lawyers, it's that simple.

5.   *What about ethics?*

Law students are unconcerned about legal ethics primarily because they don't think that they will become unethical lawyers. Students think of unethical lawyers as the sleazeballs who chase ambulances (think Danny DeVito in *The Rainmaker*) or run insurance scams (think Bill Murray in *Wild Things*) or destroy evidence (think Al Pacino's crew in *The Devil's Advocate*). Students have a hard time identifying with these lawyers. When students think of life after graduation, they see themselves sitting on the 27th floor of some skyscraper in a freshly pressed dark suit (blue, black, or gray) with a starched blouse or shirt (white or light blue) doing sophisticated legal work for sophisticated clients. Students imagine—wrongly[76]—that such lawyers do not have to worry much about ethics, except, perhaps, when the occasional conflict of interest question arises.

If you think this—if you think that you will not have any trouble practicing law ethically—you are wrong. Dead wrong. In fact, particularly if you go to work for a big firm, you will probably begin to practice law

---

75.   As one participant in the ABA Litigation Section study of corporate defense litigators said:

> [Law firm partners live] in a cannibalistic world. They don't act differently toward their adversaries than they do toward each other. If you are a great lawyer, but don't bring in fees, you are fired. The only common value among a firm of 300 lawyers is money. There will be no other common values.

Quoted in Austin Sarat, Enactments of Professionalism: A Study of Judges' and Lawyers' Accounts of Ethics and Civility in Litigation, 67 Fordham L.Rev. 809, 826 (1998).

76.   It was precisely because so many blatant ethical violations were being committed by so many "talented partners at major establishment law firms" that the American Bar Association's Section of Litigation convened a task force of legal scholars and social scientists to study the ethics of big firm litigators. The illuminating and disturbing report may be found in Report, Ethics: Beyond the Rules, 67 Fordham L.Rev. 691 (1998), followed by analyses by a number of scholars.

unethically in at least some respects within your first year or two in practice. This happens to most young lawyers in big firms. It happened to me, and it will happen to you, unless you do something about it.

I mean three things when I speak of practicing law ethically. First, you generally have to comply with the formal disciplinary rules. As a law student, and then as a young lawyer, you will often be encouraged to distinguish ethical from unethical conduct *solely* by reference to the formal rules. In many other ways, subtle and blatant, you will be encouraged to think that conduct that does not violate the rules is "ethical," while conduct that does violate the rules is "unethical."

Defining ethics with reference to rules puts tremendous power in the hands of the organized bar that writes those rules. And many lawyers want the absence of disciplinary measures and adherence to the profession's own ethics rules to be sufficient to qualify a lawyer as "ethical," simply because it is *easy* to avoid disciplinary measures and to adhere to at least the letter of the formal rules.

It is important to learn and follow the formal rules, except on the rare occasions when a good person would engage in conscientious disobedience. But you should also understand that the formal rules represent nothing more than the lowest common denominator of conduct that a highly self-interested group will tolerate. For many lawyers, "[e]thics is a matter of steering, if necessary, just clear of the few unambiguous prohibitions found in rules governing lawyers."[77] But complying with the formal rules will not make you an ethical lawyer, any more than complying with the criminal law will make you an ethical person. Many of the sleaziest lawyers you will encounter will be absolutely scrupulous in their compliance with the formal rules. Complying with the rules is usually a *necessary*, but never a *sufficient*, part of being an ethical lawyer.

The second thing you must do to be an ethical lawyer is to act ethically in your work, even when you aren't required to do so by any rule. To a substantial extent, "bar ethical rules have lost touch with ordinary moral intuitions."[78] To practice law ethically you must practice law consistently with those intuitions. For the most part, this is not complicated. Being an ethical lawyer is not much different from being an ethical doctor or mail carrier or gas station attendant. Indeed, long before you applied to law school, your parents had probably taught you all that you need to know to practice law ethically. You should treat others as you want them to treat you. Be honest and fair. Show respect and compassion. Keep your promises. Here's a good rule of thumb: If you would be ashamed if your parents or spouse or children knew what you were doing, then you should not do it.

77. Frenkel et al., supra, at 703; see also Robert W. Gordon, The Ethical Worlds of Large–Firm Litigators: Preliminary Observations, 67 Fordham L.Rev. 709, 732 (1998); Carla Messikomer, Ambivalence, Contradiction, and Ambiguity: The Everyday Ethics of Defense Litigators, 67 Fordham L.Rev. 739, 743 (1998).

78. Id. at 675.

The third thing you must do to be an ethical lawyer is to live an ethical life. Many big firm lawyers ignore this point. So do many law professors who, when writing about legal ethics, tend to focus solely on the lawyer at work. But being admitted to the bar doesn't absolve you of your responsibilities outside of work—to your family, to your friends, to your community, and, if you're a person of faith, to your God. To practice law ethically, you must meet those responsibilities, which means that you must live a balanced life. If you become a workaholic lawyer, you will be unhealthy, probably unhappy, and, I would argue, unethical. I would be surprised if the belief system to which you subscribe—whether it be religiously or secularly based—regards a life dominated by the pursuit of wealth to the exclusion of all else as an ethical life, or an attorney who meets only his responsibilities to his clients and law partners as an ethical person.

It is hard to practice law ethically. Complying with the formal rules is the easy part. The rules are not very specific, and they don't demand very much. You may, on rare occasions, confront an extremely difficult conflict of interest problem that will require you to parse the rules carefully. You may even confront a situation in which some ethical or moral imperative compels you to *violate* the rules. But by and large, you will have no trouble complying with the rules; indeed, you are unlikely to give the rules much thought.

Acting as an ethical lawyer in the broader, non-formalistic sense of being honest and fair and compassionate is far more difficult. Practicing law ethically involves habitual and instinctive conduct in a everyday world occupied with the mundane. It is unlikely that one of your clients will drop a smoking gun on your desk or ask you to deliver a briefcase full of unmarked bills or invite you to have wild, passionate sex. These things happen to lawyers only in John Grisham novels. Your life as a lawyer will be filled with the kind of things that drove John Grisham to write novels: dictating letters and talking on the phone and drafting memoranda and performing "due diligence" and proofreading contracts and negotiating settlements and filling out time sheets. And because your life as a lawyer will be filled with the mundane, whether you practice law ethically will depend not upon how you resolve the one or two dramatic ethical dilemmas that you will confront during your entire career, but upon the hundreds of little things that you will do, almost unthinkingly, each and every day. You're going to have to act almost instinctively.

What this means, then, is that you will not practice law ethically—you *cannot* practice law ethically—unless acting ethically is habitual for you. You have to be in the *habit* of being honest. You have to be in the *habit* of being fair. You have to be in the *habit* of being compassionate. These qualities have to be deeply ingrained in you, so that you can't turn them on and off—so that acting honorably is not something you have to *decide* to do—so that when you're at work, making the thousands of phone calls you will make and writing the thousands of letters you will write and dealing with the thousands of people with whom you will deal, you will *automati-*

cally apply the same values in the workplace that you apply outside of work, when you are with family and friends.

Here's the problem, though: After your start practicing law, nothing is likely to influence you more than "the culture or house norms of the agency, department, or firm" in which you work.[79] If you are going into private practice—particularly private practice in a big firm—you are going to be immersed in a culture that is hostile to the values you now have. The system does not *want* you to apply the same values in the workplace that you do outside of work (unless you're rapaciously greedy outside of work); it wants you to replace those values with the system's values. The system is obsessed with money, and it wants you to be, too. The system wants you— it *needs* you—to play the game. No one will tell you, as one lawyer told another in a Charles Addams cartoon, "I admire your honesty and integrity, Wilson, but I have no room for them in my firm."[80] Instead, the culture will pressure you in more subtle ways to replace your values with the system's.

In a thousand ways, you will absorb big firm culture[81]—a culture of long hours of toil inside the office and short hours of conspicuous consumption outside the office. You will work among lawyers who will talk about money constantly and who will be intensely curious about how much money other lawyers are making. The lawyers in your firm are not unique. Thirty or forty years ago, talking about income and clients and fees " 'just [wa]sn't done,' " even among Wall Street lawyers. Today, "[t]he legal profession ... has become extraordinarily self-conscious about making money," and "the new legal journalism [has] hone[d] this self-consciousness to a sharp comparative and competitive edge."[82] Just about every issue of the *National Law Journal* or the *American Lawyer* includes at least one article about how much money some lawyer somewhere is making. Several times a year these journals publish extensive surveys of lawyers' incomes, focusing in particular on the incomes of associates and partners in big firms. These surveys are pored over by lawyers with the intensity that some boys bring to poring over the statistics of their favorite baseball players.

79. Michael J. Kelly, Lives of Lawyers: Journeys in the Organizations of Practice 18 ("[T]he culture or house norms of the agency, department, or firm play a dominant role in the way a lawyer practices. The organization profoundly affects the lives of lawyers."); see also Frenkel et al., supra, at 698 (discussing research showing that "the settings in which lawyers work are among the most powerful, contextual factors shaping enactments of professionalism.").

80. Actually, someone might tell you this. See Gordon, supra, at 718: "An associate

who raises an ethical objection, or even just a question, about what a partner or client wants is taking a risk of being perceived as a difficult or obstructive person.... An associate whose ethical fastidiousness poses the risk of displeasing or even losing the client will not last long."

81. *See* Messikomer, supra, at 759 (describing how big firm associates absorb "knowledge, techniques, norms, rules, and behavioral patterns" through "a process of 'osmosis' ").

82. Kelly, supra, at 170 (1994).

Big firm culture also reflects the many ways in which lawyers who are winning the game broadcast their success. A first year male associate will buy his suits off the rack at a department store; a couple years later, he'll be at Brooks Brothers; a few years after that, a salesperson will come to his office, with tape measures and fabric swatches in hand. Similar ostentatious progress will be demonstrated with regard to everything from watches to cell phones to running shoes to child care arrangements to private social clubs. When lawyers speak with envy or admiration about other lawyers, they do not mention a lawyer's devotion to family or public service, or a lawyer's innate sense of fairness, or even a lawyer's skill at trying cases or closing deals, nearly as much as they mention a lawyer's billable hours, or stable of clients, or annual income.

It is very difficult for a young lawyer immersed in this culture day after day to maintain the values she had as a law student.[83] Slowly, almost imperceptibly, young lawyers change. They begin to admire things they did not admire before, be ashamed of things they were not ashamed of before, find it impossible to live without things they lived without before. Somewhere, somehow, a lawyer changes from a person who gets intense pleasure from being able to buy her first car stereo to a person enraged over a $400,000 bonus.

As the values of an attorney change, so, too, does her ability to practice law ethically. The process that I have described will obviously push a lawyer away from practicing law ethically in the broadest sense—that is, in the sense of leading a balanced life and meeting non-work-related responsibilities. When work becomes all consuming, it consumes all. If you are working all the time, you won't, you can't, meet any other responsibilities that require any appreciable commitment of time or energy. This much is obvious. However, absorbing the values of big firm culture will also push a lawyer away from practicing law ethically in the narrower sense of being honest and fair and compassionate. In the highly competitive, money-obsessed world of big firm practice, "[m]ost of the new incentives for lawyers, such as attracting and retaining clients [and, I would add, billing copious amounts of hours], push toward stretching ethical concerns to the limit."[84]

83. Several researchers involved in the Ethics: Beyond the Rules project, supra, noted the "lack of connection" between the daily work of big firm litigators and "the lawyer's moral sense." Frenkel et al., supra, at 706. In other words, the researchers found that the ordinary "moral sense" that lawyers use to guide their personal lives has little carryover to their professional lives; the researchers also found that "moral sensitivity beyond [complying with] the rules ... is more apparent in associates than partners." Id.

84. Gordon, supra, at 735. See also Mark C. Suchman, Working Without a Net: The Sociology of Legal Ethics in Corporate Litigation, 67 Fordham L.Rev. 837, 860 (1998) (reporting the opinion of big firm litigators that many features of the incentive system within big firms, such as "billing pressures ..., competitive compensation, emphasis on rainmaking, and the favorable treatment of aggressiveness in evaluation," are "designed to reward behavior that [is] at best unrelated to ethicality, and at worst destructive of it.").

Unethical lawyers do not start out being unethical; they start out just like you—as perfectly decent young men or women who have every intention of practicing law ethically. They don't become unethical overnight; they become unethical just as you will (if you become unethical)—a little bit at a time. And they don't become unethical by shredding incriminating documents or bribing jurors; they become unethical just as you are likely to—by cutting a corner here, by stretching the truth a bit there. It will start with your time sheets. One day, not too long after you start practicing law, you will sit down at the end of a long, tiring day, and you just won't have much to show for your efforts in terms of billable hours. It will be near the end of the month. You will know that all of the partners will be looking at your monthly time report in a few days, so what you'll do is pad your time sheet just a bit. Maybe you'll bill a client for ninety minutes for a task that really took you only sixty minutes to perform. However, you will promise yourself that you will repay the client at the first opportunity by doing thirty minutes of work for the client for "free." In this way, you'll be "borrowing," not "stealing."

And then what will happen is that it will become easier and easier to take these little loans against future work. And then, after a while, you will stop paying back these little loans. You will convince yourself that, although you billed for ninety minutes and spent only sixty minutes on the project, you did such good work that your client should pay a bit more for it. After all, your billing rate is awfully low, and your client is awfully rich.

And then you will pad more and more: every two minute telephone conversation will go down on the sheet as ten minutes, every three hour research project will go down with an extra quarter hour or so. You will continue to rationalize your dishonesty to yourself in various ways until one day you stop doing even that. And, before long—it won't take much more than three or four years—you'll be stealing from your clients almost every day, and you won't even notice it.

You'll also become a liar. A deadline will come up one day, and, for reasons that are entirely your fault, you won't be able to meet it. So you'll call your senior partner or your client and make up a white lie for why you missed the deadline. And then you'll get busy and a partner will ask whether you proofread a lengthy prospectus and you'll say yes, even though you didn't. And then you'll be drafting a brief and you'll quote language from a Supreme Court opinion even though you'll know that, when read in context, the language does not remotely suggest what you are implying it suggests. And then, in preparing a client for a deposition, you'll help the client to formulate an answer to a difficult question that will likely be asked—an answer that will be "legally accurate" but that will mislead your opponent. And then you'll be reading through a big box of your client's documents—a box that hasn't been opened in twenty years—and you'll find a document that would hurt your client's case, but that no one except you knows exists, and you'll simply "forget" to produce it in response to your opponent's discovery requests.

After a couple years of this, you won't even notice that you're lying and cheating and stealing every day that you practice law. None of these things will seem like a big deal in itself—an extra fifteen minutes added to a time sheet here, a little white lie to cover a missed deadline there. But, after a while, your entire frame of reference will change. You will still be making dozens of quick, instinctive decisions every day, but those decisions, instead of reflecting the notions of right and wrong by which you conduct your personal life, will instead reflect the set of values by which you will conduct your professional life—a set of values that embodies not what's right or wrong, but what is profitable, and what you can get away with. The system will have succeeded in replacing your values with the system's values, and the system will be profiting as a result.

Does this happen to every big firm lawyer? Of course not. It's all a matter of degree. The culture in some big firms is better than in others. At the same time, you should not underestimate the likelihood that you will practice law unethically. And, although big firms and big firm lawyers are not all alike, they are *becoming* more alike. One of the most consistent findings of the social scientists involved in a recent ABA study of the ethics of big firm litigators was that the cultures of individual firms are weakening, leaving a "void of guidance to junior lawyers."[85] This void, in turn, is being "filled by other powerful systemic or environmental influences," especially influences from outside the firm.[86] In other words, the distinctive cultures of *individual big firms* are influencing young lawyers less and less, while a generic *big firm culture* is influencing young lawyers more and more.[87] That is why, no matter which big firm you join, there is a good chance that working at the firm will make you unhealthy, an even better chance that it will make you unhappy, and a very large chance that it will make you unethical—at least if you accept that practicing law ethically includes practicing law in a manner that permits you to meet your responsibilities to someone besides your firm and clients.

[In the remainder of the article Schiltz encourages students and young lawyers to "avoid working in large law firms—or in firms that act like law firms." He argues that the costs outweigh whatever benefits there may be to work in large law firms. Concluding that the only true benefit of big firms is money, Schiltz advises readers to "seek alternatives to private practice—and especially to big firm practice." They will be happier and healthier, in general, in public sector and corporate counsel positions. Students who choose large law firms despite this advice should shop carefully for firms that maintain an ethical culture, go to them with their eyes open, be prepared to resist the temptations to cut corners, and "develop the habit of acting ethically."]

---

85. See articles in Report: Beyond the Ethics Rules, supra: Frenkel et al., at 705; Gordon, at 717; Nelson, at 792; Sarat, at 824–25, 827–28; Suchman, at 857, 864.

86. Frenkel et al., supra, at 705.

87. Id.; Douglas N. Frenkel, Ethics: Beyond the Rules—Questions and Possible Responses, 67 Fordham L. Rev. 875, 880 (1998); Suchman, *supra* note 173, at 868.

D.   SOME FINAL THOUGHTS

Whose Morality?

This ancient question has lots of answers but no single answer. The content of the answer varies greatly depending upon whether the inquirer is thinking in philosophic, religious or anthropologic terms. The major strands in Western philosophy are familiar to most law students. One prominent stream of thought, undergoing a renaissance in recent years, stems from Aristotle and his concept of human flourishing. The basic idea is that reflection and discourse about the conditions and circumstances that lead to human flourishing will lead to a broad range of agreement concerning such matters as virtue and vice, good character, presumptive moral principles and practical judgment.[1] A second prominent strand, stemming from Kant, attempts to build an elaborate superstructure of rights, duties and moral rules from simple foundations, such as Kant's principle that human beings are not to be used solely as means. A third strand, originating in Hobbes and Locke, is often lumped together under the rubric "social contract theory." Johns Rawls' egalitarian principle of justice as fairness, derived from the point of view of a detached observer standing behind the "veil of ignorance," is an influential modern version of social contract thought.[2] A fourth major school of moral philosophers emphasizes the consequences of action or inaction—"the greatest good for the greatest number." A prominent modern version of utilitarian consequentialism, stemming from Bentham and Adam Smith, is committed to an economic approach to issues of law and justice.[3]

At a high level of abstraction any of these philosophic traditions can be consistent and satisfying, but each is elusive and frustrating to a person with a particular history, background and role who confronts a messy situation in which two or more moral principles appear relevant. Philosophy then becomes both too abstract and too conflicted—a Babel of contra-

---

1. See Alasdair MacIntyre, After Virtue (1982), and MacIntyre, Whose Justice? Which Rationality? (1988); Martha Nussbaum, The Fragility of Goodness: Luck and Ethics in Greek Tragedy and Philosophy (1986); John Finnis, Natural Law and Natural Rights (1980).

2. John Rawls, A Theory of Justice (1971). See also Ronald Dworkin, Taking Rights Seriously (1978) (a theory of rights applied to judicial decision-making), and Dworkin, Law's Empire (1986) (the objective of law is not to report consensus or provide efficient means to social goals, but to answer the requirement that a political community

act in a coherent and principled manner toward its members); David Gauthier, Morals by Agreement (1986) (deriving an ethical system from a principle of rational cooperation that should be accepted by self-interested individuals).

3. See Richard A. Posner, Problems in Jurisprudence (1992) and The Economics of Justice (1981). See also Robert H. Frank, Passions Within Reasons (1988) (the role of moral sentiments in rational choice). Other modern consequentualists, following John Stuart Mill, do not emphasize economic consequences.

dictory approaches and assertions all couched in esoteric jargon.[4] Most of us at that point retreat for guidance to the commitments we have made and the community from which we draw our image of ourselves.

Robert Fulghum expresses this approach in a popular, secular form:[5]

Most of what I really need to know about how to live and what to do and how to be I learned in kindergarten. Wisdom was not at the top of the graduate school mountain, but there in the sandpile at Sunday school. These are the things I learned:

Share everything.

Play fair.

Don't hit people.

Put things back where you found them.

Clean up your own mess.

Don't take things that aren't yours.

Say you're sorry when you hurt somebody.

Wash your hands before you eat.

Flush.

Warm cookies and cold milk are good for you.

Live a balanced life—learn some and think some and draw and paint and sing and dance and play and work every day some.

Take a nap every afternoon.

When you go out into the world, watch out for traffic, hold hands and stick together. . . .

For most Americans, this sort of popular morality derives from the religious and cultural values explicitly or implicitly conveyed in home, church, school, college and, for budding lawyers, law school. Religion is the neglected stepchild of the academic world even though for most Americans it is one of the most powerful influences on moral development. Moreover, social scientists tell us that most Americans are believers and take their religion seriously enough to participate on a regular basis.[6] For many of us a religious tradition, fostered in the home and in church or synagogue, provides a moral compass that is directional to a greater or lesser degree.

Although it is trendy in moral philosophy to talk about dialectic rationality—mature, responsible, intelligent adults sitting around a table calmly and endlessly discussing the aims of life—in practice agreement on many specific matters of morality seems impossible to achieve (e.g., abor-

---

4. See Alasdair MacIntyre, After Virtue (1982) (the Enlightenment project of providing a shared, rationally justifiable, secular basis for morality has failed).

5. Robert Fulghum, All I Really Need to Know I learned in Kindergarten: Uncommon Thoughts on Common Things 4–5 (1988).

6. See Andrew M. Greeley, Religious Change in America (1989); Phillip L. Berman, The Search for Meaning (1990); Christopher Lasch, The True and Only Heaven: Progress and Its Critics (1991).

tion, assisted suicide).[7] And the concept of dialogic exercise signifies a detached rationality that lacks the warmth, fervor and commitment that can be supplied either by religious experience and belief or by absorption in a secular cause that builds strong ties among its adherents. People who do important things usually are fired by the kind of enthusiasm that flows from being committed to narratives of human aspiration, suffering and redemption that have implications in terms of moral behavior.

Man is a rational animal, but the image of man as only a rational decision-maker does not describe most people's experience. Human beings are seldom as rational and free as most modern philosophical ethics assume, an important point discussed below. Stanley Hauerwas, drawing on the work of Iris Murdoch, argues that how we view the world is more fundamental than deciding particular moral questions.[8] Moral virtue, according to Hauerwas and Murdoch, is not so much the result of making ethically correct decisions as it is a matter of orienting ourselves according to what is good, beautiful and true. We create our world as well as live in it. It is thus a world in which "reality" is elusive and our imagination of reality is central. Murdoch refers to "unselfings," moments in which through an act of will the self is denied—forgotten, if you will—allowing us to discover an essential component of reality, the reality of the other. Freedom is living in accordance with reality, but that means we must take responsibility for imagining the reality of others, which requires the humility to "unself." The truly moral life may be located in these moments of "unselfing."

Social scientists tell us that Americans find it difficult to express ideas concerning moral values.[9] Religious terms such as sin, grace and repentance have been banned from the secular public forum, crippling our moral language. By default, this leads to heavy reliance on the language and symbols of either managers or therapists, such as in the profusion of "self-help" books that crowd the bookstores.

Anthropologists tell us that most human beings get a sense of self, community and hope from membership in a community. Carol Greenhouse's study of how Baptists in a Georgia community think and act in dealing with disputes concludes that "people tend to explain their morals by claiming membership in a community—a family, an ethnic group, a

---

7. The existence of moral disagreement is sometimes taken, erroneously, as establishing the truth of relativism or subjectivism. But the fact that rational people can disagree on some matters does not prove that the world is governed solely by subjectivism, force or irrationality. See Isaiah Berlin, The Crooked Timber of Humanity (1991). Human beings, located within history, exchange reasons and arguments about things that are good and bad, sound or unsound. This effort to persuade (a search for truth) is not equivalent to manipulation and unreason. See Martha Nussbaum, Human Functioning and Social Justice, 20 Political Theory 202 (May 1992).

8. Stanley Hauerwas, Vision and Virtue (1974), drawing on Iris Murdoch, The Sovereignty of Good (1970).

9. See Robert N. Bellah et al., Habits of the Heart: Individualism and Commitment in American Life (1985).

region of the country, or in the case of her Baptists, a congregation."[10] As Thomas L. Shaffer puts it, "We account for our morals, unintentionally, by naming what we belong to."[11] Shaffer argues that most people at the moment of moral choice do not engage in the sort of "ethical dilemma" thinking that pervades teaching of moral and legal ethics—discussion of a moral quandary based on highly abstracted and limited facts.[12] Instead, people remember or discover who they are, a psychological homecoming, and then, having remembered or discovered that they belong to a community or are living out a story, act as if they were members of that community or engaged in that story. Moral action is founded not on "principles" or on "choice" as much as it is on the commitments of participation in community. As deTocqueville said, America is "a society built not on obedience [to principles] but on participation."[13]

Moral life is simpler if one is brought up in a single community in which one moral language expresses a relatively coherent set of ideals, commitments, roles and expectations. Today we must cope with multiple moral traditions: with a Western tradition that is highly eclectic, diverse and pluralistic, and also with a multicultural world in which the cacophony of religions and philosophies is compounded by voices expressing the old divisions of class, race, ethnicity and sex and newer ones of sexual preference and "life style."

Is Role Relevant?

A basic criticism of legal ethics by some moral philosophers is the argument that the nature of law practice itself, when conducted in faithful adherence to official standards, is inherently amoral or immoral. That is, a good person, observing the ordinary morality of people generally, cannot also be a good lawyer who observes professional requirements. When an abstract vision of ordinary morality is compared with the stereotypical description of legal ethics, lawyers look bad. Lawyers appear to be partisan rather than disinterested, as ordinary morality would prescribe, guileful rather than open, grasping rather than generous and duplicitous rather than truthful. Things that lawyers do as a matter of course, such as asserting the statute of limitations to bar a "just" claim or assisting an immoral cause, become morally questionable.

One response to this criticism is that the moral philosophers have built their edifice on a shaky foundation: The law and ethics of lawyering is much less single-minded than the straw figure that the moral philosophers have sought to destroy. First, ethics rules provide lawyers with a great deal of moral choice in selection of clients, control of procedure and tactics,

10. Thomas L. Shaffer and Mary M. Shaffer, American Lawyers and Their Communities: Ethics in the Legal Profession 25 (1991), discussing Carol J. Greenhouse, Praying for Justice: Faith, Order, and Community in an American Town (1986).

11. Id.

12. Robert M. Cover makes a similar point. See Cover, Nomos and Narrative, 97 Harv. L.Rev. 4.10 (1983) (normative behavior is communal in character).

13. Quoted in Shaffer and Shaffer, supra, at 26.

opportunities for moral suasion of clients, withdrawal from representation of a client who will not take a lawyer's advice and, in the versions adopted by most states, disclosure of a client's confidences to prevent serious harm to courts and third persons. But this argument does not respond to the basic point that the lawyer's traditional role permits and generally commits lawyers to a partisan presentation on behalf of clients that puts client interests first.

A more fundamental response to the philosophers' critique of the lawyer's partisan role rests on a skepticism about whether the abstract universalism of the moral philosophers fairly reflects the contextuality and complexity of moral action. The universalism generated by Kantian and Benthamite premises—that all human beings are of equal value—may lead to silly conclusions such as that a mother's preference for her own child, as against the claims of a distant child in Somalia, is morally unworthy. Ordinary morality, however, involves conceptions of doing the right thing in the family, the neighborhood, the workplace and as a citizen in a range of communities (local, state, national and international). Moral actors are also located in time, space and circumstance. Any meta-ethics that ignores these brute facts is simplistic, unrealistic and predicated upon misconceptions about moral action.

The idealized ordinary person of some moral philosophers has no personal history and thus acts in problematic situations without constraining commitments to others. She confronts stipulated facts that are perfectly comprehensible at the point of fateful decision. Her ethical repertoire is clearly apparent to her, and she is readily able to determine the relative priority of her values in whatever circumstances may be presented. Her ethical choices are never subject to being second-guessed. This idealized ordinary person does not exist in this world.

In the real world actors have personal histories which determine their position in life at any moment of ethical choice. Having a position in life limits one's options in taking action and therefore limits one's ethical options. People in the real world operate in a web of commitments to others. Having commitments to others—children, family members, fellow believers, friends, co-workers, co-adherents to a cause, etc.—makes one a partisan, whether willingly or unwillingly. Information relevant to a decision arrives disjointed and is often contradictory. Having fragmentary information means that ethical choices are often based on factual assumptions that turn out to be wrong. Among other consequences, this uncertainty often requires decisions modulated by concern that one should, as Oliver Cromwell said, "think it possible that you may be mistaken." So far as competing values are concerned, most people discover that their repertoire of values is not fully apparent to them until the moment of decision, and even then remains disorganized and often internally discordant. Perhaps most important, in the real world people have to answer to others for the consequences of what they have done. Accusation and recrimination are agonizing possibilities that must be considered at the time of action.

Circumstances such as these have the result that, as a practical matter, values that we affirm as fundamental in the abstract often turn out to be incompatible in concrete application. Isaiah Berlin tellingly expounds the incommensurability of values:

> [S]cientifically minded rationalists declared that conflict and tragedy arose only from ignorance of fact [and] inadequacies of method . . . so that, in principle, at least, . . . a harmonious, rationally organized society [can be] established. . . . But if it is the case that not all ultimate human ends are necessarily compatible, there may be no escape from choices governed by no overriding principle, some of them painful, both to the agent and to others.[14]

Thus the real world of ordinary people, as Berlin argues, may offer "no escape from choices governed by no overriding principle."[15] Lawyers' ethics should be compared with those of real world people rather than idealized cardboard figures.

Some of the classic "hard cases" of legal ethics—defending a person that the lawyer knows is guilty, pleading the statute of limitations against a person who has a good claim and interjecting the lawyer's own moral and prudential values into advice given the client[16]—have analogs in ordinary life: The parent who is confronted with a police officer who believes the parent's child has stolen merchandise from a store; the situation in which one person says to another, concerning an old grievance, "Can't we just forget about it?"; and the many situations where business or family advice is offered, often unsolicited, to colleagues, friends and family members. In all these situations, for good reasons, ordinary people have difficulty doing what some moral universals say is the right thing.

Doing the right thing in law practice is no easier. Defending the guilty, pleading the statutes of limitations and giving hard advice are often the right things to do, even if they involve a conflict in values. Trying to do the right thing, when it is impossible to do so without conflict of values, is one of society's necessary but messy jobs. However, no one is compelled to become a lawyer or, generally, to represent a particular client. If doing so is repugnant in a particular case, one should withdraw. If doing so is repugnant as a more general matter, one should leave the profession. But can the ethical problems arising from circumstance, background and com-

---

14. Isaiah Berlin, The Crooked Timber of Humanity 234–35 (1991).

15. The contextuality and complexity of moral decision-making makes it difficult to state or agree upon a set of rationally ordered principles. But the existence of rational disagreement should not be viewed as establishing the dominance or inevitability of unreason. Power alone does not govern the affairs of human beings; persuasion by rational argument remains central.

16. The governing rule of legal ethics is clear in all three cases. A lawyer retained or appointed to defend a guilty person has an ethical obligation to provide effective assistance in defending the case; if a client wishes to assert the defense of statute of limitations, the lawyer has an ethical duty to interpose the statute; and, with regard to interjection of personal moral and prudential values, professional rules give the lawyer the authority and at times the duty to be assertive.

mitment be escaped in any station in life other than as an inmate in an insane asylum?

Does the Legal Profession Provide Sure Moral Guidance?

The professional rhetoric of lawyers and bar associations carries the implication that a lawyer can find sure guidance in facing problems encountered in law practice in the traditions and ethics of the legal profession. At the individual level, the moral example of professional mentors—teachers, practitioners and judges—is an energizing source of guidance and aspiration. At the collective level the resonance of images and stories, such as those suggested by the Holmes and Choate quotations at the beginning of this chapter, helps form a lawyer's professional persona. But the guidance from rules of formal ethics is less sure and more troubling.

First, an unthinking obedience to professional rules that state a clear duty involves a moral simplification that may lead to wrongdoing. Consider, for example, the blanket obligation to report of Model Rule 8.3 or the limited disclosure options of Model Rule 1.6. Would a truly moral lawyer conform woodenly to those prescriptions? Reliance on a handbook of rules is tempting but results in a simplified moral framework that fails to include some moral aspects of a particular situation.[17] A good lawyer who is also a good person may be faced with some situations in which civil disobedience of the profession's edicts may be the truly moral choice.

Second, the profession's rules fail to give guidance in many problematic situations. Sometimes the rules are self-contradictory, with one rule pointing in one direction and another in a different direction. Sometimes the ethics rules are contradicted by other law, especially agency law, criminal law, procedural law or regulatory law, containing provisions that permit or require a lawyer to take action that the profession's rules appear to prohibit or vice versa.[18] More frequently, the ethics rules fail to tell a lawyer what to do but leave it to the individual lawyer's discretion. Whether to accept a client, whether to conform to a client's direction on a matter of procedure or tactics, whether to try to persuade the client to take a particular course of action, whether to withdraw when the client rejects advice or wants assistance that the lawyer finds repugnant and whether to disclose a client's future crime or fraud—the ethics rules leave these decisions to lawyer discretion. Such guidance as exists in these situations comes from the ideology and practice of professional subcultures of which the lawyer is part: the criminal defense bar, legal services lawyers, plaintiff's personal injury lawyers, outside or inside counsel to large corporations, etc. But even within a legal subculture, ideology and practice are highly variable and often rest on unexamined assumptions.

---

17. See John Ladd, The Quest for a Code of Professional Ethics: An Intellectual and Moral Confusion, reprinted in Geoffrey C. Hazard, Jr. and Deborah L. Rhode (eds.),

The Legal Profession: Responsibility and Regulation 105 (2d ed. 1988).

18. See the discussion of client fraud at p. 282 above.

Third, the profession's messages are influenced by the self-interest of the profession itself. In the 19th century the moral framework of American lawyers was heavily influenced by the "lawyer as gentleman" in a largely white, Protestant, capitalist culture.[19] In the 20th century efforts to adapt the profession to a more competitive world in professional services and to make the profession more accountable to consumers and to the public were generally resisted by the organized bar.[20] Every group that has a strong collective identity tends to view the world from a special vantage point. The tendency of individuals and groups to believe that what is in their own interest is also in the general interest is a constant danger. Thus a skeptical evaluation of the profession's rules, rather than an uncritical obedience, is called for.

Finally, the profession's preference for clients is itself limited by the responsibilities of lawyers to courts, other legal institutions and third persons. Whose interests must be considered?

Who Are the Relevant Others?

Each of us exists in a world in which individual uniqueness is shaped by social and cultural forces. The structure of our world is determined by such objective or external factors as our sex, age, race, religion, nationality, circumstances of birth and upbringing, education and family status at any given time. It is also determined by our occupation in life. Thus, it is one thing to be male, another to be female; to be a child, a young aspiring professional, or a retired person; to be a Caucasian in the Far East or an Asian in the United States; to have had supportive nurturing as a child or to have suffered privation or abuse; and to be married with responsibilities for children or not. Similarly, it is one thing to be a lawyer and another to be a teacher, a business manager or a blue-collar worker. These and other aspects of circumstance may have moral significance in a specific situation.

The world of the self is determined by internal factors as well. In aggregate these constitute a person's subjective viewpoint—the world as it appears from inside one's station in life. People having substantially the same background and education, and engaged in essentially the same vocation, respond very differently to different kinds of ethical problems, as anyone knows who has participated with other committee members in deliberating upon such a problem. These differences in "personality" can be crudely correlated with various personal background factors. For example, some feminists and many commentators assert that many men respond to ethically charged situations in ways different from most women.[21] People who are verbally articulate usually respond in different terms than people

19. See Thomas L. Shaffer and Mary M. Shaffer, supra, cc. 2–4 (discussing and critiquing the American tradition of the "lawyer as gentleman").

20. See Richard Abel, American Lawyers (describing and critiquing the professional project to increase the status, authority and income of lawyers).

21. See, e.g., Carol G. Gilligan, In a Different Voice 25 (1982).

who express themselves dramatically or in body language.[22] Nurture as well as nature also has important effects on development, character and personality.

A person, however, is not simply a summation of his or her life experience. Stated one way or another, this is the problem of free will—the realization that, whoever and whatever one of us may be, an element of subjective freedom is involved in every ethically significant decision. The response to an ethically problematic encounter on the part of one specific person thus is a product of the unique mind and spirit which that person brings to that unique encounter.

These aspects of one's station in life—objective circumstance, personal history and unique occasion for action—apply both to lawyers and to nonlawyers.[23] Every lawyer has such a station in every moment of practice. Being a lawyer entails having clients and having clients in turn entails special ethical responsibilities. In addition to professional identity as a lawyer, every lawyer practices in a context that has its own legal subculture. Within each legal subculture, substantial variation is found: Although corporate lawyers tend to have some characteristic attitudes different from those of criminal lawyers, lawyers in each subgroup are not all cut to the same pattern. Everyone who practices law gives the vocation a personal definition.

To recognize station in life and personal subjective viewpoint, and their relevance to ethical choice, is not to reject the notion that there are general ethical principles that speak to situations in life. We believe that foundational ethical principles, or at least a universal ethical perspective, can be identified.[24] A society cannot exist at all, let alone flourish, without some generally accepted rules against harming other people, stealing, lying, breaking of promises and the like. Language itself is dependent upon some degree of truth-telling. Moreover, if ethical perspectives were not shared, we could not make ethical comparisons, whether in terms of station in life or personal experience or otherwise.

Another aspect of a universal ethical perspective is that, in the absence of other considerations, all people should be treated equally. Of course, other considerations are always present, so that the ethical universal never has unqualified application. But that does not diminish the ideal of universal equality.

Ethical responsibility requires consideration of who are the "relevant others" for whom an actor should have ethical concern. A second dimen-

---

22. See Herman Melville, Billy Budd (published posthumously in 1924) (portraying and contrasting an inarticulate person's response to evil with the response of a "rational," educated actor).

23. Nonlawyers also have stations in life, as accountants or mechanics, homemakers or breadwinners, parents or children, neighbors or strangers. They combine various personal attributes in infinite variation, each one in his or her own way of life. They encounter ethical problems similar to those encountered by lawyers.

24. See James Q. Wilson, The Moral Sense (1993) (arguing that empirical studies suggest a core of near universal moral attitudes).

sion consists of the established and recognized rules governing the situation—the rules of the game. A third dimension consists of time, including time past and the future. Another factor, that of uncertainty, modifies these other dimensions. All real-world ethical problems have these dimensions: pre-existing rules, a placement in time and actors functioning under conditions of uncertainty. Thus, ethical analysis is more complicated than generally conceived.

Ethically conscious actors are aware that the world is full of such relevant others. Many of them are much in need of our benefactions, including legal services from those who practice law.[25] The principle of moral equity provides no basis for choosing which is most deserving. The triage problem thus plays out in infinite variation. Explaining the triage problem is the basic insight of economic analysis: Human needs, or at least human wants, forever outrun available resources to meet them. The principles of economics, of course, do not exhaust ethical analysis. But ethical analysis that is unmindful of economics fails to take account of relevant others.

And yet, we should pause before relying on the calculating rationality that suggests the moral superiority of weighing a response to a neighbor in need against the claims of real and hypothetical others who are not present. The parable of the Good Samaritan was a response to a lawyer's question: "Who is my neighbor?" The answer in narrative form was that everyone in the community, regardless of class, race or religion, is a neighbor whom we should treat with the care and respect that we give to ourselves. Jesus was not engaged in a philosophic analysis of problems of triage but was vividly portraying the ideal of reaching out to those in the community whose need confronts us face-to-face. We are present, we see the need, we have the capacity to help, and we should respond.[26]

The person who stops first to ponder the conflicting and more distant claims of the engagement for which he is heading or the alternate uses of his time and money may end preferring the convenience and profit of not becoming involved. A terrible truth about human rationality is its tendency to find rationalizations for what is convenient and profitable. Rejecting the passionate response to the immediate needs of the injured and helpless victim in order to serve some more abstract good may involve a terrible paradox. At what point does the calculated rationality of such a person so diminish her humanity that she is no longer able to recognize or serve the larger good?

25. Is it immoral to choose to become a corporate lawyer rather than a public defender or a legal services lawyer? Charles Fried, The Lawyer as Friend: The Moral Foundations of the Lawyer–Client Relation, 85 Yale L.J. 1060, 1076–80 (1976), argues that individual autonomy provides a moral justification for choosing a type of practice one prefers rather than one that satisfies utilitarian considerations of "the greatest good to the greatest number." Is he right?

26. Recall the Jewish story of "repairing the world" by picking up bits of glass and the Christian statement to the effect that he who does good to "the least among us" also does it to God. See p. 1064 supra.

Everyone Is Accountable

The simple binary choices of moral quandaries such as that involving Kohlberg's husband, druggist and sick spouse postulate complete autonomy in making the decision whether or not to steal the drug (see p. 36 supra). That kind of freedom rarely if ever exists in the real world. Rather, every actor is in some way accountable to someone beyond those whose interests are immediately involved, whether it be family members, a co-worker, an employer, a governmental authority or the court of public opinion.

Accountability means having to answer to someone else for what one has done—explaining and justifying the course of action that has been chosen. When contemplating action, the actor must calculate whether the justification will be convincing to the relevant audience. Such a calculation must include an estimate of how the facts will look to that other person. Accountability often turns not on questions about the governing norms, but on questions of fact. Questions of fact can arise whether accountability takes the form of legal responsibility or discussion within a family or organization as to how a relative, neighbor or co-worker should have been treated. The calculation about accountability must also include an estimate of how the balance that was struck by the actor between the competing interests—stealing versus helping a sick spouse—will be regarded by those to whom the actor is accountable.

One statement can be made with certainty: The problem of choice will *not* look precisely the same in retrospect as reviewed by the actor's professional group or by external bodies as it did to the protagonist at the moment of choice. All forms of review involve an element of second-guessing in which hindsight bias is an established fact.[27]

The professional ideal of independent judgment involves a sphere of autonomous authority.[28] Nevertheless, a lawyer who is a member of a firm is directly accountable to her partners or associates for ethically debatable decisions. More than one law firm has fallen apart when such a decision did not sit well with colleagues. Accountability for a solo practitioner is less direct but nevertheless real. A solo practitioner depends on "reputation" for a continued flow of referrals, and reputation is the community's informal system of accountability. Also, all lawyers in principle must answer to the state's disciplinary agency. When a breach of ethics also involves violation of criminal or tort law, for example, in misappropriation of client funds or a departure from ordinary care, lawyers are also accountable to the criminal and civil law.

Accountability to legal authority is especially significant in legal ethics. In most forms of law practice a lawyer is an agent for the client.[29] As an

---

27. The findings of psychologists concerning "hindsight bias" are discussed at p. 302 supra.

28. See M.R. 5.4(c); Model Code, Canon 5.

29. An exception, or perhaps only an apparent exception, is a lawyer who also holds authority as a principal. The most common instance is a government attorney who is a legally constituted public official, such as a prosecutor or an attorney general. The merger of the function of lawyer and public official presents a problem often referred to

agent for a client, a lawyer owes legal and ethical duties to the client. Not all lawyers equally understand that an agent also owes legal and ethical duties to the third person with whom the lawyer deals on behalf of the client.[30] The principle of agency accountability is not merely a legal concept; it is an ethical concept as well.

Two things are clear about an agent's accountability. First, an agent may not be fully chargeable with the principal's purposes. The agent rarely has the same knowledge of relevant facts as the principal and only limited knowledge of the principal's purpose. Moreover, ethical and legal conceptions of loyalty allow substantial deference to the principal's choices.

The other aspect of agency accountability, however, is that at some point and degree of involvement, an agent is equally chargeable with the principal for an ethically problematic choice. In legal terms, this is the liability that is described as "aiding and abetting." In the practice of law, a similar limitation is expressed in the canon that a lawyer's zeal on behalf of a client must be "within the bounds of the law."[31] In the language of ordinary ethics, the same idea is expressed in the proposition that it is not a defense simply to say "they made me do it" or "I was only doing my job." Ethically conscious actors are aware that while political authority is a source of ethical justification or excuse, and often an impetus to doing good, it is also an impetus to complicity in doing evil.

The fact of accountability in all real world relationships thus implicates problems of politics. Politics *is* the allocation of power and authority. Politics in this classical sense is not everything there is to ethics, but ethical analysis unmindful of politics is incomplete. These complications come into view, however, only if we include political authority among the "relevant others" who are involved in real world ethical dilemmas.

In summary, real-world ethical problems have unavoidable complications arising from the number of relevant others whose interests are involved in resolving such problems. The resulting complexity would be unmanageable without rules and conventions that impose priorities and give preferred position to various "relevant others." For lawyers, the qualified preference is given to a client, but not in disregard of the interests of "relevant others" who are not clients. For those in other stations in life, such as parent or business manager, there are counterpart rules of qualified preference. One of the functions of legal rules and institutions is to establish, maintain and circumscribe such rules of preference.

In Closing

When lawyers or future lawyers gather for ceremonial occasions, such as a Law Day banquet or a law school graduation ceremony, speakers call

---

in terms of "who is the client?" See Chapter 8 above.

30. See generally Restatement (Second) of Agency § 343 et seq. (tort liability); Lucas v. Hamm, 56 Cal.2d 588, 15 Cal.Rptr. 821, 364 P.2d 685 (1961) (malpractice liability

of will drafter to intended beneficiaries); United States v. Benjamin, 328 F.2d 854 (2d Cir.1964) (criminal liability).

31. See M.R. 1.2(d), Model Code, Canon 7.

forth the kind of rhetoric found in talks at other ceremonies marking beginnings and endings: some aspiration, some nostalgia, perhaps even some pretense. Pretense can be a bad thing, of course, but there are many worse things than having ideals we know we do not fully live up to—active participation in evil, for example, or acquiescence in evil committed by others.

The lawyer's morality of duty consists primarily of observing the limits of law in counseling and advocacy for clients. The moral tradition of the profession, reflected in part in the crime-fraud exception to the attorney-client privilege and the ethical prohibition on assisting a client in criminal, fraudulent or illegal conduct, is to take legal strictures seriously and to observe them. But a truly moral life goes beyond conceptions of duty. The morality of aspiration of many lawyers builds on the idea that justice is not solely an ideal that is dependent upon the state, acting through the formal institutions of the law.[32] Maintaining and improving the formal institutions of justice is a responsibility that every lawyer should undertake. But it is not enough. Justice also flows from how people, including lawyers, treat each other every day. In the broader sense, justice is a gift that good people give to each other by how they act in everyday encounters.

Karl Llewellyn, a teacher and mentor of one of the authors, used to tell his students: "Technique without compassion is a menace; compassion without technique is a mess." Both are necessary to a successful and happy professional life.

Some years ago the National Institutes of Health did a study of the quality of medical care delivered to patients by a large group of general practice physicians. The study was designed to shed some light on what characteristics were highly correlated to high quality medical care. Thousands of bits of information about the physicians and the circumstances of their practice were fed into the computers along with an objective evaluation of the patients' files. On almost every item the study came up with negative results: Most differences between physicians—age, ethnicity, experience, medical school, size of practice, etc.—did not seem to matter. But significant findings emerged on a tantalizing series of items that tell something about what it takes to be a good physician. The physicians who always delivered good medical care subscribed to and read medical journals; they attended out-of-town medical education meetings (attending local ones was not significant); they responded to their patients' emergency needs and requests; and they worked long hours.

What does this study tell us? The good physician cares about medicine, possessing an intellectual interest in and continuing curiosity about this area of human knowledge. He cares about his patients. And he cares about his own self-integrity and performance as a physician. The result is an

---

32. Lon L. Fuller distinguished the "morality of duty" and the "morality of aspiration" in Fuller, The Morality of Law (1964). See also the report on the lawyer's role drafted for an AALS–ABA Joint Committee, Professional Responsibility: Report of the Joint Conference, 44 A.B.A. J. 1159 (1958); and Robert P. Lawry, The Central Moral Tradition of Lawyering, 19 Hofstra L.Rev. 311 (1990).

internalized value system that finds doing good work rewarding and doing sloppy work a source of shame and guilt.

The same things are true of the good lawyer: She cares about the law, maintaining throughout her career an intellectual interest in it and a desire to improve it. She cares about her clients and suffers with them if they suffer. To a lesser degree, she also cares for and considers the interests of third persons who are affected by why she does for her client. Finally, she cares about herself as a professional—a skilled, principled and compassionate professional who delivers honest work for honest pay.

Law graduates sometimes delude themselves into believing that work can be separated from the rest of life, that "doing time" in hateful professional work for big bucks will be made up by the enjoyments of leisure and personal life, now or in some future stage of life. The problem is that being a good professional takes too much time and attention; it cannot be separated from the rest of life. Work turns out to be too important a part of one's self and one's life.

An African–American spiritual has it right:

O you gotta get a glory in the work you do,
A Hallelujah chorus in the heart of you.
Paint or tell a story, Sing or shovel coal,
But you gotta get a glory Or the job lacks soul.[33]

33. Quoted in Caroline Royds, Prayers for   Children 36 (1988).

INDEX

CLIENT FRAUD
General, 282–309
Hindsight bias, 302
Lawyer codes
Canons, 283
Model Code, 283–285
Model Rules, 285–286
O.P.M. fraud, 304
Restatement on, 288
State ethics rules on, 288, 302
Withdrawal upon discovery, 287–288, 463

CLIENT FUNDS AND PROPERTY
See also Attorney Liens; Lawyer–Client Contracts; Lawyer–Client Relationship; Fee Disputes
General, 553–556
Accounting, to client, 555
Advance fee payments, 501
Attorney liens, 565–566
Audits, 556
Client protection funds, 555
Commingling, 553–555
Fees, 489–521
IOLTA accounts, 556
Retainer fees, 501
Trust accounts, general, 553–556

CLIENT PROTECTION FUNDS, 555

CLIENT TRUST ACCOUNTS, 553–556

COACHING
See Witnesses

CODE OF JUDICIAL CONDUCT, 17, 926

CODE OF PROFESSIONAL RESPONSIBILITY
See Model Code of Professional Responsibility

CODES
See also Canons of Professional Ethics; Model Code of Professional Responsibility; Model Rules of Professional Conduct
General, 3–5
Source of moral guidance, 1223
Violation of, as basis for malpractice, 171
Uniform codes for all lawyers, 453

COFFEE, JOHN C., JR.
Plaintiffs' class action lawyers, 824–832

COHEN, GEORGE M.
Class actions, 848
Malpractice insurance, 175

COMMINGLING FUNDS
See Client Funds and Property; Client Trust Accounts

COMMUNICATION WITH CLIENT
See also Attorney–Client Privilege; Confidentiality
Class, members of, 544

COMMUNICATION WITH CLIENT
—Cont'd
Duty to keep client informed, 470–473
Insurance representation, 637
Plea bargain offer, 484
Settlement offer, 474–476

COMMUNICATION WITH REPRESENTED PERSON OR PARTY, 533–551
See also Represented Person or Party

COMPETENCE
See also Admission to Practice; Continuing Legal Education (CLE); Effective Assistance of Counsel; Legal Education; Malpractice
General, 149–202
Definition of, 150
Discipline for neglect, 151–152, 916, 922–923
Extent of incompetent lawyering, 149–151
Lawyer codes on, 151–152
Malpractice remedy, 154–176
Model Rules and Model Code, 151–152
Measures to assure, 151–154

COMPULSORY BAR MEMBERSHIP, 961–965
History, 961–962
Political activities, 962–965

CONCEALING EVIDENCE
General, 39–61
Contraband, 53
Dead Bodies case, 57–59
District of Columbia, 56
Model Penal Code, 53
Physical evidence, 39–61
Witness availability, 551

CONFIDENTIALITY
See also Attorney–Client Privilege; Conflict of Interest; Disclosure; Perjury; Whistleblowing
General, 203–336
Bodily harm threatened, 310–332
Centrality of to bar, 131–133, 249–250
Client consent to disclose, 271
Client fraud, 282–310
Confidentiality principle, general, 267–272
Duty of lawyer to an organizational client, 209–221
Exceptions,
Self-defense, 272–282
To prevent bodily harm or death, 310–332
To prevent client fraud, 282–310
Implied authority to reveal information, 271
Joint representation and, 623
Model Code, 269
Model Rules, 270
Policies underlying, 333–336
Professional duty, 276–336
Publicly available information, 271
Remedies for breach, 272
Tarasoff duty to warn, 325–333
Using confidential information, 270